Writing and Speaking
in the Technology Professions

IEEE Press
445 Hoes Lane
Piscataway, NJ 08855

Writing and Speaking in the Technology Professions

A Practical Guide

Second Edition

Edited by

David F. Beer

University of Texas, Austin

A Selected Reprint Volume

IEEE Press

A JOHN WILEY & SONS, INC., PUBLICATION

Published by John Wiley & Sons, Inc., Hoboken, New Jersey.

For general information on our other products and services please contact our Customer Care Department within the U.S. at 877-762-2974, outside the U.S. at 317-572-3993 or fax 317-572-4002.

Wiley also publishes its books in a variety of electronic formats. Some content that appears in print, however, may not be available in electronic format.

Library of Congress Cataloging-in-Publication Data is available.

ISBN 0-471-44473-1

Printed in the United States of America.

10 9 8 7 6 5 4 3 2 1

Contents

PART III Text and Graphics: Presenting Information Visually

PART IV Manuals and Procedures: Giving Directions that Work

PART V Proposals: Writing to Win the Customer

PART VIII Listening, Meeting, and Teamwork: Working with Others to Get Results

PART IX Global Communication: Conveying Meaning Internationally

Preface

The articles in this Second Edition were published in the *IEEE Transactions on Professional Communication* over the past two decades and consist of hands-on and practical advice from communicators in the technical workplace or academia. Forty-six of these articles are new to this edition, but if you are familiar with the First Edition, you will soon notice that I have preserved several articles I consider seminal and classic. Unlike in the world of technology, many effective communication tools never become obsolete, and solid advice given some years ago on how to produce, for example, a winning proposal can be as relevant and helpful now as it was then.

You may well ask why this is an anthology rather than a textbook. The main reason is that I want to provide guidelines written by engineers and others who are involved in communicating in their everyday work. Thus you will find articles here by people well acquainted with industry, whether in science, technology, or a branch of engineering. Some authors are working engineers themselves. Another reason this is not a textbook is that there is no shortage of textbooks directed at students who need to learn technical writing skills applicable to a very wide range of fields and careers. Most of these texts assume the reader is training to be a technical writer. Few are directed specifically at engineers or technicians and their workplaces.

You will find the majority of articles to be relatively short and to the point. They not only contain insightful and practical information, but are also models of clarity and coherence. The information within each article is accessible: it is easily retrieved by a busy reader looking for advice on how to communicate in a variety of situations and modes. In brief, the articles are practical and "user friendly," rather than theoretical or scholarly additions to the publish-or-perish pool.

People have needed to communicate on technical matters at least since the building of Stonehenge and the Pyramids, and the amount of technical communication now taking place is staggering. Whether they like it or not, engineers and other technical people must communicate on a daily basis in writing, speech, and graphics, through a variety of means. With the modern development of advanced technologies, in fact, the need has become even more critical—and complicated. It is unlikely that this need will diminish in the future, and all indications are that it will increase. Thus, if you want to be a success in technology, you must inevitably master the skill of efficient communication.

The selections in this anthology are separated into ten parts. The first six parts deal with written communication and follow a logical sequence. Thus, Part I contains information and help on the initial stages of the writing process. The material here is as applicable to a one-page memo as to a book-length proposal. These opening articles will give you practical advice on how to plan your document and begin writing it clearly and to the point while effectively conveying your message to your selected audience.

Part II covers the structure of some technical documents and also the overall formation of a report. You will find an interesting and useful approach to writing the whole document in the first article, which suggests setting up specs for your report before you write it. The second article also looks at reports as a whole, while the next four focus on quite specific genres of writing: the bad news message, job applications, recommendations, and technical articles to be published. Finally, the section deals with two topics we rarely think of: how to go far beyond the ways we normally use a style guide, and the question of just how objective and honest our technical writing really is.

Part III takes up some formatting and visual aspects of technical writing. Not only will you find information here on such basics as margins, fonts, and headings, but also on choosing appropriate graphics and incorporating them into your text when needed. Other visual/verbal combinations, namely lists, abbreviations, and symbols, are also covered. From this section you will get some excellent ideas on how careful use of these tools can improve the economy, appearance, and success of your documents.

Parts IV and V contain practical advice on how to write manuals and proposals. The usefulness of many products depends on how well written the accompanying manuals are. Moreover, a company's success may depend on how many winning proposals it submits. Although a proposal can be as brief as a one-page suggestion, many manuals and proposals are lengthy documents, and most technical professionals are likely at some time in their career to be part of a team working on such a document. Being aware of the "larger picture" will make you a much more useful member of that team. Thus Parts IV and V provide many insights into how to put together effective manuals and proposals, whether you are writing alone or as part of a team. You will also find your questions on how to focus, organize, and design these documents answered here.

It has been said that there is no such thing as a good writer—only good rewriters. This may well be true. At any rate, few of us would be foolhardy enough to write something to be read by others, whether a one-page letter, e-mail, five-page report, or five-hundred page proposal, without first carefully reviewing and testing it to ascertain its quality. The articles in Part VI will enable you to approach the task of editing your drafts methodically and confidently. The first four articles in this section deal with revising and editing your writing in general. The remaining three focus on some interesting possibilities for document improvement, such as collaborating with others, using an outline to reorganize a completed piece, or starting a report at the beginning of the project it deals with and developing it as the project progresses.

Because many people in engineering and the sciences find they have to communicate verbally as much as in writing, Part VII contains a collection of articles showing how you can give effective oral presentations. These selections, like all others in this book, are practical rather than theoretical. From them you will get help in successfully planning, organizing, and delivering both short informal talks and longer, highly technical presentations. You will also find guidelines on how to handle an audience unfavorably disposed towards what you have to say, and the concluding article is in effect a checklist of everything you need to consider before getting up in front of an audience. In Part VIII, the first two articles deal with listening, and it is worth noting the word *effective* is key to this activity. We all have to do a lot of listening, but as these articles reveal, much of our listening is inefficient and does not lead to real understanding of what we are hearing. If we can eliminate the barriers to efficient listening, we will become much better communicators, while enabling others to do the same. The next article will enable you to prevent a meeting from deteriorating into the lengthy, ineffective exercise in frustration and boredom that we are all familiar with. You will also find guidelines on how to organize a technical seminar in this section, plus four articles dealing with various aspects of team communication under differing circumstances and using different technologies.

Part IX considers a number of issues involving international technical communication. The global world is upon us, and its language generally—but not always—is English. All kinds of problems can occur in this world, along with many opportunities and challenges. You should, as one article stresses, become familiar with the varieties of international English and the cultural implications they reflect. Other articles in this section will give you further insight into international English, including the use of it, editing it, and some problems involved in evaluating and translating it. One article will also remind you that not every culture organizes its technical documents the way we do.

The final section of the book, Part X, focuses entirely on electronic communication. E-mail is taken for granted today, but as the first two articles show, there are several important facets of using e-mail that we tend to forget. Then an article on online documentation recommends not only deep audience analysis but also an on-going relationship with users of the documentation. The rest of this section's articles are devoted to communicating on the Web and cover corporate usage, editing, disabled users, and international users. Some of these articles may seem a bit "academic" since they present the results of research, but in each case the research points to practical applications.

Many people have contributed directly or indirectly to this anthology. First, of course, are the authors of the articles themselves. Next, I must acknowledge all the engineers I have worked with at the University of Texas and in industry. They have enabled me to get a clear picture of the kinds of communication skills technical people need, and thus have helped me decide which articles to select. My friends and colleagues in the Electrical and Computer Engineering Department at the University of Texas at Austin have contributed to the book in the same way, as have my students throughout the years. My fellow members of the IEEE Professional Communication Society have been an encouragement and help, and meeting them each year at the IEEE International Professional Communication Conference is always both an educational and pleasurable experience. My thanks also go to the staff of the IEEE Press and their excellent assistance. My wife Ruth and our daughter Natasha have, as always, been a source of encouragement—and have helped me keep my priorities straight.

DAVID F. BEER

Austin, Texas
April 2003

PART I

Getting Started: Writing the First Drafts

"Can Engineers Write?" Joan Knapp asks in the title of this section's opening article. The answer is, of course—provided engineers are given the training and practice anyone needs to do a complex task well. Thus the articles in this section will show you some of the best ways to start writing a technical document and some practical ways to proceed once you have started.

Preparing to write your report

In response to her own question, Knapp takes you through ten stages of writing an engineering report. She describes five kinds of people most likely to read your reports and shows how your writing must to a great extent be determined by who you are writing for. Her emphasis is on research reports, operation manuals, proposals, and feasibility studies, but what she says applies to many other kinds of technical writing as well.

The art of prewriting

While Knapp takes an overall view of the challenges faced in writing an engineering report, Ronal Nelson specifically focuses on preparing to write a document, an activity often known as "prewriting." He also expands on some of Knapp's most important points, breaking his topic down into five practical categories. Nelson's two-page worksheet will enable you to methodically approach several different aspects of preparing to write a report.

Gathering your thoughts

In their article on issue trees, Joann Dennett and Michael Hseih show how your report content can be efficiently organized before you begin writing by borrowing the idea of decision trees from some other scientific fields. This concept, when used by the engineering writer, becomes an "issue tree," a device that helps in the process of producing a well-organized and effective report. Rather than the linear approach to prewriting, writing, and revision, the issue tree calls for initially brainstorming your subject on paper, showing subtopics, logical relationships, analyses, important and less vital information, and possible conclusions. This approach will not only help you overcome writer's block but will also enable you to stay focused on your topic and have all your data lined up before writing your report.

Who is your reader?

In the fourth article Ruth Savakinas gives pointers on finding out who your audience really is. The pay-off for careful audience analysis prior to writing is a reduction in the need to rewrite. This article's title is a reflection on how we tend to rush into written work too quickly, without allowing time for thoughtful "pre-writing," and hence fall into the trap of writing first and afterwards doing a lot of re-aiming and re-writing.

Where should you start?

The Piersons take a look at the life of a report as it usually evolves, and advise you not to simply start at the beginning and work through to the end. The authors show the practical wisdom of writing a report "from the inside out," completing the body of the report first and then concentrating on the beginning and ending parts, including not only your introduction and conclusion but also the title and abstract.

Clarity counts

We all agree (I hope) that writing must be clear and that busy readers should easily understand our documents. As Ronald Dulek points out, we are aware of the need for clarity, but defining it and making sure our documents are clear is often a challenge. Dulek examines the numerous elements of clarity and concentrates on three of the most important ones: writing unambiguously, making information accessible to a variety of readers, and using language appropriate to the corporate situation. This article provides an insightful synopsis of what everyone needs to remember about writing clearly and is also a fresh look at some elements of clarity that are rarely considered.

Is my grammar correct?

Alan Manning raises the question of what constitutes correct grammar—a concern that has been the source of debate ever since the first grammarians set their opinions down on paper. With recent tendencies towards descriptive rather than prescriptive grammar, the "rules" have become even fuzzier. Nevertheless, violations of long-entrenched usage standards can jolt a lot of readers and cause them to have unflattering opinions of the writer. Manning takes a 1990 study of questionable usage and compares it a similar study made in 2001. He then develops an interesting "botheration scale," showing how certain errors cause more reader botheration than others. Turning this around, you will come to see that not all grammar and usage errors are equal, and that some can be taken more lightly than others.

Industrial and academic writing

Whether we like it or not, much technical writing is taught in English departments by instructors with little knowledge of industry. This, as Don Bush shows, creates two cultures—academic writing and industrial writing. Both cultures have the same goal: to improve communication. However, they often approach this goal in different ways, and Bush makes some intriguing comparisons and contrasts on a number of levels. This article will be useful to any technical writers who received their initial training as writers in a liberal arts department, and who will surely find themselves agreeing with Bush that more "cross-fertilization" is needed between the two cultures.

Can Engineers Write?

JOAN KNAPP

Abstract—**Writing skill is an important element in engineering success. To supplement engineering curricula that provide little help in developing writing ability, this article describes ten steps in report writing that apply to research reports, operation manuals, proposals, and feasibility studies. The steps are (1) analyze your audience; (2) classify the report; (3) design the report; (4) do the research; (5) write a rough draft of the body of the report; (6) write a conclusions section; (7) write an introduction; (8) write an executive summary or abstract; (9) revise the report; and (10) add missing elements.**

CONGRATULATIONS, graduates! Engineering school has taught you all you need to know to guarantee a successful career, right? Maybe not. You haven't learned how to write a report. However, the fact that you got through engineering school means that you can surely handle such trivialities as writing assignments, doesn't it? Perhaps. But recent studies, such as the major study of graduate adequacy conducted by Colorado School of Mines in 1978, suggest that many graduating engineers are deficient in communication skills, particularly writing. The studies also conclude that those skills are necessary for a successful career.

"My son never writes home–he's an engineer."

The experience of practicing engineers bears out the correlation between writing skills and successful careers. Engineers who write well advance in rank, eventually reaching management levels. Those who cannot write tend to be passed over for promotions and remain in routine jobs. Junior engineers may find writing requirements minimal during the first year or two of practice, but as they gain expertise, they are increasingly required to communicate that expertise. Those who can do so are promoted to more challenging, better paying positions.

Reprinted with permission from *Colorado Engineer,* Summer 1983, vol. 79(4), pp. 4–8; copyright 1983 by Colorado Engineer, Boulder, Colorado.

The author is an Information Developer with the Field Engineering Division, IBM Corporation, 3131 28th Street, Boulder, CO 80301; (303) 441-2367.

Unfortunately, the usual engineering curriculum offers little or no help in developing students' writing abilities. Since grades depend on tests involving calculations only, students have no incentive to improve their writing. Further, constant emphasis on mathematical rather than verbal material may actually decrease ability to communicate verbally over a four- or five-year period. And, finally, many students adopt a defeatist attitude toward writing; because they don't write, they assume they can't.

Yet most engineers have the potential to write well. Indeed, because they have been trained to think logically, engineering students often have the capability of becoming better writers than humanities students. What they need is instruction and practice.

Although this article cannot substitute for the supervised practice and detailed instruction offered in a writing class, it is addressed to senior students with the intent of providing a method and some guidelines for report writing. To simplify the process of planning and writing a report, I have divided that process into ten steps and I discuss each step as it commonly applies to engineering reports.

1. Analyze your audience. Nobody gets up in the morning, looks out the window, and says, "What a nice day! I think I'll write a report." Poems may be written on such occasions; reports are not. Whether it be a handwritten memorandum or a handsomely bound proposal, a report is a communication needed and directed by an audience.

Thus, when you are asked to write a report, your first step should be to ask three questions: Who will read the report? For what purpose are they reading it? Are they engineers? Based on the answers to those questions, readers usually fall into one of five audience categories:

a. Expert	Other engineers, preferably in the same field, who read the report for information relating to their own projects
b. Executive	Managers, usually lacking an engineering background, who read the report to make executive decisions
c. Technician	People usually lacking an engineering background, who read the report for direction in using products and systems designed by engineers

Reprinted from *IEEE Trans. Prof. Comm.,* vol. PC-27, no. 1, pp. 10–13, March 1984.

d. Lay	People lacking an engineering background, such as special-interest groups, who read the report for non-engineering reasons
e. Combined	A group such as a government agency, comprising engineers and non-engineers, who read the report to make decisions

Placing your reader in one of these categories helps you structure the report to fulfill readers' information needs and also helps you select the level of language that will communicate best. For instance, if you're reporting to the Sierra Club on the cost/benefit ratio of a water project, you should avoid highly technical language where possible and insert simple definitions for the terms you have to use. If, on the other hand, you're reporting to an engineering firm on thermodynamic analysis of an engine, nontechnical language would be both inefficient and insulting.

2. Classify the report. The foregoing examples suggest the second step you should take in writing a report. Not only must you analyze the audience and their purposes, but you also must classify the report and its purposes to decide what format you will use. The more common reports engineers write are physical research reports, operation manuals, proposals, and feasibility studies. Although in-depth directions for writing these reports cannot be given here, a brief description of the purpose and format for each type follows.

• *Physical research reports* are written to describe research projects, such as stress tests on metals. They follow a rigid format: introduction, problem statement; materials; methods; results; discussion; summary; and conclusions.

Students who have written lab reports are familiar with this format, but a report written in a work situation differs from that in the academic situation in four ways. First, the practicing engineer is not writing for a professor who knows the answers but for people who don't know the answers and are primarily interested in answers. Second, if new testing methods are used or if a physical system is modeled via equations, those features must not only be described but also justified. Third, as in all professional reports, a title page, table of contents, lists of illustrations and symbols, and other reader aids are required. And fourth, different language levels are needed in different sections of the report. These distinctions are illustrated in the discussion of feasibility reports.

• *Operation manuals* for water and sewer systems, for power plants and other industrial complexes, and for specialized tools and instruments are written to tell the user how to operate and maintain these systems and products. A manual must include a brief introduction, stating its purpose; a set of performance directions; and a set of debugging procedures. Theoretical sections presenting principles of design and descriptions of mechanisms may be included, but they should be firmly separated from sets of instructions.

When writing a manual, use clear, simple language; keep sentences short; supplement the text with plenty of drawings; and separate individual instructions by using numbers and white space. Current research at American Bell suggests that effective use of white space can increase speed of comprehension by as much as 50 percent.

• *Proposals* are written to propose that a project be undertaken. Projects may range from practical (better parking facilities) through R&D (research and development of a space shuttle) to pure research (a method of soils testing). Because of this diversity of projects, no firm directives for format or language levels can be given. But since proposals are the most audience-oriented of all reports, great care should be taken to analyze the audience and to present a report as persuasive and attractive as possible for that audience.

The proposal begins with a statement of the problem (good parking facilities, a space shuttle, or adequate methods of soils testing do not exist) and then presents the immediate background to the problem, the benefits that will come from solving it, and the feasibility of the solution. It describes the methods to be used, the facilities available, the tasks to be done, and a schedule for doing them. The competence of the persons or organizations doing the work must also be demonstrated: What are their qualifications? How much previous experience have they had? What references can they supply? Finally, costs and method of payment must be specified.

More than any other type of report, a proposal must be visually attractive and inviting to the reader. Use headings and white space generously. Supply helpful, attractive graphics. Indicate different sections of the report clearly (index tabs at the outside edge are often helpful). And, finally, select a binding that is both durable and convenient for distributing sections of the report to various audiences.

As a junior engineer, you will probably not be asked to write a proposal. But you may be asked to write a section of a proposal, and you will benefit from knowing how a proposal works. The kind of report you will most commonly be asked to write is a feasibility study.

• *Feasibility studies* are written to answer three questions: Is a given project physically practical? Is it economically practical? Is it suitable from the viewpoint of those who will be affected by it? These questions require definite answers supported by factual evidence. This requirement, in turn, demands that the writer reverse the research process, beginning with conclusions and organizing facts to support them.

To illustrate, suppose you are asked to report to the Boulder City Council on the feasibility of a walkway over the intersection of Broadway and College Avenue. You would have to research the rationale for the walkway and various walkway designs to decide on a practical solution; your report would then present that decision supported by data. The most common error made by beginning writers of feasibility reports arises from confusion with physical research reports: Writers report what they have done rather than what they have discovered.

Because the ability to write a feasbility report is important to your career, this hypothetical example is used to illustrate the remaining steps in writing a report. You have defined your audience: the Boulder City Council. Although they aren't engineers, they will give the report to the city engineer or an outside expert. You are therefore writing for a combined audience. You have classified the report as a feasibility study. What is your next step?

3. Design the report. Most report-writing textbooks suggest that you begin research at this point. But much research and writing can be avoided if you first brainstorm the subject, examining possible approaches and arriving at the most practical, and then discuss these approaches with your clients to find out what they want to know and in what detail. Perhaps the city council already has a design in mind and is partly committed to it. If it's a good design, your report can support it with the modifications you suggest; if not, your report must show why another design is superior. You should also find out what dollar figure they have in mind: If they're thinking $200,000 and you're thinking $500,000, your report will not be useful. Third, you should find out what kinds of information they're most interested in. If they're not much interested in environmental impact, you can limit your research accordingly. And, finally, you should find out how massive a report they are expecting.

On the basis of this information, design the report. If the council is expecting a 25-page report, decide what proportion should be given to structures, what proportion to materials, and what proportion to environmental impact. Within the structures section, decide how many designs should be presented, what graphics are needed, what major and minor factors should be considered, and in what detail they should be described. You now have a format that prevents you from gathering facts willy-nilly and trying to fit them together to produce a report.

4. Do the research. Since research is a separate activity, only two suggestions for doing it are presented here.

First, begin with the obvious. Measure traffic flow to see whether the project is justified. Measure street width, maximum vehicle heights, and walkway grades to determine whether users of the walkway would feel as though they were climbing Mt. Everest; if so, the street may have to be lowered. Draw up preliminary specifications (final specifications will be made in the final report) and calculate costs. Determine who will be affected by the structure and how their views can be sampled.

Second, if library research is involved, take notes on cards that can be arranged according to topics and then rearranged within topics to provide supporting information for conclusions. You may find a note-card system convenient for recording and storing all information obtained through research. It provides a place to file bits of information and also helps you draw up an outline for each topic.

5. Write a rough draft of the body of the report. Since you have already designed the report, you can write any section when it has been researched. If you find the original report design inadequate, modify it, but don't let research alter the basic structure you designed to respond to your audience's needs.

Guide your reader through each section of the report. Suppose you've finished researching a section on design and have identified the most practical one. Do you describe the unsatisfactory possibilities and then, with great flourish, present your solution? Quite the opposite. Begin with the solution and support it through comparison and contrast with other possibilities. If it has disadvantages, admit them, but remember that you are the authority and that your audience is interested in answers.

At the beginning of each section, tell the reader what points you discuss. Listing these points displays them clearly and guides your writing so that each point can be the subject of a separate paragraph.

Paragraphs are the basic building blocks of writing. Each must be restricted to a single topic summarized in a topic sentence, usually the first sentence in the paragraph. The remainder of the paragraph develops the topic through factual evidence, explanation, or examples. Logical ordering of this material and transitions between ideas are necessary so that the reader experiences each paragraph as a structured body of information.

The sentences that compose paragraphs are also structured entities. Sentences usually contain a single thought or two related thoughts; in the latter case, the writer supplies the connection through punctuation and connecting words. Engineers tend to use too many short, unconnected sentences. Combining them improves the reader's logical grasp of the material and also improves the flow of the paragraph.

Two final suggestions are offered for writing rough drafts: First, don't be afraid of including too much detail. Extraneous material can always be edited out, but if your original draft doesn't contain the logical connections needed by your reader, you may find it difficult to supply them in later drafts. And, second, double-space your writing, use only one side of the page, and leave generous margins. These practices allow you to cut and paste to move subsections and to insert additional material and transitions without rewriting when you revise the report.

6. Write a conclusions section. Although individual

sections of your report present conclusions for that section, you need to gather those conclusions into a cohesive whole. Doing so requires formulating general statements from particular conclusions and arranging these in a hierarchy, with the most important (or logically prior) conclusions first. For example, state that the walkway is structurally feasible and why before stating that design A is the most practical design.

Since the conclusions section may be read by people who do not read the entire report, it must be self-sufficient and fairly detailed. It may be placed at either the beginning or the end of the report.

7. Write an introduction. Now that you have finished the report, you can write an introduction stating subject, purpose, scope, and plan of development. An introduction is not an overview of the subject of the report; rather, it is an overview of the report itself. Thus, conclusions, historical background, and literature reviews do not belong here.

Introductions frequently begin with a problem statement: "Two people, four students, and six dogs were injured at the intersection of Broadway and College Avenue in 1982." The remainder of the introduction explains how the report addresses the problem.

Beginning writers sometimes attempt to write the introduction before they have written the report—a virtually impossible task. Once the report is complete, however, writing the introduction should present no problem.

8. Write an executive summary or abstract. An executive summary presents the substance of the report in abbreviated form to an executive audience; an abstract presents this information to an expert audience. Abstracts and summaries are usually limited to a page or slightly more, but no rules about length or amount of detail apply to all reports. The best plan is to read well-received reports on similar topics and structure the abstract or summary accordingly.

Like the conclusions section, the summary or abstract must be self-sufficient and must be written at the language level appropriate for the targeted audience. Although you may have been writing for an engineer throughout the body of the walkway report, an executive summary for the city council demands a shift to language appropriate for a lay audience. But beware that a shift in level isn't accompanied by a shift in tone. Don't "talk down" to this audience; just use different terms.

9. Revise the report. Revision is such a complex process that specific directions for it cannot be given. A practicing engineer I consulted in writing this article offered this suggestion: "Put the report down for a couple of days and then come back and analyze it for clarity and concentration of ideas. Among other activities, this analysis may result in adding, deleting, and moving material; adding concluding statements and transitions between sections and subsections; checking topic sentences of paragraphs to see that they present a logical line of reasoning; adding transitions within paragraphs; checking sentences for subject-verb agreement, noun-pronoun agreement, and parallel structure; correcting punctuation and spelling; and substituting active for passive voice where appropriate.

10. Add missing elements. To add missing elements, consult a report-writing textbook and past reports in the company files. The elements to be added include letter of transmittal, title page, table of contents, list of illustrations, glossary, list of symbols, appendixes, list of references cited, and bibliography. Rules for documentation of sources depend on the firm or agency you are working for. All these additions take time but they are minor considerations compared with the conceptually demanding task of writing the report.

Finally, select an attractive binding, sign your name, and prepare to bask in the satisfaction of a job well done.

Preparing to Write the Document: A Worksheet for Situational Analysis in the Workplace

RONALD J. NELSON

Abstract—**Difficulty with writing may be attributable to lack of preparation. This article presents a worksheet which helps authors facilitate writing projects by identifying important preliminary considerations, the potential readers of the document, relationships of the writer to the audience and the document, the purpose of the document, and strategies to employ to achieve that purpose. Each of these categories is discussed in detail, in terms of the entries to be made on the form. The result of this kind of preparation is a methodical approach and a product that will have value to others.**

PROFESSIONALS IN THE WORLD of work often struggle with their writing. One of the likeliest reasons for this difficulty is ineffective writing courses in colleges. In an article in *The Bulletin,* Dan Dieterich identifies, with disarming directness, a major problem with the writing courses that are intended to prepare students for the working world: "Most of the student writing now done in college writing courses is a waste of time.... It is usually written to no one and accomplishes nothing." [1] This waste is, regrettably, carried over into professional life, in which writing sometimes leads only to miscommunication and frustration.

Despite the difficulty of overcoming poor writing habits, people in a work setting can write more effectively. But it is necessary to prepare for doing so. I have devised a worksheet for facilitating each writing project by channeling writers' thoughts in ways that can make messages flow with maximum impact.*

We, and our objectives, are best served if we write directly and sincerely from one human being to another on the basis of a careful analysis of the particular writing situation at hand. To achieve this end, we need to break down the complexities of writing situations into manageable units: the points to be considered prior to writing the actual memorandum, correspondence, proposal, news release, report, or other document. The worksheet shown in figure 1 contains many of these elements. (The worksheet has been printed on two sides of a single page, so that it can be removed and copied for use as necessary.)

Dr. Nelson, Assistant Professor of English at James Madison University, holds a B.A. in economics and M. A. in English; he received the Ph.D in English from the University of Nebraska in 1978. He has published in the fields of technical writing, art, and literature; his extracurricular interests include juggling and "New Orleans trumpet" playing.

* Other worksheets have been prepared by Carosso [2], Mathes and Stevenson [3], and Pearsall. [4]

Completing the worksheet need not be done in the indicated sequence. For example, a person may have a general idea of the subject but not be ready to settle on a definite title at the start of the project. Certain categories might require some brainstorming with others—for example, a person might need to check on who the secondary readers are likely to be—before completing the forms. It is, of course, advantageous to fill out the worksheet completely before getting down to serious writing.

At first, the worksheet will seem difficult to use because of its novelty and its mental demands on the writer. After using it several times, however, a person gets into the flow of the process, and it requires less time and energy to complete. Any investment at the start is likely to pay handsome dividends by saving time and effort during the writing of the document, as well as creating a more useful finished product.

The worksheet is designed to make the user reflect on what is to be written. By having to consider consciously the various factors involved in preparing a convincing document, the writer is likely to produce a high-quality finished product. If the writer is unclear about any aspect of the task at hand, it should be possible to clarify matters with someone in a position to know.

The factors that the writer needs to identify and cope with before getting down to the actual writing are grouped under five categories on the worksheet:

- Preliminary considerations
- The reader(s)
- The writer
- The purpose of the document
- Strategies to employ to achieve that purpose

These five factors are discussed in the following paragraphs.

PRELIMINARY CONSIDERATIONS

The identifying information in the right-hand corner is mostly self-explanatory. *Project Number* and *Name,* of course, allows for easy filing of and access to the worksheet. As more and more projects are completed, the writer's personal files will become increasingly valuable as a storehouse of information that is likely to be useful for future projects.

Reprinted from *IEEE Trans. Prof. Comm.,* vol. PC-33, no. 1, pp. 12–18, March 1990.

Worksheet

(page 1)

PRELIMINARY CONSIDERATIONS:

Deadline ______________________ Project Number/Name ______________________

When Completed ______________________

Writer's Name ______________________ Department/Unit ______________________

Subject ______________________

Title ______________________

Format ______________________ Means of Distribution ______________________

THE READER(S) Name Title Department/Location IH/IV/E

Initial Reader(s) ______________________

Primary Reader(s) ______________________

Secondary Reader(s) ______________________

Homogeneous Group(s) ______________________

Diverse Group(s) ______________________

Factors to Consider Primary Secondary

General Category of Audience ______________________

Level of Expertise ______________________

Daily Concerns ______________________

Specific Knowledge of Project ______________________

Interest/Commitment ______________________

Personality ______________________

THE WRITER:

Relationship to Primary Reader ______________________

Tone to Adopt ______________________

Vocabulary Level to Employ ______________________

Political Considerations ______________________

Figure 1. Worksheet for the Professional Writer (sheet 1 of 2)

Worksheet

(page 2)

PURPOSE OF THE DOCUMENT:

Primary: To inform ____________ To affect ____________ To effect action ____________

Secondary: To inform ____________ To affect ____________ To effect action ____________

Specific Response Expected: Primary ____________________ Secondary ____________________

STRATEGIES TO EMPLOY TO ACHIEVE PURPOSE(S):

Sources to Consult

People ____

Written Sources ____

Other Sources ____

Specific Techniques to Employ

Introduction ____

Thesis Statement ____

____

____

Organization for Body of Document ____

____

____

Conclusion ____

____

____

NOTES:

____

____

____

____

Figure 1. Worksheet for the Professional Writer (sheet 2 of 2)

It is useful to remind oneself of the *Deadline* for a project and to attempt to complete the assignment well before the deadline. The category *When Completed* is included for a record of how well the writer has met the deadline. Repeatedly just making a deadline should be a message to the writer that better time management is in order.

The *Subject* of the project will most often be a short phrase—for example, "Office Furniture." The *Title* line for an internal memo might read "A Study of the Office Furniture Requirements in Our Needham Branch." The title will be much more detailed than the subject and will be clearly related to the unifying idea (thesis statement) in the document.

The *Format* may be a letter, memorandum, proposal, progress report, bulletin, analytical research report, news release, environmental impact statement, instructional manual, trip report, among others. The *Means of Distribution* may be hand delivery, external or internal mail, fax machine, or whatever method is used to convey the document to the initial or primary reader.

THE READER

It is essential for the writer to be clear on who the intended audience is. As Mathes and Stevenson point out, the task of identifying the reader(s) can be difficult, since there may be audiences in addition to the person addressed, including "unknown or unanticipated audiences." [3] With their "egocentric organizational chart," these authors have simplified the task somewhat, using concentric semicircles to assist the writer in targeting potential readers in varying degrees of proximity to the writer.

Trzyna and Batschelet offer an equally good way to identify readers: "Start by listing all of the people who will be dealing with your report. Begin with yourself and any people with whom you work daily: the people who share your ideas, your hopes, your way of talking about your work. Next list the people in your audience who work closely with your group: managers, supervisors, and members of other departments who are working on projects related to yours. Then list even more distant personnel and administrators who might need to read or evaluate your reports or proposals." [5] In general, identify close audiences with whom you have daily contact and distant audiences who might be interested in the document.

The writer must identify *Initial, Primary,* and *Secondary Readers* so that the needs of those people can be met. (Sometimes initial and primary readers are one and the same.) The person's name (correctly spelled), title (accurately phrased), department (if internal), and location (if external) must be ascertained. Whether the audience is internal horizontal (IH), internal vertical (IV), or external (E) will also have to be determined. Material intended for internal consumption may be quite different from that intended for external audiences, given the impact of business relationships. Similarly, horizontal is sometimes quite different from vertical communication—for example, in matters of tone and amount of detail included.

The intended readers may be a *Homogeneous Group,* such as computer operators, salespersons, or genetic engineers. For such groups, the writer may assume a certain common level of vocabulary, knowledge, and experience. For a *Diverse Group,* however, one must have in mind the varying backgrounds, emphases, and value systems of the readers. An environmental impact statement, for example, must be comprehensible to a wide range of readers: those concerned with the physical, biological, historical, economic, human, social, and esthetic implications of a project.

There could be many *Factors to Consider* for each reader; the complexity of the task, however, precludes absolute thoroughness. The best a writer can do is to focus on a number of aspects related to the audience and try to approach the particular reader(s) from a position of knowledge rather than ignorance.

The *General Category of Audience* can be thought of in many ways. For example, Kenneth Houp and Thomas Pearsall divide readers into the lay audience, experts, executives, technicians, and combined audience. [6] Michael Keene uses the same audience types as Houp and Pearsall, but he distinguishes "complex audiences" (a person who is both an expert and an executive, for example) from "multiple audiences" (several people who fall into different categories). [7] Rebecca Carosso, on the other hand, offers seven categories: experts, technicians, operators, professional nonexperts, students, general readers, and children. [2] Trzyna and Batschelet suggest the following four categories: the general reader, technicians, technical specialists, and executives/managers. [5] By categorizing readers in some standard fashion, the writer can begin to focus on the reader's probable training, responsibilities, needs, and role in the organization.

Determination of the *Level of Expertise* should give the writer important clues to the amount and type of background information and detail to include or exclude, as well as the vocabulary level to employ. Factors about the person's education—academic degrees or lack thereof, field of specialization, and years out of school [8]—will be important considerations. Other factors, like years with the company, reputation for competence, and even age, will help the writer to address the reader appropriately.

The reader's *Daily Concerns* must be taken into account as well. Generally, "Will his [or her] daily concerns and attitudes enable him to react to your report easily, or will they make it difficult for him to grasp what you are talking about?" [3] How the reader spends the day will suggest that person's needs. The document will become useful inasmuch as the writer addresses and satisfies the reader's needs.

to specific (deductive reasoning), specific to general (inductive reasoning), less important to more important, more important to less important, chronological, spatial (physical relationship of parts, left to right, clockwise, and so forth), and problem-method-solution.

Of course, each paragraph should have a topic sentence (often leading off the paragraph), followed by examples, quotations, data, or whatever it takes to establish the main idea in the paragraph. The combination of topic sentences should be roughly equivalent to the thesis statement.

A space for NOTES has been provided on the form for recording any other essential, but uncategorized, information.

CONCLUSION

Producing convincing, solid writing is not easy. But the task can be made easier by adopting a favorable attitude toward the task at hand and by employing the worksheet to advantage. Not the least of the rewards for using such an approach is the pleasure of having worked methodically at a document and creating a product that will have value to others.

NOTES AND REFERENCES

1. Dieterich, D., "Real Readers for Real Writers," *The Bulletin 49,* 2 (1986), p. 28.
2. Carosso, R. B., *Technical Communication,* Belmont, CA: Wadsworth Publishing Company, 1986.
3. Mathes, J. C., and Stevenson, D. W., *Designing Technical Reports,* Indianapolis: Bobbs-Merrill, 1976.
4. Pearsall, T., *Teaching Technical Writing: Teaching Audience Analysis and Adaptation,* Anthology No. 1, Association of Teachers of Technical Writing, 1988.
5. Trzyna, T. N., and Batschelet, M. W., *Writing for the Technical Professions,* Belmont, CA: Wadsworth Publishing Company, 1987.
6. Houp, K., and Pearsall, T., "Analyzing your Audience," in *Reporting Technical Information,* New York: MacMillan, 1984.
7. Keene, M. L., *Effective Professional Writing,* Lexington, MA: D. C. Heath and Company, 1987.
8. Mathes and Stevenson [3] remind the reader that the half-life of an engineer is about 5 years. Thus, a person 5 to 10 years older than a recent graduate is likely to have only a superficial knowledge of current happenings in the field. They further suggest that, to assess a reader's competence in your field of specialization, you might ask yourself if the person could participate in a professional conference on the subject.
9. Middleman, L. I., *In Short: A Concise Guide to Good Writing,* New York: St. Martin's Press, 1981.
10. Wilkinson, C. W., *et al., Communicating Through Letters and Reports,* Homewood, IL: Richard D. Irwin, Inc., 1980.
11. Middleman [8] discusses information theory, in which *information* is defined as "the reduction of uncertainty," and notes that anything which interferes with that reduction is called *noise.* He goes on to say, "Information informs, but noise annoys."
12. Bostwick, B. E., *Resume Writing,* New York: J. Wiley, 1976.
13. Hayes, R., "Political Realities in Reader/Situation Analysis," *Technical Communication,* First Quarter 1984, p. 17.
14. Markel, M. H., *Technical Writing Essentials,* New York: St. Martin's Press, 1988.
15. Zimmerman, D., and Clark, D., *The Random House Guide to Technical and Scientific Communication,* New York: Random House, 1987.
16. Winkler, A. C., and McKuen, J. R., *Rhetoric Made Plain,* New York: Harcourt Brace Jovanovich, 1974.

In *The Writer's Pocket Almanack,* R. John Brockmann and William Horton present a number of "Broken Quill Awards," two of which follow:

You can include a page that also includes an Include instruction. The page including the Include instruction is included when you paginate the document but the included text referred to in its Include instruction is not included.

IBM memo

3.3.12.3.2.2.10 POINTER SEQUENCE
See paragraph 3.3.12.3.2.1.12.

Australian Defence Department manual

Issue Trees: A Tool to Aid the Engineering Writer

Joann Temple Dennett and Michael Hseih

Abstract— **This paper surveys studies of the process model for understanding writing, focusing in particular on problem-solving strategies in the writing process. It then presents a case study of the use of issue trees—a hierarchal network of goals not unlike the decision trees used in management science and artificial intelligence—to guide the writing process of the second author as he wrote a technical report. A good issue tree shows the relationships between various pieces of information: which information is central and which is supportive or incidental. Issue trees offer engineers a visual view of their writing plan. By building a hierarchal issue tree to illustrate the logical links of the proposed writing task, the engineer can put an overlay of "technology" on the task of writing—an overlay that may "trick" the unwilling writer into writing, and writing well.**

Introduction

THE PROCESS by which we write has been a major focus of rhetorical and educational research in the last two decades. As early as 1965, in fact, Rohman [1] offered the idea that the writing process could be viewed in three stages—prewriting, writing, and rewriting. Many beleaguered composition teachers, shell-shocked from endless hours of picking nits in student writing, welcomed the pedagogical shift from critiquing only the written product to concentrating classroom effort on helping each student unveil the actual process by which he or she produced the writing. This philosophical shift began with Janet Emig's doctoral research at Harvard University [2]. She showed in her case study that the composing process did involve three major efforts, even though her 12th grade subjects did little prewriting or rewriting. During the following decade, more and more researchers hopped on the process bandwagon [3-10]. Many described an essentially three stage process—often in different words, such as Murray's "prevision, vision, and revision," Britton's "preparation, incubation, and articulation," and the segmented sections of prewriting, writing, and postwriting described by Koch and Brazil as eight discrete steps. Experiencing, discovering, and making formal choices were seen as part of prewriting. Forming, making language choices, and "languaging" were part of writing, and the distinctly different tasks of criticizing and proofreading were grouped into postwriting.

Most of these early models were essentially linear, based on theories about the nature of somewhat static components of what was actually a dynamic process. Perl [11] addressed this failing. She observed the recursive nature of writing quite clearly, noting that "composing always involves some measure of both construction and discovery. . . . Writers know more fully what they mean only after having written it."

Arguing that "current research on the composing process is pre-theoretical, that is, that it lacks a coherent, process-oriented theory from which to generate and test hypotheses," Matsuhashi [12] concluded:

> Clearly, the goal of much writing process research must be towards model-building: towards the construction of an abstract system which characterizes the writing process and which directs us to regularities or patterns in observational data.

Models have come a long way in a steady evolution from the simple linear version to a complex recursive one. In 1981, for example, the Document Design Center [13] combined and integrated the strategies inherent in technical writing into a process model that leads the writer through the process.

The first researchers to begin to successfully capture the basic dynamic recursiveness of the writing process in a necessarily static model were Flower and Hayes [14]. They used the protocol technique—recording detailed transcripts of writers thinking aloud while they wrote—and observed writers commenting on problem-solving and strategy. Emig's study of eight 12th-graders had pioneered the protocol technique; ten years later, Flower and Hayes described the process as capturing:

> . . . a detailed record of what is going on in the writer's mind during the act of composing itself. . . . We ask [the writers] to work on the task as they normally would—thinking, jotting notes, and writing—except that they must think out loud. They are asked to verbalize everything that goes through their minds as they write, including stray notions, false starts, and incomplete or fragmentary thought [14, p. 368].

Flower and Hayes developed their model to reflect what they saw as a complex interaction among the writing process, the writer's self, and the rhetorical problem being addressed. They found that writers set goals about both content and process. This goal setting is both recursive and constant, and as such, it directly affects the entire composing process. In short, Flower and Hayes reported evolving goals that "grow into an increasingly elaborate network of goals and sub-goals as the writer composes" [14, p. 377].

They described the writing process as "a goal-directed thinking process, guided by the writer's own growing network of goals"—a network that is hierarchal "in the sense that new goals operate as a functional part of the more inclusive goals above them" [14, p. 378]. This hierarchal network of goals is not unlike the decision trees used in management science and artificial intelligence [15], and, in fact, Flower adapted

Manuscript received November 1993, revised January 1994.

Joann Temple Dennett is with the School of Journalism and Mass Communication at the University of Colorado, Boulder, CO 80309 USA.

Michael Hseih is a student in the Department of Electrical Engineering, University of California, Irvine, CA USA.

Reprinted from *IEEE Trans. Prof. Comm.*, vol. PC-37, no. 2, pp. 88–96, June 1994.

such decision trees, called them issue trees, and promoted their use as a writing tool in a basic composition textbook [16]. Other texts also focused on the teaching process. In her textbook, *Contemporary Composition,* Maxine Hairston clearly agreed that the writing process is a good pedagogical tool [17]. In his 1987 overview, Steven Lynn writes that Hairston "has something solid to teach—a writing process, patterns of various kinds of writing, precepts of what makes writing more or less successful" [18].

Not everyone has agreed with this cognitivist approach. Michael Carter, for example, noted that the process movement of the seventies "was founded on information-processing theory, which . . . offers a view of human performance as based on domain-general processes." Carter argues for a "pluralistic theory of expertise, one that reflects the value of both general and local knowledge" [19]. Joseph Harris also criticized the Flower and Hayes focus on the logic shared by writer and reader; the focus variously called reader-based prose, writing for your reader, and meeting reader expectations. However, his concluding argument that "Flower's reader-based prose is really another name for a privileged form of discourse" can be seen to support the role of issue trees in facilitating "privileged" discourse, which he defines as "hierarchal in structure, issue-centered, organized around concepts rather than events, and [containing] transitions and conclusions (but not always assumptions) . . . made strongly explicit" [20].

Underlying the utility of issue trees is the Flower and Hayes conclusion that "good writers are simply solving a different problem than poor writers." This is probably nowhere more apparent than in the frequent question in composition classrooms: "How many words does it have to be?" Students writing to a specified word count have a clear, but hardly evolving, goal, and they are undoubtedly "solving a different problem" than their colleagues who are answering a specific question for a specific audience.

Recognizing that there are differences in the problems different writers are trying to solve clearly suggests that helping writers pose the right problem may be a valuable first step in helping them write better. Issue trees address this directly; they serve as a non-rhetorical solution to the rhetorical problems of organizing material, and they can be a powerful tool in casting the writing task as a problem to be solved.

Any problem-solving involves thinking, of course, and as Jacques Barzun [21, p. 176] observed, "Thinking means shuffling, relating, selecting the contents of one's mind so as to assimilate novelty, digest it, and create order." Research indicates that we go about this assimilation, digestion, and creation in different ways. Citing technical experts from Aristotle to Einstein, IBM's G. T. Smith [22, p. 20] argues for a sharp distinction between image thinkers and verbal thinkers, ". . . it is not uncommon for scientists, engineers, and mathematicians to think without words." This presents teaching problems. She observes,

> . . . when a student tells us he knows what he is thinking but can't express his thought, we are apt to challenge him and urge him to think more clearly and logically, convinced as we are that no one can think without language . . . [22, p. 19].
>
> Image thinkers also claim that not only is their thought accompanied by concrete representations other than words, but that they perceive these representations in gestalt, that is, all images present at the same time as if projected on a screen [22, p. 23].

This certainly presents a problem for interpreting thought into the sequential framework of language, but it also offers a useful insight into the "writer's block" often encountered by engineers and scientists—a useful insight that reflects a divergence, if not a difference, in the composing process, a divergence that can be corrected by using familiar problem-solving processes.

Attacking a problem with a standard, familiar problem-solving technique often makes the writing task easier for engineers. This paper explores the utility of using issue trees as such a technique, and it offers real-world examples of their application.

Case study research is virtually the only mechanism available to assess cognitive processes such as composing or problem-solving. Case studies, of course, do not carry the rigorous force of classical, repeatable experimental research. Nonetheless, they do contain useful clues about the general situation that emerge in the naturalistic reporting style reminiscent of interpretive journalism, which intermingles observed fact and suggested conclusion in a readable, story-like style.

The observations reported in this paper are the result of such a naturalistic case study. Both authors were involved in the writing process described in detail in the last sections of this paper: the first author as teacher and writing coach, the second author as a fledgling technical writer using a tool new to him in this context—issue trees.

Gist and Goal: A Tool to Help with Prewriting

Good technical writing should attempt to deal first with why the writer is bothering to write and to whom he or she is writing. Linda Flower [16, pp. 215-216] discusses this basic beginning, suggesting that the writer provide the gist and goal to appropriately complete the following thought: "What I am writing about is (gist) because what I want to do is (goal)." Thus, a powerful way to start prewriting is to determine and explicitly state the gist and goal of the proposed writing. This is a direct extension of rhetorical work from Aristotle to Bitzer [23]. It argues that the task of a technical writer is to provide information about a specific topic that logically addresses the specific goal and audience defined by the project. It further incorporates the purpose of the project. Once the statement of gist and goal has been written, it should be posted prominently—at the top of the issue tree, above the computer, on the blackboard, or, in the case of a collaborative effort, where all collaborators can see it. In view of the ongoing nature of the problem-solving process, the gist and goal may evolve as the writing progresses. But, this evolution should be conscious. If the gist and goal are changed, they should be physically rewritten and the new results posted or somehow shared among collaborators.

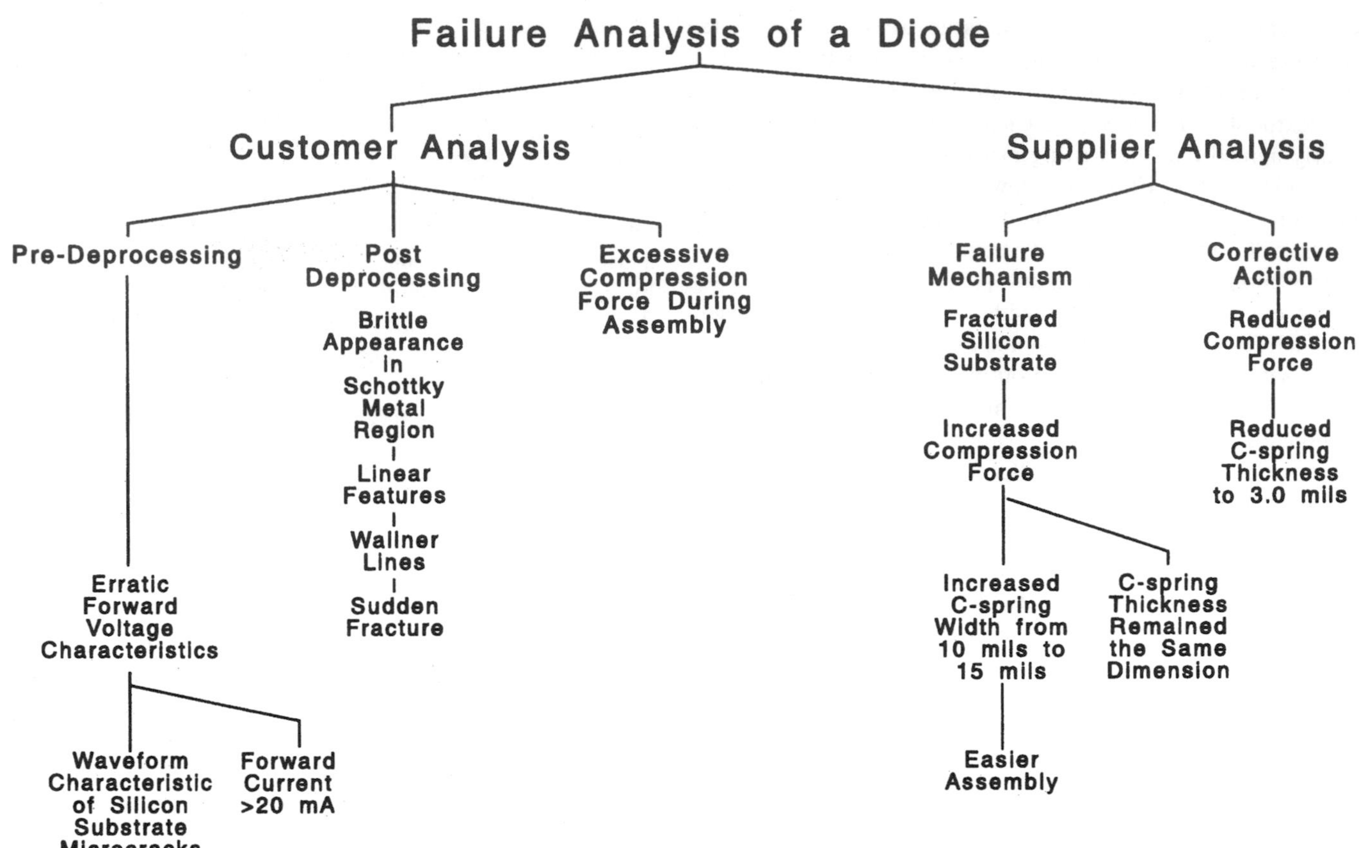

Fig. 1. This issue tree was written to help members of an industrial engineering team focus on their subject: Analyzing the failure of a diode received from a supplier. (Courtesy StorageTek)

ISSUE TREES: A TOOL TO MOVE FROM PREWRITING TO WRITING

With the gist and goal firmly in mind, the writer is ready to begin prewriting organization—an organization process that many typically begin by constructing an outline. However, standard outlining practices often only further confound people who find writing a difficult, even alien, task.

Substituting hierarchal issue trees for outlines has many advantages. Whereas a standard outline helps organize the material you already have, an issue tree helps you identify both the information you need to gather and the logical structure you need to tie it together for your reader. A good issue tree always shows the relationship between various pieces of information, and, most importantly, shows which information is central and which is supportive or incidental.

Issue trees offer engineers a visual view of their writing plan—a view that often seems to bypass the "writer's block" so often experienced by technical professionals who must write as the final step of their engineering efforts. By building a hierarchal issue tree to illustrate the logical links of the proposed writing, the engineer can put an overlay of "technology" on the task of writing—an overlay that may "trick" the unwilling writer into writing, and writing well.

Fig. 1 shows how the decisions that formed the issue tree kept members of an industrial engineering team focused on their subject. The electronics reliability engineer who wrote the final report from this issue tree reported clearly on the analysis of the failure of a diode received from a supplier. The conclusion of the report (Fig. 2) is as clear and succinct as the writing that supported it.

CASE STUDY: ITERATIVE GOAL SETTING AND ISSUE TREES

The following case study illustrates in detail the process of using an issue tree—a process experienced by the second author while a summer student visitor at the National Center for Atmospheric Research (NCAR) in Boulder, CO. This case study of the second author's use of issue trees illustrates how issue trees can facilitate the writing process of the novice engineering writer. The graphical (hierarchal) look of the trees is apparently an important consideration. The second author undoubtedly speaks for many of his engineering colleagues when he states, "After all, the clearest way to represent information is in graphical form."

Michael was assigned to work with data from state-of-the-art radars at NCAR. A final paper reviewing the summer's research results is a requirement of the summer program. Since NCAR seeks to provide a valuable research experience for the summer visitors, both NCAR and the National Science Foundation, the sponsoring agency, take the requirement of a final paper very seriously.

Electronics Reliability

Failure Analysis Report

Failure Analysis of a Diode

Conclusion: The diode failures are attributed to a supplier process defect. Evaluation of the forward voltage characteristics revealed erratic or "jittering" waveforms when the forward current approached 20mA. These waveform deformations are characteristic of microcracks in the silicon substrate. Subsequent deprocessing of the diode revealed a brittle fracture appearance in the diffusion region. The fracture surface contained linear features with fine ledges, known as "Wallner lines", perpendicular to the linear features. The presence of Wallner lines is evidence of a sudden fracture rather than a delayed fracture. It was suspected that a sudden or excessive compression force present during device assembly attributed to the fracturing of the silicon substrate.

Four failing diodes that exhibited similar erratic V/I breakdowns were submitted to the supplier per request of the supplier's Reliability Department. Conclusions of their analysis confirmed the customer's findings. The supplier indicated that excessive compression forces at the C-bend/Au button/die interface was fracturing the silicon substrate. The increased compression force was the result of an engineering change that increased the C-spring width for easier assembly purposes. The C-spring width was changed from 10 mils to 15 mils while the thickness remained at 3.5 mils. A corrective action has been implemented by the supplier to reduce the compression force at the interface by reducing the C-spring thickness to 3.0 mils.

Fig. 2. The conclusion of the report written from the issue tree in Fig. 1. (Courtesy StorageTek)

The first author has taught a technical-writing seminar for the summer student visitors for several years. We begin each seminar with a self-assessment of individual writing processes. Michael had never used an issue tree before encountering the concept in the summer writing class at NCAR. On his self-assessment, he described his process: "I haven't written an outline in years. Usually I write a rough draft in the first sitting and then revise it for as long as the time available." Given that he is an undergraduate in electrical engineering, the "time available" for writing tasks was undoubtedly limited and often produced less-than-adequate results. The time available for writing a report on research done in NCAR's ten-week summer internship was also severely limited, and less-than-adequate results were not an acceptable option. Michael agreed that another approach was worth trying.

His prewriting relied heavily on issue-tree development, and his overall writing process followed the steps good writers apparently use in developing coherent documents; that is, it was an iterative process involving the three major stages of prewriting, writing, and rewriting.

Michael's Use of Issue Trees

The issue tree helped Michael use his time more effectively. The first issue tree, Fig. 3, represents Michael's "first thinking—where should I start?" He was getting a general sense of his topic and thinking in terms of a comparison—comparing two sets of data with similar categories. Therefore, he focused on what made each one different, as can be seen in the details describing the Nexrad and CP-2 Doppler radars. This first tree has only four levels, of which the first two are actually probably one. It is a simple beginning. Recognizing this, Michael did not write from Fig. 3; it was strictly a prewriting tool. After more thought, he generated a new tree, Fig. 4. This tree is still a compare/contrast structure but with four actual levels of detail and an important structural change: Michael chopped the top off his first tree and "just started with Doppler radar." Narrowing his topic in this way was an important first step in focusing his writing.

Michael describes his subsequent efforts that spanned the next three to four weeks: "I started writing from this tree [Fig. 4], got about half way into it and then started a new tree [Fig. 5]." This is a big change. There are now six levels in Michael's issue tree. Nexrad and CP-2 have dropped to the fourth level. The focus is now on the parameters that Doppler radar can measure—reflectivity, radial velocity, and spectrum width—and what atmospheric phenomena these parameters suggest—hydrometeors, wind shear, tornadoes, and turbulence.

Michael explains: "In this version of the issue tree, I focused on the three quantities that radar measures and why we want to measure them. That led me to realize that my focus should really be on hydrometeor detection."

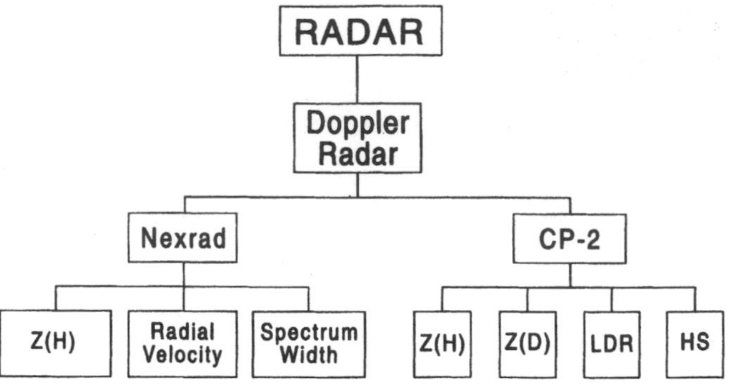

Fig. 3. This issue tree represents Michael's first thinking when he was just getting a general sense of his topic.

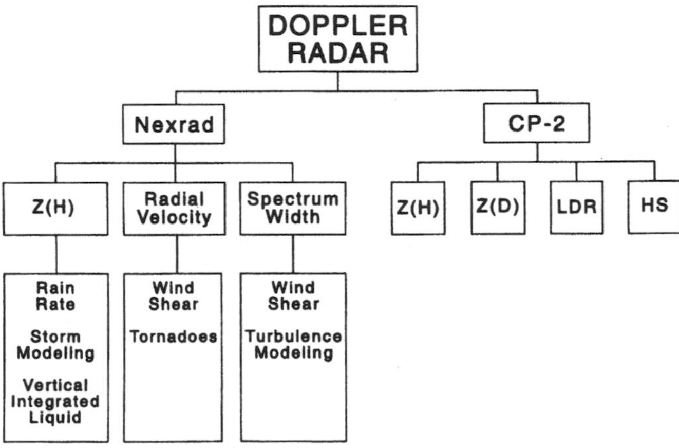

Fig. 4. This is Michael's second issue tree. He began to write from this tree but quickly found its hierarchy too limiting.

At this point, he wrote what would become the opening sentences of his final version:

> Pulsed-Doppler radar is used in meteorology to collect information about the state of the atmosphere. This paper is concerned mainly with the detection of various types of hydrometeors, which are water particles in solid or liquid state.

Discussing the issue tree in Fig. 6, Michael notes: "I wasn't real sure how the structure of the tree would work. Both radars do the same three things: that is, measure reflectivity, measure radial velocity, and measure spectrum width; but CP2 does more with reflectivity. Also there are three different kinds of reflectivity readings."

In Fig. 6, his fourth issue tree, Michael moved Nexrad and CP-2 up to level 3 and tried to distinguish their detecting capabilities. Look at the tree nodes on level 4: tornadoes, wind shear, Z(H), and atmospheric turbulence are on one side, and Z(H), Z(D), LDR, and HS are on the other side. Tornadoes, wind shear, and atmospheric turbulence leap out as nonparallel and misplaced in a listing of the parameters a radar can detect and measure. This specific confusion is symptomatic of a general confusion Michael was sorting through at the time. His first major effort of the 10-week summer project was to document and understand the mathematics that defined the measurable parameters. How these measurable parameters then related to physical phenomena was yet another mathematical hurdle. As he explains:

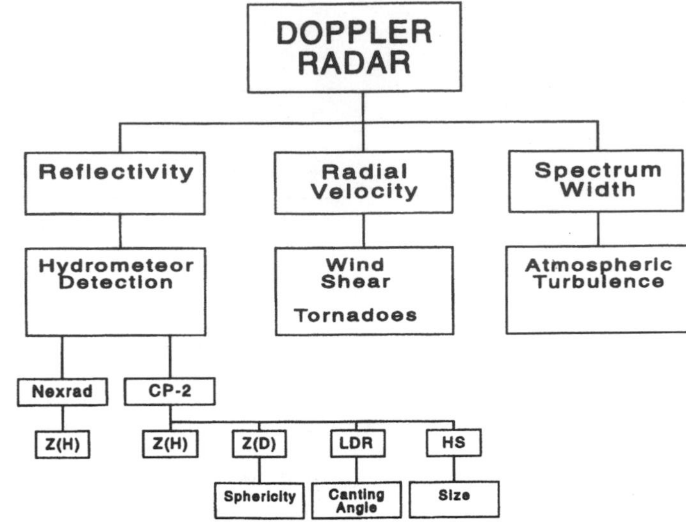

Fig. 5. The next tree changed the focus to the parameters that a Doppler radar can measure and began to explore why meteorologists want to measure these parameters.

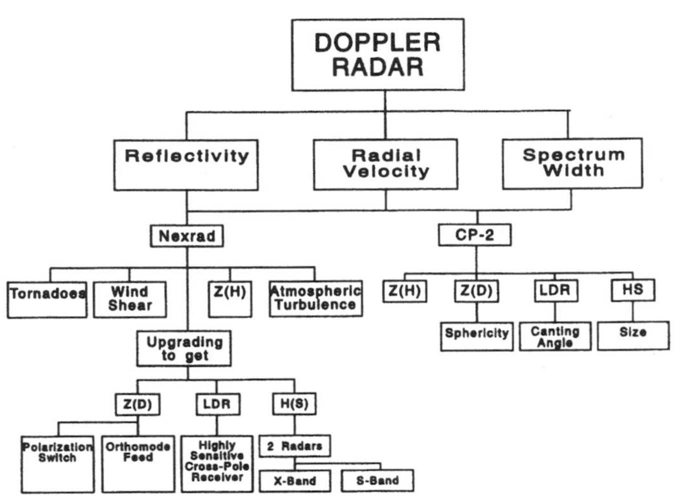

Fig. 6. This issue tree highlights an ongoing confusion about the parameters which a radar can detect and measure.

> At first, I approached the math from the standpoint that it would make relationships between different reflectivity measurements clearer, and make the concept of reflectivity itself clearer. Then the equations started taking up the majority of the pages, and I realized that I should explain the concepts without the math. Those who would take my word for it would read on more smoothly; those who wanted to check my mathematics could do so. I did put in the simplest equations concerning ZHV, ZDR, LDR, and HS because they are very basic to the relationships between the different measurements and take up little space, not interrupting the flow of the paper.

Abandoning his decision to force the reader down the same mathematical discovery path he had followed, Michael gathered all the mathematics and theory and moved them to an appendix. Thus, readers who already understand the parameters and those who don't really need a detailed definition are not confronted in the main text with information such as the following:

> Reflectivity is defined as the sixth power of the drop diameter summed over all drops in the unit volume, or drop size parameters are found from the differences in measured reflectivity factors due to Rayleigh and Mie scattering characteristics.

Citing principles of writing for the reader [24, 25], Michael noted that readers who need a definition can easily turn to the appendix; others can comfortably accept that the author is correct, refer to Table 1 of his text (a summary relating specific radar parameters to specific hydrometeors), and keep reading.

At this point, Michael devised a whimsical analogy equating the radar signatures meteorologists use to deduce information about hydrometeors to hypothetical dragon footprints that suggest only the height and weight of the creature that made them. Initially overwriting this analogy, he spent several hundred words explaining how "seasoned travelers in dragon country" would react on finding footprints. He finally edited this part down to a paragraph:

> We don't know exactly what it [the presumed dragon] looks like and we cannot guess as to what type of dragon it is. What color is it? Is it airborne? What is its wingspan and maximum airspeed? More importantly, what does it like to eat?

Wrapping up this analogy, he returned to his topic: hydrometeors.

> We need more information than just the tracks our dragon leaves. Similar ambiguities are present in the meteorological realm. We see a large thunderstorm, but where in the storm will it hail, and to what extent? Where will it snow? Are there dangerous icing conditions that require the issuing of warnings to airplane pilots? It is here that the additional capabilities of the NCAR CP-2 radar come into play.

Fig. 7, the fourth issue tree, is also where Michael decided to put in the last section on upgrading. "I did this," he said, "to make one system resemble the next but I didn't write the new section, yet I just sketched out what I thought it would take to make the upgrade." In the issue tree of Fig. 6, this appears as "Upgrading to get" with Z(D), LDR, and HS under that heading. Michael explains: "I refined this into the issue tree in Figure 7 and wrote from that." In Fig. 7, the upgrading is now the more specific upgrading of Nexrad to CP-2 capabilities, and the capabilities themselves have better superordinate titles—Dual Wavelength instead of the "two radars" of Fig. 6; Polarization Switch and Orthomode Coupler are now one instrument-based topic.

Michael points out, "Notice that I still haven't thrown away 'spectrum width' and 'radial velocity' and 'reflectivity.' They're still dangling around out there at a very high hierarchal level with nothing noted under them, and, in fact, they came

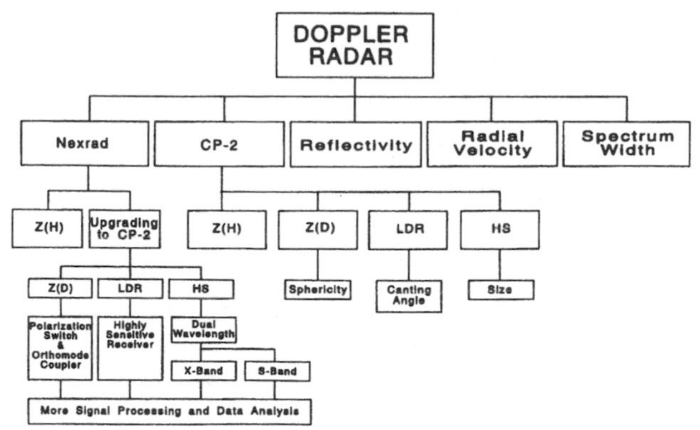

Fig. 7. A new section on upgrading appears in this issue tree.

back full-blown into the paper on the final issue tree [Fig. 8]." In Fig. 8, there are now seven levels of hierarchy, seven levels of detail. The Nexrad/CP-2 comparison is at level 4 under the organizing concept of meteorological phenomena.

Discussion

How does Michael's process compare to other successful technical writing processes? In a random survey of 180 members of the Society for Technical Communication (STC), McKee reported on a wide variety of advice offered to beginners by the professionals [26]. "First write an abstract or summary and then draw" the outline from this, suggests Arlene D. Schaller, technical writer and editor for Rohm and Haas, Philadelphia. Brainstorm and then do a rough-words outline, suggests Peter D. Rush, Chairman of Humanities at Kalamazoo Valley (MI) Community College.

Use a tape recorder, advises S. A. Miles, Vice President, Miles-Samuelson, Inc. of New York. This prevents writing block, he says: just free-associate into your microphone, play it back, and take notes on what you said. Then you're ready to start writing. A similar approach is advocated by William Baron, Specialist, Market and Sales Services of the Wyman-Gordon Company, in Worcester, MA.

Franklyn L. Squires, Senior Quality Control Analyst for General Dynamics, Oakdale, CT, presents a more traditional suggestion. He prefers index cards, with each section or chapter rating a separate card. Keeping the cards in random order as research goes on clearly separates the research and organization problems. He suggests not even thinking about ordering the cards until at least 75 percent of the content of the writing is on the cards.

Janet Robidoux, Application Analyst, Control Data Corporation, St. Paul, MN, suggests a table of contents, but admits that "by the time the manual is finished, any similarity between the first table of contents and the last is purely coincidental. Primarily it serves as a checklist so that all subjects are covered." Michael Monsour, an electric adjustor at 3M in St. Paul, MN, decides on the sections of his report, gathers material, numbers the source material in some seemingly logical order, and then picks up a packet and starts drafting.

These limited glimpses suggest that technical writers may not compose by processes identical to those of the academy

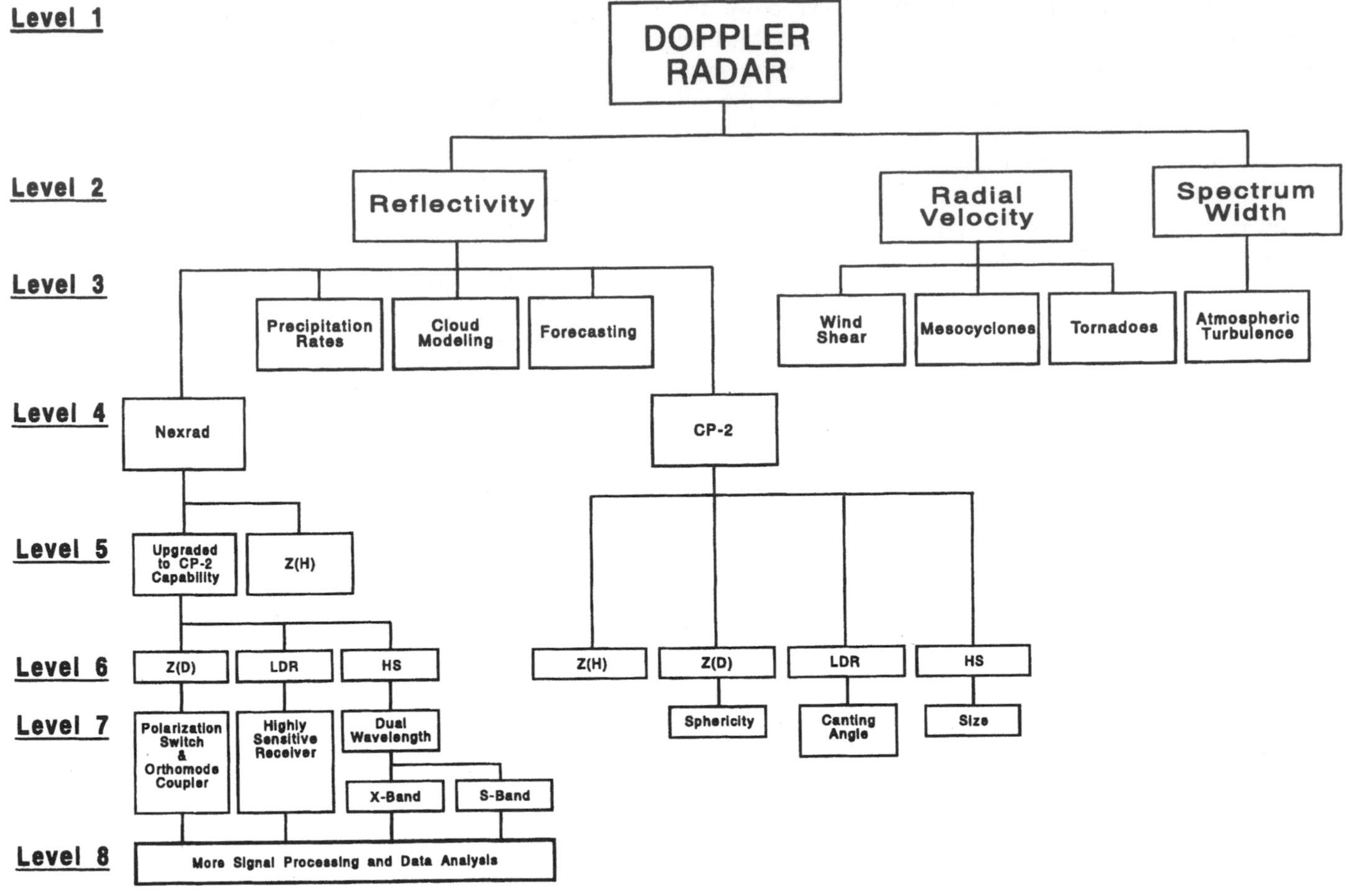

Fig. 8. The final issue tree served as a template for the final article.

or those that researchers first studied. Susan Nicholas [27] suggests this may be true; however, both Selzer [28] and Mair and Roundy [29] report results to the contrary. Selzer observed and reported on the composing process of a single engineer, Kenneth E. Nelson. Selzer found that Nelson "performs distinct planning, arranging, writing, and revising activities . . . he places special emphasis on planning and arranging at the expense of revision" [28, p. 179] Selzer concluded: "The most striking thing about Nelson's composing habits is how closely they approximate the habits of professional writers and skilled academic writers whose composing processes have been studied by other researchers" [28, p. 184].

Mair and Roundy surveyed 70 writers by questionnaire and interview. They deliberately excluded technical editors and professional technical writers. Instead they concentrated their effort on technicians, engineers, and researchers. They found [29, p. 10] that the 70 writers they surveyed "all engage in a composing process similar to that of other writers." Nonetheless, they add,

> Technical composition does differ from composing in other fields. . . . The composing process is more deliberate and strategies more clearly defined: audience, purpose and form guide planning, writing, and revising. The situational nature of writing also influences composing. [29, p. 12]

Some of the differences that Mair and Roundy mention include such factors as the form of the writing task. This form often dictates the length of the document itself, as well as the length of the prewriting and rewriting stages. Short communications merited short prewriting and short rewriting efforts. Longer documents required longer prewriting, and experienced writers often used strategies to facilitate this process. The researchers grouped these strategies as "first-order" and "second-order." First-order strategies included audience considerations, purpose of the document, and reference to standard or "classic" forms of technical writing. Second-order strategies often involved an ordering device to help with structure.

Hints of the utility of issue trees appear in such statements as the following:

> Although the list, expanded to an outline, was the most common ordering device used, writers also mentioned utilizing diagrams when describing systems, or a combination of diagrams and flow charts when describing processes, indicating the form-specific nature of this second-order strategy. [29, p. 8]

Michael credits the iterative issue tree with keeping his writing process on track. Discussing his experience with using issue trees to organize the NCAR paper, he said, "I think I wrote less . . . it [the issue tree] helps you cut and paste as you write. It is a really useful writing tool and it certainly helps with lateral thinking."

The issue tree also helped Michael stay focused on his topic: remote sensing of hydrometeors. A look at the first paragraph of each section in his final report shows how Michael used his final tree to divide his paper into major sections: INTRODUCTION, THE NEXRAD SYSTEM, THE PROBLEM, THE NCAR CP-2 RADAR SYSTEM, and CONCLUSIONS [30]. And, in the continuing recursive writing process, he made a final change from final tree to final text: he moved the meteorological parameters noted in level three of his final issue tree, Fig. 8, to his conclusions.

From levels 1 and 2 of the tree in Fig. 8, Michael wrote the introduction.

> INTRODUCTION: Pulsed-Doppler radar is used in meteorology to collect information about the state of the atmosphere. This paper is concerned mainly with the detection of various types of hydrometeors, which are water particles in solid or liquid state. Pulsed-Doppler radar measures three meteorologically relevant quantities: reflectivity, mean radial velocity, and spectrum width.

He then followed the first major branch of his tree from levels 4 through 8 to write about the first radar.

> THE NEXRAD SYSTEM: The NEXRAD radar system comprises 137 WSR-88D radars strategically spaced to provide virtually complete coverage of the conterminous United States. Each WSR-88D radar has an effective range of 50 kilometers with variable range resolution from 150 to 300 meters, and an azimuthal resolution of 10. Each of the three Doppler radar quantities measured by the Nexrad system provide several products useful to meteorologists.

He continued on this first side of the issue tree, addressing levels 5, 6, and 7 as they related to the upgrading process.

> THE PROBLEM: While the WSR-88D system provides a wealth of useful and accurate information, it cannot tell us everything we may wish to know about cloud structures. In particular, it is not able to reliably differentiate between different types of hydrometeors; rain, sleet, hail, and ice crystals. This is because different types of hydrometeors may give identical reflectivity readings. It is analogous to finding a footprint of some large, vaguely reptilian creature.

Moving back to level 4 on the second major branch of his tree, Michael next discussed the CP-2 system.

> THE NCAR CP-2 RADAR SYSTEM: While conventional (non-polarimetric) Doppler radars transmit and receive in one polarization form—horizontal, vertical, or circular— polarization diversity radars such as the NCAR CP-2 employ polarimetric techniques to observe size, shape, orientation (a measure of how far off the axis of polarization a nonspherical particle is aligned, also known as canting angle), and phase state of particles in the observation volume. The unique feature of the CP-2 radar is its ability to measure reflectivity. . . . The CP-2 radar system produces four sets of data to show the contents of any observed cloud structure. . . .

And, in the above-noted final change of his issue tree, Michael returned to pick up the ideas of level 3 in his conclusions.

> CONCLUSIONS: From the CP-2 radar parameters, we can infer a great deal about the characteristics of any given cloud structure.

Conclusion

Flower notes that ". . . the wedding of composition with rhetoric, psychology, and now reading has called on us to theorize our understanding of composing in more reflective and testable ways." Concluding this paper, she wrote, "The ultimate reason for my research is intervention . . ." [31].

We can only say that, in this case study at least, the intervention strategy of issue trees was clearly productive. Michael's writing process on this task was clearly iterative and problem-solving, as he developed a series of issue trees to guide his process as it moved back and forth among prewriting, writing, and rewriting.

In retrospect, Michael says the following:

> I think the best thing about the issue trees is that they "clean up" the structural organization of the paper. Before, I'd plop myself down and write a rough draft, then revise again and again, sort of filtering my paper through more and more refinements. Come to think of it, maybe "filter" isn't the right analogy for my previous writing efforts, since sometimes I would end up putting things back in that I had taken out. Anyway, the graphical (hierarchal) look of the trees is the important part. Which makes sense: after all, the clearest way to represent information is in graphical form. In the process, I would come up with ideas in my head, put each of them in individually, cut and paste, etc. With the trees, I'm not dealing with each little revision close up in its little section of my paper. I have a broad view of ALL of my paper, how each section fits, vertically and horizontally, with the whole.

And that may be the key to why issue trees work so well with the visually oriented engineering writer.

References

[1] D. B. Rohman, "Pre-writing: The stage of discovery in the writing process," *College Composition and Commun.*, vol. 16, no. 2, pp. 106–112, 1965.

[2] J. Emig, "The composing processes of twelfth graders," Urbana, IL: National Council of Teachers of English, 1971, Research Report No. 13.

[3] P. Elbow, *Writing Without Teachers*. New York: Oxford University Press, 1973.

[4] W. R. Winterowd, "'Topics' and levels in the composing process," *College English*, vol. 34, no. 5, pp. 701–709, 1973.

[5] D. H. Graves, "An examination of the writing processes of seven-year old children." *Res. in the Teaching of English*, vol. 9, pp. 227–241, 1975.

[6] E. W. Nold, "Alternatives to mad-hatterism," in *Linguistics, Stylistics, and the Teaching of Composition,* D. McQuade (Ed.), Akron, OH: University of Akron, 1979, pp. 103–117.
[7] A. N. Applebee, "Trends in written composition." Paper presented at the Midwest School for Improvement Forum, Milwaukee, WI, October 1979.
[8] D. M. Murray, "Internal revision: A process of discovery," in *Research on Composing: Points of Departure,* C. R. Cooper and L. Odell, (Eds.), Urbana, IL: National Council of Teachers of English, pp. 85–105, 1978.
[9] C. Koch and J. M. Brazil. *Strategies for Teaching the Composition Process.* Urbana, IL: National Council of Teachers of English, 1978.
[10] J. Britton. "The composing processes and the functions of writing," in *Research on Composing: Points of Departure,* C. R. Cooper and L. Odell, (Eds.), Urbana, IL: National Council of Teachers of English, 1978, pp. 13–28.
[11] S. Perl, "The composing processes of unskilled college writers," *Res. in the Teaching of English,* vol. 13, 1979, pp. 317–336.
[12] A. Matsuhashi, Producing written discourse: A theory-based description of the temporal characteristics of three discourse types from four competent grade 12 writers. Unpublished doctoral dissertation, State University of New York at Buffalo, 1979.
[13] "The process model of document design," in *Simply Stated,* newsletter of the Document Design Center, American Institutes for Research, 1055 Thomas Jefferson Street NW, Washington, D.C. 20007. Reprinted in *IEEE Trans. Prof. Commun.,* vol. 24, no. 4, 1981, pp. 176–178.
[14] L. S. Flower and J. R. Hayes, "A cognitive process theory of writing," *College Composition and Commun.,* vol. 32, 1981, pp. 365–387.
[15] D. Wojick, "Planning for Discourse," *Water Spectrum,* Winter 1975–76, pp. 25–29.
[16] L. Flower, *Problem-Solving Strategies for Writing.* 3rd ed. San Diego, CA: Harcourt, Brace, Jovanovich, 1984.
[17] M. Hairston, *Contemporary Composition,* 4th ed. Boston, MA: Houghton, Mifflin, 1986.
[18] S. Lynn, "Reading the writing process: Toward a theory of current pedagogies," *College English,* vol. 49, no. 8, 1987, pp. 902–910.
[19] M. Carter, "The idea of expertise: An exploration of cognitive and social dimensions of writing," *College Composition and Commun.,* vol. 41, no. 3, 1990, pp. 265–286.
[20] J. Harris, "Rethinking the pedagogy of problem-solving," *J. of Teaching Writing,* vol. 7, no. 2, 1988, pp. 157–165.
[21] J. Barzun, "The process model of document design," *IEEE Trans. Prof. Commun.,* vol. 24, no. 4, 1981, p. 178.
[22] G.T. Smith, "Difference in the thinking-writing process," *J. Tech. Writing and Commun.,* vol. 2, no. 1, 1972, pp. 19–32.
[23] L. Bitzer, "The rhetorical situation," *Philosophy and Rhetoric,* vol. 1, 1968, pp. 1–14.
[24] J. Dennett, "Writing for Your Readers—What the Research Shows," 1992, Applied Technology Council, Redwood City, CA.
[25] G. Gopen and J. Swan, "The science of science writing," *Amer. Scientist,* vol. 78, 1990, pp. 550–558.
[26] B. K. McKee, "Do writers use an outline when they write?" *Tech. Commun.,* vol. 19, no. 1, 1972, p. 10.
[27] S. Nicholas, "A video observational study of the writing process of college students in a non-academic situation," Doctoral dissertation, Oakland University, 1983. *Dissertation Abstracts Int.,* vol. 44, 1983, 03-A.
[28] J. Selzer, "The composing processes of an engineer," *College Composition and Commun.,* vol. 34, no. 2, 1983, pp. 178–187.
[29] D. Mair and N. Roundy, "The composing process of technical writers, a preliminary study." Paper presented at the College Composition and Communication Conference, Dallas, 1981. (ERIC Document Reproduction Service No. ED 200994).
[30] M. Hseih, "The Dragon's Footprints: Microwave Radar Remote Sensing of Hydrometeors with the NEXRAD/WSR-88D and NCAR CP-2 Radar Systems," 1992, National Center for Atmospheric Research, Boulder, CO.
[31] L. Flower, "Cognition, context, and theory building," *College Composition and Commun.,* vol. 40, no. 3, 1989, pp. 282–311.

Joann Temple Dennett teaches science writing at the University of Colorado, Boulder, CO 80309 USA. A frequent lecturer in industry and government on writing technique, she has published in a wide variety of media, from popular newspapers and magazines to reference books and engineering reports. Dr. Dennett is an associate editor of IEEE Transactions on Professional Communication.

Michael Hseih is a student in the Department of Electrical Engineering at the University of California, Irvine, CA USA.

Ready, Aim—Write!

RUTH C. SAVAKINAS

Abstract—**This paper details a methodical audience identification approach called a 'pre-write,' which will greatly reduce the need for rewriting a document. To pre-write, the writer must write a statement of the purpose of the document and a statement identifying both the intended audience and the implications of writing to that audience. Five questions the writer must answer about the audience are given, and information on audience identification and the needs of particular audiences is included.**

[Author's note: To educators, pre-writing is the first of the six steps used to teach the writing process and includes group discussions, reading of models, and practice in research and organizational methods. In technical communication, the phase known as pre-writing encompasses all activities that occur before the first draft is begun—for example, performing research, taking notes, and preparing outlines. The pre-write method I present in this paper, which focuses on writing about technical subjects, may be applied by anyone preparing to write. This pre-write method involves identifying the document's purpose and intended audience.]

WHEN WE WRITE, we want to feel confident that our readers understand—perhaps even enjoy—what we have written for them.

If we know our readers, we may interview them to discover what they want in a document. When we cannot communicate directly with our audience, or when our audience is not clearly defined, we can use other methods.

Many test the readability of their writing by applying a formula such as Gunning's Fog Index. A technical writer or editor or a colleague may be asked to review a document for accuracy and clarity; this is also a readability analysis. A nontechnical person may also provide valuable feedback as to whether the material is understandable. Instructional or procedural materials can be tested for usability by a representative sample of the intended audience. However, since these methods are applied after writing, considerable rewriting may be necessary. It is obviously preferable to do the best possible work the first time.

PRE-WRITE VERSUS REWRITE

Complex technical writing is likely to be very difficult to read. Readability further decreases when the writer does not define major ideas for the reader and when the written document is not relevant to the reader's experiences and interests. These two impediments can be eliminated if you clearly define your purpose and your audience; this definition is what I call a *pre-write*.

You can dramatically increase the clarity and luster of your writing, and reduce the need for tedious rewriting, by following this simple pre-writing approach.

WRITE YOUR PURPOSE

Whether you write a memo or a book, always consider your reasons for writing before you begin:

- What is the subject of your document? Will you introduce a theory, propose an improvement, explain a technique, describe a process, or report the results of your research?
- Where will your document appear? You may be writing a report that will be circulated within your company, an article that will appear in a commercial publication, a research paper that will be published in a professional journal, or a procedure that will be used in training.
- Why are you writing? Is your purpose to instruct, inform, persuade, or inspire?

The subject and purpose of your document must be clear to you if you hope to make it clear to your audience. As to the subject, think about the breadth (which topics) and the depth (how much detail) of coverage needed. Doubtless you will slant the material in one way if your purpose is informative, in quite another if your purpose is persuasive. You must also consider your goals and aims in writing the document.

With your goals and aims in mind, write your purpose clearly in a statement of a few short sentences. Keep this statement nearby and refer to it often as you write. This reference ensures that you communicate the document's purpose to your reader and that you maintain your focus on the purpose of your writing.

IDENTIFY YOUR AUDIENCE

When you write to a friend, the letter is easy to write because you know the person you're addressing. Also, you usually write the way you speak. Writing or speaking to someone you don't know isn't as easy, and you can't al-

Ruth Savakinas is a senior technical writer with the Applied Technology Division of Computer Sciences Corporation in San Diego, California.

Reprinted from *IEEE Trans. Prof. Comm.*, vol. 31, no. 1, pp. 5–7, March 1988.

ways be sure that you're communicating clearly. If your audience does not understand what they have read, or becomes so lost or bored that they don't finish reading what you have written, it may be that you did not truly write it to and for them. To write to and for your audience, you must get to know them.

To identify your audience, there are five questions you must answer:

- Who will be reading your document?
- What prior knowledge do these readers have about the subject?
- What do these readers need to know?
- Why will these readers read your document?
- How will these readers use the information you provide?

Who the Readers Are

Your readers may be administrators and executives, or your supervisors and colleagues. They may be professionals from various fields of science and engineering, or professionals from a single field of science or engineering. They may be nontechnically trained individuals, or the general public (a mixture of these categories of readers).

You may have direct access to your audience. Or you may have access to audience profiles maintained by your company's market research or personnel departments, or your professional society. If not, consult library sources to learn some things about the profession(s) and to become familiar with the educational level of your readership.

If most of your readers are in a specific profession, you can consult the Occupational Outlook Handbook published by the U.S. Department of Labor's Bureau of Labor Statistics to become acquainted with the profession. This handbook describes the nature of the work, the working conditions, training and other qualifications, opportunities for professional advancement, average earnings in the profession, and related occupations. If, for example, you are writing about an automotive electronic modification to an audience of automobile mechanics, this handbook reveals that although knowledge of electronics was quite a narrow specialization in the past, today's mechanics must be familiar with basic electronic principles.

Another helpful source is the Statistical Abstract of the United States, published annually by the Bureau of the Census of the U.S. Department of Commerce. Among the many subjects about which this book provides data is educational attainment by profession. Continuing our study of automobile mechanics, we learn that more than half (52 percent) graduated from high school and that 24 percent attended college.

The average educational level is an important factor both in the choice of vocabulary and the sentence structure, and in the psychological approach of your writing. Knowing the educational level will help you answer the questions pertaining to what readers already know and what they need to know.

What the Readers Know

Note the educational level of your anticipated readers and the specific educational background required in the profession. (Amount of experience also affects the readers' knowledge; however, such data may not be available to you.) Compare this information with the subject and purpose of your document to determine the relationship between the two. For example, the subject may be of a general nature given the readers' background or it may concern a highly advanced topic within a narrow, specialized branch of the profession.

This comparison will also help you to assume a specific level of experience at which to aim your document: you must decide if you will write to the beginner, the reader with intermediate-level experience, or the expert.

Let's assume you are introducing a new plating process. The new process is similar to a plating process that has been used by your company's production technicians for several years. Your technicians' familiarity with the existing process eliminates the need to explain steps common to both processes; instead, your document can refer to these similarities and focus on the differences.

What the Readers Need to Know

Now that you have an idea of who your readers are and what they know, you can decide how much background information to include. You can also determine what level of detail is necessary to ensure that your readers will understand your document.

If you are preparing a report for administrators and executives, you should condense the subject into an exact statement of the purpose and the outcome; they want the gist of the subject, not the minute details. Be logical, assume an appropriate tone and attitude, avoid overly technical language, and omit opinion. In writing for your supervisors and colleagues you should also remain factual and brief, but for this audience jargon and implication are usually acceptable.

Professionals from different fields of science and engineering want precise details; they want to know about procedures and measurements used, applications of results, and any sources of error. Though a high-level vocabulary can be used, field-specific terminology should be avoided. With readers from one profession of science or engineering, field-specific vocabulary is appropriate. These readers are interested in precise details; however, they also want you to locate the problem and indicate its importance in the field.

Readers in the nontechnical audience will require full

background information and explanation of any uncommon terms and concepts. Be diplomatic, clarify goals, and motivate your audience.

When writing for a general audience, you should decide what your readers' need to know based on the level of experience at which you are aiming. Beginners require extensive coverage of topics and a great amount of detail; assume no prior knowledge on the part of these readers, and introduce all basic concepts and terminology to them. Those on the intermediate level also need detail, but they want to know about the unique aspects of the subject and also want a good reference section. Experts require detail only on the extremely technical aspects of the subject and prefer an extensive reference section. No matter which audience you are addressing, all readers want and need a carefully organized document. Give them concrete information and clear examples. Vary your vocabulary, sentence length, and sentence structure to maintain their interest.

Why the Readers Are Reading

Two people may read the same document for entirely different reasons: an engineering technician may read about computer architecture to gain an understanding of it; an engineer may read about it to find ways to improve its efficiency.

Few people read technical documents for pleasure or relaxation. More commonly, they read such documents to learn. They may be reading to increase their knowledge of the field or to improve their job performance. Some are motivated to read by financial reasons, such as those seeking promotion within their occupation or seeking to change occupations. Many simply need to learn how to operate a new piece of equipment.

Motivating psychological needs and desires may also differ. Some readers may be motivated by the need for personal fulfillment or discovery, or by the desire for achievement or prestige. Others may be motivated by the need for security or preservation, or by the desire for status or freedom from pressure. Considering the likely or possible motivating factors may cause you to alter your writing approach.

The subject and purpose of your document, and your knowledge of your intended audience, will all help you decide why readers are reading and how they will be using the information you present.

How the Readers Will Use the Information

When readers are seeking to increase their knowledge (whether in an effort to gain a promotion, to change occupations, or to learn for the pleasure of learning), be sure to show how your document fits into the literature in that field. If a reader is reading to improve job performance, examine the information and omit anything that is irrelevant.

When you are writing instructions for operating a piece of equipment or for performing a task, remember that your reader will want these instructions logically grouped and presented in 'bite-size' chunks (procedure steps). Decisions for grouping and presenting such instructions must also include environmental considerations, that is, the work area in which the document will be used.

WRITE ABOUT YOUR AUDIENCE

The last step in pre-writing is to write about your readers. It is important to actually write down your answers to the five questions above, on paper. The result will be a fairly clear picture of your audience. As you answer the questions about your readers, you should also write about the implications those answers will have for your writing approach; write about how you will focus or slant the material to meet your readers' needs.

USE YOUR 'PRE-WRITE'

Your pre-written statements of purpose and audience identification will help keep you 'on target' as you write, and help your readers understand—perhaps even enjoy—what you have written.

So, ready, aim—write!

SUGGESTED ADDITIONAL READING

1. Gowers, E., *Plain Words*, New York: Knopf, 1954.
2. Gunning, R., *The Technique of Clear Writing*, Rev. ed., New York: McGraw-Hill, 1968.
3. Klare, G. R., and Buck, B., *Know Your Reader: The Scientific Approach to Readability*, New York: American Book, 1954.
4. Leonard, D. C., and McGuire, P. J., ed. *Readings in Technical Writing*, New York: Macmillan, 1983.
5. McGehee, B., *The Complete Guide to Writing Software User Manuals*, Cincinnati: Writer's Digest Books, 1984.
6. Sides, C. H., *How to Write Papers and Reports About Computer Technology*, Philadelphia: ISI Press, 1984.

Beginnings and Endings: Keys to Better Engineering Technical Writing

—MARCIA MARTENS PIERSON AND BION L. PIERSON

Abstract—*Engineers face many technical writing tasks that have many features in common: title, abstract, introduction, problem formulation, methods, results, and conclusions. But it is often very difficult to actually write these segments in the same order they appear in the finished product. Instead of this linear approach, we recommend a modular approach starting with the core sections, the methods and results that researchers know best, and working backward and forward to pick up the beginnings and endings. We show how the beginning and ending sections build on the core sections and offer strategies to improve them.*

Index Terms—*Abstracts, conclusions, introductions, modular writing approach, technical writing strategies, titles.*

Manuscript received April 1997.
This paper is based on a presentation given at the 57th Annual American Society of Engineering Education North Midwest Section Meeting, St. Cloud, MN, October 5–6, 1995.
M. M. Pierson is with Engineering Publication and Communication Services, Iowa State University, Ames, IA 50011-3060 USA.
B. L. Pierson is with Aerospace Engineering and Engineering Mechanics, Iowa State University, Ames, IA 50011-3231 USA.
IEEE PII: S 0361-1434(97)08925-X.

CONVENTIONAL wisdom says that engineers as a group dread writing. Yet the results of a recent survey of practicing aerospace engineers and scientists [1] show that practicing engineers spend a significant portion of their time creating their own technical documents or working on those of others. For example, "the average number of hours spent per week producing technical communications varied from a mean low of 19.6 hours to a mean high of 23.3 hours," depending whether the engineers worked in design or development, "and a mean low of 14.9 to a mean high of 19.6 hours" if they worked on technical communications received from others. Add to that engineering academics who write proposals, journal articles, project reports, and conference papers, to say nothing of lectures and class handouts, and we see that the need to write well is pervasive.

Engineering and writing have been inextricably linked from the early Roman times [2] as shown in the earliest translations of the Roman architect Vitruvius [3] and of the Roman engineer Frontinus [4]. Both stressed the need to keep a written record of what had been done so that those who came later could follow their steps. Early in this century, the famous scientist Charles Steinmetz [5] had a particularly clear view of the value of good engineering writing. He was concerned among other things with how well research reports communicate knowledge to particular audiences. Even these early engineers felt responsible not only for practicing engineering but also for documenting it and making their knowledge available to others. That goal is still important today and is amplified by the knowledge that how well engineers conduct research, write, and publish has a great impact on the advancement of their careers as well as on the advancement of knowledge.

While the fields of engineering and the language to discuss them have expanded enormously over the centuries, the need to communicate engineering knowledge is still at the heart of the engineering profession both in industry and academia. We

Reprinted from *IEEE Trans. Prof. Comm.*, vol. PC-40, no. 4, pp. 299–304, December 1997.

want to look at the major problems we see in the technical papers we edit as the editor of an international scientific journal and as a technical editor in an engineering college. We first consider the overall writing process and how to get started. Then we explore the four parts of technical writing that seem to give authors the most difficulty: title, abstract, introduction, and conclusions. These beginnings and endings play a critical role in the overall success of any technical paper [6], [7]. Our recommendation is to adopt a modular approach for writing a technical report or article. By that we mean to pull the sections out of their normal order and work on them in the order of ease for the author. The discussion focuses on determining the purpose of each of these beginning and ending components, the order in which they might be written, and strategies for writing each one.

Getting Started

J. H. Mitchell [8] says that "most research and writing projects begin with a problem and end with a solution." Thus to get started, writers need to develop a working problem statement. This is simply a qualitative statement of the main message or messages in the paper under construction. What will the publication of this paper accomplish? For instance, we might state the problem for this paper as follows: researchers frequently have trouble writing technical papers because they get bogged down in the beginnings and endings. Such a working problem statement will help keep the writer focused on the main objective while working on each of the components.

With a working problem statement in hand, researchers can do the literature review and examine what people currently know and where the issues are. Until researchers know something about past work, they will find planning the research, assessing how their ideas fit with previous work, and determining the likely contributions difficult at best. Abstracting journals are the place to start. A subject search gives the scope and key players on any given topic. From there, an author search will yield the specific articles most likely to be of interest. Checking the references in these articles will likely add a number of other authors and titles of interest.

After researchers have compiled a list of articles, the next question is how to deal with them. Before writing can begin, information must be gathered and thoughts assembled. One method we find helpful in the beginning stages of writing is to label a piece of paper or a computer file with the various sections of the paper. Generally, researchers know what should be included in a technical paper: 1) title, 2) abstract, 3) introduction, 4) problem formulation, 5) methods, 6) conclusions, and 7) references. The task is to enter salient points or quotes from the literature under the proper heading with bibliographic information noted. The order of the information under each heading is not critical at this point because entries can be rearranged later.

Once the notes are taken, researchers typically think that the best way to write the paper is to start at the beginning and write till they come to the end. That approach is a logical and linear way to think, but it is not necessarily the most effective way to work through the writing process. Facing a blank piece of paper labeled introduction or abstract can be daunting. Rather we recommend a modular approach in which we separate the sections of the paper and work on them in the order that is easiest for the writer.

Methods and Results

When the research or project is complete, researchers know the most about the problem that has just been solved, the methods used to solve it, and the results achieved. Thus it seems auspicious to begin with the problem formulation and the methods used to solve the problem—What worked? What didn't? and Why?—and describe the process used to get to a solution. Reviewing their laboratory notebooks or computer files shows how they tackled the problem—the false starts, the twists and turns, and the triumphs. Beginning with what they know best gets writers off dead center and into the fray. At this creative stage, writers do not need to worry too much about the grammar, but rather they need to concentrate on tracking the research.

When a draft of the methods is complete, writers can go on to the next section and show the results achieved. The questions they need to ask themselves include: What did I find out that I didn't know before? What do the data indicate? How do my results compare with those of others? After these questions are answered, writers need to go back to the laboratory notebook or computer files to document the results. Tables and figures can be used to display the results and to show comparisons with other methods. Once a draft of the results is finished, the bulk of the paper is well under way. This achievement will give writers the confidence to tackle the next section, which might be either the introduction or conclusions.

Writing the Introduction

For many situations, the introduction will be the best place to start. The purpose of the introduction is to encourage the reader to read the whole article. It explains why there is a need or a problem and how the author will deal with it. The introduction usually motivates the present study, provides a literature review, and explains how the current work fits with what has gone before. In addition, a brief summary of the findings is frequently included. What better time to write the introduction than when the results section has just been completed. The importance of the work and how it fits in with the larger scheme of research in this area should be the clearest at this time.

Much has been written about the function of introductions. Menzel, Jones, and Boyd [9] indicate that "the first sentence of the introduction is a kind of a road map, a brief indication of the direction the argument will take and the nature of the goal." Rada [10], on the other hand, touts the role of introductions as assuring the likelihood that a reader will move on to the body of the article. Miles [11] states that the introduction "usually gives an overview of the problem confronted, the theory behind the methodology used, and a statement about the significance or importance of the current research," while Mills and Walter [12] cite four specific functions of the technical introduction: to state the subject, purpose, scope, and plan of development.

The common themes in the literature indicate that the introduction contains the problem statement, shows what has been done on the problem in the past, and relates the current work to past history. As writers do research, they are all indebted to the researchers who have preceded them. We like to think of this progression of knowledge as a pyramid, with each higher level resting on the base of the previous one. If the research area is well-developed, writers can cite survey papers for the earlier works and then spend more time reviewing the last ten years of research. Having shown their place on this pyramid, they can indicate their methods of development and indicate briefly what they have found. Questions for writers to ask themselves include: Is my approach an incremental contribution or a new way of approaching the problem? Specifically, how does my work differ from previously published work? Be explicit about this; do not make the reader guess what is new. End the introduction by stating the importance of the research.

Some authors, such as Mills and Walter [12], recommend including the organization of the paper. For example, "This report will be divided into five major parts: . . ." While perhaps useful for a long report, this information already appears in the table of contents. We do not recommend that writers end the introduction with such a paragraph unless the guidelines call for it. Such a paragraph is a weak ending to an important section; it is usually filler and does not advance the work. A better method is to end the introduction with a clear statement of the importance of the research and then use subheadings to indicate the structure of the remainder of the paper.

Writing the Conclusions

When the introduction has been drafted, the next section to tackle is the conclusions. Writers have written about their vision of the project, the methods they have used, and the results they have obtained. Now it is time for them to step back, ask themselves the following questions, and assess what they have learned. What does the research mean? Why is it significant? What contributions does it make, i.e., what value has it added to the body of knowledge in the field? How will others be able to use it? Where do we go from here?

Authors of technical writing books and technical society publication guides offer a variety of thoughts on the function of conclusions. For example, Marder [13] notes that "conclusions give a sense of completion to the report" and "conclusions and recommendations (either positive or negative) comprise the value received for the money spent." "Conclusions," notes the American Institute of Physics [14], "are convictions based on evidence. If you state conclusions, make certain that they follow logically from data you presented in the paper, and that they agree with what you promised in the introduction." Lannon [15] lists the functions of conclusions as a "summary of information in the body, comprehensive interpretation of information in the body, and recommendations and proposals based on the information in the body."

From our perspective, authors need to make a distinction between a summary that deals with the process of the research and a conclusion that focuses on the contributions of the research. For a long report, writers may want to summarize the work briefly and then analyze the significance of the research in a final section titled Summary and Conclusions. However, a conclusion should not simply restate what was done, and writers should avoid the trap of repeating a lot of what was stated in the introduction. Thus the summary ought to be kept to a minimum and instead the emphasis should be placed on interpreting the results and especially on identifying the contributions. It may be advantageous to list the main conclusions with bullets or numbers so that readers can identify them immediately.

Most journal articles should not include a summary. Rather the conclusions should delineate the significance of the research. What do we know now that we did not know at the beginning? How good are the results? Writers should be as quantitative as possible when they state their conclusions. For example, use "The XYZ method achieved a 15.7% reduction in manufacturing time," rather than "the XYZ method works well." The IEEE Power Engineering Society [16] suggests several additional questions for authors to answer at the end of the conclusions: "What are the advantages and limitations of the work?" and "What are the recommendations for further work?" Perhaps the paper has several small contributions or maybe a big one. Whichever it is, the conclusions section is the place to wrap up the package and deliver it to the reader.

Developing a Title

The title provides the first hook for the reader. Not only are titles important for their content but also for their visibility, especially when they appear in an abstracting journal. Finding the right words and phrases is crucial to bringing the reader into the article itself. Our strategy for writing titles is to jot down key words and play with them to see how they might go together. While writing the paper, we keep a list of alternatives so that a number of possible titles are available, either to use as is or as a springboard for a new title.

What makes a good title? Make it short and make it snappy sums up the thinking of many technical communicators [9], [17]. An exception is Jones [18], who indicates that unlike literary books, whose titles are short to arouse interest, report titles are primarily informative and concerned more with completeness than conciseness. He does advocate being as brief as possible, but up to 40 or 50 words may be used. Many other technical writers advise making the title brief while still descriptive. Marder [13], for example, suggests that a title "is a phrase announcing the essence of the report," but it should not be a summary of the report's contents. Since many journals limit the length of titles, authors should check the guidelines. Even if guidelines pose no restrictions, a good goal for title length is recommended by the American Mathematical Society [19], which asserts that "A title of more than ten or twelve words is likely to be miscopied, misquoted, distorted, and cursed." Jones [18] also suggests that the title may begin with the words "Report on..." or "A Study of...." Most current writers on technical writing recommend instead using key words to start the title [9], [17]. The American Mathematical Society [19] is more explicit than that when they advise authors to "make the title as informative as possible, but avoid redundancy, and eschew the medieval practice of letting the title serve as an inflated advertisement."

To shorten a draft title, cut the words that are not essential. As an example, consider the title, "An Investigation into the Effects of Residential Air-Conditioning Maintenance in Reducing the Demand for Electrical Energy." Clearly, the author is considering the relationship between residential air conditioning maintenance and electric power demand. A more compact title would simply be "Role of Air-Conditioning Maintenance on Electric Power Demand." This new title reflects the relationship between the two parts of the subject and reduces the number of words by half.

Most importantly, the title should reflect the focus of the paper and allow an editor to place the paper in the appropriate category in an abstracting journal, conference attendees to know whether they want to hear the paper, or managers to know if a particular report is of interest for the problem at hand. Titles then are critical—they need to have the keywords that will help a researcher make the first cut, e.g., is the paper about linear or nonlinear programming? control theory? artificial neural networks? Also pick some of the title words to distinguish your work from previous papers. For example, if in the past a particular problem has only been solved using linear methods and you are solving the problem with nonlinear methods, make sure you include the word *nonlinear* in your title. Consider inventing a new word to make your title stand out, e.g., "Optimal Aerocapture Trajectories"—aerocapture is not in the dictionary, but it conveys the main focus of the paper.

Once a title is chosen, take time to proofread it and check for spelling, grammar, and capitalization. For example, "articles (a, an, the), coordinating conjunctions (and, but, or, for, nor) and prepositions, regardless of length, are lowercased unless they are the first or last word of the title or subtitle. The *to* in infinitives is also lowercased" [20].

Writing the Abstract

Abstracts are often the hardest part to write and yet are the most important. Thus we recommend leaving it till last so writers have their whole text in front of them. Abstracts play a role both within the paper and outside it. As part of the paper, abstracts give a brief overview and help the reader know and judge the value of a particular piece of scientific writing. Outside the paper, the abstract serves as a filter for classifying papers. Abstracts of journal articles appear in abstracting journals and in this form they help readers decide if they want to see the whole paper or not. For reports, the abstract gives the first clue to an agency whether the work is worthwhile and whether they will look beyond the abstract. To get a paper read, authors must take great care to give enough information in the appropriate language (buzz words if you will) so that researchers can quickly decide if they will read the full paper.

Authors writing about abstracts provide a variety of recommendations. Menzel, Jones, and Boyd [9] admonish writers "to present a clear, concise summary, preferably in one paragraph, of the purpose and most import results of the investigation together with a minimum of the theory it is based on" to be used in abstracting journals. Booth [17] advises authors "to state briefly what you did. Then the main results.... State the conclusion in the last sentence." Marder [13] calls abstracts a "thumbnail (sketch) of the report itself."

Regardless of the words used to describe an abstract, the abstract is critical in getting a researcher's work out to the scientific community. In our view, the abstract contains some elements of an introduction, problem statement, methods, results, and conclusions. A sentence for each of the main areas may be all that is needed. The abstract may be quite brief, perhaps 100–200 words or less. This means the writer has to be concise. Also the writer should state the relevant facts as objectively as possible and avoid self-praise and overt advertising. We like to think of writing an abstract as including five parts: 1) the context of the work, 2) the problem statement—specifically what the scope is, 3) the methods—how the work was done, 4) the results—what discoveries were made, and 5) the conclusions—the significance and contributions of the work.

In writing abstracts, do not include references; the abstract should be able to stand alone. Likewise, avoid acronyms unless the word or word cluster is cumbersome and is used more than once. Then identify it the first time it is used in the abstract and again the first time it is used in the body of the paper.

Conclusion

Writing a technical paper using a modular approach is not the norm, but it does have some advantages. Writing first what a researcher knows best builds confidence and gets the creative juices flowing. By the time researchers get to the tougher sections, such as the abstract, most of the ideas that they need are already in hand. The task then is to pick out these salient points and key words and weave them together to tell the story in miniature.

If writers stopped with discrete modules, of course, the paper might not hold together as an organic whole. Therefore, the writer's last task, once all the sections are in place, is to look critically at how they fit together. Questions to ask include: Does each section perform its appointed task? Is the order logical? Do the ideas flow together or are better transitions needed? Does the same material appear more than once? Can the writing be tightened and made clearer? Does the writing fit the audience? For example, if it is for technical peers, is the background condensed and the methods, results, and conclusions amplified? If it is for the boss in industry, is the problem statement clear and the big picture painted in broad strokes? Is there enough detail to back up the generalities but not so much as to discourage the reader? Does the title contain the key words that will hook the reader?

We have talked little about the quality of the writing itself because that is not our primary focus here. But since the quality of the writing is very important, we offer a suggestion for writers once they have done their best. That is to ask for some peer review from colleagues or an editorial service. Getting feedback from an impartial reader will help a writer see the places where readers go astray and where reader's questions are unanswered.

The format of the paper is another detail that needs attention. If you are writing a journal article, consult the journal to see how they want the document to appear. Pay attention to heading styles and how references should be cited and listed. These guidelines will also specify number of pages, how to deal with tables and figures, and so on. Putting your paper in the recommended format is a subtle way of saying to the editor that this paper is prepared especially for that journal. These details **are** noticed by journal editors.

As we take a long view of technical articles, we see that the writer has three key places to hook the reader—each one reveals a little more about the topic, like layers of an onion: for example, 1) the title gives readers key words to catch their interest; 2) the abstract gives a mini overview of the whole paper, kind of a teaser that gives more detail than the title; and 3) the introduction gives the scope of the problem and the objectives of the research, the background and how it relates to past work, and the nature of the data and analysis. Along with the conclusions, these beginnings are crucial for engaging readers' attention. Most seasoned researchers do not read all papers straight through. They start with the title, of course, then the abstract, the conclusions, a quick scan of the references, next the introduction, and then maybe on to the body of the paper. Will the beginnings and endings of your paper survive this sequence of inspection? Writers who can master these sections will boost their chances of publishing their articles and having others read them.

References

[1] T. E. Pinelli, R. O. Barclay, M. L. Keene, J. M. Kennedy, and L. F. Hecht, "From student to entry-level professional: Examining the role of language and written communications in the reaculturation of aerospace engineering students," *Tech. Commun.*, vol. 42, no. 3, p. 497, 1996.

[2] H. Petroski, "Engineers as writers," *Amer. Scientist*, p. 419, Sept.–Oct. 1993.

[3] Vitruvius, *The Ten Books on Architecture* (translated by Morris Hicky Morgan). New York: Dover, 1960, p. 4 (originally published 1st century B.C.E.).

[4] Frontinus. *The Two Books on the Water Supply of the City of Rome* (translated by Clemens Herschel), 2nd ed. New York: Longmans, 1913 (originally published 97 A.D.).

[5] C. P. Steinmetz, *Engineering Mathematics: A Series of Lectures Delivered at Union College*, 3rd ed. New York: McGraw-Hill, 1917, pp. 290–292.

[6] J. E. Harmon and D. R. Hamrin, "Bibliography on communicating technical research information," *IEEE Trans. Prof. Commun.*, vol. 36, pp. 2–6, 1993.

[7] M. J. Charney and J. H. Williams, "From start to finish: Approaches to introductions and conclusions in technical writing textbooks," *IEEE Trans. Prof. Commun.*, vol. 33, pp. 220–225, 1990.

[8] J. H. Mitchell, *Writing for Professional and Technical Journals*. New York, 1968, p. 6.

[9] D. H. Menzel, H. M. Jones, and L. G. Boyd, *Writing a Technical Paper*. New York: McGraw-Hill, 1961, pp. 16 and 336.

[10] J. Rada, Jr., "Anatomy of a technical introduction," *The Editorial Eye*, vol. 17, pp. 2–4, 1994.

[11] T. H. Miles, *Critical Thinking and Writing for Science and Technology*. San Diego, CA: Harcourt Brace Jovanovich, 1990, p. 156.

[12] G. H. Mills and J. A. Walter, *Technical Writing*, 4th ed. New York: Holt, Rinehart, and Winston, 1978, pp. 226, 241, and 242.

[13] D. Marder, *The Craft of Technical Writing*. New York: Macmillan,1960, pp. 195, 239, and 336.

[14] AIP Publication Board, *AIP Style Manual*, 4th ed. New York: Amer. Inst. Physics, 1990, p. 4.

[15] J. M. Lannon, *Technical Writing*, 2nd ed. Boston, MA: Little, Brown and Co., 1982.

[16] *IEEE Power Engineering Society Publication Guide*. Piscataway, NJ: Tech. Council and Pub. Dept., IEEE Power Eng. Soc., 1995, p. 9.

[17] V. Booth, *Communicating in Science: Writing and Speaking*. Cambridge, U.K.: Cambridge Univ. Press, 1984.

[18] W. P. Jones, *Writing Scientific Papers and Reports*, 8th ed. (revised by M. Keene). Dubuque, IA: Wm. C. Brown, 1981, p. 199.

[19] *The Manual for Authors of Mathematical Papers*. Providence, RI: Amer. Math. Soc., 1990, p. 1.

[20] *The Chicago Manual of Style*, 14th ed. Chicago, IL: Univ. Chicago Press, 1993, pp. 282–283.

Marcia Martens Pierson is an editor in Engineering Publication and Communication Services at Iowa State University. She received the B.S. and M.A. degrees in English from Iowa State University and Columbia University, respectively. She works with both faculty and students to prepare papers, proposals, contract reports, newsletters, departmental annual reports, conference proceedings, and other documents for the College of Engineering at Iowa State.

Bion L. Pierson is a Professor in the Department of Aerospace Engineering and Engineering Mechanics at Iowa State University. He received the Ph.D. degree in aerospace engineering from the University of Michigan and the M.S. and B.S. degrees also in aerospace engineering from Iowa State University. His primary research interests are in trajectory optimization, numerical methods in optimal control, and control and dynamics of aerospace vehicles. He is the editor of the international journal *Optimal Control Applications and Methods*, published by John Wiley and Sons, Chichester, England.

Could You Be Clearer? An Examination of the Multiple Perspectives of Clarity

Ronald E. Dulek

Abstract— **Clarity is a favorite topic of every writing aficionado—from the armchair editor to the psycholinguist. Each expert tells us: clarity is good. Despite this unanimity of opinion, however, few recognize the important, complex factors that affect readers and writers' perceptions of clarity. This article examines three of the most important such factors: precision, document accessibility, and corporate language context. Each factor is defined and examined in terms of its influence on clarity. The result is a better understanding of the multiple factors we need to consider before we pass judgment on a document's clarity.**

Introduction

CLARITY is the standard of professional prose. Advocates wave, salute, line up behind, and defend it with a fervor reminiscent of the return of a victorious army. Yet despite the hoopla in its favor, including 388 articles dealing with clarity published in the last five years [1], the past two decades have seen few revolutionary ideas about how to achieve clarity. In fact, if one believes research results by Bennett and Olney [2] or testimony from practicing professionals such as Davies [3], clarity problems seem to have gotten worse. In cynical moments one is tempted to paraphrase Mark Twain: "Everyone favors clarity, but no one does anything about it."

Approaches toward clarity over the past twenty years follow one of two directions. The first, the Cheerleader Approach, encourages clarity at all costs. Clarity is seen as an unquestioned good for which everyone should strive. And the goal is easy to attain—simply "be clear." Lewis [4], McTague [5], and Northey [6] are among the many espousing this attitude toward clarity.

The second approach views clarity as a skill problem: A message is unclear because the writer is unaware of the strategies needed to make the message clear; once the writer learns these strategies, the clarity problem disappears. Johnson [7], Reinold [8], and Tibbetts [9], as well as numerous texts, exemplify this approach.

Three Perspectives of Clarity

Over the past 14 years I have served as a writing consultant to a number of major national and international firms. During this time I have examined thousands of documents written by managers and technical specialists. Many of these messages were already clear; others needed to be clearer. But few were unclear solely because writers lacked the desire or skill to create such a message. Instead, clarity problems developed from complex audience, technical, or organizational concerns.

Manuscript received December 1991.
R. E. Dulek is with the University of Alabama, Tuscaloosa, AL 35486.
IEEE Log Number 9200128.

My experience indicates that three important issues shape a writer's attitude toward clarity: the importance of precision; the need for document accessibility; and the corporate language context in which the message is sent and read. Each issue affects how the writer constructs and phrases the message.

The main problem that seems to arise is that writers seldom consider all three issues simultaneously. Instead, much like politicians who pass legislation that advantage some constituencies but disadvantage others, writers often focus on one issue and overlook the other two. The result is a document that appears patently clear from one point of view but ridiculously unclear from another. A brief examination of each issue provides needed insight into this complex problem.

Perspective 1: Precision

Precision is the "backbone" of good technical writing. Fifty years ago Rhodes declared that the "prime requirements of a good report are precision and clarity"[10]. Ever since Rhodes' definition appeared, scholars and practitioners alike have sought to clarify precision. Ulman and Gould [11], Zimmerman and Clark [12], and others believe precision derives from the honest use of data, to which Roze [13] adds that this data must be transcribed accurately and Alley [14] adds that it must include all relevant data, not just that which supports a certain conclusion. Neufeld [15], on the other hand, equates precision with clear, accurate interpretation of data, to which Houp and Pearsall [16] add a strong emphasis on objectivity.

By far the most frequently emphasized definitions of precision, however, are language-based. Writers advocate language that is "utterly clear" [17]. Mills and Walter [18], Brusaw, Alred and Oliu [19], Bjelland [20], and a host of others call for language that is impartial, objective, unemotional, unambiguous, detached, to the point, and precise. Each stresses the importance of exactitude, of limiting interpretation to one meaning. Earl Britton [21] summarizes all of the above definitions by noting:

> [T]he reader must be given no choice of meanings; he must not be allowed to interpret a passage in any way but that intended by the writer. Insofar as the reader may derive more than one meaning from a passage, technical writing is bad; insofar as he can derive only one meaning from the writing, it is good.

"Utterly clear" thus becomes "utterly precise."

Reprinted from *IEEE Trans. Prof. Comm.*, vol. PC-35, no. 2, pp. 84–87, June 1992.

These calls for precision are not voices crying in an academic wilderness. Precision is a vital, important aspect of effective professional prose. A recent real-life incident involving a bid specification demonstrates precision's importance at even the most minute level.

An architect wrote the following specification as part of a call for bids on a major construction project:

> **Countertops:** Post-form plastic laminate with hardwood bull-nosed edges, thickness 1 9/16."

This project involved construction of 250 of these countertops. The architect intended to convey the message that the entire countertop would have a thickness of 1 9/16".

Bidding on the multi-million dollar project was fiercely competitive, with the eventual winners placing bids at "rock-bottom" prices. When construction began, contractors and suppliers sought all possible avenues to minimize costs. The countertops became one such path. Suppliers delivered the following: a one-half inch thick countertop with a 1 9/16" bull-nosed edge. The suppliers claimed that these countertops met the specifications of the call for bids.

A variety of threats, counterthreats, and legal entanglements followed, with the argument's final outcome turning on the comma after the word "edges." This comma made the attached phrase nonrestrictive—i.e., without the comma, the final phrase would have read "bull-nosed edges that are 1 9/16 inches thick; with the comma, the phrase referred to the entire statement. An out-of-court settlement required the suppliers to provide thicker, more expensive countertops at a total extra cost of over $450,000.

Precision in this case, as demonstrated by the presence of a comma, proved important to all involved. Without precision, proposals, contracts, letters of agreement, and many other forms of written documentation become a shambles of meaningless verbiage. Precision *is* essential for effective professional prose.

Perspective 2: Document Accessibility

Accessibility involves making information available to a broad array of readers. Writers concerned with accessibility view documents democratically. They believe a message should be understandable to many—if not all—readers. Administrative, managerial, and bureaucratic masses, not just the technical elite, should be able to read, understand, and, if appropriate, act upon the information. Words associated with this viewpoint include audience analysis, reader adaptation, interpretation, and, recently, discourse analysis.

Writers who strive for accessibility often seem at odds with advocates of precision. Sanders [22] and Whitney [23] call for increased "elegance" to overcome writing that is technically flat, a frequent complaint about precise messages; Savakinas [24] and Nagle [25] argue for elimination of "field specific" terminology and insertion of understandable, acceptable terms to overcome highly specialized, extremely precise language; and Hill [26] and Wu [27] encourage adaptation to and consideration of one's audience in order to make information available to a broader, more diverse group of readers.

Yet while these arguments may at first seem to counteract efforts for precision, a closer look reveals the criticisms are aimed not at precision, but at precision's by-products—i.e., specialized, technical language and narrowly focused readers. Each of these writers recognizes the need for precision. But each also recognizes that precision alone is not enough. A precise document fails to achieve maximum potential if it is read by only one or two readers.

William Empson, the literary critic who championed the ambiguity of the English language, provided special insight into the problems faced by writers who strive too much for precision. Empson [28] defined the problem thus:

> English is becoming an aggregate of vocabularies only loosely in connection with one another, which yet have many words in common, so that there is much danger of accidental ambiguity . . . It is to combat this that so much recent writing has been determinedly unintelligible from any but the precise point of view intended.

Empson's key phrase, "determinedly unintelligible," summarizes the complex task those seeking precision face. As writers strive for precision they also strive for words with singular, specialized meanings. The result is a passage that achieves the singularity of meaning called for by Britton, but whose singular meaning is shared by only a select few. Hence, the aforementioned criticisms.

Writers achieve accessibility by modifying messages in one of two ways: structurally or stylistically. Abstracts, cover letters, executive summaries, and introductions are among the many structural modifications used to make information available to generalized, lay audiences. On some occasions, the report's body does the job, with appendices containing complex, technical, and highly specialized information.

Stylistic modifications are an equally effective means of achieving accessibility. The vast majority of stylistic modifications occur at the word level, with general words replacing those with highly specialized meanings. Thus a trade-off occurs: precision is sacrificed to breadth. A writer who wants to refer to a "Mandrel type bench grinder with 12 inch wheel capacity, located in the grinding room" may instead refer to it as a "Mandrel type bench grinder in the grinding room," a "Mandrel bench grinder," a "bench grinder in the grinding room," or even just a "bench grinder." The choice depends on the need for technical detail and on the reader's ability to interpret the more general description.

At the sentence level, modifications involve stylistic shifts. Language patterns of everyday speech replace objective, scientific, laboratory-like prose. Short, simple, subject-verb-object sentences appear, as do active rather than passive sentences. Passage styles thus become more forceful, personal, and sometimes colorful. These changes increase sentence impact and create what Brenda Rubens [29] labels as "user friendly" or "conversational" sentence patterns.

Perspective 3: Corporate Language Context

Corporate language context consists of the words, phrases, syntax, and general language patterns used within a particular business. In many ways, corporate language context is the language fingerprint that identifies a company as distinct from others. It is a business's beliefs expressed in language.

Writers who understand corporate language context know that in order to function they must use accepted corporate language patterns in their day-to-day activities. These patterns may not be the most precise or even the most accessible, but they are the ones used within a particular company.

In many ways, corporate language context defines clarity within a particular company. Documents are not measured against external standards of clarity but against the patterns, rules, and syntax of the company. An excellent example of corporate language context is occurring right now in a major Fortune 500 company. The CEO has created a list of 85 words that are not to appear in any report sent to him. The terms are mostly specialized financial terms.

Since the list was created by the CEO, the words on it have become taboo not only when writing to the CEO, but also when writing to anyone else in the corporation. And anyone who uses these words, even in conversation, receives strange looks from others in the corporation and is regarded either as an outsider or as "naive."

The concept of a corporate language context should not, however, be oversimplified. It is not a one business/one language relationship. The language context may be infinitely larger or smaller than a given company. Language context may be industry-wide—experts in computers, paper, telecommunication and various other industries use specialized terminology unique to their areas; it may be functional—accountants, engineers, marketers and statisticians have field-specific terminology they share with few, if any, outsiders; or it may be departmental—language contexts that identify individuals as accepted members of a particular corporate subset.

An interesting example of this latter usage occurred while I was conducting a training session for the marketing division of a large computer company. The marketers in this company used the word "migrate" in most of their written messages. I had never previously seen this term used within this company—nor by other marketers in other firms. A brief inquiry revealed that these marketers used "migrate" as a substitute for "change," a word that had highly negative connotations to readers being asked to switch from one computer system to another. Interestingly, the term was introduced to the marketers through internal corporate trainers who taught these individuals before they went into the field.

A final important observation needs to be added about corporate language context: the corporate context may define how acceptable clarity is. Organizations do not always prefer clarity. Alesina and Cukierman [30] studied "dynamic electoral models" to explore the issue of ambiguity among national politicians. Their results showed politicians preferred ambiguity over pinpoint precision. Anyone who has worked with government agencies knows that at times political realities shape the language used. Perfect clarity is not always the preferred method of operation. An upper level administrator in one large organization I worked for made the following comment: "Clarity isn't my biggest problem; you don't have to teach me how to write clearly. I need to master 'bureaucratic obfuscation.' Now there's a skill that's useful." If we are fortunate, this perspective is not widely held.

Conclusion

To say that the term clarity is more complex than we at first realize is, by this point, a bit obvious. Yet the statement's truth cannot be ignored. Clarity is a multi-faceted term with many different perspectives. Technical editors who criticize others for being unclear and managers who attack subordinates with the same invective mistakenly assume their suggestions are easily understood. Unfortunately, such understanding is neither always easy nor present. Unless the editor or manager directs the criticism to a particular clarity issue, such as precision, accessibility, or corporate language context, the listener may freely interpret the comments in any of a number of different ways.

Clarity needs clarification. Scholars, researchers, and writing practitioners need to examine the term's many different meanings and create and test hypotheses as to what people mean by "be clear." The result of these efforts may be the development of a "Language of Clarity," one that will provide a practical terminology for editors, managers, and other writing experts to use when describing this supposedly simple concept. The presence of such a vocabulary might ultimately provide a way for people to tell others how to write more clearly. An accomplishment such as that would be worthy of praise.

References

[1] This figure was obtained through ABI/Inform. The dates checked were Oct. 1986 to Sept. 1991.

[2] J. C. Bennett and J. R. Olney, "Executive priorities for effective communication in an information society," *The Journal of Business Communication*, vol. 23, no. 2, pp. 13–22, Spring 1986.

[3] J. E. Davies, "Teaching managers to write," *Personnel Management*, vol. 19, no. 1, pp. 26–29, Jan. 1987.

[4] H. G. Lewis, "The future of 'force-communication': Power communication," *Direct Marketing*, vol. 53, no. 2, pp. 69–70, Jan. 1991.

[5] M. McTague, "How to write effective reports and proposals," *Training & Development Journal*, vol. 42, no. 11, pp. 51–53, Nov. 1988.

[6] M. Northey, "Learn to be a better communicator," *CA Magazine*, vol. 122, no. 3, pp. 58–60, Mar. 1989.

[7] T. P. Johnson, "How well do you inform?" *IEEE Trans. Prof. Commun.*, vol. 25, no. 1, Mar. 1982.

[8] C. Reimold, "Business writing—Clear and simple," *IEEE Trans. Prof. Commun.*, vol. 24, no. 4, pp. 184–85, Dec. 1981.

[9] A. Tibbetts, "Ten rules for writing readably," *IEEE Trans. Prof. Commun.*, vol. 25, no. 1, pp. 10–13, Mar. 1982.

[10] F. H. Rhodes, *Technical Report Writing*. New York: McGraw-Hill, 1941, p. 4.

[11] J. N. Ulman and J. R. Gould, *Technical Reporting*. New York: Holt, Rinehart, and Winston, 3rd ed., 1972.

[12] D. E. Zimmerman and D. G. Clark, *Guide To Technical and Scientific Communication*. New York: Random House, 1987, p. 34.

[13] M. Roze, *Technical Communication: The Practical Craft*. Columbus, OH: Merrill Publishing, 1990, p. 9.

[14] M. Alley, *The Craft of Scientific Writing*. Englewood Cliffs, NJ: Prentice-Hall, 1987, p. 20.

[15] J. K. Neufeld, *A Handbook for Technical Communication*. Englewood Cliffs, NJ: Prentice-Hall, 1987, p. 107.

[16] K. W. Houp and T. E. Pearsall, *Reporting Technical Information*. New York: Macmillan, 1984, 5th ed., p. 8.

[17] T. E. Pearsall, *Teaching Technical Writing: Methods for College English Teachers*. Washington, DC: Society for Technical Communication, p. 1.

[18] G. H. Mills and J. A. Walter, *Technical Writing*. New York: Holt, Rinehart and Winston, 1978, 4th ed., p. 7.
[19] C. T. Brusaw, G. J. Alred, and W. E. Oliu, *Handbook of Technical Writing*. New York: St. Martin's Press, 1976, p. 7.
[20] J. Bjelland, *Writing Better Technical Articles*. Blue Ridge Summit, PA: TAB Books, 1990, p. 139.
[21] W. E. Britton, "What is technical writing? A redefinition," in *Technical Writing in A Corporate Culture*, C. Barabas. Norwood, NJ: Abley Publishing, 1990, p. 137.
[22] S. P. Sanders, "Practice, proficiency, professionalism," *IEEE Trans. Prof. Commun.*, vol. 29, no. 2, pp. 15–18, June 1986.
[23] M. A. Whitney, "Combining elegance and readability: Walker Gibson's tough, sweet, and stuffy," *IEEE Trans. Prof. Commun.*, vol. 20, no. 4, pp. 222–226, Dec. 1987.
[24] R. C. Savakinas, "Ready, aim—Write!" *IEEE Trans. Prof. Commun.* vol. 31, no. 1, pp. 5–7, Mar. 1988;
[25] J. G. Nagle, "Avoiding linguectomy," *IEEE Trans. Prof. Commun.*, vol. 31, no. 3, pp. 99–100, Sept. 1988.
[26] J. Hill, "The power of the word," *IEEE Trans. Prof. Commun.*, vol. 31, no. 3, pp. 97–98, Sept. 1988.
[27] V. W. Wu, "The problems that I have with writing," *IEEE Trans. Prof. Commun.*, vol. 31, no. 4, pp. 181–183, Dec. 1988.
[28] W. Empson, *Seven Types of Ambiguity*. London, UK: Chatto and Windus, 1947, p. 236.
[29] B. Rubens, "Personality in computer documentation: A preference study," *IEEE Trans. Prof. Commun.*, vol. 29, no. 1, p. 58, Dec. 1986.
[30] A. Alesina and A. Cukierman, "The politics of ambiguity," *The Quarterly Journal of Economics*, vol. 15, no. 5, p. 845, Nov. 1990.

Ronald E. Dulek is Professor of Management Communications and Chair of The Management and Marketing Department at The University of Alabama. He has published five books, numerous academic articles, and consults regularly with industry and government.

The Grammar Instinct

Interface

—Feature by
ALAN D. MANNING,
MEMBER, IEEE

Manuscript received February 4, 2002;
revised March 15, 2002.
The author is with the
Department of Linguistics,
Brigham Young University,
Provo, UT 84602 USA
(email: alan_manning@byu.edu).
IEEE PII S 0361-1434(02)04968-8.

S. Pinker
The Language Instinct: How the Mind Creates Language
New York: HarperCollins
(Perennial Classics ed.), 2000.

Index Terms—*Editing, grammar teaching, language change, usage.*

Back in 1990, Leonard and Gilsdorf presented 45 instances of questionable usage, in full-paragraph contexts, to both academics and working business executives. These usage elements included sentence fragments, assorted punctuation problems, pronoun–antecedent (dis)agreement, and various examples of questionable word choice. Their intent was to assess the "botheration level" of each usage "error"; their conclusions were that

1) academics are (nearly) always bothered by usage "errors" more than executives and

2) usage elements that bothered survey respondents the least were evolving over time into acceptable English usage [1].

Just over ten years later, these same researchers have followed up on their original study and have drawn similar conclusions from the more recent data [2].

> Most of us acknowledge that language is arbitrary, its signification deriving from the general agreement of its users, and that language changes with its users' practice .... Standing in the language's midstream, we as teachers are responsible for teaching written English that is correct for our time. It would seem futile to try to persuade students that the Standard English of, say, 1930 (which some outdated textbooks still purvey) is still the Standard English expected by present and future employers (p. 440).

Gilsdorf and Leonard (G&L) propose that recent changes in usage acceptability might be due to the increased influence of email informalities and the globalized use of English among nonnative speakers. They acknowledge, however, that this influence cannot be demonstrated or measured using the findings of their study (p. 441).

Setting aside for now the problem of ongoing language change and its causes, this interface will focus on the problem of predicting what will remain unchanged in language-usage rules and propose an explanation for why certain rules will remain unchanged. This problem is critically important for anyone who is mentoring the writing of younger people, people whose primary audience will not follow our rules, but rather the rules of the next generation of readers.

VARIABLES AND CONSTANTS OF USAGE

The ten most bothersome items in G&Ls' 1990 study were essentially the same items ranked most bothersome in their 2001 study. Most of these involved sentence structure or punctuation problems that directly impact perceived sentence structure, as in these examples:

a. *He focused all his energies on his personal goals he never wavered from his chosen path.*

   RUN-ON SENTENCE Average score: 4.49 on a 1-to-5 "botheration" scale.

b. *When the time came for the representatives to sign the contract however the bid was withdrawn.*

Reprinted from *IEEE Trans. Prof. Comm.*, vol. PC-45, no. 2, pp. 133–137, June 2002.

UNPUNCTUATED PARENTHETICAL EXPRESSION Average score: 4.36 out of 5.

(p. 450).

In contrast, five of the ten least distracting usage items (the ones possibly changing in acceptability over time) involve problems of word choice:

> *The line supervisor was anxious to receive her Employee-of-the-Month Award.*
>
> ***ANXIOUS*** as a synonym for ***EAGER***. Average score: 2.15 out of 5.
>
> *The data supports his recommendation.*
>
> ***DATA*** as singular. Average score: 2.37
>
> *... the Biltmore is still the most unique resort in Phoenix.*
>
> ***MOST*** or ***VERY*** used as qualifier with ***UNIQUE***. Average score: 2.5.
>
> *Terry initially supported the project but later became somewhat disinterested in it.*
>
> ***DISINTERESTED*** as synonym for ***UNINTERESTED***. Average: 2.66.
>
> *The supervisor had no objection to us leaving.*
>
> ***US*** rather than ***OUR*** (objective versus possessive) with *-ing* verb. Average: 2.72 .

[2, p. 451]

Note that the degree of "botheration" rises somewhat (but is still slight) as the usage issue moves from pure word choice to a semigrammatical issue of pronoun case.

The other five of G&L's ten least bothersome usage items are based on traditional "grammar rules." These items are not evidence of language change but rather evidence for the opposite, a resistance to language change. Such "rules" are historically based on attempts to change English usage so that it would conform to presumed rules of good logic and/or the word structure of Latin. In logic notation, a conjunction cannot begin an expression and a double negative does mean a positive, for example. In Latin, it is impossible to split an infinitive or end a sentence with a preposition. English on the contrary has manifest such forms since the dawn of its written history. Continuing acceptance of such forms is evidence for resistance to change, even in the face of strong social pressure. Most (though certainly not all) readers are merely willing to ignore contrived "school marm rules" that fail to match their instincts about acceptable written English.

AN ARBITRARY LEXICON AND A UNIVERSAL GRAMMAR

G&L themselves recognize that usage teachers must rely on students' implicit "language sense" (p. 464). Their reliance on that instinctive sense, as well as their data given above, provides evidence against what G&L stated earlier, however, that "language is arbitrary, its signification deriving from the general agreement of its users ..." This cannot always be so, or we would not expect to find consistent resistance to change in matters of sentence structure, nor such strong relative openness to change in matters of word choice. If all language forms, words and sentence structures alike, were equally arbitrary, they should be equally subject to changing usage.

Considerable light is shed on this problem by Steven Pinker's now classic *The Language Instinct*, first published in 1994 [3]. Pinker attempts, more or less successfully, to do for the science of linguistics what Carl Sagan did to popularize astronomy and physics. Mainstream linguists researching the problem for the last 40 years have generally come to agree that most of what people know about language use cannot be taught but is rather built on a biological, universally human instinct for language behavior.

For a lay audience, this is a counterintuitive conclusion, however. Most people believe that parents teach their children to speak, and it seems unclear—if language is just like upright posture and opposable thumbs, a genetically programmed human trait—why languages like English and Chinese can be so different from each other. For that matter, it seems unclear why we would ever disagree with other writers about "usage errors" at all, if there were a universal grammar instinct.

Pinker notes that, while the proposed universal language "engine" is invisible to most people,

> ... the trim packages and color schemes are attended to obsessively. Trifling differences between the mainstream and the dialect of other groups, like *isn't any* versus *ain't no, those books* versus *them books*, and *dragged him away* versus *drug him away*, are dignified as badges of "proper grammar." But they have no more to do with grammatical sophistication than the fact that people in some regions in the United States refer to a certain insect as a *dragonfly* and people in other regions refer to it as a *darning needle*, or that English speakers call canines *dogs* whereas French speakers call them *chiens* (p. 16).

Pinker thus allows that the marriage between individual words and their meanings can be as arbitrary as a shotgun wedding, with evident strangeness if we think too hard about it. If the word for dog in Spanish can be *perro*, but *goh* in Chinese, then it is no more or less surprising that we can drive on a *parkway*, but park in a *driveway*, eat jumbo *shrimp*, or *blue*berries that are more purple than blue, or *cran*berries that are not cran at all [3, p. 75]. The usage-questionable phrases like *most unique*, noted above, are no more or less unreasonable than this. *Unique* does not have to always mean "only object in its class" any more than *shrimp* has to always mean "small."

This is not to say that we should not make students aware of the (current) social consequences of using phrases like "them books." As writing mentors we need to be equally aware that rules of the purely lexical "dragged vs. drug" variety are essentially fads of social prestige, like the stars on the bellies of Dr. Suess's Sneeches, and they are very prone to pass out of fashion.

Unlike the passing fads of vocabulary, every phrase of every language has to work from a fixed set of grammatical functions. Following Pinker's metaphor, popular makes, colors, and models of automobile change from year to year, but they are (nearly) all driven by the same piston-engine technology that Henry Ford started with. This is equally true of even one language, like English, as it becomes a series of "different" languages across a long span of time.

For example, there are probably no two languages more different than English and Kivunjo, a language spoken in Africa. The equivalent of the English sentence "He now does eat it for her," is a single (highly inflected) verb, *naikimlyiia*. (Most of) the inflections on the Kivunjo verb nevertheless mark out the same grammatical functions as the English sentence:

> a subject/specifier (*n*)*a* = (focus) he,
> a time modifier *i* = now,
> a direct object *ki* = it,
> an indirect object *m* = her,
> a verb *lyi*(*i*) eat (for),
> an indicative mood marker *a* = does (the "head" of the proposition expressed).
> (p. 121).

What is universal here are the four grammatical functions: subject/specifier, object(s), modifier(s), and head. The first three functions may or may not be present, but every phrase in every language must have one defined "head." Every verb phrase has to have a verb in it, and every noun phrase has to have a noun in it, and so on.

> For example the N[oun] P[hrase] *the cat in the hat* refers to a kind of cat, not a kind of hat; the meaning of the word cat is the core of the meaning of the whole phrase .... The same goes for verb phrases: *flying to Rio before the police catch him* is an example of flying, not an example of catching, so the verb *flying* is called its head. Here we have the first [universal] principle of building the meaning of a phrase out of the meaning of the words inside the phrase. What the entire phrase is "about" is what its head word is about (p. 99).

Following Pinker's analysis, what would never pass out of fashion would be matters of usage that directly impact the universal constants of phrase and sentence structure and a reader's ability to determine these in a piece of writing. Pinker discusses at some length a kind of sentence known as a "garden path" sentence:

1) *The horse raced past the barn fell.*
2) *The man who hunts ducks out on weekends.*
3) *The cotton clothing is usually made of grows in Mississippi.*
4) *The prime number few.*
5) *Fat people eat accumulates.*
6) *The tycoon sold the offshore oil tracts for a lot of money wanted to kill JR* (p. 211).

Although these sentences violate no traditional usage rule, they are still structured in a way to cause serious readability problems. These readability problems are readily explained using the theory of universal grammatical functions. In each case, a reader is easily fooled into misidentifying the head of the sentence (an auxiliary verb or main verb marked for tense). In the first sentence, *raced* seems like the main verb, but that first analysis is undone when the second tensed verb *fell* is read. The reader has to go back and reparse the sentence, re-identifying *raced* as the head of a phrase modifying *horse*, and so on.

Usage Errors not Created Equal(ly)

Recall the examples of usage which, in G&Ls' study, were unchangingly bothersome:

a. *He focused all his energies on his personal goals he never wavered from ...*

This can appear to be a well-formed sentence, with the phrase [that] *he never wavered from* ... (mis)interpreted as a relative-clause modifier of *goals*. This interpretation is possible, that is, until the last three words are noticed, following the word *from: ... his chosen path*. In this, this sentence is exactly parallel to the garden-path sentences Pinker describes. The difference here is that no backtracking reinterpretation can rescue the run-on sentence, unless it is reanalyzed (and therefore repunctuated) as two sentences, with two separate main verbs as two separate heads.

In the above example, the reader has two main-clause heads to separate. In the following example, no main-clause head can initially be found:

b. *When the time came for the representatives to sign the contract however the bid was withdrawn.*

Here, the word *when* causes the reader to assume that subsequent words belong to a relative clause = a modifier in some other, main clause. The subject and head of the main clause cannot be identified until the end of this modifying clause is found. The difficulty comes in locating the end of that modifying clause: *however* can also mark the beginning of yet another, subsubordinate clause. The reader runs out of words and eventually realizes that the *when*-clause must have ended after *however*. This is where the comma should have gone. Again, the lack of punctuation is a problem precisely because it creates a phrase/sentence that cannot be easily parsed into its universal grammatical functions.

G&L note another aspect of their data for which they do not give full explanation. Different errors of same type (academically speaking) do not all provoke the same level of botheration [2, p. 463]. My proposed misanalyzed-head model of strong usage errors explains this. If a punctuation error is technically wrong but does not cause the misanalysis of the main-clause head, it will be less noticeable than any error which does cause main-clause misanalysis.

So, for example, item (c) below provokes somewhat less difficulty, though it is technically the same as (b) above:

c. *The chairman fired five department heads among them Jerald DeStephano.*

This is another "unpunctuated parenthetical expression" (p. 472), but it was only rated by executives with a 3.56 botheration level, as opposed to the 4.32 (executive) rating given to sentence (b) (p. 471). This is because, in sentence (c), the analysis problem does not adversely affect identification of the main-clause head (*fired*). Rather, the problem is confined to the assignment of the modifier phrase *among them Jerald DeStephano.* It is unclear at first whether the phrase attaches directly to *heads*, the noun it is next to. It does not, which is why the comma is still notably missed. Instead, the phrase attaches as modifier in the verb phrase.

As a final example, the following sentence fragment (d) was rated the most bothersome (4.38 rating) of any item by executives.

d. *Although the Department of Transportation has implemented rules making it legal for employers to test employees for drugs if he or she works in the airline, trucking, gas pipeline, or maritime industries.*

Like item (a) above, the subordinating conjunction *although* causes a reader to suspend search for a main-clause head, until the subordinate clause comes to an apparent end. The end of the whole item is reached before any clause-end marker is found. In contrast, item (e) below is less bothersome to executives (3.69) even though it likewise contains a sentence fragment (p. 450).

e. *Small companies suffer in a tight labor market. One of their problems being that they can't compete for qualified personnel.*

The apparent difference is the presence of an easily identified main clause, prior to the fragment. The fragment itself lacks any misleading candidate for main-clause head, and so is readily attached to the existing main clause, despite the technically erroneous punctuation.

Conclusion

A language-universals analysis greatly clarifies the findings of Gilsdorf and Leonard. It supports their claim that not all academic usage rules should carry equal weight in actual professional discourse. Many older rules of word choice are outmoded and can always be safely ignored. Others can be set aside depending on the age or academic background of readers. What must be continually dealt with, however, are matters of usage that impact the ready interpretation of a sentence's grammatical functions. As Pinker's garden-path sentences show, this problem must be (and will always be) a matter of concern, regardless of whether there is a formal usage rule to cover the case or not.

It is worth noting that the best students need no formal training in order to write well-formed sentences. They use commas or other punctuation properly, even if they do not consciously know the difference between a preposition and a participle. This is likewise in keeping with the hypothesis of an innate language-learning capacity. There is strong evidence that this unconscious and relatively effortless language learning ability fades away by the time a person reaches puberty [3, pp. 293–296].

In many ways, written English is a related but different language than spoken English. Those writers who need help with commas are probably in the same boat as adult, nonnative English speakers who need ESL courses and help putting the right tense on verbs in conversation. Classroom instruction can help in either case, but it is a sure sign that a person was not given adequate exposure to the language form they are trying to learn at an early-enough age.

Acknowledgment

I wish to thank Joann Temple-Dennett for initially suggesting this topic to me.

REFERENCES

[1] D. Leonard and J. Gilsdorf, "Language in change: Academics' and executives' perceptions of usage errors," *J. Bus. Commun.*, vol. 27, no. 1, pp. 137–158, 1990.
[2] J. Gilsdorf and D. Leonard, "Big stuff, little stuff: A decennial measurement of executives' and academics' reactions to questionable usage elements," *J. Bus. Commun.*, vol. 38, no. 4, pp. 439–475, 2001.
[3] S. Pinker, *The Language Instinct: How the Mind Creates Language*, Perennial Classics ed. New York: HarperCollins, 2000.

Alan D. Manning (M'97) received his Ph.D. (linguistics with a minor in technical writing) from Louisiana State University (LSU) in 1988. He has taught linguistics, literature, and writing courses at LSU, Stephen F. Austin University, and Idaho State University before joining the Brigham Young University linguistics faculty in 1994. He serves as a feature editor for the IEEE TRANSACTIONS ON PROFESSIONAL COMMUNICATION.

Books Available for Review

The following books were available for review in the IEEE TRANSACTIONS ON PROFESSIONAL COMMUNICATION when this issue went to press. If you want the most current list or would like more information about reviewing a book in 1000-1500 words, please visit http://www.d.umn.edu/~kriley or contact Book Review Editor, Kathryn Riley, at kriley@d.umn.edu. If you would like to suggest another book for review, please provide her with a title and brief description.

Geoffrey Cross. *Forming the Collective Mind: A Contextual Exploration of Large-Scale Collaborative Writing in Industry.* Cresskill, NJ: Hampton Press, 2001. (272 pp.)

Amita Goyal Chin. *Text Databases and Document Management: Theory and Practice.* Hershey, PA: Idea Group, 2001. (248 pp.)

Sandra W. Harner and Tom G. Zimmerman. *Technical Marketing Communication.* New York: Longman (Allyn & Bacon Series in Technical Communication), 2002. (236 pp.)

Brian R. Holloway. *Technical Writing Basics: A Guide to Style and Form, 2/e.* Upper Saddle River, NJ: Prentice Hall, 2002. (210 pp.)

Johndan Johnson Eilola. *Designing Effective Web Sites: A Concise Guide.* Boston: Houghton Mifflin, 2002. (122 pp.)

Jeannine M. E. Klein. *Building Enhanced HTML Help with DHTML and CSS.* Upper Saddle River, NJ: Prentice Hall PTR/Hewlett-Packard, 2001. (380 pp.)

Daniel G. Riordan and Steven E. Pauley. *Technical Report Writing Today, 8/e.* Boston: Houghton Mifflin, 2002. (598 pp.)

Maris Roze and Simon Maxwell. *Technical Communication in the Age of the Internet, 4/e.* Upper Saddle River, NJ: Prentice Hall, 2002. (305 pp.)

Kim J. Vicente. *Cognitive Work Analysis: Toward Safe, Productive, and Healthy Computer-Based Work.* Mahwah, NJ: Lawrence Erlbaum, 1999. (392 pp.)

Kristin R. Woolever. *Writing for the Technical Professions, 2/e.* New York: Longman, 2002. (516 pp.)

Comparing the Two Cultures in Technical Writing

Don Bush

Abstract—**Veteran technical writers and editors sometimes suspect that the professors who teach technical writing and editing are too deeply immersed in their academic culture to translate effectively into the classroom the world of work culture in which technical writing and editing are practiced. In fact, the two cultures are remarkably alike, sharing the same goal—to improve communication. Differences arise primarily in the approaches taken to achieve that common goal. Drawing upon the author's 25 years of experience as a technical writer and editor and his more recent experience as a Visiting Professor in a university writing program, this paper discusses the different approaches that industry and academe take to such topics as grammar, rhetoric, audience, editing, artwork, decision making, and collaborative writing.**

Introduction

AFTER 25 years as a technical editor and teacher at McDonnell Douglas, St. Louis, MO, I had the honor last year to be selected to teach a semester of technical writing and technical editing as Visiting Professor in the Writing Program at the University of New Mexico, Albuquerque.

Thus I had a chance to compare the two cultures, industry and academia. Perhaps because academia was new to me, I found it free and refreshing, and also stimulating. But also, I found the two cultures remarkably alike, sharing the same goal—to improve communication—and fighting the same battles against circumlocution, diffuseness, redundancy, prolixity, tautology, and tediousness. I felt right at home.

But here are a few of the differences I found in my excursion into a different world.

Grammar

Industry esteems rigid grammar. Most companies have style manuals, which are so costly in terms of ongoing employee time and corporate money that the text should be illuminated with floral designs in gold leaf. These overrated compilations, instead of covering company-specific items, try to teach grammar, generally in the form of questionable prohibitions (*data is*, *hopefully*, *none are*).

English teachers, despite their stereotype, are not at all sticklers for prescriptive grammar. They know that most rules cannot be applied across the board. They prefer *It's me* to *It's I*, because that's the way educated people speak. They know about linguistics. Linguistics describes what educated grammar actually is, rather than prescribing what it should be. A key principle is that the spoken language *is* the language. Teachers are thus surprisingly more likely to accept "slang" or "jargon," depending on the audience.

Industry editors generally reject "common usage" in favor of rules. However, they themselves have already learned to overlook split infinitives and sentence-ending prepositions. Also, for instance, they will never use *440 hertzes* (like *blitzes*, or *waltzes*), because *hertzes* "sounds funny." What they mean is that it's not common usage.

Rhetoric

As you might expect, English teachers do indeed know about writing. Using tropes descended from Aristotle and the precepts of 18th century rhetoricians like Hugh Blair and George Campbell, they can show students how to make prose not just more euphonious, but also more precise and visual, and thereby more technically accurate. In industry, you can spend years without once hearing the word "metaphor," even though the form is common in engineering copy (*umbilical*, *female* connector, *rubber* airplane, *glass* view, *hands on*).

English departments also know semantics. They know how to use labels to develop organization and consolidate ideas, and, conversely, how to avoid labels that stereotype.

The schools are continually seeking out the rhetorical features that communicate better. What about finite verbs? Periodic sentences? Compound rather than complex sentences? The theme–rheme concept? This is where the college people really do seem smart.

Splendid examples of this new rhetorical study can be found in *Style: Ten Lessons in Clarity & Grace*, by Joseph Williams, and the Modern Language Association's book on editing, *Line by Line*, by Claire Kehrwald Cook. This is the technology of writing.

Approach to Writing

In industry, the approach to creative writing is to copy what people did last year. There is good reason; last year's report survived the formidable approval cycle. Another popular form of invention is to copy the competition.

English teachers are different. They are more like modern artists, often seeking the new, the original, just because it is new and original. "Let's try a new phrase." "Have we thought about whether four columns is the best solution?" "What's another word for ANNUAL REPORT?" I found this attitude refreshing.

Industry, on the other hand, seems to be dedicated to making every technical report just as dull as the last one,

Manuscript received February 1, 1991.
The author is a retired consultant in technical writing and editing.
IEEE Log Number 9144343.

Reprinted from *IEEE Trans. Prof. Comm.*, vol. PC-34, no. 2, pp. 67–69, June 1991.

semicolon by semicolon. Even the cliches are programmed in: few reports escape extolling "state-of-the-art advances" or "total Corporate commitment." The writers claim to abhor cliches, but they cling to them with their dying breath. They even use them in their mixed metaphors: "The odds are stacked against us." "We plan to probe all facets of the problem." Such examples are more common than you think. Watch for them in a corporate brochure near you.

In pursuit of sales "zing," industry imposes instant panaceas: active voice, present tense, "positive" words, "you," partial sentences, ellipses, dashes–slashes, and bongs or meatballs. Results are proudly totted up by a computerized style checker. If only writing were that easy!

In short, instead of revering rhetoric, industry tends to ape advertising. To be sure, technical writers can learn from advertising a lot about readability, with devices like short words, short paragraphs, frequent subheads, and thesis-first "deductive" organization.

But industry has already been influenced too much by poor advertising. Today, the popular business writing style is hype, which, unfortunately, is easier to acquire than to eradicate.

AUDIENCE

Both industry and academia talk a lot about audience, but there are differences. Once the audience is defined, industry proceeds to write down to the public, aiming the copy at the dumbest dolt and then descending two more notches. Writers therefore frequently either: 1) include no technical detail at all, which makes the material chummy but valueless; or 2) over-explain with multiple steps and repetition, which, ironically, makes even simple things hard for the dolt to follow.

This is how computer manuals become too long, too vague, too expensive. It is a current problem for industry, and teachers should apply themselves to helping. They could well use their research to define specific styles to fit various "publics" (to borrow a PR term), such as technicians, managers, scientists, assembly-line workers, computer operators, housewives, non-native English speakers, other ethnic groups, and students at all levels.

Unfortunately, teachers are generally forced to use audience studies in the opposite way, to tailor their textbooks and class material to one-size-fits-all. They know their audience includes at least a small percentage of future scientists, for instance, so they feel the need to discuss Aristotle and the analysis of persuasion.

STARTS

One difference between industry and academic writing is the starts. An academic article will likely start "This paper . . ." Even letters may begin "This letter addresses." The justification is reader orientation.

However, in some journals, like *PMLA* (*Publications of the Modern Language Association of America*), or in magazines where authors are paid money, like *Scientific American* or *Smithsonian*, the reader is propelled into the story with no self-conscious preliminaries: "An important window to the universe is being closed in the interests of commercial television."

EDITING

In industry, editing is stiff and unyielding, and proud of it. Too often, the sole object is "consistency," and writing quality is evaluated versus the style manual. Technical editors are thus chosen not for their talent, but for their obdurateness.

As mentioned, editors use strict grammatical rules, leading to such gaffes as changing the singular engineering *design criteria* to a *design criterion* and arousing customer suspicion that the opus was not really authored by a cognizant engineer but by some unknowing amateur.

Companies commonly adhere to their own style even when it differs from the style of their customers. Ironically, on the campus, editing is more attuned to the real world.

ARTWORK

But teachers are not perfect. The *Technical Writing Teacher* is a journal written by and for teachers. Unfortunately, it is replete with classroom exercises where, for instance, students sit back-to-back and create prose to describe a pattern on a hidden piece of paper.

Technical writers would never do that. They would draw a picture. Tech writing uses artwork.

DECISION MAKING

Both businessmen and teachers hate to make decisions. Industry, faced with a deadline, may go to press with two versions, which to me is appalling, but admittedly practical. Teachers, on the other hand, may make no decisions at all. (To their credit, they may still be asking questions.)

Some textbooks, for instance, may offer a profuse variety of ideas, but no value judgments, leaving the misleading message that every concept is equally OK. Teachers often dismiss judgments as "situational," which is the academic equivalent of "TBD."

You can tell a bad stylebook by the number of decisions it defers. No stylebook should use the word "situational."

A NEW DIMENSION

In the past ten years or so, teachers have added a new dimension to technical writing: history.

For instance, they have developed the canon that Chaucer, because of his classic description of an astrolabe, was really a technical writer. Now, this may seem a bit like engineering students claiming that St. Patrick was an engineer because he devised the first worm drive. No. Research in Chaucer and others elevates the profession, gives it a heritage, and helps dispel the view of some teachers (and engineers) that technical writing is merely a matter of filling out engineering forms.

Teachers have similarly "canonized" Aristotle. Now, Aristotle was principally concerned with oratory, not technical writing, but he was strong on logic and persuasion, and literally wrote the book on Rhetoric.

To my surprise, however, in a fascinating class I audited at

UNM on "How to Teach Technical Writing," one bright graduate student proposed that it was not necessary to teach Aristotle. Instead, he argued, you can teach technical writing by using Milton. "Hence, vain deluded joys."

Teaching

One difference I found in teaching technical writing in college is that I needed to cover many routine things that engineers in industry know automatically: format, figure numbers, decimal numbering, lists of figures and tables, the processing of artwork, and so on.

I think the ideal course should also include standard abbreviations, the SI units, and the Greek alphabet (with explanations of *three-sigma* probabilities, *alpha* as angle of attack, and so on). It should also cover proposal storyboards, desktop publishing, and printing costs. It should explain, as time allows, trade-off studies, life-cycle costs, statistical reliability, and other common engineering terminology. It should not neglect the need for non-sexist language. Can you believe that some inexperienced technical writing teachers have trouble finding enough to teach?

Students should also know about controversies in grammar and how to bargain with the grammar experts universally found in business. That may be all the grammar instruction you need. And it's interesting.

I myself like to review the etymology of words used in engineering. Students enjoy discovering the derivation of *symposium* and *matrix*. Did you know that *duct* and *ductile* are both cognates of *education*?

I also make students write resumes to business firms and review books on technical writing topics.

These are all bridges between the two cultures. A course like this combines student interest and corporate practicality, and has a flavor distinctly different from freshman English.

By the way, English teachers correctly lament that industry is too often in a hurry. But, unfortunately, they sometimes act as though editors have a full fortnight to fix each faulty paragraph. Courses somehow need to prepare students to edit proposals of 1000 pages.

Collaborative Writing

In the past, writing—especially good writing—has been considered a lonely procreation. Also, industry has been slow to adopt the idea of paying two bodies for work that can be done by one. (Unless, of course, the work can be done twice as fast.)

In contrast, most teachers today see values in group participation. They envision writers exchanging ideas and actually brainstorming computer manuals, although perhaps not sitting side-by-side at the keyboard in cozy four-handed duets.

Briefly, the difference is that teachers tend to advocate communication, whereas industry sees time and cost advantages in holding fewer meetings.

Conclusion

For my own part, I lean toward more communication, particularly in one area: between industry and the universities. I am aware that the academic world is itself a "real world," devoted to education rather than training, and should not always adopt the "practical" precepts of business. But, nevertheless, both sides can learn a great deal from each other. As we know, professional societies are proof of this premise.

Differences between the two cultures are actually in shades of gray. Many technical writers already know about the ongoing research from the campus, and many teachers are active in the real world, away from the ivory tower.

However, we still need more cross-fertilization. Students and teachers should be invited to work in industry, to learn about costs and time and practicality. And even more important, industry should be encouraged to attend classes, to learn about freedom and invention and the language of the 21st century. In this way we can disseminate among ourselves our own technology in technical writing and pursue the mutual education we need to improve the products of our profession.

Don Bush was a proposal analyst and technical writing teacher for McDonnell Aircraft Co., for 25 years, where he was chief editor on successful proposals for the F-15, F-18, and AV-8B Harrier aircraft, the Harpoon missile, and the Space Station. Earlier, he was a reporter for the Kansas City *Star* and the Tulsa *World* and a public relations supervisor for Beech Aircraft Corp. and Southwestern Bell Telephone Company. He is a Fellow of the Society for Technical Communication and has been a frequent speaker at their annual conferences. His articles have appeared in *Technical Communication*, the *Technical Writing Teacher*, *Issues in Writing*, the *Editorial Eye*, and technical writing journals in England and Japan. He is coauthor of *Technical Writing, Principles and Practice* (Chicago: SRA, 1982). He retired from McDonnell in 1987 and now lives in San Diego, where he teaches part-time at San Diego State University and collects books on writing and editing.

PART II

Construction and Content: Putting Documents Together

This section focuses on how to organize and present certain kinds of writing. (Manuals and proposals are covered in separate sections.) A variety of topics are covered, from how to create a specifications document for a report you are going to write, to organizing a final copy. We also look at some unique aspects of certain documents, namely the bad news message, job application materials, recommendations, and technical articles for publication. Next you will see how important a style guide can be and how it can be used for more than just looking up "rules." The final article questions just how objective technical and other documents really are.

Organizing your report

Creating a document that will help you better produce another one might at first seem a bit redundant to a busy writer, but Liz Wing shows how writing up a blueprint, or document specification, for the work you have to produce can save a lot of time and also result in a much more effective final draft. The document specification Wing describes covers everything that will impact the document to be written and also enables its authors to estimate how many hours each task will take to complete. Although the example the author provides is for a software user guide, her approach can be applied to other kinds of documents also.

Writing your report

Since the second article deals with the structure of technical reports in general, it will help you prepare a variety of documents. Gael Ulrich's advice is universal, although you may want to modify parts of her suggested outline to suit specific documents. The weight each part of a report should carry is portrayed graphically in a table, and the comments on report length and style are to the point. A final comment on foggy writing is also worth noting, for as Ulrich observes, your fine engineering work may go unnoticed if it is not communicated effectively.

Communicating negative messages

Not all news is good news, and sometimes we cannot avoid the need to write bad-news messages. Thomas Wiseman shows you how to do this by avoiding the weak links that can form the transitions from one part of the message to another and which can unnecessarily further alienate the reader by adding to the negative tone of the message. The five guidelines he cites for composing bad-news documents are fundamental, and his practical advice on making a message no more negative than it need be will be of considerable use to those of you who sometimes have to communicate negative information.

Getting a job

Ron Blicq offers a compendium of what you should know about the documents needed to get a job. The most obvious are the resumé and letter of application, and these are discussed and illustrated fully. Blicq also considers other aspects of the job hunt, such as application forms and the dynamics of the job interview, and stresses that audience analysis is as important in writing to get a job as it is in other kinds of technical writing.

The recommendation letter

Alan Wilcox also emphasizes audience analysis in the article following Blicq's. A letter of recommendation needs a clear focus, and you should carefully identify your reader before you begin to write. The "general-purpose outline" Wilcox offers, together with his two examples of recommendation letters, will be of considerable help if you are asked to write such documents.

Publishing for growth

The next article shows why it is worth transforming some of your technical reports into published articles. Richard Manley, Judith Graham, and Ralph Baxter write specifically for engineers and scientists who may not yet have considered the advantages to their company and to themselves of publishing technical articles. The authors consider the difficulties involved, including the question of proprietary information, and then provide steps you can take to organize papers for submission. Finding out what editors want and what kinds of articles different journals look for are also important steps in the process.

A writer's best friend: the modern style guide

Perhaps the most useful document you can have nearby when writing is a style guide. This has always been true, especially since many companies give few standards for their writers to go by. As Perkins and Maloney show, a style guide is a primary and essential tool for single or team writers—but its usefulness can be extended beyond the mere application of "rules." It can also become an important tool for training new employees and for helping create both paper reports and Web pages.

How objective is your document?

Although the title of this article by Edmond Weiss might seem quite a mouthful, the author raises a fascinating question that can impinge upon all our writing. He asks whether all forms of communication are not to some extent clever forms of lying. Weiss closely develops this idea, analyzing various aspects of history, education, vocabulary, corporate culture, and "spin," showing how they all may help determine the final objectivity of a document, whether or not we are truly conscious of it. This has broad implications for technical writers who pride themselves on their completed documents being scientifically objective. However, Weiss also helps you recognize how difficult it is to be totally objective in your writing, and enables you to admit that at times you won't want or need to be.

Creating a Doc Spec

Interface

—Feature by
LIZ WING

Manuscript received February 8, 1999; revised February 24, 1999.
The author is with Nortel Networks, Research Triangle Park, NC 27709, USA.
IEEE PII S 0361-1434(99)04921-8.

Joyce Lasecke, "Stop Guesstimating, Start Estimating!" *Intercom*, November 1996.
Eric Layman, "Creating a Documentation Plan," *Intercom*, January 1997.
JoAnn T. Hackos, *Managing Your Documentation Projects*. New York: Wiley, 1994.

***Index Terms—** Documentation specification, estimating writer effort, levels of edit, subject matter experts (SMEs).*

All technical documentation projects benefit from a good content plan or doc spec. The doc spec is a blueprint for a document. It identifies the product, users, source materials, and subject matter experts (SME). It also provides a preliminary outline of topics, and it estimates the effort to produce the document.

Although the doc spec I describe here is for a printed software user guide, you can adapt your doc spec for other types of documentation, including hardware manuals and training guides. The doc spec template is simply a tool that leads you through the document planning and estimating process. Your customized doc spec captures the who, what, when, why, and how of your project.

Planning the Content

To create a customized doc spec, consider the unique processes, products, timelines, and constraints of your organization. A good doc spec includes most of the following kinds of information, which your template can reflect with headings and sections. (In this discussion, I include several examples from my own work with doc specs.)

Product Information Briefly describe the product. What does it provide the user? What problems does it solve? What new capabilities does it offer? The software products that I document provide automated capabilities for the telecommunications industry, particularly in the area of directory and operator services. My doc spec would briefly summarize the ways the product affects existing services, or it might list the key concepts the product introduces.

Audience Describe the users of the product. List any assumptions about the users' capabilities here. Most users of my guide work for the companies that provide local telephone service. These users are responsible for planning and maintaining operator networks. So my guide would assume that users are familiar with how basic call processing and operator queuing are performed at their telephone switch.

Subject Matter Experts List the SMEs from whom you will receive product and user information, including engineers, programmers, product testers, marketers, designers, managers, and customers. Also list their areas of expertise. Most of my SMEs are software designers, architects, and project managers. The list might also include experts in marketing and product verification from outside our organization.

Source Material List the product source documents, such as high-level design descriptions, functional or requirement specs, and marketing information. At my company, the software designers are required to write their own functional design specs. These, in turn, provide me with good source information to expand on or refine.

Reviewers List the reviewers of your document, their role and location. Include anyone who has an interest in the technical accuracy and usability of your document. My doc spec would list appropriate SMEs, one or two specialists in related areas within the company,

Reprinted from *IEEE Trans. Prof. Comm.*, vol. PC-42, no. 2, pp. 128–131, June 1999.

a technical editor, and, if possible, a customer. Reviewers will receive drafts and attend a technical review of the document. Those who cannot attend the review give me their comments on the hard copy.

Schedule Based on your organization's delivery timeline, list the dates for major document milestones. These dates specify when you will deliver the first draft, when you need comments returned, and when the technical review will take place. To create my document schedule, I start with our software release date and work backward. I plan for at least one technical review two to four weeks before the software release date. Then I give my reviewers two weeks before the review date to read the draft. This, in turn, determines the delivery date of my first draft.

Document Contents List the user tasks and give details on the document's purpose and content.

- *User tasks:* What tasks or procedures does the user need to perform with the product? To implement a new capability, my users often need to provide the telephone switch with specific data. My user guide needs to lead the user through the datafill process.
- *Purpose of document:* How will the user use the document? Knowing the purpose helps you refine the scope. What is the key information the document must provide? What should the user be able to do or understand after reading the document? My doc spec would list the major questions the user guide will answer, and it might briefly associate each question with a key feature of the product.
- *Preliminary outline:* Based on your user analysis and document purpose, evaluate the available product source material. List the expected chapters or main sections and describe or outline them. Consider the key topics that will make up each section. I usually devise the broad chapter names first. These are general categories such as overview, software description, call flow scenarios, and so on. Then I flesh out each category with a hierarchy of subtopics that are specific to the product.

Estimating the Effort

This part of the doc spec estimates the writer effort to produce the document. First, using your preliminary outline, estimate the length of the document in pages. Then, consider all the variables of the project to select a realistic formula for calculating the number of writer hours.

Page Estimate Consider how detailed the information must be. Will it have conceptual descriptions or step-by-step procedures (or both)? How much original information (not found in the source material) will the writer create? How much of the source material is usable and fits the purpose? Will it need extensive editing and reformatting? Will the document contain appendices of reference material? My preliminary outline might reveal that my user guide needs both conceptual (descriptive) and reference (alphabetical) information to adequately document the product. By researching the source material, I can estimate how complex a topic is and how many pages are needed to adequately explain it.

Also consider the number and complexity of graphics such as software and hardware architecture diagrams, process-flow scenarios, examples of screens for entering data, and printouts of user reports. In good user documentation, illustrations are plentiful. My user guides contain numerous network diagrams, call processing flows, and sample user datafill.

An experienced writer, using previous projects, can judge the number of pages a document will have. A novice writer can examine documents from similar products to use as a model.

Project Variables The amount of time a writer spends on a document depends on several variables.

- *Type of information:* Determine which procedures the document will include. Are they simple or complex? How many major concepts does the product introduce? Can these be explained better through text or through illustration? For example, a phone call travels through many steps before arriving at its destination. In my user guide, a particular call flow might be conveyed with a graphic that shows step numbers and directional arrows.
- *Research and training:* Even an experienced writer needs time to learn about a new capability or product. This learning can include interviewing SMEs, studying source material, attending software code inspections, and taking classes on related products. On my documentation projects, I study the design specs to learn the unique terminology of the product. Then, through one-on-one interviews with SMEs, I am able to translate the concepts into a logical narrative.
- *Number of reviews:* Producing a quality document requires at least one technical review. Will the review be a sit-down inspection with all reviewers present, or an informal exchange of comments? Each review takes time for reviewers to read the draft and provide comments; the comments take time to incorporate. Turnaround time and major revisions increase the effort. After the review, I typically need one or two weeks to rewrite and refine the content. In some cases, the book may need a second review.
- *Stability of product:* Consider how much the product is likely to change before the final re-

lease. When a document is developed in parallel with the product, changes can occur during the testing phase or near the end of the project cycle. Major changes or additions to the document increase the effort.

- *Document testing:* The writer needs to verify the accuracy of the user interface, such as the appearance of screen displays, the validity of data values, and the syntax of user commands. How much hands-on experience will the writer have with the product? For example, will the writer have a chance to install, configure, or otherwise interact with the product? To test my user guide, I use a command line interface at the telephone switch to check my datafill examples. Also, I like to have another team member test my written procedures.
- *Document editing:* Determine the level of edit the document will receive and build in adequate turnaround time. A substantive edit can take several days, depending on the page count. If your organization does not have a full-time editor, it is a good idea to have another writer copyedit your book for consistency, clarity, and corporate style.

Formula To estimate writer effort, consider the variables along with your estimated page count. In technical documentation, standard formulas for writer hours vary from three to six hours per page. This formula is affected by the constraints of the project, such as the availability of SMEs, the project timeline, the complexity of the material, and the writer's skill. These circumstances determine the number (i.e., 3–6) to use in your formula.

Example Estimate This part of the doc spec calculates the hours for the typical writer tasks. The sample book, shown in Table I, will contain mostly descriptive text and illustrations. The estimated page count is 200 pages, with one technical review scheduled. Based on the constraints of the project, a four-hour-per-page formula is chosen:

$$200 \text{ pages} \times 4 \text{ hours per page} = 800 \text{ hours (20 weeks)}.$$

To determine whether one writer has time to complete the documentation, compare the estimated weeks of writer effort to the weeks available in your timeline. In some cases, the book may require more than one writer, or the book's scope may need to be reduced.

Table I shows a breakdown of the total number of hours estimated for each task. The tasks are listed in rough chronological order; however, in practice, some tasks run through the entire project.

TABLE I
ESTIMATE OF EFFORT FOR A 200-PAGE SOFTWARE USER GUIDE

WRITER TASK	HOURS
Researching source docs, learning about product, producing doc spec	140
Attending software code inspections	20
Interviewing SMEs	40
Creating book structure with authoring tool	40
Writing new content and creating graphics	160
Editing and reformatting existing content from source docs	180
Delivering first draft to reviewers	10
Conducting one technical review	10
Copyediting per corporate standards, style, and page layout	40
Testing user interface in lab	30
Incorporating comments from technical review and copyedit	80
Producing final version with index and glossary	50
TOTAL HOURS	800

REFERENCES

[1] J. Lasecke, "Stop guesstimating, start estimating!," *Intercom*, vol. 43, no. 9, Nov. 1996.

[2] E. Layman, "Creating a documentation plan," *Intercom*, vol. 44, no. 1, Jan. 1997.

[3] J. T. Hackos, *Managing Your Documentation Projects*. New York: Wiley, 1994.

Liz Wing is a senior technical writer at Nortel Networks, where she plans and writes user documentation for telecommunications products. On every project, she creates a doc spec to give management a realistic estimate of the scope and effort to produce the documentation. She has presented her sample doc spec template at local and international STC gatherings. Her paper, "Using a Doc Spec for Printed Books," appeared in *1998 Proceedings of the Society for Technical Communication 45th Annual Conference*.

Write a Good Technical Report

GAEL D. ULRICH

Abstract—A _good_ technical report can have an important effect on a wide range of people. Here are some techniques to help you prepare, choose a suitable structure, provide the right amount of information in the right places, and make your points with clarity. An informal style—using "I" and "we," for example—is acceptable for technical reports and publications. To improve your writing, read good writing by others and invite criticism of your own; practice is important.

IN the beginning, the story goes, God, after creating humankind, was defining the professions. "Anticipating that squabbles would ultimately develop between chemists and chemical engineers, He decided to settle the issue once and for all, dictating to His typist, 'All a chemical engineer does is *right*.' Unfortunately the typist misspelled the last word" [1]. At times, many of us might agree that all a chemical engineer does is *write*. Some feel we don't even do that very well and that we're getting worse. In a recent survey of educators and industrialists, for instance, some respondents complained that language skills among chemical engineering graduates had deteriorated severely in recent years. Others, according to the reporter, felt simply that the skills were not better than before—abominable [2].

I have heard some managers in industry claim that communication skills are more important than technical competence. I do not agree. Communication would be unnecessary if there were no technical result to report. (It does, indeed, require exceptional writing or speaking skill to camouflage an inept or incomplete engineering job.) But I do agree with a variant of the managers' statement: "Many exceptional engineering jobs go unappreciated because of poor writing or speaking." With this in mind, let us consider the elements of effective writing.

PHILOSOPHY OF TECHNICAL REPORTING

Unlike politicians, engineers should write with the hope that readers will find their errors. It is much less embarrassing and painful for an engineering mistake to be found in print before it appears in fact. Thus, a technical report should be designed with clarity as the major goal.

Basic honesty is a key ingredient of clear writing. If there is no concrete result or recommendation, say so. Perhaps your most important contribution will be to expose a question or a mistake. Such honesty may not always pay off immediately, but a reputation for integrity is worth the wait. Reports intended to reveal rather than obscure will be better understood by others and, when deserving, will be defended by them.

MECHANICS OF REPORT WRITING

An outline does wonders to initiate the writing process. Professional or experienced writers often outline their work mentally, not formally. However, judging from the indictment in the first paragraph of this chapter, you should prepare a written outline if you are a student or an engineer. As an example, a skeleton outline of this chapter is shown in the box. (Of course, the real outline is scribbled on three sheets of paper with numerous insertions and marginal notations.) As you prepare your outline, think about the audience. Van Ness and Abbott [3] caution that readers of most technical reports

1. Are busy or at least believe so.
2. Have a background similar to yours but know much less about the project in question.

Other reader characteristics may prevail under various circumstances. In fact, the abstract and summary of a report are often designed for administrators and business people with nonengineering backgrounds.

"Joe, we need your report. Is it about ready?"

Extracted and reprinted with permission from chapter 9, "Report Preparation," of the author's new text *A Guide to Process Design and Economics for Chemical Engineers;* copyright 1984 by John Wiley and Sons, Inc., New York.

The author is a Professor of Chemical Engineering at the University of New Hampshire, Durham, NH 03824; (603) 862-3655.

Reprinted from *IEEE Trans. Prof. Comm.*, vol. PC-27, no. 1, pp. 14–19, March 1984.

Outline
Chapter Nine
REPORT PREPARATION

I. Introduction
  (Attention) "Skills no better than before–abominable."
  A. Importance of communication skill.
    1. More important than technical skills? Hogwash.
    2. "All an engineer does is write (right?)."
  B. Philosophy of writing.
    1. Honesty.

II. Mechanics of report writing
  A. Outline.
    1. Reader identification.
    2. Who, What, When, Where, Why, How?
    3. Write conclusions first.
    4. Review literature or calculations.
    5. Write thoughts on sheets of paper.
  B. Structure.
    1. Cinnamon roll.
    2. Dangers of rigid format.
    3. Sample outline.
      a. Purpose of section.
        i. Present technical information.
        ii. Define, recommend, encourage, promote action.
        iii. Data repository.
      b. Sample format (see Table I)
  C. Length.
    1. Long enough to reach the ground.
    2. 50-mile hike.

III. Style and technique.
  (Interest) Hydrochloric acid to clean pipes.
  A. First person, humor, informal versus formal.
  B. Fog Index.
  C. How to improve.
    1. Practice, practice, practice.
    2. Invite criticism.
    3. Read good writing appreciatively.
    4. Read bad writing critically.

Some suggestions by Bolmer [4] for preparing a speech are also appropriate for prose. At each juncture, ask the magic questions: Who? What? When? Where? Why? How? The answers will usually lead you to the next step. Bolmer also suggests writing or identifying the conclusions first (asking the same questions) to provide focus in the outline. Next, review your notes and write prominent thoughts, quotations, and ideas on slips of paper. Do not then cast them into the air and pick them up randomly from the floor. Instead, organize them as your mind directs. In the shuffle, some ideas might appropriately land in the wastebasket.

Report Structure

Composing a report is much like baking cinnamon rolls. A cook does not put dough in one pile, raisins in another, cinnamon and sugar in a third, and then bake the ingredients separately. Neither does one place all the materials in a blender and atomize them into a uniform mass. Instead, individual elements are assembled wisely and in proper proportion to yield an interesting, attractive, and tasty result. So is a report organized to provide mental nourishment, impetus, and satisfaction.

I see three primary purposes of a design report:

1. To present technical information.
2. To serve as a repository of data.
3. To promote or define action.

The first two might be viewed as the dough, the third as cinnamon and raisins. Unfortunately, I cannot give you an exact recipe for composing a report. A rigid outline for all reports and situations is stifling. However, for a beginner, a skeleton format may be helpful. The format illustrated in

TABLE I
SAMPLE FORMAT FOR A TECHNICAL REPORT

Division	Section	Purpose: Present Information	Purpose: Data Repository	Purpose: Promote or Define Action
I. Beginning procedural section (front matter)	Letter of transmittal Title page Table of contents Abstract			
II. Summary	Summary			
III. Body	Introduction (background, literature survey, theory, etc.) Method of approach (procedure) Results Discussion of results Conclusions Recommendations			
IV. Concluding procedural section (back matter)	References Appendix			

Table I is discussed in detail. As you read about each section, think which of the foregoing purposes is satisfied. (I have provided space in Table I to keep score; I divulge my ratings later.)

I like to think of a report as containing four divisions: a beginning procedural segment, the summary, a body, and an end procedural segment.

• *Front Matter*
The beginning procedural segment usually contains a *letter of transmittal, title page, table of contents,* and *abstract*.. It is much like the pages at the beginning of this book numbered in lowercase roman numerals. (This section is known as "front matter" in the publishing business.) In many reports, especially brief ones, some of these components are unnecessary. In a short or letter report, the title, abstract, and beginning of body may appear on the first page.

• *Summary*
The *summary* is an isolated section because it is often circulated separately to a wider audience that includes managers and nontechnical readers who are concerned with action and recommendations rather than computational detail. Because of its political impact and importance in decision making, the summary should be written most carefully, emphasizing vital conclusions and recommendations. Supporting data must be summarized and presented clearly and interestingly to a less sophisticated reader. Illustrations should be used effectively but sparingly. Since the summary is based on the broader report, it is, of course, written last. It appears, however, near the front of the finished document as shown in Table I.

• *Body*
Asking who, what, when, where, why, and how leads smoothly to an efficient outline for the report body. An *introduction* of some sort is necessary to bring the reader "up to speed." Historical or chronological structure is ofttimes effective in this section. If appropriate, *literature survey, theory,* and other topics may be folded into an introduction or inserted as separate sections.

To evaluate your report, a technical reader must understand how you derived the results. A section on *approach* or *procedure* serves this need. It should be written in a way that permits a reader to duplicate experiments or calculations independently if necessary. In a design project, pivotal assumptions and bases should be included and, where appropriate, explained. More common assumptions are listed in the appendix or not at all. Detailed calculations should not be placed here or in the appendix. They belong in your files. Representative sample calculations should be in the appendix.

A key structural role is played by the *results* section.

Information vital to the final conclusions and recommendations is found here. Peripheral data should be in the appendix or in your files. Inclusion of unnecessary detail obscures vital results.

The results section is followed by the *discussion* or *discussion of results*. This is where logical conclusions are exposed. Many authors fail to develop and manipulate their data enough. One table in my book, for example, was assembled from ten sources. I spent hours arriving at a format, days defining the details. This single table required more than a week's hard labor. The original ten sources could easily have been reprinted directly but I wanted focused data, not diffuse data. Many engineers do not invest enough energy in massaging results. They are satisfied with detailed tabulations of numbers when refined charts or curves would tell the story better.

The *conclusions* and *recommendations* sections represent the apex of your report. As you outline these sections, think, analyze, and ask the magic questions. Skilled technical writers, not unlike popular authors, often use suspense to create a climax. Since preceding sections have created a focusing effect, this segment can be concentrated and brief. Often conclusions and recommendations are combined into a single section. Sometimes recommendations are presented as a numbered list of statements.

How you say it *does* make a difference. We could imagine someone walking down a corridor, stopping at each door, knocking, and politely stating, "My senses perceive a conflagration at the extremes of this structure. I advise you to depart with haste." A real messenger would, of course, race up and down the hall screaming "Fire! Fire!" Provocations and emotions created by screaming "Fire!" in a technical report sometimes cause regret. On the other hand, we want readers to sit up, take notice, and, in many cases, act. Of the two approaches illustrated, a tone nearer "Fire!" is suggested.

- *Back Matter*

The final procedural section will not be opened by many readers, yet it serves a fundamental role in supporting the report. Not only should we be considerate of our more technical readers who will read this section but also want to help them find any mistakes that might be present.

References can be presented in any logical, consistent format so long as they are clear and unambiguous. The format used in this book should be acceptable in most reports. As a reader, I find article titles informative and recommend their inclusion. Sometimes, authors try to impress readers by citing exhaustive lists of nonpertinent references. This creates the same result as unnecessary detail in the text—foggy and misleading communication.

Efficiency and clarity are traits of an effective *appendix*. Sometimes, students dump their raw calculations here to prove the work was done and to impress the teacher. As a reader, I am confused, discouraged, and angered by this strategy. Writers often fail to separate the wheat from the chaff. In almost every case I have seen, computer printout is chaff and should not be included in the report. Raw calculations are also chaff and should remain in your files. They do serve nicely, nonetheless, as a useful outline for preparing the appendix. Illustrative and sample calculations selected critically from your work provide effective support to more focused information found in the report body. An effective appendix demands the same kind of creativity as any other part of the report. Sometimes even good authors are careless with this section.

By the way, in my opinion, purpose 1 (to present information) applies to the letter of transmittal, title page, and table of contents in Table I. The abstract, summary, discussion of results, and conclusions accomplish the same end and promote or define action (purpose 3) as well. Purposes 1 and 2 generally suit the introduction and approach sections. Action is promoted and defined primarily in recommendations. References and the appendix serve as data repositories.

I reemphasize that the outline is only a suggestion; the nature of the project—and your personality—shape the structure of the report. This reminds me of my first 50-mile backpacking trip. I had listened to a man who frequently hiked in California's Sierra Mountains. He stressed the importance of lightweight packing and illustrated it by telling how he took only three pair of socks. He wore two pair and carried the other. When camping for the evening, he changed socks and washed out the sweaty ones; laying them on a warm stone. The next morning, they were dry and ready for the day's hike.

I tried the same technique on a trip in the Appalachian Mountains in New England. What succeeded in dry California failed miserably and odorously in the Northeast. (Where does one find warm rocks in the rain?) Consider the situation in designing a report. Is yours a three-sock or a nine-sock project?

Report Length

The question of report length might be answered the same way Abraham Lincoln answered a query about a man's legs. He said they should be long enough to reach the ground. A report should be long enough to tell the story.

Length is also somewhat dependent on audience and other circumstances. Many of us, infatuated with our own writing, tend to inflate its length. The old saying "Length of a graduate thesis is inversely proportional to the data it contains" is boringly valid at times. It's as though there was a minimum weight limit. Even though I am considered sparing with words, a ruthless but respected critic eliminated about 20 percent of what was originally drafted for this chapter. The improvement was worth the pain.

STYLE AND TECHNIQUE

Some years ago, a New York plumber discovered that hydrochloric acid was dandy for cleaning clogged drains. He sent his suggestion to the National Bureau of Standards.

"The efficacy of hydrochloric acid is indisputable," the Bureau wrote back, "but the ionic residues are incompatible with metallic permanence."

"Thank you," replied the plumber. "I thought it was a good idea too."

Finally, someone at the Bureau wrote, "Don't use hydrochloric acid! It eats hell out of the pipes!"

No doubt, crisp language communicates ideas efficiently. No one knows how many years scientific and technological progress has been retarded by foggy writing. Communication professionals have been criticizing the characteristically formal impersonal language of science for years. Yet, we still encounter unpleasant examples in our professional literature. Fortunately, promising trends are evident and we find more humor and use of first person in modern technical prose. Van Ness and Abbott wrote [3]:

> For many years the dominant attitude with respect to scientific and technical writing was that it should be impersonal, because science and technology were said to be impersonal. This forced adoption of the passive voice and promoted the lifeless syntax, the witless style, to say nothing of the grammatical mistakes of technical prose. We repudiate the whole of it. Not only does habitual use of the passive voice make for dull writing, it forces a convoluted style almost impossible for an engineer to make concise, precise, and grammatical. *I* and *we* are not four-letter words; they are entirely acceptable in technical reports and publications. We do not suggest that every sentence start with *I* or *we*; one seeks variety. If you are too humble or shy to bring yourself to write *I*, use *we*, in the sense of you, the reader, and I, the writer. *One* also has its place. Do not think you can avoid responsibility for what you write by adopting an impersonal style. No way; your name is on the title page. Take some pride in it; you are the expert.

The entire article is a useful guide for engineers.

I remember speaking, not long ago, with a student who went to work at DuPont. As a new recruit, he spent his first month on the job in a writing course. Instructors emphasized informal personal style because it makes written communication so much more effective. If the largest U.S. chemical corporation believes in it, we should feel free to promote it.

In the following example, the information about a project is written at different levels of formality:

> This experiment was designed to define the relationship between temperature, time, and location in the curing of a polyurethane automobile bumper. It was initiated because of failures in certain applications.

> About five percent of the bumpers we manufacture for the new Z cars are dropping from the vehicles at subfreezing temperatures. In a crash program to salvage our contract with Studebaker, Jean Doe assigned Dan Jordan and me to analyze the curing process and isolate any flaws.

Unfortunately, not all organizations tolerate informal technical documents. You may find the need to aim your language somewhere between that befitting an automobile purchase agreement and that in a letter to an intimate friend. However, grammar, punctuation, spelling, clarity, and precision of writing at any level of formality can be improved. As guides to the technical rules for good English expression, references 5 and 6 are recommended.

A recent article in *Science 82* [7] discusses the Fog Index used by Douglas Mueller, a writing consultant. It is a measure of writing clarity. As reported in that article, big words and long sentences are the two major culprits. The Fog Index puts these factors into a simple formula that tells how many years of schooling are needed to read a sample easily. The first letter to the plumber has a Fog Index of 26. To understand it requires a Ph.D. and seven years of postdoctoral study. The second letter, with a Fog Index of 6, should be clear to a sixth grader.

The article continues to describe how to calculate a Fog Index. My 12-year-old son Thatcher, intrigued with the challenge, computed indices for two important recent documents created in our family. A selection from the preface of this book scored 15, low enough for students with 12 years of grammar and high school and three years of college. My wife's recent book on colonial history rated 11. According to *Science 82*, she wins.

> At what Fog Index should a writer write? "A low one," says Mueller. The nation's largest daily newspaper, *The Wall Street Journal*, got that way by lowering its Fog Index to 11. *Time* and *Newsweek* also average 11. *The New Yorker* usually comes in under 12. Technical journals range a lot higher, but most are notoriously hard reading, even for specialists. Good technical memos, according to a recent study at Bell Laboratories, average only 14. "The truth is," says Mueller, "no matter what Fog Index your readers can tolerate, they prefer to get their information without strain." Mueller says he's never met anyone, in any field, who couldn't lower his Fog Index to 15. "Einstein could. It's easy. Just keep your average sentence length under 20, cross out every useless word, and never use a Big Word unless you absolutely need to. Remember: The less energy your reader wastes on decoding your language, the more he'll have left for your brilliant ideas" [7].

Some examples, prominent and otherwise, were also given. From a business letter:

> We might further mention that we would be glad to furnish

any one of these whistles on a trial basis, to the extent that if the smaller size was not adequate enough, it could be returned in lieu of the purchase of a larger size, depending upon actual operation and suitability of your requirements for signal distance and audibility. (Fog Index: 28)

Translation:

> If your whistle isn't loud enough, send it back and we'll give you a bigger one. (Fog Index: 6)

From the scientific journal *Nature*:

> The current fashion for environmental impact assessment (EIA) is partly explained by the continuing force of the environmental protection movement in Western countries. That movement is now under severe pressure from economic recession, and there are signs that impact assessments themselves will play a decreasing role in planning and development. Certainly, this is the message that emerges from the U.S.A., where the emphasis is switching back to the costs of environmental protection. (Fog Index: 17)

Opening of the Gettysburg Address:

> Fourscore and seven years ago our fathers brought forth on this continent a new nation, conceived in liberty and dedicated to the proposition that all men are created equal. Now we are engaged in a great civil war, testing whether that nation or any nation so conceived and so dedicated can long endure. We are met on a great battlefield of that war. We have come to dedicate a portion of that field as a final resting place for those who here gave their lives that that nation might live. It is altogether fitting and proper that we should do this. (Fog Index: 10)

Matthew 6:9–13 (King James version):

> Our Father which art in heaven, Hallowed be thy name. Thy kingdom come. Thy will be done in earth, as it is in heaven. Give us this day our daily bread. And forgive us our debts, as we forgive our debtors. And lead us not into temptation, but deliver us from evil: For thine is the kingdom, and the power, and the glory, for ever. Amen. (Fog Index: 4)

Knowing the facts of good style does not necessarily create good writing. A reporter is said to have asked a famous football coach the secret of his success. He said there were three reasons: (1) practice, (2) practice, (3) practice. (A bystander added, "But it helps if the players are big and fast.") By analogy, to improve writing skills, you should write, write, write. (But it helps if you have grown up in an articulate family, studied debate for eight years, and taken a minor in English.)

Not only must you write, but also you should swallow your ego and invite expert criticism. In a less threatening vein, read quality writing by others and try to understand why it is good. When it is necessary to read bad writing, read it critically, noting errors and problems in margins as you observe them. Rewrite passages to see if you can improve them. (If the writer is your professor or a corporate vice president, it might be wise to destroy the marked copy.)

REFERENCES

1. Leesley, M. E.; Williams, M. L., Jr. "All a Chemical Engineer Does Is Write," *Chemical Engineering Education*. Fall 1978; 12(4): 188–192.
2. Ricci, L. J. "Chemical Engineers' Education Goes Downhill," *Chemical Engineering*. April 2, 1979; 86(9): 94–98.
3. Van Ness, H.C.; Abbott, M. M. "Technical Prose: English or Techlish?" *Chemical Engineering Education*. Fall 1977; 11(4): 154–159.
4. Bolmer, J. "Tips on Talking in Public." *Chemical Engineering*. Sept. 21, 1981; 88(19): 143–146. Also in *IEEE Transactions on Professional Communication*. March 1982; PC-25(1); 40–42.
5. Hodges, John C.; Whitten, Mary E. *Harbrace College Handbook*. 7th ed. New York: Harcourt Brace Jovanovich; 1972.
6. Strunk, W., Jr.; White, E. B. *The Elements of Style*. 3rd ed. New York: Macmillan; 1978.
7. Dunkle, T. "Obfuscatory Scrivenery (Foggy Writing)." *Science 82*. April 1982; 3(3) 82–84.

How to Avoid the Transitional Ax in Indirect Bad News Messages

Thomas L. Wiseman

Abstract—**Professional communicators and managers can soften the tone of bad news messages by avoiding "transitional axes," which are words and phrases that sever one section of the message from the next section. These words destroy any potential for goodwill between the sender and receiver of the message. The sender can avoid transitional axes in at least three ways: 1) by using verbally keyed transitions such as repeated words, synonyms, specific naming, abbreviations or generic nouns; 2) by using cognitively keyed transitions that employ word- and thought-association to create implied connections; 3) by using traditional connectors such as conjunctions and conjunctive adverbs. Each of these techniques avoids use of the transitional ax and facilitates the exchange of bad news.**

Introduction

An "indirect" bad news message is distinctly different from a routine or "direct" bad news memo or letter. In the indirect bad news message, the writer wishes to say "no" firmly, yet maintain the goodwill of the reader. The purpose of such a message, as Bowman and Branchaw explain, is to present "negative information in a way that will help your readers accept it" [1]. In direct bad news messages, however, the writer's sole purpose is to deliver the bad news in clear and pointed language. For example, when you fire a worker for documented reasons, you probably have no need (or inclination) to maintain the goodwill of the receiver of the message. That is direct bad news. On the other hand, if budget problems force you to lay off an efficient and productive employee, you might want to soften the bad news as much as possible to maintain the person's goodwill, or at least not create any unnecessary ill will.

Other common "no" letters requiring an indirect format are refusals to extend credit, grant discounts, make adjustments, contribute to causes, or lengthen contract terms [2]. As P. V. Anderson notes, "The indirect pattern often works better in situations where the audience is likely to treat the main point as unwelcome or bad news, at least if the writer or speaker does not prepare the audience for it beforehand" [3]. There is a fairly conventional and reliable structure to help writers who must present such indirect bad news messages: 1) a neutral or positive buffer to open the letter or memo; 2) a reasons section that provides solid evidence for *why* you are going to say no; 3) a short and unquestionable statement giving the bad news; 4) a closing neutral or positive buffer to soften the impact of the bad news.

The weak seams in almost any indirect bad news message are the transitions from one section of the message to the next. In fact, these transitions mark the stress points where writers are most likely to defeat their purpose by using words such as "however," "but," "on the other hand," and others that loudly herald in the bad news or create a negative tone. Because such a term cuts off the earlier positive message and tone, I refer to it as a "transitional ax."

In a message where you wish to give bad news firmly yet maintain the goodwill of the audience, just one of these words can undercut even the most careful use of positive language, complex sentence structure, minimum space given to bad news, and other textual and structural devices commonly used to avoid breaking down the relationships between the message sender and the receiver. In this paper, I will outline three methods of avoiding the transitional ax: 1) verbally keyed transitions (such as repetitions, synonyms, substitutions, abbreviations, and generic nouns; 2) cognitively keyed transitions (word-associations semantically related to the main topic); and 3) conventional and forward-pressing transitions like "because" or "for this reason."

Coherence of Tone Needed

Let us first review the basic structure of an indirect bad news message: 1) neutral or positive buffer; 2) reasons, facts, or evidence for the negative decision; 3) the bad news message itself; 4) positive or neutral buffer to close the message. Although some add a section for "alternatives" and one for "good will closings," these two sections are optional because often there are no alternatives to offer and a good will close can be adequately handled in the closing buffer section. Within this structure, writers should keep in mind K. J. Harty's five guidelines for writing bad news letters [4].

1) Whenever possible, be indirect rather than direct.
2) Cushion bad news with a positive or neutral opening.
3) Try to anticipate and sympathize with your reader.
4) Talk directly to the reader by using personal pronouns and terms the reader will recognize.
5) Exploit the length of the letter—brevity is inappropriate in bad news letters.

Based upon Harty's guidelines and upon the indirect structure itself, we may infer that the writer's sympathy and understanding of the reader's situation ultimately determine the coherence of tone and the effectiveness of the letter. As writers, it is not our intention to "pretend to be able to manipulate the reader's response," as D. Brent suggests [5]. Although Brent opposes the idea, we might well see a certain Rogerian argumentative approach in the indirect bad news letter. Brent himself summarizes Rogerian argument thusly: ". . . the communicator [strives] to establish an atmosphere of trust by attempting to understand, as honestly as possible, the other's point of view, and by concentrating on areas of shared values before discussing areas of disagreement" [5]. This concept seems extremely close to the buffer-reasons-bad news-buffer approach to writing an indirect bad news letter.

Verbally-Keyed Transitions

In the opening buffer, strive to make a "neutral, noncontroversial statement closely related to the point" of the message

Manuscript received October 25, 1990.
The author is with the Department of Humanities and Social Sciences, Southern College of Technology, Marietta, GA 30060.
IEEE Log Number 9041447.

Reprinted from *IEEE Trans. Prof. Comm.*, vol. PC-34, no. 1, pp. 20–23, March 1991.

[6]. This opening buffer is best when it is brief, relevant, positive, yet does not "falsely suggest that good news will be forthcoming" [7]. It also is vital to avoid saying "no" in this early buffer. At stake in this opener is the tone and overall effectiveness of the entire message, so you must choose your words thoughtfully and place them carefully. More importantly, it is crucial to avoid the transitional ax when you begin to move your thoughts from the buffer to the reasons section of the message.

A word like "unfortunately" immediately severs the buffer from the reasons section. In context, such a word cuts one section away from another. In indirect bad news messages, these ax words are not transitional at all: they are actually antitransitional because they mark abrupt and rhetorically ineffective changes in tone and content in the message. For example, consider the following buffer and potential transitional axes that would point to the second paragraph:

BUFFER	Thank you for presenting your proposal to Coleman, Inc.'s Board of Directors on Wednesday, June 20, 1990. Your coverage was thorough and enlightening, and we can understand why several other major corporations are using this information management system.
TRANS. AX	However, . . . Unfortunately, . . . On the other hand, . . . But . . .

If your purpose is to turn down the proposal and still maintain the goodwill of the reader and her firm, you must find a less ominous transition to substitute for any of these ax words.

K. Rolland has observed that "most readers are satisfied with a convincing explanation for a rejection" [2]. But the writer must make an effective transition from the opening buffer to the reasons section of the letter if he is to convince the reader of the justness of the company's decision. How to do it? First, in the reasons section you could repeat a word that appears in the buffer. In the example, you could repeat the key words "major corporations" or "information management system," depending upon the emphasis of the second paragraph. Such repetition of key words or phrases—and the thoughts they carry—creates an organic and implied transition between the two paragraphs. The example bad news opener and reasons might then read something like this (transitions in italics):

BUFFER	Thank you for presenting your proposal to Coleman, Inc.'s Board of Directors on Wednesday, June 20, 1990. Your coverage was thorough and enlightening, and we can understand why several other major corporations are using this information management system.
REASONS W/ TRANSITIONS (Repeated Key Words)	These *other corporations* have pinpointed specific *information management* needs and objectives. We are currently in the process of doing that. We are focusing on several of the matters that you examined in your proposal: these areas include documentation design, in-house documentation, spreadsheet availability, and accessibility. We are also interested in system networking for all mid-level managers.

There are, of course, many ways of creating coherence in your message with verbally keyed transitions. In an analysis of business writing, M. P. Jordan mentions "full and partial repetition, substitution, synonyms, generic nouns, naming and abbreviations" [8] as means of "re-entering" a topic that has already been introduced to the receiver of a message. He views "the writer, having introduced a topic for description, as then having to use the many means of 're-entering' that topic into the text so that he can describe it further" [8]. Jordan's paradigm contains only techniques that contribute to "the progressive writing of the text" [8] rather than those he calls "anaphoric (referring back)" [8]. For this reason, his analysis is extremely relevant to a discussion of transitional axes in bad news messages, which invariably reverse the thought flow or impede its progress.

Use of synonyms as transitions is a common technique in composition courses, as are the other "basic re-entry" formulas Jordan mentions. By "substitutions" he means relative pronouns like "which" or "that" or other words that refer back to an antecedent. Use of "generic nouns," "naming," and "abbreviation" are merely different forms of repetition, substitution, and synonyms. In the previous example. "These other corporations" in the reasons section would represent substitution ("these"), generic nouns ("corporations"), and partial repetition ("other corporations") picked up from the buffer. "Information management" is also a partial repetition of the "information management system" in the buffer.

Cognitively-Keyed Transitions

Such techniques are quite clear and can be useful. As Jordan points out, however, you also have access to a second, more sophisticated, strategy of transitions for more complicated messages. You can create subtle transitions, he says, by using "associated re-entry," which "occurs when the writer chooses to discuss something associated with the topic rather than discussing the topic itself" [8]. An associated re-entry word, the use of which in this paper I have called "cognitively keyed transitions," can be "any nominal group which the readers will associate with the topic" [8].

In our sample bad news message, the word "proposal" is clearly the topic and the "trigger" word, which generates the semantic connection [8]. Any words that the reader logically associates with the proposal itself or with information management systems (the subject of the proposal) can serve as transitional words—as cognitive keys—to get you from section to section in the message. Notice that the definite article serves to indicate whether the reader should be familiar with the association or not. As Jordan points out, "most of the associated re-entries . . . generally contain the definite article, indicating that readers should know or expect the existence of that re-entry in association with the topic being discussed" [8]. In moving from buffer to reasons in our example bad news message, then, we might use words that our readers would associate with the proposal in a positive but neutral tone (transitions set in italics):

BUFFER:	Thank you for presenting your proposal to Coleman, Inc.'s Board of Directors on Wednesday, June 20,

	1990. Your coverage was thorough and enlightening, and we can understand why several other major corporations are using this information management system.
REASONS with TRANSITIONS (Cognitive Keys)	*The data* cited make it clear that more and more firms are active in the field. The need for a system like the one you described is a priority for the larger corporations. The main point that American firms are behind businesses of other nations was well presented. We are currently in the process of *upgrading our* IMS in the areas of *document design*, *in-house documentation*, *spreadsheet availability*, *and accessibility*. A *system* is also needed to provide electronic networking for mid-level managers in our 72 branch offices throughout the world.

Early in the paragraph the word associations should be familiar to the reader and are signaled by the definite article "the," except in the case of "a system." Later, however, as we move into unfamiliar word-association, the indefinite article appears or there is no indicator at all. This movement tracks the movement from the known information to that which is not known (and which will lead to the bad news itself). The rhetorical flow of thought from the buffer to the reasons sections is smooth and avoids the transitional ax.

Moreover, the cognitively keyed transitions within the reasons section are unobtrusive and move quietly from neutral and shared information to what, we suppose, would be the logical evidence for saying "no." As readers, we infer that the proposal in question did not cover the specifics mentioned after "upgrading our IMS" and the material following "A system" in the third from the last line. Such implied transitions are effective in making your bad news message coherent and forceful without being offensively blunt.

Forward-Pressing Transitions

In addition to verbally keyed and cognitively keyed transitions, you may choose to use a forward-pressing conjunction or a conjunctive adverb to push your message across forcefully yet tactfully. Perhaps the safest and simplest conjunction for our model case would be "and." After the buffer, you could simply say, "*And* we are focusing on several of the matters that you examined . . . ." If you wanted a more formal link between the two sections, you could use a conjunctive adverb like "Moreover" or "Furthermore," both of which clearly indicate that you are merely adding more to what you have already said. These transitional words are neutral and reassuring in that they suggest that the thoughts and tone will remain relatively unchanged. A phrase containing a forward-pressing word could work just as well: "*We are also* focusing on several of the matters that you examined." Having made a smooth and effective bridge between your first two sections, you could then proceed to fill in the details and evidence that make up the reasons section.

Stressing the effectiveness of these verbal connectors, S. Baker notes that they tighten a message because they "tie things together [while] pointing back as they carry the reference ahead" [9]. Thus, whether you have used verbally keyed, cognitively keyed, or conventional transitions, you have avoided the transitional ax that might have severed your early buffer from the reasons section. You can now move on, secure in knowing that your reader or listener is still with you. But now comes the toughest part: how to get from the logic and common sense of the reasons section to the potential emotionalism of the bad news section.

The Crucial Transition

No other point in the message is as vulnerable to the transitional ax as is the seam between your reasons and bad news sections. Once again, you can avoid the ax by using repeated key words, word associations, or forward-pressing transitions. Part of the difficulty throughout the indirect bad news message, but crucial at this point, is that you carefully consider what information the reader already knows and what is new to him or her. Researchers have called this arrangement the "given-new contract," in which sender and receiver agree "that while communicating they will share a 'mental world' where all parties know what is given information and what is new" [10].

As important as the given-new contract might be, however, it has little but theoretical value if the transitions between sections of the message are weak. This is especially true of the transition between the reasons and the bad news sections. Once you are aware of the several "safe" means of transition, you can make the movement with reasonable assurance of success. For our model message, consider the following transition from reasons to bad news (transitions set in italics):

BUFFER:	Thank you for presenting your proposal to Coleman, Inc.'s Board of Directors on Wednesday, June 20, 1990. Your coverage was thorough and enlightening, and we can understand why several other major corporations are using this information management system.
REASONS WITH COGNITIVE TRANSITIONS	*The data* cited make it clear that more and more firms are active in the field. The need for a system like the one you described is a priority for the larger corporations. The main point that American firms are behind businesses of other nations was well presented. We are currently in the process of *upgrading our* IMS in the areas of *document design*, *in-house documentation*, *spreadsheet availability*, *and accessibility*. A *system* is also needed to provide electronic networking for mid-level managers in our 72 branch offices throughout the world.
BAD NEWS	*For this reason*, we have accepted the proposal of a company that specializes in electronic networking.
CLOSING	I have mentioned *your proposal* to Mr. Darren Witherspoon, CEO of Hawkings Environmental Design, which is an international *corporation* with major activities in the areas *you mentioned*. If

TABLE I
How to Avoid the Transitional Ax in Bad News Letters

To avoid these transitional ax words . . .		**Change sentence and use** . . .	
However	1) **Verbal transitions**	[Or] . . .	2) **Cognitive transitions**
But	• Synonyms		• Related concepts
Yet	• Word repetitions		• Word association
Nevertheless	• Proper nouns		• Thought coherence
On the other hand	• Relative pronouns		
All the same	• Abbreviations		
Just the same	• Substitutions		
Even		[Or] . . .	
On the contrary		3) **Conjunctions or Conjunctive Adverbs**	
Although		• Therefore	
Despite		• And	
In spite of		• Consequently	
Unfortunately		• For this reason	
Regrettably		• Because	

> you would like, I can arrange a suitable time for you to present *your material* to Mr. Witherspoon and his Board of Directors.

The forward-presenting transition, "For this reason," is one means of moving from the reasons to the bad news. You could also use a repeated key word to exit the reasons section such as "*A system* for *international electronic networking* has been offered in the proposal of another company, and we have accepted that proposal." Or you could employ a cognitively keyed transition such as "*These features* are offered in the proposal of another firm, which we have accepted." Note that in each case the bad news is clearly implied and not explicitly stated.

If, however, you feel that the reader or listener would have doubts about the finality of the decision, you could state it firmly but tactfully. In this case, the implied bad news seems quite straightforward and unequivocal. The bad news, as many authors have suggested, should be brief, positively phrased (what you did rather than what you did not do), and not at the beginning of the sentence. In the closing buffer, you can use a cognitively keyed transition to move from the bad news, then tell the reader or listener what you have done for him or her. It is important to close on a positive side note if at all possible, so you must avoid repeating the bad news, apologizing for your decision, anticipating problems, or revealing any doubt that you still have the goodwill of the receiver of the message [6].

Summary

In indirect bad news messages, then, you have several workable options to the transitional ax. And you seek to avoid ax words because it destroys the tone of your message and can cause ill will between you and the receiver of your information. Perhaps the most obvious transitions to substitute for ax words are the basic verbally keyed transitions like repetitions, synonyms, naming, and abbreviations. You may also wish to use cognitively keyed transitional word associations. In addition, you can use conjunctions or conjunctive adverbs like "because" and similar words that do not impede the thought-flow. It is quite possible, too, to use combinations of these three techniques which are summarized in Table I. By using any of these methods to avoid the transitional ax, you will find that your indirect bad news messages are more coherent, more positive in tone, and ultimately, more effective in doing a difficult job well while maintaining goodwill.

References

[1] J. P. Bowman and B. P. Branchaw, *Successful Communication in Business*. San Francisco, CA: Harper & Row, 1980, p. 151.

[2] K. Rolland, "Letters can say no but keep or make friends," in *Printer's Ink*, vol. 229, October 7, 1949, pp. 46–53; Rpt. in *Strategies for Business and Technical Writing*, K. J. Harty, Ed. New York: Harcourt Brace Jovanovich, 1980, pp. 161–165.

[3] P. V. Anderson, *Business Communication: An Audience-Centered Approach*. San Diego, CA: Harcourt Brace Jovanovich, 1989, p. 255.

[4] K. J. Harty, "Some guidelines for saying, 'No'," *The ABCA Bulletin*, vol. 44, pp. 23–25, 1985.

[5] D. Brent, "Indirect structure and reader response," *J. Business Commun.*, vol. 22, no. 2, pp. 5–9.

[6] C. L. Bovee and J. V. Thill, *Business Communication Today*. New York: Random House, 1986, pp. 210–211.

[7] M. E. Guffey, *Essentials of Business Communication: Instructor's Edition*. Boston, MA: PWS-Kent, 1988, p. 145.

[8] M. P. Jordan, "The thread of continuity in functional writing," *J. Business Commun.*, vol. 19, no. 4, pp. 5–22, 1982.

[9] S. Baker, *The Complete Stylist and Handbook*, 3rd ed. New York: Harper and Row, 1984, p. 62.

[10] T. L. Kent, "Paragraph production and the given-new contract," *J. Business Commun.*, vol. 21, no. 4, pp. 45–66.

Thomas L. Wiseman received the B.A. degree in English *summa cum laude*, in 1971, from the Pennsylvania State University, University Park, and won an NDEA Fellowship to Tulane University, New Orleans, LA, where he received the M.A. and Ph.D. degrees in English, in 1974 and 1979, respectively.

He has taught undergraduate technical and business communications at Southern College of Technology since 1985. He is also a member of the graduate faculty and teaches courses in technical journalism, management communication, technical research and theory, and technical editing. He is a part-time writer and editor with the U.S. Forest Service's Regional Office in Atlanta, GA. His most recent publication is "Difficulties in reporting the acid rain story," which appears in the Fall issue of the *Humanities and Technology Review*. He is currently working on a textbook/reader dealing with environmental journalism. His primary research interests are in mass communication and audience analysis.

Dr. Wiseman is a member of the Association of Teachers of Technical Writing, American Business Communications Association, Council of Biology Editors, Society for Technical Communication, Georgia Poetry Society, Georgia Press Association, and the Humanities and Technology Association.

Job Hunting: Sharpening Your Competitive Edge

RON S. BLICQ, SENIOR MEMBER, IEEE

Abstract—**A job seeker who tailors each resume and application letter to capture the interest of a particular employer is far more likely to elicit a response than a job seeker who simply sends copies of a standard resume and letter to every employer. In a highly competitive job market, careful orchestration of the whole employment-seeking process is essential, from resume preparation to personal presentation during an interview.**

UNTIL recently, engineers seeking a job or wanting a new challenge simply sought help from an employment agency or turned to the "Careers" section of a prominent newspaper or an engineering journal. They then applied to the employers who advertised positions of particular interest to them and expected the normal application-interview process to follow. But today the scenario has changed so greatly that scientists and engineers have to use entirely different tactics.

N. A. Macdougall, president of the Technical Services Council, writes [1]:

> In normal times, only 58 percent of jobs are advertised. Even fewer are advertised today, and some employers rely upon speculative applications. The vice-president of a chemical company says: "We never advertise any more. We rely upon marketing contacts and people who apply to us directly."

He also quotes the head of recruitment for a major oil company [2]:

> "Only 20 percent of jobs the company fills are from advertisements...we hire what we need today. If we lose someone, we will consider replacement. We no longer do long-range hiring.
>
> "Large employers get so many applications that they have to play the odds. Resumes which have obscure dates, don't explain summer jobs or miss data just get rejected. We can't afford the time to follow up. Little things can get you knocked out."

To see these remarks in the proper perspective, one needs to take a broad view of the whole employment process. Figure 1 shows the four stages a *successful* job applicant goes through, from making the initial contact to attending interviews and ultimately receiving a job offer.

Received April 12, 1984; revised July 11, 1984.

The author teaches technical communication at Red River Community College; Box 181–Postal Station C, Winnipeg, Manitoba, Canada R3M 3S7; (204) 632-2292.

If an employer has, say, 60 applications to consider for a particular vacancy, 59 of the applicants will be unsuccessful, some being eliminated at each stage. Most of them will be eliminated in the first two stages, since an employer will want to invite no more than eight to ten applicants for screening interviews and four or five for selection interviews. This means about 50 of the original 60 applicants are eliminated solely on the evidence they provide *on paper*, either in their resumes, letters of application, or application forms.

You cannot afford to be one of the 80 percent eliminated in this way. Consequently, *the impression you create when presenting your credentials to a prospective employer becomes critical if you are to be selected for an interview.*

This article examines the major factors one has to consider today when applying for a job. It emphasizes the written aspects, since applicants initially are judged almost entirely on the written documentation they provide. It also includes comments on presenting a confident, informative image during a job interview.

PREPARING A RESUME

For decades we have become accustomed to seeing and using the traditional format for our resumes (sometimes referred to as "curriculum vitae") in which the information we want to present is divided into five parts each preceded by an appropriate heading and listed in the following order:

1. Personal Information
2. Education
3. Experience
4. Extracurricular Activities
5. References.

This traditional arrangement is well recognized and still widely used. I do not describe it here because many books discuss the traditional resume in depth (e.g., [3]). Instead, I describe an alternative resume format which was highlighted at specials sessions of two technical communication conferences held in 1981 [4] and 1983 [5].

A major problem with the traditional resume is that its sequence tends to focus the reader's attention on the applicant's personal information and education which, although of interest to employers, often are not the factors they

Reprinted from *IEEE Trans. Prof. Comm.*, vol. PC-27, no. 4, pp. 201–210, December 1984.

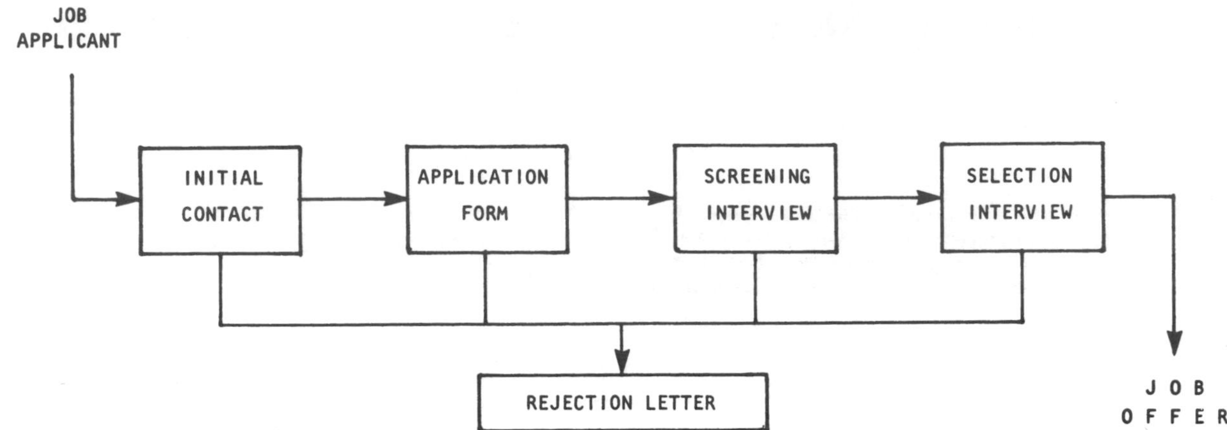

Fig. 1. The employee selection process.

most want to know. Today's technical employers are much more likely to be interested in *specifically what the applicant has done and special capabilities he or she has demonstrated that make him or her a particularly attractive choice.*

A contemporary resume directs its readers' attention to the skills and capabilities that will be of most value to a particular employer. It does this by using the "pyramid" method of writing described in the April 1982 issue of *Manitoba Technologist* [6], in which the resume opens with a summary statement that describes (a) what the applicant is particularly qualified to do or has extensive experience in doing; (b) what kind of work he or she wants to do; and, sometimes, (c) how the applicant's expertise can be used to the prospective employer's benefit. (Ideally, of course, there is a logical connection or development between these pieces of information.) This short paragraph is no longer than two or three sentences; it is titled Objective or Aim.

The second piece of information addresses the question a prospective employer is most likely to ask after reading the Objective, i.e., "What experience have you gained that specifically qualifies you to achieve this objective?"

The Experience section comes next and is divided into two compartments: first Related Experience and then Other Experience. This immediately focuses the reader's attention on those aspects of an applicant's work history that are especially relevant to the position being sought.

Moving the Education section much further down into the resume can be difficult for an applicant to accept if he or she has advanced degrees. Essentially it means taking a firm, objective look at all of one's qualifications *from the potential employer's point of view.* (The only times that education should be brought forward in a contemporary resume are when the job being sought calls for the applicant to have an extensive academic background and when the application is for a position in an academic institution.)

The remaining sections of the resume then follow, so that the complete list of headings becomes

1. Objective or Aim
2. Related Experience
3. Other Experience
4. Education
5. Extracurricular Activities
6. References

A two-page resume prepared in this contemporary format is shown in Fig. 2, in which the persons and circumstances are a composite designed to illustrate the methods for listing various information. The numbers in the margin are keyed to the following comments.

1. These essential details replace the Personal Information compartment of the traditional resume. Human rights legislation prevents job applicants from having to provide any more information about themselves (such as age, sex, weight, and ethnic background) than is shown here. However, if there are certain details they still feel they want to include, these can be inserted at the end of the Extracurricular Activities section.

2. The positions described with each Experience compartment should be listed in reverse order, the most recent experience being described first and the earliest experience described last. The most recent and most relevant experience should be described in considerably greater depth than early or unrelated experience (compare the descriptions of Dennis Hartley's Southcentral Contractors' experience with his Bowlands Stores' experience). The applicant should take great care to discriminate between factors he or she feels are most interesting and those an employer would particularly like to read about, and should concentrate on the latter.

3. The employer's name is listed first, underlined, and followed by the city and state. The person's position or job title is identified next, and then a description of

Resume

DENNIS G. HARTLEY, P.E.

(1) 310 -- 408 Medwin Street
St. Cloud, Minnesota, 56301
Tel: (612) 548 1612

OBJECTIVE

After four years supervising the installation and testing of wire and fiber optic telephone communication systems, I returned to college to obtain an M.S. in electronics engineering with a major in fiber optics. I am now seeking employment where I can apply my knowledge and experience in fiber optics engineering.

RELATED WORK EXPERIENCE

(2) June 1982 to September 1983 and May 1984 to date — Ebby, Little and Associates, Engineering Consultants, St. Cloud, Minnesota. Supervising engineer, responsible for installation, testing and analysis of tandem wire and fiber optic telephone communication links between Brainerd and Little Falls, Minnesota. Currently carrying out performance tests on installed links.

(3) September 1973 to August 1979 — Southcentral Installation Contractors Inc., Lincoln, Nebraska. For first four years, member of team installing high voltage transmission lines and transformer stations along power grid between Weekaskasing Falls, Nebraska and Bismarck, North Dakota. After 18 months appointed crew chief in charge of team installing interconnecting and distribution systems to townsites along the route; responsible for:
(4) hiring, training and supervising local labor; ordering and monitoring delivery of parts and materials; arranging and supervising subcontract work; and preparing progress and job completion reports.
From June 1977 to August 1979, assigned as supervisor of team working under contract to Ohio Utilities Corporation, installing and testing fiber optic links between towns up to 28 miles apart.

OTHER WORK EXPERIENCE

January 1967 to February 1971 — United States Air Force. Enlisted serviceman with Construction and Maintenance Directorate. For first two years, member of crew installing basic antenna systems and associated structures. For final two
(5) years, site technician responsible for maintenance of transmission lines and antennas at a midwestern USAF base. Attained rank of corporal.

June 1963 to December 1966 — Bowlands Stores Inc., Duluth, Minnesota. Stock clerk in grocery store No. 16. Full time for two summers and June to December 1966; part time while attending high school.

2/...

Dennis G. Hartley - page 2

EDUCATION

(6) Master of Science in Electronics Engineering, with major in fiber optics, University of Minnesota, 1984.
Bachelor of Science in Electrical Engineering, University of Montrose, Montrose, Ohio, 1982
Graduate Electrical Engineering Technician, Walter Halstadt Community College, Reece, Minnesota, 1973.
Graduate of Winona Collegiate, Duluth, Minnesota, 1967.

ADDITIONAL ACTIVITIES/INFORMATION

Member, Institute of Electrical and Electronics Engineers Inc. (IEEE), 1973 to date. Secretary, St. Cloud, Minnesota Section, 1982-83.
Awarded Orton R. Smith Scholarship for proficiency in applied mathematics, Walter Halstadt Community College, 1972, and Ohio Power
(7) and Light Scholarship for achievement in communications engineering, University of Montrose, 1980.
Technical paper: "Accuracies of Computer Data Transmissions Attainable at High Baud Rates Over Fiber Optic Communication Links," in Communications Technology, 13:07, July 1984. (Paper based on thesis written as part of M.S. program, University of Minnesota.)
Military courses attended while in USAF:
Transmission Line Installation Techniques, 1967.
Supervisory Skills Development, 1969.
First Aid and Safety Methods, various courses, 1968-71.
Junior Leader, Duluth, Minnesota, YMCA, 1962-67, teaching swimming and aquatic activities to boys age 9-15. Awarded Red Cross Bronze Medallion, 1965.

REFERENCES

The following persons have agreed to provide information regarding my qualifications and work capabilities:

(8)

Martin F. Ebby, P.E.	Philip M. Karlowsky
Project Coordinator	Contracts Manager
Ebby, Little and Associates	Southcentral Installation Contractors Inc.
360 Rosser Avenue	1335 Westfair Drive
St. Cloud, Minnesota, 56302	Lincoln, Nebraska, 68528
Tel: (612) 544 1867	Tel: (402) 632 1450

Fig. 2. A contemporary resume.

what the job involved. If several positions have been held within the same firm, each is named and its duration stated so that the applicant's progress within the firm is clear.

4. Each position should draw attention to the personal responsibilities and supervisory aspects of the job, rather than just list specific duties. Verbs should be chosen carefully so they make the position sound as comprehensive and self-directed as possible. Verbs such as these are effective choices:

   coordinated
   monitored
   presented
   planned
   directed
   implemented
   supervised
   organized

   If a paragraph grows too long (and this paragraph is rather long), it can be broken into subparagraphs:

   ...appointed crew chief responsible for
   - installing interconnecting and distribution systems
   - hiring, training, and supervising local labor
   - ordering and monitoring delivery of parts and materials
   - arranging and supervising subcontract work
   - preparing progress and job completion reports.

5. Single-spaced typing should be used as much as possible to keep the resume compact. At the same time there should be a reasonable amount of white space on each side and between major paragraphs to avoid a crowded effect. A resume preferably should not exceed two typewritten pages (employers want to find the facts quickly; they do not want to wade through a mass of details) although it is acceptable to attach an extra page or pages containing, for example, a list of publications one has authored

6. Education can be listed either in chronological or reverse sequence. If a resume is to be sent out of the state, or if the applicant was educated out of state, it is best to identify the city and state of each educational institution attended.

7. Employers *are* interested in a job applicant's accomplishments and extracurricular activities, particularly those describing community involvement and awards or commendations.

8. When choosing people to supply references, always ensure that (a) the person's relevance is readily apparent (there should be a connection between the referee and the job applicant's previous work experience or community involvement); (b) the referee's full address and telephone number are listed (most requests for a reference are made by telephone); and (c) the referee knows the applicant is naming him or her in the resume (so that the referee will be prepared if a prospective employer calls).

Never overlook the importance of a resume's appearance. To a prospective employer the immediate impression created by the resume says a lot about the quality of work the applicant does. It may cost a bit more to have your resume typed by a professional stenographer on a high-quality typewriter and then duplicated properly, but the result can pay handsome dividends in the form of invitations to attend interviews.

And do not be afraid to use a display technique that enhances the professional quality of your resume. A soon-to-be-published textbook [7] describes how an engineer printed the two pages of his resume side by side on an 11″ × 17″ sheet and then folded the sheet so that the resume was on the inside. On the outside front he printed only his name and the single word "Resume" (Fig. 3). On the outside back he printed a cross-reference chart showing along one axis specific tasks in which he had experience and along the other axis projects he had been involved in. At the intersection point for each pair of entries he drew a small circle and then blacked it in to show his degree of involvement, as shown in the example in Fig. 4.

Another engineer, hearing that a sudden resignation had created a vacancy in a local company and was to be advertised the following day, prepared a one-page resume overnight (which he typed himself) and took it to the company shortly after door-opening time the following morning. He asked for, and gained, a two-minute interview with the manager of the department where the new employee would work. When he faced the manager he announced that he had all the capabilities to fill the position, that he could save the company *X* hours per month by using a special technique he had developed and used on previous tasks,

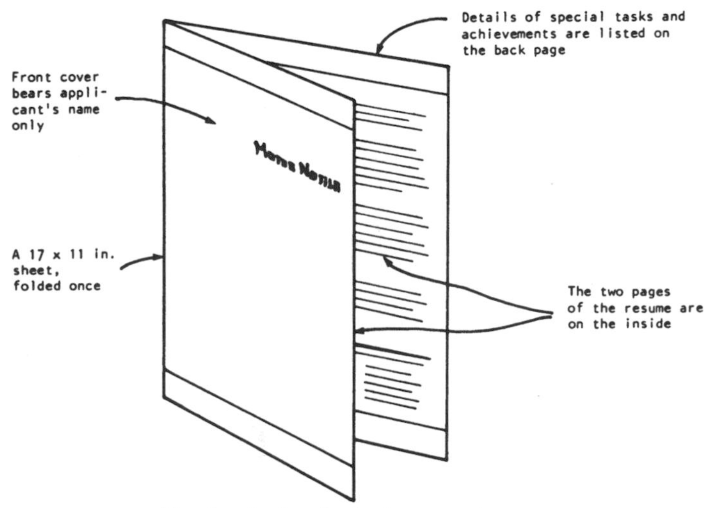

Fig. 3. An imaginatively prepared resume.

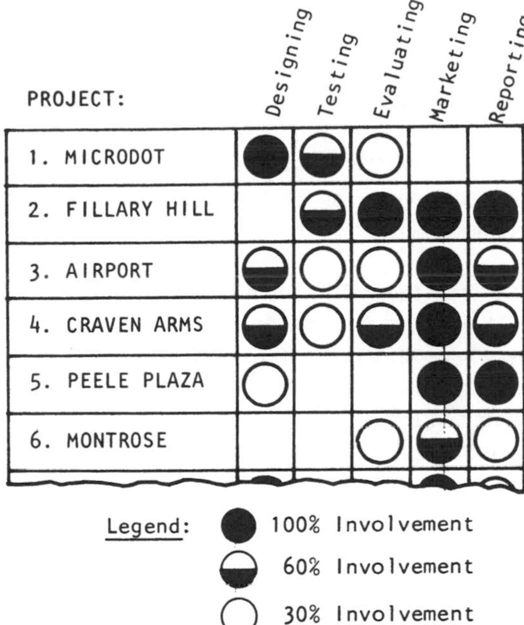

Fig. 4. A cross-reference chart showing the applicant's involvement in various activities.

and that he had summarized what he could do for the company on the resume he had handed to the manager.

His resume, like his opening remarks, was oriented totally to the company's requirements. It was titled

RESUME PREPARED FOR ABC COMPANY

Its opening paragraph (the Objective) was introduced by the heading

How I Can Improve ABC's...

and then he listed three areas in which he would apply his expertise.

The next heading was

Previous Experience/Achievements in...

and was followed by four short paragraphs that identified with facts and figures what he had achieved elsewhere.

After two interviews he was hired the same day and the company withdrew the advertisement it had planned to place. His job-hunting tactics, and those of the engineer described earlier, point up two important aspects of current resume writing:

- Originality of presentation and approach can help capture a reader's attention, providing they focus on the potential employer's needs and are not brash.
- The days when a single resume could be prepared, duplicated, and mailed to numerous employers are over. Now it is much wiser—indeed, essential—to prepare an individual resume for each employer, in which the emphasis and focus shift depending on the particular employer's requirements. These changes are most evident in the Objective and Related Experience sections of the resume.

WRITING A LETTER OF APPLICATION

Although some resumes may be delivered personally, the majority are mailed with a covering letter. Because potential employers will probably read the letter first, it must do much more than simply introduce the resume. It needs to state your purpose for writing (that you are applying for a job) and demonstrate that you have some very useful qualifications that the reader should take the time to consider. As such it becomes a letter of application to which you have attached a resume containing more definitive information.

A strong, interesting, well-planned application letter can prompt an employer to place yours among those whose authors he would like to see in person. On the other hand, a dull, unemphatic letter may cause the same employer to drop it onto the pile of "also rans" because its style and approach seem to imply you are a dull, unemphatic person. In today's highly competitive employment environment you cannot afford to let your letter be dropped onto the "also ran" pile.

Every business letter—and a letter of application essentially is a business letter—should follow the "pyramid" method of writing. That is, it should open with a brief summary that defines the purpose of the letter and then offer strong, positive details to suport the opening statement. Finally, it should close with a brief remark that identifies what action is to be taken next.

This means that an application letter can be divided into three parts:

- An *initial contact,* which states that you are applying for a job and briefly identifies what special qualifications you have that make you a particularly suitable candidate. (The intent should be to capture the reader's interest in the first one or two sentences.)
- An *evidence* section, which provides details and solid facts to support your contention that you are well qualified to hold the position. The facts you quote should be selected for their relevance to the position sought and their pertinence to the reader. (Remember that the most interesting experiences from your point of view may not be the most interesting to the reader.)
- A *closing statement,* which, rather than just closing the letter with a polite remark, *opens the door* to the next step (the employment interview).

There are two types of application letter: Those written in response to an advertisement for a job that is known to be open, or at the employer's specific invitation, are called "solicited" letters. Those written without an advertisement or invitation, on the chance that the employer might be interested in your background and experience even though no job is known to be open, are referred to as "unsolicited" letters. The overall approach and shape of both letters are similar, but the unsolicited letter generally is more difficult to write.

The Solicited Letter of Application

The main advantage in responding to an advertisement, or applying for a position that you know to be open, is that you can focus your letter on facts that specifically meet the employer's requirements. This has been done by Dennis Hartley in the letter illustrated in Fig. 5, which he has written in response to an advertisement for a project group leader with experience in installing, maintaining, and testing fiber optic transmission lines.

The following comments are keyed to the circled letters in this application letter.

A. For a letter that will have a personal address at the top, it is better to adopt the modified block style shown here rather than the full block style in which every line starts at the left-hand margin. Because the modified block style helps balance a personal letter on the page, it provides a more pleasant initial impres-

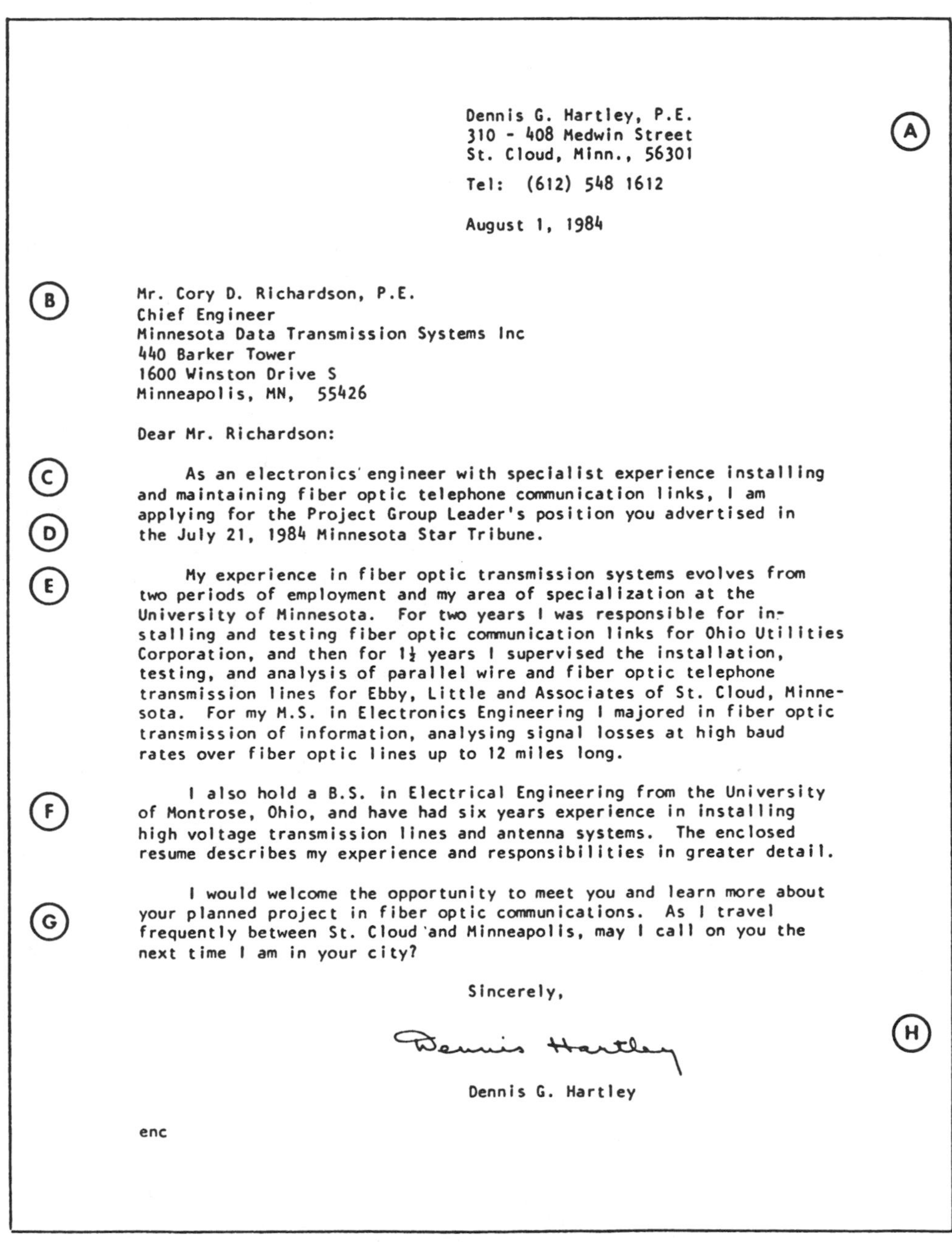

(A)

Dennis G. Hartley, P.E.
310 - 408 Medwin Street
St. Cloud, Minn., 56301

Tel: (612) 548 1612

August 1, 1984

(B)

Mr. Cory D. Richardson, P.E.
Chief Engineer
Minnesota Data Transmission Systems Inc
440 Barker Tower
1600 Winston Drive S
Minneapolis, MN, 55426

Dear Mr. Richardson:

(C) (D) As an electronics engineer with specialist experience installing and maintaining fiber optic telephone communication links, I am applying for the Project Group Leader's position you advertised in the July 21, 1984 Minnesota Star Tribune.

(E) My experience in fiber optic transmission systems evolves from two periods of employment and my area of specialization at the University of Minnesota. For two years I was responsible for installing and testing fiber optic communication links for Ohio Utilities Corporation, and then for 1½ years I supervised the installation, testing, and analysis of parallel wire and fiber optic telephone transmission lines for Ebby, Little and Associates of St. Cloud, Minnesota. For my M.S. in Electronics Engineering I majored in fiber optic transmission of information, analysing signal losses at high baud rates over fiber optic lines up to 12 miles long.

(F) I also hold a B.S. in Electrical Engineering from the University of Montrose, Ohio, and have had six years experience in installing high voltage transmission lines and antenna systems. The enclosed resume describes my experience and responsibilities in greater detail.

(G) I would welcome the opportunity to meet you and learn more about your planned project in fiber optic communications. As I travel frequently between St. Cloud and Minneapolis, may I call on you the next time I am in your city?

Sincerely,

(H)

Dennis Hartley

Dennis G. Hartley

enc

Fig. 5. A *solicited* application letter.

sion. Each line of the applicant's name, address, and telephone number, and the signature block at the end of the letter, should start at the page centerline.

B. Whenever possible, personalize an application letter by addressing it by name to the personnel manager or the person named in the advertisement. This gives you an edge over applicants who address theirs impersonally to the "Personnel Manager" or "Chief Engineer." If the job advertisement does not give the person's name, invest in a telephone call to the advertiser and ask the receptionist for the person's name and complete title. (You may have to decide whether it is better to send your letter and resume to someone in the personnel department or to a technical manager who is more likely to be aware of the quality of your qualifications and how you could fit into his or her organization.)

C. The first line of each paragraph may be indented about five spaces or may start flush with the margin.

D. This is the *initial contact*, in which Dennis summarizes the key points about himself that he believes will most interest his reader and states that he is applying for the advertised position. Note particularly that he creates a purposeful image by stating confidently "I am applying... ." This is much better than writing "I wish to apply... ," "I would like to apply... ," or "I am interested in applying... ," all of which create weak, wishy-washy images because they only imply interest rather than purposefully apply for a job. An equally confident opening is "Please accept my application for... ."

E. The *evidence* section starts here. It should offer facts drawn from the resume and expand on the statements made in the first paragraph. Broad generalizations such as "I have 13 years experience in a metrology laboratory" should be replaced with shorter-term descriptions that indicate the applicant's exact role and responsibilities and stress the supervisory aspects of each position. The name of a person for whom an applicant worked on a particular project can be usefully inserted here because it adds credibility to the role and responsibilities the applicant describes.

F. The *evidence* section should cover the key points an employer is likely to be interested in and draw the reader's attention to the attached resume. It may be divided into two paragraphs if a single paragraph seems to be too long.

G. This paragraph is Dennis's *closing statement*, in which he effectively draws attention to his interest in the position by referring to facts about the company's operations. He avoids using dull, routine remarks such as "I look forward to hearing from you at your earliest convenience" or "I would appreciate an interview in the near future," both of which tend to close rather than open the door to the next step.

H. Contemporary usage suggests that most business letters should end with a single-word complimentary close such as "Regards," "Sincerely," or "Cordially," rather than the more formal but less meaningful "Yours very truly."

The Unsolicited Letter of Application

An unsolicited application letter has the same three main parts as a solicited letter and looks very much the same to the reader. To the writer, however, there is a subtle but important difference, in that it cannot be focused to fit the requirements of a particular position an employer needs to fill. This means the job applicant has to take particular care to make the letter sound both positive and directed. Here are some guidelines to help you shape a letter that you are submitting "blind."

- Make a particular point of addressing your letter by name and title to the person who would most likely be interested in you. This may mean selecting a particular department or project head, who will immediately recognize the quality of your qualifications and how you would fit into the organization, rather than the personnel manager. Never address an unsolicited letter to a general title such as "Manager, Human Resources," because, if the company does not use such a title and you have not used a personal name, it will likely be the mail clerk who decides who should receive your precious letter.

- Try to find out enough information about a firm that you can visualize the type of work it does and how you and your qualifications would fit the company's needs. This will enable you to focus your letter on factors likely to be of most interest to the employment manager or selected department head.

- Try to make your initial contact positive and interesting even though you are not applying for a particular position. For example, Dennis Hartley might modify the opening he wrote for his unsolicited letter to this:

  As an electronics engineer with an advanced degree in fiber optics, I am seeking a position where I can use my ten years' experience in installing, testing, and maintaining both wire and fiber optic transmission lines. Have you any openings in your Project or Design Departments?

  My experience in fiber optic transmission systems evolves from... .

COMPLETING AN EMPLOYMENT APPLICATION FORM

Filling in a series of company application forms can become a boring and repetitive task, yet any carelessness on an applicant's part can create a negative reaction from readers. Each company or organization usually uses its own specially designed form which, although it asks for generally the same basic information, may vary in detail. Consequently these suggestions apply primarily to the *approach* you should take rather than suggest what you should write.

- Always carry a personal data file with you so that you can search for accurate details such as dates, telephone numbers, and names of supervisors.

- Treat every application form as though it is the *first* one you are completing—write carefully, neatly, and legibly. Never let an untidy application form subconsciously prepare an employer to meet an untidy worker.

- Use words that describe the responsibility and supervisory aspects of each job you have held rather than list only the duties you performed.

- Particularly describe extracurricular activities that show your involvement in the community or in which you held a teaching or coaching role.

- Pay particular attention if there is a section on the form that asks you to comment on how your education and past experience have especially prepared you for the position. Think this through very carefully before you write so that what you say shows a natural progression from past experience to the job you are applying for. If you can, and if they fit naturally, add a few words to demonstrate how the position fits your overall career plan. This can be a particularly difficult section to write so do not be afraid to obtain an opinion of its effectiveness from an objective third party.

ATTENDING A JOB INTERVIEW

The key to a good interview is thorough preparation, by both the applicant and the interviewer. We tend to take it for granted that an interviewer comes well prepared—that he or she will have read the applicant's letter and resume thoroughly, will have clearly identified the type of person needed for the particular position, and will have prepared certain questions to ask. A good interviewer frames questions so that they elicit properly developed answers from the applicant, rather than laconic "yes" and "no" answers. Without adequate preparation by the interviewer, the interview may stumble along with no apparent sense of direction and have awkward pauses, resulting in a generally weak exchange of information.

Your role as a job applicant is to prepare thoroughly for the interview. This means researching information about the company, preparing answers to questions you anticipate will be asked, and developing a short list of questions that you want to ask.

Pre-Interview Preparation

Learning something about the employer means identifying the size of the company and where other offices exist, its principal products and services, specific projects or jobs it has handled, the number of people it employs, its involvement in community activities, and so on. Armed with this knowledge you will be able to ask intelligent questions during the interview and subtly demonstrate that you are a knowledgeable individual who is not treating the interview casually.

Preparing answers to questions you may be asked is more difficult because you have no way of knowing what types of questions the interviewer is likely to throw at you. There are, however, certain questions which frequently surface that you can prepare for:

1. What makes you want to work for our organization?
2. How do you think you can contribute to our company?
3. Why do you want to leave your present employer?
4. What do you like (or dislike) most about your present job?
5. What prompted you to leave (name of company) on (date)?
6. What salary are you looking for?
7. What do you expect to be doing in five years? ten years?

It is important to think about such questions before the interview so that you will be able to answer them directly and confidently. An unprepared job applicant who hesitates before answering them may create the unfortunate impression that he or she is a hesitant, unsure person.

Many job applicants ask "Why would an interviewer want to know what salary I want when he or she already knows the company has a fixed salary range that I would have to fit into?"

The answer is simply that the interviewer uses the question to assess how you value yourself and how well you have prepared for the interview. An ill-prepared job applicant may reply hesitantly, "Oh, between $22,000 and $26,000, I guess," whereas a well-prepared applicant will reply confidently, "With my experience I believe I should be getting $26,500." If you fear that the salary you want to quote may be too high, you can always add the qualification "...depending, of course, on the opportunities for advancement and the fringe benefits your company offers."

If you are well prepared you will attend every interview with certain questions in mind. Your interviewers expect this and so, toward the end of the interview, will ask, "Now, do *you* have any questions?"

Often you will find that most of your questions have already been covered during the discussion and that you have only one or two more you want to ask. But at this point, under the pressure of the moment, you may find you cannot remember what they were!

To overcome such a mental block you should jot down brief notes defining the questions onto a small card and carry it with you in a pocket or purse. Then, if you are not sure what you need to ask, you can produce the card and quickly check what remains to be covered. If you feel that a card is too much like a crib sheet and looks unprofessional, remember that to the interviewer the reverse is more true: It shows that you have done your homework and have prepared properly for the interview.

Creating a Good Initial Impression

You are being evaluated from the moment you step into the interview room. Perhaps the interviewer considers that the interview does not begin until you are both sitting down and have exchanged opening remarks, but subconsciously he or she is forming an opinion of you right from the start. Consequently you should

- Walk in briskly and cheerfully.
- Shake hands firmly, because a limp handshake creates an image of a limp, indefinite applicant (an image you cannot afford to create).
- Repeat the person's name as you are introduced and look him or her directly in the eye.
- Sit when invited to so do, pushing yourself well back in the chair, making yourself comfortable, and avoiding folding your arms across your chest (which psychologically suggests that you resist questioning).

Participating Throughout the Interview

The interviewer will want to set you at ease and establish a comfortable atmosphere conducive to a good exchange of information and so, during the initial part of the interview, often will ask questions about you and your personal interests which you can answer easily and readily.

To learn as much as possible about how you think and react, an interviewer expects you to give thoroughly developed answers to questions. An effective interviewer will pose questions and subsequent prompts in such a way that you are carried easily from one discussion point to the next and are automatically encouraged to provide comprehensive answers. But if you find yourself face to face with an inexperienced or inadequately prepared interviewer, the responsibility is solely yours to develop your answers in greater depth than the questions seem to call for.

For example, the interviewer may ask, "How long did you work in a mobile calibration lab?"

You might be tempted to reply "Three years," and then sit back and wait for the next question. You would do much better to reply, "For three years total. The first year and a half I was one of four technicians on the Minneapolis-to-Sioux City circuit. And then for the next year and a half I was the lab supervisor on the Fort Westin-to-Manomonee route."

An answer developed in this depth often provides the prompt (i.e., piece of information) from which the interviewer can frame the next question.

Sometimes you will face a single interviewer, while at other times you may face an interview board of two to five people. In a single-interviewer situation you will naturally direct your replies to the interviewer and should make a point of establishing eye contact from time to time. (To maintain continuous eye contact would be uncomfortable for both you and the interviewer.) In a multiple-interviewer situation you should

1. Direct most of your questions, and your responses to general questions, to the person who apparently is the chairperson. (But if an answer is long you should occasionally take time to look briefly at and talk momentarily to other board members.)
2. If a particular board member asks you a specific question, address your response to that person.
3. If a board member has been identified as a specialist in a particular discipline, direct questions to that board member if they especially apply to that field.

In certain interviews—often when applicants are being interviewed for a high-stress position—you may be presented with a "stress" question. A stress question is designed to place you in a predicament to which there may be two or even more answers or courses of action that could be taken. You are expected to think *briefly* about the situation presented to you and then to select what you believe is the best answer or course of action. Often you will be challenged and expected to defend the position you have taken.

The secret is not to let yourself be rattled and to defend your answer rationally and reasonably even though the questioner's challenging may seem harsh or unreasonable. Remember that the interviewer is probably more interested in seeing how you cope in the stress situation than in hearing you identify the correct answer.

Other points you should consider during the interview:

- If you do not know the answer to a question, it is far better to say you don't know than to try bluffing your way through.

- If you do not understand the question, again don't bluff. Either say you do not quite understand or, if you think you know what the interviewer is driving at, rephrase the question and ask if you have interpreted it correctly. (Never imply that the interviewer posed the question poorly!)

- Use humor with great care. What to you may be extremely funny may not match the interviewer's sense of humor.

- Bring demonstration materials to the interview if you wish (such as a technical proposal or report you authored, or a drawing of a complex circuit you designed) but be aware that you may not have an opportunity to display them. If the topic they support comes up during the interview, introduce them naturally into your response to a question. But remember that the interviewer does not have time to read your work, so the point you are trying to make should be readily identifiable simply by viewing the demonstration item. Never force demonstration materials on an interviewer.

- Do not smoke unless the interviewer also smokes and invites you to do so.

Finally, the most important thing to do during an interview is to *be yourself*. If you try to be the kind of person you think the prospective employer is looking for, you are likely to create a false impression which somehow rings hollow to the interviewer. An interviewer gains a much better impression of you if you answer questions firmly and confidently because you know the answers represent what you truly believe.

REFERENCES

1. Macdougall, N. A. "Job Hunting: Getting In the Door." *Design Engineering* (Canada). January 1983; 29(1): 28.
2. Macdougall, N. A. "An Employer's View of the Job Market." *Design Engineering* (Canada). January 1984; 30(1): 28.
3. Blicq, Ron S. *Technically-Write!: Communicating in a Technological Era.* 2nd ed. Englewood Cliffs, NJ: Prentice-Hall Inc.; 1981: p. 54.
4. The IEEE Professional Communication Society Conference on Communications with/for/by Government, Arlington, VA, September 16–18, 1981.
5. The IEEE Professional Communication Society Conference on The Many Facets of Computer Communications, Atlanta, GA, October 19–21, 1983.
6. Blicq, Ron S. "Tips for Writing Sharper Letters and Reports." *Manitoba Technologist.* April 1982; 12: 2.
7. Blicq, Ron S. *Administratively-Write!: Communicating in a Business Environment.* Scarborough, Ontario: Prentice-Hall Canada Inc.; 1985.

How to Write a Recommendation

ALAN D. WILCOX, MEMBER, IEEE

Abstract—**Writing an effective recommendation requires an understanding of the reader and his specific needs. A "recommendation outline" is presented here which will meet those needs and also ease the burden of preparing the recommendation itself. In addition to the outline, two sample letters of recommendation are presented.**

MANY times in your professional career you will be asked to write a recommendation for someone. Perhaps a good friend, a colleague, or a business associate is changing jobs and would appreciate your written evaluation of his or her performance. In the academic milieu especially, many students ask for recommendation letters.

Faced with this situation, and after agonizing over a number of letters, I located some of the standard "form letter" recommendation sheets used by various schools and companies. Unfortunately, these letters seemed inadequate to express my assessment of the candidate, and I ultimately abandoned them entirely. They were useful in one sense though: I gathered an inkling of what employers and personnel managers consider important. What I really needed was my own general-purpose outline to easily write an effective recommendation.

THE READER

Who is going to read the recommendation? The personnel manager, the department head, and the direct supervisor will probably see the recommendation, and it should be written with their needs clearly in mind. They need to see your friend as you do: as a real person with real strengths and weaknesses. After an interview they already have a "best manners" impression, but they need more substance. Perhaps they need to verify facts or clarify some uncertain points from the interview itself.

Well, if they need "strengths and weaknesses," it should be no trouble to put together a recommendation, even a recommendation with substance. The agony begins here. Consider what is really important to an employer: He needs to know whether your friend would not only be able to do the required work but also whether he or she would fit into the company and succeed as a long-term addition to the staff.

Several key factors seem to be of great interest in evaluating the potential employee and whether he or she will succeed: social competence, work competence, and a suitable blend of character attributes. These factors are shown as part of Table I. My impression is that a recommendation addressing these issues will be of great value. This is especially true if you have been candid and accurate in your presentation of the facts.

Received April 16, 1984; revised July 3, 1984.
The author is an Assistant Professor of Electrical Engineering at Bucknell University, Lewisburg, PA 17837; (717) 523-0777.

SOME POINTS TO REMEMBER

To help you write a recommendation that will help both your friend and the personnel manager, keep a few points

TABLE I
Outline of a Recommendation

Introduction	...is applying for a position as...and I would like to recommend him to you.
Background	Have known him for...
	In a relationship as...
Description	Career goals and interest in the field
	Relevant hobbies, activities, talents
	Social Competence
	Works well with others
	Is cooperative, congenial
	Is understanding, open minded
	Communicates well with others
	Work Competence
	Able to see and solve problems; gets results
	Speaks and writes effectively
	Understands technical fundamentals
	Has specific related experience
	Is up to date in field of expertise
	Can plan and organize work
	Does quality work: accurate and thorough
	Character Attributes
	Honest, sincere
	Industrious, willing to work hard
	Enthusiastic, motivated, self-starting
	Initiative, ambitious
	Sound, practical judgment
	Imagination, vision, creativity
	Independent thinker, problem solver
	Logical
	Perceptive
	Positive attitude, desire to be effective
	Emotionally stable
	Intelligent, quick learner
Conclusion	Because of (all the above), ...would be suitable for this job.
	Would welcome phone call to discuss further.

Reprinted from *IEEE Trans. Prof. Comm.*, vol. PC-27, no. 4, pp. 211–214, December 1984.

in mind:

1. You are writing to a person, not to "whom it may concern." Ask your friend to give you the name and address of the person you should write. Then, when you write, keep him in mind and what he needs to know about your friend so he can make an informed hiring decision.
2. The hiring decision is based on the skills and character of your friend. He or she has various qualities, and the personnel manager needs to know what they are. Perfection is neither required nor expected! The relevant issue for the reader is to put the right person in the job.
3. Ask your friend what you should include in the letter. For example, he or she might be particularly competent

Bucknell University
Lewisburg, PA 17837
March 29, 1984

Prof. John Smith, Chairman
Biomedical Engineering Department
Xxxx University
Xxxxxx, Xxxxx

Dear Professor Smith:

Susan Xxxx is applying for summer employment and has asked me to write to you about her job qualifications. She is interested in two openings: Analysis of Heart Wall Motion and Computed Tomography. I can highly recommend her to you as an excellent selection to add to your summer staff for work in either of these two positions.

Sue attended my Introduction to Digital Systems class last fall and was one of my top students. I found her to be hard working and diligent to do the work assigned. Although her background is computer science, she did as well in this electrical engineering course as the EE students themselves. This semester she is in my Advanced Digital Systems class, and she is doing just as well as before.

Computer software is one of her strong areas, particularly in being able to relate it to the processing hardware. For example, she did a special project for me last semester in which she built a hardware multiplier circuit. In addition to doing the circuit design, she wrote the system software to interface the computer to the multiplier. This semester she's designing and building a small computer system using her own processor architecture.

I have no doubt that she can do application programming for you in FORTRAN. She has already programmed in that and other high-level languages in her studies at Bucknell. She learns quickly, and I know that she can successfully relate what she already knows to your job.

You will enjoy having her work with you this summer.

Very truly yours,

(signed)
Alan D. Wilcox, P.E.
Assistant Professor

Fig. 1. Recommendation letter for a student summer job.

in a special field, and your discussion of this skill would reinforce what others might describe. Also, if the interview falls somewhat short, your clarification of some of the weak points will be beneficial.

4. Be honest about the qualities of your friend. If you write only in glittering superlatives, the recommendation says much less than if you are candid and down to earth. Give specific examples of what your friend has

Micro Resources, Inc.
Lewisburg, PA 17837
June 29, 1984

Mr. George Sherman, Engineering Manager
Computer Devices and Circuits, Inc.
Philadelphia, PA 19019

Dear Mr. Sherman:

I am writing in response to your June 4th inquiry about Ted Land, one of my former engineers. Based on my knowledge of his work, I am sure that he is fully qualified to be employed as a Senior Engineer, and I recommend him highly.

During the three years he was with our company, from 1978 to 1981, I worked closely with him when he developed a new, highly efficient, miniature switching power supply for our line of computer products. He was very methodical in planning his work and in his approach to solving the technical problems of the power supply. His attention to engineering detail helped us get the supply into production in near-record time with a minimum of changes from the prototype model he designed and built. Two novel ideas he had when working on the project also resulted in patents.

In addition to the power supply, he designed a water-level measuring system which went into production in 1980. He planned the entire project and did all the design and development of the system components. He was quite enthusiastic about the product and was here at the plant many evenings investigating new design approaches.

He is a very intense person and prefers to work alone rather than in a team effort. For that reason, when he was working for me with four other engineers, I made a special effort to give him assignments that required little direct involvement with others. I was pleased to discover, though, that he did get along well and went out of his way to assist the less-experienced engineers.

From what I have seen of Ted, I believe that he would be an ideal person for the job you described in your letter. Feel free to call me if you would like to discuss any points in greater detail.

Yours truly,

(signed)
Edward S. Johnson
Engineering Group Leader

Fig. 2. Recommendation letter for an engineer.

done that might be relevant to the new job. Avoid vague and unsubstantiated generalities.

HOW TO WRITE THE RECOMMENDATION

Once you feel comfortable with an understanding of the needs of the reader, the recommendation can be written by following the general outline shown in Table I. Certainly not all the items in the figure apply to everyone, but they should help give direction to your writing so it meets the needs of the reader.

For example, Fig. 1 is a letter I wrote for one of my students who was seeking summer employment. The letter follows the general thrust of the outline and provides as much information as possible to the reader. Hardware and software expertise were job requirements so I illustrated Sue's experience by examples of her work for me.

Figure 2 is a recommendation letter an engineering group leader wrote for one of his former team members. During the time Ted was working for him, Ted successfully designed a number of products, and the description of these achievements can help the prospective employer make a decision. Note that Ted does need some special attention: he's inclined to work alone. Balanced by the other information given, that is not really a negative factor in the recommendation. Overall, Ted comes across as a highly competent engineer who is a real person.

SUMMARY

Writing an effective recommendation requires an understanding of the reader and what specific information he or she needs to find in your letter. The recommendation outline in Table I can help meet those needs and also ease the burden of writing the letter. In addition, you can complete the task knowing you've made a positive contribution to the success and future of your friend.

Some Guidance On Preparing Technical Articles For Publication

RICHARD MANLEY
JUDITH GRAHAM
RALPH BAXTER

Abstract—**Writing for publication in the professional literature brings prestige to the author and recognition to his employer. Yet in many organizations, few technical articles are written for publication in the professional literature. This paper discusses some of the elements involved with writing technical papers for publication within a technical corporate environment. It outlines some of the major incentives and barriers to publishing and offers suggestions for addressing the barriers from both the author's viewpoint and that of management. Those elements composed the foundation of a workshop designed to encourage technical professionals to write for publication. The workshop included exposition of the reasons to publish, addressed barriers to publication, discussed skill building, and contained company-specific briefings on internal release procedures and management support for writing.**

MANY ENGINEERS AND SCIENTISTS carry out their research and analysis projects in the corporate world, on internal development projects or on contract projects awarded by some outside agency or sponsor. Often these project professionals write documents describing the solution to a technical problem or recommending some action based on their analysis or study. Yet few of the technical professionals who write these business documents take the next step and prepare articles for the technical community at large.

Business documents have a specific purpose: to present the results of the research, study, or analysis, cast in terms of a solution to a particular problem. Although the research and analysis itself may prove exceptionally worthy, the documents are usually the means to satisfy the initiating inquiry. In many organizations, detailed discussion of the substance of technical analyses is often relegated to an appendix of the business report.

Richard Manley is Technical Program Manager for the MITRE Institute, the educational and training unit of the MITRE Corporation.

Judith H. Graham is President of Graham Associates, a Virginia consulting firm specializing in technical and business writing instruction.

Ralph C. Baxter is President of New Dominion Services and Professor at George Mason University (Fairfax, VA).

Engineers and scientists often record results informally in briefing charts, technical memoranda, working papers, or occasionally a technical report. These documents see limited distribution, often only within the sponsoring organization, and concern themselves with procedure and analysis as an adjunct to reporting results.

Documents like these may contain answers that reveal insights developed by the researchers or point to some new area of analysis that might fall beyond the scope of the current investigation. Unfortunately, because the documents themselves are often company confidential or even classified in a national security sense, their circulation is further limited. Yet the researchers have done good work and the investigators take pride in their accomplishments. Most would be pleased that the technical community is interested in the paths they followed and in sharing the insights they gained.

Clearly, the investigators can benefit professionally by disseminating their work to as large an audience as possible [1]. Publication demonstrates command of a specific area, exhibits the company's involvement in the particular field, and shows active participation in the technical community. In many cases, technical publications provide a means for the ideas and work of the staff to gain exposure to the management of their own organizations. Yet few authors of in-house technical publications take the next step. That is, few extract the seminal ideas from their work and prepare an article for publication in the professional literature of the field.

MITRE Corporation's in-house technical training and education wing is the MITRE Institute. The staff of the Institute recognized that barriers within the corporate environment can prevent disseminating technical work in a form suitable for communication to the larger community. Our work led us to design a workshop to guide aspiring authors

Reprinted from *IEEE Trans. Prof. Comm.*, vol. 32, no. 1, pp. 5–11, March 1989.

in surmounting those barriers over which they have some control and in managing those over which they have less.

This paper discusses some of the elements involved in writing technical papers for publication within the corporate environment. It outlines some of the major incentives and barriers to publishing and offers some suggestions for addressing them from the viewpoints of both authors and management. These elements then became the foundation of a workshop designed to encourage technical professionals to write for publication within our company's specific environment.

SOME MAJOR ELEMENTS IN PREPARING TECHNICAL ARTICLES

Writing technical papers for publication involves a number of activities that are strongly influenced by many factors both within and beyond the direct control of authors. We considered the following list of topics to be a comprehensive and useful one for the purposes of our workshop:

- Understanding why/why not to write professional papers
- Identifying an appropriate conference or publication
- Classifying publications
- Analyzing the elements of journal articles
- Using research resources
- Gaining public release authority for the work
- Clarifying management support

WHY PUBLISH

In an intense technical environment such as ours, deadlines, briefings, and new projects all have high priority. In the face of these demands, it is often necessary to remind the technical staff of the benefits that can accrue to those who write about their work in the literature of a professional field. Our staff members have found the following benefits in varying degrees when they write for publication:

- New insights
- Expert feedback on the reported work
- Professional interest in sharing results
- Prestige
- Personal/professional gratification
- Renewed research funding
- Management awareness of the value of individual work to the field

Among the most compelling reasons to publish is that writing a succinct, clear paper aimed at one's colleagues helps the author generate new insights into his work. Putting one's thoughts down on paper seems to discipline the thought process. Reconstructing the steps that were taken to achieve some set of analytical results and developing those novel or innovative portions of the analysis in greater depth allow an author to revisit work with the benefit of hindsight. Thinking about the facts and drawing them together in a logical arrangement—which often differs from the chronological order—and then setting them down tends to yield a fresh perspective and new understanding [2].

When the manuscript is submitted to a publication for consideration, many publications and all scholarly journals have it carefully reviewed by experts in the area. The author clearly benefits from the feedback his colleagues can offer regarding the context of this writing. They often point out new information, ask questions that lead to new insights, and offer recommendations that can clarify thinking.

Of course, once the author has completed his paper and finally views his work in print, he feels a sense of personal accomplishment and professional gratification. Adding to this is the fact that colleagues and associates are now aware of the author's contribution to a particular field and tend to hold the author in higher regard for the capabilities which the paper demonstrates.

In some cases, renewed funding for research projects depends at least in part on reporting results to the community. Many research organizations consider it a part of their responsibility to disseminate their findings once the material has been released for public distribution. Papers written about the company's research results demonstrate its presence and capabilities in a field that the company considers important enough to fund with research dollars.

Management awareness of an individual's contribution to a field on behalf of the company is still another important benefit. Most professional staff in large organizations have only limited exposure to their upper management. But publishing distinguishes the individual author and sets him apart as one who may be furthering corporate goals by writing on topics that the management considers worthy.

Some organizations have formal programs that recognize authors of technical papers. In our organization, management strongly encourages publication of technical work. In an annual "Best Paper Contest," MITRE awards a substantial cash award for the year's best contribution to the literature of a field; papers published in refereed journals or proceedings earn lesser but considerable incentive awards. The writers are featured in the company newsletter and are usually photographed with company officers presenting the award and offering their appreciation. The newsletter usually briefly describes the winning paper and lists authors who received the incentive awards. The Corporation's publishing awards program has features similar to that introduced some years ago at Motorola and reported by Marsh [3], and to that described by Anderson [4].

WHY NOT PUBLISH

The path that leads from an idea for a paper to an actual publication of an article is usually a long, unclear, often confusing one. It demands patience and clear communication with one's management and company organizations as well as sponsors and with the publication's editorial staff. Technical people fail to write technical papers on work-related topics due to a host of difficulties. Reasons given for failing to write for publication seem to fall into two main categories:

- Lack of information about writing opportunities and procedures
  - Difficulty in choosing a topic
  - Difficulty in identifying an appropriate forum for the article
  - Difficulty in keying the article to the forum
  - Low odds of acceptance squelching motivation
  - Critical reviewers
- Lack of skills and resources for formal writing
  - Lack of basic writing skills
  - Little business time for writing
  - Minimal financial incentive preventing use of personal time on such endeavors
  - Uncertainty about management policy, difficulty of security review, controls denying discussion of seminal results, uncertainty about release of data
  - Lack of support resources (management, secretarial, editorial, research)

ADDRESSING OBJECTIONS

Writing Opportunities

Most staff members write in association with their jobs. Nearly all staff have some writing responsibilities for documenting their work and the results that they achieve. Most papers written by the technical staff can be classified as technical business papers; they represent a body of knowledge upon which the author can draw for a technical article.

The general format of a technical business paper opens with a brief executive summary aimed at decision makers, focusing on the results and how they impact the business. Other sections of the business report develop the procedure, elaborate on the nature of the problem, discuss results in relation to other work or the limitations of the current work, and sometimes include appendixes that explain technical details. But the primary purposes of the business paper are to report some results in a business context and to provide some recommendations for action based on the results. The procedures and methods used, the study's relation to other work, and the technical details mainly provide little interest compared with the results.

Usually, readers of the literature of a professional field are most interested in those very parts that are subordinate in the business paper. So, in using a business report as a source document for a technical article, a major step is to change its emphasis. The author must often recast the article to clarify and focus on those aspects of the work that are of primary interest to technical colleagues who read a particular publication and are the likely audience for the article. It is also important to keep the publication's editorial policy in mind and target one's writing to accommodate it.

Selecting a Specific Topic

Each project or related work usually contains dozens of possible ideas for technical papers if evaluated carefully. The individual author and his management should review his work assignments together and glean a set of promising topics; the set can be narrowed down further as each is better understood. A major criterion for choosing one topic over another may very well be related to the corporation's overall strategic goals.

The company management usually has a clearly articulated strategic plan for the company's growth in the near future. Often, a component of the plan involves establishing some credentials in new fields of interest to the company. If an aspiring author is familiar with, or working in these fields, he can further his firm's reputation and distinguish himself by writing on such specific topics. Technical papers may be strategic for their subject matter, but good timing is also very important. Papers that appear late are usually of little value to the corporate strategic plan.

Even if no new fields are to be conquered, writing about one's work in the technical disciplines is important to advancement of the field. Authors should work closely with management and technical experts to select topics that are both interesting to the members of the profession and yet likely to pass corporate release approval, declassification procedures, and the review process. A case study, a novel application of a well-known approach, or a description of a new model for a process may all be appropriate topics. The author must keep in mind the operative constraints—the audience's fields of interest, the editorial policy of the targeted publication, corporate goals and policies, sponsor goals and policies, and the availability of resources to deal adequately with the chosen topic.

Outlet Opportunities

According to the New York Times, more than 40,000 professional journals and business/trade publications document work in nearly every field imaginable. Although the literature of electrical engineering and computer science represents a small portion of that total, it offers many opportunities to recast the business report as a technical paper or article, including the following:

- Professional journals
  - National societies (e.g., *Proceedings of the IEEE, Journal of the Association of Computing Machinery*)
  - Subsocieties (e.g., *IEEE Transactions on Computers*)
  - Special interest groups (e.g., *IEEE Transactions on*

Software Engineering, ACM SIGSOFT Notices, IEEE Computer magazine)
- Conference proceedings
  - National conferences
  - Regional conferences
  - Special interest group/subsociety meetings
- Broader interest publications (e.g., *BYTE, Defense Electronics*)
- Trade journals (e.g., *PC Week, Electronic Business*)

A comprehensive list of IEEE journals appears in *IEEE Spectrum* and in the membership materials distributed by IEEE. Similar lists appear in ACM publications.

SOME CHARACTERISTICS OF AN ARTICLE

Journal Article

Understanding the characteristics that various classes of professional publications expect for articles helps to target the writing. The journals and transactions of the various professional societies are the most scholarly. Journal articles convey information to other practitioners in a particular field, people already familiar with the subject matter of the technical material. The introduction to a journal article typically includes a rationale for the work based on a set of technical objectives and features a literature review of related work. The journal article differs from the business paper in that it contains not only the results, but also details on how they were reached. The discussion section focuses on the results and their significance to other work in the area. Detailed technical aspects of the work inappropriate for the body of the paper often appear in an appendix. Michaelson [5] describes several formats that journal articles might take.

A journal's editorial policy may appear in the publication itself. It describes the subjects covered by the publication, acceptable length, writing style, and format expected. Although reviewers' comments and correspondence with the professional journal offer expert feedback, authors face difficulty in gaining acceptance for their papers in such publications. Because space in them is at a premium, stiff competition and delays in publication are commonplace. The length of the manuscript is crucial for a journal. Usually, only those that meet strict length limits are accepted.

The author and editor of the journal have a critical relationship in preparing an article for a technical journal. The editor judges whether an article should be included in the publication. Normally, the editor assigns the article to a group of peer reviewers for comment and critique. When they complete the review, the editor returns the article to the author with suggestions and reviewers' comments. Because most authors dislike criticism of their work, they often take it personally even when the legitimate comments are helpful. Experienced authors, however, view such feedback as valuable free advice from leading figures in the field. Not only does the critique lead to a better paper; it sometimes points out other relevant technical issues or resource materials that can shed further light on the topic.

Special Interest Group Publication

Special interest group (SIG) publications offer another outlet for technical writing. Usually less scholarly than the transactions of the parent society, SIGs are likely to be more timely and relevant to a specialized readership. Often the SIG dedicates a particular issue of its publication to a special theme. Articles in theme-related issues include tutorials on the basic technology of the topic, a review of the state of the art in one or several aspects of the field, and reports of likely new directions the field might take based on recent results. For example, in 1988, the IEEE *Software* magazine published separate issues focusing on the special topics of parallel processing, CASE, and fourth-generation languages, respectively. Most publications promote their special theme issues well in advance. Their advance promotion efforts should give authors enough time to find an issue that relates to their work. Articles appearing in IEEE special interest magazines are peer-reviewed and edited.

Conference Proceedings

Conferences are an excellent forum for technical authors to begin the process of writing for publication. The oral conference presentation is usually accompanied by a paper that presents the material and makes the presenter's points in writing. The conference paper provides an opportunity for the author to assemble thoughts in an organized way and to prepare a paper describing the work with somewhat less demanding editorial standards than the journals call for. Conference papers often report on work in progress or tentative results.

Most conferences issue a call for papers well in advance of the conference itself and usually request that only an outline or an abstract be submitted to the program committee for consideration. On the basis of this material, the program committee determines whether the paper relates to the theme of the conference and decides to reject or accept the author's submission for the conference session and publication in its proceedings. However, the review and inclusion policies vary greatly from conference to conference. An author can benefit from having the points of the paper discussed during the presentation at the conference. A paper appearing in the conference proceedings can then incorporate elements of the discussion, be revised, rewritten formally, and submitted to a journal for consideration.*

In nearly every area of electrical engineering and computer science, conferences take place on a more or less regular

* *Ed. note*: IEEE policy expressly prohibits "double publication"—that is, publication of the same paper in both the proceedings of a conference and in a journal. It is acceptable, however, as Dr. Manley suggests to enhance the paper with additional material and submit it for journal consideration.

basis, usually annually. The professional societies almost always sponsor an annual meeting at the national level that focuses on the special interests of the subsociety as distinguished from those of the profession as a whole. Regional and local chapters of the subsocieties hold annual conferences with a topical theme that usually changes from year to year.

Notices announcing upcoming conferences usually appear in the last sections of IEEE publications under the heading "Call for Papers." Some conferences may have more extensive promotional campaigns, particularly if the likely participants come from different disciplines. Additional promotional techniques include mailing announcements to targeted mailing lists and running extended advertising copy in society publications or in the publications of related societies. Some conferences have such an impact, either by their sheer size or by the topic they deal with, that even the popular media will report on the plans (for instance, Comdex).

Other Outlets

Technical writers can turn to other outlets as well. The magazines published by the various societies of the IEEE (such as *Computer, MICRO,* or *Software*), special interest group letters of the ACM (such as SIGADA, or SIGPLAN), other special interest journals such as *BYTE,* and trade journals like *PC Magazine* all appeal to various audiences. Articles in the IEEE magazine format and ACM letter format publications are peer-reviewed. Each publication maintains its own editorial policy but, by and large, articles that report research results from a practical viewpoint or describe applications of new technologies or procedures to existing problems merit publication. Of course, the audiences of such articles vary widely from publication to publication. They vary in education, interest focus, and expectations of style, currency, and level of technical detail; the author who is aware of these characteristics can successfully target an article for a particular publication.

SKILLS AND RESOURCES

Writing Skills

For most researchers, the memory of college writing assignments has faded dimly into the past. Most of their current work is documented in briefings and short information papers with a decidedly business thrust. As Eisenberg [6] points out, the technical writing professional needs technical writing skills.

Many corporations have recognized that technical writing skills are vital for their staff. They often run courses that deal with technical writing principles and offer practice for the attendees. These courses can be developed internally by the company or can be offered as professional development courses outside the office. Technical writing courses are offered by local community colleges as well as by the extension services of state universities. Specialized consultants are also in business to teach technical writing and overall communication skills to the technical professional. The IEEE Educational Activities Department offers self-study courses in writing and communication; the "Put It In Writing" Program (7) offers a videotape and workbook designed to build technical writing skills. There are many other quality courses available as well.

Research Resources

Many organizations maintain a library which houses a collection of reference material relevant to their work. Most industrial libraries maintain a close working relationship with local public or university libraries or have access to documents from distant sources through an interlibrary loan system. Most staff members realize that the library exists and maintains a collection of reference works, but many don't known that modern computer technology has made the library a formidable reference identification and retrieval system. Many industrial libraries maintain online data base services designed to match researchers' topic areas and keywords to documents that address them in the literature. A particularly powerful system is the online citation index, designed to track the citation history of technical papers as they are themselves cited in the literature. This allows the researcher to follow a seminal idea first discussed in a technical paper into succeeding years, and to find those paths of research that built upon the original idea. Also, most libraries have a collection of "how-to-write" books, the corporate writing style standard and other style manuals, journal guides, as well as many journals themselves. Corporate libraries can also obtain copies of citations that an author finds of interest.

In recent years, authors have become increasingly aware of copyright issues. Before a copyrighted article can be excerpted or a figure used in an article, the copyright holder must grant permission. Libraries and information services departments usually encourage authors to secure copyright permission through them. Because they have blanket agreements with many publishers and the experience of seeking permission from many others, they can save the author time and effort.

TIME PROBLEMS

One way authors can deal with time constraints and delays is to write a technical paper as the project progresses, using the "incremental approach" outlined by Michaelson [5}. The writer constructs an outline from project plans and details it as the project progresses. Each writing increment takes only a short while because each time the writer visits the manuscript, he produces only small increments, written while the material is fresh in mind.

From a broader viewpoint, timing the completion and publication of a technical paper can be important to a company and its strategy for asserting its presence in a particular field. Articles and papers that fit a corporation's publication plan reflect well on the author. They provide additional exposure to management and enhance the author's standing in a field where the company has an interest.

COMPANY POLICY

Gaining Public Release

Before employees can offer to write about their work for the general community, document control authorities in the company must usually approve the original paper for public release. This is particularly important in research fields dealing with material that is classified in either a company confidential sense or a national security sense. Although this practice relates to the safeguarding of sensitive information, it also helps assure the company that its sponsoring agencies are aware of information being disseminated. Nothing is more embarrassing for an agency than to discover some new issue in the technical press and note its discovery attributed to work performed under its own sponsorship.

In our organization, each paper must go through a prescribed release process; a time lag of six weeks is usually required for approval. Our procedures require an author to file a standard form with the document control office. This office then acquires the approval signatures from the internal corporate management chain, the technical release office, and the sponsor's project officer. This public release step can cause some delay; it's always prudent to allow plenty of time for this process.

There are several ways to lessen the impact of the delay. First, co-authoring with a member of the sponsoring agency allows many potential obstacles to be dealt with by the co-author. Experience shows that sponsoring agencies usually expedite material that members of their own organization submit. Also, keeping one's own management apprised helps speed the signature process through the internal organization. Good planning and consultation with management early in the preparation process will shorten turnaround time and help eliminate potential snags that could send the author back for a major rewrite. Another tactic is to submit a suitably sanitized draft of the paper to the acceptance committee for review purposes only, noting that the complete paper will be forthcoming only after release approval. It is not uncommon for public release approval to be denied when a paper reports results in the context of a sensitive project or program. Another approach may be to obscure the sensitive nature of the project by reporting the elements in a hypothetical, unclassified context. The author could discuss only small parts of the work without revealing the motivation for it, or plan to discuss only those parts that are most likely to be declassified [8].

What Managers Can Do

Management can play a strong role in encouraging technical professionals to write about their work. By carefully structuring assignments and understanding the benefits of publishing, they can take several steps to enable and encourage the technical staff to prepare papers for publication:

- Recognize that writing about technical work enhances the company's reputation and prestige
- Include writing for publication in project planning and coordinate professional writing with business reports
- Encourage incremental preparation of manuscripts
- Brainstorm with staff to identify fertile topics for papers within the technical work program
- Realize that writing is an important part of professional development
- Include professional writing and publication as part of the corporate strategic plan
- Acknowledge and reward those who successfully publish technical papers
- Keep sponsoring organizations apprised of the professional writing agenda
- For classified or sensitive projects:
  - — Plan to gain release of suitable results
  - — Identify elements of the work that are not sensitive

Management is an important force for the technical author. By taking a proactive role, the manager can help guide the author's work and encourage preparation of a paper that meets corporate strategic goals, enhances the department's reputation and builds the author's esteem. A helpful manager can provide unique guidance on the author's choice of subject and approach and help prepare the way for release of technical data that the author may want to include.

MITRE'S PUBLISHING WORKSHOP

MITRE management was concerned that, although our work program continues to show steady growth, the staff has not kept up with contributing to the technical literature at a commensurate rate. Over the last two years, our Washington facility prepared nearly 1400 technical business papers, supported by a great deal of interesting and useful work. But it seems that little of this information reaches the wider technical community. Of the business-oriented documents produced during the last two years, staff members requested releases of only about 50 for public distribution; only 70 papers were published in technical journals or conference proceedings.

Why the discrepancy? As detailed above, new authors don't fully appreciate the benefits of technical publishing; they face uncertainty, obstacles, and setbacks. They wonder what to write about or how to locate an appropriate publication or conference, worry that their work may lack sufficient interest or quality (and thus be rejected), and struggle to find the time and resources to prepare articles suitable for publication. We felt that a short course or workshop that would address these areas would help eliminate some barriers and encourage more staff to publish their work.

Workshop Approach

The MITRE Institute collaborated with two local writing consultants to develop and deliver such a one-day workshop. The program emphasizes some of the incentives and barriers discussed in this paper. The course shows participants how, what, and where to publish. We also developed a notebook of resource materials to which prospective authors could refer. One goal of the workshop is to offer guidance on how to prepare the technical article from the body of knowledge on which a business report is based.

Our business reports are the product of a general process that is more or less consistently applied across the company. Although report topics vary greatly, within the electrical engineering, systems engineering, and computer science fields most of our business reports share a common format and expository style and their preparation usually begins as a response to a sponsor's question or expressed need. For this reason, the process of preparing technical articles for publication based on corporate business reports can be somewhat standardized for our organization as a whole, and a workshop that offers guidance on the process is generally applicable to the work of most of the technical staff.

We opened the workshop to the entire technical staff at our Washington facility. The workshop participants realized that attending the publishing workshop would benefit them professionally and personally. They perceived that the course materials would help them prepare for publication and they attended because they wanted to. Sanders [9] observes that many people receiving technical writing training these days are college-trained professionals. All the professionals attending our workshop were formally trained in a technical discipline and had many years of experience. The average experience of the class was nearly 17 years since the bachelor's degree; no one with fewer than four years of experience attended. As a key aspect of the workshop, we coordinated its offering date with a call for papers from a local ACM conference that dealt with an area of computer science in which many of our staff were experienced and qualified to contribute.

Several speakers were invited to share with the participants their experiences with publishing technical articles based on their work for the corporation. We also invited representatives of the Information Services (library) and Security/Document Control departments to discuss their respective services and how authors might make particular use of them.

Participants found the expository portions of the workshop to be of greatest benefit. Few were aware of the considerable number of outlets for publishing, or that targeting articles is a well-developed strategy, or that so many potential topics were hidden in their work, or that writing can forward both the organization's goals and their own. Most believed that if management would offer support in a more proactive way, they would be more inclined to support corporate goals by writing technical papers for publication.

CONCLUSION

Technical professionals can meet the challenge of publishing their work by familiarizing themselves with the process of preparing technical papers based on the work they perform in their jobs. By understanding that the business report can serve as a resource for the technical article, by recognizing the barriers to publishing and how to overcome them, and by becoming familiar with the nature of the various types of technical articles and their various outlets, technical authors have the tools they need to prepare an article for publication.

This familiarization process can be expedited through conducting a short workshop designed to expose aspiring authors to the elements of preparing a technical article for publication in the professional literature. The workshop helps to demystify a process that appears arcane and obscure to many technical professionals.

REFERENCES

1. Corbin, N. C., "The Importance of Competent Technical Communications to Career Advancement," *Proc. IEEE Professional Communications Conf.* (1985), pp. 17–20.
2. Michaelson, H. B., "How Writing Helps R&D Work," *IEEE PC-30,* 2 (June 1987).
3. Marsh, J., "Motorola's Silver Quill Program to Encourage Writing about Work for Publication," *IEEE Micro Magazine* (June 1985), pp. 53–57.
4. Anderson, D. T., "Company Incentive Program for Getting Engineers to Write," *IEEE PC-26,* 4 (December 1983), pp. 170–171.
5. Michaelson, H. B., *How to Write and Publish Engineering Papers and Reports.* Philadelphia: ISI Press, 1986.
6. Eisenberg, A., "The Importance of Writing Skills for the Engineer," *IEEE Potentials* (February 1984), pp. 24–28.
7. Joseph, A., *Put It In Writing,* Cleveland: International Writing Institute, 1986.
8. Michaelson, H. B., "Publishing Classified Papers," IEEE *Institute* (January 1987).
9. Sanders, S. P., "What Is Communication Education and Training?" *IEEE PC-30,* 1 (March 1987), pp. 45–46.

Today's Style Guide: Trusted Tool with Added Potential

Abstract—*Style guides, the primary tool of technical editors, are as important as ever; actually, their increased uses and benefits can redefine the activities of editors. Specifically, style guides can be used to train new employees, to generate buy-in of subject-matter experts, and to define the process flow of document and product generation. Additionally, because they have the potential to control many style decisions and to integrate a variety of skills, computer-driven styles and Web style guides reinforce these increased uses and benefits and suggest the emergence of even more. Thus technical editors' roles may be expanded to include additional training functions, new marketing dimensions, and innovative research in multimedia design and development.*

—JANE PERKINS AND CASSANDRA MALONEY

Index Terms—*Style guides, technical editing, Web design guides.*

Manuscript received October 15, 1997.
J. Perkins is with Clemson University, Clemson, SC 29631 USA.
C. Maloney is with the Proposal and Presentation Team, NationsBank, Atlanta, GA USA.
IEEE PII S 0361-1434(98)01975-4.

TODAY, corporate and industry-wide style guides are as essential for editing as they have ever been. But their uses are also expanding, especially as their development and application are shifted from final editing rounds of document production to the genesis of product development. This shift, most apparent in editing for information-intense industries such as software development, has many influences:

- Cross-functional teams blur writing and editing responsibilities and optimally urge people to talk and share their knowledge and work tools (like style guides).
- Graphical user interface (GUI) design has software developers searching for standards and guidelines.
- Usability testing advocates encourage user-tested standards integrated throughout product and document development cycles.
- Outsourcing contractors and third-party vendors require guidelines to maintain in-house standards.
- New technologies such as the World Wide Web incite "everyone" to create home pages and, therefore, to need standards of good and usable design.

Stimulated by these influences, writing, design, and editing changes raise questions about style guides: Who needs to use style guides? When in the development process are they needed? What should style guides include? What are their purposes and functions? How are changes in style guide use affecting editors and professional communicators?

These style guide questions suggest expanded possibilities—that build on traditional editing skills—for editors and professional communicators. Therefore, we will first recount "established" uses and benefits of style guides, and then contrast these with additional uses and benefits that have been

Reprinted from *IEEE Trans. Prof. Comm.*, vol. PC-41, no. 1, pp. 24–31, March 1998.

presented in recent publications. Because a common denominator or impetus for changes in style guide use is the computer, we will highlight some of these influences as we extend this discussion to our analysis of Website style guides. The phenomenon of creating for the Web, with its integration of many skill areas, offers a unique opportunity for studying emerging uses and benefits of style guides. Similar to the development of *The Chicago Manual of Style* for paper-based publications, new style guides are being created now for Web publishing. For both corporate style guides and industry-wide style guides, current developments indicate new dimensions of editing, which make that essential editing stand-by—the style guide—a hot tool for technical communicators.

Traditional and Expanding Uses of Corporate Style Guides

Even with the many changes listed above, the primary responsibility for editing documents, hard copy and/or online text, including user manuals, product specifications, proposals, reports, and conference presentations and proceedings, continues to fall within technical editors' territory. To get these jobs done, corporate style guides, usually in the form of three-ring binders of site-specific guidelines, are employed. Although these style guides, especially the volumes that detail obscure and little-used concepts, often gather dust as they line the shelves of editors' cubes, their agreed-upon standards are essential for producing corporate documents of quality. And often these internal corporate style guides are supplemented by more generic industry-wide guidelines and with the old standby, *The Chicago Manual of Style*. Technical editors are well aware of the absolute necessity of these style guides for fulfilling traditional editing needs:

- to create coherence within a document;
- to align documents within a division and an organization;
- to ensure consistency across time and locations; and
- to provide time-saving standards so that writers aren't always starting over to "reinvent the wheel."

These purposes support a definition of style guide most recognized by technical communicators: "a rule-driven document that sets the parameters for consistency and acceptability for all written materials produced by an individual or group" [1, p. 244]. However, beyond these traditional uses, researchers are noting additional benefits of style guides—those that are less about applying "rules" and more about orchestrating work. These expanded uses include training new employees, generating buy-in of subject-matter experts, and defining the process flow of document and product generation. Designing style guides to be less about rules and more about helping employees create documents broadens the technical editor's role.

Training New Employees Although the potential of style guides for training new employees may have long been apparent to writers and editors, this use has recently been emphasized in articles extolling style guides. Hagge discusses the normative effect of style guides in his research of style manuals sponsored by professional disciplinary associations in the sciences. He argues that "such manuals reflect underlying conventions that communities of scientists have ratified as normative for the production of texts in that discipline" [2, p. 129]. Because norms suggest a discipline's, or group's, or company's agreed-upon standards of behavior—or in the instance of style guides, approach to writing and communication forms—newcomers must learn these norms or conventions. Style guides, therefore, are appropriate tools for communicating an organization's norms, especially to newcomers: "Writers in a discipline, especially neophytes, are often expressly encouraged to use the manual associated with their discipline" [2, p. 134]. Allen situates the use of style guides for training new employees specifically in corporations when he describes the ways in which style guides can save corporate dollars. He explains that a "corporate style guide, used as a training guide, reduces the actual time required to train the new employee" and also, to some extent, replaces a human trainer with a written document [3, p. 286].

As style guides' training purposes become more acknowledged and important, technical writers and editors may want to evaluate their style guides to see if they support this use. What should style guides look like—in content and organization—if they are to be used, not solely as traditional reference documents, but also as tutorials?

Generating Buy-In of Subject-Matter Experts In addition to their use for training, style guides—and more specifically the way they are created—can engender the cooperation of subject-matter experts. If the primary purpose of a style guide is to control consistency, one person can create the standard and editors can apply it. If a style guide originates as part of a group's norming process, it results from agreement among its users. And while editors still use the guide to ensure standards of consistency, its broader purposes—including training, educating, and even identifying group members and their roles and responsibilities—are often as significant. The power of the corporate style guide, or its ability to generate compliance, depends in large part on how and by whom it was created.

Many corporate style guides are created by a single author or perhaps by a team of technical writers assigned to the task. Single authorship seems to equate with style guides that serve primarily to ensure consistency. Washington describes such a single-authorship experience. Although she gathered information and suggestions from selected prospective users and cycled the style guide through reviewers, she, alone, "was given *carte blanche* in developing the Guide" [4, p. 553]. Her goal was to establish consistency among corporate documents, and while helpful to its users, the style guide was designed to be The Standard.

A single-authored style guide usually has a different influence than a guide which is created and backed by subject-matter experts. Although gaining the support of management is recognized as critical [3]–[5], inclusive methods aimed at subject-matter experts broaden the accepted use and, therefore, the benefits of style guides. Allen advises thinking of style guides as "always in some stage of development" [3, p. 289] and soliciting revision and update suggestions from users. Le Vie cautions that style guides are more easily implemented when "Consequences for noncompliance are corrective and not punitive" [5, p. 23]. Additionally, technical writers may benefit from sharing some of their "authority" and expertise for style guide creation. Even though technical writers are the language experts in most companies, they may learn of new style guide needs and develop more buy-in if they work as part of a cross-functional team of style developers.

As technical writers and editors—those most often responsible for producing style guides—realize the value of building co-workers' ownership in the corporate style guide, they will design more inclusive methods of creation. What processes, then, for the development and maintenance of corporate style guides are most inclusive? Who will benefit from contributing to their creation and revision? And how can diverse corporate members be best convinced of this value?

Defining the Process Flow of Document and Product Generation Style guides can also be used to define the process flow of document generation, including document components, coordination of contributors, cycles of edits, and schedules and deadlines [3]. The use of style guides to define development processes pushes their use from the end of document production, the final edit, to the beginning stages of pre-planning. Le Vie explains that use of style guides shifts responsibility to subject-matter authors, such as the engineers in research and development, and away from resting solely with the writers and editors. Le Vie writes, "Placing and enforcing compliance closer to the information source allows writers and editors to add value to a project rather than serving as high-priced desktop publishers" [5, p. 20]. Hackos believes that a "higher level of process maturity" [6, p. 56] in an organization results from establishing a publications process, with the first critical step depending on the integrated development of publications standards. These standards, or corporate style guide, may include information on the "publications-development life cycle" [6, p. 302].

When it includes information that helps subject-matter experts make decisions and explain those decisions in writing, the style guide is integrated into the overall development process, and it thus adds significant new value. How can style guide use be integrated with product design and development? In what ways is the technical editor's job affected?

Applying Computer-Driven Styles

Because style guides can provide help in addition to rules, the uses of style guides are expanding and thereby affecting the roles of technical editors and communicators. Additionally, the technical editor role is affected because of computer-driven styles and, in particular, the World Wide Web.

Computers offer style guide developers and users new opportunities, while requiring new decision-making. Although editors may think of computer-driven style options as features separate from style guides, these style options can also be considered significant components of a style guide. Software capabilities that allow the creation and application of "styles," "macros," and "templates" encompass many style guide decisions. For example, from the definitions of these terms used in Microsoft Word's online help, it is clear that their use provides the same benefits as traditional hardcopy style guides; they offer consistency, ease, and speed [7]:

- Styles for characters and paragraphs: "a collection of formats—such as font, point size, and indents—that you name and store as a group. When you apply a style to selected text, Word applies all formatting instructions in that style at once."
- Macro: "a sequence of actions that is named and stored."
- Template: "a blueprint for the text, graphics, and formatting that is the same in every document of a particular type."

Computer-driven style capabilities, similar to online help features, are often meeting grounds where technical editors and writers come together with computer engineers, usability specialists, graphic designers, and marketing specialists. These style domains and their interfaces—sometimes contested turf, sometimes an advantageous blend—are seldom ignored or considered unimportant. For these many style creators, the appeal and benefits of offering computer-driven style capabilities extend beyond the traditional ones of assuring consistency and of saving time, energy, and money. For some style creators, computer-driven styles are appealing because they provide a challenge to develop new style features; for other style creators, the appeal comes with added control for enforcing writers'/users' application of styles. If computer-driven styles are applied as a matter of course—say as a policy within an organization—the style creators have more pervasive control... and more responsibility. That responsibility could rest, at least in part, with technical editors.

In a paper-based publishing world, technical editors may be involved in formulating style guides in ways similar to their involvement with the creation of electronic templates. However, editors' responsibilities may also change when styles go electronic. If electronic styles, such as templates, are applied, editors may gain more compliance, which may be more automatic and less resisted. With that ease and habitualized application, editors may be perceived less as the "style police." They may be freed to spend less time, for example, measuring with their pica rules to see if standards are being followed and more time considering the design or update of page formatting to be inscribed into a template. This shift in responsibilities also reinforces the technical editor in the role of corporate trainer. With new computer capabilities, such as templates, users often turn to the creators for help with their use and application. The line between enforcing a corporate standard and training corporate employees is blurred.

For both their creators and users, computer-driven styles are advantageous because they can generally be updated more easily and, therefore, more frequently; updating electronic styles is far easier than copying, binding, and distributing. This speed is certainly important in work environments where change and a fast pace are motivating forces. As the editors of *Wired*, who wrote *Wired Style: Principles of Usage in the Digital Age*, explain, "technology is pushing us forward, toward the cultural and linguistic frontier. Techies invent terms daily; fresh slang sweeps through the online community within hours; new media shifts how we use words...Our mantra is not *How has it been?* but *How will it be?*" [8, p. 83]. In such mercurial environments, editors and their style guides may go the way of what Clement Mok, an acclaimed information architect, describes as the direction for graphics standards manuals:

> Companies still need graphics standards manuals, but now the way they are maintained and updated can accommodate the mobility of a company's identity and take into account that more people shape corporate communications. Some companies have replaced their forty-pound graphics standards manuals with simple pamphlets updated on a quarterly basis, making them available to everyone in the company—Digital technology has spurred streamlined, direct communication, and some companies have dispensed with printed manuals altogether... [9, p. 68]

Expanding style guides electronically in the form of styles, macros, and templates raises some new issues and possibilities for technical editors and writers. The range of their decision-making may include issues such as the following:

- What should be built into computer-driven styles, macros, and templates and what still needs to be included in more traditional corporate style guides?
- If a hardcopy needs to be developed, what should be included? What should be duplicated in both the electronic and hardcopy style guides?
- How will updates be managed and coordinated, especially if both electronic and hardcopy style guides are used?

Although the application of computer-driven styles is familiar to most technical editors and writers as part of their expertise, the creative, up-front decision-making and design may offer new areas of rewarding and valued work.

Creating Web Style Guides

Nowhere are computer-driven styles more significant, more in demand, nor in a more malleable infancy than in Web design. The Web sites being developed to offer guidelines may be portents of style guides' future. They integrate new multimedia capabilities and suggest new uses and benefits.

Typically, a URL (Uniform Resource Locator, the term for a WWW address) will bring up a Web style guide in minutes. These guidelines for Web design are delivered in the same volatile medium in which their users will apply the information learned from them. Although the Web style guide sites listed below are popular and often referenced examples, we can provide no guarantee that you will be able to access them in the same form in which we reviewed them during the spring and summer 1997. In general, however, the list should continue to be a good resource, especially those sites with corporate or university sponsorship. Of the many Web sites we considered, we selected the following for review:

- Apple Web Design Guide http://applenet.apple.com/hi/web/web.html
- Berkeley Digital Library http://sunsite.berkeley.edu/Web/guidelines.html
- Composing Good HTML http://www.cs.cmu.edu/tilt/cgh/
- IBM Web Design Guide http://www.ibm.com

/ibm/hci/guidelines/web/web _guidelines.html

- Microsoft Internet Workshop http://www.microsoft.com/ workshop/
- Sun Microsystems Guide to Web Style http://www.sun.com/ styleguide/
- System Magic HTML Style Guide http://www.sysmag.com/ web/html-style.html
- Web Wonk: Net Tips for Writers and Designers http://www.dsiegel.com/tips/
- Yale Style Manual http://info.med.yale.edu/ caim/manual/

We analyzed these sites, focusing on the creators' purpose of the style guide for its audience/users, the features and content included, and similarities with and differences from traditional style guides. Uses and benefits of many of these Web style guides are similar to those of traditional hardcopy style guides; the Web style guides are intended to ensure coherence within a site (or electronic document), align linked sites (or multiple publications) with each other, and develop some industry standards, thus promoting an ease that comes from consistency in design decisions. However, we also believe that many of these Web style guides are expanding the uses and benefits of traditional style guides in ways similar to those we described earlier. These uses include training, buy-in, and processes.

Training Many of the Web style guides we reviewed stated as their goal: to help Web authors develop effective, well-designed and informative sites. For example, Apple wants to offer "suggestions for creating Web pages that are usable and effective." Although training is clearly a primary purpose, these Web style guides offer a variety of approaches. Some Web style guides provide theories of Web design and others offer step-by-step how-tos. Various guidelines include, for example, traditional graphic design issues, introductory computer programming information, or technical computer discussions of optimal delivery methods.

Aimed at novice authors of this new medium, some Web style guides have evolved to include theory and training on the "correct" way to design Web pages. This information, or the standards professed, provides a form of communication to members of a new industry. These members are from many different professional areas and not everyone has training or experience in effective documentation or page design. For example, *Web Wonk: Net Tips for Writers and Designers* not only explains the correct way to use white space between paragraphs but it explains what white space is and how professional authors use it in traditional paper publications. The creators of this Web style guide are using their paper-based expertise as a basis for instruction in Web design for authors who are not familiar with traditional layout skills.

Decisions about the training content depend, of course, on who the Web style guide creators are targeting. For example, those developed by Sun, Microsoft, and IBM may be for internal use, third-party vendor use, and the use of potential customers world-wide. The creators of these guidelines are training the users of a burgeoning new field and interest area. The user audience, for both the Web style guide creators and those the authors/users are targeting, may be diverse and complex in many ways: their knowledge of technology, their skills in writing and designing, their different purposes for these styles, their location in the world, and the world-wide locations of their potential audiences. Thus because of the wide range of audiences/users of this new medium, the training function of Web style guides is complex in new ways and is often expanded to include theories and step-by-step assistance that are not the norm of most paper-based style guides. Technical editors, therefore, may be expected to assume new training dimensions as part of their positions.

Buy-In While creators of corporate style guides are becoming aware of the significance of generating agreement among style guide users as part of a group's norming process, Web style guide creators are also concerned with user buy-in. However, Web style guide buy-in is motivated by larger industry factors such as developing and maintaining market share for a company's products. This additional use reflects the Web's potential as a marketing tool, especially in creating brand definition and loyalty. In general, this buy-in comprises two, related types:

1) the acknowledged expertise of an industry leader
2) the literal buying power that comes from attracting users to a Web site

Companies, such as Microsoft, IBM, and Apple, vie for user buy-in through their Web style guide sites. Their sites promote the correct way to use the companies' products, help users understand product features, and ensure consistency of design application with users, thus helping to establish their dominance in Web know-how. These companies frequently update their sites to provide visitors with the latest information and to encourage their return for browsing new products and information.

Microsoft Internet Workshop is designed to instruct Web authors and to entice them into frequent returns for new information and digital elements, such as graphics, templates, and fonts. For this Web style guide site, Microsoft classifies information into five major categories:

1) Authoring—focuses on content and using HTML to present information effectively.
2) Design—includes information on Web technologies, tools, color management, typography, and Web design.
3) Programming—covers development of ActiveX controls and Internet communications technology.
4) Server—explains how the server side of Web operations works.
5) Gallery—contains a library of electric images, fonts, style sheets, and other Web elements that can be downloaded.

Although the Microsoft Internet Workshop site is expansive, these categories are written to appeal to specific groups of users: programmers, designers, authors, and administrators. For example, administrators would probably want to see the information in "Server" before browsing "Design." Microsoft is aiming to build their Web reputation by targeting specific users and addressing their needs.

Compared to Microsoft's site, IBM Web Design Guide is a collection of principles and guidelines in a more traditional format. The interface has more of a step-by-step feel because its interface uses a notebook metaphor, similar to the tabbed reference guides that all writers have. This IBM Web style guide site defines principles and guides:

- Principles are the goals which guide design decisions. They reflect knowledge about human perception, learning, and behavior.
- Guidelines are based on principles, but are specific to a particular domain of design.

Developed by IBM's Human Computer Interactive Group, this site's purpose is to promote buy-in from Web authors. It walks Web authors through the process of creating a Web site, using IBM's prescribed methods. And, as an authority in this new field, the Web style guide site provides "Principles" and "Guidelines." If Web authors use its standards, IBM achieves buy-in and is considered an authority, and IBM also enhances its potential to have a market share in this developing industry.

Apple's Human Interface Web Design Guide is geared more toward the theory of information. Apple says, "this Web site contains information about general human interface principles that you can apply to designing Web pages." Although they may be targeting a more limited audience of users, Apple is still addressing ways to make Web sites more enjoyable and usable, while establishing their own Web presence and expertise. As the Web-design authority, the Apple site talks theory and offers generalizable information.

The potential to stimulate user buy-in through Web style guides expands the purposes and benefits of these guides beyond their traditional uses, especially since the Web is attracting authors/users who may be new to both the Web and to all kinds of writing and page-design concepts. Web style guides are not, then, only about hints for proper use of discrete stylistics: "use a comma after all items in a series." The nature of the Web and its potential to manage information in new ways result in a demand for Web style guides that address the whole, inclusive design process. By becoming the recognized authority for this new communication medium, companies can create both direct and indirect marketing opportunities. And technical editors who create Web style guides are influenced by these buy-in or marketing aims.

Processes Because Web designing with its many interrelated capabilities is new to many of the authors/users who visit these Web style guide sites for help, Web style guides typically cover similar topics of needed information. They provide authors/users with guides to the whole complex, interactive design process. Rather than presenting this information—as does the site Composing Good HTML, which formats information in a linear, long paper—sites such as Web Wonk, Berkeley Digital Library, IBM, Yale, and Sun Microsystems provide linked indexing methods, usually as some type of clickable table of contents. Creators of Web style guide sites need to model the innovative design capabilities they are explaining. Therefore, technical editors involved in creating these Web style guides need to learn the newest Web design features and include them in their style guides. They have the added opportunity and responsibility to push the research edge in multimedia design and development processes.

The Web Wonk site, for example, helps users by providing tips that address a variety of Web publishing issues. Web Wonk believes that "these tips will help you be a better communicator on the Net." The tips not only cover spelling in cyberspace but address setting links ergonomically, and many issues in between.

Berkeley Digital Library addresses many of the new issues and standards that Web authors face, such as:

- contextual information
- accessibility
- structure and organization
- navigation
- format and editing
- markup language
- images

The site's clickable table of contents is a run-down of the complexity of the Web design process and the issues involved.

To address the complex combinations of new capabilities and required skills of Web designers, IBM uses a tabbed reference guide metaphor. Author/users are given five sections of information that break down the Web design process into stages:

1) Proposal
2) Plan
3) Design
4) Production
5) Maintenance

Once users have selected a major section, they are provided with additional embedded topics; in Design, users can select structure, visuals, navigation, and so on. Each stage, of usually no more than three screen lengths, further chunks the design process.

Yale's Style Manual, one of the first style guides developed for the Web, provides a great amount of detailed information. Their aim to include all aspects of the Web design process results in a large and complex site: "However, few existing resources have attempted to approach Web page and site design as a challenge that combines traditional editorial approaches to documents with graphic design, user interface design, information design, and the technical authoring skills required to optimize the HTML code, graphics, and text within Web pages." The site is very detailed because of their inclusive aim, the many updated additions as new electronic features are made possible and further research is conducted, and the decision to include actual papers and bibliographies for Web authors who want additional research information.

Because the Web environment offers a different delivery method from its traditional paper-based counterparts, Sun Microsystems Guide to Web Style, for example, includes a "Quick Reference" with many topics that would not be necessary for non-Web design, including Links, Image Maps, Navigation, Security, Netiquette, and Java. And within more traditional reference pages, such as Page Length, it provides information about Web page length as opposed to hardcopy page length. It reports research findings, which suggest that people in general will not read a long Web page. Sun has found that online readers want short, clearly segmented chunks of information because they will not scroll down the page. Part of the value of Web style guide sites, such as the Sun Microsystems Guide to Web Style, is in the research and expertise of the creators who are familiar with the process of designing for this complex, new publishing field. The Sun creators offer a simple caveat for the information they provide: "This is a cookbook for helping people create better Web pages. The guidelines presented here represent the opinions and preferences of a small group of people within Sun who have created some Web pages, and have looked at many more."

Web documents give author/users the ability to create sites that combine hyperlinks, sound, pictures, and multimedia elements. Each one of these elements forces authors/users to rethink standards of effective communication and to need additional answers. The creators of Web style guides—including technical editors—not only consider complex design and delivery processes but try to address emerging issues and standards.

Traditional Editing with New Twists

The use of Web style guides for developing training, buy-in, and processes further supports the changing role of technical editors. However, while innovative technological capabilities often result in expanded possibilities and roles, much of what technical editors do depends on their traditional expertise and experience. For example, Web style guide creators must make decisions that balance their control of style decisions against authors'/users' flexibility—the traditional style guide decision, with some added twists.

Because of the technology, authors/users cannot control all aspects of their Web documents; users' browsers impose many constraints and possibilities. New versions of browsers, such as Netscape and MS Explorer, also allow Web authors to develop style sheets that can be attached to documents. Style sheets control additional aspects of the document and how it is displayed. Web authors can control multiple style aspects in three ways:

1) linking text to a style sheet,
2) embedding a style block in text, and
3) using inline styles.

The Web Wonk and Microsoft Internet Workshop help Web authors consider not only the site as a whole but all the small details, such as font size, type, color, and placement. However, even with the use of style sheets, Web documents may not appear as the author intended them to. The readers/users have the ability to change their display and that will affect the document. If styles are important to Web creators, they may have to be concerned in new ways with appealing to their users.

Most of the sites we reviewed are intended for general use and contain information that can be applied to most Web development projects. However, as companies start to develop intranet sites—sites confined to internal users—technical editors and publication departments will develop internal Web style guides. Intranet style guides will help companies develop an internal Web identity, similar to and consistent with a paper-based corporate identity. Intranet style guides will help in that goal. The System Magic HTML Style Guide is an example of one organization's style guide for its employees. It has also been published on the Web as an external tool. System Magic provides its corporate users with different classes of guidelines:

1) Rules that must be adhered to for the Web page to satisfy System Magic's standards.
2) Suggestions for Web design processes that have been successful.
3) Preferences that are the author's personal choices.

As an internal style guide, System Magic defines what authors should use for tools, standards, files and links, document structure, and writing style. And yet, by using the different classes of guidelines, authors can have flexibility in developing a Web page but still help define a consistent corporate identity. While Web technology adds new dimensions to balancing style guide control, the basic issue is one with which technical editors are quite familiar.

Expanding Roles for Style Creators

Thus when the creation and application of style guides shifts from the final stage of document production and the adherence to rules to the genesis of product development and includes teams of creators with complementary expertise and needs—as often occurs in the creation of Web sites—the role of technical editor expands. And while style guides continue to ensure consistency and standards, they increasingly provide training functions, promote buy-in opportunities, and define development processes. With these expanded uses and benefits of style guides, the technical editor's role also gains new responsibilities and opportunities, including those of trainer, marketing specialist, and researcher in the use and application of new technologies, especially computer-based, multimedia capabilities. Today, the work of style guide creators—including technical editors—may be far from routine; they are in prime location for solving problems or for generating new approaches and possibilities.

References

[1] P. MacKay, "Establishing a corporate style guide: A bibliographic essay," *Tech. Commun.*, vol. 44, no. 3, pp. 244–251, 1997.

[2] J. Hagge, "Disciplinary style manuals as reliable guides to scientific discourse norms," *Tech. Commun.*, vol. 44, no. 2, pp. 129–141, 1997.

[3] P. Allen, "Save money with a corporate style guide," *Tech. Commun.*, no. 2, pp. 284–289, 1995.

[4] D. Washington, "Developing a corporate style guide: Pitfalls and panaceas," *Tech. Commun.*, no. 4, pp. 553–555, 1991.

[5] D. Le Vie, "Developing a documentation style and template guide for a large company," *InterCom*, pp. 20–23, Jan. 1997.

[6] J. Hackos, *Managing Your Documentation Projects.* New York: Wiley, 1994.

[7] *Microsoft Word*, Version 6.0.1. Microsoft Corp., copyright 1983–1995.

[8] C. Hale, Ed., *Wired Style: Principles of English Usage in the Digital Age.* Singapore: HardWired, 1996.

[9] C. Mok, *Designing Business—Multiple Media, Multiple Disciplines.* San Jose, CA: Adobe, 1996.

Jane Perkins is an Assistant Professor of English at Clemson University, Clemson, SC, where she teaches undergraduate and graduate courses in professional communication. She received the Ph.D. degree from Iowa State University in rhetoric and professional communication and has published in IEEE Transactions on Professional Communication, *The Journal of Business and Technical Communication*, *Studies in Technical Communication*, and *The Bulletin of the Association of Business Communication*. With Nancy Blyler, she is co-editing a collection of essays, *Narrative and Professional Communication*. She writes ethnographies of workplace communication.

"Professional Communication" and the "Odor of Mendacity": The Persistent Suspicion that Skillful Writing is Successful Lying

Edmond H. Weiss

***Abstract*—From the time that rhetoric first differentiated itself from philosophy there has been a widespread belief that the craft of rhetoric is, to a considerable extent, the art of deception with impunity. As early as the *Gorgias* dialogue and as recently as a proposed rule from the Food and Drug Administration, one finds those who argue that even the skills of technical and scientific communication are, in effect, artful forms of misrepresentation. These critics indict not only those who sell and apologize—easy targets—but also those whose avowed purpose is merely to make messages clearer. Can it be true that all forms of communication skill, even those that enhance clarity and precision, are merely elegant forms of lying? Does the word *rhetoric* deserve its tainted historical connotation? Or, even worse, is writing itself an inherently self-serving (that is, misleading) way of adapting to one's environment.**

Writers as Deceivers[1]

In the autumn of 1992, the Food and Drug Administration publicized a proposed rule limiting the roles of professional writers in pharmaceutical companies. The draft directive, never actually enacted, was worded as follows:

> "Independent scientific and educational articles about a company's drug or directly competing drugs should not be written by medical writers employed by the firm, including freelance writers hired by the firm for specific projects. In addition, medical writers employed by the firm should not ghostwrite, edit, or otherwise influence the content of articles, purporting to be independent, on the company's drugs or directly competing products written by others [1]."

The context of this proposal is interesting. By law, pharmaceutical companies may advertise their products only for "approved indications," that is, conditions and regimens officially approved by the FDA. But they are allowed to distribute reports and publish papers describing "unapproved indications," that is, other uses of the drug not yet approved. It is no secret that substantial portions of drug revenue come from these other, unapproved uses and that the reports and papers are, in reality, a sophisticated form of advertising with disclaimers to the contrary. Thus, to contain this "illegal" advertising somewhat, the FDA hoped that, by eliminating writers from the creation of these documents, the resulting messages would be less commercial and more "informational." After all, how could a professional medical writer "purport to be independent"?

Note that the proposed policy did not mention or restrict public relations or advertising writers, whom we would naturally suspect of overzealousness; it specifically indicted "medical writers," persons whose professional goal is to make biomedical literature as clear and intelligible as possible. The implication is unmistakable: such writers would enable companies to write "objective" scientific reports that would, with impunity, overstate the virtues of their employer's products in a way that could not happen if scientists wrote the documents alone. Apparently, lying well about science is a specialized skill; writers have it, but scientists do not.

Plato, Quintilian, and Such

Interestingly, Plato's judgment of medical writers anticipated the FDA's. In *Gorgias* he observed:

> Socrates: Then, when the rhetorician is more persuasive than the physician, the ignorant is more persuasive with the ignorant than he who has knowledge? Is not that the inference?
> Gorgias: In the case supposed: yes.
> Socrates: And the same holds of the relation of rhetoric to all the other arts; the rhetorician need not know the truth about things; he has only to discover some way of persuading the ignorant that he has more knowledge than those who know [2, screen 28:177]?

In Plato's judgment, one who *knows* the object of discussion has no need of language skill, whereas those skilled in rhetoric rely instead on "flattery and cookery," what we nowadays called "audience adaptation":

> Socrates: In my opinion then, Gorgias, the whole of which rhetoric is a part is not an art at all, but the habit of a bold and ready wit, which knows how to manage mankind: this habit I sum up under the word "flattery"; and it appears to me to have many other parts, one of which is cookery, which may seem to be an art, but, as I maintain, is only an experience or routine and not an art . . . and the art of attiring and sophistry are two others: thus there are four branches, and four different things answering to them [2, screen 36:177].

Manuscript received November 1994; revised May 1995.

The author is with the Graduate School of Business Administration, Fordham University, New York, NY 10023 USA.

IEEE Log Number 9414001.

[1] This paper appeared earlier in a substantially different form as "The Odor of Mendacity: Root Causes of Poor Corporate Communication," in the *Proceedings of the Seventh Conference on Corporate Communication*, Fairleigh–Dickinson University, May 1994.

Reprinted from *IEEE Trans. Prof. Comm.*, vol. PC-38, no. 3, pp. 169–175, September 1995.

The classic (and classical) rejoinder to this indictment is to point out, first, that just because good communicators *can* deceive does not mean that they *will*. This position (what Lanham calls the "weak defense" [3]) holds that a communicator need not be the "good man (with) not only outstanding skill in speaking but in all the virtuous qualities of character defined by Quintilian. Rather, a communicator may be expected to exhibit the same distribution of virtue and depravity as any other group. The competent "technical communicator" may be relied upon to provide a useful service—be a mediator—for Plato's "ignorant": "The technical writer's professional expertise is to take the objective truth of technical data and translate it into language that persuades reader of the data's truth in the context in which it would be used [4, p. 64]." And a second argument, (Lanham's "strong defense" [3]), what might be called the ethical foundation of rhetoric, is the view that the contest between persuasive parties is the most philosophically reliable route to the truth, and that rhetoric, far from being the enemy of science and philosophy, is its benefactor and enabler.

But no one really doubts the position of the "strong defense." Even Plato chooses to work in dialogues and his Socrates is full of verbal wit and artifice—rhetoric, in its less exalted sense. The real issue is whether communication skill, no matter what the ultimate purpose, can ever be employed "artlessly," that is, without the communicator's regard for his or her own interests. In short, is it possible ever to write or speak without wishing to glorify oneself or one's employer, or, at the very least, to ingratiate oneself with one's audience?

The Odor of Mendacity

The problem is, partly, writing itself. Writing is learned as a way of adapting to pressures placed upon us, mainly by teachers, later bosses—people who have the power to injure us if our writing displeases them.

A principal objective of nearly everything we write—from grade-school essays through the 40 years of correspondence, reports, and studies that make up a career—is to create the impression that we worked harder and better than we actually did. From the time we first begin to write our little school reports, what we are mainly trying to do is make ourselves look good, that is, *to look better than we are.*

Those young people who are good with words learn quickly the rewards of their gift. Not only do the various tests of intelligence favor those with the best vocabularies, but even teachers who should know better can be taken in by a child who says *myriad* instead of *many*. The facile student, unprepared for an exam, hopes for an "essay test."

The idea takes hold in us at an early age that facility, the ability to cover pages with little effort, is almost a magic ring of invisibility that allows one to escape punishment for chapters unread and research not finished.

Most of the bad writing we see every day, I now suspect, derives from this either deliberate or habitual attempt to impress, to ameliorate the unpleasant facts of a situation, or to lead us to unwarranted conclusions. In short, to appease the audience through exaggeration and overstatement.

The people who try to mislead us like this are nearly always acting in a manner considered professional or businesslike. They have been *taught* to communicate this way, typically by people they admire, often by their professors. Moreover, most attempts to disabuse them of these habits count for nothing when compared to the apparent rewards offered by their superiors for more of the same. In fact, many students of "business communication" wish they could be *more facile at impressing and misleading, not less.*

Cezar Ornatowski notes that writing students who work are far less naive about clarity and truthfulness than those who have no bosses to appease:

> [The skeptical reactions of the working students contrast with] the naiveté of the nonworking students, who take at face value—often with a vengeance—the stylistic injunctions to be clear and direct . . . [to write reports] that would never fly in the complex game of tradeoffs and judgment calls that defines the communicative dynamics of real organizations [5].

What Ornatowski fails to appreciate is that the nonworking students are not seekers after clarity and truth at all; they are seekers after *his approval*!

This quest to please, flatter, accommodate, minimize, or exaggerate lends a vague aroma to much conventional corporate writing, a sickly sweet smell noticeable when one reads or listens closely. I call it the "odor of mendacity," borrowing Big Daddy's phrase from *Cat on a Hot Tin Roof.* "Didn't you notice," he asks his son in Act III, "a powerful and obnoxious odor of mendacity in this room?" In part he is reacting to outright lies being told him about his failing health; the lies are meant to comfort, but they are still lies. But he is also talking about the unceasing chorus of praise and affection he hears, much of it aimed at influencing his Last Will. (His son, Brick, like Lear's daughter Cordelia, will not tell him the flattering lies; unlike Cordelia, though, Brick is rewarded, though partly through his wife's deception.)

By the "context of mendacity" I mean that set of impulses and objectives that Big Daddy's family (and Lear's older daughters) pursue with such ardor that it affects every phrase: self-promotion, self-indemnification, unearned reward, amelioration of embarrassing or unpleasant truth. And I fear that these are the primary forces that impel people to write in the workplace.

The Techniques of Mendacity

Bad writing is normal but not natural. We *learn* it from our first days at school, and, more important, we are usually rewarded for mastering it.

A powerful motivator is the pervasiveness of vocabulary tests as measures of general intelligence. The influence of this construct, "verbal aptitude," can only be appreciated when we realize that, in America at least, IQ is actually an index of middle-classness. Someone who understands that *mordant: dulcet* is as *bitter: sweet* will not only score well on ITBSs and CATs and SATs; he or she will have access to better education, which, where we live, usually means access to the professions.

This is not to object to the teaching of vocabulary. Every teacher of writing feels indignant on meeting adults with advanced degrees who cannot define words like *incontinent* (in either sense) or distinguish *perversion* from *perversity*. Quite the contrary. Few things are more pleasing than a robust vocabulary in the command of a writer or speaker who makes intelligent choices and uses just the right words.

The problem is with "official" vocabulary, the notion that people who say *prioritize* are smarter than people who say *rank*, or that people who write *utilize* are better than people who write *use*. Although it is surely innocent enough to encourage students to use the words they have just learned in writing and speaking as soon and as often as possible, it is only a small step to convincing these students that good writers use *implement* in place of *begin* . . . all the time.

Beginning in high school, gaining momentum in what Sidney Hook called the "tertiary" schools, is a second main force for bad writing: the premium on length. From about puberty onward, the first requirement in nearly every written assignment is minimum length, expressed in number of words or number of pages. Whatever other virtue a paper may have, if it is too short it fails. The understandable equation of length with substance or hard work affects students through to graduate school, where, except for certain hard sciences, no one receives a Ph.D. without delivering a dissertation with heft. (And the "softer" the science, the more paper is expected: social psychologists must write more than chemists; doctors of education must write more than even economists.)

Schools teach, reward, and inculcate the habit of writing long, at every level and in nearly every discipline. In contrast, few students are ever punished or scolded for prolixity. So that the good students learn quickly to write *make a selection with respect to* instead of *select* or *should it prove to be the case that* in place of *if* . Unconsciously, our students learn a short list of rules that double or triple the lengths of sentences, without affecting their substance. This new skill, applied to the habit of impressive vocabulary, creates the style of writing that is usually called "professional" or "official."

For most university students, even including the best ones, the goal is to finish, to get on with whatever benefits accrue to the matriculated. The hard way to finish is to read, study, remember, assimilate, evaluate, and report. The easier way is to develop a certain facility in writing and use that as a substitute for honest work in any course that will allow it. The temptation is nearly irresistible.

Interestingly, the professors who teach reluctant students to write these days are frequently from separate and independent Departments of Communication. What is best about this arrangement is that today, far more often than in past, the person teaching Basic Composition is genuinely interested in the topic and may even know something about it. This contrasts with the harried, somewhat disaffected graduate students of literature who were forced to teach it in my youth.

But what is worst is that this discipline called Communications is not always an entirely "ethical" one. Unlike its ancestor, Journalism, Communications appeals not only to those who wish to learn the craft of truthful, understandable reporting, but also to those mountebanks and casuists that Plato warned us about in *Gorgias*, those who consider truthfulness and integrity relatively unimportant in the pursuit of advantage and rhetorical "effectiveness"—winning, prevailing, looking good. If "audience adaptation" is the first principle of "effective communication," then, necessarily, truth and honor must be lower on the list.

Corporate Mendacity

At first, mendacity is deliberate, a learned technique for presenting one's self and one's company favorably. We master it on the job by imitating the speech of our bosses; we acquire flamboyant methods of deception from the advertising department, subtler ones from our attorneys, who teach us the craft of "avoiding exposure," rather than doing good. Eventually, we internalize these techniques and language; they become second nature.

Corporate mendacity is sustained by three communication precepts, each of them ethically suspect:

- First, short of outright lies, one should always put the most favorable interpretation on one's self and one's employer (*The Precept of Spin*).
- Second, it is always more cost-effective to reduce one's liabilities through legal contrivances than through more honorable actions (*The Precept of Exposure*).
- Third, it is better to win an argument than to learn the truth (*The Precept of Campaign*).

Spin

The Precept of Spin teaches us that it is always possible to put things in a better light without actually lying. And, for many, the main goal of business communication is to make themselves (and often their superiors) look as good as possible—typically, better than they are. With the right spin, errors can be turned into innocent mistakes, false promises into misunderstandings, sloppy performances into tolerably good work, larcenous prices into standard fees . . . all by writing about them effectively in an "official" style.

Covering up the sins of persons and companies has developed into a high self-defensive art, once called "Apologia"; coming just short of using the word *truth,* Ware and Linkugel observe:

> Strategies of denial are useful only to the extent that such negations do not constitute a *known distortion of reality or to the point that they conflict with other beliefs held by the audience* (emphasis added) [6, p. 275].

Firms that escape scandal and go on to prosper are the objects not only of research but admiration. Writing of Toshiba's disgrace and redemption, J. Hobbs, who characterizes the episode as an "image crisis," writes:

> The Toshiba case study illustrates the importance of reestablishing identification with the public after a crisis. In this case, identification can be defined as a perceived joint interest between the public and the corporation [7, p. 341].

Note how communication, spin, can ameliorate even larceny and treason. And note how Toshiba's decision **not** to deny the truth of the charges is regarded, with appreciation, as a winning communication strategy.

"Spin Doctors" are people who think they can turn bad news into good news. For example, recently a major American telecommunications company announced that it will lay off 15,000 employees, but that these layoffs will include generous severance packages and other compensations. In the broadcast words of a company representative: **We decided with our heads but we're implementing with our hearts.** This sentence is an illustration of pure professional spin: it is the clear work of "professional communicators" who toiled for hours or days to find the right bromide. What is astonishing is that its authors expect that the widespread agony and desperation brought on by their profit-motivated action will somehow be ameliorated with this bit of greeting-card sentimentality.

Most of the spin in corporate writing is not so slick or smarmy as this example. Indeed, most of it is artless and inconspicuous. "Unfortunately, the plan was rejected . . ." or "Due to budgetary constraints . . ." or "Hopefully, there will be a minimal impact . . ." or "there is insufficient knowledge with respect to this option . . . ."

Much of it is an elaborate vocabulary for communicating the rejections, reversals, and embarrassments that are inevitable in government and business.

The closest most business communicators come to outright lies, however, are their schedules, deadlines, and promised delivery dates. Because so much depends on low costs and quick schedules, people whose work entails budgeting and scheduling are drawn into patterns of self-serving estimates and "acceptable" deceit, couched in official style. This deceitfulness eventually affects nearly everyone whose job is to meet tight deadlines, stay under budget, or keep fixed schedules. It is an attitude that eventually corrupts the communication of those who must promise more than they can deliver or who must compete in arenas where they are unqualified.

For example, because it is nearly impossible to make airplanes takeoff and land exactly when we want them to, the writing and speech of airlines tends be the most noxious with mendacity.

Experienced air travelers have learned to dread most messages from the airlines, because airport announcements are nearly always bad news: big delays or cancellations. "Due to late arriving equipment . . ." the agent begins. Moreover, when things are going wrong, airline personnel are elevated to new heights of mendacity. During open-ended delays, travelers are told to "remain comfortably seated," as though saying it would cause comfortable seating to appear in airports. When travelers ask for a revised departure time, they hear something like "I'm showing a 10:30 departure." Not surprisingly, frequent flyers suspect that much of the evasiveness and mendacity of airline speakers is intended to prevent us from switching to other airlines while there is still time.

The Precept of Spin encourages us to think that with a few passive verbs (to obscure agency), a sprinkling of *hopefullys* and *regrettablys*—even the use of *we* or *The Company* in place of the more accurate *I*—the lapses and larcenies will go away. The lowliest technical employee will write "QA is currently unable to verify these outstanding issues due to system requirements" and hope that the obscure language will obscure the failure.

Exposure

The Precept of Exposure teaches us that it is just as good to be "not guilty" as to be "innocent." That is, "deniability" is at least as worthwhile as never having done something wrong.

This attitude is a product of lawyerism: NOT law—which has always prized justice, but lawyers, who, even from Biblical times, have earned their largest fees by obstructing justice. It is not just legal jargon that is at issue; new students of writing often think mistakenly that replacing technical vocabulary with familiar vocabulary will make matters clear or "plain." On the contrary, most effective lawyers, far from being the chronically bad writers that the public thinks them, know how to be clear or unclear at will. And their usual tactic is to be as unclear as they can be in defining their clients' obligations.

The lawyer's way of reviewing a business document is to "soften," that is, obscure the commitments of the client while sharpening the promises of the other party. Ironically, lawyers are the only large group in North America who understands the distinction between *shall* and *will* (at least in the third person) and they use this knowledge to differentiate the elements in a contract into commandments (theirs) and remarks about the future (ours).

Responsible, well paid lawyers want to keep their clients safe. "Reducing exposure" is the term-of-art, but this term-of-art is really a euphemism for protecting people from the proper consequences of their misdeeds. Corporate attorneys try to do it before-the-fact, hedging all their clients' promises, building in smokescreens to obscure future problems that are already known. And they earn even bigger fees after-the-fact, putting absurd "interpretations" on their clients' nonfeasance, misfeasance, and malfeasance.

Because this strategy is so often effective in contracts and official documents, executives and managers try to imitate it in their ordinary business and technical communications as well. The chronic abuse of *hopefully* is not just a problem of grammar; the term is reprehensible because it usually means nothing more than "don't hold me to this, but . . . ." Such ideas as the "flexible specification" and the "guideline" are little more than a habitual, mendacious way of appearing to state predictions and requirements in a way that is not binding!

Too many business professionals believe that it is generally cheaper and easier to write or speak one's way out of trouble than to do things honorably the first time. This deliberate, deceitful vagueness shields us in advance from being wrong or missing a target. One cannot appreciate fully the business professionals' distrust of clear, simple assertions and predictions unless one realizes how terrified many are of having to admit a mistake later on.

Again, the airlines, more than any other organizations in the private sector, believe that a resilient smile and the right string of lawyerish sentences can distract us from what actually happens. Why else would any decent-thinking person say "We have lost our connection capability" when he or she could just as easily say "We cannot make our connection"? Why "Due to a crew unavailability situation . . . ," instead of "Because we lack a crew . . ."?

In 1988, for example, several organizations began to publish accounts of how often various airlines reached their destinations "on time." (That is, according to the lawyers, within 15 minutes of the scheduled arrival, not counting delays caused by bad weather.) Inevitably, the airlines that fared best in these comparisons began publishing the results in huge newspaper ads. How did the airline I used most frequently respond to its chronically poor showing? **By lengthening the estimated time for all its flights.** A 55-minute flight was scheduled as an 85-minute flight, and the company's "on-time performance" has improved dramatically. (A representative of that particular airline told me that I should applaud their new policy of more honest estimates!)

Campaign

Unlike scientists and scholars, business and government people believe that consistency and persistence are greater virtues than accuracy and humility. Ours is a society in which candidates for leadership must not admit to having been wrong and certainly not to having changed their mind. We are even hard on people who complain that they were deceived, implying that folks of good character are never misled about anything.

The *Precept of Campaign* holds that anything can be proved through an aggressive program of assertion and promotion, and, more important, that the ability to wage such a winning campaign is far more useful than the ability to establish what is true. The corporate professional's attitude is put nicely by Michael Gilbert, who says that the first rule of arguing is "Never admit defeat unless you are absolutely convinced, and even then keep your mouth shut and wait till Monday" [8, p. 21]. Viewed calmly, this is good advice; too often, in the heat of debate, we feel overwhelmed by an argument that is not as good as it seems at first. But viewed more cynically, it is one of the core causes of corporate mendacity.

Often, the purpose of corporate discourse is to resolve matters of fact or assign praise and blame. When the driving force is to have one's way, the whole range of tainted language, specious arguments, and material fallacies parade themselves as analysis and research. The typical feasibility study, for example, is a politically motivated proof that a *foregone* conclusion was reached *after* objective evaluation of risks and benefits. Indeed, many (if not most) of the "technical" documents produced during the life (or "life cycle") of a new plan or system are after-the-fact rationalizations of decisions reached through suspect means.

In many cases like these, technical communication has a kind of Mandarin function, lending scientific or philosophical respectability to decisions reached through less legitimate means.

Technical Communication

On the surface, the techniques criticized above seem the province of those professions that place a higher premium on winning and selling than on advancing the truth. Technical communicators, who are supposed to be a "bridge" [4], should be, by skill and professional commitment, less guilty of the infractions.

But to the extent that professional communicators, even technical writers, are self-conscious of their messages, making deliberate choices of phrase and image, they are probably incapable of presenting matters in ways that do not advantage themselves or their sponsors. This observation applies not only to those whose art is selling but also to those whose profession is editing away distractions so that the "objective truth" can get out unimpeded. As Sanders puts it, "[There are] ethical problems that technical writers face when they act as anonymous spokespersons for a variety of businesses, research laboratories, and the government." [4]

There are always employers and clients to satisfy. Even the dispassionate presentation of technical facts and designs can help our sponsors perform monstrous acts. Steven Katz [9, p. 256] offers us the plain, understated memo of a Nazi engineer, in which he explains how to modify a truck to serve as a transportable gas chamber. "For easy cleaning of the vehicle, there must be a sealed drain in the middle of the floor. . . . During cleaning, the drain can be used to evacuate large pieces of dirt." The memo, printed entirely in Katz's paper, is not only blood-chilling (as it describes the effects on the truck's suspension of having the "merchandise" suddenly shift to the doors), it is **an exemplary bit of technical writing**.

As Katz sees it, the underlying evil in all this is that *expediency is elevated to a philosophical principle.* Effectiveness, adaptation, clarity, understandability . . . these innocent virtues we associate with the best technical writing are "the ethic of expediency that enables deliberative rhetoric and gives impulse to most of our actions in technological capitalism as well . . ." [9, p. 256] In other words, direct, clear, attractively presented business information, when presented dispassionately in the service of one's employer, can constitute the most dangerous lie of all.

Lying as Adaptation

Writing clearly and directly is relatively easy. It is easier than solving a partial integral equation; easier than removing a spleen; much easier than landing an airplane on an aircraft carrier. How is it, then, that people who can do these quite difficult things cannot write a readable letter of transmittal or announce a delay in departure? Those of us who teach writing to people in the learned professions are forever mystified by this paradox.

The answer is that **writing and speaking are social behaviors, performed by human beings, in stressful environments, and that, quite often, our models of correct rhetoric are just biologically inadequate**. Probably, most learned people could be clearer and more honest, but choose not to be.

These writers want to be impressive; they want, more than anything else, to cover their inadequacies and obscure their shortcomings. And their style of writing—difficult, oblique, puffed-up, smarmy, hackneyed, saccharine, or even inappropriately "clear and simple"—is the product of choice, not just habit or ineptness.

Some, like David Nyberg, even propose that our mendacity is a survival tool. In 1993 he published a sustained attack on the homely virtue of truth-telling. This witty and provocative work argues that clever lying is an advanced technique of biological adaptation:

> . . . a healthy, livable human lifetime of relationships with others is to me inconceivable without deception . . . I think deception is in our nature, and it is there for some reason: the mind does not evolve in ways harmful to itself [10, p. 2].
>
> It's the artfulness we have evolved for avoiding both truth telling and lying at the same time that interests me most—the varnishing, the adding and subtracting, the partial display and concealment of what one person takes to be the truth while communicating with another. As a communicative strategy, deception is so often rewarded that it would seem to have become unavoidable and indispensable. It may actually serve to promote and preserve emotional equilibrium on a personal level, and a civilized climate for communicating with each other and living our lives together on a social level [10, p. 53].

Although Nyberg distances himself from all sorts of transparently evil deceivers, his position is clear. People who always write and speak the "unvarnished truth" are less civilized, less evolved, than those who have mastered the rhetorical arts of deception. Compulsive truth-telling is a symptom of mental deficiency, as we see when we consider the example of Forrest Gump.

A more recent essay by Loyal Rue says that there are "noble lies" meant to protect humankind from the nihilist fears that haunt us, the fear that:

> . . . the universe is blind and aimless; it has no value in and of itself; it is unenchanted by forces, qualities, characteristics that might objectively endorse any particular human orientation toward it [11, p.3].
>
> Noble lies [are used] to unify the group by eliciting conformity with an integrated myth; that is, by bringing individuals to a point where their consciousness is organized by the meanings of the myth [11, Appendix 3].

The truth is that which "conforms with myth"! Rue's position supports Nyberg's: the relentless pursuit of truth is incompatible with a long happy life.

Ethical Solutions

So writing, even technical writing, is inevitably flawed by the self-serving motive of the writer, learned as a child, reinforced and rewarded at work. To counter this inclination, teachers of writing make occasional remarks about ethics and truth, but spend far more time on effectiveness, expediency. Katz observes: "When expediency becomes an end itself or is coupled with personal or political or corporate goals that are not also and ultimately rooted in humanitarian concerns, as is often the case, ethical problems arise [9, p. 272].

But does Katz offer a realistic solution to the problem?

> We should question whether expediency should be the primary ethical standard in deliberative discourse, including scientific and technical communication, and whether, based on Cicero's advocacy of a rhetoric grounded in knowledge of everything and Quintilian's definition of the orator as 'a good man skilled in speaking,' we can and should teach the whole panoply of ethics in deliberative discourse in our rhetoric and writing courses . . . [9, p. 272].

But how can professors whose every public utterance is shaped by the speaker's desire for tenure be expected to teach such a course? (Shall the professing of ethical discourse be limited only to those who have achieved tenure and who are, therefore, free to honor their conscience)? And how many of us can offer a grounding principle more ethically satisfying than those that currently guide our courses: effectiveness, clarity, persuasiveness, and expediency.

Moreover, the Quintilian solution begs the question and is unrealistic. When we write at work, "goodness" is a constraint, not a goal. How "good" we are determines how far we will stray from the truth. And, as everyone knows, changes in one's income and job security can easily recalibrate one's ethical compass.

The key, I think, is to shift "slightly but significantly" from the emphasis on the writer's virtue to the less-personal issue of **justice**. In a widely read paper on ethics and technical writing, Philip Rubens defines objectivity as the "**fair treatment** of facts and phenomena." [12, p. 18]

Good writing, ethical communication, may be understood in this context as the pursuit of fairness and justness, **even if it is inconsistent with the personal goals of the communicator**. So, we do not expect writers to be selfless. And we do not expect motivated communicators to be scrupulously honest. But we can insist that all writing be fair to the parties it affects.

Justice, justice, shall you pursue.

Acknowledgment

The author thanks to S. Sanders and K. Rappaport for their assistance with the current version.

References

[1] Source: FDA, Div. Drug Marketing, Advertising and Commun., Nov. 1992.

[2] Plato, *Gorgias.* (Jowett Translation), Electronic Classical Library II, 1995.

[3] R. Lanham, *The Electronic Word: Democracy, Technology, and the Arts.* Chicago, IL: University of Chicago Press, 1993.

[4] S. P. Sanders, "How can technical writing be persuasive?" in *Solving Problems in Technical Writing,* Beene and White, Eds. New York: Oxford, 1988, pp. 57–78.

[5] C. Ornatowski, "Between efficiency and politics: Rhetoric and ethics in technical writing, *Tech. Commun. Quart.,* vol. 1, no. 1, pp. 91–103, 1992.

[6] B. L. Ware and W. A. Linkugel, "They spoke in defense of themselves: On the generic criticism of Apologia, *The Quart. J. Speech,*vol. 59, pp. 273–283, 1973.

[7] J. D. Hobbs, "Treachery by any other name: A case study of the Toshiba public relations crisis," *Manage. Commun. Quart.*, vol. 8, no. 3, pp. 323–346, 1995.
[8] M. Gilbert, *How to Win an Argument.* New York: McGraw-Hill, 1979.
[9] S. B. Katz, "The ethic of expediency: Classical rhetoric, technology, and the Holocaust," *College English,* vol. 54, no. 3, pp. 255–275, 1992.
[10] D. Nyberg, *The Varnished Truth.* Chicago, IL: University of Chicago Press, 1993.
[11] L. Rue, *By Grace of Guile.* New York: Oxford University Press, 1994.
[12] P. Rubens, "Reinventing the wheel?: Ethics for technical communicators," reprinted in *Technical Communication and Ethics*, Brockmann and Rook, Eds. Washington, DC: Soc. for Tech. Commun., 1985.

Edmond H. Weiss is affiliated with the Graduate School of Business Adminstration at Fordham University, New York, NY.

PART III

Text and Graphics: Presenting Information Visually

As an effective writer you will sometimes need to consider strategies that can make your information even more accessible to your readers, such as page organization, font choice, graphs, tables, lists, and symbolic material. This section deals with some of these visual tools and how you can use them to your advantage, and also takes a look at some of the technicalities involved in transferring large graphics from hard copy to the computer screen.

Do you always need graphics?

While most of the papers in this section deal with the graphic nature of specific writer's tools—headings, graphs, tables, safety labels, and math symbols—Thomas Williams and Deborah Harkus consider the question of whether you should always plan on using visuals in your documents. This is a decision you should make only after careful thought, and the authors give a great deal of insight into how to make the right choice of when or when not to use a graphic. They also discuss what the most appropriate graphic might be for a given context, and how much detail or color a graphic should contain. As the authors point out, your editing tasks do not stop with text but must also be extended to any graphics you might employ.

Formatting your headings

We all know headings are essential in a document of any length and that they can be useful and necessary even in a single-page memo. Thomas Williams and Jan Spyridakis consider the visual aspects of headings in considerable depth, looking at how their appearance can enhance their usefulness as indicators of a text's structure and content. The results of the authors' studies reveal some important factors in the formatting of headings and their hierarchical status, and also show how readers perceive the format and usefulness of headings as information indicators.

Charts and tables tell the tale

The third and fourth articles in this section look at graphs and tables. First, Jean-Luc Doumont and Philippe Vandenbroeck recognize what they feel to be "poor graph literacy" among engineers and others and then discuss how to select the right kinds of graphs for your documents. The authors show how different kinds of graphs and charts should be chosen on the basis of need and intention, and discuss various graphical displays you can employ to improve the effectiveness of your work. Eva Dukes' article on table construction then illustrates how well-arranged tables can also present information efficiently. Since tables are so useful as communication tools, Dukes' six pointers for table construction, her cautions on pitfalls to avoid, and her illustrations make this a valuable article.

Warning your reader

Another kind of visual that stands apart from written text, particularly in operator manuals, procedures, and instructions, is the safety alert. If you write such documents, you will need to design warning labels to reveal hazards, prevent injury, and avoid litigation. Some of Christopher Velotta's timeless advice on word choice, symbols, colors, and readability can be applied not only to safety labels but also to other kinds of notations and labels you might want to visually separate from your text for emphasis, such as directions, headings, pointers, or captions.

Sensible math symbols

Barry Burton provides guidelines on what to watch for when your writing includes mathematical symbols. Although his guidelines are for editors, many technical writers can benefit from Burton's observations on eliminating unneeded symbols, defining or redefining symbols, and following standard grammar when using them. As always, you should use symbols (and the same must be said for all graphics, lists, labels, and acronyms) only after you have first spent some time evaluating the technical level of your readers.

From paper to computer screen

In this section's final article we move to the world of computer graphics. In a written document, a good technical illustrator can provide graphics of almost unlimited dimensions, especially in foldouts, if need be, but how can you present such large and complex visuals effectively on a relatively small computer screen? This is the question Janet Lincoln and Donald Monk set out to answer. First they look at some general concerns involving the computerization of printed graphics and then give seven techniques whereby large and complex graphics can be transferred to a computer screen. These techniques are discussed and illustrated in depth by the authors, and by the end of their article you will have a solid idea of how to transfer oversized graphics to a computer screen without negatively affecting their readability and usefulness.

Editing Visual Media

—THOMAS R. WILLIAMS AND DEBORAH A. HARKUS

Abstract—*The principal obligation of the editor charged with editing visual media is to understand the strengths and the limitations of both text and visuals so as to make informed media choices. The following paper compares and contrasts visual and verbal media in an effort to provide the reader with some practical guidance in making media choices. This paper also offers a set of practical guidelines for the use of visuals that is intended to ensure that the visuals chosen and their utilization result in both efficient and effective communication of the kinds of ideas best suited to presentation in pictorial form.*

Index Terms—*Information design, media choice, technical editing, visuals, visual editing.*

Manuscript received November 20, 1997.
The authors are with the Department of Technical Communication, University of Washington, Seattle, WA 98195 USA.
IEEE PII S 0361-1434(98)02044-X.

IN editing visual media, as in editing text, the boundaries between the responsibilities of the editor and those of the author greatly overlap. The author, of course, is charged with the responsibility of translating thought to symbol so that those thoughts can be conveyed to the reader. The editor serves as a surrogate reader in an effort to ensure that the author has succeeded in that task. But, in a most fundamental sense, author and editor both are engaged in the process of crafting a message that will be both intelligible and useful to the reader. Both author and editor, consequently, concern themselves with the rhetorical dimensions of a document, and one of those dimensions—a critical dimension, in fact—is media choice—or, specifically, when and where to use a visual and what kind of visual to use.

Of course, the editor's responsibilities also include traditional "picture editing" tasks such as sizing, cropping, and assessing the reproduction quality of art submitted by the author or illustrator. Nevertheless, it is in serving as a check on media choice, by assuming the role of reader, where the editor can make the most significant contribution to the usefulness of the message to the reader.

There is, we believe, a strong and, perhaps, quite understandable text bias among writers—a general reluctance to use pictures—that arises partially out of habit and partially out of a belief that words are the appropriate medium for any serious discourse. Understandably, writers are most comfortable with words. And, as is the case in other domains, people confronted with problems to solve fall back on strategies and tools that have worked in the past whether or not those strategies or tools are optimal. In the domain of writing, this "set" or "Einstellung" effect [1] often results, we believe, in the notion that if enough words are thrown at it, virtually any communication problem can be solved.

If, however, you, as a reader, have experienced the frustration of having to wade through a cumbersome and seemingly interminable verbal description in a printed document, you have also probably found yourself screaming at the conveniently absent author to "give me a picture!" And, despite the claim

Reprinted from *IEEE Trans. Prof. Comm.*, vol. PC-41, no. 1, pp. 33–45, March 1998.

that "a picture is worth 10,000 words," anyone who has played the game Pictionary can attest to the fact that there are some ideas that are very difficult to represent pictorially—this sentence, for example. Simply, as Salomon [2] notes, pictures and text are symbol systems, and symbol systems differ in, among other things, the kinds of ideas they are best equipped to express. This would not pose much of a problem for us were it not that, despite the fact that some ideas are extraordinarily challenging to represent in some symbol systems, there is nonetheless considerable overlap among symbol systems in the ideas they can represent. In other words, the same idea often **can** be expressed symbolically, even if somewhat crudely or awkwardly, in more than just one symbol system. The practical implication of this fact, of course, is that the communicator must then choose from among the available media the one best suited to the delivery of information in a form that will be both intelligible and useful, given the user's needs and preferences. And, while, unfortunately, the **correct** choice is not always clear-cut, the consequences of a poor choice can make the reader's job much more difficult.

A poor choice of medium affects the reader's efforts to comprehend in at least two significant ways. First, as already suggested, the medium may just be too inadequate to express with either much precision or efficiency the idea the author wishes to communicate. For example, abstract concepts such as "freedom" and "justification" are difficult, if not impossible, to express pictorially, as are conditional relationships such as "If you ride your bicycle to work and it rains later today, I'll pick you up in the car to take you home." Conversely, perceptual concepts such as "orientation," "texture," and "color" are difficult to express linguistically. Second, should the message be provided via a symbol system different from the one in which the reader finds it useful to represent meaning internally, then he or she must translate the message into the preferred—or, as Salomon [2] notes, "task required"—symbol system. Such translations require the diversion of mental resources and open the door to misinterpretation of the message.

In the article that follows, we focus, consequently, on providing the reader with a look at the most fundamental differences between text and visual and at the implications of those differences for media choice. It is in understanding those differences, we believe, that the editor will be best equipped to evaluate the author's media choices and to articulate media-choice problems to the author. Finally, we limit our comments in the paper that follows to "representational" visuals—visuals that resemble what they are intended to signify.

Some Fundamental Differences Between Pictures and Text

When expression of the same idea is possible, as it often is, in either system, then on what basis is the editor to choose? To determine which system is likely to be both the more explicit and the more efficient requires first an understanding of the fundamental differences between the two systems. Those differences include

1) differences in how symbols in each system evoke their referents;
2) differences in the nature of the referents they evoke;
3) differences in the structure each symbol system imposes on the information it carries; and
4) differences in the degree to which information carried in either system can be processed perceptually.

First, pictures and text often differ in the way in which they evoke their referents. Both text and pictures are symbols or *coding elements* that serve as substitutes for other things: their *referents*. Words evoke their referents somewhat arbitrarily in the sense that it is only through the agreement of those who speak the language of which the word is a part that the word means what it does. There is nothing intrinsic to the word *sphere* that would suggest its referent; it is simply agreed among English speakers that the specific combinations of letters comprising the word *sphere* and the sounds they represent stand for an object (or class of objects), namely, a sphere. Conversely, pictures—specifically realistic or representational pictures such as photographs and illustrations—evoke their referents by resembling them. Given that much of the meaning we derive from our environment is derived perceptually, it seems logical to assume that preserving the perceptual qualities of a referent in the form of the symbol standing in for it might result in some cognitive processing efficiencies. In fact, there is considerable evidence in cognitive science that reductions in the articulatory distance between a sign and its referent reduce the mental workload involved in accessing the sign's meaning [3].

Second, pictures and text also differ in the **kinds** of referents they evoke. Words (with the exception of proper nouns) typically evoke very broad and inclusive "equivalence" categories, while pictures typically evoke very narrow "identity" categories [4]. The word *sphere*, for example, evokes not just a specific referent but an entire class of referents that claim membership in the category or concept *sphere* by virtue of possessing certain critical attributes. The discursive system, however, provides us with a complement of very powerful tools consisting of modifiers and a set of strict syntactical rules constraining the permissible ways in which ideas can be linked to one another. Those tools allow us to be quite explicit about the bounds of virtually any concept we wish to convey. For example, I can narrow the category *sphere* to a specific Penn Championship, Extra-Duty Felt, Optic Yellow, number 7 tennis ball that I hit over the fence and into the woods last Saturday during my weekly game with my neighbor Jim.

Conversely, as Knowlton argues, iconic signs such as representational pictures "cannot, in isolation, signify a concept;" they can only "exemplify" certain members of an equivalence category [4]. A picture of the aforementioned tennis ball, for example, is much more likely to evoke the concept Penn Championship, Extra-Duty Felt, Optic Yellow, number 7 tennis ball than it is to evoke the concept *sphere*. Of course, it may be possible to broaden the concept evoked by subtracting from it some of its figural detail—the brand, the number, the color, etc. But still, it is only possible to suggest the bounds of a concept pictorially. And what kind of a ball would the editor choose to picture if the intent were to convey the more general and inclusive idea *ball*, or *sports equipment*, or *geometric form*?

This problem is compounded by the fact that pictures can be used much the same as verbal figures of speech. A picture, for example, can be used metaphorically, as when pipes and valves are used in a biology text to explain the human circulatory system. The sign picturing a knife, fork, and spoon in an airport signifies not silverware but a restaurant (synecdoche). Even when pictures appear to be representational, then, they may be used to denote something other than what they literally depict.

Third, pictures and text differ in the kinds of structures they impose on the information they present [5]. There is considerable evidence from the field of cognitive science that people store information in schemas [6]–[8], hierarchical memorial structures, constructed on the basis of experience, that both organize what we already know about a particular domain and, as well, provide "slots" or "placeholders" to organize new, incoming information. Text, however, because of its linear structure, is in its most fundamental sense a list of ideas and a set of instructions (metadiscourse) to the reader as to how to reconstitute the rich relationships among those ideas that the writer originally saw in his or her schema, or view of the domain. To a considerable degree, pictures and other visual forms such as diagrams are not constrained by the sentential structure of text and can thus preserve the author's complex view of the relationships that exist among ideas. In diagrams, and even to some extent in representational visuals, space provides a metaphor for logical or functional relationships: related information is put in the same location. This greatly simplifies the search for related information and reduces the burden on the viewer's memory.

Finally, text and pictures differ in the degree to which their meaning can be apprehended through "pre-attentive" perceptual processes [9]–[11]. In the early stages, perceptual processing occurs "in parallel." What that means in a practical sense is that much of the processing we perform on the visual world occurs rapidly, simultaneously, and unconsciously. At the pre-attentive stage, enormous amounts of processing take place. The lines, contours, and boundaries suggested by contrasts in hues, values, or light intensities are combined to reveal objects—objects separated from one another and separated from their backgrounds. Consequently, when we look at a figure, we typically do not see the individual lines composing it unless we consciously attend to them. We see ready-made figures or combinations of lines. Of course, pre-attentive processing occurs during our apprehension of words as well. We combine many visual elements to see letterforms, and we (at least for familiar words) combine letterforms to see whole words. The difference, however, is that in pictures much of the **meaning** of a visual resides in the perceptual qualities that are apprehended at this stage of processing. Meaning derived from words requires additional processing—importantly, processing that must occur at a conscious level, that takes place serially, and that requires considerable conscious attention and effort on the part of the reader.

In summary, then, pictures hold the promise of considerable efficiency in delivering certain kinds of messages because they can deliver those messages **directly**. Processing the meaning of a picture is much the same as processing the meaning of the thing the picture signifies. For example, from the perspective of the human perceptual system, the actual visual image of, say, the Statue of Liberty (the referent) and a photographic image of the Statue of Liberty (the sign) are fundamentally the same: in both cases their recognition/interpretation draws on virtually identical perceptual processes.

Pictures (and, of course, diagrams), because their composition is not constrained by the linear structure of text, also are often more efficient at representing nonlinear relationships among objects or ideas than is text. Those relationships might be either logical, as in an organization chart, or spatial, as in a map or photograph. A picture of a machine, for example, may directly depict a complicated set of spatial relationships among that machine's components. A verbal description of the same set of relationships would necessarily, because of the sentential structure of text, take the form of a list.

On the downside is the fact that pictures do not map unambiguously to the concepts they are intended to evoke. Pictures have much difficulty expressing broad, inclusive concepts because they typically evoke only exemplars of those concepts. A picture of a border collie, for example, is likely to be interpreted as a picture of a border collie, not dog, or mammal, or animal, or quadruped, or pet. Moreover, what a picture depicts may not be what it is intended to denote: pictures, like words, can be used as figures of speech.

The practical implications of these observations, of course, are that words and pictures work best in concert, each assuming the communications functions they are best equipped to perform. For pictures, that lies in the expression of information in a form that can be processed perceptually. For words, that lies in the conversion of "vague, amorphous, and fleeting thoughts into controlled and easily retrievable propositions" [12].

"Representational" Visuals

As noted previously, not all pictures resemble what they are intended to denote. A number of informal taxonomies have been offered [4], [12]–[14] to logically categorize visual media on the basis of their "representationality" or lack thereof. For present purposes, however, we find it convenient to distinguish simply between "representational" graphics—those graphic forms that realistically depict what they are intended to represent—and "nonrepresentational" graphics—those graphic forms that do not. In the former category—the topic of this paper—we include photographs and illustrations; in the latter we would include such visual forms as graphs, charts, tables, and diagrams.

By far the most common function performed by representational visuals is depiction (others being simplification and reification [15]). The goal of depiction is generally to teach the identification of things through recognition of an object's critical attributes. But **why** are pictures a useful medium for the communication of this kind of information? Again, it is because visuals convey that kind of information directly. The word *appearance*, in fact, refers to the sensory impression conveyed by an object. In a sense, the appearance of an object is the aggregate or "gestalt" of an object's visual sensory qualities: its color, shape, size, orientation, and texture. If what we desire to communicate are the perceptual attributes of an object, those objects are preserved in a picture in a form amenable to direct perceptual processing.

Simply stated, if the meaning one wishes to communicate resides in the perceptual attributes or qualities of an object, then one should use a medium that can convey those attributes without translation into another symbol system. For example, it is possible to characterize the hue, intensity, and saturation of a color by specifying the constituent wavelengths and wave amplitudes of light that combine to create it. That form of information is not likely, however, to help the homeowner trying to find the right color for the downstairs bathroom. What is important here—where, to the homeowner, the meaning of the color resides—is in the sensory impression it conveys. We can communicate that sensory information quite easily by providing it in a form amenable to direct sensory processing: a sample or "chip" of the actual color. In addition to color, some of those purely perceptual qualities often best communicated directly include shape, orientation, position or location in space, texture, pattern, size, and arrangement.

Fig. 1. View from the top of a ski jump. ("Droodle" picture; adapted from R. Price, *Der Kleine Psychologe*. Zurich, Switzerland: Diogenes, 1975, p. 105; Reprinted with permission.)

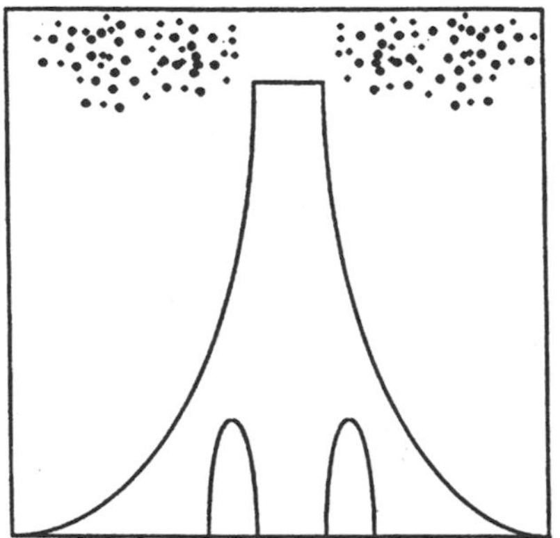

Editing Representational Visuals: Practical Considerations

Provide a Context or Frame of Reference The meaning of some pictures, like text, is ambiguous in the absence of a frame of reference. The same crude drawing might be used to evoke either a mailbox or a loaf of bread depending on the objects depicted with it. What is being depicted by Fig. 1? The ambiguity of this visual message could easily be resolved by including relevant, recognizable items, by labeling the picture, or by providing explanatory text in the passage preceding the picture.

Conversely, text also can be ambiguous or difficult to decipher, and, in those instances, can sometimes be clarified by pictures [16]. In fact, it is not unusual at all to find readers frequently shifting back and forth between text and visual media, using their interpretation of one medium as a check on their interpretation of the other. This use of visual media in particular has been referred to as the "confirmatory function" of visual media [17].

Provide Means for the Viewer to Decipher Scale Often the size or relative size of an object is a critical, or defining, feature; it may even be the only feature that allows the reader to distinguish one item in the picture or illustration from another. If the reader is already familiar with the object (a #10 pan-head screw), a text label may well be adequate. If the reader is a novice and is not likely to know what a "pan-head" screw, much less what a #10 pan-head screw is, consider how he or she will attempt to identify it—largely on the basis of appearance and size (see Fig. 2). Appearance, as already noted, can be conveyed visually. Realistically depicting the screw will allow it to be discriminated from fasteners that are not pan-head screws. But how does the novice discriminate the #10 from the #8 or #12 pan-head screw? The answer in the present case, of course, is that he or she won't be able to in the absence of something that provides a scale. In less critical situations, it may well be adequate simply to juxtapose an object with an object the size of which is likely to be familiar.

Ensure that the Level of Detail is Adequate for the Task As obvious as this suggestion may seem, it is perhaps the most commonly violated. An attempt to fit as much information as possible into a small space sometimes increases the willingness of the editor to shrink a very large visual—an exploded parts diagram, for example—to fit a very small piece of paper. While the pattern and order of connection of the components may be preserved in doing so, the critical details of the components themselves are often lost (see Fig. 3).

Provide a Familiar Perspective or Viewpoint Unusual perspectives need to be learned and are sometimes learned with great difficulty. It takes considerable training, for example, to understand aerial photographs—most of us have little experience seeing our world and the objects in it from the air. The familiar grocery store in our neighborhood or the maple tree next door suddenly appear much less familiar when we see them from above. [18]. Consequently, provide the viewer with a point-of-view that is familiar. Similarly, provide a perspective that is consistent with the perspective you wish the viewer to assume. Note, for example, in Fig. 4 that the perspective provided, while "familiar," is nonetheless one that casts the viewer in the role of observer rather than performer. If the viewer is expected to perform the tasks being illustrated, the perspective should be the reverse of the one provided. In other words, the view of the object being depicted should be the one the reader would see if he or she were removing the drive shaft coupling rather than observing someone else doing it. The view provided in Fig. 4 obligates the

Fig. 2. Showing scale. (Reprinted with permission of Sears, Roebuck and Co.)

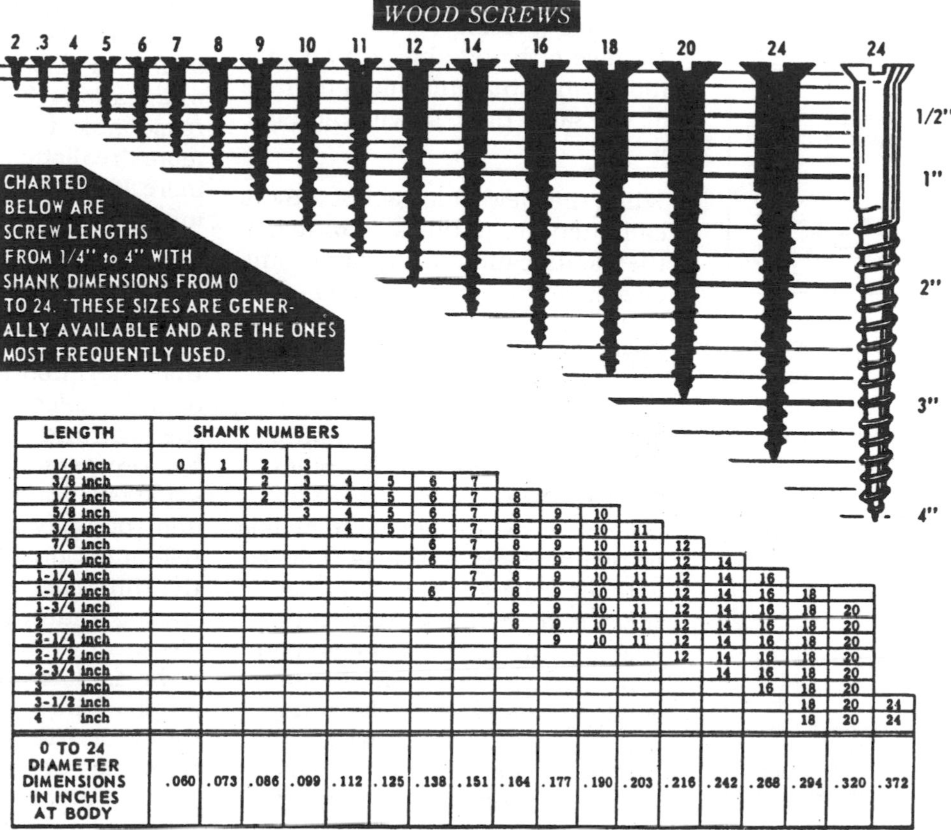

LENGTH	SHANK NUMBERS																	
1/4 inch	0	1	2	3														
3/8 inch			2	3	4	5	6	7										
1/2 inch			2	3	4	5	6	7	8									
5/8 inch				3	4	5	6	7	8	9	10							
3/4 inch					4	5	6	7	8	9	10	11						
7/8 inch							6	7	8	9	10	11	12					
1 inch							6	7	8	9	10	11	12	14				
1-1/4 inch								7	8	9	10	11	12	14	16			
1-1/2 inch							6	7	8	9	10	11	12	14	16	18		
1-3/4 inch									8	9	10	11	12	14	16	18	20	
2 inch									8	9	10	11	12	14	16	18	20	
2-1/4 inch										9	10	11	12	14	16	18	20	
2-1/2 inch													12	14	16	18	20	
2-3/4 inch														14	16	18	20	
3 inch															16	18	20	
3-1/2 inch																18	20	24
4 inch																18	20	24
0 TO 24 DIAMETER DIMENSIONS IN INCHES AT BODY	.060	.073	.086	.099	.112	.125	.138	.151	.164	.177	.190	.203	.216	.242	.268	.294	.320	.372

viewer to transform the picture by mentally rotating the object pictured in it.

Focus the Viewer's Attention on the Important Parts of the Visual Goodman [19] characterizes visual media as being "replete." What he means, essentially, is that almost every aspect of a picture contributes to its message. The unfortunate implication of that fact for the communicator using a visual medium is that the visual may communicate to its viewer much more than the editor intends or the viewer needs. Several devices exist for the editor to ensure that the reader focuses on the intended message. The first, and most conventional, perhaps, is cropping. Cropping is simply the act of excising any "deadwood" from a picture much as the editor would delete any superfluous verbiage from a paragraph. It is important, however, that the editor examine carefully his or her communications goals for the picture. What is "deadwood" in Fig. 5? The answer, of course, is that without first defining what it is the picture is intended to communicate, it is impossible to tell. If the intent were to provide enough feature information so that the viewer could recognize the man were he or she to see him on the street, then anything other than the part of the photo that coveys his appearance is probably superfluous. If the intent were to convey the idea of an intense meeting between a man and woman, then the entire foreground in the picture contributes very little to the message and could be cropped out. If, however, it were important to convey the sense that this meeting is a private meeting, then, perhaps, nothing in this picture is superfluous.

Fig. 3. Would you be able to identify a "grounding lug" on the basis of information this visual provides? (Reprinted with permission.)

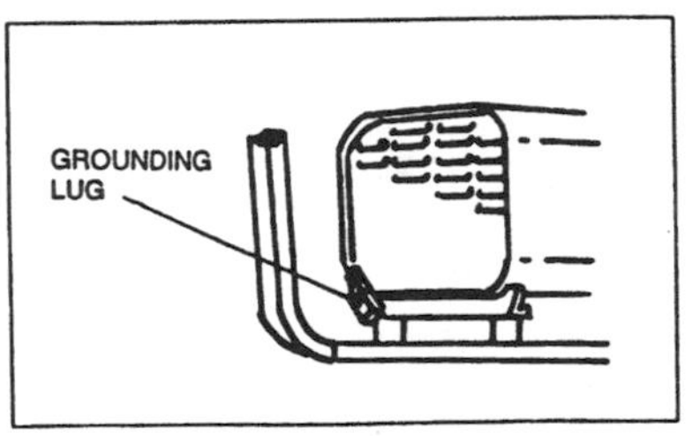

Fig. 4. Is the point of view provided in this illustration consistent with one the "doer" would assume or is the viewpoint that of an "observer?" (Reprinted with permission.)

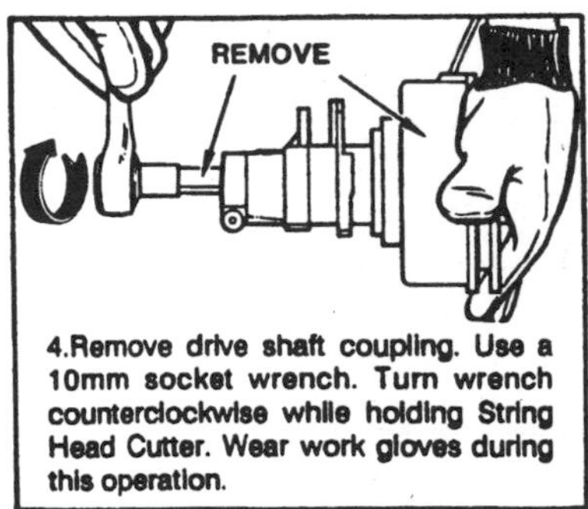

A final caution about cropping, however. Remember that a picture that does not provide the needed contextual information runs the risk of being misinterpreted or not interpreted at all.

A second method of focusing the reader's attention is "ghosting." Ghosting (see Fig. 6) has the advantage of being able to provide more contextual information while, at the same time, de-emphasizing it.

When the viewer needs not only to call attention to but also to teach the identification of the important elements in a picture, labels or "callouts" (see Fig. 7) are often useful.

Ensure that the Relationship Between Visual and Relevant Text is Clear Again, this suggestion seems intuitively to belong to that category of things that "go without saying." Unfortunately, there is a wealth of real-world examples in which this commonsense notion has been ignored. Confusion is most likely to happen in instructions in which the procedural or "action step" information is numbered to reveal the sequence in which the steps are to be performed. If those action steps are accompanied by visuals, and those visuals or "figures" are numbered, unless each action step is provided a separate figure, figure numbers are necessarily different from the numbers of the steps they illustrate.

Such conflicts between step and figure numbers are a potential source of confusion for the reader. On the other hand, grouping spatially the operational steps with the relevant figure and discarding a superfluous figure number largely eliminates any possible confusion over which step or steps belong with which figure. See, for example, Fig. 9.

Choosing Among Photographs and Illustrations While both photos and illustrations are "representational" in the sense that they resemble what they denote, there are significant differences between them. Photographs certainly are unmatched in their ability to veridically preserve the rich figural detail in an object or scene. The question confronting the editor is whether that rich detail serves a legitimate communications function. It seems reasonable to assume that the more "realistic" a visual is, the more likely it is to be useful or informative. Perkins [18] calls this assumption into question, as does Winn [15]. Winn notes that the general consensus in cognitive psychology today seems to be that the important correspondence to effect is the one between the sign and the viewer's **internal representation** of the ideas signified, not between the sign and the objective qualities of its referent. Consider, for example, the difference to an electrician tracing a fault in an automobile's electrical system between using a wiring diagram or a color photograph of the actual wiring harness. Certainly the photo is the more "realistic" of the two "pictures." Just as certainly, the rich detail it provides is not nearly as informative as is a simplified, and perhaps less confusing, diagram. Or consider the difference between an aerial photo of a city and a much less "realistic" bus route diagram. As these examples suggest, uninformative realism may simply confuse.

Dwyer [20] assessed differences among four renderings of the human heart that differed only in the amount of figural detail. Dwyer concluded that whether the additional detail was helpful to the learner depended on the time and effort the learner was willing to expend studying the detail as well as on the extent of the learner's prior knowledge. When viewing time was limited, excessive realistic detail seemed to divert learners' attention away from more important information. Conversely, rich, realistic detail was helpful when viewing was self paced and when the learner brought extensive relevant prior knowledge to the learning task.

While color photographs are the medium of choice for the editor who does, indeed, wish to convey lots of realistic detail, illustrations provide the editor with another, if somewhat different, complement of advantages. The first, and perhaps most obvious, is that, in a sense, an illustration is a visual that has already been "edited." Extraneous detail typically has been eliminated simply by not having been rendered in the first place. Moreover, the critical features can be enhanced to make it easier for the viewer to perform the kinds of visual discriminations the editor wants the viewer to be able to perform. Consider a typical "field guide." Many of the trees, birds, insects, or minerals

Fig. 5. How much of this scene is "superfluous?"

Fig. 6. Note how "ghosting" de-emphasizes background, but, at the same time, provides contextual information. (Reprinted from D. D. Baals and W. R. Corliss, *Wind Tunnels of NASA*, Washington, DC, 1981.)

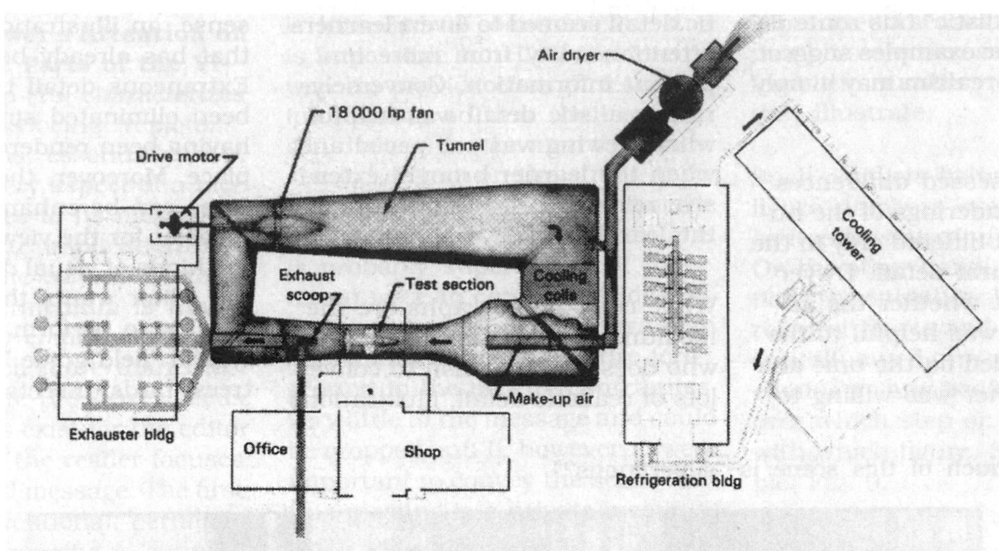

Layout of the Lewis altitude wind tunnel, showing equipment necessary to purge combustion products, control air pressure, and reduce air temperatures.

Fig. 7. Callouts are an easy way to provide text labels for components of a photo or illustration. (Reprinted with permission of Sears, Roebuck and Co.)

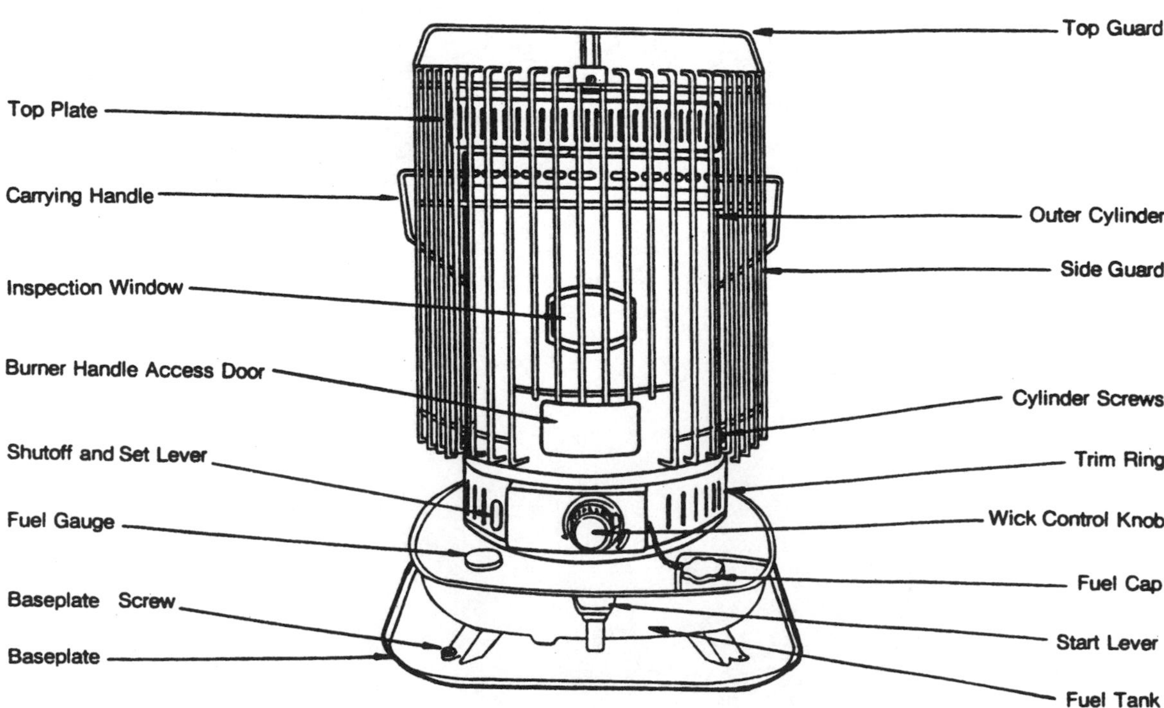

depicted in them look quite similar. Illustrations, however, can highlight—even exaggerate—the critical, or defining, differences among very similar species or samples.

Illustrations, again unlike photographs, also can provide “impossible,” or at least “difficult” views. See, for example, Fig. 10.

In fact, certain forms of illustrations have been developed especially to provide views that photographs typically cannot. Often, the point is to reveal the internal structure or arrangement of the elements comprising the objects being depicted as well as the appearance and orientation of the elements themselves. Cross-sectional, cutaway, and exploded views are common; see Figs. 11 and 12.

While similar in many respects, cross-sectional views, cutaways, and exploded views also differ subtly in both the kinds of information they emphasize and in the kinds of tasks they best support. Cross-sectional views slice through a fully assembled object and thus provide the viewer, in a simple sense, with a visual representation of a theory of operation. Cross-sectional views, consequently, are often useful when the editor's goal is to explain how something works. Exploded views (sometimes called exploded diagrams), on the other hand, provide (or should provide) realistic representations of the component parts and their spatial orientations relative to the larger object and to each other. Moreover, because they imply a sequence for the assembly of the object of which they are a part, exploded views are often very useful when used to support assembly or disassembly tasks. Cutaway views also provide information about structure, but they preserve the critical spatial relationships that exist between a component and the exterior form of an object. Cutaways are consequently helpful in providing information about where, relative to a larger object, something is located.

The Question of Color Whether or not to use color is a decision frequently made on the basis of cost. Color does indeed cost more, especially when the output medium is paper. Additional costs notwithstanding, however, color can serve a variety of important functions in a publication. Winn [21] suggests five: directing attention, delimiting shapes and areas, clarifying complex ideas, creating affect, and facilitating identification.

Indeed, the human visual system is especially sensitive to color, and the judicious use of color optimizes a natural ability in humans to detect and identify images [22]. Moreover, color, particularly when it contrasts with its surroundings, demands our attention. The human visual system uses color information to define forms and to allow us to distinguish between those forms and their backgrounds. Color simplifies by helping us to organize our world—to group logically related things or ideas on the basis of an easily apprehended perceptual attribute. People also generally prefer color to black and white.

It is in facilitating identification, however, that the editor needs to exercise the most judgment. The basis for making those judgments, simply, is whether or not color is a critical attribute of the object being pictured given the task the viewer is assumed to want to accomplish with the information being conveyed. The color of a lemon, for

Fig. 8. Emphasis through shading. (Reprinted with permission of Apple Computer, Inc.)

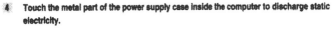

4 Touch the metal part of the power supply case inside the computer to discharge static electricity.

Always do this before you touch any parts, or install any components, inside the computer.

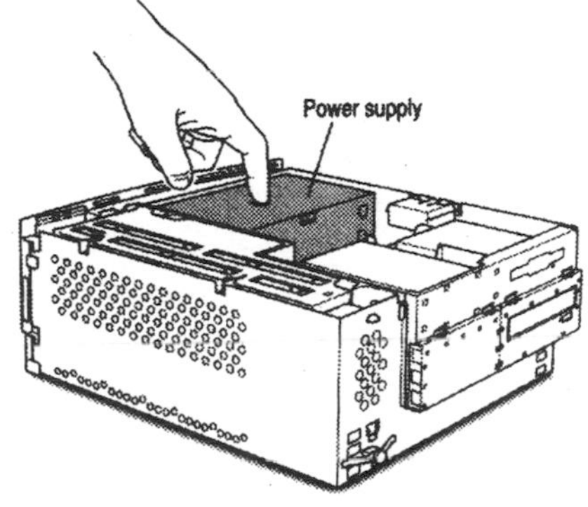

Fig. 9. Operational steps are grouped clearly with related visuals. (Reprinted with permission of Sears, Roebuck and Co.)

3. The rip fence must be PARALLEL with the sawblade and miter Gauge grooves . . . Move fence until it is along side of groove. Do NOT LOCK IT. It sHould be parallel to groove. If it is not;

A. Loosen the two "Hex Head Screws."

B. Hold fence head tightly against bar . . . move end of fence so that it is parallel with groove.

C. Alternately tighten the screws.

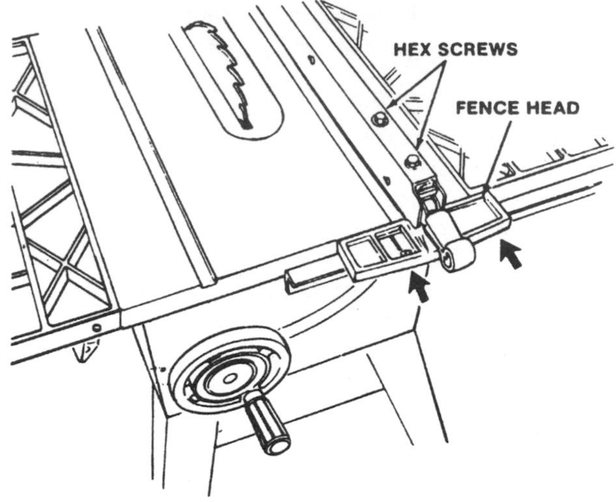

ADJUSTING RIP SCALE INDICATOR

1. Turn ELEVATION HANDWHEEL clockwise until blade is up as high as it will go.

   IMPORTANT: BLADE must be SQUARE (90°) to TABLE, in order to ALIGN rip fence.

2. Using a rule, position fence on right side of sawblade 2 in. from the sides of the teeth . . . tighten lock handle.

3. Loosen screw holding the indicator . . . adjust so that it points to "2" on the rip scale . . . tighten screw.

   NOTE: If you cannot adjust indicator so that it points to "2", loosen the screws holding the front guide bar and move the guide bar.

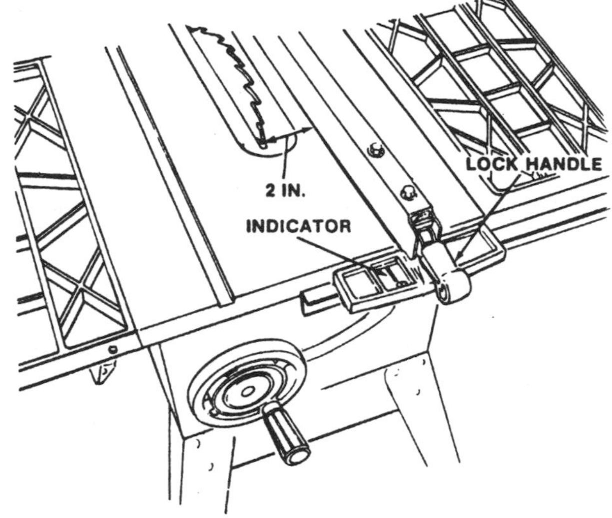

Fig. 10. An "impossible" picture. (Reprinted from C. M. Yeates, T. V. Johnson, L. Colin, F. P. Fanale, L. Frank, and D. M. Hunten. *Galileo: Exploration of Jupiter's System.* Washington, DC: NASA, 1985.)

Figure 1. The Galileo spacecraft—orbiter and probe—on the way to the giant planet Jupiter and an in-depth exploration of the complex jovian planetary system.

Fig. 11. Cutaway illustrations preserve critical spatial relationships between a component and the external form of an object. (Reprinted from D. R. Lord, *Spacelab: An International Success Story.* Washington, DC: NASA, 1987.)

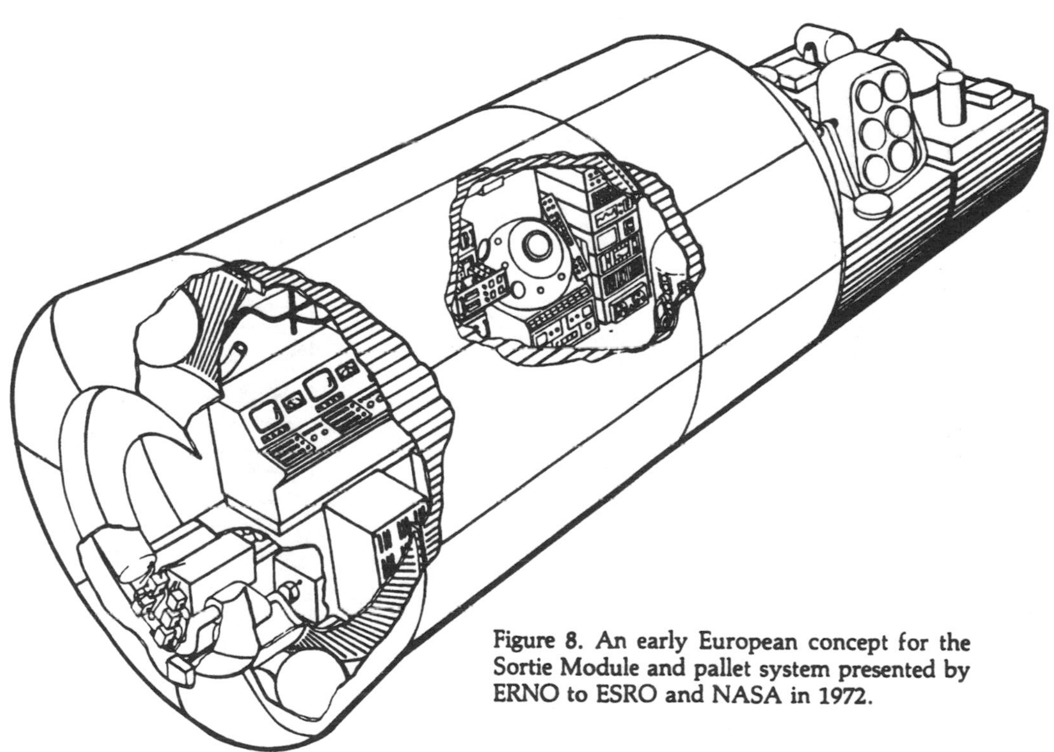

Figure 8. An early European concept for the Sortie Module and pallet system presented by ERNO to ESRO and NASA in 1972.

example, may be unimportant unless the viewer needs to be able to discriminate between a lemon and a lime. Simply, the question the editor needs to ask is whether color provides the viewer with important or useful information—given his or her understanding of how the viewer is going to use the information.

Conclusion

In a most fundamental sense, both text and visuals are systems that allow us to represent information symbolically. Despite the fact that both systems allow for the communication of many of the same ideas, each system is especially well suited for the communication of **some kinds** of ideas and, conversely, poorly suited to the communication of some others [2]. Consequently, one of the more challenging tasks the editor confronts resides not in deciding **how** to use a visual, but in deciding first **whether**, and if "yes," then, **what kind** of visual to use. Those decisions need to be informed by an understanding of the basic differences between text and visual and by an attempt to discern what kind of symbolic representation will be the most useful to the reader/viewer given the nature of the task he or she wishes to accomplish with the information provided.

Acknowledgment

Pictionary is a registered trademark of Pictionary Incorporated, Seattle, WA.

Penn is a registered trademark of Penn Racquet Sports, Phoenix, AZ.

Fig. 12. Exploded diagrams are especially helpful in support of assembly and disassembly tasks. (Reprinted from C. M. Yeates, T. V. Johnson, L. Colin, F. P. Fanale, L. Frank, and D. M. Hunten. *Galileo: Exploration of Jupiter's System.* Washington, DC: NASA, 1985.)

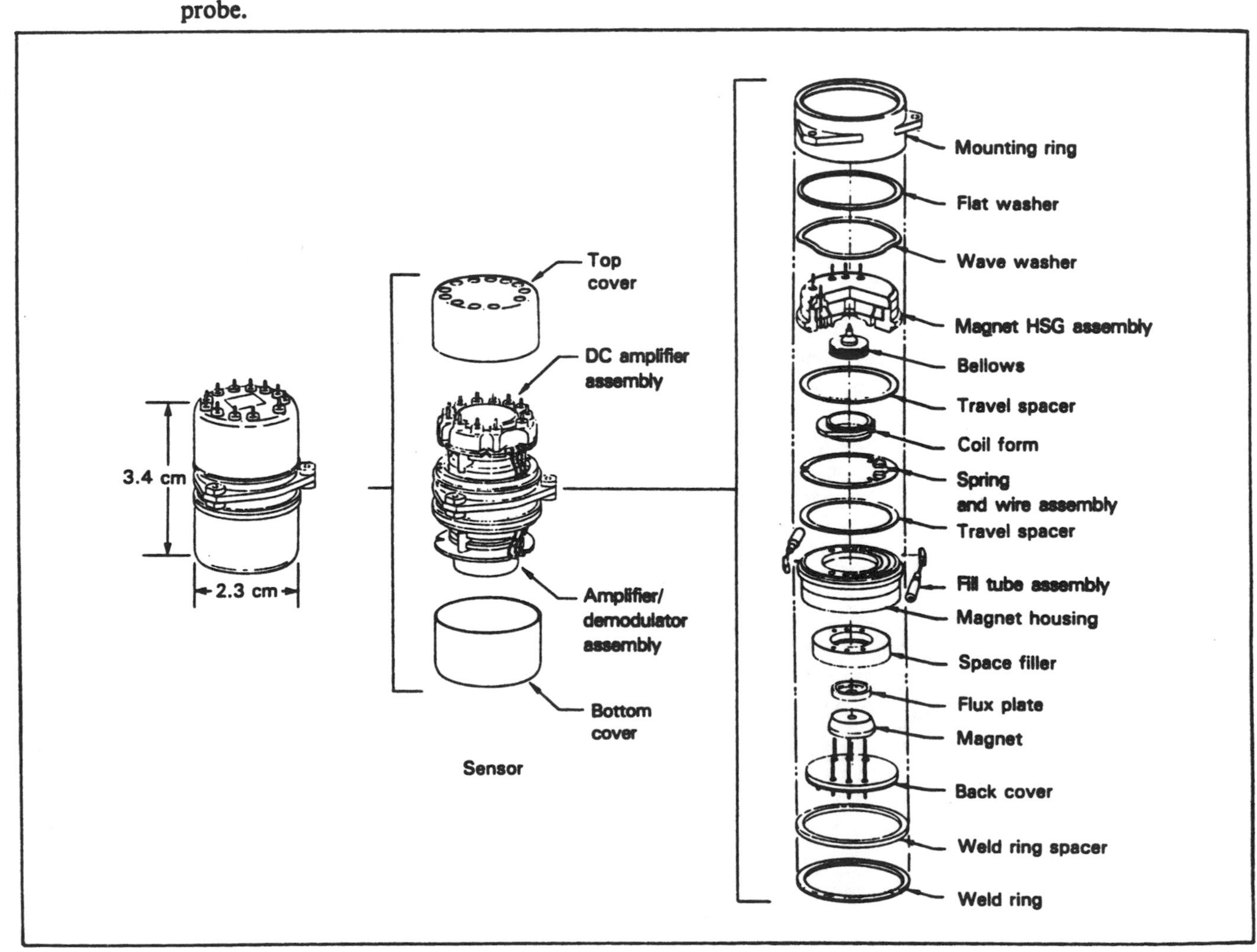

REFERENCES

[1] A. S. Luchins, "Mechanization in problem solving," *Psychological Monographs*, vol. 54, no. 248, 1942.

[2] G. Salomon, *Interaction of Media, Cognition, and Learning.* San Francisco, CA: Josey-Bass, 1979.

[3] W. P. Banks and J. Flora, "That there are no iconic signs," *Phil. and Phenomenol. Res.*, vol. 23, pp. 278–290, 1977.

[4] J. Q. Knowlton, "On the definition of 'picture,'" *AV Commun. Rev.*, vol. 14, pp. 157–183, 1966.

[5] J. H. Larkin and H. A. Simon, "Why a diagram is (sometimes) worth ten thousand words," *Cogn. Sci.*, vol. 11, pp. 65–99, 1987.

[6] P. W. Thorndike and F. R. Yekovich, "A critique of schema-based theories of human story memory," *Poetics*, vol. 9, pp. 23–49, 1980.

[7] J. M. Mandler, *Stories, Scripts, and Scenes: Aspects of Schema Theory.* Hillsdale, NJ: Lawrence Erlbaum, 1984.

[8] T. R. Williams, "Schema theory," in *Technical Communications Frontiers: Essays in Theory*, C. Sides, Ed. St. Paul, MN: Assoc. Teachers Tech. Writing, 1994.

[9] Z. Pylyshin, *Computation and Cognition: Toward a Foundation for Cognitive Science.* Cambridge, MA: MIT Press, 1984.

[10] A. Treisman, "Features and objects in visual perception," *Sci. Amer.*, vol. 255, pp. 114–125, 1986.

[11] W. D. Winn, "A theoretical framework for research on learning from graphics," *Int. J. Educ. Res.*, vol. 14, pp. 553–564, 1990.

[12] B. A. Hunter, A. Crismore, and P. D Pearson, "Visual displays in basal readers and social studies textbooks," in *The Psychology of Illustration: vol. 2: Instructional Issues*, H. A. Houghton and D. M. Willows, Eds. New York: Springer-Verlag, 1987.

[13] J. Doblin, "A structure for nontextual communications," in *The Processing of Visible Language*, vol. 2, P. A. Kolers, M. E Wrolstad, and H. Bouma, Eds. New York: Plenum, 1980.

[14] K. L. Alesandrini, "Pictures and adult learning," *Instruct. Sci.*, vol. 13, pp. 63–77, 1984.

[15] W. D. Winn, "The role of graphics in training documents: Toward an explanatory theory of how they communicate," *IEEE Trans. Prof. Commun.*, vol. 32, pp. 300–309, Dec. 1989.

[16] J. D. Bransford and M. K. Johnson, "Contextual prerequisites for understanding: Some investigations of comprehension and recall," *J. Verb. Learning and Verb. Behav.*, vol. 11, pp. 717–726, 1972.

[17] D. E. Stone and M. D. Glock, "How do young adults read directions with and without pictures," *J. Educ. Psychol.*, vol. 73, no. 3, pp. 427–436, 1981.

[18] D. N. Perkins, "Pictures and the real thing," in *The Processing of Visible Language*, P. A. Kolers, M. E. Wrolstad, and N. Bouma, Eds. New York: Plenum, 1980.

[19] N. Goodman, *Languages of Art: An Approach and a Theory.* Indianapolis, IN: Bobbs-Merril, 1968.

[20] F. M. Dwyer, *A Guide to Improving Visualized Instruction.* University Park, PA: Penn. State Univ., Learning Services Div., 1972.

[21] W. D. Winn, "Color in document design," *IEEE Trans. Prof. Commun.*, vol. 34, pp. 180–185, Sept. 1991.

[22] L. G. Thorell and W. J. Smith, *Using Computer Color Effectively: An Illustrated Reference.* Englewood Cliffs, NJ: Prentice-Hall, 1990.

Visual Discriminability of Headings in Text

Thomas R. Williams and Jan H. Spyridakis

Abstract—**Headings in text provide critical signals that help a reader discern a writer's structural treatment of a topic. Today, writers and editors have powerful formatting and typographical tools available in word processing and desktop publishing software that can be applied to headings to visually reveal or signal the structure of text, and thus the author's perspective. The results of the studies presented in this article, however, suggest that 1) visual discriminations among headings are easier for a reader to make when headings vary on fewer rather than more formatting and typographical dimensions, 2) size is the most powerful visual cue to a heading's hierarchical position, 3) relative size differences among different levels of headings of about 20% are more discriminable than are absolute size differences, and 4) formatting cues are perceived by readers consistently but not necessarily conventionally.**

Introduction

WRITTEN discourse, at least discourse that conforms to rhetorical conventions, has structure. And while a specific structure may be varied to accommodate differences in an author's purpose or perspective, ideas are generally cast in superordinate, coordinate, or subordinate roles in relation to other ideas in a text.

Meyer [1] suggests that such hierarchies result from writing plans through which both the organization of the ideas and the allocation of different degrees of emphasis to those ideas are implemented. In general, the more important, more inclusive, ideas are presented higher in the content structure and the less important, supporting details are presented lower in the content structure. Moreover, there seems to be a reasonable level of consensus among researchers investigating the effects of text structure on comprehension that there are relatively few basic structures; there is likewise considerable consensus on what those structures are.

Meyer and Rice [2], for example, identify five basic groups of relations: collection, causal, response, comparison, and description. Similarly, Anderson and Armbruster [3] identify six groups: description, temporal sequences, explanation, compare-contrast, definition, and problem-solution. A single passage, of course, may employ several of these organizational schemes, yet the top-level structure of a passage is likely to employ only one.

Competent readers are particularly sensitive to such top-level structures, or rhetorical predicates, and, in their attempts to decipher text meaning, construct mental representations of a text's structure (or "text schema") that they believe will be similar to the structure intended by the writer [1], [2], [4]–[14]. These text schemata [15] guide our processing of text through our knowledge of conventionally used discourse structures. In fact, only when the reader's purpose in reading a text is quite inconsistent with the writer's purpose in structuring a text, or when the reader has considerable expertise in the topic domain addressed by a text, is he or she capable, without enormous difficulty, of ignoring the writer's structural plan.

Meyer argues that readers search for the writer's organizational plan or top-level structure in their attempts to subsume large chunks of information and tie such information into a comprehensible whole. This same perceived top-level structure is also employed by the reader to guide retrieval. During retrieval, superordinate information is retrieved first, and subordinate information is recalled only if its links to the superordinate information are intact.

In fact, a reader's knowledge of, and facility with, the use of text structures is predictive of subsequent comprehension and retention of text information [16]. Moreover, readers of well-organized passages generally agree on the relative importance of different pieces of information contained in them [9] and prefer passages that are highly organized to those that are not [17], perhaps because the structure of such passages is easier for readers to discern.

Readers use a variety of cues or signals provided by text in their attempts to discern its structure. Of interest here are structural cues that may affect a reader's selection and retention of superordinate content and his or her ability to make inferences from that content at the time of comprehension. These signals attempt to pre-announce or emphasize content and/or reveal content relationships.

Relevant Studies

One specific type of signal is headings, which occur as short phrases or topical labels and announce superordinate content before the reader encounters the actual content. During encoding and processing, headings should prime a reader's prior knowledge and assist him or her in activating the appropriate hierarchical framework or text schema to accept new information. This new information "instantiates" the reader's schema by fleshing it out—by filling it in with specific details. Likewise, at the point of retrieval, headings held in memory serve as guides to the reader in his or her attempts to access stored information.

While many have studied the effects of different types of signals, we review here only the findings on headings from studies that have investigated headings alone or as a variable in factorial research designs where heading effects are separable from effects of other signal types. These studies have used a variety of text bases differing in length, difficulty, familiarity, and structure. Subjects have ranged from elementary school

Manuscript received January 1992.

The authors are with the Department of Technical Communication, University of Washington, Seattle, WA 98195.

IEEE Log Number 9200127.

Reprinted from *IEEE Trans. Prof. Comm.*, vol. PC-35, no. 2, pp. 44–70, June 1992.

students to adults. Performance tasks have varied from immediate and delayed, cued and free recall; to forced choice tests; to search and retrieval tasks; and to preference measures.

Many studies have assessed the effects of headings—their presence and their phrasing—on content retention and recall, and on reader preference. Hartley, Morris, and Trueman [18] assessed headings phrased as questions or statements placed in the margin of a short expository text (300 words) and found that only headings phrased as questions improved immediate and delayed recall scores of remedial second grade readers. With a somewhat longer text (400 words), both question and statement headings improved factual recall with both immediate and delay tests when those headings were underlined, yet question headings aided low ability, primary school readers more than statement headings [19]. Dee-Lucas and Di Vesta [20] had college students read a 500 word passage, with or without headings. Subjects who read passages preceded by headings recalled significantly more information from the passage than did subjects who read passages without headings. Krug, George, Hannon, and Glover [21] tested the effects of headings versus no headings in 600-word expository passages read by college students. They also found that subjects recalled more from headed texts.

Hartley and Trueman [22] used a considerably longer text (1,000 words) and observed again that the presence of headings improved the recall of high-school age subjects while the phrasing of headings (statements versus questions) had no effect. Holley, Dansereau, Evans, Collins, Brooks, and Larson [23], assessing the effect of headings with college age readers on a 2,400 word expository text, found that headings improved immediate recall slightly and improved delayed recall greatly. Klare, Shuford, and Nichols [17] found no content retention differences on an immediate, multiple choice test among Air Force personnel reading headed versus non-headed excerpts (1,200 words) from aircraft mechanics manuals. They did, however, find a reader preference for headed passages. The nature and length of the text as well as the type and timing of the test appears to influence the recall findings: positive effects for headings are found for expository texts of greater length, particularly in delayed, factual recall tests.

Others have assessed the effect of headings with different dependent measures. Swarts, Flower, and Hayes [24] examined misleading headings and found that they impeded adults' prediction of content following the headings and the matching of content to the headings. However, with a search task, they found no significant differences between headings in clear prose versus clear prose without headings. Charrow and Redish [25] had adult subjects read consumer warranties with standardized headings or no headings and found no difference in subject performance (number of correct answers to a questionnaire and amount of time to answer the questionnaire): They did note that subjects preferred the headed texts.

Spyridakis [26]–[29] ran three studies on signaled expository texts with college students. The factorial designs included headings, previews, or logical connectives (i.e., transitions) singularly or in combination in six texts that varied in length, content complexity, and familiarity. Forced-choice tests assessed the comprehension of factual and inferential as well as subordinate and superordinate content. No significant effects for headings occurred with the easiest passage—a short (600 words), familiar, and easy-reading-level (grade 9) passage. Another text, which was also relatively short, equally familiar, but more difficult by reading level (grade 11), exhibited a disordinal interaction where headings created higher scores alone and with previews, but lower scores when mixed with logical connectives. A third passage of similar length to those cited above contained less familiar content and exhibited a more difficult reading level (grade 16); it showed significant main effects for headings and a heading/logical connective interaction on the inference scores. The interaction again indicated that headings supplied more help when they appeared without logical connectives and vice versa.

When even longer (1,029–1,142 words) unfamiliar passages were used, the positive effects of headings in particular became clear. With one passage, headings alone aided subjects with superordinate inferential information on an immediate test. Also, heading/logical connective interactions occurred on the superordinate and subordinate content measures in the immediate test: in both cases, headings or logical connectives resulted in higher scores when the passages contained one or the other, but not both. With the delay test, the positive effect of headings became even more evident: subjects who read headed passages maintained and sometimes increased comprehension after two weeks—subjects who read unheaded passages showed reduced comprehension. The one disordinal interaction of headings and logical connectives again revealed that subjects performed better with headings or logical connectives alone and poorer when they were both present.

One final passage showed very few significant results: it was the longest passage, of low familiarity, and of high difficulty. One must wonder whether a passage can become so difficult that even headings will be insufficient in aiding readers in designing hierarchical frameworks of superordinate information to accept lower level information.

Very few studies have assessed the effect of different physical dimensions of headings. Hartley and Trueman [22], [30] conducted six studies in which they varied the position of headings (outside the margin versus left justified); they found that position had no effect on recall or search and retrieval tasks with children of different ability levels.

Summary of Existing Studies

Despite some seemingly contradictory findings in the headings research, a model of heading effects in expository technical prose nonetheless begins to emerge. If a passage is quite simple—due to its shortness, high familiarity, or ease in terms of readability—then proficient adult readers may not need or benefit from headings. Conversely, if a passage is difficult—due to its length, its low familiarity, or its difficulty in terms of readability—then readers will need textual guidance and will benefit from headings. However, if a passage is too difficult, a reader may need much more help than headings alone can provide.

If readers, then, do use headings in their attempts to discover the structure an author has imposed on a piece of writing, it stands to reason that headings should be constructed and presented so as to effectively reveal that structure. Headings do, it appears to us, possess semantic and visual attributes that can signal a text's structure. Semantically, a heading entitled "Formatting" in a manual for a word-processing application would logically, and without much difficulty, be interpreted as more inclusive, and therefore, superordinate, to a heading entitled "Indenting Paragraphs" contained in the same manual. Visually, that superordinate/subordinate relationship might be represented in a variety of ways. The superordinate heading might be set in a larger type size, it might be set in upper case letters, it might be centered, or it might be underlined. In fact, it is not at all uncommon to see several, if not all, of these different treatments applied simultaneously to headings in the same document. For example, a main heading might be presented in all caps, centered on the page; the immediately subordinate heading might be upper and lower case, centered and underlined; the third level heading might be moved to the left margin; the fourth level heading might be distinguished from the third by removing the underline, and so on.

The Present Study

We sought in the present study to determine how readers actually perceive various physical attributes of headings. The questions addressed in the present study were 1) how effective physical formatting conventions are in revealing text structure and 2) how uniformly such formatting conventions are interpreted. Do subjects consistently assume certain format dimensions to be superordinate to others? Is, for example, upper case a stronger cue to superordinate status than underlining, or is centering a head assumed to make it superordinate to one that is underlined?

To answer these questions we presented subjects with a card-sorting task, each card stack consisting of different combinations of heading treatments. All headings were word-like but meaningless. If headings are visually discriminable by physical attributes alone, it should be a fairly simple task for subjects to sort the cards in a hierarchal order; if physical attributes alone do not provide easily discriminable cues as to the relative level of headings in a text hierarchy, then a set of cards containing different heading treatments should be difficult to sort and, consequently, take more time.

One might logically expect that the typographical and formatting combinations available to an author to reveal the relative level of a heading provide a powerful complement of tools. Intuitively, it would also seem that the greater the number of visual attributes that differ among headings, the easier such visual discriminations would be for the reader to make. In fact, to some extent this is true—the more visually different headings are, the more easily the reader will discriminate among them—*if* the reader's task is simply to determine whether those headings are the same or different. However, if the reader must decide how those headings relate to one another hierarchically, he or she may have difficulty interpreting what those different dimensions are intended to signal. A good deal of evidence suggests that the process of discrimination in such situations is actually easier when it is based on fewer dimensions [31]–[36]. Moreover, for such cues to be effective, they must be interpreted uniformly. Consequently, if visual discriminations are easier when made on fewer dimensions or if those conventional formatting cues used to signal heading levels are not uniformly decoded, then the traditional methods writers have employed in formatting headings to reveal hierarchical levels may actually confound the reader's attempts to discern text structure.

We deemed an ancillary question to be of potential interest as well: if size alone (one dimension) proved to be an effective condition in facilitating discrimination among the cards in the sorting task, would an absolute difference in type sizes (for example, cueing hierarchical level among all heads by changes of three or four points) or a relative difference (for example, changing head sizes by, say, 30%) best facilitate those discriminations? A brief examination of our preliminary stimulus materials suggested to us that relative size differences were more discriminable than absolute size differences.

Our hypotheses, then, were that 1) the fewer dimensions on which subjects had to make discriminations, the faster they would make them, 2) relative size differences would be easier to discriminate than absolute differences, and 3) the "conventions" used in formatting headings are far from conventional—although readers should uniformly or consistently interpret formatting changes intended to cue differences in the hierarchical levels assigned to headings, they might view the hierarchical importance of various heading treatments differently from what we conventionally expect.

Methods

Subjects

The subjects consisted of 30 male and female pre-engineering students recruited from two introductory technical writing classes offered by the Technical Communication (TC) Department of the College of Engineering at the University of Washington. Participation in the study fulfilled a course requirement, which could also be satisfied by writing a two-page paper on a topic assigned by the course instructor.

Materials

Materials for the first treatment, intended to address the question of differences in the visual discriminability of headings varying in the number and type of dimensions, consisted of seven sets of 16 5″ × 7″ index cards, each of which exhibited both a heading and a paragraph of laser printed text. In order to ensure that readers would be unable to process the headings semantically, both the headings and text were composed of "greeking" (non-word combinations of letters that visually resemble words). Thus, for example, one-word headings used as stimulus materials in this study included "Wonxvaogn," "Zxcvbnmie," and "Uqerqwfjs." The number of cards in each set (16) was chosen initially somewhat arbitrarily. We believed that too few cards would be inadequate to present the subjects with a challenge and might result in no discernible task differences, while too many might make those tasks extraordinarily difficult. In a pre-trial, three volunteers tested our stimulus materials and confirmed that our estimate of 16 cards would present the subjects with a manageable challenge.

In the first treatment, headings were formatted so that the kind and the number of dimensions varied. Dimensions that were varied included size, position (centered, flush left, indented, embedded), underlining (present or absent), and case (upper or upper-and-lower). Not all combinations, however, could result in 16 heading variations. For example, in looking at two-dimension possibilities, varying size with position (centered, flush left, indented, or embedded in text) allows an unlimited number of combinations because of the relatively unlimited number of different type sizes available, while varying position with case (uppercase and upper-and-lower) allows only 8 (4 × 2) combinations, eight fewer than the number of cards required in each stack. In fact, however, given the principal research question we chose to address, which is the effect of the number of dimensions, not the kind, the fact that all combinations were not possible was not an important methodological limitation. Finally, so that we also could analyze the effects of different kinds of dimensions, we included one set of cards using all four dimensions. Consequently, we limited our stimulus materials in the first treatment to the following conditions, consisting of seven card-stacks: one variable (size); two variables (size and position; size and case; size and underline); three variables (position, case, and underline; size, case, and underline); and four variables (size, position, case, and underline).

Materials for the second treatment, a task intended to address the question of the effects of relative versus absolute size differences in headings, consisted again of 16 5″ × 7″ cards, each containing a greeked heading preceding a greeked paragraph. Each heading, however, was printed in a different size, and each heading differed in size by three points from both the next larger and the next smaller heading in the set. Thus, headings were set in sizes from 12 to 57 points in increments of three points. These 16 cards were then separated into four sets: 12 to 21 points, 24 to 33 points, 36 to 45 points, and 48 to 57 points. The four headings in each of the four sets thus differed in absolute size by three points from others contained in the same set. However, the relative sizes among the headings in each set differed. A 15-point heading is 25% larger, for example, than a 12-point heading, but a 57-point heading is only 5.6% larger than a 54-point heading. Mean differences in the sets were thus 20.7% for headings sizes 12 to 21 points, 11.2% for headings sizes 24 to 33 points, 7.7% for headings sizes 36 to 45 points, and 5.9% for headings sizes 48 to 57 points. Our reasoning was that if absolute size differences are sufficient to cue visual discrimination effectively, then there should be no difference in the times required to sort the four different sets of cards. However, if relative size differences are better at facilitating those discriminations, then subjects should be able to sort the set containing headings disposed in the range of 12 to 21 points more rapidly than they would be able, for example, to sort the set containing the headings in the range of 48 to 57 points.

Procedure

Each subject came to the TC usability lab at his or her scheduled time. When the subjects arrived, a trained student assistant read them an introduction stating that they would be sorting headings in several sets of cards in the order that they believed would reflect order of importance, placing most-important cards on top and least-important cards on the bottom. The sequence of the card stacks and of the cards within a stack was randomized for each subject to control for order effects. For each sorting task, subjects were told when to begin and were asked to say "done" when they felt they had completed the task successfully. Using a stopwatch, experimenters recorded each subject's sort times for each card stack to 0.01 second. Subjects were first presented with the seven sorting tasks requiring them to sort 16 cards differing on both the number and kinds of formatting dimensions. Subsequently, they were asked to sort the four sets of four cards, each varying only in size. Again, the order of presentation of the cards and stacks was randomized to control for order effects, and, again, the times were measured with a stopwatch.

Two independent raters reviewed the subjects' protocols for card stacks and individually ranked and recorded which heading dimensions and position levels subjects perceived as superordinate to other dimensions or levels. On the few stacks where the raters disagreed, the raters discussed their differences and arrived at one answer, or the tie was broken by a third rater. Raters discarded subject data when subjects appeared to have switched sorting strategies during the sorting task.

One-factor, repeated measures analyses of variance (ANOVAs) were performed on the resulting time data, as were multiple comparisons using Fisher PLSD tests, to ascertain which conditions differed. Friedman analyses of variance and Wilcoxon matched-pair sign-tests were used to determine whether subjects hierarchically perceived different heading dimensions consistently.

Results and Discussion

Visual Discriminability of Dimensions

For the seven card-stacks varying in type and number of dimensions, the ANOVAs on the time data revealed significant differences among the card stacks, $F(6, 180) = 6.626$, $p = .0001$. The general pattern in the results revealed that the fewer dimensions a card stack contained, the faster the subjects performed. Moving down the column of mean time in seconds in Table I, note that the times increase with the number of dimensions, starting with 98.21 seconds for the one-dimension card stack and increasing to 143.28 seconds for the four-dimension card stack.

The Fisher PLSD tests identified which means cited above significantly differed from other means; only results significant at $p \leq .05$ are discussed. The results of the Fisher tests confirm what the data appear to show—the fewer the dimensions, the faster the card stacks were sorted. The one-dimension card stack was sorted significantly faster than the two-dimension, three-dimension, and four-dimension card

TABLE I
CARD STACK DIMENSIONS AND MEAN PERFORMANCE TIMES

Dimensions		Mean Time	SD
No.	*Type*	*(Seconds)*	
1	Size	98.21	32.80
2	Size/Position	126.00	50.51
2	Size/Case	121.80	10.06
2	Size/Underline	110.39	39.74
3	Size/Case/Underline	121.95	43.65
3	Position/Case/Underline	143.12	48.40
4	Size/Position/Case/Underline	143.28	71.18

stacks. Two of the two-dimension card stacks (size/case; size/underline) were sorted significantly faster than the three-dimension card stacks, and all two-dimension card stacks were sorted significantly faster than the four-dimension card stack. One of the three-dimension card stacks (size/case/underline) was sorted significantly faster than the four-dimension card stack.

Discriminability of Size Differences

The ANOVA on the time data for the second treatment—sorting cards on the basis of size alone—also proved to be statistically significant, $F(3, 90) = 11.93$, $p = .0001$. In general, the results revealed that the greater the relative differences in heading size, the more rapidly the headings were sorted. Note in Table II that as the relative size differences decrease, the mean time in seconds increases.

Again, Fisher PLSD tests were conducted to ascertain which means differed from other means and only comparisons at $p \leq .05$ are discussed. The card set with the smallest relative difference in heading size (5.9%) took significantly longer to sort than the other three card sets, all of which had larger relative size differences among their headings. Also, the card set with a 7.7% relative size difference in headings was significantly slower to sort than the card set with the 20.7% relative size difference. There appears to be a somewhat consistent pattern in the results that supports the hypothesis that relative, not absolute, differences in heading sizes provide the most easily discriminable cues to hierarchical level. Were that not the case, one would expect the mean sorting times for the different stacks to be quite similar.

Hierarchical Perceptions of Heading Dimensions

Analyses were conducted to ascertain whether subjects used the different heading and position variables as cues to hierarchical position in a consistent fashion in the card stacks. Specifically, we wanted to determine whether most subjects perceived specific heading variables as more important than others or whether such perceptions were mixed across subjects. Eight of the nine analyses proved significant at $p \leq .03$: Friedman analyses of variance were conducted when card stacks contained more than two variables, and Wilcoxon matched-pairs signed-rank tests were used when card stacks contained only two variables.

Table III reveals the results for the four heading treatments (size, position, case, and underline). Subjects consistently

TABLE II
HEADING SIZE DIFFERENCES AND MEAN PERFORMANCE TIMES

Head Size *(Points)*	Relative % Difference	Mean Time *(Seconds)*	SD
12–21	20.7	9.09	3.83
24–33	11.2	11.14	5.79
36–45	7.7	14.07	7.58
48–57	5.9	17.61	12.49

perceived heading size as the most important marker of superordination in their ordering of the card stacks, a heading treatment that was always significantly higher in mean rank than all other treatments except for the case variable in stack F. Case was perceived as secondary to size in three stacks (B, D, and F), and this difference was significant for stacks B and D. In stack E, case and position were significantly more important than underline, yet case and position were essentially equivalent in rank. In card stack F containing all four variables, again the relative importance of the variables, from most to least important, was size, case, position, and underline, though size and position, which significantly differed from each other, did not significantly differ from case.

In summary, 1) type size is always perceived as the most important cue to hierarchal status; 2) underline is always perceived as the least important cue; and 3) position and case are deemed secondary to size, yet position and case are generally considered to be equally important treatments.

While changing size alone in a heading appears adequate to signal the heading's level, one other formatting variable—position—does, by itself, allow the writer to signal at least four different heading levels (headings may be centered, flush left, indented from the left, or embedded in the text). This is not the case, of course, with either case (two possible levels) or underline (two possible levels). Consequently we analyzed the sorting protocols of the subjects on those tasks in which position was used as a formatting variable to determine if position cues are interpreted uniformly.

Table IV reveals the findings and significant effects for the four position treatments. As column three reveals, subjects consistently perceived centered headings as most important and embedded headings as least important. When all four position treatments were presented (stacks H and I), flush left or indented headings ranked second or third in importance; their relative differences ranging from 2.25 to 2.67 is essentially the same, not meeting the necessary critical differences between mean ranks for the given treatments. Flush left and indented headings were significantly different from centered and embedded heads in all instances. It is interesting to note that subjects consistently perceived centered headings as most important and embedded headings as least important but were somewhat split as to the intermediary importance of left versus indented headings. Although it is common practice to assign flush-left headings a role superordinate to indented headings, many of our subjects actually did the reverse. While position as a structure revealing cue can provide the writer/editor with up to four head levels, readers' inconsistency in interpreting the relative importance of flush-left and indented headings might

TABLE III
MEAN RANKS AND STATISTICS FOR HEADING VARIABLES

Card Stack	n	Mean Ranks for Treatments				Statistic	$p \leq$	Crit. Diff.^
		Size	*Position*	*Case*	*Underline*			
A	29	1.24	1.75	—	—	$z = 2.79$	.005*	
B	29	1.38	—	1.62	—	$z = 1.30$	.19	
C	30	1.26	—	—	1.70	$z = 2.56$	.01*	
D	27	1.48	—	2.17	2.35	$\chi_r^2 = 12.64$	.01*	.579
E	20	—	2.00	1.58	2.42	$\chi_r^2 = 7.41$	.03*	.673
F	29	1.97	2.81	2.22	3.00	$\chi_r^2 = 13.14$	.01*	.812

* Significant p level for accompanying statistic.
^ Critical difference needed between mean ranks for significant multiple comparison, overall $p \leq .10$. See J. D. Gibbons [37].

TABLE IV
MEAN RANKS AND STATISTICS FOR HEADING POSITIONS

Card Stack	n	Mean Rank for Positions				Statistic	$p \leq$	Crit. Diff.^
		Center	*Left*	*Indent*	*Embed*			
G	21	1.00	2.00	—	—	$z = 4.47$	.001*	
H	24	1.21	2.67	2.25	3.88	$\chi_r^2 = 52.55$	.001*	.614
I	18	1.00	2.50	2.61	3.89	$\chi_r^2 = 45.27$	.001*	.709

* Significant p level for accompanying statistic.
^ Critical difference needed between mean ranks for significant multiple comparison, overall $p \leq .10$. See J. D. Gibbons [37].

militate against the use of both heading treatments in the same document to reveal heading position in a hierarchy.

CONCLUSIONS

Critics of technology have long argued that the adoption of technological advances invariably comes at some cost. One might reasonably argue that the introduction of powerful word-processing and desktop publishing systems is yet another example of such a trade-off. While the formatting capabilities of these new tools relieves the writer or editor from the formatting constraints imposed by the inflexibility inherent in the typewriter, they also provide those same writers and editors with both the ability and, we believe, the temptation, to overuse those capabilities. There is an old saying to the effect that if you give a child a hammer, he or she will suddenly discover a million things that need hammering. We believe that we have seen manifestations of similar revelations among communicators. The provision of the capability to easily bolden, italicize, outline, shadow, and underline—singly or in combination—the headings on which the reader depends to discern the structure of a piece of written discourse, does not carry with it the obligation to use those capabilities.

The studies we have reported here, in fact, suggest that using fewer formatting dimensions is more useful to the reader and that using more is likely only to confuse. The flip side of our technological trade-off, of course, is that we do now, because of the computer, have the ability to convey visually as many levels of headings as we need by using only one formatting cue: size. Further, subjects consistently discern the hierarchy signaled by size variations. Our results suggest that if size is used, size differences between heading levels of roughly 20% are the most helpful to the reader.

Finally, given that some writers may resist using larger and larger heads to satisfy their needs, we suggest that writers choose heading treatments that, by varying the fewest formatting dimensions, will allow for the creation of the number of heading levels the writer requires.

ACKNOWLEDGMENT

The authors wish to acknowledge the assistance of Cynthia Dahl and Ruth Hansing, students in the Technical Communication Department at the University of Washington, Seattle, for their considerable efforts in helping to conduct this study.

REFERENCES

[1] B. J. F. Meyer, "Text dimensions and cognitive processing," in *Learning and Comprehension of Text*, H. Mandl, N. L. Stein, and T. Trabasso, Eds. Hillsdale, NJ: Lawrence Erlbaum Associates, 1984.

[2] B. J. F. Meyer and E. Rice, "The interaction of reader strategies and the organization of text," *Text*, vol. 2, no. 1–3, pp. 155–192, 1982.

[3] T. H. Anderson and B. B. Ambruster, "Studying strategies and their implications for textbook design," in *Designing Usable Texts*, T. M. Duffy and R. Waller, Eds. Orlando, FL: Academic Press, 1985.

[4] B. K. Britton, B. J. F. Meyer, R. Simpson, T. S. Holdredge, and C. Curry, "Effects of the organization of text on memory: Tests of two implications of a selective attention hypothesis," *J. Exp. Psychol.: Human Learning and Memory*, vol. 5, pp. 496–506, 1979.

[5] D. B. Eamon, "Selection and recall of topical information in prose by better and poorer readers," *Reading Research Quart.*, vol. 14, pp. 244–257, 1978.

[6] W. Kintsch and J. Keenan, "Reading rate and retention as a function of the number of propositions in the base structure sentences," *Cognitive Psychology*, vol. 5, pp. 257–274, 1973.

[7] W. A. Kintsch and T. van Dijk, "Toward a model of text comprehension and production," *Psychological Review*, vol. 85, pp. 363–394, 1978.

[8] W. A. Kintsch, "Reading comprehension as a function of text structure," in *Toward a Psychology of Reading*, A. S. Reber and D. L. Scarborough, Eds. Hillsdale, NJ: Lawrence Erlbaum Associates, 1977.
[9] G. McKoon, "Organization of information in text memory," *J. Verbal Learning and Verbal Behavior*, vol. 16, pp. 247–260, 1977.
[10] B. J. F. Meyer, *The Organization of Prose and Its Effects on Memory*. Amsterdam, The Netherlands: North Holland, 1975.
[11] B. J. F. Meyer, "Organizational aspects of text: Effects on reading comprehension and applications for the classroom," in *Promoting Reading Comprehension*, J. Flood, Ed. Delaware: International Reading Association, 1984.
[12] J. R. Miller and W. A. Kintsch, "Readability and recall of short prose passages: A theoretical analysis," *J. Exp. Psychol.: Human Learning and Memory*, vol. 6, pp. 335–353, 1980.
[13] R. B. Miller, F. L. Perry, and D. J. Cunningham, "Forgetting of superordinate and subordinate information acquired from prose material," *J. Educ. Psychol.*, vol. 69, pp. 730–735, 1977.
[14] D. J. Richgels, L. M. McGee, R. G. Lomax, and C. Sheard, "Awareness of four text structures: Effects of recall of expository text," *Reading Research Quart.*, vol. 22, pp. 177–196, 1987.
[15] L. W. Brooks and D. F. Dansereau, "Effects of structural schema training and text organization on expository prose processing," *J. Educ. Psychol.*, vol. 75, pp. 811–820, 1983.
[16] B. J. F. Meyer, D. M. Brandt, and G. J. Bluth, "Use of top-level structure in text: Key for reading comprehension of ninth-grade students," *Reading Research Quart.*, vol. 16, pp. 72–101, 1980.
[17] G. R. Klare, E. H. Shuford, and W. H. Nichols, "The relation of format organization to learning," *Eduction Research Bulletin*, vol. 37, pp. 39–45, 1958.
[18] J. Hartley, P. Morris, and M. Trueman, "Headings in text," *Remedial Eduction*, vol. 16, pp. 5–7, 1981.
[19] J. Hartley, J. Kenely, G. Owen, and M. Trueman, "The effect of headings on children's recall from prose text," *British J. Educ. Psychol.*, vol. 50, pp. 304–307, 1980.
[20] D. Dee-Lucas and F. F. Di Vesta, "Learner-generated organizational aids: Effects on learning from text," *J. Educ. Psychol.*, vol. 72, pp. 304–311, 1980.
[21] D. Krug, B. George, S. A. Hannon, and J. A. Glover, "The effect of outlines and headings on readers' recall of text," *Contemporary Educ. Psychol.*, vol. 14, pp. 11–123, 1989.
[22] J. Hartley and M. Trueman, "The effects of headings on text recall, search, and retrieval," *British J. Educ. Psychol.*, vol. 53, pp. 205–214, 1983.
[23] C. D. Holley, D. F. Dansereau, S. H. Evans, K. W. Collins, L. Brooks, and D. Larson, "Utilizing intact and embedded headings as processing aids with nonnarrative text," *Contemporary Educ. Psychol.*, vol. 6, pp. 227–236, 1981.
[24] H. Swarts, L. S. Flower, and J. R. Hayes, *How Headings in Documents Can Mislead Readers*, Document Design Project, Washington, DC, DHEW, Tech. Rep. 9, 1980.
[25] V. R. Charrow and J. C. Redish, *A Study of Standardized Headings for Warranties*, Document Design Project, Washington, DC, National Institute of Education, Tech. Rep. 6, 1980.
[26] J. H. Spyridakis and T. Standal, "Headings, previews, logical connectives: Effects on reading comprehension," *J. Technical Writing and Communication*, vol. 16, no. 4, pp. 343–354, 1986.
[27] J. H. Spyridakis and T. Standal, "Signals in expository prose: Effects on reading comprehension," *Reading Research Quart.*, vol. 12, no. 3, pp. 285–298, 1987.
[28] J. H. Spyridakis, "Signaling effects: Increased content retention and new answers," *J. Technical Writing and Communication*, vol. 19, no. 4, pp. 395–415, 1989.
[29] J. H. Spyridakis, "Signaling effects: A review of the research," *J. Technical Writing and Communication*, vol. 19, no. 3, pp. 227–240, 1989.
[30] J. Hartley and M. Trueman, "A research strategy for text designers: The role of headings," *Instructional Science*, vol. 14, pp. 99–155, 1985.
[31] U. Arend, K. P. Muthing, and J. Wandmacher, "Evidence for global feature superiority in menu selection by icons," *Behavior and Information Technology*, vol. 6, pp. 411–426, 1981.
[32] R. Remington and D. Williams, "On the selection and evaluation of visual display symbology: Factors influencing search and identification times," *Human Factors*, vol. 28, pp. 407–420, 1986.
[33] M. G. Samet, R. E. Geiselman, and B. M. Landee, "Human performance evaluation of graphic symbol-design features," *Perceptual and Motor Skills*, vol. 54, pp. 1303–1310, 1982.
[34] A. Treisman, "Features and objects in visual perception," *Sci. Amer.*, vol. 255, pp. 114–125, 1982.
[35] A. Treisman, "Features and objects: The fourteenth Bartlett Memorial Lecture," *Quart. J. Exp. Psychol.: Human Exp. Psychol.*, vol. 40A, pp. 210–237, 1988.
[36] A. Treisman and G. Gelade, "A feature integration theory of attention," *Cognitive Psychology*, vol. 12, pp. 97–136, 1980.
[37] J. D. Gibbons, *Nonparametric Methods for Quantitative Analysis, 2nd Ed.* Columbus, OH: American Sciences Press, Inc., 1985.

Thomas R. Williams received the Ph.D. in educational psychology and the M.C. and B.A. degrees in communications from the University of Washington, Seattle.

Currently he is an Assistant Professor of technical communication in the Department of Technical Communication at the University of Washington. His research interests are text and graphics variables and their effects on comprehension and recall.

Jan H. Spyridakis is an Assistant Professor in the Department of Technical Communication at the University of Washington, Seattle. She received the B.A. and M.A. degrees in English and the Ph.D. degree in curriculum and instruction.

Her research interests include the refinement of research methods in technical communication and the assessment of document and screen design variables and their effect on readers and users of various informational media.

Choosing the Right Graph

***Abstract*—** *When it comes to graphing data, most professionals show little method or creativity. They typically limit themselves to a small repertoire of graph types and select from it on the basis of habit, if not sheer ease of production. Similarly, the many books on graphing devote much attention to graphical integrity and readability, but little or none to graph selection. We developed a methodology to help engineers, scientists, and managers choose the "right graph" on the basis of three criteria: the structure of the data set in terms of number and type of variables, the intended use of the graph, and the research question or intended message. The first and third criteria allow one to construct an effective two-entry selection table.*

—JEAN-LUC DOUMONT,
SENIOR MEMBER, IEEE,
AND PHILIPPE VANDENBROECK

***Index Terms*—** *Data sets, graphs, variables.*

Manuscript received November 12, 2001; revised November 28, 2001.
J.-L. Doumont is with JL Consulting, B-1950 Kraainem, Belgium (email: JL@JLConsulting.be).
P. Vandenbroeck is with Epiphany, B-3001 Leuven, Belgium (email: philippe@wholesys.org).
IEEE PII S 0361-1434(02)02338-X.

Written documents and oral presentations are essentially sequential. Even if they are constructed along a hierarchical (tree-like) structure, they have a beginning, a middle, and an end, either in space (documents) or in time (presentations). As a result, they lend themselves well to methodologies that specify "what goes where." Introductions, for example, provide some context first, then establish the problem or need, state what was done to address the need, and finally announce what the document attempts or contains—all in a systematic sequence.

Graphical representations, by contrast, are in essence nonsequential. While the most quantitative of them usually embody a sequence of numbers, they do not suggest a viewing sequence, with a beginning and an end. On the contrary, they are meant to be perceived and interpreted globally, all at once. There lies their specific "competitive advantage," in comparison to verbal communication (text). If there is a viewing sequence, it is in the level of granularity (first the global trend, then the local variations) rather than in any spatial arrangement (for example, first the top, then the bottom).

Graphs, being nonsequential, seem to resist methodologies altogether. The well-known books of Edward R. Tufte, such as *The Visual Display of Quantitative Information* [1], offer authoritative guidelines on graphical integrity and readability, illustrated by very diverse examples, but no method to go from data to graph. More quantitative books, such as those of William S. Cleveland in the United States [2] or Jacques Bertin in France [3], attach similar importance to a statistically sound encoding of data and propose powerful graphical representations, but they still fail to help readers choose the right graph in a given situation. Clearly inspired by programming languages, Leland Wilkinson's recent book, *The Grammar of Graphics* [4], takes an original object-oriented approach to (re)constructing graphs and, as such, reviews a repertoire of representational "objects," but still lays no explicit link between graph type and, for example, intended message.

Reprinted from *IEEE Trans. Prof. Comm.*, vol. PC-45, no. 1, pp. 1–6, March 2002.

Our own training and consulting experience reveals a poor graph literacy on the part of engineers, scientists, and managers. These professionals and others typically use the same few graph types for all their data sets, regardless of the amount and nature of their data. When asked how else they could graph the same data, they usually do not have a clue. Yet when shown a different graphical representation (new to them or not) of the same data, they recognize it as insightful; they just "didn't think of graphing it that way."

As part of a training effort about the visual representation of data, then, we developed a methodology to help engineers, scientists, and managers go from data to graph. The training aimed at broadening their repertoire of graph types, but especially at enabling them to choose the "right graph" from that repertoire in any given situation. This selection method is the object of the present paper.

Three Criteria for Choosing a Graph

We have found that the effectiveness of a visual representation can be gauged against the following three criteria that can usefully guide the choice of graph type:

- the structure of the data set, that is, the number and type of variables;
- the intended use of the graph, from analysis to communication; and
- the research question or, conversely, the intended message.

The choice of representation can also be influenced by the tools used to produce the data, such as the physical layout of the experiment, or used to produce the graph, such as hardware (printers) or software (graphing applications).

The Structure of the Data Set In quantity (number of variables) and in quality (type of variables), the structure of the data set is an obvious first criterion for choosing the optimal graph. Yet many professionals seem to lack the vocabulary to describe the structure of their data, let alone use this structure to elect a graph type. A useful reference on data structure is Pyle's *Data Preparation for Data Mining* [5].

Variables can be either continuous or discrete. Continuous variables represent series of numbers that can assume (in theory) all possible values, such as measurements of the temperature. They run along either an interval scale, with an arbitrary zero, such as degree Celsius, or a ratio scale, with a absolute zero, such as Kelvin. Discrete (also called "grouping") variables represent series of "labels," dividing the data into groups. They are located along either a nominal scale, such as gender (the values male and female cannot be ordered), or an ordinal scale, such as dosage (the values control, low, medium, and high can meaningfully be ordered).

The structure of the data set, in terms of number of continuous and of discrete variables, is not a given. Like any structure, it is a view of the mind. For example, if measurements have been made at both 30°C and 80°C, the variable temperature can be considered either continuous (with, as it happens, two actual values only) or discrete (with "30°C" and "80°C" being then labels more than numerical values). Similarly, concentrations of substances *a*, *b*, and *c* in a given solvent could be considered either three continuous variables or a combination of one continuous variable (concentration) and one discrete one (substance, with labels *a*, *b*, and *c*). The other two criteria will dictate which of the possible structures is most effective in a given situation.

The Intended Use of the Graph The intended use of the graph, in particular its intended audience, is a second criterion for selecting a graph. Audiences are sometimes described as the three Ps—personal, peer, and publication—but we prefer to think of the corresponding use of the graph, ranging from analysis or answering questions for oneself (personal) to communication or conveying messages to others (publication), possibly with discussion (peer) somewhere between pure analysis and pure communication. In practice, graphs that allow a rich analysis may not excel at conveying a message effectively and vice versa.

The intended use of the graph also influences the level of care bestowed upon its final production. Graphs designed for communication usually require or deserve more care. Realistically, graphs should not be perfect: they should be **optimal** for their intended use.

The Research Question At the analysis end, the research question or, conversely, the intended message at the communication end is another obvious criterion. Professionally, graphs are not drawn to store (or, worse, decorate) data, but to answer questions, either for oneself or for an audience. Again, no graph type is absolute; each makes answering some questions easier and other questions harder.

Research questions are complex and multiple, yet they can be grouped in the following four generic categories:

- **comparison** among individual data,
- **distribution** of data along a scale,
- **correlation** between variables, and
- **evolution** over time of a variable.

One fifth category, almost at a metalevel compared to the above four, is the comparison among **groups** of data. As such, it is a comparison of different comparisons, distributions, correlations, or evolutions, and usually involves more complex displays. It results, of course, from the presence, in the data set, of a discrete variable.

Graphical displays usually encode a discrete variable in the form of either subsets or categories. Graphs with subsets distinguish among the various groups of data on a single view, using a visual difference such as color, plotting symbol, line thickness, or dash pattern (Fig. 1(a)). Graphs with categories display the various groups of data in separate, juxtaposed views (Fig. 1(b)); these views then use the same scales to allow meaningful comparisons.

When the data set involves more than one discrete variable, the resulting graphs can use multiple subsets (for example, with both different colors and different plotting symbols), multiple categories (for example, with views juxtaposed horizontally and vertically), or both subsets and categories.

The Impact of the Data Model

In two-dimensional (2-D) space, such as a sheet of paper or a computer screen, the data set is typically rendered as a table of values, whether numbers or labels. The way this table is built always reflects an underlying data model, which we may sometimes impose, but which is usually hard-wired in the software application we use. The data model has a major impact on the way we structure our data set and, therefore, on the graphs we will be able to construct or, conversely, the research questions these graphs will be able to answer. The three most common data models encountered in graphing applications focus on cells, columns, and variables, respectively.

The cell-oriented data model, the archetype of which is Microsoft Excel, considers all "cells" of a "spreadsheet" homogeneously: it allows users to write any information in any cell without specifying any a priori relationship between cells (Fig. 2(a)). With some work, it can produce compact and orderly tables, yet it does not lend itself easily to graphing several views of the same data set or to accommodating additional data. (Excel's predecessor, *Microsoft Chart*, was clearly designed for graphing data sets limited to a single continuous variable [6].)

The column-oriented data model, as used for example by SPSS Science's SigmaPlot, is a constrained spreadsheet. It organizes data in columns, each identified by a column head, but does not associate each column univocally with a variable (Fig. 2(b)). Like the cell-oriented model, it encodes discrete variables implicitly, by repeating existing columns as many times as necessary. While it allows easier graphing of continuous variables than an unconstrained spreadsheet, it does not encourage users to think in terms of discrete variables and thus to compare groups of data.

The variable-oriented data model, at the heart of statistical applications such as Insightful's S-Plus, strictly associates one column of the table with one variable of the data set (Fig. 2(c)). While it yields longer, more redundant, and possibly less insightful tables than the other models, it encourages users to think in terms of data structure, not graph structure, and thus allows a more flexible analysis of the data set. Equally important, it accommodates additional continuous or discrete variables easily, by simply adding as many columns to the table.

Without surprise, graphing applications designed on cell- or column-oriented models have felt the limitations of their initial model as they attempted to add more capabilities. Recent versions of Microsoft Excel, for example, have thus incorporated more variable-oriented features, such as pivot tables.

A Simple Selection Table

Using the first and third selection criteria above—structure of the data set and research question—as

Fig. 1. Graphical displays typically distinguish among the groups of data defined by a discrete variable with either subsets (a) or categories (b).

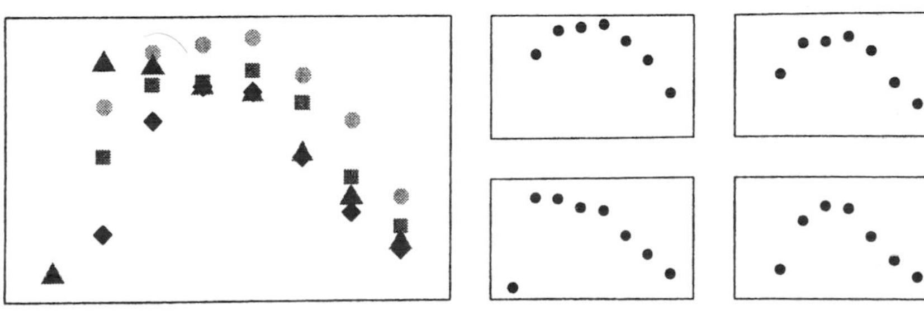

(a) Graph with subsets

(b) Graph with categories (same data set)

entries, one can turn a sequential repertoire of graph types into a much more useful selection table. A simple example of such a table is shown as Fig. 3, with graph types commented below. It could easily be extended to include more graph types or to show explicitly the corresponding graphs with subsets or with categories.

Bar charts and **dot charts** are maybe the two most basic representations of quantities along a numerical scale. Bar (or column) charts encode the data as lengths. To allow a meaningful comparison, they must be drawn along a linear (not logarithmic) ratio scale, starting from zero. Partial bars indeed mislead the viewer, even when accompanied by an explicit scale. Dot charts, by contrast, encode the data as positions along a scale, marked by dots. While somewhat less intuitive than (properly drawn) length representations, they can be used with any scale and can thus better resolve closely grouped data. They also more easily accommodate additional information, such as subsets or whiskers (error bars). They have been much promoted by William S. Cleveland [2].

Histograms encode data as positions along a scale in the horizontal direction and corresponding frequencies as lengths in the vertical direction. While fairly intuitive to interpret, they are very sensitive to the origin and width of the intervals used to group data: a different choice of grouping intervals (wider, narrower, or simply shifted) may yield a very different picture of the distribution.

Box plots and related graphical representations provide a summary of the distribution of the data. Traditional boxes, with whiskers and a central point, are five-point summaries, corresponding for example (definitions indeed vary) to percentiles of 10%, 25%, 50% (median), 75%, and 90%, but they can easily be extended to be nine-point summaries or to show individual extremes or outliers. Summaries are limiting, of course, especially for complex distributions, such as multimode ones. For small data sets, they are best replaced by individual data (sometimes called point plots). For large data sets, by contrast, they allow easy comparisons between groups of data, each summarized by one box.

Scatter plots, encoding the data as positions along two scales, reveal the shape and strength of the relationship between two continuous variables, as well as the presence of possible outliers. Three-dimensional (3-D) scatter plots, using three scales in a perspective view, are direct and sometimes useful generalizations, but are usually more difficult to visualize. A better alternative for three or more continuous variables may be the matrix plot, a juxtaposition of 2-D scatter plots—one for each pair of

Fig. 2. A data set structured along two continous variables (XY) and one discrete variable (Z, with values a,b, and c) can be rendered in tabular form along three different data models. The cell- and column-oriented models encode discrete variables implicitly, as additional lines or columns. The variable-oriented model, while heavier to read as a table, encodes discrete variables explicitly; as a consequence, it is a more powerful and more flexible starting point for graphing the data set and, especially, for comparing groups of data.

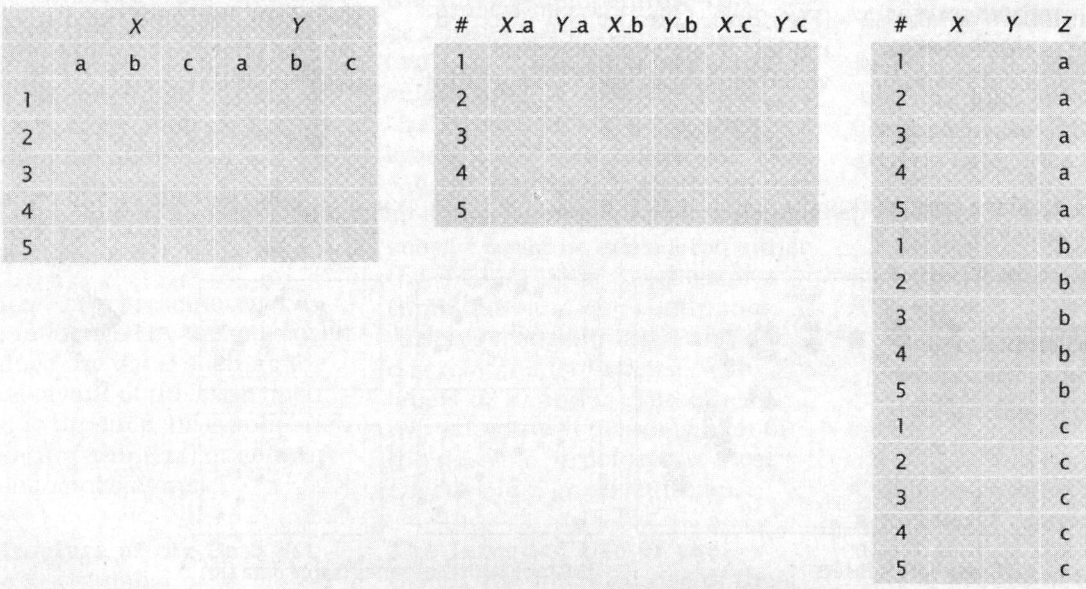

variables—not unlike a chart of distances between cities.

Line plots, which are, in essence, sequenced scatter plots with connected dots, reveal the evolution of one variable versus another, typically time. Multiline plots compare the evolution of several variables expressed in the same units, so they can be graphed along the same scale, while multipanel plots relate the evolution of several variables along different scales.

Conclusion

The methodology we developed to help engineers, scientists, and managers chose the "right graph" for their contents, audience, and purpose proved successful in the companies where we introduced it. Training participants, many of whom graph data daily for analysis and regularly for publication, found it simple, innovative, and useful.

Still, the usefulness of the selection table depends largely on the relevance of the proposed graph types for the intended audience. We believe the success of our training programs comes partly from adapting each time the repertoire of graph types and the corresponding selection table to the specific graphing needs of the client company.

Fig. 3. A simple two-entry table to select candidate graph types on the basis of the structure of the data set (columns) and the research question (lines). The table can easily be extended to include more graph types.

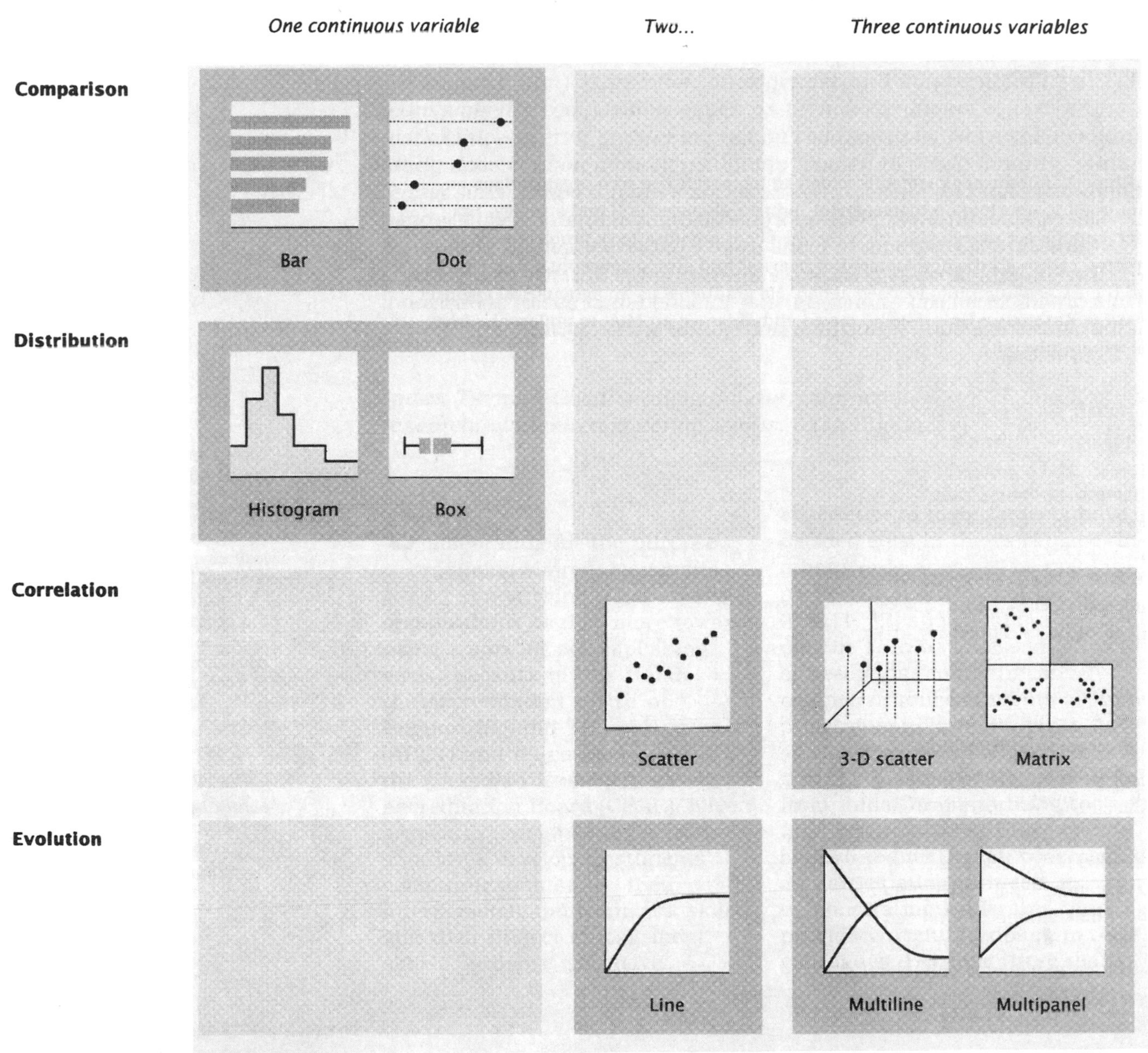

REFERENCES

[1] E. R. Tufte, *The Visual Display of Quantitative Information*. Cheshire, CT: Graphics, 1983.
[2] W. S. Cleveland, *The Elements of Graphing Data*. Pacific Grove, CA: Wadsworth & Brooks/Cole, 1985.
[3] J. Bertin, *Sémiologie Graphique*. Paris, France: Mouton-Gauthiers-Villars, 1973.
[4] L. Wilkinson, *The Grammar of Graphics*. New York: Springer-Verlag, 1999.
[5] D. Pyle, *Data Preparation for Data Mining*. San Francisco, CA: Morgan Kaufmann, 1999.
[6] S. Lambert, "Presentation graphics primer," *MacWorld*, May/June 1984.

Jean-luc Doumont (S'90–M'93–SM'00) teaches and provides advice on professional speaking, writing, and graphing. He also trains trainers and facilitates any process that requires structuring and effective communication. For over 15 years, he has helped audiences of all ages, backgrounds, and nationalities structure their thoughts and construct their communication. He graduated as an engineer from the Université Catholique de Louvain,and obtained a Ph.D. in applied physics from Stanford University.

Philippe Vandenbroeck consults widely in high-tech research organizations on data quality, information management, project management, and strategy. His interventions are designed to increase the client organization's problem-solving repertoire through the development of relevant and strong conceptual frameworks and their translation into focused action. He graduated as an agricultural engineer from the Katholieke Universiteit Leuven and obtained an M.A. in philosophy from the same university.

Table Construction: Do's and Don'ts*

EVA DUKES

Abstract—**A table is a tool frequently used to arrange technical data in a meaningful way. A good table summarizes information by avoiding the unnecessary repetition of unit symbols, test conditions, or other data compressible into stub, column, or spanner heads. Whereas poor table construction tends to confuse the reader, sound table construction helps readers understand the significance of technical information in a minimum of time.**

BECAUSE FAMILIARITY breeds contempt, most of us believe that we can construct a proper table without giving it much thought. Alas, this is seldom so.

Basically, a table is a simple tool for listing exact data for purposes of comparison and analysis. However, when the data are numerous and complex, table construction becomes an art: it needs refinement to attain clarity.

THE BASIC TABLE

As Voltaire once said [1], "If you would dispute with me, define your terms." In the same spirit, let us first agree on naming the parts of a table. Figure 1 [2] shows a rather simple table, comparing it with a graph. Mary Fran Buehler has compared the two by saying, "A graph may not give so much data, or such exact data, but it gives an instant picture of relationships and trends in a way that a table cannot." (Of course, a table may also show trends [3]—as when all, or most, of the figures in a column can be grouped in ascending or descending order.) Figure 2 [2] shows a more complex structure, identifying all the essential parts of a table.

The following points are important rules for constructing and reading a table:

- Information always reads *down* from the boxhead, all the way to the end of the table.
- Information should also read *down* from the stub head.
- But information controlled by the stub head reads *across*.

* A shorter version of this article was published in 1983 in *Guide for RCA Engineer Authors*, and is used courtesy of General Electric Company.

Eva Dukes is a technical writer and editor with experience in training and supervising personnel in communication skills.

THE INVISIBLE BOX

The easiest way to visualize the structure of a table is to think of it as a box. For typeset tables, or those set on the more sophisticated computer-aided publishing equipment, the box is created easily, perhaps automatically. But every table has a box structure—even if the box is not drawn, as in the typewritten or word-processed table. Drawing vertical lines is not cost effective, and even the top and bottom rules (above the boxhead and below the last line, or row, of data) are not essential. That is why many government specifications and other style guides insist that these rules be omitted.

Figure 3 is a boxless table. Underscoring has been used to differentiate the heads from the body of the table; italics, if available, may also be used for this purpose. Note that the underscore for each column head extends from the beginning of the longest word in the head (in this case, *Column*) to the end of that word; lines above or below the longest word are centered in regard to it or, in some cases, flush left to it.

The line underscoring the spanner head extends from the beginning of the longest line in the first column head it spans to the end of the last column head it spans. The spanner head itself is centered over that bar.

Styling a table with a box differs significantly in one respect from styling one without a box. In the former, column heads should be centered vertically as well as horizontally within their own boxes [3]. This vertical centering is difficult to achieve on an ordinary typewriter or word processor. In this case (the boxless table), column heads should be aligned horizontally with the bottom of the lowest column heads under the spanner head (as in figure 3). That is, the heads should be "flush bottom" in the invisible box for the header. In this way, each head is close to the data it controls.

Even in the most crowded table, there should be a space (at least one pica) between the underscores of each pair of column heads and between the underscores of the stub head and the first column head. The latter space may be a little larger than the between-column-heads spaces, which should be equalized (unless good design dictates otherwise).

Reprinted from *IEEE Trans. Prof. Comm.*, vol. 32, no. 1, pp. 36–40, March 1989.

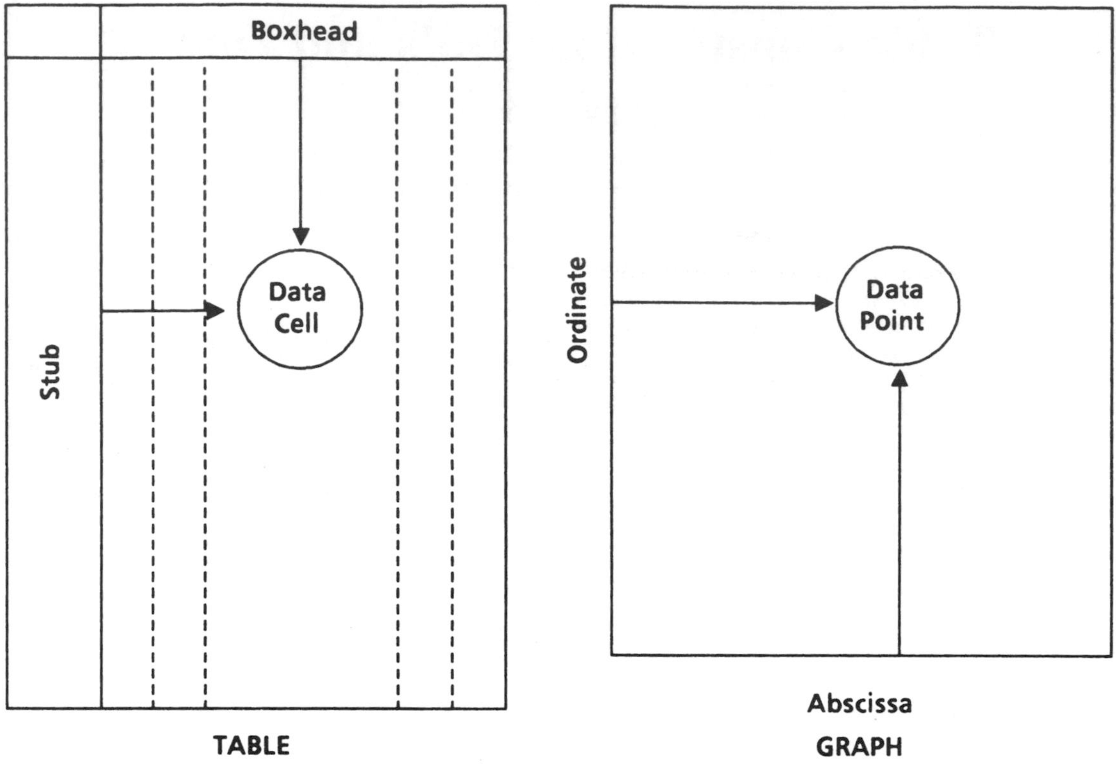

Figure 1. Structure of Tables and Graphs

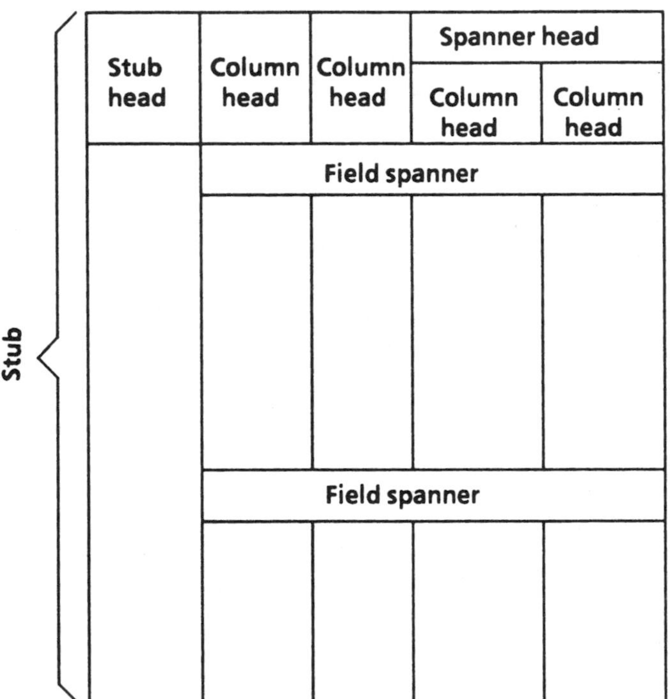

Figure 2. Major Parts of a Table

			Spanner Head	
Stub Head	Column Head	Column Head	Column Head	Column Head
		Field Spanner		
		Field Spanner		

Figure 3. The "Boxless" Table

Table 0
Temperature Constants (°C)

Liquid	Boiling Point	Freezing Point
Water	100	0
Ethylene glycol	197	-20[a]
Glycerol	290	0[b]

[a]In 44% by volume (antifreeze) solution
[b]Gradually solidifies

Figure 4. Table Footnotes

USEFUL POINTERS

Rules of Construction

As pointed out above, information always reads down from the boxhead, all the way to the end of the table; information from the stub head also reads down; information reads across from the stub column. The following examples illustrate these points:

Do this:

Liquid	BP (°C)	FP (°C)
Water	100	0
Ethylene glycol	197	−20

Don't do this:

Characteristics:	BP (°C)	FP (°C)
Water	100	0
Ethylene glycol	197	−20

Independence From Text Material

A table, like a figure, should be able to stand alone. The caption, heads, and (if necessary) footnotes should tell the whole story, in case the reader skips the surrounding text.

Avoiding Clutter

Applying the law of paucity does wonders for clarity. Therefore, never repeat a unit symbol if you don't have to.

Do this:

Boiling Point (°C)
100
197
290

Don't do this:

Boiling Point
100°C
−20°C
0°C

If the table you are constructing also lists freezing points, and especially if it is complex and has other spanner heads, you might introduce a spanner head here, too. Then you can avoid repeating °C even once.

You might do this:

Temperature Constants (°C)	
Boiling Point	*Freezing Point*

rather than this:

Boiling Point (°C)	*Freezing Point (°C)*

There are creative ways to shift material from one part of the table to another to achieve maximum paucity and clarity. It helps to ask yourself: "How much data does this description apply to, and what is the clearest way to show that?" A lengthy description that applies to a small amount of data—a few entries, perhaps, or one column—could be placed in a footnote.

Footnotes

Since the data in tables are usually numerical, many editors like to use lowercase letters to refer to footnotes (figure 4).

The footnotes themselves should be placed flush with the left margin of the table, not the left margin of the page, and directly following the table, not at the bottom of the page. That is, they fall within the box.

A footnote may be used to indicate a shift in units of measurement or in conditions:

Degree of Hardness (at 20°C)[a]
9
5 (at 10°C)
2

[a] Unless otherwise indicated.

	Amsterdam	Brussels	Frankfurt	Madrid	Paris	Rome	Vienna	Zurich
Amsterdam		126	285	1092	303	1033	752	563
Brussels	126		239	966	177	931	729	518
Frankfurt	285	239		1156	361	813	466	304
Madrid	1092	966	1156		789	1300	1494	1169
Paris	303	177	361	789		915	774	397
Rome	1033	931	813	1300	915		750	806
Vienna	752	729	466	1494	774	750		436
Zurich	563	518	304	1169	397	806	436	

Figure 5. Matrix of Distance Between Cities

Consistency

Small inconsistencies hurt the appearance of a document and may interfere with comprehension. For instance, when identical or comparable column heads appear in different form in the same table or in tables within the same document, the reader is left to wonder if the information contained in the columns is the same or different.

It is important to use a consistent convention for handling missing, inadequate, or negligible data. Many editors use the word *none* or *N/D* (no data) or leave an empty space for missing data and insert a dash (or double hyphens) for inadequate or negligible data. *N/A* may be used for *not applicable*.

Alignment

Usually, numerical data are aligned on the decimal point, or wherever the decimal point would be if one were given. In the case of numbers less than 1, insert a zero before the decimal point (0.95, not .95). It is not advisable to add zeros after the decimal point unless you known that this is warranted by the degree of accuracy of the measurement.

Legibility

Tinker analyzed the results of 238 legibility studies [4]; the following of his observations are particularly applicable to tables:

- Arabic numerals are easier to read than Roman numerals.
- Lowercase type is easier to read than all capitals type.
- Leaving a space every five or ten lines down a column aids legibility; five is better.
- The smallest type recommended is 10 points. Although 8-point type may be readable, it does not fulfill the legibility requirements for micropublishing.

If at all possible, it is best to set a table vertically rather than horizontally, so that it will fit on a right-reading page. Similarly, avoid foldouts if possible.

COMMON PITFALLS

Lack of a Stub Head

Authors often omit a head for the stub column because the entries in this column are so disparate that a common denominator is not easily found. This in itself points to a weakness in the table. If a common denominator cannot be applied—even a ''portmanteau'' word like *parameter*—you should consider revising the table.

Misuse of the Field Spanner

It makes no sense to use only one field spanner; two is the minimum. If you have only one, you are using the field spanner for information that should go into the caption or into the boxhead of the table.

The field spanner spans all column heads but should not extend into the stub column.

THE INFORMAL TABLE

Informal tables are essentially lists. Data may be arranged in tabular form to give the reader a better overview, even though the material does not lend itself to full tabular treatment. Such informal tables may have no stub column; they may merely present data for comparison under adjacent column heads, such as the following [5]:

Advantages	*Disadvantages*

Much of the advice given above applies to informal tables as well as to formal tables—for instance, the principles of alignment, legibility, and so forth.

THE MATRIX

The matrix is a special type of table that makes each item in the stub column interact with each item in the column heads.

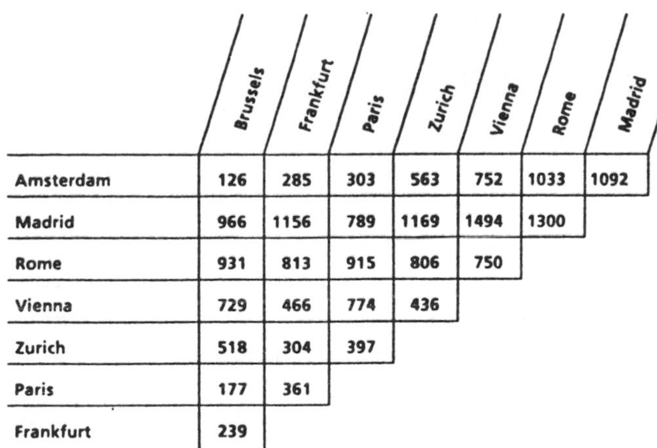

	Brussels	Frankfurt	Paris	Zurich	Vienna	Rome	Madrid
Amsterdam	126	285	303	563	752	1033	1092
Madrid	966	1156	789	1169	1494	1300	
Rome	931	813	915	806	750		
Vienna	729	466	774	436			
Zurich	518	304	397				
Paris	177	361					
Frankfurt	239						

Figure 6. Simplified Matrix

	Dollars	Yen	Francs	Pounds
Dollars		125	6.08	0.563
Yen	0.00803		0.0490	0.000454
Francs	0.164	20.4		0.0926
Pounds	1.78	220	10.8	

Figure 7. Nonsymmetrical Matrix

In figure 5, a matrix of distances between cities, the same entries may be found in the stub column and in the column heads. The diagonal block of entries is blank because, obviously, the distance between Amsterdam and Amsterdam, or Paris and Paris, is zero. Each entry occurs twice—for instance, under both Brussels—Frankfurt and Frankfurt—Brussels; therefore, this matrix can be read across and down *or* down and across.

A simpler presentation of the same information is shown in figure 6. This matrix has no blank spaces and no repetitions (at the cost of having a peculiar stepped appearance). The economy has been effected by a rearrangement of the stub and column heads.

Similar matrixes can be drawn for, say, currency conversion factors (figure 7). In a case like this, however, there is no repetition of data, because dollars expressed in yen is not the same as yen expressed in dollars.

Thus the matrix fits the definition of a table: an arrangement of data that makes the data easier to read and to understand.

REFERENCES

1. Voltaire, F. M. A., private communication (via an instructor who knew Voltaire's writings well).
2. Buehler, M. F., "Table Design—When the Writer/Editor Communicates Graphically," *Proceedings* 27th ITCC, 1980, pp. G-69 to G-73.
3. Arnold, C. K., "The Construction of Tables," *IRE Trans. Engineering Writing and Speech EWS-5,* 1 (1962), pp. 9-14.
4. Tinker, M. A., *Legibility of Print,* Ames, IA: Iowa State University Press, 1963.
5. Buehler, M. F., "Report Construction: Tables," *IEEE PC 20,* 1 (1977), pp. 29-32.

Safety Labels: What to Put in Them, How to Write Them, and Where to Place Them

CHRISTOPHER VELOTTA

Abstract—**Current standards developed by organizations like the American National Standards Institute and the Westinghouse Electric Corporation can help technical writers design effective safety labels. According to such standards, safety labels should contain a signal word, a hazard alert symbol, a specific color, a symbol or pictograph, a hazard identification, a description of the result of ignoring the warning, and a description of how to avoid the hazard. In addition, the safety label should be clear, concise, forceful, descriptive, and well-organized. Finally, safety labels usually should be placed in the operator manual and on the product, and they should appear before the operator encounters the hazard. Considerations involved with this placement include reading distance, viewing angle, and available space on the product.**

WITH legal precedents that often seem to contradict themselves, the consumer products industry is facing a dilemma concerning how to construct effective safety labels and how to avoid product liability suits. For example, Joseph G. Manta cites many cases where the courts have found that a failure to warn was not the *proximate* cause of injury; therefore, the companies in question were not liable for the injuries: "plaintiff has the affirmative burden of establishing causation between the failure to warn and the injury." According to Manta [1], the focus can now be diverted "from the defendant and its product to the plaintiff and his conduct and knowledge."

However, Harry M. Philo quotes The Metal Forming Subcommittee of the Machine Tool Builders Association's Accident Prevention and Safety Committee as reporting, "The proper use of warning signs can also reduce possible exposure to product liability suits." Philo himself asserts that [2]

> If there is a failure to warn, then in every instance that failure is a cause of the injury or death complained of unless the injured person was attempting suicide, was blind or blindly intoxicated, or was intentionally undertaking an unreasonable risk.

Although he does not cite specific cases, Philo argues that the law should be moving toward holding the defendant liable in instances of failure to warn, but he believes that "neither lawyers, judges, nor the law are up to date when it comes to the law and warnings."

Chris Velotta is a technical writer at NCR Corporation, E&M—Wichita.

This unstable legal climate does little to guide a company in the process of constructing effective safety labels and in avoiding product liability suits. Current research in this area seems to offer the most hope for a standard set of guidelines to follow. For example, Michael Ursic's study of 91 undergraduates showed that a product with a safety label projects a significantly safer image than a product without a safety label: "Therefore, it seems that a safety warning, instead of causing a person to perceive a product as more dangerous, may cause an individual to believe that the product is safer." This finding should help reassure marketing specialists who are worried that putting safety labels on a product will cause consumers to perceive that product as hazardous [3].

Although this development is encouraging, because now safety labels are thought to enhance a product's image, the rest of the problem is yet to be solved. What techniques can we use to ensure the effectiveness of safety labels? In the previously mentioned study, Ursic manipulated three variables—pictograms, signal words, and capital letters—to find out if they affect a consumer's perceptions of a product and also to see if they increased a consumer's recall of a safety label. The results of these manipulations showed that the subjects did not demonstrate any increased perceptions of product safety and effectiveness or any increased recall of the safety label. Unfortunately, these results do not offer any immediate guidelines to follow, but Ursic is quick to point out that a great deal more research needs to be done in this area, such as in the effects of color or in the way a safety label affects the way a consumer uses the product.

The potential contribution that such research could offer to those who design safety labels seems boundless. For example, the American National Standards Institute (ANSI) has already developed a set of guidelines for constructing effective safety labels. In addition, many corporations have developed their own suggestions for designing safety labels. One such organization is Westinghouse Electric Corporation (WEC).

To assist those who must design effective safety labels, this paper discusses "Specifications for Product Safety Signs and Labels," ANSI Draft Z535.4, 1984 [4] because ANSI is widely respected in the consumer products industry and because many organizations follow its standards.

Reprinted from *IEEE Trans. Prof. Comm.*, vol. PC-30, no. 3, pp. 121–126, September 1987.

This discussion is supplemented with material from the WEC *Product Safety Label Handbook: DANGER, WARNING, CAUTION* [5], which corroborates the ANSI standards in many instances. The WEC handbook contains a disclaimer that bears repeating, and it applies to both the quoted material from the handbook and to any other suggestions contained in this article:

> Westinghouse makes no representations or warranties, express or implied, including warranties of merchantability or fitness for purpose as to the accuracy, completeness, or legal sufficiency of the recommendations or information contained herein. Westinghouse assumes no liability arising out of any use of this book.

Also presented are sample safety labels from The Charles Machine Works, Inc. (CMW), because they were developed after much research into current practices and because they exemplify the proper use of ANSI guidelines.

Because constructing effective safety labels is a complex process, I must limit my discussion to a few main stages of the process. The areas covered include what to put in safety labels, how to write them, and where to put them. Other stages that are worth further investigation include the identification of hazards, the specific layout and design of safety labels, and the differences between safety labels in the manual and safety labels on the product itself.

WHAT TO PUT IN SAFETY LABELS

Before actually assembling the ingredients of an effective safety label, the technical writer should first determine what levels of warnings to use (DANGER, WARNING, CAUTION, or NOTICE) and what situations to use them in. These decisions should be easier to make if the technical writer uses the following definitions from the September 1986 revisions [6] to the ANSI Z535.4 Draft, "Specifications for Product Safety Signs and Labels":

- DANGER: indicates an imminently hazardous situation which, if not avoided, will result in death or serious injury. This signal word is to be limited to the most extreme situations.
- WARNING: indicates a potentially hazardous situation which, if not avoided, could result in death or serious injury.
- CAUTION: indicates a hazardous situation which, if not avoided, may result in minor or moderate injury. It may also be used to alert against unsafe practices.*

Based on these definitions, the difference between DANGER and WARNING is in the possibility for occurrence and in the extremity of the hazard. For example, the hazard is *imminent* in the definition of DANGER but is only *potential* in the definition of WARNING. In addition, death or serious injury *will* result in the definition of DANGER but they only *could* result in the definition of WARNING. DANGER's definition also indicates that it should only be used in "the most extreme situations"; however, the definition of WARNING does not carry this restriction. To see this difference, compare the following safety labels developed by CMW:

> DANGER: TURNING SAW can kill or cut off arm or leg. STAY AWAY.
> WARNING: MOVING PARTS can cut off hand or fingers. DO NOT TOUCH.

Whereas both safety labels warn against serious hazards, the danger from a turning saw is more emphatically threatening and more extreme than the danger from moving parts in general. Therefore, DANGER is the appropriate choice for the turning saw, and WARNING is used correctly for moving parts.

Compared to DANGER and WARNING, CAUTION discusses minor injuries and warns "against unsafe practices." For example, the following safety label from CMW accomplishes both objectives:

> CAUTION: FALL POSSIBLE. People may slip or trip and fall from operator's area, causing broken bones. KEEP AREA CLEAN.

The injury being described here is minor compared to a lost life or hand as described in the previous DANGER and WARNING examples. In addition, this CAUTION warns against the unsafe practice of having a messy work area.

Finally, NOTICE is used only with alerts that warn against property damage. NOTICE is inappropriate when any type of potential injury is involved. The following example from CMW shows an appropriate use of a NOTICE:

> NOTICE: If engine does not start in three tries, find out what is wrong. Correct the problem. Overheating the starter can damage it.

Using these definitions as a guide, the technical writer can now decide what to put into individual safety labels.

Seven basic elements of an effective safety label have been described by WEC in the *Product Safety Label Handbook: DANGER, WARNING, CAUTION:*

- The signal word
- The hazard alert symbol
- The color
- The symbols and pictographs

* DANGER or WARNING should not be considered for property damage accidents unless personal injury risk appropriate to these levels is also involved. CAUTION (and NOTICE) are permitted for property-damage-only accident hazards and for unsafe practices.

- The hazard identification
- The result of ignoring the warning
- The description of avoiding the hazard

Signal Word

The four signal words listed in the handbook are DANGER, WARNING, CAUTION, and NOTICE. In their respective safety labels, these words are larger than the rest and are the first words in the label. This word catches the operator's attention and orients him or her to the possibility and extremity of the hazard. By defining this set of words and advising the operator to learn them, the technical writer will be helping the operator to easily recognize the severity of individual hazards. Based on the nature of the hazard, the technical writer should use the signal words consistently. For example, after reading a few safety labels and the definitions of the signal words, operators will quickly become aware that DANGER signals imminent and extreme hazards while CAUTION signals minor injuries and unsafe practices.

Hazard Alert Symbol

Immediately preceding the signal word is the hazard alert symbol, which consists of an exclamation point inside a triangle, ⚠. This symbol should be used with the signal words DANGER, WARNING, and CAUTION but not with NOTICE. The symbol is recognized internationally and is a reminder to be alert. It combines with the signal word to attract the operator's attention to the safety label and the hazard being warned against.

Color

Encompassing both the hazard alert symbol and the signal word is the color field. (In a NOTICE, the color field includes only the signal word because the hazard alert symbol is not used.) Each level of safety label has its own distinct color. According to both the WEC handbook [5] and the ANSI Z535.4 Draft [4], DANGER should have a red background with white lettering, WARNING should have an orange background with black lettering, and CAUTION should have a yellow background with black lettering. The handbook adds that a NOTICE should have a blue background with white lettering. This consistent color-coding increases the operator's ease in distinguishing among the different levels of hazard being warned against in an operator manual.

Symbols and Pictographs

The technical writer should also add an appropriate symbol or pictograph to give the operator an immediate idea of the hazard. The symbol or pictograph should consist of a universally recognizable graphic that displays the potential injury involved with the hazard. Designing an effective set of symbols or pictographs is a complicated process that is best left to experts in symbol recognition. Experts have developed symbols for many common hazards, and technical writers can incorporate these symbols in their own safety labels. One such set of symbols is in the WEC handbook. ANSI Z535.3, "Specifications for Safety Symbols," also presents guidelines for symbol use.

Hazard Identification

The next task in constructing a safety label is to describe the hazard. This description should be "the first verbal message following the signal word." Bold type and all capital letters can emphasize the type of hazard being warned against [5]. Some examples from CMW safety labels include ROLLOVER POSSIBLE, DEADLY GASES, and HOT PARTS. This segment can be its own sentence (as in ROLLOVER POSSIBLE), or can be part of a sentence (as in "HOT PARTS can cause burns"); but it should always come first in this section of the safety label. Therefore, the technical writer should not say, "Burns can be caused by HOT PARTS," but rather "HOT PARTS can cause burns."

Results of Ignoring the Warning

Bold type and upper- and lower-case letters can make this section easy to read, and it should not be separated from the first segment of the verbal message. It tells the operator what harm a rollover, for example, will cause or what harm deadly gases or hot parts will cause. For example, in a CMW safety label, "DEADLY GASES" is followed by "Breathing exhaust gases can cause sickness or death," which describes the result of ignoring the warning.

Description of How to Avoid the Hazard

A final and important element in a safety label, this segment should be separate from the rest of the verbal message; it can either start a new sentence or come after a skipped line. In addition, this segment can contain either bold or regular type. At CMW, for example, bold type and all capital letters were used:

> DANGER: DEADLY GASES. Breathing exhaust gases can cause sickness or death. BREATHE FRESH AIR.

In this example, "BREATHE FRESH AIR" describes how to avoid the hazard of deadly gases.

HOW TO WRITE SAFETY LABELS

After deciding what ingredients to include in a safety label, the technical writer should decide how to write the verbal message. The writing style should allow the technical writer

- To say as much as possible in as few words as possible
- To say it forcefully and directly
- To say it in a way that is as well-organized as possible

Concise Messages

To say as much as possible in a safety label that has limited available space, the technical writer should first be sure not to waste any words. Only then will there be enough room to effectively communicate the warning. For example, the WEC handbook offers a helpful guideline in this area: avoid using adjectives unless they provide crucial information in the safety label. Most writers are already familiar with this principle; an example is *very,* which is commonly known to carry little meaning and is, therefore, not often used. Another guideline from the handbook describes the proper use of prepositions: do not use strings of words where one preposition will convey the same meaning. For example, *in the event of* does not convey any more meaning than *if*; therefore, *if* should be used instead.

Another way of pruning unnecessary words is to write in a telegraphic style. The WEC handbook suggests usually eliminating the articles *a, an,* and *the* in addition to eliminating pronouns such as *that, this,* and *they* and all forms of the verb *to be*. This technique is illustrated in the following safety label from CMW:

> CAUTION: HOT PARTS can cause burns. DO NOT TOUCH UNTIL COOL.

Four words could be added to this safety label by including the missing article, the missing form of the verb *to be,* and the missing pronouns. However, the following rewrite shows that these insertions do not add any meaning to the safety label.

> CAUTION: *THE* HOT PARTS can cause burns. DO NOT TOUCH *THEM* UNTIL *THEY ARE* COOL.

When the operator needs quick access to the information, as in safety labels, every word should carry meaning. Therefore, the telegraphic style is appropriate for writing safety labels.

Forceful Messages

Not only should every word carry meaning, but the entire message should be forceful. Writing the message in active voice helps ensure that the message comes across forcefully; there is a clear connection between the cause of the hazard and the effect of the hazard. The following example from CMW shows an effective use of active voice:

> CAUTION: BATTERY ACID can cause burns. DO NOT SPILL.

Writing the first sentence of this safety label in passive voice would add two unnecessary words to the message and would reduce the force with which the message comes across to the operator:

> DANGER: Burns can *be* caused *by* BATTERY ACID. DO NOT SPILL.

Using strong auxiliary verbs will supplement the active voice and will help ensure that the operator knows the true nature of the hazard. For example, if a hazard "will" happen as the result of a certain action, the auxiliary *will* should be used as opposed to *may,* and *can* should be used as opposed to *could* to increase the forcefulness of the message. Finally, technical writers should avoid using contractions because, for example, *don't* is much less forceful than *do not.*

Direct Messages

In addition to being forceful, safety labels should be direct. A direct message starts with appropriate word choice. Nouns should carry precise and easy-to-understand meanings. For example, in "LEARN HOW TO USE ALL CONTROLS" from a CMW manual, *CONTROLS* is the correct choice because it encompasses the entire range of levers, pedals, and switches that an operator should know about. Using jargon can also cloud the issue and diminish the directness of the communication; *machine* is much more direct and easy to understand than *modularmatic trenching unit.*

When telling the operator what action to perform, the technical writer should choose verbs with precisely the intended meaning. For example, "FEEL FOR LEAKS WITH CARDBOARD" could mislead operators into using their hands to *feel* for leaks and could leave operators wondering what to do with the cardboard. The CMW version, "CHECK FOR LEAKS WITH CARDBOARD," eliminates this ambiguity because of correct choice of the verb. In addition, the technical writer should choose the simplest form of the verb: *utilize* and *recognize* do not say anything more than *use* and *know,* and the operator will more readily understand the latter, more direct verbs.

Choosing the most precise modifiers can also increase the directness of a safety label. In an example from CMW, the true nature of the hazard is clear and direct: "Striking *electric* lines may cause death." Rewriting this warning with a less precise modifier shows the ineffectiveness of such ambiguous constructions: "Striking utility lines may cause death." The operator may have no idea that electricity flows through the lines and may think instead that water flows through the lines, which would be a much less severe hazard.

The technical writer should also strive for detailed descriptions of the results of the hazards. Operators are more likely to avoid moving parts if they read the direct warning from CMW that such parts "can cut off hand or fingers" than if they read the indirect rewrite that "MOVING PARTS can cause serious injury."

Organized Messages

One final stage for the technical writer is to organize the safety label. The previously discussed order of the seven elements of a safety label shows a progression from general (signal word) to specific (how to avoid the hazard). The WEC handbook goes on to suggest that using a chronological order will help the operator understand how to avoid the hazard. A safety label from a CMW manual illustrates this concept: "LEARN HOW TO USE ALL

CONTROLS and OPERATE ONLY FROM OPERATOR'S POSITION." After reading this line, operators should be aware that they ought to learn how to use the controls before operating the machine.

Another way to ensure effective organization is to pay attention to line breaks and to keep the style consistent from one sentence to the next. A line like "TURNING SAW can cut off arm or leg" should appear all on one line to invest the communication with the proper impact; and "STAY AWAY" should not be broken after "STAY" so that operators do not misunderstand and think that they should stay near the hazard.

Finally, the technical writer should use parallel grammatical constructions throughout the safety label to set up a recognizable pattern for the operator to follow. For example, the following CMW safety label exhibits a consistent use of active voice, imperative mood:

> CAUTION: HOT PARTS can cause burns. DO NOT TOUCH UNTIL COOL.

Changing the second sentence to passive voice, indicative mood, decreases the label's readability and shows inconsistent organization, which is harder for the operator to follow:

> CAUTION: HOT PARTS can cause burns. THEY SHOULD NOT BE TOUCHED UNTIL COOL.

WHERE TO PUT SAFETY LABELS

Typically safety labels appear in two places:

- In the operator manual
- On the product

When placing a safety label in an operator manual, the technical writer should determine when and where a hazard could occur and then include a safety label immediately before the section of the instructions that deals with the hazardous situation. Placing a safety label on the product involves that consideration plus several others, such as where the operator will be located in relation to the safety label and the available space on the product.

Placement of safety labels depends a great deal on the sequence of steps needed to operate the product. To ensure that the operator will see a safety label before encountering a hazard, the technical writer should think chronologically through the operation procedure. If technical writers rely on what they think they know about using the product or on memory to identify potential hazards, "shop blindness" can cause them to gloss over some potentially hazardous situations. Such omissions can be avoided if the technical writer actually performs the operation and takes notes on every step.

After defining the hazards, the technical writer usually should locate a spot close to each hazard and then place a safety label in those places. In this way, the operator will be able to observe the label while using or maintaining the product. However, some instances require that the operator observes the safety label before coming close to the hazard. For example, a safety label warning against breathing exhaust gases should not be placed on an exhaust pipe but on a part of the machine that is visible and at a safe distance from the exhaust gases. Some instances require a pair of labels: one outside the hazardous area and another that functions as a reminder inside the hazardous area—for instance, a hazardous voltage warning on the back of a stereo amplifier and the complementary warning inside the stereo amplifier.

Technical writers should also consider the operator's position in relation to the safety label. Such factors as reading distance and viewing angle can affect whether or not the operator can easily see the safety label in time to avoid the hazard. As noted, the safety label should not require the operator to get too close to the hazard; therefore, the technical writer should determine how large to make a safety label so that the operator can read it at a safe distance. Fortunately, handbooks such as the one produced by WEC offer tables that specify reading distances for different sizes of safety labels. To help provide a proper viewing angle, the technical writer should place the safety label so that the operator can look directly at it and have a perpendicular viewing angle. The farther the viewing angle varies from perpendicular, the less readable the safety label becomes. In fact, the WEC handbook states that "A viewing angle more than 60 percent from the perpendicular will decrease readability."

In the rare instance that the product offers the exact amount of space needed for a safety label of appropriate size, the technical writer can consider this stage of the process completed. However, more often than not the product will offer either too much or too little space. Too much space is not a difficult problem to deal with; it is only important to remember not to try to make the safety label fit the available space. Instead, writers should follow the previously referred to tables, which specify safety label sizes for various reading distances. One exception is the product which is used under inadequate lighting conditions, for which the safety label may need to be larger to increase readability.

If the product offers too little space for a readable and complete safety label, the technical writer should make certain modifications to the safety label. The techniques described so far should help ensure that the safety label contains all the essential information in the minimum space. However, if space is extremely limited, the technical writer should not sacrifice readability for information. If operators cannot read the safety label, they will not receive any information at all. Therefore, when available space requires that some information be left out, the technical writer can create a readable safety label that warns of the hazard and its effects and then refers the operator to the operator manual for further information about the hazard.

CONCLUSION

Although the courts still have not conclusively defined what constitutes an effective safety label, current standards can help guide technical writers in designing safety labels. Organizations such as ANSI and WEC have developed such standards, but further research in this area can provide even more support for constructing effective safety labels. In spite of the fact that safety labels are–of necessity–short, their construction is a complex process. Stages of this process involve including the appropriate information, writing in an appropriate style, and placing the safety label in an appropriate location.

REFERENCES

1. Manta, J. G., "Proximate Causation in Failure to Warn Cases: The Plaintiff's Achilles Heel," *For the Defense,* October 1984, p. 11.
2. Philo, H. M., "New Dimensions in the Tortious Failure to Warn," *Association of Trial Lawyers of America,* 1981, p. 17.
3. Ursic, M., "The Impact of Safety Warnings on Perception and Memory," *Human Factors,* 26:3, 1983, p. 680.
4. "Specifications for Product Safety Signs and Labels," *Draft ANSI Z535.4,* August 1984, p. 11.
5. *Product Safety Label Handbook: DANGER, WARNING, CAUTION,* Westinghouse Electric Corporation, Trafford, PA, 1981.
6. The ASNI Z535 Committee voted for these revisions in its meeting of September 16-18, 1986.

Editing Math: What to Do With the Symbols

BARRY W. BURTON

Abstract—**When faced with mathematical material, editors with limited technical training often address only superficial concerns such as format and punctuation. A few simple guidelines, however, can help us do a more complete job. We first delete superfluous symbols, then make certain that the remaining symbols are defined properly, redefined where necessary, and used according to the rules of grammar.**

WHAT often makes many ordinarily courageous, capable technical editors trained in the liberal arts cower in humility and submissiveness? Math. Technical editors are faced daily with reports, articles, presentations, and other material packed with mathematical symbols and expressions. And many editors have a distressingly poor background in mathematics. This deficiency often leads to a feeling of inadequacy that may prevent the editor from delving too deeply into the mathematical portions of the document for fear of making a mistake that could mislead the reader or hold the writer up to ridicule. As a result, some may concentrate only on formatting the displayed expressions to conform to the organization's style guide (if one even exists). Some may address nothing more than punctuation. In either case, the job may fall short of professional standards.

But how can we do a more professional job without going back to school and getting a degree in mathematics? Quite easily, in fact. Many of the issues raised by the use of math symbols allow themselves to be addressed by editors with minimal mathematical background. Here I will discuss what to do with mathematical symbols. Once problems with math symbols have been cleaned up, many of the other math problems become more manageable. The meaning of the math may sometimes be beyond us, but the editing can be done proficiently and professionally if we approach it systematically.

The discussion below briefly describes four simple steps in addressing the symbols in a mathematical document: eliminating superfluous symbols, defining the remaining symbols, redefining the symbols where necessary, and using the symbols in parallel constructions. Formatting of displayed expressions, punctuation, and fitting expressions grammatically into sentences are not discussed. These concerns are covered by definite and easily applied rules found in many style manuals, though those rules differ from source to source. Some very popular style guides, such as *The Chicago Manual of Style* [1] and *Mathematics into Type* [2], adequately deal with these subjects.

All the examples used here are real, taken from scientific journals. They were remarkably easy to find, evidence that these easy-to-fix problems are widespread.

Barry W. Burton is with Burton Literary Services, Los Alamos, NM 87544.
IEEE Log Number 9035636.

Delete Unnecessary Symbols

In most organizations, policy dictates that the author is responsible for the accuracy and relevance of the information—math included—in his or her document. It is, however, up to the editors to enforce this policy. They must ensure that the mathematical symbols and expressions used are relevant to the discussion and help achieve the writer's goals. It makes no sense to spend time editing a document to make it readable if some of the material should never have been included to begin with.

An easy way for the editor to begin is by deleting unnecessary symbols. Many sources, including mathematicians themselves, agree that writers of mathematical material should use symbols only when necessary [3], [4]. Writers are often so wrapped up in the formal language of mathematics that they get carried away and throw in symbols they don't need. Superfluous symbols cluttering the page can make the text forbidding to nonspecialists, confuse other workers in the writer's field, and distract the reader from the document's important points.

Mathematical symbols are just names of things or abbreviations of those names. For instance, a writer may use the abbreviation $s_s(f)$ to represent the speed of sound in a fluid instead of writing it out longhand every time the term is needed. This shorthand can be a useful space saver when the term is used more than a few times. But if the term is used only once, inclusion of the symbol is gratuitous and, without a verbal definition in context, can be confusing. A symbol shouldn't be used at all unless it appears often enough to make it a worthwhile shortcut for the reader to learn it. Introducing gratuitous symbols can even be misleading: the extra emphasis placed on an idea when a symbol is assigned to it suggests that the thing being symbolized is more important that it may really be. Such misplaced emphasis can distract the reader from the writer's point.

One-time symbols are easy to find. By listing all the math symbols during the first editing pass, then checking each one off when it appears a second time, the editor can

- spot gratuitous symbols,
- keep track of the definitions of symbols, and
- find symbols that aren't defined at all.

An editor doesn't need a complete understanding of mathematical material to identify unnecessary symbols. This dictionary definition exemplifies a typical problem:

A topological space is a set X along with a collection T of

Reprinted from *IEEE Trans. Prof. Comm.*, vol. 33, no. 2, pp. 62–65, June 1990.

distinguished subsets of X called *open* sets which satisfies: 1) each member of X is contained in some open set, 2) the intersection of two open sets is open, and 3) the union of a subcollection of open sets is open.

Here the first symbol, X, represents a particular set. That symbol appears twice more in the passage, distinguishing the set X from all other sets and avoiding confusion in the discussion. Just as each person has a name that sets him or her apart from everyone else, so this set is distinguished by its name, X. The reader doesn't care, however, what a particular set is called if the name isn't needed to show that it's unique. As far as the editor should be concerned, the important thing about X as a symbol is that it's used more than once. The introduction of X as a symbol in this example is fully justified because it's needed more than once and serves as a useful shorthand.

On the other hand, in the same paragraph the symbol T identifies a collection of special subsets called open sets. An editor need not even know what a distinguished subset or an open set is; he or she should note only that the symbol T is used once to define something and is never seen again. Readers shouldn't be asked to expend any more energy than necessary, so they shouldn't be required to learn the definition of T if that knowledge isn't going to help them understand the material.

One-time symbols such as T in the example above can usually be deleted without any loss of meaning and without confusion. At other times, the grammatical structure of the sentence requires that a phrase or even the whole sentence be rewritten. In either case, the correction should be fairly simple.

Just because a symbol appears only once doesn't necessarily mean it's superfluous. This expression is a good example: "Because the mesh is fine enough to approximate the derivative, $\partial u/\partial x$, both elements described above give about the same shear stress." A partial derivative is usually identified by a "curly d," ∂, as in $\partial u/\partial x$, but an editor who is unfamiliar with the notation may want to delete the $\partial u/\partial x$ in this case as superfluous. Discussion with the author, however, just might reveal that the $\partial u/\partial x$ is needed to keep the reader from confusing this particular derivative from some other one, perhaps $\partial w/\partial x$, or from the corresponding regular derivative, given by du/dx. Such misunderstandings often result from the editor's imperfect mathematical background. No rule is foolproof, but one-time symbols almost always prove to be gratuitous. If the $\partial u/\partial x$ in this example serves only to indicate that the derivative is a partial one, the sentence could be rewritten to make that point without the symbol being used.

The most common type of unnecessary symbol usually appears in a construction similar to the following:

In order to study the properties of multilayer shielding, we put a source in an iron cyclinder and placed it at a distance $d = 40$ cm from the wall in a cubic tank filled with pure water.

Scientific writing often contains this kind of tautology, which might be called a "mathematical stutter." The word is first spelled out, then given as a symbol in a mathematical relation. In this example, the author assigns the symbol d to distance, giving "... a distance $d = 40$ cm ..." An editor who is alert to the mathematical stutter can easily delete the symbol and recast the phrase as "... and placed it 40 cm from the wall ... ."

Define the Symbols

Once the confusion of superfluous symbols has been eliminated, the editor must ensure that the remaining symbols are defined properly. The following excerpt illustrates how unidentified symbols can render an equation ineffective:

The frictional pressure difference ΔP_f in the return tube is

$$\Delta P_f = \rho v^2 F \frac{L}{2D} .$$

This passage tells us that the frictional pressure difference is denoted by ΔP_f and that the writer persumably knows how to calculate it. But we can't calculate it, and neither can the readers, at least not with only the information at hand. The writer's thoughts would be clearer were she to explain the meanings of the symbols in the formula, in this case, that ρ is the fluid density, v is the liquid velocity in the tube, L/D is the length-to-diameter ratio of the tube, and F is a friction factor. By defining the variables, the writer would not only demonstrate that she knows what she is doing but also make the mathematics more accessible to the readers.

Sometimes a symbol almost always represents the same quantity, such as m for mass, v for velocity, or ρ for density. But just because a symbol has a standard definition doesn't mean that the writer is using it in that sense. Even when all the symbols in a document are universally known, the author still must identify them, partly because not all readers know the standard definitions of all the symbols they might see and partly because they can never be sure whether the writer means for the symbols to represent the standard quantities or some other quantities unique to that document. For instance, most technical editors would recognize the equation $W = \int F\, ds$ as the definition of physical work, W, where F is the force and ds is the infinitesimal distance over which the force is applied. A writer might think it unnecessary to explain such a self-evident equation, but some readers need to be reminded and others need to be reassured that this is really the familiar work equation and not something else that just happens to look like it. Symbols, no matter how familiar, should always be defined.

Redefine the Symbols

We have all seen documents filled with such a proliferation of symbols that we can't keep them straight. It's not just us. The readers, even other mathematicians, have the same problem. Many symbols have more than one meaning, and writers often attach entirely new definitions to familiar symbols. In some long or complicated documents, a single symbol can represent different quantities in different contexts.

Sometimes a symbol introduced near the beginning of a document doesn't reappear until many pages later. Just because a symbol is defined early on doesn't guarantee that readers will remember that definition when they finally see it again. Also, many readers jump from one section to another, skipping the material in between, looking for specific information. Since they don't read the entire document in the usual front-to-back way, they miss many symbol definitions. The editor must help the readers recognize symbols wherever they find them.

A glossary of symbols can to some extent mitigate the confusion. Glossary definitions, however, are necessarily short (and therefore incomplete) and, relegated to a separate part of the document, taken out of context. Besides, if a given symbol has several meanings, a glossary can't tell the readers which meaning is used on which page.

An editor can solve some of these problems by using what might be called "strategic redundancy," that is, by redefining symbols at important locations throughout the document. A location can be "important" when

- the symbol is first used,
- the symbol is reintroduced after a long intervening discussion, or
- the symbol is redefined to represent a new quantity.

It's not easy to say just how large a gap between appearances of a symbol is tolerable. It depends partly on how well known the symbol is. Some symbols, those having standard definitions, for instance, can be defined only on their first appearance with no trouble later on; others may need to be redefined several times. Consultation with the author (often several consultations) can provide answers to many editorial questions about usage of certain symbols in a given scientific field. As a rule of thumb, though, if the editor, as advocate for the reader, needs to be reminded what a symbol means, it might be time to redefine it.

We seek not merely to redefine a symbol but to do it so subtly that the reader doesn't realize its being redefined. For example, without being too obvious one can write "the C^1 norm $\|f\|$ is small" or "both the matrix T and its Hermitian conjugate T^* are zero." In the first case, we managed to sneak in a redefinition of a previously defined $\|f\|$; in the second case, we inserted a reminder that the universal notation for the Hermitian conjugate of a matrix uses an asterisk. By applying a little thought and attention to consistency and context in which the symbols appear—just as one does with verbal phrases—an editor can redefine most symbols without attracting much attention.

Use the Symbols in Parallel

The versatility of modern mathematics can be attributed to its symbolic nature. That same symbolism, however, readily leads to abuses of the underlying grammar, and without proper grammar the math can become incomprehensible. Symbolic notation requires parallelism for the same reason that verbal phrases do: the underlying grammatical structure should support the overt meaning.

Some common symbols can be one of several parts of speech depending on how they fit into a sentence. Problems with the grammar of symbols occur most often when the writer uses a symbol twice in the same sentence without regard to changes in its position (and hence its part of speech) [4]. The difference is usually the presence or absence of the verb "to be." For example, the symbol $=$ is pronounced either "equal to" or "is equal to," the symbol $>$ is pronounced either "greater than" or "is greater than," and the symbol $\in$ is pronounced either "in" or "is in." Just which interpretation is read into a symbol depends on its position in the sentence.

This phrase exemplifies the problem: "For $x > y$, Farber showed that $u > v$." When the symbols are spelled out, this sentence reads, "For x greater than y, Farber showed that u is greater than v." Here we pronounce the symbol $>$ as both an adjective and a verb in the same sentence. The ideal version of this sentence would use the same part of speech in both places; that is, the verbal definitions of the symbol would be parallel. Probably the simplest way to make the definitions parallel is to recast the sentence in an if-then structure. The writer could just as easily have written "according to Farber, if $x > y$, then $u > v$," which is parallel with "is greater than" used in both places. The if-then construction always leads to parallel definitions of symbols.

Another way to tackle the problem is simply to avoid it by using the symbol only once. We can write out the first clause: "For x greater than y, Farber showed that $u > v$." This trick solves the problem, but it also raises the question of why we don't just write out the entire sentence, not using any symbols at all. Avoiding symbols altogether is often an acceptable tactic in writing for the general public, but most readers of scientific material need a technical explanation, one that calls for symbols. The editor must therefore balance the precision of verbal descriptions with the conciseness of symbolic notation. The if-then construction may help us out of this dilemma, but its repeated use results in very tedious reading. Occasionally replacing one symbol in a pair with its verbal counterpart can introduce a little variety and keep the text from being too repetitive.

Correcting nonparallel constructions involving symbols implies that the editor knows how to pronounce those symbols. Learning the symbols is a simple matter of consulting reference works. Mathematical and technical dictionaries [5]–[7] and even some writing style guides [1], [8] list the most common symbols and their definitions. Unfortunately, most sources assume that the reader is already familiar with the symbols' meanings and offer only the briefest of definitions. A few, on the other hand, go into more detail. The Chemical Rubber Company's *Standard Mathematical Tables* [9] offers complete definitions of almost all the symbols an editor is ever likely to run into, although it assumes some mathematical background. Two reference works that explain a few of the most common symbols are *The Technical Editor's and Secretary's Desk Guide* [10] and *The McGraw-Hill Style Manual* [11]. Schenkman's *The Typing of Mathematics* [12] discusses in considerable detail the meanings and uses of the most common mathematical symbols. A review of these works can be time well spent for a technical editor who is unsure of his or her grasp of mathematical notation.

Summary

The lack of a rigorous mathematical background often leads technical editors to address only superficial issues such as formatting and punctuation when editing documents with many mathematical symbols embedded in the text. This practice can result in the publication of poorly edited documents. With some effort, however, editors can edit more effectively, tackling complex and pertinent issues without fear of making some apocalyptic mistake. Editors can attack the problems caused by poor use of symbols first by deleting unnecessary symbols, then by ensuring that the rest of the symbols are properly defined, redefined where necessary, and used according to the rules of grammar. By following these four easy steps, editors can clarify and focus the discussion of even a document that is replete with mathematical symbolism.

Acknowledgments

I wish to thank M. L. DeLanoy and L. C. McFarland, Los Alamos National Laboratory, for their constructive review of an early draft of this manuscript.

References

[1] *The Chicago Manual of Style,* thirteenth ed. Chicago, IL: The University of Chicago Press, 1982.

[2] E. Swanson, *Mathematics into Type.* Providence, Rhode Island: American Mathematical Society, 1971.

[3] E. J. Podell, "Mathematics must be effective in technical communication," *IEEE Trans. Prof. Commun., PC-27,* no. 2, 1984, pp. 97–100.

[4] N. E. Steenrod, P. R. Halmos, M. M. Schiffer, and J. A. Dieudonné, *How to Write Mathematics.* Providence, Rhode Island: American Mathematical Society, 1973.

[5] *James & James Mathematical Dictionary.* New York: Van Nostrand Reinhold Company, 1968.

[6] W. Karush, *Webster's New World Dictionary of Mathematics.* New York: Webster's New World, 1989.

[7] *McGraw-Hill Dictionary of Scientific and Technical Terms,* S. Parker, Ed., third ed. New York: McGraw-Hill Book Company, 1984.

[8] M. E. Skillin and R. M. Gay, *Words Into Type,* third ed. Englewood Cliffs, NJ: Prentice-Hall Inc., 1974.

[9] *Standard Mathematical Tables,* S. Selby, Ed., twentieth ed. Cleveland, OH: The Chemical Rubber Company, 1972.

[10] G. Freedman and D. A. Freedman, *The Technical Editor's and Secretary's Desk Guide.* New York: McGraw-Hill Book Company, 1985.

[11] *The McGraw-Hill Style Manual: A Concise Guide for Writers and Editors,* M. Longyear, Ed. New York: McGraw-Hill Book Company, 1983.

[12] R. Schenkman, *The Typing of Mathematics.* Santa Monica, CA: Repro Handbooks, 1978.

Displaying scientific graphics on computer

—JANET E. LINCOLN
AND DONALD L. MONK

Abstract—*Complex scientific graphics that reproduce well on paper may be difficult to display on computer because of the limited size and resolution of standard desktop monitors. This paper describes several methods for computer display of such large, dense graphics that preserve the usability of the graphics and support the ways users need to interact with the figures. Building on a simple structure of base panels and overlays joined by hypertext links, these methods provide ways of reorganizing figures into smaller graphical units that can be displayed easily, yet communicate all the information the original figure was designed to convey.*

Index Terms—*Computer displays, graphics, technical figures.*

Manuscript received September 1996; revised February 1997. This work was supported by a consortium of U.S. Government and international organizations, including the Armstrong Laboratory, the Air Force Office of Scientific Research, the Army Research Laboratory, the Naval Command, Control and Ocean Surveillance Center, the Defense Technical Information Center, the Federal Aviation Administration, and NATO/AGARD.

J. E. Lincoln is with Hudson Research Associates, Stuyvesant, NY 12173-9720 USA.

D. L. Monk is with Armstrong Laboratory, Human Engineering Division, Wright-Patterson AFB, OH 45433-6573 USA.

IEEE PII: S 0361-1434(97)04355-5.

SCIENTIFIC research reports and other technical materials often rely heavily on graphics to communicate important information. When publications of this kind are converted to electronic form, special attention must be given to the graphics to ensure proper translation from paper to screen. Complex scientific figures with many panels, extensive detail, or dense labeling may not reproduce well on a standard computer monitor. The problem is the small screen size and the relatively low resolution of most displays. Small monitors (13–15″) are still the standard for most desktop computer systems, and software producers are reluctant to design a product that requires a larger display. Moreover, not even the full dimensions of a small monitor will be available for the display of artwork, since some screen real estate must always be reserved for basic interface elements. Given the low resolution of conventional computer monitors (typically about 72 dots per inch), the display area available is simply inadequate to reproduce some large or complex graphics at an acceptable quality.

For scientific graphics, more is at stake than just a good-looking figure. Figures play a critical role in much scientific and technical material. Often, they are central to a report, providing the substantiating data for points summarized only briefly in the text. They may even communicate information that is not discussed in the text at all. To fill this role, an electronic figure must not only be readable, it must also be usable—that is, it must support the way users need to interact with the information in the figure.

Although there are many excellent books on the design of quantitative graphics [1]–[7], these sources are aimed primarily at scientists and others who are looking for the best way to graph a given set of quantitative data. They do not deal directly with the special problems that arise when existing printed graphics are converted to another medium. Nor do they address how to take advantage of the unique aspects of computerized display, such as the potential for interactivity.

Recently, as part of the Computer Aided Systems Human Engineering (CASHE) program (a multiagency government program that is developing automated tools to help designers integrate ergonomics data into system

Reprinted from *IEEE Trans. Prof. Comm.*, vol. PC-40, no. 2, pp. 78–91, June 1997.

design), we converted approximately 1500 scientific and technical figures from printed to electronic form during the creation of a large ergonomics database for CD-ROM [8]. Drawing on our experiences and the insights we gained, this article summarizes some general issues in computerizing printed graphics and describes a set of figure display methods that can be used to present complex and oversized graphics successfully on a small computer screen.

Considerations in Electronic Figure Display

When scientific and technical figures are converted for electronic display, the following basic requirements should be met to insure that the information value of the figures is preserved:

- The figures should be readable on screen. While this may be an obvious requirement, it is not a trivial one, given the complexity of many printed scientific figures.
- Image quality should be preserved throughout common user manipulations. Figures should remain sharp and clear when the user resizes the figure on screen. Figures should print out well.
- The usability of the figure should be maintained (or even improved). That is, the on-screen display should enable users to extract the information they need from the figure. For example, a perfectly readable, high-quality data graph might still be hard for the user to interpret if the figure is too large to be viewed without scrolling.
- Consistency with the printed documents is important, especially if both the printed and electronic versions of the document will remain available. Any manipulation of the figures to accommodate computer display should preserve a reasonable correspondence between printed and electronic versions and maintain the original figure numbering scheme. Discrepancies between the two versions can create confusion among readers as well as headaches for those wishing to cite figures in other works.

The first two of these criteria are related to display format and image data structure; that is, how the electronic images are created, stored, and rendered. These issues are addressed briefly in the section that follows. The last two criteria concern figure design and interface issues: what is included in a particular graphic and how the user interacts with it on screen. These issues are the main focus of this article and are discussed in the remaining sections.

Image Data Structure and Format

In converting printed figures for electronic display, screen image quality is a primary issue that has a strong impact on usability. Often, when paper documents are converted for computer access, the printed artwork is simply scanned to produce digitized images for display. Scanning is relatively inexpensive. It is the only feasible way to reproduce continuous-tone artwork, such as photographs. It is also good for illustrations with large areas of fine detail or nonrepetitive patterning. However, scanning does not always yield a high-quality reproduction for some other types of graphics, including the line art typical of most scientific and technical documents. For example, scans of black-and-white data graphs may pick up spurious gray tones, and the small type typically used for axis labels and legends may appear fuzzy. Unless careful alignment is maintained during scanning, horizontal and vertical lines and edges may become ragged.

Scans also entail several other disadvantages that are related to the data format used to manipulate and store the image. Scanning generates a bitmap of the original figure. A bitmap represents an image as a matrix of tiny dots or pixels and records the value of each pixel. The more dots per inch (dpi) used to represent the figure, the greater the resolution and thus the finer the detail that can be reproduced.

Bitmaps can produce a high-quality image provided the resolution of the bitmap matches the resolution of the display or output device. However, converting an existing image file from one resolution to another degrades image quality. One consequence is that bitmapped images displayed on screen can become grainy or blotchy when they are enlarged or reduced in size. Another consequence is that it can be difficult to obtain both a good screen image and a sharp printout of the figure. The reason is the large difference in the resolution of a computer display (70–100 dpi) and the resolution of most printers (300–600 dpi for a standard desktop laser printer). Bitmaps that are optimized for screen display print out poorly at the higher printer resolutions. Bitmaps created at a higher resolution to support good printout may yield an unsatisfactory screen image and require longer to display because of the computations required to step down the resolution.

One solution is to scan the artwork twice and store duplicate versions of each figure, one at a lower resolution for screen display and one at a higher resolution for printing. This solution is often impractical, however, because of another drawback of bitmapped images—the large size of the image files. File size increases with the size of the figure, the level of resolution, and the number of different colors or gray levels supported. A full-screen, high-resolution figure with maximum color depth can require megabytes of storage. Such large image files can rapidly eat up disk space. They also require more computer memory for display and may display more slowly.

One way to avoid these problems is to use one of the many commercial drawing or CAD/CAM packages to redraw the figures in vector format for electronic use. In vector graphics, a figure is described in software code in terms of basic components or objects such as lines, arcs, rectangles, and ellipses. What is stored for a vector graphic thus is not a representation of the image itself, as with a bitmap, but rather a set of instructions for recreating the image by drawing the objects that comprise it. The vector graphics approach is especially well-suited for the type of line drawings and data graphs that predominate in scientific documents. It offers several advantages that are well known [9]–[11]:

- Screen images remain sharp with vector graphics, even when users resize a figure by zooming in or zooming out.
- Vector graphics print out at high quality at any printer resolution.
- Except for very complex figures, vector graphics files generally are significantly smaller than high-resolution scanned versions of the same artwork and therefore require less disk storage space.
- Alphanumeric text in vector graphics is stored as ASCII strings with attributes, and can be readily located by text-search routines in response to user queries.

As noted earlier, scanning is the only real option when printed photographs or other illustrations with subtle color gradations are converted for electronic display. However, for line drawings such as data graphs and schematics, redrawing the figures on computer will provide a much higher quality screen image. Redrawn (not scanned) bitmapped images optimized for the resolution of the display hardware yield a superior screen display and may be the best solution if the artwork is strictly for screen viewing and will not be printed out or resized on screen. Otherwise, redrawing in a vector graphics format is a good compromise that offers a crisp screen display as well as a high-quality printout.

Although redrawing the artwork for electronic display yields a much higher quality product, this process is also much more expensive than scanning the printed figures, because of the time and expertise required to recreate each figure on computer. Whether the higher quality justifies this additional cost will depend on the goals and constraints of the individual project. For the CASHE database project, the quality of the figures was critical because much important information is communicated through data graphs or precisely labeled mechanical or anthropometric illustrations. Therefore, to ensure high-quality displays and printouts, we chose to hire a graphics studio to redraw all the printed figures as vector graphics for the CASHE CD-ROM.

Figure Design

Image quality is only one aspect that must be considered in transferring printed figures to computer displays. Even more important is preserving the usability of the figures. Any lengthy scientific document is likely to have at least a few figures that will not fit in a single screen on a small monitor in their original configuration because they are too large, contain too many panels, or are too detailed or densely labeled. Depending on the original page size, format, and type of subject matter, a printed document may contain a significant minority of such "problem" figures.

One figure we encountered, for example, contained 12 separate data graphs plotting vibration comfort-limit contours for different axes of vehicle vibration and different body-vehicle contact points. Another printed graphic, an anatomical drawing of the human eyeball, had 55 text labels and over 25 sets of lines and arrows delineating various anatomical and optical features. Arbitrarily splitting up such complex figures or simply "shoe-horning" them into the available display area can destroy their usability and make it impossible for the user to perceive the relationships the figure was designed to convey. For instance, dividing the 12-panel vibration figure into 12 separate graphics would make it much harder for users to compare different aspects of the data, such as whether horizontal or vertical vibration is tolerated better, or whether vibration of the seat pan is more uncomfortable than vibration of the footrest.

When a figure is too large or too dense to fit in the allocated graphics viewing area, the information it contains must somehow be condensed or parsed into complementary units that can be displayed separately without loss of context and meaning. In what follows, we describe several methods for reorganizing or restructuring complex figures so they can be displayed in a relatively small screen area. All of the display methods utilize a simple system of base panels and overlays joined by hypertext links. To make it easier to understand how each display method operates, we will first describe these three basic building blocks and define their general characteristics and relationships.

Each figure to be displayed is organized as a set of one or more *base panels* (see Fig. 1). A base panel is a data graph, schematic, or some other portion of the graphic that is displayed as a single unit in the designated figure viewing area. Although a figure may contain more than one base panel, only one panel may be displayed in the viewing area at a time.

• Each base panel of the figure may have one or more *overlays*. An overlay can contain text, data points, curves, or other graphic elements. Overlays have transparent backgrounds and are displayed by stacking them over the base panel like acetates.

• Because only one base panel of a figure can be viewed at a time, one panel must be designated as the "default" panel that is displayed whenever the figure is opened on screen. If a figure panel has overlays, one or more overlays may also be designated as defaults; these overlays will then be displayed whenever the base panel is first called up.

• Base panels and overlays are joined together by hypertext *links* that allow the user to control what is displayed on screen. A link is a directional electronic connection between one graphical element (the link origin or source) and another (the link destination). Activating a link by clicking a "hot spot" in the source graphic invokes an operation defined by the type of link. Three types of links are used: "Add," "Replace," and "Remove" links. "Add" and "Remove" links join base panels and overlays. An "Add" link displays the designated overlay on top of the base panel (and any other overlays already present). A "Remove" link removes the designated overlay but leaves the rest of the display (including other overlays) unchanged. "Replace" links connect base panels to other panels or to overlays. A "Replace" link removes the panel (or overlay) currently in view and displays the designated panel (or overlay) in its place.

• Link markers are employed to alert users to the presence of a link and to indicate the location of the "hot spot" that must be clicked to activate the link. Link markers can be buttons, icons, or an embedded region of the artwork. They can be located on any panel or overlay, though of course they will be visible only when the panel or overlay is being displayed and when they are not obscured by a higher overlay.

These simple building blocks—base panels, overlays, and the hypertext links among them—can be organized in several different ways to allow interactive display of complex scientific figures.

Split Panels Method The simplest and most obvious means for dealing with a complex multiple-panel or multipart figure is to divide the figure into pieces and treat each piece as a separate graphic. This simple method works well for printed figures with two or more panels that are fairly independent of one another. Fig. 2 shows a graphic that can be handled in this way. Although the two panels of the original figure are related (both deal with color temperature), each remains completely understandable when presented alone.

Each new panel becomes a separate figure component with its own figure number and caption. To maintain consistency with the printed version, figures that have been split will generally be numbered Fig. 1a, Fig. 1b, and so on, instead of being renumbered as Fig. 1, Fig. 2, and so forth.

Merged Panels Method If splitting figures apart cannot solve display problems, merging the parts together sometimes will. In behavioral science research, for example, figures sometimes plot the data for each individual experimental subject in a separate graph, even though the graph axes are the same for all subjects. Figures such as these can sometimes be simplified for electronic display by replotting the data sets from all the original graphs onto a single set of axes. For this solution to work, figures must contain a limited number of graphs with a limited number of data curves or points per graph, so that the original data sets remain fully distinguishable from one another when they are superimposed in the composite figure. Fig. 3 shows an example of a two-panel figure handled using this method. Because each original panel had only a single curve and the curves remain well separated spatially when they are superimposed, the resulting composite figure is still quite readable.

Data Overlay Method Many times, the data graphs of a multiple-panel figure contain too much material to be merged as described above, even though their axes are identical. In these cases, it may be possible to display the figure on screen as a base

Fig. 1. General structure of an electronic figure.

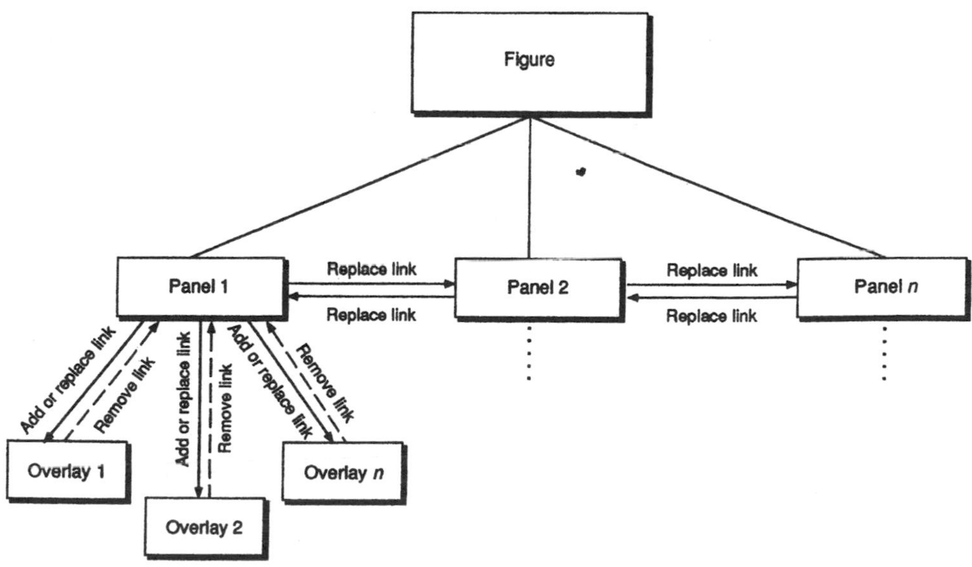

panel with several data overlays. Fig. 4 shows how a printed figure with three graphs plotting similar data for three subjects can be presented on screen using data overlays. The base panel contains an axis box and axis labels. Accompanying it is a set of three transparent overlays, each showing the data curve for one subject. Each data overlay can be viewed separately or the overlays can be stacked as desired to compare the data for different subjects. Functionality is actually improved over the paper version, since the user can see the different sets of data superimposed instead of comparing them across separate panels, yet can still view each data curve separately if desired.

In data overlay figures, the base panel is linked to each overlay by an "Add" link that opens the corresponding overlay on top of the base panel. Each overlay contains a "Remove" link that closes the overlay when activated.

Check boxes make good link markers for data-overlay figures because these toggle-type controls are already familiar to most users. The check boxes can be arranged at the top of the figure as a "menu" of available options. Clicking an unfilled check box opens the corresponding overlay, while clicking a filled check box removes that (and only that) overlay when the user no longer wants to display it. The check box labels can also serve as a legend for the stacked data curves. Users can simultaneously stack as many of the available overlays as desired (or remove all of them). Depending on the structure and purpose of the figure, all overlays can be displayed along with the base panel when the figure is first accessed (i.e., all overlays can be defaults) or only one overlay (or a subset of overlays) can be displayed initially.

Explanatory Overlay Method Overlays can also be used to simplify some complex figures that contain long explanatory labeling, insets, or other material that augments the main figure. The core graphic comprises the opaque base panel.

Fig. 2. Graphic handled using the split-panels method. The printed figure is reproduced on the left. In the electronic version, each panel of the original figure is presented as a separate figure, as shown on the right.

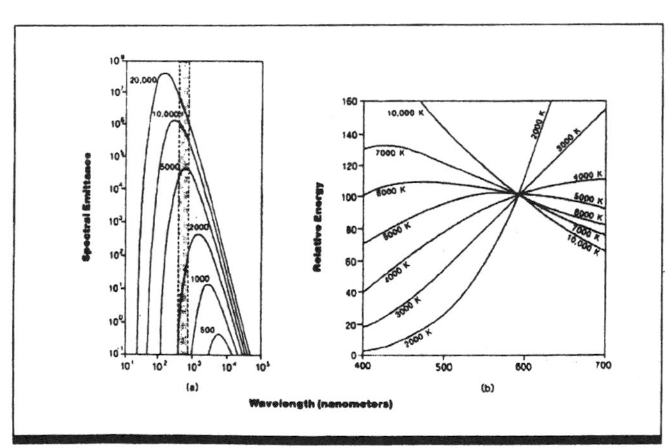

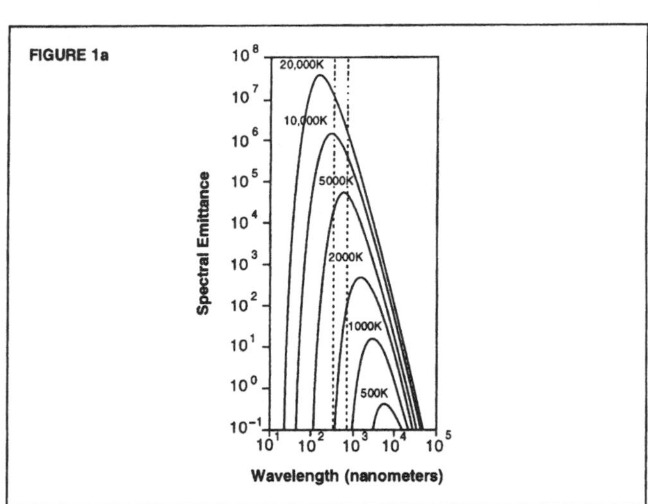

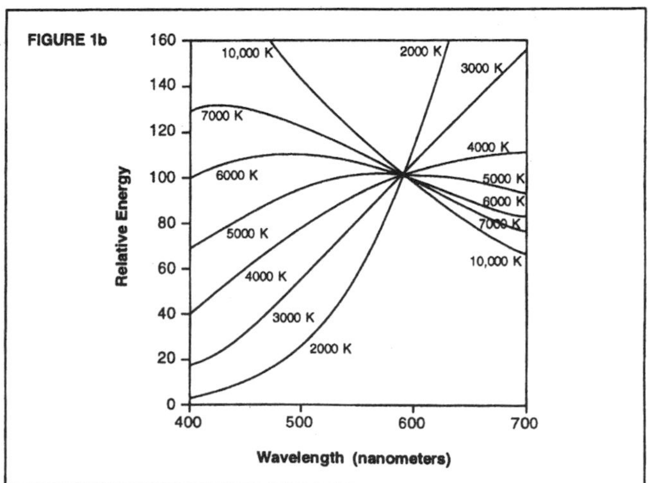

The supplementary text and/or graphic material is organized into one or more transparent overlays that appear on top of the base panel like pop-up boxes.

The base panel is displayed when the figure is opened. There are no default overlays (that is, no overlay is opened when the base panel is first accessed). To display an overlay, the user clicks an embedded link marker in the base panel, which may be a label, a specific region within the artwork, or a special button. The overlay is closed by clicking in the overlay to activate a "Remove" link. Only one overlay can be viewed at a time. Clicking a new link marker in the base panel when an overlay is already in view removes the current overlay and displays the new one (that is, the links from base panel to overlay are "Replace" links).

Fig. 5 shows how a graphic can be handled using the explanatory overlay approach. The original figure is a fairly complex Venn diagram with a definition of each region embedded in the figure. In the on-line version, only the diagram itself and the key for its three major components are portrayed in the base panel. The user can click any region of the diagram and display a text box that defines that region and explains its significance. The area the user clicked is rendered in reverse video to signal the region to which the text box applies. The overlay can be closed by clicking this highlighted region (which is actually part of the overlay) or by clicking anywhere in the text box. A prompt at the bottom of the figure alerts users to the availability of the overlays and explains how to access them.

Linked Panels Method Figures containing several panels of distinct but closely related graphical information can be presented as a connected set with links that allow users to move easily from panel to panel. Fig. 6 shows a graphic to which this method can be applied. The two panels of the original figure plot the same set of skin sensitivity data in two different ways—one panel on linear coordinates and the other panel on log-log coordinates. These multiple panels are kept as a single unit and are linked, instead of being broken into separate figures, to emphasize their interrelatedness and to alert users to the presence of different views of the same information. Linking also speeds users' access to the different panels by eliminating the need to return to a figure menu or some other higher level figure selection tool to switch among panels.

One base panel of the set is designated as the default and is the panel displayed when the figure is opened. "Replace" links join the panels and allow users to move freely among them. The entire set of linked panels comprises the figure and carries a single figure number.

Fig. 3. Graphic drawn for electronic display using the merged panels method. The two panels in the original figure (left) show data for two different observers. The printed panels were merged into a single panel for electronic display by redrawing both data curves onto a single set of axes (right).

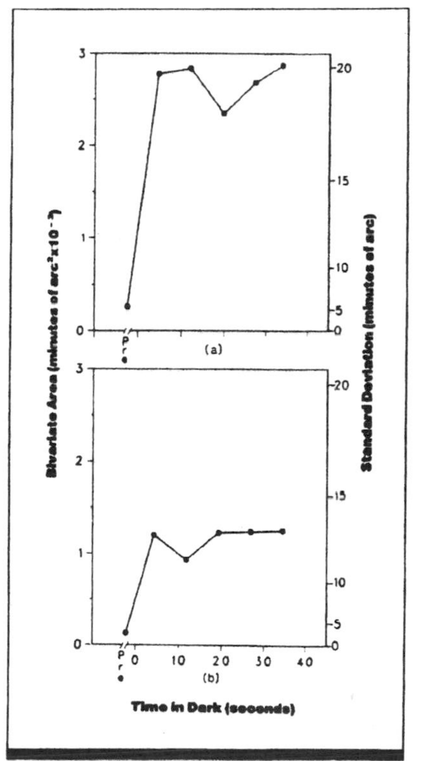

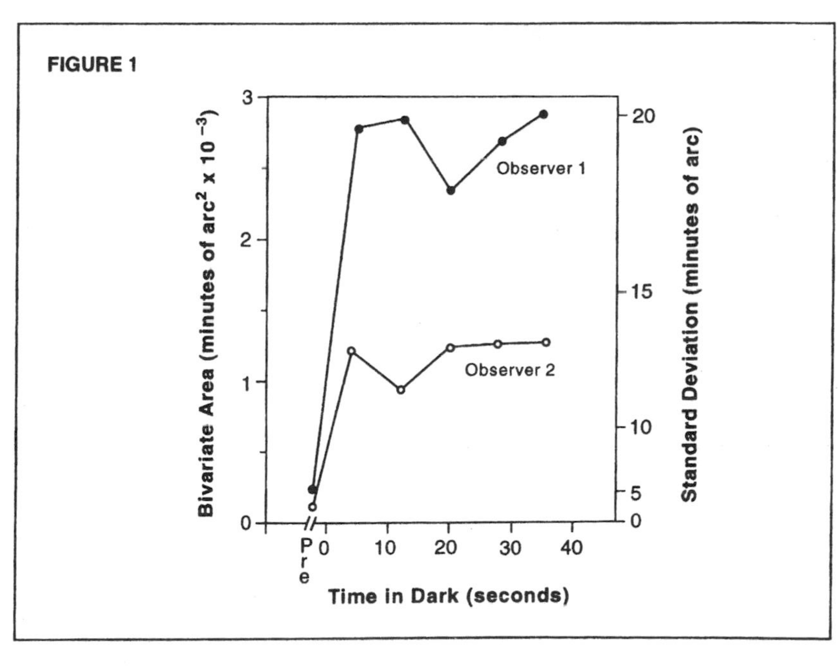

Radio buttons are convenient link markers for panels of equal importance. These can be styled as a radio-button "menu" of available items at the tops of the panels to allow users to switch easily among them. Each panel has one filled radio button (indicating the panel currently in view) and one or more unfilled radio buttons (identifying other available panels). Clicking an unfilled radio button activates a "Replace" link that removes the current panel and displays the selected panel.

The complex drawing of the eyeball mentioned earlier was actually made much more usable by adapting it to this display method. The original figure showed a human eyeball densely labeled with various anatomical and optical structures and dimensions. For the electronic version, three individual linked panels were created. The same basic drawing of the eyeball was repeated in each one. However, the labeling was divided into three cohesive groupings focusing on different aspects of the information and was distributed among the three panels. One panel defined the basic structures of the eye, another listed the anatomical dimensions of various structures, and the third portrayed the optical constants of the eye. Because the amount of information in each panel was reduced, the labeling was easier to read and the user could focus more readily on a specific kind of information about the eye.

Preview-and-Zoom Method Multiple-panel scientific figures that have too many panels to be suitable for a data-overlay or linked-panels treatment can be handled by previewing the panels to aid user selection. To display these figures, each individual panel of the multiple-panel figure is drawn up as a separate base panel. In addition, a special preview or index panel is created to serve as a selection device. Fig. 7 provides an example of such a figure. The original graphic is a complex six-panel figure showing subjects' motion detection performance under several related conditions. In the restructured version used on-line, there is a preview panel containing thumbnail sketches of the six data panels. In addition to providing an overview of the available panels, the preview also contains enough information to allow users to make general comparisons among the data in the different panels. The thumbnail panels in the preview are also link markers. When the user clicks one of these reduced panels, a zoomed, full-size version of the corresponding data panel is displayed.

Navigation links are provided to allow users to browse through the full-size data panels or return to the preview to select a new data panel. Fig. 7 shows an example of how such links might be implemented. The arrows at the lower right in the zoomed panel advance users to the previous or next data panel in the set, while the square button in the center returns them to the preview panel.

Each set of preview-and-zoom panels is treated as a unit and carries a single figure number. The preview panel is the default panel and is displayed when the figure is opened. Data panels are accessible only via the preview panel. Only one of the

Fig. 4. Graphic portrayed using the data overlay method. The printed three-panel figure is shown on the left. For electronic display, the figure was drawn as a base panel with three overlays, each containing the data curve from one original panel. In the example on the right, the first and third overlays are currently displayed, as indicated by the filled "check boxes" at the top of the figure. The check box "menu" also serves as a legend. Users add or remove overlays by clicking the check boxes.

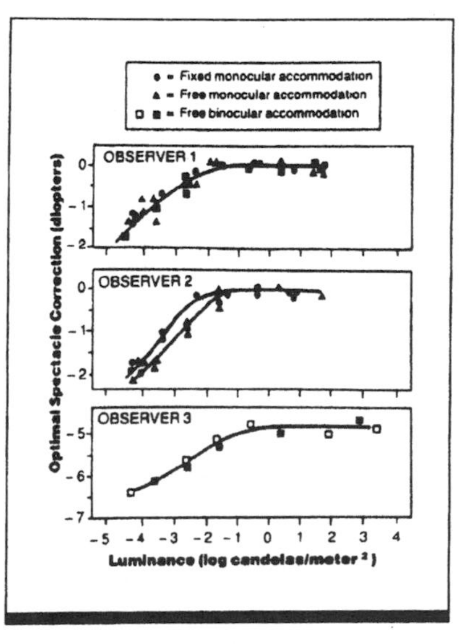

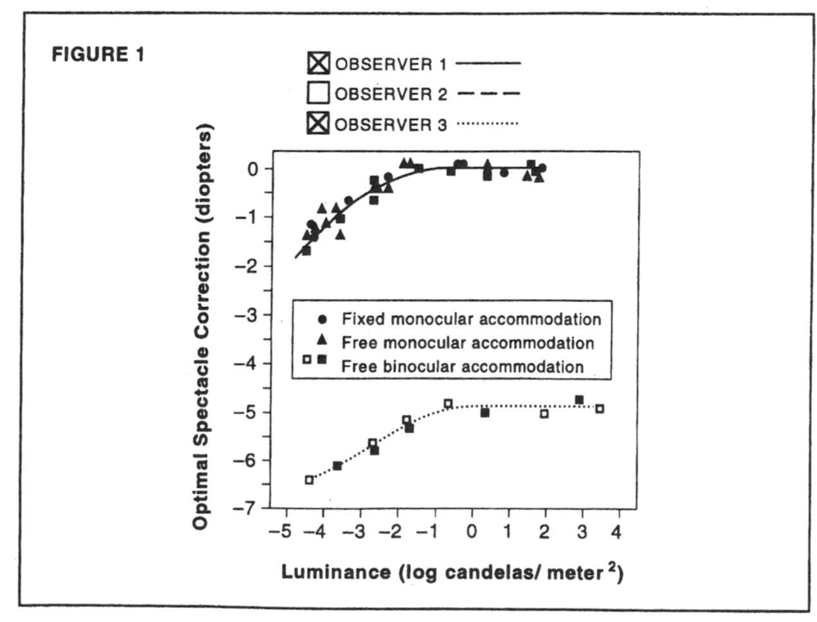

Fig. 5. Graphic to which the explanatory overlay display method was applied. The printed figure is reproduced at left. At right is the electronic version, showing the display after the user has clicked on the rectangle labeled TIS_b, which has been highlighted. The small drop-shadow box is an explanatory overlay that defines the meaning of the highlighted region. The overlay can be removed by clicking anywhere in the drop-shadow box or the highlighted region.

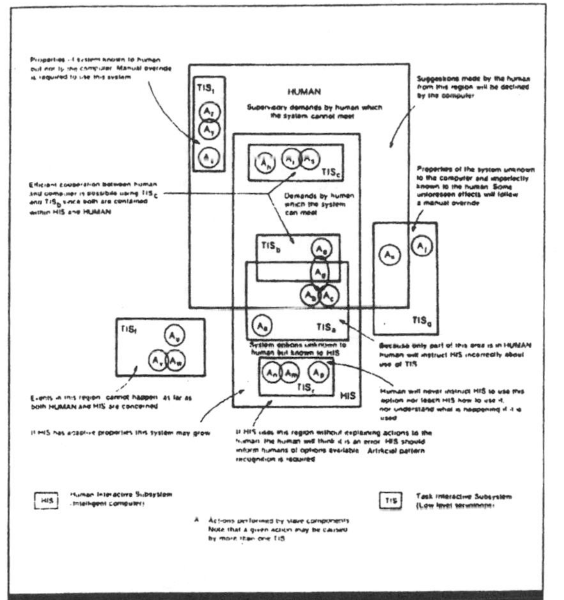

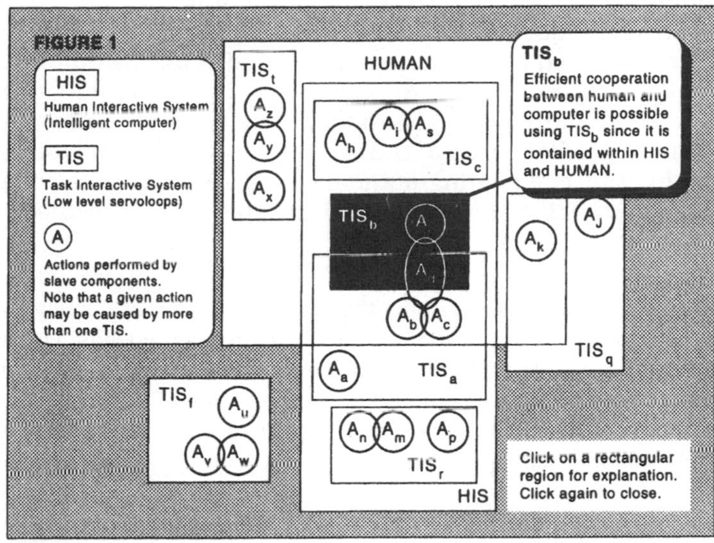

Fig. 6. Graphic displayed using the linked panels method. The printed figure (left) presents the same experimental data plotted on linear axes (top panel) and log axes (bottom panel). To display the figure on line, it was drawn as two separate linked panels (right), only one of which is displayed at a time. "Radio-button" controls at the top of the display list the available panels. The filled radio button indicates the panel currently in view. The user removes the current panel and displays the alternate panel by clicking the unfilled radio button.

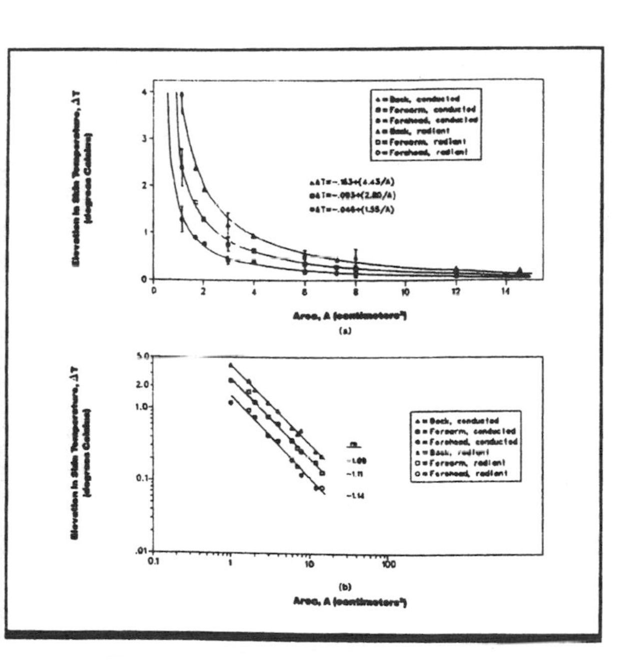

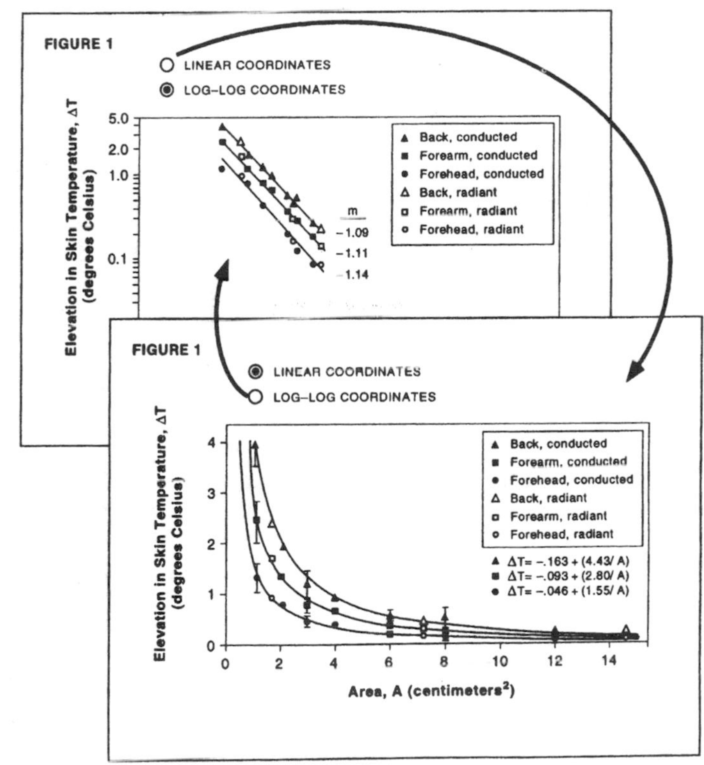

figure panels (the preview or a data panel) may be displayed at a time (i.e., all links between panels are "Replace" links).

Combination of Techniques The display techniques described above can be combined to accommodate especially complex figures. An example is shown in Fig. 8. This figure, originally published in a U.S. military human engineering standard, presents specifications for hand cranks to promote ease of use by human operators. Part of the figure consists of drawings that define various crank dimensions and illustrate several crank styles. The figure also contains a table that lists government-mandated minimum, preferred, and maximum values for various hand crank dimensions in both metric and common (U.S.) units and for two different load levels. For electronic display, a combination of the split-panels method, linked-panels method, and explanatory overlay method can be combined to create a graphic set that not only fits within the standard figure display area but improves the usability of the material.

First, the original figure is split into two separate figures. The drawings illustrating crank styles, which form a coherent unit and are not necessary for understanding the other elements, are put into one figure. The

Fig. 7. Graphic handled using the preview-and-zoom display method. The printed figure (left) contains six panels graphing data for two types of motion and three motion speeds. On screen, the user is presented with a preview panel (upper right) that presents an overview of the information with "thumbnail" versions of the six data panels. When the user clicks one of the reduced panel icons, a full-size version of the data panel is displayed (lower right). Buttons in the lower right corner of the data panel allow the user to page to the next or previous data panel in the series (arrows) or return to the preview panel (center icon).

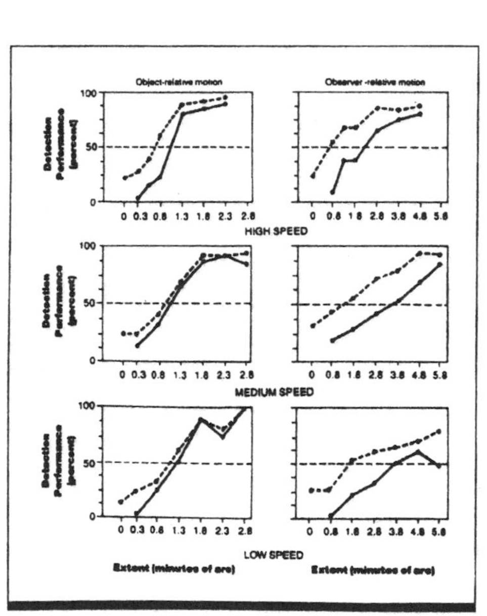

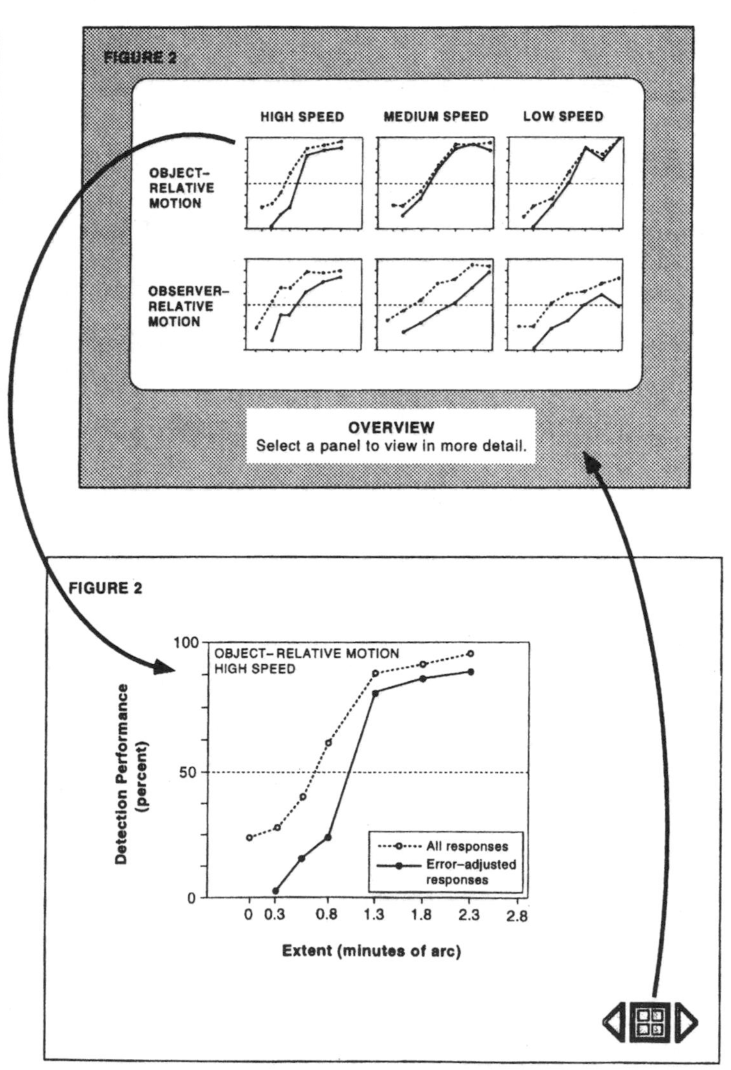

other figure consists of the remaining dimensional drawings and table of specifications. These elements are organized as a set of 13 panels joined by "Replace" links as in the linked-panels method. Twelve of the panels show identical drawings of basic crank dimensions. Instead of simply illustrating how the dimensions are defined, however, each panel inserts into the drawings one of the 12 sets of official values for the dimensions from the original data table (see Fig. 8). For example, one panel shows minimum values for light loads in metric units, while another shows preferred values for heavy loads in common units, and so forth. The panels thus serve as filters on the tabled data that allow users to focus on the particular class of values they need. Users can configure the visible figure panel to display the desired data using three sets of radio buttons at the top of each panel.

The thirteenth panel contains the complete table of standard values. The table panel is linked to all 12 pictorial panels through a "Show Table" button at the bottom of each panel, which executes a "Replace" link. The table panel is enhanced with multiple explanatory overlays that help users interpret the tabular information. When the table is displayed, users can click any control dimension listed in the column headings to open a small illustration box showing how that particular dimension is defined (see Fig. 8). A "Return" button at the bottom of the table allows users to return to the pictorial crank-dimension panel from which the table was originally accessed.

In the printed document, users who need to know specified values for particular hand-crank dimensions have to shift attention back and forth between the pictorial and the tabular portions of the figure to fully understand what each dimension represents and to locate the specific value corresponding to that dimension. This is not too burdensome for the figure used in the example, because the pictorial illustrations and the value table appear on the same page in the printed version. However, there are other cases in the same military standard where the illustrations defining given dimensions and the table containing the mandated values for these dimensions are separated by several pages, forcing users to shuffle back and forth to match definitions with values. By applying the method described here—incorporaing the tabular data into the dimensional drawings while preserving the data table as a separate unit with its own pictorial overlays to define individual measurements—the on-line version makes the information easier to use and allows users

Fig. 8. Graphic displayed on-line using a combination of display methods. The printed figure is shown on the left. For electronic display, the graphic was divided into two separate figures. One figure (bottom right) illustrates various types of hand-crank controls. The other figure (top two panels on the right) shows control dimensions and their government-mandated values. The panel at the top center is one of 12 pictorial panels illustrating the official values for various control dimensions. Three sets of "radio buttons" at the top of the panel allow users to specify the exact set of values desired, which determines which of the 12 panels will be displayed. The user can display the full table of values (upper right panel) instead of the pictorial panel by clicking the "Show Table" button. The table panel has explanatory overlays (drop-shadow box with illustration) that define the dimensions listed in the table column headings.

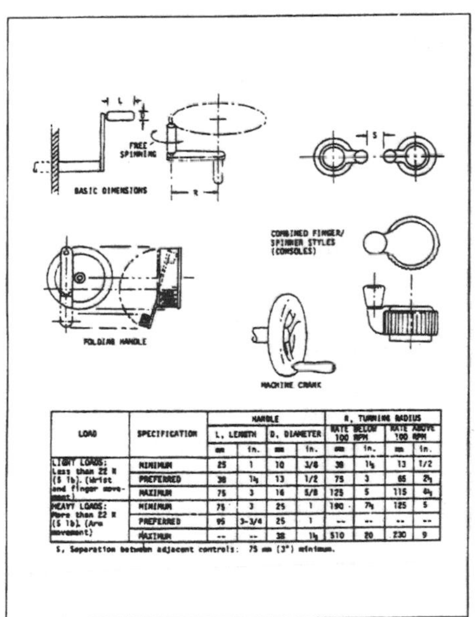

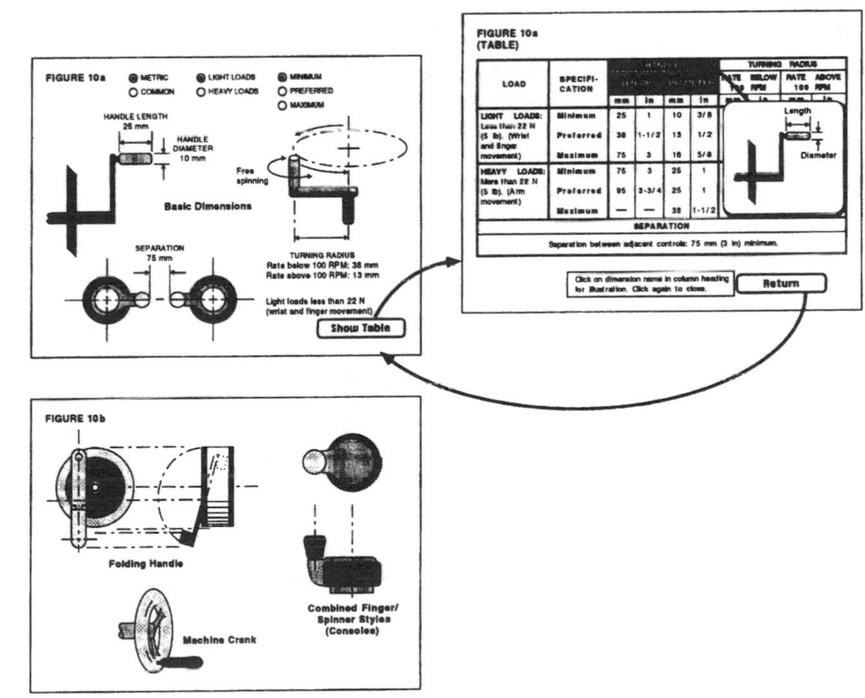

to obtain all the information they need from either the table panel or the pictorial panels.

Clipped View This "method" is a fall-back that can be used as a last resort when figures are difficult to parse into information units small enough to fit in the allotted display area and cannot be adapted to one of the other display techniques described above. This type of display requires that figures be presented in a scrollable field or window. The figure is drawn to a readable scale and is clipped when it is brought into the viewing area. Users must scroll to see all portions of the figure. If figures are displayed in a resizable window, then users with large monitors can increase the window size so the complete figure is visible. When a zoom function is available, users with small monitors can zoom out to reduce the figure so it can be viewed in its entirety, although detail will be lost. Users can also print out the complete figure for viewing if printing is supported.

Figure Production and Display Implementation

This section describes in very general terms a production process for implementing the electronic figure display methods outlined above. Because programming details will vary depending on the software (commercial or proprietary) used to develop the final product, primary emphasis will be on the editorial procedures involved in preparing figures for electronic display.

Implementing the suggested display methods involves seven production steps:

1) Determining maximum display size
2) Defining link marker style
3) Reviewing and analyzing the figures
4) Preparing electronic graphics files
5) Creating links
6) Updating text and captions
7) Checking and proofreading

Determining Maximum Display Size The first step that must be accomplished is to establish the maximum screen area available for figure display. The maximum display area will depend on the design of the user interface for the particular application and how it handles graphics. Although the maximum figure display area can be as large as the entire screen, typically it is less, to accommodate menus, buttons, and other interface elements that need to remain visible for navigation and control functions.

Defining Link Marker Style It is also helpful to determine a general style for link markers early on so that any necessary labels can be defined during figure review. Link markers should be styled consistently for each display method. Markers for links that perform the same function should look the same and should appear in the same location in each figure. Any necessary on-screen user prompts to explain figure operation should also be standardized as much as possible in design and location.

Reviewing and Analyzing the Figures The next step in figure processing is to review each figure in the printed document to determine whether or not it can be presented adequately in the available screen area in its printed form. This initial sort will identify "problem" figures that need special treatment to remain readable and usable on screen.

Two elements enter into this judgment: 1) the size of the printed figure; and 2) the complexity (amount of detail) of the figure. Very large figures clearly present problems, and a decision must be made as to whether the figure can be reduced sufficiently in size without loss of quality. Figure density is also important. The resolution possible with solid ink lines on paper in offset printing is several orders of magnitude greater than the resolution of electronic displays. Thus details that appear perfectly clear on printed artwork may disappear or run together on screen because there are not enough pixels to resolve them.

Once the "problem" figures are identified, each must be examined individually to determine which of the special figure display methods should be applied. The reviewer must analyze how the user needs to interact with the figure:

- What is the purpose of the figure and the primary meaning it is intended to convey?
- What graphical elements do users need to see on screen at the same time in order to understand and interpret the information portrayed?
- What comparisons do they need to be able to make?

On the basis of this analysis, a display method is selected that best suits the content and purpose of the figure and preserves its usability. Input from a subject-matter expert is important at this stage. Someone who understands the content of a given figure and how it will be used should review the proposed graphic design to make sure the functionality and tutorial intent of the figure have not been compromised.

Once the display method is determined, individual instructions must be prepared for each problem figure to guide the preparation of the electronic files. These instructions should define:

- Which figure display option is being used for the given figure.
- How many panels, overlays, etc., should be created and how the elements in the printed graphic should be divided up among these designated subunits (color coding can be helpful in communicating which graphic elements belong in each subunit, especially for the explanatory overlay method).
- What labels should be used for the link markers.

- How to position, style, and label any nonstandard link markers or prompts.

Preparing Electronic Graphics Files Once a display method has been determined for each graphic, the electronic versions of the figures must be created. The individual instructions prepared for each figure during the figure review are used to guide creation of the required base panels and overlays for each figure. Even if the figures are scanned, rather than redrawn completely, an artist's help will probably be required to clean up the scanned artwork and divide figure content appropriately among panels and overlays for the more complex figure treatments.

Printed figures are usually copyrighted. Unless the publisher of the on-line product owns the copyright to the figure, permission must be obtained from the copyright holder to reuse the figure in the electronic version. The copyright holder may make certain stipulations on the figure's use (such as the requirement that users not be allowed to print out the figure or that a copyright notice accompany the printout).

Creating Links After the artwork is completed, the links among panels and overlays must be generated. The precise mechanics for accomplishing this task will depend on the software environment. Among the elements that must be specified are the source and destination of each link as well as the position coordinates, presentation style (such as check box or radio button), and label text for each link marker.

Updating Text and Captions Depending on the display method used, the structure of some figures may be changed in the electronic version. The original printed figure captions must be reviewed and corrected if necessary before they are put on-line. For example, graphics that have been divided into more than one figure using the split-panels method need a separate caption for each new figure, and the original caption must be split accordingly. Any references to figures in the running text also must be checked to make sure they are still accurate for the electronic version.

Checking and Proofreading Adequate checks at each production step help to assure the quality of the final product. Electronic figures must be examined to verify that the correct display method has been applied, that all required base panels and overlays have been created, and that the content of each panel and overlay is correct. If the figures have been completely redrawn, each must be carefully proofed to make sure it has been drafted accurately. If the figures have been scanned, the bitmaps must be checked for clarity and completeness. Type, source, and destination must be verified for each link, and the accuracy of link marker style, placement, and labeling must be confirmed. Any changes made to figure captions or figure references in the running text must be proofread.

Areas of Application and Development Environment

The methods described in this article were used successfully to prepare computerized versions of the many scientific and technical figures incorporated in the CASHE electronic database. Of the 1500 graphics in the database, roughly 350 would not fit on screen in their original format. Slightly over half of these complex or oversized figures could be handled using one of the simpler methods described above (split-panels method or linked-panels method). The remaining problem figures required one of the more complicated display approaches. Only four figures had to be displayed in clipped form because none of the other methods could be applied.

Although these display techniques were developed to aid in transferring complex printed scientific figures to the computer screen, they can serve equally well for graphics created directly for computer display. The methods work best for data graphs, charts, schematics, and other figures that can be broken into meaningful subunits for electronic display. They are not very useful for photographs, pictorial drawings of complex scenes, and other similar artwork that have no natural subdivisions.

Proprietary software was written to implement the figure display methods in the CASHE database because of the scale of the effort and other product requirements. However, the methods can be implemented using almost any commercial software package that supports hypertext linking between graphic elements. Among the many suitable hypertext, electronic publishing, and multimedia packages are HyperCard (Apple) and SuperCard (Allegiant) for the Macintosh computer; Hyperties (Cognetics) and HyperWriter (Ntergaid) for PC's; and Director (Macromedia), and Oracle Media Objects (Oracle), which are available for either platform.

It will be much easier to implement the data overlay and explanatory overlay methods when the software used also allows layering. For example, creating a three-overlay data-overlay figure when layering is supported requires only four separate graphic elements—one for the base panel and one for each overlay. Creating the same functionality without layering would require seven separate graphics—one for each possible combination of overlays (plus base panel).

The World Wide Web is expanding explosively as a medium for communicating scientific and other information. Early Web browsers did not allow "hot spots" to be embedded within graphics, so that awkward and difficult workarounds would have been required to implement the four interactive methods (data overlays, explanatory overlays, linked panels, as well as preview and zoom) on the World Wide Web. Now, however, most browsers do allow links within graphics and are beginning to incorporate support for the platform-independent programming language Java. These advances make it easier to apply the methods described here to display figures on the World Wide Web.

Summary

Although computerization of scientific documents can make access and retrieval easier, printed scientific materials sometimes contain graphics that are too large, too complex, or have too many panels to reproduce well on a computer screen in their printed form. Several methods can be used to restructure such complex or oversized graphics so they can be displayed easily on a standard-sized computer monitor without compromising their readability and usability. These methods include:

- Splitting existing panels into separate figures.
- Merging existing panels by regraphing the data onto a single set of axes.
- Transferring the data from two or more existing panels onto overlays that can be stacked on top of each other or viewed separately.
- Separating insets, dense labeling, or other explanatory material into overlay boxes that remain hidden until the user chooses to display them.
- Dividing existing graphs into individual panels that are displayed separately but are linked to one another so users can jump rapidly between them
- Displaying multiple panels separately but providing an index panel that allows general comparisons among graphs and speeds access
- Clipping the graphic within a scrollable window

These methods preserve all the functionality of the printed figure so users can extract the information they need from the electronic version. By taking advantage of the interactivity possible with computer display, they sometimes even increase the usability of complex figures by allowing users to tailor the display of information to their individual needs.

The display methods are straightforward to employ, have been applied successfully to many types of scientific figures, and can be implemented using a number of commercial software packages.

Acknowledgment

The authors would like to thank Kenneth Boff, Alan Straub, Roy Livingston, and Gae Xavier for helpful comments and suggestions during the preparation of this article. They are also grateful to Glenn Johnson for drafting the artwork.

References

[1] J. Bertin, *Semiology of Graphics* (translated by W. J. Berg). Madison, WI: Univ. of Wisconsin Press, 1983.
[2] W. S. Cleveland, *The Elements of Graphing Data.* Monterey, CA: Wadsworth, 1985.
[3] H. T. Fisher, *Mapping Information: The Graphic Display of Quantitative Information.* Cambridge, MA: Abt Assoc., 1982.
[4] S. M. Kosslyn, *Elements of Graph Design.* New York: Freeman, 1994.
[5] C. F. Schmid, *Statistical Graphics: Design Principles and Practices.* New York: Wiley, 1983.
[6] E. R. Tufte, *The Visual Display of Quantitative Information.* Cheshire, CT: Graphics Press, 1983.
[7] ——, *Envisioning Information.* Cheshire, CT: Graphics Press, 1990.
[8] *Computer Aided Systems Human Engineering: Performance Visualization System.* [CD-ROM], Wright-Patterson AFB, OH: Armstrong Lab., Human Engineering Div., 1995.
[9] S. Feiner, S. Nagy, and A. van Dam, "An experimental system for creating and presenting interactive graphical documents," *ACM Trans. Graphics*, vol. 1, pp. 59–77, Jan. 1982.
[10] G. Apperson and R. Doherty, "Displaying images," in S. Ropiequet, Ed., *CD ROM: Optical Publishing*, vol. 2. Redmond, WA: Microsoft, 1987.
[11] I. Ritchie, "Hypertext—Moving toward large volumes," *Comput. J.*, vol. 32, no. 6, pp. 516–523, 1989.

Janet E. Lincoln received the Ph.D. degree in experimental psychology from New York University, New York, NY. She is Director of Hudson Research Associates, an ergonomics consulting firm. One of her primary interests is the problem of how to communicate scientific research findings effectively to those without a scientific background. Her work has focused on developing printed and electronic reference products for design engineers that will help them to understand and apply human perception and performance research relevant to system design.

Donald L. Monk is a Program Manager at the Armstrong Laboratory, Crew Systems Directorate, Human Engineering Division, located at Wright-Patterson AFB, OH. As Manager of the Computer Aided Systems Human Engineering (CASHE) project, he is trying to improve the cross-disciplinary communication of technical information. Mr. Monk is also active in the design, development, and application of multi-crew-member information systems and design support systems for the Air Force.

PART IV

Manuals and Procedures: Giving Directions that Work

The seven articles in this section deal with writing clear instructions. The instruction manual is perhaps the one technical document most of the public is familiar with, and there is no shortage of complaints about the frustration poorly written instructions can cause. These complaints are made as frequently about online instructions as they are about paper ones. From the following articles, however, you will learn there is no mystery to writing clear instructions and procedures: planning, prewriting, analyzing, organizing, formatting, editing, and testing will all ensure that your procedures are dependable and user-friendly.

The overall view

In the opening article Lidia Lopinto takes an introductory look at conceiving, organizing and producing a manual. Her eight steps for this process, which are as valid now as they ever were, conclude with the need to review your completed document for accuracy. Her final words remind you that few manuals can be engraved in granite—they will always need to be revised and updated.

Producing the usable manual

Next, James Gleason and Joan Wackerman investigate the difference between effective and poor computer manuals and from their findings derive the most successful ways for you to link machine and user. Dividing a manual into two parts, operator manual and reference manual, is yet another example of foreseeing your readers' needs. The authors' emphasis on testing and retesting instructional material opens a theme to be further developed later in this section.

Using graphics in your instructions

Complicated instructions call for complex formatting which must nevertheless be clear to the user. In their in-depth study, Angelique Boekelder and Michael Steehouder look at five visual formats you can use to present instructions or procedures: the flowchart, logic tree, yes/no tree, decision table, and list. The authors compare the pros and cons of each format and then describe an experiment they did to measure the relative effectiveness and efficiency of these tools—specifically for complex tasks that require the user to "switch" back and forth between the instructions and the equipment involved. The five formats are compared and the authors show that generally flowcharts, yes/no trees, and logic trees are more effective than decision tables or lists. They also stress that users prefer to stay with one format when following instructions, and that user preference plays a significant role in how instructions should be graphically presented.

Can manuals be slimmed down?

You've probably seen the old cartoon where an employee about to use a new computer is handed a user manual almost as big as the computer itself. John Craig looks at ways to reduce the size of such tomes, specifically those used for the in-house computer system of a large government organization. His approach, which involves an intensive audience analysis in the prewriting stage of large manuals, helps a writer identify what material to include and what to leave out. Craig describes the three components of this approach—preliminary analysis, needs assessment, and design for learning—and discusses each in detail, with the result that you are indeed helped in the process of creating "an efficient, well-tested manual that meets the real needs of a user."

Saving costs and time

Gary Bist first looks at the costs involved in writing different manuals for similar products, and then suggests ways to design documentation that can be used for two or more products. He also shows how to produce and maintain both a printed and online manual for the same product. This article has plenty of practical advice on how to create such documents, and also considers the trade-offs that may have to be made. As with any innovation, there might be risks, yet they may well be worth it if the results are increased efficiency and productivity.

Embedding screen pictures in manuals: pros and cons

Surprisingly little research has been done on whether screen captures improve learning on the part of computer manual users. This article, by Mark Gellevij and others, looks into the question extensively, citing what limited previous research there is, and pointing out that the use and placement of screen captures in manuals have been paid only marginal attention by researchers. The authors then describe their own in-depth study of the topic and show what they have found regarding the relative effectiveness of manuals that employ full-screen captures, those that use partial-screen captures, and those that rely solely on text. Their conclusions are interesting and perhaps surprising: they find no convincing evidence for the desirability of including screen captures in manuals. The authors do, however, give useful advice on how best to include screen captures if the manual writer wishes to do so.

Testing your manual

In the final article of this section Marshall Atlas describes how you should test your technical manuals once they are completed—the "user edit." Once again, although the article was written some years ago, it gives timeless advice: you are never going to know how useful your instructions are if you don't watch someone try to follow them. One wonders if those writers of instructions that accompany countless "Assembly Required" items bought by the public ever do this. And as this article reminds you, if instructions can possibly be misinterpreted, someone will do so. By following Atlas's advice on testing your manual both informally and formally, you will be able to expose the flaws and ambiguities often missed by a manual's authors—people already familiar with the process.

Designing and Writing Operating Manuals

LIDIA LOPINTO

Abstract—**A manual should communicate the design engineers' intentions for the operation of a process. To do this, it must be accurate, detailed, and logical, and it must be completed in time for the startup. Steps in preparation are structuring the manual; gathering and organizing information; making an outline; writing a draft; checking for technical accuracy; reviewing for consistency, style, and format; cross referencing and making an index; and distributing and accumulating updates and corrections.**

An operating manual is a key document for training personnel in the operation and maintenance of a new plant. If made available before the startup, it can help avoid costly operating errors. After the startup, it becomes a source of reference for experienced personnel and a source of instruction for replacement personnel.

To serve these purposes, the manual should cover startup, routine operations, trouble-shooting, normal and emergency shutdowns, and equipment maintenance and repair. For those learning the process, the information must be technically accurate, clearly written, and in logical sequence. For those familiar with the process, it should also be indexed and arranged for ready access to specific items. Its format should allow easy revision as the process is modified and new insights are gained about operations.

THE INFORMATION REQUIRED

Before the writing of an operating manual can begin, the process must be clearly conceived by the designers and be at least partially documented in process flow diagrams and engineering drawings.

Generally, the task of preparing the manual is assigned prior to the completion of the engineering work. This makes preparation difficult because not all of the information needed has been developed and finalized. However, there is an advantage to such scheduling: The missing information can be requested while there are still engineering labor-hours remaining in the budget.

The project engineer is usually responsible for the preparation of the manual. If the project is small, the project engineer may actually write it. If the project is large, another person may do the writing, with the project engineer coordinating the flow of information from the various engineering groups.

Reprinted with permission from *Chemical Engineering,* July 11, 1983, vol. 90(14), pp. 77–78; copyright 1983 by McGraw-Hill, Inc., New York.

The author is editor and publisher of *The Engineering Software Exchange* newsletter, 41 Travers Avenue, Yonkers, NY 10705; (914) 963-3695.

Certain information must be available, at least in preliminary form, before preparation of the manual can begin, including process-flow and piping-and-instrument diagrams, control-panel design, a statement of the control logic for routine and emergency operations, and operating and maintenance manuals from equipment suppliers.

A systematic procedure for preparing the operating manual includes these steps:

- Designing the structure
- Gathering and organizing information
- Making an outline
- Writing a draft
- Checking for technical accuracy
- Reviewing for consistency, style, and format
- Cross referencing and making an index
- Distributing and accumulating corrections and updating.

DESIGNING THE MANUAL'S STRUCTURE

Many engineers make the mistake of plunging into the writing of a manual without a plan. Because a manual is in

Reprinted from *IEEE Trans. Prof. Comm.,* vol. PC-27, no. 1, pp. 29–31, March 1984.

many ways analogous to a complex computer program, it makes sense to first prepare a preliminary structure, i.e., a flowchart.

The structure is not an outline (which comes later) but a flowchart of the types of information that will be presented. This can be done early in the design stage because details are not yet required. Having a structure, the details can be filled in more easily later. Time and work will be saved by securing approval of the structure by those responsible for the design of the plant. If the structure must be rearranged at a later date, ensuring the consistency of the parts can be a burdensome task.

Although the structure of the manual depends on the type of process and the specifications and needs of the operator of the plant, a proven approach to this structuring might be called "modular design."

By this approach, the manual is divided into modules, each devoted to a specific group of equipment. Each module is self-contained, providing all the essential operating and maintenance information for each equipment group. The idea behind this approach is to divide the manual into manageable parts that can be easily referred to by those concerned only with portions of the process.

A module typically contains the following:

Summary A brief statement of content.
Introduction A discussion of the process design concept.
Description A detailed description of the construction and arrangement of the equipment.
Routine operation A detailed discussion of how the equipment is to be operated and controlled.
Troubleshooting A description of procedures for pinpointing and diagnosing equipment malfunctions.
Maintenance A compilation of procedures for disassembling equipment and replacing parts, plus testing and lubrication schedules.
Emergency operation Detailed procedures for handling emergencies such as a runaway reaction, loss of cooling water, fire, leaks, and overheating, and for shutting down the process, with a description of the operation of automatic controls.
Appendix Parts lists, spare-parts lists, drawings and figures, and manufacturers' literature illustrating equipment and describing its operation and maintenance.

An obvious way to organize the modules is according to their sequence in the process. The first module of the manual encapsulates all the other modules, generally taking the form:

- Process design philosophy—explains why the process was chosen and gives the rationale behind the design.
- Overall process description—describes, with the aid of an overall process flow diagram, the main process flows, the physical and chemical changes occurring, and the instrumentation.
- Following in order—the overall table of contents, general operating instructions, maintenance philosophy, summary of controls and alarms, cross-reference index, equipment list, instrument list, environmental records, and general emergency procedures.

GATHERING AND ORGANIZING INFORMATION

After the manual has been structured, the next tasks are to gather all the information and organize it under the major headings. Arranging the information alphabetically or according to the process sequence will help pinpoint what may be missing. Those responsible for this material should be made accountable for supplying it by a specified date, and systematically prompted via memorandums or phone calls.

SETTING UP THE OUTLINE

The next step is to make a list of subheadings for each of the major headings. This is more easily done if the information that has been gathered has been separated into file folders designated by the major headings. The subheadings, with the information belonging with each, should next be organized into a logical sequence.

STARTING THE WRITING

After the material has been organized and carefully reviewed (so that one becomes familiar with all the technical details), the writing can begin, and it will be easier because of the systematic approach that has been followed to this point.

REVIEWING FOR ACCURACY

Each section of the first draft should be reviewed by the engineers who designed that portion of the process. Because a lot of time can be wasted if all the reviewers act as literary critics, it should be pointed out to them that they are to check technical accuracy and not style. The manual should be clear, logically ordered, informative, and useful; it need not be a literary masterpiece.

REVIEWING THE FINAL DRAFT

After the results of the accuracy review have been incorporated into a final draft, the manual is ready for a final review. Now, items to be checked include consistency of units, terms, and nomenclature; correctness of crossreferences; completeness of sentences; logical structure of paragraphs; and proper spelling.

CROSS REFERENCING

Each listing in the table of contents should be keyed, by

means of numbers, to the section of the manual it covers. Generally, these numbers overhang the left-hand side of the table so they can be picked out easily. They should not be page numbers because such a system can become meaningless as the manual undergoes revision.

A cross-reference index will be helpful to the reader who is familiar with the process and who needs specific information. An alphabetically arranged index will enable this person to find the information wanted without going through the entire table of contents.

CORRECTING AND UPDATING

Upon distributing the manual, it is important to have a system for receiving corrections and changes. One way is to send out forms, along with the manual, on which reviewers can make entries.

Changes can be made easily if the manual has been written with, and stored in, a word processor. If the manual is available to a user via a word processor, that person can quickly gain access to any section of it by means of the search routine for key words.

ACKNOWLEDGMENT

I thank Dell Archer of Engelhard Industries for his contributions to this article.

Manual Dexterity—What Makes Instructional Manuals Usable

JAMES P. GLEASON AND JOAN P. WACKERMAN

Abstract—**This paper discusses how properly designed instructional manuals can meet the needs of operators of home computers, office systems and word processing equipment. It also details several ways that structure and content presentation can help you produce more effective manuals.**

PICTURE a woman returning to office work after a 25-year hiatus. She recalls her 20-page Smith-Corona typewriter manual and then looks at her new word processor manual, which is more than two inches thick. It's immediately obvious to her that things have changed in the past few years.

How much will this new manual help her? Because today's market offers greater function and flexibility to less sophisticated users, manuals like this must meet her needs, but must also work for a variety of users with different word processing backgrounds.

As a new product developer, how can you ensure that the documentation you develop is going to meet the users' requirements? How can you make sure that your manuals will be simple, easy to use, and appropriate for your target market?

WHAT MAKES AN EFFECTIVE MANUAL?

There are a number of factors that distinguish the best and most popular manuals from the ones that people throw in the corner and never look at. Consider the following:

- *Organization* Good manuals have a structured format, a complete index, sections set off by tabs, and a table of contents.
- *Content* The material focuses on operator tasks, contains practice exercises, provides clear illustrations, and is concise.
- *Appearance* The presentation is attractive and colorful, with plenty of white space, and is "packaged" in booklets that are small and easy to handle.
- *Language* The text is conversational and easy to read, geared toward an eighth-grade reading level.

Reprinted with minor changes from *Conference Record* of the IEEE Professional Communication Society Conference held in Atlanta, GA, October 19–21, 1983; Cat. 83CH19160-4, pp. 142–144, IEEE Service Center, 445 Hoes Lane, Piscataway, NJ 08854; copyright 1983 by the Institute of Electrical and Electronics Engineers, New York.

Jim Gleason is a technical writer for IBM Corporation, Dept. F98/962-3, 740 New Circle Road, Lexington, KY 40511; (606) 232-7967. Joan Wackerman is area manager of training systems for Courseware, Inc., 427 N. Lee St., Alexandria, VA 22314; (703) 684-1000.

On the other hand, operators do *not* like documentation that

- Is inaccurate
- Has too much information or detail
- Has a demeaning or childish tone
- Is formal, stiff-sounding, or full of jargon
- Has poor printing qualities (broken type and so on)
- Is poorly organized (the information is of no use if you can't find it).

In providing the best documentation, manuals must be as usable as possible. That is, they must enable your users to do what they want to do with the equipment. That usually means two different kinds of documents need to be available: an operator guide (for training) and a reference manual. Also, you might want some sort of job aid, such as a quick-reference card, to summarize keys, functions, and probably the most common procedures.

Why so many kinds of documents? First, the operators need a training manual to take them step-by-step through the equipment's uses. This kind of documentation needs practice exercises. On the other hand, the reference manual should be organized in a more traditional sense around system features and functions. As a rule, it should also provide a greater level of detail.

One recent trend that is becoming increasingly popular among equipment manufacturers is toward customer problem-solving and repair. In most cases, this means the manufacturer provides some sort of problem determination

Reprinted from *IEEE Trans. Prof. Comm.*, vol. PC-27, no. 2, pp. 59–61, June 1984.

guide and the operator uses it to isolate machine problems. On the positive side, this approach can significantly decrease system downtime for things like operator error. On the other hand, the guide itself may be difficult to use. The same criteria for usable manuals apply here—maybe more so, as these guides are usually very task-oriented and instructions must be followed exactly.

Further, if the operators are expected to repair some part of the machine, not only must the manual be explicit and usable, but also the task must be practical. Make sure that the operators are not expected to do anything beyond their technical ability.

KEEP THE CONTENT BRIEF

How do companies keep manuals small and friendly when there are complex features to cover? One way is to divide one manual into separate booklets, based on different procedures or tasks. These booklets can be contained in a ringed binder or in one box, similar to the reading kits available in schools.

Another, and perhaps better, way is to ensure that the manual spells out only the content that the user needs to know to do his or her own tasks. For example, in word processor documentation, users need to know how to enter text on the machine, edit the text, and then print it out. In this case, the first portion of the manual must address only those areas. (Often the hardest battle for the author is preventing the engineers from putting every detail about how the system operates into the manual.)

Users want only brief, boiled-down, step-by-step keystrokes for the operations they want to do. Thus, one way to keep your content slim is to identify the series of tasks your users will perform and then list the step-by-step procedures for doing these tasks on the equipment.

Avoid covering all functions of the machine in an operator's manual. As they become more experienced, operators will tailor their machines to their own specific applications and will learn how to do many of the functions by experimentation. The place for detail is in the reference manual.

Practice exercises should be short and interspersed systematically throughout the structured format. They should be clear and procedural and provide feedback to the operators as to what they did right or wrong.

Illustrations should be as simple as possible. Good technical artists know how to take a complex piece of equipment and represent it simply. Authors of good manuals use their artists' expertise (or ask for their advice) to produce these simplified illustrations. Remember that the reason for having illustrations is to clarify an idea and to avoid using a large number of words to explain a concept. All illustrations should reduce the number of words required and should stand alone—that is, they should make sense together with the caption and the callouts.

The organizational structure should be very apparent to the user. The operator's manual should be sectioned according to common performed tasks or the ways people use the equipment. This is in contrast to organizing by functions or what the machine can do—an approach more appropriate to organizing engineering materials. Where possible, the task sections should be separated by tabs. Further, these sections should be broken into elements that are the same for each section. For example, you might want to have a preview, a system overview, the main content, practice exercises, and then a review.

By following this format with each section, the user quickly becomes accustomed to your manual and can use it more effectively. Further, users *like* a structured format. It makes them feel comfortable and they can skip sections they know they won't need.

Once they work through a few sections and know what to expect under each kind of heading, they can successfully skim for the information they need. Whether we like it or not, users will skim and will also skip sections. That's the way people use manuals; they are often impatient to do something and need information quickly. For this reason, it is important that a manual remain somewhat modular, especially for equipment with many and diverse functions. Every user will not use every function.

A structured format forces you as a writer to provide only information that fits the format. This prevents rambling, unnecessary content, and excessive detail.

The index must be complete and must be approached from several directions: features of the machine, functions of the keys, tasks the operator wants to do, and so on. Users must be able to find information for a variety of reasons. The most popular documents let the users quickly find the pages they need.

APPROPRIATE LANGUAGE

It is fairly well known that jargon should be avoided in technical documentation. Terms must be as simple as possible, and their use must be consistent; the reader should not find a variety of terms for the same concept. Further, when successful writers introduce a new term, they try to tie it to something that the user already knows. For example, you might contrast the way a particular key on a word processor works with a similar key on a typewriter.

There is some new documentation on the market now that attempts to be conversational, but ends up being demeaning. It's not easy to write a readable document without becoming patronizing—that is, using childish language or telling the customer to do something that sounds too elementary. For example, several users recently complained that, in a particular operator's manual, the text told them they were "doing a great job and should take a break." The users found this somewhat presumptuous and resented it.

A good rule of thumb is to read the manual aloud. If you feel it sounds patronizing or demeaning, others probably will too.

MANAGING DEVELOPMENT

If you are managing the writing or development process, you need to do several critical things to turn out a set of documents that really work.

First and foremost, you need to ensure that the materials are tested, retested, and tested again. Do not allow your writers or yourself to become ego-involved with the manuals to the extent that you cannot change them when the data say you should. The manuals must work.

As you begin the documentation process, use an instructional designer or an experienced document designer to give input to your format. It is worth hiring a consultant for a day or two for this. The format will act as a blueprint or specification for your writers. It will give you the tool you need to ensure that the documentation produced is relevant. The document should be designed not only for what the machine can do but, more important, for what the users will do with it.

Once you have your format designed, meet with your writers and show them a model section of a manual, using your format. Also show them some good examples of existing documentation that is similiar. Next, train your writers to write to the format. Make sure that the editor is part of your team all along the way. Involve him or her in the design of the format and the writing of the prototype section. Then ensure that as the authors begin to write, they frequently submit outlines and drafts to the editor.

Give writers immediate and frequent feedback on what they are doing right and wrong. The more specific you are about what is and is not working, the better your final product will be.

Stay close to your users. Interview them and find out how they use or intend to use the equipment.

We do not go into detail here about how or why to write at lower reading levels. There are many guidelines available on how to do this. Briefly, they recommend using short, simple, concrete words and writing in short sentences. Ask someone to calculate the readability of your document or send it through a computer program that analyzes reading level.

The important thing to emphasize is that it does not hurt to aim for an eighth-grade reading level for any document. Brighter people are not offended by simply written material. They just read it faster.

Arrange to have one editor, if possible, edit all your documents for a particular piece of equipment. This will help related documents appear more consistent. Ensure that this editor understands your desire to use terms consistently and to keep the language simple, clear, and readable. Again, make him or her part of your team.

MAKING IT LOOK GOOD

We all know that we are drawn to documentation that is attractive. But what makes it attractive? A variety of characteristics come into play, such as color, novelty, and simplicity.

How do you develop a creative, attractive package? If you are a writer or manager, let your artists be creative—brief them on your overall direction and give them a chance to select typography, layouts, and covers. Tell them what type of reaction you want the user to have upon seeing the package and let them come up with ideas. It is wise to have at least two artists working on ideas in parallel before you decide on one direction.

Take time to make sure there is plenty of white space and the layout is clean, simple, and useful.

The most recent finding is that users like documentation that is small. They like the smaller 6-in. × 9-in. size as opposed to the traditional 8.5-in × 11-in. manual. Why? It is less intimidating. Also, when they are operating a piece of equipment and using the documentation, they often put the manual on their laps. It is awkward to use the machine if the book is too large.

GETTING THE POINT ACROSS

Let the final test of how the material should look and read rest upon customers or users. Keep as close to the users as you can.

As a writer, you provide the most important (and, in many cases, the only) interface between the designers and engineers who developed the equipment and the operators who must use it. Unless the documentation you produce is the most informative and usable possible, you do both groups a grave disservice.

Selecting and Switching: Some Advantages of Diagrams Over Tables and Lists for Presenting Instructions

—ANGELIQUE BOEKELDER
AND MICHAËL STEEHOUDER,
Member, IEEE

Abstract *– Instructions for operating a control panel were presented in five different formats: flowchart, logical tree, yes/no tree, decision table, and list. Subjects had to choose one out of eight buttons, depending on the settings of the control panel. The results show that the decision table resulted in more errors, and that both the decision table and the list took longer than the three other formats, which did not show mutual differences. It turned out that the subjects valued most the format they had been using, except for those who had worked with the list. It is suggested that the users' ease of orientation for a diagram's format, both during reading and after "switching" between equipment and instructional text, explains the differences between the formats.*

Index Terms *– Diagrams, document design, tables.*

Manuscript received March 23, 1998; revised September 10, 1998.
A. Boekelder is with the Baan Company, Barneveld, The Netherlands (e-mail: aboekelder@baan.nl).
M. Steehouder is with the University of Twente, Enschede, The Netherlands (e-mail: m.f.steehouder@wmw.utwente.nl).
IEEE PII S 0361-1434(98)09152-8.

A procedure explains how to do something. More formally, it is an ordered sequence of steps that have to be carried out to reach a goal, to solve a particular problem, or to construct a product [1]. A procedure may consist of simple actions to achieve a goal, but the actions may also be elaborated by adding conditions and specifications about when, where, and how to perform them. If a procedure is presented on paper or on a screen, it is usually meant to support task performance, from operating a machine to preparing a meal. The procedure functions as an "instruction."

One of the factors that makes instructions complicated is that some steps depend on certain conditions, as in the following example:

> If the top left switch is in ON position and meter 1 reads less than 3, and display A shows STOP and meter 2 reads 100, then press button 6. But if the top left switch is in ON position and meter 1 reads less than 3, and display A shows RUN, then you should press button 7.

Such complex conditional structures can be simplified by formatting the text appropriately, in particular by using bulleted lists, tables, or diagrams such as flowcharts and logical trees. The spatial position of the elements (top/bottom, left/right), together with graphical symbols, such as bullets, lines, boxes, and arrows, replace verbal conditionals such as *if, then, while, unless*, etc.

Many publications about professional communication recommend

Reprinted from *IEEE Trans. Prof. Comm.*, vol. PC-41, no. 4, pp. 229–175, December 1998.

using tables, decision tables, or flowcharts for presenting complex conditions. For instance, Jansen and Steehouder [2] show that flowcharts were more effective than unformatted text ("prose") for informing citizens about a government regulation. Overhoff and Molenaar [3] argue that laws and regulations can be designed and controlled more effectively by converting them into decision tables instead of bureaucratic prose. They recommend decision tables as a tool for jurists who construct and/or evaluate government bills. In a technical context, Horton's [4] chapter on visualizing procedures contains useful advice and convincing examples for applying graphic formats, ranging from simple bulleted lists to complex flowcharts.

Literature Review

Rationales for Graphics What characteristics make graphics useful for presenting instructions? The following important advantages may play a role.

1) Graphics help selection of relevant information: In many instructions, particular steps are only relevant under certain conditions and can therefore be skipped if these conditions do not hold (as in the example at the beginning of the article). In particular cases, some of the conditions do not have to be verified, for example:

- If an instruction is of the form *"If A or B, then perform action C, otherwise, do D,"* and condition A turns out to be the case, it is not necessary to verify condition B; action C has to be performed anyway.
- If an instruction is of the form *"If A and B, then perform action C, otherwise do D,"* and condition A turns out not to be the case, it is not necessary to verify condition B; action D has to be performed anyway.

If a procedure has to be efficient (saving time and effort), the reader may profit from "partial processing" of the instructions—i.e., jumping over all the elements that are irrelevant in the specific situation. However, in ordinary texts, it is often difficult to identify these irrelevant elements. Readers have to read and understand the complete procedure before they can decide which elements can be skipped. Experiments by Holland and Rose [5] show indeed that readers checking conditions in ordinary texts do process all the text, without saving time and effort by partial processing.

Certain graphical formats, however, such as flowcharts and decision tables, are supposed to enable partial processing much more easily. Depending on whether a condition holds or not, the reader may proceed by a different "route" to the next condition to be verified or to the outcome of the procedure (the action to be performed). Experiments [6] have confirmed that readers are able to take advantage of graphical formats and that graphic formats take less time for verifying conditions than prose texts. However, if this effect is intended, it is very important that the sequence of the conditions is the most efficient [7].

2) Graphics reduce the syntactic complexity of the instruction: Experiments by Holland and Rose [5] suggest that the complexity of instructions outlined above is determined by four factors:

- The number of conditions. The more conditions, the more difficult the instruction is.
- The number of embeddings. The conditions may be coordinated (*"A and B and C"*) or subordinated (*"A and B or [C and D]"*). If they are subordinated, sentences can easily become ambiguous, e.g., *"Press button A if the red light is on or counter X reads 4 and the switch is in the ON position."*
- The relation between the conditions. Conjunctions (*"A and B"*) seem to be easier to understand than disjunctions (*"A or B"*).
- Negations (*"A and not B"*). These are especially important if certain expressions are used, such as *unless, provided,* or *except.*

In graphical presentations, complex instructions are split up in single steps, connected by a spatial arrangement of lines and/or arrows. This means that almost all of those four factors are eliminated. Only the number of conditions remains a relevant factor. If the reader adopts a "switching" reading style (see below), even this factor almost becomes irrelevant, because the reader has to read and perform only one element at a time. The number of conditions would only affect the time needed to perform the task, not the difficulty.

3) Graphics help readers process procedures step-by-step: A common experience of readers of technical material is that when they start to work with the equipment or the software after reading a long procedure, they find that they have forgotten the first step, and they have to return to the text and reread it. In many cases, it would be easier to switch from the text to the equipment immediately after reading one step, then perform the action, switch back to the instruction to read the second step, etc.

This issue of switching is not restricted to instructions for equipment. In a thinking aloud experiment by Steehouder and Jansen [8], readers had to read a text about a government regulation to discover what this regulation would mean in their particular situation. In this case, the time when they started to apply the information to their own situation was very important. When they switched from reading to applying too early, they made mistakes because they had not yet read all relevant information. When they switched too late, they had already forgotten the exact content of the text, or they confused the relevant and irrelevant information.

Graphical formats may help readers to switch at the right moment. An experiment by Boekelder and Steehouder [9] suggests that spatial and graphical separation between steps in a text influences the switching behavior of users of technical equipment. However, the facilitating effect of graphic presentations on switching has not yet been investigated in detail. It was tested in the experiment described below.

Of course, graphic formats have some disadvantages as well. They are more laborious to design, and they take up more space on paper or on the computer screen. In documentation for nontechnical people, problems may occur if readers are not used to graphics. Although no evidence has been found that this would affect the effectiveness or the efficiency of the instructions, it might nevertheless influence the appreciation of the documentation by the readers, and, consequently, their willingness to read it carefully.

An important disadvantage of graphic formats might be that some types have a negative effect on the understanding of the procedure by the reader. The overview of the procedure may be lost when readers apply a switching reading strategy, particularly because they skip a number of steps that are irrelevant in their particular situation but might be very important for understanding the big picture. This loss of understanding explains why flowcharts in particular seem to be less suitable when a procedure has to be learned [10].

Differences Between Graphical Formats Perhaps due to the fact that the "graphical approach" never has been challenged seriously, there is less empirical research in this field than is necessary to understand its effects in detail. Most of the research on tables has to do with searching for numerical data in tables, for example, the many detailed experiments by Patricia Wright in the early 1970s. However, in relations to conditions-and-action information, the research is quite limited, although unambiguously supporting the superiority of graphics to prose. Wright and Reid [10] compared instructions in several formats: ordinary ("bureaucratic") prose, flowchart, table, and list. Subjects in the experiment had to answer questions about a fictitious space voyage, using one of the instructional formats. They concluded that, for complex problems, flowcharts and tables were more effective (they led to fewer errors) than both prose and list. For simple problems, there were no differences in effectiveness, but the table format turned out to be more efficient: it took less time to find the answer.

In another experiment, Wright [11] compared prose, table, and logical tree formats for explaining to examination candidates which questions they should answer. In this experiment, the advantages of the graphical presentations were less clear. A table or a logical tree did not produce fewer errors than prose, and the prose version even took less time than both graphical formats. Wright explains this by pointing out that in this experiment the instructions **did not contain irrelevant information**, which the instructions in the previous experiment did. In other words, the advantages of graphical presentations seem to lie primarily in the fact that they help readers apply partial processing; they select from the instructions what is relevant for their actual situation.

In an ingenious and very carefully conducted experiment (that regrettably never has been published), Holland and Rose [6] used three formats for presenting instructions of the type "*If A and B or C and D, then press button X*"—where *and* and *or* were systematically alternated, and negations (*not-A, not-B, etc.*) were also considered. The instructions were presented in prose, algorithm (flowchart), and question list formats. The latter consists of a sequence of questions such as: *Does A apply to you? If yes, go to nn, if no go to mm*, where *nn* and *mm* were either the next question to be answered, or the final instruction *to push button X*.

The results of their experiment showed that both flowcharts and lists were more effective and more efficient than prose. Both were equally effective, but flowcharts were more efficient. Holland and Rose conclude that both lists and flowcharts enable the reader to partially process the instructions easily. Moreover, their results show that moving from one question to the other takes less time if the questions are linked graphically (as in the flowchart) than if they are connected verbally (by cross-references like "*Go to nn*").

Michael and Hartley [12] present an overview of eleven experiments (including the Wright and Reid experiment) that compared flowcharts with other formats. They conclude that flowcharts yield better results than other formats in the following cases:

- if there are complex combinations of conditions;
- if there are complex problems;
- if it is important to separate relevant information from irrelevant information;
- if it is not necessary to memorize the instructions or the problem to be solved;
- if the flowchart is oriented from left to right and from top to bottom (however, as far as we know, no experiments have been done in cultures with a right–left orientation of the alphabet, so this conclusion may be limited).

Michael and Hartley indicate that the most important drawbacks of flowcharts are that they are more complex to design than prose and that sometimes readers have difficulties in reading flowcharts.

Switching Between Instructions and Equipment In the experiments reviewed here, the effects of graphical formats (table, flowchart, list) have always been tested in situations were the conditions could be verified either by applying information from memory (in the experiments of Holland and Rose, e.g. "*If you are married and over 45* ··· "), by realizing what the subjects want ("*If you want to* ··· "), or by applying task information (e.g., in the experiments by Wright "*What means of transport is to be used if* ··· "). However, users often have to verify the current state of external equipment (meters, switches, codes in displays, etc.), as in the example at the beginning of this article. This may complicate the situation in two respects.

First, readers have to decide at what moment they should switch from the instructional text to the equipment, and back. Users may decide first to read the entire instruction, and then verify the state of the equipment. However, it is more likely that they read step-by-step and verify each step immediately after reading, as is suggested by another unpublished experiment of Holland and Rose [5]. Graphical formats may influence the switching behavior of readers because they show the edges between the steps better than continuous prose.

Secondly, since readers are drawn away from the instruction to inspect the equipment, it is important that when returning to the text, they can find the exact place where they have to proceed. The format of the text should facilitate their orientation at that moment. Graphical formats clearly support this process better than continuous prose. However, it is not clear which of the graphical formats is preferable in this respect.

Research Design

Research Purpose The purpose of the experiment reported here is to explore the relative effectiveness and efficiency of several graphical formats for tasks that include

- the need to verify a number of conditions, and
- the need to switch from the instructional document to the equipment to be used for the task.

Overview Two different control panels of a fictitious spacecraft were presented alternately on a computer screen. The panels consisted of a number of switches, check lights, meters, and displays, and a numbered row of eight buttons at the bottom. The subjects had to click one of these buttons with the mouse, depending on the settings of the meters and the texts of the displays. Which button to click for a particular panel setting was explained by instructions on a second screen. The format of these instructions differed between subjects; each subject was confronted with either flowcharts, logical trees, yes/no-diagrams, decision tables, or lists.

The subjects were able to look at either the instruction or the control panel by pressing or releasing the space bar. The mouse clicks and the actions of the space bar were registered in a log file.

Five Instructional Formats Compared in the Experiment In the experiment, five graphic formats of an instruction were investigated. (The original materials used in the experiment were in Dutch.)

- A flowchart (Fig. 1): a series of yes/no questions, connected with arrows. For instance: *Is the top left swift ON? Yes/no.* The reader has to follow either the *yes*-arrow or the *no*-arrow to reach the next question and eventually the outcome. In this flowchart, all yes-arrows point to the right, all no-arrows point down (the last one with an angle to the right).
- A logical tree (Fig. 2): again a series of questions, connected with arrows, but in this cases, the questions are not yes/no-questions but questions with two alternatives. For instance: *What does the display A show? RUN/STOP.* As with the flowchart, the reader has to follow the appropriate arrows to reach the next question or the outcome. In this logical tree, all lines point down, and no arrows are used.

The difference between a flowchart and a logical tree is not often made in the literature as we do here—usually, the terms are used without a clear distinction (as well as the term algorithm). It seems that those formats are mostly considered as equivalents. There seems to be no sound base for hypothesizing about differences. An exception is the experiment by Barnard *et al.* [13]: form-fillers needed more time to answer questions such as *Are you married? Yes/no* than questions of the type *I am single/married.* The latter type, however, is not a question, and the answers are by definition complementary, at least in most countries (one is either single or married, but in the case of the display it is theoretically possible that there are more possibilities than RUN or STOP).

If we would find any differences between the flowchart and the logical tree, then there may be two explanations. The differences might be caused either by the layout (two directions versus one direction) or by the formulation of the questions (yes/no versus alternatives). Therefore, we decided to include a third type of graphic in our experiment:

- A yes/no tree (Fig. 3): this has the graphic form of the logical tree, but the *yes/no* questions of the flowchart.

- A decision table (Fig. 4): this consists of columns indicating parts of the equipment and rows that represent the setting that these parts can have. By choosing the right row from left to right, the reader reaches the appropriate outcome in the rightmost column.
- A list (Fig. 5): this consists of vertically ordered numbered actions, each followed by a number of conditions, after which either a route-instruction ("*Go to number* ⋯") guides the reader to the next question, or the appropriate outcome is given.

A continuous prose version is

Fig. 1. Flowchart.

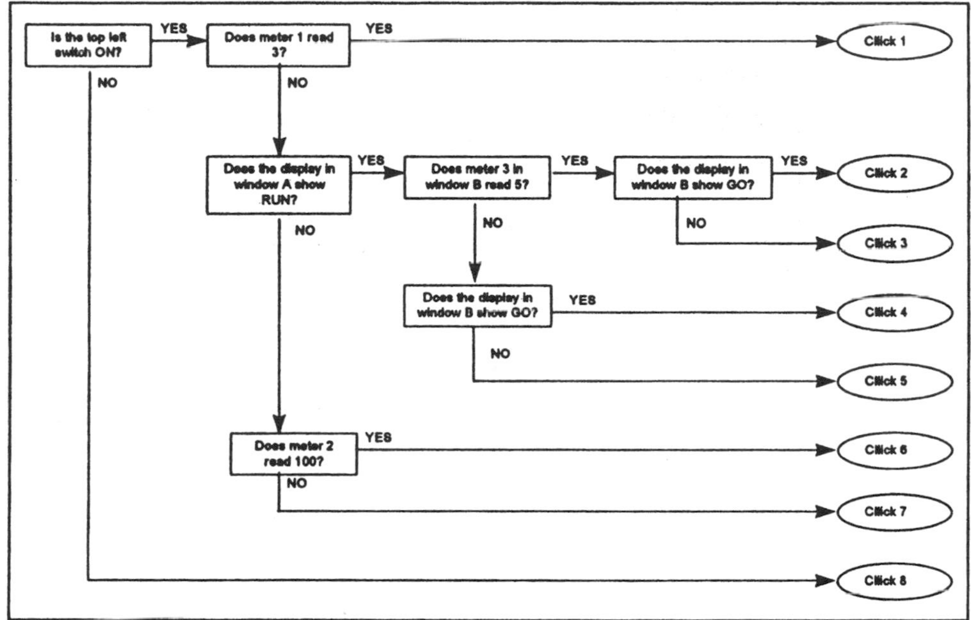

Fig. 2. Logical tree.

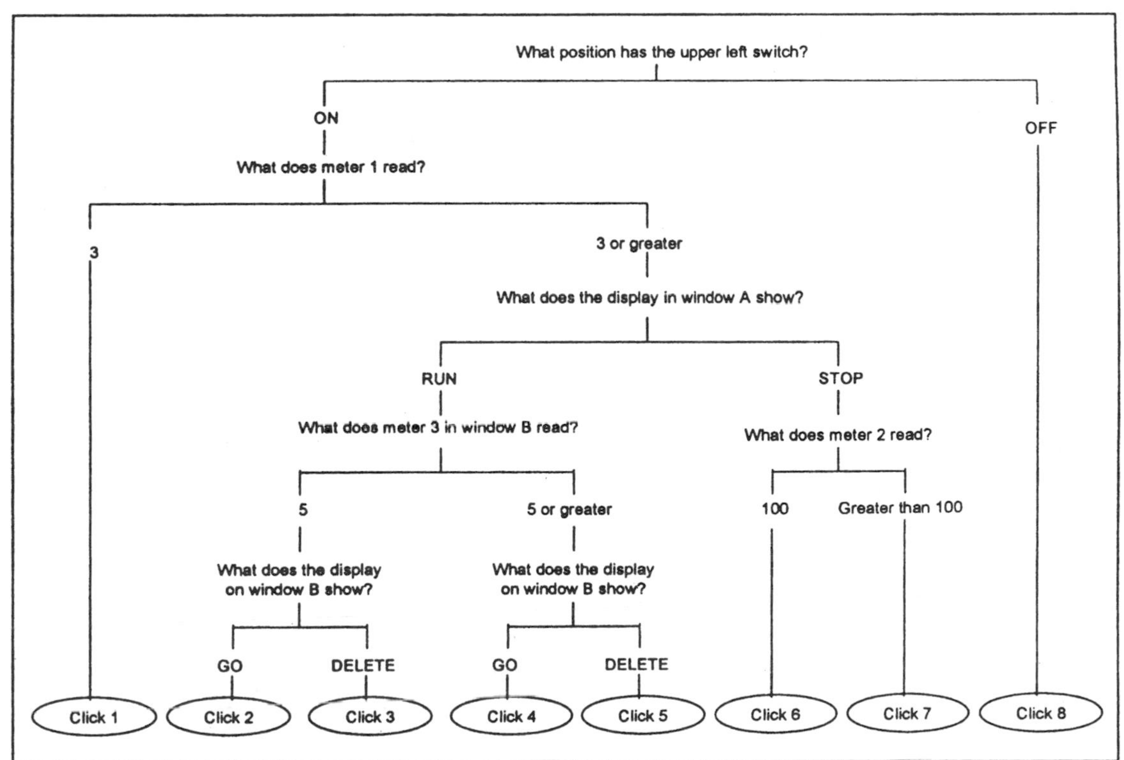

outside the scope of this study because of the unanimous results of the experiments reported in the literature [12]. Graphical formats proved to be more effective and efficient than prose in all experiments. Thus it does not make sense to investigate this again.

Control Panels Two different control panels were used in the experiment (see Fig. 6(a)–(c)). Each panel was shown with five different settings (i.e., a combination of positions of meters, windows, indicators, etc.), which resulted in ten cases. Three cases required verification of two elements before

Fig. 3. Yes/no tree.

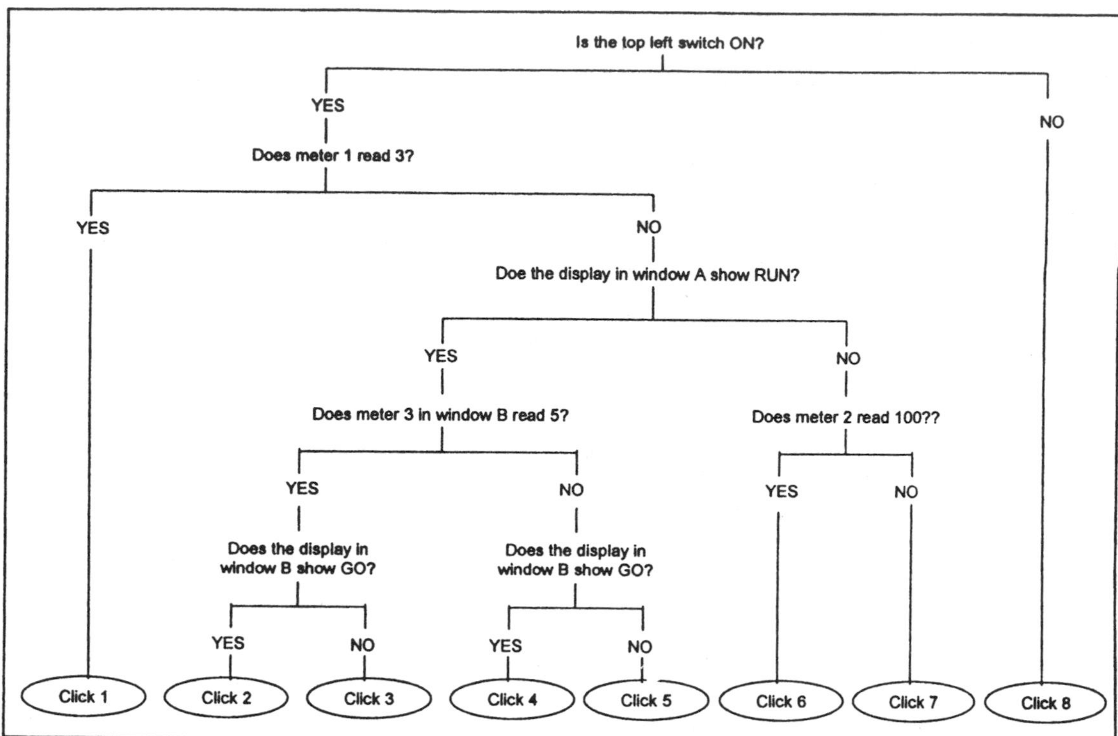

Fig. 4. Decision table.

<table>
<tr><th>Is the top left switch read ON?</th><th>Does meter 1 read 3?</th><th>Does the display in window A show RUN?</th><th>Does meter 3 in window B read 5?</th><th>Does the display in window B show GO?</th><th>Does meter 2 read 100?</th><th>Click</th></tr>
<tr><td rowspan="7">YES</td><td>YES</td><td>–</td><td>–</td><td>–</td><td>–</td><td>button # 1</td></tr>
<tr><td rowspan="6">NO</td><td rowspan="4">YES</td><td rowspan="2">YES</td><td>YES</td><td>–</td><td>button # 2</td></tr>
<tr><td>NO</td><td>–</td><td>button # 3</td></tr>
<tr><td rowspan="2">NO</td><td>YES</td><td>–</td><td>button # 4</td></tr>
<tr><td>NO</td><td>–</td><td>button # 5</td></tr>
<tr><td rowspan="2">NO</td><td>–</td><td>–</td><td>YES</td><td>button # 6</td></tr>
<tr><td>–</td><td>–</td><td>NO</td><td>button # 7</td></tr>
<tr><td>NO</td><td>–</td><td>–</td><td>–</td><td>–</td><td>–</td><td>button # 8</td></tr>
</table>

a button could be clicked. Three cases required verification of four elements, and four cases required verification of five elements. This variation would make it possible to investigate whether the subjects partially processed the instructions. Cases that only require two verifications would require less time than settings that require four or five verifications.

The control panels were displayed on a screen in front of the subject. After the subject had clicked one of the buttons, the message *next assignment* was displayed. After the subject clicked OK, the next status of the control panel was shown.

Subjects Subjects were 99 students (36 female, 63 male) at the University of Twente. 71 of them were engineering students; 28 were social sciences students. The subjects received NFL 10 (approx. $5 US) for their cooperation. The subjects were randomly assigned to one of the graphical formats.

Procedure The experiment was fully controlled by a computer program except for a questionnaire. The introduction to the experiment (see Fig. 6) was displayed on the screen. The introduction was formatted in short paragraphs, which were displayed one after another. By clicking *Continue* the subject could proceed to the next paragraph. *Click on OK to start the first assignment* was displayed at the end of the introduction.

There were two different procedures (one for each panel) that indicated which of the eight buttons had to be clicked. The instructions (in one of the formats discussed above) were presented on a second computer screen, left in front of the subject.

Only one of the screens was visible at any one time during the experiment. When the subjects wanted to look at the instructions, they had to press the left screen's space bar. At the same moment, the control panel at the right was made invisible. When the space bar was released, the instructions became invisible, and the control panel was visible again. So the subjects were able to look at either the instructions or the control panel, not both. This experimental setting made it possible to keep track of reading times, as well as of the exact moments and frequencies of switching between instruction and control panel. It turned out that (after little practice) switching between the two screens was very easy.

The subjects were presented in turns with one of the control panels that had a different setting of the switches, the meters, and the lights each time. The subjects had to decide which of the eight buttons on the bottom of the control panel had to be clicked with the mouse. After clicking, a different task—unrelated to this experiment—had to be carried out. (A different control panel was presented for this in-between task, along with ordinary prose instructions. The subject had to click some button and key in some codes.) When this task was

Fig. 5. List.

A Look at the top left switch
- If the switch is ON, go to B
- If the switch is OFF, click button # 8

B Look at meter 1
- If it reads 3, click button # 1
- It it reads greater than 3, go to C

C Look at the display in window A
- If its shows STOP, go to D
- If it shows RUN, go to E

D Look at meter 2
- If it reads 100, click button # 6
- If it reads greater than 100, click button # 7

E Look at window B
- If meter 3 reads 5 and the display shows GO, click button # 2
- If meter 3 reads 5 and the display shows DELETE, click button # 3
- If meter 3 reads greater than 5 and the display shows GO, click button # 4
- If meter 3 reads greater than 5 and the display shows DELETE, click button # 5

Fig. 6. (a) Sketch of control panel #1 with settings that require five elements to be verified and button #5 to be clicked; (b) sketch of control panel #1 with settings that require two elements to be verified and button #1 to be clicked; and (c) sketch of control panel #2.

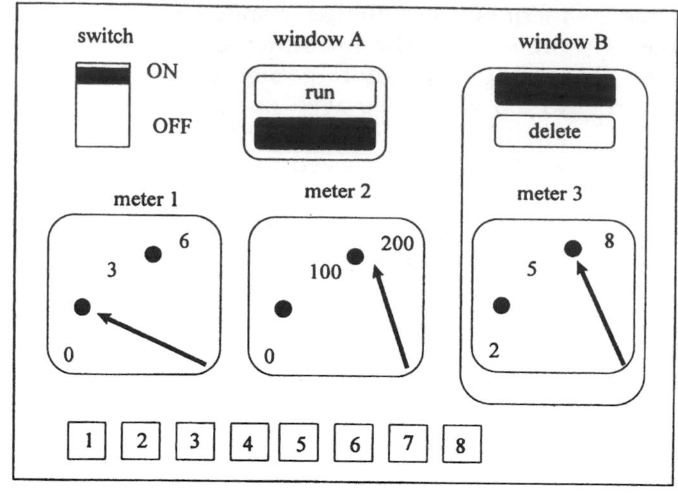

(a)

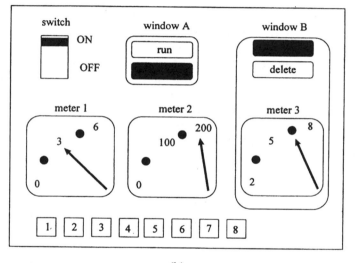

(b)

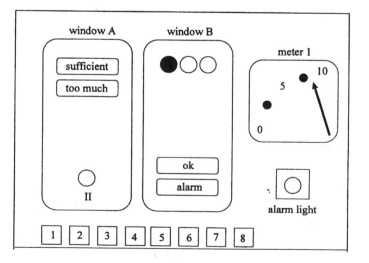

completed, the next assignment appeared on the screen.

All the subjects' actions were logged by the computer: pressing and releasing the space bar, as well as clicking one of the buttons with the mouse. The log files were converted into a record that showed exactly when and for how long the instructions were read and which buttons were clicked at the end of each assignment.

Each subject completed ten different assignments, five for each control panel (see Fig. 7 for some examples). Each assignment started with different settings of one of the control panels.

The first assignment of the test was the same for all subjects; this task was used to practice and has not been included in the analysis of the results. The order of the other nine assignments was varied between the subjects.

The format of the instructions was a between-subjects variable. Each of the subjects was confronted with only one of the five formats.

Results

Effectiveness The first question to ask is: how accurate are the results of the different formats? After all, time differences are only relevant if the number of correct answers is equal. The number of errors (wrong buttons clicked) per format is shown in Table I. A one-way ANOVA showed a difference ($F = 3.550, df = 4, p < .01$). Tukey's test showed that the number of errors made with the decision table differs from the number of errors made with the logical tree, the yes/no tree, and the list. Thus the decision table produces less accurate results than the other graphical formats.

Efficiency The efficiency of the formats can be expressed in two measures: task time (= time between starting a new assignment and completing it by clicking one of the buttons) and reading time (= time during which the space bar is pressed down, i.e., the time that the instruction could been seen, and the panel was hidden).

The mean task times (in seconds) are presented in Table I. A one-way ANOVA showed a significant difference ($F = 5.201, df = 4, p < 0.001$) between the formats. Tukey's test showed that the list was less efficient than the logical tree and that

Fig. 7. Introduction of the experiment (translated fragment).

Several control panels of a spacecraft will shortly appear on the screen you are currently watching. The panels contain buttons that can be clicked with the mouse. Imagine you are the commander of the spacecraft and you have to handle the buttons for several tasks.

The procedure is as follows. When the control panel appears, the meters and switches are in certain positions. This indicates a particular situation. You have to react on this situation by clicking one of the buttons numbered 1 to 8, at the bottom of the control panel. You can find which button you should click in the instructions that are presented on the left screen.

After you have clicked the button, the next control panel will appear on the screen.

TABLE I

Number of Errors, Mean Task Time, and Mean Reading Time Per Assignment (Standard Deviations in Brackets)

	Flowchart n=19	Logical tree n=19	Yes/no tree n=18	Decision table n=22	List n=21
Mean number of errors per assignment	.7 (1.4)	.5 (.7)	.6 (.7)	1.8 (2.1)	.5 (1.0)
Mean task time per assignment	23.1 (4.7)	23.8 (3.8)	24.4 (5.1)	28.3 (6.9)	29.3 (6.5)
Mean reading time per assignment	12.1 (3.8)	12.2 (1.9)	13.0 (4.0)	15.1 (4.0)	17.2 (4.3)

the decision table was less efficient than the flowchart.

The mean reading times (in seconds) are also presented in Table I. Again, a one-way ANOVA showed a difference ($F = 7.050, df = 4$, $p < 0.001$). Tukey's test showed that the list was less efficient compared to the flowchart, logical tree, and yes/no tree.

The analysis so far has been presented for each assignment without considering the number of elements that had to be verified to decide which of the buttons had to be clicked. As stated above, some tasks required two, some required four, and some required five verifications. Table II presents the task times for the assignments by the number of verifications required.

An analysis of variance with repeated measures yielded significant time differences between the five graphical formats ($F = 5.61, df = 4, p < 0.001$), and between the three types of assignments ($F = 226.96, df = 2, p < 0.001$). Tukey's test showed that:

- For assignments that required two verifications, the list was less efficient than the flowchart and the logical tree was less efficient than both the flowchart and the yes/no tree.
- For assignments that required four verifications, the list was less efficient than both the logical tree and the flowchart.
- For assignments that required five verifications, no differences were found.

Table III shows the mean reading times for the assignments, by the number of verifications that had to be verified.

An ANOVA with repeated measures showed significant differences between the reading times for the five graphical formats ($F = 7.47, df = 4, p < 0.001$) as well as differences between the three types of assignments ($F = 219.74, df = 2, p < 0.001$). Tukey's test showed that:

- For assignments that required two verifications, both the list and the decision tree were less efficient than the flowchart or the yes/no tree.
- For assignments that required four verifications, the list was less efficient than the flowchart, the logical tree and the yes/no tree.
- For assignments that required five verifications, the list was

TABLE II

Mean Task Time Per Assignment When Two, Four, or Five Verifications Were Required (Standard Deviations in Brackets)

	Flowchart n=19	Logical tree n=19	Yes/no tree n=18	Decision table n=22	List n=21
Assignments requiring two verifications	12.9 (3.5)	15.6 (4.2)	13.0 (2.1)	18.6 (7.1)	17.6 (4.3)
Assignments requiring four verifications	23.1 (5.3)	23.6 (5.0)	24.4 (7.7)	28.4 (8.6)	31.3 (11.7)
Assignments requiring five verifications	28.0 (6.5)	28.1 (5.1)	29.3 (6.2)	33.1 (8.1)	33.7 (7.4)

TABLE III

Mean Reading Time Per Assignment for Assignment That Required Two, Four, or Five Verifications (Standard Deviations in Brackets)

	Flowchart n=19	Logical tree n=19	Yes/no tree n=18	Decision table n=22	List n=21
Assignments requiring two verifications	5.8 (2.1)	6.6 (2.2)	5.2 (1.7)	8.3 (4.3)	8.8 (2.9)
Assignments requiring four verifications	11.9 (3.9)	11.9 (3.3)	13.5 (5.4)	15.0 (5.8)	18.8 (8.2)
Assignments requiring five verifications	15.3 (5.3)	15.3 (2.6)	16.6 (4.9)	18.6 (4.8)	20.3 (4.9)

less efficient than both the flowchart and the logical tree.

Preferences After the experiment, the preferences of the subjects for the various formats were collected. The subjects were asked to rank printed examples of the formats by preference: the best one in the first place (1 point) and the worst one in the last place (5 points).

The results are presented in Table IV. These results indicate that the subjects preferred the format they had used during the experiment. The only exception to this is for those who had used the list. They preferred the flowchart and the yes/no tree to the list.

Conclusions

The results of the experiment show clear differences between the five graphical formats. The decision table yielded more errors than all the other formats. This can be explained by the fact that it requires cognitive processing in two directions: rows and columns. It seems that readers sometimes choose the wrong row (or "lose" their row), so that they come to the wrong outcome. Despite the fact that a decision table requires relatively little space, it is evidently not the most appropriate format. Our conclusion that working in two directions is more difficult than working in one direction is consistent with the results of an experiment by Wright and Fox [14], who asked subjects to look up numbers in a "matrix table."

The differences in the efficiency measures (task times and reading times) show that the list format (and to some extent also the decision table) are less efficient than the other formats. For the decision table, this may also be explained by the bidirectional orientation: users have to orient themselves twice within the table, which takes extra time. The fact that the list is less efficient than the other formats suggests that verbal cross references ("*Go to* ··· ") are more difficult to follow than the graphic features (arrows and lines) in the diagrams.

No significant differences were found between the flowchart, the logical tree, and the yes/no tree. Apparently, neither the direction of the lines and arrows made any difference, nor the type of question (yes/no versus open). But it should be taken into account that the open questions in this experiment had only two answers. If the number of possible answers increases ("*What color is the sign: red, green, blue?*"), then the differences between the flowchart and the logical tree become more substantial. In order to make a choice between three or four options, two yes/no questions are needed, while only one open question is needed to offer the same number of alternatives. Other experiments [15] suggest that one choice of four alternatives can be made more quickly than two choices of two alternatives each. Consequently, in such cases, a logical tree may be more efficient.

As to the subjects' preferences for the formats, it is interesting to see that this depends on their previous experience. The format they worked with was valued most, except for the list. It is striking that even the subjects that had worked with the table preferred it to the other formats, despite the difficulties they seemed to have with using it (of course, the subjects were not aware of the fact that the table turned out to be less effective than the other formats). These results indicate that users' preferences for certain visual formats may not reflect their ability to use them effectively. Thus it might be unwise to base design decisions on preferences of users. On the other hand, users' preferences may be important as to

TABLE IV

Mean Preference Ranking of the Five Graphic Formats Related to the Format the User Used During the Experiment

	Ranking of the flowchart	Ranking of the logical tree	Ranking of the yes/no tree	Ranking of the decision table	Ranking of the list
Subjects who had used the flowchart	**1.7**	3.0*	2.7*	3.7*	3.8
Subjects who had used the logical tree	2.7*	**1.5**	2.2	4.4*	4.3*
Subjects who had used the yes/no tree	2.3	3.0*	**1.6**	3.9*	4.3*
Subjects who had used the decision table	2.3	3.4*	2.7*	**2.1**	4.5*
Subjects who had used the list	**2.3**	3.0*	2.5*	4.2*	3.1

bold = most preferred format (=lowest number) in the row
* = differs significantly ($p<.05$) from the most preferred format in the column

their willingness to use and follow instructions—which is why we still consider them as relevant.

Our results indicate that it is important that readers of instructions can orient themselves in the chosen format. Two types of orientations were important in the experiment First, it was important that the reader was able to "follow" the route from one verification to the next. As we have seen, this was more difficult with the two-dimensional decision table, and it took more time with the list. But since the subjects had also to switch between the instruction and the control panel, a second moment of orientation was important. Suppose the reader reads one step (*"Does the counter read 3?"*), then switches to the control panel to verify this, and then returns to the instructions to read the next verification. The reader has to orient him- or herself to find the place where he or she left the instruction. This switching problem may be of little influence when it is easy to remember the complete instruction as a whole. However, if the instructions consist of many steps, it seems likely that the influence will be more substantial.

Our data do not allow for any conclusions to be drawn about the relative influence of both types of orientation problems. A considerable number of subjects turned out to be able to complete their task after one (long) period of studying the instruction. They inspected the control panel, switched to the instruction, and returned to the control panel and clicked on the button immediately. Other subjects switched more frequently between control panel and instruction. More research is needed to find out how important the influence of both types of orientation is.

What conclusion can been drawn for the design of instructions in practice? Our experiment suggests that flowcharts, yes/no trees, and logical trees are more appropriate for instructions than decision tables (which yield more errors) or lists (which take more time and are appreciated less by users). As long as the individual verifications have only two outcomes, these three formats seem to be equally appropriate, but it seems important to restrict instructions to one format, since users prefer the format they have become familiar with.

References

[1] P. F. Merrill, "Structured outline representations for procedures or algorithms," in *The Technology of Text. Principles for Structuring, Designing and Displaying Text, Volume I*, D. H. Jonassen, Ed. Englewood Cliffs, NJ: Educational Publications, 1985, pp. 233–251.

[2] C. Jansen and M. Steehouder, "Improving the text of a public leaflet," *Inform. Des. J.*, vol. 4, pp. 10–18, 1984.

[3] R. W. Overhoff and L. J. Molenaar, *In de Regel Beslist. Een Beschouwing over Regelgeving met Behulp van Beslissingstabellen [Deciding Conform the Rules—Observations on Legislative Drafting Using Decision Tables]*. The Hague, The Netherlands: SDU, 1991.

[4] W. Horton, *Illustrating Computer Documentation*. New York: Wiley, 1991.

[5] V. M. Holland and A. M. Rose, "Understanding instructions with complex conditions," Document Design Project Tech. Rep. 5, Washington, DC, Amer. Inst. for Res., 1980.

[6] ——, "A comparison of prose and algorithms for presenting complex instructions," Document Design Project Tech. Rep. 17, Washington, DC, Amer. Inst. for Res., 1981.

[7] C. J. M. Jansen and M. F. Steehouder, "The sequential order of procedural instructions. Some formal methods for designers of flow charts," *J. Tech. Writing and Commun.*, vol. 26 no, 4, pp. 453–471, 1996.

[8] C. Jansen and M. Steehouder, "Improving the text of a public leaflet," *Inform. Des. J.*, vol. 4, pp. 10–18, 1984.

[9] A. Boekelder and M. Steehouder, "Switching from instructions to equipment: The effect of graphic design," in *Visual Information for Everyday Use: Design and Research Perspectives*, H. J. Zwaga, T. Boersema, and H. C. Hoonhout, Eds. London, U.K.: Taylor & Francis, 1998, in press.

[10] P. Wright and F. Reid, "Written information: Some alternatives to prose for expressing the outcomes of complex contingencies," *J. Appl. Psychol.*, vol. 57, pp. 160–166, 1973.
[11] P. Wright, "Decision making as a factor in the ease of using numerical tables," *Ergonomics*, vol. 20, pp. 91–96, 1977.
[12] D. Michael and J. Hartley, "Extracting information from flowcharts and contingency statements: The effects of age and practice," *British J. Educ. Technol.*, vol. 22, pp. 84–98, 1991.
[13] P. Barnard, P. Wright, and P. Wilcox, "Effects of response instructions and question style on the ease of completing forms," *J. Occup. Psychol.*, vol. 52, pp. 209–226, 1979.
[14] P. Wright and K. Fox, "Presenting information in tables," *Appl. Ergon.*, vol. 1, pp. 234–242, 1970.
[15] P. Wright, "Presenting people with choices: The effect of format on the comprehension of examination rubrics," *Progr. Learn. and Educ. Technol.*, vol. 12, pp. 109–114, 1975.

Angelique Boekelder graduated in Text Linguistics at Tilburg University, The Netherlands (1986–1992). From 1993 till 1997, she was a Ph.D. student at the University of Twente, where she did research into the field of instructional design. Since 1997, she has worked as a technical author with Baan Company, a major IT company producing ERP software.

Michaël Steehouder (M'98) is an Associate Professor for Professional and Technical Communication at the Communication Studies Department of the University of Twente. He has published several textbooks and a number of articles on professional communication, and he was (co-)editor of several conference proceedings. He is the Editor-in-Chief of *Tekst[blad]*, a Dutch journal on professional communication, and an Associate Editor of IEEE TRANSACTIONS ON PROFESSIONAL COMMUNICATION.

Using a Structured Design Analysis To Simplify Complex In-House Computer Manuals

John S. Craig

Abstract—**As an organization's in-house computer system becomes more complicated, user manuals can quickly become so large and complicated that they become unusable. Redesigning a computer user manual to be both comprehensive and usable can be a question of finding what information to keep and what to cut. To produce a more efficient and portable computer user manual, a structured, three-stage design analysis was added to the pre-writing strategy. To find what information users really needed, a needs assessment was used as part of the three-stage procedure. The portable manual was designed for a large government organization whose employees are in a highly mobile environment.**

Introduction

TECHNICAL writers who write computer user manuals must produce documents that are complete and accurate, and they must be careful not to exclude important information that would affect the outcome of a user's task. By contrast, the more text used, the more the document will cost; additionally, presenting too much information can make a user manual ineffective.

This paper outlines a three-stage procedure used to create a user manual for the city of Denver's Department of Safety in-house computer system. Department of Safety computer users require the skills and the reference material sufficient to access information from a variety of in-house systems that keep the records for a variety of concerns ranging from offenses, citations, DUI (Driving Under the Influence), DWAI (Driving While Ability Impaired), accidents, gun registration, juvenile records, field contacts, active prisoners, and released prisoners. Along with the in-house systems, users must also have access to data from the National Crime Information Center computer (NCIC) and the Colorado Crime Information Center computer (CCIC). To complicate matters, users need to know how to operate several personal computer software programs, including word processors, spreadsheets, and data base management systems.

As the number of in-house computer applications grew, the original user manual expanded into several hundred pages and multiple volumes. Its content was elaborate, covering in-house computer queries, log-on procedures, screen displays, descriptions of fields, an introduction, an extensive index, troubleshooting, hundreds of codes (vehicles, guns, and others), and basic information on operating keyboards, printers, and other peripherals. An additional concern was personal computers; their use was increasing in the organization, but there was no comprehensive instructional or tutorial material in the existing manuals to aid PC users.

Manuscript received July 1991; revised September 1991.
The author is at 7777 Yale, Denver, CO 80231.
IEEE Log Number 9105411.

The challenge was to develop a single "portable" manual that could be moved from one work site to another, or used to operate a computer terminal in a car, if necessary, yet be detailed enough to instruct or inform a user on the most significant information. To add to the challenge, there was a diverse audience—police officers, fire fighters, sheriff deputies, and civilians—each with different needs. What information *needed* to be added, kept, or excluded from the elaborate manuals was assessed through three stages: Preliminary Analysis, Needs Assessment, and Design for Learning.

In planning to write referential or instructional material, the technical writer is interested in the same objective as the instructional designer: analyze the needs of the learner in a given instructional situation. Adding traditional instructional design methods, such as performing a needs assessment and defining a learning objective, to the pre-writing strategy can create a more effective document design strategy. By adding these two methods the writer can discover the needs of specific user groups, provide cost analysis, define what the user needs to learn, and establish an iterative usability test.

Overview Of The Three-stage Design Analysis

A detailed analysis of what users needed was required to solve the problem. To identify what information should be retained from the elaborate manuals and what information should be added, the needs assessment and a design for learning were added to a traditional technical communication audience analysis procedure to create a more comprehensive pre-writing strategy. The strategy is outlined below.

Preliminary Analysis
- Breaking the Audience Into Groups
- Analyzing Existing Information
- Relating Training to Documentation

The Needs Assessment
- Analyzing the Problem
- Problem and Clarification Phase
- Survey Phase

Design for Learning
- Matching Needs with the Groups
- Defining the Learning Objective
- Design Strategies
- Testing the Document

The remainder of this paper details the stages in this process. As the procedures are explained the reader should see why

Reprinted from *IEEE Trans. Prof. Comm.*, vol. PC-35, no. 1, pp. 7–12, March 1992.

some information was kept, some was deleted, and some information was added to create the new portable manual.

Preliminary Analysis

An effective analysis of a writer's audience will define who the audience is, what they presently know about the subject, what they need to know, and how they will react to the information presented.

Breaking the Audience into Groups

For this project, the audience analysis began with an egocentric organization chart. An egocentric organizational chart differs from a conventional organization chart in two ways: it identifies individual roles (i.e., civilians in Records and officers in the Radio Room) rather than complex organizational units; and it defines readers in terms of how close they are to the writer [1]. The chart uses four levels of distance from the writer: 1) audiences in the writer's group, 2) audiences in close proximity to the writer, 3) audiences elsewhere in the organization, and 4) audiences outside the organization. The farther away a user is from the writer in an organization, the more difficult communication may be because terminology that is assumed to be understood by users in the writer's group may not be understood in other parts of the organization or outside the organization.

Each level or degree of distance may define a need for different information (see Table I).

TABLE I
EGOCENTRIC CHART

Audience in Own Group	Data Section (officers/civilians) Records (civilians)
Audience Close to Group	Radio (civilians/officers) Identification (civilians/officers) Detectives (officers) Administration (officers/civilians)
Audience Elsewhere in Group	Street police officers Arson (firefighters, civilians) Firefighters District Police Technicians
Audience Out of Organization	None

Analyzing Existing Information

After analyzing the egocentric chart, a search was made for existing program and user documentation, instructional material, tutorials, or any analysis done by previous instructional designers. This search produced the following items:

- **Program Documentation:** data flow diagram, structure chart, flow chart, programming code, data dictionary.
- **Training Material:** needs assessment, task analysis, learning hierarchies, learning objective descriptions, training guides.
- **Existing User Documentation:** older versions of system documentation and current user manuals that may contain too much or too little information for a user.

Relating Training to Documentation

A thorough training program can help limit the amount of information necessary in a reference manual. The writer should consider what, if any, computer courses are offered in-house and if those courses are mandatory.

By itself, training must provide practice, steady-paced learning in comfortable, undisturbed surroundings, and a sense of accomplishment for the student. With positive results, the student is more likely to proceed through other phases of learning, such as attending additional tutorials; reading electronic manuals; and using help systems—interactive job aids, simulations, intelligent tutors—collectively known as "embedded training."

Embedded training is a continuing aspect of online instruction that is an integral part of a product or system [2]. The more elaborate the embedded training systems are, the less reference material the writer may need to provide. An analysis of online help messages, online codes (vehicle codes and so on), and all embedded training systems will tell the writer what instructional material is missing and what referential documentation is needed.

One objective of computer training is to provide the student with enough knowledge so that he or she can continue to learn whenever they are using a computer. The structure and availability of training should profoundly affect the decision regarding what should be included in documentation and tutorials. Analysis of successful training guides made sure that the important information in the guides was included in the manual. Important online help messages were assessed and included with additional detail in the manual (i.e., the percent sign "%" is a wild-card character that can be used to search for names and partial license plate numbers). The Department's strong commitment to training gave computer users the knowledge needed to find codes through online help. Any codes that could be accessed online were deleted from the proposed portable manual.

Needs Assessment

Needs assessment is a systematic effort that gathers opinions and ideas from a variety of sources regarding performance problems or new systems and technologies [3]. The assessment is done through interviews, surveys, and small group interactions. It involves as many concerned sources as the writer can budget. It is conducted in stages: what the assessor learns in the first stage influences the questions asked and data examined in later stages [4]. From this process the writer can assess the sources' opinions about the ideal goal (optimals), what is happening now (actuals), feelings, causes, and solutions. If properly completed, the needs assessment can show trainers, writers, and managers a variety of organizational, system, and managerial problems.

A needs assessment can be designed to discover problems that will affect the user's performance: incentive problems (motivation); improperly designed systems (managerial); and missing tools, machines, or facilities (environmental) [5].

When users are questioned on their feelings and opinions about existing systems, they may let the writer know, in passionate terms, that they don't care to learn a particular application. They also may point out that existing system errors make their job difficult, or that they don't have access to machines, or a place to learn. On the other hand, they may reveal little about how they feel. Problems that writers or trainers can't solve should be forwarded to management.

Analyzing the Problem

The needs assessment can be done through one-on-one interviews, phone interviews, or surveys. When possible, the assessor should document the source of the information. The purpose of conducting a needs assessment is to seek information about the following topics [6].

- **Optimals**—What should be happening? What is the ideal situation? What should users do and how well should they do it?
- **Actuals**—What is going on now? Opposed to the ideal situation, what is happening in the field? Users may not be as forthcoming with the shortcomings of their performance.
- **Causes**—What is causing the problem? Is it prerequisite skills, supervision, lack of equipment, motivation? Is there a problem that written material will solve? If there *is* a performance problem, will written material alone solve it or will training be required?
- **Feelings/Priorities**—How do people feel about the problem? Is the new system something that will help them in their job, or is it something that they will dread or not use?
- **Solutions**—Can a writer help solve the problem? What else can solve the problems?

Problem Clarification Phase

This phase of the needs assessment specifically defines the problem and presents evidence that there is a problem. The analysis in the portable manual project came from interviews with personnel working in mainframe operations support, management, personal computer operations support, systems analysts, and inventory control specialists. This phase used an eight-step, problem-solving approach.

- Description of the problem.
- Evidence that there is a problem.
- What would happen if the problem is left alone?
- What would happen if nothing is done?
- What are the costs?
- Possible aspects of the problem.
- Optimals/Actuals.
- Possible solutions.

These eight steps are described below along with some example analysis.

- **Description of the problem.** A lack of knowledge concerning the use of personal computers and in-house computer systems.
- **Evidence that there is a problem.** Who says there is a problem and what can a writer do to solve the problem? If a writer can't solve the problem, who can?
- **What would happen if the problem is left alone?**

  Example analysis: If the problem were left alone poor use of personal and in-house computers would continue. User ignorance concerning clearing warrants, copying files, backing up files, proper directory and file creation, proper word processing techniques, and hardware use would continue (Interview Source: Jones in Operations).
- **What would happen if writers did nothing?** If nothing would change by creating user documentation, then writers or trainers aren't needed to solve the problem. The problem may only be solved by management assessing environmental or motivational concerns.
- **What are the costs? Will the problem cost more to solve than it will cost to leave it alone?** Costs can be assessed not only in monetary terms, but in terms of lost time, duplicated effort, destroyed equipment, outside organizational training, and the possible costs arising from potential injury or loss of life.

The example given in the boxed exhibit on the following page is more elaborate in its detail. This kind of analysis can demonstrate to management how writing referential documentation and tutorials can significantly reduce costs of an organization. Pseudonyms replace real company, interview sources, and product names.

Not all costs can be measured in dollars, and the report on intangibles can detail those costs. If management wants more information concerning costs, the needs assessor should cite monthly or yearly costs. For example: "Training users on personal computer systems off site: $22,000 a year versus in-house training: $14,000 a year."

- **Possible aspects of the problem.** Is there a skill, information, or motivational deficiency? Are tools/equipment and facilities available for the user to complete his or her job?
- **Optimals/Actuals.** By matching optimals with actuals, the writer can clearly contrast what the user should be doing to what is actually being done. The match may show a performance gap that the writer can close with written referential documentation, written procedures, and tutorials. See the smaller boxed exhibit on the following page for a detailed example of this stage in the needs assessment.
- **Possible Solutions.** Is the solution something a writer can do? Will computer-based instruction or quick-reference guides solve the problem? Will referential documentation or written tutorials solve the problem, or will training be necessary?

When considering possible solutions, the author may see ways to solve problems other than the original proposed solution. When the project began, designing a portable manual was believed to be the best way to solve crucial documentation and training problems, but quick-reference guides showing how to log-on were also found to be an excellent way of helping the user.

Survey Phase

The survey phase was done by questioning the users who

Needs Assessment: What are the Costs?

Example Analysis: It will cost more not to solve this problem than to leave it alone. Most of the cost rests in duplicated effort and time lost as users show other users how to operate personal computers. There is some loss in money due to the equipment failures listed below.

A service maintenance contract covers all ABC equipment for $11,000 a month (J. Doe, Management). Ace Supply Co. and Advanced Co. repair other brands under a monthly budget of $600. Over the past year those figures have not changed (Source: Jones, Operations).

There are 23–25 hardware problems a month. Defective equipment causes most hardware problems. Operator error is rarely involved in any kind of hardware problem (Source: Jones, Operations). Hardware problems that are not operator-related include hard disk failure, read-write errors, burned out chips, inoperative controllers, failed monitors. Software problems that are causing complaints and frustration for users are due mostly to Xbase errors (scrambles data when files aren't closed properly).

Lost Time: Lost data when hard disks are erased (each disk that is accidentally wiped out takes 1–2 hours to restore, depending on the size of the hard disk). Keyboards improperly cleaned and inoperable. Time cleaning keyboards under usual maintenance procedures vs. time cleaning keyboards that were rendered inoperable due to user ignorance. Lost time when users forget their passwords. (1 hour a week is devoted to wiping out forgotten passwords). 52 weeks × $18 (hourly rate of the Operations individual who does UNIX security clearances) = $936 a year.

Duplicated Effort: A survey question should ask how much time users use to train others or explain material that could be put in a computer user manual.

Destroyed Equipment: Floppy disks destroyed by improper use. Floppies cost approximately $0.80. The number of destroyed floppies is unknown.

Training Costs: Computer Skills Training Center has trained six users in the past. Their fee is 199$ per person, per training session. These users had an average of three sessions, costing 597$ per person. Training users on the word processor at the Computer Skill Training Center would cost approximately $175 per three-hour session. Training users in the same material in-house would cost what the training coordinator is paid, development of written tutorials, and $7000 to purchase additional personal computers and software.

Intangibles: Safety concerns for all officers and the public. Improper use of NCIC-CCIC could lead to serious legal concerns and safety of officers and the public viz. improper "clearing" of individuals with outstanding warrants. There will be a loss of good will and image if users are given personal computers and not shown how to use them.

Needs Assessment: Optimals/Actuals

Optimal: Log into main-frame from dumb terminal and log into main-frame from personal computer through emulation. The logon procedure must be documented and quick reference cards would help. An emulation process allows a user to enter a mainframe. Menus can be created for users to enter any personal computer application. [Source: Jones, Operations]

Matching the optimal with the actual.

Actual: Many users don't know the difference between a personal computer and a dumb terminal. Most users don't know how to emulate the system with a personal computer. [Source: Jones, Operations and personal observation].

were outlined in the egocentric chart. A questionnaire or survey is an analysis tool that has several advantages: it reaches many people; it guarantees anonymity for those who want to express sensitive opinions; it allows respondents time to ponder questions; it shows users you care about their opinion; and it is easy to score and analyze if properly constructed [8].

The way a question is written is critical. Questions can be open-ended or structured. Open-ended questions allow the respondents to express their opinions or attitudes toward a subject in their own words: "If I had access to a PC I would be interested in learning . . . ," or "The biggest problem with our current user manual is . . . "). Structured questions provide the respondent with a more constrained response. Questions can elicit yes/no answers, rankings, agree–disagree ratios; or they may rate or compare items [9].

A survey should be sent to a sample population, a portion of the audience that can be a representative example of the larger audience. In smaller organizations, the entire user base can be surveyed. For the portable manual project, users were randomly chosen from each layer of the egocentric chart.

The survey assessed the feelings, opinions, and needs of people from each level of the audience. Users were asked to rank the three systems they used the most, the system they had the most trouble with, and the system they would like to know more about. From 24 systems or topics, respondents selected the systems or topics they needed in a portable computer manual. The users were asked to voice their opinions about how much they would use personal computers in their jobs in the future, how much they would use a portable manual, what they had to teach other users, opinions concerning past problems, and what they would like to learn.

The survey showed that each agency had its own needs. The survey also outlined the most used systems, the most troublesome systems, what topics should be included, and what topics could be minimized or eliminated based on their users' experiences with the existing manual, training, and training guides. The users expressed positive sentiments concerning the future use of personal computers in their job (over 90%). Each agency had its own opinion on how much a portable manual would help them (Police 70%, Sheriff 100%, Fire 50%). Some open-ended questions allowed the users to express in their own words their opinions and feelings.

The survey showed a greater need for learning word processing than we originally thought existed, and a strong desire from the users that a single user manual contain referential and tutorial material on the department's standard word processor. One user voiced a strong opinion about the lack of technical support for personal computers at a police department district station. This information was forwarded to management.

Design For Learning

This stage in the writing strategy moves from gathering information to analyzing audience needs, defining learning objectives, and, finally, designing the manual itself.

Matching Needs with Egocentric Chart Audience

By matching the needs and the relative computer "access" of the ten audience groups listed in the egocentric organizational chart, we discovered the general topics to include in the manual. Information found from the survey combined with analysis of the needs of the audience groups gave a more detailed breakdown of users' needs. A single manual could be developed to satisfy the query needs of all of the users if the manual covered these topics:

- log-on procedure for queries
- in-house systems
- NCIC-CCIC systems

- basic operation of personal computers
- WordStar reference and tutorial

Table II matches the users' needs to the four audience levels identified in the egocentric chart.

By matching the needs of the users with the audience groups, the writer can combine user groups with similar needs. Some of the audience groups have exact needs and access. By combining some groups, the audience fields can be simplified from ten to seven: Data Section, Records, Radio, Identification, Detectives/Administrators, Arson/Fire fighters, Street Officers/District Technicians. This match defined the "optimal" situation. When budget and time allow, the ideal situation would be the creation of a customized user manual for each of the seven user groups.

Defining the Learning Objective

An instructional designer defines the objective of the lesson before instruction occurs to specify what the learner should be able to do after instruction. Defining the learning objective takes the mystery out of the educational objective. After defining who the audience is and what they need to know, the writer should then establish what the user should learn from his or her writing.

Users of computer manuals are learning from referential or instructional material. Defining what the user needs to learn may aid the writer later in establishing usability tests. The Gagne–Briggs "SLOAT" method of defining the learning objective [9] specifically defines the **S**ituation, **L**earned Capability, **O**bject, **A**ction, and the **T**ools/Constraints that the user needs to learn. Serving as a guideline for developing instruction, SLOAT can help measure what the student should know after using instructional material. Here is an example of how the Gagne–Briggs "SLOAT" method helped define a learning objective.

The Learning Objective: Either at a Department of Safety AT&T terminal or personal computer (situation), a Department of Safety employee will generate a query response or a WordStar word-processed document (learned capability) by displaying the query on screen or by printing a WordStar document (object) using only a portable user manual (tools/constraints).

Defining the learning objective clearly illustrated the most important instructional goals for the documentation:

- how to log-on to three systems
- how to make in-house and NCIC-CCIC computer queries
- how to format a disk on a personal computer
- how to create a directory
- how to save a document in WordStar and how to print the document.

Design Strategies

The portable manual needed to contain the smallest amount of information but still provide information on the most significant subjects for users. To create a more portable manual than the original "elaborate" version, "minimalist" design strategies were used.

The main objective of a minimalist manual is to condense text and other passive elements of the manual with the single goal of trying to enrich the training experience by giving the learner more to think about and less to overcome [10]. This design strategy has the additional advantage of saving printing costs.

TABLE II
MATCHING THE NEEDS WITH THE AUDIENCE GROUP

Audience Description	Needs	Access
	Audience in Own Group	
Data Section	All systems, PC	Query and Entry
Records	Offenses, Accidents	Query and Entry
	Audience Close to Group	
Radio	NCIC-CCIC,* Arrests, Contacts	Query and Entry
Identification	NCIC-CCIC, Arrests, Jail Management	Query and Entry
Detectives	All systems, PC	Query
Administration	All systems, PC	Query
	Audience Elsewhere in Group	
Street Police Officers	All systems, PC	Query
Arson	NCIC-CCIC, Offenses, Contacts, Arrests, PC	Query
Firefighters	NCIC-CCIC, Contacts	Query
District Police Technicians	All systems, PC	Query
	Audience Out of Organization	
	None	

*NCIC—National Crime Information Center, CCIC—Colorado Crime Information Center.

The design of the portable manual focused on real tasks and practical activities. Verbiage was slashed by eliminating all repetition, previews, reviews, descriptions of screens, index, introduction, and appendix.

Other key design features employed in the manual included:

- Secondary features of the manual (overviews, introductions, summaries, etc.) were cut.
- Information gained from iterative testing was immediately implemented in the document.
- Special keyboard and printer instructions were combined into one section called "Hardware."
- Codes that could be accessed online were cut from the manual.
- Screen displays, glossaries, and field descriptions were cut.
- Readers were referred to what they already knew by continuously linking new information to old information.
- All entry, modification, and deletion processes used by data entry personnel were cut for audiences requiring only query information.
- "Troubleshooting" was eliminated. Phone numbers for the data processing department were provided and users were encouraged to use this phone support.

Testing the Document

Testing a document's efficiency at the end of the writing

cycle may be too late [11]. In contrast, an iterative approach can find problems and give the writer the time to make changes. With the iterative approach the tester provides users with tasks and focuses on problems the users have completing the tasks. Problems are fixed as quickly as possible, and the product is retested. The process continues until the problems are solved or the remaining problems are considered trivial.

For the portable manual project, one test and two evaluations were used to gauge the accuracy and opinions of the users. Testing began as soon as a skeletal version of the portable manual was developed.

Test 1: This test judged the elaborate manual versus the portable manual by comparing the time it took users to perform tasks, accuracy of the answers users obtained in performing tasks, and whether the user could perform the task at all. The tasks tested covered a broad spectrum: log-on procedures, various in-house queries, DOS commands, and basic word processing techniques.

When the test was complete, changes that needed to be considered were written in a comments section on the test. An example comment follows.

> **Example Comment:** Add to log-on section about the necessity of using small letters in the hunt group. Put more detail in table of contents, especially number of pages. Separate F6 and F8 section on bringing function keys back up in the printer section. Change the term "Function Keys" to "Orange Boxes on the Screen" in the printer section.

Evaluation 1: The first evaluation was separated into four parts. The first part used yes and no answers. The users evaluated seven topics in the portable manual: completeness, unnecessary information, use of examples, ease of use, inconsistencies, logic in the presentation of information, and the accuracy of headings and the table of contents.

In the second part, using a scale ranging from 0–10, the user evaluated the accuracy of the information presented, how easy the language was to use, and how much an index would have helped.

To evaluate the quantity of information covered, the third part of Evaluation 1 asked the to user answer questions by responding 1) too much, 2) too little, 3) adequate (information). This question covered the main topics: log-on procedures, department queries, NCIC-CCIC queries, DOS commands, word processing.

In part four, using open-ended questions, the users gave opinions concerning their perception of the most serious problem with the manual, what they would change, the section used the most, and the section used the least.

Evaluation 2: Analyzed the word-processing tutorial section. The user was asked to identify the agency they worked for and how much experience they had with the word processing package before the tutorial. Then they judged the tutorial on a scale of 1–5 and were asked about the length, whether they finished it, sections they had trouble with, and whether they felt the tutorial should be included in the user manual.

Problems found in the testing were documented in a log. Changes to the manual were noted at the bottom of each entry of the log.

CONCLUSION

Creating an in-house computer manual presents unique challenges to a writer. By breaking the development of the manual into three stages (Preliminary Analysis, Needs Assessment, and Design for Learning) the writer can clarify significant organizational needs and training issues:

- user groups
- the possible need for different versions of the manual
- what material from other sources can be used in the new manual
- costs if writing isn't done
- who to write for
- an iterative testing method
- training needs
- concerns for management

Following this three stage process will help the writer create an efficient, well-tested manual that meets the real needs of a user. It justifies the writer's work by citing specific cost factors, and it casts the writer in the role of a valuable communication analyst who is capable of finding motivational, environmental, and cost issues in the organization.

ACKNOWLEDGMENT

The author would like to acknowledge Dr. C. Beck at the University of Colorado, at Denver for his help in preparing this article.

REFERENCES

[1] J. C. Mathes and D. W. Stevenson, *Designing Technical Reports: Writing for Audiences in Organizations.* Indianapolis, IN: Bobbs-Merrill, 1976, p. 123.

[2] M. Mullins, "Embedded training: A bibliography," *Technical Communication,* vol. 36, no. 1, p. 19, First Quarter, 1989.

[3] A. Rossett, *Training Needs Assessment.* Englewood Cliffs, NJ: Educational Technology Publications, 1987, p. 62.

[4] ——, *Training Needs Assessment.* Englewood Cliffs, NJ: Educational Technology Publications, 1987, p. 67.

[5] S. Thiagarajan, "How to avoid ID," *Performance and Instruction Journal,* p. 5, May 1984.

[6] A. Rossett, *Training Needs Assessment.* Englewood Cliffs, NJ: Educational Technology Publications, 1987, pp. 75–76.

[7] —, *Training Needs Assessment.* Englewood Cliffs, NJ: Educational Technology Publications, 1987, p. 203.

[8] D. H. Jonassen, W. H. Hannum, and M. Tessmer, *Handbook of Task Analysis Procedures.* New York: Praeger, 1989, p. 391.

[9] R. M. Gagne, L. J. Briggs, and W. Wager, *Principles of Instructional Design.* New York: Holt, Rinehart, and Winston, 1988, p. 139.

[10] J. M. Carroll, *The Nurnberg Funnel: Designing Minimalist Instruction for Practical Computer Skill.* Cambridge, MA: M.I.T. Press, 1990, ch. 4.

[11] J. S. Craig, "Approaches to usability testing and design strategies: An annotated bibliography," *Technical Communication,* vol. 38, no. 2, pp. 190–194, second quarter, 1991.

John S. Craig received the M.S. degree in Technical Communication from the University of Colorado, Denver. He is a Computer Systems Analyst and Trainer with the Department of Safety, Denver, CO and is currently researching usability testing methodologies for technical documentation. His latest publication on usability testing and design strategies appeared in *Technical Communication.*

Single-Source Manuals

Gary Bist

Abstract—**Because corporations today face fierce international competition, they must produce and maintain high-quality documentation—but at minimal cost. Optimizing a writer's time and effort will no doubt become a key study area as we try to do more with less, without sacrificing quality. One way to increase a technical writer's productivity is to design documentation so that it covers a broader product area. This approach gets more use (or reuse) of the text. This paper describes the productivity and cost benefits of creating single-source manuals, that is, two or more manuals output from the same set of source files created and updated by one writer. It also describes how to create single-source manuals based on an actual case.**

Why Write Single-Source Manuals?

PRODUCTIVITY is one of the key business issues of the 1990s [1]. To remain competitive in a global economy, corporations and individuals need to continually examine their efficiency and determine where they can improve their operations [2]. This article describes how to write a single-source manual to reduce costs and improve writer productivity. It has a how-to section focusing on an example of one single-source manual that could have been derived from two separate existing books or designed as a single-source manual for two products initially. The article also describes the process for maintaining the set of files and presents three types of output from them that are appropriate to different situations. The three types of output are the following:

- one manual that is used by two (or more) products
- two (or more) manuals that can be used by two (or more) products
- a printed manual and online documentation for the same product

One practice in technical communication that drives up costs is to write different manuals for largely similar products. This situation doubles not only the number of writers to be supported, but the printing, stocking, and distribution costs as well. In such cases, one way to increase productivity is to create a single-source manual, that is, one set of files that would cover both products and is written and maintained by just one person. Table I presents a comparison of these two scenarios using costs based on the actual production of a typical reference manual. The assumptions for this cost comparison are that two writers working at the same rate could produce two manuals in 12 months. One writer producing a single-source manual (in this case, one physical book) suitable for two products would take longer to produce the manual, but overall costs (including just one cost for printing, stocking and distribution) would be lower.

Manuscript received July 1993, revised January 1994.
The author is with IBM Canada Ltd., North York, ON, Canada.
IEEE Log Number 9402280.

Choosing a Candidate for Single-Sourcing

Just as a programmer analyzes modules of software to factor out common functions and write a concise program, so you can analyze the structures of manuals and map their common topics to factor out all the common information [3]. This concept of factoring out information repeated in different manuals into a more concise information equation is critical in selecting manuals as candidates for single-sourcing. The mapping exercise will also tell you what sections are unique to each manual and how large those sections are. As mentioned previously, you can either create a single-source manual from two different existing books or design a single-source manual for two products initially. Since the design issues would be similar for either case, for the purposes of this article I will choose the former and show how two existing manuals could be merged into one set of files.

What is the criterion once some candidates for single-sourcing are evident? Two manuals for two similar products that have 80% identical information are good candidates for being combined into a single source. To determine what percentage of the content is similar, do two passes on the books. On the first pass, analyze the structure of each and map the topics of one to the other. On the second pass, look at the common sections to compare them for detailed content and for differences in writing styles. The degree of variation will tell you how much work will be needed to create a style that will be acceptable to the audiences of both products. These two steps are described in detail below.

Step 1: Mapping One Manual to Another

The simplest way to map the topics of one manual to another is to compare their tables of contents. As an example, we will here look at two software reference manuals for the Structured Query Language (SQL) that we found could be combined into a single source. (The examples shown in this paper are taken from a published common manual, the *SQL Reference for IBM VM Systems and VSE.* This manual describes two similar products used on two computer systems.) Fig. 1 shows that the topics of each manual map almost one-to-one, with only a minor change in order.

The topics that may not map 100%, such as "Referential Integrity" to "Maintaining Integrity," are areas to investigate, as they may just be titled slightly differently but be very similar in meaning. In fact, on the first pass, this will be your biggest challenge: to examine areas that have similar titles to see if they are in fact the same. At the conclusion of the first pass, you will have a list of sections that fall into one of three categories:

Reprinted from *IEEE Trans. Prof. Comm.,* vol. PC-37, no. 2, pp. 81–87, June 1994.

TABLE I
COST OF PRODUCING TWO MANUALS VERSUS A SINGLE-SOURCE MANUAL

	Two Manuals, Two Writers		Single-Source Manual	
Activity	**Time**	**Cost**	**Time**	**Cost**
Writing	12 months	$252K	14 months	$147K
Printing	1 month	$ 18K	1 month	$ 9K
Stocking	1 month	$ 2K	1 month	$ 1K
Distribution	1 month	$ 4K	1 month	$ 2K
Total	15 months	**$276K**	17 months	**$159K**

SQL Reference for VM

Introduction
- Static SQL
- Dynamic SQL
- Interactive SQL
- Relational Database
- Tables
- Keys
- Primary Keys
- Referential Integrity
- Indexes
- Views

Language Elements
- Characters
- Tokens
- Identifiers
  - SQL Identifiers
  - Host Identifiers
- Naming Conventions

SQL Reference for VSE

Concepts
- What is a Relational Database?
- Types of SQL
  - Static
  - Dynamic
  - Interactive
- Objects in a Database
  - Tables
  - Views
- Using Indexes on Tables
- Maintaining Integrity
- Keys
  - Primary and Foreign
- Conventions Used for Names

Components of the SQL Language
- Characters
- Tokens
- Types of Identifiers
  - SQL
  - Host

Fig. 1. Partial table of contents of two similar manuals.

- map directly from the first manual to sections in the second manual
- map closely, but will require adjustments to allow them to be shared between the two products
- are unique to each manual

With this list, you can quantify how much information is common and can be shared and how much is unique to each product.

Step 2: Merging Sections

On the second pass, compare each mapped section for writing style and approach. On the first pass, you might conclude that you have an easy task if many sections are found to cover the same topic. However, two manuals may share considerable content, but the style may vary considerably. This can mean substantial effort in adjusting the material so that it can be presented to both audiences. For example, Fig. 2 shows two paragraphs on the same topic, but the difference in approach is obvious.

The writer of the first paragraph was concerned with the benefits of referential integrity; the second writer, with precisely defining the term and its relationship to other similar terminology.

First Manual's Paragraph on Referential Integrity

Referential integrity is a powerful feature for maintaining data integrity. The database maintains the rules, making them effective for all application programs and interactive users. This results in the consistent use of the rules established for your data. The programming effort is reduced, because programmers do not need to write application logic to support referential integrity rules. There is no risk that an application program or interactive user will bypass the rules.

Second Manual's Paragraph on Referential Integrity

Referential integrity is the state of a database in which all values of all foreign keys are valid. A foreign key is a key that is part of the definition of a referential constraint. A referential constraint is the rule that the non-null values of the foreign key are valid only if they also appear as values of a primary key. The table containing the primary key is called the parent table of the referential constraint, and the table containing the foreign key is said to be a dependent of that table.

Fig. 2. Two manuals' views of the same information.

Referential integrity benefits those writing applications programs using a relational database by:

1 Maintaining data integrity for you
2 Applying consistent use of rules established for your data

Five terms necessary to the understanding of referential integrity are:

Primary Key	A unique key that is part of the definition of a table
Foreign Key	A key that is part of the definition of a referential constraint
Referential Constraint	The rule that the non-null values of the foreign key are valid only if they also appear as values of a primary key
Parent Table	The table containing the primary key of the referential constraint
Dependent Table	The table containing the foreign key

Referential integrity is the state of a database in which all values of all foreign keys are valid.

Fig. 3. Combined information in a common manual.

To estimate the amount of effort required to merge two distinct styles, select a few passages that deal with the same topic and try to combine them; then extrapolate the effort required to update these few samples to calculate the conversion of the entire text. The paragraphs in Fig. 2, for example, might (after a period of careful consideration and some trial-and-error) be combined as in Fig. 3.

The person or persons with DBA authority are charged with the task of controlling the SQL/DS database manager and are responsible for the safety and integrity of the data.

The person or persons with DBA authority are charged with the task of controlling the VSE database manager and are responsible for the safety and integrity of the data.

Fig. 4. Sentences with specific product names.

The person or persons with DBA authority are charged with the task of controlling the database manager and are responsible for the safety and integrity of the data.

Fig. 5. One sentence with no product name.

Merging of content is also challenging when sentences use a specific product name. For example, Fig. 4 has a sentence from each manual with a specific product name: SQL/DS in the first instance and VSE in the second. (SQL/DS is a trademark of International Business Machines.) The best way to merge product-specific sentences is to use generic sentences. The previous sentence, for example, can appear in both manuals by simply removing the product name, as shown in Fig. 5.

(There will be some cases in which product-specific sentences are unavoidable; these cases are discussed later.)

Designing a Structure

Before you begin any style changes, estimate the effort for designing a new structure for the single-source manual. To do this, return to your mapping of the two tables of contents, and determine how easily you can create a new table of contents for the single-source manual. If the new table of contents seems self-evident, then the work to design the new structure will be minimal. However, if it does not appear naturally, you should add an additional week or two to your estimate to define the structure. In the example in Fig. 1, a table of contents for the *SQL Reference for IBM VM Systems and VSE* might look like Fig. 6.

This revised table of contents is the first view of the combined manual. Assuming you will be having the manual reviewed simultaneously by the two groups of product experts who would have reviewed the two individual books, show them this structure early on to give them a picture of the entire "new" manual. Also share with them your reasoning for the headings selected and their order. If changes in headings and order are recommended, it is best to make those structural changes at this time, before extensive rewriting begins.

The Process

Once you have determined from analysis that a single-source manual will be more beneficial than two separate ones, have estimated the work effort, and established the design of the structure, then the writing starts. Whether you are creating a single-source manual for the first time or updating an existing one, the process is similar to working with a manual

SQL Reference for VM and VSE

Concepts
- Definition of a Relational Database
- Types of SQL
  - Static
  - Dynamic
  - Interactive
- Objects in a Database
  - Tables
  - Views
- Indexes on Tables
- Referential Integrity
- Keys
  - Primary
  - Foreign

Language Elements
- Characters
- Tokens
- Types of Identifiers
  - SQL
  - Host
- Naming Conventions

Fig. 6. The table of contents for a single-source manual.

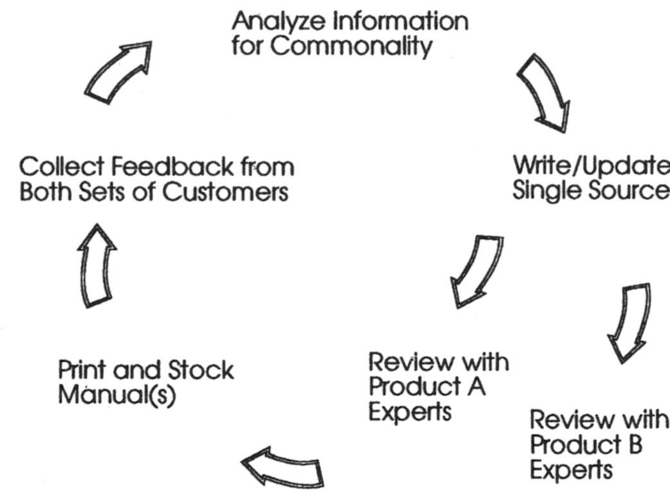

Fig. 7. The process of writing a single-source manual.

for one single product. However, there are several important differences, which are evident in Fig. 7.

For one thing, the manual is reviewed twice, once by each set of product experts who are concerned with it. This means more meetings for you to attend and more perspectives to consider. You must consider the feedback from both sets of reviewers and assess where comments are applicable to shared sections of the manual and where they are unique to one product. Any textual or graphics changes that are made to the shared sections of the manual must be acceptable to both sets of reviewers, usually meaning that there must be more compromises by everybody. You should expect these reviews to take considerably longer than those done for manuals tailored specifically for each product. Before presenting the reworked manual for the first time, discuss it with the product experts. Show them its relative advantage over the system of two separate manuals; specifically, demonstrate that it makes good business sense [4]. Present the cost savings in low-level detail so that it is clear the amount of money saved in the long term justifies the effort. Then tell them what is expected of them: to review the single-source manual in the spirit of compromise, accommodating "their" manual with "the other" manual. Emphasize the positive aspects: they can gain from the input of the other group's expertise.

INCLUDE SQLCA Declarations

In this section, the description of the SQL Communication Area (SQLCA) given by the INCLUDE SQLCA declarations is shown for each of the host languages.

Report Program Generator (RPG) Language

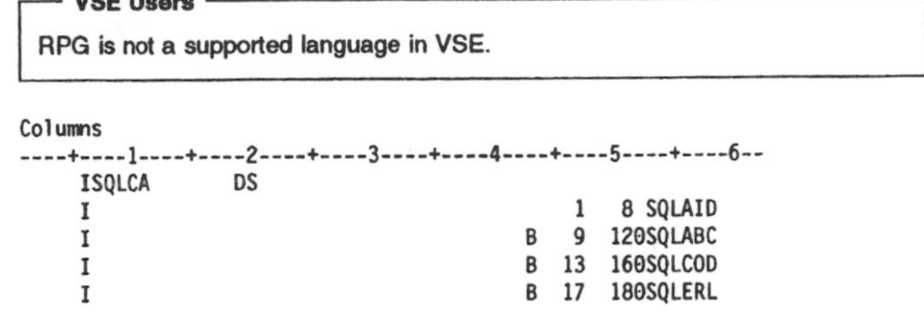

VSE Users

RPG is not a supported language in VSE.

```
Columns
----+----1----+----2----+----3----+----4----+----5----+----6--
     ISQLCA       DS
     I                                         1   8 SQLAID
     I                                     B   9  120SQLABC
     I                                     B  13  160SQLCOD
     I                                     B  17  180SQLERL
```

Fig. 8. Example of product differences in an explicit common manual.

THE THREE TYPES OF SINGLE-SOURCE MANUALS

A single-source manual can be either explicit or implicit, with implicit having two variations. An explicit single-source manual names both products on the cover, and inside explicitly identifies any information unique to one. An implicit single-source manual can be either of the following:

Variation 1. Two books created by one writer using a single-source file, with conditional statements embedded in that file to indicate for each section whether it is to be used for both versions or just for one. When the source file is printed, two manuals are created from it, with each appearing to be unique to one product.

Variation 2 Two forms of the same information, usually hardcopy and online, with conditional statements embedded in that file to indicate for each section whether it is to be used for hardcopy or online presentation. Variation 2 could encompass many information elements, however, such as images, audio, and video.

(You must, of course, have word processing software that enables you to add these conditional statements and create this configurable documentation [5].) Another way of viewing explicit or implicit single-source manuals is that in the former the reader interprets the conditionals, and in the latter the word processing formatter interprets them.

Which type of single-source setup should you choose to do? If almost all the information is common, write an explicit single-source manual, since the coding needed to hide the unique information in an implicit manual is difficult to maintain over time. If as much as 15-20% of the information differs between the products, and these differences are interspersed throughout the manuals, then an implicit manual (Variation 1) is a better choice, since in such cases it would be frustrating for readers to have the flow continually interrupted by identifiers for product-specific information. Note that although the implicit manual (Variation 1) will save on writing costs just like the explicit manual, it has the disadvantage of not saving on printing, stocking, and distribution costs.

The strategy for creating Variation 2 of the implicit manual is usually self-evident: your objective would be to have your hardcopy information and online information all in one set of files for easier maintenance and, as in Variation 1, to share information between the hardcopy and online presentation where possible.

The Explicit Single-Source Manual

The book we have referred to in this paper, *SQL Reference for IBM VM Systems and VSE,* is an example of an explicit single-source manual. As shown in Fig. 1, the two original manuals had many common sections and a similar order. But how do you distinguish the occasional differences between the two sources? It is advisable to consider this design question before you start to write. In most cases, you will find one of the sources has more material than the other. For example, a software product that is designed for two computer operating systems will usually have more features on one of the systems. It is therefore most efficient to identify those places where one product does not have a certain feature. Once these places are identified, create a standard "eye-catcher"—for example, a box with a consistent heading to it—that states that this feature is not applicable to Product B. An example is shown in Fig. 8.

Users will quickly learn the meaning of this visual cue and recognize that it consistently identifies one product as being excluded from a set of additional features.

As a rule, an explicit single-source manual is easier to maintain than an implicit one. Write the manual as if you are writing for one product, and whenever there is a product difference, state that the following section is not applicable to Product B. Seems easy. But consider this possibility: only Product A currently has a certain function, but Product B will have it in another year. You must thus be very careful to keep track of the product differences. Each time a new release of the manual is issued, some "eye-catchers" will disappear as some functional differences are eliminated, and others will appear in new areas. A subtle twist on this issue concerns version differences too. Your manual may have to specify version levels of Product A and Product B, in which case distinctions in functions will reach a finer granularity.

One advantage that the explicit single-source manual offers is the possibility of one review that includes both sets of product experts. This option is available because the product differences are explicitly stated and therefore each set of experts can clearly see what is unique to their area. If both products are being developed and released in approximately the same time frame and in the same physical location, you should consider this option to minimize the number of review meetings. It also makes consensus decisions on the common information easier, since the product experts can hear each others' points of view and compromise where necessary.

Variation 1 of the Implicit Single-Source Manual

As stated earlier, there are two versions of the implicit single-source manual. Let us look first at the variation in which two books are created out of one single-source file by using conditional statements embedded in that file to indicate whether a given section is to be used for both versions or just for one.

When the differences between the products are extensive and subtle, an implicit single-source manual enables the writer to share as much common information as possible without inserting frequent and distracting "eye-catchers." This type of manual is not as simple to create or maintain as the explicit single-source manual, yet is still a better choice than creating two separate manuals using two different writers. Alternatively, one writer might write both manuals even if they are not single-sourced. As with the explicit single-source manual, it is advisable to consider the design of this type of manual before you start to write it. Just as programmers who produce complex software spend considerable time thinking about the implementation and maintenance of their code, so a writer who will code and maintain the conditional statements used in a set of files—no small task—should set up a structure that minimizes the coding required. Like the programmer, consider applying "functional decomposition" to the files; that is, break the information into manageable chunks that describe the specific functions of each product, and insert the conditional statements where those functions differ. Conditional statements that control formatting are specified using Boolean logic, either including or excluding text. Depending on what proportion of text is to be shared, you may find it more efficient to specify common text directly, or to not specify it (that is, to have it included in both manuals by default).

Note that these conditional statements will be "buried" within hundreds or thousands of lines of text: in such an environment, it is very easy to forget the logic. Therefore, create "eye-catchers" similar to those described for explicit single-source manuals but seen only in the internal files, so that you are visually reminded of which product is associated with the text you are currently working on. An example of the source file for an implicit single-source manual is shown in Fig. 9.

Another way to manage product differences is to establish a file-naming convention in which files are identified as containing either unique information for a specific product or common information. Once the naming convention is established, you can create master files that call the appropriate set of files. For example, we might define our convention as pppaxyyy where:

ppp identifies the type of product. Using our previous example, this would be "sql."

```
////////////////////////////////
/// Start of a VM-Only Section ///
////////////////////////////////
.CONFIG 'UNIQUE' ON
.WHEN 'VM' INSERT
A distributed relational database consists of a set of tables and other
objects that are spread across different but interconnected computer
systems.  Each computer system has a relational database manager to
manage the tables and other objects in its environment.  The database
managers communicate and cooperate with each other in a way that allows
a given database manager to execute SQL statements on another computer
system.
.CONFIG 'UNIQUE' OFF
////////////////////////////////
//// End of a VM-Only Section ////
////////////////////////////////
```

Fig. 9. Examples of product difference specified in a file.

```
SQL Reference (VM) - Master File      SQL Reference (VSE) - Master File
/* Introduction   */                  /* Introduction   */
.imbed sqlrmint script                .imbed sqlrsint script
.imbed sqlrcsta script                .imbed sqlrstyp script
.imbed sqlrcdyn script                .imbed sqlrcsta script
.imbed sqlrcitr script                .imbed sqlrcdyn script
/* SQL Components  */                 .imbed sqlrcitr script
.imbed sqlrmrel script                /* SQL Components  */
.imbed sqlrctbl script                .imbed sqlrsobj script
.imbed sqlrcvws script                .imbed sqlrctbl script
.imbed sqlrcidx script                .imbed sqlrcvws script
.imbed sqlrckey script                .imbed sqlrcidx script
:
```

Fig. 10. Example using a file naming convention.

a identities the manual. This would be "r" for Reference.

x identifies if the file is unique or common. This would be m, indicating it is unique to VM; s, indicating it is unique to VSE; or c, indicating common information.

yyy indicates subject matter. For example, "tbl" could identify the file as containing information on database tables.

An example is shown in Fig. 10.

Variation 2 of the Implicit Single-Source Manual

The aim of creating a single source is to write once and use this same information repeatedly for a variety of uses. Variation 2 produces two forms of the same information. Usually one form is intended for the printed page (or hardcopy information) and one form is intended for screen display (or online information). Since there is a large cost benefit to online documentation over hardcopy, it is advantageous to use the same source but increasingly to optimize the output, so to speak, for online. Like Variation 1, some tags must distinguish the hardcopy information from the online so that a program can extract the right information for the right form; that is, with one condition the hardcopy manual is produced and the online information hidden, and vice versa.

In a recent article, Chet Ensign [6] applied Variation 2 to files coded with the increasingly popular Standard Generalized Markup Language (SGML). SGML is a non-proprietary markup language that has tags that indicate what sections are, as opposed to what the text will look like. Encoding the documentation with these tags separates structure from presentation or, in other words, makes structure and presentation

```
<help id=hlp_CREATE_VIEW_Stmt>
<ledi purpose>
<p>The CREATE VIEW statement creates a view on one or more tables or
views.
<ledi invocation>
<p>This statement can be embedded in an application program or issued
interactively.  It is an executable statement that can be dynamically
prepared.
<ledi syntax>
<syntax style="space"
     view="full">
<synlbl>
<kwd>CREATE VIEW
<var>view-name
<group seq
     opt>GRPLBL
   <delim>(
   <group>GRPLBL
      <repsep>,
      <var>column-name
   </group>
   <delim>)
</group>
<kwd>AS
<var>fullselect
<group opt>GRPLBL
    <kwd>WITH CHECK OPTION
</group>
</syntax>
```

Fig. 11. Identifying online help text.

Purpose

The CREATE VIEW statement creates a view on one or more tables or views.

Invocation

This statement can be embedded in an application program or issued interactively. It is an executable statement that can be dynamically prepared.

Syntax

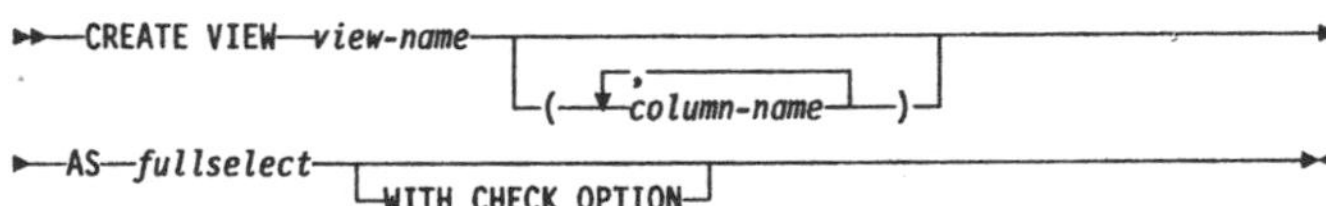

Fig. 12. An online help panel generated from the help identifier.

independent of each other. This means a variety of presentation styles may be created from the source, such as a style for devices such as display screens or for printed appearance. These styles are generated from a document type definition (DTD) file, which determines the definition of the output. Fig. 11, an example of SGML markup, shows how you can identify text in a file so that the DTD would recognize it appropriately as online help text.

This source code then can be extracted and converted with a suitable DTD file to output the online help panel shown in Fig. 12.

Note that if the identifier were for a print output (for example,< print id=prt_CREATE_VIEW_Stmt>) and another DTD were used to create a printed copy, the same source could take advantage of variations in fonts, indentation, and highlighting. In this way, a single source is tailored for the selected output medium, as shown in Fig. 13.

To the writer, this means that all information, hardcopy and online, can be logically grouped together for easier main-

Purpose

The CREATE VIEW statement creates a view on one or more tables or views.

Invocation

This statement *can be embedded* in an application program or *issued interactively*. It is an executable statement that can be dynamically prepared.

Syntax

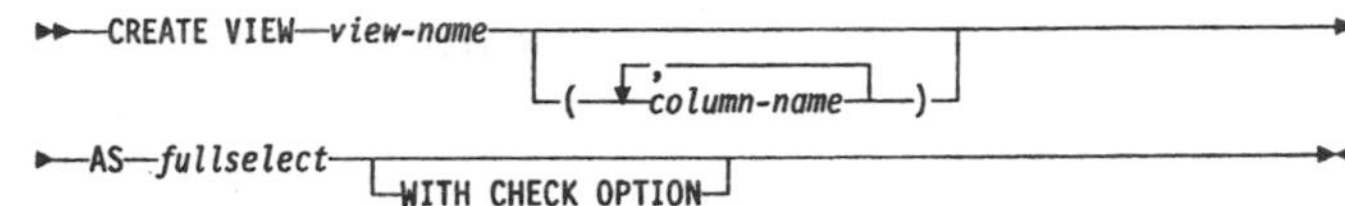

Fig. 13. Print output generated from the print identifier.

```
//////////////////////////////////
/// Start of a VM OR VSE Section ///
//////////////////////////////////
.CONFIG 'BOTH' ON
.WHEN 'VM' OR 'VSE' INSERT
A distributed relational database consists of a set of tables and other
objects that are spread across different but interconnected
.CONFIG 'BOTH' OFF
//////////////////////////////////
//// End of a VM OR VSE Section  ///
//////////////////////////////////
//////////////////////////////////
/// Start of a VM-Only Section /////
//////////////////////////////////
.CONFIG 'UNIQUE' ON
.WHEN 'VM' INSERT
-including connections among a set of VM machines -
.CONFIG 'UNIQUE' OFF
//////////////////////////////////
//// End of a VM-Only Section //////
//////////////////////////////////
//////////////////////////////////
/// Start of a VM OR VSE Section ///
//////////////////////////////////
.CONFIG 'BOTH' ON
.WHEN 'VM' OR 'VSE' INSERT
computer systems.  Each computer system has a relational database manager
:
```

Fig. 14. Example of complex conditional statements leading to errors.

tenance. In the example in Fig. 13, all information on the CREATE VIEW statement would be in one place, and the writer would simply update one file to ensure that the hardcopy and online information remained current and consistent with each other.

Maintaining the Implicit Single-Source Manual

The maintenance of an implicit single-source manual tends to be higher than it is for explicit manuals. As releases go by and writers change, the coding complexity grows. Again using the analogy of coding, the older a program, the more layers of code are added by people with little or no knowledge of the original design. Added complexity usually introduces errors. For example, if you start using sophisticated Boolean logic (AND, OR, exclusive OR, NOT) in your files at the sentence level, it is likely that you or a subsequent writer will forget the logical twists occasionally and accidentally add or omit text. Fig. 14 shows an example in which there appear to be more conditional statements and "eye-catchers" than text!

Writers working with implicit single-source manuals should apply one rule they learned from writing to coding conditional statements: keep it simple.

MANUALS FOR MORE THAN TWO PRODUCTS

Occasionally, an organization can have more than two similar products with a large percentage of shared information—for example, computer software that can be used on several operating systems. A single-source manual for all the products might at first appear to be a good way to meet our objective of increasing operational efficiency [7]. However, the greater the number of manuals combined, the greater the complexity in design, reviews, and maintenance. For instance, there will be more product differences to monitor and more meetings to attend, possibly in distant locations. If the manual is to be implicit, the coding becomes exponentially more sophisticated—a point to consider since one day this manual will be handed to another writer and the knowledge transfer will be no simple matter.

Should the complexity become too great, single-sourcing will become inefficient, not just because it will overtax the writer, but because several groups of product experts will find they must change their individual plans to suit the schedule of one shared manual. It is possible to compromise on content, style, and publication dates with two products, but this becomes much more difficult when three or more are involved. As a rule, a multiple single-source manual will be successful only if all of the products are in one location and there is a high degree of cooperation among the participating groups.

WORKING WITH A GROUP OF WRITERS ON A SINGLE-SOURCE LIBRARY

A large product often comes with an entire library of manuals (plus, in the case of computer products, online information). The example we have been using here, the *SQL Reference for IBM VM Systems and VSE*, is part of a library of information on a relational database product that is available on both the VM and VSE operating systems. All the other manuals that form this library are similarly available for users of either system. All the writers of this library have created single-source manuals. This situation implies, of course, that the writers needed to work as a team to create standards that they all complied with while writing. This teamwork is extremely important, because from a user's perspective a set of manuals is a unified set of information; users should not perceive any discrepancies in moving from one book to the next. If you are working with a group of writers on a library of single-sourced manuals, there must therefore be a high degree of "buy in" from everybody. Once the process is set up, there must be considerable cooperation, since the broad range of user audiences for a library (ranging from executive to clerk, from expert to novice) requires tradeoffs in documentation design. Creating a single-source library will quickly reveal how cooperative a team is.

CONCLUSION

Today, knowledge-based corporations compete with other similar corporations stocked with highly skilled personnel in an international market. One area that distinguishes a successful corporation in such an environment is the ability to increase efficiency in operation by using innovative methods [8]. The single-source manual is an innovation that can significantly boost a technical writer's productivity while reducing a product's documentation maintenance cost, since the writer's time and effort, and the publishing and distribution expenses, are divided over two products. Like most innovations, there are tradeoffs to consider. However, if a corporation has two similar products with similar documentation, it should consider the long-term cost savings and increased operational efficiency of single-source manuals.

ACKNOWLEDGMENT

The author would like to thank Frank Pellow for the original design of the manual used in the examples for this paper. In addition, Brad Cassells, Marilyn Pontuck, Ross Robertson, and Jimmy Chui were helpful in reviewing, and Anne Stilman provided editorial guidance. All of these people are employees of IBM Canada Ltd.

REFERENCES

[1] A. P. Carnevale, *America and the New Economy.* San Francisco: Jossey-Bass, 1991.

[2] E. M. Goldratt and J. Cox, *The Goal: The Process of Ongoing Improvement,* Croton-on-Hudson, NY: North River Press, 1986.

[3] J. Fisher and D. Gipson, "In search of elegance," *Comp. Language,* vol. 17, no. 11, 1992, p. 42.

[4] C. Pickering, "Preparedness training" *CIO*, vol. 6, no. 5 (1992), pp. 24–25.

[5] M. A. Verber and E. D. Zwicky, "Configurable user documentation—or how I came to write a language with a future conditional," LISA V, *Proc.* of the Fifth USENIX Large Installation System Administration Conference, September-October, 1991, pp. 153–154.

[6] C. Ensign, "SGML by evolution," *Tech. Commun.*, vol. 40, no. 4 (1993), pp. 387–393.

[7] M. Treacy and F. Wiersema, "Customer intimacy and other value disciplines," *Harvard Business Review*, vol 71, no. 1 (1993), p. 85.

[8] P. Drucker, "The new society of organizations," *Harvard Business Review*, vol. 70, no. 1 (1992), p. 97.

Gary Bist is a technical writer at the IBM Canada Laboratory. He has written documentation for a variety of software products, including database and image software, and word processing software for non-English language national languages. In addition, he has published articles about the technical writing profession, often focusing on techniques to improve information quality and writing efficiency.

The Effects of Screen Captures in Manuals:

A Textual and Two Visual Manuals Compared

—MARK GELLEVIJ,
HANS VAN DER MEIJ,
TON DE JONG,
AND JULES PIETERS

Abstract *—This study examined the use of screen captures in manuals. Three designs of manuals were compared, one textual and two visual manuals. The two visual manuals differed in the type of screen capture that was used. One had screen captures that showed only the relevant part of the screen, whereas the other consisted of captures of the full screen. All manuals contained exactly the same textual information.*

We examined the time used on carrying out procedures (manual used as a job aid) and the results on retention tests (manual used for learning). We expected to find a trade-off between gain in time and learning effects. That is, we expected that higher scores on the retention tests involved an increase in time used and, vice versa, that gains in time would lead to lower retention test scores. We also explored the influence of manual design on user motivation.

For job-aid purposes, there were no differences between manuals. For learning, the full-screen captures manual and the textual manual were significantly better than the partial-screen captures manual. There was no proof for the expected trade-off. More learning was ***not*** *caused by an increase in time used. We found no effects on user motivation.*

This study does not yield convincing evidence to support the presence of screen captures in manuals. However, if one wants to include screen captures, this study gives clarity for the type of screen capture to choose. The use of full-screen captures is preferable to partial ones. Finally, we conclude that documentation designed to expedite the execution of tasks does not necessarily hamper the learning that may result.

Index Terms *— Documentation, motivation, screen captures, usability, visualizations.*

Manuscript received February 11, 1999; revised March 17, 1999.
A summary of this article appeared in the *IPCC 98 Proceedings* (pp. 439–451).
The authors are with the University of Twente–Faculty of Educational Science and Technology, 7500 AE Enschede, The Netherlands
(email: gellevij@edte.utwente.nl).
IEEE PII S 0361-1434(99)04914-0.

Nowadays, the use of visuals in user manuals for the computer industry seems to be a must. Designers devote much time and energy to creating attractive manuals. Often this is done by including various screen captures throughout the manual. These screen captures are presented for more than merely a decorative function. They can show, for example, a required start-screen or the correct result of an action. Designers face important questions such as when (for which type of information) and

Reprinted from *IEEE Trans. Prof. Comm.*, vol. PC-42, no. 2, pp. 77–91, June 1999.

which screen captures (full or partial) to use in their documentation.

Handbooks on technical documentation reveal very little about the use of screen captures. Price and Korman [1] treat the topic in one paragraph, stating that screen captures should be used for two purposes: 1) to show the results of action steps taken and 2) to show the object to act upon in the next action step. The only design guideline they offer is to use callouts to draw the users' attention to key parts of a window. Similarly, in *Dynamics in Document Design*, Schriver [2] does not discuss the role and design of using screen captures in technical documentation. She just gives several general guidelines on combining the use of words and graphics in document design.

The most extensive discussion on screen captures comes from Horton [3]. Among other things, Horton questions whether screen captures always have a purpose that justifies their cost. Horton also mentions that screen captures offer visual relief on pages full of text and states that "when used appropriately and placed wisely, they make procedures easier to learn and quicker to follow" (p. 148). What actually is "appropriate" and "wise" is described in three guidelines (p. 148):

1) In tutorials, screen captures should be offered to let the user imagine how to use the system.
2) Screen captures should be used to let the user verify the display, especially when the target group is the novice computer user.
3) If only part of the screen is important, only that part should be shown. The pages "should not be cluttered with what the users already know."

In short, research and advice about the use of screen captures in technical documentation are limited. The questions when and which screen captures to use in manuals are, for the bigger part, unanswered by the literature.

The "when" question concerns the types of information whose presentation can be supported by the use of screen captures. A common and valuable classification into types is the distinction between conceptual and procedural information. Conceptual information offers explanations and supports goal setting. Procedural information supports direct or indirect user actions and can be divided into action information, error information, and coordinative information [4]. Screen captures can be used to support the presentation of all these information types, for example, by showing a target screen (goal setting), the outcome of an action step (action information), or a specific button (coordinative information).

The question "where" to use screen captures is about the appropriate place of a screen capture on a manual page. Screen captures can be placed on the left of the text, on the right, or in the flow of the text.

Asking "which" screen captures to use often boils down to asking whether to use full- or partial-screen captures. Should the designer present everything that is shown on the screen, or is a display of only the relevant part better? The main difference between full- and partial-screen captures concerns the use of context. Full-screen captures show the complete interface. Partial captures show little (e.g., the active window) or no context (e.g., a single button).

So far, we have only talked about design issues of screen captures in manuals. However, our primary drive to focus on screen captures is that we think they can improve documentation. They can, for example, support locating a specific menu or object and make checking the correctness of a screen easier. Using screen captures for such specific goals will facilitate a bridge between what is written in the manual and what is seen on the computer screen. Documentation can be used in mainly two ways: for learning how to work with a program and for carrying out tasks. Improving documentation therefore means two things: to speed up task execution and to improve learning.

Whether the presence of screen captures speeds up task execution is a question that has been studied by Van der Meij [4]. In a study comparing a visual and a textual manual, he found a significant positive effect of screen captures on task execution time. He offers three explanations for this. One, the connection between what is written and what is shown on the screen is now presented in a single source: the manual. Users may thus have fewer difficulties in handling the two separate sources. Two, there is no need for the user to translate the text into an image because the way it should look is already printed in the manual. Three, fewer switches between manual and screen are needed. Because of the screen captures, the manual becomes more self-contained. In general, these arguments all share the core idea that screen captures reduce coordination problems.

Van der Meij [4] also mentions some drawbacks of screen captures. One of these is user passivity. The presence of the screen captures may discourage users to study the interface and reduce the need for users to search and examine the screen very closely. Another drawback is that the redundancy of both screen captures and text may be disadvantageous because the user has to process the same information twice, which imposes an undesirable heavy cognitive load.

This raises the intriguing question of the existence of a trade-off. Is what is gained from using screen captures for speeding up task execution also a loss for learning? When screen captures reduce cognitive effort and speed up task execution, they may simultaneously fail to maximally activate the user in using and exploring the interface, and thereby fail to support learning. In other words, users benefit from the manual as a job aid but suffer a loss for learning due to decreased cognitive effort. To give a specific example, when a screen capture in a manual is used to support locating a button on the interface, the user will be quicker in finding that button than without that screen capture. In the meantime, there is no need to search the interface for the relevant button. Consequently, the user will gain less knowledge of the interface as a whole.

Thus, it seems fair to predict that screen captures in manuals cannot serve both goals: to speed up task execution and simultaneously, to improve learning. For this study, a main question is whether this prediction holds. We predict that faster training leads to lower learning. In addition, we look at a design issue of screen captures. More specifically, we examine the role of full-screen captures versus partial-screen captures.

Three manuals (tutorials) were compared: a textual manual (Text), a manual supporting procedural information with partial-screen captures (V-Part), and a manual that supported procedural information with full-screen captures (V-Full). The textual manual was designed according to minimalist principles and heuristics [5] and formed the basis for the two visual manuals. Partial-screen captures were added to the action steps in the V-Part manual, whose design was inspired by Stuur's visual steps approach [6]. A partial-screen capture showed that part (or parts) of the screen the user needed to perform the action step. Examples of partial-screen captures are: menus, dialogs, or parts of windows. Full-screen captures were added to the action steps in the V-Full manual, whose design was inspired by the *Visual Learning Guide* manuals by Gardner and Beatty [7]. A full-screen capture showed the complete interface. Example pages of the three manuals can be found in Appendix A (Text), B (V-Part), and C (V-Full).

The main goal of the study was to find out if these manuals have a different effect on speed of task execution and learning, and whether faster training leads to lower learning.

We expected that the manual with full-screen captures would lead to the quickest task execution. Because of the lack of visual support in the textual manual, we expected this one to be the slowest. For learning, we expected the opposite. As users of the textual manual were expected to devote the most effort on getting to know the system, the largest effect on learning was expected there. For users of the manual with full-screen captures the need to actively examine the system was expected to be the lowest. Consequently, learning effects were expected to be worst for that manual. We expected the manual with partial-screen captures to take the middle position for both speed on task execution as well as learning effects.

We examined two levels of learning: learning to perform the same tasks as trained with the manual (trained tasks) and tasks that were different than trained with the manual (untrained or transfer tasks). For example, a manual can contain information on how to make a bulleted list: the trained task. Matching untrained tasks can be making a bulleted list in multiple levels or making a numbered list.

To examine the effects of manual type on the job-aiding purpose of the manual, we measured training time. The total training time consisted of time that users needed to read explanations, carry out procedures, and explore the program. To find out whether the visual manuals gave visual relief and were viewed as more attractive, user motivation was measured.

Method

Subjects Seventy-three Dutch students from the Faculty of Educational Science and Technology participated in the experiment. The mean age of the experimental group was 21.2 years (SD = 2.4 years). The subjects were classified as intermediate or experienced computer users on the basis of their score on the Computer Self-Efficacy Scale questionnaire. It was expected that subjects with less computer experience would benefit more from screen captures than would experienced users. Subjects were randomly assigned to one of the three experimental conditions: Text, V-Part, or V-Full. Table I shows how the subjects were distributed. Classification of subjects into levels of computer experience served two additional purposes. One, it made clear that the subjects' level of experience was average or above average; they were certainly not beginners. Two, it made it possible to check that subjects were indeed randomly distributed over the three conditions.

Materials

Computers: The sessions were held in a computer room with 20 IBM compatible Pentium Pro 166 computers with 32 MB of RAM. During the experiment, all subject actions with the computer program were logged automatically.

SimQuest and Motion Application: Subjects learned to use the SimQuest authoring tool version 1.1 [8]. SimQuest uses an object-oriented approach, which means that a collection of ready-made elements can be used to create an application or program. With SimQuest, the teacher or designer creates a learning environment that offers a set of simulations, assignments, and explanations that enable learners to explore a specific domain. A main component in the subject's education (educational science and technology) is learning how to systematically design instruction using various media. As SimQuest is a state of the art tool for designing multimedia instruction, it was expected that the subjects would be very interested in learning to use it.

The SimQuest application used to exemplify the creation of a simulation environment in the manuals dealt with the physics domain of motion. The application lets the students explore the relationship between initial velocity, velocity at a certain point and time, and acceleration. Subjects are shown various simulations with moving motorcycles, trains, cars, scooters, and others. Assignments make it possible for the student to check the correctness of any discovered relationship. Explanations such as videos and textual information introduce and discuss the variables used in the simulations and assignments. Main tasks trained in the manual concerned modifying and creating simulations, assignments, and explanations.

Manuals: The manuals were written in English, and all contained exactly the same text. In order to avoid differences in reading, we attempted to keep the layout of the three manuals as similar as possible. Even so, the presence of screen captures led to manuals of different sizes. The text manual consisted of 32 pages. The V-Part had 54 pages containing a total of 231 partial-screen captures, and the V-Full had 58 pages, containing a total of 87 full-screen captures.

Each chapter in the manual consisted of two sections (see Fig. 1): a guided section with a brief task description and detailed action steps to accomplish the task, and an exploratory section, which offered

Fig. 1. Example of a guided section ('Adding interface elements') and an exploratory section ('Try it yourself') in the manual.

Adding interface elements

To be able to use the interface, you have to add an interface element to the interface. The necessary interface element for this is available in the Library window. You can find it in the folder: Interface elements. You need a Start button to let the scooter move.

1 In the *Library window*, select the folder **Interface Elements**
2 Select the subfolder **Dynamic Widgets**
3 Select **Action Button**
4 Drag **Action Button** from the *Library window* and drop it into the *interface*

Try it yourself

As you can see, you cannot stop the car (apart from closing the window). If you want to exercise modifying interfaces more, you can now add a stop-button to the interface.
Do not forget to save your work afterwards!

TABLE I
DISTRIBUTION OF SUBJECTS PER CONDITION

	Computer experience		
Manual	Intermediate (m/f)	Experienced (m/f)	Row total (m/f)
Text	10 (0/10)	15 (3/12)	25 (3/22)
V-Part	10 (1/9)	15 (5/10)	25 (6/19)
V-Full	9 (1/8)	14 (6/8)	23 (7/16)
Column total	29 (2/27)	44 (14/30)	73 (16/57)

m = male, f = female

one or more exercises comparable to the task practiced in the guided section. In line with the minimalist approach [5], these exploratory sections are an important feature in the manual.

Questionnaires and Tests: The subjects received a questionnaire with general questions about gender, age, and previous experience with authoring tools. Nineteen participants (7 males and 12 females) stated that they had used an authoring tool at least once. In addition, there were 20 questions to classify the subjects as intermediate or experienced computer users. For this purpose, the Computer Self-Efficacy Scale [9] questionnaire was translated into Dutch. This questionnaire used a five-point agree–disagree scale.

An electronic questionnaire, based on Keller's ARCS theory [10], asked the subjects about their motivational state. The four motivational elements from the ARCS theory (Attention, Relevance, Confidence, and Satisfaction) were captured in four SimQuest-specific questions, which were shown (every 15 min) in an automatically appearing window (see Fig. 2). Subjects were asked to answer the questions by moving the sliders, which always displayed the middle, neutral, position when presented.

Two tests were used to determine learning effects: an immediate test and a delayed test. The items in the tests had two levels of difficulty:

- Items that measured trained tasks (exercises that were the same as practiced with the manual); and
- Items that measured untrained, also known as transfer tasks (new tasks that were different from practiced tasks).

Table II shows the number of test items in the immediate and delayed test.

Procedure The experiment consisted of three sessions: practice, an immediate test, and a delayed test. Before the practice session, the subjects answered the questionnaire on gender, age, previous

Fig. 2. Pop-up motivation questionnaire.

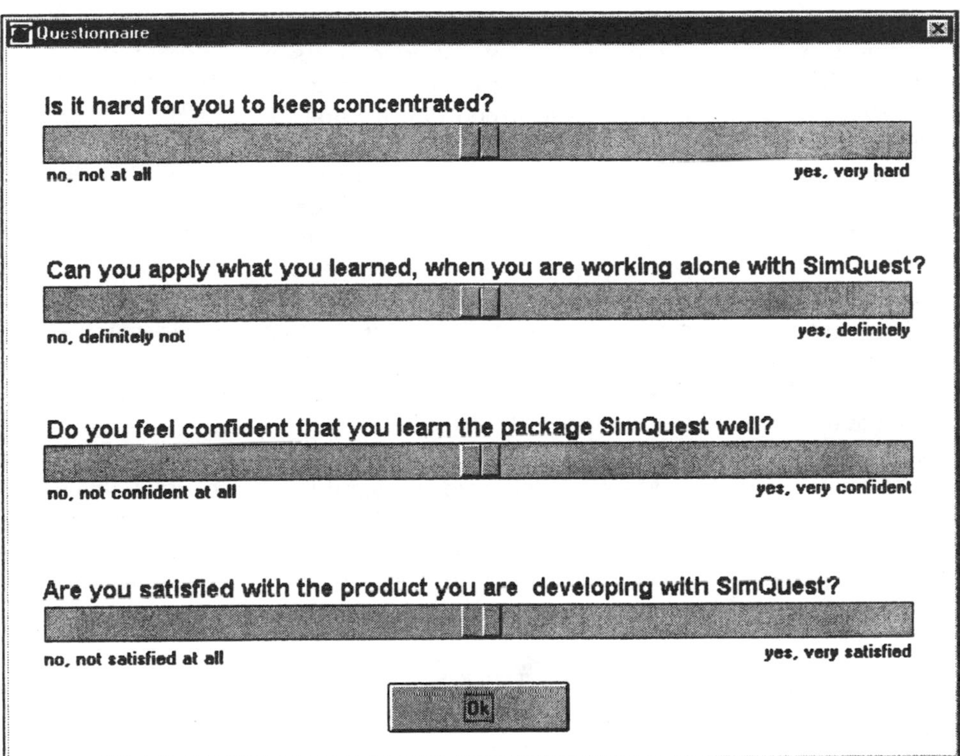

TABLE II
NUMBER OF ITEMS IN IMMEDIATE AND DELAYED TEST

	Immediate test		Delayed test	
	Trained	Untrained	Trained	Untrained
Number of test items	18	23	19	23

experience with authoring tools, and computer experience.

The practice session lasted 4 hours maximally. It was held from 9:00 A.M. to 1:00 P.M., with two coffee breaks of 15 min. At the start of this session, the subjects were told that their task was to learn how to work with SimQuest. They were told to work on their own, using only the manual for support. During practice, every 15 min a pop-up screen appeared asking the subjects the four questions about their current motivational state. The subjects could stop practicing when they felt they were able to comfortably use SimQuest.

The immediate test session took place the same day, starting at 2:00 P.M., and lasted a maximum of 2 hours. The subjects were asked to try to do their best without the use of a manual. They were also told that some things in the test would be rather different from what they had practiced that morning. They were further told that this session would end at 4:00 P.M., but that they could leave when they were finished.

The delayed test session took place one week after the first test session. The subjects could work a maximum of 2 hours on this test. As with the immediate test, they were not allowed to use their manual.

Coding and Scoring

Computer Experience, Gender, and Previous Use of Authoring Tools: The questionnaire on computer experience used a five-point disagree-agree scale. Subjects with a mean score lower than 3 were classified as intermediate users, subjects with a score of 3 or higher as experienced users (see Table I). Female subjects were scored as 1, and male subjects as 2. Subjects who stated that they had used an authoring tool at least once before were scored as 1 and subjects that never used an authoring tool before as 0. Computer experience, gender, and previous use of authoring tools were all variables at a nominal level.

Time: During practice, all subjects' actions were logged. These logs allowed us to determine training time for guided and exploratory sections. Time used for coffee breaks was subtracted.

Time used on the guided parts showed a direct effect of manual type on task execution. It showed how long subjects took to complete the reading of the short explanations and to carry out the action steps. Time used on exploratory parts showed the time users spent in exploration. Both in guided and exploratory sections, subjects had to save their work as a last action. Saving was therefore taken as the transition to the next section.

A MANOVA showed no significant relations between time and computer experience, time and gender, or time and previous use of authoring tools. Therefore, there was no need to correct for these three variables when examining differences on time.

Motivation: The data of the motivation pop-up questionnaire consisted of a maximum of 12 repeated measures. The first measurement was removed because it was used for practice. After the ninth measurement, the number of subjects that answered the questionnaire dropped below the pre-set criteria of 85% (it was 84%). Therefore, only measurements 2–9 were used in the analysis. Examination of the instruments' reliability showed that the questionnaire was highly reliable (see Table III).

Tests were performed to determine if the results on the four measures could be combined into one value indicating the subjects motivational state. Table IV shows the correlations between the four items. Pearson correlations indicate that the four indeed share a fundamental basis. Therefore, the scores for the four measures were combined into a composite score for motivation.

A MANOVA showed no significant relations between motivation and gender, and motivation and previous use of authoring tools. A significant relation was found between motivation and computer experience ($F(1, 72) = 4.60$, $p < 0.05$). Computer experience will therefore be treated as a covariate when testing for

TABLE III
RELIABILITY OF MOTIVATION MEASURES

	Cronbach's Alpha
Attention	0.95
Relevance	0.96
Confidence	0.94
Satisfaction	0.95
Motivation (combination of the four factors)	0.96

differences on motivation between manuals.

Learning Effects: For each trained or untrained item, a subject could receive a score of 1 if the item was performed correctly or a score of 0 if executed incorrectly.

A MANOVA showed no significant relations between learning effects and computer experience, learning effects and gender, or learning effects and previous use of authoring tools. Therefore, there was no need to correct for these three variables when examining differences on learning.

Results

Time: Table V shows the means and standard deviations of the time users spent in dealing with the guided and exploratory sections of the manuals.

No statistically significant differences for practice time between manuals were found on guided sections of the manuals. One explanation is that all texts provide sufficient coordinative information. The action steps clearly explain what to do and where to act. The screen captures may therefore have been redundant, offering no vital or new information. Inaccurate or unclear screen captures may even lead to confusion, and consequently to delay. Another reason might be the transparency of the interface. The interface may have been so easy to use, that (extra) coordinative information was not necessary at all. Yet a third explanation may lie in the specific content of the guided sections. These sections contain procedural (doing) as well as conceptual (reading) information, and the recorded time reflects the processing of both information types. Clearly, this somehow moderates any time gain of screen captures because they mainly support the handling of procedures. A better view of the effects of screen captures on time requires a filtering out of all reading time.

The three conditions differed considerably in the time subjects spent on exploratory sections. Subjects with the text manual spent almost twice as much time exploring the program as did users of V-Part manual. This difference was statistically significant ($F(2, 72) = 3.37, \ p < 0.05$; with a Tukey HSD-test at 0.05). Users of the text manual thus appeared more willing to devote time on trying things themselves than users of the V-Part manual. This may signal a difference in motivation, although this could not be proven statistically (see next section). The statistically significant difference on time used on exploratory sections continues to exist when time on exploratory sections is taken as a proportion of the total training time ($F(2, 72) = 3.39, \ p < 0.05$; with a Tukey HSD-test at 0.05). The mean proportion of time used on exploratory sections of the total training time varied between 0 and 24%.

Motivation: An ANCOVA with computer experience as covariate showed no significant effect of manuals on motivation ($F(2, 72) = 0.781$). Experienced users were more motivated. Regression analysis showed that 7% of the variance on motivation could be explained by computer experience ($F(1, 71) = 5.29, \ p < 0.05$).

Despite the fact that there were no statistically significant main effects of manual type on motivation, the results consistently favor the V-Full manual (see Table VI). These results give an indication of the possible visual relief that this type of manual is supposed

TABLE IV

CORRELATIONS BETWEEN MOTIVATION MEASURES

	Attention	Relevance	Confidence
Relevance	0.41*		
Confidence	0.58*	0.73*	
Satisfaction	0.47*	0.55*	0.74*

* p<.001

TABLE V

MEANS (STANDARD DEVIATIONS) OF TIME IN SECONDS USED ON GUIDED AND EXPLORATORY SECTIONS

	Manuals		
	V-Part	Text	V-Full
Guided sections	7583 (1071)	7483 (1243)	7427 (1184)
Exploratory sections	596 (597)	1133 (834)*	936 (767)
Total	8179 (1104)	8616 (1169)	8362 (1223)

* p<0.05 compared to V-Part

to offer when compared to the text manual.

Examinations of the results in the course of time showed results that pointed in the same direction, favoring the V-Full manual. Fig. 3 shows the flow of measurements on motivation. It can be seen that the V-Full manual is the best motivator on all factors, all the time, but not significantly so. A repeated measures test found no proof in favor of one of the three manuals ($F(2, 60) = 0.596$).

Surprisingly, there are no clear differences between the V-Part and text manuals. In other words, there seems to be no extra benefit in offering partial-screen captures in comparison to plain text. Indeed, there may be an opposite effect. As motivation slightly drops over time using the V-Part manual, it may well be that partial-screen captures tend to de-motivate.

Learning Effects: All subjects, regardless of the manual with which they had practiced, performed quite well on the items that measured trained tasks. On the immediate test as well as the delayed test, more than 87% of the tasks were performed correctly (see Table VII). This ceiling effect is troublesome because it strongly limits the chances of finding any significant differences on trained tasks.

The untrained tasks were performed somewhat less well (see Table VIII). Both the V-Full and the text manual outperformed the V-Part manual on the delayed test ($F(2, 71) = 5.56$, $p < 0.01$), with a Tukey HSD-test at 0.05). The difference between V-Full and V-Part suggests that the V-Full users have gained a better understanding of the program. Explaining the difference between the text and V-Part manuals is more difficult. One account may be that the text manual forces

TABLE VI

MEANS (STANDARD DEVIATIONS) OF MOTIVATIONAL FACTORS (SCALE 0–100, DEFAULT SCORE WAS 50)

	Order of conditions		
Attention	V-Part 64.21 (25.36)	Text 67.59 (20.44)	V-Full 70.65 (18.84)
Relevance	V-Part 64.31 (22.49)	Text 66.19 (13.57)	V-Full 69.38 (13.84)
Confidence	Text 67.98 (11.58)	V-Part 68.91 (17.17)	V-Full 72.23 (10.98)
Satisfaction	Text 62.89 (9.95)	V-Part 63.02 (19.92)	V-Full 66.86 (11.89)
Motivation	V-Part 65.11 (17.05)	Text 66.16 (11.21)	V-Full 69.78 (11.94)

Fig. 3. Development of motivation in the course of time where high scores indicate high motivation. (The neutral [default] score was set at 50.)

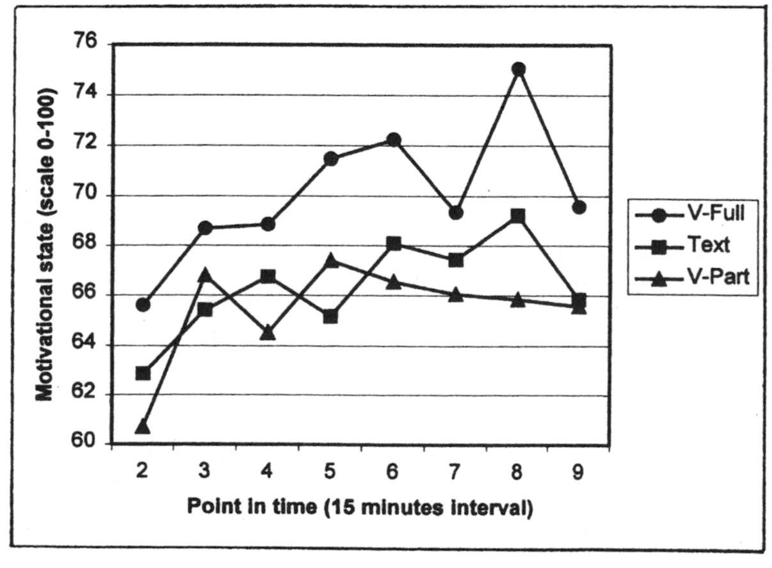

users to more actively explore the program. The results on time, where significantly more time was spent on exploratory parts by text users than V-Part users, supports this explanation. Apart from devoting more time, it could also be that the partial-screen captures interfere with understanding the program. On the one hand, the information given by the partial-screen captures may have been too limited to support users to learn to understand the program. On the other hand, the partial-screen captures may have confused users who actively constructed their own understanding of the program and therefore disturbed that construction process.

Trade-Off Between Time and Learning Effects: Examinations of Pearson correlations between training time and learning effects revealed an intriguing pattern (see Table IX).

The correlations for total training time show that there is a negative relationship (immediate test) or no relationship (delayed test) with the scores on the retention tests. This means that shorter training time leads to higher test scores respectively, that there is no relationship between training time and test scores. Correlations on guided sections are all negative, except for the V-Full manual on the delayed test, where the correlation is nil. From theory, it was expected that a gain in time would work against learning. Therefore, we expected the correlations to be positive. Instead, the results show that **shorter** training time leads to **more** learning, and **longer** training time leads to **less** learning. These findings clearly contradict a trade-off between training time and learning.

It is interesting to see that there were no main differences between manuals in this respect. Manuals like these, designed—among others—to shorten training time do not obstruct learning. On the contrary, there is some indication that users benefit.

This finding made us reconsider the need to take training time into consideration as a correcting factor when considering effects

TABLE VII

MEANS (STANDARD DEVIATIONS) OF TEST-SCORES ON TRAINED TASKS

	V-Part	Text	V-Full
Immediate Test (max. 18)	15.68 (3.92)	15.84 (4.89)	17.13 (1.29)
Delayed Test (max. 19)	16.76 (4.11)	17.32 (2.46)	18.32 (1.09)

TABLE VIII

MEANS (STANDARD DEVIATIONS) OF TEST-SCORES ON UNTRAINED TASKS

	V-Part	Text	V-Full
Immediate Test (max. 23)	13.36 (5.44)	14.68 (5.13)	14.87 (4.30)
Delayed Test (max. 23)	11.96 (4.86)	15.40 (4.76)*	16.00 (3.88)*

* $p<0.05$ compared to V-Part

TABLE IX

CORRELATIONS OF IMMEDIATE AND DELAYED TEST SCORES WITH TIME ON GUIDED AND EXPLORATORY SECTIONS

	V-Part	Text	V-Full	Total group
Immediate Test				
Guided sections	-0.59**	-0.41*	-0.15	-0.41***
Exploratory sections	0.16	0.32	0.23	0.26*
Total time	-0.49*	-0.20	-0.00	-0.24*
Delayed Test				
Guided sections	-0.45*	-0.07	0.01	-0.21
Exploratory sections	0.40*	0.31	0.53*	0.42***
Total time	-0.22	0.15	0.35	0.06

* $p<0.05$, ** $p<0.01$, *** $p<0.001$

of manuals on learning. An ANCOVA with total training time as covariate still showed a significant effect of conditions for untrained test items on the delayed test ($F(2, 71) = 5.23$, $p < 0.01$). In other words, time did not interact with the main effect found for learning.

Conclusion

The experiment does not make it perfectly clear whether screen captures are a necessary feature for the improvement of documentation. Looking at the results, there is proof that a design in which partial-screen captures are coupled to action steps is not a good solution. On several measures, the subjects who had worked with the V-Part manual performed worse than the other subjects.

When the V-Full and text manuals are compared, there is no proof that one leads to more learning than the other. Also, in time used on guided and exploratory parts, no differences were found between the V-Full and text manuals. The use of full-screen captures suggests a motivating influence. The experiment has not proven this assertion, however.

Another important finding of this study is that the use of screen captures does not lead to a trade-off between gain of time and benefits for learning. The results show that better performances on the tests cannot be asserted to an increase in training time. Therefore, it can be concluded that documentation designed to expedite the execution of tasks does not necessarily hamper the learning that may result.

One might conclude that devoting much time and resources on presenting screen captures in manuals is not worth the effort. A closer look at the experiment cautions against such a conclusion. There are several arguments to show that it may be too early to tell.

An important premise for this experiment was that we wanted to have a situation that was close to reality. It can be argued that learning how to use a computer program with a manual as the only source of information, and for 3 hours in a row, is a not realistic situation. Learning a computer program at home or at work may go quite differently. It may take four half-hour sessions over a period of two weeks instead of one long session. Using a visual manual instead of a textual one in this case, where you have to restart several times, may then have its benefits.

A final consideration is that the subjects who participated in this experiment may not represent computer users in general. As students and our faculty must and do use computers quite a lot, their computer experience (and level of formal educational training) is probably higher than that of average computer users. For real novices, differences between using textual and visual manuals may again be stronger.

Looking at the types of manual used in the experiment, a few remarks can be made. It was surprising to see that there were no differences in time on task, especially because Van der Meij [4] found quite strong effects. This may very well be explained by the manuals used in both experiments. Van der Meij used manuals that were meant for job-aiding purposes only. That documentation consisted almost completely of procedural information whereas the tutorial in this experiment was a balanced combination of conceptual and procedural information. As the focus of a tutorial is primarily on learning, or better, in getting to understand the program by doing, reading, and exploring, less gain in time can be expected.

A second remark pertains to the difficulty of the tests in combination with the quality of the manual. The results for learning show that subjects were very capable of performing the tasks on which they had trained and even on those they did not, both in the immediate and the delayed test. These results indicate that the tests may have been too easy or that the manual did its job well in teaching the subjects how to use the program. Too well, perhaps? If this is indeed the case, benefits from screen captures can only be small.

Also, the two designs of the visual manuals were in a way unsophisticated. In each manual, only one type of screen capture design was used, full or partial. These screen captures should support various user activities. For example, a screen capture may focus the user's attention at the start of a procedure, may help the user in identifying and locating screen objects during task execution, and may ease verifying a screen state at the end of a procedure. Functions such as these may require different screen capture designs. A visual manual in which screen captures are presented in a way that their roles and designs are optimally attuned to one another may function much better than the visual (or textual) manuals tested in this study. Van der Meij and Gellevij [11] have proposed a framework for research in this fashion. That framework, created after we completed this study, distinguishes four roles and four design dimensions for screen captures in manuals. With this framework, we think it is possible to fine-tune roles and designs for screen captures in a more sophisticated way.

Manuals quite often not only serve the purpose of instructing and supporting users. Visually attractive manuals can very well be part of the selling strategy for software packages which could be a legitimate reason to choose a visual manual. If the marketing department makes that decision, they should, as this experiment suggests, opt for presenting full- rather than partial-screen captures.

APPENDIX A: TEXT EXAMPLE PAGE

The SERVIVE project — SIMQUEST V-September

Adding explanations to the application

Before you can start editing your explanation, you must:

- drop it from the library and drop it into your application
- give it a meaningful name.

Dragging and dropping an explanation

You already decided which explanation element you are going to use, you can take it from the library and put it into your application.

1 In the *Library window*, select **Video**
2 Drag **Video** from the *Library window* and drop it into the tabsheet *level 1* of the *Application window*

Naming an explanation

To keep it clear what your elements contain, you can give the explanation a meaning full name. The video fragment this explanation is going to contain is about a motorbike.

1 In *level 1* of the *Application window*, select **Video**
2 Click your right mouse button and choose **Rename**
3 Type `Motorbike`, and click **OK**

Editing an explanation

To be able to create or edit your explanation you should:

- open the explanation editor,
- specify the content, and
- specify the learner description.

Opening the explanation editor

First you have to open the explanation editor.

1 In *level 1* of the *Application window*, select **Motorbike**
2 Click your right mouse button and choose **Edit**

Check if the editor appears on the screen.

Specifying the content

You use the Specification tabsheet to specify which video file must be presented.

1 Select the **Specification** tabsheet
2 Click **Select video**
3 Select the folder **motion.res**
4 Select the subfolder **video**
5 Choose **Optr-rem.avi** and click **OK**
6 Click **Apply**

Specifying the learner description

You can offer your student a short description of the explanation's content that they can read before they decide to start the explanation. This description is called the learner description. The learner description will be shown to

Appendix B: V-Part Example Page

Adding explanations to the application

Before you can start editing your explanation, you must:

- drop it from the library and drop it into your application
- give it a meaningful name.

Dragging and dropping an explanation

You already decided which explanation element you are going to use, you can take it from the library and put it into your application.

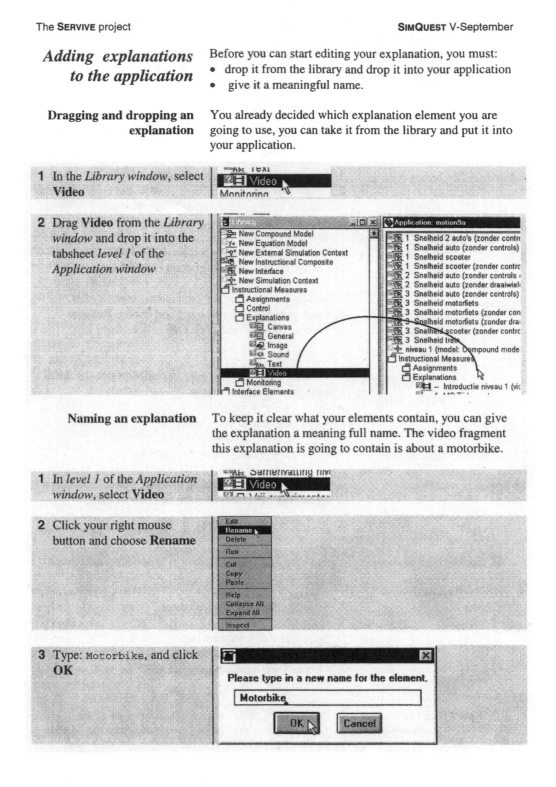

1 In the *Library window*, select **Video**

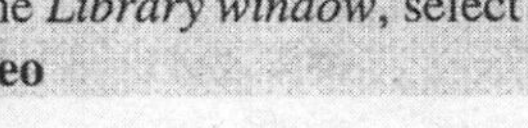

2 Drag **Video** from the *Library window* and drop it into the tabsheet *level 1* of the *Application window*

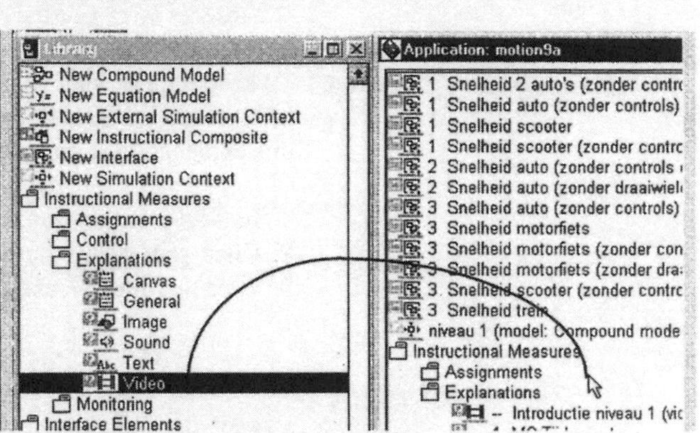

Naming an explanation

To keep it clear what your elements contain, you can give the explanation a meaning full name. The video fragment this explanation is going to contain is about a motorbike.

1 In *level 1* of the *Application window*, select **Video**

2 Click your right mouse button and choose **Rename**

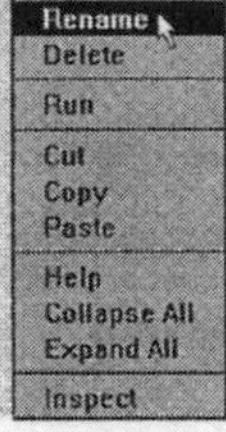

3 Type: `Motorbike`, and click **OK**

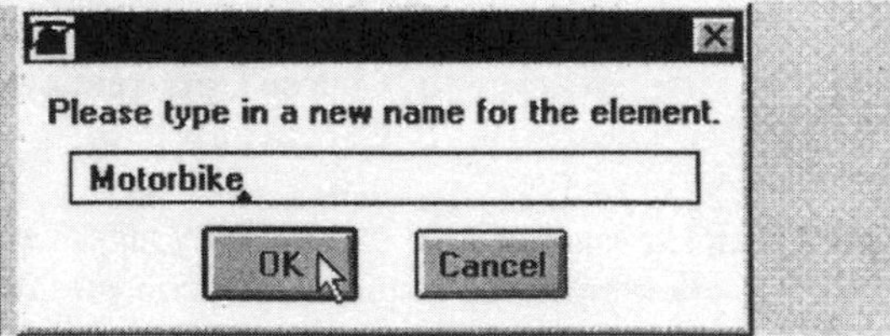

APPENDIX C: V-FULL EXAMPLE PAGE

The SERVIVE project — SIMQUEST V-September

Adding explanations to the application

Before you can start editing your explanation, you must:

- drop it from the library and drop it into your application
- give it a meaningful name.

Dragging and dropping an explanation

You already decided which explanation element you are going to use, you can take it from the library and put it into your application.

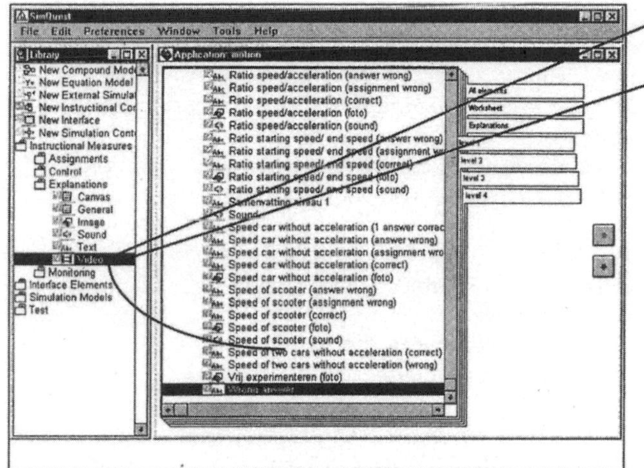

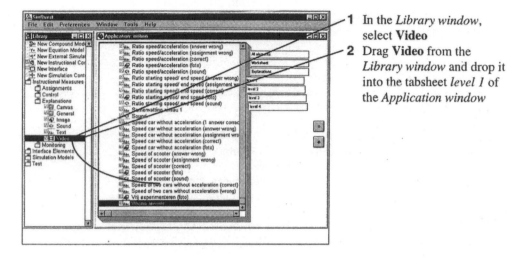

1 In the *Library window*, select **Video**

2 Drag **Video** from the *Library window* and drop it into the tabsheet *level 1* of the *Application window*

Naming an explanation

To keep it clear what your elements contain, you can give the explanation a meaning full name. The video fragment this explanation is going to contain is about a motorbike.

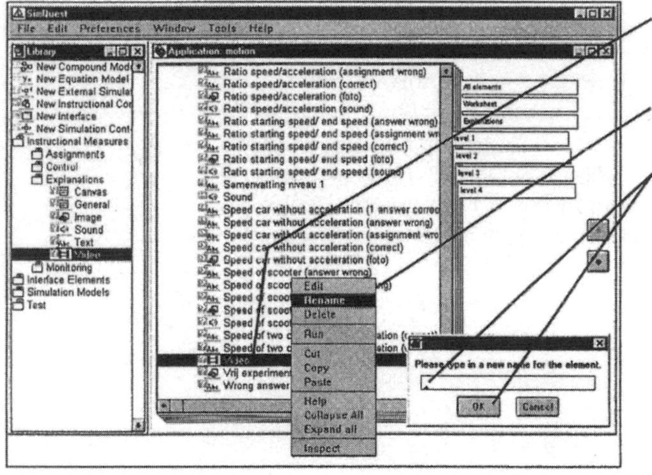

1 In *level 1* of the *Application window*, select **Video**

2 Click your right mouse button and choose **Rename**

3 Type: `Motorbike`, and click **OK**

Acknowledgment

We would like to thank D. Farkas for his valuable help on the study and the review of this paper.

References

[1] J. Price and H. Korman, *How to Communicate Technical Information*. Redwood City, CA: Benjamin/Cummings, 1993.

[2] K. A. Schriver, *Dynamics in Document Design*. New York: Wiley, 1997.

[3] W. Horton, "Visual literacy—Dump the dumb screendump," *Tech. Commun.*, vol. 40, pp. 146–147, 1993.

[4] H. van der Meij, "Optimizing the joint handling of manual and screen," in *Minimalism Beyond the Nurnberg Funnel*, J. M. Carroll, Ed. Cambridge, MA: MIT Press, 1998, pp. 275–310.

[5] H. van der Meij and J. M. Carroll, "Principles and heuristics for designing minimalist instruction," *Tech. Commun.*, vol. 42, pp. 243–251, 1995.

[6] A. Stuur, *Windows Voor Kinderen: Deel2 [Windows for Children: Part 2]*. Utrecht, The Netherlands: Bruna Informatica, 1996.

[7] D. C. Gardner and G. J. Beatty, *Visuele leermethode Windows 3.1 [Windows 3.1: The Visual Learning Guide]*. Utrecht, The Netherlands: Bruna Uitgevers B.V., 1994.

[8] T. de Jong and J. van Joolingen, Eds., *SimQuest: An Authoring System for Integrated Simulation Environments SERVIVE Project (ET1020)*. Enschede, The Netherlands: Univ. Twente, 1998.

[9] C. A. Murphy, D. Coover, and S. V. Owen, "Development and validation of the computer self-efficacy scale," *Educ. Psychol. Meas.*, vol. 49, pp. 893–899, 1989.

[10] J. M. Keller, "Motivational design of instruction," in *Instructional-Design Theories and Models*, C. M. Reigeluth, Ed. Hillsdale, NJ: Erlbaum, 1983, pp. 383–434.

[11] H. Van der Meij and M. R. M. Gellevij, "Screen captures in software documentation," *Tech. Commun.*, vol. 45, pp. 529–543, 1998.

Mark Gellevij works at the Department of Instructional Technology of Twente University, Enschede, The Netherlands. After graduating from this department, he worked as a technical writer in trade and industry. He is now working on his doctoral thesis about designing user support for complex software environments. His paper "Screen Captures in Software Documentation," coauthored with Hans van der Meij, has recently been selected as the winner of an award of Distinguished Technical Communication in the Society for Technical Communication's outstanding article award competition for 1998.

Hans van der Meij works at the Department of Instructional Technology of Twente University, Enschede, The Netherlands. His main areas of interest are information seeking behavior and technical documentation. In the latter area, he has published 16 chapters and 33 articles. One of his articles, coauthored by J. M. Carroll, received an Award for "Distinguished Article of 1995" from the Society for Technical Communication. Hans also received the "Best Transactions Paper Award for 1997" from the IEEE Professional Communication Society. His studies in technical documentation combine theory, practice, and empirical research. He currently conducts inventories on the roles and designs of screen captures, procedures, warnings, and indexes.

Ton de Jong is Professor of Instructional Technology at the University of Twente, Enschede, The Netherlands. He received the Ph.D. degree from the Eindhoven University of Technology, Eindhoven, The Netherlands, on the topic "Problem solving and knowledge representation in physics for novice students." He specializes in problem solving and discovery learning with computer simulations.

Jules M. Pieters is Professor of Instructional Technology (appointed 1991), Faculty of Educational Science and Technology at the University of Twente, Enschede, The Netherlands. After graduating in Experimental Psychology at the University of Nijmegen, he wrote his doctoral thesis about the role of psychomotor control and language in spatial localization (1980). He joined the faculty in Twente in 1980. Currently, he is Dean of the Faculty of Educational Science and Technology. Pieters is codirector of the research program in Cognitive Tools and Instructional Design. He is involved in research projects on knowledge acquisition and transfer and on designing learning environments.

The User Edit: Making Manuals Easier to Use

MARSHALL A. ATLAS

***Abstract*—Possibly the simplest way to make a technical manual easier to use is a "user edit"—that is, having an inexperienced user try to work with a machine, using only its manual as a guide. His errors and hesitations should tell you where the weak points are. This report describes how to set up such tests, what to be careful of, and some of the benefits you can expect.**

NEARLY everyone who uses or services a complex machine—whether computer, copier, or fork-lift truck—sooner or later needs an instruction manual to figure out what to do next. Such manuals must be carefully written. It is not enough that they be technically accurate, grammatically correct, and easy to read; they must also be "usable," that is, the reader must be able to find and use the instructions quickly, easily, and without error.

One of the best tools for improving manual usability is the "user edit"; it is fast, cheap, easy, and powerful, yielding a lot of information for very little effort. Unfortunately, this technique has not been well-documented; even the U.S. Army, which uses it extensively, describes it only in very sketchy detail [1]. As a result, writers are likely to regard the user edit as either a piece of folklore or a new discovery. Indeed, when we first tried it, we had to learn most of the rules from scratch; our purpose here is to give others the headstart we lacked.

The user edit is based on a very simple idea: Find someone who knows nothing about your machine and have him work with it, using only your manual as a guide; his errors and hesitations should tell you where the weak points are. To get more detailed information, it is also a good idea to ask users to talk while they work, telling what they are trying to do, what they are looking for, what gives them trouble, and what they suggest to make the manual better.

This procedure yields so much information that you will often need to test with only one or two users. Furthermore, you can often afford to be quite casual; for example, even though your best bet is to test *typical* users of your product (people who work for other companies), you can still get good results by testing users who are much less typical (like people who work for you or your company). However, there are two things you should *not* be casual about:

1. Be sure the manual and the machine are as complete as possible. Anything you don't test is almost certain to cause you trouble later.

2. Take detailed written notes: They will be your only source of information. The best way we have found is to write on a copy of the manual, just as if you were editing it. Have at least one person do nothing but take notes (someone else can set up the machine, talk to the user, etc.). Better yet, have the writer of the manual take the notes; that way he can get a feeling for how severe each problem is (i.e., how much harm it can do, and how much work it will take to correct it) and get some practical experience with users as well.

Manuscript received November 7, 1980.

The author is a research psychologist. This paper was written during his association with the Information Development Dept., IBM Corp. Boulder, CO. His current address is Army Research Institute Field Unit, P. O. Box 6057, Fort Bliss, TX 79916.

INFORMAL TESTING

The simplest way to run a user edit is to have the user read the manual one page at a time, carrying out the instructions as he reads them. The main disadvantage to this procedure is that it does not test whether he can *find* the appropriate instructions when he needs them. Nonetheless, it can help locate the following:

Problems of Content; in particular:

Missing instructions Unless you know exactly what you're looking for, it is extremely difficult to read a manual for missing information. The presence of something wrong is likely to be much more obvious than the absence of something necessary, simply because an incorrect item is right there for you to look at, while a missing item must be supplied from memory. A user edit, on the other hand, makes the job simple—if a vital instruction has been left out, the user will be unable to perform the task. Period.

Misleading instructions Instructions can be accurate and detailed and still be confusing. This is most likely to happen when the procedure being described is so complicated that a diagram is necessary to make it clear.

Badly designed instructions Some instructions are well-written but represent a poor use of the machine, producing unnecessary steps and a greater risk of error. By watching a user, you can often find out (especially if you have a human factors specialist observing the test) which procedures are unnecessary or awkward, and alter or eliminate them.

Problems of Style

Writers can often develop styles that are easy to read but still not usable. For example, one common mistake is to place warning statements only at the beginning or the end of each *set* of instructions. Such warnings are often ignored, because users expect a set of instructions—including warnings—to be presented in order. It is better to place each warning statement just before (or after) the event it is warning about.

A user edit can help uncover stylistic errors but it may not uncover all of them. With practice (and help from whoever is running the test) users can adapt to the writer's style. For this reason, the manual should be formally edited for consistency; that is, once the user edit has found a stylistic error, an editor should check the manual thoroughly for similar errors. Likewise, the editor should check for consistency of content,

Reprinted from *IEEE Trans. Prof. Comm.*, vol. PC-24, no. 1, pp. 28–29, March 1981.

especially because writers sometimes omit vital instructions (e.g., how to gain access to some part of the machine). A casual edit should also be done before the first user test—indeed, before, the manual is complete. That way, the editor can warn the writer early, before his more obvious mistakes spread through the book.

FORMAL TESTING

Testing a manual page by page can improve the usability of every section and still leave a badly flawed book. To be usable, the information in a manual must also be

- *Complete*

An informal test can find out whether information is missing from a section, but may not discover that a whole section is missing. The writer should check his work against a formal list (preferably one devised with the aid of engineers and human factors specialists) of the jobs a typical user should be able to do.

- *Accessible*

In real life, the user will seldom take time to read the manual page by page. Instead, he will need to find answers to specific questions with the aid of the table of contents, index, cross-references, and tabs. For this reason, you should give some of your users a formal test; that is, instead of asking them to work the manual page by page, give them a set of typical user problems to solve. For example, a copier user might be asked to make transparencies, add toner, and clear paper jams. This kind of test can locate

Directory problems Entries in the table of contents and the index can often be

A. *Misleading* For example, an entry called "Troubleshooting" could suggest that all problems are solved in this section; an entry like "Solving Other Problems" might be better. A formal test may show that users are turning to the wrong part of the book.

B. *Cryptic* For example, "Check Paper Path" may not be meaningful to all copier users; "Clearing Paper Jams" is more to the point. In general, avoid technical jargon and have each section heading refer to what the user will want to do, not to the part of the machine he will have to do it with. In a formal test, users will either turn to the wrong section or give up entirely. In either case, you have a good clue to what the trouble is.

Cross-reference problems Sometimes titles can be clear and correct, and yet users may still end up in the wrong place. For example, the user may turn to the "Control Panel Lights" page whenever a trouble light comes on. A sensible way to handle this problem is to add cross-references ("see page —") to send him to the right location.

Getting a representative set of test items is not always easy, but it may be well worth the effort. If you can, consult a human factors specialist. If you are lucky, he may have already developed the items you need.

CLOSING REMARKS

The user edit is a simple but powerful tool for making technical manuals easier to use. Although you get the best results by being careful—testing typical users, using well-designed test problems, and having human factors consultants—you can still get a lot of useful information even if you are less thorough. Like any other kind of edit, the user edit works well as part of an edit-revision cycle. For example:

1. Run a user edit with one or two users.
2. Fix the errors you find.
3. Check for similar errors and fix those.
4. Have an editor formally edit the manual.
5. Revise to correct any errors found.
6. Run another user edit. Et cetera.

The repeated process of editing and revision refines the test procedure. The important thing to remember is that this is an *editing* tool, not a scientific one. Although the final document will not be perfect, it will be much more usable than it was in the beginning.

ACKNOWLEDGMENT

My thanks to Jeff Brand, Kathy Dowling, and Charlotte Mackey, who helped me design and run the tests on which this report is based.

REFERENCES

[1] E. E. Miller, "Designing Printed Instructional Materials: Content and Format," Technical Report RP-WD(TX)-75-4, Human Resources Research Organization, El Paso, TX, Oct. 1975.

PART V

Proposals: Writing to Win the Customer

Few technical documents need more careful preparation than a proposal. You can annoy a lot of customers if you sell equipment accompanied by unclear instructions, but a poorly written proposal will guarantee that you never get those customers in the first place. The articles in this section, with their emphasis on meeting the requirements of the customer-audience, offer you a great deal of help on how to write winning proposals. The fact that some of this material has been around for a while should not put you off, since the rules rarely change when it comes to putting together effective proposals that you can be proud of.

The overall picture

T. M. Georges' one-page synopsis gets to the point right away: your proposal will succeed only to the extent that it meets your customers' needs. Georges' article could just as well end this section as begin it, since the author's fifteen questions can serve either as a preliminary outline or final checklist for your proposal. His closing comment on packaging introduces a theme further developed by other authors in this section.

When brevity counts

The next article looks at short proposals whose formats have not been mandated in a Request for Proposal (RFP). This article will be useful if you have an idea for an unsolicited proposal and decide to write it up. Bernard Budish and Richard Sandhusen illustrate a short proposal in the form of a one-page letter, which even omits headings. Their article analyzes why long proposals often fail and encourages you to use short proposals early in the negotiation process when feasible.

Longer proposals

Not all proposals are one page long, of course, and the next three articles focus on writing a substantial document in response to an RFP. First Robert Greenly presents ten strategies for putting together such a proposal, from preliminary organization to final packaging. He suggests preparing proposal drafts even *before* you receive an RFP. Since large proposals are usually not read in their entirety by all evaluators, section summaries assume great importance, as do carefully presented data and graphics. This article also introduces you to the mechanics of setting up a proposal room and using techniques such as storyboarding (presenting sketches of material on panels) to generate and review your proposals.

Telling the story as a team

Storyboarding is investigated in depth in the next article by Robert Barakat. Long formal proposals require detailed planning and efficient teamwork if they are to succeed—that is, win the bid. Barakat defines and describes storyboarding, showing how it enables you and other members of a team to concentrate on individual tasks and yet work together to produce a unified document. The process is broken down into five steps: outlining, creating storyboards, supporting the message, illustrating storyboards, and reviewing. Everyone on the team is involved in each step so no matter how lengthy your final document might be, it will be highly organized and coherent.

The very large proposal

The next article, also by Robert Barakat, describes with telling graphics the way you might want to plan the composition of an extremely large proposal. Since such documents may consist of several volumes, each volume and even sections of volumes must be approached methodically and in detail. To help you do this, the author suggests seven strategies that can be implemented at specific points in the proposal planning phase. He includes a flowchart of actions you can take before you receive the Request for Proposal and gives valuable advice on the formatting and packaging of the final document. He also reminds you of a point that can't be stressed too often: illustrations are not just for decoration but must be part of your message or sometimes even the message itself. Barakat's own graphics in this article are excellent examples of what he means.

Asking the customer questions

Annette Reilly looks at a different facet of producing a winning proposal: procuring information not fully provided in an RFP, and putting yourself in the place of a proposal evaluator. How do you get more specific information on the customer's needs after an RFP has been issued? And how do you ask clarification questions (which may be made public) without divulging your own approach to your competitors? Reilly's article looks at the intricacies of this problem and considers the rhetorical subtleties involved in asking open questions in a highly competitive environment. Her ten guidelines for writing such questions will show you how to obtain information from your potential customer while presenting further evidence that you have the best answer to that customer's needs.

Being evaluated

Clark Beck's article emphasizes in-depth reading of an RFP, particularly the "technical exhibit" section that outlines what you as the bid winner will be required to do. Your proposal will be judged on how you respond to this section and on whether you convince the proposal evaluators that you are the best person or company for the job. In a research proposal you may have some leeway in your approaches to the problem, but only a meticulous study of the RFP will tell you just how much freedom you have. Beck's five suggestions for final format and his comments on what will be looked for during the technical evaluation perceptively summarize the stages of a proposal's life just prior to the decision on whether it becomes the winner.

Job-hunting for proposal writers

The final article, by Sherry Hamilton, is based on the sad but persistent fact that plenty of cutbacks continue to be made in industry and that it is always a good idea to be flexible in your career path. Specifically, Hamilton looks at the opportunities existing in nonprofit organizations such as colleges and universities for someone with corporate proposal-writing experience. She then makes a number of comparisons and contrasts between nonprofit and industrial proposals, such as their aims, reviews, and editing processes, and points out the different attitudes of corporate and nonprofit colleagues toward proposals. She concludes with the reminder that there are several job titles besides "proposal writer" in the nonprofit sector that nevertheless describe positions involving a significant amount of proposal writing.

Fifteen Questions to Help You Write Winning Proposals

T. M. GEORGES

Abstract—**Providing the answers to these 15 questions can help ensure that your proposal is complete and oriented to your customer. The questions can also be used as a guide for reviewers and as a checklist for completed proposals.**

WHEN you write a proposal, you are usually offering to do some work or provide some product at a specified price for a specific customer. Your proposal has the best chance of succeeding if your product closely matches your customer's needs, if your price is one he can afford, and if you can deliver your product on time.

Here are a few questions to ask yourself while you are writing your proposal. The questions force you to think about the most important things your prospective customers will look for as they read and evaluate your proposal. Make sure your proposal answers all these questions clearly.

Keep in mind that many of your readers are busy executives who are buried in paper and will be able to take only a few minutes to digest your message. Be sure they can find what you want them to find in those few minutes.

1. Who, specifically, are you writing your proposal to?
2. Suppose you were that person and had to review your proposal and decide whether to buy your product or service. What information would you look for first to help you make that decision? Is that information up front and easy to find?
3. What specific need or problem does your product or service address?
4. How will your product or service make your customer's life easier?
5. What best qualifies you to supply your product or service over any of your competitors?
6. Have you convinced your customer that you can actually supply the proposed product or service?
7. Are the costs of your product or service clearly spelled out?
8. How might you break down costs so your customer can select parts of your product or service that best suit his needs?

Received September 28, 1982.
The author is a communication consultant, 340 Norton St., Boulder, CO 80303, (303) 530-2692.

9. What extra-cost items, not included in your proposal, are likely to be needed?
10. What products and services that some readers might expect are *not* included in your proposal? Should you list them explicitly?
11. If you are offering a service, how will your customer know when the job is done?
12. Do you clearly state how long it will take to deliver your product or service? If your product is a large or complex one, should you provide a delivery timetable with milestones?
13. If you are proposing a research program, do you clearly state what you are going to do and how you will know the job is done? Do you avoid using vague words like "investigate" and "develop" unless you couple them with specific processes and goals?
14. If you are selling a product, what after-sale arrangements do you offer for training, maintenance, parts, and service?
15. Have you relegated most of the technical details and specifications to clearly labeled appendices, where interested readers can easily find them?

You can use these questions in three ways:

- You can answer them before you begin work on your proposal, to form its core outline. The more detailed and specific your answers, the easier it will be to flesh out your outline.
- You can use them as a checklist for your completed proposals.
- You can attach them to copies you submit for approval to speed the review process.

Your careful answers to these questions will help you package the information your customers are looking for and will help them make their decision quickly. The way you present your product tells your customers a lot about the kind of work you do. It pays to show them right at the start that you know how to take their needs into account.

FOR FURTHER READING

Georges, T. M. *Business and Technical Writing Cookbook—How to Write Coherently on the Job*. Boulder, CO: Syntax Publications; 1983.

Reprinted from *IEEE Trans. Prof. Comm.*, vol. PC-26, no. 2, p. 84, June 1983.

The Short Proposal: Versatile Tool for Communicating Corporate Culture in Competitive Climates

BERNARD ELLIOTT BUDISH
RICHARD L. SANDHUSEN

Abstract—**Proposals, applicable in a broad range of corporate communication situations, are typically overwritten, poorly researched documents that force recipients to search for ideas of pertinent concern and rarely accomplish their objectives. This paper suggests short proposals, introduced early in the negotiation process, as replacements for formal proposals, or as interim documents leading to more productive, persuasive formal proposals.**

SITUATIONS in which corporations communicate to, through, and among their diverse internal and external publics can differ appreciably. Some are subtle and complex; others simple and straightforward. Some are welcome, as when the firm apprises customers, suppliers, or financial intermediaries of a new product or project venture. Others are sought, as when the firm solicits favorable publicity for a newsworthy venture. Still other situations are unwelcome, as when the firm confronts hostile stockholders, employees, or citizen action groups.

The degree of risk associated with communication failure also differs appreciably from situation to situation. In some situations, the risk is negligible; in others, terminal—as such diverse groups as air traffic controllers, professional football players, and corporate raiders continue to discover.

Regardless of context, content, degree of complexity or risk, however, most corporate communication situations exhibit common characteristics that help define their essential nature and suggest strategies for success. Invariably, each involves an exchange of information, a negotiation, implying varying degrees of accommodation among the participants and, if successful, culminating in a "win-win" outcome in which all parties perceive gain. The seller gains the order, the buyer the product benefit; union members get their pay increase, the company an increase in productivity; the company gets its funds, its stockholders a share of the profits. In addition to perceiving gain, each party to a successful negotiation also accepts a commitment to maintain the conditions that produced this gain. As cases in point, recently negotiated agreements to reduce atomic stockpiles or sell the New York Post would be little more than scraps of paper without such commitments.

Bernard Elliott Budish is Professor of Management at Fairleigh Dickinson University.
Richard L. Sandhusen is a member of the adjunct faculty in the Marketing Department at Fairleigh Dickinson University and is completing a dissertation in the Doctorate of Professional Studies program at Pace University.

Another characteristic common to negotiation situations is the early appearance of a proposal, offered by one party to be accepted, rejected, or countered by the others. Typically, this proposal, written or oral, presents one party's interpretation of the situation which precipitated the negotiation—a problem, an opportunity, a grievance—and makes an offer designed to address this situation. Frequently, this proposal, and the response it engenders, is the best motivator and measure of a successful outcome to the negotiation: if the proposal is read and clearly understood by all parties, and written and sequenced to perform its persuasive purpose, it can be the single most important element in generating a mutually satisfactory outcome. Alternatively, if it is rejected, or diverts the negotiations into unproductive bickering over messages and meanings, it can be the key element in ensuring failure.

Unfortunately, most proposals don't succeed in achieving their persuasive purpose. Hillman, for example, sampled a diverse population of multipurpose proposals and concluded that "approximately 90 out of 100 proposals are rejected." [1] This ratio is documented in other studies in the generally sparse literature on proposals. For example, surveys of government procurement sources by Wexler and Carmel indicate that 75 percent of all proposals submitted are either "inadequate or nonresponsive," with another 15 percent judged as only "barely adequate." [2] Another study by Department of Defense procurement officials found that, of a representative sample of 1103 proposals surveyed, fewer than 15 percent were deemed worthy of further consideration. [3] An informal survey undertaken by the authors among partners at four "Big 8" accounting firms further reinforces this conclusion. Each partner was queried as to the success ratio of proposal submissions designed to generate new business. The consensus: even when representatives of the accounting firm had consulted with prospective client personnel prior to proposal submission, and the proposal itself had been prepared with the

Reprinted from *IEEE Trans. Prof. Comm.*, vol. 32, no. 2, pp. 81–85, June 1989.

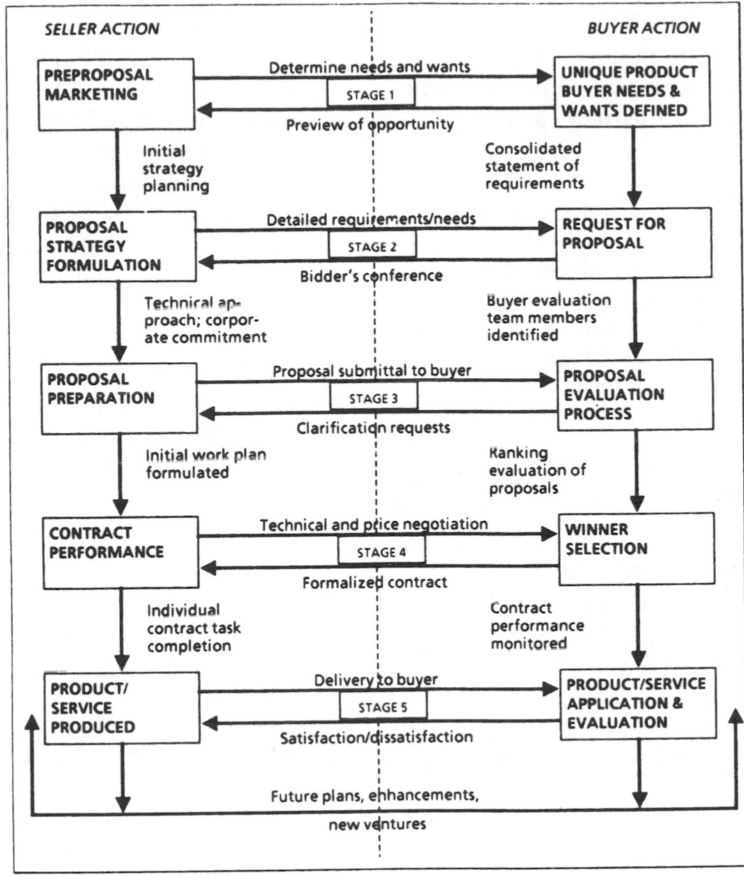

Figure 1. Proposal Preparation Process

assistance of communication specialists—the usual scenario—the rate of success was never above 20 percent.

Aggravating the impact of this high failure rate are high direct and indirect costs involved in the preparation of a typical formal proposal. Figure 1, for example, depicts a five-stage model of buyer and seller actions identified by Horowitz and Jolson as the typical sequence followed by industrial firms and government procurement agencies in the proposal preparation process. [4] At each stage, direct costs of the process itself, plus indirect costs of human resources that could be productively employed elsewhere, can accumulate dramatically.

Is this high cost of preparing proposals a necessary cost? This paper suggests not. Specifically, we suggest an alternative proposal preparation process that employs interim short proposals to address expensive problems endemic in the traditional process of preparing formal proposals. Typically, these short proposals obviate the need for long formal proposals, or ensure that they are used much more productively and profitably.

WHY LONG PROPOSALS FAIL

To understand the value of short proposals in the negotiation process, as well as characteristics and components of these proposals, we first examine problems implicit in the preparation of long proposals that are effectively addressed by short proposals.

One obvious problem is the sheer length and complexity of the process, as illustrated in figure 1. Given competitive pressures and time constraints, this frequently means that insufficient time is devoted to important information-gathering activities required to ensure a document that is responsive to receiver needs. For example, regardless of proposal context or content, the following information is invariably required in preparing a proposal calculated to lead, persuasively, to a mutually beneficial outcome:

- The roles of people who will read and receive the proposal. Some, for example, will influence decisions leading to an agreement; others will actually make the decisions; still others will have to live with these decisions. The proposal must speak, persuasively, to each role.
- The goals and needs of recipients assuming these diverse roles in the decision process. Again, proposal content and structure should address this diversity in presenting a cogent, compelling rationale for accepting the proposal offering.

Much more often than not, however, roles, goals, and needs of proposal recipients are addressed, if at all, in a scattershot manner, with great amounts of data and information piled high, often almost at random, in the apparent assumption that individual readers will select information of interest. This self-selection assumption is implicit, for example, in this excerpt from a proposal preparation training course offered to managers and partners at a large accounting firm:

> A written proposal should be a document that covers in complete detail all the prospect needs to know about the firm and its approach to the prospect's problems. It is available to be studied at the reader's convenience, to be picked up, put down, and possibly picked up again later. If a part of the written proposal is not immediately clear at first, the prospect can reread it several times. Also, the written proposal can be read at various times by different readers and then discussed later.

Also reflective of this perception of the reader as willing to leaf leisurely through the proposal, selecting items of interest from a sort of literary smorgasbord, are the weighty, elaborate formats for formal proposals suggested in the proposal preparation literature. Herewith, three examples, from these three sources: *What Makes a Good Proposal* (F. Lee and Barbara I. Jacquette) [5], *Guidelines for Preparing Proposals* (Meador) [3], and a content analysis by the authors of characteristics of formal proposals submitted by accounting firms:

- Sellers are not responsive to buyer's needs. (Reflect little knowledge of customer's business, fail to do technical and marketing homework, do not follow Request for Proposal requirements etc.)
- The message is poorly stated. (Wordy and repetitious, lacks innovation and creativity, jumbled and crowded, writing style dwarfs substantive content, conclusions unsupported by data, inherently dull, too much boilerplate or technical overkill, etc.)

HOW SHORT PROPOSALS SUCCEED

The short proposal that addresses communication problems implicit in the traditional proposal preparation process is a versatile, multifaceted document with a useful life that begins well before it is actually written. Specifically, it comes into being at the point during the negotiation when the first substantive point of agreement is arrived at. Typically, this first point of agreement implies a cooperative effort to arrive at a solution, and can include an agreement to resolve a dispute.

Examples of these early points of agreement that trigger the short proposal preparation process include the following:

Jacquette	*Meador*	*Accounting Firms*
Summary	Cover letter	Transmittal letter
Defense	Title page	Table of contents
Biographies	Table of contents	Abstract
Budgets	Proposal summary or abstract	Engagement services (tax, audit, management services)
Organizational arrangements	Introduction	Engagement benefits
Competencies	Statement of the research problem or program	Engagement team resumes
Feasibility	Objectives and expected benefits of the project	Firm's profile
Study importance, utility	Description of the project	Practice clients in area
Venture creativity, originality	Timetable for the project	Fee estimate
Appropriateness to client focus	Key project participants	Appendixes
Leverage prospects	Project budget	
Appendixes	Administrative provisions and organizational chart	
	Alternative funding	
	Postproject planning	
	Appendixes and support materials	
	Bibliography and references	

More often than not, a formal proposal is a ponderous, lengthy, uninteresting document, often pieced together with inventoried boilerplate in the hope that individual recipients will plow through it in search of items of personal interest. Realistically, this is almost invariably an invalid assumption, as suggested, for example, by the response to queries among proposal recipients pertaining to "major areas of weakness" in currently submitted proposals: [4]

- From an employer to employee representatives: Let's agree to clarify issues separating us in these negotiations.
- From a corporate raider to stockholders of a target company: Let's agree to the possibility, at least, that this company can be made much more productive and profitable.
- From a company representative to a prospective cli-

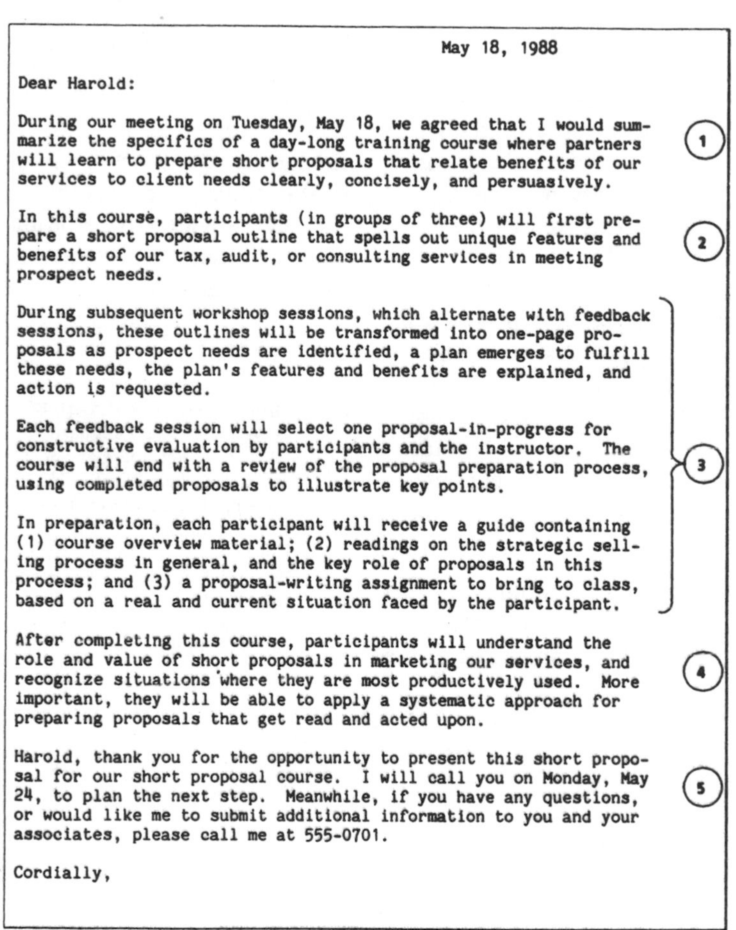

May 18, 1988

Dear Harold:

During our meeting on Tuesday, May 18, we agreed that I would summarize the specifics of a day-long training course where partners will learn to prepare short proposals that relate benefits of our services to client needs clearly, concisely, and persuasively. (1)

In this course, participants (in groups of three) will first prepare a short proposal outline that spells out unique features and benefits of our tax, audit, or consulting services in meeting prospect needs. (2)

During subsequent workshop sessions, which alternate with feedback sessions, these outlines will be transformed into one-page proposals as prospect needs are identified, a plan emerges to fulfill these needs, the plan's features and benefits are explained, and action is requested.

Each feedback session will select one proposal-in-progress for constructive evaluation by participants and the instructor. The course will end with a review of the proposal preparation process, using completed proposals to illustrate key points. (3)

In preparation, each participant will receive a guide containing (1) course overview material; (2) readings on the strategic selling process in general, and the key role of proposals in this process; and (3) a proposal-writing assignment to bring to class, based on a real and current situation faced by the participant.

After completing this course, participants will understand the role and value of short proposals in marketing our services, and recognize situations where they are most productively used. More important, they will be able to apply a systematic approach for preparing proposals that get read and acted upon. (4)

Harold, thank you for the opportunity to present this short proposal for our short proposal course. I will call you on Monday, May 24, to plan the next step. Meanwhile, if you have any questions, or would like me to submit additional information to you and your associates, please call me at 555-0701. (5)

Cordially,

Figure 2. Sample Short Proposal

ent: Let's agree that you can use our services to solve a pressing problem or meet a pressing need.

Note that these agreements are arrived at early in the negotiating process, they are generalized, and they are couched in a spirit of further inquiry, not finality. Invariably, they are points much easier to agree on than agreements arrived at during later, more irrevocable stages of the process. For example, a prospective customer can agree on the need for a certain type of product, without agreeing that the product should be purchased from the seller company.

This early agreement aspect of the short proposal highlights a significant difference between it and its long proposal counterpart; thus, while the long proposal is largely perceived as a document for summarizing data relating seller services to buyer needs, the short proposal is perceived as, among other things, a device for accumulating the data in the first place. Typically, for example, the proposer will suggest the short proposal as a device for gathering and pulling together data required to solve a problem.

The short proposal might end with a preliminary presentation of the accumulated data, and a clear exposition of information that will be required to formulate a final proposal. So used, the short proposal serves as an interim document between the preliminary agreement and the final settlement, generally ensuring that the final proposal will be a more focused, pertinent document than the typical scattershot version.

Alternatively, the short proposal, with minor modifications, might also serve as the final agreement, thereby streamlining and simplifying the negotiation process, increasing the likelihood of a win-win outcome, and dramatically reducing associated direct and indirect costs.

That this short proposal, although viewed mainly as a preliminary, interim document, will indeed double as the final proposal is usually a strong probability, given inherent qualities that make it a much more efficient, interesting, persuasive document than its long, boring counterpart.

Figure 2, a one-page short proposal for a short proposal course, illustrates these short proposal qualities:

- *Structured and sequenced logically and economically:* The main reason the short proposal is short is that it dispenses with most of the headings (see above) included in the typical long proposal—often gratuitously, inflexibly, and with little concern for reader needs. The short proposal reduces this laundry list of topics to the four or five of real reader concern, and sequences them logically in terms of reader interests. In figure 2, for example, the sequence includes (1) needs agreement to put the ensuing discussion into context; (2) a concise proposal of what will be done to facilitate agreement—the plan; (3) a brief discussion of how the plan works; (4) a summary of benefits, and (5) a description of action to be taken by the sender and receiver of the proposal.

- *Easier to read:* The fact that the short proposal has many fewer topic categories than the long proposal is usually sufficient, in itself, to ensure that it will be read in its entirety by all involved in the final decision; that it will be more effectively targeted to audience goals, needs, and roles; and that it will be more effectively comprehended. Aiding this efficient comprehension is the simple, direct writing style of short proposals.

The short proposal serves, initially, as the stimulus for further inquiry into areas of mutual concern. Then, data emerging from this inquiry are organized and presented in the short proposal format designed to facilitate quick, efficient comprehension by all parties to a mutually satisfactory agreement.

Frequently, the short proposal, with minor additions and modifications, becomes the long proposal; alternatively, it can help provide a base of understanding which makes the long proposal, if necessary, a much more efficient, productive document.

REFERENCES

1. Hillman, H., *The Art of Writing Business Reports & Proposals,* New York: The Vanguard Press, 1981.
2. Wexler, J. A., and Carmel, C. A., *How to Create a Winning Proposal,* Santa Cruz, CA: Mercury Communications, 1977.
3. Meador, R., *Guidelines for Preparing Proposals,* Chelsea, MI: Lewis Publishers, 1985.
4. Horowitz, H. M., and Jolson, M. A., "The Industrial Proposal as a Promotional Tool," *Industrial Marketing Management 9,* 1980, pp. 101–109.
5. Jacquette, F. L., and Jacquette, B. I., *What Makes a Good Proposal?,* Washington, DC: The Foundation Center, 1973.

Technical Writing and Illustrating Strategies for Winning Government Contracts

ROBERT B. GREENLY

Abstract—**Procurement of government systems, equipment, and services is a complex process. It normally begins with the government advertising its intention to solicit bids for the supplies or services sought. The government issues a Request for Proposal, or RFP, which is a detailed statement of the requirements, the specifications, the elements required in the contractor's bid, and the relative criteria against which bids will be evaluated. The technical writer's task is to organize, structure, and package the proposal into a coherent, readable, and salable whole. Here are ten writing and illustrating strategies that can help create winning proposals.**

THIS ARTICLE gives guidance to technical writers, engineers, proposals specialists, and managers who compete for government contracts. If you follow the recommendations of this article you can

- Improve your company's win/lose ratio,
- Reduce the long hours you and your staff typically invest in the preparation of proposals, and
- Make proposal assignments a welcome challenge.

Contracts, including those from the government and those from industrial enterprises, are awarded on the basis of written proposals and supporting marketing activities. Contracts are won by offering the best proposed solution to the "problem" posed by the Request for Proposal (RFP). The name of the game is to score the highest number of points with the proposal evaluation committee, often called the SSEB, or Source Selection Evaluation Board, in U.S. Government procurements.

When you have developed your strong team and excellent solution to the "problem," then you must use modern and appropriate writing and illustrating techniques—"on-the-walls visualization," storyboards, the graphics-driven writing process, what have you, that best *communicate* that message to the evaluators. Modern writing and illustrating techniques are what this article is all about.

Robert B. Greenly is a Program Acquisition Leader at the Lockheed Missiles & Spaces Company, Inc.

STRATEGY 1—START EARLY

A key to winning contracts is to get started *before* the RFP is released. The official release is signaled when the procurement is announced in the *Commerce Business Daily*, a U.S. Department of Commerce publication.

Savvy proposal specialists know, however, that *Commerce Business Daily announcements are too late*. Initial drafts should be prepared *before* the formal CBD advertisement. The usual excuse is, "We can't do anything until we have the RFP," which is not true. You can make your own "strawman" RFP, one that anticipates what will appear in the real thing. You know for example, that it will ask about your experience, facilities, organizational structure, and your cost and schedule control system. So get started on these first drafts. Resumes are another area where the real RFP probably will shed no additional light. Set up interviews with key personnel and "customize" their resumes to the requirement.

Experience shows an unmistakable correlation between starting early and winning. Starting from scratch at RFP release is not an impossible position to be in, but it is dangerously close to it. If you start at RFP release your chances probably hinge on the favorite stumbling or falling out-of-favor before the contract is awarded.

STRATEGY 2—STRUCTURE YOUR PROPOSAL IN THE CORRECT SEQUENCE

Treat the RFP as a series of questions. It asks about your technical approach, management plan, experience, facilities, etc. Answer the questions in the same sequence in which they are asked. The RFP will state what needs to be included in the proposal and the order in which things are asked for is the *required* order of a high-scoring proposal response. In the absence of RFP directions, order your proposal headings in the sequence of the statement of work (SOW) headings or in the sequence of the specification topics. Resist the temptation to restructure the order of things, no matter how elegant your restructuring might seem. It takes less time to evaluate a proposal whose organization is familiar than one which is not. A predictable organization takes the drudgery out of the evaluator's job by putting things in the expected order, the order in which things are spelled out by the RFP.

In the management section the traditional approach is to

Reprinted from *IEEE Trans. Prof. Comm.*, vol. PC-28, no. 2, pp. 157–162, June 1992.

describe the parent corporation, then the company or division within the corporation, then the program or project. The last part, the project structure, is the real heart of the matter. I contend that the usual narrative sequence of corporation-company-project is wrong. Customers are most interested in who is going to do *their* work. The order of discussion should place the project, (the evaluator's real interest) *first*, company organization *second*, corporate structure *last*. Corporate organization may be an important and necessary part of the overall writeup, but it does not really deserve the lead-off position.

STRATEGY 3—BEGIN EVERY VOLUME AND EVERY MAJOR SECTION WITH A SUMMARY

The higher the proposal evaluator is in the customer's organization, the less of the proposal he reads. The older, more experienced evaluators are likely to skim rather than read with great care. For these reasons, summaries take on magnified significance. Every volume, every major section and, indeed, the total proposal should have a summary. Summaries also serve to verify in the writer's mind that all the pertinent questions: Who? What? Why? When? Where? and How? have been answered.

For example, a writer can develop a summary by asking: Who will perform the work? What are the expected results? When will significant milestones be reached? Where will the work be done? Why are we best qualified among all of the potential bidders? How will we manage the work? Answering questions such as these, first in isolated sentences, then in a smoothly connected narrative is one journalistic formula for creating effective summaries.

STRATEGY 4—WRITE YOUR PROPOSAL USING THE LANGUAGE OF THE RFP

You should thoroughly study and *understand* the RFP in

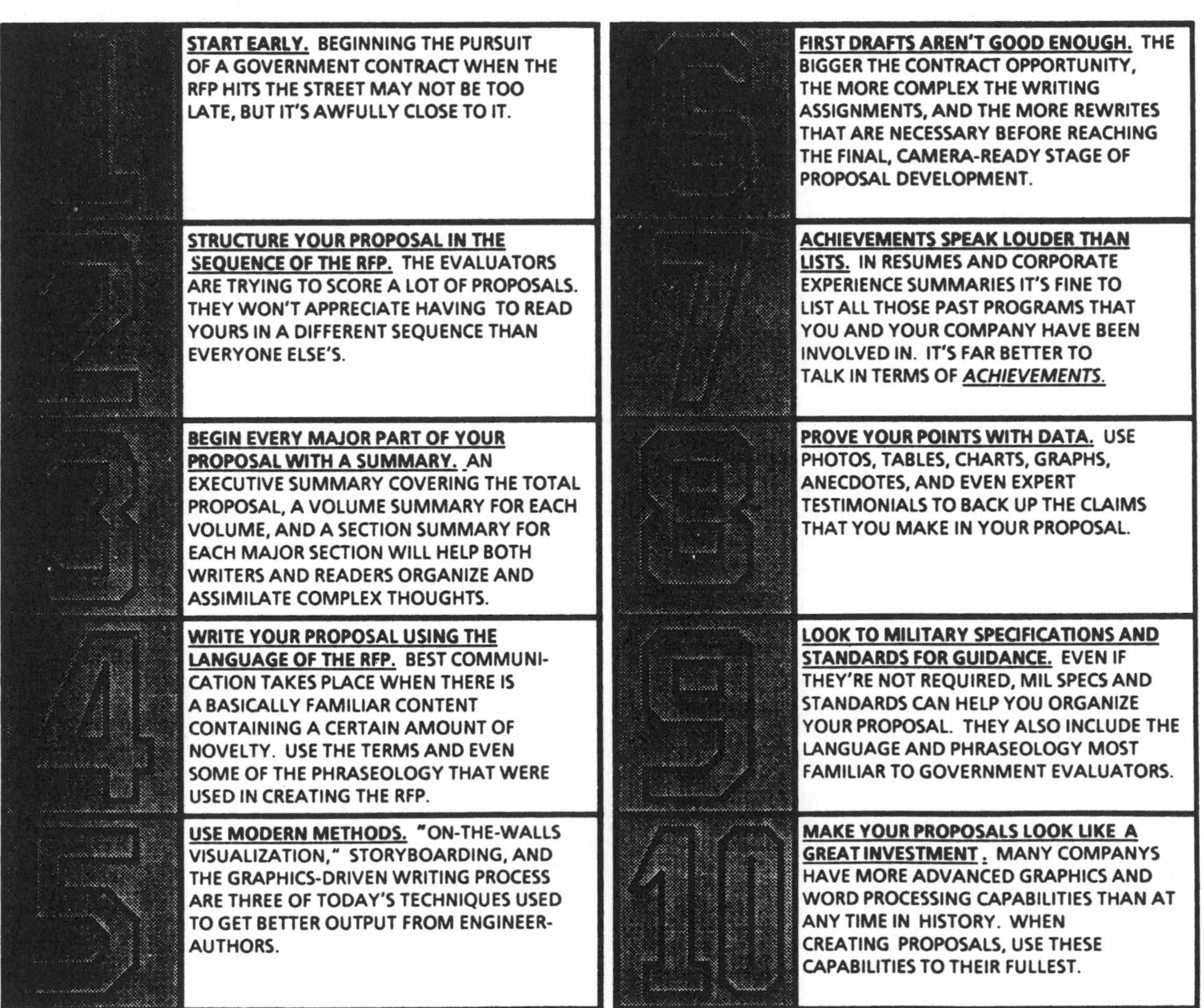

1
START EARLY. BEGINNING THE PURSUIT OF A GOVERNMENT CONTRACT WHEN THE RFP HITS THE STREET MAY NOT BE TOO LATE, BUT IT'S AWFULLY CLOSE TO IT.
2
STRUCTURE YOUR PROPOSAL IN THE SEQUENCE OF THE RFP. THE EVALUATORS ARE TRYING TO SCORE A LOT OF PROPOSALS. THEY WON'T APPRECIATE HAVING TO READ YOURS IN A DIFFERENT SEQUENCE THAN EVERYONE ELSE'S.
3
BEGIN EVERY MAJOR PART OF YOUR PROPOSAL WITH A SUMMARY. AN EXECUTIVE SUMMARY COVERING THE TOTAL PROPOSAL, A VOLUME SUMMARY FOR EACH VOLUME, AND A SECTION SUMMARY FOR EACH MAJOR SECTION WILL HELP BOTH WRITERS AND READERS ORGANIZE AND ASSIMILATE COMPLEX THOUGHTS.
4
WRITE YOUR PROPOSAL USING THE LANGUAGE OF THE RFP. BEST COMMUNICATION TAKES PLACE WHEN THERE IS A BASICALLY FAMILIAR CONTENT CONTAINING A CERTAIN AMOUNT OF NOVELTY. USE THE TERMS AND EVEN SOME OF THE PHRASEOLOGY THAT WERE USED IN CREATING THE RFP.
5
USE MODERN METHODS. "ON-THE-WALLS VISUALIZATION," STORYBOARDING, AND THE GRAPHICS-DRIVEN WRITING PROCESS ARE THREE OF TODAY'S TECHNIQUES USED TO GET BETTER OUTPUT FROM ENGINEER-AUTHORS.
6
FIRST DRAFTS AREN'T GOOD ENOUGH. THE BIGGER THE CONTRACT OPPORTUNITY, THE MORE COMPLEX THE WRITING ASSIGNMENTS, AND THE MORE REWRITES THAT ARE NECESSARY BEFORE REACHING THE FINAL, CAMERA-READY STAGE OF PROPOSAL DEVELOPMENT.
7
ACHIEVEMENTS SPEAK LOUDER THAN LISTS. IN RESUMES AND CORPORATE EXPERIENCE SUMMARIES IT'S FINE TO LIST ALL THOSE PAST PROGRAMS THAT YOU AND YOUR COMPANY HAVE BEEN INVOLVED IN. IT'S FAR BETTER TO TALK IN TERMS OF ACHIEVEMENTS.
8
PROVE YOUR POINTS WITH DATA. USE PHOTOS, TABLES, CHARTS, GRAPHS, ANECDOTES, AND EVEN EXPERT TESTIMONIALS TO BACK UP THE CLAIMS THAT YOU MAKE IN YOUR PROPOSAL.
9
LOOK TO MILITARY SPECIFICATIONS AND STANDARDS FOR GUIDANCE. EVEN IF THEY'RE NOT REQUIRED, MIL SPECS AND STANDARDS CAN HELP YOU ORGANIZE YOUR PROPOSAL. THEY ALSO INCLUDE THE LANGUAGE AND PHRASEOLOGY MOST FAMILIAR TO GOVERNMENT EVALUATORS.
10
MAKE YOUR PROPOSALS LOOK LIKE A GREAT INVESTMENT. MANY COMPANYS HAVE MORE ADVANCED GRAPHICS AND WORD PROCESSING CAPABILITIES THAN AT ANY TIME IN HISTORY. WHEN CREATING PROPOSALS, USE THESE CAPABILITIES TO THEIR FULLEST.

Technical writing and illustrating strategies for winning government contracts.

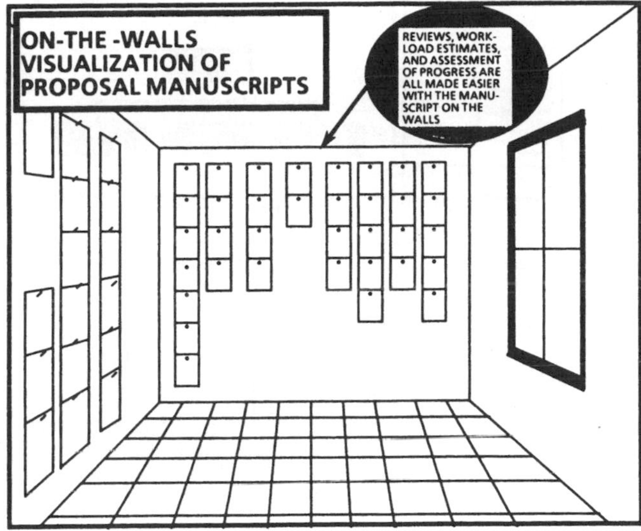

Fig. 1. On-the-walls visualization of proposal manuscripts.

order to see clearly what is required and how the various requirements are connected. You should have a mind's eye view of how your capabilities match up with the requirements, especially in ways that show that you are *uniquely* capable of providing a solution. You should then write your response, answering the requirements using language that is familiar to the evaluator. Use many of the same words and some of the phraseology used in the RFP itself. Add supporting rationale and examples in the form of line drawings, photos, charts, tables, graphs, anecdotes, and even testimonials.

STRATEGY 5—USE MODERN METHODS

On-the-walls-visualization, the taping or pinning of the proposal (or any writing project) to the walls is the way to get the most out of manager, editor, and engineer-author reviews. A proposal room, like Fig. 1, with lots of wall space is the place to do it. Work progress and the magnitude of the workload are made more apparent, permitting you to better prepare for and schedule additional help, temporary typists and outside illustrators, for example.

Storyboarding, the communication technique originated in Hollywood, is another way to create proposals that are superior textual/visual entities. Five elements make up each storyboard module: title, theme sentence, narrative, graphic, and caption. The sequential steps of the process are illustrated in Fig. 2.

Storyboarding begins with the creation of theme sentences, compelling statements that summarize each subsection of the proposal. Narratives and captioned illustrations are then developed which support the themes. A storyboard control form like the one shown in Fig. 3, facilitates this development. The form is designed for quick, hand-lettered and hand-drawn entries. For the finished proposal, the storyboarded material is formatted into a paired-pagc spread, as illustrated in Fig. 4.

Storyboarding makes the writing dramatically easier. It can be an effective process for improved communication, but be forewarned that successful storyboarding can involve a Herculean *planning* effort in the early stages of the proposal's preparation. This is because storyboarding is a method that attempts to describe, by use of themes, highly technical and complex matters, often before a clear idea of these matters exists. Writing the themes can be a very tricky and difficult assignment. ''Off-the-mark'' themes, a hazard of the storyboard method, can be disastrous to the proposal's chances for success. Hundreds of person-hours can add up to nothing if the central point is missed. But theme sentences done well—even though they are more work in the beginning—can save you much work in the later stages of the proposal's preparation.

A variation of the storyboard method called the graphics-driven writing process places initial emphasis on *first* doing the illustrations and data exhibits (summaries of all the relevant parametric data), and doing the writing *last*.

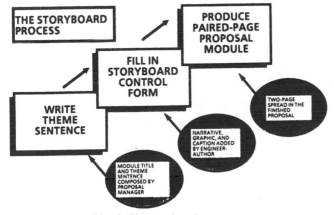

THE STORYBOARD PROCESS
WRITE THEME SENTENCE
FILL IN STORYBOARD CONTROL FORM
PRODUCE PAIRED-PAGE PROPOSAL MODULE
MODULE TITLE AND THEME SENTENCE COMPOSED BY PROPOSAL MANAGER
NARRATIVE, GRAPHIC, AND CAPTION ADDED BY ENGINEER-AUTHOR
TWO-PAGE SPREAD IN THE FINISHED PROPOSAL

Fig. 2. The storyboard process.

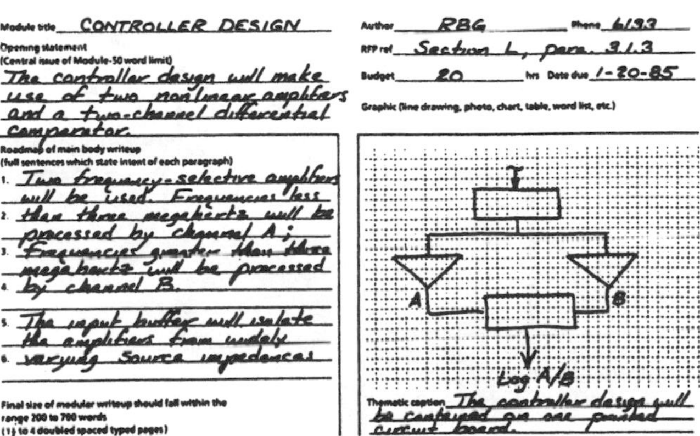

Module title CONTROLLER DESIGN
Author RBG Phone 6193
Opening statement
(Central issue of Module-50 word limit)
The controller design will make use of two nonlinear amplifiers and a two-channel differential comparator.
RFP ref Section L, para. 3.1.3
Budget 20 hrs Date due 1-30-85
Graphic (line drawing, photo, chart, table, word list, etc.)
Roadmap of main body writeup
(full sentences which state intent of each paragraph)
1. Two frequency-selective amplifiers will be used. Frequencies less
2. than three megahertz will be processed by channel A;
3. Frequencies greater than three megahertz will be processed
4. by channel B.
5. The input buffer will isolate the amplifiers from widely
6. varying source impedances
Final size of modular writeup should fall within the range 200 to 700 words
(1½ to 4 doubled spaced typed pages)

Thematic caption The controller design will be contained on one printed circuit board.

Fig. 3. Storyboard control form.

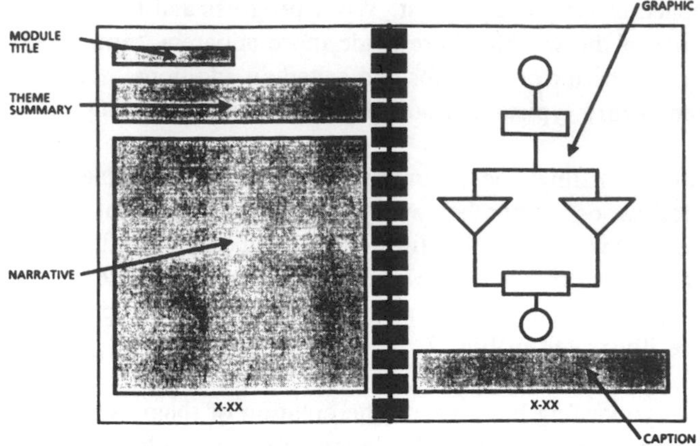

Fig. 4. Paired-page storyboard format as it might appear in the finished proposal.

While storyboarding might be summed up by "Do all the theme sentences first," the graphics-driven writing process is oppositely polarized; it says "Do all the illustrations first." Simply put, the graphics-driven approach, illustrated in Fig. 5, consists of four steps.

1) Create graphic data exhibits that support your proposal: tables, drawings, photographs, flow diagrams, schematics, equations, etc. Consolidate these graphics onto generously-sized, profusely-illustrated proposal pages, even foldouts. Figure 6 is an example.
2) Sequence and format these parametric graphics such that they answer the requirements of the RFP.
3) Review the illustrated pages for responsiveness, completeness, accuracy, and clarity. Rework and reposition the graphic elements if required.
4) Write accompanying proposal text that talks to the graphics.

If you have an aversion toward foldouts, as some do, the graphics-driven writing process still has merit. It can be an effective tool for developing better first and intermediate drafts. If you want a conventional-appearing final proposal, you can cut the graphics apart and place them in the

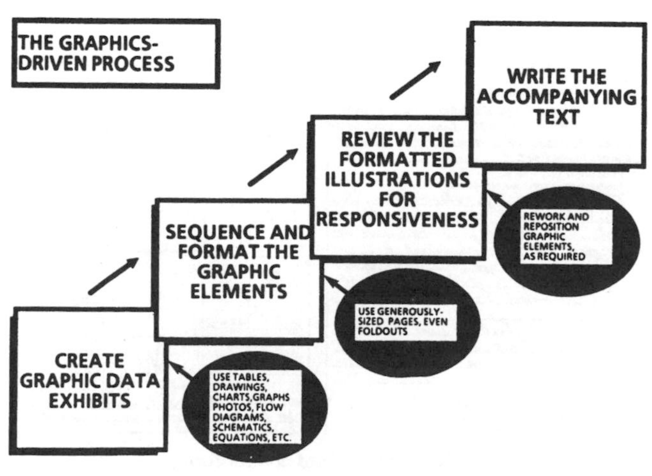

Fig. 5. The graphics-driven process.

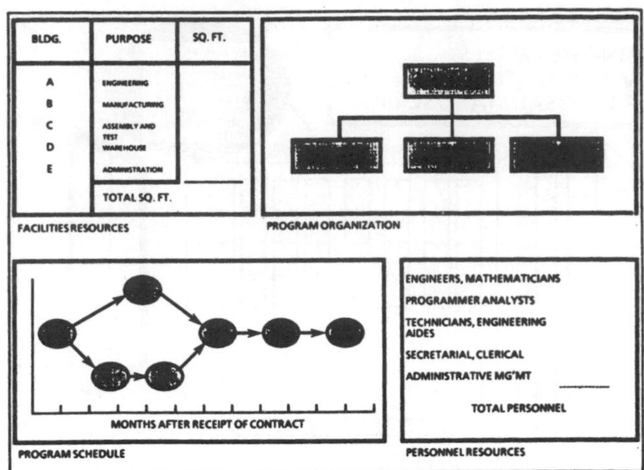

Fig. 6. An example of the graphics-driven approach to proposal preparation.

text, "river raft"* fashion as was typically done before. You'll probably have a better proposal having followed the "do the graphics first" discipline.

The number of hours spent writing will decrease when using the graphics-driven writing process. First drafts have been shown to be of markedly higher quality because well-thought-out graphics give better focus and purpose to the writers. But illustrator hours may increase as much as two-fold because of the greater emphasis on graphics. After a bit of practice and with one or two "pacesetters" on the proposal team who are adept at thinking graphically, the graphics-driven process can be very effective.
Figure 7 compares the relative levels of planning, writing, graphics design, and production efforts for the graphics-driven writing process, the storyboard method, and the conventional, i.e., river raft way of doing things.

STRATEGY 6—FIRST DRAFTS AREN'T GOOD ENOUGH

General Douglas MacArthur wrote complex letters and reports, setting down his thoughts clearly and accurately on his first attempt, and only rarely making corrections. Most of us are not that gifted. Most good writers will rewrite everything that they create several times and few would even dare to send out the first draft of an important proposal, letter, or memo. A proposal whose parts come together, cover-to-cover, for the first time on the day before delivery is destined to contain many errors and will likely receive a low score.

Rewriting is a vital part of the proposal writing process. How many proposal drafts should you plan for? Experience shows that elaborate proposals, those involving larger contract amounts, require the most rewrites. Small proposals for contracts less than one million dollars and containing only a few thousand words can usually be finalized in two rewrite cycles following the initial draft. (A "re-

* "River raft" format is effectively a scroll with unpredictable figure placement. It is the traditional format of most textbooks.

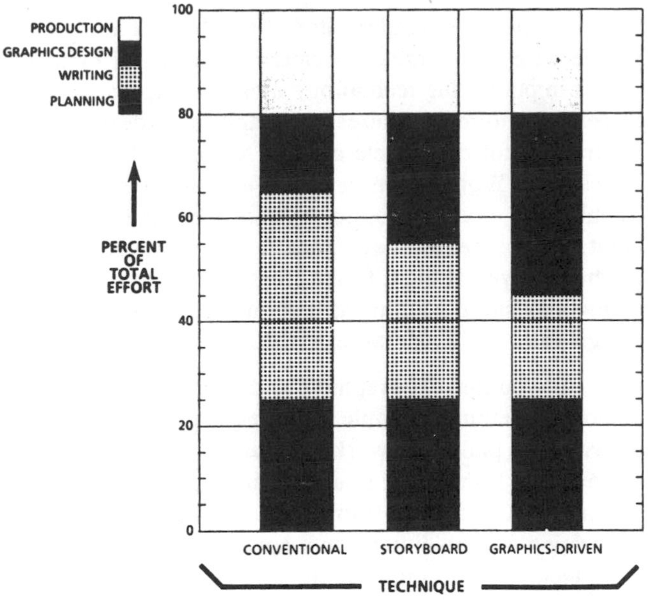

Fig. 7. Levels of effort in three methods of proposal preparation.

write" is defined here as a complete pass through a review, edit, and correction process.) Large, complex proposals for contracts of 100 million dollars or more with many volumes and books containing tens of thousands of words may have to be rewritten as many as seven times before reaching the camera-ready, ready-to-print stage.

Figure 8 summarizes the recommended number of proposal drafts that you should plan for. In cases where an earlier proposal, study report, or research and development report can be used as a point-of-departure document, your proposal effort can hit the ground running and the height of the bars in Fig. 8 might be reduced by one or two draft cycles.

At the risk of stating the obvious, the reverse interpretation of Fig. 8 is not necessarily true. A proposal rewritten seven times is not automatically worthy of a billion dollar contract.

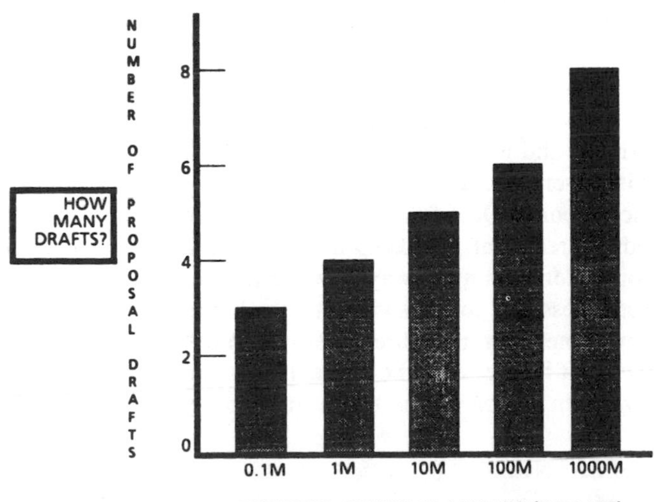

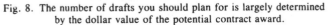

Fig. 8. The number of drafts you should plan for is largely determined by the dollar value of the potential contract award.

STRATEGY 7—ACHIEVEMENTS SPEAK LOUDER THAN LISTS

Evidence of recognized superior prior work from customers, e.g., testimonial letters, awards, early completion of high quality work within budget, etc., can be especially effective towards achieving a top score for the experience section of your proposal. Don't just list what you have done, state the *significance* of what you have done. Also, company experience should not be restricted to the management volume. It should be infused throughout the proposal to substantiate and explain claims. For example: "......using a similar technique on the ABC Project, we were able to reduce the time needed to prepare a failure modes analysis from 56 hours to 1/2 hour."

Likewise, in resumes, do not just list where you worked and what you did. Tell *how well you did* each of your assignments. And, in doing so, lean heavily on action verbs: "designed," "directed," "created," "caused," etc.

STRATEGY 8—PROVE YOUR POINTS WITH DATA

Visual impact and style, while important, are qualities that can only count as secondary (but they can be decisive). What really matters, is relevant parametric data, absolute proof that your proposal is quantitatively superior to all others.

Graphically-oriented proposal specialists can often visualize a proposal graphic filled with parametric data before hard data exist. They sometimes know what point the data should make even before the actual data have been gathered. A case-in-point is to summarize the company's facilities and resources in a way that not only states floor area, but also helps show diversified functions, capabilities, and resources. Instead of merely stating that one million square feet of floor space is available, create an interesting table, like the one illustrated below, that shows the allocation of space and the various purposes that are served.

Building	Purpose	Square feet
A	Administration	------
B	Electronic Data Processing	200,000
C	Engineering	350,000
D	Manufacturing	------
E	Word and Graphics Processing	200,000
	Total Sq. Ft.	1,000,000

Few people will have all of the needed detailed data entries at their fingertips. But, somebody does. The point is, tables can be constructed in the proposal draft without having the actual data at hand. By inserting blanks and fake data a busy, highly-paid engineer need not ponder over the numbers. Someone else can be given the data fill-in assignment: "Find out what the right entries should be," or simply, "Fill in the blanks."

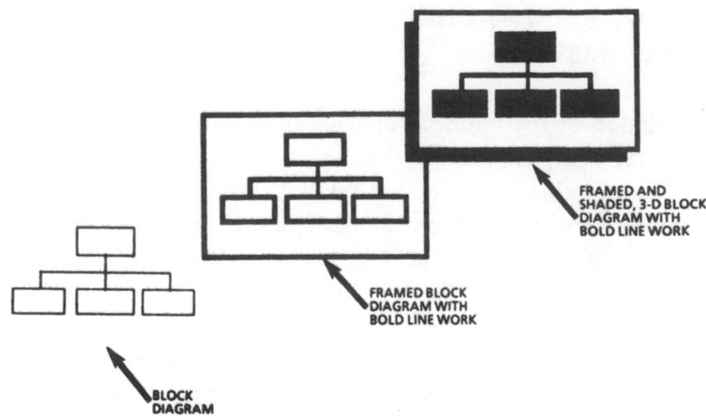

Fig. 9. Progressively greater highlighting of a block diagram.

STRATEGY 9—LOOK TO MILITARY SPECIFICATIONS AND STANDARDS FOR GUIDANCE

Mention Mil specs and standards to engineers and their thoughts turn to higher costs. But consider the work that has gone into these documents, some having been revised many, many times. For the most part, they are well-organized and comprehensive and provide valuable guidance on management, engineering, manufacturing, logistics support, and other topics. They can be useful and valuable references *even when they are not requirements of the RFP*. MIL-STD-881, for example, is all about work breakdown structure. If you want to organize a proposal, report, program, or even a company, applying the WBS technique can bring order out of chaos.

STRATEGY 10—MAKE YOUR PROPOSALS LOOK LIKE A GREAT INVESTMENT

Let's face it, even good proposals are not the most stimulating reading. Proposals are plagued by a sort of flatness of style that typifies books-by-committee, and most are under-illustrated. More and better illustrations are what proposals need. Albert Einstein rarely thought in words. Ideas came to him in images, and only later did he try to express these in words.

Following Einstein's lead, instead of verbalizing, use illus-

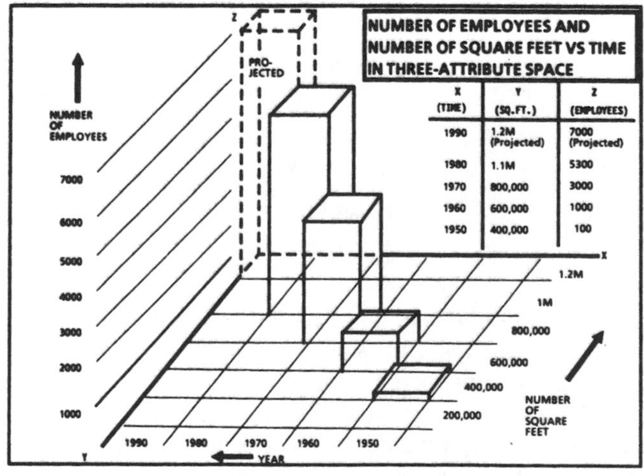

X (TIME)	Y (SQ.FT.)	Z (EMPLOYEES)
1990	1.2M (Projected)	7000 (Projected)
1980	1.1M	5300
1970	800,000	3000
1960	600,000	1000
1950	400,000	100

Fig. 10. Number of employees and number of square feet vs time in three-attribute space.

trations to heighten reader interest and break the monotony of otherwise dull reading. Because of a flood of rapid advances in publishing technology most companies have the proper tools to make interesting graphics. (I designed the illustrations for this article using a Xerox 8010 "STAR" Professional Workstation, a powerful computer-based graphics and word processing system.) In the space of only about two decades we have gone from hot-metal line casters that set type at eight to ten lines per minute to laser photocomposition equipment that handles intermixed text and graphics while operating at 1000 lines per minute.

How can you make a graphic stand out? Figure 9 is an attention-demanding example. Here an organization chart is drawn using plain line work, then using bold lines and a surrounding frame, and finally, using bold line work, shading, a surrounding frame, and a "shadow," giving the illustration a three-dimensional appearance. You can use these techniques to improve the overall visual impact of a proposal or to highlight graphics of key importance.

Sometimes, three dimensions are more interesting than two. Many scientists and engineers rarely venture beyond two-dimensional plots in their technical illustrations. Yet, an additional dimension can be helpful in the study and understanding of complex relationships. Three-dimensional illustration is often the "natural way" when data have X, Y, and Z components: height, width, and depth; x-position, y-position, and altitude; range, bearing, and elevation; speed, weight, and amplitude (as in vibration analyses); volume, weight, and cost; wear rate versus load versus velocity.

Three-dimensional graphics should be exploited. For example, returning to the facilities and personnel resources depicted in the upper left corner of Fig. 6, we might try to visualize how to illustrate a company's facilities and personnel resources, showing how these parameters have changed over the years. With a little research and using the graphics capability of our in-house computerized system, we can show these relationships in one three-dimensional illustration, Fig. 10, even projecting into the future. I call this technique "illustrating in three-attribute space."

CONCLUSION

Writing and illustrating strategies will not, on their own, win government contracts. Much more is required than just the proposal. Qualifying past performance is often an overriding credential. But keep in mind that the most qualified contractor does not always get the job. Just as the race is not necessarily to the swift, nor the battle to the strong, government contracts are often won, not by the most qualified, but by the one who presents himself most persuasively, in person and in his written proposal.

REFERENCES

Greenly, R.B., *How to Win Government Contracts*, Van Nostrand Reinhold Company, Inc., 1983.

Storyboarding Can Help Your Proposal

ROBERT A. BARAKAT

Abstract—**Storyboarding is an efficient technique that provides proposal managers and writers a disciplined, yet flexible, framework for planning, developing, and reviewing proposal text incrementally and sequentially. The technique facilitates intragroup communication so that all team members are aware of the "message" being developed to sell an approach to a customer's problem. A major benefit of storyboarding to proposal teams is that it encourages consistency which, in turn, ensures that the proposal complies with the customer's requirements and the bidder's win strategy.**

PREPARING PROPOSALS can be an interesting, challenging, and satisfying experience, especially when the proposals turn out to be "winners." Usually, winning proposals are the result of careful and thoughtful planning by proposal managers who know what they want from proposal teams and can communicate ideas clearly to them. Everyone is working to the same objectives, plan, and schedule; all goes smoothly.

Unfortunately, not all proposal development efforts are well planned or well executed. Many a proposal manager has burned the midnight oil trying to undo the confusion resulting from misdirections, ineffective communication, or foggy thinking. For example, writers will write their sections with only a hazy idea of what they need to accomplish, groping for direction and guidance at a time in the proposal development effort when they should be operating from a firm base. In addition, proposal managers often devise outlines that are inadequate for their intended purposes. Often they simply mimic the Request for Proposal (RFP) in a fashion that satisfies the RFP requirements but does little to sell the substantive content of the deliverables in the proposal.

Storyboarding is a technique that can make the process more effective and efficient because it gives proposal managers more control over the development process.

WHAT IS STORYBOARDING?

Storyboarding is an efficient and effective technique for controlling and coordinating the *incremental* and *sequential* development of technical and management information for proposals into a coherent story. It involves writing ideas and phrases on sheets of paper or cards and placing them, in order, on a wall in a dedicated proposal control room. This technique enables a team of writers to work together in laying out a blueprint for the message they want to convey to the evaluators. It ensures that all topics to be covered in the final proposal are included and treated in the most effective manner possible, and that each topic relates to the total proposal theme and win strategy (figure 1).

Storyboarding is the focal point of proposal planning. From it stem the pieces of the overall proposal message which, when properly assembled, constitute the final version of the proposal. The storyboarding phase is a critical transition that links the planning with the writing. Inadequate planning at this transition period affects all later stages of the proposal development effort.

As a tool for developing mammoth proposals, storyboarding can be indispensable because it helps the proposal manager and team to devise complete outlines of items to be covered in the actual proposal. Storyboarding allows writers to focus their attention on individual writing tasks instead of the potentially overwhelming whole proposal project. Further, the technique allows proposal managers and writers to plan, visualize, review, adjust, and revise the proposal's organization and contents well before any draft writing begins. Additionally, storyboarding encourages, through reviews, intragroup communication and facilitates, among writers, a common understanding of what should be considered and included in the final version of the proposal. It is this last point that makes the process efficient.

To create effective storyboards, writers still have to outline, select topics, write thematic sentences, develop key thoughts, and conceive illustrations to support the thesis or central message. Each of these elements, including rough sketches of relevant illustrations, is placed on the storyboard. Once completed, the storyboards can be reviewed quickly, revised or discarded, as necessary, even before writers generate rough-draft text.

Working in this fashion, writers will discover that rewrite times are cut considerably and the entire proposal development cycle is also shortened, because reviews and revisions take place earlier than on conventionally developed proposals. Figure 2 depicts the several steps in the storyboarding process.

Robert A. Barakat is Director of Training and Staff Development for Arthur D. Little, Inc.

Reprinted from *IEEE Trans. Prof. Comm.*, vol. 32, no. 1, pp. 20–25, March 1989.

PROPOSAL STORYBOARD

SECTION NO. & TITLE: TRAINING 5.16 (SOW 3.11)

TOPIC: TRAINING DESIGN/DEVELOPMENT/IMPLEMENTATION

RFP REQUIREMENTS: DETAILED DESCRIPTION OF OUR APPROACH TO TECHNICAL TRAINING FOR DATA PROCESSING PERSONNEL

PROPOSAL: XYZ PROGRAM
VOLUME: 1
NO. PAGES: 5
AUTHOR: RAB
EXT: 2250
DATE: 6/6/87

STRATEGY: EMPHASIZE THE BENEFITS TO THE AIR FORCE OF USING THE ISD MODEL TO DEVELOP TRAINING. ALSO, STRESS THE ADVANTAGES OF PERFORMANCE-BASED TRAINING.

THEMATIC SENTENCE: WE USE AN EIGHT-STEP ISD MODEL BASED ON THE CLOSED-LOOP MODEL USED SO SUCCESSFULLY BY THE AIR FORCE TO DEVELOP PERFORMANCE-BASED TRAINING FOR DATA PROCESSING PERSONNEL.

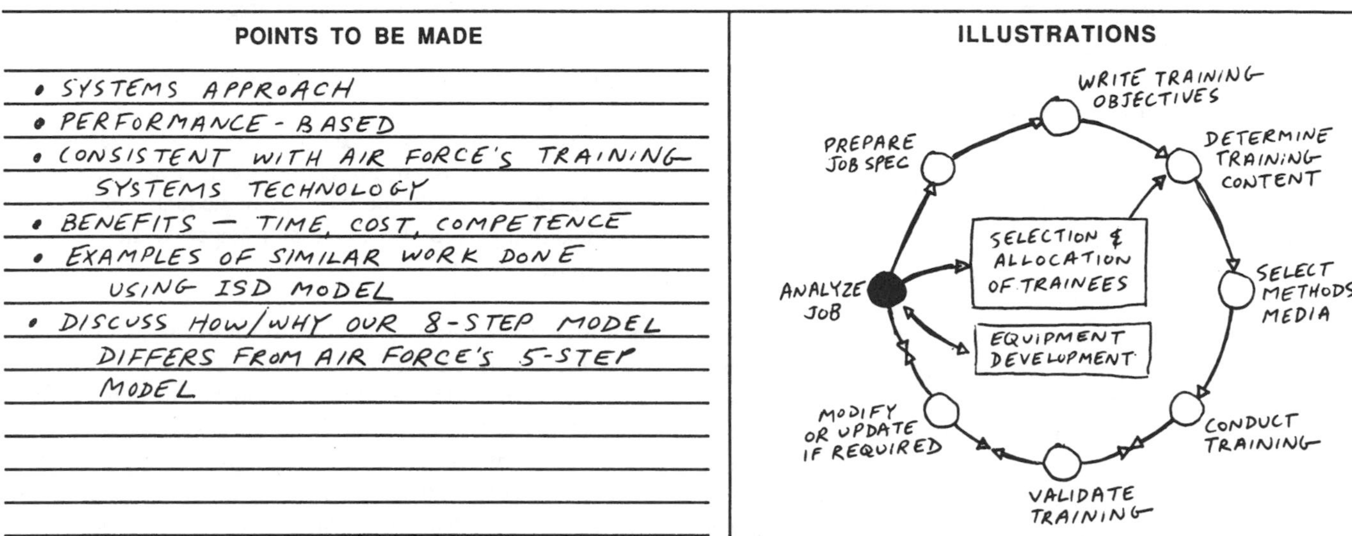

POINTS TO BE MADE

- SYSTEMS APPROACH
- PERFORMANCE-BASED
- CONSISTENT WITH AIR FORCE'S TRAINING SYSTEMS TECHNOLOGY
- BENEFITS — TIME, COST, COMPETENCE
- EXAMPLES OF SIMILAR WORK DONE USING ISD MODEL
- DISCUSS HOW/WHY OUR 8-STEP MODEL DIFFERS FROM AIR FORCE'S 5-STEP MODEL

ILLUSTRATIONS

Figure 1. This completed storyboard illustrates a representative form as well as examples of information placed in each block.

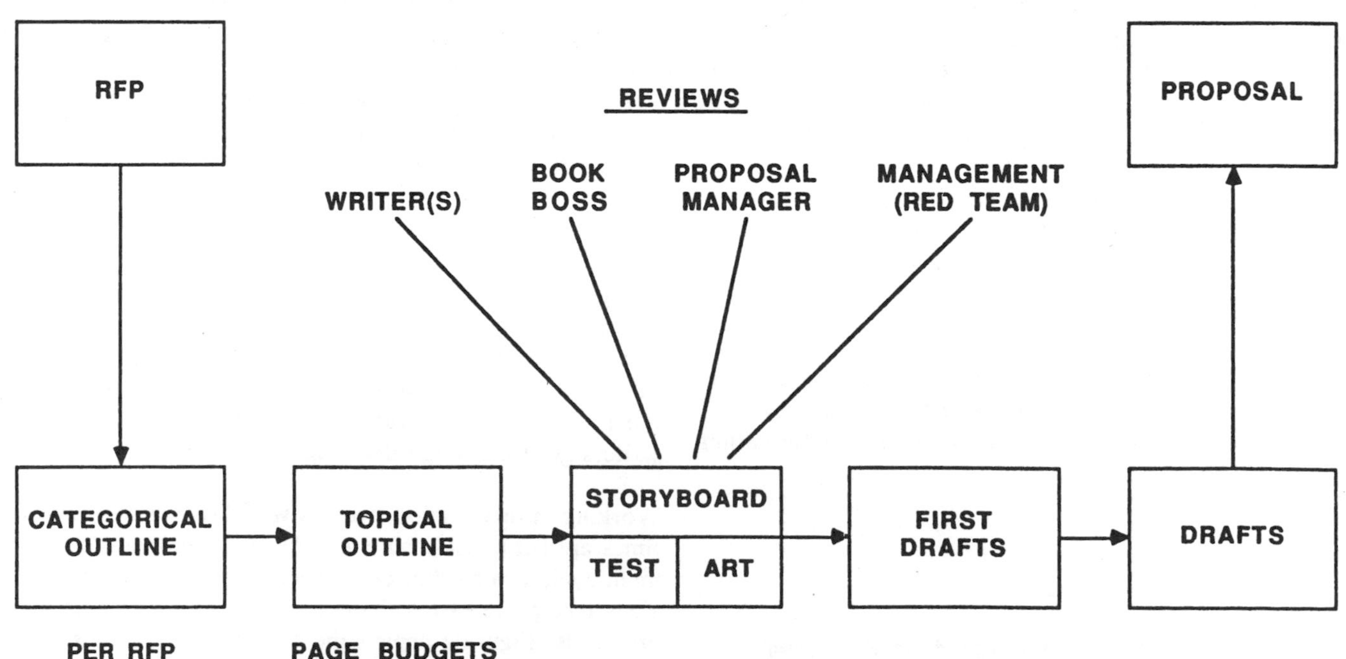

Figure 2. Storyboarding is an integral part of the proposal development process that helps managers plan and control the group writing process.

STEP ONE—OUTLINING THE PROPOSAL

As the preliminary step to creating a storyboard, the proposal manager and selected team members must devise two types of outlines:

- Categorical outline (of the RFP requirements)
- Topical outline (for each proposal section)

Categorical Outline

Typically, this outline specifies who is to write each section and subsection, as well as the appropriate RFP references to which they respond. The categorical outline, therefore, should include only highest-level categories. Figure 3 illustrates portions of a categorical outline subdivided to third-level headings. It is critical that a proposal manager or a designated individual check and recheck the categories against the RFP requirements before distributing the outline to individuals responsible for each volume who, in turn, distribute it to writers.

Since categorical outlines divide thoughts and ideas into discrete categories subordinated with letters or numbers, the proposal manager can rank these categories by their relative importance. In addition, categorical outlines help ensure that all topics are covered. Completeness is what proposal managers must strive for when devising this outline.

However, the categorical outline does not specify *how* writers are to treat the headings. This is the primary function of the topic or topical outline.

Topic or Topical Outline

Transforming a categorical outline into a more detailed topical outline makes the headings more specific and helps the writers flesh out the contents of their sections. In the process of performing this transformation, writers will realize they can formulate a message that they can weave into their narratives to emphasize the win strategy. Care must be taken not to create an outline that is too long or exceeds reasonable page allocations, if these are considered at this time in the proposal development effort.

Topic headings are not difficult to create. Once formulated, they serve as aids for writing thematic sentences and as guides for ensuring that the narrative conveys the exact message intended. Writers simply ask themselves one or both of these questions: "What about this topic?" or "What do I really want to tell the evaluators of this section or subsection?" The following examples illustrate the process:

- *Example:* Operator Training
  What about it?
  We will use the U.S. Air Force-approved Instructional System Development model to design, develop, evaluate, validate, and implement XYZ System operator training.

1. INTRODUCTION AND SUMMARY
2. HARDWARE DEVELOPMENT AND INTEGRATION
   2.1 Hardware Development
      2.1.1 End Item Design and Development (SOW 3.4.1)
      2.1.2 Fabrication (SOW 3.4.2)
      2.1.3 Factory Support Equipment
      2.1.4 Maintenance Support Equipment (SOW 3.5.1)
   2.2 Hardware Integration
      2.2.1 Planning and Control
      2.2.2 Integration (SOW 3.4.1.2)
   2.3 Interface Development
      2.3.1 ICDs
      2.3.2 Joint Operating Procedures

•
•
•

4. TEST AND EVALUATION
   4.1 Test Planning and Conduct (SOW 3.4.1.2; 3.7)
      4.1.1 Test Schedule
   4.2 Development Test and Evaluation (SOW 3.4.1.2)
   4.3 Development Integration Testing (SOW 3.4.1.2.2.2)
   4.4 Test Hardware Requirements
   4.5 Test Documentation
   4.6 Test Facilities
5. SUPPORTING ACTIVITIES
   5.1 Reliability (SOW 3.9.2)
   5.2 Maintainability (SOW 3.9.3)
   5.3 Standardization (SOW 3.9.14)

   •
   •
   •

   5.16 Training (SOW 3.11)
   5.17 Technical Publications (SOW 3.12)
   5.18 Quality Assurance Program (SOW 3.8.5)

Figure 3. A bare-bones categorical outline responds exactly to the RFP requirements but says nothing about how each item is to be treated.

- *Example:* Material Control
  What about it?
  Material control is accomplished through a totally integrated data system that monitors and controls the flow of material.

It is important that writers create headings that are specific, informative, and descriptive. Once created, the authors' messages become clear and coherent. It is important to keep in mind the bidder's position on the topic as well as the topic itself. For example, "Reduction of data base errors" is better than "Data base errors," and "How to simplify operator training and make it more effective" is better than "Operator training."

The topical outline is not an expanded version of the categorical outline. It specifies precisely the manner in which writers will approach their topics. A thorough and complete outline allows writers to achieve consistency and coherency throughout their narratives. Figure 4 illustrates a carefully conceived and executed topical outline.

STEP TWO—CREATING STORYBOARDS

The storyboard process begins in earnest when writers formulate thematic sentences that state the central message of their sections. These sentences make a challenging, refutable statement that stimulates the reader to say "Prove it!", and then read on for the details used to support the writer's claim. Thus, thematic sentences contain a good deal of "punch" and specific evidence in support of their

5.18 QUALITY ASSURANCE PROGRAM

5.18.1 Organizing for Control of Quality

5.18.1.1 The Importance of the QA Organization
- QA assures quality, reliability, and safety of product
- Safety is designed in; QA assures it is built in (i.e., not degraded during build)
- Our QA was in place for the build of over 500 units for the XYZ Qual Program

5.18.1.2 The QA Engineering Function
- Establishes and reviews criteria
- Assures personnel awareness of quality requirements
- Assures timely and effective corrective action

5.18.1.3 The Quality Control Function
- Analyzes material
- Inspects and tests parts, material and assemblies

5.18.2 Planning for Control of Quality

5.18.2.1 Our Policies and Procedures
- Policy 20.1 provides access to vice president and general manager for resolution of quality issues
- Operating procedures in place and approved by local DCAS

5.18.2.2 QA Engineering Quality Planning
- All required inspections and tests are identified. Instructions can be used as is or with slight modification
- No new inspection equipment is necessary
- Results of XYZ Qual Program have been used to firm up criteria

5.18.2.3 The Quality Assurance Program Plan
- Defines quality role to other departments to assure timely inter-department coordination of tasks

5.18.3 Implementing the Quality Program

5.18.3.1 Design Review and Approval
- Assures quality requirements are incorporated in the design
- Assures manufacturability, inspectability of item

5.18.3.2 Control of Purchases
- Assures selection of qualified suppliers
- Assures quality requirements are imposed on suppliers

Figure 4. A topical outline that answers the question "So what?" is likely to stimulate authors to write interesting and sales-oriented narratives.

assertions. Working together at different levels, the proposal manager, book bosses (persons responsible for individual volumes), section leaders (persons responsible for individual volume sections), and writers can produce effective thematic sentences that guide both the writer and the reader.

The following are some suggestions for formulating effective thematic sentences:

- Ask yourself a series of questions about your topic. *Example:* Suppose the topic is "transportability of hazardous waste." Take some time to think about the topic, then ask:
  "What about the transportability of this hazardous waste?"
  "Who needs it?"
  "Is it required by the RFP?"
  "Does the waste present any dangers during transit?"
  Write down all the questions and answers as to *how and why* the company can achieve this requirement.

  Some of these points may have come up in your thinking:

  — We are certified by the DOT to transport hazardous waste over public roads to our EPA-approved hazardous waste treatment facilities.
  — We use double and triple bagging procedures and sealed barrels that minimize risks, yet remain cost effective.
  — Our staff is well trained to handle any emergency that might arise, including spills.

  Now formulate a thematic sentence based on these points and rework the sentence until you have a persuasive or refutable statement. The final sentence might read

  "Our company is fully certified by the DOT to transport carefully packaged hazardous waste over public roads to our EPA-approved waste treatment facilities, where our trained staff can handle any emergencies that might arise."

- Keep the sentences short, preferably 25 words or less. The impact on the reader will be greater. If you need to write a longer sentence, do so. Occasionally, two sentences might be necessary.
- Use words that demonstrate a clear line of reasoning, like these:

because	moreover
since	consequently
therefore	otherwise
however	furthermore

- Take a position by using qualitative words, like these:

better	optimal
benefits	fastest
advantage	most
limitations	smaller

- Make the sentences an argument:
  Irrefutable, weak: "The widget has been designed to meet the requirements."

  Refutable, strong: "We have adopted Model A of the widget design because it contains components capable of withstanding extreme conditions in all environments in which it will be deployed."

- State the purpose of the unit:

  "The widget must be capable of withstanding EMI and still transmit signals, without degradation, to satellites."

In summary, the thematic sentence is derived from the win strategy, expresses the key topic of the section, addresses the RFP requirement, and makes a challenging statement that stimulates the reader to say: "Prove it!" When writing the narrative, writers should keep this sentence in mind at all times because it is their guide—and the readers—to the section. It may be used as a standalone headline at the beginning of the section or as the opening sentence of the section's first paragraph.

STEP THREE—SUPPORTING THE MESSAGE

The thematic sentence represents the point of reference for developing the key thoughts of the narrative. Once this sentence is finalized and written on the storyboard, writers must begin to jot down convincing facts to support the statement. The facts selected must relate directly to the statement. Writers must think carefully about how they formulate and organize the supporting facts. By asking and answering a series of questions about the statement, writers will come up with a random list of facts which then can be logically sequenced for maximum impact on the reader.

For example, "Our company uses data from the System Test of the XYZ Program units because these units are similar to those proposed for the Widget System Program." The points to support the thematic sentence (above) could include the following:

- We can provide early estimates.
- We can conduct tests to verify our analysis.
- We can generate inputs for Electric Power Analysis CDRL requirements in conjunction with similar data regarding the Widget System Program requirements.

Although it is not essential, writers should compose their points in complete sentences rather than in short phrases or single words. By doing so, they will more clearly define their points and also help the storyboard reviewers.

Usually at this point, writers should begin to think about the graphics they will need to illustrate their points. Placing rough sketches of illustrations on the storyboard forms is an effective means of developing text and illustrations simultaneously.

STEP FOUR—ILLUSTRATING STORYBOARDS

The next major step in developing storyboards involves the creation of illustrations such as flow charts and tables. It is important for writers to understand that graphics are powerful vehicles for conveying complex ideas, concepts, information, and messages to evaluators. For maximum impact, graphics have to be designed with the reader in mind. Getting the evaluator's attention is one function that graphics serve; there are others:

- Reinforcing a message or parts of a message conveyed in the text
- Conveying a complex idea or concept that would otherwise require hundreds of words to describe

In addition, illustration captions offer writers another opportunity to sell their messages. Therefore, captions should relate to the entire concept being sold, identify the particular feature that forms part of that concept, and have punch as a selling point. For example:

- *Instead of* "Figure 2.1—Subsystem Block Diagram"
  Try "Figure 2.1—The key feature of this subsystem is the microprocessor."
- *Instead of* "Figure 2.4—Master Program Flow Diagram."
  Try "Figure 2.4—A highlight of our program flow is our ability to identify and minimize risk areas."

The figure captions used with this paper are further illustrations of the above points.

STEP FIVE—"RED TEAM" REVIEWS

The storyboarding technique provides proposal managers and writers a means of developing proposal text incrementally within a well-defined review process called the *Storyboard* or *Red Team Review*. This review helps control and channel the efforts of writers and simultaneously enhances the effects of the win strategy. This review also encourages intragroup communication and ensures that the win strategy is addressed throughout the proposal.

Storyboards should be kept in a dedicated proposal control room where the current version of the proposal plan is instantly visible to all team members. Posting the storyboards on the control room wall also allows individual writers to comment on other parts of the proposal. Reviewers can best perform their task because they can visualize the organization and flow of the proposal. If the storyboards need to be reorganized or if the proposal manager wants to experiment with different organizations, then the storyboards can be rearranged easily and quickly until the most effective organization is obtained.

The first formal team review should be conducted within a week or so after storyboards are assigned and before draft writing begins. Reviewers should check each storyboard and group of storyboards for the following:

- Compliance with the RFP requirements
- Presentation and placement of the win strategy
- Coherence and relevance
- Consistency among thematic sentences, illustrations, and strategy
- Proper sales message
- Effective use of illustrations
- Logical ordering of storyboard modules
- Oversights, misinterpretations, and inconsistencies among storyboards

Storyboard reviews are group reviews that take place in two stages:

- Continuous reviews by the proposal manager, book bosses, and writers
- Management Red Team reviews by representatives not associated with the proposal development effort

This latter team puts their final stamp of approval on the storyboards or recommends revisions before draft writing takes place.

Typically, each review team has an appointed chairperson who is responsible for setting review dates, compiling agendas, maintaining order, recording action items, stimulating discussions, and resolving conflicts. However, these reviewers should remember that storyboards are simply plans for the writing to follow. Reviewers' comments should be limited to content, viewpoint, and organization. Nitpicking of grammatical and stylistic faults is to be avoided since these can be fixed easily after draft writing is completed. Some writers might find it difficult to compose relevant, challenging thematic sentences, especially if they have never written them before, so reviewers should offer suggestions for improving the sentences. Also, suggestions for improving the illustrations should be offered.

However, vague comments like "needs work" or "rewrite" are not helpful and should be avoided. Clear, concise, and incisive suggestions will help writers improve their storyboards and, ultimately, their narratives.

IN SUMMARY

Storyboarding is a technique and a process which proposal managers and writers can use to their advantage. In fact, when storyboarding is used to its full potential, proposal teams are able to telescope an otherwise tedious, inflexible proposal development effort into a neat, coherent, and winning proposal. Since storyboarding exploits the creative and management skills of the entire proposal team, it provides control over the planning and writing without sacrificing flexibility and early reviews. Each proposal team member has a common set of guidelines for developing text and illustrations.

Writers benefit because storyboards allow them to focus their knowledge and creativity on developing the appropriate message for their respective sections. Proposal managers have a baseline for measuring performance of the writers, as well as a means for ensuring cross-fertilization among team members. The Storyboard or Red Team Review, in particular, is valuable to the proposal manager because it is a means for quickly pinpointing any text that is weak, unsupported, or redundant. Similarly, the reviewers no longer have to read through completed rough drafts to check the writers' message; this can be accomplished before or during the review cycle. Editors benefit because they receive text that is well thought out and complete.

Developing Winning Proposal Strategies

Robert A. Barakat

Abstract—**Winning proposals are usually the result of careful planning during the prebid and proposal planning phases. For multivolume proposals typically submitted to the U.S. Government, the overall proposal strategy the proposal manager conceives and implements represents the master blueprint that serves as the basis for strategies for individual volumes and sections within these volumes. Although the overall proposal strategy is critical for producing a credible proposal, success can come from following additional strategies the proposal manager must devise and implement at key points during the proposal development schedule: Will-to-Win Strategy; Customer Development Strategy; Assessing the Competition; Pricing Strategy; Tactics and Themes; Proposal Presentation Strategy; Review Strategy.**

Introduction

For organizations that sell services, ideas, or products, the proposal is the primary vehicle used to acquire new business. For customers, the proposal is the major source of information about the seller's capabilities to perform a job. Thus, for the seller, the proposal is a critical sales document that, if planned and written effectively, will provide the basic information the customer needs to decide which organization to select for a specific project.

Because proposals are sales documents, sellers must carefully and thoughtfully devise an overall proposal strategy that differentiates their organizations from competitors for the same project. This overall proposal strategy provides the general outline of what is being offered, but it does not provide the specific details of the offering. The detailed description is developed in the strategies for each volume, and these strategies, in turn, are developed further in individual section strategies. Large proposals, such as those submitted to the Department of Defense, may consist of several volumes, each of which may cover a variety of disciplines and topics. Each volume is like a proposal within a proposal. Similarly, an individual section within a volume is like a proposal within a proposal.

Like the overall proposal, volumes and sections must be planned, scheduled, orchestrated, and made consistent in style and content with the overall proposal being submitted to the customer. Fig. 1 represents a simple form proposal managers and teams may use to develop the proposal, volume, and section strategies.

Proposal writers should be guided by an overall strategy, which should be devised either in preparation for the bid/no bid decision or very early in the proposal development process. Without a proposal and volume strategy to guide them, writers might discover that their narratives are excellent technical documents but do little to sell the organization's approach or the solution proposed to satisfy the customer's needs.

For many sellers, an overall strategy and detailed volume and section strategies are not always essential, especially if they are selling a product that exists already. For example, automobile, appliance, or electronic equipment manufacturers can present a set of test data that demonstrates the reliability, performance, quality, and maintenance history of the product. Therefore, for manufacturers to sell their products, they need only demonstrate—with facts—how and why their products surpass those of the competition.

For organizations that sell services, however, strategies are essential because the promise to deliver an intangible cannot be supported with hard facts other than previous experience on similar work. For example, an organization selling engineering design services to the Department of Defense often cannot point to an existing product because that product does not exist. Consequently, these sellers must develop and submit proposals that describe what they believe the actual product will look like. In other words, the description of the proposed concept serves as a surrogate for the real thing.

Given that their product does not exist, these sellers must make implied or stated promises in their proposals that the concept can be transformed into an actual product that meets customer-specified requirements and specifications. In such situations—and they are typical in the defense industry—the promises sellers present in their proposals become more suspect in the eyes of the customer's evaluators. To overcome what might be an inherent skepticism among the evaluators, organizations participating in this market must devise well-defined strategies to be used at all levels of the proposal.

The proposal manager, usually with the help of marketing department representatives and the core proposal team, develops the overall game plan—the overall proposal or win strategy—and ensures that the individuals responsible for each volume and section, as well as the writers, use it as a basis for the strategies in their respective parts of the proposal. Implementing the strategies, however, can be a nightmare for an unorganized proposal manager, especially when team members might be constantly second-guessing. Allowing team members free rein to do what they prefer undermines the entire proposal development effort. Getting it back on track might require a Herculean effort at a time when proposal managers can least afford it, usually during the latter stage of the proposal development process.

The following quote by a proposal manager is from a "Lessons Learned" document compiled after a mammoth, winning proposal development effort. It illustrates the prob-

Manuscript received March 8, 1990; revised May 9, 1991.
The author is with Arthur D. Little, Inc., Cambridge, MA 02138.
IEEE Log Number 9102034.

Reprinted from *IEEE Trans. Prof. Comm.*, vol. PC-34, no. 3, pp. 130–139, September 1991.

Overall Proposal Strategy ______

How are we going to win?

Volume Strategy ______

How are we going to win in this volume?

Section Strategy ______

How do I implement the volume strategy in this section?

Section Theme Statement ______

Why should the customer choose us?

Used with permission of Shipley Associates

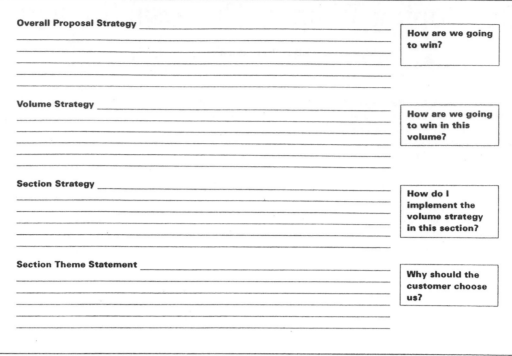

Fig. 1. A simple form that may be used to develop strategies.

lem described above:

> As a fundamental high-priority strategy, I established that we must, at every single possible point in the proposal, highlight our [related program] experience and with as much *specificity* as we could. I found several pockets of resistance to this strategy ranging from people independently concluding that our page count would not allow us to fulfill this strategy and also present our technical solutions. In several instances, I found team members telling me (or worse, not telling me) that "of course [the customer] knows our record; it is not necessary to beat it to death in the proposal."
>
> However, I had correctly assessed that the evaluation would be conducted by [the customer] newcomers and young officers who did not directly, or at all, know about or understand the fine work we had done in the [related program] R&D phases. That, in fact, many of these expected evaluators knew us only in the mode of the last few years when we have done only sustaining engineering or support, and in fact, had for a few reasons developed a highly negative image of [our company]. It was for these, as it subsequently turns out, correct assessments, that I insisted on frequent and specific highlighting of our [related program] experience. It took me one hell of a lot of effort to make this happen, including, on some occasions, direct authoritarian orders to make it happen [1].

One way proposal managers can ensure that their strategies are used correctly in key proposal sections is to assign a team member to track each strategy as the text evolves. This individual would report directly to the proposal manager on the status of the strategies. To do this effectively, he or she should have complete access to all proposal sections as they are being developed.

Although the overall proposal strategy is a critical factor that guides and directs writers, there are several additional proposal strategies a proposal manager should consider devising in preparation for the proposal planning phase during the period before the Request for Proposal arrives. These strategies are discussed in their approximate order of creation and include the following:

- Will-to-Win Strategy
- Customer Development Strategy
- Assessing the Competition
- Pricing Strategy
- Tactics and Themes
- Proposal Presentation Strategy
- Review Strategy.

Will-to-Win Strategy

This is a critical strategy for proposal managers to devise because they are building a cohesive and enthusiastic proposal team. To build and motivate that team to work effectively and efficiently, the proposal manager has to get them "psyched up" to win. Even though this strategy might never be committed to paper, the proposal manager can do several things to motivate the team members to give their all, plus a little more, if necessary.

To devise an effective will-to-win strategy, proposal managers must understand individual team members. Because a proposal manager has probably worked with these same people on previous proposal efforts, he/she will know something of their individual peculiarities. This knowledge gives the manager an advantage in selecting an appropriate motivational technique. For example, knowing the strengths of individual team members allows the proposal manager to assign work that will make them most productive and, as a benefit, give them a sense of satisfaction.

A proposal manager might also consider convening brief, informal, stand-up meetings each morning or late afternoon to present progress reports and accomplishments. Such meetings also allow individuals to share ideas, information, and insights which might not otherwise be expressed or even solicited. In addition, it is always effective to conduct a few hours of training for the proposal team to prepare them for the task ahead. This training is especially useful for individuals who have never worked on a proposal. Typically, training covers schemes for organizing sections; how to transform a categorical outline to a topical outline; basic writing skills; storyboarding; thesis sentence formulation; and graphics, including how to write captions.

Setting up a dedicated proposal area equipped with desks, computers for word processing, and a library is always helpful. Team members will be able to share a common experience, discuss issues, and assist each other as the need arises. The proposal manager should have an office in the immediate area so that he/she will be accessible to team members when they have questions or need some guidance.

Proposal managers must work with and through people to achieve an objective. Although proposal managers cannot do everything themselves, if they are not careful, they might end up doing everything anyway. Caution is called for, especially with regard to being too dictatorial. Authoritarian behavior could turn the team off completely, which could obstruct the ultimate objective: to win new business. Moreover, the proposal manager should not hesitate to delegate responsibility and authority to individuals in key roles.

Gaining the respect and loyalty of the team is equally critical; it ensures that writers will use the proposal, volume, and section strategies. People will always second-guess the proposal manager's wisdom; this reaction is inevitable because someone is bound to think he or she knows better. By identifying and addressing potential people-related issues beforehand, proposal managers will be prepared to resolve them before they get out of hand.

Customer Development Strategy

In the first phase, sometimes referred to as "long-term positioning," marketing and other representatives, such as engineers, systematically gather information about the program to be bid. The goal is to develop a positive relationship with the customer and to get the customer to know more about the seller's organization. This strategy presents the guidelines by which marketers and others attempt to influence the customer—to presell the program before the RFP is issued. If the seller's representatives do their work properly, then the customer's evaluators should not be surprised by the proposal's contents when they receive and evaluate it. If an organization's marketing staff reads about the program in the *Commerce Business Daily* (*CBD*) for the first time, then it is probably too late to bid on the program. Preselling the customer is essential, and it must be done long before the *CBD* announcement is made.

Usually the proposal manager and the marketing organization work together to identify individuals within the customer organization who are concerned with the program. Also, individuals within the seller's organization, such as marketing representatives, must be identified and given the responsibility of contacting the customer's representatives periodically. In addition, they must be informed of the exact message they are to transmit to their contacts, as well as how and when.

Usually, this contact plan is put into effect long before the RFP is issued and before an organization's management has given the go-ahead to bid for the job. In a sense, it is a logical follow-on to the marketing plan that bidders should have in place. However, the plan for a particular program must be more intensive and program-specific. Also, it is a logical extension of the various marketing plans that are devised for related programs; that is, the marketing organization tracks candidate programs for months or even years so they are able to presell solutions to a client's problem well before a final request for proposal is issued or, in some instances, before a draft RFP is issued to the industry for comments.

Assessing the Competition

Assessing the competition requires a thorough audit of the environment in which the organization will compete; that is, the seller's position in relation to all competitors for the program. Typically, a brainstorming session of knowledgeable individuals is convened to identify the organization's strengths and weaknesses, successes and failures, as well as those of the competition.

Some questions that are usually raised include the following:

- **What does the customer really think about us?** Does the customer believe we have the capabilities to do the job? What is our standing in relation to our competitors for this program? Is our reputation solid, improving, or declining in the mind of the customer?
- **What does the customer think about each competitor?** Do we know what our competitors' strategies are for this and previous programs? In fact, do we know who the competitors are?
- **What benefits does the customer get by awarding the job to us?** Do we offer more or less value than our competitors? What are the pivotal proposal features and benefits that will prompt the customer to buy our services? Have we offered them before to the same customer? Were we successful or did we stumble?
- **What are our biggest weaknesses and what can we do to neutralize them?** How can we capitalize on our strengths so they dovetail with the customer's needs?
- **Are we followers or leaders in this market?** When the customer has a problem does he turn to us for advice or help?

Whether consciously or unconsciously, the customer's proposal evaluators constantly compare one bidder with others throughout the evaluation process. Proposal managers cannot leave this process to chance because evaluators have many preconceived notions about each bidder, some false, some true. During the brainstorming session, the team will have to identify and list the good, the bad, and the ugly things they know about their own organization and its competitors.

Although there are several techniques for assessing the

Discriminator
Our track record in contract research and development spans 103 years of success in product development for commercial and U.S. Government clients, many of whom still look to us for advice and counsel.

Aha! Discriminator
When NASA was implementing the Apollo Program, we were selected to design and build fifteen experimental instruments that, ultimately, were placed on the lunar surface. Thus, we have more experimental equipment on the lunar surface than any other private sector firm.

Oh-Oh! Discriminator
We understand your problem, because we have helped solve it for other organizations in both the private and public sector.

Ho-Hum! Discriminator
As the oldest and largest consulting firm in the world, we have been providing professional advice and counsel to organizations throughout the world—on technology and management issues, and in contract research and development.

Ghost Story
Unlike our competitors for this program, we propose conducting the program without a teaming arrangement because we believe it is more cost effective and efficient to complete the tasks in a single, fully equipped facility using our own experienced, dedicated professional staff.

Fig. 2. These examples illustrate the various D/A/G list items Beveridge and Velton consider critical for a successful competitive assessment.

competition, Beveridge and Velton's D/A/G discipline is one of the most effective and efficient [2]. D/A/G stands for *Discriminators*, *Ahas*!, and *Ghost Stories*. These are defined and discussed below in summary form. Fig. 2 illustrates examples of several discriminators and a ghost story.

Discriminators are just differences; they do not imply value judgments nor do they have any emotion associated with them. Later, the *Ahas*!, *Oh-Ohs*!, and *Ho-Hums*! provide the emotion for the *Discriminators*. When an *Aha*! *Discriminator* agrees with the customer's needs, it provides impact because it strikes an emotional chord in the evaluator's mind. In fact, the *Aha*! *Discriminators* can swing the evaluators to favor a bidder's approach.

However, bidders have to be careful about using what Beveridge and Velton call *Oh-Oh*! *Discriminators*. These are the ideas that strike the wrong chord; that is, these might identify one activity to be done one way, when the evaluators might think it should be done another way. Thus, what the bidder might consider an *Aha*! *Discriminator* could be interpreted by evaluators as an *Oh-Oh*! *Discriminator*, and cause the bidder to lose points to the competition. Too many of these *Oh-Oh*! *Discriminators* could damage the bidder's chance of winning.

Beveridge and Velton also believe there is a set of what they call *Ho-Hum*! *Discriminators* that are bothersome to evaluators. Their reaction to these might be "So what?" or "Who cares?" Many losing proposals are heavily larded with these *Ho-Hum*! *Discriminators* because the brainstormers did not separate them from the important *Ahas*! and *Oh-Ohs*!

Although *Ho-Hums*! should not be included in proposals, it is possible to turn them into *Ahas*! by modifying or changing the proposed approach to the customer's problem. But proposal managers should not include *Ho-Hums*! just to fill white space; too many could bore the evaluators, which could reduce the score card's points.

Ghost Stories are another vehicle for putting emotional value into the proposal and into the way evaluators score it. These *Ghost Stories* identify potential problems. Bidders use these to try to shoot down their competitors. Telling a *Ghost Story* about the competition will plant in the evaluator's mind doubts about the other bidder or bidders. Or, if one bidder tells a *Ghost Story* about another bidder who does not counter it in his own proposal, then chances are the "teller" will win some points. Bidders should take advantage of every opportunity to plant doubts about the competition in the minds of the evaluators.

Generating the D/A/G lists is important for three reasons. First, it forces the brainstorming team and the proposal team to think about the important differences that set their organization apart from the competition and the competition from them. Second, the discipline allows proposal managers to sharpen their understanding of the benefits deriving from the differences. The more *Aha*! *Discriminators* a brainstorming team can raise and support, the greater the chances of defeating the competition. Third, the more *Ghost Stories* they can bring out of the closet about the competition—who might not counter them in their proposal—the more doubts that can be planted in the minds of the evaluators about those other bidders.

Generating the D/A/G lists is a preproposal task that allows proposal managers to identify the important competitive factors in their respective proposals, and all the benefits of the approach being proposed. Usually, the process requires two or more iterations before the lists can be fine-tuned. Everything should be written out on flip charts, taped to the wall, reviewed and refined by the team. The final step is to organize the list. Once completed, the proposal manager will have a formidable armory of ammunition to include in the proposal.

There are four rules to observe. First, never ignore an *Oh-Oh*! It could raise its ugly head and lose points for the bidder. Second, if the team thinks the competition might raise a *Ghost Story* about them, then raise it in the proposal and counter it as specifically as possible. Third, use *Ghost Stories* about the competition liberally throughout the proposal. They can hurt the other bidders and help the organization that raises them. Fourth, it is necessary to devise a detailed plan specifying the sections in which these messages will be placed, then carefully monitor their use.

Pricing Strategy

This is the strategy proposal managers devise for offering a customer an affordable product, system, or service. Price is the figure given to the customer and should be based on what it costs to provide the service—but it is not necessarily the same as the cost. This strategy also identifies and addresses the various cost risks or uncertainties associated with doing the job. Ultimately, this strategy is conceived in light of the cost proposal's purpose: to convince the customer that the proposed price represents a reasonable estimate in relation to the scope of work.

The pricing strategy is difficult to devise if the proposal manager does not have up-to-date information about the program. The quality and quantity of that information is a function of how well the Customer Development Strategy is conceived and executed and how effectively the cost volume manager obtains information. If the marketing people have little credibility with their customer contacts, then the information might be misleading or too vague to be useful. For example, marketing representatives should have a rough estimate of the customer's budget for the program, which is especially important for the seller's pricing exercise. Since obtaining that information is sometimes difficult, organizations must put people into the field who know the customer and have a trusting relationship with them.

With valid budget information available, the cost volume manager and his/her estimators can conduct a preliminary cost analysis and estimate, referred to as a "cost bogey." The cost bogey will determine the ultimate pricing strategy. For example, if the marketing representatives know the customer's budget is limited, then the pricing strategy should reflect that fact. On the other hand, if the customer is less concerned with price and more with another requirement, such as reliability and safety, then emphasis should be on spending more for quality assurance, design, testing, materials, and manufacturing [3]. These exercises also include analyses of the Statement of Work and other documents connected with the program bid package issued by the customer.

The pricing exercise is a critical one that the proposal manager, upper management, and cost volume manager must develop and guide. Because others conduct the exercise, it is important to understand their costing biases. Some will overbid; others will underbid. If proposal managers do not watch the estimators carefully, they might submit an improper bid. The individuals who do the costing and set the price must understand that the evaluators use the cost volume to cross check the technical proposal to determine whether or not the bidder has a thorough understanding of the problem. For example, the level of engineering effort, as indicated by the engineering hours, will either substantiate or cast doubt on the seller's understanding of the customer's requirements or problem.

Therefore, consistency between the proposal text and the manpower/cost estimates is necessary. For example, proposal evaluators will compare each task in the technical volume with its cost. If anything appears out of line, then the seller will lose points. So, cooperation, as well as communication, between the technical people and the cost estimators is critical.

Proposal managers should provide a reasonably complete pricing strategy before submitting it for review. It must be clearly arranged for the reviewers to understand it as a guide for their specific sections. If it is not, then the proposal manager runs the risk of letting some team members second-guess him or her or the chief estimator. Whatever proposal managers do, they should not let anyone arbitrarily change the numbers.

Of course, the pricing strategy has to be adjusted periodically as the program is more clearly defined and as team members better understand the tasks to be performed. As the proposal manager develops the technical approach or concept, the pricing strategy will become more definitive.

Tactics and Themes

The term *strategy* is sometimes misunderstood by proposal managers. What some perceive to be a strategy is nothing more than a competitive assessment that identifies an organization's strengths and weaknesses and those of its competitors. By proposal strategy I mean an overall game plan that identifies the seller's objectives to be achieved, key messages and selling points to be stressed, the anticipated customer requirements, and the seller's capabilities to conduct the program successfully. As I stated above, the proposal strategy should be devised well before any formal proposal development effort begins, usually during the period before the customer's Request for Proposal is issued. Fig. 3 illustrates a series of critical, preparatory activities that should be completed well before the final RFP is received. In addition, the proposal strategy should derive from the organization's strategic plan and the strategic plans of the program managers and the marketing department who identify the programs they will pursue during a given year.

How clearly one defines strategies depends on how clearly one identifies key issues, which are areas of concern or unresolved problems for either the seller or the customer. Issues are identified by examining the program requirements, specifications, customer wishes, and biases. Emphasizing these issues and how they will be resolved, especially if they are related to critical program requirements, is important because they might be the decisive factors—the discriminators that distinguish bidders from one another—evaluators use to select a winner.

These issues, once identified and articulated, must be addressed in the overall proposal strategy as well as in volume and section strategies. Typically, each issue will be translated into a tactic or several tactics, each with a slightly different purpose and thrust. Ultimately, the purpose of tactics is to achieve the objectives specified by a strategy by covering all facets of key issues. In addition, tactics focus the evaluators' attention on the bidder's proposed resolution of various issues. Fig. 4 presents key issues and the strategies and tactics that respond to each issue.

Thematic headings are then created and express, in capsule form, the contents of a section. For example, this headline was used in a recent winning proposal:

> **We can provide successful subcontract management because our organization includes both subcontract technical monitoring and subcontract administration functions. Our Sub-Contract Technical Manager is a full-time position whose sole function is to manage subcontractors. He has total responsibility for overall subcontractor cost, schedule, and technical performance.**

This sample heading was then followed by several paragraphs describing the organization's critical subcontractors, procurement planning and source selection policies/proce-

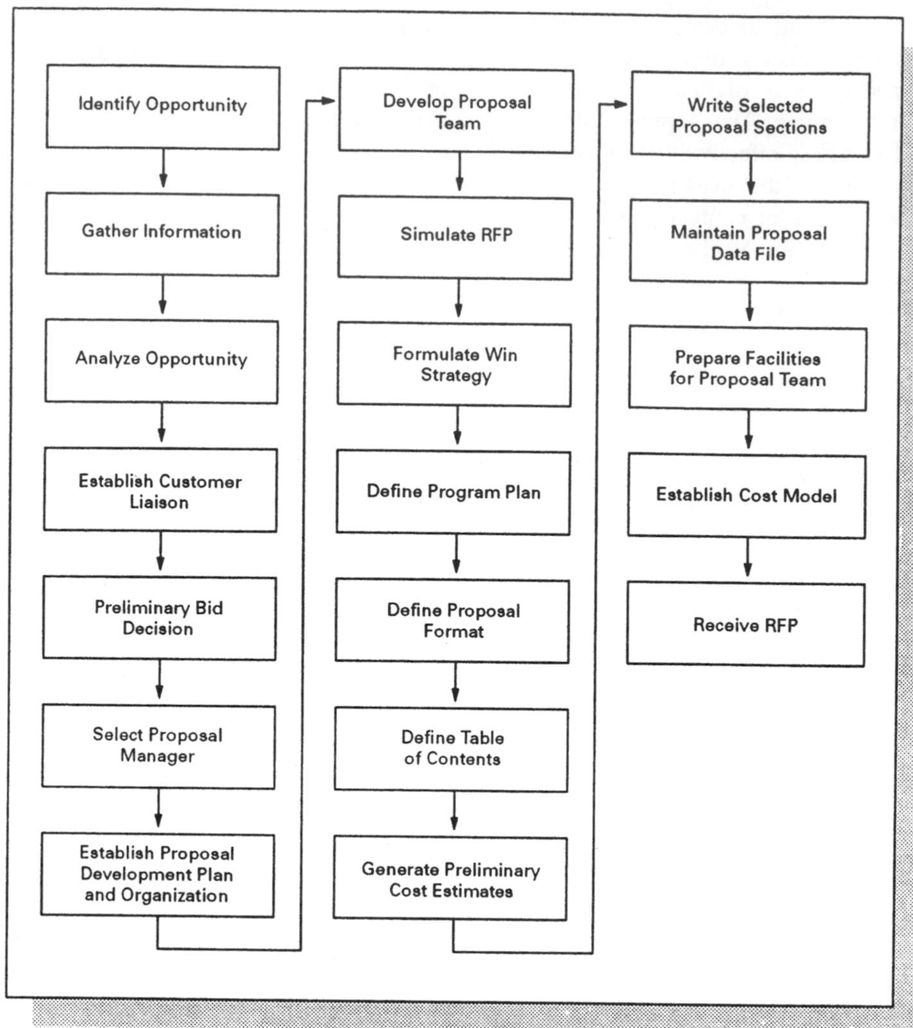

Fig. 3. Typical activities that must be completed before the RFP arrives are shown here.

dures, and the organization's subcontractor management methods to the program for which they were currently bidding. In a sense, these thematic headings are the primary vehicles for driving home the section's message, stimulating the reader to continue reading, and for swaying the evaluators to the bidder's point of view or solution to the customer's problem.

Once thematic headings have been created, theme statements must be devised. Their purpose is to summarize and provide an overview of the section's contents. They must be concrete, concise, factual, readable, action-oriented, and reflect the proposal strategy. Theme statements contain the section's critical message that will capture the evaluators' attention and, at the same time, hammer home to them the bidder's selling point [6].

The headline noted above, for example, was supported by the following theme statements:

> As a major C^3 prime contractor, we are experienced in the handling of major subcontractors. Table 1.2-1 summarizes our approach to the areas of concern that our experience tells us need to be addressed in the management of subcontractors for the [program]. Our subcontract planning, selection, and management techniques are those that have been developed, refined and proved over a long history at similar contracts, such as [related programs].

These statements were then followed with facts and points in a descending order of importance (i.e., the most important facts or points first and the least important last) to support the claims the seller was making about subcontract management.

Proposal Presentation Strategy

The presentation strategy formats and organizes the proposal so that it helps sell the bidder's solution or approach to the buyer's problem. *Presentation*, as used here, means the overall appearance of the proposal: illustrations and headings; cover and page stock; colors; and the like. Each of these aspects must be carefully selected for maximum effect upon the evaluators and to build maximum credibility for the proposal. Excess cost or the appearance of excess cost in the presentation should be avoided.

The proposal manager should consider the merits of using a modular format whereby the proposal is divided into discrete topics. Each topic or module is presented on two pages with text on the left page and artwork on the right. The

Key Issues	Strategies	Tactics
a. It seems clear that we do not enjoy any competitive edge over the competition with [customer]. As a matter of fact, we may be in worse shape reputation-wise than the competition.	a. Illustrate our past performance everywhere we possibly can and not just confined to the "boilerplate" section of the proposal.	a. Several entries in columns (2) and (3) (above) address this issue.
b. We may be viewed as a black-box house, but not necessarily a good systems house.	b. Show we have rounded out our skills with two other respected and complementary team members.	b. Specifically, a total systems solution and how we will validate or change it.
	• Demonstrate [program] wherever possible where we have put together a team composed of old [related program] "smarts" and "new blood."	• Demonstrate our analytical and system engineering and operational analysis capability by detailing as specifically as we can—taking the evaluator by the hand—to show him how we arrived at solutions at the end of the exercise to form the understanding of the problems we show at the beginning.
	• Present [program] as a "communications problem" not a data processing problem. Does [the client] want a data processing house to solve its communications problem? Or does it want a communications house to solve it?	

Fig. 4. This excerpt from a list of key issues illustrates the method for translating issues into tactics.

"river raft" format might also be suitable, whereby the proposal text flows continuously with artwork dispersed at irregular intervals. Both formats are illustrated in Fig. 5.

Illustrations are more than space fillers or afterthoughts. Writers should think of them as part of the message or, in some instances, the message itself. Illustrations and their captions should be conceived with the same care as narratives because they can have the same or greater impact as narratives.

The proposal manager should look over previous proposals, especially for the way thematic headings and theme statements are written and positioned for each section and subsection. Are they written to catch the readers' attention and challenge them to read on for more details? Do the headings and theme statements capture essential information? Do they permit the reader to selectively skim the proposal? And what of the captions for illustrations? Do they convey a message and, thereby, help convey the proposal's message?

Selecting the proper cover and page stock is the responsibility of the proposal manager and the technical publications representative, possibly the proposal's head editor. For example, high-gloss, coated stock can interfere with reading. Substituting dull-coated stock is a reasonable alternative if lighting might be a problem for the evaluators. Colors, in particular, must be pleasing to the eye and, thereby, enhance the credibility of the proposal. Overall, the choice of colors must create a balanced, harmonious effect that appeals to the evaluators' aesthetic sense and, hence, their perception of the proposal's credibility. The choice of colors must make all submissions for the same program stand out as unique and immediately recognizable as the product of one organization.

Credibility is an important aspect of persuasive communication. Not only does the physical appearance of the proposal build credibility but so does the "appearance" of the argument on the printed page, including headings, thematic statements, and paragraph organization. For example, the proposal manager and the editors must decide early in the proposal development cycle whether they will use an ascending (climactic) or a descending (anticlimactic) order for the arguments being communicated. Each order has its merits. The ascending order captures the readers' attention and, by the use of dynamic language, builds receptivity for the most important argument that follows. The anticlimactic order, which is structured like a newspaper report, immediately captures the reader's attention and interest, and gives the evaluators the section's key message. The anticlimactic order is an effective structure because it provides essential information, such as a conclusion, recommendation, or resolution to an unresolved issue. Evaluators get tired of reading every word of every section of the proposals they are evaluating. The seller can help them by providing key information in capsule form—as a visual device to gain their attention so they focus on the important ideas—at the beginning of a section, gaining extra points as a result.

In addition, the proposal manager and chief editor should consider a "writing strategy" for the writers to follow. This strategy provides the primary means for implementing the proposal volume and section strategies. The writers can also use the writing strategy as a guide for the thematic headings, theme statements, and narratives they will produce. It should also help them avoid the pitfall of being technically arrogant, which could lead the evaluators to believe the writers are sloppy thinkers and, therefore, do not understand the needs of the customer. Writers can destroy credibility when they adopt a technically arrogant tone or write at a level that is too complex for the evaluators. However, they can build credibility when they communicate in words for which the evaluators share common meanings.

The proposal manager might even consider using a personal computer-based software program that allows writers to periodically compute the readability level of text using the Flesch–Kincaid formula (DoD MIL-M-48784B), the Flesch formula, or the Fog formula. Although readability indexes are not the solution to awkward writing, they can help writers better match their narratives to the reading capabilities of evaluators; that is, if one has or can guess that information.

Review Strategy

Any major proposal development effort includes several different reviews conducted by specially constituted teams. Conducting these periodic reviews can help a bidder improve the chances of winning. A number of sound reasons support the need for these reviews. For example, U.S. Government procurement agencies report that approximately 75% of the proposals they receive and evaluate are nonresponsive or inadequate; 15% are barely adequate; and only 10% can be properly considered in the zone of consideration. In many

Modular Format | **River Raft Format**

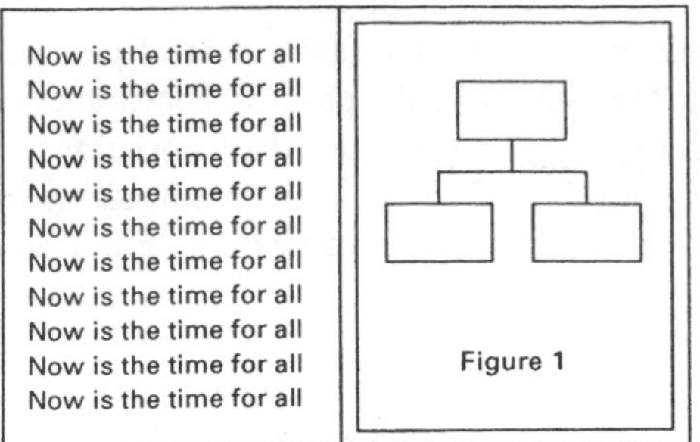

Text on left page and illustrations on right

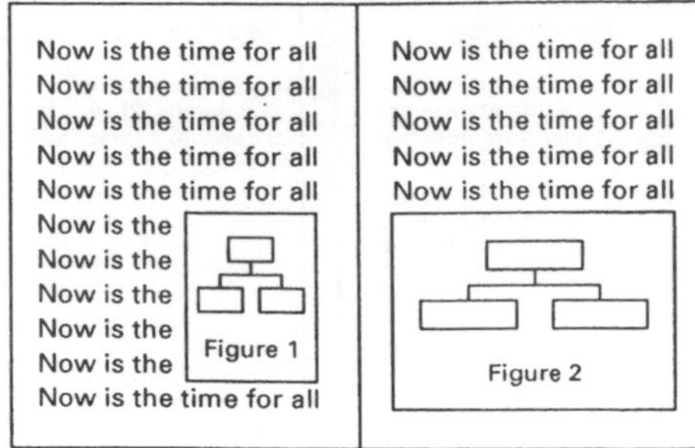

Integrated text and illustrations

Fig. 5. Either format is equally effective for proposals.

TABLE I
THESE REVIEWS ARE TYPICAL FOR LARGE SYSTEM ENGINEERING PROJECTS

Type of Review	Purpose	When Scheduled	Participants	What is Reviewed
Strategy	Do we have a winning strategy?	Before kick-off	Marketing; proposal management team, review board	Win strategy document
Storyboards and outlines	Review contents, tone, and emphasis	During the first ten days of proposal development	Author; proposal management team; review board; editors; illustrators	Storyboards and outlines
System design	Evaluate design and approach	Design freeze-point	Proposal team; review board; technical review committee; proposal management team	Proposed design baseline; management plans and approaches
Review board	To "score" draft proposal	When complete draft proposal available	Review board	Draft proposal; review board scores proposal and makes suggestions
Cost reviews	To establish proposed price	Initial (after baseline freeze); final management review (before submission)	Senior management and staff; proposal management team	Cost estimates
Final management review	To determine if proposal should be submitted; establish a price	End of proposal development phase	Senior mgr.; business area mgr.; proposal mgr.; technical mgr.; marketing specialist; estimating mgr.; contracts administrator; other specialized staff	Marketing environment; technical aspects; risk assessment; program management; cost/price; contracts

instances, the buyer must choose on the "least objectionable" rather than the "best" basis.

Unfortunately, many proposal managers consider reviews an added burden to their already overtaxed schedule. However, reviews can be a source of considerable benefit to the proposal manager and the proposal if they are

- held to a reasonable number;
- staffed with knowledgeable people who do their homework;
- conducted at the proper points in the proposal development process to be of some value.

Management is responsible for staffing, organizing, and preparing for the reviews. The proposal manager, however, is responsible for including the reviews in the proposal development schedule and providing reviewers with all the required materials. Table I specifies several types of reviews, their purpose, timing, participants, and the subject of the reviews.

An effective review team understands, appreciates, and assesses all aspects of a proposal, including the adequacy and risks of proposed solutions. Moreover, they offer ways to improve the strategy, organization, and coherence of the proposal's contents. The internal review team simulates the evaluation process conducted by the procurement agency's Source Selection Evaluation Board or, in the case of commercial customers, the process used by an individual or a team. By simulating the customer's evaluation process and by

Volume I **Date** XX–XX–XX

Section Whole Volume **Reviewer** AEW

There is much good material in this volume. To make it a winner, I think we should do four things. These are:

1. Rewrite Section 1.0 (Introduction and Summary) from the customer's point of view. Throughout the proposal we point out that we are in a unique position – having a head start on the [program] and being an [program] associate contractor. The customer is not interested in that. He is interested in what, if any, benefits that fact brings to him. How does it benefit him? Since we know so much about the job, can we not tell him with confidence that we will meet the schedule, the cost goals, the reliability requirements? Can we not assure him a trouble-free contract? Can we not comment on manpower and facilities availability – and show him how the [related program] and [program to be bid] requirements do not overlap? I understand that the schedule is tight. That we could not meet it without a head start. Can we not show him just what the head start is enabling us to do and what the schedule would be if we didn't have it? (throws doubt on the competition capability). My comments on section 1.0 give some suggested words to begin with. Why don't we make a list of the management considerations the customer would address and try to hit them in this summary.
2. The authors of section 1 should read sections 2, 3, and 4 and incorporate significant details from those sections into the program plan discussion.
3. All sections should be edited for the following:
   a. Win strategy items. The individual authors have incorporated a certain amount of drum beating. Any one individual instance of this is not objectionable—but the whole is repetitious and embarrassing.
   b. Duplication. I did not make a list, but I did notice some; e.g., between the Produceability Studies write-up and the one on Equipment Fabrication. There are two other sections on Produceability Considerations.
4. Rewrite subsections 4.1, 4.2, 4.5, 4.10, 4.11, 4.13, and 4.15 to make them specifically applicable to the [program].

Fig. 6. These comments illustrate the level of detail that reviewers should provide.

applying the customer's stated evaluation criteria, the internal review team can score the proposal, detect weaknesses, assess whether the proposal is responsive to the stated criteria, and recommend changes or modifications to correct weaknesses and strengthen the proposal.

The review of the proposal win strategy is particularly important to the proposal team; therefore, it must be reviewed by a proposal review board (i.e., sometimes referred to as a Tiger Team or Red Team). The purpose of this review, which is conducted in time for the proposal "kickoff" meeting, is to permit management to determine whether the proposal manager has devised the best winning strategy and to ensure that the bidder's approach responds to and complies with the customer's requirements. In addition to the regular review team members, other management representatives who participated in the strategizing process, or who have valuable inputs from lessons-learned, may be invited to attend and to participate.

Ideally, the win strategy should include the following elements:

- Tone
- Issues to emphasize and deemphasize
- Guidelines on how to interpret the RFP
- Bidder's strengths and weaknesses
- Other items the proposal team can use to guide and direct them as they plan and write their individual proposal sections.

Because the strategy statements represent the initial proposal baseline, they should be detailed and well documented. The statements, of course, must be tied in with the evaluation criteria as stated in the RFP. The more complex these criteria are, the more critical is this formalized assessment.

The proposal manager is responsible for arranging and conducting the win strategy review. As a minimum, the following individuals should attend the review sessions:

- Proposal manager
- Business area (or operations) manager
- Technical manager
- Volume leaders
- Proposal review team
- Marketing representative
- Business development manager
- Proposal development manager.

The reviewers should address the following questions:

- Do we know who the real customer is?
- Who are the evaluators and what are their biases?
- Does our win strategy cover all key issues?
- Do we know our strengths and weaknesses? Do we capitalize on our strengths and neutralize our weaknesses?
- Who are our competitors? What are they offering? What are their strengths and weaknesses?
- Do we understand the evaluation criteria? Does our strategy focus on the important criteria?
- What is the central message to be conveyed in the proposal?
- Do we link features with benefits?

Answering these and other questions will result in an overall proposal strategy, which will be distributed to the proposal team. However, the final version will evolve as the proposal development effort continues and as more information comes in from marketing representatives. Indeed, the development might require several reviews, and each is well worth the time spent.

The review team not only reads, evaluates, and scores the proposal, but also annotates it, prepares deficiency reports, debriefs the proposal team, helps team members rewrite their sections, reviews the rewrites, and follows up to ensure that the deficiencies are corrected. Fig. 6 is one of nine pages that a thoughtful, knowledgeable reviewer submitted.

In addition, early reviews conducted by the review team can result in the following considerations:

- exploring teaming possibilities to bolster weaknesses;
- establishing a customer contact plan;
- establishing a plan to present briefings to the customer to solicit reactions to the bidder's preferred approach and to trade ideas;
- establishing plans to influence the RFP;
- identifying documents the bidder does not have but which will influence the bidder's strategy.

Some Final Words

This article describes several strategies that comprise an overall blueprint for a winning proposal strategy. Obviously, they are not the only strategies a proposal manager can use; others might work equally well. However, the methods presented here offer a deliberate and thoughtful scheme for planning the proposal development effort so that customer-critical issues are identified and addressed throughout the proposal via an overall strategy translated into detailed substrategies.

Planning a proposal is not easy. Consequently, the proposal manager must think of strategies as more than simply a few paragraphs stating the key factors based on a competitive assessment, customer requirements, and the organization's capability to do the job. The overall proposal strategy is more comprehensive and wide ranging. It emphasizes the many factors that contribute to winning, including, among others, the extraordinary interpersonal skills a proposal manager must exercise to motivate the proposal team. Without the proposal team's cooperation and respect, a proposal manager's strategies, no matter how carefully crafted, might be ignored in what could turn out to be a losing, and expensive, proposal effort.

Acknowledgment

The author wishes to thank F. Giggey, proposal manager extraordinaire, for his guidance on this concept.

References

[1] F. Giggey, Ed., *Lessions Learned for [program]*. 1980.

[2] J. M. Beveridge and E. J. Velton, *Creating Superior Proposals*. Talent, OR: J. M. Beveridge, 1978.

[3] Shipley Associates, *Managing Winning Proposals*. Bountiful, UT: Shipley, 1987.

[4] R. A. Barakat, "Storyboarding can help your proposal," *IEEE Trans. Professional Commun.*, vol. 1, pp. 20–25, 1989; also R. A. Barakat, "Writing to win new business," in *Project Management*, to be published; see also several articles on proposal development in *IEEE Trans. Professional Commun.*, vol. 2, 1983, especially J. M. Killingsworth, "A bibliography on proposal writing," pp. 79–83. For a detailed description of the proposal development process, see H. Kerzner and H. Thamhain, *Project Management Operating Guidelines: Directives, Procedures, and Forms*. New York: Van Nostrand Reinhold, especially ch. 7, "Bid Proposals," pp. 101–202, 1986.

Robert A. Barakat is a graduate of the University of Pennsylvania, the University of Texas, El Paso, and Suffolk University, Boston, MA.

He is Director of Training and Staff Development for Arthur D. Little, Inc., Cambridge, MA. His current research and business interests include proposal development, cross-cultural management and communication training, business graphics, and team-building techniques for multicultural tasks groups.

Clarification Questions That Work

ANNETTE D. REILLY

Abstract—**In technical marketing to the government, the purpose for writing clarification questions is to improve the firm's chances of preparing a winning proposal. Written clarification questions are a valuable means of obtaining information from the potential customer once the RFP has been released. Well-worded clarification questions can also persuade the government to accept one approach and to suspect competitors' approaches. Since the government releases all written clarification questions and answers, they provide valuable competitive information to all bidders. Thus, clarification questions must simultaneously present a position to the government, and conceal it from competitors.**

WITHIN THE GOVERNMENT PROCUREMENT cycle, clarification questions are an important step in developing a proposal (figure 1). Potential bidders submit clarification questions to the government as soon as they have reviewed the government's Request for Proposal (RFP). They may continue to submit additional questions to the government until their proposals are submitted, or as specified in the RFP.

The government may also ask clarification questions, but at a later stage in the procurement process. After proposals are submitted, the government issues clarification requests and deficiency reports (CRs and DRs) to obtain clarifications and corrections in the vendors' proposals. However, this article considers clarification questions only as a technical marketing technique used by potential contractors.

The potential contractor's purpose for submitting clarification questions is to improve its chances of preparing a winning proposal. Since contact between the government and vendors is limited after the RFP is released (FAR 15.612 (e)(2)), written questions are a valuable means of obtaining information from the potential customer, either in the form of amendments to the RFP, or as direct answers to the questions.

The opportunity to ask clarification questions in a negotiated procurement produces a complex rhetorical situation. Understanding the rhetorical situation and applying strategic writing and editing guidelines will produce better clarification questions. This article briefly discusses the rhetorical factors influencing clarification questions. It then presents editorial guidelines to improve them. These guidelines are also useful in preparing questions for interviews, marketing presentations, legal proceedings, and other situations.

Annette Reilly works for Martin Marietta Data Systems in Greenbelt, MD, as a documentation and proposal manager for systems integration projects.

RHETORICAL SITUATION

The immediate audience for clarification questions is the government agency that issued the RFP. Reading the RFP and comparing it to any previous drafts or other RFPs the agency has issued adds to a firm's understanding of its audience. The firm needs to consider the audience's strengths and biases in technical areas, its efficiency, and its relative interest in the technical, management, and cost factors of the procurement.

With this audience profile in mind, the immediate purpose for clarification questions is to obtain information that was not in the RFP. Clarification questions usually seek information in the following areas:

- Does the RFP lack information needed to prepare a good proposal?
- Are there discrepancies between sections of the RFP that hinder preparing a consistent response?
- Does the RFP limit the solution to one vendor's product?
- Does the RFP require outmoded technology or technology beyond the state of the art at fixed prices?

Thus, the purpose of asking clarification questions is not only to obtain information, but also to persuade the government to favor one approach and to draw away from competitors' approaches.

However, the government is not the sole audience for clarification questions. In the interest of fairness, the government contracting officer distributes all clarification questions and their answers to all bidders. Thus, the clarification questions will be read by competitors, and a prudent company will weigh carefully what sensitive information its questions disclose to them. Conversely, although a firm is unlikely to see its competitors' proposals, it will see their questions. The proposal team can learn more about the competition by studying the complete question and answer packet:

- How many serious competitors are there?
- Do the questions suggest that the competitors misunder-

Reprinted from *IEEE Trans. Prof. Comm.*, vol. 31, no. 2, pp. 93–95, June 1988.

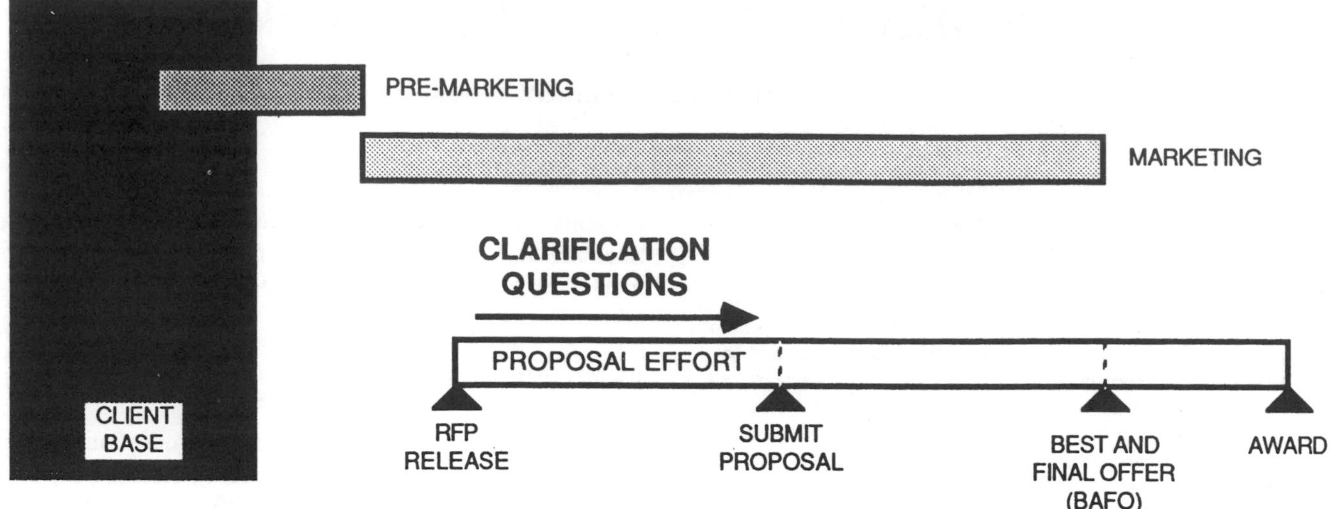

Figure 1. The Business Development Process

stand the requirements, or are they sophisticated analysts?

- Do the revisions the competitors want in the RFP suggest weaknesses in their approach?
- Did no other bidder question a requirement that is difficult for the proposal team to meet, indicating a weakness in its approach?

In short, clarification questions must simultaneously present a firm's position to the government, and conceal it from its competitors. Skillful editing can improve the chances that the questions will achieve their purposes.

EDITING GUIDELINES FOR CLARIFICATION QUESTIONS

In many respects, the task of preparing a set of clarification questions is similar to other editorial projects. The editor or proposal manager assigns members of the proposal team to review all sections of the RFP, collates and edits their questions, and arranges for internal reviews of the package. For competitive reasons, questions are usually submitted on plain paper as an attachment to a cover letter. The questions are arranged in order of RFP reference, or grouped by topic if they are voluminous. Each question needs references to an RFP paragraph and page number; the government is prone to ignore questions with incorrect or missing references.

Beyond this general procedure, here are some specific guidelines for editing clarification questions.

Ask Direct, Concise Questions

Edit to pare each question to the essentials; omit lengthy explanations. Circumlocutory indirect requests are easily overlooked, or condensed by the government so that the real question is evaded. Reword comments into questions. For example, the technical staff may submit items like "Section C.6.4.2.5 requests an unreasonable manpower requirement." The editor needs to find out what staffing level the firm considers reasonable, why the firm wants that level, and what question will persuade the government to amend the requirement. The question might be worded, "May the offeror determine the level of staffing required to meet the 4-hour response requirement?"

Don't Repeat the Requirements

Restating the RFP wastes space. Summarizing the RFP runs the risks of misinterpreting it or of drawing competitors' attention to an advantageous interpretation. Avoid preaching to the government about what the requirements mean.

Ask One Question at a Time

Burying multiple questions in a paragraph makes it unlikely that each question will be answered. Moreover, a rapid-fire series of short questions in one paragraph, in an adversarial style, may not endear a firm to the customer.

Use the Indicative, Not the Subjunctive

Suppose the question is asked, "Would the government consider the use of offsite test facilities?" Even if the answer is yes, the firm has no assurance that the government will actually accept the offsite approach after hypothetically considering it. An improved wording is, "Are offsite test facilities acceptable to the government?" Or, more subtly, "Will travel costs to offsite test facilities be reimbursed by the government?"

Don't Disclose the Solution

Watch out for questions that explain a technical approach. For example, the question, "Can the requirement for 24-hour coverage be met by equipping an Acme Corporation technician with a beeper?" lets competitors know that the firm doesn't plan to bid three technicians on 8-hour shifts. Also, never mention the company or product name in a question; the government is sometimes remiss in editing them out of the response package.

Don't Disclose Weaknesses

The comment, "Our operating system does not provide the automatic time-out feature," is unlikely to win any change in the requirement, and pinpoints a vulnerability in the solution. Requests for softening requirements are more effective if they point out that the requested feature is either commercially unavailable or vendor-specific.

Justify the Request from the Customer's Point of View

The changes and clarifications you request should be justifiable on the grounds of reducing cost, simplifying evaluation, allowing full and open competition, and the like. Good questions show the government that the firm thoroughly understands the requirements and intends to provide the best solution.

Ask for a Specific Answer

A general question may produce a great deal of unwanted information. Asking, "What does the government mean by 'dynamic reconfiguration' capabilities?" may produce a wish list that far exceeds what a firm has to offer. Instead, the question can be worded, "Which of the following dynamic reconfiguration capabilities does the government require?" taking care to cite only those that the firm is prepared to provide—and which its competitors may not have.

Include the Desired Answer in the Question

Avoid either/or questions. "Should configuration drawings be provided for all 654 sites, or in generic form for each of the five standard configurations?" can be asked only if either answer is acceptable. Otherwise, ask, "Should configuration drawings be submitted for each of the five standard configurations?" Rather than asking, "How many copies of the documentation would the Navy like?" the question should ask, "Should the offeror submit two copies of all referenced documentation?"

Don't Ask Needless Questions

Weigh each question carefully. Is it worth the risk of alerting others to pitfalls in the RFP by asking about them? Can the firm justifiably proceed on its best judgment of what the government wants? Or will a mistaken assumption cause more trouble later? When in doubt, remember that the only dumb question is an unasked question.

Applying these guidelines asks more of an editor than a cursory check of page references and pronoun antecedents; it means substantive revisions of draft clarification questions. The guidelines are more readily applied when a firm has a well-developed technical approach and a clearly understood competitive position, and when the technical editor is familiar with the firm's approach and strategy.

Although this ideal situation is rarely achieved, careful scrutiny of clarification questions and responses is even more valuable when the firm's marketing position is not as strong as might be desired. An astute editor can alert management to possible problems by asking questions about draft clarification questions. Anticipating the answers to clarification questions before submitting them allows a firm to assess alternative approaches, perceive its comparative weaknesses, and determine how to exploit its strengths. As a byproduct, the process of reviewing the draft questions can itself contribute to building a productive proposal team early in the marketing cycle. Thus, clarification questions are an important step in technical marketing, for they contribute to

- Developing a technical approach
- Understanding the customer and the competition
- Building the proposal team

Good clarification questions can lead to a winning proposal—the ultimate step in the new business cycle.

Proposals: Write to Win

CLARK E. BECK

Abstract—**Knowing ahead of time what a proposal evaluator looks for will help increase your chance of writing a winning proposal. Winning proposals contain (1) a proposed line of investigation, (2) a method of approach to the problem, (3) recommended changes (if appropriate), (4) logical work units, and (5) estimated completion time. Other tips include writing directly and specifically and making the proposal complete and easy to read.**

ARE you involved in any facet of technical proposal writing? If so, knowing how it will be evaluated might suggest how to write to enhance its chance of success. This article is written from the perspective of one who requests and evaluates technical proposals.

Winning proposals require the best of all four forms of writing: exposition, description, narration, and persuasion. As an instrument of persuasion, it must be aimed directly at the interests and objectives of the customer. Company interests, prejudices, and conflicting goals must be avoided in the proposal. The writer must achieve a customer-oriented tone and resist a natural tendency to offer personal views.

Only a small percentage of proposals are winners in technical circles—as in social circles. But proposal preparation represents no small investment of time, money, and facilities. Some degree of success must be achieved to justify continued investments in proposal writing.

Research-and-development proposals are among the most difficult to write, and often they are the most difficult to evaluate. The reason? The limited knowledge available—for both the writer and the evaluator. In early research work there is usually no universally agreed and predetermined best way or approach. Both the preparation and the evaluation are based on predictions and estimates, usually with a host of unknown complicated factors. Writers and evaluators understandably feel that theirs is a difficult task.

PROPOSAL REQUEST

The request for proposal (RFP) includes a section that outlines the work for which the proposal is solicited. This section is most important to the proposal writer. Often called the "technical exhibit," it offers the *only* specific guidance and criteria about the work the winner will do. Your proposal *must* respond to this section better than all other competitors. Keep in mind that (1) the work described in the technical exhibit *will* be done (there is no need for your proposal to convince anyone that it should be done) and (2) *someone* will do the work. Your proposal must persuade the evaluators that *you* should be the one to do it. Sometimes a problem develops at this point. The possible problem is a combination of communication and understanding. The technical exhibit was written by one who presumably knows what is wanted (the result) but may not know for sure the best way to achieve it. If it had been known, the request would not be for a research proposal but for hardware. A list of specifications would have been provided with the request for you to design, assemble, fabricate, or build the item to satisfy the given specifications.

Manuscript received August 2, 1982.

The author is a technical manager in the Flight Dynamics Laboratory, Wright-Patterson Air Force Base, OH 45433; (513) 255-2274.

If the technical exhibit is not well written or if you, as a proposal writer, misinterpret some part of that technical exhibit, the result could be disastrous. You may write an excellent proposal—offering the best possible solution—but for the wrong problem!

Don't read the technical exhibit just once and charge into the proposal preparation. Study the technical exhibit to see if there could be something more (or different) really asked for. The sender and the receiver may be on different wavelengths.

PROPOSAL CONTENTS

A technical exhibit might have more than one possible interpretation; your proposal does not have that luxury! A technical proposal must be specific and complete. A competitor with a more specific proposal will make you look bad. If your proposal is incomplete or vague, the evaluators are likely to consider you incapable.

Your technical proposal has to stand alone as advocate and defender during the evaluation process. Only information contained in the proposal is going to be considered during the evaluation. If your company is recognized as the leader in the specific technology needed to solve the problem, state that fact, with justification in the proposal to increase your chance of being favorably reviewed.

Several acceptable proposal formats exist; however, any good research proposal includes

1. *A proposed line of investigation* Brief but specific. The customer is entitled to know exactly what steps you plan to take. Restate the specific problem and define the specific solution you expect to offer.
2. *A method of approach to the problem* An especially important element in research. Often the probability of

Reprinted from *IEEE Trans. Prof. Comm.*, vol. PC-26, no. 2, pp. 56–57, June 1983.

success depends on how you approach the problem. Convince the evaluators that you plan to spend the money you will receive in a manner that offers the highest probability of success.

3. *Recommended changes* Perhaps not an obvious proposal inclusion. In research work, however, your company experts may know (or infer) that a part of the work requested in the technical exhibit has already been done and will contribute nothing to the solution of the problem. Also, some work that needs to be done may have been omitted from the technical exhibit. In these cases, the evaluators will appreciate your recommendations to improve the effort or decrease the cost. After all, one evaluator will probably be assigned to monitor the program; its degree of success will affect his or her future.
4. *Logical work units* A list of logically sequenced phases with reasons why they optimize chances of success.
5. *Estimated completion time* A timetable to indicate when results will be available and to define the proposed expenditure of funds and labor.

Your proposal should not merely offer to conduct an investigation in accordance with the technical exhibit. Even unqualified companies can say "yes, yes" and still not be able to produce. Clearly state in the proposal what, how, why, and when things will be done.

TECHNICAL EVALUATION

Once submitted, your proposal is on its own. In the evaluation arena each proposal is examined thoroughly and a winner selected. Rarely is there a prize for "place" or "show."

The criteria for evaluation certainly vary, but two broad categories cover much of the technical information of interest to evaluators: (1) qualifications of the organization and (2) the scientific/engineering approach.

Qualifications

1. *Specific experience* List the specific, related, and pertinent experience of the company and the personnel who will perform the proposed work.
2. *Technical organization* Consider three aspects of organization:
   (a) How the proposal is organized. Often the proposal format and appearance indicate how reports will be presented.
   (b) How the personnel, resources, and facilities working on the program will be organized.
   (c) How the company is organized. Do the researchers on this program have access to top management in the company?
3. *Special equipment and facilities* Indicate that all necessary equipment and facilities needed to complete the program are available.
4. *Analytical capacity* Ensure that adequate computational and analytical skills necessary for this program are available.
5. *Level of effort and support* Be sure that enough person-hours will be dedicated to this program. Is the mix of the time and skills proper to complete the program? Will the company adequately support its personnel working on this program? How much of the total program effort must be obtained from other divisions of the company—or subcontracted from other companies?

Scientific/Engineering Approach

1. *Understanding of the problem* The proposal must reflect a good understanding of the problem. The first step in the solution of any problem is a complete and in-depth understanding of the real problem.
2. *Soundness of approach* There may be more than one way to approach the problem. The proposal must show justification and sound technical reasons for the one offered.
3. *Compliance with requirements* The technical exhibit often calls for specific requirements such as reporting schedule and format. The proposal should indicate clearly that all such requirements will be satisfied.
4. *Special technical factors* If there are any special benefits that favor your company's doing the proposed work, mention them in the proposal. When two proposals are essentially equal, consideration of items in this category could make a difference.

SUMMARY

Advice for writing a winning proposal includes

1. Be sure you understand the problem.
2. Address the problem directly; be specific.
3. Write descriptively.
4. Make the proposal easy to read.
5. Make the proposal complete and self-supporting.
6. Include all pertinent information; leave nothing for the evaluators to assume (they aren't supposed to, anyway!).

Finally, recognize that the evaluators will infer from the quality of writing in your proposal the quality to expect in a final report.

Commentary

Broadening Employment Horizons: Transferring Proposal Writing Skills from For-Profit to Nonprofit Organizations

Sherry Shebley Hamilton

Abstract—**When faced with the need to seek employment, technical communicators with expertise in proposal writing may want to extend their job-seeking horizons beyond the for-profit world and also consider nonprofit organizations as potential employers. The skills required of proposal writers and the situations in which they work are similar whether the writer is employed by a for-profit corporation or a nonprofit organization such as a private college or social service charity. In developing proposals, writers employed in either setting use similar proposal formats, rely on good interpersonal skills while working under deadline pressures, and work with teams of experts from a variety of fields. The article concludes with information on careers with nonprofit organizations, including typical salaries, benefits, and job titles.**

CONSIDER the following information about the American workplace:

- Each year, 500 000 families in the United States relocate because of job transfers. In 85% of the transfers, the woman is the "trailing spouse," who must find employment in the new location [1].
- "Despite the economic recovery, massive downsizings continue at one brand-name behemoth after another. Rarely a week passes without the announcement of yet more cutbacks .... In the year's [1994's] first quarter, employers announced an average of 3106 cutbacks per day" [2].
- From 1990 to 1993, American corporations saw a $22 billion decline in federal defense contracts and purchases of hard goods such as electronics and communication equipment, aircraft, space systems, ships, and weapons [3]. Since 1991, layoffs at just four of the country's major defense contractors have totaled more than 65 000 workers [2].
- "Many technical communicators have already been affected [by cutbacks] or know someone who has been affected by decisions to downsize. Some even suspect that they will be the next ones to fall victim to such decisions, even though the field's future appears promising" [4].

Manuscript received May 1995; revised October 1995.
The author is with Boise State University, Boise, ID 83725 USA.
Publisher Item Identifier S 0361-1434(96)03653-3.

When it comes to careers, Americans must constantly be prepared for change, whether by choice or by change in a spouse's or one's own work situation. This article outlines a career option for technical communicators who specialize in proposal writing and who are or will be seeking new employment.

During the past 11 years, I have worked as a proposal writer for nonprofit organizations, including two private colleges and two social service agencies. In comparing the proposal writing process in for-profit corporations and nonprofit organizations, I find the two situations to be similar, such that a writer with a corporate background should be able to transfer his or her skills successfully to a nonprofit setting.

Despite recent declines in government spending for defense and the concomitant layoffs at major defense contractors, corporate proposal writers can find new job-hunting territory by looking into employment opportunities with nonprofit organizations. Nationwide, there are more than 3600 colleges and universities and over 6000 social service, health/medical, and cultural nonprofits. Because the bulk of these organizations employ proposal writers or fund raisers for whom proposal writing is a significant component of their work, nonprofits provide a ready job market that many technical communicators may not have explored. In the following pages, I will:

1) describe proposal writing in a corporate setting
2) compare proposal writing in a nonprofit organization with that in a corporation
3) outline the benefits, salaries, and job titles typically available to proposal writers in nonprofit organizations

Proposal Writing in a For-Profit Corporation

Researchers in technical communication have written extensively about proposal writing in corporations. "In business and industry, no kind of technical document is more important than the proposal. Any company that must seek out and

Reprinted from *IEEE Trans. Prof. Comm.*, vol. PC-39, no. 2, pp. 99–102, June 1996.

win contracts depends on effective proposals for its very survival" [5]. "Proposals are the bread and butter of many engineering firms" [6]. Further, as companies face growing competition for government contracts, they are emphasizing the qualities traditionally associated with effective proposal writing—a focus on audience needs [7]; the use of language that is persuasive, direct, and unexaggerated [6], [9]; and the segmentation of material into easily comprehended units [10].

Because of the importance corporations place on effective proposal writing, this genre is covered in many technical writing texts and courses. Freed and Roberts examine the varied proposal formats presented in 40 technical communication textbooks for college students, derive a generic proposal format, and describe three basics types of proposals—analytic, service/product, and bids [10]. Hays defines common proposal terms in a glossary as a reference for teachers of proposal writing [11]. Norman and Young describe methods for incorporating the peer-review process into proposal writing instruction [12], while Werner suggests using an RFP (request for proposals) as a means of helping students understand proposal development in an actual job setting [13]. Butler outlines a four-week program to teach proposal writing as a process of developing and reworking ideas to reach a solution, rather than first posing a solution, then developing supporting evidence [5].

The proposal writing process in corporate settings, particularly collaborative writing efforts, has been the subject of much study as well. Proposal writers often work in teams or serve as leader/editors for writing teams composed of engineers and other knowledge experts [14], [15]. These teams may be as small as 3 or 4 members, but on large projects may involve 40 to more than 100 writers. As one veteran proposal writer observed, "It's like writing a book with 25 authors" [6]. Frequently, this collaboration occurs in a "pressure cooker" atmosphere under the constraint of fast-approaching deadlines. Moreover, proposal writers serving as team leaders and editors "generally ha[ve] no formal authority over the individuals assigned to the team, so resolving conflicts requires good interpersonal skills." Team members "must elect to cooperate" [14].

McIsaac and Aschauer have conducted what is perhaps the most thorough study ever of proposal writing in a corporate setting. They spent eight months observing the proposal writing process and interviewing 18 employees of a Silicon Valley engineering firm (given the pseudonym AJI) that seeks and implements government defense contracts. In addition to reporting on collaboration at the engineering firm, McIsaac and Aschauer [6] reported several other findings:

- **The scope of the proposals written.** AJI engineers developed proposals as long as 1000 pages in 30–45 days, working 12- to 15-hour days during this time. The company spent \$500 000 to develop an average-length proposal and up to \$1 million for a large one; however, the reward for such an investment could be a contract worth \$30 million or more.
- **The traits of the writing.** In-house proposal evaluators at AJI found that engineers were effective in describing the technical aspects of a system, but that some were suspicious of persuasive writing, believing that a "design should win on its own merits" (p. 550). In early proposal drafts, evaluators also observed a lack of attention to the audience.
- **The storyboard writing strategy.** AJI writing teams used storyboards in the initial phases of developing proposals. First, team members selected the portions of the RFP to which they would respond, wrote their ideas on large scribble sheets, then pinned these to the walls. Second, they circulated around the room and wrote suggestions for improvements on blank sheets pinned next to the scribble sheets. Third, writers reviewed the suggestions and incorporated them into their writing. The storyboard technique fostered collaboration and helped writers reduce the number and improve the quality of early drafts.
- **The proposal review process.** AJI developed an independent "Red Team" to review each proposal in its latter stage. A typical Red Team member would be a senior engineer who had the technical expertise to judge a proposal critically and who had written several proposals. The Red Team used both objective and qualitative measures to score proposals and could demand that sections with low scores be reworked before the proposal was submitted.

Proposal Writing in Nonprofit Organizations

While technical communication researchers have examined proposal writing at length in for-profit corporations, most of the writing about proposals in nonprofit organizations has been of the "how-to" variety. However, my purpose here is to compare the proposal writing process in for-profit and nonprofit settings and to describe nonprofit career possibilities for proposal writers seeking employment.

Proposals are as important to nonprofit organizations as they are to corporations. For colleges and universities, grant-winning proposals mean that new equipment to upgrade laboratories can be purchased, new research facilities built, and new curricula launched. For hospitals, grants help to purchase modern equipment such as MRI's or to add facilities such as a new children's wing. For social service agencies, grants can mean the difference between providing meals to half of the needy people in a neighborhood or to all who are eligible for assistance.

Corporations seeking contracts and nonprofit organizations seeking grants use similar proposal formats. For corporations and nonprofit organizations, government RFP's often dictate the form of a proposal. In these situations, proposals may run into the hundreds of pages, as was common at the engineering firm AJI [6]. Depending upon the preferences of foundation and corporate grantors, nonprofits may follow an RFP-type format requiring answers to specific questions. However, nonprofits most frequently use much shorter proposals written in the form of a letter. Freed estimates that over 90% of the proposals written in corporate settings are also in letter format, ranging from 5–15 pages in length [16].

Proposal writers in both corporate and nonprofit settings work in a high-stress atmosphere of meeting constant deadlines. Government RFP's for nonprofits are often released only 30–45 days before the deadline for submitting a proposal, so these writers may work 12- to 15-hour days as well. Proposal writers at nonprofits may be able to schedule projects with more certainty than are corporate proposal writers because foundation and corporate grantors tend to set deadlines that occur at the same time each year. However, a former colleague of mine once finished drafting a proposal as she sat next to her husband's hospital bed in order to meet a foundation deadline.

Collaborative proposal writing is as common in nonprofit organizations as it is in corporations. For example, during the five years I wrote proposals at private colleges, I worked with several teams of faculty members to prepare proposals seeking grants for computers and scientific equipment or to develop new curricula. These teams usually comprised 3–5 faculty members from one discipline, but the teams could be as large as 15–20 faculty members representing such disciplines as art, biology, English, history, mathematics, physics, and computer science. Although I was responsible for guiding and completing the proposal writing process, I had no authority over other team members and relied on negotiation and other interpersonal communication skills to maintain cooperative working relationships.

Reviewing and editing proposals is perhaps not as formal a process at nonprofits as at companies such as AJI with its Red Team editing approach [6]. In my experience at private colleges and social service agencies, the chief executive officer of the organization was usually the final stop for a proposal before submission to a grantor. Before reaching this stage, faculty team members, the provost, and my department head had all reviewed the proposal for accuracy, persuasiveness, and attention to audience characteristics.

As observed with engineers at AJI, faculty members I worked with—particularly those from scientific disciplines—were suspicious, to some degree, of persuasive language. On occasion, faculty members have accused me of writing puffery when my goal was to point out the strengths of the college's academic programs. Once I asked a biology faculty member to help me write a paragraph to persuade a donor of the importance of supporting an on-campus natural history museum. Like some AJI engineers, he apparently believed that a project should win support "on its own merits" [6] and stated that the need for the museum was as obvious as the need for city parks.

Careers for Proposal Writers in Nonprofit Organizations

Proposal writers at colleges and universities and other nonprofit organizations enjoy benefits and salaries comparable to those available to technical communicators, including proposal writers working in corporate settings. Ninety-three percent of all nonprofits offer their employees medical benefits [17], while 98% of technical communicators reported receiving medical benefits in a 1994 salary survey [18]. In 1994, the median annual salary for directors of corporate and foundation relations (a typical job title for a proposal writer) at all educational institutions was $45 186 [19]. At universities granting doctoral degrees, the median salary for this job title was $57 538 [19]. Top proposal writers at social service, cultural, environmental, and health organizations earned an average of $53 466 [17]. These salary figures compare with an average salary of $51 125 for a technical communicator at the senior management level and a median salary approaching $40 000 for all technical communicators [18], [*Chronicle of Philanthropy* 1994, Society for Technical Communication Salary Survey 1994].

As is true of all salary surveys, individual salaries vary widely depending upon the size, type, and location of one's employer. In nonprofit organizations, salaries for proposal writers are typically higher at large educational institutions and hospitals than at small social service, environmental, cultural, and health organizations. Geographically, salaries tend to be higher at nonprofits located in the urban areas of the northeastern states and California [18].

The following are some common job titles for proposal writers and fund raisers for whom proposal writing is a significant duty:

- **Director of corporate and foundation relations.** Typical duties include researching grant opportunities available from corporations, foundations, and government agencies; visiting with personnel from these organizations; writing proposals (often in collaboration with faculty members or other subject-matter experts); and writing reports on the use of grant funds. Supervisory duties are often limited to managing volunteers and clerical staff.
- **Grant writer.** Usually this position is entry level and involves researching grant opportunities and writing proposals and funding reports.
- **Director of development.** In larger nonprofits, the director of development may supervise proposal writers and other fund-raising professionals. At smaller nonprofits, the director of development may research grant opportunities and write proposals, in addition to managing special events, direct mail campaigns, and public relations. At educational institutions, the director of development may be known as the director of institutional advancement or the director of college or university relations.

Conclusion

While technical communicators may initially overlook nonprofits as potential employers, the opportunities are rich and varied and should be considered in a job search. In addition to salaries and benefits comparable to those available in corporations, proposal writers in nonprofits may experience a renewed sense of purpose as they help find resources enabling their organizations to fulfill missions of public service.

Technical communicators seeking further information about careers in nonprofit organizations may wish to begin their search by contacting the National Society for Fund Raising Executives (NSFRE), 1101 King Street, Suite 700, Alexandria, VA 22314, (703) 684-0410. The NSFRE has 13 500 members and 125 local chapters nationwide. The organization offers professional education for fund raisers and publishes the *ESS*

Employment Opportunities Newsletter, which is included as an insert in the *NSFRE News*. Published eight times per year, the *NSFRE News* is available at an annual subscription rate of $40 for nonmembers.

The following publications also provide listings of employment opportunities with nonprofits as well as information about current issues in the fund raising profession:

- *Chronicle of Philanthropy*, 1255 23rd Street NW, Washington, DC 20037, subscription rate: $67.50 per year
- *Contributions*, 634 Commonwealth Avenue, Suite 201, Newton Centre, MA 02159, subscription rate: $24 per year
- *Fund Raising Management*, 224 7th Street, Garden City, NY 11530, subscription rate: $54 per year
- *NonProfit Times*, 190 Tamarack Circle, Skillman, NJ 08558, subscription rate: $59 per year
- *Nonprofit World*, 6314 Odana Road, Suite 1, Madison, WI 53719, subscription rate: $79 per year, single copies available for $15

REFERENCES

[1] "Relocation blues," Employee Relocation Council Report 1994 in the *Idaho Statesman*, pp. 1a–2a, Apr. 9, 1995.

[2] "The pain of downsizing," *Business Week*, pp. 60–68, May 9, 1994.

[3] Bureau of the Census, *Statistical Abstract of the United States: 1994*, 114th ed. Washington, DC: U.S. Gov. Printing Office, 1994.

[4] P. M. Smudde, "Downsizing technical communication staff: The risk to corporate success," *Tech. Commun.*, vol. 40, no. 1, pp. 35–36, 1993.

[5] D. R. Butler, "Government projects and teaching the technical proposal," *The Tech. Writing Teacher*, no. 1, pp. 44–51, 1987.

[6] C. M. McIsaac and M.A. Aschauer, "Proposal writing at atherton jordan, inc.: An ethnographic study," *Manag. Commun. Quart.*, vol. 3, no. 4, pp. 527–561, 1990.

[7] M. Cole, "Guiding the reader: Proposals and persuasion," *Tech. Commun.*, vol. 39, no. 1, pp. 53–56, 1992.

[8] R. C. Freed and G. J. Broadhead, "Using high-affect goals in teaching proposal writing," *J. Adv. Composition*, vol. 7, no. 1–2, pp. 131–138, 1987.

[9] T. Whalen, "Improved proposal writing: Unity, coherence, and emphasis," *Bull. Assoc. Business Commun.*, vol. 49, no. 4, pp. 14–15, 1986.

[10] R. C. Freed and D.D. Roberts, "The nature, classification, and generic structure of proposals," *J. Tech. Writing and Commun.*, vol. 19, no. 4, pp. 317–351, 1989.

[11] R. Hays, "The trade jargon of proposal writing: A brief glossary," *The Tech. Writing Teacher*, vol. 11, no. 2, pp. 94–99, 1984.

[12] R. Norman and M. Young, "Using peer review to teach proposal writing," *The Tech. Writing Teacher*, vol. 12, no. 1, pp. 1–9, 1985.

[13] W. W. Werner, "An RFP for research reports," *The Tech. Writing Teacher*, vol. 16, no. 2, pp. 120–122, 1989.

[14] T. R. Bacon, "Collaboration in a pressure cooker," *Bull. Assoc. Business Commun.*, vol. 53, no. 2, pp. 4–8, 1990.

[15] D. Safford, "What I didn't teach in technical writing," *Teaching English in the Two-year College*, vol. 15, no. 1, pp. 53–58, 1988.

[16] R. C. Freed, "A meditation on proposals and their backgrounds," *J. Tech. Writing and Commun.*, vol. 17, no. 2, pp. 157–163, 1987.

[17] "Non-profit chiefs' pay up 4.8% in year," *Chronicle of Philanthropy*, p. 31, June 28, 1994.

[18] Society for Technical Communication, *Technical Communicator Salary Survey*, Arlington, VA, 1994.

[19] "Salaries for senior college fund raisers up 3.6%," *Chronicle of Philanthropy*, p. 33, Jan. 25, 1994.

PART VI

Revising and Editing: Refining Your Documents

Few of us joyfully approach revising a paper, but if your report is worth writing, it is worth editing. Only a rare writer can produce a flawless document the first time around, yet even if you never expect to be a great writer you can still train yourself to become an effective re-writer. These seven selections provide numerous and timeless pointers on how to edit, improve, and even perfect your written work.

Editing in layers

The first article provides a unique approach to the mundane task of editing. Roger Masse shows how you can systematically improve and perfect your editing by dividing it into separate levels: content, structure, style, format, mechanics, tone, and policy. A table outlines these levels and suggests questions to ask at each. Although aimed primarily at technical writing students, if you follow Masse's suggestions you will find that you can develop a methodical and thorough system for editing your own and other writers' documents.

Editing beyond the basics

Laurel Grove points out that in a lot of companies editing means no more than mechanically correcting sentence structure, grammar, and a few other basics. She quickly adds that this is far from enough, and can in fact be a waste of time and money. To produce quality documents, much more comprehensive editing is called for, and Grove describes how this can be done. She first lists the six steps involved in comprehensive editing, and then illustrates with charts the difference between "mechanical" and comprehensive editing. Her article's subheadings are in question form and the answers reveal the effectiveness, advantages, and attributes of the kind of editing she encourages. Grove concludes with the interesting question of how to identify job applicants who might have the characteristics to become good comprehensive editors.

Team editing

The idea of having a colleague help you proofread is expanded in Charles Stratton's discussion of collaborative writing. Although collaboration might constitute plagiarism in a freshman English class, it is often desirable and necessary in industry, where documents can be hundreds of pages long. However, you can improve on the traditional division of labor, as Stratton shows, by stratifying tasks rather than by assigning them individually. Such stratification enables individuals to work where their strengths are while a project manager coordinates their efforts.

The outline as editor

Like Stratton, Dietrich Rathjens focuses on perfecting longer documents. You might have thought of an outline as something to write first and then use as a blueprint for the rest of the paper, but it can also be a useful tool if you apply it to a document after completing a draft. Rathjens gives five steps to follow if you wish to use this kind of "reverse engineering" to analyze and restructure your document to improve its final coherence and impact.

Start early—avoid the rush

You can avoid a lot of last-minute revision, Herbert Michaelson points out, if you begin writing up a project report in the early stages of the project and develop your report as an integral part of the project. Writing a report concurrently with on-going research and development will create both a better report and a better project. If you start the writing process early, much of your document will be completed as the project is, and you will have more time for editing and perfecting a final report you can be proud of. Moreover, the process of writing can sometimes reveal flaws in the way your project is going, and thus help you get back on track.

Defining and improving the revision process

Although at first glance you might think Alice Philbin's and Melissa Spirek's article belongs in the Manuals and Instructions section of this anthology, the authors' study of how 20 technical communicators from different industries approach the process of revising their manuals is of use to any technical editor. The question immediately arises of what revision really means to working technical communicators. Few detailed definitions exist, according to the authors, and thus they look at the various definitions used in industry before they make four suggestions on how the revision process can be improved. They also find that there is often confusion about the meanings of "update" and "revision." You will find this study quite detailed in its research and enlightening in what respondents in the study have to say.

Editing by pencil or by software?

David Farkas and Steven Poltrock realize that many people still prefer to edit the printed copy of a document by hand. This, of course, is the way it has been for centuries. More and more, however, editors are finding there are benefits to marking copy on the computer, and many electronic editing tools now exist. Yet, as the authors point out, even in large companies there is plenty of resistance to online editing and some experts feel there are as many liabilities as advantages to the practice. This article is important because it looks at the two sides of the argument from both the organization's and the editor's perspective, and even evaluates the ergonomic advisability of spending more time at a computer. Since the authors feel editing on the computer is eventually going to be the norm, however, they end their article with a look at some of the techniques used in online editing and discuss what factors you should consider when looking for good editing software.

Theory and Practice of Editing Processes in Technical Communication

ROGER E. MASSE

Abstract—A conscious and organized study of editing processes can introduce basic editorial values to technical communication students. Through research and practice, students can learn systematic methods of editing with levels of edit (or types of edit) for written manuscripts and with editorial dialogue for conferring with writers. This work can lead to development of individual theories and practices of editing.

TECHNIQUES for editing in technical communication can be learned in practice on the job but, without guidance, the self-taught editor could be severely limited. To be really good, to meet the challenges of editing well, to effectively help someone else communicate technical information clearly and consciously, the editor needs to develop a broad understanding of the theory and practice of editing. This foundation for developing basic editorial values can be learned from courses or workshops that are organized to teach editors how to edit efficiently and effectively. These courses can be structured to help students examine research on editing, practice editing, and develop their own theories and practices of editing.

For the graduate students who take my Advanced Workshop in Technical and Professional Communication, I have developed such a course to provide the foundation for understanding and using editing processes. The advanced workshop is limited to ten graduate students from any discipline, including technical communication. While the students work on the writing they need to do in their particular fields and on writing processes for their manuscripts, they also learn much about editing for peer evaluation of each other's work. The editing helps students in all fields learn how editors work and how their own writing can be critiqued. And as they learn to edit the writing of other students, they also learn what to examine in their own writing.

To learn the theory and practice of editing, my students and I concentrate on two main activities:

1. Developing and using levels of edit and editorial dialogue in editing workshops
2. Developing theories of editing process through research and experience.

The author is an Associate Professor of English, New Mexico State University, Box 3443 University Park, Las Cruces, NM 88003; (505) 646-3931.

The first activity is accomplished within the editing workshop by all the students; the second activity is accomplished by the graduate students who are majoring in technical communication.

DEVELOPMENT OF EDITING TECHNIQUES IN THE GROUP

In the group workshop, my students and I develop and use levels of edit and examine and use editorial dialogue to edit manuscripts written by the students.

Levels of Edit and Types of Edit

To develop techniques for editing papers in our workshop, my graduate students and I examine several articles on editing. Some of those articles are nicely collected in a 1981 issue of *Technical Communication*, a special issue on technical editing [1]. The issue contains useful articles by Lola Zook, Don Bush, Alberta Cox, Harold Osborn, Eva Dukes, Lee Shimberg, and Mary Fran Buehler. We concentrate on Buehler's essay [2] and on one that Buehler wrote in 1977 [3].

Buehler's essays provide us with an organized approach to editing through the concept of "levels of edit." The concept, which Buehler developed for editing at the Jet Propulsion Laboratory (JPL), involves defining types of editing and then combining them into different levels according to the amount of editing needed in a manuscript. The types of editing activity include coordination, policy, integrity, screening, copy clarification, format, mechanical style, language, and substantive. These nine types are combined into five levels, which are used according to what is needed for a publication at JPL. A level 1 edit, for instance, would involve all nine types of editing while a level 5 edit would mean only two types of editing would be needed on a manuscript.

Most of Buehler's "tag" words for the types of editing are easily understood though overlapping seems to exist. For a "coordination edit" an editor coordinates or schedules and monitors production processes for a manuscript. For a "policy edit" the editor ensures that the manuscript reflects the company's policy on parts of a report, references, and units of measurement. For an "integrity edit" an editor checks that the parts of a publication match. A "screening edit" is a minimal editing of language and graphics. "Copy clarification" refers to legible copy. For

Reprinted from *IEEE Trans. Prof. Comm.*, vol. PC-28, no. 1, pp. 34–42, March 1985.

a "format edit" the editor marks a manuscript for correct format. In a "mechanical style edit" the editor checks for correct and consistent usage. For a "language edit" the editor considers all aspects of language. For a "substantive edit" the editor reviews the manuscript for content, coherence, emphasis, subordination, and parallelism.

The concept of levels of edit provides an approach for almost any editing situation. Buehler demonstrates its use for manuscripts at the Jet Propulsion Laboratory; I modify the concept to give students a tool for evaluating manuscripts written by other students in the workshop and for later use in their professional lives. I also modify the concept to structure my graduate workshop. Editing experiences in workshops have shown me that editors need organized approaches to editing, especially when ten people are doing the editing with one writer. Because a "shot gun" approach to editing only confuses a writer, I have my students determine main areas that need emphasis in editing a manuscript. If the editing is not organized, beginning editors cover various areas in a manuscript in a hit-or-miss fashion as they jump from a content weakness to a subject-

TABLE I

LEVELS OF EDIT AND QUESTIONS FOR EACH TYPE

Content—Knowledge of subject matter and transfer of that knowledge, information, or message

1. Is information or a message being transferred to the reader?
2. What is the message?
3. Are specific details provided to explain or prove generalizations?
4. Have the best materials been selected to explain the message?
5. Are the ideas fully explained?
6. Are unnecessary materials included?

Structure—Organization of whole piece of writing, of each section, and of each paragraph with clear beginnings, middle parts, and endings

1. Can a definite structure be seen?
2. Is that structure logical?
3. Is another structure better for the material?
4. Does the introduction set up all the parts?
5. Do the middle sections fulfill the promises of the introduction?
6. Is there logical coherence between the parts?
7. Does the conclusion summarize all the parts?

Style—Pattern of sentences and use of words

1. Is the writing clear?
2. Is the writing concise?
3. Is the writing strong?
4. Are the style of sentences and use of words appropriate to the subject?
5. Does the style interfere with the intended message?
6. Is the language appropriate for the intended audience?
7. Does the writer use effective parallelism, subordination, and coordination?
8. Is there an absence of wordiness, compound phrases, and redundancy?
9. Is there good use of agents for action to avoid passive constructions?
10. Is there good use of specific verbs, adverbs, and adjectives to suggest action?
11. Is the diction clear, concise, and connotative?

Format—Specialized physical arrangement and appearance

1. What format is used?
2. Is the format appropriate for the material?
3. Is that format the correct format for a report, a memo, an article, a proposal, a thesis, or a class paper?
4. Are the graphic aids effectively prepared and placed?
5. Are the headings used correctly and spaced correctly?
6. Is the material referenced correctly?
7. Are footnotes or citations used correctly?
8. Is the bibliography or list of references set up correctly?
9. How can the general appearance of the writing be improved?

Mechanics—Use of language according to established rules of grammar

1. Is the grammar of all the sentences correct?
2. Are the sentences structured correctly?
3. Are all the words spelled correctly?
4. Are punctuation marks used correctly?
5. Are typical errors avoided such as subject-verb disagreement, dangling modifiers, incorrect pronoun reference, pronoun-antecedent disagreement, incorrect parallelism, and poor subordination?

Tone—Voice or persona of the writer

1. Is the tone appropriate for the subject and the audience?
2. Is the writer present in the writing?
3. Should personal pronouns be used?
4. Is a persona created for the writer in the writing?

Policy—Conventions that the writer should follow for a journal, company, or organization

1. What policy conventions should the writer be following for the publishing agent or for the intended audience?
2. Are those conventions followed?
3. Is the writing non-sexist?
4. Is the writing free of other prejudices, biases, and imbalances?

verb disagreement to a format inconsistency to a graphics problem to a parallelism error to a paragraph misplaced to a word misspelled. If ten people are using the hit-or-miss approach at once, the writer understandably feels overwhelmed and totally confused. Therefore, to organize editing sessions early in a semester, I have my students develop guidelines for editing. After they have read Buehler's essays, we decide main areas to examine for editing a manuscript.

Invariably, we come up with seven areas or types of editing: content, structure, style, format, mechanics, tone, and policy. For each type, we then define the type and develop questions such as those in Table 1.

Loosely using Buehler's concept of levels of edit but reversing it, we decide that a level 7 edit includes all types of edit, a level 6 edit includes any six types, a level 5 edit includes any five types, and so on. Then, for an editing workshop, students read a manuscript written by another student, determine which types of edit and how many types need to be worked on, comment in writing in the text of the manuscript, and provide an overall reaction to the writing with suggestions on what needs the most work.

In the workshops, we then agree on which types of edit in a manuscript need the most work and which level of edit we will be involved with. Usually as a group we concur that a level 3 or 4 edit is needed. Very rarely do we decide that a level 7 edit is needed because by the time that we are editing papers in the course, students who are writing manuscripts are quite aware of what editors will be concentrating on and work hard in their writing on the areas that we will be examining.

Then, if a manuscript needs a level 2 or 3 or 4 edit, we decide which area needs the most work and concentrate on that area until it has been fully discussed with the writer by all the editors. We also examine other areas of editing that need more work. Near the end of the editing session, we may make comments on minor revisions needed in the remaining types of edit. In this way, we organize the editing session so that the most important types of editing are concentrated on for that particular manuscript and so that the writer is not overwhelmed with disorganized comments.

Editorial Dialogue

Organizing the editing sessions is not enough. To produce worthwhile editing sessions in the workshops, I have my students learn to use editorial dialogue to confer with a writer. Before any editing is done, the students read articles published by Mary Sigurdson Hageman, Louise Merck Vest, and Patrick M. Kelley [4].

The articles on editorial dialogue provide techniques that allow the workshop editors to work on talking *with*, not *at*, the writers. Editorial dialogue helps the editors work at making an editing session not a hatchet job but a team effort as editors and writer discuss together the editing that is needed in a piece of writing. Editorial dialogue helps the editors and writers work as partners as the editors suggest changes to improve the writer's manuscripts. As explained by Hageman, Vest, and Kelley, editorial dialogue emphasizes empathy and mutual respect in the editor-author relationship. Editorial dialogue makes use of Richard L. Johannesen's components of dialogue, which include the following [4; pp. W 39–40, W 64–65, W 107–108]:

- *Genuineness*—Being yourself and expressing what you think and feel, not what you think you ought to express
- *Accurate empathic understanding*—Comprehending and understanding the other person in a relationship
- *Unconditional positive regard*—Affirming the other person as a partner in dialogue
- *Presentness*—Being consciously and actively present in a dialogue and concentrating on the other person
- *Spirit of mutual equality*—Seeing the other person as an equal
- *Supportive psychological climate*—Communicating without preconceptions.

These components of dialogue can be used in an editing session through the following techniques [4; pp. W 107–108]:

1. *Receptive listening*—The editor actively listens to the writer and asks questions and the writer actively listens to suggestions.
2. *Guide for analysis*—The editor uses a guide [such as the questions for levels of edit] to check what has been done and the writer uses a guide to see what needs work.
3. *Notetaking*—The editor takes notes as the writer talks so that the writer's words can be used in a revision.
4. *Role mirroring*—Both the editor and the writer take the other's role to understand problems.

To use editorial dialogue, the student editors and I work to build a positive relationship with a writer to help the writer successfully transfer information to readers. The editorial dialogue allows us to make our editing sessions a team effort that is also a humane effort, and the concept of levels of edit allows us to organize our criticism and suggestions.

DEVELOPMENT OF INDIVIDUAL THEORIES OF EDITING PROCESSES

In addition to working on team editing, the technical communication students research editing processes to lead to a description of their own theory of the editing process. They are given the following assignment:

> Study editing processes in technical and professional communication to develop a knowledge of theory on editing process and to develop your own theory on editing process.

Complete the following reading and writing assignments:

1. Read articles and books on editing.
2. Write an essay for technical communication professors, writers, and students (or for publication) on your literature search and on your theory of editing process in technical and professional communication. Include a literature review of the reading materials with the explanation of your own theory of editing process. Either make the literature review a separate section of your essay or integrate it into the explanation of your theory.

The word "theory" is used in this assignment to mean a proposed explanation, perhaps conjectural, to explain the operation of certain acts or behaviors. It is used in the sense of a looking at, a contemplating, a speculating of how something operates or how something is done. It is a view, a perception of reality, an attempt to describe reality—the reality being the editing process.

For their research on editing processes, I give students a bibliography for beginning their literature searches. The bibliography, which is presented in the appendix, contains titles of articles and books on editing. I also urge students to use the lists of references at the end of the articles and books for titles of other sources. I urge them to check technical communication journals, such as *Technical Communication, The Technical Writing Teacher, Journal of Technical Writing and Communication, IEEE Transactions on Professional Communication,* and *Proceedings of ITCC*. I tell them to check the Society for Technical Communication publication *Technical Editing: Principles and Practices*, edited by Lola Zook [5]. I suggest that they have computer searches done. In addition I suggest that they consider their editing practices in past and present editing jobs and their editing practices in their present work in our workshops. I suggest that they examine other people's editing processes.

The students then combine their research with a description of their editing processes. Often students are able to use their own experiences at jobs as technical writers and editors to explain their theories of editing processes. For instance, one student combined research with her own editing experience at the Atmospheric Sciences Laboratory to explain her theory of editing process. Her process includes four stages: (1) reviewing—determining the areas to be edited; (2) repairing—making necessary changes during each type of editing; (3) conferring—discussing the manuscript with the author; and (4) evaluating—reviewing the edited product. Another student described her editing process in three stages: (1) getting in shape, which includes developing editorial attitudes, editorial competency, and editorial thinking; (2) finding the problems, which includes reading through a manuscript twice, first for understanding of content and second for locating possible problems; and (3) solving the problems, which includes suggestions to the writer to ensure the transfer of information to an audience.

A third student explained that her editing process consists of understanding the nature of editing, finding and correcting barriers in a manuscript through three readings, and convincing authors of needed revisions. A fourth student developed a theory based on the concept that an editor must discover facts on content, structure, and style in a manuscript to be able to explain what is wrong with a manuscript and how it can be improved. She developed an editing process that has five stages: (1) Read the manuscript to obtain a general idea of content and to underline grammatical errors to discover if a pattern of grammatical errors exists; (2) outline the manuscript by finding out what the structure is and by commenting on it; (3) edit the manuscript for content by indicating what needs more support and for structure by indicating where logic could be strengthened; (4) edit the manuscript for composition to suggest objectively revisions in style and emphasis in sentences and paragraphs; and (5) comment to the author on major and minor problems in the manuscript and suggest possible revisions. A fifth student looked for ways to achieve professional attitudes and to develop workable editing techniques. He discovered that editors are not mere proofreaders, that an editor has a responsibility to ensure clear communication, and that an editor needs to become personally involved in editing decisions. He developed a systematic method for editing that involved understanding content, discovering organization, and analyzing and solving the writer's problems with content, structure, and style [6].

The research and development of individual theories of editing thus go beyond simply teaching editing skills. The students develop a broad understanding of the scope of editing and are thereby prepared for the editing challenges they will meet in their future jobs.

SUMMARY

The work in editing ensures that graduate students become aware of editing processes through experience and research, through practice and theory. By developing and using levels of edit and editorial dialogue in editing workshops and by researching and examining their own and other people's techniques, the students develop their own theories of editing processes. Thus, through their group editing and their individual editing experiences and research, the graduate students learn basic editorial values and editing techniques that they can use to help others communicate well.

REFERENCES

1. *Technical Communication*. Ed. Frank Smith. Fourth Quarter 1981; 28(4).
2. Buehler, M. F. "Defining the Terms in Technical Editing: The Levels of Edit as a Model." *Technical Communication*. Fourth Quarter 1981; 28(4):10–14.
3. Buehler, M. F. "Controlled Flexibility on Technical Editing: The Levels-of-Edit Concept at JPL." *Technical Communication*. First Quarter 1977; 24(1):1–4.
4. Hageman, M. S.; Vest, L. M.; Kelley, P. M. "Editorial Dialogue: An Alternative Writer-Editor Relationship." *Proceedings of the*

28th International Technical Communication Conference. Washington, DC: Society for Technical Communication; 1981: pp. W 38–40. Kelley, P. M. "Charting a New Course for Technical Writing and Editing: Technical Writing and Editing as Dialogue." *Proceedings of the 29th International Technical Communication Conference*. Washington, DC: Society for Technical Communication; 1982: pp. W 62–65. Vest, L. M.; Hageman, M. S. "Developing an Alternative Writer-Editor Relationship: A Workshop in Editorial Dialogue." *Proceedings of the 29th International Technical Communication Conference*. Washington, DC: Society for Technical Communication; 1982: pp. W 106–109.

5. *Technical Editing: Principles and Practices*. Ed. Lola M. Zook. Washington, DC: Society for Technical Communication; 1975.
6. The students cited include Marie Richardson, Mary Lou Vocale, Martha Delamater, Susan Bagby, and Robert Toland.

APPENDIX: SELECTED RESOURCES ON EDITING PROCESSES

A

Abshire, Gary M.; Culberson, Dan. **The Art of Technical Writing and Editing.** Report 05.225. Boeblingen, Germany: IBM Corporation; 1978.

Adams, Tom. **Be Your Own Editor.** *Industrial Supervisor*. 1980; 44: 6.

Amsden, Dorothy Corner. **Exercise Your Visual Thinking.** In *Proceedings of the 29th International Technical Communication Conference*. Washington, DC: Society for Technical Communication; 1982: pp. W 12–15.

——. **Get in the Habit of Editing Illustrations.** In *Proceedings of the 27th International Technical Communication Conference*. Washington, DC: Society for Technical Communication; 1980: pp. W 147–154.

Applewhite, Lottie. **An In-House Editorial-Tutorial Program for Developing Communication Skills.** *Technical Communication*. First Quarter 1983; 30: 5–7.

——. **An Individual Development Program.** In *Proceedings of the 29th International Technical Communication Conference*. Washington, DC: Society for Technical Communication; 1982: pp. E 14–16.

Atkins, Eldred E. **At the Outset of Technical Editing.** *Electronic Engineer*. November 1969; 28: 29–30.

Atlas, Marshall, A. **The User Edit: Making Manuals Easier to Use.** *IEEE Transactions on Professional Communication*. 1981; PC-24(1): 28–29.

B

Bagby, Susan A. **Editing as a Matter of Fact.** In *The 577 Papers: Writing Processes, Editing Processes, Written Products*, Volume II. Eds. Roger E. Masse and Martha Delamater. Las Cruces, NM: Technical Communication Programs, New Mexico State University; 1983: pp. 125–137.

Barnow, Renee K. **Setting and Cleaning a Table: How an Editor Can Get Out of the Kitchen.** In *Proceedings of the 29th International Technical Communication Conference*. Washington, DC: Society for Technical Communication; 1982: pp. W 18–21.

Batchelder, Susan K. **Friends or Foes? The Relationship Between Writer and Editor.** In *Proceedings of the 30th International Technical Communication Conference*. Washington, DC: Society for Technical Communication; 1983: pp. W&E 73–74.

Behnke, Lynn. **Stranger in a Strange Land: My First Year as an Editing Manager.** In *Proceedings of the 29th International Technical Communication Conference*. Washington, DC: Society for Technical Communication; 1982: pp. C 11–14.

Bennett, John Barnard. **Editing for Engineers.** New York: Wiley-Interscience; 1970.

Boomhower, E. F. **Producing Good Technical Communications Requires Two Types of Editing.** *Journal of Technical Writing and Communication*. Fourth Quarter 1975; 5: 277–281.

Brett, Carlton E. **Editor's Bootstraps.** *Journal of Technical Writing and Communication*. Fourth Quarter 1971; 1: 307–316.

Briggs, Nelson. **Editing by Dialogue.** In *Technical Editing: Principles and Practices*. Ed. Lola M. Zook. Washington, DC: Society for Technical Communication; 1975: pp. 56–61.

Briles, Susan M. **Designing a Training Program for a Technical Editing Department.** In *Proceedings of the 29th International Technical Communication Conference*. Washington, DC: Society for Technical Communication; 1982: pp. C 15–18.

Brogan, John A. **A Pitfall for Professionals.** In *Technical Editing: Principles and Practices*. Ed. Lola M. Zook. Washington, DC: Society for Technical Communication; 1975: pp. 87–91.

Bronson, Judith Gunn. **Prevention of Donkeyism: The Role of the Medical Author's Editor.** In *Proceedings of the 28th International Technical Communication Conference*. Washington, DC: Society for Technical Communication; 1981: pp. W 10–13.

Buehler, Mary Fran. **Defining Terms in Technical Editing: The Levels of Edit as a Model.** *Technical Communication*. Fourth Quarter 1981; 28: 10–15.

——. **Situational Editing: A Rhetorical Approach for the Technical Editor.** *Technical Communication*. Third Quarter 1980; 27: 18–22.

——. **Controlled Flexibility in Technical Editing: The Levels of Edit Concept at JPL.** *Technical Communication*. First Quarter 1977; 24: 1–4.

——. **Patterns for Making Editorial Changes.** In *Technical Editing: Principles and Practices*. Ed. Lola M. Zook. Washington, DC: Society for Technical Communication; 1975: pp. 1–6.

Burr, William. **Why Technical Editors Act That Way.** Report 64-825-1195. Oswego, NY: IBM Corporation; 1964.

Bush, Don. **The Trouble with Definitions.** In *Proceedings of the 30th International Technical Communication Conference*. Washington, DC: Society for Technical Communication; 1983: pp. W&E 28–31.

——. **Content Editing, an Opportunity for Growth.** *Technical Communication*. Fourth Quarter 1981; 28: 15–19.

——. **Strategies for a Technical Editor.** *Technical Writing Teacher*. 1979; 7: 19–23.

——. **Semantics (Words are Chameleons).** In *Technical Editing: Principles and Practices*. Ed. Lola M. Zook. Washington, DC: Society for Technical Communication; 1975:

pp. 33–37.

Butcher, Judith. **Copy-Editing.** Cambridge, England: Cambridge University Press; 1975.

C

Carmichael, Edna. **Management's Responsibility in Training the Technical Communicator.** In *Technical Editing: Principles and Practices.* Ed. Lola M. Zook. Washington, DC: Society for Technical Communication; 1975: pp. 82–86.

Cathcart, Margaret E. **Training the Technical Editor.** In *Proceedings of the 30th International Technical Communication Conference.* Washington, DC: Society for Technical Communication; 1983: pp. RET 13–15.

Cederborg, Gibson A. **The Role and Rationale of Technical Editors.** *Journal of Technical Writing and Communication.* Fourth Quarter 1975; 5: 283–286.

Clements, Wallace. **Jargon and the Technical Writer.** In *Technical Editing: Principles and Practices.* Ed. Lola M. Zook. Washington, DC: Society for Technical Communication; 1975: pp. 38–41.

——; Waite, Robert G. **A Guide for Beginning Technical Editors.** In *Proceedings of the 26th International Technical Communication Conference.* Washington, DC: Society for Technical Communication; 1979: pp. W 32–36.

Coggshall, Gordon. **Using the Core Sentence to Edit Poorly Written Technical Manuscripts.** *Technical Communication.* First Quarter 1980; 27: 19–23.

Colby, John. **Paragraphing in Technical Writing.** In *Technical Editing: Principles and Practices.* Ed. Lola Zook. Washington, DC: Society for Technical Communication; 1975: pp. 42–46.

Corrigan, Anne M. **The Technical Editor as Teacher: How to Explain What's Wrong and Why.** In *Proceedings of the 27th International Technical Communication Conference.* Washington, DC: Society for Technical Communication; 1980: pp. R 167–170.

Cox, Alberta. **Copy Editing—The Final Word.** *Technical Communication.* Fourth Quarter 1981; 28: 18–20.

——. **The Editor as Generalist as Well as Specialist.** In *Technical Editing: Principles and Practices.* Ed. Lola M. Zook. Washington, DC: Society for Technical Communication; 1975: pp. 7–10.

D

Dalla Santa, Terry M. **Managing the Editing Function on Large Publication Tasks with Short Flow Times.** In *Proceedings of the 30th International Technical Communication Conference.* Washington, DC: Society for Technical Communication; 1983: pp. W&E 21–24.

Delamater, Martha. **Editors: Trolls or Fairy Godpersons?** In *The 577 Papers: Writing Processes, Editing Processes, Written Products,* Volume II. Eds. Roger E. Masse and Martha Delamater. Las Cruces, NM: Technical Communication Programs, NMSU; 1983: pp. 111–123.

De Quattro, James. **Getting It Right with the Author.** In *Proceedings of the 26th International Technical Communication Conference.* Washington, DC: Society for Technical Communication; 1979: pp. W 46–48.

Dukes, Eva P. **Some Authors I Have Known.** *Technical Communication.* Fourth Quarter 1981; 28: 27–30.

——. **The Art of Editing.** In *Technical Editing: Principles and Practices.* Ed. Lola M. Zook. Washington, DC: Society for Technical Communication; 1975: pp. 62–66.

——. **The Simple Joys of Editing.** *Technical Communication.* Third Quarter 1972; 19: 7–8.

F

Farkas, David K.; Farkas, Nettie. **Manuscript Surprises: A Problem in Copy Editing.** *Technical Communication.* Second Quarter 1981; 28: 16–18.

Fearing, Bertie E. **The Education of an Academic Journal Editor.** In *Proceedings of the 29th International Technical Communication Conference.* Washington, DC: Society for Technical Communication; 1982: pp. E 41–43.

Fourdrinier, Sylvia. **The Editor as a Teacher.** In *Technical Editing: Principles and Practices.* Ed. Lola M. Zook. Washington, DC: Society for Technical Communication; 1975: pp. 67–70.

G

Gamer, Roy W. **Improving the Effectiveness of Technical Documentation through Analysis.** In *Proceedings of the 30th International Technical Communication Conference.* Washington, DC: Society for Technical Communication; 1983: pp. MPD 13–15.

Garber, Reeta. **Terminal Oversight: The Editor and the Word Processor.** In *Proceedings of the 31st International Technical Communication Conference.* Washington, DC: Society for Technical Communication; 1984: pp. ATA 50–52.

Genin, Michael S. **Editing Report Art Differs from Editing Presentation Art.** In *Proceedings of the 31st International Technical Communication Conference.* Washington, DC: Society for Technical Communication; 1984: pp. VC 53–55.

——. **Turning Adversaries into Allies—Avoiding Tension in an Author-Editor Relationship.** In *Proceedings of the 26th International Technical Communication Conference.* Washington, DC: Society for Technical Communication; 1979: pp. W 59–60.

Gibson, Martin L. **Editing in the Electronic Era.** Ames, IA: Iowa State University Press; 1979.

Griffin, C. W. **Theory of Responding to Student Writing: The State of the Art.** *College Composition and Communication.* October 1982; 36: 296–301.

H

Hageman, Mary Sigurdson. **High Touch in the Workplace: Integrating Scientific Research and Scientific Writing (and Editing).** In *Proceedings of the 31st International Technical Communication Conference.* Washington, DC: Society for Technical Communication; 1984: pp. WE 112–113.

——; Vest, Louise M.; Kelley, Patrick M. **Editorial Dialogue: An Alternative Writer-Editor Relationship.** In *Proceedings of the 28th International Technical Communication Conference.* Washington, DC: Society for Technical Communication; 1981: pp. W 38–40.

Hallinan, Edward J. **Practical Writing and Editing Techniques.** In *Proceedings of the 31st International Technical Communication Conference.* Washington, DC: Society for Technical Communication; 1984: pp. WE 34–36.

Harrington, J. Y. **Editing Computer Manuals.** *Technical Communication.* Fourth Quarter 1980; 27: 14–17.

Hartley, James. **The Role of Colleagues and Text-Editing Programs in Improving Text.** *IEEE Transactions on Professional Communication.* March 1984: PC-27(1): 42–44.

Hasch, Jean; Chepeleff, Val. **Wearing the Production Editor's Hat.** In *Proceedings of the 29th International Technical Communication Conference.* Washington, DC: Society for Technical Communication; 1982: pp. G 23–26.

Haughness, Norman. **The Technical Editor as Tact-ician.** *Technical Communication.* Third Quarter 1968; 15: 18–19.

Heffner, Maxine. **Stalking the Troublesome Hyphen.** In *Technical Editing: Principles and Practices.* Ed. Lola M. Zook. Washington, DC: Society for Technical Communication; 1975: pp. 53–55.

Henderson, Arnold C. **Editing for the First Half-Second: The Perceptual Process and the Technical Editor.** In *Proceedings of the 28th International Technical Communication Conference.* Washington, DC: Society for Technical Communication; 1981: pp. W 49–52.

Heiken, Jody H.; Norton, Diane D. **Mechanized Editing: We Won't, We Can't, We Did!** In *Proceedings of the 31st International Technical Communication Conference.* Washington, DC: Society for Technical Communication; 1984: pp. WE 128–131.

J

Jack, Judith. **Teaching Analytical Editing.** *Technical Communication.* First Quarter 1984; 31: 9–11.

——. **Teaching Technical Editing: A Structured Approach.** In *Proceedings of the 30th International Technical Communication Conference.* Washington, DC: Society for Technical Communication; 1983: pp. RET 11–12.

Jackson, Purvis M.; Dunkle, Susan B. **A Systematic Approach to Editing.** In *Proceedings of the 31st International Technical Communication Conference.* Washington, DC: Society for Technical Communication; 1984: pp. WE 121–124.

Jarmon, Brian. **Coping with Crash Editing.** In *Proceedings of the 27th International Technical Communication Conference.* Washington, DC: Society for Technical Communication; 1980: pp. W 9–12.

K

Kantrowitz, Bruce M. **Recipe for a Cooperative Technical Editing Program.** In *Proceedings 1978 of the Council for Programs in Technical and Scientific Communication.* Ed. David L. Carson. Troy, NY: Council for Programs in Technical and Scientific Communication; 1979: pp. 62–68.

Keedy, Hugh. F. **Musings of an Engineering Professor on Leave as a Technical Editor.** In *Proceedings of the 28th International Technical Communication Conference.* Washington, DC: Society for Technical Communication; 1981: pp. W 64–67.

Kelley, Patrick M. **High Tech/High Touch: A Trend in Technical Writing and Editing.** In *Proceedings of the 31st International Technical Communication Conference.* Washington, DC: Society for Technical Communication; 1984: pp. WE 106–108.

——. **Charting a New Course for Technical Writing and Editing: Technical Writing and Editing as Dialogue.** In *Proceedings of the 29th International Technical Communication Conference.* Washington, DC: Society for Technical Communication; 1982: pp. W 62–65.

Kellner, Robert Scott. **A Necessary and Natural Sequel: Technical Editing.** *Journal of Technical Writing and Communication.* First Quarter 1982; 12: 25–33.

Koski, Raymond; Mann, Gerald A. **The Editor's Role in Reducing Future Shock.** *Technical Communication.* Second Quarter 1974; 21: 2–5.

L

Layton, Edward. **Editor-Author Relationships: Both Can Win.** *IEEE Transactions on Professional Communication.* September 1973; PC-16(3): 57–59, 172.

Leavitt, William D. **The Proof of Your Editorial Pudding Is in Its Tasters.** In *Proceedings of the 30th International Technical Communication Conference.* Washington, DC: Society for Technical Communication; 1983: pp. MPD 16–18.

Lehr, Dolores. **Three Roles of a Technical Editor.** In *Proceedings of the 31st International Technical Communication Conference.* Washington, DC: Society for Technical Communication; 1984: pp. WE 65–66.

Lien, Patricia L. **Text Editing on the LLL Octopus.** In *Proceedings of the 27th International Technical Communication Conference.* Washington, DC: Society for Technical Communication; 1980: pp. C 209–212.

Lindberg, Helen. **Keeping a Sense of Humor.** In *Proceedings of the 26th International Technical Communication Conference.* Washington, DC: Society for Technical Communication; 1979: pp. W 87–91.

Love, Earl A. **An Abrupt Awakening: Or, an Editor Comes of Age.** In *Proceedings of the 26th International Technical Communication Conference.* Washington, DC: Society for Technical Communication; 1979: pp. W 92–94.

Lynch, Denise. **Easing the Process: A Strategy for Evaluating Compositions.** *College Composition and Communication.* October 1982; 33: 310–314.

M

Mann, Gerald A. **Minimal Editing: How Much Is Too Much?** In *Proceedings of the 27th International Technical Communication Conference.* Washington, DC: Society for Technical Communication; 1980: pp. W 5–7.

Masse, Roger E. **Editing in Technical Communication: Theory and Practice in Editing Processes at the Graduate Level.** Las Cruces, NM: NMSU; 1984. ERIC document ED 229 790.

—— Ed. **The 577 Papers: Writing Processes, Editing Processes, Written Products, Volume I.** Las Cruces, NM: Technical Communication Programs, NMSU; 1982.

——; Delamater, Martha. Eds. **The 577 Papers: Writing Processes, Editing Processes, Written Products, Volume II.** Las Cruces, NM: Technical Communication Programs, NMSU; 1983.

Mazzatenta, Ernest. **GM Research Laboratories Improve Chemistry Between Science Writers and Editors.** In *Teaching Technical Writing and Editing—In-House Programs That Work.* Ed. James G. Shaw. Washington, DC: Society for Technical Communication; 1976; pp. 55–61.

McCarron, William E. **Confessions of a Working Technical Editor.** *The Technical Writing Teacher.* Fall 1978; 6: 5-8.

McCormick, Barbara S. **How to Function as a Schizoid Editor.** Washington, DC: Society for Technical Communication; 1977.

McDonald, John W. **Taking the Noise Out of Technical Writing.** In *Technical Editing: Principles and Practices.* Ed. Lola M. Zook. Washington, DC: Society for Technical Communication; 1975: pp. 28-32.

McGough, David L. **Production Editor: Key to New Effectiveness.** In *Technical Editing: Principles and Practices.* Ed. Lola M. Zook. Washington, DC: Society for Technical Communication; 1975: pp. 71-76.

Meckel, Susan R.; Sauer, Kathleen H. **Five Concepts for Effective Interaction Between an Artist and Editor/Writer.** In *Proceedings of the 29th International Technical Communication Conference.* Washington, DC: Society for Technical Communication; 1982: pp. G 38-40.

Mott, Wesley T. **Editing Business and Institutional Publications: A Course for the Working Editor.** *The ABCA Bulletin.* 1981; No. 1: 3-7.

Myers, Barbara Y. **A Classification of Author-Editor Relationships: Toward Team-Centered Relationships.** In *Proceedings of the 31st International Technical Communication Conference.* Washington, DC: Society for Technical Communication; 1984: pp. WE 116-119.

Mullins, Carolyn J. **The Computer as Nitpicking Copy Editor.** In *Proceedings of the 27th International Technical Communication Conference.* Washington, DC: Society for Technical Communication; 1980: pp. C 197-199.

O

Osborne, Harold F. **Intuition, Integrity, and the Decline of Editing.** *Technical Communication.* Fourth Quarter 1981; 28: 21-26.

——. **Criticism and Creativity.** In *Technical Editing: Principles and Practices.* Ed. Lola M. Zook. Washington, DC: Society for Technical Communication; 1975: pp. 17-19.

P

Peterson, Dart G. **Developing the Editor-Author Relationship.** In *Proceedings of the 23rd International Technical Communication Conference.* Washington, DC: Society for Technical Communication; 1976: pp. 85-86.

Power, Ruth M. **Who Needs a Technical Editor.** *IEEE Transactions on Professional Communication.* September 1981; PC-24(3): 139-140.

R

Rathbone, Robert R. **Communicating Technical Information.** Reading, MA: Addison-Wesley; 1966.

Richardson, Marie. **The Editor Won't Let You.** In *The 577 Papers: Writing Processes, Editing Processes, Written Products,* Volume I. Ed. Roger E. Masse. Las Cruces, NM: Technical Communication Programs, NMSU; 1982: pp. 75-91.

Rohne, Carl F. **Editing the Small Study Proposal.** In *Technical Editing: Principles and Practices.* Ed. Lola M. Zook. Washington, DC: Society for Technical Communication; 1975: pp. 77-81.

Rosner, Mary. **Sentence-Combining in Technical Writing: An Editing Tool.** *The Technical Writing Teacher.* Winter 1982; 9: 100-107.

Ross, Peter Burton. **Slash for Quick Editing.** *Technical Communication.* Third Quarter 1977; 24: 11-14.

Rutter, Russell. **Starting to Write by Re-Writing: A Unit on Teaching Editing and Revision.** *The Technical Writing Teacher.* 1980: 8: 22-26.

S

Sealine, Barbara A. **Using Interpersonal Communication Skills as a Managing Writer/Editor.** In *Proceedings of the 27th International Technical Communication Conference.* Washington, DC: Society for Technical Communication; 1980: pp. M 133-140.

Shear, Marie. **Fixing Rotten Writing: A Cameo Case History.** *The Journal of Business Communication.* 1981; No. 2: 5-14.

Shimberg, H. Lee. **Editing Authors' Style—A Few Guidelines.** *Technical Communication.* Fourth Quarter 1981; 28: 31-35.

Shipley, L. J; Gentry, J. K. **How Electronic Editing Equipment Affects Editing Performance.** *Journalism Quarterly.* Fall 1981; 58: 371-374, 387.

Sideras, George. **Creativity in Technical Editing.** In *Proceedings of the 18th International Technical Communication Conference.* Washington, DC: Society for Technical Communication; 1971: pp. 6-10.

Simons, John L. **The Technical Editor as a Decision-Maker.** In *Proceedings of the 27th International Technical Communication Conference.* Washington, DC: Society for Technical Communication; 1980: pp. W 27-30.

Sims, Robert L. **Advantage of Dialogue from a Management Perspective.** In *Proceedings of the 31st International Technical Communication Conference.* Washington, DC: Society for Technical Communication; 1984: pp. WE 114-115.

——. **Dialogue: The Key to Professionalism in Technical Communication.** In *Proceedings of the 30th International Technical Communication Conference.* Washington, DC: Society for Technical Communication; 1983: pp. W&E 35-37.

Smith, Frank R. **The Education of a Society Journal Editor.** In *Proceedings of the 29th International Technical Communication Conference.* Washington, DC: Society for Technical Communication; 1982: pp. E 110-111.

Smith, Herbert J. **Training the Technical Editing Student in Interpersonal Skills.** In *Proceedings of the 30th International Technical Communication Conference.* Washington, DC: Society for Technical Communication; 1983: pp. RET 52-54.

Smith, Patricia N. **Here, Edit This!** In *Proceedings of the 28th International Technical Communication Conference.* Washington, DC: Society for Technical Communication; 1981: pp. W 92-94.

Sommers, Nancy. **Responding to Student Writing.** *College Composition and Communication.* May 1982; 33: 148-156.

Stocker, Deborah J. **Managing a Successful Editorial Group in a Multidisciplinary Consulting Firm.** In *Proceedings of the 31st International Technical Communication Con-*

ference. Washington, DC: Society for Technical Communication; 1984: pp. MPD 87–89.

Stohrer, Freda F. **Training Apprentice Editors.** In *Proceedings 1978 of the Council for Programs in Technical and Scientific Communication.* Ed. David L. Carson. Troy, NY: CPTSC; 1979: pp. 62–68.

Stratton, Charles R. **Ambiguity: An Exercise in Practical Semantics.** In *Technical Editing: Principles and Practices.* Ed. Lola M. Zook. Washington, DC: Society for Technical Communication; 1975: pp. 47–52.

Swain, Deborah E. **Dynamic Online Editing: A Proposal.** In *Proceedings of the 31st International Technical Communication Conference.* Washington, DC: Society for Technical Communication; 1984: pp. WE 132–135.

Swaney, J. H.; *et al.* **Editing for Comprehension: Improving the Process Through Protocols.** Washington, DC: American Institutes for Research; 1981. ERIC document ED 209 642.

T

Taylor, P. **How to Get Along with Authors.** *The Editorial Eye.* January 1981; 53: 6–7.

Thralls, Charlotte. **Editing of Professional Reports: A Rhetorical Modes Approach.** In *Proceedings of the 27th International Technical Communication Conference.* Washington, DC: Society for Technical Communication; 1980: pp. 199–203.

Toland, Robert. **Attitudes and Method: Complements of an Editing Process.** In *The 577 Papers: Writing Processes, Editing Processes, Written Products,* Volume II. Eds. Roger E. Masse and Martha Delamater. Las Cruces, NM: Technical Communication Programs, NMSU; 1983: pp. 139–152.

V

Van Buren, Robert; Buehler, Mary Fran. **The Levels of Edit,** 2nd edition. JPL 80-1. Pasadena, CA: Jet Propulsion Laboratory, California Institute of Technology; 1980.

Van Eps, Barbara J. **Editing Computer-Based Education Lessons.** In *Proceedings of the 28th International Technical Communication Conference.* Washington, DC: Society for Technical Communication; 1981: pp. W 114–116.

Vaughn, David E. **A Logical Approach to Editing Proposals, Reports, and Manuals.** In *Technical Editing: Principles and Practices.* Ed. Lola M. Zook. Washington, DC: Society for Technical Communication; 1975: pp. 20–27.

Vest, Louise M. **Toward Human-Centered Technology: '...A Sense of Obligation.'** In *Proceedings of the 31st International Technical Communication Conference.* Washington, DC: Society for Technical Communication; 1984: pp. WE 109–111.

——; Hageman, Mary S. **Developing an Alternative Writer-Editor Relationship: A Workshop in Editorial Dialogue.** In *Proceedings of the 29th International Technical Communication Conference.* Washington, DC: Society for Technical Communication; 1982: pp. W 106–111.

Vocale, Mary Lou. **Overcoming the Manuscript: An Editing Process.** In *The 577 Papers: Writing Processes, Editing Processes, Written Products,* Volume I. Ed. Roger E. Masse, Las Cruces, NM: Technical Communication Programs, NMSU; 1982: pp. 57–73.

W

Wagner, Carl B. **The Technical Side of Technical Editing.** In *Proceedings of the 29th International Technical Communication Conference.* Washington, DC: Society for Technical Communication; 1982: pp. W 112–115.

Wales, Ruth W. **A Taxonomy of Editing Tasks.** In *Proceedings of the 29th International Technical Communication Conference.* Washington, DC: Society for Technical Communication; 1982: pp. W 116–117.

Wall, Florence E. **Requirements and Responsibilities of a Technical Editor.** *Journal of Chemical Education.* October 1953; 31: 516–521.

Weil, Benjamin. **Technical Editing.** Westport, CT: Greenwood Press; 1975.

Whittaker, Della. **Editor? Teacher?** In *Proceedings of the 22nd International Technical Communication Conference.* Washington, DC: Society for Technical Communication; 1975: pp. 407–408.

Wood, M. **The Sharp Pencil: Editing Corporate Jargon.** *Editors Workshop.* July/August 1981; 2: 5.

Z

Zimmerman, Muriel. **Reducing by Design: A Checklist for Editors.** In *Proceedings of the 30th International Technical Communication Conference.* Washington, DC: Society for Technical Communication; 1983: pp. W&E 18–20.

Zook, Lola M. **Technical Editors Look at Technical Editing.** *Technical Communication.* Third Quarter 1983; 30: 21–26.

——. **Editing and the Editor: Views and Values.** *Technical Communication.* Fourth Quarter 1981; 28: 5–9.

——. **Even an Editor Can't Have Everything.** *The Editorial Eye.* January 1981; 53: 2–3.

——. **Lessons Learned—Not Always By Choice.** In *Proceedings of the 27th International Technical Communication Conference.* Washington, DC: Society for Technical Communication; 1980: pp. W 31–36.

——. Ed. **Technical Editing: Principles and Practices.** Washington, DC: Society for Technical Communication; 1975.

——. **Training the Editor: Skills Are Not Enough.** In *Technical Editing: Principles and Practices.* Ed. Lola M. Zook. Washington, DC: Society for Technical Communication; 1975: pp. 12–16.

When the Basics Aren't Enough: Finding a Comprehensive Editor

Laurel K. Grove

Abstract—**In today's competitive markets, organizations may be tempted to reduce costs by cutting staff or hiring less skilled, and thus less costly, staff. At the same time, and for the same reasons, the need for higher quality in reports and manuals grows. As companies begin to invest in quality, they are finding that "good" is no longer good enough. To achieve excellence, staff must have the right skills. This paper describes how to find technical editors who can make documents more than just good, editors who can think about the content of the message, not just its presentation.**

IN MANY companies, the term *editing* means reviewing for effective sentence structure, correct grammar, and proper format. This kind of mechanical editing is good and necessary, but it can also waste time and money and result in inadequate documents. To solve some of these problems, a more technically oriented kind of editing, comprehensive editing, is useful. Comprehensive editing centers on an editorial review for technical content, completeness, and coherence. Methods for comprehensive editing have been described by Bush [1], Zimmerman [2], Van Buren and Buehler [3], Cheney and Schleicher [4], and Brouns and Grove [5].

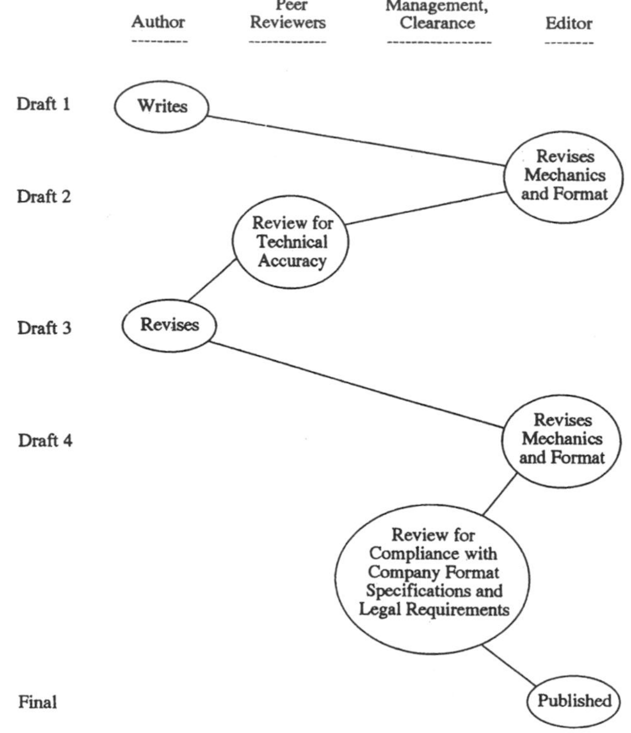

Fig. 1. Document production process using mechanical editing.

What is Comprehensive Editing?

Comprehensive editing involves six steps:

1) reading the document through quickly
2) studying the outline or structure of the document
3) thinking about the document
4) reading the document carefully; asking whether the discussion is complete; whether there are technical discrepancies; and whether terms are defined clearly
5) writing comments on the document
6) meeting with the technical author

After the author has decided on revisions, the editor checks format, spelling, grammar, and other mechanical aspects, then sees the document through to publication.

Why is Comprehensive Editing More Effective than Mechanical Editing?

As Figs. 1 and 2 show, one obvious difference is in who has most control over the document. In the mechanical editing process, the technical staff—the author and the peer reviewers—have only two opportunities to revise a draft; in the comprehensive editing process, the technical staff members have three.

Mechanical editing has four drawbacks:

- *It is inefficient.* In mechanical editing, when editors get documents, they typically read them through once, correcting grammar, punctuation, spelling, sentence structure, word usage, and document format. Unfortunately, checking mechanics and format carefully at this early stage is inefficient. The technical staff will inevitably revise the document in response to peer review comments or during their own reviews, and these revisions often include rewriting some sections. The result is that the document has to be completely re-edited.
- *It focuses on superficial problems*. While the editors are checking mechanics, they cannot see the entire document as a unit. Even if each independent sentence is coherent, the document may lack overall unity; it may not adequately define or describe technical terms, concepts, and processes; and it may not be written in a tone and style

Manuscript received May 1994; revised, June 1994.
The author is with Battelle, Pacific Northwest Laboratories, Richland, Washington 99352, USA.
IEEE Log Number 9404906.

Reprinted from *IEEE Trans. Prof. Comm.*, vol. PC-37, no. 3, pp. 171–174, September 1994.

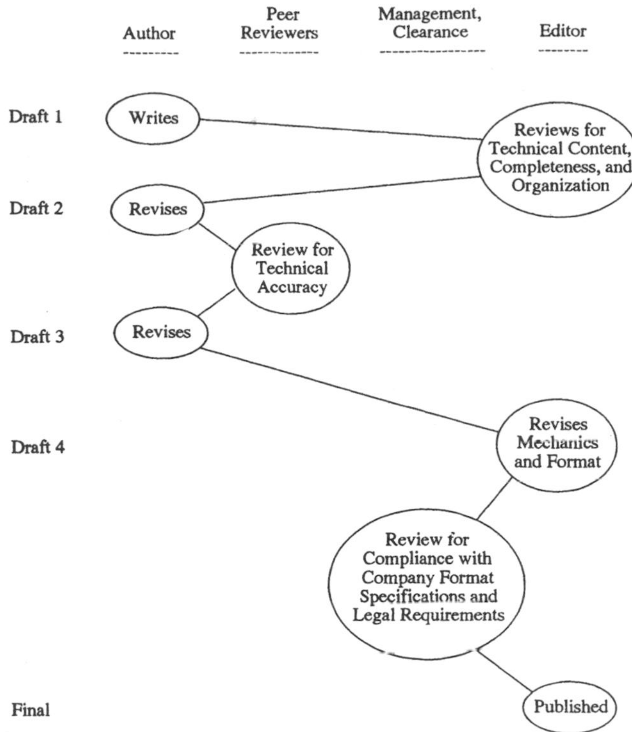

Fig. 2. Document production process using comprehensive editing.

appropriate for the audience. In short, the document may be inadequate.

- *It can lead to a faulty analysis of the audience.* Because the technical staff members focus on research and development, when they write user's manuals, for instance, they often forget that the user does not know all that they do. If the editors concentrate only on getting the commas right, they lose sight of such gaps in the content. When mechanical editors don't understand the technical material they are editing, they generally assume that the technical author is right and do not question the issues. Unfortunately, authors are not always right; many published documents contain errors of oversight on the author's part. Even the peer reviews required by many companies miss errors, especially if the reviewers are involved closely in the same project.
- *It can lead to conflict with the technical staff.* After doing this mechanical editing, the editor meets with the technical staff to review all of the editorial changes marked. These conferences can be long and stressful [6]. The technical staff members feel as though they have no control over their own work and that the editor is making arbitrary changes; the editor is often frustrated, being left with many questions that the technical staff did not or could not adequately answer.

The comprehensive editing process evolved in part as a way to improve the overall quality of the document and to prevent unpleasant and time-consuming author conferences. Comprehensive editing is audience-oriented, rather than rule-oriented. Whereas the mechanical editor may concentrate on parsing sentences, the comprehensive editor thinks about whether a reader will understand the ideas.

During their first editorial review, comprehensive editors essentially ignore the mechanics and format of the report. Instead they focus on content, coherence, and completeness. They look at the document as a whole, at the concepts being expressed, rather than focusing on the words.

What Are the Advantages of Comprehensive Editing?

Individual engineers or researchers rarely get to see the large and complex projects they are working on as whole entities. Often, no single member of the technical staff has a broad enough perspective to recognize what readers would need to know or what the content of written procedures should be. As a result, the input from individual contributors is likely to be based on mistaken assumptions and therefore be inconsistent and uninformative [7]. Because technical staff members focus on their own areas of expertise, they do not and, in fact, cannot catch what might in the context of the larger project prove to be errors or inconsistencies. For this reason, a comprehensive editor is needed.

With comprehensive editors prompting technical staff on technical issues, the technical staff members tend to check the content of their documents more carefully. In addition, the technical staff members learn to apply the editor's suggestions to future writing; their writing abilities improve. As a result, editors and technical staff use their time more efficiently, the technical staff members feel more confident about the report, and the company releases a higher-quality product.

What Are the Attributes of a Comprehensive Editor?

One reason that much editing is merely mechanical is that it is relatively easy to find someone good at the basics (commas, headings, grammar, consistency). For comprehensive editing, an editor must be a critic. But being an editor/critic is not easy. According to Jacobi [8, p. 63],

> It takes understanding, decisiveness, a lot of courage, and a lot of tact. It takes someone whom the writer can respect but need not fear; someone who can flatter you without fawning, encourage you with full awareness of the forces he sets in motion, and squelch you where you need to be squelched, but without rancor; someone who can tell you that you are being pedantic and get away with it.

Editors sometimes limit themselves to mechanical editing because they are unfamiliar and uncomfortable with the technical context of the material they edit. They may have been cowed by what Isay calls the first rule of scholarly editing: "*You have to understand the research*" [9, p. 40]. In fact, there is very little that cannot be understood by an intelligent person who makes the effort; even if an editor may have to accept the author's technical assertions, he or she will still be able to point out where an author is obfuscating, begging the question, and fudging answers [8]. Even without enough technical knowledge to make the implicit assumptions and consequent logical leaps, an intelligent editor can still follow the explicit descriptions. Nonspecialist editors can indeed work with specialized engineers' and scholars' writing, "assuming they keep alert, work with care, and use appropriate reference resources" [10, p. 1].

Thus, the primary attributes of a comprehensive editor are not technical; rather they are tactfulness, negotiating skills, analytical ability, and general knowledge.

Tactfulness and Negotiating Skills

Tactfulness and negotiating skills are important to all technical editors. In part because editing is generally considered a support service, editors who wish to convince technical staff (or management) that changes are appropriate and necessary need to be diplomatic, not belligerent. Tactful editors are not judgmental, even though much of the job is to make judgments [9]. Above all, tactful editors know how to make it clear that they are not judging the technical author as a person but rather trying to help find the best way of getting the author's message across. More than anything else, tactful editors must know the difference between disagreement over style and being right or wrong, and they must offer solutions, not just criticism [11].

The editor's negotiating skills also apply to the problem of scheduling and communication planning. Editors use this skill to ensure that they are not expected to do impossibly long jobs in impossibly short times, and to ensure that they know what is expected of them and that their authors know what they will provide. They also use these skills in working with their support people. Thus comprehensive editors arrange to get the best support they can with the resources they have. They ensure that the work done for them is good and that their support staff will be willing to continue to cooperate and provide good work.

Analytical Ability

As in other disciplines, analytical ability is the skill of breaking down a problem, an issue, or an argument into its component parts. This ability allows the comprehensive editor to examine the flow and logic of a document (or even a sentence) and find flaws that might mislead the reader. Logic is crucial to sound argument and persuasion, and so it is essential to clear writing. An editor must be as alert to logic as to technical points, uncovering writers' errors in logic as well as in their grammar [12].

Analytical skills also help the editor ensure that all parts of processes are described and examine a text methodically, as an integrated unit rather than as a sequence of unconnected sentences. By taking text apart, the editor can determine the relationships among the parts and decide what should remain, what should be eliminated, and what should be fixed.

Because of their analytical skills, editors can tell technical staff where their presentation is weak and where it needs cutting, clarification, or condensation [8]. The editor frequently asks questions such as, "What does this mean?" It is unacceptable for an editor to accept the author's text uncritically [8].

General Knowledge

The editor must have a general knowledge about the world, knowing how things usually work, so that when anomalies occur, they are apparent. In scientific technical writing, the knowledge required of the editor as generalist is usually simple: the fact that gravity pulls things toward the earth, heat rises, water flows downward, gases are heated liquids and solids are cooled ones. With such basic knowledge, the comprehensive editor has some idea whether what is described in a document is intuitive. If it isn't, the editor looks for an explanation (in the document) of why things work in some different way—like water flowing upward because it is being pushed from below.

General knowledge is necessary because the editor might be the only person who reads the whole document before it is published; technical staff members often read only what is in their immediate area of concern. As a result, it is the editor who must notice that, although in Chapter 4 Freda said a production accident had no effect, in Chapter 7 George said the same accident accounts for a discrepancy in the data. Especially if Freda and George have used slightly different terms to describe their contradictory conclusions, a report might be published without anyone's noticing the discrepancy, until the outside client or, worse, a hostile reader finds it and complains. Thus, general knowledge enables the comprehensive editor to recognize the same idea when it is called by different names and to make it recognizable to others, preventing such embarrassment.

An advantage of hiring editors who are generalists is that they can work on anything that needs editing. A generalist can write an overview draft that the technical person might be unwilling to attempt. The editor who is a generalist can ghostwrite in a variety of specialties for a variety of technical people; write summaries and introductions that suit non-specialized audiences; recognize breaks in thought; and recognize where technical staff members have suddenly started skirting an issue or waffling because they are unwilling to commit to a position.

In short, general knowledge enables the editor to be detached enough to see the big picture, to understand how the parts fit together. Whereas analytical skills help the editor separate parts, general knowledge helps the editor put them together. Having both these attributes, the editor is able to see both the forest and the trees.

How Do You Identify These Skills in Job Candidates?

Unfortunately, a résumé does not necessarily indicate whether a candidate has the desired characteristics. Although many courses teach the basics of editing, there is no single course that can turn a student into a comprehensive editor. In fact, detailed, specialized studies may be an obstacle, because they inherently teach the student about old methods rather than burgeoning ones [13]. Just as specialization is often detrimental to cultural survival [14], the comprehensive editor is best served by maintaining versatility [13]. The most desirable candidate might then be the one who has studied in the most areas (or rather learned in them); someone who has the self-motivation to read in a variety of literatures would be a good candidate [15]. What is beneficial is the breadth of the candidate's knowledge and familiarity with technical concepts (not necessarily or merely with the terms); this is one case in which being a dilettante can be advantageous.

To identify good candidates, make your standard editing test more than just a test of copyediting skills. Zimmerman et al. [16] have suggested a technique of measuring editing skills by examining the number of times a candidate stops in reading a piece of material and the reasons for those stops (if for a grammatical point, an issue of communication effectiveness, or a question of content). In reviewing the test, see how the candidate treats ambiguity. Does the candidate just follow rules and force the text to conform? If so, although the person may be a satisfactory mechanical editor, he or she is not a good prospect as a comprehensive editor. The comprehensive editor must distinguish fact from opinion, check facts, be skeptical, improve the style, and develop the organization and clarity of the document [17]. Therefore, those are points to watch for in the test response.

In addition to testing, try to get a feel for what a candidate thinks the job of an editor is. Good candidates will see editing as being about meaning, not just about following rules. They recognize editing as being enormously challenging and creative. Therefore, talk to candidates about where they would draw lines and cut corners when time and money are tight. Ask what they consider to be the most important things to get right. Ask how they would solve problems in working with technical staff. Comprehensive editors recognize that the editor mediates between the technical author's needs and the reader's needs, simplifying communication and ensuring that the message the reader gets is the one the author intended to send. Their responses will reflect those priorities, emphasizing content over mechanics to prevent errors that would embarrass the company or the technical staff.

Although technical communications is a very broad field and no single set of attributes ensures success in all aspects, a set of particular skills required for comprehensive editing can be defined. The prospective editor can hone these skills, and the manager who needs to hire a comprehensive editor can select for these skills, as a means of improving the quality of communications.

ACKNOWLEDGMENT

This paper benefited from discussions with Virginia (Brouns) Harrison.

REFERENCES

[1] D. Bush, "Content editing, an opportunity for growth," *Tech. Commun.*, vol. 28, no. 4, pp. 15–18, 1981.
[2] D. E. Zimmerman, "Teaching content editing," in *Teaching Technical Editing*, C. D. Rude (Ed.), ATTW Anthology 6. Lubbock, TX: Association of Teachers of Technical Writing, 1985.
[3] R. Van Buren and M. F. Buehler, *The Levels of Edit*, 2nd ed., JPL Publication 80-1. Pasadena, CA: Jet Propulsion Laboratory, 1980.
[4] P. Cheney and D. Schleicher, "Teaching comprehensive editing: A proposal for university writing programs," in *Teaching Technical Editing*, C. D. Rude (Ed.), ATTW Anthology 6. Lubbock, TX: Association of Teachers of Technical Writing, 1985.
[5] V. L. Brouns and L. K. Grove, "Comprehensive editing—A solution to some typical editing problems," in *Proc. 35th Int. Tech. Commun. Conf.*, pp. WE119–WE121. Washington, DC: Society for Technical Communication, 1988.
[6] K. Garstka and M. D. Romans, "The writer/editor relationship: A docudrama," in *Proc. 34th Int. Tech. Commun. Conf.*, pp. WE77–WE80. Washington, DC: Society for Technical Communication, 1987.
[7] A. M. Selvin, "A changing role: Communicators as problem solvers," in *Proc. 36th Int. Tech. Commun. Conf.*, pp. MG79–MG81. Washington, DC: Society for Technical Communication, 1989.
[8] E. Jacobi, *Writing at Work*. Berkeley, CA: Ten Speed Press, 1985.
[9] J. Isay, "Editing scholars and scholarship," in *Editors on Editing*, Rev. ed., Gerald Gross (Ed.) New York: Harper, pp. 240–246. & Row, 1985.
[10] P. S. Taylor, "Do scholars need editing?" *The Editorial Eye*, vol. 14, no. 7. pp. 1–3, 1991.
[11] M. Cunningham, "Finding rules for substantive editing," *The Editorial Eye*, vol. 15, no. 8, pp. 1–3, 1992.
[12] B. O. Boston, "Editing logically II," *The Editorial Eye*, vol. 12, no. 4, pp. 6–8, 1989.
[13] L. Zook, "Working as a communicator: Then and now," *The Editorial Eye*, vol. 15, no. 4, pp. 1–3, 1992.
[14] M. D. Sahlins, "Evolution: Specific and general," in *Evolution and Culture*. Ann Arbor, MI: Univ. of Michigan Press, 1960, pp. 12–44.
[15] K. H. Wolf, "Educating editors," *European Science Editing*, vol. 47, pp. 18–19, 1992.
[16] D. E. Zimmerman, A. A. Day, M. Tipton, and F. Willging, "Using the signal stopping technique as a measure of editing skills," in *Conf. Rec, IEEE IPCC '92—Santa Fe, NM*, 1992, pp. 793–796.
[17] D. L. Stephenson, "From the editor's notebook: The facts tell the story," in *Proc. 37th Int. Tech. Commun. Conf.*, Society for Technical Communication, 1990, pp. ET46–ET49.

Laurel K. Grove has been a technical communicator specializing in comprehensive editing for nine years. She finds excitement and intellectual challenge in her work in environmental sciences, which came as a fairly easy transition from her prior career as an archaeologist.

Collaborative Writing in the Workplace

CHARLES R. STRATTON

Abstract—**More and more, technical experts are teaming up to produce technical documents. Dividing the workload horizontally, with each team member handling a separate chapter or section, doesn't work very well. Stratifying the project vertically, with a project team leader, a data gatherer, a writer, an editor, and a graphics person, is a more efficient and more effective method of collaborative writing. The process is quicker and the product is better because team members get to do what they are best at.**

MORE AND MORE often in business, industry, and government agencies, technical experts are teaming up to write reports, proposals, articles, and other technical documents. This is not at all surprising when we consider the widespread application of the project team approach to research, development, and engineering design. Recently, Andrea Lunsford and Lisa Ede surveyed 1200 working professionals in management, engineering, behavioral science, chemistry, and communications to seek data on collaborative writing in on-the-job contexts. Of their 530 respondents, "87 percent reported that they sometimes wrote as part of a team or group." [1] I began writing professionally in 1960 and joined the Society for Technical Communication (then the Society for Technical Writers and Publishers) in 1962. At that time, the collaborative or project team approach to writing, editing, and producing technical documents was well established, so well established, in fact, that it wasn't even a topic for discussion. Corporate authorship was the overwhelming norm.

The days of the single person handling all aspects of product development are long gone, and the days of the solitary author for technical documents are long gone, as well. Perhaps the model of the solitary writer never had any validity in business, industry, and government agencies. This article is an outgrowth of my experiences with multiple-author documents over the past 34 years and offers some suggestions for efficient and effective collaborative writing in the workplace.

THE HORIZONTAL DIVISION MODEL

My first experience with collaborative writing was as a college student. Professor Jones would assign three or four students to research a topic and write a report. The only model we knew was one of horizontal division (figure 1). If we had four students on the team, we made sure we had four chapters or sections in the report. Joe wrote chapter 1, Skip wrote chapter 2, Mary wrote chapter 3, and Harold wrote chapter 4. What could be more natural than equitable division of responsibility? Each of us researched one subtopic, outlined one chapter, wrote one draft, edited one copy, and typed one final draft. Our idea of teamwork was to get together once at the beginning and once toward the end of the project, to compare notes.

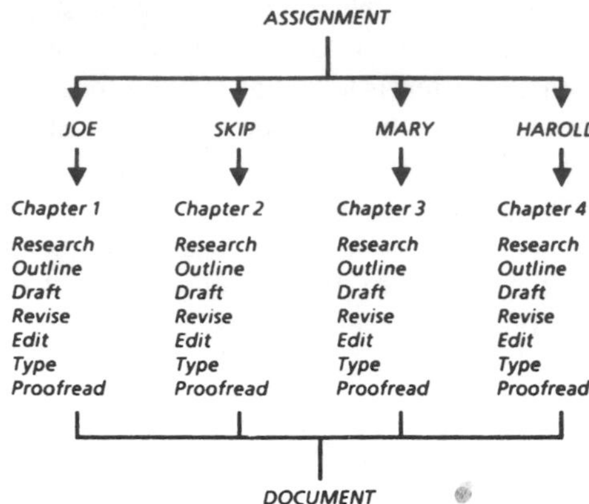

Figure 1. Collaborative Writing by the Horizontal Division Model

At best, this procedure led to a mediocre report. We would wind up with a patchwork quilt, good swatches of material but of different colors and textures and with very obvious seams. Joe's chapter was well organized and developed but poorly edited. Skip's chapter was lengthy but dull as the hood of an old pickup. Mary's chapter was well crafted but incomplete. Harold's was complete and concise but as pompous as Howard Cosell. Terminology was inconsistent from chapter to chapter. Illustrations abounded here and were absent there. There was lots of duplication, a few holes and, above all, inconsistency. And this was under the best of circumstances; most of the time, it was worse.

Unfortunately, this horizontal division model still seems to be very popular in business, industry, and government agencies—probably because managers aren't aware of any other way to improve on the solitary writer model. Lunsford and Ede found that 72 percent of their respondents used the horizontal division model at least occasionally in their writing; 24 percent, of the respondents used this organizational pattern "often" or "very often." [1]

Charles R. Stratton is a Professor of Technical Communications at the University of Idaho.

Reprinted from *IEEE Trans. Prof. Comm.*, vol. 32, no. 3, pp. 178–182, September 1989.

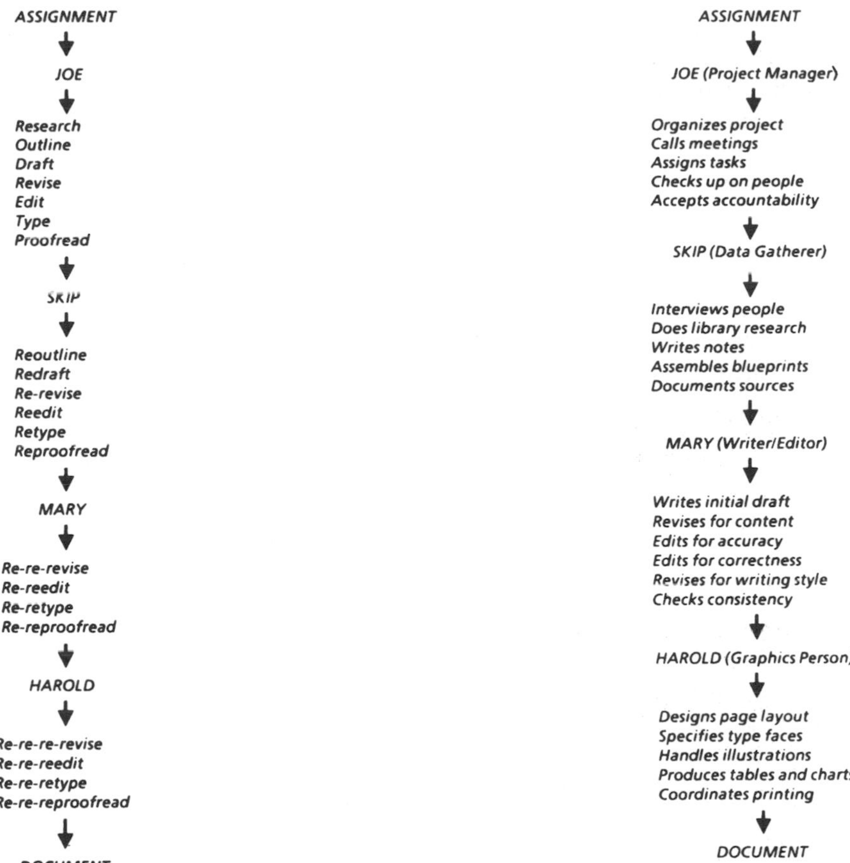

Figure 2. Collaborative Writing by the Sequential Model

Figure 3. Collaborative Writing by the Stratification Model

THE SEQUENTIAL MODEL

Early in my writing career, in the computer center of a big-ten university, I was exposed to the sequential model of collaborative writing (figure 2). In this model Joe started the ball rolling. (By this time, Joe was a technical expert—a software engineer.) Joe got the ball rolling by organizing the material, writing a draft, revising it, editing it, and having it typed up. In other words, Joe prepared what he viewed as a final draft, or pretty close to it. Joe would then give his version of the document to Skip, who by now was a technical editor. Skip regarded Joe's stuff as raw data and would promptly reorganize it, rewrite it, re-revise it, and re-edit it, much to Joe's chagrin. Skip would then pass his version to Mary, who had become a publications manager. She would say, "Ehhh, this isn't quite what I had in mind," and she would re-reorganize, re-re-revise and re-re-edit. (She didn't re-rewrite, because she was a manager, and managers don't do any writing.) Finally, the document got to Harold, the programming manager. He would take one look at it and give it back to Joe, saying "The publications people really screwed this thing up. See if you can straighten it out."

After two or three trips around this circuit, the document finally got printed and distributed. The end product was nearly always better than that produced by the horizontal division model. At least it was consistent. More than that, though, each person in the sequence contributed to the *entire* document, and, as a result, the document communicated more effectively. However, the sequential process was every bit as time consuming and inefficient as the horizontal division process. And it polarized the shop. Joe no longer talked to Skip, Skip was mad at Mary, and Mary muttered a lot about Harold and Joe. Each person in the sequence regarded each other person in the sequence as a barrier to efficient and effective communication—a hurdle that had to be jumped in order to get a document published. The sequential way of doing things was effective but not at all efficient.

THE STRATIFICATION MODEL

Finally, I landed in the service publications division of a Fortune 500 corporation. Here, we produced documents with the vertical division model, or stratification model (figure 3). Joe functioned as project manager; Skip gathered data and drafted the document; Mary revised and edited; and Harold handled format, layout, and production. Each did what he or she was really good at; all worked together, right from the start; everyone had a sense of ownership (or authorship) in the document; and the team was both effective and efficient. Here's how we divided up the duties.

Project Team Leader

Top management at the company was convinced that every project that involves more than two people needed a project manager or project team leader. This included writing projects. I agree. If the project team leader never writes a single word, he still earns his keep. The project team leader organizes the project; calls and chairs team meetings; assigns various data-gathering, writing, and revising tasks; checks up on people; keeps the project on schedule; referees disagreements; and basically accepts accountability for the project.

The critical skills for a good project team leader are ability to see the big picture, effectiveness in working with other people, and knowledge of (which usually means several years' experience in) the organization as a whole. This person need not necessarily have a job title of supervisor or manager. The project team leader can be any member of the team who has decent organizational and managerial skills.

Data Gatherer

The data gatherer or data supplier is the person who assembles all the basic information that is to go into the document. Often, the data gatherer (or data supplier) is the technical expert who knows most about subject matter of the document. In this sense, he functions much as Joe did with the sequential model, only he stops short of organizing, revising, and editing. This person might write notes, outlines, and drafts from his own knowledge, or he may assemble blueprints, specifications, and pertinent copy from other documents. He stops short of writing copy, however.

The requisite skills for a good data gatherer are knowledge of the subject matter, thoroughness, and accuracy. Ability to interview people and care in documenting sources are useful skills as well.

Writer

Following the organizational framework set by the project team leader and using the data supplied by the data gatherer, the writer generates the first draft of the document. The writer's chief job is to get some words down on paper—words that the other team members can work with. The writer is the person who translates data into copy.

A good writer needs to be able to compose text rapidly and have an easy way with words and sentences. A writer also needs a great deal of audience empathy, a sensitivity—preferably gained first hand—to the needs and natures of the people who will read the document and use the information it contains. Above all, the person who writes the draft must like to write.

Editor

The editor is the detail person. The editor is also the consistency person. The editor may do some revising; more often, if the editor sees a need for revision, he sends the draft back to the writer with suggestions or instructions, as the case may be. Mostly, the editor checks writing mechanics, usage, consistency in terminology, and the like. The editor also views the document with a detachment more like that of a reader, not having the immediate and close involvement with it of either the data gatherer or the writer.

The most important skill for an effective editor is extreme politeness. Other requisite skills include a thorough knowledge of grammar, mechanics, and usage; a sense of effective writing style; a good deal of audience empathy; and an ability to pay close attention to detail. The chief function of the editor is to move the document from good to excellent.

Graphics Person

The graphics person handles all the visual aspects of the document, including type face, spacing, and margins; page layout; headings and subheads; tables, charts, and illustrations; and the cover and title page. Often, too, the graphics person will handle printing and distribution of the document. In some cases, the graphics person will do all the work personally; in others, this individual will coordinate with photographers, illustrators, typesetters, paste-up people, and printers.

A good graphics person needs an artistic sense of theme, balance, and composition. A good graphics person also needs a thorough knowledge of the techniques of publications production and, of course, drafting skills and computer skills.

ADVANTAGES OF STRATIFICATION

The chief advantage of stratifying the collaborative writing process lies in specialization. Each person involved in developing the document gets to work in his or her area of expertise and interest. More important, the entire document benefits from each participant's specialty. The best manager organizes the entire project. The most facile writer drafts the entire document. The most careful editor edits the entire document. And the most artistic team member handles the visual aspects of the entire document. The end product is stronger and more consistent than that produced by individuals working under the horizontal division model.

A strong secondary advantage of stratification, however, lies in the immediate coordination of efforts by the project manager. Each person contributing to the document's production works in the same administrative unit, rather than being in separate sections or even separate divisions of the organization. Each is but one step from the boss. This tends to eliminate the competition between technical people and writing/editing people, or between writing/editing people and publications production people that is inherent with the sequential model. Moreover, with the project team, each participant—manager, data supplier, writer, editor, and graphics person—has a much stronger sense of involvement or authorship with the document than with either of the other methods of collaborative writing.

MIX AND MATCH

Obviously, not every collaborative writing project needs five individuals to function in these five roles. (In fact, in many writing arenas, an individual technical writer has to wear all five hats.) A single person may double up as writer and editor, or project team leader and editor, or data gatherer and graphics person. Similarly, a given person may not fill the same role with every writing project; he or she may be project team leader for one, writer for another, and editor for a third. When I wrote for the advertising department of one of the country's largest manufacturers of heating and airconditioning equipment, I saw many instances where Joe was boss and Skip was worker on one project, while during the same time period, Skip was boss and Joe was worker on another project.

Ideally, each person on the team should perform the function he or she is most skilled at. If all people working on a collaborative writing project are equally skilled at all functions, the choice usually is made on the basis of who wants to do what. (The same is true, I guess, if all people are equally unskilled.) Or sometimes, upper management will designate one team member to be project team leader, and the team leader will assign the other tasks. The important things are to have all the roles filled and to have each remain more or less discrete.

VARIATIONS ON THE THEME

Perhaps the most common variation is to eliminate the overhead and try to get along without a project team leader. I advise against it. For a team with a pretty good writer and a document whose verbal message is more important than the visual, the editor can often double up as project team leader. However, it's important for the editor to keep the two roles distinct. For a document such as an annual report or sales promotion piece, where the visual message is as important as or more important than the verbal, the graphics person might double as project team leader.

Some years ago, I was working as a technical writer with several service engineers who functioned as data suppliers. One of the engineers, however, had a flair for writing and got very testy when I tinkered with his copy. We talked about the problem and decided to shift roles. From time to time, he would fill the role of writer as well as data supplier, and I would then function as editor (which mostly meant suggesting that he make certain changes, rather than going ahead and making them myself.) This worked pretty well, so long as we both kept our roles straight. Once in a while, he would ask me to function as engineer, designing a part or a special tool or developing a service procedure, so that I got to be data supplier now and then.

In another situation some years later, I again switched roles with an engineer. I would gather the data and write the rough draft. He would then edit it, filling in all my technical holes and correcting my technical misconceptions. Although he edited mainly for content, he would take great delight in finding an occasional typographical error or terminological inconsistency. This role switching gave us a more tightly organized and more audience-empathic document and at the same time saved the engineer lots of time and frustration.

In a classroom situation, I had a mediocre student who—among other shortcomings—just couldn't edit the mechanical errors out of his own writing. He missed the project team's organizational meeting and drew, by default, guess what role? Editor. Jerry was a good sport and gave it a try. Much to his surprise (and mine), he found that he could do an excellent job of spotting and correcting the errors in other people's writing. He turned out to be a good editor, and by separating the writing and editing roles he became much better with his own work.

CONCLUDING COMMENTS

Research supports the notion that collaborative writing is both more effective and more efficient than individual efforts. That is, it produces better documents with less time spent. In an article in *Research in the Teaching of Writing* [2], Ann Ruggles Gere and Robert D. Abbott discuss collaborative writing in middle and high school and state that

> Existing research on writing groups supports their efficacy in improving critical thinking, organization, and appropriateness of writing ... in improving usage in writing ... and in increasing the amount of revision done ... .

Gere and Abbott go on to cite some 17 books, articles, and doctoral dissertations that support their observations. Lunsford and Ede's research supports the efficacy of collaborative writing as well. [1] In their survey, they asked, "In general, how productive do you find writing as part of a team or group as compared to writing alone?" Fifty-nine percent of their respondents answered "very productive" or "productive."

My own experience also supports their observations. Of the nearly two million words of scientific and technical information I have published, some were written in isolation, some with prewriting collaboration, some with postwriting collaboration (as with this article), and some with collaboration at all three stages of the writing process. Consistently, the greater the level of collaboration, the better my writing has been accepted and the less it has required revision.

In spite of this strong research and anecdotal evidence, however, I don't see much by way of teaching multiple authorship techniques in college writing classes. In what little I do see, the collaboration is limited pretty much to the horizontal division model. I suspect that the reluctance is simply due to the difficulty of evaluating the contribution of each individual student in a collaborative writing project. (It is possible to do so, however. See my article "A Project Team Approach to Technical Writing in the Classroom." [3]) To be sure, I see a fair amount of pre-writing collaboration (group discussion of topics, or brainstorming) and even more postwriting collaboration (peer review, or group editing), but not much in the middle. (See Dene Thomas [4] for a discussion of prewriting collaboration in the classroom and Kenneth A. Bruffee [5] for some suggestions regarding postwriting collaboration. Also, see Bruffee [6, 7] for discussions of some of the epistemological and pedagogical implications of collaborative writing.)

Of the several methods of collaborative writing with which I have had experience, both as a writer and as a teacher of writing, stratification is the most effective and the most efficient. It combines the advantages of specialization with the advantages of project integration. Sequencing of writing tasks without integration is a fairly effective way to collaborate, but it's not very efficient. You can get a decent writing product that way, but it takes a lot of time and effort. Horizontal division of writing tasks is neither efficient nor effective. It takes a lot of time, and the end product is not all that good, because (of course) horizontal division isn't really collaboration at all. It's just individual effort masquerading as a joint effort.

Collaborative writing is fun. Most people enjoy doing what they're good at and welcome respite from chores they're not so good at. Some people like to honcho projects but hate the details. Others like to do the work but escape the pressures of authority and accountability. A person who's not very good with words can contribute substantially in the visual department or as a data gatherer. Job satisfaction is an increasingly important commodity in today's work place.

Collaborative writing is flexible. People can learn to become good writers without having to take on total responsibility for a major document all at once. The project team approach allows for more efficient allocation of human resources. Individuals can fill different roles in different mixes at different times. Workers don't stagnate. People can find out where their strengths and weaknesses are in a matter of weeks rather than years.

In short, collaborative writing makes sense—especially under the stratificational model—and I recommend it as an efficient and effective method of producing technical documents in business, industry, and government agencies.

REFERENCES

1. Lunsford, A., and Ede, L., "Why Write ... Together: A Research Update," *Rhetoric Review 5*, 1 (Fall 1986), pp. 71-81.
2. Gere, A. R., and Abbott, R. D., "Talking About Writing: The Language of Writing Groups," *Research in the Teaching of English 19*, 4 (December 1985), pp. 362-381.
3. Stratton, C. R., "A Project Team Approach to Technical Writing in the Classroom," *Technical Communication 20*, 2 (2nd quarter 1973), pp. 9-11.
4. Thomas, D. K., *A Transition from Speaking to Writing: Small-Group Writing Conferences,* unpublished doctoral dissertation, University of Minnesota, 1984.
5. Bruffee, K. A., *A Short Course in Writing,* 2nd ed., Cambridge, MA: Winthrop, 1980.
6. Bruffee, K. A., "Writing and Reading as Collaborative Social Acts," in *The Writer's Mind: Writing as a Mode of Thinking* (Janice N. Hays, et al., ed.), Urbana, IL; National Council of Teachers of English, 1983, pp. 159-169.
7. Bruffee, K. A., "Collaborative Learning and the 'Conversation of Mankind,' " *College English 46*, 7 (November 1984), pp. 635-652.

Reverse Engineering: The Outline As Document Restructuring Tool

DIETRICH RATHJENS

Abstract—**Outlining is usually thought of as an important tool for the initial stage of document development. However, it can also be used to greatly increase the efficiency of restructuring a longer document or developing a composite text from several sources. This essay proposes and details a five-step procedure to effect such a "reverse engineering" of documents.**

OUTLINING is a fundamental part of technical writing, part of a process that normally moves from researching and noting ideas, through outlining and writing, to revising. Each of these steps is essential. Outlining, however, exerts the greatest influence on this process because it indicates the degree to which the necessary research and notation have been completed, and it defines the structure and scope of what is to be written.

Although not all engineering writers use outlines, those who do find that arranging concepts (super-, co-, and subordinating them) into an outline serves the following functions:

- It establishes the relative importance of the concepts.
- It ensures continuity of thought.
- It lends proper structure to the document.
- It promotes document completeness.

Assigning ideas to first-, second-, and lower-order headings means defining each section's limits and ensuring document coherence. It is also a *de facto* placement of emphasis.

Consecutively listing coordinate headings is a means of developing continuity, so that the concepts in one section follow from the foundations laid in preceding ones. This helps to create a smooth transition, a logical flow from one concept or subject to another.

Next, the outline gives a good picture of the scope of each section. We can compare each one's length and level of detail with those of the others. This can point up anomalies among (and within) sections, such as greatly varying lengths or single subordinate headings.

Finally, outlining helps us determine the (in)completeness of the presentation. The outline is the document in skeletal form; it is easy to use this structure for checking integrity, to preclude insufficiencies in the completed text.

These points show the importance of outlines within the context of the incipient stage of document development.[1] Yet this is only taking advantage of half their usefulness. Outlines can also be used to excellent effect when revising, or even trying to understand an ineptly structured document. They can save the writer, editor, and reader much time, as well as greatly increase the efficiency of that revision or attempt at understanding. In fact, the longer the document, the more time is saved.

This procedure is based on the concept of reverse engineering, a process of disassembling a (usually complex) device for the purpose of gaining a better understanding of how it functions or what new developments have been incorporated into it. The concept and procedure can be applied analogously to the basic restructuring or analysis of any document, by engineers and technical writers as well as editors. The procedure is simple and highly efficient; it consists of five steps, detailed in the following paragraphs.

Step 1: Make an outline that accurately reflects the structure and content of the original document.

It would be understandable, indeed even seem sensible, to begin a revision by turning to page 1 of the document and starting to edit words, sentences, and paragraphs. Three problems are associated with this intuitive, "brute force" approach.

First, it provides no overview of the task's magnitude, for use in budgeting time. Further, although it may ensure proper word choice, sentence construction, and paragraph development, it has little or no impact on overall coherence and continuity.

Dietrich Rathjens developed the Technical Writing Program for the Department of English at San Jose State University (California), where he teaches courses in technical writing and editing.

1. For additional information on outlining at this stage, the following articles are recommended:

   Hall, H.A., "MARCO—A New Technique for Outlining Technical Publications," *STWP Proceedings*, 14th International Technical Communications Conference, May 1967.

   Landreman, D.M., "A New Look at Outlining—The LSN/SN Approach," *STC Proceedings*, 21st International Technical Communications Conference, 1974, p. 88.

Reprinted from *IEEE Trans. Prof. Comm.*, vol. PC-29, no. 3, pp. 19–22, September 1986.

Second, any emendations made at this level may be vitiated later, when it becomes apparent that certain sections should be deleted or vastly restructured. The interrelation of a document's sections may render some already-edited parts superfluous or redundant.

Third, it is difficult to be sure whether you can delete certain sentences or paragraphs, or where they should be repositioned, without memorizing the entire document. Only after completing the initial edit do you know that a matter is discussed repetitiously in several parts of the document. At that point, you still have the job of combining all references to the subject into one section, deleting some, and rearranging others. This approach is like going into a labyrinth blindfolded.

More fundamental than the word-level, sentence-level, or paragraph-level edit is the structure edit. Thus, the first task is to make an outline. Even in the absence of numerical designations for sections or paragraphs, this can be done quickly by using the existing section titles and subheadings. Each numerical designation or head/subhead in the original text must have a corresponding entry in the outline.

At this stage of the edit, it may be tempting to correct in passing certain flaws, errors, or solecisms. However, this is inadvisable for two reasons:

- It can cause confusion later, in trying to correlate the revised headings of the outline with sections of the original text.
- It lessens the efficiency and speed of the outlining task.

The only concern should be the document's structure, not editing its contents or making *ad hoc* changes to the outline being developed.

Step 2: Delete those sections of the outline that do not contribute to the document's unity or purpose.

The finished outline, reflecting the original text, gives a complete perspective of the document, its structure (or lack of structure), and the interrelationship of its sections. It is now easy to ascertain which headings have little or no relation to the document's purpose; these should be deleted. However, do not renumber or change the heading designations (first-order, second-order, and the like) in the outline.

Ineptly structured documents are often carelessly written (and vice versa). Therefore, if a document has been found to require this kind of reverse engineering, it is highly likely that some sections can be deleted. This simplifies the task, because the shorter the outline, the better the overview and the better the editor's ability to manipulate headings.

It is important to remember that this step (and the two following) pertain only to the outline. Put the original text aside; do not try to effect in the document the structural changes you are making in the outline. It is shown below that this is unnecessary and time-wasting.

Step 3: Restructure the outline.

The (reduced) outline will lend itself to quick and efficient manipulation. You should now consider the importance, and, therefore, the placement, of each heading. Is it properly subordinated? Coordinated? Superordinated? If the original text was not well structured, then even after deleting irrelevant or redundant material from the outline, rearrangement—possibly even additions—will be required.

The goals of this rearrangement are the same as those of any careful outline construction: coherence and continuity. Logically grouping the headings of the outline gives the existing ideas coherence. Determining the order of the heading groups, and the headings within each group, gives continuity.

The heading designations of the before restructuring outline merely serve as "tags" that help locate the corresponding paragraph or idea in the document (which you have set aside). You need not be concerned with their rank; a third-order heading, for example, would not necessarily persist as such.

As you restructure the concepts in the original outline, you must give each heading a designation that reflects its place in the new structure. To distinguish between the original and the new designation, place the former in brackets, after the new heading.

It is generally agreed that, when subordinate headings occur within a section or subsection, there must be more than one of these (the rule of double subordination). This rule may be suspended during restructuring; single subordinates are of no consequence in this step. They will, indeed, prove helpful in the next step.

Step 4: Determine what is missing in the outline.

Two phenomena in the outline highlight missing information:

- The relative brevity of some sections
- The occurrence of single subordinates

If one or more sections of the new outline are unusually short (that is, have far fewer subheadings than the other sections), this probably indicates that those topics have not been adequately covered. This assumption is based on morphological considerations: most outlines will have few if any subheadings in the introduction and conclusions, but the central sections will often be similar in length and development. A cursory look at the tables of contents of several books will substantiate this.

Single subordinates in the original outline could have several meanings:

- This is a minor point, which should be deleted (case 1).
- There is at least one other subordinate missing (case 2).
- This subordinate should be incorporated into the next-higher-order heading (case 3).
- The subject's importance is actually commensurate with that of the next-higher-order headings; it should be made one of these (case 4).

Consider the following hypothetical outline:

Section	*Contents*
1.0	PURPOSE AND SCOPE
1.1	Purpose
1.1.1	Need for Evaluation
1.2	Scope
2.0	CONTRACT AND TECHNICAL DIRECTION
2.1	Contractual Direction
2.2	Technical Direction
3.0	MANAGEMENT TASKS
3.1	Program Plans
3.2	Reviews
3.3	Reports
3.3.1	Milestone Report
3.3.2	Status Report
3.3.3	Red Flag Report
4.0	STANDARDIZATION PLAN
4.1	Nonstandard Parts
5.0	PRODUCTION GOALS
5.1	Design to Unit Production Cost
6.0	SYSTEMS ANALYSIS TASKS
6.1	Design Verification
7.0	SYSTEM EFFECTIVENESS
7.1	Reliability, Maintainability, Producibility
7.2	Integrated Logistics Support

Section 1.1.1 illustrates case 1, above; this heading should be eliminated from the outline. Section 4.1 corresponds to case 2; the subordinate headings should be *4.1, Standard Parts,* and *4.2, Nonstandard Parts.* Section 5.1 corresponds to case 3; designation 5.1 and its heading should be deleted, and the title of section 5.0 should be *COST/PRODUCTION GOALS.* Section 6.1 illustrates case 4; it should be redesignated section 7.0. (This means that the first-order designation for all subsequent sections will be increased by one; section 7.0 will become 8.0 and so forth.)

When you have eliminated single subordinates of the case 1, case 3, and case 4 types, any single subordinates remaining in the revised outline will reflect case 2. When you have thus identified the topics that require more information, you should try to supply the missing headings. Do not try to write the text to accompany these headings. Either write it later or, if you are coordinating the work of others, tell those responsible of the urgent need for specific information. You should now proceed to the final step.

Step 5: Restructure the original text according to the revised outline.

The revised outline will probably consist of some unchanged (original) headings and some changed headings; each changed heading should be followed by the original designation in brackets. Using the original headings as signposts, find the corresponding text in the original document. Then cut and paste (either literally or on a word processor), arranging the text in the order given by the outline. Where there are new headings without any corresponding text (that is, instances where you have identified the need for more information), leave space after each to call attention to the incompleteness.

It is likely that there will be text left over, corresponding to those sections that were deleted from the original outline because of irrelevance or redundancy. Discard this text.

The cut-and-pasted text can now be edited. Incorporate the new text for the headings created in step 4, either by writing it or editing material supplied by others. The entire editing process should be simple and straightforward because the sections that would have provided the most confusion have already been eliminated. Your editing will now have purpose and efficiency. Also, you will be able to ensure consistency, as well as specify layout and format, in this one pass. This certainly would not have been possible before the basic restructuring of the document.

The procedure described above may be more readily understood if illustrated with two realistic examples:

- *Case 1*—You are under time constraints to revise an unstructured (and haphazardly written), 300-page product description into a technical proposal for a potential customer who is interested only in certain aspects of the product described.
- *Case 2*—You must produce a coherent, encompassing report on a subject that has been covered in several books and numerous articles.

Case 1

The unmanageable 300-page document could be turned into a manageable 10-page outline by following step 1. This step seems to take up valuable time, especially if done thoroughly and meticulously in ensuring parity between the numbering of sections in the original text and that of the outline's headings. It is tempting to think of the number of pages that could be edited (even superficially) in this amount of time. However, it soon becomes apparent that the outlining actions are much more trenchant than any editing could have been, and that this seeming detour is actually the start of a remarkable shortcut.

Deleting inappropriate headings (step 2) is easily effected because of the outline's relative brevity. The 10-page outline suggested above may now be only seven or eight pages long. Also, the next step (in effect, the original task in miniature) is easily managed because of the overview afforded by the outline.

Determining what is missing can be a complex task, depending on your knowledge of the product being offered and the customer's needs. This step often requires the assistance of staff members in engineering or marketing organizations. It should not result in a noticeable lengthening of the outline; rather, the outline should only indicate those concepts that must be presented (or presented in greater detail). A copy of the restructured outline will indicate the desired level of detail to the person charged with writing the new sections.

The restructuring of the original text (step 5) can be done by rote if sufficient care was exercised in step 1. Then, only the editing (for grammar, punctuation, style, and so forth) of the document remains to be done—a simple job, requiring only one pass.

Case 2

Here, the task is more complex, producing a complete report by integrating sections from various sources. Although the course is not as linear as in case 1, above, it is still fairly simple. In step 1, you make an outline of each book, using first-order headings for chapters, second-order headings for sections, and so on. (It is possible that the table of contents of each book will serve this purpose; at least it will facilitate outlining the book.) The articles can be treated as one book, with a first-order heading for each, because articles usually compare with chapters in a book, in both level of detail and length.

Because the original texts all pertain to the topic of the report, step 2 will consist of eliminating redundancy among the outlines. Compare two outlines at a time. If both address the same concept, choose the more detailed discussion; then delete the superfluous section from the other outline. This process is continued until all outlines have been compared and all redundancies deleted.

You can now effect step 3 by integrating the remaining sections of the various outlines into a new, composite outline. Since you chose the more detailed discussion for each concept presented more than once, you may have some inconsistencies in length and level of detail between these discussions those that did not result from such a choice. Step 4 will probably consist of noting those sections that are much briefer than others in the new outline. This will lead either to further research on the concepts they cover, or at least to a notation that no more information is currently available.

Developing the report from the composite outline should not be difficult if step 1 was done methodically and carefully. It comprises cutting and pasting texts in the order prescribed by the new outline. Editing for continuity and for consistency in style should, then, require only one pass.

The advantages of using an outline for the reverse engineering of one or more documents should be apparent. Of prime importance is the order imposed on the task, which provides a perspective of the entire project. This perspective, in turn, allows for the effective budgeting of time. Each step taken toward completion of the project is the most efficient one; the tasks are streamlined, each sharply focused.

The most important advantage, however, is the saving of time. Proof of the time saved, and a full appreciation of it, requires a comparison with the usual (brute force) method of revision. The time saved is in direct proportion to the length of the original document. For documents of several hundred pages or more, therefore, this method becomes imperative.

How Writing Helps R&D Work

HERBERT B. MICHAELSON
LIFE MEMBER, IEEE

Abstract – **An engineer author can develop better perspectives and even new technical concepts when writing a report of project work done in an R&D laboratory. These new insights eventually help the engineering work in subtle but powerful ways. An illustrative example is given.**

INTRODUCTION

Writing can be surprisingly productive for an author, especially where development work is being reported. The benefits of good writing can indeed be subtle. Although many engineers readily admit acquiring new ideas while writing manuscripts, others are not always aware of the insights born of writing. Regardless, such new understandings eventually are reflected in the engineer's own work and achievements. Composing a report or paper, then, sets up interactions among the author, the manuscript, and the work itself.

The relation between writing and thinking is summarized nicely by a brief comment in the famous book on the elements of style by Strunk and White [1]:

> Fortunately, the act of composition, or creation, disciplines the mind; writing is one way to go about thinking, and the practice and habit of writing not only drain the mind but supply it, too.

This is especially true of any report on a research and development (R&D) project that was, during the development cycle, plagued with changes of pace and new directions of thinking. In preparing such a report, the engineer must retrace the thread of development work to construct an intelligible description of what was done, what was found, and what was contributed to the state of the art. In thinking the whole process through, the author may discover limitations and omissions in the data base.

The author is a consultant in technical communication in Jackson Heights, NY.

This paper shows how creativity in writing can actually help the work. It also cites an illustrative example of how a frustrated attempt to describe completed development work produced instead a new engineering concept.

CREATIVITY IN WRITING

Although the discipline of formal writing can expand a writer's own technical ideas, there are also some negative aspects. All writing, of course, is not creative. Much depends on the author's attitude.

The bored author who considers writing a tiresome but necessary evil will inevitably produce a bored, tired manuscript, mechanically written and lacking in imagination. Even though such a paper is clear, correct, and accurate, it can be deadly dull. The author's negative feelings have quenched any spark of creative effort.

The engineer who wants to be known for contributions to the field adopts a different approach to writing. Such an author carefully reviews the methods and results of the development project, identifies the portions of the work that were novel and innovative, and emphasizes those items in the manuscript. This kind of critical probing of the engineering work can produce not only new patterns of thinking but also a more interesting paper.

The mechanisms of thinking that produce sudden bursts of insight are poorly understood. Regardless of how these creative forces operate, they seem to be at play in an engineer's reporting of R&D work. When writing a paper at the completion of a laboratory project, many an author senses a new interpretation or sees a defect in the results and goes back to the laboratory for additional data, a more thorough analysis, or a modified design.

One theory of the subconscious to explain this kind of spontaneous thinking was favored by several scientists, including Helmholtz and Poincaré: While the mind is occupied with a conscious activity (for instance, composing a manuscript), new ideas and relationships are being generated at the same time in the unconscious. According to this theory, fresh, creative thinking consists of ideas rushing pellmell into the conscious mind from a mental arena below the writer's threshold of awareness.

Reprinted from *IEEE Trans. Prof. Comm.*, vol. PC-30, no. 2, pp. 85–86, June 1987.

Whatever the thought mechanism, an author's attempt to sort out the facts and set them down in a manuscript in logical order does tend to yield a fresh perspective and new understandings.

INTERACTIONS BETWEEN AUTHOR AND PERSONAL COMPUTER

Because of the proliferation of computers in industrial laboratories, many engineers now compose reports and papers on a personal computer (PC) or workstation instead of on a typewriter. The interactions between writer and machine tend to stimulate creativity in writing in several different ways – an unexpected fallout from the new technologies.

The obvious benefits of using a PC are fast corrections and insertions, automatic formatting, spelling checks, and freedom from proofreading the revised papers. Less obvious, however, are the machine's influences on the writer's intellectual output and therefore on the engineering work.

Composing on a PC effects some definite changes in the engineer's writing habits. Writing habits, of course, cannot be separated from thinking habits. The modifications of the writing process are due to the speed of the machine. For example, fleeting ideas are part of every writer's composing process; the mind generates new ideas, in fact, far faster than a writer can inject them into a typewritten or handwritten paper. The computer quickly records such thoughts before they are lost from short-term memory. Simplification of the mechanics of writing allows more attention to the intellectual process. Further, the PC does a rapid, legible job of modifications and additions to the text and does it easily; this capability gives the author more time (and more inclination) to refine the technical content of the manuscript.

The machine affects a writer's thinking in another way. For the PC user, "writer's block" tends to disappear because of a psychological reaction: the machine forces the attention of the user and in effect invites an author to take control of the writing situation. In addition, the computer has certain functions that aid the user's reasoning power. Engineering ideas can be explored and tested with programs that build models and do simulations, to confirm and extend technical concepts. Often the calculation and simulation functions can be carried out on the same computer or computer terminal as the writing function. Programs that facilitate moving back and forth between these functions have facilitated the creative process enormously.

In addition, when connected to a communication network, the PC or workstation permits quick interaction with other people. This, of course, is a decided advantage in any kind of cooperative writing project. Co-authors in separate buildings can trade notes or send revised manuscripts almost instantaneously on the network. Here, again, the speed of transmission becomes an actual stimulus to information exchange and to a free play of thinking.

Another excellent function of the PC is its use for writing a report or paper in increments – a technique described some years ago in these *Transactions* [2]. This method consists of writing a manuscript in segments as the development work on the project proceeds. The writer stores successive increments of the paper on disk or in system memory. The insights derived at various times during the writing are thus applied to engineering work. Instead of first beginning to think of writing a paper at the end of the project, the author can print out a completed draft, ready for revision and editing.

Writing in increments is not a theory. It has been used successfully by hundred of engineers to prepare papers for publication while design or development work was still in process. The writing was part and parcel of the development cycle instead of an afterthought.

ILLUSTRATIVE EXAMPLE

Industrial research and development usually takes place in an atmosphere of change. Even with the best of planning, modifications are necessary to meet new requirements or improved approaches to the work. These may be dictated, for example, by changes in marketing strategies or by news of competitive developments in another company.

Or else, an engineering project may get off to an awkward start for one reason or another and require new thinking. Here is an example of such a situation, in which writing actually helped the work.

Many years ago, when applications of electronic computing were beginning to develop commercially, a programmer at an IBM laboratory designed an ingenious system for solving a traffic problem at a given street corner. The problem dealt with variations of pedestrian traffic throughout the day, a specified number of vehicle right-hand turns per hour, a need for periodically adjusting the traffic signals, and so on. When the program was completed, the programmer's manager asked him to prepare a report describing its operation for the customer. Writing the document was a frustrating job and, as a direct consequence of these frustrations, the author first began to realize the complications of the mathematics on which the program was based.

When the report was half finished, the programmer suddenly had a new idea and abandoned the writing. He started over again from scratch and worked out a new program for the traffic problem. This program generated a graphic printout representing the street corner, with built-in parameters and variables. The program was successful and later became widely used by traffic engineers.

REFERENCES

1. Strunk, W., Jr., and White, E. B., *The Elements of Style*, Third Edition, Macmillan Publishing Co., Inc., New York, 1979, p. 70.
2. Michaelson, H. B., "The Incremental Method of Writing Engineering Papers," *IEEE Transactions on Professional Communications*, *PC-17*, No. 1, 1974, pp. 21-22.

The Paradox of Revision: A Study of Writing as a Product in the Revision of Manuals

Alice I. Philbin and Melissa M. Spirek

Abstract— **Businesses need not do much that is expensive, radical, or new to improve their documentation, and a product-oriented approach is much more likely to be used in the workplace instead of the writing-as-a-process approach. These are the two findings that emerged from our study of the revision of manuals as described by practicing technical communicators. We conducted in-depth interviews with 20 technical communicators from six different types of industries to explore and understand their concept and use of the revision process. The study describes the understanding technical communicators have of revision in their corporate cultures and then discusses the need for an improved understanding of product-based writing among educators of technical communicators.**

THE broad idea of "revision" is easily documented as a salient concept for technical communicators in both the industrial and academic arenas. Technical communicators in the workplace dedicate numerous hours to revising manuals and rank revision as an important topic for communication training. Similarly, many technical communication educators devote a segment of their course curricula to revision. Despite the importance of revising manuals as a key activity for technical communicators, very little information exists about how technical communicators revise manuals in the workplace.

INTRODUCTION

The Problem

Diane Haugen has explored the process of revision [1]. She observes that practicing editors can profit from academics' research on the writing process. Although we agree with her conclusion, this paper focuses upon the contention that academics and practicing technical communicators can also learn from technical communicators' revision processes in the workplace. Specifically, the purpose of this paper is to respond to the void in the literature on revision from the viewpoint of the practicing technical communicator. In this study, we present practicing technical communicators' definitions of revision and, based upon their insights, offer businesses and educators several recommendations for improving their documentation revision process. Our literature review describes three categories of influential revision studies. These three categories of studies are then used as the bases for generating the three research questions that guided the current investigation.

Studies of Revision Comparing College-Level and Workplace Writers

One of the three studies examines the revision process as it is practiced by college students and professional writers such as instructors and journalists. Journalists and students were in the sample of the writers studied by Faigley and Witte [2]. In this study, experts were found to differ from inexperienced writers in their revising steps. Experts were more likely to "bring a text closer to fitting the demands of the situation" [2, p. 411]. Differences between expert and novice writers when revising were also the findings of Hayes, Flower, Schriver, Stratman, and Carey [3], who proposed a cognitive processing model of revision. Finally, the Flower–Hayes [4] team built upon their earlier research by testing the cognitive model in a second study to see how helpful the model could be to beginning students of writing.

Studies of Revision in the Workplace

Revision has also been examined as a part of the collaborative writing process among professionals such as managers, engineers, and academics who write for various occupational requirements. Tomlinson's interviews with professional writers demonstrated that metaphors are useful when describing the revision process. Her study is important because she notes that too often academics "lump together as revision a variety of processes that have little more in common than their timing—they occur after some set of initial decisions, statements, and efforts at text" [5, p. 75].

Odell and Goswami [6] edited a collection of studies of writing and revision in varied professional settings. In addition, Broadhead and Freed [7] compared and contrasted the revising processes of two company vice-presidents and management consultants who were employed in the same firm. An analysis of eight writing samples provided support for the conclusion that cultural and personal characteristics were reflected in the professionals' respective proposals.

The definitive study of occupational writing and collaboration, Ede and Lunsford's *Singular Texts/Plural Authors* [8], first argued that writers compose and revise in teams even when the writers think they do not. It is the foundation of many later works that refer to revision as a part of collab-

Manuscript received March 1995; revised November 1995.

A. I. Philbin is with the Program in Scientific and Technical Communication, Bowling Green State University, Bowling Green, OH 43403 USA.

M. M. Spirek is with the Department of Telecommunications, Bowling Green State University, Bowling Green, OH 43403 USA.

Publisher Item Identifier S 0361-1434(96)02280-1.

Reprinted from *IEEE Trans. Prof. Comm.*, vol. PC-39, no. 1, pp. 30–37, March 1996.

orative writing, works such as Barabas' *Technical Writing in a Corporate Culture* [9] and Lay and Karis's *Collaborative Writing in Industry: Investigations in Theory and Practice* [10]. These major works, the bases of much of the current written communication pedagogy, test and expand on Flower and Hayes's [11] observation that writing is a dynamic and fluid process.

Studies of Technical Communicators as Writers

Although a few scholars have investigated the writing step of revision and others have investigated the writing process in the workplace, a smaller group of studies has explored technical communicators' revision of manuals in the workplace.

In a survey of 420 technical communicators, Scanlon and Coon [12] found that over half of their participants thought that revising should be included and emphasized as a critically important topic for a basic college course in technical communication. However, the term *revision* was not defined, nor was its application in an industrial setting discussed. A study by Gerich [13] focused upon revision among the technical communicators in a scientific laboratory. She found that the technical editors' three main responsibilities were consistent with "the three primary skills of expert writers: detect problems, diagnose their causes, and determine strategies to fix them" [13, p. 59].

We found only one article, Haugen's "Editors, Rules and Revision Research" [14], that examines the discrepancy between the writing process as taught in the classroom and as it is practiced in the workplace. Her case study described clearly the product-oriented nature of the writing her participants practice at work. Haugen's article is quite important, for she discusses in detail the literature of revision and its paradoxes; however, she does not directly test her contentions about this discrepancy between the classroom and workplace for the technical editor. Even more important, however, is her conclusion that the workplace should adopt the university classroom's writing-process model.

Although we found a limited literature that examines, compares, or contrasts the writing practices of technical communicators in different industries, we found no studies of revision as a specific task of technical communicators or editors who write manuals for a variety of industries. Not only is there very little direct study of writers of manuals as revisers, but also the study of revision practices among technical communicators is made even more thorny because, typically, process-oriented researchers tend to describe revision as inextricably linked to the other steps of the writing process. Yet the technical communicators themselves claim to spend a large amount of time at work on revision; it is an area that merits examination if only to improve the speed of the process. In studying this issue, we attempt to search for common themes and typologies in order to provide a better understanding of technical communicators' revising of manuals. We agree with Clair, McGoun, and Spirek, who argue that "typologies can guide research toward elegant and useful theories which may illuminate the sources of and solutions to a problem" [15, p. 211]. In short, our study results in a classification or typology of the technical communicators' views of their revision process.

Our study explored three research questions:

- How do technical communicators who write manuals primarily in a business setting define the term *revision*?
- What are the actual procedures technical communicators follow to revise a company manual? This question suggests as well our curiosity about how the structures and policies of particular types of businesses influence the technical communicators' manual revisions.
- What are the implications of our study for educators of technical communicators and for practicing technical communicators?

METHOD

Sample

A purposive sample was selected for this study. The Society for Technical Communication's biennial Profile is a fairly definitive report about the work compensation and attitudes of technical communicators. We attempted to imitate the distribution patterns of the *Profile 92* [16] in the subject recruitment. The *Profile 92* classified technical communicators by a category called "Employer Operations," a term for the type of industry in which a worker is employed. Our own experience indicates that a worker may be employed in several categories at once. For example, he or she may compose documentation for telecommunications software, thus crossing into two or three of the STC's categories of software documentation, hardware documentation, and telecommunications. Nonetheless, the categories in the STC membership survey provided the most reasonable basis for our subject selection because the STC survey was completed by 420 respondents.

We identified 30 alumni who worked in the various types of firms described in STC's biennial Profile member reports. We phoned potential subjects and were able to arrange interviews with 20. With about half in the computer hardware and software industries, and with the others somewhat evenly distributed among the other STC Profile categories, our sample corresponded to the workplace. As shown in Table I, there were 15 women and 5 men; 2 of the women could have been classified as minorities, although the STC Profile does not report on race or ethnic distribution. The sample of 11 B.A. and 9 M.A. graduates was fairly representative of the profession. As in the STC data, most of our interviewees were writers primarily; 15 of the participants performed writing only, 5 had supervisory responsibilities but wrote as well, and 1 worked as a freelance communicator.

Procedure

We used an interview schedule because a detailed survey instrument would have interfered with the inquiry. We designed an instrument that would elicit baseline data about revision through a dialogue. The schedule presented the concept of revision as a series of topics in a simple three-part, 13-item topic outline. The first 3 items asked about the process of

TABLE I
SAMPLE DEMOGRAPHICS

Sequence	Interview Description	Sex	Education	STC Categories*	Company Type
INT01	Statistical Process Control Manufacturer	F	M.A.	CSH	International
INT02	Computer Documentation & Training Manuals	F	M.A.	CSH	National
INT03	Communications Corporation Computer Documentation	F	B.A.	CSH	International
INT04	Database and Accounting Software	F	B.A.	CS	National
INT05	Accounting Software Manufacturer	F	M.A.	CS	National
INT06	Free-Lance for Procedures and Newsletters	F	M.A.	O	Metropolitan
INT07	Engineering Firm	F	B.A.	E	International
INT08	Research Company with a Communications Franchise	M	B.A.	T	International
INT09	Manufacturing Company	F	M.A.	E	International
INT10	Automobile Manufacturer	M	B.A.	CS	International
INT11	Automobile Manufacturer	F	M.A.	CS	International
INT12	Defense Contractor and Designer of Training Systems	F	M.A.	A	National
INT13	Defense Contractor and Designer	F	B.A.	A	National
INT14	Federal Unit of a Computer Systems Company	M	M.A.	TR	International
INT15	Refrigeration Company	F	M.A.	O	National
INT16	Heavy Manufacturing	F	B.A.	O	International
INT17	Engineering Company	F	B.A.	ET	International
INT18	Acoustics Firm	M	B.A.	T	International
INT19	Manufacturer of Computer Hardware	M	B.A.	CH	International
INT20	Bank	F	B.A.	O	Regional

Note. The STC survey combines the categories of computer software and computer hardware. The group above was separated with computer software (CS), computer hardware (CH), and computer software and hardware (CSH).

*STC Categories CSH -- computer software and hardware, CS -- computer software, CH -- computer hardware, A -- aerospace, T -- telecommunications, TR -- training, O -- other.

revision and the personnel who initiate revisions of documents within the interviewees' firms. The second set of 3 items focused on the technical communicators' roles, decisions, and actions during revision. The third set examined the collaborative aspect of revision by asking about the roles of peers, other writers, supervisors, users, constraints, and subject matter experts in the process. The interviews were tape-recorded and lasted about one hour.

Coding

This study used an interdisciplinary approach adopted from the ethnographic traditions of technical communication and mass communication. Thus the coding categories emerged from the patterns provided by the interviews. The procedure we used was that provided by Fielding and Fielding [17], who mandated that the frequency and themes offered by the participants be used for the analysis. As suggested by Walzer and Gross [18], we chose to use the participants' own words, including their colloquial and sometimes substandard usage for descriptions and for categories.

We assigned each interview a sequence number as a means of protecting the technical communicators' identities. The interview sequence number remained with its participant for all coding and recordkeeping. All interviews were transcribed, and all identifications of the speakers or their firms were removed from the transcripts. Two separate readers coded each transcript. We compared the coding and determined the ultimate classification of each type of item. We did not force consensus; rather, as subject-matter experts, we collated and interpreted the codes that the trained volunteers assigned [19].

FINDINGS

Research Question 1: How do technical communicators who write manuals primarily in a business setting define the term revision *?*

The technical communicators shared a view of the term *revision* because all of the participants stated they were aware of revision as part of their writing process. Within that orientation, the participants described revision as either a part of a product package or as a part of a solo product, the document itself that is sold as a product. Specifically, most of the technical communicators described their writing in conjunction with a product, and the remaining participants described their writing as the product itself. Half of the

TABLE II
How the Sample Views Revision

Interview Sequence	Dynamic/ Continuous	ISO 9000	Task Importance	Writing As A Solo Product	Writing With A Product/ Package
INT01	YES		Primary		
INT02	YES		Primary		
INT03	YES		Secondary		YES
INT04	YES		Secondary		YES
INT05	YES		Primary		YES
INT06	YES		Primary	YES	YES
INT07		YES	Secondary		YES
INT08	YES		Secondary		YES
INT09	YES		Secondary	YES	YES
INT10	YES		Secondary		
INT11	YES		Secondary		
INT12			Primary		YES
INT13	YES		Primary		YES
INT14	YES		Primary		YES
INT15			Primary		YES
INT16			Secondary		YES
INT17			Secondary		YES
INT18			Secondary		YES
INT19			Primary		YES
INT20	YES		Primary	YES	

participants described the revision process as the primary focus of their jobs, and half described it as a secondary job task. Even though 13 of the participants referred to revision as a dynamic and continuous process, invariably they talked about it as part of a product orientation, as shown in Table II. All of the participants defined revision by describing a product as opposed to a process orientation toward writing.

We turned to Voss and Keene's textbook definition [20] for a validity check of this distinction between product and process writing. They define the product approach as that which "... expects each student to figure out where and how things went wrong in that specific assignment, generalize from those instances, carry the generalizations over to the next assignment, and then see how to apply those generalizations to that next assignment's (different) specific situation [20, p. 1]." In contrast "(t)eaching writing as a process means 'opening up' what goes on between the instant someone conceives of a writing task (for example, when a student receives an assignment) and the time that person declares emotional and psychological closure on the task (for example, when a student gets a grade)" [20, p. 1]. Thus our ultimate finding is the unmasking of the paradox of revision, an activity that is performed one way (as a product orientation with its implied deadlines) but described another (as an open-ended process).

From the participants' comments and vocabulary, we built a typology of definitions. We explored how the participants defined revision and then we looked through the sample for patterns as the participants described their revision processes at their firms. Two major definitions of revision emerged.

Definition One—Revision as a Comprehensive Act: Revision as a term for a comprehensive act categorized 13 of the distinctions made by the 20 interviewees. The technical communicator of an international engineering firm captured the essence of revision from the comprehensive perspective:

> By revision here, we will mean engineering changes or design changes in a product that occur over time, and those changes need to be reflected in the support information—particularly hard copy manuals (INT18).

One technical communicator of the sample of 20 mentioned her company's compliance with ISO 9000. Her revision definition was also consistent with those of the majority of the sample. But importantly, her comments were the only ones to show that the ISO 9000 standards shaped her clarification of the revision concept:

> Before ISO, we didn't have a procedure for maintenance. Say I completed a manual and we got a user comment form which said "page 36 has wrong information" then I might just go off on my own and correct it on my own schedule, and do it the way I felt best. Now with these ISO procedures, we have very specific ways that we go about revising manuals (INT07).

The other 19 respondents either did not mention ISO 9000 or said it had no effect on their revision patterns.

Definition Two—Revision and Updating as Related Concepts: In contrast to the conceptual clarification of revision as a term for a comprehensive act, 7 of the interviewees independently and spontaneously defined the term revision by referring to updating as a key concept. Three relationships between revision and updating emerged.

In some cases, revision and updating had the same meaning. For example, 2 of our interviewees, both with international computer firms, referred to the terms similarly:

> Revision is a matter of updating things. Because they're into such technical things. Software changes by the day. Support agreements change by the day. Legal things change all the time so they're in a constant struggle to get it up to date and out to the customer (INT01).

This was also the view of the technical communicator of an international statistical process control manufacturer:

> Since I've been there, I've written from ground level a 1000-page book and I am currently revising a 1500-page book. When I say I'm revising, I should say updating (INT14).

In both cases, the emphasis is on information as the driving force for a language or style change.

A second relationship emerged as 3 of the participants described the terms *revision* and *update* as unique and independent concepts. A technical communicator working for an international automobile manufacturer defined this view aptly:

> When I think of revision, I think of revising a draft after somebody has reviewed it or before I give it to somebody to review, whereas I think you mean it more as what we call updating (INT11).

A similar description was also offered by a technical communicator at a medium-sized database and accounting software manufacturer:

> When you ask what revising is to me, at our company, there's two types. One is when a document is already printed and for some reason we decide to update it while the current product is still shipping . . . . (T)he owner is a visionary on a daily basis. This makes it interesting in terms of revision. We have to be technical enough to study the product every day and see what changes have been made. When development of a new product occurs, revision starts with an old product (INT04).

These quotations show that our technical communicators were comfortable using the terms *revision* and *update* separately to refer to different tasks they perceived to be parts of the text-preparation process.

In yet a third definition, interviewees described revision as subordinate to or as part of updating. Two participants offered this clarification. For example, a technical communicator at an international communication research company said:

> When you say revision I assume an existing document for an existing product, and there's a new version coming out. The revision would be an update of the existing document to reflect whatever changes have been made to the new product. It also could be that the product was stagnant, but since the document and the product have been released to the field, customer comments or errors in the document have been reported back to the tech pubs group and a revision is made to update those problems (INT08).

In heavy manufacturing, we found the same type of distinction. For example, a writer in an automotive factory elaborated on the relationship between revision and updating:

> I like to consider an update as a time when you have to update whatever documentation you have because of a change in the system. That's what constitutes an update. To me a revision is revising or making changes or treatments to a document for the purpose of making it more readable, more usable (INT10).

Clearly, this communicator sees revision as an aspect or subset of an information- or production-driven update.

Research Question 2: What are the actual concerns technical communicators confront as they revise company manuals?

Interviewees reported three main concerns as they revise documentation: defining the type of revision (language-based or information-based) for supervisory, cost management, and task hierarchy purposes; understanding the genesis or organizational purposes for the revision; and determining the accountability for reviews.

Type of Revision Needed: Two different types of revision were mentioned by the participants. The distinction is consistent with two of Schriver's [21] test categories for evaluating text quality. Schriver's two categories are called text-focused and reader-focused, while we preferred to categorize the revision responses as language-based and information-based.

Language-based revision refers to the traditionally editorial or copy-editing aspects of revision. The writer examines the text for clarity, accuracy, arrangement, word choice, and other traditionally editorial functions. Roundy describes this aspect of revision as being one of "mechanical accuracy" [22]. Participants described language-based revision as checking for "good" grammar, accurate punctuation, and conventional usage. This revision includes any acts related to the improvement of the document primarily as a piece of writing and secondarily as a product.

Information-based revision describes the transformation of the document by the addition or deletion of information. This category is consistent with Coney's view of the manual reader as a receiver of information [23]. The information might be a revised engineering specification, some new lines of computer code, a list of new product features, debugging or troubleshooting procedures, or a complete redesign of the document's appearance for various reasons, including conformity with the firm's design requirements, the maintenance of a competitive position within its market, or the satisfaction of the design preferences of the firm's decision-makers.

Genesis or Purpose: The revisions were initiated by internal and external personnel. An internal revision is initiated by an employee, whereas an external revision is initiated by someone outside the company, for example, a customer, a vendor, or a consultant. These categories are not mutually exclusive. For example, a technical communicator employed by a major defense contractor and designer of training systems noted that a language-based revision is requested within the organization (internal revision), or an information-based revision can also be requested either internally or externally. That is, the military client may make a request (external), or an engineer employed by the firm might request a revision (internal).

An internal language-based revision was described by 7 of the technical writers, and 1 of the 7 also mentioned an externally generated language-based revision. In addition, 2 of these 7 technical writers emphasized that language-based changes are not the sole grounds for revision at their firms. "They are thrown at me and I forget about them" (INT05). "We don't do revisions for typos" (INT19). These two responses would indicate that language-based revisions tend to be subordinate to information-based revisions.

The technical communicators reported that a number of people were directly involved with the revision process. An internal information-based revision was described by 15 of the participants. As shown in Table III, 10 of these 15 technical communicators described an internal information-based revision as they also reported that they completed an external information-based revision. The information-based revisions were initiated by someone external to the com-

TABLE III
HOW THE INTERVIEWEES DESCRIBE THE REVISION PROCESS

Interview Sequence	Language-Based Revision Internal	Language-Based Revision External	Information-Based Revision Internal	Information-Based Revision External	Testing	Revision Accountability
INT01				YES	YES	Customer
INT02	YES		YES	YES		Customer; Proofreader
INT03			YES	YES		Sales; Engineers; Marketing
INT04			YES	YES		Customer
INT05			YES	YES		Technical Support
INT06	YES	YES		YES		Customer
INT07			YES	YES	YES	Customer
INT08			YES	YES	YES	Customer
INT09			YES	YES		Customer
INT10	YES		YES			
INT11	YES		YES			Editor
INT12	YES			YES		Writer; Engineers
INT13	YES		YES			Engineers
INT14				YES		Engineers
INT15			YES	YES		Engineers; Technical Support
INT16						Engineers
INT17	YES		YES			Writer
INT18			YES	YES		Customer; Engineers
INT19			YES			Engineers
INT20			YES	YES		Government Regulated

pany—usually the customer. A total of 14 of the sample of 20 technical communicators practiced external information-based revision. Formal channels for customer input such as comment cards and 800 numbers were mentioned by 12 of the interviewees as the means by which the customers were encouraged to provide feedback about the product and its documentation.

Accountability: Most of the technical communicators mentioned multiple groups of reviewers. Engineers and technical support personnel were the most likely to review a revised document. Table III demonstrates that we found that the customers made up the second most-consulted group, whereas, for example, the writers, editors, and peer reviewers were the third-most likely to be consulted.

Other factors contributed to the interviewees' picture of revision as practiced within their corporate cultures. For example, 14 of the participants reported that their revisions were related to product-driven deadlines. Over half of the interviewees reported that the writer would work on the revision either alone or with an editor, and 6 said that technical support personnel or engineers must approve the revision. Four interviewees reported that multiple department heads contributed to the revisions, and 1 communicator reported that the company's marketing representative was the key individual who contributed and approved revisions before their release.

Research Question 3: What are the implications of the interviews for both those who educate technical communicators and those who are employed as technical communicators?

1) *More studies of writing as a product orientation.* Of our 20 interviewees, only 1 spoke of writing in a process frame of reference. Our study would seem to indicate that even though the process approach helps students learn to write, the product-oriented, deadline-driven method prevails in the technical communication settings of our interviewees. It would appear that academics would need to address this discrepancy. We need to extend a certain amount of respect to a product-orientation toward writing as we introduce our technical communication students to writing within the world of commerce. Studies are needed of the full dimension of the product orientation so we can prepare students better for the transition from college writing and its attendant process basis to corporate or business, that is, product- and deadline-oriented writing with its orientation toward a task hierarchy. There is a major difference between the fluidity inherent in a process approach and the task-analyzed orientation of the product approach. Our students deserve to understand how to navigate between the two approaches.

2) *Some awareness of discrepancies in product- and process-based writing.* Students need to be aware of the discrepancies between their college-level writing classes and the world

of business. Numerous studies have established the benefits of the process orientation in the education of college students; nonetheless, when these young professionals enter the world of business they need to understand the importance of deadlines, contracts, multiple reviews, and the effects of the institutional or corporate contexts upon the editing and production of documents. In order to engage students with their texts, instructors may find it useful to use the process-based approach to writing, but the results of this study suggest that after college and in industry, despite talk of the writing process, the approach is almost totally product-based.

3) *More testing of writing.* Only 3 of our participants reported any testing of their manuals. In each case, the testing through beta and usability tests occurred too late in the product development cycle to be truly beneficial to the design of the manuals. At least 4 of our 20 interviewees mentioned that their manuals accompany the firm's products to the products' testing but that the manuals themselves were never actually tested as a component of the product testing. When we asked why that was so, the interviewees volunteered that testing the manual with the products had not even been considered. At best it seems inefficient not to test the manuals when a firm's engineers intend to use them as part of a product test anyway. Companies need to understand the value added to their sales and product service that can occur if manuals are tested [24].

4) *Quality assurance of communications.* Quite a few of the companies have quality-assurance mechanisms for their documentation in place, but they fail to use them. For example, at least 4 interviewees described their contact with customer hot line or service personnel whom they saw to learn about the product. However, none of the information developed by the technical communicators during these visits was ever used. Other participants described service classes they attended in which they interviewed product users; they then explained that the classes helped the writers to learn about the products but that no system was in place so that the technical communicators could incorporate the information from the service classes into their documentation. Similarly, the technical communicators were neither encouraged nor permitted to follow up on the contacts they had made with actual product users during the service classes they attended, but we know that such follow-ups are cost-effective methods of information development. Several other participants described interviews with all kinds of subject matter experts: engineers, technical experts, technical support and hotline service personnel, users, and the rest. In all cases, the interviews had occurred because the technical communicators had sought the information despite the objections of supervisors and coworkers.

Thus a major implication of these data is that a business need not incur great costs to improve its documentation. Rather, if technical communicators would be permitted or even encouraged to incorporate the existing informal communication channels of a given business culture into their revisions of their manuals, marked improvements of the written products would be possible.

Conclusion

The four recommendations we make should be of interest to both industry and academe for they are based on the actual narratives of 20 working communicators. Our participants have cautioned us that both researchers and supervisors of communications need to improve their awareness of writing as it actually (not ideally) occurs. We are in complete agreement with the observations made by Morgan [25] that additional workplace research be pursued and by Brown [26] that teachers give consideration to workplace technical communicators' writing processes because our findings echo these researchers' concerns.

Morgan [25] concludes her study of classroom and workplace team writing processes by observing that workplace writers and academics need to continue to collaborate in order to learn from each other. In a similar vein, Brown [26] calls for a rethinking of communication training because oftentimes the university "course is divorced from important realities of the workplace" [25, p. 407]. Our study responds to the plea that additional research be completed with those who face workplace realities as we ask teachers to make their students aware that discrepancies will occur between the approaches taken to writing in the classroom and writing at work. Other researchers have reported in some detail about the types of pedagogies that can bring the concerns of workplace technical communication into the classroom, so we exclude that list from our recommendations. Instead, our study reminds teachers and managers alike that some 20 years into process pedagogy, our interviewees describe businesses still strongly committed to various forms of writing as a product orientation. We see no evidence that it is in the interests of these firms to change their orientations. Thus it falls to those who train the technical communicators both in colleges and at work to prepare the writers to address successfully the range of challenges posed by this discrepancy.

Acknowledgment

The authors wish to thank Janet Parenti Scouten for her assistance with preparing the tables and Sundeep R. Muppidi for his assistance with editing the text.

References

[1] D. Haugen, "Editors, rules, and revision research," *Tech. Commun.*, vol. 38, pp. 57–64, 1991.

[2] L. Faigley and S. Witte, "Analyzing revision," *College Composition and Commun.*, vol. 32, pp. 400–414, 1981.

[3] J. R. Hayes, L. Flower, K. A. Schriver, J. F. Stratman, and L. Carey, "Cognitive processes in revision," in *Advances in Applied Psycholinguistics*, 2nd ed., S. Rosenberg, Ed. Cambridge, MA: Cambridge Univ. Press, 1987, pp. 176–240.

[4] L. Flower, J. R. Hayes, L. Carey, K. Schriver, and J. Stratman, "Detection, diagnosis, and the strategies of revision," *College Composition and Commun.*, vol. 37, no. 1, pp. 16–55, 1986.

[5] B. Tomlinson, "Tuning, tying, and training texts," *Written Commun.*, vol. 5, no. 1. pp. 58–81, 1988.

[6] L. Odell and D. Goswami, Eds., *Writing in Nonacademic Settings.* New York: Guilford, 1985.

[7] G. J. Broadhead and R. C. Freed, *The Variables of Composition: Process and Product in a Business Setting.* Carbondale, IL: So. Ill. Univ. Press, 1986.

[8] L. Ede and A. A. Lunsford, *Singular Texts/Plural Authors: Perspectives on Collaborative Writing.* Carbondale, IL: So. Ill. Univ. Press, 1990.

[9] C. Barabas, *Technical Writing in a Corporate Culture: A Study of the Nature of Information.* Norwood, NJ: Ablex, 1990.

[10] M. M. Lay and W. M. Karis, Eds., *Collaborative Writing in Industry: Investigations, Theory and Practice.* Amityville, NY: Baywood, 1991.

[11] L. S. Flower and J. R. Hayes, "A cognitive process theory of writing," *College Composition and Commun.*, vol. 32, pp. 176–240, 1981.

[12] P. M. Scanlon and A. C. Coon, "Attitudes of professional technical communicators regarding the content of an undergraduate course in technical communication: A survey," *Tech. Commun.*, vol. 41, pp. 439–446, 1994.

[13] C. Gerich, "How technical editors enrich the revision process," *Tech. Commun.*, vol. 41, pp. 59–70, 1994.

[14] D. Haugen, "Editors, rules, and revision research," *Tech. Commun.*, vol. 38, pp. 57–64, 1991.

[15] R. P. Clair, M. McGoun, and M. M. Spirek, "Sexual harassment responses of working women: An assessment of current communication oriented typologies and perceived effectiveness of the responses," in *Communication and Sexual Harassment in the Workplace*, Gary L. Kreps, Ed. Cresskill, NJ: Hampton, 1993, pp. 209–233.

[16] *Profile 92.* Alexandria, VA: Society for Technical Communication, 1992.

[17] N. G. Fielding and J. L. Fielding, *Linking Data.* Beverly Hills, CA: Sage, 1986.

[18] A. E. Walzer and A. Gross, "Positivists, postmodernists, Aristotelians, and the Challenger disaster," *College English*, vol. 56, no. 4, pp. 420–433, 1994.

[19] J. Kirk and M. L. Miller, *Reliability and Validity in Qualitative Research.* Beverly Hills, CA: Sage, 1986.

[20] R. E. Voss and M. L. Keene. *Starter Kit: The Heath Guide to College Writing: Things All Beginning Teachers of Writing Need to Know.* Lexington, MA: Heath, 1992.

[21] K. Schriver, "Evaluating text quality: The continuum from text-focus to reader-focus methods," *IEEE Trans. Prof. Commun.*, vol. 32, no. 4, pp. 238–255, 1992.

[22] N. Roundy, "A program for revision in business and technical writing," *J. Business Commun.*, vol. 20, no. 1, pp. 55–66, 1983.

[23] M. B. Coney, "Technical readers and their rhetorical roles," *IEEE Trans. Prof. Commun.*, vol. 35, no. 2, pp. 58–63, 1992.

[24] J. C. Redish and J. A. Ramey, "STC continues studies of value added," *STC Intercom*, vol. 41, no. 3, pp. 1, 6, Oct. 1994.

[25] M. Morgan, "Patterns of composing: Connections between classroom and workplace collaborations," *Tech. Commun.*, vol. 38, pp. 540–545, 1991.

[26] R. M. Brown, "Rethinking the approach to communication training," *Tech. Commun.*, vol. 41, no. 3, pp. 406–415, 1994.

Alice I. Philbin is director of the Program in Scientific and Technical Communication, Bowling Green State University, Bowling Green, OH. She has published a textbook, she presents papers regularly for STC, and she studies the career trends of technical communicators using interdisciplinary methodologies.

Melissa M. Spirek is an assistant professor in the Department of Telecommunications at Bowling Green State University, Bowling Green, Ohio. She has published and presented multiple articles on the topic of cognitive and emotional responses to the media.

Online Editing, Mark-Up Models, and the Workplace Lives of Editors and Writers

David K. Farkas and Steven E. Poltrock

Abstract—**Although editors make extensive use of the computer in their work, most editors still mark changes on paper using traditional editing symbols. There are, however, compelling reasons for editors to begin marking copy on the computer. In this article we consider online editing from the perspective both of editors and their employers. We then focus on one aspect of online editing: the mark-up models embodied in various editing tools. We demonstrate that the different mark-up models and their particular implementations have major implications for the editing process, including the quality of edited material and the worklife satisfaction of editors and writers. We conclude by recommending that the technical communication community exert its influence on software developers and corporate technology planners to encourage the development and adoption of online editing tools that will be congenial to editors.**

SIGNIFICANT writing projects in the workplace are generally carried out by a group of people working together [1]. Typically, a team of writers will contribute components of the eventual whole. In the process, they are likely to informally edit each other's contributions. The draft may also undergo review by higher-level subject-matter experts, whose focus will be technical accuracy and appropriateness for the intended audience [2], [3]. Very often, a professional editor will apply his or her communication expertise to the document.

Today's computer technology can provide impressive support for many group-writing activities. Writers can easily share fully formatted drafts over computer networks, either within their building or across continents. The computer can also serve as a project librarian, keeping track of who has (and has had) each section of the document and controlling who can change certain components. The review process is also reasonably well supported: features such as hidden text, pop-up notes, and special annotation footnotes allow reviewers to comment on the author's draft. Soon it will be commonplace for reviewers to embed audio and even video clips anyplace in the author's document where they want to comment.

There is, however, one part of the review process in which computer support is considerably less effective: editing. Consequently, although almost every stage in the preparation of typical workplace documents is digital, most editors, as we shall see, continue to work with paper and pencil. This situation and the prospects for change are the starting point for this article. We review the role of the editor in workplace writing and the status of both general computer use and online editing. Then we consider how organizations and editors view online editing, concluding that online editing will gradually take hold in the workplace. If this is so, the nature of the online editing tools that will be used becomes important both for editors and the writers who work with them. Therefore, we show some of the ways that the fundamental operation and features of these tools can affect both the quality of edited material and the workplace lives of editors and writers, and we suggest that the technical communication community should take an active role in determining the character of the tools that will be developed and adopted.

Manuscript received October 1994; revised February 1995.

D. K. Farkas is with the University of Washington, Seattle, WA 98195 USA.

S. E. Poltrock is with Boeing Computer Services, Seattle, WA 98124 USA.

IEEE Log Number 9411542.

The Editor's Role in Creating Documents

Editors serve a variety of roles in preparing documents, including helping to plan the document, coordinating the work of writers, and supervising production; however, their fundamental and defining role is to improve the document by marking changes in the draft they receive from the author [4], [5]. These changes include making large-scale organizational changes and rewriting whole passages, but editors—unlike reviewers—are responsible for style, grammar, usage, and mechanics, and so they mark a large number of small-grained changes. For this reason, a key characteristic of any online editing tool is how the mark-up process is handled. As we shall see, there are major challenges in creating software that can effectively deal with large numbers of small-grained changes.

In addition to marking changes, editors—much like reviewers—must write messages to the author. These may be queries for more information, justifications of what they have done, or proposals setting forth how the editor would like to deal with some difficulty in the document. In most cases, the author has ultimate responsibility for and intellectual "ownership" of the document. Authors therefore reject some changes and make new changes. Also, they will send their own messages back to the editor, messages that the editor may reply to. Editing, then, entails a dialog between editor and author, a dialog that may continue through several cycles. After the editor-author dialog, the editor (or the editor's assistant) will incorporate the agreed-upon changes into the document in preparation for final formatting and printing. Or, the author or the person doing the production work will incorporate the changes.

Authorial review can be a difficult and troublesome part of the editor's job. Many editors establish excellent relationships with authors; on the other hand, there are inherent tensions

Reprinted from *IEEE Trans. Prof. Comm.*, vol. PC-38, no. 2, pp. 110–117, June 1995.

stemming from one person's making corrections in the work of another. Indeed, this relationship is often characterized by suspicion, disrespect, and antagonism. From the author's point of view, the sins of editors include making unnecessary and arbitrary changes, introducing errors and unintended meanings, and not adequately explaining why changes were made [4, pp. 338–345], [6, pp. 47–64]. Editors, of course, do not defend introducing errors or changing the meaning of the document without querying, but they expect to be recognized as the project's communication experts [7]. Tarutz's book on technical editing provides numerous glimpses of writers' frequent suspicion of and antagonism toward editors. She notes, for example, that most writers "approach editors cautiously and skeptically," and "have a lingering bad taste from previous edits" [6, p. 54]. She portrays an editor who asks, "Why do writers hate me?" [6, p. 47].

In Duffy's survey of 28 expert editors, the ability to establish a collaborative relationship with the author ranks as number 6 in a list of the 39 most important editorial skills—more important than the ability to find and correct errors of grammar, syntax, and punctuation [8]. Speck's bibliography of the literature on professional editing [9] shows that relations with authors is a constant theme. Because relations with authors is an important and problematic aspect of the editor's work, an important consideration in the design or selection of an online editing tool is how the tool is apt to affect editor/author relationships.

How Editors Use Computers

Most editors make some use of the computer in their work. A survey of "writer-editors" by Rude and Smith [10] showed 63% of the respondents using the computer as part of their editing work. Duffy's survey showed 78% of his expert editors using the computer. The computer tasks performed are varied, including formatting, checking spelling and grammar, performing search and replace operations, generating an index, and sending and receiving drafts. Most likely the amount of computer use by editors will continue to increase.

Editors work differently in different settings and have individual habits and preferences; therefore, there are innumerable specific scenarios for how editing is carried out. Following is one scenario that entails significant use of the computer. It is not, however, complete online editing because the editor is still marking changes on paper. In this scenario, the editor

1) Receives a draft from the author over a computer network or on disk.
2) Prints a copy and skims or reads to become familiar with the material. The editor may take some notes at this stage.
3) Performs a computerized spelling check (and perhaps a grammar check) and makes changes in the online version. (Here we assume that the editor has been authorized to make minor changes "silently"—without marking them for the author to review.)
4) Makes any necessary major organizational changes online and writes a message to the author explaining these changes. It is easier to re-arrange large sections of an online document than to mark these changes on a print copy. Also, the author is better able to visualize the re-structuring when he or she sees the changes executed.
5) Prints a copy of the document and makes one or more major editing passes, marking the changes with a pencil on the print copy. This is the heart of the editing process.
6) Returns the paper copy to the author and negotiates the final changes.
7) Keyboards the changes into the computer in preparation for final formatting and bookbuilding or gives the paper copy to a formatting/production person, who will keyboard the changes while doing the production work.

This scenario shows that an editor can use computer technology while marking changes on paper. This fact, no doubt, helps explain the loyalty of many editors to the red pencil. On the other hand, the use of the pencil, the only non-digital part of the entire publications process, is a return to an earlier era and, as we shall see, is inefficient in some important respects.

Neither Duffy's survey nor Rude and Smith's provides a precise view of the prevalence of online editing; clearly, however, online editing is atypical among these respondents. Of Rude and Smith's respondents, about 15% edit online. When Duffy's 28 expert editors were asked to list the computer tools they employ, only two listed an online editing tool (DocuComp from Advanced Software, Sunnyvale, CA), and one of these editors commented that DocuComp was only usable for documents that contained few editorial changes.

Alred, Oliu, and Brusaw offer a negative assessment of online editing, an assessment that we believe is widely shared: "The potential advantages that online editing offers cannot compensate at this time for its liabilities" [11, p. 293]. In this comment, they are referring primarily to difficulties in marking copy on the computer and in visualizing and navigating an online document, issues we address later. Princeton University Press is seeking to widely implement online editing, but nonetheless "red pencils still rule in the editorial department" [12, p. 235]. Boeing and Microsoft are two large, technologically sophisticated organizations that have been looking at online editing for quite a few years, but hardcopy editing remains the rule at both companies.

While online editing has achieved only limited acceptance, there clearly is interest in it and pressure for its adoption. In the following sections, we look more closely at this situation by examining both the perspective of organizations and the perspective of editors on the use of online editing. We believe that from both perspectives the advantages of online editing are considerable, although the benefits accrue more assuredly and directly to organizations.

The Organization's Perspective Regarding Online Editing

Online editing potentially offers organizations greater speed in preparing documents, better version control, better archiving, increased productivity, improved systems integration, and other benefits. Online editing, however, must not degrade quality and must fit within the organization's overall operation.

Speed

The speed with which a proposal, product catalog, or manual update can be prepared is often crucial. Formerly, when deadlines were tight and collaborators were physically separated, paper drafts were often sent back and forth among authors, reviewers, and editors by Federal Express or even courier. In the era of fax, the physical distance separating collaborators is a less important issue, but even now valuable time is lost and errors may be introduced when agreed-upon changes marked on the paper copy are keyboarded into the digital version. Online editing in its most current implementations makes it possible to incorporate agreed-upon changes in the manuscript instantly and without introducing errors. In fact, with currently available tools, such as Aspects (Group Logic, Arlington, VA), authors, reviewers, and editors can simultaneously change a document and view a continuously updated version of the document.

Version Control to Prevent Mistakes

One major difficulty in creating complex documents is simply keeping track of where the various parts are in the writing, review, and editing cycles and controlling who is working on what. At times, organizations mistakenly assign writers and editors to work on sections of a document that managers have already decided to delete from the final version. Worse yet, draft chapters containing serious factual errors are inadvertently included in a printed document; and occasionally writers or editors, following a personal agenda, make surreptitious changes that appear in the published version. In paper environments, project librarians check drafts out, check them back in, and in general attempt to maintain version control. As noted earlier, in an all-digital environment, the computer can be used to provide effective version control: the computer can keep track of who has (and has had) each section of the document, limit the distribution of certain sections, withhold all but "read-only" access to parts of the document an individual is not authorized to change, and display the changes made by each individual.

Efficient Archiving

Organizations must often archive the complete life histories of documents. They must archive not only all published versions, but all drafts, review comments, and even personal notes. Such archiving may be necessary to support an old version of a product, trace responsibility for a mistake, or determine the date on which a patentable idea was conceived. Archiving paper material is time-consuming, requires expensive storage space, and still leads to serious problems of information retrieval. Archiving and retrieving digital material is much easier and cheaper.

Increasing Productivity While Maintaining Quality

Naturally, organizations are concerned with the productivity of individual editors and the efficiency of the editing process. An online editing tool that significantly slows down the editors or the authors who review edited copy is not acceptable. Similarly, while organizations might not have the same sensitivity to document quality that editors do, serious quality-control problems caused by a clumsy editing tool will likely be unacceptable. Some online editing tools have failed in the marketplace for these reasons; newer tools may prove superior to current tools and to paper editing as well in regard to both productivity and document quality.

The Requirement of Overall Systems Integration

Necessarily broad, *systems integration* refers to all the ways an online editing tool fits the organization's existing technologies and operations, including the kinds of documents they prepare and their writing and publishing processes. It includes such issues as staffing, training, and budgets. The need for systems integration within an organization can easily lead to the rejection of a particular online editing tool and possibly all available online editing tools. For example, an organization may reject tools that cannot be tightly integrated into its electronic publishing system or electronic mail system, that cannot gracefully handle elaborately formatted documents, or that cost too much. For all these reasons, editors cannot simply assume that tools they like and that authors like will automatically be adopted by their organizations. Editors may have to make a strong case for preferred tools within their organizations and encourage the commercial development of tools that both satisfy themselves and fit the needs of their organizations.

Other Values

Organizations should inherently value the quality of workplace life and want their employees to work comfortably, feel pride in their work, and enjoy positive human relations. In any case, deficient workplace quality ultimately hurts productivity. Another priority valued in organizations is respect for the environment; online editing reduces the amount of paper and toner consumed in large organizations, thereby both protecting the environment and reducing costs.

The Editor's Perspective Regarding Online Editing

Because editors have a stake in their employers' success, they share an interest in efficiency, accuracy, and cost reduction. Presumably, they support technologies that protect the environment. Editors, however, also have their own concerns. They are naturally concerned with the comfort and healthfulness of their work environment. Also, they care about the operation of their tools—whether these tools make possible high-quality editing, and whether they make the job more complex and difficult.

Comfort and Health

Online editing increases the number of hours each week that the editor spends at the computer, raising questions about health and comfort. Back pain, carpal tunnel syndrome, eye fatigue, and (in the opinion of many) monitor emissions are major societal problems. These questions should be and are being addressed through such means as ergonomic office furniture and keyboards and low-emission monitors with more legible displays. Ergonomic problems associated with computer use persist, of course, and this makes editors understandably wary.

The computer is nevertheless the center of the professional workplace, and many kinds of workers spend long hours staring at the screen. If online editing tools become highly efficient, editors (like newsroom journalists a decade or more ago) will probably have little success citing increased time at the computer as a reason for rejecting these tools. Fortunately, editors are apt to engage in professional activities such as interviewing and project management that limit time at the computer. Also, editors can significantly reduce time at the screen by reading from a print copy when they first familiarize themselves with a document and switching to the computer screen when they begin marking up the document. Paper thus becomes a useful temporary interface but is not really part of the main flow of the process of preparing a document.

Typos and Reading Errors

It is also possible that the screen's inferiority to paper in regard to resolution and other viewing factors can cause editors to miss typos and make other character-level errors. Evidence regarding reduced performance is mixed. Horton reviews a variety of conflicting studies and concludes that "with careful design of screen displays, reading speed and accuracy can approach those of paper" [13, p. 246]. No doubt the quality of displays will continue to improve. Furthermore, an important but often unnoticed point is that the editor is not restricted to a particular set of font and display variables when reading from the screen. Contemporary word-processing software allows the editor to zoom in on the document (effectively increasing font size), view text in ultra-readable screen fonts, change the text color, and in general create a customized reading and editing environment. Most editors, we assert, would miss fewer typos working in their preferred on-screen reading environment than they would reading a document in 9-point Times Roman type produced by an ink-jet printer on both sides of low-quality, show-through paper. The ability to create a custom on-screen reading environment also alleviates part of the comfort and health problem discussed earlier.

Visualization and Navigation

Visualization refers to how well an editor can visualize the structure of a document; navigation refers to how easily an editor can find a portion of the document (e.g., the editor needs to look quickly at the fourth section of Chapter 11). Without adequate visualization and navigation, online editing becomes impractical.

Like many other editors and non-editors, the editors surveyed by Rude and Smith cite superior visualization and navigation as major reasons for working on paper. This belief is certainly not surprising: we are all comfortable with such print elements as tables of contents, running heads, and page numbers; furthermore, the heft and physicality of paper help people gauge the size of the whole document, sense their current location within it, thumb through it readily, and keep several pages open at once.

On the other hand, perhaps because the visualization and navigation issue pertains not just to professional editors but to all those who use computers to prepare documents, the visualization and navigation capabilities of word processors and electronic publishing systems have improved greatly in the last decade. For example, contemporary word-processing software provides means for visually gauging the approximate size of the document and one's location in it, can display different portions of the document in separate windows, and offers such special views of the document as the outline view and thumbnail images of multiple pages. Editors, moreover, can instantly jump to any word, phrase, or page and can easily find every element in a manuscript that shares a certain formatting characteristic (boldface, a certain heading level, etc.). Finally, monitors on desktop machines are becoming larger, and monitors that can display a full 8-1/2 by 11 page (or larger) are not rare. It may well be that some of Rude and Smith's respondents were not considering the capabilities of the best software and hardware when they judged in favor of paper, and significant improvements have occurred since the survey was conducted.

Those who laud the heft and physicality of paper almost always assume a document that is very manageable in size, not a physically cumbersome document requiring multiple volumes. We assert that, objectively considered, visualization and navigation in the best word processors clearly exceed visualization and navigation in paper when documents are even moderately long. Furthermore, there is at least one study in the research literature that lends strong support to this view [14].

Marking Copy

The way the editor marks copy is crucial. It bears upon productivity, document quality, and job satisfaction. It has major implications for editors' relationships with authors. Consequently, in assessing any online editing tool, editors will doubtless give much weight to this aspect of the tool. We examine mark-up in the next section. For now we can say that editors will make rigorous demands regarding mark-up, both because of its importance and because the mark-up model embodied in traditional paper editing is efficient in four important respects.

- The traditional symbols are fairly easy for editors and authors to learn, and a workable subset (e.g., the symbols for deletion, insertion, transposition, and some other basic operations) is both familiar and highly intuitive.
- The traditional symbols represent a rich repertoire of editing operations, enabling editors to mark changes rapidly.
- There is no difficulty distinguishing the editor's hand-entered work from the author's printed draft. The author easily sees what has been changed.
- Because of the rich, well-designed symbology, the careful editor can make fairly extensive changes without making the marking so complex that the author will have difficulty reviewing the changes. At some point, however, it is best for the editor to simply re-write a passage and ask the author to compare the new one with the original.

Prospects for the Future

Editing is almost always an organizational activity, performed within or for companies. Consequently, the organization's perspective is apt to be influential. We expect that the organizational agenda will result in a gradual but steady increase in the amount of online editing. Furthermore, although many editors are wary (or even hostile) regarding online editing, the benefits, we believe, of editing online and working entirely in a digital environment should continue to win over more editors. There is certainly anecdotal evidence of editors who have become enthusiastic proponents of online editing. For example, Lynnette Porter, who works actively as a freelance editor, reports positive experiences using a range of online editing techniques; and Joann Een, an editor for the Seattle-based training company Catapult, endorses the online editing tools in Microsoft Word and declares online editing to be "more efficient than manual editing."

If online editing is apt to become prevalent (and perhaps dominant), an important question is, What will the tools be? Will there be many tools or just a few? Will they be standalone tools or will they exist as part of word processing and electronic publishing applications? Will some tools become optional add-ons, possibly created by third-party developers? Most important, what will be the features of these tools, and how well will the features fit the work of editors and writers, as well as the agendas of their organizations?

Editors and writers certainly have a stake in the nature of these tools, and if they are to influence the tools they use, they will first need to understand the key differences among these tools and the implications of these differences. Clearly, the nature of a tool significantly affects the user of the tool, but the nature of this relationship is not easy to determine. In the next section we look at what is perhaps the most fundamental characteristic of any online editing tool: the mark-up model it embodies.

Implications of Mark-Up Models

It is hard to overestimate the importance and centrality of mark-up in any online editing tool. It is how the editor works and how the document is changed. Mark-up is also a key means of collaborating with the author. Michael Shrage observes that "all collaboration relies on a shared space" [15, p. 153] and writes about the computer's potential to create better shared spaces among collaborators in many domains. The mark-up model embodied in any online editing tool, the particular implementation of the model, and the features associated with it collectively make up much of the shared space between editors and writers.

To provide a full survey of mark-up models or online editing tools is beyond our scope. Rather, our goals here are simply to delineate the concept of a mark-up model, illustrate the most important models, and argue that the choice of a mark-up model and, more generally, the choice of an online editing tool have many important, subtle, and hard-to-predict implications. Also please note that the names of particular products are used only as examples of the models these products embody; we have made no attempt to discuss all product features or to evaluate these products. Finally, we assume that any useful online editing tool will enable two-way messaging between editor and author, although this facility may lie outside the mark-up model. In most instances, whatever means reviewers use to send comments to writers (e.g., hidden text or an annotation feature) will serve for messaging between writers and editors.

Mary had a savage <del little lamb.

Fig. 1. A typical implementation of the comment model.

The Silent Editing Model

Silent editing means simply that the editor works on the author's draft using the normal features of a word processor. This is the simplest model—almost the lack of a model. It requires no special tool or technique. This model is effective when the author fully trusts the editor (or has limited concern for the manuscript). This model, however, causes frustration and likely antagonism if the author wishes to check the editor's work against the original carefully, for doing so requires the author to read both versions sentence by sentence, an excruciating task.

Editors may enjoy working in this untrammeled manner, but the practice is dangerous, even when authors will permit it. First, this model causes the editor to work in the manner of an author and likely results in less regard for the author's original text and, hence, over-editing. Second, because this model is "destructive," the editor cannot readily recover the author's wording once it has been changed.

Silent editing is routinely and effectively used in a very limited form and in conjunction with some other model. The editor is authorized to make minor, utterly unarguable changes silently, thus simplifying the workspace shared by editor and author and reserving this workspace for weightier issues. Even here, however, the author must trust the editor's judgment regarding which changes to make silently.

The Comment Model

The comment model is embodied in pop-up notes, temporary footnotes, hidden text, and special symbols placed within the text. It was also the basis for the unsuccessful product MarkUp (Mainstay Software, Agoura Hills, CA), in which the editor marked changes on a virtual "acetate" layer created by the editing tool.

In its most rudimentary form, such as pop-ups and hidden text, the editor is simply writing brief notations indicating desired changes, as in Fig. 1.

The notation indicates the editor's intention to delete "savage." This model can work reasonably well, especially for editing manuscripts that are short or in need of few changes, but it is too labor intensive for many settings.

In its more sophisticated form, software can execute the marked changes. Online editing is performed in this manner at the Princeton University Press [12] using the XyWrite word processor and custom programming. Even in this more sophisticated form, however, a significant amount of extra keyboarding is required to mark the proposed changes.

~~A little lamb~~ Mary had a little lamb whose fleece was white ~~like~~ as snow. And everywhere that Mary went ~~T~~the lamb~~,~~ ~~moreover,~~ was sure to go ~~everywhere that Mary went~~.

Fig. 2. The edit trace model.

The Edit Trace Model

The edit trace (or "compare") model is the dominant model in current online editing software. It has been implemented in DocuComp and in various word processors.

In the edit trace model, the editor works like an author, deleting, adding, and moving text using all the usual features of the word-processing software. The computer, however, can compare the editor's new version to the author's original version, and so permits the author to view the draft with the editor's changes juxtaposed on it by means of such typographic attributes as strikethrough to show deletion and underlining (or boldface) to show insertion. The edit trace model is shown in Fig. 2. Microsoft Word includes a useful feature that enables the author to jump from one of the editor's mark-ups to the next.

In a less sophisticated variation of this model, only a change bar appears in the margin where the editor has changed the text. The author must look at the original version to see the unedited passage.

The edit trace model could easily win favor among editors because of the ease of making changes. On the other hand, this mark-up model is apt to encourage heavier editing and less regard for the author's original text. If this is indeed the case, there may be significant implications for the quality of edited documents, the editor's standing within the organization, and the editor's relationships with authors. In this way, the edit trace model is like the silent model but far more feasible because the editing is not destructive.

There are three different ways that editors can view the "trace" made by the computer. In the first, the editor stops and begins a distinct compare operation. In the second, the trace appears in real time as the editor works. In the third, a second scrolling window continuously shows the trace. The second and third options are apt to limit heavy editing and are therefore more desirable than the first.

Because this mark-up model uses typographical attributes rather than a complete, highly refined symbology, changes are not economical or easy to interpret. For example, in Fig. 2 there is significant visual complexity just to show the change from an uppercase "T" to a lowercase "t." With traditional paper editing, only a single slash mark would be drawn over the upper-case "T."[1] This difficulty may hinder editors, and it can be quite difficult for authors. Conceivably, it can make authors careless about reviewing their edited drafts and/or less willing to work with editors. An implementation that used traditional editing symbols rather than typographical attributes would be better.

Most implementations of the edit trace model have another deficiency: they show that a block of text has been deleted and they show that a block of text has been inserted, but they do not communicate the concept of moved text. Hence, when text is moved beyond the confines of a paragraph or page, the editor must provide messages to indicate the move. Otherwise, the author is apt to see the deletion and ask, "Why did the editor take that out?" Seeing an insertion, the author might say, "Why is the editor putting this in twice."

Traditional Model Adapted for the Computer

The traditional paper mark-up model can be adapted for the computer screen. One approach is that of Red Pencil, a clever DOS product that allows the editor to apply a nearly complete set of traditional editing symbols directly to a document. Using the mouse or keyboard, the editor highlights a word, phrase, or passage and issues a command to add a particular editing symbol to the highlighted text. Once marked in this way, the document can be transmitted to the author for review. The author can then remove and add new editing marks to the document. When the process is complete and the final changes have been made, all the marked changes are executed with a single command; and so, as with the edit trace model, there is no manual keyboarding of editing changes.

Red Pencil has not been successful in the marketplace. This is partly because Red Pencil was never designed to deal with elaborately formatted text and partly because Capsule Codeworks (Redmond, WA), the very small software company that developed Red Pencil, has had trouble keeping up with changes in computer hardware and software environments, leading to limitations in systems integration.

Another implementation of the traditional model is becoming feasible due to the advent of a technology that lets the computer recognize both human handwriting and basic editing symbols: the editor uses "digital ink" to mark a simple subset of the traditional editing symbols, along with the words the editor means to insert in the draft. The digital ink looks like a simple bitmap but is much more powerful [16]. For, when the author has reviewed the editor's changes, the editing symbols (known to computer scientists as "gestural commands") can be executed. The editor can also enter messages to the author, such as "Please improve this passage." These comments remain as digital ink and are ultimately deleted.

MATE is a research prototype that uses digital ink, although the editor writes with a stylus on a pressure-sensitive tablet rather than directly on the screen [17]. One excellent feature of MATE is a second window, which scrolls in conjunction with the main window and shows what the document looks like with the changes executed. This second window is a major benefit to both editors and authors, especially when text has been heavily edited. The two windows are shown in Fig. 3. One capability that is not present in MATE but that can be implemented with digital ink is the automatic "neatening" of editing symbols.

[1] Complex changes in formatting may, in fact, surpass the capabilities of an edit trace tool or result in typographic markings that are too complex for anyone to deal with. Therefore, when an editor wishes to show complex formatting changes in a text element—for example, a list or table—the best procedure is often to duplicate the element, reformat the new instance, and let the author simply compare the two.

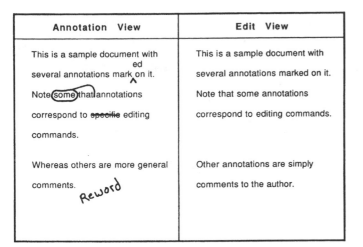

Annotation View	Edit View
This is a sample document with several annotations mark on it. (inserted: ed) Note (some) that annotations correspond to ~~specific~~ editing commands.	This is a sample document with several annotations marked on it. Note that some annotations correspond to editing commands.
Whereas others are more general comments. Reword	Other annotations are simply comments to the author.

Fig. 3. A passage edited in MATE. One window shows the changes marked in digital ink; the other shows the passage with the editing commands executed.

Much of the ~~background~~ knowledge & ~~and~~ guidelines for **structure** ~~kiosk~~ **plan** ~~design~~ comes from the field of exhibit **plan** ~~design~~ (e.g., Klein, 1988; Konikow, [Au: Spell 1] 1984; Miles & Alt, 1988). [Au: Date 1] Indeed, a major principle of exhibit **plan** ~~design~~ is to create displays that attract attention & ~~and~~ invite participation. However, the many technology components & ~~and~~ the nature of the interaction possible with interactive systems poses many new challenges even for experienced exhibit designers(FN: 2).

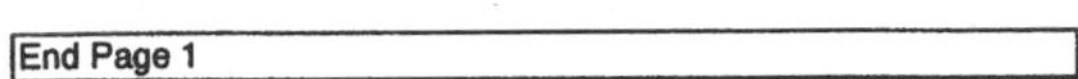

Fig. 4. Copy marked with PenEdit. The rounded rectangle indicates a footnote. The squared-off rectangles indicate queries to the author.

PenEdit (Advanced Pen Technologies, Upper Saddle River, NJ) is a promising new online editing tool that emulates many aspects of traditional paper editing. In PenEdit, the editor uses an electronic pen to place the traditional deletion symbol and certain other editing symbols directly on the computer screen. Text can be inserted both with the pen or with a keyboard; text appears on the same line as the author's text, but in a distinctive "handwriting" font. Text marked by PenEdit is shown in Fig. 4. This process encourages restrained editing, and in one published account a pencil-and-paper editor describes the new process favorably [18]. If authors have computers that run PenEdit, they can view the editor's changes and respond to them on the computer; the less expensive procedure is for editors to ask authors to review printouts of the marked copy. Editors and authors can also view a "clean" version of the manuscript, in which all the changes have been executed.

Because PenEdit currently runs in a special pen-based operating system and because manuscripts need to be imported into PenEdit, organizations using PenEdit must address some systems-integration issues. This product, however, is under active development by people who are attuned to the needs of professional editors.

A special section of *Byte Magazine* [19] that discusses digital ink is notable for emphasizing that digital ink and voice recognition are complementary technologies. In the scenario that emerges from this section, editors use both digital ink and voice commands. Crane and Rtischev offer this example: "While editing on the screen, you might say the following: Move this sentence [indicating what 'this sentence' refers to by simultaneously circling the sentence] to the beginning of this paragraph [simultaneously circling the paragraph] . . ." [20, p. 100]. Assuming that the oral "move" command would also create some traceable record of the move, the combination of pen and voice input might be a very efficient implementation of the traditional mark-up model.

Whether implemented on paper, in Red Pencil, or with digital ink (possibly augmented by voice commands), the traditional mark-up model encourages restrained editing. Editing changes take more time to mark than they do with the edit trace model, and the editor is always reminded that he or she is altering another person's document. Restrained editing is favored by most experienced editors and reduces conflicts with authors. Furthermore, to the degree that the rich vocabulary of traditional editing symbols is retained, authors and editors can interpret the editor's markings more readily than they can in the edit trace model.

The Role of the Technical Communication Community

No one can know just how editing will be performed in the future. We believe, however, that online editing will be prevalent if not dominant, and we have tried to show that in regard to just one design issue (albeit a central one), the number of design options is great and the differences among them significant.

A key question is whether online editing will improve the quality of edited documents and the worklives of both editors and the writers who work with them. There is at least the potential for a "win-win" situation in which these tools will please editors, writers, and their employers. To ensure that good tools will be developed and to ensure that the best of these are adopted, editors and the technical communication community in general should try to exert some influence. We can, for instance, help software developers understand the work of editors (as well as informal editing) and make clear which features are necessary and useful and which will create problems. We can also influence the technology planners in our own organizations.

The basis of this influence is our own understanding of the still-uncertain issues surrounding online editing. Therefore, we have great need for research such as the survey of Rude and Smith [10] and that of Duffy [8], which had the explicit goal of contributing to the development of better tools for editors. Also important are detailed and sensitive case studies, such as that of Kincade and Oppenheim [12]. We hope as well that this analysis focuses attention in a useful manner.

Finally, we note that editing is just one of an enormous number of collaborative activities that are moving online [21]. Online editing, however, is a relatively early and fairly challenging test case for computer-supported collaboration. If effective tools for online editing emerge and are accepted, the prospects for computer support of collaborative work in many other domains brighten and there may be lessons to share with others whose work is moving online.

REFERENCES

[1] L. Ede and A. Lunsford, *Singular Texts/Plural Authors: Perspectives on Collaborative Writing.* Carbondale, IL: Illinois University Press, 1990.

[2] J. Paradis, D. Dobrin and R. Miller, "Writing at Exxon ITD: Notes on the writing environment of an R&D organization," in *Writing in Nonacademic Settings*, L. Odell and D. Goswami, Eds. New York: Guilford, 1985.

[3] S. Kleimann, "The reciprocal relationship of workplace culture and review," in *Writing in the Workplace: New Research Perspectives*, R. Spilka, Ed. Carbondale, IL: Southern Illinois University Press, 1993.

[4] C. Rude, *Technical Editing.* Belmont, CA: Wadsworth, 1991.

[5] D. Haugen, "Coming to terms with editing," *Research in the Teaching of English*, vol. 24, no. 3, pp. 322–33, 1990.

[6] J. A. Tarutz, *Technical Editing: The Practical Guide for Editors and Writers.* Reading, MA: Addison-Wesley, 1992.

[7] C. Gerich, "How technical editors enrich the revision process," *Tech. Commun.*, vol. 41, no 1, pp. 59–70, 1994.

[8] T. M. Duffy, "Designing tools to aid technical editors: A needs analysis," *Tech. Commun.*, vol. 42, forthcoming, 1995.

[9] B. W. Speck, *Editing: An Annotated Bibliography.* New York: Greenwood, 1991.

[10] C. Rude and E. Smith, "Use of computers in technical editing," *Tech. Commun.*, vol. 39, no. 3, pp. 334–342, 1992.

[11] G. J. Alred, W. E. Oliu, and C. T. Brusaw, *The Professional Writer: A Guide for Advanced Technical Writing.* New York: St. Martin's, 1992.

[12] D. Kincade and L. Oppenheim, "Marking it up as we go along: Into editorial production's electronic future," *J. Scholarly Publishing*, vol. 25, no. 4, pp. 233–42, 1994.

[13] W. Horton, *Designing and Writing Online Documentation.* New York: Wiley, 1994, 2nd ed.

[14] D. E. Egan, J. R. Remde, L. M. Gomez, T. K. Landauer, J. Eberhardt, and C. C. Lochbaum, "Formative design-evaluation of superbook," *ACM Trans. Inform. Syst.*, vol. 7, no. 1, pp. 30–57, 1989.

[15] M. Shrage, *Shared Minds: The New Technologies of Collaboration.* New York: Random House, 1990.

[16] D. Mezick, "Pen computing catches on," *Byte Mag.*, pp. 105–112, Oct. 1993.

[17] G. Hardock, G. Kurtenbach, and W. Buxton, "A marking based interface for collaborative writing," in *Proc. ACM Symp. User Interface Software and Technol.*, Atlanta, GA, Nov. 3–5, 1993, pp. 259–66.

[18] P. Hilts, "I sing the editor electric," *Publisher's Weekly*, p. 43, Jan. 3, 1994.

[19] "Pen and voice unite," *Byte Mag.*, pp. 98–120, Oct. 1993.

[20] H. D. Crane and D. Rtischev, "Pen and voice unite," *Byte Mag.*, pp. 98–102, Oct. 1993.

[21] R. M. Baecker, Ed., *Readings in Groupware and Computer-Supported Collaborative Work: Assisting Human-Human Collaboration.* San Francisco: Morgan-Kaufmann, 1993.

David K. Farkas is an Associate Professor in the Department of Technical Communication in the College of Engineering at the University of Washington. He has also taught technical communication at West Virginia University, Texas Tech University, and the University of Minnesota, where he received a Ph.D. in British literature. His main area of interest is information design, including multimedia and the advisory interface of computer systems. He also works in the area of computer support for collaborative writing. Farkas has a long-standing interest in online editing software and supervised the design of a prototype online editing tool in 1987.

Steven E. Poltrock leads a project supporting collaborative authoring in the Research and Technology organization of Boeing Computer Services. He worked as a programmer and engineer in the aerospace industry before obtaining a Ph.D. in Cognitive Psychology at the University of Washington. He conducted research in perception, cognition, and mathematical psychology at the University of Denver and Bell Laboratories. His research focus is groupware technology and its application to collaborative document preparation.

PART VII

Oral Presentations: Speaking Effectively to Groups

Many professionals are required to present information orally as well as in writing, and if you are in management or marketing you may speak before groups even more frequently than you write. The articles in this section, therefore, offer well-tested ideas on how to prepare and make successful oral presentations. Some topics, such as controlling nervousness, keeping audience attention, and using notes or visual aids are discussed in more than one article, so you will get a variety of help on the primary concerns we all have when giving a presentation. The final two entries deal with visuals: the use of photos (and by implication other highly detailed graphics) in presentations, and the practical aspects of producing a video to help present technical information.

Preparing the presentation

In the first article, Richard Lindeborg points out that there is really no substitute for careful outlining and revision when you prepare an oral presentation. Fortunately, as we all know, word processing has made this easier than ever before, and Lindeborg gives several useful pointers on how to expediently use this technology to organize your thoughts and stress your main points in a logical and coherent manner.

Delivering your message

Although Bert Decker focuses on helping managers and executives speak in public, his insights can help all of us who have to do so. In the author's words, when you give a presentation you are "both the delivery system and the message itself." An oral report involves verbal, vocal, and visual elements, not just turning written words into spoken ones. Decker's concluding pointers on maintaining eye contact with your audience and using visual aids are taken up in more depth in some of the remaining articles in this section.

The overall view

Next, Ronald Rosenburg looks at high-tech presentations in government and industry, covering the spectrum from audience analysis, planning, and rehearsing, to handling visuals, conveying confidence, and providing handouts. In his own words, "Achieving a successful presentation begins with the consideration of three things: what to say, how to say it, and how to conduct the presentation to convince an audience that you mean it." Rosenburg provides plenty of material to help you do this, and his tips on conducting the presentation are particularly useful.

Practice, practice, practice?

Most experts stress the need for practice before making a presentation, but Susan Dressel provides an anecdote illustrating the possible dangers of overpreparing. You could tie yourself into a straightjacket if you plan every syllable and action in advance, give your talk in a robot-like manner, and leave little flexibility to respond to cues from your audience. Some preparation is needed, however, and Dressel's fellow contributor to this article, Joe Chew, has some useful ideas on how to practice your presentation in such a way that your confidence, spontaneity, and personality will all work for you when you get up to talk.

Handling the mob

No one wants to face an unfriendly audience, but it can happen, often through no fault of your own. Gilda Carle's narrative of how one speaker handled an awkward situation is instructive and reassuring. Several articles in this section stress eye contact with an audience, and as Carle shows, you can use visual contact or "eye-alog" as an effective tool for softening negative attitudes among listeners. Eye contact alone is not enough, however—responding to hostile listeners also involves appreciating their point of view and talking with them in language they can relate to.

Problems in presenting the proposal

Michael Warlum looks at oral presentations you sometimes have to make in support of proposals, first analyzing why so many proposal presentations are ineffective and then describing the steps taken by the Boeing Company to remedy problems such as poor audience analysis and a failure to establish a clear goal, with the resultant failure to stress key points. Warlum' s comments on borrowing storyboards from the proposal team to ensure an accurate presentation of the proposal show a further use of these aids discussed by Greenly and Barakat in their articles in Part V of this anthology.

Do not overdo the graphics

You have probably attended presentations where the visuals were so overdone that they practically obscured the message. Thomas Walsh takes up this problem in his short article by considering the use of photographs compared to line drawings to illustrate an idea. Although he uses photos of church facades to show that sometimes a much simpler diagram might better make the point, his message can be taken as a warning to always use the simplest and least complex graphics needed to support your presentations. Sometimes photos or other highly detailed illustrations might be needed for your presentation, but you should carefully consider your purpose before substituting them for less detailed visuals.

Making a film

Technical materials can now be presented in more than one medium due to the emergence of new technologies over the years. Video is one of these, and Danny Dowhal and his fellow authors show you how to team up to produce a technical video. Their approach is methodical—they take you from the planning stages, to writing the script, to the actual production, editing, and distribution process. One essential question they confront right away is "How much is it going to cost?" They also outline how the work can best be divided up among team members, and illustrate a sample timeline for the project. Their list of details to remember is insightful and practical, and as they state in their conclusion, a good video can make technical information both highly accessible and transferable.

A Quick and Easy Strategy for Organizing a Speech

RICHARD A. LINDEBORG

Abstract—**Organizing thoughts—arranging ideas in an effective or logical order and stressing them appropriately according to their importance—is an important part of writing an effective speech on a technical subject. However, it takes so much time and effort to organize material manually and revise it until it is clear that many writers give up before producing a clearly written speech. Writing in a modified outline form on the word processor helps solve this problem. The outline form, coupled with the simplicity and speed of making changes on the word processor, makes it easy to respond as you write to the visual feedback of your writing, almost forcing you to express ideas in a well organized, simple, and clear manner. For many writers, the speed and ease of the word processor is the only thing that makes repeated revision possible. On the word processor, you can experiment repeatedly with the visual display of the text and keep revising until the display—and the text—reflects the best organization of the material and the natural cadences of the spoken word. The result is a speech that guarantees that the listener will understand the message and stay awake through the speech.**

THE development of a speech can be like the development of the land masses of the earth. Theory says the land masses came from a single, primeval continent and then drifted apart. Similarly, the idea behind a speech may be unified, with a fairly simple shape. As the speech develops, this grand, unified idea fragments, with the pieces slowly drifting apart. Finally, the speech resembles the geography of the earth: ideas are scattered like islands around the surface, but four-fifths of it is all wet.

The speech may include unbelievably massive Eurasian ideas that you could never hope to traverse in the lifetime of a single speech; huge ideas, resembling the American continents, held together by narrow Panamanian isthmuses of ideas; African ideas—full of potential, but politically unstable in places and largely undeveloped; Australian ideas— beautiful but embellished with flora and fauna found nowhere else; and Antarctic ideas—easy to define, but impossible to warm up to. You need an atlas just to find your way around a speech you thought was going to express an idea directly.

Curing Bad Organization

If you have experience writing anything, let alone speeches on technical subjects, you already know that good writing is hard work. Good writing requires good organization and much rewriting. You need knowledge of how to organize the speech, and you need to have the time and energy to organize, reorganize, write, and rewrite. Textbooks, journals, and teachers provide the knowledge of rhetoric required to produce a well-organized, clearly written speech. The word processor greatly reduces the time and energy required.

Richard A. Lindeborg is with the Forest Service, U.S. Department of Agriculture.
IEEE Log Number 9037664.

Simplifying and organizing used to take stacks of index cards, a good outline, and—if you could spare the time—many drafts. But now, with the aid of a word processor, you have the ability to change the outline as you go along, making repeated revisions to the text and the way it is displayed on the page. Revisions that were once too much trouble to contemplate can be done quickly. This helps you organize the material and keep it simple, resulting in a speech that is easier for the speaker to deliver with conviction and easier for the audience to understand.

The Quick and Easy Way

One writing technique that works well on a word processor is typing the speech in a modified outline form, breaking down every thought into manageable phrases, and determining where in the outline the idea belongs. This controls the complexity of every phrase and its position in the speech. Fig. 1 shows a passage from a speech on research and development (R&D) developed using this technique.

Place the most general or most important phrase or sentence first within each related group of phrases or sentences. This method of organizing will produce a speech in what is called the deductive style of writing, where the general idea is stated first, followed by more specific ideas. This style of writing is most common in journalism, where it is important to get the main ideas to the reader or listener quickly. The deductive style works well in speeches on technical subjects because it allows the speaker to make his or her point quickly. Hearing the main point up front allows the listener to place the supporting evidence in perspective and evaluate the supporting ideas as the speech progresses.

As you write in outline form, place each phrase on its own line or two of type, separated from other phrases and indented to show its relationship to the phrases preceding it and following it. Despite breaking sentences into phrase lines and indenting the phrases different amounts, you can still punctuate most of the material as you would in traditional manuscript typing. Standard punctuation makes the outline easier to follow. It also helps produce a traditional written text of the speech if you want to distribute the speech to the press, the audience, or others.

Experimenting with ways of arranging material in phrase lines and in outline form would be cumbersome without a word processor, but it could be done. The amazing thing is not that a speech can be done in outline form, but that this

Reprinted from *IEEE Trans. Prof. Comm.*, vol. PC-33, no. 3, pp. 133–136, September 1990.

The United States is not among the leaders in the percentage of Gross National Product devoted to R & D.

Last month, Business Week listed the figures as 1.8 percent of GNP for the United States,

versus 2.6 percent of GNP for West Germany and 2.8 percent of GNP for Japan

That is for nonmilitary R & D.

These two strongly competitive nations are outspending us by 50 percent in R & D.

Research is too important for us to allow it to suffer this neglect.

Fig. 1. Sample page of the outline form used for speeches. Three levels of indentation are used. The outline shown here is printed on a laser printer, using desktop publishing software. The left margin is wide to allow space for revisions and the speaker's delivery notes.

particular method of outlining allows the physical act of writing (the act of keyboarding) to dictate the writing style of the speech. On the screen, ideas that are not expressed in short, simple clauses and phrases grow to multi-line entries that are obviously not in character with the other material on the display screen. Splitting complex ideas into simpler, shorter parts is easy and quick on the word processor. Other ideas may nest deeper and deeper in the outline, indented farther and farther to show their subordination to main ideas. On the screen, this symptom is an obvious signal that something is terribly wrong with the organization of that part of the speech. The word processor makes it easy to add, delete, and rearrange points until the problem is corrected. Properly organized material fits the outline. Nothing else does. Without the word processor, you might not notice these problems. Even if you did notice them, there is a good chance you would shrug your shoulders and move on, rather than take the time to split up ideas onto separate index cards or rewrite a handwritten outline.

After you have written the speech in this outline style, you can print it out using a large, easy-to-read typeface and clear formatting. Fig. 1 is an example of output printed on a laser printer using desktop publishing software. This sample is printed in 12-point type (boldface except for minor points) on the upper one-half to two-thirds of the page. This point size is large enough for most speakers to read without stooping or squinting at the text. A 3-inch margin on the left keeps the number of words on a line within reason and allows room for

R & D in the world

R & D in the United States

R & D in this industry

R & D in this company

Progress in conducting an R & D project

Steps needed to gather this data

This week's work assignments

Fig. 2. Seven levels of ideas for a speech on R&D. The final speech should probably use only three levels of ideas. Which three levels to use depends on who the speaker is and who will be in the audience. The points generated for possible inclusion in the speech should be sorted. Those that seem to fit within the three levels selected for the speech should be arranged in outline form. The other ideas should be set aside in case the structure of the speech changes.

changes or for the speaker to add delivery notes. Restricting the text to the upper half of the paper allows the speaker to read the text without lowering his or her head. This is good for two reasons: it helps the speaker maintain eye contact with the audience; and it allows unrestricted flow of air past the vocal chords. A speaker with a lowered head will mumble into the lectern.

Getting Started

No one should give a speech without having an objective. Before replying to an invitation, develop a list of reasons for accepting or declining the invitation and a list of points that might be covered in a speech to the particular audience involved. If these lists reveal a good reason for speaking, accept the invitation. Otherwise, refuse it.

Once the engagement has been accepted, the speaker, the speech writer, and one or two technical experts can meet to discuss ideas for the speech. The important thing is to have several minds involved in generating ideas. If you are writing the speech for yourself, you may also be the technical expert. In this situation, you should meet with a couple of your peers. The participants should start this meeting by discussing the characteristics of the audience, their interests, motivations, preconceptions, and biases relative to the topic. They should discuss the occasion, the strengths and weaknesses of the speaker, and strategies to tie the listeners' purposes and priorities to those of the speaker. They should continue developing objectives for the speech, start on a list of major topics to cover, think of specific points to make, and start a list of topics that need to be researched in order to write the speech. Properly arranged relative to your strategies, all of these points become the outline for the speech.

Arranging Ideas

Whether you jot down ideas at home or meet with a group to toss out ideas, you may get confused about the relationship between the general ideas. Some ideas are obviously global in scope; others seem like trivial details; most are somewhere in between. Depending on the stature of the speaker and the nature of the audience, some global ideas may be too general to belong in the speech. Similarly, many of the details may be too specific to be of interest in the speech.

Fig. 2 shows several levels of points for the material considered for inclusion in the speech on research and development. The president of a trade association, speaking at a national convention, might use world research and development as the main theme for a speech, U.S. research and development in several industries as the main points, and U.S. research and development by several companies as specific examples. The head of research for a single company, speaking to the board of directors, might use U.S. research and development in that one industry as the main theme, research and development by several companies in that industry as the main points, and individual research projects in those companies as specific examples. A leader of a research team within a company, speaking to other team leaders, would speak in even narrower terms.

In general, one of the first things you as a speech writer need to do with a list of ideas is to come to grips with how to organize the individual ideas into tiers of points, each tier subordinate to the one above. You should try to include no more than three levels of ideas in a single speech. Your first step is to determine which levels are proper for the speech you are writing. Temporarily move items that seem too global or too trivial to the end of your list, and move the remaining ideas around until they seem to form a logical structure for the speech. This kind of shuffling can be done with index cards, but it is easier and more efficient on a word processor.

Use the main topic in the title of the speech, the introduction, and the conclusion. Use each of the main points as the heading for a section of the speech, and present each as the first group of thoughts in its section. Finally, use the specific examples within each section, following each with as much explanation as is appropriate for the audience and the occasion. This strategy puts the overall speech in the deductive style—starting with the most general ideas and moving to the most specific. This style is well suited for talks on technical subjects.

As you try to arrange ideas this way, it may become obvious that you have some related details with no main point to put them under or a main point with no details under it. These holes in your outline will enable you to come up with the missing items or, in some cases, show you that your ideas are leading you to a totally different structure for the speech than you originally envisioned. One explanation for this kind of "drift" is that you are straying from your topic. In this case, you can file the irrelevant portions of the outline for use in some future speech on that topic. Another explanation is that an unexpected, but entirely acceptable, approach to the topic has forced itself on you. The new approach may require you to reassess the value of all your ideas. You will be glad that you saved all the ideas, rather than throwing the ones that at first seemed to be outside the scope of the speech. This kind of shift in emphasis is fairly common in the early stages of organizing a speech.

Filling in the Blanks

Once you seem to have the overall structure of the outline in place, you can work on adding supporting points, working in illustrations, and writing an introduction and conclusion. At the same time, you can use the outline as a template for the writing style of the speech. You have to put any new piece of material someplace in the framework that already exists. Like a paleontologist assembling a dinosaur, you have a sack of bones and a mental picture of what the beast should look like. If a bone doesn't fit, perhaps it belongs to another dinosaur.

As the outline fills in, it becomes easy to see what ideas are properly placed, what ideas are in the wrong place, and what ideas have no place. Indent subordinate ideas under the main ideas to making relationships clear. Use short phrases on separate lines to keep the ideas clear and make them easy for the speaker to deliver.

Ideally, you should be able to begin each idea on its own page. If you use 12-point type with an extra half line of space between lines and one and a half spaces between phrases, you can fit a bit more than 20 lines of writing on a full page, or 13–15 lines on two-thirds of a page. A page usually provides enough room for a phrase or sentence summarizing the idea that will follow on that page, plus room for phrases or sentences supporting that topic. When you organize the page this way, the entire page is in the deductive style, moving from the most general phrase to the most specific.

As you add a point to the speech, you can actually see, as you type the words into the word processor, whether or not they are phrased properly. Bureaucratic expressions, overly technical language, sentences that are too long and complex—all become painfully obvious as soon as you type them. They just get too long. As the machine wraps a sentence to the third line, you know something is wrong. The structure is getting too complex.

When you are faced with an idea that has become a long, complicated monstrosity, first try to break it into parts. You can break it into equal parts, indented the same amount but separated by a blank line, or you can break it into unequal parts, some indented more than others. Most of these long sentences are fairly easy to break down; identifying them is hard when you type in paragraph form, but easy when you type in outline form. Other long sentences seem to defy cleaving into parts. Generally, these are the bureaucratic boulders that have no place in the pea gravel of your speech. You can find ways to crush the essential boulders so they can be used, but you should load up most of these bureaucratic boulders and ship them off to other speech writers, who might still have use for them.

Review and Revision

After you have produced the basic speech, let the speaker review it and suggest changes. If you are the speaker, then you will have to review it yourself or let a peer review it. You then work the changes into a revised version of the speech. This process of review and revision can be repeated as needed. You should give the technical people who have been doing the research for the speech an opportunity to review it, as well as anyone who needs to review policy issues. The word processor makes it easy to work new material into the speech between reviews.

If you are writing for someone else, do not be disappointed if the speaker makes changes. The final speech should be the speaker's creation; the speech writer and the technical staff should support, not override, the speaker. This relationship between the speaker and those producing the speech is similar to the relationship between a research scientist and the scientific writers and editors who transform research findings into readable reports. The speech writer, like the scientific writer or editor, helps put the ideas in a simple, well organized form; but the ideas—the essential part of the speech or article—belong to the speaker, just as the ideas in an article belong to the scientist.

Summary

If you go astray in crafting a speech, you can wind up like Mary Shelley's famous medical scientist. You finish grafting together all of the parts that are handed to you and wind up with something that is full of ideas but virtually uncommunicative. You are stuck with a monster whose heart is in the right place, but whose behavior is socially unacceptable. And as Dr. Frankenstein found out, it takes more than good intentions to make the public accept your point of view.

Outlining and revision are the only ways to avoid the problems of poorly organized speeches—but methods of organizing and writing take so long that many people quit before the job is one. Working in a modified outline form on a word processor makes the task fast enough and easy enough that you can actually take the time to do it.

When you take the time to organize and rewrite, you can produce speeches that use direct language; present major ideas clearly and concisely; follow a clear outline for combining major ideas with background, evidence, or example; and avoid jargon, technical language, and bureaucratic double-talk.

The word processor gives you a quick and easy way to organize your thoughts and revise your speeches. Organizing and rewriting are essential. The speed and ease of writing on the word processor make it practical to keep revising until the structure is logical and the writing clear enough to keep "continental drift" from fragmenting the grand, unified idea behind your speech.

Richard A. Lindeborg is a program analyst and a former speech writer for the Forest Service, U.S. Department of Agriculture. He has an M.S. degree in journalism from Syracuse University, Syracuse, NY, and has taught technical writing at Colorado State University, Fort Collins, CO, and Baker University, Baldwin, KS.

A Good Speech Is Worth a Thousand (Written) Words

BERT DECKER

***Abstract*—Management often thrusts the role of speaker on people untrained in that art. Although they know that printed words are effective for communicating information and data, they seldom realize that spoken words may have little to do with the effectiveness of a presentation. More important to believability are the visual and vocal characteristics projected by the speaker. Several suggestions are given for becoming a more effective speaker.**

TO obtain desired results and actions, information processing professionals must be able to communicate. Speaking effectively and delivering plausible presentations can make the difference and is a good place to start.

In any management situation, it's critically important to touch the emotions and the senses. Listeners will not react and won't be moved if they are given nothing but literal information. Unfortunately, managers often ignore the basics. They don't realize how their own nerves help cause those "blahs."

While technology has catapulted organizations into an information maelstrom, the human capability of communicating has moved at a snail's pace. For each technological advance that distances one person from another, there is a corresponding increase in the need for human contact.

The most important skill any manager can have is the ability to verbalize and motivate people—to put ideas into action. Yet fewer than one percent of the business people in America have done anything to improve their skills.

Thomas A. Murphy, former chairman of General Motors Corp., once said, "Few of us are trained in public speaking; it isn't how we got where we are. But when you reach the general-management level, you are thrust into that role."

There is nothing complicated about speaking. It comes naturally to everyone, but too many business people approach it the wrong way.

NOT A WRITTEN REPORT

If there is one critical concept that the majority of business people have not realized, and one essential for verbal effectiveness, it is that a presentation is not a written report.

Reprinted with permission from *Data Management,* September 1983, vol. 21(9), pp. 30–31, 55; copyright 1983 by Data Processing Management Association, Inc., Park Ridge, Illinois.

The author is president of Decker Communications, Inc., 999 Sutter Street, San Francisco, CA 94109; (415) 775-6111.

The printed word is the most effective tool for getting across data and information. People can read four times faster than they can speak. Business traditions are based on the rational, logical approach of the sequential printed word; so is the educational system. But a live, verbal presentation is much more than a linear progression of words delivered through the mouth.

When a person is speaking, many other things are going on. Studies have proven that when nonverbal messages are inconsistent with words—even contradictory—people believe the nonverbal over the words. The speaker is the medium of the message; and to a very large extent, the speaker *is* the message. If a speaker grasps a lectern, gazes up at the chandelier, displays signs of nervousness, and begins a speech with "My associates, my good friends, ... ," no one in the audience will believe he or she is their friend. Actions speak louder than words.

RICH BRAIN, POOR BRAIN

One way to understand speaking is to recognize that it is largely a right brain function. So are seeing and listening to a speaker.

"... And that government of the people, by the people, for the people, shall not perish from the earth."

Reprinted from *IEEE Trans. Prof. Comm.,* vol. PC-27, no. 1, pp. 32–34, March 1984.

Much has been written in the last four years about right brain/left brain processing. What is important for the business executive to understand is that everybody thinks in both modes, but by knowing what is to be accomplished, the speaker can achieve more success by using the strongest mode for the goal at hand.

The right brain handles intuition, emotion, and holistic methods of the thinking and decision-making processes. This is where such inputs as sound, color, movement, and patterns register.

The left brain (usually located in the left side of the cerebral hemisphere) processes information analytically, logically, and linearly. Reasoning and scientific data are stored and categorized by the left brain. The written word—reports, budgets, analyses, arguments, and even written speeches—is processed through the left brain.

Recent studies have indicated that top executives are largely guided by right brain activities—they score high on intuition and prefer oral reports to written reports because they can "get a feel" for the person presenting. "Seeing the whole picture" is a right brain function, and the best managers operate from that perspective.

Speaking is not a ping-pong game of words. People communicate mind-to-mind in person, not word-by-word. It's not just the words, but *how* those words are said. More than that, it's how the person looks, sounds, and everything he or she does. They all register—either positively or negatively. So it's important to know what counts the most for the message to be accepted.

THE THREE V'S

There are only three elements to any spoken communication:

- Verbal—the words or content—what is said
- Vocal—the voice expression, resonance, tempo, and inflections
- Visual—all that is seen by others: How the speaker looks, eye contact, posture, gestures, and facial expressions.

Dr. Albert Mehrabian of UCLA startled the traditional world of communication (in both education and business) with the discoveries published several years ago in his book *Silent Messages*. One of the foremost communication researchers in the country, Mehrabian measured the impact and believability of the spoken message according to these three elements.

His important findings: verbal—only 7 percent; vocal—38 percent; and visual—a whopping 55 percent. These figures contradict what has been taught in the schools and has carried over into business communication.

BECOMING EFFECTIVE

Very few managers are operating at their optimum level of communicative ability. Most managers block their message, get bogged down in the detail of words or facts, and forget that they are both the delivery system and the message itself. Even those managers who are outstanding decision-makers, administrative whizzes, and financial geniuses often fall short when they stand up to speak.

Following is some personal advice on how to go about becoming a more effective speaker, to deliver ideas with impact.

DON'T READ A TALK

Hiding behind the security of a written script may make *you* feel better, but not your audience. More important, it's not very effective.

When you are speaking from notes or extemporaneously, personally making your point, the audience can see that it comes from you. A written speech might be analytically correct, but most people will assume the words aren't yours. Voice takes on a reading-aloud incantation—often a monotone—and your eyes are chained to the page too long.

Don't Think They're Going To Get It Just Because You Said It!

Most managers erroneously think that because they give five major points in a presentation, their audience will remember them all. Not so!

You'll actually be lucky (or skilled and effective) if they remember your point of view, your key statement, and perhaps one or two supporting points. The truth is, they'll remember a good story or an anecdote. They'll remember a vivid litle detail—such as the color of the socks you said you wore on your first job interview. Abstract facts and data will go in one ear and out the other.

Since nobody can go back and reread your statements, you have to make sure the audience gets your main points. Don't try to overload them. Remember *KISS'M*: Keep It Simple, Stupid—and Memorable.

Be The Host, Not The Roast

When you're at the lectern, you're in charge of your audience's well-being. You are momentarily the host—not the main course they want to devour—so don't let your nervousness show.

If you have butterflies (all speakers do) don't assume everyone knows it. As a matter of fact, they don't. If you think your voice is quavering or your knees are shaking, chances are nobody else notices or cares. Simply release your knee lock and let your natural energy carry you through animated gestures and movement.

Look at your listeners the same way you would in your office, with "extended eye communication." This goes beyond the traditional notion of eye contact: Look at one person for four to five seconds, then move on to someone else at random, covering all corners of the group. By looking at people with extended eye communication, you show you're interested in communicating personally with them. They feel it, and you feel it.

Get Feedback

Speak as often as you can and use both audiotape and videotape to find out what others are hearing and seeing. Forget about asking friends and associates how you did. Most will say "Wonderful!" and mean it—they're too close to you and your goals to appraise objectively.

And don't tear yourself down in audio or video replay. Most speech teachers are counterproductive in telling people what *not* to do rather than pointing out their strengths as well as their weaknesses. Use the tools available. We are in an electronic age and there is no better learning tool than video, when used constructively by professionals.

Discovering bad habits in yourself does no good unless you know what to do about them, what specific steps to take for your style of speaking. You are your own best teacher.

Use Visuals, Be Visual

Since 85 percent of what we know has come through our eyes, it's obvious that we learn more from what we see than from what we hear or touch; people remember images far longer than facts. They will remember the image of you, too—animated or flat, energized or rigid, enthusiastic or dull.

As visual aids, overheads (transparencies) are probably the most versatile presentation tool, with 35-mm slides and flip charts also used for the right situations.

Keep simplicity in mind: One thought per page, three lines per page (or slide), bold graphics and color. Visual aids should highlight key points, not tell the whole story. Never put yourself in the dark or half-hidden behind equipment. You are the host. Think of your visual aids as a good waiter—there to assist you, not replace you.

Self-Confidence!

These are just a few essential guidelines for speaking effectively.

Tips, techniques, and ideas are great. Anyone can find a million more in books, but if you don't use them, they're about as valuable as a mail-order course on tap dancing if you don't get up to dance.

What counts is experience and self-confidence. Speak at every opportunity, get the kind of expert feedback that's immediately useful for your environment, and keep extending yourself.

The Engineering Presentation—Some Ideas on How to Approach and Present It

RONALD C. ROSENBURG

***Abstract*—Achieving a successful presentation begins with the consideration of three things: what to say, how to say it, and how to conduct the presentation to convince an audience that you mean it. Determining what materials, topics, and details to use must be based on an analysis of the potential audience, their sentiments, interests, technical disciplines, and possible responses to what would be presented. Presentation material must be put into a unified, professional, and easily understandable format and thoroughly rehearsed so that it can be delivered in a manner that instills confidence that the subject has been well-researched. The author presents some strategy, guidelines, and pitfalls, based on experience, for consideration toward these ends.**

MOST of the time we are given only one chance to present our ideas. If this is not done effectively at that time, the success of any future communication on the same subject could be jeopardized or, even worse, willingness of the audience to ever listen again to a particular speaker who "came across" as ill-prepared, boring, or incompetent could be destroyed.

For communication between speaker and audience to be successful, it must be the culmination of a preparation process started long before, one which included a carefully thought-out "speaker–audience interaction scenario." Such a scenario hypothesizes the type of audience expected, their sentiments, prejudices regarding the subject, orientations (political beliefs or group structure, for example), technical disciplines, personal interests, and questions that might be raised.

Based on the results of this audience analysis, you can determine *what* and *how much* must be said to satisfy both your and the audience's needs. When this is accomplished, organize the information into a suitable format and take it through as many full-scale dress rehearsals or dry-run presentations as necessary to become confident of convincing the audience that you know what you are talking about. To help achieve these goals, some guidelines, pitfalls, and ideas on strategy, based on experience, are presented.

PREPARING THE PRESENTATION

Determining What to Say

1. Thoroughly research what the presentation is to cover, from a general and a contractual viewpoint. Know what your audience *has* to see and hear and what information they *would like* to receive.

2. In researching your contractual documents, *extract all of the categories you are obliged to cover*. You may be surprised at some of the items at a subtler level that are specified in an applicable military specification. For example, in preparing an aircraft avionics presentation, I compiled material on the major and commonly thought-of topics such as displays, signal acquisition techniques, and processing capability but was surprised to find that I also had to address such topics as fungus control and acoustic noise limitations.

3. *Cover all areas*, even if very briefly, and specify them on your agenda. It's better to be complete and include them than to be criticized later for their omission. Your audience may know of the topic, however obscure, but generally they will not know what they are supposed to evaluate or question you on. They will depend on you for that information. If you cover it with details *you* feel are satisfactory, the chances are that no one will want any more.

4. After formulating ideas as to what is expected and what must be covered, contact representatives of your potential audience for further information and confirmation of your own ideas and plans. Again, find out what *they expect* to see and hear and what they would *like* to hear. You can readily gain the appreciation of your audience if you "just happen" to talk about an area they are interested in, or one they may have to cover in a future presentation of their own.

5. *Research your audience's past correspondence* on the subjects you will be covering and be knowledgeable enough to discuss them in depth. Understand their reasons for generating such correspondence so that you will be able to direct any discussion that may arise.

6. It is very important that your presentation *answer your audience's specific questions and concerns*. If possible, gear the material and language of the presentation in that direction. Have viewgraphs presenting *data* that address their specific questions. Try to think about other questions your presentation may raise, and be prepared to answer them.

7. *Thoroughly research all current and past problem areas*. Don't let your audience be first to introduce you to them. Get the latest and complete story on any problem. If it

Received April 7, 1983; revised August 25, 1983.

The author is a senior project staff engineer at the Grumman Aerospace Corporation, C11-40, Bethpage, NY 11714; (516) 752-3651.

Reprinted from *IEEE Trans. Prof. Comm.*, vol. PC-26, no. 4, pp. 191–193, December 1983.

involves hardware, go to the manufacturer for first-hand information on the nature of the problem and on what is being done to correct it. Maybe even include a discussion of those items in your presentation. In this case, however, ensure that for every problem you have either a solution or a direction you will take toward its resolution.

Putting the Information in Presentable Form

At this point in the preparation, even the most well-versed person, with a wealth of information to present, has, at times, fallen flat on his or her face!

1. At the outset, generate a detailed fact sheet covering the subject of the presentation. For example, if a work status is to be presented, outline all efforts to date; if it is a design concept, list design requirements, assumptions, trade-offs, and rationales. Review your material for correctness, clarity, and applicability. Next, extract only the highlights of this information to use as viewgraph points, making a separate (general) viewgraph for each subtopic and ensuring that there are no more than six points on each viewgraph.

2. In general, *have two viewgraphs per subject*—one general and one detailed. You may never use the latter, but it could be a lifesaver should the need for more information suddenly arise. The general viewgraph should contain only terse statements of fact to key your memory on what to say. The detailed viewgraph, on the other hand, should be slightly "overstuffed," especially with pertinent backup data that cannot be easily memorized. For example, the design review requirements for a particular Air Force avionic development contract called for the contractor to summarize the overall design requirements together with his concept for each. In this case, the general viewgraph contained a summary of the eight major requirements and was backed up by eight detailed viewgraphs presenting laboratory and analysis data. Although the speaker was quite knowledgeable, he was not ready for the barrage of inquiries with respect to "hard numbers." He was able to recover, however, with the help of one of the detailed viewgraphs he hadn't really planned to present.

3. *Make good quality viewgraphs*. Audiences tend to lose interest in faintly observable, hand-written viewgraphs. This is followed by loss of interest in the presentation itself. Make sure that viewgraphs are typed, all with the same typewriter.

4. *Prepare viewgraphs well in advance*. It is better to redo one or two of them than to not have any completed on time. Even having to do all of the viewgraphs over (as a result of, say, a dry run) would not cost much, especially compared to the business that might be lost by not getting your point across. Remember, *you only get one chance at the final presentation—have everything perfect for that time*.

5. *Always have an introductory viewgraph* before you get into the main part of your presentation to clearly tell your audience *what you intend to cover*. Never start off right into the "meat" of the subject as I saw one person do in an attempt to review changes made to a receiver design. The all-important *reasons for* the changes were lost, together with most of the audience, in an explanation *of* the changes. Close with a viewgraph telling the audience *what you have told them*.

6. *Have at least one dry run with the final presentation material*, and have as many knowledgeable people as possible present to critique it.

Notwithstanding the fact that the value of the dry run has been proven over and over again, I have found from personal experience, and through discussions with others involved in various presentations, that many organizations appear to be lax in this important area. Dry runs are always planned but often, due to lack of time, are cancelled or reduced to only a quick last-minute review. *Dry runs should be mandatory for all presentations*.

7. In the dry run, go through each viewgraph in *exactly the same order and manner you will formally present it*. Don't skip areas because you think they are of lesser importance. What you might think is insignificant or will be easily understood by your audience may be just the area that causes problems. Don't wait until the actual presentation to find out about it.

CONDUCTING THE PRESENTATION

1. The most important thing to remember is that *you must, from the outset, instill in your audience confidence that you know what you are talking about*, that you will be proceeding in the right direction with your work, and that, ultimately, you will give your customer what he or she wants.

This is extremely important, for the degree of success you achieve will manifest itself in the effectiveness and ease with which you are able to conduct your work in the future.

2. *Know your audience*. If your audience will contain a majority of people from a particular area (flight crews, for example), expect many questions and discussions in that area (displays and "knobology," in this example). Be prepared so that you will have to defer only a minimum of questions. The more you answer during the presentation, the fewer action items you will have to worry about later.

3. *Don't dwell on what may be boring or not universally interesting topics*. People tend to go into unnecessary detail explaining things they are very knowledgeable about. I attended a presentation to the Air Force in which one speaker went into a long and precise technical explanation of an avionic system. His knowledge of the subject was excellent but the details he presented were unnecessary. When he finished, a number of Air Force personnel gave him a standing ovation, partly because of his expertise, but mainly because he finally finished! *Avoid this pitfall*.

4. *Don't engage in arguments or any other confrontation with your audience.* Stay calm and unflustered—postpone (if necessary) touchy discussions to splinter groups.

This advice may sound unnecessary but I was, unfortunately, witness to such a confrontation during an initial engineering design presentation, where the thrust was really to establish the confidence I spoke of earlier. Needless to say, it did not help us toward that goal; nor did it help the people scheduled to speak next.

5. *Speak loudly and actively throughout the presentation.* Too many people start loud only to become inaudible either toward the end of the talk or toward the end of each sentence.

6. *Have handouts* consisting of at least a topic outline of your presentation if not a copy of your entire set of viewgraphs. Handouts of data are also desirable.

7. *Have enough handouts.* Make sure that there are enough to go around. I knew one individual who was insulted and subsequently appeared hardened to the presentation because he didn't receive a copy of the handout. Such a person may be rare but sometimes this may be the voice that counts.

8. *Never allow your presentation to be a reading of your viewgraphs.* A person who does this only proves two things: that he or she can read and that he or she is the wrong person to give the presentation.

9. *Always maintain a "lecturer" stature during your presentation.* You should strive to maintain a speaker–listener relationship with your audience in which *you* are the one giving the information for their review. Do not fall prey to a barrage of questions that puts you on the defensive. This will destroy your presentation and violate item 1. Once you lose the speaker or lecturer role, it is difficult to fully regain.

A FINAL COMMENT

After all is said and done, remember that your audience is human, also. They are just as anxious to learn about the subject you are presenting as you are to teach them. The easier you make it for them, the easier your task will be, and the more favorable an impression you will make. Always try to *put yourself in their place*, both when you prepare and when you deliver your presentation.

Authenticity Beats Eloquence

SUSAN DRESSEL
Associate Editor, *PC Transactions*
with JOE CHEW

Just last month, a new engineer spoke up in a staff meeting to explain the advantages of a design modification he had recommended. He made his point effectively, drawing a few helpful diagrams on the board and providing an example that clarified a technical detail for several managers in the group. The engineer spoke clearly, confidently, spontaneously. His explanation took about $3\frac{1}{2}$ minutes.

A few days later, the project manager asked the engineer to present his explanation as part of a briefing scheduled for some customers in another 2 weeks.

The engineer prepared his drawings more thoroughly and had the audiovisual lab make some nice transparencies for overhead projection. Although his explanation at the briefing took more than 5 minutes, it was not nearly so complete, cohesive, and effective as his extemporaneous effort in the staff meeting.

At the staff meeting, his attention was fixed sharply on helping others understand his point. At the briefing, his attention seemed to be on his own performance as a speaker. Although he spoke well, he had lost an authenticity far more valuable than the studied eloquence that he, like many other speakers, had attempted.

In preparing his more structured presentation, the engineer locked himself into a script and audiovisual material, on the assumption that all listeners would interpret his words just as he intended. Under this assumption, he was unlikely to notice a puzzled look on a listener's face. And being tied to his script, he couldn't offer spontaneous explanations or examples. He was no longer an authentic person communicating with others.

In his levity-laced contribution to this column, Joe Chew advises speakers to rehearse "in the interest of spontaneity." The purpose of rehearsing, don't forget, is to ensure that you have all the main points in the right order and well supported, NOT to ensure that you have all the words committed to memory.

Joe Chew, guest contributor to Dr. Dressel's column, is a Senior Technical Writer with Softcom, Inc., a Hayes Research and Development Company, San Francisco.

Knowing that you are in control of your subject and the message you want your audience to understand, you will have more confidence. That confidence allows you to deliver your message spontaneously. Just as Joe's personal style and voice come through in the following sample of his writing, your own authentic personality should come through to your audience when you speak. Now listen to Joe.

A FEW WORDS OF ADVICE TO SPEAKERS

You may be one of those enviable souls who can stand up at a moment's notice and make an extemporaneous discourse on anything. If you are, congratulations; we look forward to hearing you, and you can look forward to basking in a room full of envy. Maybe you'll even get a promotion.

Most of us, though, get a bit rubber-legged at the thought of giving a talk. Some butterflies in the stomach. A little sweat on the palms. In fact, if that's all you suffer, you're lucky. Willard Scott passed out on the set of The Today Show a few years ago; upon being revived, the old trouper shocked a lot of people by revealing that he'd been having violent attacks of stage fright for years. (A little stress is actually a good thing; it gets your blood up, so to speak, so you can perform at your best. Serious speaker paralysis is something different.)

If you're a hard-case talkaphobic, it will probably take more than encouragement to turn you around. Being convinced that nobody wants to hear you, or even cares about your subject matter, and that it's a moot point because you just couldn't go through with it anyway, is a bad-news problem. But if you just have a little case of opening-night jitters, there are a few simple and effective things you can do.

Rehearsing probably does the most good for the most people. Now don't write out a script and memorize it by saying it over and over. The only memory work needed here is to store and retrieve your main points and supporting points in the order you plan to use them. You won't have trouble finding the right words when you're in control of what you want your listeners to understand. You ought to have this control established at least by the night before your talk. A quick flip through your slides

Reprinted from *IEEE Trans. Prof. Comm.*, vol. PC-30, no. 2, pp. 82–83, June 1987.

just before the talk is fine, but frantic last-minute cramming will just get you even more keyed up without really helping.

When you have control of sequence and support for your points, you'll need to see if you can sustain that control while talking and applying some of the pointers below. For a live audience, why not try your local chapter of IEEE? If you're not quite ready for them, the bathroom mirror is always handy; so is the rear-view mirror of your car if you don't mind some curious stares from fellow commuters. You can give your talk to the television set, where there are always some confident (if lobotomized) models to emulate, or try it out on your Significant Other if constructive sarcasm is more to your taste. Some people get an ego boost from a dog that barks at all the right times; others prefer the noncommittal bubbling of goldfish. Run through it at least once somehow.

Having demonstrated that you can talk while remembering what you're supposed to be talking about, how can you help yourself further? In a word: relax. An internal attitude of self-confident defiance is helpful to some people: "If they don't like it, to heck with 'em." (Of course, being able to say that and make yourself believe it indicates that your problem was not too severe in the first place.) Yoga, TM, and other mental disciplines or relaxation techniques are great if you're into that sort of thing; there are those who swear by a martini.

Probably, though, the best thing to do is to take a deep breath and dive right in. Once you move into the technical material, you'll get yourself squared away.

Relaxed? Check. What now? Believe it or not, the hardest part is over. You're already in control of your material, so the part you will be judged on – the substance – is in place and ready to go. So here are those pointers we promised.

Speak up.

A seemingly basic and trivial requirement, yet often neglected, especially when someone in the front row asks a question. Don't shout; just get a feel for how your voice carries (or, rather, doesn't carry) and crank it up accordingly.

You're probably not going to use the training technique Demosthenes supposedly came up with, which involved a mouthful of pebbles and a beachful of crashing waves to outshout. (Four of five dentists surveyed disapproved of this technique anyway.) But you don't need that much power just to make your voice carry across the room.

Speaking loudly, addressing the room in confidence, is also a self-fulfilling prophesy. You become what you act like. If you're shy, BLUFF shamelessly. What they don't know won't hurt you.

Stand tall.

Let them see you. Stand in a relaxed but upright posture; don't crawl behind your visual aids. And here's an eye-contact trick: look 'em right in the bridge of the nose. They can't tell the difference, and you'll achieve that magic eye contact without paralysis.

Don't hide rhetorically, either.

In his collection of stylistic essays, *On Writing Well*, William Zinsser reminisced about an old editor of his, an individual allergic to equivocation. "Don't go peeing down both legs," he would say. If you have something controversial to bring up, think it through, decide if it's right, and figure out a fair way to put it across. Then say it.

Be informal – engage your audience.

Life is not long enough to sit there listening to some droning nebbish read a paper verbatim – but you only have to think back as far as your last professional conference or convention to come up with some horrible examples. Use crib notes if you have to. But don't read; talk.

Stay in charge.

Balancing this goal with the previous one is quite a trick sometimes, and unfortunately nothing helps except practice and a strong personality. Try gently but firmly to keep the presentation on track even as you briefly explore sidelines that attract people's interest.

SUMMING IT UP

The Three Rules of Public Speaking:

- Be forthright.
- Be brief.
- Be seated.

Handling a Hostile Audience—With Your Eyes

GILDA CARLE

Abstract—**This paper defines a method for turning confrontation between a speaker and a hostile audience into engagement of common concerns by effective use of eye contact, as well as vocabulary related to the audience's perceptive style.**

DAN WESTON, an engineer with the Clifton Power and Light Company (CPL), stood before the local Kiwanis Club. It was his job this evening to inform the 30-member audience about CPL's new power lines, soon to be constructed in this community. Until yesterday, CPL was looked on as a community asset, providing hundreds of jobs and less expensive electricity. However, just one day before Weston's presentation, the Clifton News published a study linking electromagnetic radiation from power lines with cancer. The Clifton Power and Light Company was the enemy. And, for this audience, Dan Weston was Clifton Power and Light.

As Weston was completing his introductory remarks, he sensed an undercurrent. As an experienced member of the Power Company's speakers bureau, Weston knew that he should discard his prepared outline dealing with the design modifications of the new structures. Instead, his two most pressing objectives were to let his listeners know he understood their concerns, and to get their attention for the information he had come to share. How would he achieve these goals?

According to the *Book of Lists* [1], people consider public speaking their number one fear. Fear is certainly to be expected when a hostile audience can turn public speaking into public persecution. But audience opposition and anger must be confronted as soon as possible [2]. If antagonism is allowed to germinate, additional resentment builds, and with the slightest provocation, an entire auditorium can become unmanageable.

Many public speakers open their presentations with a prepared *monolog*—one that bridges the audience's agenda with their own. Other presenters immediately immerse the audience in participative *dialog* to build enthusiasm and activate involvement. But both *monolog* and *dialog* heavily rely on words to get their meaning across. And because as little as 7 percent of our information is communicated through words alone [3], Weston chose to concentrate at first on communicating with facial and body expressions, particularly with his eyes. Before he uttered a single word, Weston conducted *eye-alog*, prolonged empathetic eye contact. More penetrable than monolog, and more disclosing than dialog, eye-alog can help to establish rapport and cooperation—especially among hostile parties.

Dr. Gilda Carle is President of InterChange Communications Training, Yonkers, New York.

SECRETS BEHIND EYE-ALOG

Former President Reagan used eye-alog before he began each press conference. He looked reporters in the eyes—and then smiled and greeted them by name. This initial eye-alog told his viewers, "I'm on your side." It promoted Reagan's reputation as "the great communicator [4]." Mikhail Gorbachev is considered by many to be one of the world's best speakers. Using his hands and voice as well, he first dominates a meeting with his eyes.

America focuses much attention on the eyes with flattering eyeglass frames, tinted contact lenses, and colorful eye makeup. The vocabulary substantiates the richness of eye-alog: *gaze*, *glance*, *glare*, *gawk*, and *gape* are just a few synonyms for "look." Because eye-alog should precede dialog and monolog, the wise communicator can use it to choose an appropriate vocabulary. Neurolinguistics teaches us that "visual" communicators look up before telling us they "see" our point of view; "auditory" communicators look from side to side before explaining that they "hear" our side of the argument; and "kinesthetic" communicators look diagonally downward before admitting that they "feel" we are right [5]. Thus, by noting the direction of a listener's glances during eye-alog, a speaker can be alerted to choose words that are derivatives of *see*, *hear*, or *feel* in an effort to connect with the eye cues before him. Based on the principle that "Like likes like," this connecting of speaker's vocabulary to listener's eye-alog enhances subliminal interpersonal communication, even under hostile conditions.

WESTON'S PLAN

After his unceremonial introduction, Weston paused silently before the angry group. He divided the audience into imaginary quadrants, and for three seconds each, 12 seconds in all, he sought friendly eyes among the faces. He had an eye-alog with each—and then smiled. Finally, he

Reprinted from *IEEE Trans. Prof. Comm.*, vol. 32, no. 1, pp. 29–31, March 1989.

took a deep breath and acknowledged the fear: "By now you have read the findings of the Savitz study. You know the information is inconclusive. You also know that Clifton Power is subsidizing further research—which will take time to conduct, analyze, and report. This is a societal issue—and one we will *all* solve together. Tonight, let us openly discuss our mutual concerns. I will be glad to fill you in on the facts we currently have."

Weston had used eye-alog to establish unity and set the stage for believable dialog. With each question from the audience, he could offer a sympathetic monolog in response.

Weston conducted eye-alog for another few seconds, then smiled to some friendly audience eyes. He called upon a receptive face for question 1. With subsequent queries, when possible, he noted the interrogator's eyes and was sure to respond in *visual*, *auditory*, or *kinesthetic* terms: "I *see* what you are saying (visual), "I can *hear* how upset you are" (auditory), or "I *understand* why you *feel* as you do" (kinesthetic). Finally, when a hostile interrogator got carried away, Weston was quick to disengage eye contact with him and enter into eye-alog with other audience members.

Thus, beginning with eye-alog, Weston set the stage for each response. He read each inquirer's eye-alog and responded to questions with the most acceptable language. He used eye-alog effectively with the hostile group before him and allayed their irrational concerns. Eye-alog was the perfect prelude to the subsequent dialog and monolog that contained Weston's real agenda.

The EDM Formula for Hostile Audiences

The EDM Formula comprises the following components:

E: EYE-ALOG

- Divide the audience into imaginary quadrants.
- Pause.
- Hold an *eye-alog* with the friendliest eyes in each quadrant, three seconds each, 12 seconds in all.
- Use the SOFA:
  - *S*: Smile.
  - *O*: Open your posture to demonstrate receptivity to your audience.
  - *F*: Forward lean—into your audience.
  - *A*: Acknowledge your listeners by nodding slightly while smiling "Hello."

D: DIALOG

- Think NOT in terms of making a *presentation to* your audience; instead, think of having a *conversation with* them.
- During your conversation with the audience, especially while answering questions, use the SOFA.
- If you are close enough, note the position of the interrogator's eyes. Also note the verbs he chooses: are they visual, auditory, or kinesthetic?
- Pause.
- Mirror the visual, auditory, or kinesthetic terminology and eye-alog used by your questioner—but sweep your gaze from the questioner to other audience members.
- By disengaging the eyes of the hostile interrogator, you will publicly and gracefully empower your own authority by *conversing* with the people you are there to influence.

M: MONOLOG

- With each response, paraphrase the question to emphasize your own objectives and eliminate negative buzz words [6].
  For example:
  "Why is your company constructing those unsightly power lines by our homes, especially in light of the potential dangers to our public health?"
  Responding Monolog: "The question is ... [Use the SOFA] ... 'What are the safest and most cost-effective means that Clifton Power has at this time to transmit electricity to our homes?'
  The question is deliberately paraphrased to formulate a positive response.
- Do not offer the usual, defensive response of "Power lines are *not* unsightly ..." or "We are *not sure* that there are potential dangers in power lines ..." Instead, reposition positive questions that will prepare you for positive responses.
- Using eye-alog and dialog, you have already primed your audience to support you. Now, through monolog, you can crystallize your position and *sell* the reason you are actually there.
  For example:
  The words of the questioner above included the visually oriented terms "unsightly" and "in light of."
  Thus, monolog following the paraphrased question should incorporate *visual* terminology: "Clifton Power *views* power lines as a cost-effective means of bringing electricity into our homes ..."
- *Monolog* can therefore come to life in the audience's terms. The subconscious subtlety of familiar terminology and congruent eye-alog set the tone for dialog that will encourage acceptance of the monolog of information.

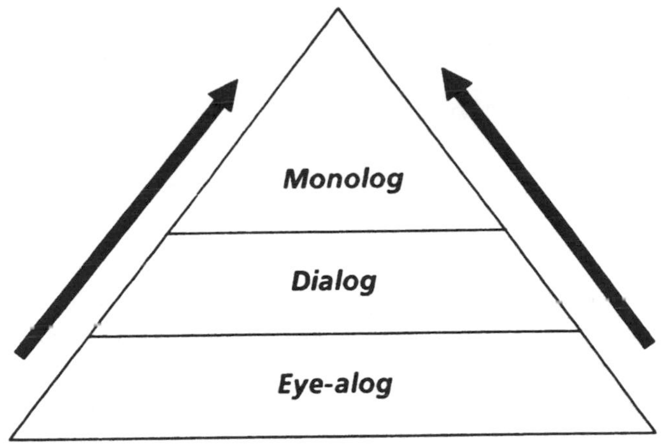

EDM Formula for Handling a Hostile Audience

The EDM formula inverts the usual tendency of speakers to begin with their prepared agenda and to monolog an audience to sleep. Especially with hostile listeners, the EDM formula establishes immediate rapport through eye-alog to be followed by dialog, and finally by monolog. Using the EDM formula, a speaker has the chance to allay audience resistance and achieve his objectives.

REFERENCES

1. Wallechinsky, D., Wallace, I., and Wallace, A., *The Book of Lists*, New York: Bantam Books, 1978.
2. Carle, G., "Coping with Corporate Rage," *Shell World*, internal publication of Shell Oil International, December 1987, pp. 28–29.
3. Mehrabian, A., and Ferris, S. R., "Inference of Attitudes from Nonverbal Communication in Two Channels," *Journal of Consulting Psychology 31* (1967), pp. 248–52.
4. Ailes, R., and Kraushar, J., *You Are the Message: Secrets of the Master Communicators*, Homewood, IL: Dow Jones-Irwin, Inc., 1987.
5. Richardson, J., and Margulis, J., *The Magic of Rapport: How You Can Gain Personal Power in Any Situation*, San Francisco: Harbor Publishing, 1981.
6. Lustberg, A., *Winning at Confrontation*, Washington: U.S. Chamber of Commerce, 1985.

Improving Oral Marketing Presentations in the Technology-Based Company

MICHAEL F. WARLUM

Abstract—**Oral presentations by a company's representatives affect its reputation and competitive position. Typically, oral presentations exhibit certain shortcomings. These can be overcome by the application of good developmental techniques. Recognizing the importance of good oral presentations, many companies are providing their employees with professional help in developing them. It is recommended that all companies address this issue.**

THE NEED FOR ORAL PRESENTATIONS IN BUSINESS DEVELOPMENT AND MARKETING

A factor vital to the health of any corporation is the constant exchange of accurate information. Although traditional, written forms of business communication remain important, the oral exchange of information occupies an increasingly important role in the functioning of today's companies.

The fast-paced business climate demands that this oral communication, whether within the company or with the customer, be clear and concise. Misunderstandings can be extremely expensive in both time and money. Contracts can, and have been, lost at this point.

Technology-based corporations are no exception to the growing emphasis on oral presentations. Management briefings, design reviews, product demonstrations, marketing and business development efforts, and other requirements for oral communication are standard practice. Oral presentations are assuming a pivotal role in government contracting decisions. Today, and for the foreseeable future, the ability to present oral information successfully is integral to corporate and individual success.

ORAL PRESENTATION PROBLEMS IN TECHNICAL MARKET DEVELOPMENT

Perhaps the greatest impediment to oral communication in the technological corporation is that most engineers and other technically educated individuals are not specifically trained to plan, produce, and deliver oral presentations. As a result, many do them poorly. Client interest declines, and proposal scores suffer.

Several barriers to effective oral communication are seen consistently in the technological community. Included among these barriers are failure to analyze the audience, develop a logical outline, use effective visual aids, or employ appropriate delivery techniques. Lack of such careful preparations usually spells poor reception.

Inattention to audience analysis lies at the heart of many ineffective oral presentations. To ensure success, certain basic facts about those in attendance must be determined. What level of detail is appropriate to the particular audience? What aspect of the subject is of most interest or relevance to the members of that audience? Are they likely to be hostile to the topic, to the speaker, to the point of view the speaker represents? Do they need to be persuaded or do they come seeking information eagerly? The answers to these and related questions about the audience have an immense bearing on how any presentation is crafted and delivered. Figure 1, a checklist for marketing speakers, can result from effective audience analysis.

As a result of their training and experience, technology-oriented presenters typically focus on technical content rather than on communication. "We'll blow them away with our technological approach," is a commonly heard statement. There are instances in the technology marketplace where such an attitude may be appropriate, others in which it can lead to disaster.

Put simply, the underlying purpose of audience analysis is to discover common ground between the speaker and the listener. What do members of the audience already know that the presenter can build upon to give new information meaning for them? If this building process does not take place, chances are that communication will not take place either.

Sometimes the presentation is not organized logically. Again, a building process has to occur. The presenter must build a case, keeping in mind that good speaking, like good writing, has a persuasive element. Too often the speaker approaches the platform with a vague idea of the

Michael Warlum is employed by The Boeing Company, Seattle, WA, where he acts as an advisor in oral presentation development.

Reprinted from *IEEE Trans. Prof. Comm.*, vol. 31, no. 2, pp. 84–87, June 1988.

SPEAKER'S CHECKLIST

Number of View Graphs: ______	Manager: ______
Duration (minutes): ______	Video Budget: ______
Presenter: ______	Video Manager: ______

Section	Treatment	Yes	No	Remedy
INTRODUCTION	All messages there? All parts explained?			
CLIENT THEME #1	Our reply			
CLIENT THEME #2	Our reply			
CLIENT THEME #3	Our reply			
CONCLUSIONS	Summation? Positive sales message?			

Next Meeting:	Action Items:

Figure 1. Checklist for Marketing Speakers

points to be covered and does so, more or less, treating each item as though it were a discrete subject, not part of a total story. The result is apt to be audience confusion. We simply cannot afford to invest hundreds of thousands of dollars on a proposal only to allow the intended listeners—a Source Selection Board perhaps—to go away with an unclear message about what we plan to achieve.

In an equally ineffective variation of this theme, a plan of organization does exist, but it is obvious *only* to the speaker. Unless care is taken to provide plenty of verbal signposts, such as "I intend to make three points. They are ..." or "To summarize, let me reiterate my major points," the members of the average business audience may lose the thread of the discussion.

In the technology-oriented presentation, visual aids have a tendency to become the presentation rather than to act as a support and enhancement to it. The use of unnecessary or inappropriate visual aids encourages the speaker to actually read the words on the charts to the audience, a task most audience members could perform more efficiently for themselves.

Many presenters pride themselves on having file drawers full of visual aids, the remains of presentations they have given over a period of several years. When faced with the challenge of a new presentation, these individuals pull a few visual aids from here and a few from there, amassing a conglomeration of disparate images. Once they have selected their visual aids, these presenters improvise some words to go with them, never actually outlining the presentation logically to ensure that the message is appropriate to their particular audience.

All too often, technical presenters neglect the rehearsal phase of presentation development completely. No matter how experienced a presenter may be, rehearsal is nearly always necessary to good performance.

Dependence on old habits, such as failing to analyze the audience, develop a logical outline, create appropriate visual aids, or rehearse and deliver the message adequately keeps presentations from being as effective as possible.

Moreover, because they have relied for so long on oral presentations that are not as successful as they could be in either content or delivery, many people do not see a need for change. Unfortunately, their presentations usually show it, and in today's demanding marketplace they frequently show it on the bottom line.

PROFESSIONAL HELP FOR ORAL PRESENTERS

To enhance their competitive stance, corporations must find ways to improve the quality of oral presentations given by their representatives. A number of companies are moving aggressively to offer oral presentation assistance to their employees. In addition to calling on the consulting services that operate in this field, firms are developing their own assistance programs.

The Boeing Company, for example, has established a group called Oral Presentation Development. Using a combination of group sessions, one-to-one counseling, customized written materials, and brief tipsheets, this group provides assistance to any Boeing employee preparing for an oral presentation, whether it is aimed at an audience within the company or outside of it. The service is based on the belief that, to be truly effective, presentation development assistance must be available every step of the way, from conception and planning to final rehearsal and delivery.

An initial step in assisting presenters is to help them analyze the potential audience. This analysis consists of identifying the individuals who are likely to make up the audience. If it is impossible to obtain actual names, an educated guess is made as to the types of people who will attend. The expectations, biases, knowledge, and level of interest of the members of the audience all have a bearing on the presentation and its thrust. If the presentation includes a request for action, the attitudes of key decision-makers likely to be in attendance are determined. The biases of the potential audience toward the presenters themselves and the firm they represent are also worthy of note, and a study is made of how the presentation will benefit the audience.

The next step is to clarify the purpose of the presentation. Presenters must ascertain why they are talking about this particular topic to this particular audience. Is the primary goal to inform, persuade, answer questions, or some combination of these? Once the purpose is agreed upon, the presenters can concentrate on stating their objective in one succinct sentence.

Out of this exercise comes a statement of the message. It is important that it be phrased in the way it will be stated to the audience, bearing in mind that subtlety is not usually appropriate to the business presentation. Richard J. Kulda of Professional Eloquence says that speakers who fail to state conclusions for their listeners can expect only about 12 percent of them to arrive at those conclusions on their own. Moreover, fully 30 percent will draw some conclusion the speaker did not intend. Conversely, if the presenter states conclusions clearly, 55 percent of the audience will draw the appropriate conclusion.[1]

With the help of oral presentation development advisors, Boeing presenters plot strategy, determining the most effective method of communicating the message. They pinpoint any shortcomings in the proposed program or product that must be addressed and anticipate probable questions from listeners, including those they hope the audience will not ask. Once these questions have been identified, the presenters can formulate effective responses.

When initial planning is complete, speakers concentrate on articulating the major points they want to express. Developing a storyboard, they organize these points into a logical structure, adding necessary subordinate points and expanding the outline to include explanatory detail. The result is the basis for the body of the presentation. Once the content and flow have been determined, appropriate closing and opening remarks are developed. Often, the actual proposal storyboards are borrowed from the proposal development group to ensure that the oral presentation reflects the technical proposal's themes and messages.

Advisors help presenters tailor their material to the time available for presentation. They treat the outlined points as time modules, link them with logical transitions, and allow ample opportunity for questions from the audience.

Presenters are urged to steer away from developing a full script. The extemporaneous technique, delivery based on an abbreviated version of the outline, promotes a conversational, unmechanical interaction between the speaker and the audience.

Appropriate visual aids are developed. They are finalized only after the content has been agreed upon, saving time, staff effort, and money by avoiding construction of art that ultimately goes unused.

REHEARSALS AND VIDEOTAPE PRESENTATIONS

In the latter stages of preparation, Boeing oral presentation development advisors assume the role of coach and critic. They attend and critique dry runs and rehearsals, videotaping them for review by the presenters when appropriate, and work with individual speakers to improve their delivery and put them at ease with their material.

The Boeing Company is by no means alone in its determination to improve the quality of oral presentations. Other companies have begun or are starting programs of their own to promote adoption by their employees of some or all of the improvement techniques described in this article. The ultimate aim of these efforts is to ensure development of carefully prepared, quality oral presentations that communicate clearly and effectively—presentations that sell.

SUMMARY

With the increased emphasis by both governmental and commercial customers on oral presentations and the growing need within technology-based companies for clarity and conciseness in verbal communication, programs of assistance, whether organized within the company or provided

[1] Kulda, R. L., *Presentation Workshop Notes*, Orange, CA, Professional Eloquence, 1973.

by outside consultants, are clearly called for. It is vital that any corporation seeking to compete effectively develop some method of assuring that oral presentations given by its representatives show the company in the best possible light. Thus we recognize that business development and technical marketing rely on a personal, verbal touch that only quality presentations can establish.

BIBLIOGRAPHY

1. Leech, T., *How to Prepare, Stage, and Deliver Winning Presentations*, New York: American Management Association, 1982.
2. Wilder, L., *Professionally Speaking*, New York: Simon and Schuster, 1986.
3. Woelfle, R. M. (ed), *A Guide for Better Technical Presentations*, New York: IEEE Press, 1975.

Illustrations in Oral Presentations: Photographs

Index Terms— *Conversational maxims, cooperative principle, instructional design, theories of perception.*

Interface

—Feature by
THOMAS WALSH

Manuscript received April 5, 1998; revised May 15, 1998.
The author is at P.O. Box 187, Grosse Tete, LA 70740 USA.
IEEE PII S 0361-1434(98)06174-8.

H. Paul Grice, "Logic and Conversation" in P. Cole and J. L. Morgan, Eds., *Syntax and Semantics 3: Speech Acts.* New York: Academic, 1975, pp. 41–58.

A picture may be worth a thousand words, but if only a hundred words are needed, that nine hundred extra words may obscure communication rather than enhance it. This is the point of Manning [1], who warns authors of instructional texts not to be too quick to scan a photograph into a document to avoid the trouble of making a line sketch. Manning bases his argument on theories of perception developed by McCloud [2], and even earlier by Peirce [3]. It seems to me that the argument might also be based on the "Cooperative Principle" of H. P. Grice in his "Logic and Conversation."

Students of pragmatics will remember Grice's claim that discourse participants attempt to be maximally cooperative by making each contribution to a discourse adhere to the four "Conversational Maxims" given as follows:

a. RELATION: the contribution is relevant.
b. MANNER: the contribution is clear, unambiguous, and concise.
c. QUALITY: the contribution is true.
d. QUANTITY: the contribution is exactly as informative as needed.

Grice points out that when one of these Maxims is violated, the listener/reader (who always assumes that the speaker/writer is being cooperative) will go to almost any length to construct a context in which the contribution will be meaningful. Thus, for example, a review of the movie *War and Peace* consisting of a statement that the movie had some "stunning snow scenes" caused readers to interpret the paucity of information (i.e., a violation of the Maxim of Quantity) as a negative review.

To the extent that a participant is unable to construct a meaningful context for a contribution appearing to violate one of the Maxims, communication breaks down. Likewise, when a reader is unable to abstract and compare the intended detail from a sequence of photographs, a breakdown in communication also occurs. Although one might argue that a photograph is not technically a linguistic contribution, surely excessive detail is tantamount to a violation of the Maxim of Quantity. As Manning suggests, to minimize the likelihood of such a breakdown, an author would do well to go to the extra trouble of abstracting the pertinent detail and presenting it in the form of a line sketch.

Manning is concerned that writers will take the high-tech expedient of scanning photos into a document, thus avoiding the relatively laborious task of making drawings. However, the same problem occurs in oral presentations when speakers use photographic slides from a database when line drawings would be more useful.

I experienced this most painfully on a recent trip to Rome. Speakers were assigned to give thumbnail sketches of various periods of art, each presentation to be followed by a walking tour to observe actual examples of the period being studied. Unfortunately, some of the speakers illustrated their lectures only with photographic slides, hoping that the audience would

Reprinted from *IEEE Trans. Prof. Comm.*, vol. PC-41, no. 3, pp. 209–212, September 1998.

be able to identify the relevant details. One speaker used literally hundreds of slides to illustrate Baroque art without ever managing to explain exactly how one might identify a Baroque church, as opposed to, say, one from the Renaissance or Early Christian periods. Two and a half hours and two hundred detailed photographs resulted in total confusion, but a half-dozen good line drawings showing what detail is relevant to each period would have done the trick in fifteen minutes.

Fig. 1. Geometric patterns characteristic of pre-Baroque architecture.

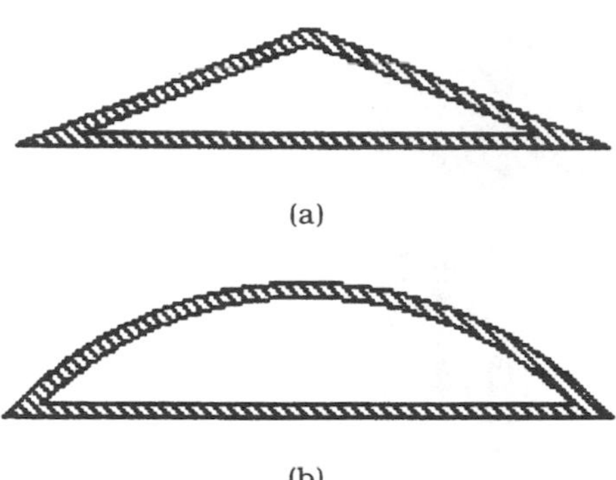

For example, one characteristic of Baroque architecture is the interruption of lines forming geometric patterns, such as the triangle or half-circle often used over openings. In pre-Baroque buildings, these patterns would usually be intact. To develop this point, it would be useful to illustrate the forms by drawings such as those in Fig. 1.

At this point, the lecturer might point this out in a photo of a pre-Baroque building such as the Renaissance church in Fig. 2 in which triangles and half-circles are intact.

In contrast, when these patterns are used in Baroque buildings, either the base, or the apex of the triangle or half-circle is often interrupted, as illustrated in Fig. 3(a) and (b).

Sometimes the interruption is caused by the intrusion of another ornament, as in Fig. 3(c) and (d).

Here the lecturer might show a photo such as that in Fig. 4, pointing out the three examples of interrupted lines. (See if you can find all three.)

After such an introduction students should be able to pick out relevant details on their own.

The psychological problem created by the use of photographic images without sufficient orientation appears to be that nonspecialists process a photograph of a building or painting holistically, as a unique entity. Without explicit instruction on what details are pertinent to the period, any details that they perceive are likely to be irrelevant. This sort of processing will result in an impressionistic, rather than systematic, comparison of successive photographs. This procedure is analogous to the classification of books by their size or color rather than their subject matter.

This is not to say that photos cannot be useful as primary illustrations. For example, the sheer complexity of a Baroque church relative to one from the Renaissance is best shown holistically in

Fig. 2. Church of S. Bernadino, L'Aquila, pre-Baroque building.

Fig. 3. Interrupted geometric patterns characteristic of Baroque architecture.

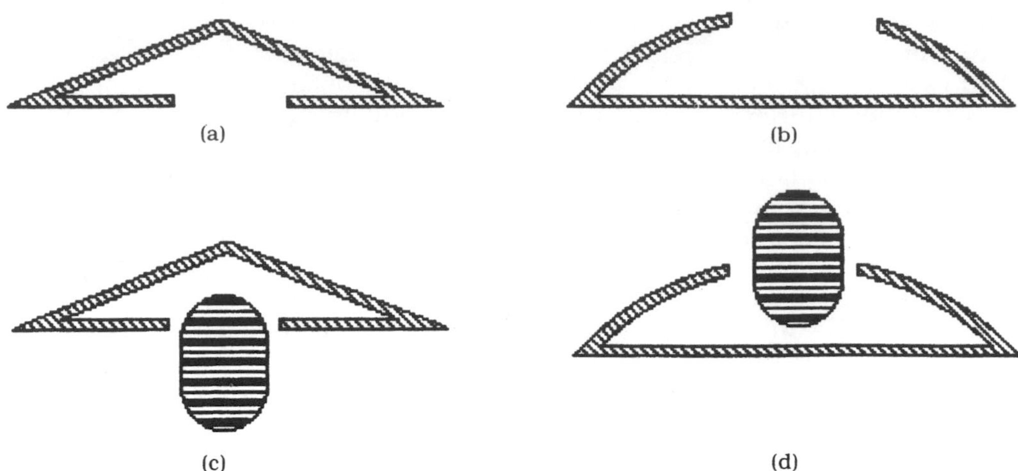

Fig. 4. Church of SS. Vincenzo and Anastasio, Rome, Baroque building.

photographs. Likewise, a ceiling in the grotesque style needs to be experienced as a whole, not as a series of separate details.

Another interesting case where photos can be more useful than line drawings occurs when artifacts are studied with regard to their **subject matter**. Thus the same lecturer who bombed on Baroque churches gave a very good photo-illustrated talk on Advent and Christmas themes in art. Assuming an audience with a Christian background, the mere mention of themes such as "Magi" and "Madonna and Child" will evoke a sufficient theoretical framework to allow works based on these themes to be processed from photos alone. That is, when a lecture deals with art works containing similar **content**, photos may suffice; when the interest lies in works with similar **form**, the abstract nature of such form does not lend itself easily to verbal or photographic presentation. Presumably, the same would hold for written material.

Thus I would extend Manning's observations regarding the usefulness of line drawings in professional writing to oral presentations, where they are at least as useful.

References

[1] A. Manning, "Interface: Scott McCloud, *Understanding Comics: The Invisible Art*," *IEEE Trans. Prof. Commun.*, vol. 41, pp. 66–69, Mar. 1998.

[2] S. McCloud, *Understanding Comics: The Invisible Art.* Princeton, WI: Kitchen Sink Press, 1993.

[3] C. S. Peirce, *Collected Papers*, C. Hartshorne and P. Weiss, Eds. Cambridge, MA: Harvard Univ. Press, 1960.

Thomas Walsh graduated from the University of Texas at Austin (B.S. degree in music, 1957) and Louisiana State University (Ph.D. degree in linguistics, 1984). He taught music in the public schools of Texas and Louisiana (1957–1977) and theoretical linguistics at LSU (1982–1997). Walsh's main interest is in phonology, and he has published several articles dealing with the interface between phonetics and phonology; he has also published textbooks in syntax and discourse analysis.

Producing a Video on a Technical Subject: A Guide

Danny Dowhal, Gary Bist, Peter Kohlmann, Stan Musker, and Heather Rogers

Abstract—**New media create new opportunities for the presentation of technical subjects, and video is one such form that is gaining in popularity. This article details how technical writers can team up to make a video on a technical subject. Based on experiences gained by the authors, it describes how to plan a video; how to write a script using visual and aural metaphors to represent technical concepts; the production process; and tips and techniques to enhance the presentation.**

Introduction

NEW media have broadened the range of presentation options for the technical writer. When creating an overview of a sophisticated product, such as a complex computer system, one medium that many writers are considering is video.[1] Why choose video either to replace or complement a manual? VCR's have gained wide acceptance in the business environment: many corporations have one in the office and routinely use it to show information of interest in the fields of technology and business. Many employees also have VCR's at home, and increasingly use them to watch videos of educational value [2]. Since one goal of a technical product such as a computer system is to reach a large audience and explain the system in conceptual terms as quickly as possible, this accessibility makes video as suitable as a manual as a presentation vehicle, if not preferable.

In addition to its accessibility, video offers a wider set of presentation options than a manual, because it is a dynamic medium that can use several channels to communicate. For example, sound, moving and still visual images, animation, a full palette of colors, and text can be integrated into an effective and memorable presentation that differs substantially from one based on the static medium of the printed page. Such multisensory or multimedia forms of information presentation have been shown to improve understanding at a faster rate, thus meeting one of a writer's goals: to increase the rate of the audience's information processing, or, in other words, to build a shorter and more efficient path to the brain [3]. The writer who wishes to get a message across quickly to a diverse audience should consider these observations by Roy Pea of the Institute for Learning [4].

1) Multimedia communication is similar to face-to-face communication.
2) Multimedia is less restricted than written text. Many people come to understand text better with broader media support for its interpretation.
3) Multimedia can place abstract concepts in a specific context (for example, refraction in physics might be depicted in a film on lens and light behavior).
4) Multimedia allows for individual differences in preferred sensory channels for learning.
5) Multimedia lets you coordinate diverse external representations (with distinctive strengths) for different perspectives.

Finally, when one considers the future of multimedia as it extends to the personal computer market, it appears that videos created today can see extensive reuse later in interactive presentations for personal computer users or as extended online help. Video, therefore, may be considered a good long-term investment in communication strategy.

Our Own Video Project: The Basis for this Paper

A small group of technical writers in our corporation met a year ago to consider producing a video. Our corporation had begun working on a complex software product that managed a set of computers, dividing up and assigning tasks to all the computer resources it controlled, so that the entire set of computers was harnessed to work as a team. Our challenge as technical writers was to create an overview of this system that could be shown to a technically and culturally diverse international audience. Video seemed the appropriate medium; however, we had almost no experience in video production. The purpose of this paper is to act as a guide (based on our lessons) to those who are in a similar situation: technical writers familiar with the print medium who are considering the option of using video to give an overview of a technical subject. In this paper, when we refer to you, we refer to a small group of individuals like ourselves, who might come together in a corporation to produce videos similar to the one we created.

How Much is it Going to Cost?

Once you have made the decision to produce a video, start by preparing a budget. Just as full-color books printed on high-quality paper will cost considerably more than black-and-white editions, so videos range in price depending on how spectacular you wish to make them. Simply stated, it is necessary to balance costs against returns, and preparing a budget creates a picture of that cost.

Our budget costs, as originally estimated, are shown in Table I. (The video was targeted to run 40 minutes, and we used

Manuscript received January 1993.

The authors are with IBM Canada Ltd., North York, Ontario, M3C 1W3, Canada.

IEEE Log Number 9209296.

[1] For further reading please refer to Ron S. Blicq, "Lights! Camera! Action! Reporting by Video," in *Proc. IEEE Prof. Commun. Conf.*, Seattle, WA, Oct. 1988.

Reprinted from *IEEE Trans. Prof. Comm.*, vol. PC-36, no. 2, pp. 62–69, June 1993.

TABLE I
Typical Costs of Producing a 40–Minute Video

Activity	Time	Cost
Structure the video	6 weeks	$18.7K
Write the script	3 weeks	10.0K
Review the script	4 weeks	12.5K
Create the animation Create the artwork	3 weeks	9.0K
Record the narrator Record the music Videotape the presenters	2 weeks	19.0K
Arrange the packaging	1 week	3.7K
Edit the video	1 week	15.0K
Duplicate the video	1 week	0.9K
Distribute the video	2 weeks	5.0K
Total	7 months	93.8K

Note: Total time does not represent time from start to finish, as tasks can run in parallel. Rather, it is an estimation of the effort required for a person.

outside sources for creating the animation, videotaping the presenters, editing the video, duplicating it, and packaging it.)

If you must justify the expense of producing a video, consider evaluating the costs of not doing so. Often, the marketing of a new technology will require many presentations by skilled personnel, involving numerous trips. A further drawback is that, while traveling, these experts are not actually working on project deliverables, and so incur a double cost to the corporation. Moreover, live presentations reach at best a fraction of the desired audience, whereas video is available to large numbers of customers, and at their convenience. This ability to capture the experts and their expertise once and then distribute it to many people greatly reduces the overall costs in the long run [5]. It must be stated that a presentation by a speaker does have one advantage that no video can match: the chance for an audience to interact with a speaker. Also, the viewer of a video may not watch the entire video, and may be less convinced, since he knows that the video is showing the product under ideal, controlled circumstances. Nevertheless, a long-term cost analysis favors the video medium over presentations by speakers. A good video will supplant the limitations that do exist with dynamic and memorable display techniques.

The Variables Affecting Video Costs

How much work you can do in-house and how much you will need to contract out to experts will be a major factor in your costs. The two main factors are:

1) **People**: Do you have individuals in your organization with some degree of skill in scripting, creating graphics and animation sequences, narrating, and recording, and who have some familiarity with the packaging of videos?
2) **Equipment**: Do you have professional quality equipment to record and edit the video?

As you work through your project, you will learn what you can and cannot do with the people and equipment you have. If you find yourself producing many videos, you may choose to invest in more and better equipment and allocate more of your own time and your colleagues' time to the production work, which will increase your capital equipment costs but decrease your production costs. However, cost is dependent on priorities: if your colleagues' regular work is critical to the corporation's profits, then taking them off their projects so that you can produce a lower-cost video would not make economic sense, and a better choice would be to utilize them just to organize and write the script.

Selecting a Video Work Group from a Writers' Group

Producing a video is a complex operation that can be costly. When putting together the group of people who will create it, begin by analyzing the strengths you have within your own personnel. There are usually a number of talented people within a technical writing group: individuals with theatrical experience, recording experience, graphics and animation skills, or organizational skills. Many times, these same people have contacts with others outside the corporation who can bring the missing elements to complete the set of skills required. We found we had most of these skills within an eight-person team, and knew whom to see and where to go to obtain the skills and services that were missing.

Look for the following skills within your group [6]:

Business Skill: Managing a video is similar to managing any project: it requires defining objectives, establishing a schedule, estimating and controlling expenses, monitoring progress, and adjusting to changes in personnel and plans as the video is developed. Business skills are necessary to see the video is planned, funded, and completed on time and within budget.

Artistic Skill: The artist's contribution is knowing how to use the medium of video to best convey the message about the product. One valuable artistic skill is the ability to visualize: to see a completed event in the mind's eye, and thereby guide its development [7]. Visualizing is helpful when creating the original script, and later, as the video is being produced, this skill ensures that the script is conveyed effectively through narration, graphics, animation, and live presentations. Other artistic skills include the ability to blend appropriate sounds and background settings to enhance the script, and coaching presenters and narrators to elucidate the storyline.

Technical Skill: Operating the cameras and microphones, setting the recording switches to the optimal levels, and advising on capital equipment purchases based on the latest developments in the video industry require strong technical knowledge. Technically skilled people are also helpful in knowing the limitations of the equipment; that is, what effects can and cannot be done with certain equipment.

Dividing Up the Tasks

Divide up the workload according to talent and interest. Start with the most important position: the director. Some experience in working in video and some training in theatre are recommended; look for your director in the group of people with artistic skills. He or she will be the final authority when several alternatives are possible as to how an idea might be presented, and will oversee the live presentations as they are videotaped.

The director can quickly identify many of the other tasks and will know what is needed and when. It will then be up to the rest of the people in the group to pick up these other tasks, which include:

- Reviewing and revising the script
- Getting and taping music if required
- Finding and recording a narrator
- Producing graphics
- Creating animation sequences
- Finding and rehearsing presenters
- Operating video cameras
- Arranging the packaging and distribution.

Make one key decision: how many of these tasks should be done in-house? This question is discussed later in this paper, but in practice, the decision becomes self-evident when the script is reviewed. At this point the video group determines what they want to achieve, and then has to consider whether they can do it themselves. If not, they must either change plans or buy the expertise from outside the corporation.

Managing the Video Production

Once group members have been chosen and the work divided, draw up a production schedule and choose a manager to ensure that the schedule is met. This is a job for a person with business skills, who can firmly yet diplomatically check that work is progressing [8]. (The director may also be the manager, or two people may share the responsibilities.) The manager would be likely to deal with some or all of the components and timelines shown in Fig. 1.

Note that a number of tasks can be done in parallel once the script has been written and reviewed. By having different people work at different tasks, it is possible to speed up completion of the video in the latter half of the production cycle.

Who Has Final Control?

Once the work begins, it is important that artistic control remain firmly in the hands of the director. Just as product managers make final decisions on the products they are responsible for, so the director makes decisions on how the video will be made. Status meetings permit discussions on how various aspects might be handled and provide input from other team members, but final decisions should always rest in the hands of one person. In particular, the group must be careful about letting people from outside take control of the direction of the video. We notified others in our corporation who had a vested interest in the video of our progress; however, they were given no voice in the group, permitting us to continue working undisturbed.

Status Meetings

Status meetings are critical to the development of a video, acting as a forum both where ideas can surface as the video is planned and produced, and where adjustments can be made to the schedule depending on recent events and resources. We used our status meetings to do the following:

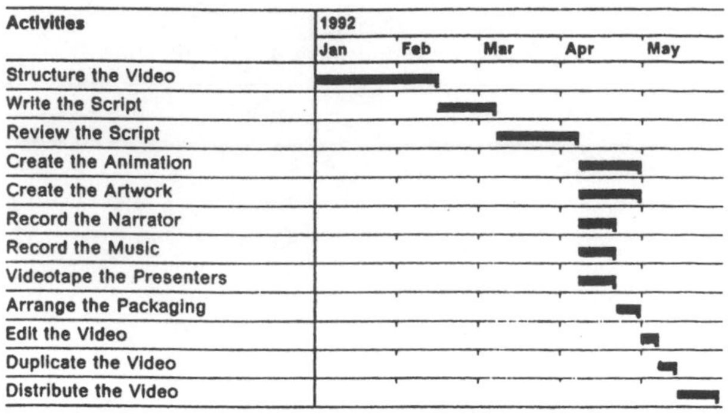

- Brainstorm
- Watch, learn from, and critique other technical and business videos
- Develop and review our script
- Refine our original ideas
- Delegate work items
- Track our progress.

We met once every two weeks for an hour, which we found to be sufficient time to address all issues.

Fig. 1. Timeline.

Writing a Script

Though video may be a new medium for technical writers, the main activity of creating one is very familiar: writing. The script is the key component to a video and a good indicator of its future success. Writing a script, however, differs from writing a book. Writers must have visual and aural sensitivity, so that their ideas can be translated into a dynamic (as opposed to static) presentation. Before you actually start to write the script, you should have a structure in place for the entire video. Imagine different modules that cover the basic ideas you wish to convey. The structure is the framework for the video.

Once you have the structure, the writing begins. A video script is a composite of several distinct scripts for a variety of experts working on the production. Different experts have their own vocabularies and concerns. For example, videographers use terms such as wipes, fades, scenes, and storylines; graphic artists refer to drop shadows, pixels, and animated sprites; actors focus on lines and diction. Three interrelated scripts emerge from the original structure: the technical script, for the cameraman and editor; the video storyboard, for the graphic artist; and the audio script, for the narrator.

The technical script provides information for the cameraman and editor. It is written with the video directions on one side and the associated audio segments on the other. Include the time (in minutes and seconds) that you intend to spend on each idea being covered in the video. Table II shows an example.

The video storyboard translates the technical script into a visual and aural format. A team member with artistic talent creates a sketch for each video scene. Like the technical script, each sketch is associated with the appropriate audio segments. This more visual format provides the graphic artist with a

TABLE II
EXAMPLE OF A TECHNICAL SCRIPT

VIDEO	AUDIO
CUT to medium shot of two circles of workstations around databases (cylinders resembling disk packs).	NARRATOR: Pieces of the network can serve as backups, should parts of the environment become unavailable. MUSIC fades out.
SOUND BITE #1 0:20	
CUT to close up (head and shoulders) of interviewee, looking off camera, talking about the product. Text superimposed at the bottom of the screen identifies the speaker and gives his/her title.	SPEAKER emphasizes the synergism of our product, how pieces join together.
SOUND BITE #2 0:20	
CUT to close up (head and shoulders) of interviewee, looking off camera, talking about the product. Text superimposed at the bottom of the screen identifies the speaker and gives his/her title.	SPEAKER focuses on how our product provides enterprises with choices.

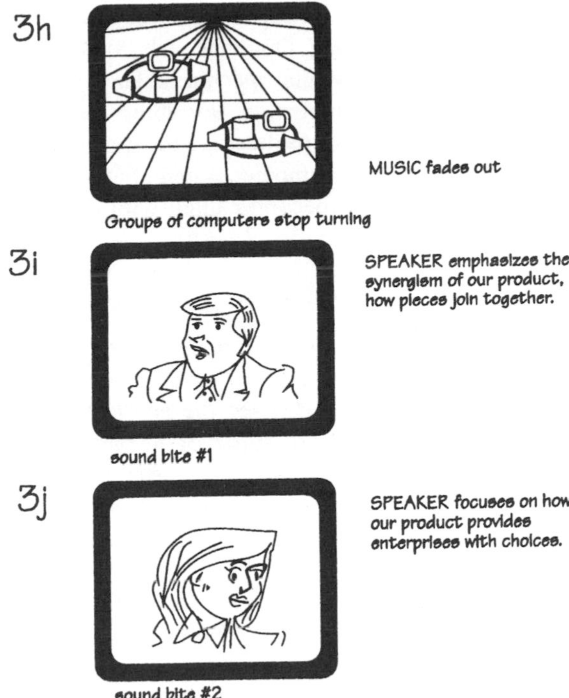
3h
MUSIC fades out
Groups of computers stop turning
3i
SPEAKER emphasizes the synergism of our product, how pieces join together.
sound bite #1
3j
SPEAKER focuses on how our product provides enterprises with choices.
sound bite #2

Fig. 2. Video storyboard.

frame of reference for each graphic or animation sequence to be created. We found that the storyboard helped us to describe the video to interested individuals from outside our team, in addition to providing our own group with a common visual representation of it prior to actual production. An example is shown in Fig. 2.

The audio script contains the dialog for the narrator, and can also contain stage directions if you are employing actors. While writing it, it is advisable to read it aloud, as the written word and the spoken word are different. We discovered that we modified our audio script as we read it aloud to others at our status meetings.

Using Metaphors

One of video's strengths as a medium is that it can effectively use metaphors to represent technical concepts. Consider using a metaphor whenever trying to explain a complex idea. For example, in our video, we wanted to show how large mainframe computers are isolated from one another and require a special encoded message to exchange information. We created a picture of a computer system within an ancient fortress. The picture turned into an animation sequence enhanced with sound as the fortress lowered its drawbridge following a special knock on its door.

Special Effects

Special effects can be an important part of a video, but they must be used carefully. If overdone or implemented poorly, they will lower the quality of the production and evoke a negative reaction from the viewing audience. However, when used tastefully and implemented well, they can make your video more appealing. One of the special effects we used was a simulated touch screen found on some personal computers. At several points in a live presentation, the presenter would touch an icon on the screen. The special effect to show how the screen was touch-sensitive was done in the editing process, by cutting from a shot of the presenter touching the screen to graphics that simulated what would happen on the screen as a consequence. This transition gave the impression that it was a real touch screen. An electronic beep was added each time the presenter touched the screen, to make the sequence more realistic.

There were several advantages to using this special effect. It provided a visual break for the audience during a long presentation. It gave visual clues about the length of the presentation remaining: five icons were shown, so the audience knew at any time what topics were still to be covered. And it added a "high tech" dimension to the video, which can be an important psychological factor when marketing a product to a technically sophisticated audience.

Animation

The cost of high-quality two- and three-dimensional animation has been reduced significantly in the past few years. While traditional ink-and-paint character animation can cost over $50,000 per minute, depending on the quality, video animation produced on a personal computer is often under $5000 per minute without a noticeable difference in quality. Since animation is a very effective presentation technique, consider adding some to any video. If used sparingly, it can be accommodated by most budgets.

Animation is well suited to explain and describe conceptual topics, such as those associated with computers. For example, it can be used to present the flow of information in a network system or show how a new paging system works. The best candidates for animated sequences are often those most difficult to document on paper. Look for a process where several events are occurring simultaneously, or that includes abstract objects, such as virtual machines. The key is action: do not waste money on animation describing a static object. For example, use a diagram to illustrate the detailed layout of a disk for storing data in a computer system, but use animation to illustrate how the disk becomes filled with data and then fragmented over time.

Producing a Video with In-House Resources

Video production is divided into three phases, as shown in Table III.

The production phase comprises the shortest part of the schedule, but consumes the largest part of the budget, requiring many people with special skills and an assortment of expensive equipment. To achieve the right balance between controlling costs and achieving quality, determine which key roles can be done in-house, and buy only the technical expertise necessary for the other tasks [9]. To many people, this phase, for example, contains much of the fun and excitement of creating a video, but do not be tempted to do it yourself if the necessary skills are not there: remember that the recorded material is permanent, and changing it later will be expensive or impossible. In our first video production, we used our own skills to plan, manage, and write the script, but assigned most of the tasks in the production and post-production phases to the video pros.

Based on our experience, the following roles can be done with in-house personnel with limited knowledge of video technology:

Pre-Production Phase

Have someone in your video work group assume the role of managing producer, which means being responsible for the budget, schedules, and finished product. The producer should ensure that all variations of the script (technical, storyboard, and audio) are written; then plan the shooting schedule with times, locations, and characters. Once the script and schedule are ready, your group should cast the talent required. In-house technical experts can best describe your product, as the enthusiasm they feel for it can seldom be portrayed authentically by actors. When casting, observe your candidates and select those who will appear most natural on camera.

Also use in-house talent for the role of the narrator, as someone familiar with your product will prove more convincing than an actor reading from a script. Issue a casting call and select the narrator from within your own set of technical writers. (It will also save you an actor's fee.)

Production Phase

A member of your work group should assume the role of director, since the group knows what needs to be said and how to say it. As stated earlier, this is the most important role. If it seems too ambitious for your chosen director to assume this role, remember that your production crew will usually provide him or her with many helpful suggestions, and translate instructions into the hoped-for wizardry.

TABLE III

Phase	Action
Pre-Production	Planning, script writing, casting, and location selection.
Production	Assembling the technical experts on location and recording.
Post-Production	Editing the tapes into one master tape; then copying the tape for distribution.

Post-Production Phase: Direct your own on-line editing session, but have a professional video editor actually make the cuts amongst the set of tapes. Guide the editor when creating the master tape by keeping your video storyboard on hand as a point of reference. Editing time is very expensive, so know exactly what you want to see in the final tape before entering the editing studio.

What Services Should be Contracted?

There are aspects of video production that should be left in the hands of professionals, especially if this is your first video experience [10]. Camera work, lighting, and editing are skills acquired over time and through apprenticeship. In the early planning stage of our video, we realized that we had neither the time to develop these skills nor the budget to purchase the necessary sophisticated equipment, so we decided to assign these tasks outside. For example, we planned our 40-minute video to include 10 minutes of animation, as we believed that this medium could explain a complex topic and provide some mild entertainment (sometimes referred to as "edutainment"). We contracted this portion of the video to a professional animator, as we lacked the necessary hardware, software, and experience to create suitable three-dimensional animation.

We also contracted professional musicians to make the soundtrack. Our computer product is designed to harmonize a company's computing environment, and we chose to use a music metaphor to show this harmony. Synthesized computer sound did not achieve the effect we were looking for, so we had music arranged and recorded by professionals. In addition to creating the right sound, this gave us a piece of signature music that we now own and that will always be associated with our product. The arrangement and recording took only two days. By getting our own original music, we avoided paying the costly copyrights and royalties associated with a previously published song.

The final service we contracted was the copying or dubbing of the master tape into VHS format (for our North American customers) and PAL format (for our European customers).

Videotaping Live Presentations

Particular technical aspects are often best expressed by experts in your own corporation, as usually these people have already presented their particular field of knowledge several times and are well prepared to be recorded. They should be taped in a professional environment like the one where they would present their material to live audiences, such as a well-appointed conference. Before taping, carefully consider the background view. For example, we placed some diagrams on flip charts which reinforced the message of one speaker and were used by him to emphasize points. Since presentations are performed before audiences, we added spectators to the scene and occasionally showed short clips of them as a group or individually to give a sense of audience involvement. It is also possible to have the audience participate; however, this tends to break the flow of the presentation, so in most cases is not advisable.

Once your background is set up, have your presenter go through a dry run. The purpose is to enable the video crew to make any final camera adjustments, for the rest of the group to make suggestions to improve the presentation, and for the presenter to adapt his or her message to the video medium. It must be remembered that presenting material to a camera is quite different from presenting it to a live audience because there is no feedback. We found that one dry run was sufficient for our presenter to adjust himself to the medium.

Then it's time to record. Two recording sessions are recommended. Set your camera slightly differently on each session; then later, when you edit, this will allow you to mix a number of different shots of the same presentation for some variety. It also allows the presenter to make some small changes in the second session and permits a few errors in delivery, since in editing you can simply use the alternate recording of the same section.

The best tool for assessing a live presentation is the line monitor, as it shows the same picture that is being recorded on tape—the camera view. The acceptability of a take should be based on the presentation on the line monitor, as it is free from any external distractions and is exactly what will appear in the final video. We based all our evaluations on this view.

Managing Live Presentations

The director must be in charge of shooting any live presentation: the video crew shooting the scene will expect their instructions to come from one person, and will be confused by orders or comments from other members of the team, even if the remarks are intended to help. Whenever members of our video work group had suggestions, we consulted privately with the director.

Including members during the recording does have some advantages, however, as they can assist the technicians move equipment around and can provide constructive feedback to the director at the end of each scene. The following questions should be considered:

- Is the scene meeting the objectives?
- Is the content correct?
- Are the important parts of the picture being filmed?
- Does the set look like the one described in the script?
- Are the lines read with proper pronunciation and natural presentation [10]?

As each scene is recorded, comments to the director can provide a valuable perspective on the scene's success. If problems are pointed out, the director may choose to immediately record one more time, since reshooting at a later date will be expensive.

Encourage Analogies: Technical subjects can often be quickly explained to a diverse audience by using analogies to the everyday world. One good analogy is worth a thousand words of detail, and we encouraged their use during our recording sessions. In one presentation in our video, for example, a presenter effectively used the following analogy to explain how his software product could be likened to playing golf:

> Like a game of golf, you could play it with one golf club; but you bring a set of clubs so that you can select the best club for the particular situation faced at the moment, such as a putter for the putting green and a driver for the fairways. Similarly, this software selects the best type of computer among a set of different types that it is managing to solve the particular problem faced at the moment. For example, a problem requiring floating-point arithmetic, which requires large computer resources, would be sent to a mainframe computer, and a problem which might be enhanced by a better visual display would be sent to a personal computer.

Details to Remember

By employing a professional video production crew, we were able to benefit from their experience and learn some tips and techniques. Here are some lessons we learned:

- *Keep a shot log.* You should maintain a record of every scene shot and take recorded. This record includes the scene name or number, the tape number, the scene start time, and the scene end time. This log will prove invaluable when it comes to locating items during the editing phase, since scenes are rarely filmed in order.
- *Record some cutaway shots.* For example, if demonstrating an activity on the computer, get shots of the hands on the keyboard and using the mouse. Or if employing an audience, take a set of individual reactions such as nodding, writing, smiling, and so on. These cutaways can be used in editing if material needs to be cut out, or if two scenes need to be joined. They provide a smoother transition than a simple cut.
- *Try to minimize background noise.* Before shooting a scene, check the noise levels by putting on a headset. In one scene we detected the hum from an overhead projector which had not been turned off. To further ensure clarity of sound when recording, place a separate microphone on the presenter to make certain you get a clear voice recording.
- *Check out the visual background.* See that the background harmonizes rather than clashes with the presentation. Use the line monitor, since what your eye sees might not be the same as the camera's view.
- *Record some room noise.* This allows for audio edits later, when you mix voice and room noise for smooth transitions. Note that you cannot go back and do this at a later time because the exact background noise in the room can never be reconstructed.
- *Get direct video output from computer screens.* If shooting a demonstration on a computer, get video output from the

computer screen itself and record it at the same time as the live presentation. This technique gives a clear computer screen image, whereas you will get one with lines and reflections if you videotape the screen itself. In addition, you will be able to focus the camera on the presenter. Later, during editing, you can cut between the computer screen and the presenter. Also remember to check the screen colors and the font size so that the lettering on the screen will be legible.

Post Production: Editing, Packaging, and Distribution

Once you have your tapes with all the live presentations, graphics, animation, and narration soundtrack, it is time for the final steps: editing the set of tapes into one master tape, and packaging and distributing copies of it.

Editing

Editing is an essential part of what makes a video interesting: it helps make smooth transitions from one topic to the next, associates ideas by placing scenes next to each other, and tightens the video by removing unwanted material. However, it costs money. The time of a film editor and equipment can easily exceed several hundred dollars per hour, so planning is important. Come prepared with your script, storyboard, and shot log, to make it easier to manage the hours of videotape you will have accumulated during shooting. Look through the "raw" (unedited) tape before editing begins, and choose the pieces you want to keep. Often the most difficult part of editing is deciding what to include and what to exclude from the final product. For example, if your script requires a 20-second clip of expert opinion on a topic, that 20 seconds may be hidden in ten minutes of tape which contains remarks about the topic. Making these decisions can take a long time. Unless you have your own editing suite, make as many of these decisions as possible before you start paying by the hour for your time with a professional editor. If you create a VHS dub of all the shots with time marks on them, this pre-editing can be done at home.

After you have made your editing decisions, choose the type of editing transition for each scene. There are many transitions available. Three of the most common are found in Table IV.

TABLE IV

Transition	Action
Cut	The switch from one image to the next is made instantly.
Fade	The visibility of the first image is reduced while that of the second image is increased, until the first image disappears.
Wipe	The first image is pushed off the screen by the second image.

While modern video editing suites are capable of an almost infinite number of variations of transitions, be careful that they do not become the center of attention. Reserve the more elaborate transitions for breaks between significant portions of the video. Editing, as a rule, should be transparent to the viewer.

Packaging and Distribution

Editing results in a Betacam master tape, which can then be copied or dubbed into VHS and PAL formats suitable for North American and European video machines, respectively. There are many packages available for the copied videotapes, from the simple black cases common in video rentals to leather boxes with cloth interiors. We selected a colored plastic case with a two-color label that included the video title, stock number, company logo, and a colored graphic that matched a scene from the tape. Distribution can usually be arranged through your present distribution channels. For example, we used our corporation's existing warehouse and ordering facilities to stock and distribute our video, in the same manner as we would stock and distribute a technical manual.

Conclusion

Prior to video, we in the technical writing field seemed better at collecting information than disseminating it. Manuals are very good as a comprehensive collection of details, but they are not the optimal means for presenting a fast overview to an audience of more than one. Video, with its multisensory appeal, makes information readily accessible and quickly transferable, and can filter out many of the low-level details by substituting metaphors that explain them conceptually. As such, it has a role to play in modeling information to make it more useful—a major demand of modern users [12]. We found we were able to convey a great deal of such useful information in 40 minutes, suggesting that video may be one answer to Edward Tufte's challenge of finding ways to increase information resolution [13].

Just as a brush and canvas do not make an artist, so buying a camcorder does not make one a videographer. Prior to creating our own project, we watched many existing industrial videos, and we felt that most were visually dull, lacked editing, and selected cast poorly, and that sometimes the topics did not suit the video medium. Our hope is that we learned what not to do from our exposure to these.

Our experience as writers, combined with our role as video critics, taught us the value of planning. We assessed the skills we had and those we lacked; then focused our activities on what we could do, and contracted the rest out to the pros. The positive feedback we have had to date indicates we made the right choices. In challenging ourselves to broaden our planning, managing, and writing skills beyond the computer manual and into the world of multimedia, after one video we are more versed in this new medium and look forward to tackling more productions in the future.

Acknowledgment

The authors would like to thank Anne Stilman of IBM Canada Ltd. for her editorial assistance. They are also grateful to Imagineering Computer Animation Inc. and Videoframe Productions Ltd. for their contributions to the finished video. They exceeded the bounds of their contracts and showed infinite patience with us, the video novices.

REFERENCES

[1] P. Drucker, "The new society of organizations," *Harvard Business Review*, p. 97, Sept.-Oct. 1992. .

[2] T. Yager, "Information's human dimension," *Byte*, p. 154, Dec. 1991.

[3] R. D. Pea, "Learning through multimedia," *IEEE Computer Graphics Appl.*, p. 59, July 1991.

[4] E. J. Garrity and J. C. Sipior, "Multimedia: A vehicle for embedding expertise," in *Proc. IEEE/ACM Int. Conf. Developing Managing*, p. 314, July 1992.

[5] D. Hon, "Butcher, baker, candlestick maker: Skills required for effective multimedia projects," *Educ. Technol.*, vol. 32 no. 5, p. 14-19, May 1992.

[6] R. Bergman and T. V. Moore, "Managing Interactive Video/Multimedia Projects," *Educ. Technol. Pub.*, p. 15, 1990.

[7] R. I. Stevens, "Implementation: The key to a successful project," *J. Systems Management*, , p. 21, June 1992.

[8] R. Bergman and T. V. Moore, "Managing interactive video/multimedia projects," *Educ. Technol. Pub.*, p. 86, 1990.

[9] N. Purdom, "Making video work for the company," *Audio Visual*, p. 12-14, Apr. 1992.

[10] R. Bergman and T. V. Moore, "Managing interactive video/multimedia projects," *Educ. Technol. Pub.*, p. 93, 1990.

[11] R. Benjamin and J. Blunt, "Critical IT issues: The next ten years," *Sloan Management Review*, p. 14, Summer 1992.

[12] E. Tufte, "User interface: The point of competition," *American Soc. Inform. Science*, p. 15, June-July 1992.

Danny Z. Dowhal is president of Imagineering Computer Animation, Inc. Past experience as a programmer, writer, illustrator, and cartoonist seemed to lead him naturally into the world of computer animation. He feels that animation gives one the ability to describe the simplest process or explain the most complex topic and at the same time entertain an audience.

Gary Bist is a technical writer at the IBM Canada Laboratory. He has written documentation and articles about a variety of computer products, including database and image software and word processing software for non-English languages. As this article suggests, he discovered that his extensive print media background served as a good base for those wishing to extend their communication skills into video production.

Peter Kohlmann is a technical writer at the IBM Canada Laboratory in Toronto. As a member of the SQL/DS development team, he has spent the last year working on a Performance Tuning Handbook for the SQL/DS product. He sees computer animation as an important way to convey complex technical concepts. He has a B.S. degree in electrical engineering from Queen's University in Kingston, Ontario.

Stan Musker is a technical writer at the IBM Canada Laboratory. He primarily writes and designs graphics for computer software running on IBM mainframes. He found that his experience with words and pictures was a valuable asset when it came time to translate concepts and themes into scripts, storyboards, and video clips.

Heather Rogers is a technical writer at the IBM Canada Laboratory. She has written manuals and various types of online help for several AS/400 software products. Most recently, she developed an online interactive tutorial for one of the lab's products, and is now working full-time on various multimedia projects.

PART VIII

Listening, Meeting, and Teamwork: Working with Others to Get Results

A lot of communication takes place beyond the written word or standard on-the-job presentation. The articles in this part will help you to become a better listener, organize and participate in successful meetings and seminars, and understand some of the communication dynamics involved in teamwork carried out under varying circumstances. You will also be able to find out how videoconferencing works, and what advantages and disadvantages it may have.

Is your boss listening?

Listening is perhaps the hardest communication skill to acquire. It plays an essential role in meetings, discussions, and any kind of teamwork, yet most of us have no training in it. As Jo Proctor points out, most communication training deals with improving writing and speaking skills, and we assume that listening just "comes naturally." Unfortunately, it doesn't. Proctor first outlines the complex nature of effective listening and then describes a series of workshops and training sessions that enabled a group of managers to become better listeners. You don't have to be a manager, however, to profit from this article—it may help you understand better why some managers do not really listen, and will also help you become a better listener yourself.

Hearing is not listening

Marion Haynes further analyses the process of listening and describes the various barriers to doing it well. Like Jo Proctor, he points out that while hearing is just a physical process, real listening involves both emotional and intellectual processes and its outcome is understanding. You will find this article full of well-organized information on the different factors that enable effective listening.

Planning and running a meeting

If you fail to plan ahead, your meeting will be unsuccessful. Thus, Eugene Raudsepp deals with specific preparatory considerations, such as the relationship between the number of attendees and the physical set-up for a meeting. Circulating an agenda beforehand can pinpoint topics and save you time. Your responsibility as the leader to establish bounds, steer the meeting, and handle "problem participants" is unavoidable. Raudsepp's article, with its final ten guidelines, encapsulates most of what you will need to run a successful meeting.

Coordinating the seminar

A technical seminar is a highly specialized meeting where you and other participants present technical material. The coordinator may be one of the speakers, but additional responsibilities fall on his or her shoulders. Thomas Ealey discusses the work involved in conducting such a seminar, and by now you will not be surprised that success depends on preseminar planning. Although your participants will be eager for information, many things can distract them. They will need comfortable facilities, supplies, frequent breaks, a dependable schedule, and reliable address systems. Ealey warns against permitting discussion during presentations and stresses the value of following up with an evaluation questionnaire.

Communication and the complex project

The more complex a team project is, the more the need for communication increases. This might seem obvious, but Tom Roberts and his colleagues found in their study that the opposite often occurs: the easier the task, the more the team members communicate. Obviously, this is not an ideal situation—a high level of communication is essential in highly complicated group tasks. Although team members may be unwilling to communicate on a project when only a few of them have adequate expertise, managers must always be alert to encouraging and facilitating communication within teams working on projects at all levels of complexity.

The cross-functional challenge

It is no secret that things can sometimes go awry in a team project and that often the root cause is poor communication. Linda Loehr looks at communication within an industrial group she designates as a cross-functional project team, and which she was permitted to observe while the team worked on a single project. As a result, she was able to identify three main areas of concern that impacted the team's communication: equity, trust, and authority. As you will learn from her carefully researched article, emanating from these three factors are communication problems that can occur in a variety of challenging settings.

Overcoming virtual reluctance

As Bernard Tan and his three coauthors remind us, modern technology permits communication to take place between people who are physically far apart and who may never meet each other face to face. When such people form a team and work together on a project entirely by means of electronic communication, some interesting problems can arise. One is that initially a "virtual team" may be quite slow in building group understanding, coherence, and decision making. You will find the dialogue technique the authors propose as a means of overcoming this problem to be highly detailed and of great help if you want to help virtual teams quickly attain mutual understanding and effectiveness.

Communicating through the videoconference

The last article in this section also deals with communication between team members who may be physically far apart from one another. First, Jan Sprey describes what can be done through videoconferencing and what kind of equipment is needed. Her discussion of actual videoconferencing procedures is particularly interesting, as are her comments on what she sees as their drawbacks. Many of these drawbacks are becoming less of a concern as equipment improves and costs fall, but Sprey's article still serves as an excellent introduction to the pros and cons of using this technology as a means of group communication.

You Haven't Heard a Word I Said: Getting Managers to Listen

Jo Procter

Abstract—**As we approach the year 2000, corporate America is focused on improving communications; yet most of the effort is directed toward improving writing and speaking. This paper describes training to encourage and improve better listening skills and attitudes. Workshops to improve interpersonal communications, negotiation, and supervisory skills have been offered to employees for a number of years. The training sessions were different from others in that they were wholly devoted to learning about listening, and managers participated in the design of the learning experiences by using case material drawn from their work situations. This focused their attention on why listening is an important part of good management, and enabled them to understand that it is their responsibility to improve their listening behavior and skills.**

Introduction

LISTENING is important: during the race for the 1992 presidential election, Ross Perot shared his success with TV viewers, "You want me to tell you how to make a million dollars? I'll tell you. Listen! Listen! Listen!" Earlier, another corporate maven, Lee Iacocca, said, "Listening can make the difference between a mediocre company and a great company." With such advice freely available to those who want to make a million dollars or just run a better business, why have experts noted that we tend to be better talkers than listeners? Corporate America's preoccupation with communications is still directed for the most part toward the improvement of writing and speaking, although it is estimated that managers spend up to 80% of their day *listening* to customers, their employees, and top management.

Improvement of listening skills is necessary if managers are to understand the work environment and culture well enough to design effective work groups [1, 2]. When managers recognize the importance of listening, they also send a clear message about the importance of their employees, who in turn increase their commitment to corporate goals. The whole effectiveness of communication, in fact, depends on listening. Communication breaks down when we won't or don't listen well. Most people assume that listening comes naturally, but it doesn't. Listening is complicated, but it is a skill that can be learned [3].

Although we use the terms *hear* and *listen* interchangeably, the processes are not the same. Hearing is a passive physical process that takes place naturally; listening is an active mental process that requires effort because it involves concentration, interpretation, evaluation, and reacting. Listening is an exceedingly complex procedure of receiving, assigning meaning, and responding.

The act of communication is dynamic, linking message elements from more than one situation. The sender integrates his/her experiences, thoughts, and feelings into a message. The content of the message is determined not only by the senders' experience and background, but also by a set of behavioral strategies intended to establish a persona. What the receivers hear is sent to the brain for assignment of meaning, and the receivers' perception of the message is structured by their field of experience and psychological frame of reference. The receivers filter what they hear until they are comfortable and feel that they understand the message. The message itself is also subject to distortion due to the limitations of language and the symbols that carry the message: non verbal (facial expressions, gestures, appearance, posture) and paralanguage (elements such as tone, pitch, rate, volume and emphasis).

Although we are not good listeners when we are born, we can be trained to become good listeners. The training model described in this paper offers organizations a procedure to provide instruction and practice in enhancing listening ability. Through this program, participants are exposed to a series of initial learning experiences followed by a set of cases specific to their work environment, which reinforce and apply the basic listening-learning.

Development of a Training Model

The workshops were designed to address general communication obstacles and to focus managers' attention on their responsibility to improve their listening skills. Interpreting what someone says is complex and difficult, largely because most people are more concerned about getting their point across than in listening to what the other person is saying.

Whenever people are together, they make an effort to be listened to. They are very seldom listened to because the person they are trying to get to listen to them is waiting desperately and impatiently to be listened to. These efforts cancel out the possibility for communication. A third of the employees who enrolled in the listening workshops said they did so because they wanted to learn how to get people to listen to them, not to learn to listen to others. Over and over participants asked, "How can I get people to listen *to me*?"

Before the earliest workshops, a self-selected group of managers met with me to discuss how we might go about training them to be better listeners. Participants agreed that if people could to be taught to be better listeners, the training must involve listening with what Reik calls the "third ear" [4].

The author is with the Faculty of Arts and Sciences Personnel Services, Harvard University, 17 Sumner Road, Cambridge, MA 02138.

IEEE Log Number 9216535.

Reprinted from *IEEE Trans. Prof. Comm.*, vol. PC-37, no. 1, pp. 18–20, March 1994.

This means listening to what speakers want to say, listening to what they do not want to say, and listening to what they cannot say without help.

Pilot

The model described here is based on workshops about listening developed for 90 managers who were trained in groups of 15. The original pilot was designed as a two-part workshop. But later it was expanded into three 3-hour sessions. The first session was an introduction to listening and to its importance in the workplace; the second concentrated on using three listening skills in managerial role-playing situations; and the third was a discussion of the cases the participants developed using their workplace for material.

A. The First Session

In the first session, participants discussed listening in terms of their own experiences and how it affected their workplace. Participants were asked to brainstorm ways in which listening is important to them and to list what it means when we say, "You're not listening to me." Participants said that the message is that "You are not important. You are not worth listening to. You are impolite. You are disrespectful. You are ignoring me. You are not trying to understand what I'm saying. You don't care about my point of view. I don't count. You are withholding information. You are wasting my time. I am wasting your time. You are listening to the words, but not the meaning. This is not the response that I want."

Naturally, no employee, customer, student, or supervisor responds well to such messages. Being listened to essentially becomes a metaphor for being accepted, valued, understood, and trusted. Thus, participants came to see that "You're not listening" means managers aren't doing their jobs.

Participants defined a good listener as someone who is interested and understanding, likes suggestions, is willing to make adjustments, tolerates criticism, and is open to change. The first session's brainstorming elicited a wide variety of practical suggestions about how to become a better listener, including the following: watch the speaker's body language, pay attention instead of thinking about what you're going to say next, look around your office, listen to your own tone of voice, and maintain eye contact. In addition, participants suggested asking themselves several questions: "What barriers stand between me and the person I am trying to listen to?" and "Do I care what the other person is saying?"

The first sessions ended with a discussion of seven kinds of obstacles to effective listening:

- Physical relations to things: "Approach" (positive) or "avoidance" (negative) behaviors to space, color, lighting, noise, and visual distractions.
- Relationships: Gender roles, ethnicity, age, degree of achievement, popularity, amount of trust.
- Personal filters: Background, experience, present feelings, and future expectations.
- Semantic: Ideas, objects, and actions referred to by more than one word.
- Time: Meaning and significance of past, present, and future as it governs work.
- Difficulty: Range, depth, constancy of information.
- Attention: Content, task, or purpose in listening, and the context in which listening occurs.

B. The Second Session

The second session took up the proposition that listening is an active process. It had the goal of understanding the employee (or customer), and letting him or her know that the manager has heard and understood his or her point of view. To do this, workshop participants learned through role playing to use the reflective, empathetic, and facilitative responses.

The reflective response does not offer solutions but rather demonstrates that the problem was heard as it was presented. Listeners repeat what they consider to be the essential parts of the speakers' message. This paraphrasing lets the speakers know that they have heard them. It requires that the listeners learn through practice to accurately paraphrase the essence of the speakers' message without changing the content.

The empathetic response is based on the idea that listeners communicate their understanding in terms of the speaker's experience, rather than in terms of their own. Listeners elaborate on the thoughts and feelings of the speaker. They amplify the stimulus statement; they respond to what is not said as well as to what is said; they integrate the verbal and nonverbal messages of the speakers in order to understand the full meaning of the message, thus bringing the message into sharper focus.

The facilitative response consists of using the five reportage questions—how, why, what, when, and where—to help clarify the situation for both the listener and the speaker and to define the meaning of the message. Listeners learn not to step into a conversation, allowing speakers enough time to clarify the statement; many speakers feel that they do not fully understand what they are feeling until they hear what they are saying.

C. The Third Session

The third session was added when early participants asked to have a forum in which they could examine their own workplace situations. Participants took responsibility for generating their own learning materials by taking notes after listening to customers/clients, employees, and supervisors, and reflecting on the causes of poor listening. From these note-taking sessions, each participant provided a synopsis (by phone, interview, or in writing), and these situations and events were combined into three cases that participants discussed in the final workshop.

Conclusion

Most people have given a great deal of thought to what they want from their listeners, and having the workshop participants help develop the workshop material was easy, convenient, and effective. Although a number of commercial listening workshops use cases drawn from situations outside the work environment, it is difficult to draw from a desert or an Arctic experience the skills necessary for an office, plant, or institutional environment. People are more likely to use what they learn within the reality they create [1]. An equally important benefit of using participants' own cases is that it helps to empower them to think for themselves and practice new behaviors and skills. They usually do amazingly well.

These 90 managers reported, three and nine months after the training, that the instruction and methods encouraged retention and self-improvement. Participants gained increased understanding of their strengths and weaknesses as listeners and built new skills and behavior.

The participants reported that they had discovered that, when they took the time to listen, they could make the manager/employee or employee/customer relationship genuinely collaborative; they increased their capacity to identify with and understand the other person, which in itself effected a positive change in that person; and that listening is a skill that takes substantial practice.

In custom-designing listening workshops appropriate for your workplace, it is critical that you understand your organizational objectives (what you want to accomplish), your audience (what are your managers' interests, needs, and perceptions? who do they need to listen to? why?), and their motivation (why would they want to learn this? how it might be helpful to them?).

References

[1] J. R. Hackman "The commitment model: From 'whether' to 'how,'" in *The Uneasy Alliance: Managing the Productivity-Technology Dilemma*, R. Hayes and K. Clark, Eds. Boston: Harvard Business School Press, 1985.

[2] R. E. Walton, "From control to commitment: transformation of workforce management strategies in the United States," in *The Uneasy Alliance: Managing the Productivity-Technology Dilemma*, R. Hayes and K. Clark, Eds. Boston: Harvard Business School Press, 1985.

[3] A. D. Wolvin, "Improving listening skills," in *Improving Speaking and Listening Skills, New Directions for College Learning Assistance*, R. B. Rubin, Ed., no. 12, June, 1983.

[4] T. Reik, *Listening with the Third Ear*. New York: Farrar, Straus, 1948.

Jo Procter is the employee communications officer in the Faculty of Arts and Sciences Personnel Services, Harvard University. She has a M.S. in Communications from Boston University and has done research and written on public relations and human resource management. She lives in Cambridge, MA.

Becoming an Effective Listener

MARION E. HAYNES

Abstract—Listening is the process of taking in information and synthesizing it into an understandable message. Clues to understanding the speaker include how things are said, what is not said, and nonverbal behavior. The difference between speaking and thinking speeds should be utilized to review, summarize, and reflect upon the speaker's points rather than to daydream. Physical distractions should be eliminated. Emotional and psychological distractions originating with the speaker or the listener should be discounted or compensated for. First impressions should be subjugated and judgment delayed until the speaker is finished. In conversation, give the other person a chance.

IT IS estimated that the average adult spends about a third of the time listening. Yet it is amazing how inefficient most people are at the process. Many reasons account for this. Among them: They don't like the speaker, they find the person boring, they feel threatened by what is being said, or they feel physically or emotionally tired.

All of these problems can be overcome by learning the techniques of effective listening. This means learning to pay attention not only to the speaker's words but also to their context, to note what's not said, to listen with a purpose, to minimize distractions, and to interpret nonverbal behavior and tone of voice.

Act Like a Listener

Listening may seem passive when you observe someone listening to another person, but it is actually a very active, engaging process. So, the starting point for becoming a good listener is to sit in a relaxed but alert posture. This means no slouching. When you get too comfortable, you may become drowsy. Next, maintain eye contact with the speaker. This says you are interested in what's going on and you are paying attention. Finally, make some verbal response such as "Uh-huh" and "I see," restate the last one or two significant words spoken, or summarize a part of what was said.

Seek Understanding

Once you've begun acting like a listener, the next step is to try to understand the message conveyed. This involves three distinct processes—hearing, listening, and understanding.

Hearing is a physical process. If you are not otherwise physically impaired, you hear sounds above a certain threshold of loudness within a certain frequency range. This is hearing.

Listening is an emotional and intellectual process. It is concerned with what you do with the information you obtain from both hearing and observing. Good listening also depends upon how you interpret what you don't hear—silences and omissions in the message. What someone doesn't say or avoids saying is often more important than what is actually said.

Understanding grows from good listening. You understand when the message takes on meaning within your own frame of reference. For example, you can understand how someone feels about an experience through empathy. Or you can understand a concept by relating it to something you already know.

Hearing is not listening. Listening is not understanding. Confusion about these concepts gets in the way of effective listening skills. Understand listening and place it in its proper perspective. Listening depends upon hearing and leads to understanding. It is the process of taking in information and synthesizing it into something that you can understand.

Good listening involves seeking the answer to three basic questions:

1. What does the speaker mean?

People take it for granted that the speaker means the same thing they would mean if they were saying the same words. But the same words mean different things to different people, in different contexts, under different circumstances. A skillful listener starts with the attitude that what the speaker's words mean to the speaker is not known and that, in order to find out, the context and circumstances must be scrutinized. A skillful listener also knows that any interpretation of the speaker's words are the listener's and are therefore his or her responsibility.

Because of different meanings, the listener demands a great deal from the speaker. It falls upon the speaker to take special pains to make meanings as clear as possible, to choose words well—to distrust them, to suspect them of vagueness and ambiguity. It also falls upon the speaker to accept his or her own interpretations of words as being personal and in need of careful clarification.

2. How does the speaker know?

After a good listener finds out what the speaker means, the next thing to work on is what reliable, factual observations have been made, or could be made, to verify the speaker's statements. The good listener wants to see data, pictures, diagrams, or demonstrations. This does not rule out abstractions and generalizations. It does, however, require that evidence supporting them be presented.

3. What is being left out?

The third basic question encourages the art of listening for what a speaker does not say. This, as a rule, refers to omitting important factual details, not drawing certain possible conclusions, or not developing certain implications of the conclusions drawn.

Reprinted from *Supervisory Management*, vol. 24, no. 8, p. 21, August 1979 with permission. Copyright 1979 by M. E. Haynes.

The author is an Employee Relations Associate with Shell Oil Co., P.O. Box 2463, Houston, TX 77001, (713) 241-6855.

Reprinted from *IEEE Trans. Prof. Comm.*, vol. PC-23, no. 2, pp. 91–94, June 1980.

Often what is not said points out that what is said is inadequate, irrelevant, or misleading. Did the speaker overstress issues in his or her favor? Was the full story presented?

Use Spare Time Effectively

When people talk, they speak at a rate of 100 to 200 words per minute. However, people think much faster, perhaps somewhere between 600 and 800 words per minute. What is done with this speaking-thinking speed differential is the key to effective listening. It can be used to become a better listener or to interfere with effective listening. Most people do not use this differential wisely, letting their minds take side trips to worry about something or to think about what they are going to do that evening or about what they will say when they get a turn to talk.

There is plenty of time for these side trips. And most people have been taking them so long that the habit is well ingrained.

But instead of taking side trips, try using this time effectively. Think about what the speaker has been saying or try to figure out where the speaker is going and what the next point may be. This will probably be easy with a well organized speaker who presents points clearly. You could also summarize what is being said or break it down into main points and supporting points. Periodically play back your summary so that it can be verified by the speaker. If you have missed some main points, they can be filled in for you.

Listen for feelings as well as content. Almost every message has a feelings dimension. Many have as a main theme the feelings being expressed and the content is simply a legitimate way of expressing them. By hearing the feelings and exploring the reasons for them, you can understand what led up to the statement. Also look for consistency or inconsistency in what is being said.

Listening is facilitated when you have a purpose for listening and concentrate on achieving it. The next time you are in a conversation with someone, take a few seconds and make a simple declarative statement of purpose. It will focus your attention on what you can get out of the conversation. When tempted to take a mental side trip, your attention can be brought back by a simple reminder of purpose.

Minimize Distractions

Distractions may come from three different sources—the environment, the listener, or the speaker.

• *Environmental distractions* include noise, people passing by, uncomfortable temperature, and poor ventilation. To improve listening, close the door, reposition seating, or, where applicable, turn off the radio. If you are a manager, have your secretary answer your phone and prevent drop-in visitors. Most calls can be returned later when you can give them your undivided attention.

• *Distractions from within* sometimes compete for attention. Instead of allowing your mind to wander, concentrate on what is taking place now—the conversation in which you are engaged—and most distractions will be shut out. You simply can't do two things at the same time, so by forcing attention to focus on the topic of conversation, other thoughts will be excluded.

When listening, you may hear something that causes an emotional reaction and distracts you from listening to all the other person has to say. Watch out for the following three reactions:

1. Defensiveness

In the course of a conversation something may be said that threatens your view of yourself. In response to that, you shift the conversation to a defense of your self-image or you allow hurt feelings to fester instead of diverting the conversation. Attention becomes focused on these feelings and because attention is somewhere else, your listening capacity suffers.

2. Resentment to opposition

It is always easier to listen to ideas similar to your own than to opposing points of view. The resentment that builds when the one to whom you are talking does not accept your ideas may get in the way of listening. Usually when opposition is encountered, the time not spent talking is spent developing a strategy and reply to overcome the opposition. Rather than listening, the mind is busy planning what will be said and how it will be said in order to make a point more clearly and destroy the opposing point of view.

3. Reactions to individuals

Sometimes a general reaction to a person will interfere with effective listening. For example, if you don't like someone, you will have difficulty listening to that person. Likewise, if you resent someone or feel threatened, these feelings will color your views of what that person may say.

There are positive filters as well as negative ones. You may so admire someone that you accept whatever is said without question. Again, a reaction to the individual gets in the way of effective listening. To improve listening ability, recognize these filters and work to set them aside.

• *Distractions from the speaker* can be caused by his or her accent, mannerisms, dress or grooming habits, language usage, delivery style, and so forth. Guard against letting a speaker's entertaining or challenging style become the focus of attention to the exclusion of content. Remember, valuable ideas can be eloquently presented and they can also be presented with a stutter, lisp, accent, or in such a lumbering style that you must fight to keep from losing interest. Probe beyond style to discover the value in the content of the message.

Delay Judgment

Most people have a habit of forming first impressions about what they are listening to. These early judgments serve as filters that color the way the remainder of the message is received. If you decide a message is good or bad, you select evidence from all that follows to back that opinion. Statements in support of a contrary viewpoint are never heard.

To overcome this problem, force yourself to delay judgment until you have heard the other person out. Often this will improve the climate of the conversation because it reflects an attitude of acceptance. Even though they may not say so, people can sense when their statements are being discounted.

Shut up and Listen

An obvious point about listening—but one often overlooked—is this: If you want to listen to someone, you must provide the opportunity for the other person to talk. Think of someone you know who chatters constantly and how frustrated you feel because you do not get a chance to say anything. Check yourself on this issue. Don't be guilty of hogging the show. Be sensitive to the other person's need for air time. The person who seems never to have anything to say may simply need an opportunity to speak or a little encouragement. If so, the best encouragement is an attentive, nonjudgmental listener.

Another common problem stems from the listener's jumping in to help the speaker. Unless the speaker actually wants help, this will usually cause some anger to develop that will have a negative impact on further communication. Why does this happen? Some listeners become impatient with speakers who are slow and ponderous. Others feel that all blank spaces in any conversation should be filled with words. So, when the speaker pauses to catch a breath, organize a response, or recall a fact, the listener jumps into the conversation. There are also some people who like to show how smart they are by jumping in to provide information or the punch line to a joke. Begin now to break the habit; eliminate this lack of courtesy. Make a pledge to be patient and to give the speaker time to speak.

Listening to How Things Are Said

Words are never neutral. They are affected by tone of voice, which accounts for 37 percent of a message's impact. Tone of voice is one of the most obvious clues to the speaker's feelings about the topic. Through tone, excitement, anger, joy, frustration, disinterest, resignation, concern, and so forth are communicated to the listener if he or she listens well.

Tone of voice can be broken down into four components—emphasis, speed, pitch, and volume.

• *The emphasis* placed on different words in a sentence—inflection in the speaker's voice—adds important meaning.

• *Speed of delivery* is another thing to observe. A speaker's delivery is slow- or fast-paced in relation to the individual's normal rate of speaking. Variations in either direction, slower or faster than normal, are significant clues to the speaker's feelings and should be noted.

An increase in speed of delivery usually signals an increase in emotional intensity. When people are excited, angry, or frustrated, they tend to talk more rapidly. A slowdown in speech delivery usually signals a resistance to address the topic. This happens in response to some perceived threat, which may be physical (such as the threat of punishment) or emotional (such as a threat to one's self-concept, ego, or sense of values). Or a slowdown in speech delivery may indicate a need to think in order to recall information and formulate responses. So, when you notice a slowdown in speech delivery, look for other data to help you draw appropriate inferences about what the other person is actually experiencing.

• *Pitch* can range from very high to very low. When experiencing stress or anxiety, the throat muscles tighten causing the voice to be at a higher pitch. When engaging in conversation, pay attention to the pitch of your own as well as the other person's voice. Allow a few minutes of related but less significant conversation at the beginning so anxiety can dissipate and both of you can relax and become comfortable. Use voice pitch as one gauge of when someone else is at ease.

• *Volume* is the final tone-of-voice dimension to observe. Some people naturally speak loudly but others use a loud, commanding voice as a mechanism of dominance. Still others, who may prefer to be less conspicuous, speak in a softer, quieter voice. It helps to know the person with whom you are conversing in order to accurately establish a reference base. However, you will be able to observe voice volume during the course of any particular conversation. If volume varies, make note of it. If volume seems louder or quieter than appropriate for the setting, make note of that. Then look for other clues that aid in forming inferences about what is being experienced.

An increase in speech volume usually indicates an increase in emotional intensity. When excited or angry, people tend to speak more loudly. Attempt to determine the reason. Then respond to the cause—not the voice volume. If loudness is in response to joy, delight, or elation, don't attempt to dampen an appropriate expression of these feelings. If loudness is in response to anger, fright, or frustration, you may choose to attempt to calm the person if you feel unqualified to deal with these feelings.

A decrease in volume usually signals feelings of perceived threat. It's as though the person talking were trying to prevent the other person from hearing what was being said or attempting to avoid saying it. Or sometimes the decrease in volume is simply caused by the speaker's not wanting to be overheard by those for whom the message was not intended. A soft voice, therefore, is only an indicator. Look for others. When coupled with slow speech delivery, it probably does reflect some feelings of threat. When coupled with fast speech delivery, it may simply mean an attempt not to be overheard. In any case, also consider other nonverbal clues such as gestures and posture before drawing inferences about meaning.

Observe Nonverbal Behavior

Most people are constantly moving. These movements reveal feelings, emotions, and reactions. Sometimes we are very much aware of body movements, as when we smile at a friend, frown, raise an eyebrow in surprise, or wink. Other times we are unaware of them.

Gestures and body movements come in clusters—the way people move toward or away from each other; the way they sit, whether tense, relaxed, on the edge, or slouched. People usually lean forward when they are involved and interested. They tend to lean back when they are not. What people do with their hands, arms, legs, and facial expressions is all part of a cluster.

Try to be particularly sensitive to any lack of congruency among the various verbal and nonverbal messages. A cluster of gestures and movements can be compared to a spoken or written sentence, while a single gesture or movement can be compared to a single word. A word, in isolation, often lacks meaning. It requires the context of the sentence for the full meaning to come through.

A word of caution about gestures. They must be viewed as indicators to be verified through other observations, either verbal or nonverbal, before they become fact. The reason is that some gestures are repeated merely because of habit while others are in response to a physical stimulus. (For example, a person might rub his or her nose from habit, because it itches, or because of feelings of deep concern.)

Let's look at some specific nonverbal behavior.

• *Eye contact* How one person looks at another is a major part of nonverbal communication. You can see interest, excitement, belligerence, warmth, and skepticism if you pay attention to the way others look at you. There are some unwritten rules about eye contact. One says that when talking, look at the person to whom you are speaking. Likewise, when being spoken to, look at the person speaking. People generally feel uncomfortable when the person to whom they are speaking does not look at them; they feel a lack of interest in what is being said. People also are uncomfortable when someone speaking to them does not maintain eye contact. A feeling of insincerity is communicated.

Direct eye contact indicates readiness to engage in the business at hand. Frequent eye contact indicates confidence. These observations let you know that the other person is interested and eager. However, when you observe your conversation partner squinting, it may indicate suspicion or doubt. Stop and check it out. Likewise, should you observe a blank, zombie-like stare, it probably indicates boredom, in which case a change of pace is called for to regain interest or the conversation should be terminated.

• *Use of hands* Next to the eyes, hands present the most expressive nonverbal communications. Open, smooth gestures are indicative of an open attitude. Covering the mouth or tugging at an ear often indicates nervousness, as does jingling keys or coins. Suspicion and doubt are communicated by touching or rubbing the nose. Running the fingers through the hair or rubbing the back of the neck suggests frustration, while thumping the fingers on something indicates boredom or impatience. Steepling, that is, bringing the hands together so they touch only at the finger tips, communicates confidence.

Touching is an important means of communication. A pat on the back; shaking, clasping, or holding a hand; or an arm around the shoulder can communicate more than many speeches.

• *Posture* How one sits during a conversation displays one's feelings about the other person as well as about the topic of conversation. Observe your partner. Is the posture tense and rigid or relaxed? This will indicate the amount of stress being experienced. If it is high, take some time to put the person at ease by talking about a nonthreatening subject.

Sitting on the edge of the chair and leaning forward indicates a readiness to move on and an attitude of cooperation. Acceptance is indicated by moving closer. Watch for these signs as indicators of agreement and conclude the conversation. Sitting erect, but not tense, indicates confidence while slouching suggests defensiveness. Turning the body away from the speaker and tilting the head forward indicates suspicion. Use these observations to know where you are with your conversation partner and alter your style or topic to utilize or overcome what you see.

Conclusion

All these components of effective listening show that it is a complex process that involves being alert to all that is heard, all that may be left out, and all that's observed. What's more, these perceptions must be thoughtfully integrated. Only then can a full understanding of the speaker's message be achieved.

Toward Better Meetings: A Psychologist's View

EUGENE RAUDSEPP

Abstract—**Meetings are potentially the best means of communication between managers and the people who report to them. Often, however, meeting time is misused and unproductive. The author suggests that in planning your next meeting you consider group size, check the meeting place before the meeting convenes, and prepare and distribute an agenda. Tips are given on guiding the discussions, handling behavior problems, establishing rules of order, and voting.**

THE RIGHT NUMBER OF COOKS

GROUP size significantly influences problem-solving and decision-making. In general, experiments have shown that as the size of the group is enlarged, members are able to participate less and become increasingly dissatisfied. Also, in larger groups a consensus is harder to achieve.

Eight participants, for example, are more likely to reach a consensus than are fifteen. In addition, the leader in the group of eight will influence decisions more than the leader in the larger group.

One obvious reason for this is that, in a large group, there is not enough time for all members to participate in the discussion, resulting in dissatisfaction with the entire meeting.

With many employees, lack of opportunity to participate and interact with others leads to the feeling that their opinions are not important, and therefore not worth presenting. Large groups also tend to disintegrate or break into factions, and spokesmen for each faction then take over the discussion.

SETTING THE SCENE

Although the importance of the meeting place's physical condition should be obvious, this factor is often overlooked. The discussion leader should personally check the conference room before anybody arrives, and see to it that

- Participants can sit sufficiently close together to develop the necessary feeling of camaraderie. The attendees should be able to see each other and the discussion leader without having to turn around.
- A blackboard and a space for the display of diagrams, charts, and maps are provided.
- The lighting and air conditioning are working well.
- The room is free from external noise and potential interruptions.

PLANNING AHEAD

The discussion leader should prepare a carefully conceived, written plan or agenda. He or she must be sure of the objectives of the meeting and should list a number of problems or questions that are to be considered. Wording of the questions is important because this determines the success of the meeting to a large degree. Effective leaders often spend as long as eight hours preparing three or four discussion areas for an important meeting!

The following sequence of steps should be the minimum for a meeting plan:

1. Statement of the problem (or problems).
2. Statement of the facts.
3. Consideration of objectives.
4. Examination of proposals in the light of the facts and objectives agreed upon.
5. Summary of the discussion.
6. Consideration of means to implement decisions.

A detailed plan or agenda guides the discussion leader and serves as a reminder of the points to bring up so that the group will gain full value. A group without either a plan or an agenda may have an interesting discussion, but may seldom reach any destination. Despite a lively exchange of ideas, the group may fail to consider the only phases of the problem that can lead to a sound conclusion.

Discussion leaders should take brief notes during the meeting or, preferably, assign someone else to do this.

Summarizing the discussion is a vital step in the meeting procedure. It should not be a rehash of all the arguments presented, but a brief review of the *results* of the discussion—a statement of points upon which agreement was reached or a solution found, as well as a listing of issues left undecided due to lack of information or unresolved disagreements. A statement is in order as to how the discussion leader proposes to supply needed information and how he or she plans to resolve the conflicts.

Disagreements need not be considered negatively. A meeting without any disagreements indicates either lack of involvement on the part of the members or a constricting atmosphere. As a rule, resolving existing disagreements is easier than breathing new life into an over-conforming, uninterested group.

The most frequent shortcoming in preparing an agenda is failure to plan carefully. Most agendas are thrown together with little attention to organizing and highlighting different aspects of the problems to be discussed. As a result, those attending the meeting are not alerted to the important parts of scheduled topics. Problems should be listed on the agenda by priority.

ADVANCE NOTICE

A question that discussion leaders frequently ask is, "Should the agenda be circulated, with supporting documents, before a scheduled meeting?" In general, this is advisable. Circulating an agenda before a meeting enhances understanding, generates thinking, and primes the whole group with the best information available. Group members who come to meetings prepared are

Reprinted with permission from *Chemical Engineering*, vol. 88, no. 6, p. 217, March 23, 1981; copyright 1981 by McGraw-Hill, Inc., New York, NY 10020.

The author is president of Princeton Creative Research, Inc., P. O. Box 122, Princeton, NJ 08540, (609) 924-3215.

Reprinted from *IEEE Trans. Prof. Comm.*, vol. PC-24, no. 3, pp. 136–138, September 1981.

better motivated and derive greater satisfaction from the sessions.

On the other hand, the major shortcoming of prior preparation is that opinions can crystallize before the general discussion takes place. This may hinder group decision-making.

The advance agenda should consist of three parts:

1. Items of information that require routine or no action.
2. Items with recommended courses of action. (Members of the group should read these items carefully before the meeting so that—if recommendations are acceptable—quick action may be taken.)
3. Items that are classified as "guidance needed," "solution needed," or "discussion indicated."

Some leaders encourage the group to prepare discussion questions, which are submitted in writing before an agenda is drawn up. This gives the members an increased sense of involvement in the meeting.

STEERING THE MEETING

Having many individuals in a group means many ideas, and many ideas can produce a sounder conclusion than a few ideas. However, this situation can also cause confusion. Here is where the discussion leader's effective presence is important. He or she maintains the group's sense of direction and keeps the meeting moving.

When the discussion is underway, the leader should regulate—not lecture. He limits his own participation to starting things and asking thought-stimulating questions (and follow-up questions) that provoke and guide the discussion. The longer a discussion leader talks at the opening of a meeting, the more passive the group becomes, and the more difficult the task of initiating and arousing the discussion becomes.

During the discussion, the group members, although naturally interested in the leader's ideas and opinions, resent being *controlled* by the leader's ideas—they want conclusions to emerge from the body of the group. The leader should draw out all the members of the group and keep their attention on essential problems so that decisions can be reached.

The leader also has the task of clarifying and interpreting the points made. Some participants state their points in a confusing and vague fashion. The leader must clarify obscure contributions by asking the confused member a few pointed questions, by uncovering the hidden premises in the speaker's statement, or by rephrasing the statement. Occasionally, clarification requires stopping the discussion and taking stock. This will make plain which issues have already been discussed and with what conclusions, what aspect of the problem is under discussion at the moment, and what points of conflict (if any) should receive attention next during the meeting.

The leader must be impartial toward the ideas and contributions offered during discussion. It is proper to acknowledge a contribution, indicating approval that the member has participated. But the leader should not indicate in any way whether he or she is in sympathy with the ideas expressed in the contribution, before pros and cons have been heard.

A leader can sharpen a group's thinking and help the members arrive at significant and effective solutions to problems if he or she poses pertinent questions at vital points of the discussion.

The high point of interest in the discussion should occur near the close of each meeting. This ensures effective decisions and provides a carryover of involvement to the next session.

How effective a group is in carrying out a decision depends on several factors. One of the most important is how clearly the goal has been defined in the discussion, and the degree to which the group directs its energies toward that goal. A responsible leader keeps a mental "goal-achievement index" in order to state at any time how much progress has been made toward a goal. This index is the chief guide in formulating an agenda for each meeting.

HANDLING MISBEHAVIOR

Three common types of problem participants are

The Commentator The discussion leader may have to deal with a flurry of whispered side-conversations, especially when a large number of people participate in a meeting. These conversations can distract and split the group. One of the most effective ways of dealing with this is to interrupt the general discussion abruptly and ask for silence. Frequently, of course, a whispered remark can be highly relevant to the discussion.

The Monopolizer Some participants tend to monopolize the discussion. This slows the pace of the meeting and also tends to divide the group. Sometimes the verbose member is incapable of submitting a contribution in a few short, clear sentences, or may present several ideas at once.

A more serious case of monopolization occurs when the speaker talks not only too long but too often. Such people also usually interrupt other speakers, confusing the discussion and annoying people.

As a rule, the monopolizer is also a bad listener; thus, there is much irrelevancy in his or her arguments. The leader should politely interrupt the speaker either by asking a question or by stating the point himself.

The Clam Diametrically opposed to the overly talkative members of the group are the sphinx-like ones who do not contribute anything. If they are hostile, or if their number exceeds two or three, their presence has a decidely adverse effect. Such people should be invited to express an opinion. After they have heard themselves speak a couple of times, they may overcome their reticence and even prove to be among the more informed and thoughtful members of the group.

RULES OF ORDER

Establishing correct meeting procedures is the best way to minimize disruptive behavior. When a series of meetings is planned, the discussion leader should devote 15 minutes of the first session to some carefully worked-out rules of order. A copy of the rules should be distributed to all members of the group and be discussed by the group leader before the regular business of the meeting.

An effective meeting guide might suggest the following rules:

- Reach all decisions by majority vote (or consensus). The discussion leader should have no preestablished decision on the problems scheduled.

- Urge everyone to participate. Voluntary expression of ideas facilitates group thinking and contributes to a lively discussion.
- Speak out one at a time and do not interrupt another speaker. Show courtesy to the speaker—refrain from private conversation.
- Be brief; present only one point at a time.
- Avoid expressions that arouse hostility, even though you will encounter many differences of opinion. Be frank and honest, but avoid emotionally tinged words and expressions that create unneccessary opposition.

When obstructive behavior occurs, calling attention to the rules should restore order.

UP FOR A VOTE

The discussion should produce something approaching unanimity; frequently, however, a vote is necessary. When the leader is reasonably sure that everything of value has been said by the group, he or she should (1) make a last summation of the discussion, highlighting the principal ideas developed, and (2) put the issue to a vote for decision, after which no further discussion on that matter is allowed.

Some rules that will further help you reach your goals follow.

TEN RULES FOR PROFITABLE MEETINGS

1. Don't call a meeting to decide something you could and should decide yourself.
2. Never get people together if a series of phone calls to individuals would serve your purpose.
3. Never invite anyone who is not essential, but make sure that everyone who would be of value to the meeting is included.
4. Insist on punctuality. If you're two minutes late for a 20-person meeting, you waste 40 person-minutes.
5. Keep the purpose of your meeting firmly in mind, and be sure it can be achieved.
6. Draft an agenda that breaks down all subjects into their simplest constituents. If well constructed, even a lengthy agenda can result in a short meeting.
7. Before sending out your agenda, read it through and examine the points that could be misunderstood. In most meetings, disagreements occur because people are not talking about the same thing. If the issues are crystal clear, the muddlers will have less chance of confusing them.
8. Circulate the agenda in time for people to read it before they come but not so far ahead that they will have forgotten about it by the time they arrive.
9. Set time limits for each section of the discussion. Make sure everyone can see a clock. A discussion, like work, expands to fill the time available.
10. See that the person in "the chair" actually acts as chairperson, i.e., that he or she states the issues, keeps to the agenda, lets everyone have a fair crack at the subject, cuts them short if they wander and sums up succinctly as soon as all have had their say.

Presenting the Successful Technical Seminar

THOMAS EALEY

Abstract—**Conducting a successful technical seminar requires careful preparation. Pre-seminar planning includes (1) outlining your material, (2) developing much more material than you think you'll need, and (3) arranging comfortable and appropriate facilities. At the beginning of the seminar you should provide a topical outline and announce plans to take a break between topics or at least hourly. After the presentation, time should be allowed not only for questions and answers but also for an evaluation to help you prepare for future seminars.**

THE knowledge explosion and the desire of most business people to enhance their careers has led to a boom in continuing education classes, usually in seminar form. The demand for highly technical seminars has created many opportunities for knowledgeable people with good communication skills, but with these opportunities come considerable challenge and usually unforeseen problems.

Whether your field is law, medicine, accounting, engineering, or computer science, you may at some point be requested to present or coordinate such a seminar, or you may even take the initiative and present one yourself. The seminar can be an opportunity to make a great impression on colleagues, your employer, potential employers, and persons who will be hiring instructors for future seminars. Unhappily, you can also cause yourself considerable embarrassment and discomfort by doing only an adequate job when expectations are high or, worse, by doing a poor job.

The people who attend technical seminars are, as a group, much different from the participants in general interest seminars, which deal with such broad subjects as motivation, basic speechcraft, or general leadership skills. Technical seminar participants have a specific purpose and a sharp focus. They are, for the most part, demanding and serious. They value their time and take great pride in their skills and talents. Most have limited time budgeted during the year for continuing education. They either have paid for the seminar personally or know what their employer has paid, and they expect their money's worth. If they feel their time is being wasted, they will certainly let you know.

The key to presenting a good technical seminar is preparation. People attend technical seminars because they feel that each hour in class has more value than many hours of independent reading and analysis. They expect you to have done the homework, the long hours of reading and analysis, so they can receive a concise presentation of the information they need. They don't expect you to cover each and every fine point within the subject area but they do want to leave feeling they can use something from the seminar in their daily work.

BASIC OUTLINE

The first steps in preparing the technical seminar are to outline the material and plan topical segments of digestible size.

The exact nature of your subject usually suggests your topical organization. A tax seminar may proceed on a numerical sequence of revenue code sections whereas an architectural seminar may proceed from foundation to roof. Don't discount an outline that seems too obvious and straightforward; your group will be able to distinguish between an erudite leader and one who tries to appear intelligent by complicating the material. If you cannot fit your material into an outline of eight or fewer topics for an all-day seminar, you need further planning and revision.

A segment should rarely run longer than one hour and you should never conduct more than two segments without taking a break. One hour is usually as long as the audience's attention span can be stretched. If you do plan to move from

Reprinted with permission from the June 1982 issue of *The Toastmaster*, published by Toastmasters International in Mission Viejo, Calif. (714) 858-8255. A nonprofit organization with 7,400 clubs worldwide, Toastmasters International teaches its members skills in public speaking and leadership.

The author is an instructor of business at Findlay College, Findlay, OH 45840, (419) 422-8313 X346.

Reprinted from *IEEE Trans. Prof. Comm.*, vol. PC-26, no. 1, p. 35–37, March 1983.

segment to segment without taking a break, schedule a short question-and-answer period and a 30-second stretch-and-yawn session to clearly mark the transition.

If you are truly prepared, you will probably develop 12 hours of material to fit your eight-hour outline. (Remember, however, you're preparing to talk to experts, so there is no such thing as being too prepared!) If this is the case, you must edit the material so your presentation fits the time schedule and is clear and concise. Any edited-out material is still useful, though—it enables you to fill any extra time you may suddenly have in your actual presentation, and it gives you the background to handle questions.

The presentation itself should be tailored to the needs of the audience and the demands made by the material. There's no one correct style for a presentation; rather, your style and format depend on each other and deserve as much thought as the material itself.

Obviously, some materials demand a lecture format, usually supplemented with handouts and projected transparencies. Remember the comments about efficiency and your group's desire to assimilate as much information as possible in the limited time available—a crisp, concise lecture can be both enlightening and efficient.

The lecture format, however, doesn't work in all instances. You may be teaching one of the newer theories of management that are heavily oriented toward democratic participation, enlightened thinking, and improved communication skills. What kind of example would you be creating if your presentation format ignored or violated your own lesson? This type of seminar calls for a combination of lecture, small group discussion, role playing, and films. No matter what your format, though, always provide your group with a topical outline at the beginning of the session. This defines the path you are following and prevents distracting conjecture on what is going to happen next.

Never insult your group by reading material to them. You may need to read specific passages or statistics, but your group will start napping or become aggravated if you do little else but read to them. Add flesh to whatever concepts or techniques you're teaching by providing emphasis, examples, anecdotes, and enthusiasm.

Always include time for questions from your audience, either by allowing questions at any time during the presentation or by calling for them at the end of your presentation. Keep in mind that taking questions throughout the seminar can be disastrous if you allow yourself to be led off the track or if you devote so much time to questions that you cannot finish your presentation in the allotted time. The best approach is to set aside specific times for questions, perhaps as you finish each major topic within your outline. This way you'll keep in touch with the group and still control the flow and continuity of the presentation.

COMFORTABLE CONDITIONS

Motivational speakers and tent preachers may enjoy "packin' 'em in," but crowded conditions and uncomfortable room temperatures aren't appreciated by people interested in capital gains taxes or the load-bearing properties of concrete. Arrange for a room that is large enough to allow each person to have an adequate table top area and comfortable seating. If necessary, place a strict limit on the number of people attending—wouldn't you rather have 40 satisfied participants than 50 disgruntled ones?

Provide a break area that is roomy and well-ventilated for smokers and has access to restrooms. Preferably this should be an area completely separate from the classroom so there'll be a true break from work.

Sound and audiovisual systems are critical and deserve a great deal of your attention. Talk with your host and the facility manager as far in advance as possible, being very specific about the type and quality of equipment you need.

When using a microphone, arrive early enough to test the mike and adjust the sound level before your audience arrives. Protest if the equipment is not delivered as promised and inquire about back-up equipment and access to amplifier controls and power sources. Someone should have immediate access to the amplifier controls during your entire presentation.

If an overhead projector or a film projector is part of your program, have the appropriate spare bulb on hand. If a film is the cornerstone of your presentation, have a splicer or a spare print ready. A good supply of grease pencils and blank transparencies allows spontaneous additions to projected displays. Whatever your setup, no one will ever complain because you are over-prepared.

FEEDBACK MECHANISM

Many seminar leaders include evaluation mechanisms in their programs. They need to know whether their presentations are accomplishing their purposes and satisfying their audiences. If your're planning to conduct more seminars, this information is invaluable.

The most commonly used evaluation technique is the questionnaire. Brief and to the point, it contains just enough questions to evaluate the major areas of presentation, organization, and setting. Designing a questionaire is not an easy job, so seek help if you are not confident in your ability to design a meaningful evaluation tool.

Remember, too, that a questionnaire isn't the only evaluation technique you can use. Consider choosing a few members of the group and asking them for a brief oral evaluation immediately after the seminar. You could ask for a written evaluation from them as a follow-up. Whatever the evaluation tool, if you have the mature ability to accept and use constructive criticism, the information will be helpful as you prepare future seminars.

When the work is done and the evaluations are in, sit back and give your seminar the ultimate test of quality. Would you want to sit through the seminar you just presented? If you can honestly pass this test, you can be sure your technical seminar was well organized and professionally presented. You can take considerable pride in having satisfied a tough audience!

Project Characteristics and Group Communication: An Investigation

—Tom L. Roberts,
Paul H. Cheney,
and Paul D. Sweeney

Abstract—*This research study examined the effects of technological complexity on project group communication. The same project teams performed three separate projects involving the development of an HTML website, the development of a local-area network (LAN), and the development of blueprints for a wide-area network (WAN). Each of the projects exposed groups to a different level of complexity. The results of the study indicated differences in group information sharing, group communication focus, and group gatekeeping activities. In each of these cases, the groups had greater communication with the less complex project task, the HTML project. The study did not find significant differences in group communication concerned with member withdrawal or group conflict.*

Index Terms—*Gatekeeping, group communication, information sharing, project complexity, project group.*

Manuscript received March 5, 2001; revised March 5, 2002.
T. L. Roberts is with Accounting and Information Systems, University of Kansas, Lawrence, KS 66049 USA (email: troberts@ku.edu).
P. H. Cheney is with the MIS Department, University of Central Florida, Orlando, FL 32816-1400 USA (email: paul.cheney@bus.ucf.edu).
P. D. Sweeney is with the Management Department, University of Dayton, Dayton, OH 45469 USA (email: paul.sweeney@notes.udayton.edu).
IEEE PII S 0361-1434(02)04972-X.

Organizations' reliance on teams and other groups has increased dramatically in the past decade [1], [2]. Many firms claim that this growing reliance on group structures has been necessary to respond quickly in dynamic business environments [3]. They believe that groups can access large and diverse amounts of information. A groups' ability to process more information than individuals can process provides potential for higher task performance [4]. Additionally, groups may be more likely to recognize valid information [5] and reject erroneous information [6].

The need to use this greater production and accuracy capability is vital to complex information system (IS) projects. As IS projects grow ever more complex, IS managers often turn to groups for development work [7]. Schuler [8] explains that individuals working with other people as a group over a sustained period of time is the best way to design and implement systems that meet society's needs. These individuals use their own specific knowledge, tools, tasks, colleagues, organizational memory, and history to assist the group effort. Most system development work is performed by multiple and, in many cases, distributed groups, each with their own standards and practices. Although these groups may not be connected in ways that help create a shared understanding, they manage to develop a reasonably coherent and stable product [9].

The deployment of groups in organizations improves the organizational response to dynamic environments only if there are quick, responsive, and accurate behaviors within the group [2]. These behaviors can only occur with proper communication within the group structure. Communication is the medium through which groups are both created and sustained and through which factors exert their influence [10]. Without question, communications is the lifeblood that flows through the veins of groups [10, p. x]. King believes a

Reprinted from *IEEE Trans. Prof. Comm.*, vol. PC-45, no. 2, pp. 84–98, June 2002.

necessary ingredient in creating a learning organization is to create a communications infrastructure that facilitates teamwork [11]. When dealing with IS projects, the challenges include selecting teams with the right number of people, skill sets, and personalities. However, one of the major issues is group communication [7], [12]. Several studies have shown that the success of information technology projects is related to effective communication [13], [14]. Thamheim and Wilemon [15] identified communicating effectively among task groups as the third most significant factor contributing to project success. Indeed, lack of successful group communication has resulted in many IS project failures [16]. In fact, without satisfactory interaction among project stakeholders, project cancellations may be inevitable, particularly for large-scale undertakings [17].

While project group communication is vital to IS project success, it has only gained considerable attention in recent years [18]–[20]. Most theoretical attention has been focused on communication between functional discipline groups such as users and system developers [21]–[23]. In most cases, these users are external to the project teams and are not directly part of the group interaction process. Like some of the earlier research, this line of work has amplified the value of group interaction and communication to success. Another related and important research focus has been IS system development team communication with end-users to gather information requirements for the new information systems. In these studies, team communication with end-users has been found to have a positive impact on performance [24]–[27].

There have been many studies considering project team communication involving group support systems and various types of media. However, a neglected area of study is the internal communication among IS project teams. This is surprising because the group interaction process is central to a group [28]. If group members are to improve the dynamics and communication within groups to solve problems, researchers and practitioners need to consider how to assist group members and gain a greater understanding of group communication [29]. For this reason, Robey and Newman [30] call for a detailed investigation of communication patterns among IS project teams. One goal of our research study is to take a look at group communication patterns among IS project groups. Each of these project groups were involved in completing multiple IS projects. In particular, we study groups who are involved in creating a small business website, setting up a local-area network (LAN), and developing the blueprint for a wide-area network (WAN). Our focus is to see if group communication differs due to the complexity of the three IS projects.

Group Communication

The most significant elements of group communication are the relationships among group members rather than individuals. Watzlawick, Beavin, and Jackson coined the phrase, "one cannot not communicate" [31, p. 49]. All behavior can be considered communication. It is clear that organizational communication must not be directed toward individuals alone, but must be carried out effectively with groups (formal and informal) that exist in the organization [32]. Group communication is more efficient if there is active interaction between members [33]. The only way two people can establish a relationship is to engage in communication [34].

For group communication, a network with a pattern of channels that link members can be developed [34]. When individuals are combined, groups develop their own characteristics. Some are composites of the characteristics of the individuals who make up the group, and some are unique to the group and may not be directly represented by any one person within the group [32]. Among these characteristics are the stylistic communication patterns developed by groups as a function of the particular parties involved [35], [36] and the dynamics of their interaction [37], [38]. Interestingly enough, context-specific and unique communication processes that develop within a group and guide knowledge sharing can be formalized [39], [40].

The direct effects of group communication can be attributed to two forms of social influence: normative influence and informational influence [41]. Group communication can be used to convey information about group norms and values. By providing group members with information about social norms governing the limits of acceptable competition and individual behaviors for their own self-interests, communication can facilitate the execution of group strategies devised during discussion [42]. Individual group members can then apply the context of the group norms to interpret messages and respond accordingly [43]. With informational influence, group communication can be used to convey information and formulate strategies for how to solve group problems or project tasks [44]. Through discussion, group members who have a better understanding of the project tasks may be able to provide less knowledgeable members with information. We believe these discussions will become even more important as the project tasks become more complex and as the range of knowledge among the project group members broadens.

Technological Task Complexity

Research on small groups has indicated that a group needs two special functions to be performed if a group is to survive. These functions include group task and maintenance, and both must be going on throughout the life of the group [45]. Hackman [46] noted that task type affects the nature of the group interaction. Task complexity refers to the extent to which operations must be performed upon the resources of the group for successful task completion [47]. March and Simon [48] characterized complex tasks by the existence of a number of subtasks to be performed while Campbell [49] defined a complex task as having a number of interrelated and conflicting components to complete. Wood [50] defined task complexity as a function of the number of distinct acts that need to be executed in the performance of the task and the number of distinct cues that must be processed during task performance. Additionally, Wood [50] stated that as the number of acts increase then the knowledge and skill requirements for completion of the tasks also increase.

IS projects are unique because they require the intense collaboration of three groups of stakeholders: IS staff, end-users, and management [17]. IS projects are group-oriented activities, organized and executed in teams and subject to all the vagaries of group dynamics, interactions, coordination, and communication [17]. The technical complexity of an IS project requires effective coordination among the group to ensure completion [17]. A complex task such as the creation of a detailed technical blueprint of a wide-area network (WAN) design may require a centralized group organization structure that includes active group discussions with rating or voting systems as the most effective approach [51]. The technical dimension of any IS development project demands that some structure be imposed on the development effort to help guide the system to successful completion [17].

The complexity and conceptual nature of systems development projects contribute to the difficulties of understanding "all possible states" of the system that may in part contribute to product flaws, cost overruns, and schedule delays [17]. These risks and uncertainties associated with IS projects are difficult to assess with any degree of reliability prior to the start of the projects. Risks may include the large size of the project, complexity of the project domain, project members being unfamiliar with the technology, unstable information requirements, and difficulties in integrating different component systems into a composite system [17].

Through pooling IS group members' skills and abilities, in theory, many of these problems can be avoided or addressed. This opinion, however, is not new. It has been assumed to be true and has been employed heavily by business for several decades even though little empirical research supports this assumption. Our opinion is that simple problems are often most quickly and effectively solved by the most competent group member and complex problems are solved best by members pooling their resources and checking for errors. Only through successful group interaction and communication can such pooling occur. Another outcome of successful pooling of resources is an increased creative output associated with group interaction and communication after initial the individual brainstorming ideas are combined.

Current Study

The current study was conducted to determine if the complexity of a technical project impacts communication within the project group. We believe that project group communication will vary depending on the complexity of the group project. Fig. 1 shows the relationship between the project tasks that were used in the study. Fig. 2 shows the research model for this study.

> H1: "Group information sharing" will be significantly different when the complexity level of the technical project varies.

Successful group communication requires the establishment of mutual knowledge [39] and is enhanced by the ability of group members to communicate directly with everyone in the group [52]. Project teams frequently encounter serious problems in sharing knowledge among group members [53]. One key problem is that if you ask any two people the same question then you may get two very different responses [54]. The individual group member's temperament, upbringing, values, and experiences are the foundation for people's different ideas about "how things should be done" [54]. This means that group members should be able to express their opinions, listen to other members of the group's ideas, and feel free to make both positive and negative comments. The success of group projects may vary greatly depending on how much collective understanding individuals have about the goals, processes, background, orientation, and thinking [54].

Information is central to group problem solving [55]. Larson and Christensen [56] argue that

Fig. 1. Types of tasks in group projects in this study and in most prior research studies.

Hands-On	Conceptual
LAN Project	*Most Prior Research*
HTML Project	WAN Project

cognitive processes such as information acquisition/search, storage, and retrieval occur at both the individual and group level. Hinsz, Tindale, and Vollrath [57] agree and use the phrase "collective information processing" which is defined as the degree to which information, ideas, or cognitive processes are shared among individuals and the group. Hirokawa and Scheerhorn [58] posit that forming a collective pool of information may be requisite for group problem-solving and decision-making. Group communication can play a promotive role in the establishment of a valid, reliable, and adequate information base by eliciting available knowledge among group members, facilitating the group acceptance of what is deemed valid, relevant, and useful information, increasing the probability of group rejection of invalid information, and by helping group members see the need to gather new information [59].

We believe that the process of group information sharing including ideas (both negative and positive) will vary depending upon the complexity of the group project task. This, in turn, will impact the group's ability to create a group information base and a sharing of knowledge.

> H2: "Group communication focus" will be significantly different when the complexity level of the technical project varies.

This communication process allows each member to focus on a specific aspect of the task and on how their role relates to others in their group [60]. Focusing is the group's ability to keep the group discussion on the group task [61]. Focusing is used when the group begins to drift from its agenda [61]. Usually, when group members are always going off the topic, it is either because some other event has become more important or because the current group topic is not as important as the group initially thought [61]. In many cases, a simple reminder from the group member may be enough to refocus the group on its original topic. However, if the groups drifts more than once, it can be taken that several members or the whole group and uncomfortable with the topic [61]. In order to focus, the group will need to organize discussions. Focusing may include looking at future group events, giving group members relevant information, introducing a topic to see what group members already know, or even detailing a group member's contribution to the group's goals thus rewarding good work [61]. We believe that a group's focus will be different depending on the complexity of the project task.

> H3: "Gatekeeping of group communication participation" will be significantly different when the complexity of the technical project varies.

The gatekeeping role in a small group includes group building and maintenance including being the expeditor [62]. Gatekeeping is behavior that helps all members of the group participate more equally by limiting those who monopolize the discussion and by encouraging participation of reticent group members [61]. With gatekeeping, efforts are made at getting quieter group members involved and controlling active members so they will allow others to contribute

Fig. 2. This diagram depicts the direct relationship between project complexity and group communication needs; as project complexity increases, group communication needs increase and vice versa.

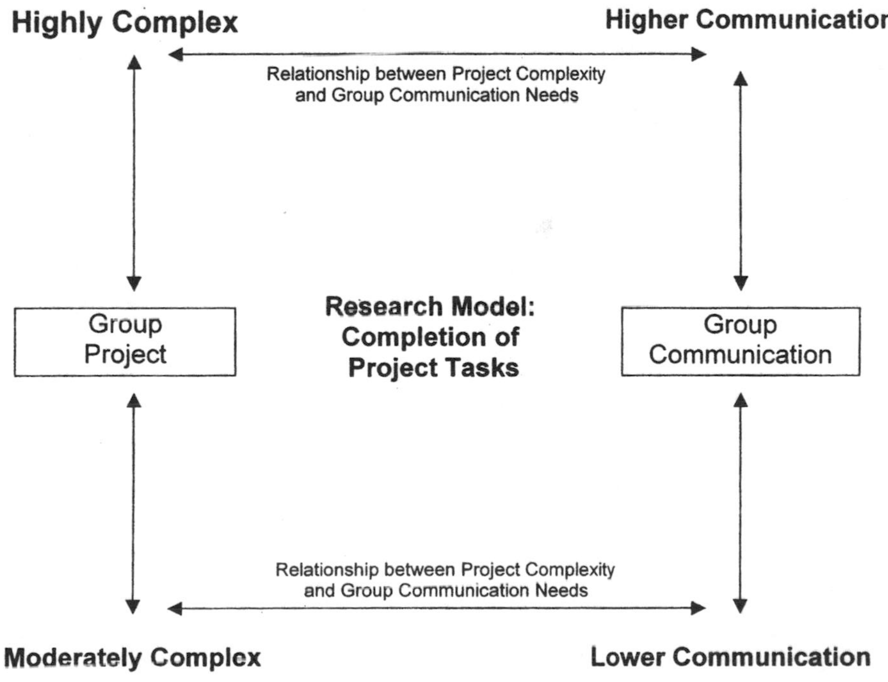

to the group. This is essential to balanced participation to the group and group success including goal achievement, group member satisfactions, and attraction to the group [61].

One potential problem with group communication is that a single person controlling the information in an organization can affect decisions by allowing certain information to flow through channels [63]. Similarly, some studies argue a few individuals within an organization can filter communication. Group success and communication may be largely dependent on the type of information available to group members [64]. We believe the gatekeeping role is essential to group projects and that it will be impacted by the complexity of the project.

> H4: "Group member withdrawal" from group communication will be significantly different when the complexity of the technical project varies.

To share ideas and influence others, individuals must communicate. For those who are reluctant to talk, communication is difficult [65]. Communication apprehension reflects both discomfort about speaking and low self-perceived competency in speaking [66] and may extend across multiple communication contexts including groups [67].

Numerous studies have investigated how people's communication apprehension affects their communication behaviors in groups. Reticent individuals interact less frequently in groups than more outgoing group members [68], and they tend to be more dissatisfied with group communication than more active group members [69]. McCroskey and Richmond [70] found that communication apprehensive individuals talked much less, chose less visible seating, tended to make irrelevant comments, and avoided disagreement.

Another problem is that reticent group members are evaluated negatively as communicators by other group members [65]. Studies have shown that reticent members are viewed as less credible and effective and that their contributions are less relevant to group success [71]. In contrast, group members willing to communicate were judged as more credible and likable [72]. Within groups, the members who participate most and presumably best understand the norms are usually the most satisfied [73].

> H5: "Group communication conflict" will be significantly different when the complexity of the technical project varies.

Conflict within a group eliminates the accumulation of blocked hostile dispositions by allowing group member's free behavior expression [74, p. 39]. It is better to define areas of conflict than to suppress them. With the conflict openly expressed, the group can work on resolving it. The goal is a resolution that is acceptable to all. Unless conflict is openly discussed, hostility can lead to blocked communication, lessening the attraction to the group and effectiveness of the group. A conflict unresolved can lead to members actually withdrawing from the group [61].

We must point out that researchers have found that task conflicts caused by disagreements regarding the specific task content can be beneficial [75]–[78], and these conflicts can improve performance [79]. Task conflict is the awareness of differences in viewpoints and opinions regarding a group task. It considers conflict about ideas and opinions concerning the task [80]. With complex tasks, groups can benefit from differences of opinion [81], [77].

De Vries [82] points out that effective project groups share ideas freely and enthusiastically and members feel comfortable expressing opinions both for and against any position. Frankness and candidness with regard to shared, open, honest, and accurate information is the norm in well-functioning project groups. Groups that meet these criteria are ideal breeding grounds for creative problem solving and complex task completion [82]. We believe that the level of group communication conflict will vary depending on the complexity of the group project.

METHOD

Data was collected from groups that were engaged in substantial information technology (IT) tasks. These tasks were part of a senior networking course at a large university. The data was gathered from students as part of a senior level business telecommunications class. The demographics of the study are presented in Table I.

TABLE I
DEMOGRAPHICS OF STUDY PARTICIPANTS

Demographics		No.
Gender	*Male*	64
	Female	36
Age	*18-21*	17
	22-25	46
	26-30	23
	>30	14
GPA	*2.00-2.49*	17
	2.50-2.99	30
	3.0-3.49	37
	>3.5	16
Race	*White/Caucasion*	61
	Hispanic	7
	Asian	19
	Black	4
	Native American	0
	Other	5
Citizen	*USA*	84
	Non-USA	16

Subjects spent the majority of the class time working in these project groups. Prior to the assignment of students to teams, demographic data was gathered and heterogeneous groups were formed based on the students work experience, education, and cultural backgrounds. Group members remained together until the three project assignments were completed. The projects were part of the required tasks for successful completion of the course. Groups were forced to have weekly in-class face-to-face meetings. Additional meetings were necessary to complete the project tasks. Projects groups scheduled their own out-of-class meetings. Finally, groups were not limited in their out of class communications. Groups were encouraged to use various methods to communicate including telephone, email, and face-to-face communication. Data was collected at three intervals during the course. Specifically, data was collected at the completion date of each of the three projects.

The researchers used fifteen items from the Watson and Michaelson [83] group style instrument to index group communication. This instrument has a significant communication component for group studies. Table II shows a list of these communication items that were used in the study. The items portrayed the various positive and negative individual communication behaviors that could be displayed by group members. The instrument uses a five-point Likert scale with anchors from 1 "to a very little extent" to 5 "a very great extent." Instrument administration was conducted without students having any definite knowledge of how the group's performance compared to other groups. The instrument was administered to a total of 100 respondents from 18 project teams. Project group size ranged from five to seven group members. The use of students may be a limitation on this study and its generalizability. However, we believe that the student population used in this study did have a knowledge understanding for these projects similar to those IS personnel in industry. Student surrogates are considered adequate to conduct behavioral studies such as this group interaction study [84], [85]. Additionally, student surrogates are used for many group experiments [86]–[88], [4], [83] and have been used for many group support system (GSS) studies [89]–[95]. Again, the focus of this study is group communication on complex IT projects and not the technical expertise of the students nor are we looking at potential outcomes.

TABLE II
MICHAELSON–WATSON SURVEY INSTRUMENT COMMUNICATION ITEMS

Item No.	Item Content
1	Some members respond only when asked.
2	Arguments carry on too long.
3	Everyone has a chance to express their opinion.
4	We listen to each individual's input.
5	In our discussions, we drift off the point.
6	Someone always makes sure that quieter group members get a chance to express their ideas.
7	Members feel free to make positive and negative comments.
8	One of our members is very good at getting less assertive members to voice their opinions.
9	Some members appear to withhold questions.
10	Some members interrupt when another is speaking.
11	We organize our communication according to available time.
12	We maintain a high exchange of ideas.
13	Encouragement is given to reticent members to express their opinions.
14	Sometimes people with good ideas don't seem to speak up.
15	One or two members tend to dominate the discussion.

Note: These items are used in the ANOVA results in Table III.

MANIPULATION CHECKS

We used individual tacit knowledge as a control variable. Tacit knowledge can be defined as the skill level an individual group member possesses concerning a given technological tool, language, or procedure that the group member acquired previously or was inherent to their natural problem-solving ability [96]. Tacit knowledge will affect the type of group interaction assuming equal task complexity and task-time duration. The controls for individual tacit knowledge were the number of required prerequisite courses for the business telecommunications courses. We measured individual tacit knowledge by summing the number of MIS courses completed prior to participation in this project. As a further check for tacit knowledge levels, a subsequent sample was gathered. Eighty-one MIS students in the same telecommunications course were asked to rate their current knowledge in performing the tasks for each of the three projects on a ten-point scale from (Not Knowledgeable) to (Very Knowledgeable). A subsequent ANOVA procedure revealed no significant differences in the amount of knowledge that students bring to each of the three projects. These results coupled with the count of completed MIS courses indicate that tacit knowledge did not play a role in the results of this study.

The treatment variable for this particular study was the task complexity related to each individual project. The projects were classified by complexity according to the number of tasks required to complete each project. Task complexity was operationalized by the number, types, and interconnected nature of the subtasks of each project. As a further check of complexity, we conducted an additional survey of telecommunications student subjects. This separate survey was taken from the same population of possible subjects. Eighty-one students were asked to rate the complexity of each project on a ten-point scale from 1 (Not Complex) to 10 (Very Complex). The results of the ANOVA procedures revealed no significant difference between the LAN and WAN projects that we had originally described as highly complex. Additionally, the results verified that both the LAN and WAN projects were considered more complex than the HTML project.

The duration was two weeks for the LAN project and six weeks for the other two projects (i.e., HTML, WAN). The order of the group performance on the three projects was random. There were three possible orders for project completion (i.e., HTML–WAN–LAN, LAN–HTML–WAN, and HTML–WAN–LAN). The study groups remained intact as they progressed through all three projects.

HTML Project

Students were required to build a commercial website. Each group built a commercial website for a carefully selected local small business to improve their business operations. The development project lasted six weeks. Each project group conducted a preliminary requirements analysis of the small business' operations. The obtained information requirements were the main components used in developing the website. Each project group presented the completed website to representatives of the small business for possible adoption.

The researchers have designated the HTML project as a moderately complex hands-on technical project. The deliverable for the HTML project was a working prototype. The wide range of complexity among the HTML projects is a concern when comparing the websites. However, constraints were put into place to attempt to limit the variability between the three projects. For instance, any active server pages (ASPs) were of a limited nature with a limit of three database tables for this particular project. The varying business needs for a website for the small businesses caused some of the websites to be much more complex than others. In addition, the researchers believe that some students brought considerable tacit knowledge to these projects by virtue of their required completion of a systems analysis and design course, a database course, and a programming course. In addition, some students were exposed to HTML and other relevant technologies through their related work experience or self-study.

LAN Project

The LAN project required the project group to install, configure, troubleshoot, and operate a network comprised of an NT Server, multiple NT Workstation, and several Windows 95 clients. The LAN project was an intense project lasting for 14 days. Project groups were given 24-hour access to a LAN laboratory with the specific instructions to install and configure a LAN network using Windows NT. Each project group started the project with four workstations, one server, and an active hub. All components were completely void of any software programs. Operating systems and additional software had to be installed by the student groups. Networking manuals and a laboratory assistant were made available to the student groups. Upon completion of the installation and configuration of the Windows NT LAN, the laboratory assistant and researchers created a number of common problems on the network. The student groups were then asked to troubleshoot the network and to restore the network to normal working order.

The researchers have designated the LAN project as a highly complex, hands-on technical project. All software and hardware components needed for this project were provided to the student groups. Each project started and finished with the same tasks. The projects were completely identical for every project team. The deliverable for the LAN project was a working LAN prototype. The researchers believe that students brought limited tacit knowledge to these projects. This course was the students' first exposure in their degree program to LANs. Many of the students made progress toward acquiring MSCE certifications as a direct result of this project experience.

WAN Project

The WAN project required the groups to design and select a WAN architecture. The WAN was required to support the transmission of full motion video, image, data, and voice. Students proposed three alternative architectures that would support such a network. Each proposed architecture was designed completely, including the specifications of each device and the media. The alternative architectures included asynchronous transfer mode (ATM), frame relay, satellite networks, circuit switching, and ISDN. Every component and its function were described for each architecture. Traffic and capacity loads were calculated. In addition, the project groups conducted a cost analysis for both the operation and development of the network. Finally, each project group selected the best architecture on the basis of cost verses capability.

The goal of the WAN project was to provide groups a problem in which the function, placement, and capability of particular telecommunications devices could be easily ascertained. The researchers have designated the WAN project as a highly complex, conceptual technical project. The projects varied depending on the WAN technology selected by each project team, however, each technology was used to solve the identical problem. The deliverable for the WAN project was a report documenting the blueprints of the WAN architectures. The researchers believe that students also brought limited tacit knowledge to these projects. This course was the student's first exposure to WANs and telecommunications hardware.

Data Analysis

An initial hierarchial linear modeling (HLM) procedure was conducted using HLM 5.04 software [97] to determine independence of individual and group responses [98]–[104]. HLM is a maximum-likelihood procedure for simultaneously estimating and testing effects involving variables (group characteristics and individual differences) operationalized at multiple levels [101]. This procedure was conducted to determine the independence of observations. This assumption was not violated and allows us to use individuals as the unit of analysis in this study.

A series of repeated measures ANOVA were conducted with the group project being the key grouping variable of analysis (HTML, LAN, WAN). These ANOVAs were conducted on each of the 15 communication items and the results of these tests are provided in Table III. Prior to conducting more specific analyses on each item, we first conducted an overall MANOVA. This analysis found a significant set of effects on communication of our grouping variable. Protected by this overall analysis, we conducted the individual ANOVAs on each of the items to see where these effects might be.

If we found a significant effect in the ANOVA, we followed this up with a series of post-hoc comparisons to determine which of the three groups differed from one another. While the ANOVA showed an overall effect, we did not know which specific means differ from one another. The results of the ANOVA procedure are in Table III. To examine this issue of specific differences, we calculated a series of post-hoc tests of differences between means. In particular, for each of the 15 items, we compared all project types with one another. For example, for item 3, we conducted three tests (LAN vs. HTML, LAN vs. WAN, and HTML vs. WAN). One problem with the use of many such post-hoc tests is the issue of the experiment-wise error rate. With 30 additional tests, for example, the probability of finding at least a few of these to be significant is quite high. Accordingly, researchers have suggested using post-hoc tests that make corrections for experiment-wise error. A post-hoc test, such as the Tukey HSD test, requires a higher standard to be met prior to declaring that a set of means. These comparisons were performed using the Tukey HSD statistic. The multiple comparisons indicated significant differences among seven items (3, 4, 6, 11, 12, 13) between the HTML project and the LAN and WAN projects at a 0.05 level of significance. Note that item 1 was significant at a 0.075 level of significance. The results of these multiple comparisons are also shown in Table III. The remaining eight items did not reveal any significant differences among the three projects.

Results

The HTML project clearly produced the most significant information sharing among group members. For example the mean positive response of 3.88 (out of 5) for the HTML project for item 12 reveals a higher exchange of ideas for the moderately complex HTML project than for either the LAN or WAN projects. The HTML project also produced significantly higher mean scores for items 3 (4.15) and 7 (3.99). These items reflect whether each group member had a chance to express their opinion regardless of whether the opinion was positive or negative. The researchers believe that this difference is most likely the result of reduced complexity with the HTML project due to fewer subtasks to be performed. Tacit knowledge could have also caused this result because group members were comfortable with the project tasks. Group members were definitely more comfortable with expressing their opinion concerning the HTML project. One thought may be that group members are less willing to interact and communicate if they are unsure of their knowledge concerning the project task. Another interesting finding was that the HTML project produced another significantly higher mean score (4.14) with regard to group members listening to everyone's opinions (item 4). Not only were group members more willing to express their opinions, but they were also more willing to listen to other group members. All group members seem to have been at the same level of competence and capability thus producing a mutual respect among the group.

The gatekeeping, series of items (6, 8, and 13), produced conflicting results when comparing the projects. Items 6 (3.29) and 13 (3.52) show the HTML project producing higher mean scores than more complex projects (LAN and WAN) for getting reticent group members to express their opinion. However, neither mean score was heavily weighted to the positive end of the Likert scale. One point that is significant here is that neither item designated a particular group member as being the individual who elicits group opinions from reticent members. Instead, the effort seems to come from the group as a whole with different members stepping up to elicit communication at different times. In support of this assertion, item 8, which states that a particular group member is good at getting less assertive group members to express their opinions, did not reveal a significant difference between the three projects. Again, a group effort seemed to more adequately address these gatekeeping communication problems for the moderately complex HTML project. Again, opinions from less assertive group members may be lost when dealing with more complex projects that have many subtasks.

The group member withdrawal, set of items (1, 9, and 14), concerning group members input to the project, failed to produce significant differences between the three projects. Group members responses indicated slight agreement with the statements "that some group members with good ideas did not speak up" (means ranged from 3.36 to 3.50), and "that some group members withheld questions concerning the projects" (means ranged from 3.37 to 3.51) for all three projects. Item 1 states "group members respond only when asked direct questions" produced no significant differences for all three projects (means ranging from 2.79 to 3.12). These results indicate that project groups will have members that hold back their communication regardless of the complexity or nature of the project. A number of potential reasons may be the reason for such member withdrawal including lack of communication skills or lack of knowledge concerning the project tasks. Group member withdrawal is a problem that many project managers should focus their efforts to improve communication.

Communication conflict was a problem for the project teams for all three types of projects. Item 2, concerning "arguments carrying on too long" did not produce significant differences between the projects. However, it did produce mean scores over 4.00 for all three projects. Project groups must have had considerable

TABLE III
ANOVA RESULTS FOR COMMUNICATION ITEMS IN TABLE II FOR THREE PROJECT GROUPS: WIDE-AREA NETWORK (WAN3), WEB DEVELOPMENT (HTML2), AND LOCAL-AREA NETWORK (LAN1)

Item No.	Mean For Project Group			ANOVA Value F	P Value P(F)
	WAN3	HTML2	LAN1		
1	3.12	2.79	3.01	2.632	.074
2	4.08	4.06	4.14	.140	.869
3	3.57^{1}	4.15^{2}	3.65^{1}	11.373	.000
4	3.48^{1}	4.14^{2}	3.63^{1}	14.433	.000
5	3.56	3.49	3.56	.143	.867
6	2.97^{1}	3.29^{2}	2.961^{1}	3.693	.026
7	3.50^{1}	3.99^{2}	3.64^{1}	9.318	.000
8	2.96	3.07	2.97	.360	.698
9	3.37	3.51	3.41	.664	.515
10	3.65	3.61	3.70	.194	.824
11	3.51^{1}	4.02^{2}	3.53^{1}	12.524	.000
12	3.36^{1}	3.88^{2}	3.54^{1}	10.231	.000
13	3.14^{1}	3.52^{2}	3.19^{1}	5.745	.004
14	3.41	3.50	3.36	.537	.585
15	3.19	3.01	3.00	.975	.379

Note: If F is significant, the superscripts reveal the significant differences for each item among project groups (1 =LAN1, 2 = HTML2, 3 =WAN3) as a result of a Tukey's Multiple Comparisons procedure.

arguments while carrying out each project. A second item (item 10), concerning "interruptions while one group member was speaking," also revealed a high range of mean scores (3.61–3.70), albeit without significant differences between the projects. Apparently, this problem existed for all three projects and may have been a cause for members withholding ideas and questions. Finally, group members slightly agreed that "some members tend to dominate the discussion" during communication sessions (item 15). The range of mean scores for this item was 3.01 to 3.19. In total, these three items reveal that conflict exists for all project groups regardless of complexity and nature. Again, one must remember that conflict concerning tasks may not be a negative impact for complex projects.

The focus area produced some interesting results. Item 5 concerning the group discussion drifting off the point produced a relative high mean score (3.49 to 3.56) for the three projects without significant differences. A very important issue for many project groups is their ability to maintain focus on the task(s) at hand. The results from the responses to this item indicate that this is a difficult task for project groups performing all levels of complex project tasks. Finally, the group's organization of their communication (item 11) did produce significant differences between the moderately complex HTML project and the two highly complex LAN and WAN projects. Groups were significantly more organized for their group communication and allocation of time for communication for the moderately complex project. The mean score (4.02) indicated that groups were highly organized and used time well for the HTML project. This is a very significant result because it may be more difficult to organize group communication when expertise is limited among a few group members or tacit knowledge is limited. A greater focus on organizing communication must be taken on more complex projects.

Summary

This study revealed that complex project tasks can impact communication patterns in information systems project groups. Task complexity did impact information sharing among group members. For technical managers, the finding that information sharing was greater with a moderately complex task as opposed to a highly complex task is very important. Managers need to place great effort on making groups understand the benefits of information sharing and make sure the communication processes are working efficiently on highly complex tasks if they expect to gain the advantages of the group pooling effect.

Task complexity also influenced groups' communication focus. Again, group communication focus dealing with communication organization and allocation of time was greater for the less complex HTML project. Technical managers need to realize that as a project becomes more complex, the need for organization of group communication becomes more important. Managers need to make sure that the group communication processes are well organized and that necessary time is allocated to facilitate group communication is allocated through meetings, discussion groups, or general intragroup communication.

Another point that is important for technical managers is the gatekeeping role of a group facilitator. The results of the study revealed that the HTML project groups did a better job of gatekeeping. Technical managers need to make sure that each project group has someone playing the facilitator role and must realize that as complexity increase that this role becomes more important.

Finally, our results did not find any differences with regard to communication involving group conflict or member withdrawal. These seem to be trouble areas for all groups. However, these results do indicate that technical managers should work at reducing these problem areas for technical groups. One important thing to remember is that some group conflict if it is about the task at hand is actually good for the group interaction process.

In general, our research has shown that the very nature of the task can produce some significant communication challenges or advantages. For practicing managers, our results suggest that special care be taken, and perhaps special nurturing or vigilance be exercised when assigning groups to complete certain IS tasks using a team structure. With all tasks (from moderately to highly complex) a special concern with communication patterns and skills is warranted.

Areas for Future Research

The results of this study lead one to believe that there is a great deal of future research that needs to be conducted on technical group communication. A first element that is of great importance is performance outcomes. We intend to look at real work groups and to see how the communication process actually leads to successful outcomes. With the abundant use of telecommunications, data networks, and video-conferencing, another large focus will to be to assess the outcome performance and communication patterns of virtual work groups. Again, there are many areas that need to be addressed.

REFERENCES

[1] R. A. Guzzo, "At the intersection of team effectiveness and decision making," in *Team Effectiveness and Decision Making in Organizations*, R. A. Guzzo, E. Salas, and Associates, Eds. San Francisco, CA: Jossey-Bass, 1995, pp. 1–8.

[2] M. J. Waller, "The timing of adaptive group responses to nonroutine events," *Acad. Manag. J.*, vol. 42, no. 2, pp. 127–137, 1999.

[3] S. A. Mohrman, S. G. Cohen, and A. M. Mohrman, *Designing Team-Based Organizations: New Forms for Knowledge Work*. San Francisco, CA: Jossey-Bass, 1995.

[4] P. H. Kim, "When what you know can hurt you: A study of experiential effects on group discussion and performance," *Organiz. Behav. Human Decision Processes*, vol. 69, no. 2, pp. 165–177, 1997.

[5] I. Lorge and H. Solomon, "Two models of group behavior in the solutions of Eureka-type problems," *Psychometrika*, vol. 29, pp. 139–148, 1955.

[6] R. Hirokawa and R. Pace, "A descriptive investigation of the possible communication-based reasons for effective and ineffective group decision-making," *Commun. Monographs*, vol. 50, pp. 363–379, 1983.

[7] D. Lyons, "IS gets a handle on teamwork," *InfoWorld*, vol. 18, no. 22, pp. 70–74, 1996.

[8] D. Schuler, "Computer professionals and the next culture of democracy," *Commun. ACM*, vol. 44, no. 1, pp. 52–57, 2001.

[9] H. Tellioglu and I. Wagner, "Software cultures," *Commun. ACM*, vol. 42, no. 12, pp. 71–77, 1999.

[10] L. Frey, *The Handbook of Group Communication Theory and Research*, L. Frey, D. S. Gouran, and M. S. Poole, Eds. Thousand Oaks, CA: Sage, 1999.

[11] W. King, "IS and the learning organization," *Inform. Syst. Manag.*, vol. 13, no. 3, pp. 78–80, 1996.

[12] S. Thomas, R. Tucker, and W. Kelly, "Compass: An assessment tool for improving project team communications," *Project Manag. J.*, vol. 30, no. 4, pp. 15–23, 1999.

[13] R. J. Boland and R. V. Tenkasi, "Perspective making and perspective taking in communities of knowing," *Organiz. Sci.*, vol. 6, no. 4, pp. 350–372, 1995.

[14] R. Hirschheim and M. Newman, "Symbolism and information systems development: Myth, metaphor and magic," *Inform. Syst. Res.*, vol. 2, no. 1, pp. 29–62, 1991.

[15] H. Thamheim and D. Wilemon, "Criteria for controlling projects according to plan," *Project Manag. J.*, vol. 17, no. 3, pp. 75–81, 1986.

[16] D. Davis, *Mini-Micro Syst.*, vol. 15, no. 9, pp. 145–151, 1982.

[17] K. Ewusi-Mensah, "Critical issues in abandoned information systems development projects," *Commun. ACM*, vol. 40, no. 9, pp. 74–80, 1997.

[18] L. Argote, P. Ingram, J. Levine, and R. L. Moreland, "Knowledge transfer in organizations: Learning from the experiences of others," *Organiz. Behav. Human Decision Processes*, vol. 82, no. 1, pp. 1–8, 2000.

[19] K. Kumar, H. Van Dissel, and P. Bielli, "The merchant of prato revisited: Toward a third rationality of information systems," *MIS Quart.*, vol. 22, no. 2, pp. 199–226, 1998.

[20] D. Wastell, "Learning dysfunctions in information systems development: Overcoming the social defenses with transitional objects," *MIS Quart.*, vol. 23, no. 4, pp. 581–600, 1999.

[21] E. Carayannis and J. Sagi, "Dissecting the professional culture: Insights from inside the IT 'black box'," *Technovation*, vol. 21, pp. 91–98, 2000.

[22] E. Carmel, *Global Software Teams: Collaborating Across Borders and Time Zones*. Englewood Cliffs, NJ: Prentice-Hall, 1999.

[23] K. Eisenhardt and B. Tabrizi, "Accelerating adaptive processes: Product innovation in the global computer industry," *Admin. Sci. Quart.*, vol. 40, pp. 84–110, 1995.

[24] R. J. Boland, "Control, causality, and information systems requirements," *Accounting Organiz. and Soc.*, vol. 4, no. 4, pp. 259–272, 1979.

[25] C. Churchman, *The Systems Approach*. New York: Dell, 1968.

[26] R. Hirschheim and H. Klein, "Four paradigms of information systems development," *Commun. ACM*, vol. 32, no. 10, pp. 1199–1216, 1989.

[27] D. Robey and M. Markus, "Rituals in information systems design," *MIS Quart.*, vol. 8, no. 1, pp. 5–15, 1984.
[28] J. McGrath, *Groups: Interaction and Performance*. Englewood Cliffs, NJ: Prentice-Hall, 1984.
[29] B. G. Schultz, "Improving group communication performance: An overview of diagnosis and intervention," in *The Handbook of Group Communication Theory and Research*, L. Frey, D. S. Gouran, and M. S. Poole, Eds. Thousand Oaks, CA: Sage, 1999, pp. 371–394.
[30] D. Robey and M. Newman, "Sequential patterns in information systems development: An application of a social process model," *ACM Trans. Inform. Syst.*, vol. 14, no. 1, pp. 30–63, 1996.
[31] P. Watzlawick, J. Beavin, and D. Jackson, *Pragmatics of Group Communication: A Study of Interactional Patterns, Pathologies, and Paradoxes*. New York: Norton, 1967.
[32] N. Spinks and B. Wells, "Communicating with groups: Prompt, purposeful, productive team meetings," *Executive Devel.*, vol. 8, no. 5, pp. 13–20, 1995.
[33] M. Voicu, "The influence of active communication on efficiency of group problem solving by students," *Revista de Psihologie*, vol. 19, pp. 193–208, 1973.
[34] B. Fisher, *Small Group Decision Making: Communication and the Group Process*, 2nd ed. New York: McGraw-Hill, 1980.
[35] T. Finholt and L. Sproul, "Electronic groups at work," *Organiz. Sci.*, vol. 1, no. 1, pp. 41–64, 1990.
[36] S. Jarvenpaa, K. Knoll, and D. Leidner, "Is anybody out there? Antecedents of trust in global virtual teams," *J. Manag. Inform. Syst.*, vol. 14, no. 4, pp. 29–64, 1998.
[37] C. Ellis, S. Rein, and S. Jarvenpaa, "Nick experimentation: Selected results concerning the effectiveness of meeting support technology," *J. Manag. Inform. Syst.*, vol. 6, pp. 7–24, 1990.
[38] M. Poole, M. Holmes, and G. DeSanctis, "Conflict management in a computer-supported meeting environment," *Manag. Sci.*, vol. 37, no. 8, pp. 926–953, 1991.
[39] A. Hollingshead, "Communication, learning, and retrieval in transactive memory systems," *J. Exper. Social Psychol.*, vol. 34, pp. 423–442, 1998.
[40] D. Wegner, P. Raymond, and R. Erber, "Transactive memory in close relationships," *J. Personality Social Psychol.*, vol. 61, no. 6, pp. 923–929, 1991.
[41] M. Deutsch and H. Gerard, "A study of normative and informational social influences upon individual judgment," *J. Abnormal Social Psychol.*, vol. 51, pp. 629–636, 1955.
[42] R. M. Kramer, "When the going gets tough: The effects of resource scarcity on group conflict and cooperation," in *Advances in Group Processes*, E. Lawler and B. Markovsky, Eds. Greenwich, CT: JAI, 1989, vol. 7, pp. 151–177.
[43] R. Spears and M. Lea, "Panacea or panopticon? The hidden power in computer-mediated communication," *Commun. Res.*, vol. 21, no. 4, pp. 427–459, 1994.
[44] K. Aquino and A. Reed, "A social dilemma perspective on cooperative behavior in organizations," *Group Organiz. Manag.*, vol. 23, no. 4, pp. 390–413, 1998.
[45] D. Forsyth, *Group Dynamics*, 2nd ed. Pacific Grove, CA: Brooks/Cole, 1990.
[46] J. R. Hackman, "Effects of task characteristics on group products," *J. Exper. Social Psychol.*, vol. 4, pp. 162–187, 1968.
[47] M. E. Shaw, *Group Dynamics: The Psychology of Small Group Behavior*. New York: McGraw-Hill, 1976.
[48] J. March and H. Simon, *Organizations*. New York: Wiley, 1958.
[49] D. Campbell, "Task complexity: A review and analysis," *Acad. Manag. Rev.*, vol. 13, no. 1, pp. 40–52, 1988.
[50] R. Wood, "Task complexity: Definition of a construct," *Organiz. Behavior Human Decision Processes*, vol. 37, pp. 60–82, 1986.
[51] C. W. Hill, "Group versus individual performance: Are $N + 1$ heads better than one," *Psychol. Bull.*, vol. 91, pp. 517–539, 1982.
[52] J. Seta and J. Schkade, "Effects of group size and proximity under cooperative and competitive conditions," *J. Personality Social Psychol.*, vol. 34, pp. 47–53, 1976.

[53] K. Fisher and M. Fisher, *The Distributed Mind*. New York: AMACON, 1998.

[54] L. Haught, "Eliminating barriers to team effectiveness," *Inform. Executive*, vol. 3, no. 2, pp. 7–9, 1999.

[55] K. Propp, "Collective information processing in groups," in *The Handbook of Group Communication Theory and Research*, L. Frey, D. S. Gouran, and M. S. Poole, Eds. Thousand Oaks, CA: Sage, 1999, pp. 225–250.

[56] J. Larson and C. Christiansen, "Groups as problem-solving units: Toward a new meaning of social cognition," *British J. Social Psychol.*, vol. 32, pp. 5–30, 1993.

[57] V. Hinsz, R. Tindale, and D. Vollrath, "The emerging conceptualization of groups as information processors," *Psychol. Bull.*, vol. 121, pp. 260–268, 1997.

[58] R. Hirokawa and D. Scheerhorn, "Communication in faulty group decision-making," in *Communication and Group Decision-Making*, R. Y. Hirokawa and M. S. Poole, Eds. Beverly Hills, CA: Sage, 1986, pp. 63–80.

[59] D. Gouran and R. Hirokawa, "The role of communication in decision-making groups: A functional perspective," in *Communications in Transition: Issues and Debates in Current Research*, M. S. Mander, Ed. New York: Praeger, 1983, pp. 168–185.

[60] D. W. Liang, R. Moreland, and L. Argote, "Group versus individual training and group performance: The mediating role of transactive memory," *Personality Social Psychol. Bull.*, vol. 21, pp. 384–393, 1995.

[61] H. Bertcher, *Group Participation: Techniques for Leaders and Members*, 2nd ed. Thousand Oaks, CA: Sage, 1994.

[62] K. Benne and P. Sheets, "Functional roles of group members," *J. Social Issues*, vol. 4, pp. 41–49, 1948.

[63] T. F. Pettigrew, "The ultimate attribution error: Extending Allport's cognitive analysis of prejudice," *Personality Social Psychol. Bull.*, vol. 46, pp. 461–476, 1979.

[64] C. O'Reilly, D. Caldwell, and W. Barnett, "Work group demography, social integration, and turnover," *Admin. Sci. Quart.*, vol. 34, pp. 21–37, 1989.

[65] B. Haslett and J. Ruebush, "What differences do individual differences in groups make?," in *The Handbook of Group Communication Theory and Research*, L. Frey, D. S. Gouran, and M. S. Poole, Eds. Thousand Oaks, CA: Sage, 1999.

[66] L. Rosenfeld, C. Grant, and J. McCroskey, "Communication apprehension and self-perceived communication competence of academically gifted students," *Commun. Educ.*, vol. 44, pp. 79–87, 1995.

[67] J. McCroskey and M. Beatty, "Communication apprehension and accumulated communication anxiety state experiences: A research note," *Commun. Monographs*, vol. 51, pp. 79–84, 1984.

[68] J. Burgoon, "Unwillingness to communicate as a predictor of small group discussion behaviors and evaluation," *Central States Speech J.*, vol. 28, pp. 122–133, 1977.

[69] C. Anderson and M. Martin, "How argumentativeness, verbal aggressiveness, and communication apprehension affect members' perceptions of cohesion, consensus, and satisfaction in small groups," *Commun. Repts.*, vol. 12, pp. 21–31, 1999.

[70] J. McCroskey and V. Richmond, "Communication apprehension and small group communication," in *Small Group Communication: A Reader*, 6th ed, R. S. Carthart and L. A. Samaovar, Eds. Dubuque, IA: Wm. C. Brown, 1992, pp. 361–374.

[71] ——, "The effects of communication apprehension on the perceptions of peers," *J. Western Speech Commun. Assoc.*, vol. 40, pp. 14–21, 1976.

[72] J. McCroskey, P. Hamilton, and A. Weiner, "The effect of interaction behavior on source credibility, homophily, and interpersonal attraction," *Human Commun. Res.*, vol. 1, pp. 42–52, 1974.

[73] V. Vanderslice, R. Rice, and J. Julian, "The effects of participation in decision-making on worker satisfaction and productivity: An organizational simulation," *J. Appl. Social Psychol.*, vol. 17, pp. 158–170, 1987.

[74] L. Coser, *Continuations in the Study of Social Conflict*. New York: Free Press, 1956.

[75] A. C. Amason, "Distinguishing the effects of functional and dysfunctional conflict on strategic decision-making: Resolving a paradox for top management teams," *Acad. Manag. J.*, vol. 39, pp. 123–148, 1996.
[76] K. A. Jehn, "A qualitative analysis of conflict types and dimensions in organizational groups," *Admin. Sci. Quart.*, vol. 42, no. 3, pp. 530–557, 1997.
[77] ——, "A multimethod examination of the benefits and detriments on intragroup conflict," *Admin. Sci. Quart.*, vol. 40, no. 2, pp. 256–279, 1995.
[78] ——, "Enhancing effectiveness: An investigation of advantages and disadvantages of value based intragroup conflict," *Int. J. Conflict Manag.*, vol. 4, pp. 223–238, 1994.
[79] K. Jehn and J. Chatman, "The influence of proportional and perceptual conflict composition on team performance," *Int. J. Conflict Manag.*, vol. 11, no. 1, pp. 56–73, 2000.
[80] A. Amason and H. Spienza, "The effects of top management team size and interation norms on cognitive and affective conflict," *J. Manag.*, vol. 23, pp. 496–516, 1997.
[81] K. Jehn and P. Shah, "Interpersonal relationships and task performance: An examination of mediating processes in friendship and acquaintance groups," *J. Personality Social Psychol.*, vol. 72, pp. 775–790, 1997.
[82] M. Devries, "High-performance teams: Lessons from the pygmies," *Organiz. Dynamics*, vol. 6, no. 1, pp. 66–76, 1999.
[83] W. E. Watson and L. K. Michaelsen, "Group interaction behaviors that affect group performance on an intellective task," *Group Organiz. Studies*, vol. 13, no. 4, pp. 495–516, 1988.
[84] M. E. Gordan, L. A. Slade, and N. Schmitt, "The 'science of the sophomore' revisited: From conjecture to empiricism," *Acad. Manag. Rev.*, vol. 11, no. 1, pp. 191–207, 1986.
[85] W. Remus, "Graduate students as surrogates for managers in experiments on business decision-making," *J. Bus. Res.*, vol. 14, no. 1, pp. 19–25, 1986.
[86] C. J. G. Gersick, "Time and transition in work teams: Toward a new model of group development," *Acad. Manag. J.*, vol. 31, pp. 9–41, 1988.
[87] C. B. Gibson, "Do they do what they believe the can? Group efficacy and group effectiveness across task cultures," *Acad. Manag. J.*, vol. 42, no. 2, pp. 138–152, 1999.
[88] D. I. Jung and B. J. Avolio, "Effects of leadership style and followers' cultural orientation on performance in group and individual task conditions," *Acad. Manag. J.*, vol. 42, no. 2, pp. 208–218, 1999.
[89] L. Chidambaram, "Relational development in computer-supported groups," *MIS Quart.*, vol. 20, pp. 143–165, 1996.
[90] D. T. Edberg and B. J. Bowman, "User-developed applications: An empirical study of application quality and developer productivity," *J. Manag. Inform. Syst.*, vol. 13, no. 1, pp. 167–185, 1996.
[91] W. W. Huang and K. K. Wei, "An empirical investigation of the effects of group support systems (GSS) and task type on group interactions from an influence perspective," *J. Manag. Inform. Syst.*, vol. 17, no. 2, pp. 181–206, 2000.
[92] B. E. Mennecke and J. S. Valacich, "Information is what you make of it: The influence of group history and computer support on information sharing, decision quality, and member perceptions," *J. Manag. Inform. Syst.*, vol. 15, no. 2, pp. 173–197, 1998.
[93] C. Saunders and S. Miranda, "Information acquisition in group decision making," *Inform. Manag.*, vol. 34, pp. 55–74, 1998.
[94] D. Stone, M. Sivitanides, and A. Magro, "Formalized dissent and cognitive complexity in group processes and performance," *Decision Sci.*, vol. 25, no. 2, pp. 243–261, 1995.
[95] B. Tan, H. Teo, and K. Wei, "Promoting consensus in small decision-making groups," *Inform. Manag.*, vol. 28, no. 4, pp. 251–259, 1995.
[96] D. Leonard and S. Sensiper, "The role of tacit knowledge in group innovation," *Calif. Manag. Rev.*, vol. 40, no. 3, pp. 112–132, 1988.
[97] S. Raudenbush, A. Bryk, Y. Cheong, and R. Congden, *HLM 5: Hierarchical Linear and Nonlinear Modeling*. Lincolnwood, IL: Scientific Software Int., 2000.

[98] D. Deadrick, N. Bennett, and C. Russell, "Using hierarchial linear modeling to examine dynamic performance criteria over time," *J. Manag.*, vol. 23, no. 6, pp. 745–757, 1997.
[99] M. Griffen, "Interaction between individuals and situations: Using HLM procedures to estimate reciprocal relationships," *J. Manag.*, vol. 23, no. 6, pp. 759–773, 1997.
[100] D. Hofmann and M. Gavin, "Centering decisions in hierarchial linear models: Implications for research in organizations," *J. Manag.*, vol. 24, no. 5, pp. 623–641, 1998.
[101] R. Hoyle, J. Georgesen, and J. Webster, "Analyzing data from individuals in groups: The past, the present and the future," *Group Dyn.: Theory, Res., Practice*, vol. 5, no. 1, pp. 41–47, 2001.
[102] K. Mossholder, N. Bennett, and C. Martin, "A multilevel analysis of procedural justice context," *J. Organiz. Beh.*, vol. 19, pp. 131–141, 1998.
[103] B. Pollack, "Hierarchial linear modeling and the 'unit of analysis' problem: A solution for analyzing responses of intact group members," *Group Dyn.: Theory, Res., Practice*, vol. 2, pp. 299–312, 1998.
[104] J. Vancouver, "The application of HLM to the analysis of the dynamic interaction of environment, person, and behavior," *J. Manag.*, vol. 23, no. 6, pp. 795–818, 1997.

Tom L. Roberts is an Assistant Professor of Management Information Systems in the Accounting and Information Systems Department at the University of Kansas. He has published in *IEEESoftware*, IEEE TRANSACTIONS ON SOFTWARE ENGINEERING, IEEE TRANSACTIONS ON ENGINEERING MANAGEMENT, *Information Resource Management Journal*, and several other top MIS journals. His research interests include systems development, networking, and group dynamics.

Paul H. Cheney is a Professor and Chair of the Management Information Systems Department at the University of Central Florida. He has over 40 publications, many of which are in the top MIS journals including *Journal of Management Information System*, *Management Information System Quarterly*, and *Information Systems Research*. His current research is in the areas of "MIS Work Environments" and "Shortage of IT Professionals."

Paul D. Sweeney is a Professor at the University of Dayton in the Management Department. He has published over 30 articles in the areas of organizational behavior especially in the global environment. He is particularly interested in the "differences in perceptions of justice across borders." He formerly taught at the University of Central Florida, Marquette University, and the University of Indiana.

Between Silence and Voice: Communicating in Cross-Functional Project Teams

Linda Loehr

Abstract—**Despite forecasts of the increasing use of cross-functional project teams in industry, too little is known about how such teams function and how they might come to function more effectively. One organization, a small manufacturing firm in the Southeast, and members of a selected cross-functional project team consented to have a researcher present during the life cycle of a single project. Reflections based on the resulting case study highlight three overarching areas of concern in cross-functional designs: first, equity as an evolving blueprint for project-team work; second, trust as the foundation upon which solid progress depends; and third, authority as the visible framework of the process and products of the team's work.**

Introduction

THE past decade has seen a resurgence of interest in work groups and project teams in organizations (see [7], [8], [19], [21], [29], [30], [12]), particularly ad hoc groups assembled for work on limited-term projects (see [23], [15]–[17]). Renewed interest in these project teams originates in the need for organizations to move quickly in response to rapid changes in technologies and increased competition in the global marketplace [34]. Many organizations are restructuring, using groups as basic framing units [1] and turning the diversity of individuals into an agent of change.

The increased use of project teams offers numerous potential contributions to organizational effectiveness. Notable, however, is the potential for communication and decision-making to occur across functions, with authority derived from an appropriate knowledge base rather than solely from organizational rank [34].

Yet some limitations constrain the project model. Functionally diverse specialists often define or frame problems according to their functional specialties [9], [29], individual levels of perceptive ability [14], and world views [22]. The resulting complexity of communication processes can result in "a virtual tangle of interdependent work relationships" [34, p. 84], manifested in unproductive power plays [10], [13], and ineffective documents, the combination of which disarm rather than inform decision makers [34].

Communication training, custom-developed for members of project teams, potentially can offset these limitations. Since the team meeting constitutes the locus of communications in project teams, training designed to enhance the process of communicating issues, negotiating positions, and documenting the progress and the product of the team's work should be tailored for the meeting setting. Yet little field research exists to inform our understanding of the processes cross-functional specialists engage in order to influence their colleagues [5] and reach consensus in group settings. Since a number of scholars predict an increase in the use of project teams in the coming decades (see [24], [11], [1]), theory-building in this area must occur to support the development of appropriate communication training.

Manuscript received October 8, 1990; revised November 15, 1990.
The author is with Northeastern University, Boston, MA 02115.
IEEE Log Number 9042234.

The case for attending to the potential of cross-functional teamwork originates in visions of a more humane and productive workplace: Bennis's [3] early prediction that the increased use of interdisciplinary task forces would topple bureaucracy; Klein's [24] idea that membership in such groups could offset the feelings of powerlessness and isolation triggered by times of turbulence and change; and Drucker's [11] vision of a "new organization" directed by teams of self-directed specialists taking individual and collective responsibility for the linking of knowledge and skills to the "joint performance" [11, p. 49] of the organization. These theorists' collective visions offer hopeful, sensible ideas for people and the organizations they comprise at a time when scarce resources and global competition demand new designs and new approaches.

Unfortunately, these visions do not provide specific blueprints for the construction of those designs. Instead, scholars offer idealistic sketches of self-directed specialists, moving together and apart, working effectively in teams, sharing action-oriented goals and a common vision, and communicating competently. Are such specialists presently at work in the world and available for hire and, if not, how might they be developed?

This paper offers a case analysis of one naturally occurring project team found in an organization working to develop such specialists. In this case, team members expressed varying degrees of dissatisfaction with the project outcome, the organizational process, and, in some instances, both the product and the process of the team's effort. Some team members indicated a loss of faith in the entire project-team concept.

This research proposes to describe and analyze what these functionally diverse team members did as they went about the work of framing problems, communicating with team members, and documenting their work. The findings, deriving from the life cycle of one project, may enhance the development of grounded theory [18], [36] and begin to provide some balance to a body of literature that has been primarily positivist in approach [30]. Additionally, the study may support the development of theory-based, communication training for members of project teams.

Case-study design requires a particular conception of generalizability. Wilson [39] offers the idea of reader or user generalizability, the concept of leaving the application of a study's findings in additional settings to the discretion of the people involved in those settings. Merriam [32] notes that the practice is common in law and medicine, fields in which practitioners determine whether or not one case applies to another. The research findings reported in this study of one cross-functional project team at work in the private sector, if generalized, should be applied in accordance with Wilson [39] and Merriam's [32] guidelines.

The Research Perspective

Since developing grounded theory involves discovering mini-theories in the data rather than "proving" a prior hypothesis, the study required special data-analysis techniques [31]. In quali-

Reprinted from *IEEE Trans. Prof. Comm.*, vol. PC-34, no. 1, pp. 51–56, March 1991.

tative research, data analysis does not consist of data reduction [31]. Rather the analysis of the data, which in qualitative research derives from the participants' multiple perspectives of reality, occurs on an on-going basis [36], [31]. Accordingly, the researcher gathered the data during a prolonged field experience [38], [31] and inductively reconstructed those multiple realities by selecting, grouping, comparing, synthesizing, and interpreting explanations of the situation of interest [25].

Conclusions drawn from this case study are derived from multiple sources: primarily, by the texts provided by the participants' perceptions of cross-functional group work, expressed in their own words in meetings and during in-depth interviews; by selected written documents related to the project, the plant, and the parent company; and, additionally, by the related literature identified during and by the field experience [18], [4].

In the tradition of qualitative research, foreshadowed problems [27] framed anticipated issues of diversity and provided an initial guide for the data collection. In this study, the following questions reflected foreshadowed problems:

- How do team members describe their perceptions of the project task during team meetings?
- How do functional specialties (or educational backgrounds) relate to the problem-setting and problem-solving processes communicated by team members?
- How do project team members function when the ideas of team members are in conflict, particularly in terms of oral and written communication processes (e.g., verbal group interactions, written documentation of work in progress)?
- How do team members use, or respond to, displays of power during the life cycle of the project?

As anticipated, team members did perceive the project task in different ways. Team members' various evolving perceptions of what it meant to be a part of a project team, however, quickly overshadowed the differing perceptions of the project task. In addition to creating the written safety plan, team members faced the multiple tasks of selecting appropriate behaviors for meetings, assuming new levels of authority, and, ultimately, speaking in the new and different voices required in a participatory work setting. Those internal-process tasks involved redefining traditional roles, often the deeply rooted legacies of education, experience, and background. The tendency of team members to define the expectations of the new participatory context by returning to traditional frames of reference complicated the multilevel challenge.

The original foreshadowed problems, while useful, focused on the symptoms rather than the source of difficulties in project-team work. Accordingly, the foreshadowed problems guiding the study required revision to reflect more closely the dynamics occurring in this project team:

- To what degree are cross-functional project-team members meant to be equal contributors when they meet as joint authors of a plan?
- From what source does the authority for equal voice derive? From position? Experience and knowledge? A combination of these attributes? Something else?
- To what extent does each project-team member possess the confidence to tap personal levels of authority in order to make contributions?
- To what degree do the members trust one another to be appropriately receptive to ideas presented? Conversely, to what degree are team members concerned that their ideas will be subject to indifference or ridicule?
- How do team members honor the trust placed in them as representatives by finding ways to offer ideas and to create a plan that will impact the safety of others?
- How do team members construct a document from the ground up if the foundation of the team, trust, is somewhat shaky?
- How are team members accountable to others in the organization if they do not first have a working knowledge of themselves and a fairly clear understanding of the roles they are expected to play?

These questions, and the framing processes driving them, revealed three overarching areas of concern: equity, authority, and trust. Since these interdependent issues involve the creation of a still-experimental organizational work design, the metaphor of building constitutes the framework for the reflections that follow: first, equity as an evolving blueprint for project-team work; second, trust as the foundation upon which solid progress depends; and third, authority as the visible framework of the process and products of the team's work.

Project Teamwork: An Invitation to the Planning Table

For several months, on scheduled meeting days, six members of a fledgling organization put aside their regular duties, their ranks, and, at times, their own points of view, to function as members of a project team. Team members represented every phase of plant operations: management, business support, and technical operations. Their titles—human resource manager, assistant to the human resource manager, operating technicians (there were two), maintenance technician, and graphic artist—bespoke their duties.

As functional specialists, individual team members accepted responsibility for expressing the safety needs and issues of their particular functional areas in a climate of mutual concern. As a group, team members faced the difficult task of assimilating those concerns and creating a safety-awareness program that would cross lines of function and position. As they framed their concerns and worked to develop such a program, team members became something more than functional specialists. Their new duties involved a process more complex than reporting safety concerns and making recommendations to address them. Ultimately, the team had to speak as one voice on the safety issues, first in the form of consensus on the elements of the plan, then in the form of a written document describing that plan and, later, in the form of informal, verbal endorsements of the plan to coworkers.

The task before them was complex and challenging; any group would have found it so. The particular responsibilities inherent in the assignment involved framing safety issues from team members' respective functional areas and assuming new levels of authority in articulating the views captured within those frames. The issue of authority itself became a dilemma as team members exhibited behaviors connoting two different concepts of authority: the traditional idea of authority as a dimension of power and control, derived from position and supported by the organizational hierarchy; and the alternative conception of authority as a natural by-product of knowledge and experience.

Coming to terms with these conflicting conceptions seemed more difficult for participants than coming to terms with fellow team members. In fact, lack of conflict characterized the group, resulting, at times, in premature consensus and a plan devoid of many ideas described during the researcher's interviews with team members. Team members seemed unready to negotiate their positions, to trust their own judgment and ideas when they deviated from those of the team leader. Yet the ideas being tested in their minds and shared in individual interviews revealed critical-thinking skills not often attributed to people in staff-level positions [41]. Having the experience of working in a participatory work setting (in the case of most team members just for one year) seemed to have thrown communication patterns into a state of transition, a place somewhere between silence and voice.

Equity: An Evolving Blueprint for Project-Team Work

Despite their wide variance in educational backgrounds, team members brought a range of highly specialized knowledge and experience to the planning table, not the least of which included varieties of experience in working with people. The combined skills, knowledge, and experience of an organizational psychologist, a trainer, a graphic artist, and three technicians provided a broad base of expertise to tap in the creation of an original safety-awareness program. Yet the complex dynamics of cross-functional teamwork, in this case, precluded the equitable sharing of ideas and expertise.

An important outcome of the examination of the construct of equity in the context of cross-functional, project-team work is a renewed awareness of the inequities that the team concept sustains. These inequities prove particularly distasteful in settings that espouse equity through participation (see [40], [20]). As important as participation can be, it does not ensure team members of equal opportunities to voice their opinions and to have those opinions considered in a meaningful way. In accordance with Witte's [40] "hard" definition, participation means performing actions that affect outcomes. In this case study, nonmanagerial team members privately expressed doubts that their participation could effect real changes. From a different perspective, the team's management representative observed that effective participation in diverse groups does not happen without some kind of sustained training effort. The process of authentic participation involves the use of learned skills.

Achieving equity in team settings begins in a complex, and sometimes painful, process of self-assessment that offers the potential for rapid growth. Until team members can learn self-assessment techniques, the process of adjusting to new and more ambiguous roles is likely to remain incomplete [42]. Through self-assessment, particularly critical during periods of technical or societal change [42], team members potentially can learn to recognize and acknowledge their own capacities for participation. Until then, others may likely resist it (see [40], [20]).

Conversely, those who promise equity through participation—but do not provide opportunities for the development of the necessary skills for full participation—are learning that the costs of unmet expectations can be high (see [40], [20]). Team members discouraged by conflicts between the rhetoric and the reality of equity-based participation may withdraw psychologically, taking with them ideas that could strengthen project work.

An additional skill needed for effective work in teams involves moving beyond the period of self-assessment into the process of connecting with other team members. Both the process of self-assessment and the process of learning to connect provide enabling devices that can support team members' efforts to merge the roles of self and group member. Again, both those who participate in cross-functional teams and those who authorize their creation need to consider the application of this critical skill.

Smith and Berg [35] describe a process of learning what to give up as individuals in order to belong to the group. Key questions, according to Smith and Berg [35] include: "How does a group determine what individuals can and cannot bring into the group except through the 'in-puts' of its members? What does it mean to be 'in'?" [35, p. 89]. The authors suggest that the answers lie in four areas of paradox:

- the paradox of identity, making the connection between individual and group identity and deciding which identity comes first;
- the paradox of involvement, examining the links between participation and withdrawal and considering the source of each behavior;
- the paradox of individuality in a situation requiring the acceptance of multi-individualities to form a meaningful collective; and
- the paradox of boundaries, defining both what the group is and what it is not.

During the course of the project, team members began the difficult process of exploring those areas of paradox, learning that equity does not come by proclamation. Team members limited that exploration, however, because in this case the areas of paradox remained unnamed and undefined. Seemingly, plant managers expected project-team members to navigate these hazy areas of paradox with neither preparations nor provisions.

Without preparation for the complex dynamics of cross-functional teamwork, participants nonetheless face issues of individual and group identity and involvement in future project-team work. If team members can find their individual voices and give names to the internal conflicts their behaviors reveal, the outcomes of grappling with paradoxical issues become potentially positive. As the inequities and inconsistencies in the philosophy and practice of cross-functional teamwork surface, they may provide a consciousness-raising function that could result in the beginnings of system self-correction. Conversely, if team members remain silent, nursing a heightened awareness of the inequities of the system, an increasing disenchantment with the team concept and its proponents may preclude even the possibility of equitable participation in future team experiences.

Mistrust: A Shaky Foundation for Progress

The lack of trust among team members constrained their individual and collective voices, restricting the sharing of knowledge, experience, and opinions. When levels of mistrust supported increasingly inequitable levels of participation, team members expressed varying degrees of mistrust in themselves, their teammates, and the team concept itself. Indications of mistrust among nonmanagerial team members ranged from mistrust of the worth of their ideas to mistrust of the system that required their generation.

While the manager on the team less often than others seemed to question his own ideas and motivations, he did reveal an element of self-doubt during private interviews with the researcher. As the manager questioned the fit between stated beliefs and the actual implementation of those beliefs in the team context, he not only expressed concerns about fellow team members, but also about the long-term success of the team concept itself.

What remained unspoken, even during the manager's periods of soul searching, was an acknowledgment of the power derived from his position as manager and its possible role in undermining the effectiveness of his teammates. Fiorelli's [13] assertion that the ineffectiveness of work teams relates to "primary issues" [13, p. 1] of power and restrictive participation warrants additional consideration. Until team members can come to trust both this manager and others in similar positions to share their power, the effectiveness of nonmanagerial team members may likely be diminished.

The paramount loss of trust among team members affected the team's ability to make decisions and create a project that might have been better than those that any of the members could create alone. At times, the sentiments of project-team members echoed the benefits of cross-functional teamwork described 15 years ago by London and Walsh [26]: the opportunity to synthesize knowledge from a variety of specialty areas, to hasten the process of information sharing, and to produce more original work than would be possible by the members of each specialty area working alone. That philosophy pervaded the team members' initial training; team members indicated that they wanted to believe it. Certainly the plant's innovative, organizational design supported the securing of these benefits. Yet meeting transcripts document a disproportionate emphasis on one member's knowledge, a protracted process of information sharing, and a final product not unremarkably different from safety plans in other manufacturing firms. Cross-functional teamwork, in this case, simply did not fulfill its promise.

Authority: A Divisive Framework for the Process and Products of Project-Team Work

Since this project team crossed lines of position as well as function, team members faced a particular developmental challenge: to create relatively equitable levels of authority for use only in the project-team setting. During team meetings, nonmanagerial team members displayed reluctance in expressing their varying perceptions of the project task and in raising questions about their roles in bringing the project to completion. Even within an organization based on the team concept, members of the management team clearly provided directives. Since one member of the management team served on the project team, team members naturally attended to the reality of the superior/subordinate relationship inherent in the group's design. The divisive elements of such relationships have been discussed in numerous accounts of teams and committees (see [40], [6], and [20]); yet this team and others within the plant continue to employ the design.

Even if the superior/subordinate relationship could have been discarded during project-team meetings, it quite likely would have been resumed when team meetings ended and the manager again assumed his position of authority. Accordingly, the manager operated within his own superior/subordinate relationship, knowing that he would ultimately report the project team's work to the plant manager. Although, as Drucker [11] predicts, middle management shrinks when project teams are in place, upper management supplants its function. The dynamics of dominance and subordination, long a part of our industrial heritage [41], continue to operate.

In this case, the substitution of teams for supervisors resulted in a degree of confusion among team members. Each—the manager included—seemingly did not know the appropriate or acceptable level of authority to exercise. As the uncertainty of nonmanagerial team members stalled progress, the management representative assumed ever-increasing levels of responsibility for directing the project. Team members largely relinquished information responsibility to the manager, reinforcing Drucker's idea that "information responsibility onto oneself is still largely neglected" [11, p. 49]. The imbalances in the use of authority that resulted reinforced existing feelings of inequity and mistrust.

In spite of private protests of these apparent imbalances, as a group the project team worked for relative harmony rather than for shared authority. Apart, individual team members expressed a variety of ideas for the safety-awareness plan that, for the most part, they withheld from team discussions. Only the management representative regularly contributed his ideas for the plan and its implementation. Other team members made comments and suggestions based on the ideas he initiated, then privately expressed dissatisfaction with their levels of involvement. Their willingness to comply with the manager's ideas despite their limited involvement and conflicting views aligns with Mayo's [28] observation: workers given an opportunity to express their views may submit more readily to authority.

The decision to work for harmony rather than shared authority conceivably can be linked to three factors: 1) an awareness that group membership brings some benefits along with its corresponding frustrations [35], 2) an instinctive fear of conflict [24], and 3) the initial training that stressed the value of consensus rather than the exercise of shared authority.

Klein's [24] assertion that people offset feelings of powerlessness and isolation by membership in groups may account for the desire for group harmony despite the reality of imbalanced power or authority sharing within the group. As long as participants maintain group membership through cooperation and relative harmony, the psychological function Klein suggests is, at least for the short term, served. The unspoken fear that conflict might destroy the team and, thereby, remove the psychological benefits of group membership may prevent the risk-taking necessary to stake the necessary claims for authority. As Pearson [33] notes, conflict originating in both personal and professional disagreements does hamper a team's effectiveness. Naturally, organizations employing the team concept would work to keep conflict levels low.

While project-team members shared a number of common goals, they did not seem to know how simultaneously to maintain harmony and to tap areas of personal authority in order to achieve those goals. These dual areas of ineffectiveness reflect researchers' concern with the lack of substantial theoretical framework for group development in general [15], [30] and cross-functional group work in particular [29].

Team members, without a doubt, shared the goal of creating an environment in which all employees could work safely. The purpose of the project, according to each meeting's agenda, focused on promoting the awareness of the need for each employee to assume an appropriate level of responsibility for creating that environment and maintaining safe operations. Team members described their shared common vision as a working environment encouraging safe practices, preventing injuries, and generating pride in the organization.

Team members, however, did not share a common vision of the ways in which that environment could be created. Team members had been taught to respond positively to the ideas of others, to disagree in a constructive manner, and to work for consensus. Observations of team members in interaction with one another during meetings indicated that they had learned most of these lessons well. But somehow responding positively to the ideas of teammates became mixed up with disagreeing in a constructive manner. Team members, with the exception of the management representative, held back major ideas or simply did not present them fully. Overall, team members' behaviors in meetings supported McCorcle's [29] linkage of ineffective team performance to a lack of knowledge of how cross-functional teams operate.

Certainly, team members had a rudimentary knowledge of conflict management. When team members disagreed in small ways, they prefaced statements of disagreement in nonconfrontational ways. When team members offered counterarguments, however, only the management representative stood his ground. Other team members seemed either uncertain that their ideas had sufficient merit or simply felt unwilling or unable to state them, much less negotiate them. Their reactions represent a natural response to the process of co-optation [40].

Team members, after all, had been taught in other contexts to follow the guidelines suggested by the manager and to work for consensus. Without a final consensus, there would have been no completed project. Yet in making the many decisions the developing project required, consensus seemed premature on many occasions. Periods of idea generation too quickly turned into sessions of idea evaluation with the management representative providing the appraisals.

Witte [40, p. 79] notes that "worker representatives" require time to think through their ideas before presenting them in groups of which managers are a part. Certainly, with meetings scheduled late in the day before and after shifts facing heavy production schedules, time posed a constraint. Yet, the team existed to prevent longer and more serious periods of lost time when injuries occurred. The team had been created as a catalyst in preventing both injuries and lost time.

Team members secured harmony at a cost: reduced project quality and lost time. As Zuboff [41] suggests, obedience can be dysfunctional when tasks involve intellective skills. Premature consensus in this case represents a special strain of dysfunctional obedience. The project resulted in a safety-incentive plan original only in the sense of its particular combination of features found in similar plans characteristic of the manufacturing industry. The management representative attributed the plan to the hard work and efforts of the entire team, heartily endorsing the product and process. Most of the other team members, speaking privately in interviews with the researcher, expressed more tentative endorsements of the plan; two members indicated that they felt the plan had only a limited chance for success.

The project team submitted the project as a written document six weeks after the date originally targeted for its completion; the plant manager scheduled the safety plan for kick-off two weeks later. The prompt implementation of a project requiring the selection and purchase of special support materials gave at least circumstantial backing to one team member's suggestion that the plant managers had predetermined the safety plan before the project began. Whether or not that observation was accurate, the management representative on the team, from the beginning, orchestrated consensus for a rewards plan in accordance with Witte's [40] description of co-optation: the manager obtained consensus by combining skill in persuasion, the authority of position, and access to information.

Each of the members of the team expressed profound relief when the project ended. Several team members indicated that they would use what they had learned from this experience to contribute more effectively in future projects, a reflection of the development of epistemic authority [2] among nonmanagerial team members.

Several team members indicated that they would prefer trying other configurations of group representation in the future. Crossing lines of specialty, they indicated, enhanced the team's efforts; crossing lines of position did not. It is interesting to note the nonmanagerial team members' closing assessments of the project focused on variables—exercising choice about procedures—in this case, the most neglected aspect of the job-design variables suggested by Witte [40].

Ultimately, the safety-project team tapped the authority (i.e., the knowledge and experience) of each functional specialist, but fell short of realizing the true collective potential of the team. The management representative served as a resource linker and a team facilitator, describing options, contacting vendors, and raising issues of implementation procedures and budgeting considerations. According to their comments, team members particularly valued the perspective and experience of the operating technicians and the maintenance technician. However, without the evolution of shared authority, team members experienced difficulties developing an authentic sense of community, managing the authority derived from their particular areas of knowledge and experience, and coming to share ownership of the project.

Team members who do not develop a shared sense of community and authority risk remaining captive to Ball's [2] emotivist view of authority. As Ball notes, from the emotivist perspective, feelings of approval or disapproval provide the means of distinguishing between legitimate and illegitimate authority. Team members dominated by the emotivist view are more likely to comply with traditional authority even when they brand authority illegitimate. It follows that such actions increase the likelihood of team members losing faith in themselves, their coworkers, and the team concept.

Yet if the team concept does not succeed, its loss will likely be remembered. As one team member privately mused, "Even if it fails, at least [I was] there when we tried it." If team members' doubts remain largely unarticulated, managers may avoid addressing them. Until team members follow the blueprint of equity, secure the foundation of trust, and establish a framework of shared authority, the new organizational structure of shared involvement and mutual gains cannot be expected to stand.

Reflective Summary

In this case, the fragmented, early training of team members did not seem to provide enough support for effective project-team work. The ideas expressed by project-team members in private interviews with the researcher indicated that, despite their frustration, team members wanted to participate and hoped to learn to do so more effectively.

Walton [37] describes the commitment approach to work design as largely conceived and delivered without a clearly articulated philosophical base. The grounded theory that may develop from this case study offers a means of beginning to focus on the assumptions and basic values and beliefs upon which project-team work is based. Such a focus can potentially inform the development of theory-based communication training for members of future project teams, training that may lessen the distance between silence and voice.

References

[1] L. M. Applegate, J. I. Cash, Jr., and D. Q. Mills, "Information

technology and tomorrow's manager," *Harvard Business Rev.*, vol. 88, no. 6, pp. 128–136, 1988.
[2] T. Ball, "Authority and conceptual change," in *Authority Revisited,* J. R. Rennock and J. W. Chapman, Eds. New York: New York University Press, 1987, pp. 39–58.
[3] W. G. Bennis, "Organizational developments and the fate of bureaucracy," *Transaction*, vol. 2, pp. 31–35, 1965.
[4] R. C. Bogdan and S. N. Biklen, *Qualitative Research for Education: An Introduction to Theory and Methods.* Boston, MA: Allyn and Bacon, 1982.
[5] S. Chase, J. H. Wright, and R. Ragade, "Decision making in an interdisciplinary team," *Behavioral Sci.,* vol. 26, pp. 206–215, 1981.
[6] E. Cohen-Rosenthal and C. E. Burton, *Mutual Gains: A Guide to Union-Management Cooperation.* New York: Praeger, 1987.
[7] T. G. Cummings, "Designing effective work groups," in *Handbook of Organizational Design: Vol. 2*, P. C. Nystrom, III and W. H. Starbuck, Eds. New York: Oxford University Press, 1981, pp. 250–271.
[8] —, "Self-regulating work groups: A socio-technical synthesis," *Acad. Management Rev.,* vol. 3, pp. 625–634, 1978.
[9] D. Dearborn and H. Simon, "Selective perception: A note on the departmental identification of executives," *Sociometry*, vol. 21, pp. 140–144, 1958.
[10] P. C. Dinsmore, "Whys and why-nots of matrix management," in *Matrix Management Systems Handbook*, D. I. Cleland, Ed. New York: Van Nostrand Reinhold, 1984, pp. 394–411.
[11] P. F. Drucker, "The coming of the new organization," *Harvard Business Rev.,* vol. 66, no. 1, pp. 45–53, 1988.
[12] P. H. Ephross and T. V. Vassil, *Groups that Work: Structure and Process.* New York: Columbia University Press, 1988.
[13] J. S. Fiorelli, "Power in work groups: Team members' perspectives," *Human Relations,* vol. 41, pp. 1–12, 1988.
[14] S. Fiske and P. Linville, "What does the schema concept buy us?" *Personality and Social Psychol. Bull.,* vol. 6, pp. 543–557, 1980.
[15] C. G. Gersick, "Life cycles of ad hoc task groups: Time, transitions, and learning in teams," Ph.D. dissertation, Yale Univ., 1985, and *Dissertation Abstracts International*, vol. 46, 1742B, 1984.
[16] —, "Time and transition in work teams: Toward a new model of group development," *Acad. Management J.,* vol. 31, pp. 9–41, 1988.
[17] —, "Marking time: Predictable transitions in task groups," *Acad. Management J.,* vol. 32, pp. 274–309, 1989.
[18] B. G. Glaser and A. L. Strauss, *The Discovery of Grounded Theory: Strategies for Qualitative Research.* Chicago: Aldine, 1967.
[19] P. S. Goodman and Associates, Eds. *Designing Effective Work Groups.* San Francisco, CA: Jossey-Bass, 1986.
[20] G. J. Grenier, *Inhuman Relations: Quality Circles and Anti-Unionism in American Industry.* Philadelphia: Temple University Press, 1988.
[21] J. R. Hackman, "The design of work teams," in *Handbook of Organizational Behavior,* J. W. Lorsch, Ed. Englewood Cliffs, NJ: Prentice-Hall, 1987, pp. 315–342.
[22] R. Herden and M. Lyles, "Individual attributes and the problem conceptualization process," *Human Syst. Management,* vol. 2, pp. 272–284, 1981.
[23] H. Kerzner, *Project Management: A Systems Approach to Planning, Scheduling, and Controlling,* 2nd ed. New York: Van Nostrand, 1984.
[24] C. B. Klein, "Group work: 1985 and 2001," *J. Specialists in Group Work,* vol. 10, pp. 88–91, 1985.
[25] Y. S. Lincoln and E. G. Guba, *Naturalistic Inquiry.* Beverly Hills, CA: Sage, 1985.
[26] M. London and W. B. Walsh, "The development and application of a model of long term group process for the study of interdisciplinary teams," *JSAS Catalog of Selected Documents in Psychol.,* vol. 5, p. 188, 1975.
[27] B. Malinowski, *Argonauts of the Western Pacific.* London: Routledge, 1922.
[28] E. Mayo, *The Social Problems of an Industrial Civilization.* Boston: Harvard University Graduate School of Business Administration, 1945.
[29] M. D. McCorcle, "Critical issues in the functioning of interdisciplinary groups," *Small Group Behavior,* vol. 13, pp. 291–310, 1982.
[30] J. E. McGrath, *Groups: Interaction and Performance.* Englewood Cliffs, NJ: Prentice-Hall, 1984.
[31] J. H. McMillan and S. Schumacher, *Research in Education: A Conceptual Introduction,* 2nd ed. Glenview, IL: Scott, Foresman, 1989.
[32] S. B. Merriam, *Case Study Research in Education: A Qualitative Approach.* San Francisco, CA: Jossey-Bass, 1989.
[33] P. H. Pearson, "The interdisciplinary team process: or the professionals' tower of Babel," *Developmental Medicine and Child Neurol.,* vol. 25, pp. 390–395, 1983.
[34] T. M. Skelton, "Designing communication systems for decentralized organizations: A new role for technical communicators," *IEEE Trans. Professional Commun.,* vol. 33, pp. 83–88, 1990.
[35] K. K. Smith and D. N. Berg, *Paralysis of Group Life: Understanding Conflict, Paralysis, and Movement in Group Dynamics.* San Francisco, CA: Jossey-Bass, 1987.
[36] A. L. Strauss, *Qualitative Analysis for Social Scientists.* Cambridge, MA: Cambridge University Press, 1987.
[37] R. Walton, "From control to commitment," *Harvard Business Rev.*, vol. 63, pp. 76–84, 1985.
[38] W. F. Whyte, *Learning from the Field: A Guide from Experience.* Beverly Hills, CA: Sage, 1984.
[39] S. Wilson, "Explorations of the usefulness of case study evaluations," *Evaluation Quarterly,* vol. 3, no. 4, pp. 446–459, 1979.
[40] J. F. Witte, *Democracy, Authority, and Alienation in Work: Workers' Participation in an American Corporation.* Chicago: University of Chicago Press, 1980.
[41] S. Zuboff, *In the Age of the Smart Machine: The Future of Work and Power.* New York: Basic Books, 1984.
[42] L. A. Zurcher, Jr., "The mutable self: A self-concept for social change," in *The Planning of Change,* 4th ed, W. G. Bennis, K. D. Benne, and R. Chin, Eds. New York: Holt, Rinehart and Winston, pp. 439–446, 1985.

Linda Loehr received the B.S. degree in English from Radford University, the M.A. degree in English from Virginia Commonwealth University, and the Ph.D. degree in human resource development also from Virginia Commonwealth. She has worked as a consultant with several corporations and is currently an Assistant Professor at Northeastern University, Boston, MA, where she teaches in the Middler Year Writing Program and in the Master of Technical and Professional Writing Program.

A Dialogue Technique to Enhance Electronic Communication in Virtual Teams

—BERNARD C. Y. TAN,
KWOK-KEE WEI,
WAYNE W. HUANG,
AND GUET-NGOH NG

Abstract—*In virtual teams, members are physically distributed and often have not met each other in person. They work together and share information via electronic communication. To address business problems in a timely way, virtual teams must quickly become effective upon formation. However, prior studies have found that virtual teams are ineffective initially because electronic communication does not facilitate building of shared understanding among team members. This study proposes a dialogue technique that facilitates building of shared understanding in virtual teams. Results from an experiment showed that virtual teams which used this technique had better relational development and decision outcome than those which did not. Moreover, these differences remained over time. Therefore, the dialogue technique appears to be useful for helping virtual teams become effective quickly so as to address business problems without unnecessary delays.*

Index Terms—*Decision outcome, dialogue technique, electronic communication, relational development, virtual teams.*

Manuscript received August 10, 1999; revised November 3, 1999.
B. C. Y. Tan and K.-K. Wei are with the Department of Information Systems, National University of Singapore, Singapore 119260 Republic of Singapore (email: btan@comp.nus.edu.sg).
W. W. Huang is with the School of Information Systems, University of New South Wales, Sydney, NSW 2052, Australia.
G.-N. Ng is with the Infocom Development Authority of Singapore, Singapore 118253, Republic of Singapore.
IEEE PII S 0361-1434(00)04486-6.

In today's highly turbulent business world, organizations are constantly seeking new business concepts to improve performance. One emerging concept is that of virtual teams [1]. Many virtual teams are formed on a project basis so as to tap the knowledge of a physically distributed work force. Members of virtual teams, who have often not met each other in person, come together to solve business problems and then disband when the work has been completed. Their work is facilitated by electronic communication, which allowed them to share knowledge and information [2]–[4].

Prior research has demonstrated that physically distributed virtual teams tend to be less effective than conventional face-to-face teams initially. However, this difference in effectiveness tends to disappear as team members develop shared understanding over time [5]–[7]. Nevertheless, if virtual teams are to address business problems in a timely fashion, they must quickly become effective upon formation. Therefore, means to enhance the initial performance of virtual teams can benefit many organizations.

This study proposes a dialogue technique to help virtual teams overcome their initial lack of performance. Based on dialogue theory [8], [9], this technique can assist newly formed virtual teams to rapidly develop shared understanding. By speeding up the relational development of virtual teams, this technique can potentially enable virtual teams to quickly become effective in carrying out their work so as to attain good decision outcome. This study employs an experiment, involving 75 subjects, to assess the usefulness of the proposed dialogue technique.

Reprinted from *IEEE Trans. Prof. Comm.*, vol. PC-43, no. 2, pp. 153–165, June 2000.

Since interventions into team processes have been found to vary in impact over time [5], [10], [11], the proposed dialogue technique is tested in a longitudinal experiment to see if it remains valuable to virtual teams over time.

DIALOGUE TECHNIQUE

Attaining shared understanding is critical to effective teamwork. To have shared understanding, team members need to know the tacit and explicit rules with which each other makes decisions. But before they can engage in a meaningful dialogue to discuss these rules, team members have to bring out the tacit rules that sometimes exist below the conscious level. Dialogue theory [8], [9] provides some suggestions on how team members can discuss their tacit and explicit decision rules, and come to an agreement. Literature on mental models [12] offers a means with which team members can surface their tacit decision rules for mutual scrutiny.

Mental Models Mental models encompass the ingrained frames of reference, generalizations, and images that reflect human understanding of the world. These models are the hidden bases for tacit decision rules [12]. Differences in mental models can cause each team member to have vastly different tacit decision rules. This is often manifested in the form of disagreements during teamwork and inability of team members to understand the perspectives of each other. To overcome these problems, team members can engage in the processes of self-reflection and inquiry [12]. During "self-reflection," each team member will trace his or her reasons and assumptions behind each decision made. A collection of such reasons and assumptions will help the team member to construct his or her underlying mental model and tacit decision rules. During "inquiry," each team member will subject his or her mental model to rigorous scrutiny by others. Shared understanding is possible if a team mental model emerges [12].

Dialogue Theory Dialogue theory offers suggestions on how team mental models can be developed. A dialogue is a sustained collective inquiry into everyday experience that people typically take for granted [9]. Its objective is to create a setting where people are more aware of the context surrounding their experience and more conscious of the thought processes that give rise to the experience.

During a dialogue session, team members bring with them a wide range of tacit differences in perspectives. This collection of different assumptions and beliefs in a team, which is rooted in different mental models, is termed a container [9]. When making decisions, the many perspectives in the container can bring about deadlocks and conflicts. If this persists and team members start displaying defensive behavior, shared understanding cannot be achieved [13] and relational development in the team can be adversely affected. Therefore, a more constructive way to manage the container of perspectives is to understand and then reconcile the different perspectives [9]. This can be achieved through a three-step process of surfacing assumptions, explaining assumptions, and reconciling assumptions [8].

When "surfacing assumptions," each team member carries out self-reflection to construct his or her mental model and tacit decision rules [12]. When "explaining assumptions," each team member illustrates his or her mental model to others, and invites others to scrutinize and help refine his or her mental model. By doing so, team members can see the bias and subtleties behind the thinking process of each other. When "reconciling assumptions," each team member picks elements from his or her mental model that are critical to the achievement of team goals. Elements commonly chosen by team members are then combined into a team mental model. At this stage, team members do not debate about whose mental model is superior. Instead, they build a common mental model that facilitates shared understanding. The more a team has achieved this, the easier it is for the team to reach a collective decision, and the more likely the decision will be implemented in the way the team wants [8]. With a clear focus, the power of the team can now be compared to a laser (a very intense and coherent beam) as opposed to an unfocused beam of light [8].

A Proposed Dialogue Technique Based on the preceding and other related literature on team building, a dialogue technique to facilitate shared understanding in virtual teams is proposed. The technique comprises three stages: small talk, infinite container, and laser generation. In the small talk stage, team members provide background information about themselves (e.g., name, gender, education, and hobbies) and share jokes [14]. The purpose of such informal and light conversation is to help team members to put aside their formal roles and mentalities [15] so as to communicate more openly with each other.

In the infinite container stage, team members list what they consider to be good communication practices (e.g., a clear goal, mutual respect, mutual complements, and no flaming) [16], [3]. They then construct their mental models and surface their tacit beliefs by recalling past experiences that cause them to list these practices. Next, team members share their mental models and clarify all questions raised. They also help each other to refine these mental models. Criticisms and defensive behavior are strongly discouraged. This stage has been termed infinite container because team members can contribute infinitely to the container of perspectives.

In the "laser generation" stage, team members collate their critical past experiences to build a team mental model that encompasses all positive communication practices to be adopted during teamwork. This model serves as team norms to guide future interaction and activities of the team. This stage has been termed laser generation because focused team norms are developed. Team members must be reminded that in the course of their teamwork, they can employ a similar approach (especially the second and third stages of this technique) to reconcile differences in opinions when these emerge.

Research Hypotheses

Virtual teams work together through electronic communication. Very often, team members may not have met each other in person. This is especially true in cases where big organizations assemble knowledgeable employees from different locations into virtual teams to address business issues. Because team members know little about each other and often do not have a history of working together, new virtual teams are typified by a lack of shared understanding. Electronic communication, where immediacy of feedback is lacking and range of cues is restricted, is not likely to encourage team members to share opinions openly and informally [17]. This may hinder attainment of shared understanding. Hence, virtual teams usually need to work together for a period of time before team members become open to and comfortable with each other so as to develop shared understanding [5], [7].

The dialogue technique can potentially facilitate shared understanding in virtual teams. Yet the impact of this technique may be moderated by the amount of time that virtual teams have spent working together. Hence, this study examines the impact of the dialogue technique and time (independent variables) on team relational development and decision outcome (dependent variables). Two aspects of relational development that are studied are team cohesion and team collaboration. "Team cohesion" is the degree of closeness that members feel for each other [18]. "Team collaboration" is the extent to which members can openly communicate and help each other to overcome obstacles and find solutions [19]. Given that many business issues confronting virtual teams do not have objective correct answers [20], two aspects of decision outcome that are examined are perceived decision quality and decision satisfaction. "Perceived decision quality" is the degree to which members think that their team decision is good. "Decision satisfaction" is the extent that members are happy with their team decision.

Team Relational Development

Members of new virtual teams bring their own unique perspectives into meetings. However, if new virtual teams start by employing the dialogue technique (via electronic communication) to systematically analyze and reconcile differences in perspectives, they may be able to attain shared understanding quickly [9]. With a common team mental model as a bond, team members should feel closer to each other [21], [22]. Having understood how each other thinks, team members should also be more willing and able to communicate freely and help each other [23], [19]. Therefore, virtual teams that use the dialogue technique are likely to have better team cohesion and team collaboration than virtual teams that do not use this technique during the initial working episodes.

Virtual teams that start off without the dialogue technique are likely to be slow in resolving their differences. They may need more interaction before they can overcome the restrictions of electronic communication to achieve shared understanding. However, after working together for some time, such teams have been reported to experience closeness [7], [24] and be able to break down communication barriers [5]. Thus, over time, virtual teams that do not use the dialogue technique may not be disadvantageous in terms of team cohesion and team collaboration.

H1a: Initially, virtual teams that use the dialogue technique will have higher team cohesiveness than virtual teams that do not use the dialogue technique.

H1b: Over time, virtual teams that use the dialogue technique will have the same team cohesiveness as virtual teams that do not use the dialogue technique.

H2a: Initially, virtual teams that use the dialogue technique will have higher team collaboration than virtual teams that do not use the dialogue technique.

H2b: Over time, virtual teams that use the dialogue technique will have the same team collaboration as virtual teams that do not use the dialogue technique.

Team Decision Outcome When team cohesion is high, team members tend to have strong motivation and morale [25]. They may work harder on their tasks, thereby arriving at better decisions [26]. Research has demonstrated that team cohesion and team performance are often correlated [27], [28]. A meta-analysis by Evans and Dion [29] confirms this observation. When team collaboration is high, team members tend to have greater synergy [25]. Their more effective information exchange may cause them to understand their tasks better and generate more creative solutions, thereby leading to better decisions. Team members who make better decisions are likely to report higher perceived decision quality [30]. Therefore, conditions that promote team cohesion and team collaboration are likely to raise perceived decision quality.

Members of cohesive teams tend to engage in more social interactions and view mutual opinions positively [26]. When making decisions, all team members are likely to participate actively so that their views are incorporated in team decisions. Since they contribute to the team decisions, team members are likely to be more satisfied with these decisions [26]. In collaborative teams, members actively build on and refine the ideas of each other when working on their tasks. This is because they have a common direction guided by shared understanding [31]. Team members are likely to be more satisfied with team decisions arising from such team synergy [32]. Therefore, conditions that promote team cohesion and team collaboration are also likely to raise decision satisfaction.

- H3a: Initially, virtual teams that use the dialogue technique will have higher perceived decision quality than virtual teams that do not use the dialogue technique.
- H3b: Over time, virtual teams that use the dialogue technique will have the same perceived decision quality as virtual teams that do not use the dialogue technique.
- H4a: Initially, virtual teams that use the dialogue technique will have higher decision satisfaction than virtual teams that do not use the dialogue technique.
- H4b: Over time, virtual teams that use the dialogue technique will have the same decision satisfaction as virtual teams that do not use the dialogue technique.

RESEARCH METHODOLOGY

The research hypotheses were tested using a longitudinal laboratory experiment with dialogue technique and time (a repeated measure) as independent variables.

Subjects A total of 75 information systems undergraduates voluntarily participated in this study. When doing their coursework, these subjects used electronic mails to communicate with instructors and with each other, to work on team assignments (shared documents and files), and to hand in and receive comments on their assignments. Also, as part of their coursework, these subjects worked on more than half of all their projects in teams (rather than individuals). Hence, these subjects had extensive experience using electronic mails and working in project teams. Their average age was 21. About half were males and half were females.

The subjects were randomly assigned to virtual teams of five members each. This team size was used because many decision teams in organizations have this size [33] and studies involving virtual teams have commonly used this size [34], [35]. The random assignment of subjects to teams helped to control for differences due to subject characteristics [36]. Eight teams used the dialogue technique while seven teams did not. Subjects revealed their demographic details and experience by completing a short questionnaire at the beginning of this study. T-tests showed that subjects under both treatments (with and without the dialogue technique) did not differ significantly in terms of age, experience using electronic mails, and experience working in project teams. A Mann–Whitney test revealed that the gender ratio of subjects had no significant difference across both treatments.

Throughout this study, members of virtual teams were not allowed to meet face-to-face. To reduce the possibility of this happening, subjects were explicitly instructed not to reveal their real names and electronic mail addresses to their teammates. Instead, they communicated using specially assigned electronic mail addresses when carrying out their tasks. Interviews with subjects conducted at the end of this study revealed that about 5% of subjects could identify only one of their teammates while no subjects could identify two or more of their teammates.

Tasks All the four tasks were adopted from [6]. For each task, each virtual team was to function as the board of directors of a hypothetical international wine-making company. Their role was to analyze business situations and make strategic decisions for the company. For the first task, team members had to resolve the problem of poor image that had plagued the company. For the second task, team members had to decide on how best to increase the product line of the company. For the third task, team members had to fight the threat of an unfriendly takeover attempt by a rival company. For the last task, team members had to work out a diversification strategy for the company to expand its operations to new places.

Such preference tasks (without correct answers) are critical because management teams are often confronted with such tasks [20], [36] and an increasing number of management teams are virtual in nature [37]. When completing each task, team members typically began by reading the business case and engaging in general discussion. Next, they would put their ideas together into alternative solutions and discuss these alternative solutions. Finally, they would select an alternative solution as the team decision through a ranking process.

Dialogue Technique In this study, all communication among team members was carried out using the PINE electronic mail software running on Unix operating system. Within such a setting, two treatments were compared: virtual teams that used the dialogue technique and virtual teams that did not use the dialogue technique. For the former treatment, each virtual team began with a warm-up session held in a different place but same time setting. During this session, team members completed a warm-up task on environmental pollution, read about the proposed dialogue technique (see Dialogue Technique, A Proposed Dialogue Technique), and applied the technique to develop a team mental model on good communication practices. The experimental administrator ensured that each team practiced the dialogue technique and answered all questions raised by team members. For the latter treatment, each virtual team also began with a warm-up session held in a different place but same time setting. They completed the same warm-up task on environmental pollution. However, instead of reading and applying the proposed dialogue technique, team members were given the same amount of time to engage in casual conversation on good communication practices. The experimental administrator observed that, although each team attempted to build some shared understanding, none of these efforts came close to the proposed dialogue technique. Regardless of treatment, each warm-up session lasted for about two hours.

Time A week after the warm-up session, all virtual teams (with or without the dialogue technique) carried out a series of four tasks (see Research Methodology, Tasks) in a different place and different time setting. Teams were given one week to complete each task. There was a one-week break between tasks. All communication among team members took place via electronic mail. Team members were not required to be online simultaneously. Instead, they could access their electronic mails at their own discretion and convenience. Such a mode of

TABLE I
QUESTIONS MEASURING DEPENDENT VARIABLES

Construct	Questions
Team cohesion (Scale: 5-point interval)	
Cohesion1	The way team members get along together is: (extremely poorly … extremely well)
Cohesion2	The way team members work together is: (extremely poorly … extremely well)
Cohesion3	The way team members help each other is: (extremely poorly … extremely well)
Team collaboration (Scale: 5-point interval)	
Collaboration1	You trust your team members enough to openly share information: (not at all … to a very great extent)
Collaboration2	You trust your team members to act responsibly in their tasks: (not at all … to a very great extent)
Perceived decision quality (Scale: 7-point interval)	
Quality1	The overall quality of the discussion is: (poor … good)
Quality2	The outcome of the discussion is: (unsatisfactory … satisfactory)
Quality3	The issues explored in the discussion are: (trivial … substantial)
Quality4	The manner in which team members examine the issues is: (non-constructive … constructive)
Quality5	The movement of team members toward the conclusion is: (insignificant … significant)
Decision satisfaction (Scale: 5-point interval)	
Satisfaction1	To what extent do you feel responsible for the team decision? (not at all … to a very great extent)
Satisfaction2	To what extent does the team decision reflect your inputs? (not at all … to a very great extent)
Satisfaction3	To what extent do you feel committed to the team decision? (not at all … to a very great extent)

operation is typical of virtual teams in actual organizations, especially those that span geographical distances and time zones [37]. On average, each team member spent four hours throughout the week to complete each task. T-tests showed that time spent by team members for each task did not differ significantly across both treatments (with or without the dialogue technique).

Pretreatment relational development and decision outcome measures were taken by asking team members to fill out a questionnaire (see Research Methodology, Dependent Variables) after their warm-up task. T-tests revealed that teams assigned to both treatments (with or without the dialogue technique) did not differ significantly in all these measures. Initial relational development and performance outcome measures were captured by asking team members to complete the questionnaire (see Research Methodology, Dependent Variables) after their first task. The relational development and performance outcome measures of virtual teams over time were captured by asking team members to complete the questionnaire (see Research Methodology, Dependent Variables) after their last task.

Dependent Variables Table I summarizes the questions used to measure each dependent variable. Team cohesion was measured with three questions from [18]. Team collaboration was assessed with two questions from [19]. Five questions from [30] were used to measure perceived decision quality and three questions from [38] were used to gauge decision satisfaction. All the original anchors and scales were retained because these questions had been thoroughly tested by empirical studies in social psychology and information systems.

DATA ANALYSIS

A 5% level of significance was used for all statistical tests.

Validity and Reliability Data for the dependent variables, collected after the first meeting and again after the last meeting, were subjected to validity and reliability analyses. Tables II and III show the results of factor analyses for data collected after the first and last meeting, respectively. For both analyses, each dependent variable corresponded to a factor with an eigenvalue exceeding 1. Moreover, each question loaded highly on its intended dependent variable. Thus, all the dependent variables had construct validity [39]. Cronbach's alpha for the dependent variables are recorded in Table IV. All the dependent variables satisfied [41] criteria for reliability at 0.7.

Hypotheses Tests Since some dependent variables were

TABLE II
RESULTS OF FACTOR ANALYSIS AFTER FIRST MEETING

Question	Factor 1	Factor 2	Factor 3	Factor 4
Quality1	0.77			
Quality2	0.84			
Quality3	0.67			
Quality4	0.74			
Quality5	0.85			
Cohesion1		0.77		
Cohesion2		0.83		
Cohesion3		0.79		
Satisfaction1			0.81	
Satisfaction2			0.75	
Satisfaction3			0.65	
Collaboration1				0.88
Collaboration2				0.75
Eigenvalue	3.45	2.37	1.74	1.59
Variance (%)	26.5	18.3	13.4	12.3
Cumulative variance (%)	26.5	44.8	58.2	70.5

correlated, a MANOVA test involving all independent and dependent variables was carried out. Results revealed significant main effects due to dialogue technique ($F = 7.07$, $p < 0.01$) and time ($F = 4.91$, $p < 0.01$). With these significant results, separate ANOVA tests could be performed for each dependent variable. All dependent variables could meet homogeneity and normality requirements of the ANOVA test. Table V records the descriptive statistics of all dependent variables. Table VI shows the results of ANOVA tests for all dependent variables.

H1a, H1b, H2a, and H2b predicted interactions between the dialogue technique and time, whereby teams using and not using the dialogue technique were expected to differ in relational development initially but not over time. The lack of interactions for team cohesion ($F = 0.26$, $p =$ n.s.) and team collaboration ($F = 0.22$, $p =$ n.s.) suggested that these hypotheses were not supported. Instead, both dialogue technique ($F = 4.34$, $p < 0.05$) and time ($F = 5.50$, $p < 0.03$) had significant main effects on team cohesion. Virtual teams that used the dialogue technique had consistently stronger team cohesion than virtual teams that did not. Over time, team cohesion also increased significantly with or without the dialogue technique. Dialogue technique also had a significant main effect on team collaboration ($F = 4.83$, $p < 0.04$). Virtual teams that used the dialogue technique reported consistently better

TABLE III
RESULTS OF FACTOR ANALYSIS AFTER LAST MEETING

Question	Factor 1	Factor 2	Factor 3	Factor 4
Quality1	0.76			
Quality2	0.79			
Quality3	0.72			
Quality4	0.70			
Quality5	0.67			
Cohesion1		0.91		
Cohesion2		0.90		
Cohesion3		0.87		
Satisfaction1			0.84	
Satisfaction2			0.88	
Satisfaction3			0.68	
Collaboration1				0.73
Collaboration2				0.89
Eigenvalue	3.15	2.70	2.14	1.78
Variance (%)	24.2	20.8	16.5	13.6
Cumulative variance (%)	24.2	45.0	61.5	75.1

TABLE IV
CRONBACH'S ALPHA FOR DEPENDENT VARIABLES

Dependent variable	After first meeting	After last meeting
Team cohesion	0.76	0.91
Team collaboration	0.72	0.84
Perceived decision quality	0.86	0.84
Decision satisfaction	0.70	0.78

team collaboration than virtual teams that did not. But team collaboration did not change over time.

H3a, H3b, H4a, and H4b predicted interactions between dialogue technique and time, whereby teams using and not using the dialogue technique were expected to differ in decision outcome initially but not over time. These hypotheses were not supported due to the lack of interactions for perceived decision quality ($F = 0.34$, $p =$ n.s.) and decision satisfaction ($F = 0.18$, $p =$ n.s.). Again, both dialogue technique ($F = 5.46$, $p < 0.03$) and time ($F = 8.42$, $p < 0.01$) had significant main effects on perceived decision quality. Virtual teams that employed the dialogue technique had consistently higher perceived decision quality than virtual teams that did not. Over time, perceived decision quality increased significantly regardless of whether virtual teams used the dialogue technique. Both dialogue technique ($F = 27.51$, $p < 0.01$) and time ($F = 9.66$, $p < 0.01$) also had significant main effects on decision satisfaction. Virtual teams that employed the dialogue technique had consistently higher decision satisfaction than virtual teams that did not. Decision satisfaction also increased significantly over time regardless of whether virtual teams used the dialogue technique.

Discussion and Implications

The pattern of results that emerged in this study points to two general conclusions. First, the proposed dialogue technique (see Dialogue Technique, A Proposed Dialogue Technique) appears to be useful for helping virtual teams, that work solely via electronic communication, to enhance their relational development and decision outcome. Second, virtual teams that have worked together

TABLE V
MEAN (STANDARD DEVIATION) OF DEPENDENT VARIABLES

Dependent variable	Dialogue technique	After first meeting	After last meeting
Team cohesion	Yes	3.25 (0.36)	3.43 (0.23)
	No	2.99 (0.22)	3.28 (0.25)
Team collaboration	Yes	3.38 (0.23)	3.35 (0.25)
	No	3.10 (0.37)	3.17 (0.28)
Perceived decision quality	Yes	5.19 (0.58)	5.56 (0.39)
	No	4.73 (0.38)	5.28 (0.34)
Decision satisfaction	Yes	3.73 (0.16)	3.94 (0.20)
	No	3.27 (0.27)	3.55 (0.26)

TABLE VI
RESULTS OF ANOVA TESTS FOR DEPENDENT VARIABLES

Dependent variable	Dialogue technique (DT)	Time	Interaction (DT x Time)
Team cohesion	F = 4.34 p < 0.05*	F = 5.50 p < 0.03*	F = 0.26 p = 0.61
Team collaboration	F = 4.83 p < 0.04*	F = 0.05 p = 0.82	F = 0.22 p = 0.64
Perceived decision quality	F = 5.46 p < 0.03*	F = 8.42 p < 0.01*	F = 0.34 p = 0.57
Decision satisfaction	F = 27.51 p < 0.01*	F = 9.66 p < 0.01*	F = 0.18 p = 0.67

* p < 0.05

for some time (with or without the dialogue technique) seem to experience better relational development and decision outcome (except team collaboration) than newly formed virtual teams. Collectively, both conclusions suggest that the impact due to time and the impact due to the dialogue technique are additive. In other words, the dialogue technique appears to give virtual teams a head start that they are able to maintain over time.

The lack of impact of time on team collaboration may be explained by examining the mediating role of trust on this causal relationship. If virtual teams are to experience improved team collaboration over time, they need to spend enough time to build up mutual trust among members. Since the process of building mutual trust may require a lot of time, the duration of this study may not have been long enough for virtual teams to develop mutual trust over time so as to enjoy better team collaboration. Also, like many virtual teams in actual organizations, the virtual teams formed for this study are ad hoc in nature. They are disbanded after they have completed all their tasks. Given the short life span of these virtual teams, members may not have put in sufficient effort to build mutual trust to the extent that they can enjoy better team collaboration.

Limitations of the Current Study Results of this study should be interpreted in the context of its limitations. One limitation pertaining to this study is the use of only four meetings to assess the impact of the proposed dialogue technique. If the virtual teams had been allowed to work together for a much longer period of time, those that did not use the dialogue technique might be able to develop enough shared understanding to match the relational development and decision outcome of those that used the proposed dialogue technique. While this idea can be tested in future research, the ability of the proposed dialogue technique to enable rapid development of shared understanding has been clearly demonstrated.

Another limitation is the use of student subjects and contrived tasks. Students may differ from members of virtual teams in actual organizations because students have less experience working in teams and solving organizational tasks [40]. Virtual teams comprising organizational decision-makers may be experienced enough to create shared understanding without using the proposed dialogue technique. Alternatively, the proposed dialogue technique may complement the experience of organizational decision-makers to help them carry out their tasks even better. As such, the value of the dialogue technique can be tested with experienced virtual teams in actual organizational settings. Nevertheless, this study demonstrates that the dialogue technique can potentially help new virtual teams to quickly become effective at their work.

A third limitation is the use of virtual teams with mostly members from the same culture. Empirical studies have demonstrated that impact of electronic communication on the behavior of virtual teams may be moderated by culture [42], [43]. When technologies (e.g., electronic communication) and techniques (e.g., the dialogue technique) go against the grain of the culture of team members, virtual teams may employ these technologies and techniques in unintended ways through an adaptive structuration process [44]. Consequently, the outcome of using such technologies and techniques becomes less predictable. In this study, the dialogue technique was used by virtual teams from a collectivistic culture which values consensus [42]. It is not known whether and how the dialogue technique may impact virtual teams from an individualistic culture where people place less emphasis on consensus.

Implications for Research

Previous research has found that relational development and decision outcome of virtual teams can only improve after team members had worked together for some time [5], [7] [10] . Over time, virtual teams had in fact attained a level of relational development and decision outcome that is comparable to face-to-face teams. This improvement in relational development and decision outcome of virtual teams over time has also been observed in this study. More important, this study demonstrates that, over and above this positive impact of time, the proposed dialogue technique can enhance relational development and decision outcome of virtual teams. Since virtual teams may function as well as face-to-face teams over time and the impact of the dialogue technique may be sustainable, it is plausible that the dialogue technique can help virtual teams to do even better than face-to-face teams in the long run. Further research is needed to test this contention.

This study measured the impact of time by assessing relational development and decision outcome after the first meeting and the last meeting. Future studies can assess relational development and decision outcome after each meeting to examine whether the improvements come gradually or whether these variables fluctuate over time. In addition, future studies can complement such quantitative measurement of variables with analyses of qualitative information gathered through electronic mail archives or interviews with subjects [45]. Qualitative information of this nature can allow researchers to attain in-depth understanding on how virtual teams actually use (or misuse) the dialogue technique in the course of their work. Such understanding can contribute to efforts at fine tuning the dialogue technique.

In this study, most of the members in each virtual team share the same cultural background. However, virtual teams in actual organizations typically consist of members from a wide range of cultures [2]. Since mental models are shaped by cultural background to a great extent [42], [46], members of such virtual teams may possess very different mental models. It is not known whether and how the proposed dialogue technique may assist such multicultural virtual teams to develop shared understanding. Therefore, although this study reveals that the dialogue technique can assist virtual teams to bridge time and distance, further research is needed to assess whether this dialogue technique can assist virtual teams to bridge their cultural differences [37].

All the tasks used in this study are preference tasks [36] that have no correct answers. When completing such tasks, members of virtual teams tend to rely very heavily on their individual inclinations (manifested through their mental models) because of the lack of common bases for team decisions. The proposed dialogue technique seems to help team members to reconcile differences in their individual inclinations in the form of team mental models. Another type of tasks that can be studied in the future are intellective tasks [36], where correct answers exist and can be determined rationally through logic. Since people usually complete such tasks using the same logical bases, the value of the dialogue technique (in helping members of virtual teams to reconcile their differences) may be diminished. Alternatively, future research can focus on negotiation tasks [36], where team members can win at the expense of each other. Under such circumstances, it is interesting to study whether the dialogue technique can help members of virtual teams to jointly maximize their outcome through win–win decisions.

Implications for Practice Meta-analyses of prior research results suggest that when teams used electronic communication to complete preference tasks, they tend to report better perceived decision quality but poorer decision satisfaction [47], [48]. Electronic communication has helped teams to focus on task activities and move toward the final deliverables. However, even if teams arrive at their decisions effectively and efficiently, the opinions of some team members may be under-represented [49]. Consequently, electronic communication raised perceived decision quality but not decision satisfaction. By guiding virtual teams toward the notion of team mental models, the proposed dialogue technique can help virtual teams to incorporate the opinions of all members into the final decisions. Virtual teams in actual organizations, who communicate solely through electronic communication, can try using the dialogue technique to raise perceived decision quality and decision satisfaction simultaneously.

Many organizations are currently flying members of virtual teams around for face-to-face meetings to help them understand and work with each other better. By enabling virtual teams to develop shared understanding quickly, the proposed dialogue technique can potentially help organizations to trim down on the costs and time needed for travel. Also, by enabling virtual teams to work effectively via electronic communication, virtual teams using the proposed dialogue technique may be able to do away with many of the costs and inconveniences (e.g., getting members from different time zones to meet at the same time) of using video-conferences and telephone conferences.

Conclusion

This study proposes and tests a dialogue technique that aims at helping virtual teams to develop shared understanding quickly. Results from an experiment show that the proposed dialogue technique can indeed enable virtual teams to quickly enhance their relational development and decision outcome. Moreover, the positive impact of the dialogue technique appears to be sustainable over a period of time. Thus, the dialogue technique may benefit the increasing number of virtual teams that are being put together by organizations nowadays [1].

In a business environment characterized by intense competition, organizations increasingly are leveraging their work force to solve business problems. An effective way to do so is to form virtual teams, comprising knowledgeable employees from all locations, to address key business issues. Given that the work of such virtual teams tends to be time critical, ways must be found to help them overcome restrictions imposed by electronic communication to become effective quickly. Although the dialogue technique proposed in this study can potentially address this problem, further research must be carried out in this direction. If virtual teams are to play increasingly important roles in organizations of the future, research targeted at enhancing electronic communication in virtual teams can create an enormous impact in organizations.

REFERENCES

[1] A. Mowshowitz, "Virtual organization," *Commun. ACM*, vol. 40, no. 9, pp. 30–37, 1997.

[2] L. M. Applegate, J. I. Cash, and D. Q. Mills, "Information technology and tomorrow's manager," *Harvard Business Rev.*, vol. 66, no. 6, pp. 128–136, 1988.

[3] M. Turoff, S. R. Hiltz, A. N. F. Bahgat, and A. R. Rana, "Distributed group support systems," *MIS Quart.*, vol. 17, no. 4, pp. 399–417, 1993.

[4] J. B. Walther, J. F. Anderson, and D. W. Park, "Interpersonal effects in computer-mediated interaction: A meta-analysis of social and antisocial communication," *Commun. Res.*, vol. 21, no. 4, pp. 460–487, 1994.

[5] L. Chidambaram, "Relational development in computer-supported groups," *MIS Quart.*, vol. 20, no. 2, pp. 143–165, 1996.

[6] L. Chidambaram, R. P. Bostrom, and B. E. Wynne, "A longitudinal study of the impact of group decision support systems on group development," *J. Manag. Inform. Syst.*, vol. 7, no. 3, pp. 7–25, 1991.

[7] J. B. Walther, "Relational aspects of computer-mediated communication: Experimental observations over time," *Organization Sci.*, vol. 6, no. 2, pp. 186–203, 1995.

[8] W. Isaacs, "Dialogue: The power of collective thinking," *Systems Thinker*, vol. 4, no. 3, pp. 1–4, 1993.

[9] E. H. Schein, "On dialogue, culture, and organizational learning," *Organizational Dynamics*, vol. 22, no. 2, pp. 40–51, 1993.

[10] K. Burke and L. Chidambaram, "Developmental difference between distributed and face-to-face groups in electronically supported meeting environments: An exploratory investigation," *Group Decision and Negotiation*, vol. 4, no. 3, pp. 213–233, 1995.

[11] J. E. McGrath and J. R. Kelly, *Time and Human Interaction: Toward a Social Psychology of Time*. New York: Guilford, 1986.

[12] P. M. Senge, A. Kleiner, C. Roberts, R. B. Ross, and B. J. Smith, *The Fifth Discipline Fieldbook: Strategies and Tools for Building a Learning Organization*. New York: Doubleday, 1994.

[13] C. Argyris, *Strategy, Change, and Defensive Routines*. Boston, MA: Pitman, 1985.

[14] P. S. George, "Team-building without tears," *Personnel J.*, vol. 66, no. 11, pp. 122–129, 1987.

[15] W. Dyer, *Team-Building: Issues and Alternatives*. Reading, MA: Addison-Wesley, 1987.

[16] R. Nath and A. L. Lederer, "Team-building for IS success," *Inform. Syst. Manag.*, vol. 13, no. 1, pp. 32–37, 1996.

[17] R. L. Daft, R. H. Lengel, and L. K. Trevino, "Message equivocality, media richness, and manager performance: Implications for information systems," *MIS Quart.*, vol. 11, no. 3, pp. 355–366, 1987.

[18] S. E. Seashore, *Group Cohesiveness in the Industrial Work Group*. Ann Arbor, MI: Univ. Mich. Press, 1954.

[19] C. E. Larson and F. M. J. LaFasto, *Teamwork: What Must Go Right/What Can Go Wrong*. Newbury Park, CA: Sage, 1989.

[20] R. L. Daft and R. H. Lengel, "A proposed integration among organizational information requirements, media richness, and structural design," *Manag. Sci.*, vol. 32, no. 5, pp. 554–571, 1986.

[21] D. W. Johnson and F. P. Johnson, *Joining Together: Group Theory and Group Skills*. Englewood Cliffs, NJ: Prentice-Hall, 1987.

[22] B. G. Schultz, *Communication in the Small Group: Theory and Practice*. New York: Harper and Row, 1992.

[23] M. L. Knapp, *Interpersonal Communication and Human Relationships*. Boston, MA: Allyn and Bacon, 1984.

[24] J. B. Walther and J. K. Burgoon, "Relational communication in computer-mediated interaction," *Human Commun. Res.*, vol. 19, no. 1, pp. 50–88, 1992.

[25] L. Chidambaram and R. P. Bostrom, "Group development: A Review and synthesis of development models (I)," *Group Decision and Negotiation*, vol. 6, no. 2, pp. 159–187, 1996.

[26] M. E. Shaw, *Group Dynamics: The Psychology of Small Group Behavior*. New York: McGraw-Hill, 1981.

[27] L. Chidambaram and R. P. Bostrom, "Group development: Implications for GSS research and practice (II)," *Group Decision and Negotiation*, vol. 6, no. 3, pp. 231–254, 1997.

[28] G. E. Littlepage, L. Cowart, and B. Kerr, "Relationship between group environment scales and group performance and cohesion," *Small Group Res.*, vol. 20, no. 1, pp. 50–61, 1989.
[29] C. R. Evans and K. L. Dion, "Group cohesion and performance: A meta-analysis," *Small Group Res.*, vol. 22, no. 2, pp. 175–186, 1991.
[30] D. S. Gouran, C. Brown, and D. R. Henry, "Behavioral correlates of perceptions of quality in decision-making discussions," *Commun. Monogr.*, vol. 45, no. 1, pp. 51–63, 1978.
[31] E. A. Locke and G. P. Latham, *A Theory of Goal Setting and Task Performance*. Englewood Cliffs, NJ: Prentice-Hall, 1990.
[32] H. Wichman, "Effects of isolation and communication on cooperation in a two person game," *J. Personality Social Psychol.*, vol. 16, no. 1, pp. 114–120, 1970.
[33] G. R. Davis, "Hardware: Offline," *Datamation*, vol. 32, no. 10, p. 109, 1986.
[34] C. L. Sia, B. C. Y. Tan, and K. K. Wei, "Can a GSS stimulate group poarization? An empirical study," *IEEE Trans. Syst., Man, Cybern., C*, vol. 29, pp. 227–237, Apr. 1999.
[35] B. C. Y. Tan, K. K. Wei, C. L. Sia, and K. S. Raman, "A partial test of the task-medium fit proposition in a group support system environment," *ACM Trans. Computer–Human Interaction*, vol. 6, no. 1, pp. 47–66, 1999.
[36] J. E. McGrath, *Groups: Interaction and Performance*. Englewood Cliffs, NJ: Prentice-Hall, 1984.
[37] M. O'Hara-Devereaux and R. Johansen, *Global Work: Bridging Distance, Culture, and Time*. San Francisco, CA: Jossey-Bass, 1994.
[38] S. G. Green and T. D. Taber, "The effects of three social decision schemes on decision group processes," *Organizational Behavior and Human Perform.*, vol. 25, no. 1, pp. 97–106, 1980.
[39] R. A. Johnson and D. W. Wichern, *Applied Multivariate Statistical Analysis*. Englewood Cliffs, NJ: Prentice-Hall, 1992.
[40] J. Nunnally, *Psychometric Theory*. New York: McGraw-Hill, 1978.
[41] G. DeSanctis, "Small group research in information systems: Theory and method," in *The Information Research Challenge: Experimental Research Methods*, I. Benbasat, Ed. Boston, MA: Harvard Business School Press, 1989, pp. 53–82.
[42] B. C. Y. Tan, K. K. Wei, R. T. Watson, D. L. Clapper, and E. R. McLean, "Computer-mediated communication and majority influence: Assessing the impact in an individualistic and a collectivistic culture," *Manag. Sci.*, vol. 44, no. 9, pp. 1263–1278, 1998.
[43] B. C. Y. Tan, K. K. Wei, R. T. Watson, and R. M. Walczuch, "Reducing status effects with computer-mediated communication: Evidence from two distinct national cultures," *J. Manag. Inform. Syst.*, vol. 15, no. 1, pp. 119–141, 1998.
[44] G. DeSanctis and M. S. Poole, "Capturing the complexity in advanced technology use: Adaptive structuration theory," *Organization Sci.*, vol. 5, no. 2, pp. 121–147, 1994.
[45] E. M. Trauth and L. M. Jessup, "Understanding computer-mediated discussions: Positive and interpretive analyzes of group support system use," MIS Quart., to be published.
[46] G. Hofstede, *Cultures and Organizations: Software of the Mind*. London, U.K.: McGraw -Hill, 1991.
[47] I. Benbasat and L. H. Lim, "The effects of group, task, context, and technology variables on the usefulness of group support systems: A meta-analysis of experimental studies," *Small Group Res.*, vol. 24, no. 4, pp. 430–462, 1993.
[48] A. R. Dennis, B. J. Haley, and R. J. Vandenberg, "A meta-analysis of effectiveness, efficiency, and participant satisfaction in group support systems research," in *Proc. 17th Annu. Int. Conf. Information Systems*, 1996, pp. 278–289.
[49] J. E. McGrath and A. B. Hollingshead, *Groups Interacting with Technology: Ideas, Evidence, Issues, and an Agenda*. Newbury Park, CA: Sage, 1994.

Bernard C.Y. Tan is an Associate Professor in the Department of Information Systems at the National University of Singapore (NUS). He received the Ph.D. degree in information systems from NUS. He has been a Visiting Scholar at Stanford University and the University of Georgia. His research has been published in *MIS Quarterly, Management Science, Journal of Management Information Systems, ACM Transactions on Information Systems, ACM Transactions on Computer–Human Interaction,* IEEE TRANSACTIONS ON SYSTEMS, MAN, AND CYBERNETICS, and *International Journal of Human–Computer Studies.* He is on the editorial board of *MIS Quarterly.* His research interests include cross-cultural issues, computer-mediated communication, and electronic commerce.

Kwok-Kee Wei is Professor and the founding Head of the Department of Information Systems at the National University of Singapore. He received the D.Phil. degree in computer science from the University of York (United Kingdom). His research has been published in *MIS Quarterly, Management Science, Journal of Management Information Systems, ACM Transactions on Information Systems, ACM Transactions on Computer–Human Interaction,* IEEE TRANSACTIONS ON SYSTEMS, MAN, AND CYBERNETICS, *Information and Management, Decision Support Systems, International Journal of Human–Computer Studies,* and *European Journal of Information Systems.* His research interests include computer-mediated communication, human–computer interaction, and electronic commerce.

Wayne W. Huang is a Senior Lecturer in the School of Information Systems, Technology and Management at the University of New South Wales in Sydney, Australia. He received the Ph.D. degree in information systems from the National University of Singapore. His research interests include group support systems, electronic commerce, and software engineering. His research has been published in IEEE TRANSACTIONS ON SYSTEMS, MAN, AND CYBERNETICS, *Journal of Management Information Systems, European Journal of Information Systems, Information and Management,* and *Group Decision and Negotiation,* as well as in conference proceedings such as ICIS, HICSS, AIS, DSI, ECIS, and IFIP.

Guet-Ngoh Ng received the B.Sc. (First Class Hons.) and M.Sc. degrees in computer and information sciences from the National University of Singapore. Presently, she is an Associate Consultant with the Infocom Development Authority of Singapore. She works in the Information Technology Division of the Prime Minister's Office. Her research interests include virtual organizations, group support systems, and electronic commerce.

Commentary

Videoconferencing as a Communication Tool

Jan A. Sprey

***Abstract*—With videoconferencing available on the desktop, the technology is becoming feasible for small- to medium-sized companies, as well as mobile workers. Videoconferencing applications range from internal company communications, educating and training remote employees, to telecommuting. It can even eliminate certain travel requirements, thereby cutting costs. In spite of several factors which are fueling the growth in videoconferencing, early projections have been overly optimistic. A literature review reveals that many technological and other barriers are preventing videoconferencing from gaining mainstream popularity. Users are primarily concerned with the costs of hardware and usage, interoperability, and poor quality. Advancements in compression algorithms and chip speed have made videoconferencing affordable to more people in the last decade. However, a video signal with quality acceptable only to some is still very costly and relatively complicated to utilize with the transport capabilities of today. Some say the turning point will not occur until hardware prices drop enough for video to become an add-on to users' PCs.**

***Index Terms*—Literature review, use of telecommuting, use of videoconferencing.**

A BROAD definition of *videoconferencing* is two or more remote locations engaging in face to face communications. But the term describes differing types of technology. The type that is the subject of this commentary is known as "two-way video" (also referred to as "compressed" or "interactive"). The enabling equipment allows a worker to accomplish some or all of the following:

- Send a live image of what is going on in the room, or send images of objects via a document camera.
- Play segments or record segments from a video tape.
- Send computer-generated images.
- Send an image and at the same time emphasize points on it by drawing on an electronic drawing tablet.
- Use slides, charts, graphs, or maps.

The entire time the user is sending they are seeing the remote site and hearing their responses, and vice versa. Two-way videoconferencing is usually accomplished using digital channels to provide video and audio communications in both directions. (When three or more locations are involved, a video bridge is employed to enable interaction among all sites.) Basic equipment includes monitors, cameras, microphones, speakers, and CODECs (to compress and decompress the video signals) integrated into conference room or desktop systems.

The camera is an analog device. It generates a signal that equates to a 90 million bits per second (90 Mb/s) stream of data. The idea is to get that 90-Mb/s video signal and the voice signal to the remote end—where the video signal appears on a monitor and the voice signal comes out of a speaker—so people can see and hear each other. Since most users do not want to pay for a data channel big enough to transmit a 90-Mb/s video signal like the TV networks, the idea is to compress the signals and transmit them over the digital network. Signals can be compressed a little bit to 45 Mb/s, or a lot, to 112 thousand bits per second (112 kb/s). The more the signal is compressed, the less video fidelity there is when the signal is expanded back up at the receiving end.

The CODEC, which stands for Coder/Decoder, is the device that does the compression and decompression—and the conversion between analog and digital. The CODEC is set at the desired transmission speed, and it compresses the signal accordingly. It does this by using a series of mathematical formulas called "compression algorithms." Typically, each manufacturer of CODECs has created its own set of proprietary mathematical compression algorithms—or customers can choose to use the set of standard algorithms developed by the International Telecommunications Union (ITU).

Fig. 1 depicts the range of the digital spectrum used in video transmission. These are the speeds which are typically used for interactive video and other kinds of video conferencing.

At the left end of the chart are the typical bandwidths used for interactive, two-way video applications. The amount of bandwidth used for this purpose today typically ranges from 56 kb/s, to the most commonly used bandwidth, 112 kb/s; on occasion as much as 1.5 Mb/s may be used. The 3.0- to 6.0-Mb/s range is typically used by satellite education services, such as PBS and the National Technological University, also known as NTU. At the higher end are speeds that are typically used for one-way video and broadcast television, although there are a few interactive, two-way video applications at these speeds. Primarily, these speeds are used for one-way video using satellite or terrestrial private line service. The viewer sees the speaker, but the speaker cannot see the viewer. 45 Mb/s is now used by many TV stations.

At this point it is important to note the distinction between group (also referred to as Conference Room) systems and Desktop video systems. Both are based on the same basic

Manuscript received November 1996.
The author is with Lucent Technologies, Basking Ridge, NJ 07920 USA.
Publisher Item Identifier S 0361-1434(97)02023-7.

Reprinted from *IEEE Trans. Prof. Comm.*, vol. PC-40, no. 1, pp. 41–47, March 1997.

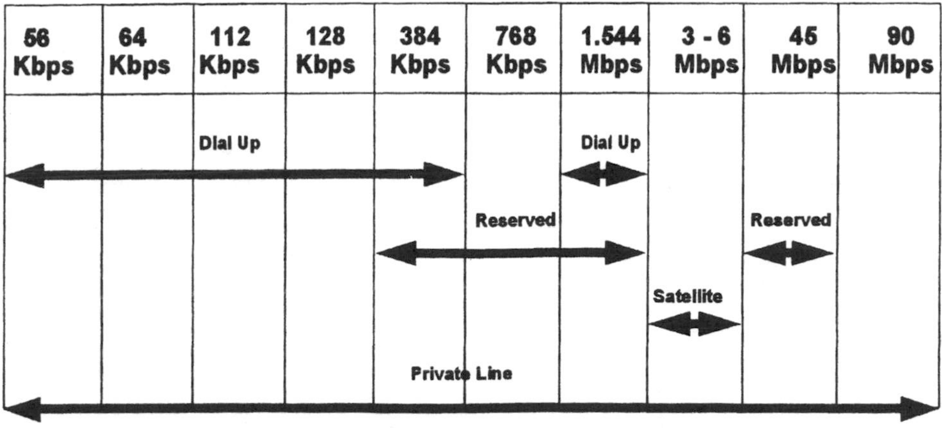

Fig. 1. Range of the digital spectrum used in video transmission.

"two-way" video technology, but they were designed to operate on different platforms. There are actually three distinct but interrelated segments of equipment [1]:

Group or Room-based systems use large television monitors and are shared among users within an organization. They are placed in specifically equipped conference rooms and workers at a site view similar groups gathered at remote sites. These systems are designed to accommodate and enhance group meetings.

Desktop systems are based on personal computers (also referred to as "personal" video). They differ from group systems in that they typically involve one-to-one communication, not one-to-many, or many-to-many communication like group systems. Participants sit at their own desks, in their own offices, and call up other participants using their personal computer in a manner much like a telephone. This relatively new type of video system is typically used in conjunction with software tools such as shared white boards or other shared applications and therefore is often a more intimate, interactive, as well as collaborative medium than the larger group video systems.

Bridging equipment or MCU's satisfy the need to join three or more locations in a videoconference. The term Multipoint Conference Unit or MCU is commonly used for this segment.

History

The first videoconferencing system was introduced by the AT&T Corporation at the 1964 World's Fair. Called the Picturephone, it allowed a user to dial up another user to make a video phone call. Although it received widespread interest, it could not be commercialized at that time due to the necessity of special transmission lines that were not widely available or cost-effective. Existing lines had less than a thousandth of the capacity needed to transmit the signals of the Picturephone. Conducting the demonstration required dedicated lines which had to be reserved in advance of their use. These limitations made it unsuitable for common usage. Finally, in 1973, AT&T discontinued selling the Picturephone. At the time, AT&T acknowledged that practical videoconferencing required an affordable, dial-up (on demand) communications network capable of supporting video [2].

Year	Units	Price per Room	Revenue (Millions)
1993	7,500	$40,000	$300
1994	12,000	$30,000	$360
1995	15,000	$25,000	$375
1996	17,500	$20,000	$350
1997	19,000	$18,000	$342

Source: Yankee Group

Fig. 2. Sales projection for group videoconferencing.

In 1982 Compression Labs., Inc., introduced an expensive group system to the market for $250 000 using $1000-an-hour lines. By 1986 prices had dropped considerably, but they were still high when PictureTel Corporation introduced an $80 000 unit using $100-an-hour lines. It took five more years for this to evolve into a $20 000 system using $30-an-hour lines [3]. With each dramatic price drop, videoconferencing use became a more viable option for more people.

Today's communications network infrastructure can provide many of the prerequisites to practical videoconferencing. Hardware has also evolved considerably. Since about 1994, videoconferencing has become much more common in large part due to the introduction of PC-based (desktop) video systems. Also called "personal" video, these systems make use of kits containing add-on boards and a small camera that can transform an existing PC into a device that delivers video to the desktop. According to a study done by Business Research Group of Newton, MA, of 301 existing users of videoconferencing, desktop video is seen as an extension of traditional videoconferencing rather than a replacement. In other words, using a desktop rather than a group system means trading resolution and performance for lower costs.

Market Size and Growth

"Room-Based" (group) videoconferencing is the most mature of the videoconferencing segments and is still in a "growth" market stage. In 1994, one source projected that the number of units sold between 1993 and 1997 would grow by 155% (see Fig. 2).

Until recently, group videoconferencing systems have been very expensive, and for this reason not practical for many

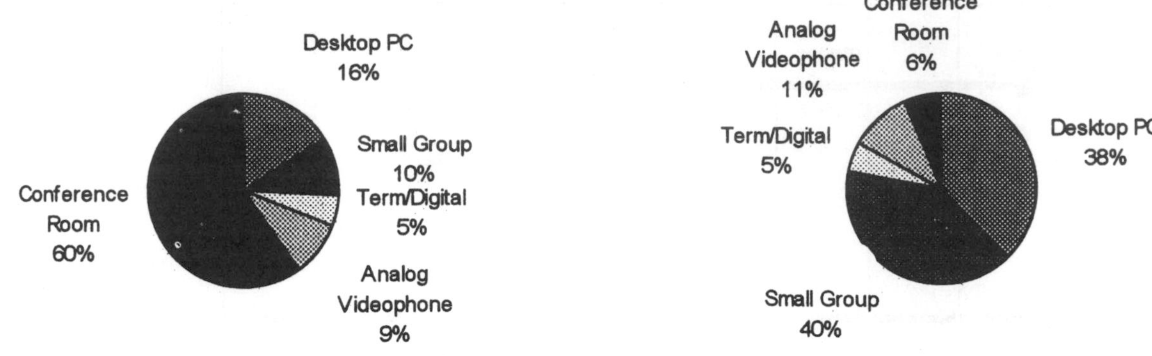

Source: AT&T–Market Intelligence

Fig. 3. Market share for videoconferencing systems.

users. According to Will Strauss, an analyst at Forward Concepts, hardware and software prices are decreasing by 30% per year [4]. A couple of reasons for the projected increase in the number of units sold are lower priced computer-based systems and the emergence of reasonably priced local and wide-area network services that will increasingly make the technology accessible to more users.

Conference Room system sales still outperform Desktop video systems, partially because the latter market is not mature. However, as shown in Fig. 3, the largest market opportunity shifts from Conference Room (fixed installations) to small group (portable systems also referred to as rollabouts) and Desktop PC systems [5].

A somewhat complicating factor in the Desktop market is that many systems run only on an ISDN line, which until recently was a service not generally available around the entire country. ISDN availability is improving, and recent figures estimate coverage to be at about 85% of the U.S. [4].

Analyst projections for future growth in the videoconferencing market vary widely for the year 1997—from $2 billion to $10.5 billion [5]. Elliot Gould, an Altadena, CA, industry analyst, from Telspan, projected sales of two-way videoconferencing on the whole would grow as high as a $7.0 billion business by the end of 1996 [6]. Considering that the market was around a half million dollars in 1994 [7], with industry growth projected by the International Teleconferencing Association to approximately average only 45% per year, it appears the actual numbers are destined to fall short of analysts' projections for the remainder of the decade.

Applications for Videoconferencing (What is it Used for?)

Some users integrate videoconferencing into day-to-day business life to help manage time and to do more with fewer employees, in addition to making communication a pleasurable collaboration with colleagues or customers. Specific ways in which videoconferencing is used include:

On-site presence: A company that looks to gain competitive advantages can accomplish the equivalent of being on a customer's site by attending meetings and/or consultations via video communications technology.

Internal company communications: There are many large companies that have locations spread out across the country or around the world. Videoconferencing provides a means for companies to communicate face-to-face with their remote departments and divisions.

Project teams: When cross departmental team members are spread out geographically, getting together for regular status meetings is very time-consuming. Videoconferencing can make workers more efficient by making it quicker to convene the meeting.

Recruitment, education, and training: Many users adopt videoconferencing as a program to create opportunities to increase revenues and/or cut costs. In order to keep employees apprised of the latest products, customer service techniques, and industry trends, U.S. firms with greater than 100 employees spent over 48 billion dollars in 1994 on traditional training [8]. Prior to implementing videoconferencing, they brought students into central sites to attend the training or sent instructors to the students at a very high cost. Implementing interactive distance learning via video makes it possible to reduce travel-time-related expenses. By reaching many students at one time, distance learning via video also enables consistent training for all employees, and they are more quickly brought up to speed due to immediate sharing of new information and ideas.

Two key trends identified in the study *Workforce 2000* are that by the year 2000 the workforce will generally be older, and new jobs in the service industries will demand much higher skill levels than jobs of today [9]. Distance learning via video will help businesses adapt to these changes by keeping the work force current as well as making training more accessible to workers.

Medical Diagnosis and Consulting: Healthcare challenges today include providing the highest quality medical care while containing costs and expenses. Videoconferencing allows doctors to provide diagnoses and second opinions on "tricky" cases in remote areas by linking the remote sites to specialists in a major medical center. This practice potentially provides better and cheaper care.

Telecommuting: As a result of the Federal Government's Clean Air Act, many states are requiring corporations to find ways to reduce the number of employees driving automobiles to their work locations. In part for this reason, many companies are encouraging telecommuting, employees working from a virtual office out of their homes. Desktop videoconferencing is often considered the cornerstone of the virtual office [10]. Employees can use a desktop videoconferencing system in order to be in contact with coworkers and participate in scheduled as well as impromptu meetings. Before the increased availability of ISDN (which provides high-speed digital transmission to the home over a special line) it was impractical to install a desktop videoconferencing system in an employee's residence. Now it is inexpensive enough for many companies to consider. Additionally, this technology can help motivate remote employees, increasing their visibility, improving their morale, and enhancing professional relationships.

Advantages (Overall Benefits)

Because of mergers, acquisitions, and globalization, communication needs have increased for many businesses. Video communications is effective in meeting these changes in communication needs by enhancing a corporation's ability to improve team work, increase productivity, and cut costs.

Better Teaming/Improved Decision Making: Video communications can effectively facilitate faster decisions in situations where workers are geographically dispersed by bringing the team together face to face. When this is required, assembling key players from multiple locations and time zones is simplified. Team members can see who's talking and quickly confer with one another. Feedback is instantaneous and all parties have the benefit of hearing information firsthand. Without videoconferencing they may make do with less personal, less effective methods of communication such as telephone conference calls or, worse, memo writing or electronic mail.

Improved Productivity: In addition, videoconferencing creates a "do it now" approach which allows for a reduction in the planning and processing time associated with most projects. This ability eliminates time delays between the need to meet and the actual meeting, reducing unproductive time and frustration. Workers can videoconference for spontaneous brainstorming sessions, "sanity checks," informal (or formal) discussion, and day-to-day needs for communication. The extraordinary lead times needed to arrange conferences otherwise are reduced.

Travel Savings: Videoconferencing allows for better use of resources by reducing hours of driving or flying, eliminating jet lag, and reducing nonproductive travel time. In addition, the greatly reduced expense of videoconferencing can increase the number of meeting participants as appropriate. Often this is the sole justification for corporations investing in videoconferencing technology.

Issues that Prevent Videoconferencing from Becoming Mainstream

The assumption of usefulness to the organization must be met before a corporation will want to deploy videoconferencing as a communication tool. There are three criteria for successful utilization: the technology must address an unmet need; it must provide better utilization of existing resources; and it must be cost-effective [11]. Beyond this, companies must overcome several barriers that stand in the way of using videoconferencing as a communications tool.

Barriers to Using Videoconferencing

Initial Investment: Prices for videoconferencing on the whole have fallen dramatically, in part because of the introduction of low-cost desktop video systems that use a PC platform. Some analysts say the turning point for widespread videoconferencing deployment hinges on price drops for desktop videoconferencing; these analysts suggest that \$300–\$500 is what users are willing to pay [4]. At this writing, an average cost for hardware and software is \$3550 not including ISDN installation and usage costs. Despite the lower price range for desktop video compared to group video (prices for group systems remain relatively high, averaging approximately \$36 000 [12]), the majority of businesses are still adopting a "let's try a couple and see how we like it" approach before they feel justified in making the investment required to put video capability on each worker's desk.

Availability of High Speed Digital Lines and Support: One mistake that is commonly made is the assumption that adequate lines required for transporting compressed video signals (facilities) are available to users. Although services are readily available, in reality, many small businesses—let's say those with fewer than 100 employees—typically do not have the existing infrastructure of high-speed lines that a larger corporation does. They do not have a large enough volume of traffic to justify paying the monthly fees for high-speed circuits. Even if a company could justify having these facilities, there is still a layer of technical support upon which their optimization relies. The whole solution implies the existence of technologically sophisticated products and personnel. There is consensus among most users that continuous access to technical support is needed [13]. If the expertise does not reside in-house, the expense of out-tasking for technical support must be added to the cost of operating videoconferencing within the business.

Using ISDN Basic Rate Interface lines has become an alternative for small (desktop) video solutions. ISDN is orderable in smaller increments and is considerably cheaper than the other digital services previously available. However, it is not yet available in all areas of the U.S. Also, the service can vary slightly (depending on which central office provides it), making compatibility an issue. The issue of incompatibility is symptomatic of any new technology in the information world, and transmission standards for ISDN are still being developed. ISDN-based systems often force the user to coordinate between the product vendor, the local phone company, and the long-distance provider to get the system working [14]. It is not unusual for users to go through weeks of finger pointing and buck passing before getting their system up and running. As such, ISDN is a relatively complicated service to understand, and one must already posses a certain level of competence on the subject or it will not be easy to use.

Quality: Due to the newness of the characteristics of video components—speed-dependent PCs, compression algorithms, digital signal processing chips, and high-speed phone lines—desktop video has relatively low resolution [10]. When these components get better and become more available, [desktop] video quality will improve accordingly. Most companies that do not have a special need for the highest possible quality are usually willing to operate at 15 frames per second in exchange for lower cost even though people are used to having the quality of broadcast television (approximately 30 frames per second). With recent videoconferencing technology improvements 30 frames per second is becoming more common than before, making video quality seem less "jerky" and more natural.

Interoperability: Since the beginning of the technology revolution, proprietary versus open standards has been a hotly debated issue. The video industry is making an attempt to specify one main standard which is called H.320. Today, unless a video system is compatible with the "H.320" umbrella standard, it will only be able to videoconference with a user of the same product. Developed by ITU-T Study Group 15 (International Telecommunications Union, formerly CCITT), H.320 outlines all phases of the procedure the technology uses to establish a videoconference call. In spite of the progress made on this standard, there are still many details it does not cover. H.320 still does not address the use of a Local Area Network (LAN) for example, so if a user's H.320 video system is a PC which sits behind a LAN, until further standards work is complete, most video systems will not transmit over that LAN.

Lack of Ubiquity: If an organization wants to use video as a communication tool it will most likely have to deploy video endpoints in each location that it expects will be involved. Unless workers at all companies universally have a video-equipped PC on their desktop and/or every business has one or more group video systems, the everyday use of video in the mainstream is not particularly practical nor likely.

A Booz-Allen & Hamilton study of 23 American corporations shows that 78% of the users surveyed said that most of their videoconferencing meetings are still intra-company. The users said that this is because of limited videoconference adoption by customer and supplier bases [15]. The slow adoption of videoconferencing abroad contributes to this lack of ubiquity. Europeans are generally slower to adopt videoconferencing because they are less enthusiastic than Americans about new technologies; and, in fact, the adoption of videoconferencing has been primarily driven by U.S. headquarters. Penetration in Asia and the Pacific is still low, primarily because videoconferencing does not fit well with the Asian culture and personality; personal relationships are still extremely important in doing business in Asia [15].

User Acceptance: The Booz-Allen & Hamilton study also finds "no correlation between the type of industry and videoconferencing usage; it all depends on the company culture, and the number and power of internal advocates" [15]. Positioning is key to whether or not workers will accept a change in the status quo and use videoconferencing, and quite often this determines the success or failure of a program.

Comfort with Hardware: The more user-friendly the hardware, the better users will be able to adapt. According to Hicks and Angiolillo, "user interfaces to [personal] visual communications products will be critical to their success" [16]. Desktop video has a graphical user interface that most PC users are familiar with, and group video manufacturers tout the well-thought-out design and layout of their products' control panels, but there are still various competency areas involved in initiating a video call (i.e., circuit speed, algorithms, and hardware particulars). Initial training is required to get started, and the lack thereof will quickly deter a potential user from trying the technology. In lieu of simplicity, it is perhaps best to offer a safety net in the form of technical support.

User Preparation: The uniqueness of this communication tool requires that meeting facilitators be trained on preparing for a videoconference. If the conference is going to be multipoint (three or more locations), the facilitator must decide what type of privileges the remote ends will have, i.e., will each endpoint only be able to listen (presentation mode), or will they have the option to be seen and heard by the other sites (voice-activated switching). Another small but significant detail involves designing viewgraphs. The typeface and line spacing must be larger for video than they are for conventional overheads, or viewing capability will be compromised.

Market Environment

Geoffrey Moore's model may help us understand users' acceptance of new technology products, including videoconferencing. The *Technology Adoption Life Cycle* describes market penetration in terms of a progression in the types of consumers it attracts [17]. It divides the market by using a bell-shaped curve that classifies potential customers according to their attitude toward technology adoption (see Fig. 4)..

Moore states that mainstream markets are dominated by the *early majority* ("they make up nearly one third of the buying population"), and he maintains that winning this segment is key to the growth of a product [17]. It appears, then, that videoconferencing consumers would have to be the *early majority* type in order for videoconferencing to be a mainstream product. They do not appear to be. When asked which groups within their organization have used videoconferencing first, 65% of the companies sampled in a Booz-Allen & Hamilton study stated that Engineering, and Research and Development were early users of videoconferencing. According to these respondents, engineers and researchers were first users because "they did not feel threatened by a new technology; they like to be pioneers" [15]. In looking at the psychological and social profiles of the current videoconferencing users, we suspect they lie solidly in the *innovator* and *early adopter* categories, and not in the *early majority*.

Comparing the characteristics of the *early majority* group to other groups we find the former are "driven by a strong sense of practicality," whereas *innovators* are "intrigued with any fundamental advance and often make a technology purchase for the pleasure of exploring the new device's properties" [17]. The *early majority* are content to wait and see how other people are making out before they buy in—they want well-established references; whereas *early adopters* are people who "find it easy to imagine, understand, and appreciate the benefits of a new technology, and to relate these potential benefits to their other concerns" [17].

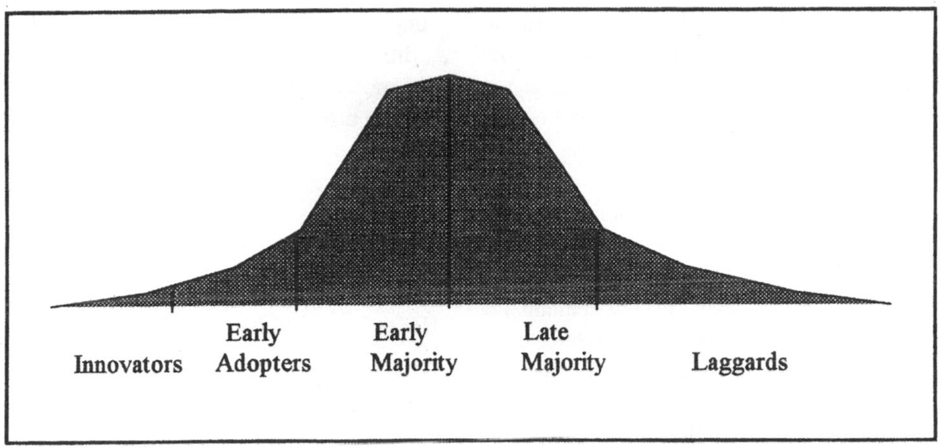

Fig. 4. Technology adoption life cycle.

The video industry as a whole has not yet managed to successfully make the transition to all of the customer segments in Moore's model, which to date has caused industry growth projections to go unrealized. A further detail to Moore's theory helps us understand why. There are "gaps" and a "chasm" between the divisions of the groups in the Technology Adoption Life Cycle model [17]. The gaps between the groups represent the idea that unless a product is presented to each of the groups in a different way than it is to the others, the marketing of that product will lose momentum, thereby *never successfully gaining that segment of the market.* The largest gap or "chasm" separates the *early adopters* from the *early majority* because this is the hardest transition in the Technology Adoption Life Cycle.

Even though the *actual* video customers and *potential* video customers may demographically look the same, they are in different groups that are separated by the chasm. In our example, the video customer (*early adopter*) buys "some kind of 'change agent' in order to get a jump on the competition and *expects* a radical difference between the old ways and the new." By contrast, the potential customers (*early majority*) "want to buy a 'productivity improvement' for existing operations. They want technology to *enhance*, not overthrow the established ways of doing business, and want it to work properly and to integrate appropriately with their existing technology base" [17].

Analogous Technology

With respect to how quickly and easily we adopt any new technology, Moore refers to *continuous innovation* versus *discontinuous innovation*, the latter being any new technology that requires a change in the way we are used to doing things before the technology was introduced [17]. An example of discontinuous innovation is microwave cooking. In this example, the improvement is in cooking food faster, but it requires a change in the way we are used to preparing it. Since one would need different cookware and modification to menus, this way of preparing food is drastically different from using a conventional oven. Since videoconferencing as a communication tool requires new equipment and new skills and knowledge, and is very different from the way the general public has communicated for so long, it fits the above description of a discontinuous innovation. Fax machines and pen-based computing are also analogous technologies because they too are discontinuous innovations.

Pen-based computing was introduced in the early 1990s and is an example of a technology that may never become very successful. These small computer devices include a special stylus with a touch-sensitive screen and use writing-recognition technology to give commands for storing and retrieving information. The concept was conceived with (as it turns out) the incorrect assumption that executives would want constant access to information but would not be likely to become comfortable with a keyboard. To make matters worse, the technology was introduced when it was only able to recognize the correct characters 95% of the time. Inevitably no one could find useful a tool that did not work accurately 100% of the time.

The fax machine is a great technology success story of the 1980s. Faxing is an easy, effective way to send information from one location to another. An important factor to its catching on was the CCITT adoption of Group 3 fax standards. Then, because of the relatively small (less than $2500) initial investment, the simplicity of installing a fax, along with the fact that it operates on something inexpensive that everyone currently owns—a plain old telephone (POTS) line—it did not take too long before fax technology caught on. The use of fax machines is now widespread enough that one can easily send a fax to almost anyone.

Geoffrey Moore might say the key to why faxing has caught on and pen-based computing and videoconferencing have not lies in the degree of success with which these products were introduced to the market. The marketing of fax technology was eventually successful enough in convincing users to change their attitudes about the way they communicate, and users realized that this product solved specific, unmet needs.

Conclusions

Overall, videoconferencing can be of great benefit to corporations as a tool to enhance communications. It can reduce costs by eliminating some travel that would otherwise be needed to conduct business, and make day-to-day communications easier, thereby improving productivity. It will not revolutionize the workplace, however, primarily because too many problems exist with the technology for it to become widely accepted.

A literature review on the subject reveals the common opinion that cost, poor interoperability, and poor quality seem to be the primary management concerns preventing mainstream adoption of videoconferencing. Today it is essentially still a first-generation product [18], and as such, users' demand for high-quality, high-performance video exceeds the technology's current capabilities, and its cost exceeds their willingness to pay.

Continuous improvement in the technology will eventually eliminate many of the objections to using videoconferencing. Perhaps the best way to solve for the problems of cost and poor quality is to achieve a transition to newer modes of transport—possibly Asynchronous Transfer Mode (ATM), an offshoot of ISDN that offers faster transfer rates, for example. This could also help eliminate the barrier created by companies having difficulty dealing with ISDN technology.

Equipment costs will be reduced, according to Alfred Riccomi, a consultant with Multimedia PC Systems in Richardson, TX, when video eventually becomes an integral part of PCs—as part of the operating system for example [4]. A number of factors are already in place making lower cost videoconferencing closer to reality: processor chips have become more powerful and the algorithms more efficient, allowing software to do more of the work.

Other barriers from the end-user perspective are ease of use and overall comfort with the hardware. Implementation of a system alone will not guarantee its popularity within the organization. Since engaging in videoconferencing is so radically different from anything users have experienced before, most users must be taught to plan, to prepare for, and to learn the basics about using the technology before they will productively use this new method of communication.

In short, the same problem exists today as did decades ago: depending on how one looks at it, technology has not advanced quickly enough, or is limited by what the communication network infrastructure will allow. It seems that if the application of videoconferencing was going to be the catalyst to effect a change in either of these areas it would have happened by now. The most promising application for desktop video seems to be as a productivity tool that permits dispersed groups to simultaneously view and alter shared documents. Additionally, this technology is ideal for telecommuting to help motivate remote employees, increase their visibility, and enhance professional relationships. Without these specific uses, however, users have yet to be convinced that they need a tiny-sized picture of the person they are talking to appearing on their PC.

References

[1] Yankee Group, Boston, MA, White Paper "The North American video equipment market," Sept. 1994.

[2] AT&T–Global Business Video Systems, "Welcome to the world of Videoconferencing," presented at Northwest Financial Customer Seminar, Aug. 4, 1994, ch. 8.

[3] W. Bulkeley, "Picture-Phone marketers target the home PC," *The Wall Street J.*, p. B1, Feb. 27, 1996.

[4] M. Brandel, "Videoconferencing slowly goes desktop," *Comput. World*, p. 81, Feb. 20, 1995.

[5] AT&T Marketing Intelligence Division, Basking Ridge, NJ, report "Visual communication industry," p. 3, Sept. 1994.

[6] D. Lyons, "Making the convergence connection," *VAR Bus.*, pp. 63–74, Apr. 1994.

[7] J. Mullich, "Videoconferencing growth focuses on sales, marketing," *Advertising Age's Bus. Market.*, pp. 21–22, Aug. 1995.

[8] Lakewood Research, Minneapolis MN, *Training*, Oct. 1994.

[9] W. Johnston, *Workforce 2000—Executive Summary*. Indianapolis, IN: Hudson Inst., 1987, p. 1.

[10] B. Machrone, "Seeing is almost believing," *PC Mag.*, pp. 238–250, June 14, 1994.

[11] A. Chute, Lucent Technologies Center for Excellence in Distance Learning, Cincinnati, OH, "Implementation issues for distance learning," presented at "A Revolution in Learning" seminar, Detroit, MI, Nov. 15, 1994.

[12] A. Knox, "Students polishing apples for cyberspace college courses," *The Star Ledger* (Newark, NJ), p. 22, Feb. 26, 1996.

[13] J. Kaplan, "Consider out-tasking before outsourcing," *Network World*, June 5, 1995.

[14] M. Desmond, "Videoconferencing coast to coast and face to face," *PC World*, pp. 179–186, Mar. 1995,

[15] Booz-Allen & Hamilton, London, England, Research Report "The outlook for travel demand; The video-conferencing survey," Oct. 12, 1994.

[16] J. Angiolillo and J. A. Hicks, "Personal visual communications enters the marketplace," *AT&T Technol.*, vol. 7, p. 18, Fall 1992.

[17] G. A. Moore, *Crossing the Chasm*. New York: Harper, 1991, pp. 9–14.

[18] P. Korzeniowski, "Videoconferencing: Crossroads ahead," *Bus. Commun. Rev.*, Sept. 1994.

Jan A. Sprey received the M.A. degree in Corporate and Organizational Communication from Fairleigh Dickinson University, Madison, NJ, and the B.A. degree in General Business from Michigan State University. She is currently a Product Manager at Lucent Technologies, Basking Ridge, NJ, the former systems and equipment division of AT&T, where she has worked in marketing, sales, and product development and support for the last 11 years.

PART IX

Global Communication: Conveying Meaning Internationally

Nowhere is the global village more evident than in American industry. Many of us rub shoulders with employees from around the world, and many of them speak English as a second or even third language. Furthermore, much of our commerce is now international, which means that a lot of technical documents are read by overseas colleagues and customers. Making sure these documents are clear and effective, whether written in English or translated to another language, is an enormous task, and the articles in this section will give you an idea of what kinds of challenges are involved in the task and some practical ways to approach them.

Tackling the varieties of international English

In her brief article Joann Dennett first reminds us of a few statistics: there are far more speakers of English as a foreign language than there are native English speakers. Practically anyone in the technology professions is going to be working and communicating with nonnative speakers, and sometimes this can be a challenge. Dennett's claim that you must accept differences in usage among various nonnative speakers is worth remembering, and her explanations of why you should are convincing.

English for special purposes

In reviewing a book on the topic, Thomas Orr describes the growth of ESP (English for Specific Purposes). This approach to English language instruction has grown over the past two decades, and is now widely used to teach specialized English to learners who will need it more for specific workplace tasks than for general conversational purposes. Thus an important element in teaching ESP is needs analysis—making sure that the English taught is closely related to the tasks to be carried out by the learners. Other factors to be considered are course design, materials selection, teaching, learning, and evaluation, and Orr provides a solid description of each. After reading this article you will have a clear idea of the nature of ESP and may even want to look at the book the author refers to.

Recognizing cultural and rhetorical differences

Kirk St. Amant cites the evidence that English is without doubt the lingua franca of the scientific world and its publications. However, the matter does not end there, since there is no one rhetorical English standard used by all global communicators. Different groups and cultures vary in what they feel is effective English and are likely to judge documents by their own cultural and rhetorical backgrounds. Thus, if you are writing a document for an international audience you should be aware of cultural preferences since they may be quite different from your own. The author gives several examples of what this means, and by citing some fifteen sources shows how "the effective use of English internationally requires a deeper understanding of the cultures using that language."

Culture and document organization

This article continues the theme of the previous one by warning us not to assume that the best way to organize a technical document is the same for all cultures. Waka Fukuoka and his co-author came to this conclusion after studying seventeen Japanese documents. They also researched some other cultures and found various ways in which nonnative English writers approach their topic and thus organize their material—and even if they are writing in English they may still follow their cultural and rhetorical norms. Although more research needs to be carried out on this subject, you should be aware that culture can affect the way information is presented and try to remember this when writing for international audiences or reading their documents.

Does simplified English make for better translations?

Anyone familiar with writing for audiences whose first language is not English has probably heard of SE (Simplified English). SE, as Jan Spyridakis and colleagues define it, is "a controlled or restricted subset of English [used] for creating documentation." Although SE may be used in its own right for nonnative readers, it has also been thought of as a starting point on which to base translations of SE documents into target languages. Little research has been done, however, on whether using SE to produce translated documents also improves the quality of the actual translations. This is what the authors explore, using aircraft maintenance documents written in SE, with Spanish, Chinese, and Japanese as the target languages. Their investigation is carefully carried out and documented, and as you will see, there is still plenty of room for further work on the topic.

Producing a document in several languages

Leo Lentz and Jacqueline Hulst look at translation from a different angle as they discuss the evaluation of multilingual documents. Basing their article on a document that was translated into six different languages, the authors consider correctness and functional errors that may occur in the translation process. They then take up some important related questions: What makes a good translation? How is a good translation achieved? Can a perfect translation by made? This is obviously a complex topic, and by seeing how Lentz and Hulst deal with these questions you will come to appreciate the multitude of factors involved in producing a document in several languages.

Editing for a global audience

If you edit documents for international audiences you will find Carol Leininger and Rue Yuan's article of great help. Even if you are not directly involved in such editing but work for a global corporation, you will still find what the authors have to say about multilingual readers to be insightful. We all know that a nonnative speaker of English may face several difficulties in truly understanding English text such as an instruction manual or set of procedures, but this article carefully categorizes and discusses each level and subdivision of possible misinterpretation and shows how they should affect your editing choices. Being aware of all the potential pitfalls will help you much more fully understand the nature of effectively editing for global audiences.

Helping nonnative speakers to publish

In this final article Shimona Kushner quickly points out that although she offers a solution to the problems of academic writers who must write and publish in English when it is not their native language, her solution could just as well be applied to nonnative speakers in industry. Her description of a writing course for graduate students would not need to be significantly changed to be useful in a company that employs foreign engineers and other skilled workers who attend conferences and are expected to publish. Such a course would also be of considerable help in improving the everyday communication activities of employees who must struggle with the English language.

World Language Status Does Not Ensure World Class Usage

Joann Temple Dennett
Associate Editor for Issues in International Communication

ONLY one-third of the world's English speakers claim English as their native tongue. The fact that two of every three English speakers uses English as a foreign language underscores recent claims that English is truly an international language, and, although nonnative speakers use English, the rhetorical patterns and expectations of their native language often differ, sometimes radically, from those of English. These differences are not always easily accommodated, possibly because of the cultural expectations that underlie rhetorical models. (For example, the goal of Aristotle's persuasive discourse is by no means universal.)

Thus nonnative writers must first understand how English rhetoric differs from that of their native language. Then, from identifying the purpose and intent of writing to casting the first sentence and eventually wrapping up the argument, they may have to force their English writing into unfamiliar patterns.

Consequently native speakers who evaluate the writing of nonnative colleagues must keep in mind not only problems with vocabulary and syntax but also the potential of larger rhetorical problems. In other words, English may be the language of the global village but the villagers are far from agreement on what is good use of the language—particularly the written language. In fact, "The world may be turning into a global village, but the villagers are at odds over what constitutes good writing," is one reported outcome of an 11-year-project that sought to compare student writing performance in 14 nations. Reporting on this study, Alan C. Purves, former President of the National Council of Teachers of English (NCTE), noted that participants "worked very hard at developing a strict international (scoring) scheme focused primarily on content, structure, and style and tone." But, nonetheless, he said " . . . it was quite clear that people in different countries valued those three (elements) in not quite the same way, or had different interpretations of them." For example, American raters looked most at content; Swedish raters looked at style [1].

Thus when native speakers begin to evaluate how well our language works as a lingua franca, we need to view English in its appropriate international context, not in the context of "proper" classroom English. Many of our colleagues who are nonnative users of English are bringing us this message. In the June issue of this journal, Professor Chia-Jung Tsui [2] of the National Chiao Tung University in Taiwan cautioned us that we might be demanding an unreasonable level of English competency from our nonnative English-speaking colleagues.

Manuscript received October 1991.
The author is with the School of Journalism and Mass Communication, University of Colorado, Boulder, CO 80303.
IEEE Log Number 9105423.

This observation is further strengthened by the two articles offered in this issue. Consider how Mahalingam Subbiah of Weber State University summarizes his argument: " . . . people from different nations think differently, learn differently, and write differently; their notions of good technical English do not necessarily have to be the same as those of native speakers of English." In his article, Professor Lou Chengzhao of Hebei University in China focuses on the difficulties of translators who work from the same language (Mandarin Chinese) to English, but who work separately from Taiwan and the Peoples' Republic of China. Professor Chengzhao reports only a slow evolution toward agreement on how to transcribe newly minted technical terms from their English origins into Chinese characters.

When we seek to evaluate the efficacy of English as a lingua franca, the difficulty at a lexical level among writers working in the same native language, Mandarin Chinese, necessarily raises many questions. For example, we must wonder how two writers or translators working in different languages can ever hope to convey accurately the substance of a theoretical discussion into yet a third language. This is a wonder we do well to remember when we read a translation or when we write a document subject to future translation. The difficulty of translation is also a fundamental message that we would do well to remember before faulting a nonnative colleague for not wielding our native language with the same finesse and skill that we do.

References

[1] "What makes writing 'good'? International panel disagrees," *The Council Chronicle,* NCTE, vol. 1, no. 1, pp.1–3, Sept. 1991.

[2] C.-J. Tsui, "English communication skills needs of professionals in Taiwan's high-technology industries,"*IEEE Trans. Professional Commun.*, vol. 34, no. 2, pp. 79–82, June 1991.

Joann Temple Dennett served in science writing and publications positions with NASA, NOAA, and NCAR, prior to starting her own consulting company. She is a Member of NFPW and NASW and a Senior Member of the Society for Technical Communication (STC) and has won awards in the STC International Technical Communication Contest. A lecturer at the University of Colorado, Boulder, Dr. Dennett has taught technical writing and lectured at Colorado State University, University of Colorado, Denver, NIST, NOAA, NCAR, and various high tech companies. She has published in a wide variety of media including newspapers, popular and technical magazines, reference books, and technical reports.

Reprinted from *IEEE Trans. Prof. Comm.*, vol. PC-35, no. 1, p. 13, March 1992.

English Language Education for Specific Professional Needs

Interface

Index Terms—ESP (English for Specific Purposes), specific needs, tailor-made instruction, workplace and academia.

—Feature by
THOMAS ORR,
AFFILIATE MEMBER, IEEE

Manuscript received March 30, 2001; revised April 18, 2001.
The author is with the Center for Language Research, University of Aizu, Aizuwakamatsu, Fukushima 965-8580, Japan (email: t-orr@u-aizu.ac.jp).
IEEE PII S 0361-1434(01)07495-1.

Tony Dudley-Evans
and Maggie Jo St. John
Developments in English for Specific Purposes: A Multi-Disciplinary Approach
Cambridge, U.K.:
Cambridge Univ. Press, 1998.

One newcomer to English-language education, with research beginning in the 1960s, is English for Specific Purposes (ESP), a discipline that has experienced remarkable growth in the last 20 years in numbers of specialists, programs, and publications as well as in quality of research and education. One good publication that describes this field and its practices is Dudley-Evans and St. John's latest book *Developments in English for Specific Purposes: A Multi-Disciplinary Approach* [1]. The text may interest technical communication trainers because it reveals how English language specialists, working primarily with nonnative speakers, address language learning needs in academia and the workplace from a nontraditional language-teaching perspective.

ESP is English language instruction designed to meet the specific learning needs of a specific learner or group of learners within a specific time frame for which instruction in general English will not suffice. Most often, this instruction involves orientation to specific spoken and written English, usually unfamiliar to the average speaker, which is required to carry out specific academic or workplace tasks, such as dissertation writing for academic purposes, doctor–patient dialog for medical purposes, technical documentation for engineering purposes, or hazardous substance labeling for safety purposes. The training may take place at a graduate school, during new employee orientation at a factory, or in a professional development seminar at corporate offices. The learners may be university or vocational school students, recent immigrants, or working professionals. And the ESP providers may be tenured university faculty, trainers/consultants from a private agency, or in-house language specialists within a major international corporation. Though ESP situations may vary greatly, approaches to ESP are quite similar.

The theory underlying ESP is that English (like other languages) is not a monolithic whole, which can be acquired in totality, but rather it consists of countless components and combinations that have evolved over time to fulfill communication needs situated within a wide range of social, academic, and work-related contexts. Some of these language contexts are common for a large portion of the English-speaking population, and other contexts are encountered by only a very small percent. But because the domains of English are vast in number and vary so greatly, it is highly unlikely that any English speaker (native or nonnative) can ever achieve high levels of competence for every possible situation.

ESP suggests that it is prudent for speakers to first master the general

Reprinted from *IEEE Trans. Prof. Comm.*, vol. PC-44, no. 3, pp. 207–211, September 2001.

symbols, sounds, and grammar of a language as well as the skills to employ them in general domains, and then obtain additional training in the specific language and skills required for any additional scenarios they may encounter in route to their career. General English language education can help learners acquire English for general contexts (e.g., ordering food at a restaurant), but ESP is needed to train learners for special contexts (e.g., courtroom debate) which can be far more complex and difficult to pick up on one's own. Consequently, ESP asserts that a one-size-fits-all approach to language education can be useful for language learning at the beginning stages, but uniquely tailored programs are far more efficient and effective for learners who require special skills to carry out highly specialized tasks for which general English may not prove sufficient.

Dudley-Evans and St. John identify the key activities in ESP as

1. needs analysis,
2. course design,
3. materials selection,
4. teaching and learning, and
5. evaluation.

They state that these do not always occur in a linear sequence, but rather activities are interdependent, and frequently overlap or occur simultaneously. Particular attention, however, is devoted to the first activity since this governs all subsequent activities and thereby distinguishes the work of ESP most clearly from English for General Purposes (EGP).

Needs Analysis

Whether creating a new university course or designing a workplace training program, the first step in ESP is to identify the specific needs of the learner. This is generally done by gathering information from learners and informed sources, via questionnaires and interviews, in order to generate a list of target tasks that the given learners will be expected to carry out. This is followed with analyses of voice or video recordings, and/or various forms of text and documentation to determine what kind of spoken or written English is required to complete the target tasks well.

This preliminary ESP research will identify a corpus of needful vocabulary, a set of spoken scripts or written texts along with useful information about their construction and usage, and a list of skills and relevant nonlinguistic information that learners must master in order to successfully accomplish the specific academic or workplace purposes for which they seek specialized training. Beyond identifying target tasks and the English required to accomplish them, one additional element of needs analysis is learner assessment. This is done prior to instruction in order for ESP specialists to determine where skill and information gaps exist so that precious time is never wasted on covering material that students or clients already know.

Applied linguists who are active in ESP research are particularly interested in needs analysis because this is where there is plenty of room for scholarly inquiry. Investigation of specific academic and workplace discourse communities [2]–[6], with their peculiar language practices and preferences, provides a wealth of information for ESP teachers who need to understand the English language as it is used in a wide range of specialized settings so that they can specify appropriate instructional content and explain it adequately to the learners who come to them for advice or for training. Genre analysis [7]–[13], in particular, is one research area that has been receiving especially popular attention in ESP circles and complements much of the work published by scholars in composition and technical communication.

Course Design

In order to meet specific needs in the best possible way, ESP specialists take into consideration a variety of instructional parameters, some of which are predetermined by outside circumstances while others are determined by the course designer. Dudley-Evans and St. John identify these parameters with questions like these:

1. Should instruction be given **intensively**, with little distraction from other concerns, or **extensively**, scheduled among other courses or work activities?
2. Should learner performance be **assessed** or **nonassessed**?
3. Should instruction address **immediate** needs or **future** needs?
4. Should the instructor's role be that of **provider** (one with primary control of the learning environment) or **facilitator** (one who shares control of the learning environment along with the learners)?
5. Should the course have a **broad focus** with less depth or a **narrow focus** with more depth?
6. Should instruction **precede** application or **run parallel** to use?
7. Should the carrier content of specific linguistic lessons contain **general** topics to stimulate and maintain learner interest or **specific** topics of direct educational value to the learner's work or studies?
8. Is the learning group **homogeneous** with similar learning needs or **heterogeneous** with a variety of different needs?
9. Will course decisions be **determined in advance** of delivery or **evolve as the course proceeds**?

Another important consideration of particular concern to ESP specialists, as Dudley-Evans and St. John point out, is good prioritization of course content. Time limits and instructional prerequisites are two important factors for decisions about which material will be included in a course and the order in which it will be presented.

Materials Selection

Most ESP instruction is tailor-made to meet the specific needs of a specific group, characterized by specific circumstances. Therefore, it is commonly quite difficult for ESP specialists to find existing textbooks that match their learners' needs exactly. Instead, for each unique set of learners, ESP teachers will usually assemble a unique collection of materials from various sources as well as create some original material of their own. This, of course, takes time, but the results in learner achievement make the extra effort for teachers and the extra cost for learners or their sponsors worth the additional investment.

Most materials used in ESP courses are authentic in nature, such as samples of real documents, video recordings of real dialogues, or other samples of language and supporting realia that language learners will actually be required to understand and use. Matching teaching materials to actual learner need is extremely important. As Dudley-Evans and St. John point out, assigning reading homework in *Time* or *New Scientist* to acquaint foreign students with the English of university courses and university textbooks will not prove effective because the content, structure, and journalistic style of popular magazines differ substantially from the didactic/pedagogic language and structure of textbooks.

Teaching and Learning

According to Dudley-Evans and St. John, ESP differs from EFL (English as a Foreign Language) not only in its rigorous commitment to identifying and addressing specific learner needs, but also in its teaching methodology. EFL, for example, which designates general English instruction for nonnative speakers residing outside English-speaking countries, usually employs what the authors call PPP (present, practice, perform). Teachers present a new language skill, students practice it, and then students go out and try to perform it, like novice swimmers who learn a new stroke, practice it poolside or in the shallow end for a while, and then venture over to the deep end of the swimming pool to see if they have successfully mastered the proper movements.

ESP, by contrast, frequently employs what Dudley-Evans and St. John call a "deep-end strategy." By this, they mean that learners, in essence, begin in the deep end of the pool to see how much they know of what is required of them and then receive coaching on specific weaknesses. This is possible in ESP because, in most cases, learners already possess some degree of general English competence and are simply seeking additional language knowledge for specialized contexts. ESP learners may even have the knowledge to perform the task already in their native language.

Russian engineers being trained by ESP specialists to produce engineering documents in English, for example, may already know how to produce similar documents in Russian, but merely require knowledge of equivalent English terms along with additional information about formatting and rhetorical differences. Providing needed input on the English being used during actual spoken or written performance is common in ESP and differentiates it from many general English curriculums where learners might begin with less background knowledge and may not even be able to use what they are learning for several years.

Evaluation

Tests should assess learner mastery of that which has actually been taught. Since the content of ESP instruction usually differs from class to class and client to client, ESP specialists generally design their own tests rather than rely on standardized exams to measure learner progress. Dudley-Evans and St. Johns offer several fine recommendations in their book for making good ESP tests, but for educators interested in even more detail about the proper design and use of quality ESP tests, another book devoted entirely to this subject has recently appeared on bookstore shelves which may prove more useful [14].

One reason ESP has gained such popularity in recent years is that general approaches to English language education have not proven very successful for students or working adults with unique academic or workplace language needs. At American universities, for example, freshman composition may be able to train students how to generate interesting topics, organize their thoughts, find their voice, and compose coherent text with grammatical accuracy, or intensive English programs may be able to teach international students how to comprehend English lectures or read English textbooks. Such general-purpose courses can help students improve their English for general academic success, but they seldom address higher level language needs such as composing successful grant proposals, managing complex pharmaceutical documentation, or negotiating business deals and constructing legal contracts.

Spoken or written language for tasks of this nature requires ESP. Consequently, business schools, engineering schools, law schools, and medical schools have begun to place language experts on their faculty who can meet the advanced language needs of their students for which general language courses in an English department are generally not equipped to address.

In the corporate world, things are not much different. In Japan, for example, when companies begin conducting business abroad, one frequent strategy for improving the English language level of key staff is to send them to a local English conversation school or set up evening classes in company offices so that EFL teachers can assist these learners "brush up"on their English. In most cases, this instruction involves reading a passage of general interest and then answering reading comprehension questions or filling out a worksheet on related grammar points. There also may be some discussion on the article topic to improve speaking skills. Another frequent strategy is to evaluate company employees via a standardized exam, such as TOEIC (Test of English for International Communication) and then send low scorers to TOEIC study seminars to help them raise their scores.

Unfortunately, none of these efforts can guarantee that Japanese engineers will be able to communicate successfully with British engineers about design or manufacturing problems and generate the necessary English paperwork that may be required during the process. Special communication needs, beyond those addressed in general English language courses, require special English training. Smarter companies hire qualified language experts who can target specific language needs with the most appropriate training to get the job done as quickly and efficiently as possible.

Professionals working in ESP and professionals working in technical communication, for the most part, have seldom crossed paths. They usually attend different conferences and publish in different journals. This is unfortunate because both groups frequently work with similar learners and deal with similar issues. Technical communication specialists, like applied linguists working in ESP, commonly address specific English communication needs that general English education is not designed to handle.

Educators and researchers in both areas would clearly benefit from greater familiarity with each others' work, and reading in each others' journals and central texts is one good way to begin. Among the potential starting points for learning about ESP, Dudley-Evans and St. John's recent book *Developments in English for Specific Purposes: A Multi-Disciplinary Approach* provides technical communication experts with one good text that provides a general overview of ESP work.

REFERENCES

[1] T. Dudley-Evans and M. J. St. John, *Developments in English for Specific Purposes: A Multi-Disciplinary Approach*. Cambridge, U.K.: Cambridge Univ. Press, 1998.

[2] K. Hyland, *Disciplinary Discourses: Social Interactions in Academic Writing*. Harlow, U.K.: Pearson Education Ltd., 2000.

[3] E. Ventola and A. Maurenen, Eds., *Academic Writing: Intercultural and Textual Issues*. Amsterdam, The Netherlands: Benjamins, 1996.

[4] H. Yli-Jokipii, *Requests in Professional Discourse: A Cross-Cultural Study of British, American, and Finnish Business Writing*. Helsinki, Finland: Suomalainen Tiedeakatemia, 1994.

[5] C. Bazerman and J. Paradis, *Textual Dynamics of the Professions*. Madison, WI: Univ. Wisconsin Press, 1991.

[6] P. Master, "Active verbs with inanimate subjects in scientific prose," *English for Specific Purposes*, vol. 10, no. 1, pp. 15–34, 1991.

[7] M. J. L. Marco, "Collocational frameworks in medical research papers: A genre-based study," *English for Specific Purposes*, vol. 19, no. 1, pp. 63–86, 2000.

[8] T. Orr, "Genre in the field of computer science and computer engineering," *IEEE Trans. Prof. Commun.*, vol. 42, no. 1, pp. 32–37, 1999.

[9] F. Christie and J. R. Martin, Eds., *Genre and Institutions: Social Processes in the Workplace and School*. London, U.K.: Cassell, 1997.

[10] B. Paltridge, *Genre, Frames and Writing in Research Settings*. Amsterdam, The Netherlands: Benjamins, 1997.

[11] C. Berkenkotter and T. N. Huckin, *Genre Knowledge in Disciplinary Communication: Cognition/Culture/Power*. Hillsdale, NJ: Erlbaum, 1995.

[12] V. K. Bhatia, *Analysing Genre: Language Use in Professional Settings*. London, U.K.: Longman, 1993.

[13] J. M. Swales, *Genre Analysis: English in Academic and Research Settings*. Cambridge, U.K.: Cambridge Univ. Press, 1990.
[14] D. Douglas, *Assessing Languages for Specific Purposes*. Cambridge, U.K.: Cambridge Univ. Press, 2000.

Thomas Orr (A'00), PhD, is Associate Professor at the University of Aizu's Center for Language Research in Japan where he studies and teaches academic and professional discourse in the fields of computer science and computer engineering. He is former Chair of TESOL's Interest Section on English for Specific Purposes (ESP) and currently Associate Editor of IEEE TRANSACTIONS ON PROFESSIONAL COMMUNICATION for submissions related to ESP, ESL/EFL, and international communication.

When Culture and Rhetoric Contrast: Examining English as the International Language of Technical Communication

Interface

—Feature by
KIRK ST. AMANT,
Student Member, IEEE

Manuscript received August 7, 1999; revised August 30, 1999.
The author is with the Department of Rhetoric, University of Minnesota, St. Paul, MN 55108 USA (email: stam0032@tc.umn.edu).
IEEE PII S 0361-1434(99)09567-3.

J. M. Ulijn, Jan M. and J. B. Strother, *Communicating in Business and Technology: From Psycholinguistic Theory to International Practice.* Frankfurt, Germany: Peter Lang, 1995.

Index Terms—*Acculturation, English-language document, rhetoric.*

We often hear the expression that mathematics is the universal language of science and technology. Yet, while mathematics can cut across certain communicative boundaries, it is not the actual language of the sciences, for that role has already been filled—by English.

In her essay "Using English as the International Language of Science," Anne Eisenberg explains that English has "vanquished its linguistic rivals to become the lingua franca of international scientific publication. It is the new Latin" [1, p. 2]. Eisenberg goes on to point out how this linguistic development is affecting the shape of modern scientific discourse. She cites key, international scientific conferences such as the 10th European Symposium on Polymer Spectroscopy and the 12th Colloquium on High Resolution Molecular Spectroscopy where the language of presentation for the entire conference was English, even though these conferences were held in countries in which English was not the official language and even though many of the conference presenters were not native English speakers [1, p. 2].

Eisenberg explains that the use of English as the language of science and technology has become so widespread that even key scientific journals, such as the international edition of *Angewandte Chemie*, while not published in an English-speaking nation, print their articles in English [1, p. 4]. (Eisenberg's claims are not alone, as Kohl et al. have pointed out, one survey of 70 native-born, Japanese-speaking engineers in Japan revealed that 44% of those engineers surveyed write exclusively in English [2, p. 67].)

But do these factors mean that professionals are now free to use a single set of English-language documents to convey technical or scientific information to an international audience? Other sources, such as Jan M. Ulijn and Judith B. Strother's book, *Communicating in Business and Technology: From Psycholinguistic Theory to International Practice*, indicate that while more and more of the world begins to speak English, a new set of rhetorical factors should be considered to ensure effective and efficient cross-cultural communication.

Rhetoric, or the concept of organizing words, sentences, and paragraphs in a particular way in order to achieve a particular end affects how credible an audience will perceive a given document, how seriously they will consider a particular message, and how they will interpret that message [3, p. 119], [4, p. 12]. Thus technical communicators need to use the rhetoric a given audience both prefers and expects. For most individuals, these rhetorical patterns are ingrained. Years of exposure to communicators in the nearby environment have taught each individual how his or her peers expect information to be presented. As Dorothy Windsor's observation of young engineering students indi-

Reprinted from *IEEE Trans. Prof. Comm.*, vol. PC-42, no. 4, pp. 297–300, December 1999.

cates, rhetorical presentation patterns, especially professional ones, are learned through a process of "acculturation:" interaction with the members of a particular professional group. In the case of Windsor's observations, engineering students in internship positions quickly adopted the presentation styles used by older professional engineers in the work environment [5, p. 19].)

Unfortunately, there is no single, universal rhetorical standard. Rather, human rhetorical expectations and preferences vary from group to group and culture to culture. Moreover, these cultural rhetorical differences can occur on a variety of levels (from the sentence to the overall document) and can affect how certain cultural audiences perceive a given English-language document.

Recent research involving translation has indicated that even when reading or speaking in another language, the reader or speaker still prefers the rhetorical patterns of his or her native culture and even judges the effectiveness of other-language documents according to these cultural rhetorical expectations [6, p. 81]. As technical documents increasingly become actual sales tools used to convince prospective international clients of the effectiveness of related technical and scientific products, the emphasis on using the "correct" rhetorical patterns with a given cultural audience increase greatly. As Jan M. Ulijn and Judith B. Strother explain in their book, *Communicating in Business and Technology: From Psycholinguistic Theory to International Practice*, "[I]nstructional manuals are used more and more as [international] marketing instruments. For instance, a Japanese client may wish to see the manual before he buys a product" [7, p. 232]. Thus professional communicators who wish to create English-language documents for a greater international audience should familiarize themselves with some of the key areas related to intercultural rhetorical preferences, especially because some of these preferences are antithetical to many of the "standard" rhetorical techniques that English-speaking (in particular American) communicators are taught or advised to use.

Certain significant cultural-rhetorical differences can occur at the sentence level. For example, many American technical communicators are taught that effective writing style involves getting to the specific subject of the sentence as quickly as possible and then introducing more general information concerning the topic. As Joseph M. Williams explains in *Style: Ten Lessons in Clarity and Grace*, 5th ed., "Your readers want to get to the subject of the main clause quickly; help them do that by keeping your introductory phrases and clauses short, by breaking them out into their own sentences, or by moving them to the ends of their sentences" [8, p. 188].

However, readers from other cultures do not necessarily share these stylistic opinions. Many Southern Europeans, for example, prefer longer sentences in written documents, especially in technical documents. As Ulijn and Strother explain, "Southern European clients expect longer sentences which include more details in technical writing" [7, p. 203]. (Instructions, for example, might not be short imperative sentences, but might instead be longer and "more articulate" sentences containing "tangents" involving different facets of performing a particular step [6, pp. 71, 77].) In some cases, this sentence length is seen as correlating with technical data: the longer the sentence, the more information it contains and thus the more reliable its content seems [7, p. 203].

Moreover, in many Southern European cultures, the reader's level of education can greatly affect his or her expectations of what constitutes "acceptable" sentence length. As Ulijn and Strother point out, many well educated Southern Europeans—those individuals who would probably be the users of high-tech or scientific products—"might expect longer sentences in user documentation to take a product seriously" [7, p. 203]. Thus the wrong rhetorical sentence style, the short sentences used by American communicators, could lead Southern European readers to believe that a particular product is either not meant for them (because it is written using a sentence style associated with a less educated class) or that the related product, "is not a serious one because the sentences in the instructions telling how to use the product are too short" [7, p. 203]. (In this case, instructions such as "Step 1—Open the front cover," might have to be rewritten to include more information—"In the factory, the machine is set according to certain specifications, and to reconfigure the machine for your own use first involves opening the front cover" (this example is based on a sample set of instructions found in [6, p. 81].)

Similarly, the kinds of paragraphs communicators use and the order in which paragraphs are placed within a written presentation establishes a framework that will affect how readers perceive the information. In American professional communication, paragraphs are generally arranged in a specific logical order where one first introduces the basics or premise of an argument, and then the following paragraphs gradually and logically build upon this original premise to prove or establish one final end or goal [9, p. 39], [4, pp. 229–231]. As Scot Ober explains in *Contemporary Business Communication*, 3rd ed., "Once you've grouped related ideas, you then need to differentiate between the major and minor points so that you can line up minor ideas and evidence to support the major ideas" [10, p. 160]. In this rhetorical system, matters not related to the logical development of the final point seem extraneous, awkward, and incorrect, for they have no purpose and will only act to confuse the reader and break the logical development of the greater argument [11, pp. 2, 33–34], [12, p. 48], [3, p. 146].

Individuals from Japanese or Latin cultures, however, often begin professional documents with a paragraph or section containing polite, solicitous comments that do not seem to relate to the logical development of the greater written presentation [13, p. 28]. For example, as William Murdick has noted, a formal Japanese business memo might begin with a statement such as, "I am pleased to hear of the success of the Marui Trading Company in its various enterprises" [14, p. 75]. Without such an introduction, a Japanese reader might perceive these documents as disrespectful or unconcerned with building long-term relationships (two key cultural concepts in Japan) [14, pp. 72–75].

Conversely, Japanese documents often do not include an introductory summary of the information presented in a given professional document (a common practice in American professional and scholarly journals). Rather, as Linda Driskill puts it, the Japanese "prefer a presentation of the data or evidence before the conclusion or recommendation, with no introductory summary" [13, p. 28]. Japanese writers tend to omit such summaries because they might encourage direct, logical debate—something the Japanese tend to avoid [13, p. 28]. Thus a document that included a summary at the beginning might create discomfort among or even offend Japanese readers who would consider such directness as ignorant or rude [14, p. 77].

Eisenberg is correct, for English is increasingly becoming the new international lingua franca. With 1.6 billion speakers around the world (only 25% of whom speak English as their native language), English has solidified its place as the medium for international exchange [15, p. 26]. But, as Ulijn and Strother, Driskill, and Murdick have pointed out, the effective use of English internationally requires a deeper understanding of the cultures using that language. As these authors indicate, effective intercultural/international communication is more than just understanding "language" but also involves understanding "rhetorical" expectations.

References

[1] A. Eisenberg, "Using English as the international language of science," in *International Dimensions of Technical Communication*, D. C. Andrews, Ed. Arlington, VA: STC, 1996, pp. 1–4.

[2] J. R. Kohl et al., "The impact of language and culture on technical communication in Japan." *Tech. Commun.*, vol. 40, no. 1, pp. 62–73, Feb. 1993.

[3] M. M. Lay et al., *Technical Communication*. Chicago, IL: Irwin, 1995.

[4] L. C. Perelman, J. Paradis, and E. Barrett, *The Mayfield Handbook of Technical and Scientific Writing*. Mountain View, CA: Mayfield, 1998.

[5] D. A. Windsor, *Writing Like an Engineer: A Rhetorical Education*. Mahwah, NJ: Erlbaum, 1996.

[6] J. M. Ulijn, "Translating the culture of technical documents: Some experimental evidence," *International Dimensions of Technical Communication*, D. C. Andrews, Ed. Arlington, VA: STC, 1996, pp. 69–86.

[7] J. M. Ulijn and J. B. Strother, *Communicating in Business and Technology: From Psycholinguistic Theory to International Practice*. Frankfurt, Germany: Peter Lang, 1995.

[8] J. M. Williams, *Style: Ten Lessons in Clarity and Grace*, 5th ed. New York: Addison-Wesley Longman, 1997.

[9] A. Lunsford and R. Conners, *The Everyday Writer: A Brief Reference*. New York: St. Martin's, 1997.

[10] S. Ober, *Contemporary Business Communication*, 3rd ed. Boston, MA: Houghton Mifflin, 1998.

[11] P. Richardson, *Style: A Pragmatic Approach*. Boston, MA: Allyn and Bacon, 1998.

[12] D. Pattow and W. Wresch, *Communicating Technical Information: A Guide for the Electronic Age*, 2nd ed. Upper Saddle River, NJ: Prentice-Hall, 1998.

[13] L. Driskill, "Collaborating across national and cultural borders," *International Dimensions of Technical Communication*, D. C. Andrews, Ed. Arlington, VA: STC, 1996, pp. 23–44.
[14] W. Murdick, *The Portable Business Writer*. Boston, MA: Houghton Mifflin, 1999.
[15] J. A. Fishman, "The new linguistic order," *Foreign Policy*, pp. 26–39, Winter, 1998–1999.

Kirk St. Amant (S'97) received his M.A. in technical and scientific communication from James Madison University. He is currently enrolled in the Ph.D. program in rhetoric and scientific and technical communication at the University of Minnesota, where he is also the Director of the Rhetoric Department's Online Writing Center (OWC). He is interested in international technical communication, especially in issues involving rhetoric and culture in the online environment.

The Organization of Japanese Expository Passages

—WAKA FUKUOKA
AND JAN H. SPYRIDAKIS
Member, IEEE

Abstract *– When document designers localize documents for readers in another country, they often assume that the organization of the material used with its original audience will be effective for readers in another country. Whether this assumption is sound depends on what organizational structure readers in other countries are accustomed to seeing. This study examines the organizational structure of 17 Japanese expository texts with the goal of determining what expository structure Japanese readers are most accustomed to reading. The results lead to implications for document designers and readers in both Japan and native English speaking countries.*

Index Terms *– Contrastive rhetoric, deductive organization, inductive organization, organization patterns.*

Manuscript received June 14, 1999; revised June 23, 1999.
W. Fukuoka is with Fuji Xerox, Tokyo, Japan (email: waka.fukuoka@fujixerox.co.jp).
J. H. Spyridakis is with the Department of Technical Communication, University of Washington, Seattle, WA 98195-2195 USA (email: jan@uwtc.washington.edu).
IEEE PII S 0361-1434(99)07231-8.

As businesses become more global, more and more expository documents, such as reports, journal articles, and procedure manuals, are crossing cultural borders. The purpose of such documents is to inform readers about topics that affect their lives at home and at work. Yet, frequently, readers find it difficult to understand translated documents written by authors from cultures other than their own. In addition to the obvious semantic and syntactic differences, documents may differ in their text structure from what the reader is used to, and these differences can cause major stumbling blocks for the reader. Knowing what text structure is commonly used by another culture can help readers set expectations for the reading experience and facilitate their comprehension. It can also help document designers restructure documents to meet the expectations of the target culture. It is with these concerns regarding reader and writer awareness of structural norms in different cultures that we undertook the study presented here.

We focused on the structure of Japanese expository documents because they are commonly believed to be organized in the opposite fashion of American English expository documents. Such contrast could have strong implications for readers and document designers in the opposing cultures. Specifically, the study investigated whether inductive organization is more common than deductive organization in Japanese expository texts, as many researchers claim. A deductively organized text moves from general-to-specific information, a structure in which a general statement is presented before supporting ideas. In contrast, an inductively organized text describes supporting ideas first and then ends with a general statement. A general statement can be a conclusive statement, a main theme, a thesis, or sometimes a summary of the passage. A general statement is not simply a banal introduction of a topic

Reprinted from *IEEE Trans. Prof. Comm.*, vol. PC-42, no. 3, pp. 166–174, September 1999.

such as "this passage is about car manufacturers."

Many researchers believe that inductive organization is somewhat of a cultural norm for Japanese expository texts: that is, the inductive pattern is more common in Japanese texts. If there is a cultural norm regarding the organization of expository texts in American English, it is deductive organization. English expository writing textbooks herald the deductive organization; students are taught to have a thesis or purpose statement in introductions (and sometimes the actual conclusion) and to use topic sentences in the beginning of paragraphs. Studies of text comprehension of native English speakers reveal that readers perform better with a deductive organization, with topic sentences appearing at the beginning of paragraphs and important information presented at the beginning of a text [1]–[4], though most research has examined paragraphs and not whole documents.

If the organizational norms for expository texts do differ between native English and Japanese speakers, it could play havoc for readers when they read documents that are translated with no changes made to the organizational structure. It could explain to a large extent why native English speakers are frustrated by what they describe as vagueness or "oblique logic" of documents written by Japanese writers [5], [6]. It may be that inductively organized Japanese texts make native English speakers, who possess well-honed structural schemata for deductively organized expository texts, feel that the information is vague and oblique, characteristics that might easily disappear with a simple reorganization to a deductive pattern. Critical for successful comprehension, structural schemata are mental frameworks that readers develop through experience with given text structures. They help readers identify a text's organization, select information to store in memory, and link new information with old information. In contrast to native English speakers who have well-developed structural schemata for deductively organized texts, Japanese speakers have well-developed schemata for inductively organized texts and might find English deductively organized documents to be too direct, abrasive, or abrupt, and in conflict with their structural schema for expository texts.

Clearly, other reasons may exist for miscommunication between the two cultures. For example, readers in either culture could be confused or even annoyed by differences in the other culture's sentence patterns, directness of language, or type of illustrations used. But the study reported here took a first step and examined one piece of the pie—organizational patterns of Japanese expository prose—with a specific goal of ascertaining whether Japanese expository texts are in fact inductively organized. After a brief review of relevant literature, we present our study of the organization of Japanese expository texts.

Relevant Literature

Literature supplying the necessary background on this topic comes from studies of contrastive rhetoric. Contrastive rhetoric studies investigate cultural characteristics of texts written in different languages. Such studies of Japanese texts have overwhelmingly found that they are inductively organized. Two approaches have been used to investigate Japanese organizational patterns: one examined English texts written by nonnative English speakers, including native Japanese speakers; the other examined Japanese texts written by native Japanese speakers.

Structure of English Texts Written by Nonnative English Speakers Some researchers believe that the text structures that writers use in their first language are transferred into texts written in the second language. Kaplan [7] analyzed the text structures of 598 English expository compositions written by foreign college students, including Japanese students. He roughly identified five paragraph structures: English, Semitic, Asian, Romance, and Russian. He described Asian writing as an indirect approach to a theme that he depicted with a spiral diagram: that is, "the circles or gyres turn around the subject and show it from a variety of tangential views, but the subject is never looked at directly" (p. 10). Although Kaplan admitted that the Asian writing diagram did not encompass the writing of Japanese students, and he later slightly modified his overall view, Kaplan's early views are often cited as having identified "the pattern" of Asian writing in many teacher-education texts and first- and second-language composition texts [8].

In a similar vein as Kaplan, Kamimura and Oi [9] compared the organizational patterns in argumentative essays written in English by U.S. high school students and Japanese college students. They found that the Japanese subjects tended to show their understanding of opposing views in a way that gives the impression that they do not stick to one opinion. Kamimura and Oi believe this pattern is similar to the circularity described by Kaplan. Kamimura and Oi stand by the assumption that when "students of different language backgrounds write in English, they are apt to transfer the rhetorical patterns of their native languages" [9, p. 1], an assumption Kaplan would agree with. Dennett [10], another researcher, would also agree. She analyzed the English business writings of five native Japanese professionals and found an inductive organizational pattern common in Japanese prose called ki-sho-ten-ketsu, an inductive organizational pattern that states supporting ideas first and then leads to a general statement. Hinds [11] quotes the definition of this pattern by Takemata [12, p. 26] (see Table I). Kaplan, Kamimura and Oi, and Dennett's assumption of transference of rhetorical patterns can be questioned because studies of the writing process would suggest that nonnative English speakers may not write English texts in the same way that they would write texts in their native languages.

Competent writers seem to effectively move among subprocesses such as planning, translating (the process of putting thoughts into written texts), and reviewing [13]. McCutchen, Covil, Hoyne, and Mildes [14] found that skilled writers possess better translation skills, performing better in sentence generation and lexical retrieval tasks, than less skilled writers. Their study concluded that writers who are more fluent in the translating process can devote more resources of working memory to the higher level processes of planning and reviewing, and thus succeed in writing better texts. However, when Japanese writers are writing texts in English, they must devote considerable working memory to the translation process, attending to syntactic and semantic demands of using a nonnative language. With working memory already heavily taxed by the translation process, they may have difficulty executing the planning and reviewing processes, and may in fact write less coherent texts in English than in Japanese. So we should not so easily assume that organizational patterns they use when writing in English necessarily mirror their native patterns.

Although the approach of examining English texts written by nonnative English speakers is a common one and may provide important implications about specific problems that Japanese writers face when writing in English, these studies do not necessarily identify text structures that represent culturally preferred structures for either Japanese writers or readers. The identification of such structures would require the examination of Japanese documents in which Japanese writers would not face an excessive translating load, in other words, documents written by Japanese writers in Japanese, as well as the examination of Japanese readers.

Structure of Japanese Texts Written by Native Japanese Speakers Several researchers who have studied native Japanese expository texts claim that they tend to be inductively organized. Hinds [11], [15] identified the ki-sho-ten-ketsu pattern in editorial columns, "Tensei Jingo," in a major Japanese newspaper, *Asahi Shimbun*. This Japanese newspaper is translated into English without changing the text organization. The purpose of the Tensei Jingo is to make readers take notice of certain societal issues; Tensei Jingo usually conveys the authors' opinions more than facts. Kubota [16] also states that "Tensei Jingo generally focuses more on involving the interlocutors than on conveying information per se" (p. 465). According to Kinosita, as cited in Kubota's study [16], "ki-sho-ten-ketsu is used primarily for literary writing and is not applicable to expository writing" (p. 469). It is a pattern adapted from classical Chinese poetry. Thus expository texts such as reports or scientific articles that primarily seek to convey factual information, sometimes conveying the author's opinion in addition to the factual information, might use organizations other than inductive structures.

Maynard [17] examined the structures of 38 opinion columns, "Column, My View," in the *Asahi Shimbun* newspaper. Her description of the purpose of the columns makes them sound very similar to editorial columns: "As explicitly indicated by the column title, writers are here expected to express their views of opinions on current events and issues with which they are familiar" (p. 392). Like Hinds, she found a tendency for an inductive organization. In her sample, initial paragraphs tended to include noncommentary sentences virtually 90 percent of the time. Also, even within individual paragraphs, sentences tended to

TABLE I
TAKEMATA'S DEFINITION OF ki-sho-ten-ketsu

ki	First, begin one's argument.
sho	Next, develop that.
ten	At the point where this development is finished, turn the idea to a subtheme where there is a connection, but not a directly connected association (to the major theme).
ketsu	Last, bring all of this together and reach a conclusion.

follow the order of noncommentary to commentary sentences.

Some have claimed that Japanese grammar and cultural communication preferences may cause this inductive tendency. Japanese is a verb-final language in which the verb is located at the end of a sentence, thus placing the commentary expression at the end of a sentence. Perhaps more importantly, "the rhetorical and stylistic preference for placing *ketsu* [a conclusion] and commentary toward the end is in agreement with ethos of interpersonal consideration and a feeling of politeness" [17]. Maynard [17] and Kinosita [18] believe that an inductive organization is a cultural characteristic of Japanese discourse. But we should be careful not to generalize Hinds' and Maynard's findings beyond the types of newspaper editorial and "opinion columns" they examined. An inductive structure may not be a common or acceptable structure for other types of expository texts, such as technical documents, scientific articles, or reports.

In fact, few studies have examined the organization of expository texts other than newspaper columns. Oi [19] examined students' argumentative essays and found 74% of Japanese subjects writing in Japanese used inductive organizations, yet 71% of American subjects used deductive organizations. Interestingly, when Japanese subjects wrote in English, 53% used a deductive organization and only 20% used an inductive organization; however, this last result is difficult to interpret because Oi did not describe the Japanese subjects' knowledge of English composition norms.

Looking at the topic from another angle, Nishihara [20] examined how two Japanese reports were modified by English-speaking editors. The editors added a summary of the conclusion at the beginning of the text or moved the general statement in the original text to the beginning of the revised text. Nishihara discussed how the ki-sho-ten-ketsu pattern, which starts with supporting ideas and ends with a general statement, is generally acceptable in Japanese texts yet the opposite organization, general to specific, is preferred in English compositions.

Kinosita [18] makes an interesting observation when he states that "the order in which ideas are presented in Western languages places greater stress on helping the other party to comprehend, and that Japanese [order of ideas] stresses development of one's own thinking" (p. 13). Kinosita [21] advocates that business documents including academic papers should state the main thesis of a passage at the beginning of the text. He also says that writers should describe their contentions explicitly without leaving any vagueness when writing technical documents; he criticizes the characteristics of a Japanese communication style, in which writers tend not to express their ideas clearly to avoid being pushy, a concept also described by Maynard [17].

In summary, several researchers who have examined the structure of Japanese texts written in Japanese claim that an inductive organization is a major, common structure for Japanese expository texts, yet they have identified this pattern in only certain types of expository texts. Specifically, they have not examined the structure of expository texts in which the primary purpose is to convey factual information to readers. We, therefore, conducted an exploratory study in which we analyzed the organization (inductive versus deductive) of Japanese expository texts, which unlike editorials or opinion essays, focus on conveying factual information to readers.

METHODS

Materials The articles for the analysis were selected from three journals so as to achieve variety and avoid the bias of sampling from only one journal that might use a consistent style across issues. Two criteria guided the selection of journals. Journals needed 1) to be written by Japanese writers in Japanese for the Japanese general public and 2) to convey factual information on business, science, or technology topics. If the articles did convey an author's opinions through a thesis or conclusion statement, this opinion needed to be based on facts presented in the article, a scenario that was not the case with the editorials and opinion pieces examined by others. Three journals were selected: *Nikkei Business*, which contains information related to business such as industrial trends or new technology; *Newton*, which contains general scientific information; and *Kagaku*, which contains both general and specific scientific information.

From these three journals, 18 articles (six articles per journal) were selected based on three criteria: selected articles needed to 1) be less than six pages long; 2) clearly discuss one theme throughout the passage; and 3) contain general information that could be easily understood so that the Japanese researcher could identify a general statement. We imposed the length restriction (less than six pages) to avoid using articles with multiple themes, a scenario we felt would be more likely in longer articles. The articles were selected from several issues of the journals. Also, articles were selected that were written by different authors (when the articles stated the authors' names) so as to avoid the bias of representing a single author's organizational strategy.

Measurement Technique The organizational structure of a passage was determined by identifying a general statement in each article and then assigning a numeric value to its location. As stated earlier, a general statement indicates a conclusion, a thesis, or a main theme for the whole text, which explicitly states what an author contends or what a passage discusses.

The method for assigning a numeric value to a general statement's location was based on a modification of Maynard's method [17]. Maynard's method of assigning a percentage to the location of a general statement within each passage was guided by the total number of paragraphs within a passage. In her method, a conclusion that appeared in the 15th of 15 paragraphs was equal to 100% and one that appeared in the third of nine paragraphs was equal to 33.3%. This method unfairly assigned a different percentage to a general statement in a passage's first paragraph, depending on the total number of paragraphs. For example, when a general statement appeared in the first paragraph of seven paragraphs, it was assigned 14%, and when a general statement appeared in the first paragraph of ten paragraphs, it was assigned 10%. To solve this problem, the method used in this study assigned 0% to a general statement appearing in the first paragraph and 100% to a general statement appearing in the last paragraph, regardless of the number of paragraphs in a passage. When a general statement appeared in a paragraph other than the first or last paragraph, its location among all paragraphs was calculated between 0 and 100%. The higher the percentage, the closer the general statement was to the last paragraph. For example, if a general statement appeared in the third of nine paragraphs, it was assigned 25% through the use of the following equation:

$$100 \div (9 - 1) \times (3 - 1).$$

The subtraction of "1" from both the total number of paragraphs and from the paragraph of interest was necessary for the first paragraph to always equal 0%.

General statements were identified in one of three ways. If the passage contained only one general statement, then a percentage for its location among all paragraphs was calculated. If a passage comprised multiple small sections with section titles, a general statement was identified within each section, a location was assigned to each general statement, and then the percentages were averaged for the whole passage. However, if a passage contained small sections that were preceded by an introductory paragraph, only one general statement within the whole text was identified. At this stage of analysis, one article from *Kagaku* was discarded because a general statement could not be identified. For the same reason, three sections from *Newton* articles and one section from a *Kagaku* article were discarded from multisectioned articles that had general statements in the remaining sections. The deleted sections did not clearly describe one theme/thesis showing the essence of the section, which was often promised in the section title. Deletion of these sections did not affect the final location percentages for the articles because the percentage was based on an average of general statement locations in the articles. The average number of paragraphs per article was 12.5.

Results and Discussion

As shown in Table II, two kinds of average percentages for the location of the paragraph containing the general statement were calculated: the total average for all passages across journals and the average for each journal. The average percentage for all passages across the three journals was 43.94%. This number is much smaller than the 86.73% found in Maynard's study [17], even given the different calculation methods. General statements in the journals in this study tend to appear earlier in passages compared to those of the newspaper columns analyzed by Maynard.

The average percentage for the location of the paragraph containing the general statement for passages in each journal indicates an interesting pattern. The average for *Nikkei Business* was 79.17%, showing a tendency for general statements to appear toward the end of the passages. In contrast, the average for Newton was 9.17%, showing a tendency for general statements to appear toward the beginning of the passages. *Kagaku* did not show a clear tendency of inductive or deductive organization with its average of 43.4%.

An examination of the content of the articles reveals a tendency that may partially explain why the journals had different average percentages. With *Nikkei Business*, five of six articles described authors' analyses of or forecasts about business situations. Although these expository articles sought to convey factual information, they also conveyed the authors' view of the information in the form of a thesis or conclusion

TABLE II
Location of Paragraph (in the Passage) Containing the General Statement

Journal	M (%)	SD
Nikkei Business ($n = 6$)	79.17	39.26
Newton ($n = 6$)	9.17	10.46
Kagaku ($n = 5$)	43.40	30.32
Total ($n = 17$)	**43.94**	**40.80**

statement. For example, one author presented information about the current business situation for domestic car manufacturing and concluded that car manufacturers need to focus on developing environmental technology to increase domestic sales. Following, in the form of a thesis/conclusion, is the general statement of the article:

> *Cars with environmental technology can appeal to domestic users because of their fuel efficiency and they will be able to revive domestic car sales.*

Another example of a thesis/conclusion general statement comes from another article in *Nikkei Business* in which the author makes forecasts about a broadcasting company and its distribution of profits:

> *Although the number of people paying to view CS broadcasting has been rapidly increasing, all the companies related to CS' business will not profit.*

In both of these examples, the authors are revealing their interpretation of the facts more than simply making the type of factual statement that occurs with articles that have main theme announcements for their general statements. In the passages with such thesis/conclusion general statements in *Nikkei Business*, the general statements appeared quite late in the articles.

With *Newton*, all six articles also reported factual information, but the general statements announced a main theme for the articles more than a thesis/conclusion emphasizing the author's view of the facts. For example, one passage reported on environmental pollution that causes hormonal disturbances in humans, describing what chemical contaminants were found, what diseases were reported, and how these chemicals are introduced into the human body. Its general statement announces the main theme of the passage without stating the author's viewpoint:

> *Chemical materials that affect hormones could cause cancer or malfunction of the human reproductive system.*

Another example of general statements that announce main themes comes from a multisectioned article in *Newton* that discusses the age of the universe. Each subsection had a main theme announcement:

> Section 1: *The age of the universe can be calculated by the use of Hubble's constant.*
>
> Section 2: *The measured values for Hubble's constant have varied and, as a result, estimates of the age of the universe vary.*
>
> Section 3: *Using the gravity lens, scientists can define Hubble's constant and therefore the age of the universe more accurately.*

These passages from *Newton* which announce factual main themes without stating the author's view of the facts, appear quite early in the articles.

Kagaku, on the other hand, included factual, expository passages with and without the authors' views on the topic (i.e., with theses/conclusions or with main theme announcements). The percentages for location of the general statement were quite varied, ranging from 9 to 80%. Thus we found no clear pattern for the location of general statements in the *Kagaku* passages.

Based on this finding, we calculated a third type of average. All passages were divided into two groups: passages with thesis/conclusion statements such as most of the *Nikkei Business* articles and passages with main theme announcements such as the *Newton* articles. The average percentage for the location of general statements in the thesis statement passages was 74.17% (SD = 37.97), and the average for the theme announcement passages was 27.45% (SD = 33.1). This result implies that Japanese authors may tend to develop passages inductively when stating their opinions based on their interpretation of the facts. This assumption corresponds to the findings of Maynard [17] and Oi [19] that Japanese texts conveying authors' opinions tend to be organized inductively, even though their passages were more purely opinion and our passages leaned more in the direction of opinions based on facts presented in the articles. In contrast, it appears that authors may develop expository passages deductively when describing facts and simply announcing a main theme.

It is noteworthy that a few passages in our study had patterns that were completely opposite of the predominant pattern in that a few passages containing thesis statements were deductively organized, and a few with only main theme announcements were inductively organized. For example, one passage in *Nikkei Business* contained a thesis in the first paragraph; yet another announced a factual main theme in the last paragraph.

The results of our study, in combination with results of earlier studies, do have some implications for readers and writers.

Conclusions and Recommendations

For many years, researchers have examined expository texts written by Japanese writers in either English or Japanese, and these researchers have usually concluded that Japanese writers organize such texts inductively. Given what we know about the writing process, it is unwise to reach definitive conclusions about Japanese organization norms for expository texts by examining texts written by Japanese writers in their second language, i.e., English. But even the studies of Japanese texts written in Japanese have found that writers organize expository texts inductively. These studies, however, have not examined texts where the goal is to convey factual information.

The study reported here took the next step and examined Japanese expository texts written in Japanese, where the goal of the texts was to convey factual information. We found that one cannot make an across-the-board statement regarding organizational patterns of Japanese expository texts. Expository texts can be organized inductively or deductively, and the author's organizational decision appears to rest on his or her goal. Although more studies are needed, our study found that passages that state a thesis or conclusion which conveys the author's view about the meaning of the factual information tend to be inductively structured and that passages that report factual information and simply announce the main theme of the passage tend to be deductively organized. Of course, there will always be a few exceptions because individual authors may have their own styles of organizing information. Some texts will not exclusively convey either an author's opinion or announce a main theme. Indeed, they may do a bit of both.

These findings have implications for readers who are native English speakers. As stated earlier, these readers are sometimes frustrated by what they describe as vagueness or "oblique logic" of documents written by Japanese writers. Native English speakers will need to realize that expository texts translated from Japanese may be organized either deductively or inductively. With this realization, they should look for clues to help them identify a text's organization early in the reading process so that they can instantiate the correct structural schema for the text at hand. If they find early in the passage what feels like an announcement of the main theme without the author taking a stand, they are more than likely reading a deductively organized passage and will be able to call up their schema for deductive structures. If, however, they cannot identify any theme announcement or thesis early on, they will need to realize that they are probably reading an inductive piece in which the author will take a stand and iterate a thesis or conclusion toward the end of the text, and then instantiate a schema for inductive structures. Native English speaking readers probably possess an inductive structural schema that they can instantiate at times, such as when an author is attempting to persuade the reader about an unpopular idea and therefore delays his or her opinion. But even this type of text usually provides thematic cues early on that help the reader instantiate a schema, clues that are often lacking in inductively organized Japanese texts that simply lead up to a thesis late in the passage. We must remember that research with native English speaking readers suggests that they comprehend deductively organized texts better than inductively organized texts. Most of this research, however, has been conducted with extremely short passages and nonadult readers.

Our findings also have implications for Japanese readers. Japanese readers would very likely possess a deductive structure schema for reading expository texts that discuss straightforward facts in that they organize such texts deductively, as shown in the study presented here. Yet there has been scant research in this area. We are uncertain though that they would call up this deductive schema if an expository text conveyed a thesis early in the text because many Japanese writers organize such texts inductively. Further, if Japanese writers place the thesis statement late in an expository text so as to avoid offending readers by not presenting their viewpoints early on, then perhaps Japanese readers would be offended if a writer placed a thesis early in the text. To be more certain about the abilities and preferences of Japanese readers with regard to inductive versus deductive organizations, tests should be conducted with adult readers of this population.

Our findings additionally have implications for document designers in both cultures, though some of our conclusions are tempered by uncertainties discussed regarding readers. If texts are organized deductively, Japanese document designers will not need to make organizational changes for native English speaking readers because this is the organization they expect most often with an expository text. But if expository texts are organized inductively, they may need to reverse the organization for these readers given what we have said about this reading population earlier. Testing of adult native English speakers with inductively organized texts presenting scientific or technical content would help provide the definitive answer to this quandary. American document designers will probably not need to make changes for Japanese readers when texts are organized deductively and are presenting factual information without an author's view of the content. But if a text conveys an author's viewpoint through a thesis in a deductively organized passage, we do not know if the document designer would need to reverse the organization because we do not know how Japanese readers would fare with such texts. Tests of Japanese adult readers with texts presenting scientific or technical content are needed to clarify what actions document designers should take, a task we undertake in our next study.

As this discussion reveals, more research is needed, both regarding Japanese cultural norms for organizing expository texts and the abilities and preferences of readers. Studies of Japanese texts should examine passages from other types of expository publications than those used in this study. These passages could be more scientific or technical, considerably longer, and serve different purposes or audiences. Readers in both cultures should be investigated to assess how well they comprehend expository texts that are inductively or deductively organized and what their preferences are. It would be most informative to discover whether the text organization that leads to the best comprehension would in fact represent the text that readers prefer.

References

[1] D. Dee-Lucas and J. Larkin, "Organization and comprehensibility in scientific proofs, or 'consider a particle p. . . ,'" *J. Educ. Psychol.*, vol. 82, no. 4, pp. 701–714, 1990.

[2] D. Kieras, "Good and bad structure in simple paragraphs: Effects on apparent theme, reading time and recall," *J. Verbal Learning and Verbal Behavior*, vol. 17, pp. 13–28, 1978.

[3] R. Lorch and E. Lorch, "Topic structure representation and text recall," *J. Educ. Psychol.*, vol. 77, no. 2, pp. 137–148, 1985.

[4] J. Gold and L. S. Fleisher, "Comprehension breakdown with inductively organized text: Differences between average and disabled readers," *Remed. Special Educ. Rase*, vol. 7, no. 4, pp. 26–32, 1986.

[5] J. Mackin, "Surmounting the barrier between Japanese and English technical documents," *Tech. Commun.*, vol. 25, pp. 346–351, 1989.

[6] F. Duffy, "Dear editor," *Intercom*, vol. 3, 1997.

[7] R. Kaplan, "Cultural thought patterns in inter-cultural education," *Language Learning*, vol. 16, pp. 1–20, 1966.

[8] C. Severino, "The 'doodles' in context: Qualifying claims about contrastive rhetoric," *Writing Ctr. J.*, vol. 14, no. 1, pp. 44–62, 1993.

[9] T. Kamimura and K. Oi, "A crosscultural analysis of argumentative strategies in student essays," presented at the Annual Meeting of the Teachers of English to Speakers of Other Languages (30th), Chicago, IL, 1996.

[10] J. T. Dennett, "Not to say is better than to say: How rhetorical structure reflects cultural context in Japanese–English technical writing," *IEEE Trans. Prof. Commun.*, vol. 31, no. 3, pp. 116–119, 1988.

[11] J. Hinds, "Contrastive rhetoric: Japanese and English," *Text*, vol. 3, no. 2, 183–195, 1983.

[12] K. Takemata, *Genkoo Shippitsu Nyuumon [An Introduction to Writing Manuscripts]*. Tokyo, Japan: Natsumesha, 1976.

[13] J. R. Hayes and L. S. Flower, "Identifying the organization of writing process processes," In L. W. Gregg and E. R. Steinberg, Eds., *Cognitive Processes in Writing*. Hilldale, NJ: Lawrence Erlbaum Assoc., 1980, pp. 3–30.

[14] D. McCutchen, A. Covil, S. H. Hoyne, and K. Mildes, "Individual differences in writing: implications of translating fluency," *J. Educ. Psychol.*, vol. 86, no. 2, pp. 256–266, 1994.

[15] J. Hinds, "Inductive, deductive, quasiinductive: Expository writing in Japanese, Korean, Chinese, and Thai," In U. Connor and A. M. Johns, Eds., *Coherence in Writing: Research and Pedagogical Perspective*. Alexandria, VA: Teachers of English to Speakers of Other Languages, Inc., 1990, pp. 87–110.

[16] R. Kubota, "A reevaluation of the uniqueness of Japanese written discourse implications for contrastive rhetoric," *Written Commun.*, vol. 14, no. 4, pp. 460–480, 1997.

[17] S. K. Maynard, "Presentation of one's view in Japanese newspaper columns: Commentary strategies and sequencing," *Text*, vol. 16, no. 2, pp. 391–421, 1996.
[18] K. Kinosita, "Differences between Japanese and Western styles of technical communication," presented at the 2nd Eindhoven Symposium on Language for Special Purposes, Aug 3–6, 1988. (Available from the author at Minami 6-6-10, Higashi Kaigan, Chigaskai 253 Japan.)
[19] K. Oi, "Cross-cultural differences in rhetorical patterning: A study of Japanese and English," *JACET Bull.*, vol. 17, pp. 23–48, 1986.
[20] R. Nishihara, "Nichiei taishou shujihou" [Contrastive rhetoric: Japanese and English], *Nihongo Kyoiku*, vol. 72, pp. 25–41, 1990.
[21] K. Kinosita, *Rikakei no sakubun gijutsu" [Compositions for science majors].* Tokyo, Japan: Chuo Koron Sha, 1981.

Waka Fukuoka is in charge of creating user manuals in English, Chinese, and Korean for Asian and Ocean countries at Fuji Xerox in Tokyo, Japan. She started her career as a technical translator and recently received her M.S. degee in Technical Communication. Her thesis focused on Japanese rhetorical norms.

Jan H. Spyridakis is a Professor in the Department of Technical Communication at the University of Washington, where she teaches courses on style in writing, research methodology, and international and advanced technical communication. Her research and consulting focus on the effect of document and screen design variables on comprehension and usability. Jan has received teaching and publication awards, and is a Fellow of the Society for Technical Communication.

Measuring the Translatability of Simplified English in Procedural Documents

Jan H. Spyridakis, *Member, IEEE*, Heather Holmback, and Serena K. Shubert

***Abstract*—This paper reports the results of a study that tested the translatability of a restricted language, called Simplified English (SE), as used in maintenance procedures in the airline industry. The study examined the effect of document type (SE versus non-SE) and procedure (procedure A versus procedure B) on the quality and ease of translation for native speakers of Spanish, Chinese, or Japanese. The results reveal that SE may be more effectively translated by native Spanish speakers than by Chinese speakers. The paper concludes with a discussion of methodological issues that researchers should consider when running such translation studies.**

***Index Terms*— Airline industry, Chinese, English, Japanese, manuals, Simplified English, Spanish, translation.**

THE use of a controlled or restricted subset of English for creating documentation is becoming more common in industry as companies attempt to improve the quality of technical documents, especially those that need to be read and understood by nonnative speakers of English. Restricted subsets of English are also being applied to documents that need to be translated into other languages, either by humans or computers. While the claims that using a restricted language makes documents more comprehensible and translatable are reasonable, empirical support is lacking.

In an attempt to provide empirical evidence as to whether, how, and to what degree a restricted language such as Simplified English (SE) can improve the comprehensibility and translatability of technical documentation, researchers from Boeing and the University of Washington conducted a two-part empirical study on SE, which is the writing standard currently used at Boeing for maintenance manuals. The first experiment, concerning the comprehensibility of SE, is reported in Shubert *et al.* [1]. Here we report on the second experiment, a pilot study on the effect of SE on the ease and accuracy of translation.

OVERVIEW OF SE

Simplified English is one of several restricted language standards that have been developed to reduce ambiguity and provide greater consistency and readability in technical documents. Proponents of SE (and other controlled languages) have claimed that using a restricted English standard makes documents easier to read and understand, and easier to translate accurately into other natural languages. SE was designed to be applied to both procedural and descriptive writing, but in practice it has primarily been applied to procedural technical documents, which we used in this experiment. What follows is a brief history and description of the SE standard. See Adriaens and Schreurs [2] for a more complete discussion of controlled languages.

The SE standard began to be formulated in the late 1970's. It was preceded by similar efforts, such as Charles Ogden's Basic English in 1932 [3] and Caterpillar Tractor Company's Caterpillar Fundamental English in 1972 [4], [5]. Caterpillar Fundamental English laid the foundation for the International Language for Servicing and Maintenance (ILSAM). ILSAM was developed to facilitate translation for international product support documentation [6]. SE was originally developed at Fokker, primarily by John Kirkman [7], and was officially adopted and modified by The Association Europeene de Constructeurs de Material Aerospatial (AECMA) for application to technical documentation in the aerospace industry [8]. SE is one of several descendants of Caterpillar's early work and ILSAM.

The SE standard was adopted by AECMA in response to requests from European airline companies to improve the readability of aircraft documentation. It is currently being used by almost all companies that produce aircraft maintenance procedures, including Aerospatiale Industrie, The Boeing Company, British Aerospace, Deutsche Aerospace, Fokker, General Electric, Lockheed, McDonnell Douglas, and Pratt & Whitney. Simplified English continues to be developed and refined by an international group, the AECMA SE Working Group, which released a new version (Issue 1) in late 1995 [9]. The Boeing Commercial Airplane Group (BCAG) has committed to comply with the SE standard in producing its maintenance manuals since it was adopted in the United States by the Air Transport Authority (ATA) and the Aircraft Industries Association (AIA). With the aid of an SE automated checker [8], the Customer Services Division of BCAG began distributing maintenance manuals written in SE in 1990.

The SE standard consists of a core vocabulary and a set of writing rules that govern grammar and style. There are also guidelines for company-defined technical vocabulary. The 1500-word core vocabulary consists of verbs, prepositions, conjunctions, adjectives, adverbs, and nouns. Words approved for the core vocabulary were chosen for their simplicity and commonality with other European languages [9]. In most cases, a given word is restricted to one meaning (to reduce lexical ambiguity), and a given meaning is represented in

Manuscript received June 1996; revised October 1996. This work was supported by The Boeing Company.

The authors are with the Department of Technical Communication, University of Washington, Seattle, WA 98195 USA, and the Boeing Co. (Holmback).

Publisher Item Identifier S 0361-1434(97)01825-0.

Reprinted from *IEEE Trans. Prof. Comm.*, vol. PC-40, no. 1, pp. 4–12, March 1997.

the vocabulary by only one word (to reduce synonymy). For example, "follow" can be used only in the meaning "to come after" and not in the meaning "obey"; and "start" is a legal SE word, but "begin" and "initiate" are not allowed.

Although the core vocabulary is limited, technical names and manufacturing processes can be added as needed. This flexibility ensures that the standard can be adapted to serve the different content domains of different companies. The goals of developing and using a highly restricted, standard vocabulary are to eliminate ambiguities and to choose the most common, simple word to express an idea to the reader. This rationale is supported by existing research on readability [10]–[15].

The writing rules of the SE standard were designed to simplify and make consistent the grammar and writing style of documents. The rules cover words, phrases, and sentences, as well as the form and content of procedures, the use of warnings and cautions, and the construction of paragraphs in descriptive writing. (See [9] for detailed SE writing rules.) In some ways, SE is very restrictive; it imposes constraints on 1) the length of sentences and noun compounds, 2) the types of verb forms that can be used (for example, no "-ing" forms, limited use of passive voice), 3) the organization of paragraphs (only one topic must be introduced in a paragraph, and it must be the first sentence of the paragraph), and 4) the expression of content (only one instruction per sentence). The "one word–one meaning" criterion can also be quite restrictive for proficient English writers, who have many synonyms at their disposal.

While it may be more difficult for writers to write in SE because of the restrictions, many companies use SE in producing documents, apparently operating under the assumption that SE accomplishes its goals of making documents easier to read, understand, and translate. Yet they seem to be doing so on the basis of intuitive and anecdotal evidence. Don Hinson raised his concerns about the "uncritical use of SE standards" in an article about issues for writers [6]. He states, "... AECMA's SE claims to be founded on readability research. It would be interesting to establish the nature, validity, and appropriateness of the research used. It would also be helpful to know of any research carried out on SE manuals in use" (p. 36). Our recent experiment on the comprehensibility of SE supports the claim that using SE improves the comprehensibility of relatively complex technical aircraft maintenance manual procedures [1]. In the current experiment, we were interested in testing the assumption that SE improves the translatability of aircraft maintenance manual procedures for native speakers of different languages. We were also interested in reassessing how procedural complexity interacts with SE.

METHODOLOGY

To test the effects of SE/non-SE, procedure, and native language on translation quality and ease, we had native speakers of either Spanish, Chinese, or Japanese translate one of four documents (SE or non-SE versions of Procedures A or B); then, raters from the same languages assessed the translations on several parameters. The specific methodology is discussed below; it is separated into the methods we used for obtaining the translations and the methods we used for rating the translations.

Translation Methods

Subjects: Subjects for the translation tasks consisted of native speakers of Chinese, Spanish, or Japanese. We used university students, rather than professional translators, as subjects for the following reasons: 1) we were interested in testing general claims about SE; 2) we believed that university students would represent novice translators and somewhat replicate the novice translator status of airline mechanics who sometimes translate portions of the maintenance procedures; and 3) we had limited funds for this pilot study.

To find subjects at the university to translate the documents, we ran advertisements in the University of Washington (UW) student newspaper. Many Chinese speakers responded and we selected those who had similar education levels (i.e., completed bachelor's degrees). Many Spanish speakers responded to the ad and we secured more by word-of-mouth and through the Internet. The Spanish speaking subjects included UW undergraduates, two UW employees (one who had completed an undergraduate degree, and one who had not), and one housemate of a student. We used all of the few Japanese speaking respondents to the ad and secured more subjects by contacting UW Asian Student Services, ESL classes, primary engineering classes, Japanese student organizations, community colleges, religious and social organizations, and Internet sources. Nevertheless, we managed to recruit only six Japanese speaking undergraduate subjects for our experiment. Therefore, we did not statistically analyze the data for Japanese speakers as we did for the other two target languages. While we had planned to use 16 subjects per language, the final subject count included 18 native Chinese speakers, 15 native Spanish speakers, and 6 native Japanese speakers.

Materials: The translation materials consisted of four documents (two procedures written in SE and non-SE), an instruction sheet and consent form for each subject, and lined tablets or blank paper.

The translation documents consisted of the same two procedures employed in the earlier comprehension experiment [1]. The procedure for selecting these documents is discussed below. With the help of a Boeing Commercial Airplane Group (BCAG) technical editor, Paul Montague, a sample of fifteen non-SE naturally occurring maintenance manual procedures was collected. Each had an SE version, written by BCAG maintenance manual writers after compliance with the SE standard, and a non-SE version, written before compliance with the SE standard.

Because we wanted only two similar procedures for the final experiment, the sample had to be reduced. After reading all fifteen procedures to ascertain the range of procedures covered, team members did a rough count of word, sentence, and paragraph length to further narrow the sample. We initially identified five similar procedures in which the non-SE version fit the following criteria: no less than 450 words, no more than 1000 words, and no more than 15% passive voice.

The procedures were typed into Word 5.0®, and the team used the Word 5.0® grammar checker to further analyze the documents. The information about number of words, number of paragraphs, percentage of passive voice, readability levels, and sentence length provided some useful criteria to help select the two final non-SE procedures, which we believed were similarly matched on the above parameters (see Table I). Furthermore, the number of steps were deemed similar in the two procedures and the topics in both were felt to be understandable by novices in the field. The final procedures chosen were Procedure A, entitled "49-15-01 APU Air Intake Duct-Removal/Installation," and Procedure B, entitled "12-15-10" no. 1, 2 and 4 Passenger Door Emergency Power Reservoir—Servicing (Gaseous)." All documents (both SE and non-SE versions of the procedures) were reformatted to exhibit similar layouts.

While we believed these two procedures were sufficiently similar given the assessment criteria, the results of the comprehension experiment indicated otherwise: Procedure A was significantly more comprehensible when written in SE than non-SE, for both native and nonnative speakers of English, than Procedure B. A re-analysis of the two procedures led us to believe that Procedure A was more complex than Procedure B. Table I above reveals that Procedure A had fewer words and sentences, but more words per sentence and more paragraphs than Procedure B. And while Procedure A had fewer passive voice constructions than Procedure B, it had a higher Flesch rating. Boeing personnel also indicated that Procedure A involved a more complex task. Given these differences, we expected to see the procedure differences surface again when translation quality was measured.

Procedure: For the translation task, subjects attended one of many three-hour translation sessions (separate sessions were held for different languages). When subjects arrived at a session, the test administrator explained the general task from a pre-written script. Subjects were then randomly assigned to read and translate one of the four English source documents (subjects were not told anything about SE or non-SE). Written instructions told subjects to preserve the meaning and style of the original procedure when possible, to use and underline any English words they did not know, and to use any English words they believed should not be translated—yet not to underline them. Subjects completed a consent form and a brief demographic questionnaire asking number of years of education, number of years living in the US, and number of years of English instruction. Subjects were paid $8 per hour for a maximum of three hours; most subjects used the entire three hours to complete the task.

Rating Methods

Raters: Three native speakers from each language (Chinese, Spanish, and Japanese) rated the translations. Raters were solicited through ads in the UW student newspaper and the Internet. The candidates submitted resumes, and the most qualified applicants were interviewed. Those chosen for the task demonstrated good communication skills in English (as exhibited in respondents' cover letters, resumes, e-mail messages, and telephone conversations). All raters were UW graduate students.

TABLE I
SELECTION CRITERIA FOR NON-SE PROCEDURES

Criteria	Procedure A	Procedure B
Counts		
Words	686	846
Sentences	32	63
Paragraphs	61	55
Averages		
Words per sentence	21	13
Characters per word	4	4
Readability		
Percent passive voice	3	11
Flesch grade level	14.7	8.8
Task Difficulty		
Stages	5	2
Steps	29	39

Materials: The rating materials included a baseline translation for each language; an English document with content ranked by importance; copies of the subjects' translations; and a rating key.

There was one baseline translation for each document (i.e., the SE and non-SE versions of each procedure in each target language). These baseline translations were provided by three Boeing employees (one native speaker per language) who were familiar with maintenance manuals. The translations were designed to provide a standard for raters to consult and to exemplify "good" translations. Raters were also given a copy of the English documents ranked for content importance. Paul Montague, a BCAG technical editor, had ranked terms, sentences, and sections with a "1" for the more important information and a "2" for the less important information.

The rating keys included five measures, two of which had two submeasures: accuracy of the translation, style match with the original document, ease of comprehension, number of major and minor mistranslations, and number of major and minor omissions.

Accuracy of the Translation: Accuracy was rated on a five-point scale with 1 equal to "highly inaccurate" and 5 equal to "highly accurate." Accuracy was defined as how precisely the translation reflected the content of the English source document.

Style Match with the Original Document: The degree to which the style of the translation matched the style of the original document was also rated on a five-point scale with 1 equal to "highly mismatches the original" and 5 equal to "highly matches the original." Style was defined as the language level, sentence difficulty, and tone of the document. This measure was based on the assumption that if a document was easy to translate, the style of the original document would be preserved in the translation, as subjects had been instructed to maintain the style of the original document when possible.

Ease of Comprehension: Ease of comprehension was also rated on a five-point scale with 1 equal to "very unclear" and 5 equal to "very clear." Raters were instructed to rate the translations for how clear and easy they were to read and comprehend. This measure was based on the rationale that a more readable translation results when the translation task is relatively easy.

Number of Major and Minor Mistranslations: The number of mistranslations and the number of omissions are traditional measures of translation quality. Mistranslations were defined as words that are inaccurately translated. Raters identified and ranked mistranslated words as either major or minor by comparing them with the baseline translations' terms, sentences, and sections ranked for importance. Major mistranslations corresponded to a 1 and minor mistranslations to a 2 on the baseline translations.

Number of Major and Minor Omissions: Omissions were defined as words that subjects left out of their translations. Raters identified and ranked omissions as either major or minor by comparing the translations with the baseline translations' terms, sentences, and sections ranked for importance. Major omissions corresponded to a 1 and minor omissions to a 2 on the baseline translations. Raters were instructed to ignore the omission of function words (such as articles). Further, the raters were trained not to assess terms that should not be translated as omissions (e.g., label on a part). The baseline translations helped ensure interrater reliability regarding what terms should or should not be translated.

Procedure: Raters were trained at an explanatory meeting and a review session (separate meetings were held with raters of the three languages). At the explanatory meeting, the administrator explained the task and provided detailed instructions. Raters read the baseline translations carefully and agreed on terms that they thought should be translated and altered the baseline accordingly (e.g., many terms were not translated in the original Spanish baseline). Further, raters gained an understanding of and agreed on how the measures were to be operationalized. After the training meeting, raters were given a practice translation to rate before the review session. The practice translation (one per language) was randomly selected from the translations completed during the experiment (the ratings of these practice translations were excluded from the analysis of the experimental data). The ratings of these translations were discussed at the review meeting and indicated that sufficient agreement among the raters had been established. The rater agreement was reconfirmed in the actual experiment. After the review meeting, raters were given copies of all of the translations for their target language. The raters were paid $240.00 each for their efforts.

After the raters returned the rated translations, the ratings of the three raters per language were averaged to provide one rating score per dependent measure for each subject. These scores were analyzed in Statview 4.0.

Results and Discussion

The primary goal of this pilot study was to investigate the claim that the use of SE in a technical procedure will improve the translatability (i.e., quality and ease of translation) of that document compared with the same technical procedure not written in SE. Another goal of the study was to assess whether there were differences in translation quality and ease between the two procedures (A and B), as we were interested in how document complexity, a factor that arose in our earlier comprehension study, might influence translatability. We were also interested in any differences in translation quality among the different target languages (Chinese, Spanish, Japanese) to determine whether SE affects translation quality equally for the three languages. To assess the issues described, we wanted to run a three-way ANOVA (SE/Non-SE × Procedure × Language); however, the small cell sizes for the Japanese speakers precluded using them in such an analysis. Instead, three 2 × 2 ANOVAs (SE/non-SE × Procedure) were run on the seven dependent measures for 1) translations from all languages combined, 2) Spanish translations, and 3) Chinese translations. Although we statistically analyzed the Spanish and Chinese translations, we were concerned about the small cell sizes and the resulting potential for large variances that might make it difficult to obtain significant findings.

Because the study reported here was difficult to conduct because of very little precedent in the literature for measuring ease and quality of translation, another goal of this study was to assess the design of this experiment and identify areas for further exploration. Because of this and the small cell sizes, we report patterns that appeared in the data as well as the results of inferential statistics.

After a brief discussion of the demographic data, the main effects of SE/non-SE and Procedure are discussed, first for all languages combined and then individually for Spanish and Chinese. This discussion is followed by a discussion of interactions.

Relationship Between Translations and Subject Demographics

The demographic profile of subjects consisted of three variables: number of years of education, number of years living in the US, and number of years of English instruction. From this data, we were attempting to identify a measure of English ability, as TOEFL scores would have been either unavailable or extremely outdated for many subjects.

To determine whether the speakers of the three languages differed, we conducted three one-way ANOVAs of native language on the three demographic variables. The ANOVAs were nonsignificant, suggesting that the speakers of the three languages were similar in number of years of education, number of years living in the U.S., and number of years of English instruction. We then correlated the demographic data with the translation ratings and found no consistent patterns. We have concluded that one may need to have a more direct measure of English ability to see how it might affect the translation quality of SE versus non-SE documents. Subjects' level of literacy in their native language and experience with scientific or technical material might also be relevant factors.

Effect of SE Versus Non-SE

We first examine the results for the effect of document type (SE versus non-SE) on the accuracy, style match, comprehension, mistranslations (minor and major), and omissions (minor and major) for the target translations.

Languages Combined: For the three languages combined, a significant main effect ($p < 0.05$) occurred only for the style match and the minor omissions measures. In both cases, the SE translations were superior, matching the style of the original document better and containing fewer minor omissions than the non-SE translations. Table II lists the means and standard deviations (in parentheses) for both the SE and non-SE documents, and the F and p values associated with the ANOVAs for the seven dependent measures.

Although significant differences were limited for all languages combined, the data do reveal an interesting pattern: subjects who translated SE documents produced higher quality translations than those who translated non-SE documents (except for major mistranslations). While these differences were significant on only two measures, the large variance on some measures, caused perhaps by combining the languages, may account for the lack of significance on the other measures. Hence, an analysis of the languages separately may be more revealing.

Spanish Translations: For the Spanish speakers, translations of the SE documents differed significantly from the non-SE documents on four measures: SE translations scored significantly higher on accuracy, style match, and comprehensibility, and contained significantly fewer minor mistranslations than non-SE translations. Table III lists the means and standard deviations (in parentheses) for both the SE and non-SE documents, and the F and p values associated with the ANOVAs for the seven dependent measures.

Beyond the significant differences between SE and non-SE means on four measures, for five measures (accuracy, style match, comprehension, minor mistranslations, and major omissions) the variances are significantly heterogeneous ($p \leq 0.05$) between the SE and non-SE translations. And the variance on these measures is consistently smaller for the SE translations than for the non-SE translations, suggesting that the SE translations are more consistent than the non-SE translations. A similar pattern is seen for the other two dependent measures, although the variances do not differ significantly. Fortunately, the heterogeneity between SE and non-SE variances is not so extreme as to invalidate the ANOVA statistics [16].

In summary, for the Spanish speakers, SE translations received significantly better ratings on four measures and showed significantly greater consistency on five measures than the non-SE translations.

Chinese Translations: The ANOVA results as well as the means and standard deviations (in parentheses) for Chinese speakers translating the SE or non-SE documents are presented in Table IV. There were no significant differences between the SE and non-SE translations. Further, the variances associated with the means are generally homogeneous, suggesting that the SE and non-SE documents were translated with equal consistency.

Comparison of Spanish and Chinese Translation Results: For both the Spanish and Chinese translations, an examination of both the significant and nonsignificant differences reveals that the SE translations were rated better than the non-SE translations on twelve of the fourteen measures: higher scores for accuracy, style match, and comprehension; lower scores for both types of mistranslations and omissions. The two exceptions are for Spanish major omissions and Chinese major mistranslations.

There were more significant differences, and larger differences between means even when there was no significance, for the Spanish SE translations versus the non-SE translations than for the Chinese translations, or for the combined languages' data (which included the Japanese subjects). One reason for

TABLE II
SE VERSUS NON-SE DOCUMENTS FOR LANGUAGES COMBINED

Measures	Means (SD)		F	p
	SE n = 19	non-SE n = 18		
Accuracy	3.72 (1.19)	3.11 (1.32)	2.15	.1521
Style Match	4.01 (.91)	3.41 (1.16)	4.74	.0367*
Comprehension	4.00 (1.20)	3.28 (1.45)	2.75	.1069
Mistranslations				
Major	10.02 (11.55)	9.37 (11.48)	0.005	.9464
Minor	7.46 (5.75)	10.57 (7.05)	2.112	.1559
Omissions				
Major	4.35 (5.86)	6.33 (10.52)	0.751	.3927
Minor	2.19 (2.62)	9.67 (11.93)	7.63	.0093*

* indicates $p \leq .05$

TABLE III
SPANISH TRANSLATIONS OF SE VERSUS NON-SE DOCUMENTS

Measures	Means (SD)		F	p
	SE n = 8	non-SE n = 6		
Accuracy	4.50 (.31)	3.56 (1.15)	5.14	.0467*
Style Match	4.71 (.28)	3.61 (.74)	23.07	.0007*
Comprehension	4.75 (.29)	3.44 (1.40)	5.56	.0400*
Mistranslations				
Major	4.38 (2.17)	4.83 (4.00)	0.09	.7617
Minor	1.17 (2.12)	10.33 (5.87)	12.79	.0050*
Omissions				
Major	2.58 (2.21)	1.13 (1.33)	1.70	.2241
Minor	1.17 (.87)	13.22 (15.31)	3.28	.1001

TABLE IV
CHINESE TRANSLATIONS OF SE VERSUS NON-SE DOCUMENTS

Measures	Means (SD) SE n = 9	non-SE n = 8	F	p
Accuracy	3.00 (1.32)	2.54 (1.51)	.51	.4843
Style Match	3.67 (.97)	3.25 (1.46)	.75	.3997
Comprehension	3.11 (1.20)	2.88 (1.55)	.15	.7034
Mistranslations				
Major	17.07 (13.68)	16.63 (14.02)	.02	.8753
Minor	11.78 (5.47)	13.96 (6.64)	.61	.4486
Omissions				
Major	6.78 (7.71)	11.79 (12.95)	1.26	.2816
Minor	3.33 (3.46)	10.13 (10.79)	3.67	.0774

this might be that English and Spanish are linguistically more similar and therefore the benefits of SE could be more obviously transferred to translations by Spanish speakers. This similarity should improve the quality of the resulting translations, and it should also have some positive effect on the ease of translation.

A finding that relates to our interpretation of the effect of the similarity of Spanish to English occurred in a study of native speakers of Arabic, Spanish, "Oriental," and "Other" recalling English texts written in different rhetorical forms [17]. Carrell found that the native speakers who possessed the appropriate schema to process the various discourse types did best on the recall test—and in her study the Spanish speaking subjects performed better than the speakers of the non-European languages.

While significantly better Chinese translations of the SE documents would have further supported our hypothesis that SE helps the quality and ease of translation, the fact that Chinese is not as linguistically similar to English as Spanish may have several explanations. The Chinese speakers may be less sensitive linguistically to the differences between the SE and non-SE, or perhaps, the English structures are changed so much in the process of translating the document into Chinese (as opposed to Spanish) that the SE/non-SE differences are not reflected in the Chinese translations. To better measure the effects of SE versus non-SE source documents on the process of translating from English into another languages, future studies will need to consider using speakers of many other languages as subjects (European and non-European) as well as perhaps assessing additional measures of quality and ease of translation.

Effect of Procedure

Beyond differences between SE and non-SE source documents, the ANOVAs assessed differences between the procedures. In our comprehension experiment, subjects reading the SE version of Procedure A performed significantly better on comprehension measures than subjects reading the non-SE version; on Procedure B, the difference was not significant. As discussed earlier, we concluded that the non-SE version of Procedure A was more complex than the non-SE version of Procedure B [1]. In analyzing the results of the current study, we were interested in assessing whether such document differences would occur in the translation results.

For all languages combined, the only significant main effect for procedure occurred for major mistranslations, $F(1,33) = 6.635$, $p = 0.02$, with Procedure A containing fewer major mistranslations M = 4.7; SD = 2.84) than Procedure B (M = 13.93; SD = 14.03). No main effects for procedure were found for the Spanish translations. For the Chinese translations, again there was a main effect for procedure for major mistranslations, $F(1,13) = 16.92$, $p = 0.0012$, with Procedure A containing fewer major mistranslations (M = 6.5; SD = 2.11) than Procedure B (M = 26.07; SD = 14.03). This result, which replicates the result for all languages combined, clearly triggered the significant effect for all languages combined. Although we were surprised to find virtually no main effects for procedures, an examination of the interactions reveals some procedure differences.

Interactions Between SE/Non-SE and Procedure

This last examination of the results concerns the interactions between SE and non-SE documents for the two different procedures.

Languages Combined: For all languages combined, the only significant interaction occurred for minor omissions, $F(1,32) = 4.70$, $p = 0.04$. As Table V reveals, the number of minor omissions for the non-SE translations of Procedure A was significantly higher (M = 14.15; SD = 15.04) than Procedure A's SE translations (M = 1.04; SD = 0.84), Procedure B's non-SE translations (M = 4.63; SD = 3.43), and Procedure B's SE translations (M = 3.03; SD = 3.16).

An examination of Table V reveals some interesting patterns. First, virtually all SE translations received better ratings than non-SE translations (see ^ on Table V for the two exceptions). However, as Table V illustrates, the differences in favor of the SE translations versus the non-SE translations were generally larger for Procedure A, the document that the comprehensibility study deemed to be more complex, than for Procedure B. While these differences were not large enough to result in numerous significant interactions, perhaps because of small cell sizes, the pattern of potential interactions in favor of the SE translations of Procedure A exists. This pattern replicates the pattern found in the comprehension study.

While much of the pattern in the means in Table V supports Procedure A as the more complex document, some does not. What is unclear from this small study is whether a source document's complexity might affect comprehensibility but not translatability or whether larger cell sizes might have made the translation results reveal more significant interactions and fully replicate the comprehension study's results.

TABLE V
MEANS FOR LANGUAGES COMBINED

Measures	Means			
	Procedure A		Procedure B	
	SE n = 8	non-SE n = 9	SE n = 11	non-SE n = 9
Accuracy	3.83	3.00	3.64	3.22
Style Match	4.54	3.41	3.76	3.41
Comprehension	4.17	3.38	3.88	3.19
Mistranslations				
Major	3.50	5.82	14.76^	12.93
Minor	6.54^	5.82	6.54	11.22
Omissions				
Major	1.08	4.75	6.73	7.92
Minor	1.04	14.15	3.03	4.63

TABLE VI
MEANS FOR SPANISH TRANSLATIONS

Measures	Means			
	Procedure A		Procedure B	
	SE n = 4	non-SE n = 4	SE n = 4	non-SE n = 2
Accuracy	4.42	3.75	4.58	3.17
Style Match	4.75	3.91	4.67	3.00
Comprehension	4.67	3.50	4.83	3.33
Mistranslations				
Major	2.41	4.75	6.33^	5.00
Minor	2.67	8.25	5.17	14.50
Omissions				
Major	1.42^	0.78	3.75^	1.67
Minor	1.00	17.42	1.33	4.83

Spanish Translations: There were no significant interactions for the Spanish translations. The means for all conditions of the Spanish translations are shown in Table VI. The patterns in the SE/non-SE data for both procedures replicate the means for the main effects shown in Table III: the translations of the SE documents were rated better for both procedures A and B, with only three exceptions (see ^ in Table VI).

Chinese Translations: There were no significant interactions for the Chinese translations. Table VII lists the means for all conditions. The translations from the SE documents were rated better (two exceptions denoted by ^ in Table VII) than the translations from the non-SE documents; however, Procedure A exhibits larger differences between the translations of the SE versus non-SE documents than does Procedure B.

The greater positive effect of SE versus non-SE for Procedure A compared to Procedure B in the Chinese data was probably responsible for the similar pattern noted in the data for all languages combined. Based on this pattern in the Chinese data and the similar results of our earlier comprehension study, we would expect that using a source document written in SE would produce relatively better translations for Procedure A than for Procedure B (assuming that more complex documents can benefit most from the goals or SE). Questions remain, however, as to why this pattern is not significant and why it is not observed in the Spanish translations. The answer to the first question may relate to the small cell sizes. To answer the second question, one might speculate that the overall translation task was easier for the Spanish subjects (because of the linguistic similarities between English and Spanish) so it might have been easier for the translators to process and more adequately translate even the more difficult documents in the time allotted and hence exhibit fewer differences between the two procedures.

TABLE VII
MEANS FOR CHINESE TRANSLATIONS

Measures	Means			
	Procedure A		Procedure B	
	SE (n = 4)	non-SE (n = 4)	SE (n = 5)	non-SE (n = 4)
Accuracy	3.50	2.25	2.60	2.83
Style Match	4.42	2.92	3.07	3.56
Comprehension	3.50	2.92	2.80	2.83
Mistranslations				
Major	5.00	8.00	26.73^	25.25
Minor	10.33	16.42	12.93^	11.50
Omissions				
Major	1.17	8.75	8.75	14.83
Minor	1.00	14.25	5.20	6.00

CONCLUSIONS AND FUTURE RESEARCH

While most of our conclusions are fairly speculative, given the exploratory nature of our study, it does appear that in certain cases using SE as a source language improves the quality and ease of translations. For the Spanish speakers, SE translations received significantly better ratings on four measures and showed significantly greater consistency on five measures than the non-SE translations. The occurrence of these findings for the Spanish translations but not for the Chinese translations may be due to the greater linguistic similarity of Spanish to English than Chinese to English. It may well be that SE will prove to be of greater benefit to translators whose native languages are linguistically more similar to English, though certainly more work is needed to reach such a conclusion with any certainty.

At this point, conclusions regarding how SE is affected by document complexity are hard to draw. In the qualitative analysis of the data, a pattern arose in the Chinese translations, showing a greater positive effect of SE versus non-SE for the more complex Procedure A compared to less complex Procedure B. It is unclear as to why such a pattern was not strong enough to be significant (though our sample was small) and why the pattern did not occur for Spanish speakers. Again, the answer may lie in the closer tie between Spanish and English; perhaps for translators whose native language is linguistically more similar to English, document complexity (as represented by Procedure A) was not sufficiently problematic to trigger the purported benefits of SE. Certainly more work is needed to solve this dilemma.

As stated earlier, another goal of this study was to assess the design of this experiment and identify areas for further exploration. Because there is very little precedent in the literature for this type of work, we feel that this study will help contribute to future studies, not only in its results, but in what it suggests about the design of translatability studies in general.

In assessing the translations, the researchers, the subjects, the raters, and the Boeing employees who provided the target translations were concerned about: 1) which words were best left untranslated in a technical document, and 2) how closely a translation should replicate the original document to be considered a good translation. In this study, with the goal of interrater reliability, these issues were decided among the raters. Another concern regarded the raters' and subjects' unspoken value judgments about simple language and how such judgments might affect the results. Speculating on how to handle these issues as a general rule for all translation studies was beyond the scope of the current experiment, though we recognize that they need to be better addressed if translation studies are to become comparable and lead to theory development. And, of course, these issues are important, not only to SE, but to the field of translation as a whole.

Future research will also need to focus on what to measure and how to analyze translations. In future studies, we would recommend a refinement of measures to more directly test both quality and, especially, ease of translation. Our greatest dilemma concerned how to measure ease of translation. We used the measure of "style match" to indirectly assess the ease of translation with the belief that if a document were easy to translate, the style of the original document would be preserved in the translation. We also reasoned that more comprehensible translations might result when the translation task was easier. Although we asked subjects how easy the task was, we did not get many usable responses. We might additionally recommend that linguistic analysis be performed to provide a better understanding of how the translations compare to the originals, e.g., one could examine the mistranslations and look for systematic causes stemming from the original documents. Such an analysis, however, was beyond the scope of the current exploratory study.

Future studies should also consider the number and type of subjects and documents to use. To make better use of inferential statistics in a study such as this one, more subjects would need to be recruited. In enlarging the total sample size, one could also seek to refine the measures of language literacy. While the means for years of education, years of English, and years in the U.S. did not significantly differ among our subjects, with a larger sample one could assess other measures of English ability as well as measures of native language literacy and experience with technical documents, to see if they interact with the effect of SE versus non-SE and document complexity. Researchers might consider using subjects who are professional translators of many different European and non-European languages, yet we must remember that, in the real world, nonprofessional translators do translate documents. Finally, future studies will have to use more and more documents, differing in length, difficulty, purpose, and so on. It is only by considering the issues discussed here that we can advance the research on the translatability of SE and further our understanding of when and whether SE contributes to the translatability of technical documents.

While our study was primarily exploratory in nature, we can suggest some ways in which a company whose documents are frequently translated might use our results. Such a company should definitely investigate using SE or a similar controlled language as a standard for authoring procedural documents that are to be translated, particularly when translations are from English to other Indo-European languages and when nonprofessional translators are employed. A company might also want to conduct its own study to assess the translatability of its documents and the benefits of using a controlled language in its specific setting. The design, results, and issues raised in the current study should contribute to such an undertaking.

Acknowledgment

The authors wish to thank Jim Hoard, Rick Wojcik, and Oscar Kipersztok, Boeing Information & Support Services, and Paul Montague, Tony H. Kuo, and Frank Tou, BCAG Customer Services Division, for their assistance with this project and for comments on an earlier version of this paper.

References

[1] S. K. Shubert, J. H. Spyridakis, H. K. Holmback, and M. B. Coney, "The comprehensibility of Simplified English in procedures," *J. Tech. Writing and Commun.*, vol. 25, no. 4, pp. 347–369, 1995.

[2] G. Adriaens and D. Schreurs, "From cogram to alcogram: Toward a controlled English grammar checker," in *Proc. COLING-92*, 1992, pp. 595–601.

[3] C. K. Ogden, *Basic English, A General Introduction with Rules and Grammar.* London, England: Paul Trebor & Co., 1932.

[4] Caterpillar Corporation, *Dictionary for Caterpillar Fundamental English.* East Peoria, IL: Caterpillar Corp., 1974.

[5] C. A. Verbeke, "Caterpillar Fundamental English," *Training and Devel. J.*, vol. 27, no. 2, pp. 36–40, 1973.

[6] D. E. Hinson, "Simplified English—Is it really simple?" *WE*, pp. 33–36, 1988.

[7] J. Kirkman, "How to communicate computerese," *Data Syst.*, pp. 14–15, July 1978.

[8] J. E. Hoard, R. Wojcik, and K. Holzhauser, "An automated grammar and style checker for writers of Simplified English," in *Computers and Writing, State of the Art.* Oxford, England: Intellect, 1992, pp. 278–296.

[9] AECMA, "AECMA Simplified English Standard," AECMA Doc. PSC-85-16598, Issue 1, Brussels, Belgium, 1995.

[10] P. T. W. Hudson and M. W. Bergman, "Lexical knowledge in word recognition: Word length and word frequency in naming and decision tasks," *J. Memory and Language*, vol. 24, pp. 46–58, 1985.

[11] M. Naveh-Benjamin and T. Ayres, "Digit span, reading rate, and linguistic relativity," *Quart. J. Exper. Psychol.*, vol. 38A, pp. 739–751, 1986.

[12] J. G. Kroll and J. S. Merves, "Lexical access for concrete and abstract words," *J. Exper. Psychol.*, vol. 12, no. 1, pp. 92–107, 1986.

[13] M. J. Lewellen, S. D. Goldinger, D. B. Pisoni, and B. G. Greene, "Lexical familiarity and processing efficiency: Individual differences in naming, lexical decision, and semantic categorization," *J. Exper. Psychol.*, vol. 122, no. 3, pp. 316–330, 1993.

[14] A.R. Dobbs, A. Friedman, and J. Lloyd, "Frequency effects in lexical decisions: A test of the verification model," *J. Exper. Psychol.: Human Perception and Performance*, vol. 11, no. 1, pp. 81–92, 1985.

[15] G. B. Simpson and C. Burgess, "Activation and selection processes in the recognition of ambiguous words," *J. Exper. Psychol.*, vol. 11, no. 1, pp. 28–39, 1985.

[16] D. C. Howell, *Statistical Methods for Psychology.* Boston, MA: Duxbury Press, 1982.
[17] P. L. Carrell, "The effects of rhetorical organization on ESL readers," *TESOL Quart.*, vol. 18, no. 3, pp. 441–469, 1984.

Heather Holmback has a Ph.D.degree in linguistics and since 1986 has been involved in computational linguistics. She has worked on general natural language processing systems and specific applications, concentrating on semantic and discourse processing. Her most recent work at Boeing includes leading a project to develop meaning-based language checking applications.

Jan H. Spyridakis is an Associate Professor in the Department of Technical Communication at the University of Washington, Seattle. Her recent work on the comprehensibility and translatability of Simplified English for Boeing BCAG is an extension of her work in refining research methods in technical communication and in assessing document and screen design variables that affect usability and comprehension.

Serena K. Shubert is pursuing doctoral studies in Educational Curriculum and Instruction at the University of Washington, Seattle, where she is continuing her research on controlled languages. Her Master's thesis in technical communcation concerns the comprehensibilty of Simplified English.

Babel in Document Design: The Evaluation of Multilingual Texts

—LEO LENTZ
AND JACQUELINE HULST

Abstract—*The aim of this study is to analyze the process of document design in a multilingual setting. In order to evaluate translation quality, a theoretical perspective is formulated as a basis for criteria for a good translation. In this perspective, the target text is considered an autonomous document. Two sets of criteria are distinguished: correctness errors and functional errors. The tools that were used to assess translation quality were expert analysis and reader-focused evaluation. For both tools a multilingual evaluation team was formed with the highest possible expertise in the target languages, in linguistics, and in usability. In this case study, the process of evaluation and the results are described.*

Index Terms—*Document design, expert analysis, multilingual communication, translation quality, usability.*

Manuscript received February 10, 2000; revised May 3, 2000.
L. Lentz is with the Department of Dutch Language and Literature, Utrecht University, 3512 JK Utrecht, The Netherlands (email: LeoLentz@let.uu.nl).
J. Hulst is with the Utrecht Institute for Linguistics UIL-OTS Utrecht University, 3512 JK Utrecht, The Netherlands.
IEEE PII S 0361-1434(00)07493-2.

How can one assess the quality of a multilingual document? This was one of the main questions in the Multilingual Communication Project carried out in the Netherlands by Utrecht University and the Dutch Ministry of Finance. There are both theoretical and methodological aspects to this question. First, we need to consider theoretical issues such as: What is "translation quality"?, What is the goal of a translation?, and What makes a good translation? When these issues have been resolved and appropriate criteria formulated, the methodological aspect becomes relevant: How can we develop procedures that will enable us to evaluate how far a given multilingual document meets our criteria? This project, which we approached on the basis of our particular interest in text and the processes that lead to the creation of texts, encompassed various aspects of multilingual communication. In this article, we report on a case study in the quality of multilingual documents, discussing theoretical principles and procedures we developed and the documents we evaluated, concluding with some reflections on document design in a multilingual setting.

WHAT IS A GOOD TRANSLATION?

In the field of document design, the notion of text quality is strongly related to usability for readers in everyday situations. The accepted view, that usability testing and reader-focused evaluation form an integral part of document design processes, is expressed in various articles in this issue. By contrast, in the field of translation practice, the role of the reader does not seem to be given much importance. A common answer to the question "what is a good translation" is that a good translation is as accurate as possible [1, p. 111]. Such a definition of "a good translation" is formulated in terms of its counterpart, the original text. This tradition has been attacked in the German literature on translation theory published since 1971 by authors like Reiss [2], Hönig and Kussmaul [3], Reiss and Vermeer [4], and Nord [5].

Reprinted from *IEEE Trans. Prof. Comm.*, vol. PC-43, no. 3, pp. 313–322, September 2000.

The result of this debate is a new theoretical framework in which a translation is seen as a text with a dual status, moving between two poles. On the one hand, it is related to its original, the SOURCE TEXT; on the other hand, it has to function as an independent text for a new audience in the target culture. If the relationship between the translation (the TARGET TEXT) and its original is given priority, the translation will be regarded primarily as a derivative product. If its function in a new environment is given more weight, however, it will be considered an autonomous document. This distinction determines both the criteria by which a translation is judged and the evaluation procedure that is followed. Since, in our view, translations are considered by their specific target audiences to be first and foremost autonomous documents, they should be evaluated in terms of whether or not they achieve their communicative goals.

This theoretical perspective implies that, in the assessment procedure, the quality of the translated text should be assessed completely without reference to the source text. This functionalist approach corresponds to current trends in translation studies [6], which in turn reflect the narrowing gap between theory and practice. In real life, readers of a translated text are likewise unable to refer back to a source text. The role of the source text is subsequent to the evaluation: it may help us understand why specific problems arose in the translated text and may even lead to the conclusion that they result from defects in the source text itself. These ideas are presented more extensively in Hulst's doctoral dissertation [7].

This case study relates to a brochure produced by the Dutch Ministry of Finance to explain to people when and how they should pay the motor vehicle tax. The development of this document is visualized in Fig. 1.

Everyone who buys a car in The Netherlands needs to know that they have to pay motor vehicle tax. This brochure contains information about the various types of vehicles, the various tax rates, the various ways people can pay the tax, and what they need to do when they sell the car. It particularly stresses the fact that, as owners, they are liable for the tax, whether or not the car is actually driven.

This document is unusual among government leaflets and brochures in that it is published in several different languages. Roughly speaking, translated brochures account for no more than 6% of all the government's information output. The decision to produce this brochure as a multilingual document (in English, French, Spanish, Turkish, and Arabic: Document 3 in Fig. 1) was presumably based on the general assumption that foreign residents also buy cars and, therefore, need to be informed about their obligations, and the more specific assumption that when they had read the brochure, speakers of Spanish, French, Arabic, and other foreign languages would be able to meet their tax obligations.

Principles: Correctness and Functionality The two principal functions of the brochure were, of course, to inform people about the regulations regarding motor vehicle tax and to tell them how they could meet their obligations. To make readers more inclined to comply with the regulations, the brochure needed to convince them that paying the correct amount on time was in their own interest. If these communicative goals were to be achieved, the brochure would need to meet a number of criteria: (a) it would have to be well-structured, (b) it would need to contain relevant information presented logically and convincingly, and (c) it would need to contain persuasive elements in terms of both content and style. These criteria were applied to the text not only on the macro-level, but also on the micro-level: every paragraph was assessed as to its adequacy in relation to the document's overall communicative goals, taking into account the

Fig. 1. Design products and processes for production of a multilingual document on motor vehicle tax.

Doc 1 → *Briefing* → **Doc 2** → *Translation* → **Doc 3** → *Evaluation I* → **Doc 4** → *Translation* → **Doc 5** → *Evaluation II* → **Doc 6**

Document Products
Doc 1 Motor vehicle tax legislation
Doc 2 Monolingual brochure in Dutch
Doc 3 Multilingual brochure in Dutch, English, French, Spanish, Turkish, and Arabic
Doc 4 New text on motor vehicle tax, in Dutch, written for foreigners
Doc 5 Translation of Doc 4 into English, German, Turkish, and Arabic
Doc 6 Revision of Doc 5, leading to a multilingual brochure published in English, German, Turkish, and Arabic

Document Processes
Briefing of the document design agency
Briefing of translators
Multilingual Evaluation Study (I)
Briefing of the document design agency
Briefing of translators
Multilingual Evaluation Study (II)

background and characteristics of the various target groups.

We distinguished two categories of error: functional errors and correctness errors. Any aspects of the text that derogated from its functional quality were classified as FUNCTIONAL ERRORS, regardless of whether they related to style, structure, or content, the deciding factor being simply whether or not they reduced functional quality. Errors that affected the correctness of the text, whether on the level of syntax, vocabulary, style, or typing or spelling, were classified as CORRECTNESS ERRORS. Correctness errors can be seen as elementary mistakes and easily corrected, very often without any need to refer to the original text.

The main argument in favor of making this distinction between functional and correctness errors is "educational" in nature. When we talked with the communication manager at the Ministry who was responsible for the brochure, we discovered that, in contrast to the functional approach taken by the Ministry in its communications in Dutch, the Ministry's attitudes toward translation were rather traditional. Correctness was seen as the most important issue, and the translation process was seen as purely linguistic: the source text was to be followed as faithfully as possible. Of course, correctness is a very important, perhaps even fundamental, requirement, but producing a text that communicates its message adequately involves much more. A linguistically correct sentence may be completely inadequate from a communicative point of view, just as not every correctness error will affect a text's functional adequacy. Of course, in many cases there may be some overlap between the two categories, but that does not diminish the conceptual power of this distinction. It allows us to see the concept of "error" as relative, and, by weighing the gravity of each error, we can arrive at a more layered picture of translation quality.

Principles: Expert and Reader-Focused Evaluation After we had identified the basic principles governing the relationship between the original text and its translations, and formulated criteria of functionality and correctness, the next step was to develop tools that would enable us to assess the quality of the translations.

The theoretical assumption that a translation has to function as an autonomous document in the reading situation suggests that two analytical traditions should be integrated: the tradition of translation studies and that of document design. Studies in document design show that one of the main determinants of text quality is the relation between the information offered by the text and the knowledge the reader brings to the reading process. Even the greatest text evaluation expert will not be able to predict more than 20% or 30% of all comprehension problems that readers are likely to experience [8]. The same applies, mutatis mutandis, to readers' capacity to make stylistic judgments. Although experts in linguistics or professional technical writers often enjoy commenting on stylistic aspects of texts, most of those aspects would pass unnoticed by ordinary readers. Such readers, we know, are incapable of unearthing all the problems that a text might potentially contain. They are experts in "everyday life," not in text structure or academic issues of text quality. Readers actually often overlook inconsistencies in texts [9], and it is not always possible to trust them when they say they have properly understood the information contained in texts. That is why we insist on a combination of expert analysis and reader-focused evaluation. Readers help us find unexpected problems regarding comprehension, relevance, appreciation, application, and acceptability of the document. Expert analysis, however, focuses on the accuracy of the translation (in terms of, say, structure, consistency, and coherence), as well as on the relationship between the intended communicative goals of the brochure and their textual realization (i.e., on the level of content, structure, and style).

To summarize, we have presented three principles that determine our perspective on translation quality:

- a translation is an autonomous document that is used independently of its source text;
- the assessment of translation quality requires that attention is paid both to correctness and to the functionality of the text;
- the assessment of translation quality requires both reader-focused evaluation and expert analysis.

However, to perform a multilingual evaluation, more is required than a set of principles. The theory should be applicable in a well-designed procedure. In the next section, we consider the problem of how to coordinate and perform a multilingual evaluation study. Although some aspects of the procedure are comparable with usability standards commonly found in the field of document design, the multilingual aspect of translated texts means that special attention needs to be paid to less frequently encountered factors.

How Do We Achieve a Good Translation?

The proper assessment of a multilingual document calls for a multilingual team of evaluators—professionals with the highest possible level of linguistic performance in the target language and training in translation quality assessment, text analysis, and reader-focused evaluation. There is no readily available body of expert knowledge that integrates all these disciplines. Therefore, we assembled our team of evaluators from university teachers and outstanding students from the Translation Studies training program, most of whom were native speakers of the target languages (English, German, French, Spanish, Turkish, and Arabic). The team was supervised by researchers from the language departments at Utrecht University. The first phase in the project involved training the team in text evaluation, translation-quality analysis, and the design of reader-focused evaluation studies. The evaluators were also responsible for convening a panel to undertake the reader-focused evaluation. Finally, all evaluators needed to understand exactly how they should report the results of the assessment. Although this may seem rather trivial, it is extremely important, particularly in a multilingual context, that all members of the team follow the same guidelines so that a coherent overall report on the complete set of translations can be produced. This meant that all members of the evaluation team had to use the same criteria in their assessments.

Simply providing evaluators with training and instruction beforehand is not enough, however. They also need coaching during the process, and the drafts of their reports need to be reviewed. Coordinating a multilingual process is an arduous task because the evaluators all make decisions relating to linguistic features in their own languages that are difficult to review. Is the German evaluator right to criticize the use of *Zeitabschnitt*? Is the Turkish evaluator right when he says that *okursunuz* uses an incorrect suffix of the aorist? Did evaluators perhaps overlook problems regarding correctness or functionality? And we were not able even to read most of the feedback given by the evaluator of the Arabic text! Only one conclusion was possible: multilingual evaluation is a process of cognitive distribution of knowledge. The linguistic judgments made by an evaluator need to be reviewed by a linguistic expert in the language in question. The reviewing and coordination of the process itself, however, as well as the drafting of the final report, need to be performed by experts in translation studies and document design. This means that there is no one single ultimate authority on all aspects of the evaluation because no single person possesses all the knowledge needed for such a multilingual evaluation.

There are two important arguments for adopting such an allocation of tasks and expertise. First, we need to guard against dilettantism. For instance, the fact that we, as authors of this article, were able to write it in English might lead us to consider ourselves expert enough to evaluate translations into English, which we are certainly not. We may claim to be experts in evaluation studies, but we could not claim expertise in the linguistics of English, let alone, say, Turkish or Arabic. In our view, the highest level of linguistic expertise is needed to be able to judge a translated text in a particular language. Second (and this is related to the previous argument), the evaluator needs to have unimpeachable authority. The Ministry of Finance called in an independent evaluator to assess the quality of the translations because it was incapable of doing so itself. However, the Ministry's lack of skills and knowledge also meant that it was also unable to evaluate the quality of the evaluation. If the evaluator had said, for instance, that the Arabic translation was very poor, the Ministry would simply have had to take the evaluator's word for it; the most it could have done was to ask the translator to account for his or her work. Every amateur or professional translator must be able to accept that the assessment made by an evaluator is based on the highest possible expertise. Consequently, high standards are necessary in all aspects of text evaluation, not only with respect to the expertise of the evaluators, but also with respect to the procedures they use. These procedures will be described in the next section.

Procedure: Expert Analysis Our functional perspective implies that the text needs to be evaluated according to the specific goals the producer has formulated. But since producers seldom formulate the goals of a text as precisely as needed, we have developed a heuristic procedure for carrying out a functional analysis. This analysis specifies the goals of the document and what is necessary for the text to meet these criteria [10]–[12]. The functional analysis of a text starts by exploring the context: what are the aims of the organization and the relevant policy goals? These questions are answered by analyzing policy documents and by interviewing the producers of the document. The second step is text-driven: what does the text tell us about the goals the authors are trying to achieve? A crucial element of this analysis is a set of four criteria that every function description has to meet:

(1) a clear indication of a speech act (e.g., to persuade, to describe, to invite);
(2) an indication of the audience;
(3) a description of the topic;
(4) an indication of the effect that is intended by the speech act.

These criteria are formulated in order to be able to evaluate the document. For example, if we know that the text has to:

(1) persuade
(2) the owners of a car
(3) that paying motor vehicle tax annually has an advantage,
(4) namely, that the cost of sending invoices is reduced by 10% and this saving is passed on to the taxpayer in the form of a discount,

then we can formulate criteria for expert analysis. The speech act of persuading implies that the text will have to present arguments in favor of the desired attitude (1). This act only makes sense to those people who are currently paying in quarterly installments and to those who are paying motor vehicle tax for the first time (2). These readers should accept the advantages as being attractive (3). Once all functions of the document have been described, we are able to formulate more specific criteria for content, style, and structure. For this persuasive function, the text had to inform the readers about the discount they get when they pay annually and emphasize the benefit of not having to worry about forgetting to pay each quarterly installment and risking fines. The style of the content unit regarding the discount should be positive and inviting, while the unit regarding fines should be presented with clear authority. We also formulated structural requirements with respect to the order in which the different functions should be presented in the text. The functional analysis thus resulted in a checklist that the expert evaluators used in their assessment of **functional** translation quality. Furthermore, they evaluated the translation from the perspective of **correctness**, focusing on grammar, lexical choices, style, and spelling.

Procedure: Reader-Focused Evaluation In both monolingual and multilingual evaluation projects, many choices have to be made regarding methodological issues. Several approaches to usability testing of documents have been developed and described [13]–[15]. For our reader-focused evaluation, we used two kinds of tools: (1) a software program (Focus) that enabled readers to give feedback on a document in the form of self-reports; and (2) a questionnaire that forced them to apply the information meant to be communicated to readers. The questionnaire also contained questions on the appreciation of the document, which were rated on a five-point scale. In this way, a drawback of the open, unstructured nature of the self-report was compensated for. That is, while the self-report provided a reflection of the reader's own agenda, the questionnaire reflected the researcher's agenda. For instance, if we did not want to miss judgments on style, we simply put some questions regarding style in the questionnaire.

The Focus software program was developed by de Jong (University of Twente) and Lentz (Utrecht University) in the context of both our research and our teaching. In our research, text evaluation is an important topic. Every year we perform a number of reader-focused studies into text evaluation. This is a time-consuming activity, especially when we use face-to-face interviews and think-aloud methods. Data collection and analysis of feedback are also complex activities, which led de Jong and Lentz to develop Focus. With this program, participants produce their feedback as they are reading the text on the screen. On the left side of the screen, the text to be evaluated is shown. Participants read the text and react to words, sentences, or paragraphs by selecting them with the mouse. This selection is copied in a box on the upper right-hand side of the screen. Participants then produce their feedback in two ways:

(1) From a list of different types of problems, they select the category that best describes their comment (e.g., *I don't understand*)

(2) They specify their comment in the next box, by writing down a remark (e.g., *What is a giro payment slip*?)

As soon as Continue has been clicked, the text selected on the left side of the screen turns blue, indicating that this passage has been commented upon and that the comment has been registered by the computer. The participant continues reading, selecting other fragments whenever a negative feeling has been aroused by the text.

In order to be able to evaluate documents that have been translated into different languages, Focus has an option to translate all commands of the interface in any western language the designer wants to use. We have had experience with evaluation studies using Focus in Dutch, English, German, and Afrikaans. We are not yet able to use Focus for languages such as Arabic or Chinese because these languages have different scripts.

The procedure of the usability test is as follows. The participants first practice with the program by reacting to a very short text. They acquire experience in selecting passages, become familiar with the different problem categories, and practice writing comments on passages they have selected in the text. Once they feel confident using the program, they first receive the document to be tested in a hard-copy version so that they can obtain a global impression of the document as a whole. This is meant to be a very short exposure to the document, the actual reading must be done on screen. During the reading and feedback process, the participants can ask the evaluator any questions they might have about the program or the procedure. In addition to the on-screen evaluation, there are, of course, many other ways participants can be invited to give feedback about the document or the program.

Focus produces both quantitative and qualitative output. The quantitative output shows the number of problems detected by the participants in the various categories. This helps the evaluator to assess what participants tended to focus on while reading the text. For instance, if almost no stylistic comments but a lot of comprehension problems are selected, the evaluator may conclude that the text is too difficult for the readers. This, of course, only provides a general indication of what needs to be revised. The qualitative output of Focus shows the specific problems readers have with the text.

Our questionnaire included three questions on aspects of appreciation of the text to be rated on a five-point scale, five questions requiring participants to apply the information in the text in practical situations in order to evaluate their understanding of the text, and ten questions on the appreciation of the Focus software program.

Focus was used for the reader-focused evaluation of the second multilingual document on motor vehicle tax (Document 5 in Fig. 1). This was a revision of the document (Document 3 in Fig. 1) we evaluated earlier on in the project. Fourteen readers with English-speaking backgrounds (British, Canadian, American, New Zealand) participated in the evaluation of the English translation. Sixteen readers participated in the evaluation of the German text. The Turkish and Arabic translation was also evaluated, but without the use of the Focus software.

Procedure: Report Results

Communicating the results of a multilingual evaluation study to readers who are probably unable to read all the languages into which the source text was translated is quite a challenge. In our final report we describe the results of the expert analysis on the accuracy of the translations, the accessibility and relevance of the information, and the relation between the source text and its translations. The results of the reader-focused evaluation are reported by describing the problems readers of the different language groups had with one particular fragment of the document. A complete overview of all problems detected was presented in a reproduction of the translation. In the fragment presented in Fig. 2, the reader problems are marked with the letter R, and the problems detected in the expert analysis are underlined and coded with C (correctness) and F (functionality).

There were two goals we tried to achieve with this kind of data report. The managers needed to be informed about the quality of the translations without having to understand the details of each problem that was detected. For them, the most important question was whether the document was correct and effective. With the report structured in this way, they were able to read our general conclusions about the quality of each translation and get their own impression by reading fragments such as those we presented in Fig. 2. The translation agency had to be informed in more detail about all problems detected. We did not expect them to be satisfied with the simple conclusion that the Arabic translation was very bad. They needed to be able to discuss translation quality in detail with every translator in order to improve their output. Moreover, the document we evaluated needed to be revised, which meant that every problem detected at micro- or macro-level had to be absolutely clear. This means that it had to be precisely identified in the text, accompanied with a clear diagnosis of the problem and, if possible, guidelines for revision.

Fig. 2. A fragment of the data report providing both reader- and expert-focused evaluations of the multilingual translation of a motor vehicle tax document.

Selling your car to an individual

In this case **(R1)** the buyer will need to have **(R2)** the registration document transferred to his name at the post office. There he will receive a Department of Road Transport warranty against liability (rdw-vrijwaringsbewijs), which he must give to you **(R3)**. This warranty <u>enables you to prove</u> **(R4/F1)** that the registration document is no longer in your name. You will not receive a refund of motor vehicle taxes for <u>the current payment term</u> **(F2)**. You may **(R5)**, however, include <u>the remainder for **(C1)** the current payment term</u> **(F3)** in the sale price.

Key to Reader Comments

- **R1** don't refer back here
- **R2** it is clearer to say: *must transfer the registration* ...
- **R3** -there should be *then* after must
-*which then becomes yours*
- **R4** awkward: *is proof that* sounds better
- **R5** boring style: too many *yous*

Key to Expert Comments

- **F1** same as R4
- **F2/F3** In the document different expressions are used for the same thing: *for the remainder of the payment term, for the current payment term, the remainder <u>of</u> the current payment term*. The last one is the best.
- **C1** *remainder <u>of</u> the current...*

Did the Principles and Procedures Result in a Perfect Translation?

A few months after our evaluation study, the Ministry of Finance published the fragment presented in Fig. 2 in the final document. The revision of the document seems to have focused on three suggestions we had presented in our evaluation study:

(1) change *taxes* to *tax*;

(2) choose one term: *quarterly payment period*, and

(3) *RDW-vrijwaringsbewijs* should be translated as *certificate of indemnification*.

These were some of the suggestions we made for lexical choices in the complete document which were accepted. Surprisingly, however, all of the problems that were unique for this specific fragment (see reader and expert comments in Fig. 2) were ignored in the revision.

With respect to the revision of the German version of the same text, the opposite happened. Three of the six "local" problems we had indicated were revised, but the only problem relevant to the whole document (choose one term: *Quartal* or *Zeitabschnitt*) was neglected. Of course, this is just a minor illustration of what happened with a small fragment of the document in the revision process. This is why we decided to perform an assessment of the complete revision of all four translations. The results very clearly show a lack of coordination. The Turkish text had improved most, by taking account of all suggestions in the evaluation report. The English and German revisions were concentrated on the level of correctness; most of the reader comments and the functional problems had been neglected. The Arabic text had not improved very much; some grammatical errors had been removed, but the overall text quality was below minimal standard requirements. This makes clear that in the process of revision probably nobody was able to review the process as a whole. The Ministry of Finance subsequently received the revised documents and was unable to check the quality of the final version. Our attempt to find a manager to take responsibility for the complete correction process following our evaluation study was not successful. This was in line with our experience in our first evaluation study. Clearly, an evaluation study alone will not lead to a perfect translation: someone has to feel responsible for the quality of the final product.

Audience Analysis Was Unavoidable Our first evaluation study concerned a document on motor vehicle tax that, years ago, had been published in six languages: Dutch, English, French, Spanish, Turkish, and Arabic (Document 3 in Fig. 1). One of our questions was related to the choice of languages: why was the document translated into these languages and not into German? We concluded that in fact nobody had really given thought to the multilingual setting. We decided to create a heuristic model for developing a translation policy to help officials see what questions are relevant when decisions with respect to translations have to be taken. These questions concern topics such as:

- the relevance of the subject for foreigners in the Netherlands;
- the sizes of the audience segments that need to be addressed in languages other than Dutch;
- particular segments that could be addressed in one foreign language;
- the multilingual setting of the final product:
  - (a) one document in four languages?
  - (b) four monolingual documents?, and
  - (c) complete translations or summaries in foreign languages?

This resulted in a new set of languages for Document 5 (Fig. 1): English, German, Turkish, and Arabic. We should also be aware, however, that every single translation may also be viewed from a multilingual perspective.

For the English text we must consider an audience of native speakers of British English, American English, and Australian English, each with their own spelling conventions and terminology. The same considerations apply to the German and Turkish texts. Arabic is used in many variants by different communities, all using their own conventions. These differences may be profound, for example, in the case of Moroccan readers living in The Netherlands, whose native language is Berber. For them, Arabic is in fact a second language, even though they belong to the vast Arabic community. Within this group, literacy in Arabic is by no means common. Of course, it makes no sense to include illiterate people in a usability study. But what level of literacy should be viewed as basic?

These are questions that are extremely relevant to the document design process and therefore should be considered at a very early stage in the process. The evaluation of multilingual documents raises questions about complex language situations that cannot be ignored by teams performing usability studies. The complex (linguistic) concept of audience comes into play here and needs to be taken into account, making decisions about multilingual documents less simple than they seemed before.

Writing and Translating Are Becoming More Integrated The evaluation process we described above also raised a number of questions concerning the relation between source text and target text. Document 3 (Fig. 1) was a direct translation of a text that had been produced for Dutch readers (Document 2 in Fig. 1). In our view, it would have been better if the document for foreigners had first been written in Dutch and only then translated into the four relevant languages. An example clearly illustrates this position. The English text of Document 3 (Fig. 1) contained the following paragraph:

> *What if you temporarily go abroad?*
>
> *If you temporarily go abroad, you are still required to pay road tax on time for the duration of your absence, regardless of whether you take your vehicle with you.* [...]

For the Dutch readers "going abroad" meant, for example, "going to England." But readers from Britain considered themselves "abroad" already—they were, after all, living in The Netherlands, and they protested that they were not required to pay British motor vehicle tax while they were in The Netherlands. For both groups, the word *abroad* had quite opposite meanings. Writing for foreigners means that the author needs to take their perspective. In other words, multilingual communication starts early in the writing process and not at the moment of translation. This has consequences for the source text. In the case of the motor vehicle tax brochure, a new source text was written in Dutch, specifically aimed at foreigners living in The Netherlands. The author of this document wrote, one could say, the first draft of a translation.

In our view, the processes of writing and translating are becoming more and more integrated. The act of writing a source text for foreigners in Dutch that will never be published in Dutch may be regarded as a first step in the translation process. As soon as an author realizes that terms like *abroad, import, export* may cause complications for foreigners, he or she is in fact entering the translation process. Conversely, the translator is entering the writing process as soon as he or she realizes that foreigners could need more (or less) information about a specific topic because things are different in their country of origin. An example may illustrate this. The statement that the transaction of buying a second-hand car should be performed at a post office caused disbelief and laughter in the German reading session. To them it seemed like buying a computer from a carpenter. In The Netherlands, many transactions unrelated to stamps and telephones can be performed in the post office, such as buying insurance, booking holidays or tickets for pop concerts, and also car registration. A German translator may feel the need to elaborate upon the concept of "post office" for German readers in order to explain why this act is performed at this place. Conversely, the translator may also decide to delete unnecessary information. For instance, in another German text, designed for people who live in Germany and work in The Netherlands, information was included about the fact that unmarried couples (heterosexual or homosexual) who officially register their partnership are regarded as married partners by the Tax Department. A German translator might want to skip this fragment because it is impossible for Germans to have legalized partnerships without marriage. By formulating discourse units that were not present in the source text or by deleting content units, the translator is entering the writing process. In this situation, both the author of the source text and the translator collaborate as equal partners in producing a comprehensible and effective document, the author anticipating on translation questions, and the translator reflecting on the result of the writing process.

We can imagine an even stronger integration of the two processes. In some cases, it might be sufficient just to formulate the basic requirements regarding content and style and indicate the goal of the translation—i.e., provide a "translation brief." The source text does not need to be produced because the translator becomes a professional writer in the foreign language. This is actually a rapidly growing trend.

This integration is one of the aspects we focused on when we developed our TRANSLATION BRIEF, a tool for Translation Quality Management. The translation brief is used by the producer of the source text who has to interact with a translation agency. It is actually a checklist with criteria for:

- the selection of a reliable translation agency;
- topics the translation assignment should specify;
- interaction between producer and translator during the translation process;
- status of the end product;
- procedures for quality control;
- planning and budget;
- format of text delivery; and
- consequences in case of errors or problems.

It is obvious that one of the most important issues in this translation brief is the shared responsibility between producer and translator for text quality. The producer shows care for quality management by giving a well-considered briefing, making clear to the translator what the aspects of a good translation are and emphasizing that interaction between translator and producer will improve text quality. The translator is then invited to produce a translation that can function as an autonomous document, which means writing and, if necessary, rewriting a text with the audience in mind. As a consequence, the translator has more freedom, but also more responsibility. Deviations from the original text will no longer automatically be regarded as translation errors, but as possible proof of the skills of the professional translator.

The checklist may also function as a quality-control tool. For instance, management can use it to check afterwards whether the translation agency used was a certified one, whether a written assignment was produced, whether the two parties actually interacted during the translation process, and whether the deadline was met on time and within budget. Obviously, these checks with respect to the process do not need specific competence in translation and document design. They provide management with the means to supervise the procedures that have been established.

CONCLUSION

Documents are often used in a multilingual setting. Usability studies in the field of document design have highlighted the importance of using a reader-focused perspective but have restricted their research too often to monolingual readers, assessing documents written in their mother tongue. The evaluation of multilingual documents requires expertise in the fields of document design, translation theory, and linguistics. Most organizations lack this kind of expertise and thus need others to assess translation quality. The linguistics departments of most universities have expertise in foreign languages, but many of them miss expertise in document design and usability testing, a shortcoming that can lead to emphasis on correctness at the cost of functionality. Integration of these different academic fields would therefore seem to be a very sensible and desirable goal.

Experience with the evaluation of multilingual documents triggers questions that are relevant for professional communication in a broader sense. Document designers are not trained to determine whether it makes sense to translate a text into four or five languages. They are not aware of the consequences and possible implications of a document being read not just by speakers of the language of the source text, but also in translated form, by speakers of other languages. Normally in usability studies, one is only dealing with a linguistically homogenous group of native speakers. Usability studies into texts in a multilingual setting, however, require a much more sophisticated approach. In moving toward a more integrated approach, the world of professional communication and document design is becoming increasingly complicated and even more challenging.

REFERENCES

[1] P. Newmark, *About Translation*. Clevedon, U.K.: Multilingual Matters, 1991.

[2] K. Reiss, *Möglichkeiten und Grenzen der Übersetzungskritik; Kategorien und Kriterien für eine sachgerechte Beurteilung von Übersetzungen* München, Germany, 1971.

[3] H. Hönig and P. Kussmaul, *Strategie der Übersetzung. Ein Lehr- und Arbeitsbuch*. Tübingen, Germany: G. Narr, 1982.

[4] K. Reiss and H. Vermeer, *Grundlegung einer algemeinen Translationstheorie*. Tübingen, Germany: Niemeyer, 1984.

[5] C. Nord, *Textanalyze und Übersetzen; Theoretische Grundlagen, Methode und didaktische Anwendung einer übersetzungsrelevanten Textanalyze*. Heidelberg, Germany: Groos, 1988.

[6] H. Hönig, "Positions, power and practice: Functionalist approaches an translation quality assessment," in *Translation and Quality*, C. Schäffner, Ed. Clevedon, U.K.: Multilingual Matters Ltd., 1998, pp. 6–34.

[7] J. W. M. Hulst, *De doeltekst centraal; naar een functioneel model voor vertaalkritiek [Focus on the Target Text. Toward a Functional Model for Translation Quality Assessment]*. Amsterdam, The Netherlands: Thesis Publishers, 1995.

[8] L. Lentz and M. de Jong, "The evaluation of text quality: Expert-focused and reader-focused methods compared," *IEEE Trans. Prof. Commun.*, vol. 40, pp. 224–233, 1997.

[9] L. Baker, "Metacognition, comprehension monitoring and the adult reader," *Educ. Psych. Rev.*, vol. 1, pp. 3–38, 1989.

[10] L. Lentz and H. Pander Maat, "Evaluating text quality: Reader-focused or text-focused?," in *Functional Text Quality*, M. Steehouder and H. Pander Maat, Eds, Amsterdam, The Netherlands: Rodopi, 1992, pp. 101–114.

[11] H. Pander Maat, "What authors and readers do with side effects information on drugs," in *Discourse Analysis and Evaluation: Functional Approaches*, L. Lentz and H. Pander Maat, Eds. Atlanta, GA: Rodopi, 1997, pp. 111–138.
[12] H. Pander Maat and L. Lentz, "Patient information leaflets: A functional content analysis and an evaluation study," in *Functional Communication Quality*, L. van Waes, P. van den Hoven, and E. Woudstra, Eds. Amsterdam, The Netherlands: Rodopi, 1994, pp. 137–148.
[13] J. Rubin, *Handbook of Usability Testing. How to Plan, Design and Conduct Effective Tests*. New York: Wiley, 1994.
[14] C. Velotta, Ed., *Practical Approaches to Usability Testing for Technical Documentation*. Arlington, VA: Soc. Tech. Commun., 1995.
[15] M. de Jong and P. J. Schellens, "Reader-focused text evaluation: An overview of goals and methods," *J. Bus. Tech. Commun.*, vol. 11, pp. 402–432, 1997.

Leo Lentz is Associate Professor at the Utrecht Institute for Linguistics UIL-OTS at Utrecht University in The Netherlands. He conducted research projects on language teaching and wrote a Ph.D. dissertation on the functions of the school curriculum as a communication document between school and government. Text evaluation is the main focus of his research. He develops evaluation methods for reader-focused and for text-focused evaluation. He has published research articles about technical writers in The Netherlands and on the development of textual features in the history of written instructions.

Jacqueline Hulst is Assistant Professor at the Utrecht Institute for Linguistics UIL-OTS at Utrecht University. Both her teaching and research activities are concentrated in the field of Translation Studies, and her speciality is Translation Quality Assessment (subject of her Ph.D. dissertation in 1995). Besides her academic activities, she also works as an advisor and consultant for intercultural and translational matters for external parties in the cultural and educational field. She is editor of *Filter*, a Dutch journal on translation and translation studies.

Aligning International Editing Efforts with Global Business Strategies

—CAROL LEININGER AND RUE YUAN

Abstract—*We define international editing as editing documents for a multilingual readership or multinational distribution. We argue that international editing embodies and represents corporate global strategies, which directly affect editing choices. We describe three global strategies—ethnocentric, polycentric, or geocentric—and four categories of editing—linguistic, socio-cultural, political, and technical—on which editors can focus to produce business and technical documents that consistently align with corporate global strategies.*

Index Terms—*Global business strategy, linguistic editing, political editing, socio-cultural editing, technical editing, textual translation.*

Manuscript received October 25, 1997.
The authors are with San Francisco State College of Business, San Francisco, CA 94132 USA.
IEEE PII S 0361-1434(98)01974-2.

TRADITIONALLY, the process of editing has been divided into levels—editors typically review documents for content, grammatical correctness, style relative to a house standard, or logic. Early in the editing process, the editor generally determines what level of editing is desired—a deep edit, a light edit, a technical edit, a stylistic edit—and devotes the requisite time to the task. While this view of editing remains part of our terminology and actions, international editing—that is, editing business and technical documents for an international audience—requires a different view of editing tasks for editors to function effectively within the corporation as well as for the edited document to accomplish its purpose. Effective international editing takes into consideration the perspectives of the readers in target countries as well as of readers in the text-producing (host) country.

Past research on international editing has generally focused on choices that help editors make business and technical documents meet international audiences' needs by taking into consideration language and culture of the target countries [1]. This research has implied that international editing choices are largely determined by individual editors who make decisions based on their own idiosyncratic knowledge and audience perception. We argue, however, that international editing should reflect corporate global strategies; these corporate global strategies directly affect editing choices. International editing choices refer to the level of detail and focus necessary when editing documents for a multilingual readership or multinational distribution. Editing focus should be aligned with global business strategies not only to enable better corporate support for international documents but also to communicate consistent global business philosophy. In this article, therefore, we will first describe four categories that outline considerations in international editing. Then, we will describe three "global strategies" (presented by Hedlund as ethno-

Reprinted from *IEEE Trans. Prof. Comm.*, vol. PC-35, no. 2, pp. 84–87, June 1992.

centric, polycentric, or geocentric [2]) that can directly affect editing. Finally, we will suggest specific categories of editing—linguistic, socio-cultural, political, or technological—on which editors can focus to produce business and technical documents that effectively support and communicate the corporate global strategies.

Considerations in International Editing

Linguistic Editing Perhaps the most common techniques of international editing fall into the linguistic category, a category that has received a fair amount of attention. Linguistic editing focuses on readability of business and technical documents for second language readers. When editing for readability, editors may be concerned with limiting vocabulary and simplifying syntax to make business and technical documents easy to comprehend. Depending on a corporation's global strategy, linguistic editing can be quite restrictive, for individuals' editing choices must follow corporate guidelines. Companies such as Caterpillar and NCR have developed their own dictionaries of Fundamental English and stylistic guidelines that depend on limited vocabulary and simplified syntax to improve readability for international audiences [3], [4].

In an article discussing writing instructional manuals for non-English speakers, Sanderlin presents guidelines that highlight syntactic concerns for writers preparing manuals for English as second language [1]. Her guidelines include:

- Use short, direct sentences.
- Use simple sentences in subject/verb/object order. Keep subject and verb close together.
- Use positive, not negative sentences.
- Change dependent clauses to separate sentences unless needed to indicate relationships between instructions.
- Use clear, descriptive English.
- Use consistent nomenclature.
- Include only essential details.
- Avoid jargon, slang, and idioms.

Following Sanderlin's guidelines, editors pay close attention to the sentence structure of the original document and change sentence structure, when necessary, to accommodate the English proficiency of second language readers. For example:

> *Original:* Release the spring-loaded plate, after making sure the corners of the paper are under the corner tabs at the front of the paper tray first.
>
> *Edited as:* Make sure the corners of the paper are under the corner tabs at the front of the paper tray. Then, release the spring-loaded plate.

The original 26-word sentence reversed the order of the steps in which paper could be placed in the printer tray. Revised into two shorter sentences, the steps are described in the order in which they would best be executed, one step at a time, a presentation that can help readers process the information more easily than they can in a longer, more complex sentence.

> *Original:* Safety glasses, which are required of all operating personnel, protect the eyes from steel shavings.
>
> *Edited as:* All operating personnel should wear safety glasses. Safety glasses protect your eyes from steel shavings.

The subordinate clause of the original sentence has been removed and the sentence broken into two shorter sentences with subject–verb directly paired; some languages do not use subordinate clauses, which can make the first construction difficult to understand quickly in English. In addition, the predicate "All operating personnel" in the first edited sentence alerts people to their own role in safety, which is then reinforced by the pronoun "your" in the second edited sentence.

> *Original:* Do not disconnect the plug from the printer.
>
> *Edited as:* Leave the plug connected to the printer.

Changing the double negative in the original to a simpler form of the directive makes the direction easier to follow. In general, negations should be avoided in instructions because they require mental gymnastics on the part of readers regardless of their primary language.

In addition to vocabulary and syntactic concerns, metaphors and clichés may also fall into the linguistic category of editing. The use of metaphors and clichés is an issue both for documents that will be read in English by second language readers and for documents that will be translated.

Ward points out some common syntactic structure reversals in Spanish/English usage that make both direct reading and translation difficult in working with second-language documents in English [5]. Examples include

- black and white (blanco y negro),
- left and right (derecho e izquierda), and
- machines run in English, walk in Spanish (pp. 223–224).

Metaphors may have different meanings on direct translation or may not signify anything in different languages. An example of a common metaphor with different meanings in German and in U.S. English is the term "a shooting star." In German, "a shooting star" refers to a positive and unending rise, while in U.S. English, a shooting star usually means that the meteoric rise has or will have a corresponding ignominious fall.

An example of a Chinese metaphor that may not be clear on direct translation is the phrase "to stick in a pin wherever there is room." In Chinese the metaphor is used to praise someone who can make use of every bit of time and space, whereas in English the remark that "Wang will stick in a pin wherever there is room" might be taken as a criticism of Wang: "If Wang can find fault, he does."

On the other hand, a metaphor that says "someone is full of wind" in the U.S. means that "they talk without substance." In Chinese, however, the same metaphor means "they don't have opinions of their own; they are unpredictable."

The use of metaphors and clichés, especially those that have conflicting meanings or do not have a direct translation, is more problematic in documents written for global use in English than those that will be translated. A good translator should know, for example, that while in the U.S. people speak of crossing their fingers to wish you luck, in Germany people say they will hold their thumbs for you. While editing English text for a multilingual audience, however, editors have to decide if the metaphor is common enough in English to be easily understood or if the metaphor introduces an element of confusion that might be better addressed by a different or more literal phrasing.

The linguistic category of editing is a concern for documents written for simultaneous translation, a growing industry. For example, in Redmond, WA, the Microsoft Corporation is breaking new ground by shipping their FrontPage product simultaneously in six languages (Chinese, English, French, German, Italian, and Japanese). To achieve this simultaneous release, the FrontPage technical writing group

- Delivers a large amount of high-quality text in short intervals.
- Remains aware of the how changes impact documentation and restrict themselves from "fine tuning" documentation because all changes to localized material are costly, both in terms of money and meeting the product deadline.
- Keeps track of unchanged documentation that can be used again. This requires tracking product development closely and setting up the documentation's file system so that text can be used again.
- Helps program management drive an early user interface (UI) freeze. Because print documentation must be done at least eight weeks in advance of a release to manufacturing (this time varies per language), writers and localizers cannot meet deadlines without an early frozen UI.
- Uses style guides that include some information about culturally-sensitive material; however, the localization team maintains and is responsible for all culturally-sensitive material. The localization team maintains style guides for this purpose [6].

The English documentation and the localization teams keep separate style guides in part because of the extremely short (six months) product cycle. The main documentation team focuses on linguistic details when writing on-line help messages and manuals in English, and the localization teams are alert to culturally-sensitive (socio-cultural) nuances.

Socio-Cultural Editing Editing in the socio-cultural category takes into consideration social role expectations and customs, such as the expected genres of documents in a particular culture and the appropriateness of content, tone, and graphics. In the example of the FrontPage product, localization teams—often based in the target countries—are responsible for determining culturally sensitive material during translation to Chinese, French, German, Italian, and Japanese.

Because socio-cultural editing crosses the boundary between traditional editing (attention to linguistic details) and writing, this category is sometimes neglected, creating cultural mistakes. Editors often have to write new content or rewrite and re-arrange existing text to accommodate cultural needs and expectations. Without corporate support, editors will not be able to focus on socio-cultural editing, because editing in this category requires editors' time and often collaboration time with the original authors.

The importance of socio-cultural editing, however, should not be underestimated. For example, in many Asian cultures, personal relationships are important in business communication. This tendency is reflected in the structure of different genres, including electronic mail messages. Gu reports that in his study of a software company in Chicago with overseas offices in Singapore and Hong Kong, 89% of the business e-mail messages sent by Chinese employees used both personal greetings at the beginning and goodwill wishes at the end of their electronic messages. In contrast, only about 20% of the electronic business messages sent by U.S. employees used either a personal greeting or a goodwill closure [7]. Gu reports that some Chinese employees tend to view their U.S. colleagues as "too businesslike" and "cold." Socio-cultural editing thus helps avoid miscommunication by emending such seemingly trivial cultural oversight.

Reorganizing information according to international readers' genre expectations is a deeper level of socio-cultural editing than sentence-level changes. In Chinese business documents, it is customary to place the most important information at the end of a paragraph and an executive summary of the document's main points at the end instead of at the beginning of the document. Consequently, when editing documents for Chinese readers, editors should use visual cues (e.g., headings, bullets, bolding) to highlight and direct readers' attention, so that they can find the most important information in the right place in the document.

Furthermore, in the Chinese culture, workplace relationships are sometimes determined more by seniority than by titles and positions. Therefore, a young manager sending a memo to a senior/elderly engineer at his subsidiary in Tianjing, China, must employ appropriate politeness strategies. Instead of addressing the engineer with his first name as a subordinate, for example, it would be more appropriate for the manager to use "Mr." with the engineer's last name. On the other hand, in business Japanese, address terms are a way of symbolizing status. Rules of status apply even to relationships between business partners. Buyers are assumed to have greater importance than sellers; sellers say "onsha" which means "your great company," to which buyers reply "otaku" or "your company" [8]. In addition, to use the local metaphor in Asian cultures, being a piece of a puzzle is more important than being a nail for a hammer (i.e., sticking out above the rest and being a target to be hammered down). Therefore, in documents such as business reports and proposals for Asian distribution, editors must ensure that the collective "we" is used instead of the individual "I" to indicate authorship. Even if an individual is the main author, it is customary for the writer to give credit to the other people involved and show group consensus.

Editing graphics is another important feature of socio-cultural editing. In Switzerland, designers of public health documents accompanied by German text portrayed stylized figures of men and women in bars and intimate settings. However, in the Turkish language versions of the same documents, designers portrayed people as naturalistic figures in more formal settings than those in the graphics accompanying the German text. The graphics were apparently chosen, or "edited" in recognition of the differences between the primarily Christian German-speaking population raised in coeducational settings and the largely Muslim Turkish immigrant population of Switzerland, many of whom still observe some separation of women and men in public. Knowledge of the cultures of the target audiences was critical to effective choice of visuals in this multilayered situation. Editors who take socio-cultural factors into consideration should be able to make more effective use of visual elements than those who assume that graphics can convey a single, universal meaning.

Political Editing We use the term "political" to refer to country-level or industry-level politics. In this category, editors consider the political implications of the language used in business and technical documents in the countries as well as the industries for which the documents are intended. To edit effectively, editors should seek to balance corresponding information about the countries involved. For example, political corruption exists in both the U.S. and the People's Republic of China (PRC), although corruption is defined and perceived differently in the different countries [9]. Bribery and "speed" money are sometimes requested and often necessary in other countries, including the PRC. Funding for lobbying or political campaigns seems to serve a similar lubricating function in the U.S. political system, and in the U.S., lobbying is as accepted as normal as "speed" money is in the PRC. The difference is in degree; for example, political actions in the PRC have more severe consequences for individuals than political actions in the U.S., a long-standing and pervasive difference between these two countries. As a result, political references in documents for international audiences need to be handled more carefully than similar references in documents intended for a U.S.-only audience.

Political editing attends to sensitive issues such as the tendency to confuse names of regions and races with names of countries. In a business proposal for establishing a subsidiary in Shanghai, a company may indicate on a pie chart that it has worldwide operations in six different countries—Taiwan included. However, to PRC government officials, Taiwan is not an individual country but is considered a part of China that is "inseparable." To edit the document politically to meet the PRC Chinese government standards, editors would change "we have worldwide operations in six different countries" to "we have worldwide operations in different countries and regions." Political editing can be very subtle but can be critical for successfully accomplishing the business purpose.

Political implications are a factor in all markets. The German government recently mandated that the East and West German dialects must be integrated into one language. This decision is officially expressed in the recent publication of a single German language guide to replace the long-standing separate volumes for East and West Germany. This linguistic integration signals a strong political change, stating definitively that there is only one Germany, not two. As another European example, the French government requires that all documentation for products being sold in France must come in a French language version that cannot contain foreign words. This requirement is especially difficult to meet when the documents entering the country contain new words, such as those developed in the computer industry, because translation of new words requires additional time. Within the same language, translations of new words can diverge in different countries. In PRC China and Taiwan, for example, the word "computer" has been translated as "calculating machine" or "electronic brain," respectively [10].

Technical Editing Technical editing can be defined as substantive editing, checking the content correctness of a document, but can also refer to the physical environments in which a document may be used. Hoft [11] has extensively outlined document production and editing choices necessary to ensure that technical terms describing physical reality fit the country being addressed (e.g., power voltages, measurement systems, technology available). A simple, familiar example is the metric system, which is used in Europe and Canada; many Canadians are bi-metric and use both the metric and English system, as are the British who ask for pints in their local pubs. Documents for readers residing outside of the U.S. are more effective when the English system of measurement is transformed to metric at the source rather than forcing readers to make the conversion.

Likewise, an awareness of the technological needs and capabilities of the target country is important in documents, visuals (such as Web site buttons), and other graphic sources (such as videos and commercials). A mundane document-based difference between the U.S. and many other countries is the size of paper placed in fax machines; a tightly printed, close margin 8.5 by 11 inch document transmitted from the United States may overflow a British or European A4-sized page at the other end of the fax line. Web site buttons may need text tags as well as graphic icons for the audience to recognize the purpose of each button. For example, a chick popping out of an egg would symbolize "life" in Chinese rather than "new" as it is intended to do in a U.S.-based Web site for small business start-ups. In the same vein, computer icons, such as manila folders, have less salience in countries such as the PRC where manila folders are seldom used for document storage (large envelopes with closure fasteners are the preferred storage for PRC documents). Finally, international texts need to consider the types of technological items in the lives of non-American readers. An internal training video script produced in the U.S. for a PRC affiliate referred to car washing as an example of machine maintenance. This is a poor example for the PRC; while car washing is a common form of low-technology maintenance in the U.S., fewer than 1% of the PRC population have cars or wash cars. A better PRC example would be bicycle maintenance, because the vast majority of PRC Chinese do clean, oil, and take good care of their bicycles.

Global Strategies and International Editing Choices

From these examples of different categories of editing—linguistic, socio-cultural, political, and technical—we hope it is clear that just as word-for-word translation does not accommodate linguistic complexity, editing for linguistic meaning alone does not necessarily produce an appropriate document or script. However, editors seldom have time to edit all four categories deeply. Therefore, we recommend aligning international editing effort with corporate global strategies for optimal use of resources. Editors would expend the most effort on international editing in corporations for which global market share is a high priority, and they would concentrate less on the needs of target countries in corporations in which the global strategy is focused more on the domestic market. Understanding a corporation's global strategies requires, again, a categorization to streamline editorial decision-making. Global business strategies can be ethnocentric, polycentric, or geocentric, depending on the market share and penetration strategies being pursued [12].

Ethnocentric The ethnocentric approach is a traditional strategy, reflecting the belief that "what worked at home will work abroad" [13]. A corporation that does not change its strategy when it begins to move beyond its local market may be ethnocentric in its international market approach. International work is undertaken much as domestic efforts would be, with the assumption that what was successful in one country will transfer to success in another. An ethnocentric corporate strategy implies that editing efforts to make documents accommodate second language readers' needs and expectations will receive little corporate support. Instead, corporations will expect and demand second language readers to accommodate their communication practices to those of the corporation. For example, some U.S. multinational corporations (MNCs) invest in English training programs in their out-of-country subsidiaries to improve employees' English communication skills, while they may not expect or encourage expatriate management staff to learn the local language of the out-of-country subsidiary. Expecting the many to accommodate to the few is an example of an ethnocentric focus on the part of a U.S. parent firm.

Editing business/technical documents for corporations that take an ethnocentric strategy to internationalization requires less attention to the socio-cultural and/or political appropriateness of documents beyond the local or home market than editing in corporations with a more international market strategy. That is, editors may still apply the editing criteria used for domestic communication to international communication.

Polycentric The opposite of an ethnocentric strategy is a polycentric strategy, in which operations are decentralized to accommodate the needs of specific countries or regions. A corporation that has experienced some success in the international marketplace and has expanded its offices and subsidiaries into target countries tends "to move toward looser coupling between units and [away] from the hierarchy ... of ethnocentrism to market solutions," becoming more polycentric in its approach to management [2].

Polycentric corporations may require documents to address specific country needs and expectations for all four editing categories identified above so that the corporations can efficiently meet their global missions in regard to expansion into new target markets. In such corporations, editing will not only involve attention to linguistic conventions but also to the socio-cultural, political, and technical appropriateness of the text for the intended local readers. This editing will be necessary even if translation into the target languages is part of the corporations' global strategies. In polycentric corporations, in fact, translation plays a large role in the localization of products and services for target markets; international editing can play a major role in reducing translation time, especially when translation into more than one language (as in the five language example of FrontPage) is expected.

Geocentric A geocentric strategy may be viewed as a balance between ethnocentric and polycentric strategies. Geocentric corporations seek to optimize their efforts internationally by focusing on commonalties so that little accommodation is required to place products or services in diverse markets. Focusing on commonalties across markets allows geocentric corporations to take advantage of economies of scale in ways that polycentric corporations with decentralized operations cannot. According to Maddox, "a geocentric orientation within the firm has been viewed as both a globally integrated business philosophy and compromise between the extremes of ethnocentrism and polycentrism" [13]. In line with Ken'ichi Omae's concept of a borderless world [14], the geocentric strategy views the world as a home market rather than a series of local markets.

In editing for corporations with a geocentric strategy, editors may take a "universal" approach, making editing choices based on the needs of the largest number of users. A heavy machinery company, John Deere, uses graphics to help meet global needs, employing the same pictures of "flatman" (a stylized human figure) accompanied by text in different languages in equipment manuals. The use of "flatman" figures is predicated on the belief that "graphics designed to be as global as possible" are a "universal form of communication," and supports a geocentric management strategy [15]. "Flatman" shows up in many places: on a tube of an anti-inflammatory drug, Voltaren™ by Ciba-Geigy AG (a Swiss pharmaceutical firm). A bent "flatman" holds its sore back on one side of the tube while the drug indications are presented in German and French on the other—the "flatman" graphic can be considered a global or universal element, and the two languages are local elements appropriate for the mid-European market. Graphics do not obviate the need for translation, although they can supplement text. An editor working with a geocentric strategy might combine text and graphics to increase the accessibility of information.

These global strategies, which reflect corporations' main business foci, have implications for editors of business and technical documents. For optimal use of corporate resources, editing choices should align with the global busi-

TABLE I

ALIGNING INTERNATIONAL EDITING EFFORTS WITH GLOBAL BUSINESS STRATEGIES

	Linguistic	Socio-cultural	Political	Technical
Ethnocentric	✓	–	–	✓
Polycentric	×	×	×	×
Geocentric	×	✓	✓	×

Editing requirements in specific categories: × = high; ✓ = medium; – = low ness strategies. Table I illustrates the specific categories of editing that best support each global strategy.

Editing for corporations with polycentric (penetration into many countries or different markets, adjusting the product as necessary for different countries) or geocentric (penetration into many countries with a relatively constant product) strategies will be more substantive than for corporations taking an ethnocentric approach, since they require medium- to high-level editing for all four categories. In polycentric corporations, however, editors should accommodate political and cultural diversity on an even deeper level than is necessary in geocentric corporations.

Implications for Editors

Aligning editing choices with corporate global business strategy is one method to insure that an editing effort is in line with the corporations' mission. By focusing on the corporate global business strategy, editors should improve their ability to obtain corporate support for appropriate personnel and resources. For example, editors in corporations with a polycentric strategy should be able to justify time spent creating international style guides, working with translators to plan major product releases, and creating new positions much more easily than editors operating in corporations that follow more ethnocentric strategies. From a broader perspective, documents edited in alignment with the global mission should more effectively meet the needs of the intended audience. Such documents may project a consistent corporate image that will help customers to understand the product, be able to use it safely, and trust its quality.

References

[1] S. Sanderlin, "Preparing instruction manuals for non-English readers," *Tech. Commun.*, vol. 35, pp. 96–100, 1988.

[2] G. Hedlund, "The hypermodern MNC—A heterarchy?," *Human Resource Manag.*, vol. 25, pp. 9–35, 1986.

[3] *Dictionary for Caterpillar Fundamental English.* Peoria, IL: Caterpillar Tractor Co., 1972.

[4] *NCR Fundamental English Dictionary.* Dayton, OH: NCR Corp., 1978.

[5] J. H. Ward, "Editing in a bilingual, bicultural context," *J. Tech. Writing and Commun.*, vol. 18, pp. 221–226, 1988.

[6] D. Sylvain, Personal e-communication. Microsoft Corp., Redmond, WA, Aug. 28, 1997.

[7] B. Gu, "A study of cultural awareness at a software company," presented at The ABC Midwest Regional Conf., Dayton, OH, Apr. 17–19, 1997.

[8] R. Mead, *Cross-Cultural Management Communication.* New York: Wiley, 1990.

[9] "China's politics of crime," in *The Economist*, vol. 340, p. 25, 1996.

[10] L. Chengzhao, "Translating English scientific and technical terms into Chinese: Comparing the practice in mainland China and Taiwan," *IEEE Trans. Prof. Commun.*, vol. 35, Mar. 1991.

[11] N. L. Hoft, *International Technical Communication: How to Export Information About High Technology.* New York: Wiley, 1995.

[12] C. Leininger, "The alignment of global management strategies, international communication approaches, and individual rhetorical choices," *J. Business and Tech. Commun.*, vol. 11, no. 3, pp. 261–280, July 1997.

[13] R. Maddox, *Cross-Cultural Problems in International Business: The Role of the Cultural Integration Function.* Westport, CT: Quorum Books, 1993, p. 53.

[14] K. Omae, *The Borderless World: Power and Strategy in the Interlinked Economy.* New York: Harper, 1990.

[15] C. Kostelnick, "Cultural adaptation and information design: Two contrasting views," *IEEE Trans. Prof. Commun.*, vol. 38, pp. 182–196, Dec. 1995.

Carol Leininger is on the faculty of the Business Analysis and Computer Systems faculty at San Francisco State University, where she researches international communication. She has a degree in Public Health and Biostatistics and worked as a statistician in the U.S. and Europe before earning a Ph.D. degree in rhetoric and professional communication from Iowa State University.

Rue Yuan is a Ph.D. candidate in rhetoric and professional communication at Iowa State University. She has published work on international business communication in the *Journal of Business and Technical Communication*. Her interests include rhetoric of organizations, writing and information technology, and writing in Asian cultures.

Commentary

Tackling the Needs of Foreign Academic Writers: A Case Study

Shimona Kushner

Abstract—**Foreign engineers and scientists must publish their research in professional journals in English, but they often lack the proficiency and skills to do so successfully. This commentary describes a course that teaches these skills to Ph.D. students before they enter the job market. The techniques described are also effective tools for teaching professionals in the workplace.**

Index Terms—**Graduate engineering education, English as a Foreign Language, Israel, teaching of writing.**

THERE is no doubt that today English is the most frequently used language of international communication. This is especially true in the fields of science and technology. For scientists and engineers around the world it is the language of numerous professional publications, international conferences, electronic mail communications, and personal oral communication. For people for whom English is not their native language, it is not only the medium of communication between themselves and native speakers, but also between themselves and other nonnative speakers from different native language (L1) backgrounds. This is clearly evident in the academic journal genre. Scientists from all over the world publish their research findings or professional communications in international journals whose language of publication is English. In fact, in some countries having an article published in an international journal in English serves not only the function of what Bazerman calls "the needs of individuals to have their representations accepted as worthy by reference groups" [1]; it can also be the determining factor for professional advancement. Publication in such forums is often viewed as more prestigious and more professionally valuable than publishing in the writer's native language.

The idea of "publish or perish" has become a basic tenet of both the academic and, in many cases, the professional worlds. This is obviously a chore for many people in the technical fields who readily admit that they find writing of any kind an unpleasant task [2]. For nonnative speakers of English, this situation is compounded by the fear of writing in a language in which they are not entirely proficient and knowing that the evaluation of their writing may not always take this into account [3], [4].

The need to publish may begin long before the writers become "officially" a part of the professional world. Advanced degree students in engineering and science often find that they must publish their research findings even before completing their studies. There are numerous reasons for this, two of which are to publicize their research for scientific or economic purposes (possible patents is a case in point) and to establish a name for themselves in their field of specialization, which will help their future prospects when, for example, they apply for post-doctoral positions upon graduation.

Problematic Prior Training

In most foreign universities, it is assumed that intelligent students who have done a lot of professional reading in English will be able to write intelligibly and successfully when they are called upon to do so as professionals. Unfortunately, this is not always the case. The task of decoding professional material in their disciplines does not usually pose great difficulty, but this ability is not always easily transferred when the time comes to write. Students and young professionals may find it difficult to glean acceptable writing conventions on their own because native speakers, being secure enough to experiment in their writing, may employ a variety of styles which may be confusing for the nonnative writer [5].

A very serious impediment to foreign professionals is the small amount of academic English instruction they have typically had. In many universities where English is taught as a foreign language, this instruction is limited to the undergraduate level alone. Furthermore, English as a foreign language (EFL) instruction in elementary and high schools tends to be primarily the language of literature and informal communication, reinforced by English input from other sources such as films, television, and popular music. Any specific writing instruction, whether in their native language or in foreign language classes, is most likely limited to the prose writing of high school compositions. A lack of academic written competency can lead to a breakdown in communication between foreign professionals and their intended audiences, a most undesirable situation. And as they do not possess the instincts that native writers have about what is and is not appropriate in

Manuscript received July 1996; revised September 1996.

The author is with the Technion–Israel Institute of Technology, Haifa 32000, Israel.

Publisher Item Identifier S 0361-1434(97)02025-0.

Reprinted from *IEEE Trans. Prof. Comm.*, vol. PC-40, no. 1, pp. 20–25, March 1997.

a particular context (a problem with those journal guidelines which recommend that authors be innovative), the writing that they produce may be in very blatant violation of either the accepted norms of the genre or of the English language, or of both.

Whether the students, or for that matter working professionals, like it or not, science and engineering are discourse technologies [6], and scientists and engineers do spend much of their professional lives involved in a variety of discourses. There is a popular misconception that these professionals work away at their research with no real need for writing as, say, the specialist in history or literature might require. That is an obvious fallacy. Recognition for research work that has been completed comes from its publication in professional journals. This can, and often does, have very direct economic implications as this publication spreads knowledge of the research findings and has the potential of investment, commercial and professional benefits.

A Solution to the Problem

How do we best provide students with the skills they will need as professionals who write? A very simple solution is to point them in the direction of the numerous writing textbooks and guides which fill the market. For the most part, these books are geared to students in either a first or second language situation who are studying at an English medium university, or to native speaker professionals. Most of these books do not deal with problems of grammar or mechanics, and, if they do, the problems are those that are common to the majority of first or second language learners and cannot, by their nature, address the specific difficulties of a particular student population in an EFL context.

The most effective solution, then, is to provide writing instruction in the academic genre at the level of study (the doctoral level) at which they are just about to enter the professional world and start publishing on their own. This instruction should provide the broadest spectrum of information and practice which will enable the students to function as successful independent writers. Since, in Sinclair's words, the English language is composed basically of "common patterns and slight variations of those common patterns," [7] combining instruction in these patterns together with the conventions of academic writing and the rules of use will give students the skills which will enable them to produce text which will be acceptable to their audience.

Setting up the Course

A basic factor that must be taken into consideration when setting up such a course is to ensure that the course is relevant. Students at this level are very pressed for time, with full programs of courses which they must take and, working as they usually do, as teaching assistants or at other jobs outside the university. The course must be based on material and practice which is meaningful for the students or else they will simply not bother [8], [9].

Another important goal is to build the students' confidence in their writing ability and raise their awareness of the writing process in general and their own writing processes in particular. They probably have already developed a *schema* derived from both their vast reading and the processes of logic that they employ in their discipline, but as foreign writers, they have understandable uncertainties about their ability to write. Giving the students the opportunity to write, providing them with a forum through which their pressing questions can be answered, and allowing them to see that their difficulties are surmountable goes a long way toward achieving this confidence-building goal.

Writing is a cognitive process related to the research which is being conducted; it is not an isolated task detached from that research. Writing involves problem solving on a number of levels—the research itself, the decision of what to include or exclude in the article, determining how much shared common knowledge exists between the writers and their audience, and the organization and mechanics of the writing. Often the act of writing down the research can and does help to put the research into perspective [10] and overcome difficulties in the logic of the work which may not have been apparent. Students have reported that by seeing a lack of coherence when putting things down on paper they realized that there was a problem in the research itself. An awareness of all these facets of writing will help the students.

Such a course must cover the different tasks which together comprise the skill of academic article writing. First is an understanding of the patterns of writing which are characteristic of the different disciplines [11]. For example, very significant differences exist between the forms that experimental and theoretical articles take; this should be examined in detail. An understanding of these specific rhetorical patterns can help to deal with and overcome individual rhetorical difficulties [12].

Professional Writing Genres

Each genre of professional writing possesses its own distinct conventions that have developed over the years [13] and are continuing to evolve in the rapidly changing technological world. These conventions relate directly to the particular genre's purpose as well as to the mode of reasoning which it employs. A grant proposal aims at convincing an outside source that the work to be done is worthy of support, whereas a lab report is a summary of work that has already been carried out. These documents differ in the audiences to whom they are addressed (the former to bodies or individuals who control funds and who may or may not be experts in the field, and the latter to people who are probably quite versed in the field's narrow specifics); they differ in purpose (one to be better than the competition and the other to document); and they differ in length (the first is normally much longer than the second). The research article is yet a different genre still, aimed at convincing people in the field of the validity and importance of work that has been undertaken. It is firmly anchored in past research but attempts to convince the audience, composed entirely of professionals, that the findings it presents are significant.

Coherence, Organization, and Clarity

Coherence, organization, and clarity are "staples" of any writing curriculum. On the macro level the acquisition of these skills in the technical and scientific disciplines may be easier than in others because the format of such writing in English has an important role in establishing coherence [14]. English expository prose has a very distinctive pattern that moves from a more general presentation of the topic or the state of the field to a very specific and orderly explication of the topic and then on to a conclusion which limits itself to only what has already been discussed in the article. Paragraphs in English also possess a distinct structure, usually beginning with a topic sentence and followed by supporting sentences, and these paragraphs are linked to each other in a linear manner. Drawing a link between the scientific method which the engineers and scientists use in their research work and the "logical" development of the text in their articles can help in the organization of the writing [15]. A conscious awareness of these patterns should also help EFL writers overcome the interference which some of them may have from the different rhetorical patterns common to the expository prose of their native languages which tends to find its way into their English writing.

However, clarity and coherence are not limited to the macro level [16]. On the micro level, nonnative speakers can and usually do have serious deficiencies. Cyril Weir found that nonnative writers reported problems with items such as grammatical accuracy, the ability to use a variety of grammatical structures, choosing the correct grammatical structure, and being limited by their small range in vocabulary—difficulties which native speakers do not possess [17]. There is a view that it is enough to expose the students to a sufficient amount of English writing in the genre for them to overcome these difficulties and become proficient writers (see, for example, Krashen's comprehensible input [18]). However, there is no doubt that drawing upon the knowledge which EFL writers already have and giving them instruction in additional, important discrete items is beneficial because it can hasten the learning process and give them the grounding that will enable them to use this information correctly and help them avoid a breakdown in communication [19]–[22].

Students at the graduate level need the most expedient method through which to eradicate the incorrect structures which may have fossilized in their writing despite years of comprehensible input. They also need to be shown that control of correct English structures is not some unnecessary fetish of the teacher's, but has direct rhetorical significance. Though a writing course of short duration cannot possibly provide all they lack, it can provide the tools with which to overcome these difficulties by formal instruction where it is most effective (like the variety of tense usage) or by acquainting them with resource materials that are available and to which they can turn, such as thesauruses and language guides.

The Technion Experience

The Technion–Israel Institute of Technology is a four-year university for engineering and science with graduate programs for both the master's and doctoral degrees. English instruction at this institution, as well as at all the other universities in Israel, occurs in the first year of undergraduate studies, meaning that by the time students reach the Ph.D. level there has been a break of at least five years since their last English instruction. All high school graduates have completed eight years of EFL instruction, but the emphasis in those frameworks is broad, covering all the four language skills (reading, writing, oral, and aural) with a heavy stress on literature.

The medium of instruction at all Israeli universities is Hebrew. The English that the students must contend with in this context is only that of textbooks and professional journals. Later, as working professionals, their primary need for English will be to read professional material in the language, but they will also need English for international contacts, if and when they arise. All faculty members agree on the importance of high English proficiency for their students, but due to time constraints, the amount of EFL instruction actually given at the universities is limited, so that the emphasis is almost solely on the most imperative skill which undergraduates (and later most professionals) need, that of reading comprehension.

The Academic Writing Course

The Technion was aware of the deficiencies that its advanced graduates had in writing in the academic genre in English. As a result, the Graduate School decided to answer this pressing need and open a writing program for Ph.D. students. Instruction was provided at this point for two reasons: this is the final stage before the students enter the academic and advanced professional world where they will be required to write journal articles; and, though still students, they are already engaged in writing articles for publication and being judged by the same criteria as "full fledged" professionals, and, even more crucial, by the same criteria as native English writers.

Aided by a small initial grant from the Wolfson Foundation (which had funded the opening of similar courses at other Israeli universities), an experimental class was opened in the spring semester of 1989. The classes met once a week during the fourteen week term for two hours of formal instruction. The curriculum was organized around the idea that the students should be expediently given an understanding of what constitutes an academic article so as to quickly permit them to implement this in the writing of their own articles. Thus the material covered included items such as the structure of such articles, the content of each article section, familiarization with resource materials such as writing manuals and guides, and text organization patterns. The assignments were the practical implementation of what was discussed in class using the students' own research results as the basis for their writing.

The students also met the instructor for individual tutorials twice during the semester. These were devoted to a discussion on a one-to-one basis of their actual written work. In this experimental stage these tutorials were spent almost exclusively on actual articles, or parts of articles, which the students were preparing for publication.

From the outset students were admitted to the course only after proving their proficiency in a one-and-a-half hour English writing examination. Students with weak written English were not admitted. Weaknesses which would preclude a student from taking the course are a consistent lack of subject–verb agreement, total lack of control of tenses, or use of completely incomprehensible sentence structures. The topics of choice on this exam are all general because it quickly became apparent that when writing on topics related to their research they display a level of proficiency which bears no relation whatsoever to their "real" ability in "free" English writing (they seem to know whole segments of text relating to their field of specialization by heart, whereas in free writing they showed less control of the language).

The class met with immediate success, and a year later the Technion Academic Senate decided to include it in the curriculum and give Ph.D. students the option of taking the academic writing Course in lieu of their second foreign language requirement (besides their first foreign language, which is English). This was an important move by the institution, which is usually reticent to add anything to the already very full subject matter curriculum (a situation not uncommon at universities [23]). As a result of this move, registration doubled immediately.

The Student Population

In accordance with the prerequsite set by the Graduate School, the original group was small and consisted of students who had all passed their qualifying examinations; that is, they were at least in the second if not third year of a three-year program. As already mentioned, this meant that they were all well into their research work and had data that they could use as the basis of their writing. But with the change in course status, the composition of the population changed radically. The students were now all in their first year (the second foreign language requirement must be completed during the first year of the Ph.D. program) and, therefore, had not yet taken their comprehensive examinations, and were, thus, at very preliminary stages in their research.

The majority of the students are native Israelis who are L1 Hebrew speakers, with a small number of L1 Arabic speakers. However, because Israel is a country of immigration, there is a constant flow of students with other L1 backgrounds depending on the current sources of immigration (for example, L1 Russian speakers from the former Soviet Union, L1 Romanian speakers, L1 Spanish speakers from South America, and L1 French speakers). We also have a fixed number of eight L1 Chinese speakers each year who are part of an exchange between Israel and the People's Republic of China.

The classes have always been composed of students from a variety of disciplines, rather than being homogeneous according to fields of specializations. This places a very great hardship on the curriculum. It forces us to search for the common themes, which can be covered while not neglecting different rhetorical styles which might be typical of individual disciplines (for example, the "classical" scientific academic article structure of introduction, materials, methods, results, conclusion, which is typical of the experimental disciplines, and the presentation of problem and solution style of organization which is found in theoretical papers). There is no doubt that it would have been much easier to teach homogeneous groups whose disciplines followed the same genre of organization. However, there was no alternative, since this was the only way to accommodate students with very disparate timetables.

It is, perhaps, interesting to note that a very big discrepency exists between the English speaking abilities of all of these students and their ability to write professional discourse in the language. Their spoken English is, more often than not, error-filled, with surprisingly basic mistakes in grammar. As a rule this is not reflected to the same degree in their academic writing.

The Curriculum

The change in the status of the course meant that new types of writing tasks had to be devised. No longer could the students be expected to write sections of their real journal articles because most of them were not far enough along in their research to be publishing. So a change in focus occurred with more emphasis placed on the analysis of authentic journal articles. Students are asked to choose and photocopy a "typical" article from a journal in their discipline. With the teacher's guidance, the students extrapolate, through discussion, the conventions of the different sections and genres. This method is preferable to having the teacher "dictate" the information because having the students look for the conventional elements on their own helps them to internalize the elements. Furthermore, the students, through their independent reading, have very broad exposure to a wide spectrum of journals in their field that may use different approaches to the writing of articles. They can report on this during the discussions and thus ensure a true representation of the variety that exists in the world of academic publications. In this way it is also possible to keep abreast of the changes that are constantly occurring in styles of writing or organization. Moreover, since the composition of the class changes from semester to semester, having the students find the conventions on their own ensures that the different disciplines represented in class are covered. This exposition provides a rich basis for the discussion and comparison of the rhetorical and discourse principles underlying the different genres, leading to a better understanding of the articles that they will write. Current research on various aspects of the academic article [24], [25] is also brought to the students' attention in order to reinforce what they themselves have found.

After the conventions of each particular section are ascertained, the students are given practice in "authentic-type" writing tasks, but not necessarily the kind which would require the use of actual data, if they do not have them. The only exception is that all students must write a real introduction section with publication in view, since no matter what the stage of their research, they have enough information to complete this task.

Since each group of students in any particular semester may be composed of different L1 or discipline backgrounds, the teacher is involved in a continual reassessment of the material covered in the curriculum so as to most effectively answer the students' needs. The difficulties evident from the free writing samples on the entrance examination are used as one basis for this reassessment, and the difficulties revealed through discussion with the students in the tutorials (discussed below) are another.

Coherence and clarity in writing are directly related to proper syntax and the knowledge of what can and cannot be done in an English sentence. As a rule, English syntax does not pose too great a problem for the L1 Hebrew speakers. However, it does pose a problem for some of the other L1 groups—Russian has a much looser sentence order than does English, and the L1 Chinese and L1 Arabic speakers often use structures in their writing that are neither coherent to the English reader nor appropriate to the technical genre. While these idiosyncratic difficulties are handled in the tutorial, general problems of syntax are covered in class. Practice is accomplished through correcting "incorrect" sentences and rearranging jumbled sentences into a coherent paragraph.

One of the most significant changes made to the curriculum after the expansion of the program was the inclusion of grammatical material, though only material with rhetorical relevance. Any individual deficiencies are dealt with on a personal level in tutorial. Based on a continuing analysis of the students' errors and reports of their own difficulties, a number of rhetorical/grammatical items were chosen to be covered in class. Some of these are the different uses of voice in the various sections of the academic article; the rhetorical, nontemporal use of tense (i.e., the use of tense where time is not the determining factor—something which is quite unfamiliar to nonnative speakers) [26]; the use of connectors to ensure cohesion; the concept of parallelism for clarity; reduced and full relative clauses which enable the writing of richer and more complex sentences; and the difference between defining and nondefining relative clauses, since their misuse can lead to a misunderstanding of what is being said.

The approach used in class is a pro-active one, where possible, having the students themselves analyze examples of written text in order to extrapolate the information and give them practice in the methods that they will have to use in the future. Because they will have to self-edit their own writing throughout their careers, practicing such techniques is invaluable. Innovative approaches are also sought for the teaching of grammatical items, some of which, despite years of instruction in school, have never been mastered. A rehash of the material in the same "old" way will not have any effective results.

The Tutorial

The teacher meets each student in individual tutorial at least twice during the semester. These are scheduled to last up to one hour each, but can and do go beyond that time limit. In these sessions the students' individual work is dicussed. Problems of organization, coherence, syntax, grammar, or vocabulary are solved through a process of negotiation. The teacher/tutor is never an editor who rewrites the student's work, but only points to those parts that are problematic, eliciting the changes from the students themselves. The goal is to make the students sensitive to the specific problems that they have with their writing so that they will be able to do this independently at a later date. The teacher must be very careful not to impose a "standardization" on the students' writing. Writing is a personal expression, and students must be encouraged to allow their individuality to shine through as long as the conventions of both the genre and the language are not compromised.

It is perhaps interesting to note that what sometimes appears to be a lack of coherence in student writing actually results from the teacher's lack of familiarity with the discipline. As the teachers are not discipline experts, the student's explanation of the difficult passages is a learning process for both the student and the teacher. This kind of activity simulates in a way the real, peer group interaction that will be an integral part of the students' professional lives later.

The tutorials are tailored to what the students themselves require. If they are in the process of writing an article, then that is the material used for the tutorial. Sometimes students need to prepare material that is going to be presented at a conference or international seminar, and they prefer to practice doing that during the session. Otherwise, their entrance examination and class writing assignments serve as material to work on.

This is the time when specific difficulties are dealt with that may not have relevance to the class as a whole. With the variety of L1 backgrounds in the class, tutorial sessions are an opportunity to delve more deeply into the problems that an individual language learner may have. For example, the L1 Arabic students tend to repeat the topic in sentence after sentence rather than use anaphoric reference as is done in English, or they tend to repeat and paraphrase whole blocks of text in order to construct their argument [27], [28]. Consider also the cultural difficulties that Chinese speakers have when they need to point to the shortcomings of previous research in the introduction to an article [29]. The tutorial is also a time during which the teacher can come to understand the composing problems that individual students have, which, if discovered to be widespread, can be dealt with in class.

One danger that must be noted here is being an editor for work actually done by the student's supervisors or collaborators. The majority of the faculty at the Technion are not native English speakers either, and they may therefore have some difficulty writing in English themselves. Because all of the articles published by the students are collaborative efforts, the question is always open to what degree the writing presented is the work of the student or the work of the supervisor. Eliciting "corrections" from the students, even if segments were written by the professors, keeps things within the realm of a learning exercise. From our experience, however, we have found that only very small segments of the writing may have actually been done or rewritten by the supervisors. The bulk remains the students' product.

Conclusion

The Ph.D. writing course at the Technion–Israel Institute of Technology successfully prepares its non-English speaking students, who will be spending their professional lives in Israel writing academic articles largely in English, in the skills and principles underlying the genre of the academic research article. The advantage of the program is its flexible format, which can be and already has been modified to suit the changing composition and needs of the students and the institution. The assessment of what needs inclusion or what must be changed is an ongoing one—based on the difficulties emerging from the student's own writing and from their own reports of what they struggle with.

By focusing on a rhetorical approach, all the necessary aspects of writing (the conventions of the genre, organization, mechanics) can be drawn together, emphasizing the interdependency of all these skills in the writing process. The individual tutorial, which is an integral part of the program, affords the learners the opportunity to deal more deeply with their own particular difficulties.

There is no doubt that the best stage for such instruction is before the students leave the university and enter the professional world. Where this is not possible (and such instruction within the university framework is, unfortunately, still the exception rather than the rule), it can be supplied at a later stage by the employer in the workplace. The distinct advantage of such instruction would be that, in contrast to what may exist at the university level, these "working-learners" are already engaged in publishable work and have "real" data which can be applied to what they learn, making the whole undertaking extremely relevant. The program can also be adapted to different time periods (it can be compressed or stretched to suit the time available). Thus non-English speaking engineers and scientists who must publish in international academic and professional forums can be provided with very important assistance in overcoming their writing difficulties and a framework in which they can receive answers to their pressing questions, helping them on their road to becoming successful, effective, and independent writers in English.

ACKNOWLEDGMENT

I would like to express my very deep gratitude to Joann Temple-Dennet for her invaluable comments and assistance, as well as to the two anonymous reviewers whose advice helped make this a better article.

REFERENCES

[1] C. Bazerman, "Foreword," in *Professional Communication: The Social Perspective*, N. R. Blyer and C. Thralls, Eds. Newbury Park, NH: Sage, 1993, pp. vii–x.
[2] S. P. Sanders, "Editorial," *IEEE Trans. Prof. Commun.*, vol. 35, p. 57, 1992.
[3] C. Kramberg-Walker, "The need to provide writing support for academic engineers," in *IEEE Trans. Prof. Commun.*, vol. 36, pp. 130–136, 1993.
[4] J. T. Dennett, "World language status does not ensure world class usage," *IEEE Trans. Prof. Commun.*, vol. 35, p. 13, 1992.
[5] Y. Kachru, "Cultural meaning and rhetorical styles: Toward a framework for contrastive rehtoric," in *Principle and Practice in Applied Linguistics*, G. Cook and B. Seidelhofer, Eds. Oxford, U.K.: Oxford Univ. Press, 1995, pp. 171–184.
[6] A. Luke, "Introduction," in *Writing Science: Literacy and Discursive Power*, M. A. K. Halliday and J. R. Martin, Eds. London, U.K.: Falmer Press, 1993, pp. x–xiii.
[7] J. M. Sinclair, *Corpus, Concordance, Collocation*. Oxford, U.K.: Oxford Univ. Press, 1991, p. 108.
[8] H. G. Widdowson, "An approach to the teaching of scientific English discourse," in H. G. Widdowson, *Explorations in Applied Linguistics*. Oxford, U.K.: Oxford Univ. Press, 1979, pp. 21–36.
[9] G. M. Blue, "Individualizing academic writing tuition," in *ELT Documents: Academic Writing: Process and Product*, P. C. Robinson, Ed. London, U.K.: British Council, 1988, no. 129, pp. 94–99.
[10] R. V. White, "Academic writing: Process and product," in *ELT Documents: Academic Writing: Process and Product*, P. C. Robinson, Ed. London, U.K.: British Council, 1988, no. 129, pp. 4–16.
[11] E. J. Schreiber, "From academic writing to job-related writing: Achieving a smooth transition," *IEEE Trans. Prof. Commun.*, vol. 36, pp. 178–184, 1993.
[12] C. Bazerman, *Constructing Experience*. Carbondale and Edwardville, IL: So. Ill. Press, 1994, p. 112.
[13] C. Bazerman, *Shaping Written Knowledge: The Genre and Activity of the Experimental Article in Science*. Madison, WI: Univ. of Wisconsin Press, 1988, pp. 6–7.
[14] A. O'Keefe, "Teaching technical writing," in *Research in Technical Communication*, M. G. Maran and D. Journet, Eds. Westport, CT: Greenwood Press, 1985, pp. 85–113.
[15] J. E. Morris, *Scientific and Technical Writing*. New York: McGraw-Hill, 1996, p. 26.
[16] R. E. Dulek, "Could you be clearer? An examination of the multiple perspectives of clarity," *IEEE Trans. Prof. Commun.*, vol. 35, pp. 84–87, 1992.
[17] C. Weir, "Academic writing—Can we please all the people all the time?," in *ELT Documents: Academic Writing: Process and Product*, P. C. Robinson, Ed. London, U.K.: British Council, 1988, no. 129, pp. 17–34.
[18] S. Krashen and T. D. Terrel, *The Natural Approach: Language in the Classroom*. Oxford, U.K.: Pergamon, 1983.
[19] J. P. B. Allen and H. G. Widdowson, "Teaching the communicative use of English," *Int. Rev. Appl. Linguistics*, vol. XII, pp. 1–20, 1974.
[20] "Introduction to grammar section," in *Methodology in TESOL: A Book of Readings*, M. H. Long and J. C. Richards, Eds. New York: Newbury House, 1987, pp. 279–281.
[21] M. Celce-Murcia and S. Hilles, "Background," in *Techniques and Resources in Teaching Grammar*, M. Celce-Murcia and S. Hilles, Eds. Oxford, U.K.: Oxford Univ. Press, 1988, pp. 1–15.
[22] M. Tomiyana, "Grammatical errors, communication breakdown," *TESOL Quart.*, vol. 14, pp. 71–79, 1980.
[23] C. Kramberg-Walker, "The need to provide writing support for academic engineers," *IEEE Trans. Prof. Commun.*, vol. 36, pp. 130–136, 1993.
[24] J. Swales, *Genre Analysis: English in Academic and Research Settings*. Cambridge, U.K.: Cambridge Univ. Press, 1990.
[25] G. E. Schindler, "Why engineers and scientists write the way they do—Twelve characteristics of their prose," *IEEE Trans. Eng. Writing Speech*, vol. EWS-10, pp. 27–32, 1967.
[26] L. Trimble, *English for Science and Technology: A Discourse Approach*. Cambridge, U.K.: Cambridge Univ. Press, 1985, p. 124.
[27] M. P. Williams, "A problem of cohesion," in *English for Specific Purposes in the Arab World*, J. Swales and H. Mustafa, Eds. Birmingham, U.K.: Univ. of Birmingham, 1984, pp. 85–98.
[28] A. J. R. Al-Jabouri, "The role of repetition in Arabic argumentative discourse," in *English for Specific Purposes in the Arab World*, J. Swales and H. Mustafa, Eds. Birmingham, U.K.: Univ. of Birmingham, 1984, pp. 99–111.
[29] G. Taylor and C. Tingguang, "Linguistic, cultural and subcultural issues in contrastive discourse analysis: Anglo-American and Chinese scientific texts," *Appl. Linguistics*, vol. 12, pp. 319–336, 1991.

Shimona Kushner is a Senior Teaching Fellow in English as a Foreign Language (EFL) at the Technion–Israel Institute of Technology, Haifa. She heads the Technion's Ph.D. Academic Writing Program and is EFL Coordinator of Technion's Pre-Academic Center. She is also the author of several textbooks specializing in English for science and technology.

PART X

The Internet: Making the Most of Cyberspace

A universe of communication was opened up some years ago with the advent of the Internet and the World Wide Web. With this brave new world came all kinds of possibilities, responsibilities, and potential hazards. The technology involved soon became highly technical, and now online documentation and Web page design demand specific skills of the technical writer or engineer. The articles in this section deal with several of the challenges, techniques, and opportunities of electronic media, from e-mail to online documentation and the Web, and should be of considerable help if you are involved, as most of us are, in these technologies.

Edit your e-mail

Although e-mail has been around for a long time, a lot of uncertainty and inconsistency still exist on the part of many of its users. You have probably received e-mail that has been hastily written, poorly formatted, or which perhaps had some content that shouldn't have been in a message that can be forwarded around the world almost instantly. Renee Horowitz and Marian Barchilon take up concerns like these and discuss numerous aspects of the sending and receiving of e-mail. Their topic is all the more important when you consider the millions of e-mail messages sent daily and how these numbers are going to do nothing but increase.

For whose eyes is it?

As the first article in this section makes clear, the wrong person reading your e-mail can have catastrophic results. Yet employees are often oblivious of how much of their e-mail is monitored by their employers—Big Brother could indeed by watching! Patricia Chociey has researched this situation and her findings are fascinating as she looks into the questions of ethics, legality, and privacy. She concludes by stressing how necessary it is for a company to have a clear e-mail monitoring policy available to its employees.

Working with the customer

This article deals with the age-old topic of audience analysis, this time as it applies to online documentation. Joanne Hackos and her co-authors state that online documentation can only be effective ultimately if it is finalized after rigorous ongoing audience and task analysis have taken place. To this end, the authors have developed a technique called "customer partnering," which goes far beyond the traditional approaches to user analysis. You will find the description of maintaining a long-term relationship between customer and information developer innovative and useful, particularly if you are involved in producing online documentation for complex applications.

Some design guidelines for a Web site

Mary Evans describes how she developed guidelines for designing Web pages at NOAA (National Oceanic Atmospheric Administration). Her article is significant because she addresses several important issues, including usability and design problems, and her description of how she developed her own guidelines for building a successful Web page are detailed and instructive. Moreover, her constant awareness of her audience and the needs of that audience make this highly researched article essential reading if you are considering building an easily accessible and usable Web page.

Creating the company Web site

Although published some six years ago, this article by Gary Ritzenthaler and David Ostroff raises questions that are still highly relevant. How is the World Wide Web best used to promote a corporation? What should be considered when creating a Web site for a company? What problems might you encounter if you have to operate such a site? Before answering these and other questions the authors provide a brief history of the Web's evolution and describe various uses to which the Web can be put. Although this article cites the experience of building an academic Web page, the potentials and pitfalls described, including security and copyright issues, will be of interest to anyone who creates Web sites for industry or other organizations.

How to edit a Web site

You are probably familiar with the concept of levels of edit when working with printed materials, but Steven Anderson and his colleagues extend the process to Web sites. Their article is based on practical experience gained by students editing a site constructed by more than one group of people. You have to admit that there are numerous Web pages out there that could benefit from a thorough edit to improve their layout, clarity, ease of navigation, and general usefulness to their audience, and this article provides excellent suggestions on how to methodically do such an edit.

Accessibility for all

Jeff Carter and Mike Markel remind us that to a large extent Web pages are inaccessible to people with disabilities. This is in spite of the fact that the ADA (Americans with Disabilities Act) has extended some of its rulings to the Web. The authors list the main categories of disability that prevent a person from using the Web easily: mobility, hearing, vision, and learning problems, and then state that some 43–54 million people in the United States suffer from such disabilities. This is an extremely large group of people who do not have normal access to the Web, and Carter and Markel survey what is being done and what can be done to remedy the situation.

The international user

In their thoroughly researched and documented article Fatemeh Zahedi and her two fellow writers review how peoples of various cultures respond differently to Web documents. Six cultural and six individual factors that come into play when the Web is used internationally are described, and then the authors show how the impact of Web pages vary according to the cultural and personal values of the users. You will find this article, with its appended propositions and extensive bibliography, to be quite revealing, particularly if you are involved in producing Web pages for international audiences.

Stylistic Guidelines for E-Mail

Renee B. Horowitz and Marian G. Barchilon

Abstract—**E-mail style has received little attention from corporations and other institutions. The absence of stylistic guidelines may create problems: communicating inappropriately with some audiences, losing sight of the message purpose, or wasting company resources in other ways. To solve such problems, technical communicators can use their unique abilities to promote e-mail formats that consider the strengths and limitations of the medium in addition to the traditional concerns with audience, purpose, and content of messages.**

WHEN business and industry address e-mail concerns, they concentrate primarily on connectivity or on privacy issues. However, companies must also address style, an area taken for granted in letter or memo writing. Firms generally regard letters as external documents, reserving memos for internal communication. Although styles differ from company to company, such variations follow well-defined conventions. Letters, for example, may be full-blocked, blocked, or semi-blocked. Memos begin with the addressee, the sender, the date, and the subject; even with slight changes in the order of these elements, they remain recognizable as memos.

E-mail, on the other hand, is used for both external and internal communication. Without clear stylistic conventions, e-mail users are left to their own devices. As a result, they may neglect to consider their audience and send messages lacking salutations or complimentary closings to international customers who expect such niceties. In other instances, they may use these formalities inappropriately, e.g., informal greetings in formal situations or polite closings for casual messages.

A literature review shows little, if any, attention to this problem. One source states the following about e-mail style:

> Because this is a relatively new form of correspondence, the conventions for it are not as well-established as those for traditional letters and memos, and you may find a variety of formats being used by organizations [1].

Worse, such variety often exists within the same organization, leading to inconsistencies in style and waste of company resources.

Moreover, employees often neglect to consider the strengths and limitations of the medium. Thus, even if company policy dictates that e-mail messages be treated as memos, screen or window space and other mechanical constraints suggest the need for further guidelines to ensure more effective and efficient styles for electronic communication.

Another source [2] finds that 70–80% of written communication by engineering managers and design engineers could be sent by e-mail. Even if this projection is high, current trends indicate that industry can expect increased reliance on electronic communication, making its effective and efficient use a major concern. As e-mail usage proliferates, therefore, companies must realize that more productive use of the medium is essential and must establish consistent guidelines for their employees. Technical writers, who are uniquely situated in the workplace to meet this need, can help companies choose suitable styles for more efficient use of electronic correspondence.

By raising such issues for technical writers in business and industry to consider, this paper encourages them to use their communication skills to establish appropriate styles for their companies. To do so effectively, technical writers must counteract the prevailing view of e-mail messages as electronic memos or telephone calls. Instead, they must influence industry to examine the effects of the medium on the message and the ways in which the medium interacts with traditional considerations of audience, purpose, and content.

Effect of the Medium on the Message

It does not take long for the e-mail user to discover the strengths and limitations of the medium. Major strengths, of course, include cost savings and speed. In lean economic times, e-mail may represent one means of improving productivity. One aerospace company, for example, now uses e-mail to send information from senior management simultaneously to all employees. Its goal is to avoid the omissions, errors, and filters of its previous system—weekly meetings of project managers, who then transmitted information with varying degrees of accuracy in a series of follow-on meetings [3].

However, in some companies, potential benefits may be lost if the medium is used without effective guidelines and users send messages indiscriminately because it is easy to do so. For example, the present writers often receive messages preceded by a dozen or more screens of distribution lists. Such sweeping use of e-mail is not uncommon. Ironically, widespread distribution originally was lauded as a way to break down hierarchic barriers to communication within a company [4]. But along with easier access, the medium allows users to waste recipients' time with messages that are too lengthy or unnecessary. Further, some e-mail messages may reflect negatively on the company. Thus, it is important for business and industry to set policy for e-mail style and usage in order to maximize productivity and prevent such potential pitfalls.

Manuscript received June 1994; revised August 1994. This paper is a revised and updated version of a paper presented at the 56th Annual Convention of the Association for Business Communication, Honolulu, Hawaii.

The authors are with the Department of Manufacturing and Industrial Technology, College of Engineering and Applied Sciences, Arizona State University, Tempe, AZ 85287-6806 USA.

IEEE Log Number 9407681.

Reprinted from *IEEE Trans. Prof. Comm.*, vol. PC-37, no. 4, pp. 207–212, December 1994.

Electronic Mail Etiquette

1. Cover only one subject per message, which facilitates replies, forwarding, and filing.

2. Use upper and lower case text, because MESSAGES IN ALL CAPITAL LETTERS HAVE THE EFFECT OF SHOUTING.

3. Be diplomatic: criticism is always harsher when written, and electronic messages are easily forwarded.

4. Be calm: you may have misinterpreted the implied criticism or missed the ironic humor in a message; don't send a message while you are still hot under the collar. (Networkers call this "flaming.")

5. To signal your humorous intent, use the "sideways smile," :-)

6. Don't use the academic networks for commercial or proprietary work.

7. Be extremely careful about executing any programs that you receive over the network, since they may contain viruses that erase or, by propagating themselves, disrupt the network.

8. Don't send anything electronically that you wouldn't want to see on page one of The Chronicle of Higher Education....

9. Don't use LISTSERVs for personal mail. It is seen by everyone on the list.

Fig. 1. Many e-mail users receive minimal stylistic information.

At times, these pitfalls are intensified by writers who see e-mail simply as another form of conversation or "talking on paper," a view that continues with the statement that e-mail "thrives because of its rapidity and fluidity: the e-mail writer performs as a speaker . . ." [5]. Here, the source fails to fully consider the purpose and the medium. The purpose, in most companies, is a business rather than a social one. For example, Nordstrom specifies that employees are to use e-mail only for "legitimate business purposes" [6]. Further, the medium makes a "talking on paper" attitude a dangerous viewpoint. Many unsuspecting e-mail users have discovered that, unlike oral conversation, e-mail messages can provide a permanent record, as evidenced by the court cases involving e-mail privacy [6].

In many instances, companies have focused on the technical aspects of electronic messaging to the near exclusion of style. For example, in examining a typical e-mail users' manual, such as the Arizona State University guide, we found 100 pages of technical information on using e-mail but only a one-page list (see Fig. 1) that addresses "Electronic Mail Etiquette." This list reminds users to be diplomatic and calm, to cover only one subject per message, to use upper and lower case rather than all capital letters, and to remember that other readers may view their messages. For further stylistic conventions, writers at this institution are on their own.

If we look carefully at the nine rules in Fig. 1, we find an attempt, conscious or not, to link the medium to audience, purpose, and content. Certainly, the guide considers audience convenience in the first rule—directing users to limit their messages to one subject—but neglects to carry it a step further and recommend one screen or window per message. Rules 2, 4, 8, and 9 also concern the audience in part. Interestingly enough, Rule 4 addresses both the receiver and sender of the message as audience.

This aspect of e-mail style, flaming (a hacker term that refers to angry or otherwise unsuitable wording), is one of the few that has received wide coverage in the literature. One source suggests, for example, that if an e-mail user must send an emotional response, it is better to start with a warning phrase such as "flame on" [7]. Another advises e-mail users to ask themselves whether they would say in person what they plan to say electronically and to "keep editing until the answer is yes" [8]. Many writers include *smilies* or *emoticons*, symbols like the one in Rule 5 above, to indicate purpose to the audience. An online file called *The Unofficial Smilie Dictionary* makes these symbols readily available [8].

Computer industry sources provide similar rules of e-mail etiquette to business users, reminding them to watch their language and giving other advice that relates primarily to audience and the medium, though the writers may not refer directly to these areas of communication:

> Scrutinize your address list. People have lost their jobs by accidentally forwarding messages to the wrong person. A little care will assure that you're not sending an employee evaluation to another employee, or a nasty note about the boss to the woman herself [9].

Despite the importance of such advice, companies do not routinely train their employees in e-mail style.

The rules in Fig. 1 represent a good beginning, but more information is necessary. In the early years of this century, when memos emerged as a new form of business communication, the major purpose was to make communication systematic, cheaper, and more efficient [10]. With the ongoing replacement of paper memos by electronic messaging, companies seem to have overlooked the original advantages of the memo format.

An examination of electronic messages at several firms shows a similar disregard for consistency in e-mail style. These messages include a series of disconnected meeting notes headed "Interoffice Memorandum," a customer-satisfaction reminder (with a long distribution list), a "While You Were Out" message, and a meeting announcement. Many of these messages are electronic memos, similar in style to paper ones. Others add personal salutations and closings to memo style, as shown in Fig. 2. (All figures in this article that show e-mail messages are modified versions of actual communications. Names and other identifiers are changed where necessary to protect privacy.)

Here, the content and purpose of the letter is business oriented, and the audience consists of two other company employees in addition to John Doe. However, the format and general tone seem to contradict these aspects of the message. This combination of memo format, informal and incomplete salutation and closing, and letter style ("Well, that's all for now") seems representative of the general confusion as to appropriate e-mail style.

Earlier studies have examined style relative to other e-mail issues. Specifically, Sproull and Kiesler [11] focused on the effects of the technology on behavior within organizations, looking at e-mail's role in empowering people by providing information. Among the data these researchers collected was information about the following eight message attributes:

```
Date:       04-Apr-1994 04:09pm EDT
From:       Sally Brown
            UXUXU
To:         John Doe
CC:         Frank James
CC:         Betty Green

Subject:    Paranoia
=====================================

John,
This is probably stating the obvious, but I don't
want to get burned in this YZY 22.0 install.

I want to make sure we document (yes, in
writing) to them a couple of things:
- all data stored between the 22.0 install and the
22.1 install/upgrade will be deleted.
-support for the system will be 8:30-5 EST only.
                    . . .

Well, that's all for now.  If I think of anything
else, I'll pass it on.

Sally
```

Fig. 2. Writer appears undecided as to appropriate e-mail style.

```
>>>MAIL 80.26<<<From:: XXXXX at ASUACAD
***Top of File***
Date:        Mon, 7 Jun 94 09:52:32 MST
From:        XXXXX@ASUACAD
To:          ZZZZZ@ASUACAD
Subject:     Source of Smith Article

From:        Mary Doe

Hi, Renee.  I hope your summer will be both
productive and restful (if those two can co-exist).
Could you tell me which issue of XYZ journal the
John Smith article you gave me was in?

Since having lunch with you, a few things have
changed slightly.  I still work 49% of the time at
the School of WWW but, in addition, Bill Jones
has hired me 50% as Program Coordinator.
We've got some good activities planned for the
year, and I hope you and I will get a chance to
get together at them and compare notes.

--Mary Doe
```

Fig. 3. Message attempts to combine styles of formal business memo and informal friendly note.

1) Length: number of lines in the text of the message.
2) Opening: number of words in the salutation.
3) Closing: number of words in the closing.
4) Positive effect: words that express positive feelings.
5) Negative effect: words that express negative feelings.
6) Politeness: courteous words.
7) Energy: format that adds emphasis to the message.
8) Topic: either work or nonwork.

The first five of these attributes can be looked at in a different way—as a departure point for examining the influence of the e-mail medium on the message and for recommending effective conventions in these areas.

Message Length

Conventions for memo and letter writing have long preferred a one-page format. With e-mail, the number of message lines available to writer and reader may vary with the software and hardware used. E-mail users often find that many communication programs use so much of the screen or window for menus and other "housekeeping" items that limited space remains for the message. Although writer and receiver can always scroll down to the next screen, restricted screen size is a limitation of e-mail that organizations should seriously consider. Writers must weigh the inconvenience to the audience of scrolling back and forth to write, to read, and to refer to previous screens or windows when responding. Research does indicate that recipients will scroll down if the message is important or interesting enough [12], but we believe both writer and reader can be served best if they limit each message and response to one screen or window, whenever possible.

Salutation and Closing

Many e-mail users indicate they are unsure of the salutation and closing format to employ. They are concerned about appearing too informal in business communications or, conversely, too formal in addressing colleagues, inside and outside the organization; to compensate, they may combine styles. The e-mail message in Fig. 3 shows a style that combines the formality of a business memo (writer-inserted From: line and closing) with the informality of a friendly note ("Hi, Renee"). Some writers circumvent this problem by using memo format for both internal and external messages. Others avoid salutations and closings; they begin with the message and end the communication when they complete the message. Still others adapt their salutations and closings to the style of the recipient, a ploy that is effective only if one is responding to an earlier e-mail communication.

These different styles may not only confuse senders and recipients, they may also offend. Here, the audience and its level of e-mail sophistication must be considered. Depending on organizational culture, people higher on the corporate ladder or international recipients may expect to be addressed formally, as may customers or potential customers of the company. On the other hand, in some business environments, coworkers may expect to be addressed personally.

Signature presents another problem, depending on the organization's e-mail program. If the program provides a clear sender name in addition to a coded ID (such as XXXXX@ASUACAD in Fig. 3), an added signature is redundant [13]. Sherblom finds such redundancy to appear more frequently in upward communications and in some horizontal communications among managers. Fig. 4 is an interesting example of memo style with added signatures, effectively illustrating Sherblom's point by addressing faculty horizontally, as colleagues. However, as Fig. 3 showed, some organizational e-mail programs give only coded ID's and addresses. Such TO: and FROM: lines are confusing to most e-mail users.

Considering these factors, we recommend a modified memo format for most internal and external messages. This format would provide the TO: and FROM: lines commonly found in memos, unless the organization's e-mail package inserts full names rather than electronically coded ID's. Fig. 5 changes the message in Fig. 2 to show an example of this format, used when a program provides only indecipherable ID's and addresses. These are not definitive rules but suggestions to

```
>>>MAIL  90.01.00<<<  From: IDMDG at
ASUACAD
***Top of File***
Date:      Fri, 1 Apr 1994 17:03:32 MST
From:      "Lattie Coor, Milton Glick, Robert Barnhill"
           <IDMDG@ASUACAD>
Subject:   Kudos
To:        A S U   F a c u l t y
<AARBH@ASUVM.INRE.ASU.EDU>

As you are aware, every 5-8 years The Carnegie Foundation
for the Advancement of Teaching issues its Classification of
Institutes of Higher Education. We want you to be among
the first to know that the Carnegie Foundation will announce
that Arizona State University will now be classified as a
Research I University.

This represents an important milestone in ASU's evolution
as a major research university. This step recognizes the
quality and productivity of the ASU faculty, staff and
students. We congratulate and thank you and your
```

Fig. 4. Message addresses faculty as colleagues, combining memo style and signature block.

```
>>>MAIL  80.26<<<  From:
XXXXX at ASUACAD
***Top of File***
Date:      Mon, 7 Jun 94 09:52:32
MST
From:      XXXXX@ASUACAD
To:        ZZZZZ@ASUACAD
Subject:   Source of Smith Article

From:      Mary Doe
To:        Renee Horowitz


I hope your summer will be both
productive and restful (if those two can co-
exist). Could you tell me which issue of
```

Fig. 5. Message no longer requires a salutation or a closing.

provide a basis for developing e-mail styles. For example, some companies may want to modify these guidelines for international audiences and set policies to respond to the expectations of that audience.

Since e-mail programs automatically date messages, this information should not be repeated. As to the SUBJECT: or RE: line, many programs ask for this information during the setup stage. They also repeat the original subject designation in your reply, unless you choose to change it.

In addition to avoiding possible confusion or offense, another advantage to the style we recommend is its response to Sproull and Kiesler's finding that e-mail senders tend to use more words for the closing than for the salutation. They attribute this difference to social and psychological factors and hypothesize that "reminders of the presence of other people are relatively weak" in e-mail communication and so people "focus relatively strongly on themselves and on what they want to say and less strongly on their audience" [11].

A bit of cautionary advice is essential here: most e-mail programs allow users to identify their most frequent addressees by nicknames to expedite sending messages. Ordinarily, these nicknames do not appear on the outgoing message but are merely for the convenience of the sender. Stories abound (possibly apocryphal) of disastrous results because some users assign derogatory nicknames to their correspondents. One such incident describes a person "who had a private shorthand for each of the computer addresses of his production team members. One day, sending a routine memo to the group, he accidentally let the nicknames—of which the mildest were 'Turkey' and 'Fruitcake'—wander into the text" [14].

Positive and Negative Words

Nicknames are not the only words that express positive or negative feelings. As Fig. 1 has shown, the use of positive and negative words within the document is one of the few areas addressed by e-mail manuals at our university. The manuals caution users to be diplomatic, telling them that "criticism is always harsher when written, and electronic messages are easily forwarded." Here, too, the medium may cause unexpected problems. We interpret the last part of the statement as a somewhat cryptic reminder that the process of sending a letter or memo conventionally gives the writer more time to consider audience and purpose and thus change the wording or withdraw the communication before it goes out. With e-mail, however, transmission involves pressing one or two keys; many programs do not offer an "Are you sure?" option before the user irrevocably and instantaneously commits the message. Sproull and Kiesler hypothesized that uninhibited e-mail messages result from the same distancing between writer and audience to which they attributed the differences in length of salutation and closing.

CEO's of several major corporations have discovered the negative effects of uninhibited e-mail messages. John Akers, former head of IBM, complained about the quality of IBM products and employees in the form of meeting notes that were later forwarded by e-mail. The manager who transmitted the information ''apparently thought he was circulating the notes just to people in his area. But, through the magic of IBM's extensive electronic-mail network, the word quickly spread through the company" [15]. Akers followed his critical talk with an e-mail message of his own that did little to compensate for his original words.

IBM recently discovered another problem resulting from the instantaneous character of the medium. Their difficulty became public when they transmitted a follow-up message that asked e-mail users who erroneously received a proprietary message to destroy it. Here, the second e-mail communication compounded the negative result of the first one because recipients considered it ludicrous [16].

Microsoft's Bill Gates, on the other hand, found his memo concerning fears for the future of the company and containing negative views of his competitors to be even more costly:

> Bill Gates may wind up in the Guinness Book of Records as the author of the world's most expensive memo. A secret memo to top staff at Microsoft Corp. was leaked to the press—and that has cost him \$315 million [17].

Gates' memo, which appears to have been distributed by e-mail, caused an 8-1/8 point drop in Microsoft stock on the day the memo became news.

In a more recent instance of an e-mail message that resulted in negative publicity for a major corporation, a Kmart senior vice-president urged high-level executives to quit if they are not ready to make the changes he wants. The message tone was harsh and emotional, including this threat: "If I trace any negativism to any of you I will personally write up and conduct a constructive-action interview and put you on probation" [18].

These are not isolated examples of problems caused by failure to weigh positive versus negative words. Many of these problems arise because people may use company e-mail for personal messages. One computer columnist emphasizes the differing views of management and employees on this subject [19]. Several years ago, Jim Seymour used the advantages of e-mail as a selling point to justify a local area network for one company. When he returned to the firm recently, employees were enthusiastic about e-mail; they used it "to set up lunch appointments, and one guy even posted a message for everyone, trying to sell his Chevy Suburban!" [19]. The same day, Seymour spoke to the company's Vice-President for Management Information Services about e-mail. This executive said, "We're going to have to put some controls on this thing." People use it to make lunch dates "and one clown actually tried to sell a used car on the network" [19].

Seymour contends that sending such e-mail notes within a company is no different than posting messages in the company cafeteria and that only Theory X authoritarian managers object to these employee morale builders. Others feel that such personal messages waste company resources [20] or happen because e-mail diminishes the conventional "boundary between work and play" [11]. These differing opinions underline the fact that many companies do not have a policy relating to personal e-mail communications. In any case, users must remember their messages may be read by persons other than the intended audience and that they have no privacy protection at all [21]. With the possibility of an unexpected audience to compound positive or negative word choices in e-mail, writers must not allow the ease of transmission to erase social conventions.

Subject Headings

Although Sproull and Kiesler's list of e-mail attributes includes "topic," they use this term solely to differentiate between work- and nonwork-related messages. Another aspect of topic, however, is the subject line of the message.

Business and technical communicators understand that the subject line of a memo should describe its content clearly enough for the audience to know immediately what the memo is about. Many memo writers, however, dash off messages with brief, general subject headings. This practice may force the receiver to skim the memo, looking for clues as to its importance.

The same considerations apply even more strongly to e-mail, for the volume of electronic messages received by both managers and employees makes it imperative that subject headings clearly indicate the content of the message. Otherwise, the message may be electronically zapped without the cursory glance most recipients give an unwanted paper memo before they throw it away. When an engineer at one major company returned from vacation, for example, he found over 1,000 e-mail messages waiting for him [22]. Although this individual established a program that set his priorities according to the job title of the sender, it also looked at message subjects. At some companies, employees are so overloaded with the e-mail equivalent of chain letters and junk mail that they have developed programs to recognize such messages and delete them [23]. Programs designed to filter e-mail are now available from major software companies [9]. Such programs may be searching for certain key words on the subject line. If the subject heading does not clearly indicate its importance to the recipient, the message will go unread. Table I lists vague subject headings and shows how they can be improved.

TABLE I
Vague Subject Headings Should be Improved

VAGUE SUBJECTS	IMPROVED SUBJECTS
Staff Meeting	Change in Staff Meeting Schedule
XX Forms	Final Test Stages for XX Forms
Travel Request	Travel Request Pilot Program
Bulletin Board	Bulletin Board Pilot Program - For Evaluation
XXX Status Report	XXX Status Report, Week Ending Jan. 21, 1994
Research	Research on E-mail Styles
Strategic Planning Retreat	Cancellation of Strategic Planning Retreat
Smith Article	Source of Smith Article Needed
Brown Bag Series	Woman-to-Woman Brown Bag Series

Conclusion

As professional communicators, we must address all of the above issues and set stylistic standards for e-mail. Computer scientists, telecommunications experts, and management-information specialists have concentrated on connectivity and other technical standards; these are certainly essential concerns. However, as shown above, stylistic issues also are important because they affect resources and productivity.

Stylistic conventions will not be easy to establish [24]. Despite government interest in and concern with the information highway, it is unlikely that we will see, or want to see, the equivalent of the 1912 President's Commission on Economy and Efficiency that attempted to codify memo format [10]. Further, through trial and error, many e-mail users have developed styles with which they are comfortable and may resist the idea of standardized formats. On the other hand, companies frequently do update the look of their correspondence, reports, and other written documents.

Today, when the concept of quality improvement no longer refers exclusively to manufactured products but includes every aspect of a company's business, firms also must establish stylistic standards for e-mail correspondence. Technical writers, who often are the catalysts for format changes to make company publications more effective, must lead the way in formulating e-mail styles. In this way, they will help industry conserve company resources and improve productivity.

REFERENCES

[1] C. R. Boiarsky, *Technical Writing: Contexts, Audiences, and Communities*. Boston: Allyn and Bacon, 1993, p. 419.

[2] F. Safayeni *et al.*, "Assessing the potential of e-mail for engineers: case study,"*J. Management Eng.*, vol. 8, no. 4, pp. 346–361, Oct. 1992.

[3] R. B. Horowitz, "Improving managerial-employee communication: A case study," in *Proc. 41st Annual Society for Technical Communication Conf.*, Minneapolis, May 15–18, 1994, pp. 409–411.

[4] L. Sussman, P. Golden, and B. Beauclair, "Training for e-mail,"*Training & Development J.*, vol. 45, no. 3, pp. 70–73, Mar. 1991.

[5] B. Redford, "Beyond talking on paper,"*Univ. Chicago Mag.*, vol. 85, no. 6, pp. 27–31, Aug. 1993.

[6] J. J. Cappel, "Closing the e-mail privacy gap,"*J. Syst. Management*, vol. 44, no. 12, pp. 6–11, Dec. 1993.

[7] J. Goode and M. Johnson, "Putting out the flames: The etiquette and law of e- mail,"*Online*, vol. 15, no. 6, pp. 61–65, Nov. 1991.

[8] G. Kawasaki, "E-mail etiquette,"*MacUser*, vol. 7, no. 11, pp. 29–30, Nov. 1991.

[9] A. Amirrezvani, Ed., "Tips for taming e-mail,"*PC World*, vol. 11, no. 11, pp. 285–295, Nov. 1993.

[10] J. Yates, "The emergence of the memo as a managerial genre,"*Management Commun. Quarterly*, vol. 2, no. 4, pp. 485-510, May 1989.

[11] L. Sproull and S. Kiesler, "Reducing social context cues: Electronic mail in organizational communication," *Management Sci.*, vol. 32, no. 11, pp. 1492–1512, Nov. 1986.

[12] M. A. Dyrud, "The role of e-mail in the organizational crisis: A case study," in *Proc. 55th Annual Convention of the Association for Business Communication*, pp. 79–92, 1990.

[13] J. Sherblom, "Direction, function, and signature in electronic mail,"*J. Business Commun.*, vol. 25, no. 4, pp. 39–54, Fall 1988.

[14] J. Solomon, "As electronic mail loosens inhibitions, impetuous senders feel anything goes,"*Wall Street J.*, pp. B1, B8, Oct. 12, 1990.

[15] P. B. Carroll, "Akers to IBM employees: Wake up!," *Wall Street J.*, pp. B1, B4, May 29, 1991.

[16] J. Austen, *Risks Dig. (Comp. Risks)*, vol. 16, no. 17, June 17, 1994.

[17] D. Kalette, "Memo costs Microsoft chief $315M," *USA Today*, p. B1, June 20, 1991.

[18] J. Muller, "If you can't stand the heat, get out of Kmart, exec tells aides,"*The Arizona Republic*, p. H2, Aug. 7, 1994.

[19] J. Dvorak and J. Seymour, "On the 10th anniversary of the PC, how much has changed?,"*PC Computing*, vol. 4, no. 8, pp. 82–83, Aug. 1991.

[20] E. Booker, "Who pays the price of chitchat?,"*Computerworld*, vol. 23, pp. 55–59, Oct. 23, 1989.

[21] J. Shieh and R. A-L. Ballard, "E-mail privacy,"*Educom Rev.*, pp. 59–61, Mar./Apr. 1994.

[22] J. S. Hirsch, "Flood of information swamps managers, but some are finding ways to bail out,"*Wall Street J.*, pp. B1–B2, Aug. 12, 1991.

[23] I. R. Valentine, "International electronic-mail services: Ready for take-off?,"*Data Commun.*, vol. 18, no. 16, pp. 145–149, Dec. 1989.

[24] J. E. Porter, "E-mail and variables of rhetorical form," *The Bulletin*, vol. 56, no. 2, pp. 40–42, Jun. 1993.

Renee B. Horowitz is a Professor in the Department of Manufacturing and Industrial Technology, College of Engineering and Applied Sciences, Arizona State University. She teaches courses in engineering communication, technical communication, and industrial management. Previously, she specialized in proposal writing at an aerospace company. She has published articles and presented papers on techniques for quality improvement in technical reports and presentations, visionary leadership, and ethical issues in the technical communications classroom. She is also the author of ''Designing Noise Audits to Improve Managerial-Employee Communication,'' a chapter in *Publications Management: Essays for Professional Communicators*, Baywood Press, 1994.

Marian G. Barchilon is an Assistant Professor in the Department of Manufacturing and Industrial Technology, College of Engineering and Applied Sciences, Arizona State University (ASU), where she teaches engineering and technical communication courses. She has published about technical communication's changing role in business and industry and is the author of ''Technical Communication Models that Ensure Productive Meetings,'' a chapter in Baywood's 1994 text *Publications Management: Essays for Professional Communicators*. She is also the Director of ASU's NSF-funded Sun Devil Bridge Program, which is designed to help underrepresented minorities achieve academic success in engineering and technology.

"Who's Reading My E-Mail?": A Study of Professionals' E-Mail Usage and Privacy Perceptions in the Workplace

Patricia A. Chociey

Abstract— **E-mail privacy in the workplace has emerged as one of the most complex ethical and legal issues confronting corporate communication in the electronic age. This paper discusses the array of legal and ethical concerns of e-mail privacy in the workplace. Building on the existing body of knowledge on the topic, the results of a research study are presented which explore the similarities and differences in e-mail usage and privacy perceptions among management level and administrative level employees. The survey, which polled 337 working professionals, confirmed the popular belief that companies are not effectively communicating their e-mail monitoring policies to their employees. Finally, recommendations are made to corporate communicators on how best to forge an e-mail communications policy that can reduce the risk of disputes, incidents, and lawsuits regarding e-mail privacy issues.**

***Index Terms*—Electronic mail, ethical issues, legal issues, usage survey.**

THERE was a time in corporate America when coworkers congregated at water coolers or exchanged voice mail messages to listen to office gossip or to share inside jokes. Today, corporate e-mail systems are revolutionizing business communication by supplanting less efficient forms of communication in the workplace. The use of electronic mail in the workplace has increased significantly in recent years. In 1995, an estimated 35 million people used e-mail—either via their company's computers or on paid networks [1]. The contentious issue of corporate e-mail privacy, the down side to e-mail's success in corporate America, beckons the attention of researchers, business leaders, and legal experts alike. Past issues of IEEE TRANSACTIONS ON PROFESSIONAL COMMUNICATION feature treatments of the complexity of issues related to electronic communication. For example, see Joe Chew's "Introduction to the Special Issue on Electronic Communication and Interaction" [2] and Susan Mallon Ross's "Electronic Mail: Legal and Ethical Concerns in United States and Canada [3]." Adding to this existing body of knowledge, this study examines the social, ethical, and legal concerns of e-mail privacy from a research perspective.

CORPORATE BIG BROTHER IS WATCHING

The dramatic increase of e-mail usage in the workplace is commensurate with the rising number of workplace cases, incidents, and disputes pointing to the ethical and legal problem of privacy for users of corporate e-mail systems. Instead of talking about personal or business-related matters over the phone or ducking into a vacant office for a word in private, employees communicate with their co-workers by sending e-mail messages to be retrieved and read by only the participants involved. The assumption is that anything sent by corporate e-mail is as private as a phone conversation or a personal meeting, and will not be read or monitored by a third party. However, some employees are learning that this assumption is wrong, and, in fact, their employers are reading and monitoring their e-mail correspondence.

Manuscript received November 1997.

The author may be reached through the Program in Corporate and Organizational Communication, Fairleigh Dickinson University, Madison, NJ 07940 USA.

Publisher Item Identifier S 0361-1434(97)02027-4.

THE LEGAL AND ETHICAL DIMENSIONS OF E-MAIL PRIVACY

The question of how private company e-mail networks should be has emerged as one of the most complex ethical and legal issues confronting corporate communication in the electronic age. The array of legal, ethical, and economic concerns that impact upon the issue has resulted in a rather unsettled landscape. Although it is illegal in some states for an employer to eavesdrop on private conversations or telephone calls, even if such exchanges take place on company owned phones, there are no clear rules governing electronic mail [4]. Presently, the Electronic Communications Privacy Act (ECPA) of 1986 is the only U.S. federal statute that addresses the issue of e-mail privacy. This law prohibits the interception of e-mail messages by parties outside of a company except where there exists proper legal authority (such as in the case of a search warrant obtained by law enforcement officials) [5, p. 819]. However, the ECPA does not address the interception of messages by parties within a company [5]. Thus the law is ambiguous about whether employers are permitted to monitor and read their employees' e-mail communications [5]. In most states, the courts do uphold the employers' right to read and monitor employees' corporate e-mail messages.

CORPORATE E-MAIL NETWORKS ARE LEGAL MINEFIELDS IN CYBERSPACE

Most employees underestimate their employers' legal right to monitor e-mail activities. In addition, employees tend to believe that their employers have no right to read their e-mail correspondences, discover abuses, and take legal action. Contrary to this opinion, employers and network administrators

Reprinted from *IEEE Trans. Prof. Comm.*, vol. PC-40, no. 1, pp. 34–40, March 1997.

argue that monitoring is justifiable, since the company owns the electronic mail system and the data it contains. They also contend that when excessive amounts of personal messages obstruct traffic on the networks, monitoring is necessary to maintain the systems.

The problem is exacerbated further when employers fail to provide employees with a written policy clearly communicating the company's expectations of corporate e-mail usage. The lack of a written policy means that neither the employers or the employees know where the company stands on privacy issues. This is dangerous for both employers and employees. Not having a written e-mail privacy policy forces employees to assume that ethical considerations will keep employers form reading their e-mail—which is not always true. It also makes employers vulnerable to lawsuits, and they also confront the possibility that employees will misuse the systems.

And employees do. Employees use their corporate e-mail network to perpetrate any number of offenses, ranging from harmless gossip to sexual harassment and theft of trade secrets. Also, abusive language containing derogatory and offensive comments are prevalent in emotional responses to business memos sent as e-mail messages.

Moreover, corporate e-mail networks are smoking guns for disgruntled employees, and they provide the most incriminating admissible court evidence used against employers and coworkers [6]. This is in part due to the fact that, unlike paper which can be systematically filed or shredded, electronic information is organized according to each user's personal system and deleted only when that individual chooses to do so [6].

Also, it is impossible to remove e-mail files completely without taking extraordinary measures because the information still exists even after a file is deleted and its name is removed from the computer's directory [7, p. 82]. Over time, new data overwrites the old, but the process is seldom absolute. Even programs designed to expunge data from hard disks are not totally effective. Network administrators and unwanted third parties can access a computer's backup system and find any file [1]. Thus as one corporate attorney commented, "E-mail is like having a video camera running all the time" [1].

Consequently, since e-mail and other on-line technology are new, corporate America and the judiciary are just beginning to contend with the legal issues associated with e-mail use in the workplace. In doing so, they decide how basic legal principles such as privacy, free speech, defamation, and libel apply to corporate e-mail privacy. To date, lawmakers and business leaders have failed to formulate an effective response to this challenge that balances the rights of employers and employees. Moreover, the number of cases involving such matters are increasing dramatically, which suggests there is a growing need for definitive legislation regarding this issue.

Study of Professionals' E-Mail Usage and Privacy Perceptions in the Workplace

Little prior research has been conducted to uncover individuals' beliefs and perceptions about electronic mail privacy in the workplace. The present study was designed to add to the body of knowledge regarding e-mail privacy issues and builds on the research study conducted by James J. Cappel, "A Study of Individuals' Ethical Beliefs and Perceptions of Electronic Mail Privacy," which explored the electronic mail privacy perceptions of students who possessed experience using e-mail in a work setting [5, p. 819].

Expanding on Cappel's research, this study is the first to explore the e-mail use of professionals in the workplace testing the interrelationships that exist among the variables of job position and monitoring policies. It primarily examines the differences in e-mail privacy perceptions and e-mail usage behaviors between two categories of personnel: managerial level employees and administrative level employees. The study addresses several questions: Are companies clearly communicating their e-mail monitoring policies and are employees aware of their companies' legal right to monitor their e-mail messages? Are there any differences in managers' and administrative employees' ethical perceptions of corporate e-mail monitoring? Are managers or administrative employees more likely to be deterred by the existence of monitoring policies from sending controversial messages? Is the age of employees a factor that affects their likeliness to send controversial e-mail communications?

The present study tests several hypotheses. The first hypothesis is that regardless of job position, employees are unaware that their employers have the legal right to monitor their e-mail correspondence. The second hypothesis is that since managers tend to be closer to an organization's decision-making process, managers, more so than administrative employees, are likely to believe that corporate e-mail monitoring is ethical. The third hypothesis is that administrative employees are less likely to be deterred from sending controversial messages than managerial level employees. Since administrative employees such as receptionists, secretaries, and other support staffers are notorious for being a part of a company's grapevine—the unofficial source for communicating information in the form of office gossip—it is expected that this traditional role will extend to their use of e-mail. Also from the standpoint of managerial level employees, managers tend to be more inhibited about stirring up controversy in the workplace because they usually have a greater stake in the company and in their job positions than do administrative employees.

Moreover, the final hypothesis predicts that age is a factor in determining the likelihood of an e-mail user's predilection for sending controversial messages: it is suspected that younger employees (under 35 years of age) will be more likely to send controversial messages than older employees (36 years of age and older). This hypothesis is based on the theory that some older employees may be less trusting of new technology and more technophobic than younger employees who grew up using PCs during the dawn of the computer age.

Procedure

A confidential, anonymous survey was administered by mail and in person in a distribution to 1000 working professionals. The survey yielded 337 usable responses, with a response rate of 33.7%, from working professionals representing both managerial level and administrative level positions from a variety of industries that currently use e-mail in their workplaces. Several telephone interviews were also conducted. The interviews were conducted over a five month period.

The first third of the survey questions asked the subjects demographic questions such as gender, age, job position, and company size using the number of employees as a measurement. The subjects were asked to identify their sex and their age. The survey also asked subjects their occupation titles and to define their job positions as either managerial or administrative.

The second third of the questions probed respondents on corporate e-mail monitoring issues. Professionals were asked whether or not their company has e-mail monitoring policies, and if they were aware of their company's legal right to monitor their e-mail correspondence. Respondents were questioned about their opinions regarding the ethics of corporate e-mail monitoring: the survey asked them if they believe corporate mail monitoring is ethical when the company has e-mail monitoring policies and if they believe corporate e-mail monitoring is ethical when the company does not have monitoring policies.

The last third of the survey relates to the respondents' e-mail usage. Subjects were asked to indicate how comfortable they felt about sending a mixture of noncontroversial and controversial messages. These items are similar to the items that Cappel used in his research [5]. For the purpose of this study, "controversial" messages are defined as follows:

1) A complaint about the employee's boss.
2) A criticism about a decision made by the company's top management.
3) An offensive joke.
4) An idea or suggestion that the employee thinks is valid but the boss thinks is stupid.
5) A complaint about a customer.
6) Gossip about coworkers or management.
7) Non-work-related messages with friends and family outside of the company.

and "Noncontroversial" messages are defined as:

1) A news report affecting the company.
2) Information about a business meeting.
3) Information about a company party.
4) A joke that is funny and not offensive.
5) Information discovered about a company benefit plan.

For the purposes of the present study, respondents were asked to assign a numeric value to their comfort level according to this scale: 1 = very comfortable; 2 = somewhat comfortable; 3 = neutral; 4 = not very comfortable; 5 = not comfortable at all. The items appeared on the survey in this format:

Various messages:	**Comfort level:**
1. A news report that will affect your company	1 2 3 4 5
2. A criticism about a decision made by the company's top management	1 2 3 4 5
3. An offensive joke	1 2 3 4 5
4. Information about a business meeting	1 2 3 4 5
5. An idea or suggestion that you think is valid but your boss thinks is stupid	1 2 3 4 5
6. Information about a company party	1 2 3 4 5
7. Gossip about co-workers or management	1 2 3 4 5
8. A joke that is funny and not offensive	1 2 3 4 5
9. A complaint about a customer	1 2 3 4 5
10. A complaint about your boss	1 2 3 4 5
11. Information you discovered about a company benefit plan	1 2 3 4 5
12. A personal message to a friend or family member outside your company	1 2 3 4 5

Results

The sample of surveys was collected from individuals who belong to organizations of various sizes, from small, local companies with as few as three employees to global corporations with employees in the thousands. Individuals from a total of 13 companies participated in the study. The respondents in the study represent a variety of industries and professional backgrounds including law, sales and marketing, research science, computer science, accounting, finance, compliance, journalism, advertising and public relations, insurance, and human resources.

The subjects in the study that fell under the "management" category range from top level management, that is, jobs with titles such as CEO, president, vice president, and director, to middle level managers. Subjects placed in the administrative category include individuals whose positions are characteristically administrative, including job titles such as receptionists, secretaries, assistants, and coordinators. Of note, these delineations were supported by the subjects' own responses to the question requesting them to identify their positions as either managerial or administrative in nature. Examples of actual job titles gathered by the study include product manager, chemical engineer, sales representatives, attorney, human resource manager, secretary, data quality analyst, and receptionist, among others.

The study's ratio of managerial respondents to administrative respondents was relatively even, with 56% of the subjects being managers and 44% of the subjects working in administrative capacities. Overall, subjects ranged in age from 23 years old to over 65 years of age with the average age range being 25 to 35 years old (see Fig. 1). A breakdown of the age range of subjects by managerial and administrative categories indicates that of the managers in the study, 34% were younger (less than 35 years of age) while 66% were older (36 years of age or more). In the study, the age of the administrative

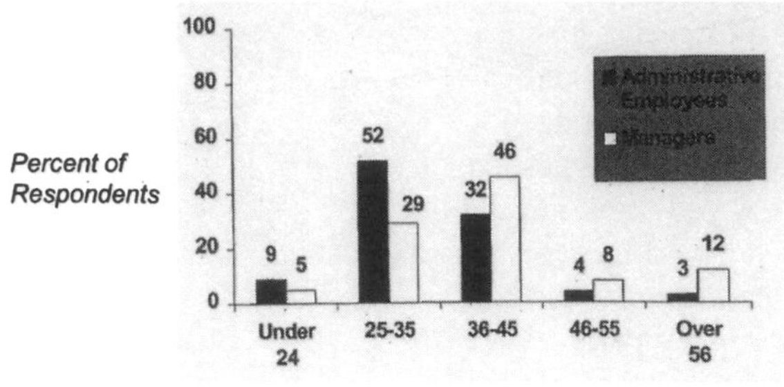

Fig. 1. Age of respondents.

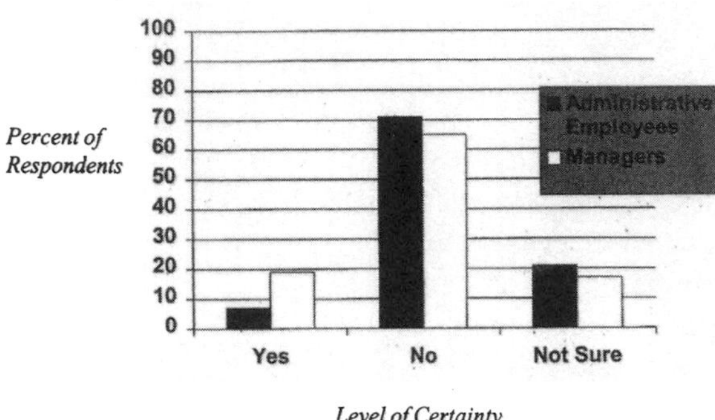

Fig. 2. Knowledge of monitoring policy.

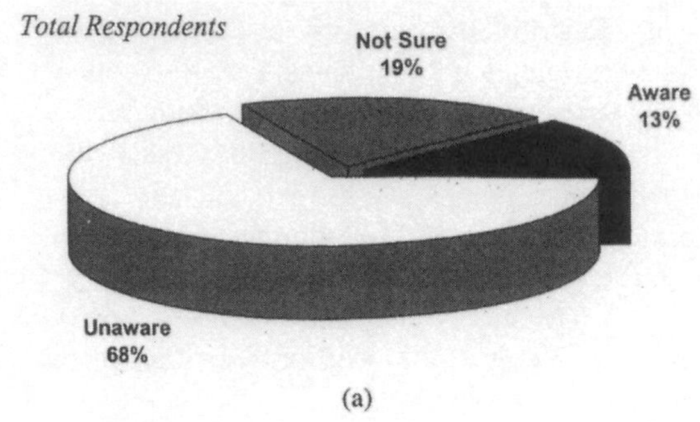

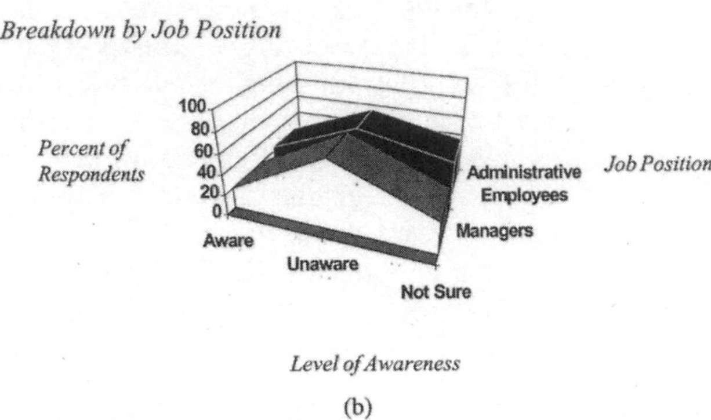

Fig. 3. (a) Awareness of employer's legal right to monitor e-mail. (b) Awareness of employer's legal right to monitor e-mail.

level employees was skewed in the opposite direction, 61% of administrative level individuals being under 35 years old and 39% being older than 36 years of age.

The results of the data, as shown in Fig. 2, confirm the first hypothesis: most employees, regardless of job position, are unaware that their companies have e-mail monitoring policies. Of the data that was collected from each of the 13 companies, the employees of only one organization responded uniformly with an answer to the question of whether or not the subjects' company has e-mail monitoring policies. This suggests that within this organization, the employer is clearly communicating the company's e-mail monitoring policies to its employees. As for the employees of the other 12 companies, there were conflicting answers to this question indicating a confusion among the employee population as to whether or not their company has monitoring policies. Overwhelmingly, this research finding supports the popular belief that companies are failing to clearly communicate their expectations of e-mail usage in the workplace to their employees.

The results in Fig. 3 demonstrate that the employees' confusion over the existence of a company monitoring policy directly correlates with employees' lack of knowledge of the fact that their employers have the legal right to monitor their e-mail correspondence. The data show that a majority (68%) of the employees polled were not aware of this fact. As an aside, the respondents should not feel poorly about their lack of knowledge concerning the legal dimension of e-mail monitoring, considering that only three out of the 17 attorneys polled in the survey were cognizant of the fact.

The research contradicted the hypothesis that managers are more likely to believe that corporate e-mail monitoring is ethical than are administrative employees. In fact, the data show that the opposite is true. A resounding 76% of managers answered "no" to both questions asking if e-mail monitoring is ethical when a company does and when a company does not have monitoring policies. By comparison, the administrative respondents were split on this issue, with 51% of the subjects agreeing that so long as the company has monitoring policies, e-mail monitoring is ethical while 39% of administrative employees also agreed that it is still ethical for a company to monitor their employees' e-mail even if the company does not have monitoring policies [see Fig. 4 (a) and (b)].

The results of the study confirm the hypothesis that managerial employees are less likely to send controversial messages that administrative employees (see Fig. 5). However, the data show that, overall, neither group is very comfortable about sending controversial e-mail messages. An average score was determined for each controversial message item. An overall comfort ability rating was then derived by averaging the total of these average scores. The overall comfort ability rating for administrative employees was 3.5, indicating they are neutral toward sending controversial messages while the overall comfort level rating for managerial employees was 4.0, indicating they are not very comfortable sending controversial messages.

A comparison of telephone interviews with administrative staffers and managerial employees suggests that e-mail is indeed becoming a favorite, new communication method for the grapevine. And administrative employees are more likely to use e-mail for this purpose. The following quotes demonstrate this finding:

> *"It used to be that I would head down to the company kitchen for the latest office scoop. Nowadays, with e-mail I don't have to leave my desk . . . and let me tell you, rumors fly by e-mail."*
>
> —Secretary, female, age 41

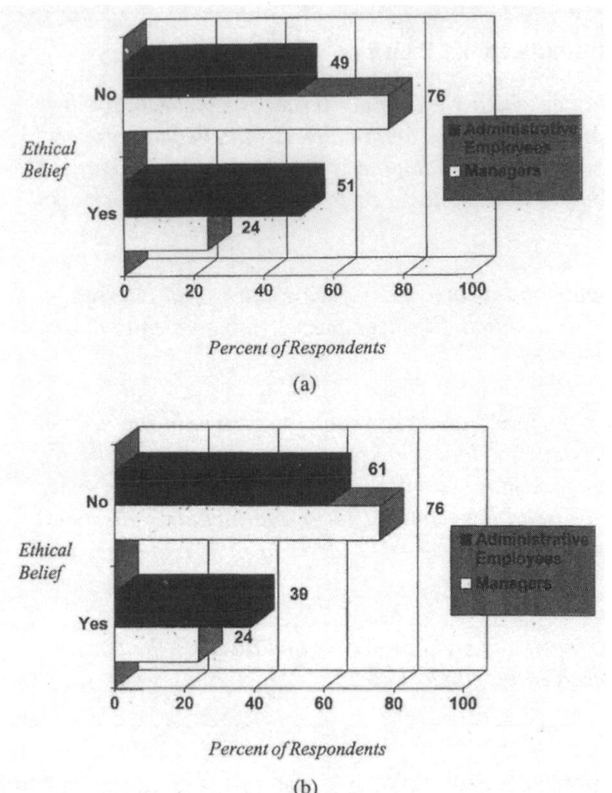

Fig. 4. (a) Is employer monitoring ethical with policy? (b) Is employer monitoring ethical without policy?

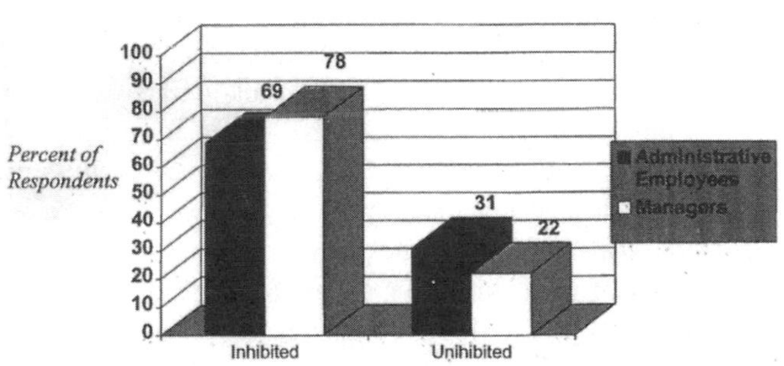

Fig. 5. Likeliness to send controversial messages.

"I know I probably shouldn't but I e-mail my friends dirty jokes at their work...the mail I get is sometimes pretty raunchy... it keeps my day moving."

—Data Entry Assistant, male age 25

"Sending anything but professional, business related communications via the company's e-mail is completely unprofessional and I wouldn't consider participating in such activity."

—Director of Corporate Communications, male age 49

"My husband once sent me a steamy note to my office e-mail and I wasn't thrilled about it. Who knows who could have read it... and... I also don't believe in making personal phone calls at the office; the same holds true for personal correspondence by office e-mail."

—Chemical Engineer, female, age 32

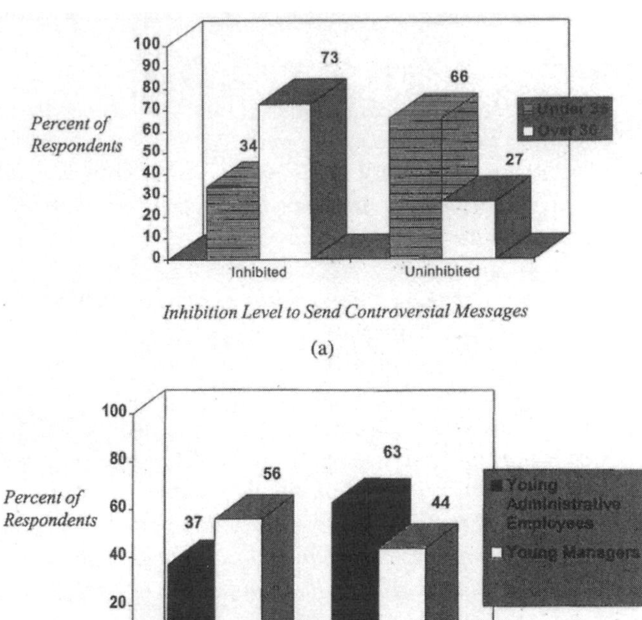

Fig. 6. (a) Likeliness to send controversial messages. (b) Comparison of young administrative employees' versus young managers' likeliness of sending controversial messages.

Surprisingly the results indicate that of those in both groups that are willing to send controversial messages, the existence of monitoring policies does not significantly inhibit these individuals from doing so. This is an interesting finding that contradicts common sense, which suggests that employees would elect to exercise caution in what they are communicating through e-mail if they know their companies are reading and monitoring their messages.

Finally, the hypothesis regarding age was confirmed. Younger employees under the age of 35 are more likely to send controversial messages than older employees over the age of 36 [see Fig. 6 (a)]. However, in comparing the e-mail usage behavior of younger administrative employees to younger managerial employees, as shown in Fig. 6 (b), the data suggests that younger administrative employees are more likely to send controversial messages than younger managerial employees.

Recommendations for Creating an Effective E-Mail Monitoring Policy

The survey emphasizes the fact that this issue remains very unsettled. Until definitive legislation is developed and public policy is formed, employers and employees must educate themselves on the issue and find ways to protect their interests. One way for employers to do this to create an effective, written e-mail monitoring policy which clearly sets standards and guidelines for e-mail usage of employees.

In the course of the research, e-mail monitoring policies from a number of organizations were obtained. Analyzing the policies, it is clear that companies are not communicating

The Company's Electronic Communications Policy

Electronic communication has become a routine part of the way in which we conduct business. Accordingly, it is important to note that, just as tangible property (e.g., equipment products, money) and intangible, intellectual property (e.g., ideas, copyrights, trade secrets) are part of the Company's assets, the Company's electronic communications are also part of the Company's assets. Protection of these assets against loss, theft, and misuse is of critical importance to us.

Electronic communication includes, but is not limited to, computer hardware and software, electronic messaging systems (E-mail), facsimiles, telecopiers, and copy machines. In addition, it encompasses communications and information transmitted by, received from, or stored in these systems.

Specifically, employees may only use passwords, access files, or retrieve stored communications within the normal parameters of their respective jobs. Employee may not use a password that makes information irretrievable by, or renders business equipment inoperable, to the Company, nor are they permitted to use the password of other employees. Employees who violate this policy will be subject to disciplinary action, up to and including dismissal from the company. This applies to all the Company's locations, operating businesses, departments, employees and outside parties that use this equipment.

While it is not our customary practice to do so, the Company reserves the right to access and disclose the contents of all electronic files, including E-mail Messages created or received by employees.

effectively their standards for employees' usage in their policy statements. In fact, the policies actually state very little about employers' expectation in this regard. The following is a model monitoring policy that is very similar to monitoring policies that were obtained from companies through this research. While the policy does state the company reserves the right to read and monitor employees' e-mail, it does not communicate any expectations on how employees are to use the system. Moreover, the policy does not specifically state that employees are prohibited from using e-mail for personal use, nor does it suggest proper conduct in terms of refraining from abusive language as well as addressing e-mail sexual harassment issues (see the top of this page).

Obviously, a policy similar to this one falls short of effectively communicating the employers' expectations of employee e-mail usage, which, at best, could breed conflict in the workplace between employees and management, and, at worst, could lead to unnecessary legal challenges by disgruntled workers.

What is the best way for companies and their corporate communicators to develop a sound e-mail monitoring policy? In developing an effective monitoring policy, corporate communicators must consider a number of policy issues. An effective policy balances the rights of the company and its systems administrators and the users' rights of employees. From an employer's perspective, there is a tradeoff between a user's right to absolute privacy and the need of systems administrators to gather sufficient information to diagnose systems problems.

There is a distinction between administrator's need to gather information on the e-mail system to diagnose problems and other perhaps dubious motives for investigating e-mail correspondence [8, p. 196]. The policy should also clearly state that the company reserves the right to monitor employees' electronic communication and also that it grants this authority to the company's systems administrators. The policy should likewise specify to what degree system administrators can examine user file to diagnose problems or for other purposes, and what rights are granted to the users [7]. Another suggestion is to include a statement concerning the system administrators' obligation to maintain the privacy of information viewed under these circumstances [7].

The policy should also incorporate a statement addressing the users' rights and responsibilities regarding the use of e-mail. In *Implementing Internet Security*, Cooper suggests the following list of topics to cover in this area of policy:

- What guidelines a company has regarding resource consumption (whether users are restricted, and if so, what the restrictions are).
- What might constitute abuse in terms of system performance.
- Whether users are permitted to share accounts or let others use their accounts.
- How "secret" users should keep their passwords.
- Statement describing how often users should change their passwords and any password restrictions or requirements.
- Whether the company provides backups or expects the users to create their own.
- Statement forbidding the duplication of copyrighted or licensed software.
- Statement on Electronic Mail Privacy (Electronic Communications Privacy Act).
- Statement on the company's policy regarding controversial mail, or postings to mailing lists or discussion groups (obscenity, harassment).
- Policy on electronic communications: mail forging [8, p. 288].

It is also recommended that these issues should be communicated in a written policy. Finally, who should be involved in creating the policy is an important consideration. Logically, the company should include personnel with technical knowledge of e-mail and computer systems, as well as management who possess the authority to implement the policy, once it is created. It may also be to the employer's advantage to include the employees in the process; employees' acceptance of such a policy may increase if they are involved its development.

Criteria for Evaluating Effectiveness of A Company's Monitoring Policy

One tool for testing the effectiveness of a company's monitoring policy is the criteria published by the Electronic Mail Association. They suggest five criteria for evaluating any policy:

- Does the policy comply with law and with duties to third parties?
- Does the policy unnecessarily compromise the interest of the employees, the employer, or third parties?
- Is the policy workable as a private matter and likely to be enforced?
- Does the policy deal appropriately with all different forms of communications and record keeping with the office?
- Has the policy been announced in advance and been agreed to by all concerned? [7]

By following these simple guidelines, companies can overcome the possibility of misunderstandings regarding e-mail monitoring and employees' use of corporate e-mail systems.

Concluding Remarks

While the debate continues, corporate communication is going to play a central and strategic role with organizations that are confronted by e-mail privacy issues. This study of professionals' ethical beliefs and perceptions of electronic mail privacy confirms the consensus that most employees are not aware that their employers can legally monitor their e-mail correspondence, and there is an increasing frequency of occasions when employees do use their corporate e-mail systems for private use. From the users' standpoint, recommendations can also be made for interpersonal communication via e-mail in the workplace. E-mail correspondence in the workplace should adhere to the same standards of professional etiquette as other forms of inter- and intra-office communication. E-mail users in the workplace should avoid using abusive language and sending messages that can be construed as harassment and slander. By abiding by these simple recommendations, employers and employees reduce the risk of disputes, incidents, and possibly lawsuits regarding e-mail privacy issues.

References

[1] M. Peyser and S. Rhodes, "When e-mail becomes oops mail," *Newsweek*, p. 82, Oct. 16, 1995.

[2] J. Chew, "Introduction to the special issue on electronic communication and interaction," *IEEE Trans. Prof. Commun.*, vol. 37 p. 193, Dec. 1994.

[3] S. M. Ross, "Electronic mail: Legal and ethical concerns in the United States and Canada," *IEEE Trans. Prof. Commun.*, vol. 37, pp. 218–225, Dec. 1994.

[4] P. Elmer-Dewitt, "Who's reading your screen?" *TIME*, p. 46, Jan. 18, 1993.

[5] J. Cappel, "Study of individuals' ethical beleifs and perceptions on electronic mail privacy," *J. Bus. Ethics*, vol. 14, 1995.

[6] L. Himelstein, "The snitch in the system," *Bus. Week*, Apr. 17, 1995.

[7] J. Cooper, *Implementing Internet Security.* Indianapolis, IN: New Riders Publishing, 1995.

Patricia A. Chociey is a professional marketing writer whose research interests include the legal and ethical issues related to electronic communication. She holds a Master of Arts degree in corporate and organizational communication from Fairleigh Dickinson University, Madison, NJ, and earned a Bachelor of Arts degree in Communication and Political Science from Boston College, Chestnut Hill, MA.

Customer partnering: Data gathering for complex on-line documentation

Abstract—*Technical communicators today must document complex applications used in complex environments. Information about users and use models is important under these conditions, especially if documentation will be presented on-line. Customer partnering, a method of information gathering that supplements surveys, contextual inquiries, usability testing, and interviews, provides one way of involving the users of complex applications in the design of information delivery systems. We used this method to help a client gather important information about user and use models and design a new information library for complex server computer systems.*

—JOANN T. HACKOS,
MOLLY HAMMAR,
AND ARTHUR ELSER, *Member, IEEE*

Index Terms—*Audience analysis, contextual inquiry, customers, participating design, usability testing.*

Manuscript received December 1996; revised January 1997.
The authors are with Comtech Services, Inc., Denver, CO 80215 USA.
IEEE PII: S 0361-1434(97)04356-7.

As technical communicators face the challenge of organizing information from different products and departments and for different audiences into integrated on-line information sources, they must perform rigorous audience and task analyses. These analyses should tell communicators how much and what kinds of information their audiences need, as well as what media to use to deliver that information. In developing on-line documentation, we have found that traditional needs analysis methods do not give us enough detailed information about the users of the products to design documentation that adequately meets their needs.

Several well-established techniques, including contextual inquiry, focus groups, and usability testing, provide valuable guidance about the information that documentation audiences need. Contextual inquiry, which involves observing customers using products in their work environments, shows technical communicators how products and documentation are used in the workplace [1]. In using contextual inquiry techniques, Holtzblatt and Beyer found a relationship between software developers and users similar to that between masters and apprentices. The software developers learned how the users did their work in ways that helped them develop software packages that better fit the workplace rather than having users fit the work into the software model [2].

Focus groups perform a similar function, but they take users out of the workplace and into a discussion of their needs with their peers. Focus groups provide insight into users' attitudes and opinions about products but do not tell communicators how the participants actually use products or documentation at work [3]. Usability testing, which allows researchers to watch participants using products, does not normally allow for long-term contact and interaction about the customers' needs.

Reprinted from *IEEE Trans. Prof. Comm.*, vol. PC-40, no. 2, pp. 102–110, June 1997.

Software development groups have also been aware of the need to involve customers in specifying requirements for system design. Customers do not want the application to dictate the way they must work any more than developers want customers to dictate how they must work. A successful requirements process helps customers and developers become partners to create "renovation and ownership" for new or revised products [4]. Successful software development managers no longer try to decide if customers should participate in the development process, but, rather, how they should participate.

Using information gathered from facilitated teams, support lines, surveys, interviews, users groups, contextual, inquiry, usability tests, and focus groups, among others, development teams have found success in using combinations of several methods [5]. Even combinations of these methods, however, sometimes fail to provide enough in-depth information to plan complex documentation sets because user input is essentially a snapshot in time. We felt we needed sustained input from users who had time to contemplate the issues in their workplace and discuss them with colleagues, so as to provide more reasoned and informed answers. In one complex information design project, we used contextual inquiry, focus groups, and usability testing to assess users' information needs. All of these techniques provided valuable direction about the kinds of product support users needed; however, we found that none of them provided us with sufficient information to design an on-line documentation library that met users' needs. To supplement these needs analysis techniques, we developed customer partnering for information products.

What Is Customer Partnering?

Customer partnering is a technique used to design information products by creating a long-term relationship between representative customers and information developers. Through a series of guided interactions, customers and developers investigate how current information products are used. They use this knowledge to specify the design of improved and new information products. Like other forms of participative design, customer partnering uses aspects of contextual inquiry and focus groups, but it provides much more detail about how the company can meet customers' needs, and it involves the customer much more deeply in the design process. Note that participative design techniques similar to customer partnering have been used in software development but rarely in the design of information products.

How We Came To Design Customer Partnering

Comtech, an information design and human performance consulting company, had been working over several years with a division of Compaq Computer Corporation that manufactures network servers. We had evaluated the effectiveness of user and service documentation and conducted usability tests on a new CD-ROM product for delivering user documentation. The first stages of the ongoing study took us to Compaq's customer sites to observe installation, customizing, troubleshooting, and repair activities. During the site visits, we observed users at work and discussed with them how they used the documentation. During visits devoted principally to installation, we observed how the documentation was used. While we learned about and reported on a rich set of details about customers use patterns, questions remained about the best course to take in redesigning the documentation and delivering it through electronic media.

We designed customer partnering to learn what Compaq's customers thought about and how they used the documentation, and to help Compaq redesign the documentation library to meet its customers' needs.

The Client's Problem Compaq decided to redesign its documentation as a result of our findings in previous large-scale field studies. During our user and task analysis for these studies, we learned that Compaq lacked insight into how its customers worked and used information. Part of the problem was the lack of direct involvement in needs analysis by the technical communicators. They needed to hear for themselves what customers' problems were, and they needed to develop answers to questions about specific design details, particularly about the best mix of paper and on-line documentation.

We had tested the usability of Compaq's documentation and had spent considerable time with its customers. We discovered that customers believed that Compaq was not paying sufficient attention to their information needs. Our analyses clearly indicated the need to redesign the documentation library but did not suggest how to satisfy all the user groups' support needs. Our analyses also indicated a need for increased user involvement in the redesign process.

Our Approach to the Problem In deciding how to design a user study that could help our client answer detailed design questions about the documentation library, we considered traditional focus groups or contextual inquiries. We felt, however, that neither of these techniques would provide the rich array of information needed. Contextual inquiry provides good information about how a customer uses a product in a particular setting, but it does not allow customers to help develop ideas and provide more thoughtful and focused feedback. Because contextual inquiry is also limited by the amount of time we can spend with a busy client, we often are unable to see the entire spectrum of behaviors users exhibit with information products.

The focus group, on the other hand, often does not allow time to concentrate on design details because participants are together only briefly and can examine problems only superficially and out of context. Neither technique allows for repeated contact between client and customer so they can collaborate in formulating ideas and opinions over time.

We needed a combination of techniques that would allow us the time to learn in depth about our client's customers while still providing an atmosphere conducive to brainstorming and collaboration. When Compaq approached us again to help them make design decisions, we suggested a new method which we call customer partnering. In concept, customer partnering is an offshoot of traditional end-user analysis techniques, including focus groups, contextual inquiry, and interviewing. We suggested that customer partnering would allow us to answer the specific design questions that were beginning to emerge.

We proposed a series of five working sessions, several weeks apart, in which the same customer team members would meet with the client team members and a facilitator. The time between sessions enabled us to process information and plan subsequent sessions to elicit the information we needed. The time between sessions also allowed Compaq to create information prototypes, based on customers' input, for evaluation during the next session. The three-month duration of the project allowed the customers to become more aware of their own information needs and to become more thoughtful and skilled in evaluating and expressing these needs.

Goals of Our Customer Partnering Project The primary goals of the customer partnering project we designed included the following:

- eliminating redundant documentation,
- providing more comprehensive documentation in areas of critical importance to customers,
- determining the kind of information customers want to have available and to what depth,
- determining the most useful mix of media for delivering documentation.

We gathered information on the physical aspects of customers' work environments, how they use documentation, what kinds of documentation they need, and how they preferred that our client address their information needs. Based on feedback from customer partners, we developed recommendations for redesigning the Compaq documentation library.

The Results of the Partnering Project At the end of our customer partnering project, we delivered a final report to Compaq summarizing our overall findings and recommendations for the redesign of their documentation. Our general conclusions were that

- customers often want to service and configure their equipment themselves rather than having to rely on outside service technicians;
- documentation should address the different needs of both novice and advanced users;
- delivery media must be matched to the type of information provided, its targeted users, and its expected use;
- customers need a process for learning if their documentation is the most current and comprehensive available.

From the general conclusions, we made strategic recommendations for our client to address its customers' needs systematically.

Part of the success of our customer partnering project resulted from our extensive understanding of customer use patterns developed over more than three years of site investigations. We do not believe that customer partnering is a technique to use initially in investigating customer needs, but only following site investigations that assist the researchers and the developers in understanding the current patterns of use. Site visits let you discover how the information is used, but can be superficial in the detailed data gathered. You start to see patterns and identify needs, but these visits are not conducive to in-depth discussions. Focus groups also provide superficial glimpses because the participants generally have not had enough time to think through the issues before the session. However, the information gathered from site visits, focus groups, and customer surveys can be used to direct the planning of a successful customer partnering venture.

How To Implement Customer Partnering

Customer partnering defines the essential relationship between a customer for a product or service and a developer who seeks to improve the quality of that product or service. However, we recommend that an individual or group skilled in partnering techniques serve as a facilitator of the customer partnering activities. In this way implementation will not be biased by preconceived notions about what the customer wants or needs or by defense of existing information products. The *client* is the information development organization that initiated the customer partnering. The *customer* represents the people who use the client's information products and volunteer to take part in the customer partnering effort. The *facilitator* is the person who designs the study, runs the information gathering sessions, writes reports about the study, and makes recommendations about information delivery methods suggested by the study.

Facilitators should be skilled in the customer-partnering technique. For projects involving information design, the facilitators should also be experts in the information design process. This knowledge is needed in designing homework assignments, helping the client understand the information gathered, and keeping the discussions focused on topics that will aid in information design. Just as with focus groups, it is often beneficial to have program facilitators who are not part of the client organization so that they can maintain a degree of objectivity during the sessions; however, customer partnering is not limited to facilitation by outside firms. Any group can use customer partnering internally to its own benefit so long as they develop expertise in the technique and engage an independent and skilled facilitator.

The facilitators in charge of a customer partnering program must first ensure that the client understands and agrees with the proposed method and its purpose. The commitment asked of customers is great, and any confusion between the client and the facilitators about the goals of the study will disrupt the focus of the meetings and quickly discourage customer partners from contributing to the meetings or even attending them. Once the purpose and method are clearly established and understood, it is time to establish criteria for selecting members of the customer partnering group and planning the partnering program.

Selecting Customer Partners Customer partners should represent a broad spectrum of the client's users. Having product users whose experience ranges from novice to experienced, who represent different sizes and types of companies, and whose use of the product varies participate in the study ensures that customer requirements and use models will be addressed during group discussions.

In addition to having the necessary experience in their field to be considered "typical" users and representing a broad range of customer company types, customer partners must also

- express interest in the project and willingness to commit to the time and schedule,
- be knowledgeable about their own documentation needs,
- reside close to the facility where the working sessions will be held, if travel budgets are not provided,
- commit to attending five to six working sessions over a period of several months,
- commit to completing "homework" assignments on their own time in between working sessions.

Adhering to these requirements may, however, add some bias to a study. Unless the area in which the working sessions are held is a large metropolitan area with many potential customer companies, it is possible to have too limited a sample of users for the sessions.

For our pilot project, we recruited customers from two critical user groups: system administrators and resellers. We created a partnering group of one reseller and four system administrators from companies operating both large and small networked systems in the Denver metro area. We were disappointed that only one reseller volunteered for the study because we had no way of knowing if the information from that person was representative of the reseller group. As a result of the low participation of resellers, this study focuses on system administration needs. Another study would be needed to address resellers' needs in equal depth.

It is also possible to introduce bias by the selection of volunteers. By their willingness to volunteer, the customers may be substantially different than the majority of users who do not volunteer. This bias, however, is endemic to all participative study techniques, including contextual inquiry and focus groups. The customer-partnering technique seeks to involve customers in product design who have a strong commitment to the product's success, who are interested in creating the best product possible. At the same time, they are selected because they represent mainstream product use; they are not the outliers. If a list of potential volunteers is suggested by the sales force, those on the list may be "good" customers in the eyes of sales; that is, they may be friendly customers, but they may not truly represent the mainstream customer.

Planning the Format and Focus of Each Working Session Careful planning of customer partnering working sessions is essential to the success of the study. Because the customers' experiences often influence the direction of conversations during the sessions, the facilitator must have a clear idea of what is to be covered during each session to stay on schedule and to maintain the focus of the group. In our project, we divided discussions of current documentation among the first four working sessions. We reserved the fifth for a discussion of prototypes and future documentation needs.

As we planned the working sessions for our customer partnering project, we planned highly focused activities that would provide specific feedback about customers' documentation needs, keep the sessions focused, and maintain participant interest. Activities we planned included asking participants to draw their workspaces with colored markers, work in groups to evaluate on-line documentation produced by our client and its competitors, and tape documentation topics to a wall-sized information organization chart.

For example, to maintain the focus of a discussion of documentation delivery media, we asked participants to complete a delivery media preferences worksheet (see Fig. 1). After participants indicated on the worksheet the documentation delivery medium they preferred for each of the server administration tasks, we led a group discussion about delivery media. Asking participants to complete the worksheet before the discussion gave them time to consider their delivery media needs for a wide range of tasks and formulate their ideas before the discussion. In our analysis of the working session, we were able to refer to the participants' worksheets and their discussion comments.

Fig. 1.

Documentation Delivery Media Preferences

Indicate whether you would like Compaq to provide online documentation or paper documentation for each task listed below by placing a check mark in the appropriate column. If you would like Compaq to provide a mixture of online and paper documentation for a task, explain which information you would like online and which you would like on paper in the space provided.

Task	online delivery	paper delivery	online and paper delivery (explain)
selecting hardware			
selecting options			
researching specifications			
installing hardware			
installing options			
using SmartStart			
choosing a configuration			
installing an operating system			
tuning the system			
troubleshooting			
correcting hardware problems			
maintaining hardware			

Comments or suggestions: ______________________________

____

____

Providing Homework for Group Participants Customer partners should be given assignments to complete between working sessions. Giving participants homework assignments enhances the working sessions in the following ways:

- Participants maintain their focus on documentation during the breaks between working sessions;
- Participants have time to think independently about the client company's product and decide what their own needs are without peer pressure or time constraints;
- Participants are able to bring concrete examples and well-formulated ideas for product improvement to the working sessions;
- Facilitators gather valuable accounts about the experiences of the partners and their coworkers in using the client company's products on the job.

Homework assignments may include polling coworkers, keeping logs of experiences with documentation, examining products or documentation produced by other companies, and designing documentation prototypes. At one session, in order to determine what type of on-line information presentation was most helpful to users, we asked the customers to bring examples of on-line documentation they particularly liked or disliked to the next working session. We found that the on-line documentation customers liked was task-oriented and organized into major task-oriented menu choices, such as installation, configuration, troubleshooting, and maintenance. Had we only asked customers to evaluate our client's existing on-line documentation, which was organized by product type and manual title, we might not have discovered customers' preference for task organization.

To ensure that homework assignments benefit the partnering venture, the facilitators must design assignments that are interesting, clear, relevant, can be accomplished in a reasonable amount of time, and that give participants a good starting point for the next working session. They must also prepare all log forms and questionnaires necessary for each assignment. Customer partners must commit to completing all of the homework assignments and must come to working sessions ready to discuss the assignments.

Facilitating the Working Sessions The relationship between customer partners and the client company develops during the series of working sessions. At the sessions, representatives of the client company are able to observe while their customer partners evaluate products, share their experiences, and talk about their needs. Client participants ask questions, present new product ideas, and solicit immediate feedback.

To guarantee productive working sessions, facilitators must prepare the necessary materials and discussion topics for each working session. Facilitators should prepare an agenda; provide equipment for running on-line, video, or audio documentation; gather the documentation that customers will evaluate during the working session; and ensure that paper, pencils, or other materials needed for working session activities are in place. Facilitators must also direct the working sessions, keep discussions focused, and prepare discussion questions and written surveys designed to elicit information on how customers currently use the products and on how they could use the products more effectively.

One main advantage of gathering information during working sessions is that the participants interact face to face over an extended period of time. Unlike focus groups, in which the participants never get to know one another, customer partnering provides enough time to allow the participants to form a coherent work group. This interaction contributes to information gathering in the following ways:

- Participants are able to play off each other's ideas and brainstorm solutions together;
- Facilitators can gauge customers' reactions to existing products and new prototypes by listening to their comments, watching their review of the products, and observing their body language;
- Client representatives can see first hand how customers react to their products.

Successful facilitation of the sessions requires a firm focus on the objectives of the partnering and the ability to promote useful conversation. The facilitator must ensure that everyone has an opportunity to contribute and that no one is permitted to dominate the discussions. If facilitation is done correctly, a rapport is established among group members that allows candid and meaningful dialog that can lead to the design of improved information products.

Duration of the Study The duration of a customer-partnering study will depend upon the complexity of the product being designed. However, a primary characteristic of customer partnering is that the interaction between customer and developer takes place over an extended period. We have found that over time, especially over a period of several months, customers grow in their understanding of the design problems under consideration. In the Compaq study, for example, we noted that the server administrators began by being positive but vague in their comments on the documentation. They told us that the existing documentation was "fine." By the fourth and fifth sessions, their opinions had changed and their articulation of their needs and the problems with the existing information had become increasingly even surprisingly, explicit.

For example, at an early session, the customers told us that the installation pamphlet was "helpful" and they would choose to use it during installation. By a later session, they became adamant that the same pamphlet was not useful and had to be redesigned. The growth in understanding comes in part from a degree of politeness. People dislike being critical in front of strangers, especially in the presence of the developers of the documentation. Unless they have very strong negative responses, they are unlikely to make an issue of minor concerns. In addition, however, users often have not formulated a clear analysis and criticism of an issue that they are asked about. They really have no opinion but will fill the gap in the dialog with vague commendations. Only after several sessions will they gain enough perspective in the issues at hand to discuss them cogently and have specific recommendations.

Users also learn from their interactions with other participants to differentiate between a "pet peeve" and a more universal issue. They tend to temper their statements of need to take into account the circumstances and patterns of use articulated by other participants.

Customer-partnering programs should consist of at least five working sessions with two to three weeks between sessions. Five sessions allow the group to become an organic unit that moves well past the usefulness of a focus group. Beyond six sessions, the sessions may begin to lose effectiveness. As the customers become more expert in the topic of the study, they cease to represent typical users. We observed this learning curve in the sessions we facilitated. Clients might usefully reconvene customer partnering groups, however, for follow-up activities (for example, for feedback on prototype documentation developed in response to the findings of the study); but for any future customer partnering programs, clients should recruit a new group of customer partners.

Recognition of Customer Participation To help encourage and recognize those customers who had participated in the program, our client gave out small gifts at several sessions, invited the participants to dinner at a nice restaurant to wrap up the study, and wrote letters of appreciation. This recognition is important because the customers receive no compensation for their participation, commit a significant amount of time, and show a willingness to contribute to the effort to improve the client's products.

Our client also provided follow-up information to the participants letting them know of progress made on the design of new information products as a result of the customer partnering sessions. Customers are very interested in knowing what has happened to their recommendations. They want to see the fruits of their labors in improved, more usable products.

We recommend that program facilitators and client companies maintain a relationship with customers after the final working session. A continuing relationship provides the client company with opportunities to ask customers for feedback on new product ideas and to modify its efforts accordingly during the development process. Customer partners might even participate in new product usability tests.

Developing Product Prototypes The time between working sessions allows the client company to develop product and documentation prototypes for customer partners to review in later working sessions. Getting customer feedback on these prototypes helps with redesign in the following ways:

- The client company receives immediate feedback on new ideas for product and documentation design and presentation;
- The client company has the opportunity to improve prototypes to meet customers' needs and preferences;
- The client's ideas are supplemented by customers' ideas for improving the prototypes.

Program facilitators, the client company, and customer partners work together to create prototypes that become the framework for the client company's new products. The client is responsible for using information gathered during the working sessions to create prototypes of new documentation and for preparing written evaluation forms designed to elicit participants' detailed evaluation of the prototypes. Customer partners evaluate each prototype and offer feedback for improving them.

Reporting the Results and Recommendations of the Working Sessions During the working sessions, the facilitator should ensure that customer responses are recorded. We have an observer attend each session to log the sessions in much the same way a data logger functions during a usability test. We also videotape the sessions for immediate review, future analysis, and presentations.

After each working session, the facilitator should summarize the findings and recommendations that result from the working session. The summary should include information about what participants like, dislike, and need from the client company. It may also include samples of products or documentation that participants bring to the working sessions, sketches participants make of their workplaces, or prototype design ideas.

At the end of the program, the facilitator should create a final report presenting the overall findings of the study and addressing its original goals. To draw on the individual working session reports but avoid redundancy, we recommend organizing the final report around an evaluation of delivery media, user experience levels, or stages of product use. For example, while our working session reports focused on what customers liked and disliked about each of our client's documents or document prototypes, our final report discussed the differences between novice and advanced users' needs and made recommendations for providing a documentation library that supports a broad range of users and uses the delivery media appropriate for each task they perform.

Benefits of Customer Partnering To The Client and Its Customers

The major benefit of customer partnering is the relationship that develops between a client company and its customer partners through repeated contact. Studies that involve one-time contact, such as interviews, surveys, focus groups, and contextual inquiry only gather participants' immediate reactions. Customer partnering, on the other hand, creates an environment for an in-depth investigation of customers' needs and preferences. As a result of the close relationship that develops between a company and its customer partners, both the client and the customers benefit. The specific benefits of customer partnering follow.

- **Customers receive a product and documentation that is custom designed to their needs.**

  Customer partners leave the program knowing that product and documentation improvements will be made with their needs in mind. They eventually receive a product that is designed specifically to meet their needs. Insofar as the partners represent the entire customer base, the new product is customized for all customers' needs. If the developers are prepared to do so, working prototypes of information products can also be delivered to the customers' sites between sessions for in-house testing, giving the developer even more detailed feedback.

- **Customers feel ownership for changes to future products and documentation.**

  As they participate in the program, partners gain a feeling of empowerment: the opportunity to give feedback directly to the client company means that they have helped design products that directly address their needs.

- **Customers learn how the process works and provide better feedback and information in the later sessions.**

  During the weeks between working sessions, the customer partners reflect at length on the product or documentation they are evaluating, complete homework assignments that help them develop their ideas, and evaluate the client company's and other companies' products or documentation. As a result, participants are able to bring to each session design recommendations, well-thought-out opinions, and examples of products or documentation they particularly like. This continuing effort on the part of the customer partners is the primary feature that makes customer partnering a richer, if different, information gathering technique than contextual inquiry or focus groups.

- **Client companies get frank and valuable information about the design of products and documentation.**

  From the relationship that develops between the client company and customer partners, the client company gains insight into customers' working styles and product needs. Most importantly, the client company receives candid feedback from customers on aspects of products they actually use and how they use them. As they get to know one another and feel comfortable with each other, participants feel free to contribute to each other's ideas and to express straightforward opinions about the products.

- **Companies get to educate their customers.**

  During the program, customer partners learn about the full range of products available to them, and they receive answers to specific, work-related questions. The development company can then use this information to help develop marketing efforts to help others learn about these products.

- **Customers' views of the client company may become more positive.**

  Customers who participate in partnering programs are impressed by the client company's dedication to improving its products and involving customer input in the redesign process. They appreciate the attention and see the client company in a new, positive light. This can, however, provide a bias that keeps them from being forthright. The facilitator must be aware of this bias and probe for issues they feel might underlie the comments being made.

- **Customer partnering benefits all involved.**

  The benefits of customer partnering to all participants are enormous. Customers feel they have direct input to products they will use, feel they have the client company's undivided attention for the duration of the program, and finally have products and documentation that more nearly meet their particular needs.

  The developer no longer has to guess about customer requirements for particular products or documentation. Rather than just hearing the "horror" stories of products and processes gone bad, hearing only from customers who love the product, or hearing nothing at all, the client interacts directly with a spectrum of typical users who can help fill in the comprehensive picture needed for good product development.

Customer partnering offers technical communicators a way to unravel the complexity of information and organize large bodies of information into *on-line documentation* that is useful for its intended audience. By involving customers deeply in the documentation design process, communicators can meet customers' information needs as effectively as possible.

References

[1] M. E. Raven and A. Flanders, "Using contextual inquiry to learn about your audiences," *J. Comput. Document.*, vol. 20 no. 1, pp. 1–13, 1996.

[2] H. R. Beyer and K. Holtzblatt, "Apprenticing with the customer," *Commun. ACM*, vol. 38, no. 5, pp. 45–52, 1995.

[3] J. S. Dumas and J. C. Redish, *A Practical Guide to Usability Testing.* Norwood, NJ: Ablex, 1994.

[4] K. Holtzblatt and H. R. Beyer, "Requirements gathering: The human factor," *Commun. ACM*, vol. 38, no. 5, pp. 31–32, 1995.

[5] M. Keil and E. Carmel, "Customer-developer links in software development," *Commun. ACM*, vol. 38, no. 5, pp. 33–44, 1995.

JoAnn Hackos is President of Comtech, a design firm she founded in 1978. At Comtech, Dr. Hackos manages a team of project managers, developers, designers, writers, and graphic artists in conducting design and development projects for companies throughout the U.S. and internationally. Comtech design projects include user and task analysis, contextual inquiry, and usability testing, as well as the design of product interfaces, documentation, and training. JoAnn is a member of the IEEE Professional Communication Society and a past president and Fellow of the Society of Technical Communication (STC).

Molly Hammar is a Communication Analyst for Comtech. She works with Comtech's information development teams on paper documentation, on-line documentation, CBT, usability testing, contextual inquiry, and customer partnering projects. She recently managed a three-month customer partnering project that included five meetings for a major client. Molly is a recent graduate of Pomona College with a bachelor of arts degree in science, technology, and society.

Arthur Elser (M'84) is a Senior Communication Analyst for Comtech. He typically works as a senior member of information development teams for traditional and on-line documentation and training projects. He has been a writer, editor, teacher, trainer, manager, and consultant in the technical communication field for over 25 years and is a member of the IEEE Professional Communication Society and a Fellow of the Society for Technical Communication (STC).

Challenges in Developing Research-Based Web Design Guidelines

—Mary B. Evans

Abstract—*Formulating design guidelines from research results can potentially offer two advantages: available empirical knowledge is distilled into a readily accessible form, and practitioners can judge the authority of those guidelines for themselves. But a case history demonstrates that challenges confront the developer of research-based guidelines for website design. First, few studies of people using the Web have yet been conducted. Second, when the process of guideline development is not systematic and designed to control bias and subjectivity, the resulting guidelines can be compromised. This paper describes the issues and problems one guideline developer encountered and suggests a guideline development process that might resolve them.*

Index Terms—*Evidence-based guidelines, research-based guidelines, usability guidelines, Web design, Web usability.*

Manuscript received November 18, 1999; revised May 3, 2000.
The author is with the Office of Response and Restoration, National Oceanic and Atmospheric Administration, Seattle, WA 98115 USA (email: mary.evans@noaa.gov).
IEEE PII S 0361-1434(00)07490-7.

John, a U.S. Coast Guard officer, is stationed in a jurisdiction with heavy oil tanker traffic. He needs to know how to choose effective response measures in the event of an oil spill. Mariama, the port manager at a large city in a developing country, oversees frequent shipments of hazardous materials to and from her port. She could use software and training materials to prepare herself to manage a chemical accident response. Karen is a student planning to do a science fair project on oil spills. She's looking for ideas and some help getting started. Near Kurt's town, fuel oil has spilled onto the beaches from a grounded freighter. He would like to learn about the spill's possible effects on local plants, animals, and habitats.

At the National Oceanic and Atmospheric Administration's Office of Response and Restoration (NOAA OR&R), we have developed software, research reports, manuals, and other products useful to John, Mariama, Karen, and Kurt. Delighted that the World Wide Web now offers a relatively cheap way for government agencies like us to offer products to a worldwide audience, we decided to construct our own website. We identified the primary audience for our site as hazardous materials responders and planners, and decided that our site should serve as a clearinghouse from which people in that audience could obtain tools and information that would help them in their work. We also hoped to serve other audiences, such as students and members of the public concerned about oil spills and chemical accidents.

Because few members of our primary audience are computer experts, we recognized that our website needed to be as usable as possible (we use Dumas and Redish's definition of a usable

Reprinted from *IEEE Trans. Prof. Comm.*, vol. PC-43, no. 3, pp. 302–312, September 2000.

The focus group, on the other hand, often does not allow time to concentrate on design details because participants are together only briefly and can examine problems only superficially and out of context. Neither technique allows for repeated contact between client and customer so they can collaborate in formulating ideas and opinions over time.

We needed a combination of techniques that would allow us the time to learn in depth about our client's customers while still providing an atmosphere conducive to brainstorming and collaboration. When Compaq approached us again to help them make design decisions, we suggested a new method which we call customer partnering. In concept, customer partnering is an offshoot of traditional end-user analysis techniques, including focus groups, contextual inquiry, and interviewing. We suggested that customer partnering would allow us to answer the specific design questions that were beginning to emerge.

We proposed a series of five working sessions, several weeks apart, in which the same customer team members would meet with the client team members and a facilitator. The time between sessions enabled us to process information and plan subsequent sessions to elicit the information we needed. The time between sessions also allowed Compaq to create information prototypes, based on customers' input, for evaluation during the next session. The three-month duration of the project allowed the customers to become more aware of their own information needs and to become more thoughtful and skilled in evaluating and expressing these needs.

Goals of Our Customer Partnering Project The primary goals of the customer partnering project we designed included the following:

- eliminating redundant documentation,
- providing more comprehensive documentation in areas of critical importance to customers,
- determining the kind of information customers want to have available and to what depth,
- determining the most useful mix of media for delivering documentation.

We gathered information on the physical aspects of customers' work environments, how they use documentation, what kinds of documentation they need, and how they preferred that our client address their information needs. Based on feedback from customer partners, we developed recommendations for redesigning the Compaq documentation library.

The Results of the Partnering Project At the end of our customer partnering project, we delivered a final report to Compaq summarizing our overall findings and recommendations for the redesign of their documentation. Our general conclusions were that

- customers often want to service and configure their equipment themselves rather than having to rely on outside service technicians;
- documentation should address the different needs of both novice and advanced users;
- delivery media must be matched to the type of information provided, its targeted users, and its expected use;
- customers need a process for learning if their documentation is the most current and comprehensive available.

From the general conclusions, we made strategic recommendations for our client to address its customers' needs systematically.

Part of the success of our customer partnering project resulted from our extensive understanding of customer use patterns developed over more than three years of site investigations. We do not believe that customer partnering is a technique to use initially in investigating customer needs, but only following site investigations that assist the researchers and the developers in understanding the current patterns of use. Site visits let you discover how the information is used, but can be superficial in the detailed data gathered. You start to see patterns and identify needs, but these visits are not conducive to in-depth discussions. Focus groups also provide superficial glimpses because the participants generally have not had enough time to think through the issues before the session. However, the information gathered from site visits, focus groups, and customer surveys can be used to direct the planning of a successful customer partnering venture.

How To Implement Customer Partnering

Customer partnering defines the essential relationship between a customer for a product or service and a developer who seeks to improve the quality of that product or service. However, we recommend that an individual or group skilled in partnering techniques serve as a facilitator of the customer partnering activities. In this way implementation will not be biased by preconceived notions about what the customer wants or needs or by defense of existing information products. The *client* is the information development organization that initiated the customer partnering. The *customer* represents the people who use the client's information products and volunteer to take part in the customer partnering effort. The *facilitator* is the person who designs the study, runs the information gathering sessions, writes reports about the study, and makes recommendations about information delivery methods suggested by the study.

Facilitators should be skilled in the customer-partnering technique. For projects involving information de-

When I found fewer studies relating to a particular design question, I looked harder, often querying colleagues in person or by electronic mail to find references on some topics. For example, I posed questions related to link placement, font size, and style to the UTEST mailing list.

(2) To interpret the studies related to a particular design question, I first reviewed each study, noting down its general methodology, the number and characteristics of the subjects, the kind of electronic system studied, the outcome of the study, relevant observations made by the authors, and any particular strengths or weaknesses of the study. I then made essentially ad hoc comparisons between the studies and summarized those comparisons.

The Research Results I Used I founded my guidelines on a total of 83 different findings obtained from 62 different studies (I used more than one finding from some extensive studies). While 88% of the studies were conducted during the 1980s and 1990s (with slightly more than half of these conducted during the 1980s), seven were conducted before 1980. Only seven of the 62 references I consulted had not been published or peer-reviewed in some way; 89% had been published in printed peer-reviewed books, journals, or conference proceedings (Table I). About a third of the findings I used were from studies of websites, intranets, or other hypertext systems; the rest were from studies of other kinds of computer systems or from research in basic science (Table II). About half (51%) of the findings I used were obtained from controlled, randomized experiments; the rest were from less rigorous studies, such as usability tests, surveys, and observational studies (Table III).

My collection of 83 findings represents a relatively small knowledge base, compared with similar efforts in related fields. In contrast, in 1986, Schriver and her colleagues at Carnegie Mellon University reviewed the document design literature, excluding all references that did not have an empirical basis, and found hundreds of relevant articles [7]. Surely one reason for the fewer findings I collected is that I worked alone and for a relatively short time. A more important reason is that, as yet, few studies of people using the Web have been conducted, since the Web has been in widespread use only since the mid-1990s. Shneiderman commented, "It will take a decade until sufficient experience, experimentation, and hypothesis testing clarify issues," and warned that meanwhile, "the paucity of empirical data to validate or sharpen insight means that some guidelines are misleading" [8, pp. 5–6].

TABLE I
NUMBERS AND TYPES OF REFERENCES USED TO DEVELOP GUIDELINES

Reference Type	No. Used
Print Book or Journal	43
Print Proceedings	11
Electronic Proceedings	1
Unreviewed Webpage	6
Unpublished Report	1

TABLE II
NUMBERS OF FINDINGS USED FOR GUIDELINE DEVELOPMENT BY MEDIUM STUDIED IN ORIGINAL RESEARCH

Medium Studied	No. Used
World Wide Web or Intranet	25
Database or Hierarchical Menu System	19
Other Computer System	14
Research in Basic Science	14
Hypertext System	11

TABLE III
NUMBERS OF FINDINGS USED FOR GUIDELINE DEVELOPMENT BY STUDY TYPE OF ORIGINAL RESEARCH

Study Type	No. Used
Controlled, Randomized Experiment	42
Research Review Article	14
Usability Test	13
Observational Study	13
Survey	1

My Guideline Presentation Format One reason to base guidelines on empirical evidence is to provide readers the information they need to judge the authority of those guidelines and decide whether and how to apply them. As Mayhew noted,

> [References] *offering only principles and guidelines for design provide little or no insight into their rationale, so the interested computer scientist and designer cannot begin to learn how to intelligently generalize and apply the principles and guidelines in novel contexts* [3, p. xiv].

Rather than offering quick answers, I wanted to make it easy for readers to review the evidence for each of my guidelines. To accomplish this for each of my design questions, I presented (a) that question, followed by (b) a brief summary of the relevant evidence, followed by (c) a bulleted list of suggestions for designers, followed by (d) a more extensive discussion of relevant research. The document containing my guidelines is available in [9].

An Example One of my design questions was **How many levels should a website contain?** Because I had found no studies of the effects of different numbers of levels in websites, I reviewed studies of people searching for information in database systems containing different numbers of levels. The findings from these studies accorded only partially with expert opinion. Generally, experts have arrived at a consensus that websites should contain as few levels as possible. Many have suggested a maximum of three levels as a rule of thumb. For example, Hackos and Stevens commented that

> *Regardless of structure most experts agree that users should not have to go through more than three jumps to find the information they need* [10, p. 147].

My review suggested a more complex situation, which I summarized as follows:

> *[Researchers] have generally found that people can complete searches faster and more accurately when the menu systems are broader (include more choices at each level of the hierarchy) and less deep (contain fewer levels). However, most of these studies have been of systems in which the names of menu options were short and the total number of options was relatively few (usually 64). In a study of a much larger system, people were able to search for information faster and more accurately when the system contained more levels, because the system had been designed to effectively guide them in finding information. The results of this study suggest that shallow, broad websites are not always better—whether or not a site has been organized in a way meaningful to its users is also a key influence on its usability* [11, p. 26].

As a guideline, I suggested that in response to these findings, Web designers (1) include no more levels than necessary in a site and (2) use other aids to help site visitors find the links of interest to them, such as including link abstracts and arranging links in meaningful groups.

What Might a Good Guideline Development Process Look Like?

I chose a research-based approach to guideline development because I saw it as a way to (a) enhance my chances of identifying design practices that would enhance usability and (b) reduce the chance that I would unknowingly promote ineffective design practices. The scarcity of studies of Web users and problems with the guideline development process I used diminished my chances of attaining these goals. Generally, those problems are drawbacks of the traditional literature review method that I adopted, which does not control for some of the kinds of bias (systematic error) that can influence the outcome of a research review.

I could not resolve the problem of data scarcity, but I wanted to know how my guideline development process might be improved. To find out, I reviewed the work of others attempting to develop research-based guidelines or draw conclusions from collections of independent studies. I found the work of biomedical researchers in the international Cochrane Collaboration (hiru.mcmaster.ca/cochrane), who are developing guidelines for medical practitioners [12], especially helpful.

My review suggested that a better method of guideline development would be more systematic, explicit, and rigorous than the one I used, and such a method might include the five steps that I list and discuss below. These steps are adapted from review procedures proposed by Light and Pillemer [6] and Mulrow and Oxman [12]. Although the current Web design knowledge base is scanty, within the near future, enough new research results are likely to have accumulated to justify an approach like the one below.

(1) **Formulate a specific design question**. When I developed my list of 16 questions, I did not adequately consider how the specificity of a given question would affect my ability to formulate an answer to it specific enough to serve as a useful guideline. A specific question makes evident both the kinds of studies that bear on it and the kind of review necessary to answer it [6]. For example, I had asked the relatively specific question, *Are site maps, site indexes, or other information overviews helpful to Web users?* This is a question about the average effect of a particular design treatment, including an information overview, that can be answered by reviewing studies that compare the usability of websites containing information overviews with websites that do not. Also, as I researched this question, I found studies comparing map-like overviews with index-style overviews in hypertext systems, suggesting an additional question about which of these two formats is best.

I asked some overly broad questions. For example, I asked, *How can I design links to make it as easy as possible for users to predict their targets?* This question is so broad that it is difficult to identify the kinds of studies to review in order to answer it. To answer this question, I reviewed studies that addressed more than one aspect of link or menu item usability, and then found it difficult to draw out a coherent guideline. A better procedure would have been to break up this overly broad question into specific questions, such as: *Can people better predict link targets when link abstracts are included with links?* (A link abstract is a short description of what the user will see after clicking a given link.) I could have answered this question by assessing studies that compared websites and other menu-driven systems that use abstracts with ones that do not. I found four such studies.

(2) **Collect as many relevant studies as possible.** Krull recommended that when an answer to a pressing design question is needed and time constraints make it impossible to complete a thorough search of the

literature, the best strategy for busy practitioners is to "limit their searches to research compilations and the most prominent studies they mention" [13, p. 172]. I followed a similar strategy, not making it a goal to collect all relevant studies, but focusing instead on finding the most important studies relating to each of my 16 questions. I spent little time searching for studies that had not been published in journals, books, or the proceedings of major conferences, and probably overlooked relevant studies in the grey literature. While this strategy is appropriate for the circumstances that Krull describes, it is not rigorous enough for guideline development. By using it, I provided an opportunity for the following sources of bias to affect my results:

- *Publication bias.* Publication bias exists if the results of published studies differ systematically from the results of unpublished studies. People comparing published and unpublished studies in a variety of academic and technical fields have found that studies with statistically significant findings have been published more frequently than studies in which the null hypothesis could not be rejected [6], [12], [14]. When this form of publication bias exists, a review like mine that includes mainly or only results from published studies would be likely to overestimate the magnitude of the effect of interest (which in my context might be, for example, the effect of link abstracts on users' search times). At least one other form of publication bias also has been documented: articles by researchers in the developing world are published much less frequently in major journals than articles submitted by researchers in highly industrialized nations [15].
- *Reference bias.* Results of at least two studies indicate that researchers tend to cite research that supports their views more often than research that does not [16], [17]. A potential effect of this form of bias is that reviewers relying heavily on the reference lists of published articles, as I did, risk obtaining a biased collection of studies.

The most effective way to minimize these sources of bias is to find as many of the studies relating to a particular design question as possible. This is easier to say than do, especially in the case of studies related to technical communication. Research relevant to this field is published in dozens of journals. Publication databases overlap each other in the cases of some journals while leaving out other journals completely, and abstracting and indexing services omit most journals that focus specifically on technical communication [13], [18], [19]. It also is more difficult to access scientific and technical research results from some regions of the world than from others; disproportionately few journals located in developing countries are included in leading citation indexes [15].

Adopting two practices might make it possible to conduct more thorough searches in the future.

- *Collaboration.* A group of researchers working together is likely to find more relevant studies related to a given topic than the same number of people working independently because a group can coordinate its work to avoid duplicating effort. International collaboration would reduce the risk of failing to find research published in languages other than English or countries outside of the industrialized world. The work of the World Wide Web Consortium (W3C) is a possible collaboration model to consider. Members of this joint effort by industry, academia, and governments collaborate to develop Web protocols and recommendations such as HTML and XML, the markup languages used to develop Web pages.
- *Databases or registers.* To make it easier to track down electronically published journal articles, Geng and van Loon [18] proposed creating a "superdatabase" linked to electronic publishing houses, which would serve as a locator for articles in electronic journals. Data such as keywords and abstracts would be presented in all major scientific languages and could be searched by anyone trying to locate articles on a particular topic. A solution that goes a step farther, in that it is intended to control publication bias, is represented by the trial registers developed by the Cochrane Collaboration. These registers make both unpublished and published information more accessible. Once a researcher is ready to begin an experimental trial of a particular medical treatment, he or she enters a brief description of that trial, along with contact information, into the relevant trial register. Separate registers exist for different topics, such as AIDS, stroke, and cancer. Later, others reviewing research related to the topic of a registered trial can contact a trial's authors to learn its outcome, whether or not the results of that trial are ever published.

(3) **Include in a review only those studies that are relevant and valid enough. Establish inclusion criteria in advance, to minimize the influence of reviewer bias.** Once I had collected studies bearing on a particular Web design question, I had to judge whether or not each of those studies was (a) methodologically valid so that I could draw valid conclusions or inferences from it, and (b) relevant enough to a particular Web design question.

In practice, both judgments were difficult to make.

First, I needed to decide just how seriously a given study must be flawed before I withdrew it from my review. An example of a study of questionable validity that I encountered was an extensive set of usability tests of nine commercial websites [20]. I judged this study to be flawed by a general lack of rigor in both design and conduct. Its authors reported many impressions and generalizations, but few quantitative results and little detail about how they conducted their study or analyzed the data they collected. Their description of the heuristic they had used to rank sites by relative usability was vague and unconvincing. They did not even report the number of participants in their study (although I eventually learned the approximate number from an email message sent by the lead author to the UTEST mailing list). Because this remains the most extensive study of Web usability that has so far been conducted and is well-known, I chose to use some of the observations made by the study's authors to develop my guidelines, but I tried to bear the study's deficiencies in mind as I considered the relative weight to accord their observations.

Second, because of necessity, I found myself more lenient than I would have preferred to be when assessing study relevance. Because so few studies of the Web were available, I did not reject studies of people using older computer systems from my review. More than half of the studies that I included in my review were completed before the development of the Web. Whether those studies were relevant enough—whether their results generalize to the Web—is a matter of judgment, and there are certainly some issues to consider. First, computer users may have changed in significant ways since some of these studies were conducted, and Web users might respond differently than the subjects of at least some of the studies I used. Second, older systems differ from the Web in that (a) systems running on desktop computers can exhibit faster system response times than typical Web response times, and (b) stand-alone systems do not offer users the opportunity to get "lost in cyberspace" (an experience often reported by Web users). Third, most of the findings I used were obtained from studies conducted in controlled settings very different from those in which most Web users work.

For example, I used a result from a 1983 study to answer the questions, *How can designers minimize page downloading times? And how important is this issue?* Barber and Lucas [21] studied telephone company clerks using terminals with different system response times. The clerks made errors most frequently when the system responded either fastest or most slowly, and least frequently when system response time was about 12 seconds. Barber and Lucas suggested that working memory is strained when system response time is substantially slower than 12 seconds, making it difficult for people to complete tasks (they also suggested that people work less carefully and therefore make more errors when system response is very fast). From the results of this and other studies, I judged that websites should be designed to minimize page downloading times. But in the absence of similar studies of people using the Web itself, I cannot be sure that Barber and Lucas' result would hold in the Web environment.

Defining in advance the criteria for including or rejecting studies for a review, rather than making ad hoc judgments as I did, has been recommended as a way to reduce the risk that a reviewer's personal biases would influence his or her selection of studies to review [6], [12]. I did not define inclusion criteria in advance, but as it happened, I also did not exclude any individual studies from my review, although I considered doing so in the case of the extensive Web study described above. Including all available studies certainly controlled for reviewer bias, but the drawback of this approach is that I may have included in my review studies that were not relevant or methodologically valid enough. If I were to repeat my guideline development project in the future, with more research on Web users presumably available, I would define inclusion criteria before beginning my research review. For example, I might exclude studies conducted before a particular date or on subjects too different from the audiences for my website, as well as studies with fundamental methodological flaws.

(4) **Evaluate studies systematically, distilling findings into the form of a guideline.** I made essentially ad hoc comparisons among the various studies relating to a particular design question, and from those comparisons, drew conclusions. By using this method, I created an opportunity for my personal biases to influence the results of my review. For example, I might have taken work by well-known researchers more seriously than work by people I had not heard of. To control for such reviewer bias, I could have decided in advance on a systematic procedure for comparing studies and combining their results [6], [12].

If I were to repeat my guideline development project, I would make two changes in order to control for personal bias. First, I would prepare and complete a summary form for each study, rather than keeping informal notes, as I had done. Using this form would help to ensure that I considered the same kinds of information about all the studies I compared. I envision that the form would contain data fields for the aspects of each study I consider to be relevant to a review, such as completion date, number of subjects and their key characteristics, short descriptions of the hypothesis tested (or the study's purpose, in the cases of observational studies), the methods used, the computer system studied, the study's key strengths and methodological flaws, and its outcome (including summary statistics such as mean effect size and standard deviation, and measures of statistical significance, when available).

Second, I also would implement a means of assigning relative weights to studies when pooling their results. Weighting studies according to a systematic procedure developed in advance is another way to control the effects of personal bias. Various numerical methods for assigning relative weights exist, such as methods for weighting the mean effect measured in a controlled experiment either by participant number or by a measure of precision such as the inverse of the variance of the effect mean [6]. I found myself using many disparate kinds of information, ranging from observations reported during small-scale usability studies to quantitative measurements made during extensive controlled experiments. To such a miscellaneous collection of data, I would apply a simple scheme for ranking studies by key factors, such as participant number, whether or not Web users were studied, and whether or not significant methodological errors had been made, rather than a numerical weighting method. My reasoning is that simple ranking can be applied to many kinds of studies, while more quantitative methods cannot. For example, I could have sorted studies into three or four categories, with the highest ranked category including recent, methodologically valid controlled experiments involving a large number of Web users as subjects, and the lowest ranked category including data such as impressions reported by researchers during observational studies or usability tests. I then could have weighted studies accordingly when combining results, giving relatively more weight to information obtained from studies in the first category when drawing my conclusions.

Of course, adopting systematic assessment procedures will not make it possible to draw out a conclusive guideline if relevant data are too scarce, as they appeared to be in the cases of some of my design questions. For example, I had asked: *How many links should be on a page? How many is too many?* In researching this issue, I found that in two early studies of people searching for target items in hierarchical menu systems [22], [23], test subjects completed searches faster when menus were shorter. These results suggested that pages should contain fewer links. But within a website, reducing the number of links per page generally requires adding more levels to the site. Visitors then must traverse more pages to find target items than they would if there were fewer pages to traverse, each containing more links. Perhaps this is why, in two recent studies of people searching for information in webpages [24], [25], people found information fastest when (a) pages within the site contained more rather than fewer links (these also were the largest pages), and (b) identical links were presented in more than one place on a webpage (for example, in a sidebar as well as at the bottom of the page). Because the available evidence did not point to a clear answer to my question, I suggested, as a guideline, that website designers (1) assume that adding more links to pages will not necessarily degrade users' performance and (2) examine the effects of link number and density in usability tests.

(5) **Test the guidelines to ensure that their effects are (a) substantial and (b) positive. Revise them when necessary.** I had considered my guideline development project to be complete once I had finished the final draft of those guidelines. But it was not long before I realized that at least one of them might need to be modified. After reviewing findings from studies indicating that slow system response times frustrate computer users and reduce their success at completing tasks, I had recommended that Web designers keep system response as fast as possible by using few graphics, minimizing the size of graphics, and taking other measures to speed page downloading. But our page visitation statistics have since made it evident that the most popular part of our website is the "Photo Gallery," a section containing large graphic files where system response is slowest. My response has been to move some of the information that we would like to convey to visitors into this section, by incorporating that information in photographic "tours" of various topics. This design decision essentially contradicts the guideline I had developed. My sense now is that the question of system response time is more complex than I had presumed it to be and that different system response times may be appropriate for different kinds of presentations within the same website.

Two general questions about my guidelines remain unanswered: (a) *Do they have a substantial influence on website usability, when applied?* and (b) *Is that influence positive?* The only sure way to answer these questions is to test guidelines to assess their effects and to build into the guideline development process a way to revise, update, or withdraw guidelines that prove ineffective. Adequately testing guidelines would require collaboration; like most practitioners, I do not have the time or resources to adequately test my guidelines by myself. (Testing also could indicate whether guidelines can be successfully applied. Some evidence suggests that practitioners may encounter difficulties when they attempt to apply software interface guidelines for a variety of reasons [26],[27].)

There are precedents for testing guidelines. Guidelines for medical practitioners have often been tested to ensure their effectiveness [28],[29]. There also has been at least one test of Web design guidelines: a two-stage experiment performed by Morkes and Nielsen [30], [31]. In the first stage, the authors studied people reading information in several versions of a test website. From their findings, they developed guidelines for writing text for webpages. In the second stage, they tested their guidelines by comparing two versions of an experimental website, an original version and a version rewritten following their guidelines. The rewritten site received a higher usability score according to the authors' scoring system.

Summing Up

Creating design guidelines based on the results of relevant research is a way to potentially reduce the effects of subjectivity on the judgment-forming process and offer practitioners the opportunity to judge guideline authority for themselves. But research-based guidelines may not prove effective if (a) those guidelines are founded on too few findings or on findings that are unrepresentative, methodologically flawed, or not sufficiently relevant to the topic, or (b) subjectivity has influenced the process of guideline development. The approach outlined above is designed to control these potential problems. It would require guideline developers to follow five steps: (1) prepare a set of specific design questions; (2) search as thoroughly as possible for evidence relevant to each of those questions; (3) use criteria developed in advance to exclude from further review any studies not judged to be relevant and valid enough; (4) use a procedure developed in advance to systematically assess relevant studies and, from them, distill out a guideline; and (5) test the resulting guidelines to learn whether they have a substantial, positive effect on website usability. Because searching for relevant research and testing guidelines are especially time-consuming operations, guideline development is best done collaboratively.

This suggested approach would be a significant departure from the standard literature review approach I used and from current practice generally. Present-day website designers are confronted with many competing sets of Web design guidelines, including my own. None of these sets of guidelines resulted from extensive collaborative effort or are based on extensive relevant evidence. Because very few tests of Web guidelines have been conducted, we cannot tell which guidelines may promote usability and which may not.

Faced with this situation, many practitioners may be asking themselves two questions: *Are existing Web design guidelines—including mine—any good? If they are, just what are they good for?*

In the case of my guidelines in particular, four drawbacks limit their usefulness. First, they may be based on studies of the wrong people, in that most are based at least partly on studies of people who may be unlike current Web audiences, using computer systems other than the Web. Second, some may be based on too little data. While I found enough research results to obtain fairly well-founded answers to some of my 16 questions, the answers to others, framed as guidelines, are likely to appear disappointingly vague to other practitioners. The guideline addressing the number of levels in a website is a case in point. More importantly, guidelines based on little data are especially likely to be misleading. Third, because of the method I used to develop the guidelines, I do not know the degree to which various sources of bias may have affected them. Fourth, I have not tested the guidelines to be sure that they are effective.

In my own work, though, I have found my guidelines to be useful design tools, despite their flaws. Although I do not always keep to them, as in the case of our website's Photo Gallery, I try to formulate rationales for the exceptions I make. Using the guidelines in this way, I have found them to be helpful decision aids for clarifying my thinking about design. They also have allowed me to recognize design areas requiring particular thought and attention, as well as usability testing.

My hope is that, by serving as a form into which existing knowledge has been distilled, the guidelines also may aid the broader Web design community to assess the state of the Web usability knowledge base and identify some of the design topics that most need to be addressed by further research. For example, a review of my guidelines document suggests that current knowledge about the following kinds of design topics may be inadequate:

- Topics for which the results of different studies conflict. This is the case for the question, *How many links should be on a page?*, as discussed above.
- Topics for which research results are ambiguous. This is the case for the topic of display polarity (whether dark text on a light background or light text on a dark background is more legible). Some studies have indicated that people can scan light text faster but report more visual fatigue when reading extensive texts in

light characters than in dark characters.

- Topics for which existing consensus may not be well-founded. A possible example is the "three levels rule," discussed above, which may be based on studies of small systems that failed to account for other factors influencing navigation success.

- Topics for which research on particular audiences is lacking. For example, none of the studies I reviewed addressed very young or elderly computer users, although these groups make up increasing large proportions of the total user population.

- Topics for which there may not be a single "one-size-fits-all" solution. This may be the case for questions about how to structure websites. Some research suggests that one kind of structure may work best for people searching a website for particular pieces of information, while a different structure may work best for people browsing within a website.

- Topics for which evidence seems to strongly support a particular design approach, but little or none of that evidence was obtained from direct studies of Web users. In these cases, results from older studies need to be confirmed by repeating them in the context of the Web. Questions about the usability advantages of link abstracts and different site structures fall into this category. Nearly all the research I reviewed on these topics was conducted on people using electronic databases or hypertext systems other than the Web.

In short, our Web design knowledge base is scanty, flawed, and full of gaps. However, research results and practitioner experience are accumulating. Visitors to our websites would be well-served if, in the near future, we were to build on our past work by taking the following steps.

- Assess what we have so far learned from our various guideline development projects and our attempts to apply the guidelines we have developed.

- Consider collaborating to apply our growing expertise and body of empirical evidence to develop Web design guidelines and test them to ensure that they are reliable.

- Apply more systematic and intentional procedures, such as those outlined in this paper, to increase our chances of developing guidelines most likely to enhance the usability of our websites.

Appendix Sixteen Web Design Questions.

Designing for Users' Technology

- How can designers minimize page downloading times? And how important is this issue?

Preparing Content for the Web

- How important is it to tailor the vocabulary used in a website to its users? If it is important, how can designers do it?
- How should text written for online reading differ from print texts? (For example, should it be equally or more concise?)

Organizing a Website

- What's the best way to organize information in a website? Hierarchical sites are the most common, but is a hierarchy always the best structure?
- How many levels should a Web site contain? Should it be relatively broad and less deep, or vice versa? And how important is this issue?

Designing Navigation Controls

- How can I design links to make it as easy as possible for users to predict their targets?
- Should designers stick with the default colors for visited and unvisited text links?
- Should links be embedded in text, or kept separate from the text in a menu or navigation bar?
- How should link menus be arranged on webpages? For example, should they be arranged horizontally across the top or bottom of the page, or as a vertical list along one side of the page?
- How can I effectively implement icons and imagemaps as links? Or is it better to just stick with text links? What are the pitfalls of image links?
- How many links should be on a page? How many is too many?
- Are site maps, site indexes, or other information overviews helpful to Web users?

Designing Web Pages

- On individual webpages, how much of the page should be taken up by white space, and how much by text and graphics?
- What are the best colors to use for page backgrounds and text? Are there background and text color combinations that should be avoided? And should designers choose dark text on light backgrounds or vice versa?
- What steps can Web designers take to ensure that text is legible?
- How do blinking text and animated graphics affect readers of websites?

REFERENCES

[1] J. S. Dumas and J. C. Redish, *A Practical Guide to Usability Testing*. Norwood, NJ: Ablex, 1994.

[2] J. Nielsen. (1998, August) Why Do People Use Something This Bad?. [Online] Available: http://www.useit.com/alertbox/980809.html

[3] D.J. Mayhew, *Principles and Guidelines in Software User Interface Design*. Englewood Cliffs, NJ: Prentice-Hall, 1992.

[4] S. L. Smith and J. N. Mosier, *Guidelines for Designing User Interface Software*. Bedford, MA: Mitre Corp., 1986.

[5] K. A. Schriver, *Dynamics in Document Design*. New York: Wiley, 1997.

[6] R. J. Light and D. B. Pillemer, *Summing Up: The Science of Reviewing Research*. Cambridge, MA/London, U.K.: Harvard Univ. Press, 1984.

[7] K. A. Schriver, "Document design from 1980 to 1989: Challenges that remain," *Tech. Commun.*, vol. 36, no. 4, pp. 316–331, 1989.

[8] B. Shneiderman, "Designing information-abundant websites: Issues and recommendations," *Int. J. Human-Computer Studies*, vol. 47, no. 1, pp. 5–30, 1997.

[9] M. B. Evans. Guidelines for Web Design. [Online] Available: http://response.restoration.noaa.gov/webmastr/thissite.html

[10] J. T. Hackos and D. M. Stevens, *Standards for Online Communication: Publishing Information for The Internet/World Wide Web/Help Systems/Corporate Intranets*. New York: Wiley Computer, 1997.

[11] M. Evans. (1998) Web design: an empiricist's guide. [Online] Available: http://response.restoration.noaa.gov/webmastr/webdesign.pdf

[12] *The Cochran Collaboration Handbook*, C. D. Mulrow and A. D. Oxman, Eds., The Cochrane Collaboration, Oxford, U.K., 1999.

[13] R. Krull, "What practitioners need to know to evaluate research," *IEEE Trans. Prof. Commun.*, vol. 40, pp. 168–181, Sept. 1997.

[14] K. Dickersin and Y.-I. Min, "Publication bias: The problem that won't go away," *Ann. NY Acad. Sci.*, vol. 703, pp. 135–146, 1993.

[15] W. W. Gibbs, "Lost science in the Third World," *Scientific Amer.*, vol. 173, no. 2, pp. 92–99, 1995.

[16] P. C. Gotzsche, "Reference bias in reports of drug trials," *BMJ*, vol. 295, pp. 654–656, 1987.

[17] U. Ravnskov, "Cholesterol lowering trials in coronary heart disease: Frequency of citation and outcome," *BMJ*, vol. 305, pp. 15–19, 1992.

[18] D. Geng and A. J. van Loon, "A technological and infrastructural challenge: A superdatabase for accessing all electronically published science and technology articles at once," in *Proc. Int. Professional Communication Conf., IPCC 98*, vol. 2. Québec City, Canada, 1998, pp. 131–136.

[19] L. K. Grove and K. S. Campbell, "Making research usable: Improving access to research results," in *Proc. Int. Professional Communication Conf., IPCC 98*, vol. 1. Québec City, Canada, 1998, pp. 45–47.

[20] J. Spool, T. Scanlon, W. Schroeder, C. Snyder, and T. DeAngelo, *Web Site Usability: A Designer's Guide*. North Andover, MA: User Interface Eng., 1997.

[21] R. E. Barber and H. C. Lucas Jr., "System response time, operator productivity, and job satisfaction," *Communi. ACM*, vol. 26, no. 11, pp. 972–986, 1983.

[22] J. MacGregor, E. Lee, and N. Lam, "Optimizing the structure of database menu indexes: A decision model of menu search," *Human Factors*, vol. 28, no. 4, pp. 387–399, 1986.

[23] G. Perlman, "Making the right choice with menus," in *Human-Computer Interaction—Interact '84. Proc. IFIP Conf.* New York: North-Holland, 1984, pp. 317–321.

[24] C. DiPierro, G. Nachman, and B. Raderman. (1999, October) Screen size and Web browsing. Univ. Maryland, Dept. Comp. Sci., College Park, MD. [Online] Available: http://www.otal.umd.edu/SHORE/bs03/index.html

[25] D. Bachiochi, M. Berstene, E. Chouinard, N. Conlan, M. Danchak, T. Furey, C. Neligon, and D. Way, "Usability studies and designing navigational aids for the World Wide Web," *Comp. Networks ISDN Syst.*, vol. 29, pp. 1489–1496, 1997.

[26] H. Thovtrup and J. Nielsen, "Assessing the usability of a user interface standard," in *Proc. CHI '91 Conf. Human Factors in Computing Systems*. Boston, MA, 1991, pp. 335–341.

[27] J. N. Mosier and S. L. Smith, "Application of guidelines for designing user interface software," *Behavl. Inform. Technol.*, vol. 5, no. 1, pp. 39–46, 1986.
[28] J. M. Grimshaw and I. T. Russell, "Effect of clinical guidelines on medical practice: A systematic review of rigorous evaluations," *The Lancet*, vol. 342, pp. 1317–1322, 1993.
[29] L. Kaegi, "Health services researchers zero in on quality, policy, and practice in a changing health care system," *J. Quality Improvement*, vol. 24, no. 11, pp. 658–671, 1998.
[30] J. Morkes and J. Nielsen. (1997, cited October 14, 1999) Concise, scannable, and objective: How to write for the Web. [Online] Available: http://www.useit.com/papers/webwriting/writing.html
[31] ——, (January 6, 1998, cited October 14, 1999) Applying writing guidelines to web pages. [Online] Available: http://www.useit.com/papers/webwriting /rewriting.html

Mary B. Evans works on website development, software documentation and usability testing, user training, and hazardous materials accident response at the National Oceanic and Atmospheric Administration campus in Seattle, WA. In June 1998, she received an M.S. in Technical Communication from the University of Washington, Seattle. She developed the design guidelines described in this article to fulfill requirements for her degree.

The Web and Corporate Communication: Potentials and Pitfalls

Gary Ritzenthaler and David H. Ostroff

Abstract—**The World Wide Web has exploded as a means of corporate communications. This paper examines the technologies employed in using the Web, including software and hardware concerns, and the uses to which the organization can employ the technology. A case study of how the College of Journalism and Communications at the University of Florida developed and is using the Web provides additional illustration of the Web's potentials for internal and external communication. The paper concludes with a brief description of organizational and legal issues which have been spawned by use of the Web.**

OVER the last two years a new publishing and communication medium known as the World Wide Web has grown from an academic experiment to a viable tool for the dissemination of all kinds of information. The World Wide Web is the latest step in the evolution of publishing on the Internet; but what is it exactly? How does one use it for corporate communication? In this paper we will describe the organizational considerations in creating a Web site, the types of uses the Web can provide for organizations, and some of the problems which must be confronted in operating a Web site. We will draw largely on our experiences with the Web site of the College of Journalism and Communications at the University of Florida.

The World Wide Web is a "wide-area hypermedia information retrieval initiative aiming to give universal access to a large universe of documents." What the World Wide Web project has done is provide users on computer networks with a consistent, simple means to access a variety of media [1]. Popular access to the Web began with the widespread availability of a software interface called Mosaic. Subsequent products, such as Netscape, and Web access by such commercial on-line services as America Online have contributed to an explosion of Web use.

The Web is a technology for sharing information that organizations can utilize for both internal and external information. In that sense, it may perform the same functions as a wide range of current information technologies: interoffice memos, product catalogs and brochures, company training manuals, and many others. Each of these existing information strategies serves its purpose well, so the Web has to provide benefits that these other technologies lack.

If we take the time to unpack the somewhat technical definition above, we begin to grasp some of the benefits the Web has over existing technologies. First, the Web is global—it provides users all around the works with the ability to find and publish information in a *consistent* way. Web documents can be displayed on any computer platform, regardless of the platform upon which it originated. The documents can include pictures, sounds, and other design elements not found in earlier Internet tools. This consistent global nature of the Web frees organizations from the constraints of time and space associated with traditional forms of corporate communication.

Second, the Web allows publishers to create links between documents in an intuitive way. (This involves links to documents at other sites around the world as well as links between local documents.) The concept of linking documents and information was originally called "hypertext." Since the Web allows a variety of media in addition to text, however, many people now refer to the concept as "hypermedia." Most current users of the Web can create links to pictures, sounds, and short video segments as well as text. Compared to footnotes or references, this is an almost effortless method of bringing background and consistency to corporate documents, and it allows the reader of those documents a measure of control not found in traditional media.

The Web, and its attendant collection of sites, has grown so rapidly as to make statistics about its size and use obsolete when published. One benchmark of its growth: in November 1993, one month after the introduction of Mosaic for Windows, Web traffic accounted for about 1% of all Internet traffic. One year later it accounted for almost 14%, the second most used service on Internet [2], and by spring of 1995 Web use ranked first, accounting for about one-quarter of all traffic [3].

The explosion of corporate interest in the World Wide Web has delighted some and enraged others. The pace of corporate homesteading on the Web would seem to be inevitable given the opportunities the Web presents for communication. The flexibility and ease of use inherent in the Web provides the potential for corporate interests to engage in many types of communication cheaply and effectively: public relations and marketing, customer service and instruction, product positioning and advertising. Each of these can be served from one properly woven Web site if some care is used organizing and developing the Web's structure and implementation. As with any corporate publishing venture, some planning is essential—a clumsily planned or executed site can hurt a company's image and hinder its development in this new marketplace. The Web is a new medium, so it presents new challenges as well as new potentials.

What Do You Need to Be on the Web?

The World Wide Web is based on a "server" and "client" system. In other words, your materials are stored on a com-

Manuscript received March 1995; revised November 1995.

The authors are with with the University of Florida, Gainesville, FL 32611-8400 USA.

Publisher Item Identifier S 0361-1434(96)02281-3.

Reprinted from *IEEE Trans. Prof. Comm.*, vol. PC-39, no. 1, pp. 16–22, March 1996.

puter called a "server." The person seeking that information uses a software program called a "browser" to access that server and display the materials. The browser locates each document by means of a unique "address" called a URL, or Uniform Resource Locator. In addition to the browser software to view Web documents you might also need an occasional "helper application" to handle the multimedia elements like sound or video.

If you wish to place documents on your own computer server you will need software. While most of the browsers are relatively low in cost (in some cases available for free), server software is more expensive. While the market remains in flux, costs in excess of $1000 are not uncommon. Many Internet Service Providers will rent access to servers. Charges are usually based on amount of space required, and the amount of traffic the server will be expected to bear.

Web documents can be prepared relatively easily. Instructions or "tags" are attached to text, images, or other document elements. They can be added using add-ons to popular word processing programs or stand-alone packages like "HTML Assistant" (HTML stands for Hypertext Markup Language, the collection of tags and rules used in developing Web documents). To a great extent, preparing these documents with HTML is much like working with a standard word-processing program. Buttons and point-and-click capabilities make insertion of the correct tags a relatively easy process.

In creating Web documents, the needs of the users must be anticipated. What some researchers have termed "flow" represents the navigational aids needed to help the user find and navigate through the documents easily. As the Web has evolved, many sites have eschewed fancy graphics for a simpler presentation.

There is another important aspect to the client/server nature of the Web that is important for the corporate communicator to know. No matter how nice a document or Web page may appear at the server end, it is the client's browser software that determines the display and presentation the reader sees. For example, one browser, Lynx, displays only text, while the early version of Netscape would display text in only one color, usually on a gray background; later versions allow for use of colored text and backgrounds.

Another limiting factor is the nature of the computer and monitor at the client's end. Picture resolution, color reproduction, etc., are not under the control of the content provider. The user's capabilities will affect the amount of information that should be reasonable included. Access to a T1 telephone line, or an in-house distribution on a LAN, and "Pentium" or Power Mac will allow for fairly rapid downloading. However, access through a dial-up 14.4 modem and a slower speed computer can mean many minutes of downloading before images are available. For moving images, an hour or more might be necessary to download only a few seconds of content. Web developers need to keep their potential users in mind when designing content for their site. Many Web page designers include the size of an audio or image file in the document, so users can determine if they wish to download the file.

Ultimately, the Web site should be carefully planned in advance. Decisions will have to be made about how to best organize information, the balance between aesthetics and functionality, and length of individual pages [4], [5]. Our experience has been that while some trial and error is inevitable making extensive changes after the Web site has been placed into service can be time-consuming.

Division of Duties

Each site will have to decide how to allocate the tasks involved in maintaining the local Web. Initially, one person will need to take the lead in developing a proposal and gathering personnel and material resources. There will be many reasons to want to assign the entire project to one person, but this temptation should be avoided if possible. Traditional information publishing processes are spread out throughout the organization and in this respect the new medium should not be any different.

A key element of the Web project leader's work should be to educate and involve as many current company employees as possible. Existing methods of information distribution can serve as models for the corporate Web, and employees currently involved in those positions will be able to explain what works and what does not to the Web developer. The company Web will improve from this interaction, and the materials it contains will be more accurate and effective. During this process of consultation and input, employees will learn about the new technology and its potentials and become more motivated to get involved, and the company will become more advanced compared to others in its field.

Depending on the size of the company's Web, the priorities it has, and the market it intends to serve the "Web leader" may be joined by other employees whose tasks range from researching good references to working with local and global groups on the best collaborations, to keeping track of the flood of information released every day on new software, new sites of interest, and other news. Given the dynamic nature of the Web and the kinds of sites that already exist, no one organizational structure will work. The priorities and resources available will dictate the organizational structure.

Four Aspects of Weaving a Web

A particular Web document might serve several purposes depending on who is viewing it, but there are some general ways to classify the functions a Web document might serve. In this review, we shall divide the types of documents one might put on a corporate Web site into four categories: internal, administrative, reference resources, and services or forums. In the following section we describe how our College of Journalism and Communications uses its site to weave our Web.

Internal documents are those pieces of information which flow throughout a company, whether it is one building or several. These include information tracking the activities of the company, its divisions, and its employees. Memos, company and department newsletters, project reports, and company training manuals are all examples of internal documents. These on-line documents can be accessible only to local users or they can be made available to the rest of the world. Most likely a combination of these two methods will work best, with sensitive documents placed in secure directories or left off the Web server entirely. The use of the Web by The College of Journalism and Communications at the University of Florida, described below, is an example of this type of use.

Administrative/PR documents are all the materials dealing with the structure of the company and its products that are open to others and any related documents to promote them. Administrative documents might include financial statements, product catalogs and promotions, outlines of the organization and biographies of key personnel, recruiting/hiring documents, and listings of the company's recent activities.

An example is @Toyota, Website of Toyota, USA [http://www.toyota.com/]. In addition to information about their cars the Website provides profiles of racing drivers, statistics about the automobile industry, and a variety of lifestyle pages, including gardening tips, sports features, and a women's-oriented collection of articles [6].

Reference documents are those documents which may be of interest to the industry at large as well as to the employees of the company. Collections of important papers in the field, relevant government documents or regulations, and specifications on important products in the field are examples of reference documents. An excellent collection of reference documents will increase traffic to all areas of the server as well as increase the company's visibility in the Web community at large.

Siemen's Telecom Reports is a bi-monthly English-language magazine sent by the German company to customers and others around the world. Since April 1995, we have been the Web site publishers for the on-line version (http://www.jou.ufl.edu/siemens/telcom.htm). The on-line version includes interviews with Siemens engineers, reports of new developments and successful applications, press releases, and breaking news about Siemens activities. An on-line index gives readers access to all articles published since 1994. As this is written, we are preparing to add sound and video clips to create a multimedia version of the printed magazine and to undertake a series of on-line surveys of users.

Services or Forums are areas that reflect special interests or projects of the company; usually they involve documents that will change from day to day or month to month. These might be joint ventures with other organizations or projects with local colleges or civic groups, or they may be developed entirely by in-house employees. Like a good set of reference documents, a top-notch collection of forums can increase traffic at the site and cultivate name recognition among Internet users.

An example is provided by CableLabs, the research and development arm of the cable television system industry. The consortium uses its site [http://www.cablelabs.com/] to provide reports to its members and to the general public, and also conducts forums that are open only to members who must use a password to participate.

Creators of a corporate Web site should consider what mixture of the above documents they want to include at their site. Limited resources will force some difficult decisions in development, and a good grasp of the priorities for the site will help to guide these decisions and suggest ways to implement compromises effectively.

A Case Study: The University of Florida College of Journalism and Communications

The College of Journalism and Communications' (CJC) Web site began serving internal and external users in December 1993 [http://www.jou.ufl.edu/]. Since then it has been overhauled, modified, and tweaked countless times. In the spring of 1995, as the Web began to explode in growth, we decided to think more formally about the structure of the server and documents stored there. Some of the ideas are still being implemented, others have been canceled or added, but in general the CJC Web continues to evolve in a positive direction.

To fulfill its mission as a medium for communication and information publishing, the developers had to focus on how we could best serve the following communities:

- users within the College
- users at the University of Florida
- residents of Gainesville and nearby areas
- journalism and communications scholars worldwide
- other global users of the World Wide Web

The structure of our Web site has changed, but these groups remain the broad target groups we are trying to reach. The first group can be served in two ways: by allowing them to communicate internal information and by allowing them to publish appropriate material to the rest of the world. The primary collections of information on the CJC server, then, consists of the following:

Internal Documents: Since every person in the building has access to a Web browser (on their office computer or through open computer labs), the server can be used as a storehouse for important internal communications as well as a way to explore global communication. On-line documents allow the producers of internal documents more options for creating the information and the consumers of those documents more flexibility in deciding when and where to read it. Documents which have been placed on the Web include council and meeting notes as well as notes from student organizations. A link to the University's Web server allow us to keep faculty and graduate students abreast of grant possibilities.

Administrative/PR Documents: In a similar vein, the college can save time for staff by placing important administrative information on line. This information includes degree requirements, course descriptions, and financial aid and scholarship information. Our handbooks for M.A. and Ph.D. students are available providing information for both current and prospective students. Placing these documents on the Web frees staff members from having to answer recurring questions, and allow those with questions to get their answers regardless of time or day.

General college documents are supplemented with information about (and by) members of the College's academic departments. For example, our Communication Research Center maintains a list of recent publications by faculty members and graduate students. Users can also send an e-mail message directly to the faculty member from the research center's Web page.

Welcome to the official WWW site of the College of Journalism and Communications at the University of Florida. More information about this site and the UF WWW servers is available. For general Internet questions, please use our Help! section.

What's New -- Sun.ONE Weekly

- A joint venture of The Gainesville Sun and the College's Interactive Media Lab.
- Check out the Interactive Media Lab brochure.

The College of Journalism and Communications

An Overview of the College of Journalism and Communications

- Academic Departments and Research Centers
- Faculty and Staff
- Television and Radio Stations
- Graduate Studies Program
- Publications

Communications Resources

- WWW Virtual Library produced by John Makulowich.
- Communications Resource Directory
- NCSA What's New page
- Computer-Mediated Communication Studies Center
- Other communications WWW sites
- Commercial WWW News Services

[Communications Page at EINet Galaxy | News:Journalism Page at Yahoo | UCI Virtual Reference Desk]

Fig. 1. The CJC web site.

The information available from the departments is not restricted to faculty-created materials. Our affiliated PBS station includes selected student résumés on its Web site, and individual students can use the university's server and personal computer accounts to place personal information on the Web.

Our Brechner Center for Freedom of Information is represented by information about the center, its staff, and programs. Further, the monthly "Brechner Report" newsletter is available to interested scholars and media practitioners.

Communications Resources: As we discussed the direction of our local Web in its early stages it became obvious that we could be a very helpful resource center for those media-related institutions (academic and commercial) that would follow us into this new territory. By providing helpful reference materials we could be both useful and pioneering. Currently we have begun emphasizing those areas in which we can make a unique contribution consistent with the mission of the College. For example, The State Media Law Sourcebook, originally published by the Brechner Center, is now available on-line, as are links to state of Florida sites maintained by the legislature and executive branch.

There are two good reasons for visiting a World Wide Web site more than once. Some sites contain reference materials.

Communication Research Center
University of Florida

The Center, a service and research unit within the College of Journalism and Communications, conducts basic and applied research on problems related to mass communication. Both master's and doctoral students work as assistants on these projects. The Center provides consultation to faculty within the College and across the University and to individuals and organizations throughout Florida. The Center has a computer-assisted interviewing system and conducts telephone polls, personal interviews, focus groups, media use and effects studies, and message-testing research. For information, write the Director, Communication Research Center, 2000 Weimer Hall, or email at crc@jou.ufl.edu.

The documents in this section provide information about the College of Journalism and Communication at the University of Florida. It highlights some of the research being done in the College by both faculty and graduate students.

- ☐ Faculty Research - July 1, 1992 to present
- ☐ Graduate Student Research - July 1, 1993 to present
- ☐ Approved and Pending Projects - These projects were submitted for UFIRB review from the College of Journalism and Communications. Faculty and students are included in the list. If the research does not involve people, the project will not be included in this list.

If you would like to view research (July 1, 1992 to present) by faculty member, choose from the list:

Laurence Alexander ... Helen Aller ... David Carlson ... Les Carson ... Bill Chamberlin ... Jean Chance
Sandra Chance ... John S. Detweiler ... Julie Dodd ... Mickie Edwardson ... Mary Ann Ferguson
John Freeman ... John L. Giffith ... Frankie A. Hammond ... K. Herzog ... Linda Hon ... Robert L. Kendall
Kurt Kent ... Kent Lancaster ... Michael Leslie ... David Malickson ... William McKeen ... Sallie Middlebrook
Jon Morris ... David Ostroff ... Howard S. Pactor ... Frank N. Pierce ... Rob Pierce ... Joseph R. Pisani
Milagros Rivera-Sanchez ... Marilyn Roberts ... Jon Roosenraad ... F. Leslie Smith ... John Sutherland
Leonard Tipton ... Debbie Treise ... Bernell Tripp ... Elaine Wagner ... Kim Walsh-Childers
Michael Weigold ... Edward G. Weston ... John Wright

Fig. 2. Communication research center page.

These sites encourage people to return because they answer specific questions or because they provide links to other resources scattered in many places. The second reason for making a return visit to a site is to check out new and interesting additions.

The developers and editors of consumer on-line services have discovered that what people like most about those services is not the information they provide, but the chance to connect with others and exchange views about a particular topic or issue. This is also the reason mailing lists and

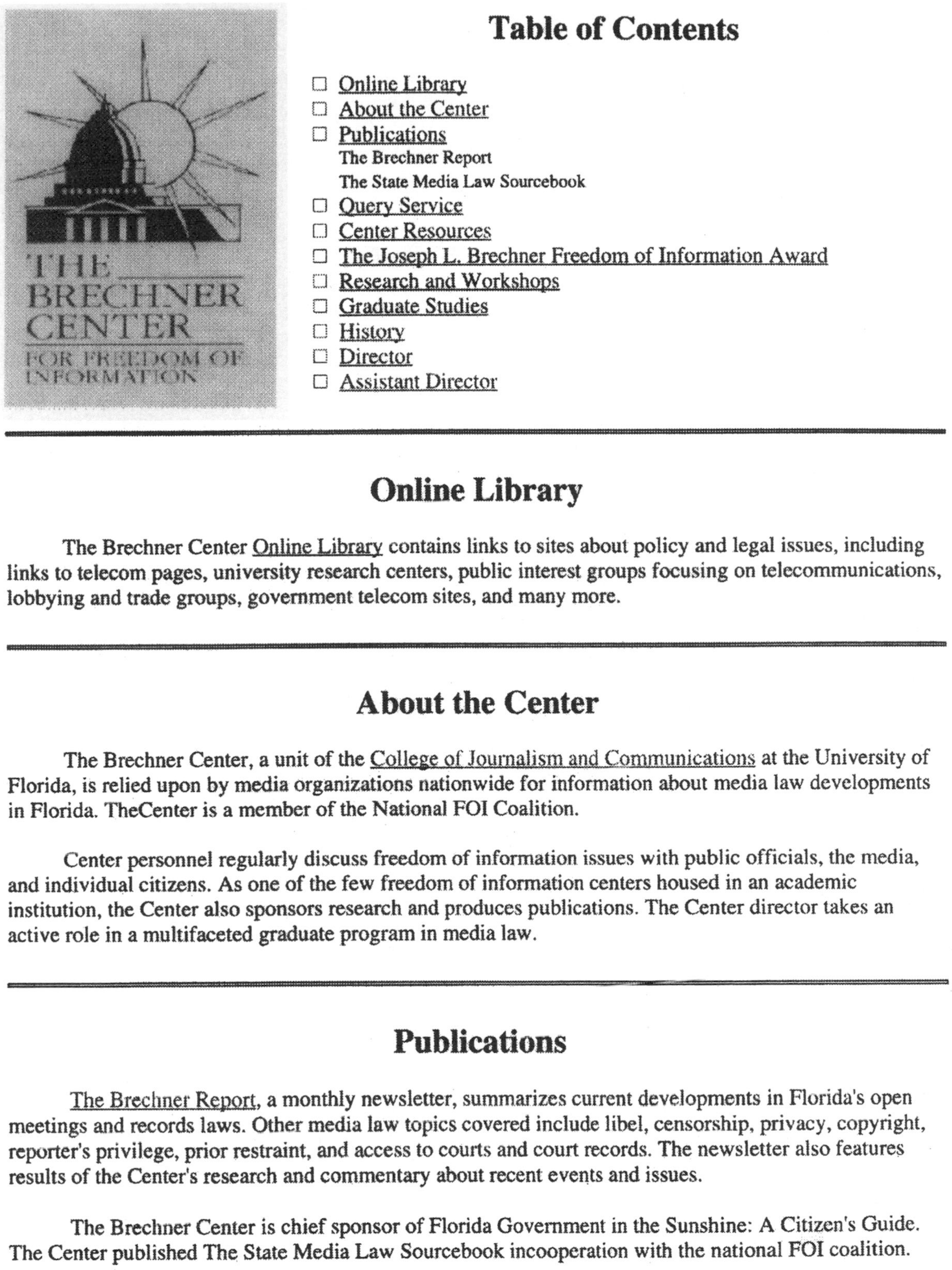

THE BRECHNER CENTER FOR FREEDOM OF INFORMATION

Table of Contents

- Online Library
- About the Center
- Publications
  - The Brechner Report
  - The State Media Law Sourcebook
- Query Service
- Center Resources
- The Joseph L. Brechner Freedom of Information Award
- Research and Workshops
- Graduate Studies
- History
- Director
- Assistant Director

Online Library

The Brechner Center Online Library contains links to sites about policy and legal issues, including links to telecom pages, university research centers, public interest groups focusing on telecommunications, lobbying and trade groups, government telecom sites, and many more.

About the Center

The Brechner Center, a unit of the College of Journalism and Communications at the University of Florida, is relied upon by media organizations nationwide for information about media law developments in Florida. TheCenter is a member of the National FOI Coalition.

Center personnel regularly discuss freedom of information issues with public officials, the media, and individual citizens. As one of the few freedom of information centers housed in an academic institution, the Center also sponsors research and produces publications. The Center director takes an active role in a multifaceted graduate program in media law.

Publications

The Brechner Report, a monthly newsletter, summarizes current developments in Florida's open meetings and records laws. Other media law topics covered include libel, censorship, privacy, copyright, reporter's privilege, prior restraint, and access to courts and court records. The newsletter also features results of the Center's research and commentary about recent events and issues.

The Brechner Center is chief sponsor of Florida Government in the Sunshine: A Citizen's Guide. The Center published The State Media Law Sourcebook incooperation with the national FOI coalition.

Fig. 3. The Brechner center page.

Internet newsgroups are so successful. Users coalesce around the interest groups focused on various topics and return again to the subjects they like, to look for new useful information and keep up with the discussion.

While we have made an initial effort in the area of forums much more might be done. Forums might be composed of student and faculty papers or projects, lists of resources related to the topic available on the Internet, and messages from visitors about the topic in question. Students might mediate Internet discussions on the topic using the Internet Relay Chat tool. This type of interaction would ensure that people think of the University of Florida's College of Journalism and

Communications as the place where something current and interesting could always be found.

The College's Information Technology Center is responsible for the technical and network-related aspects of the Web server. This includes keeping current on various problems and features of the software, learning about and acquiring upgrades as they become available, and explaining various features of the software to the faculty and staff. The ITC also assists faculty and staff with learning procedures involved in making information available via the network.

The control over most of the information has been distributed to the appropriate staff and faculty throughout the building. Shared directories are available on the college's computer network so faculty and staff can easily work with and save information to appear on the Web server. To maintain a sense of order, each academic department provides one or two faculty and/or staff advisors who monitor the information in that department's section of the information network. In some cases, a student assistant has been tapped from each department to act as a *liaison* to the ITC and to other faculty and staff advisors.

The tasks involved in maintaining and growing our Web server have been grouped into three primary jobs and an unlimited number of supplementary jobs. The primary jobs deal with the administration of the server as a whole, whereas the supplementary positions deal with specific areas of the server. The three primary positions are Administrator, Content Developer, and Research Leader. Each of these positions is a fuzzy outline of the primary focus of each individual's duties, not a hard division of thought or energy. Each of the individuals needs to be involved in all three areas and communicate regularly with the others on the best approaches and methods for completing tasks. Certain tasks cluster together, however, so the division of duties proposed here has worked out well.

Some Potential Problems

Creating and maintaining an organization's Web site is not without its problems. The Web has grown rapidly and unexpectedly and some managerial and legal issues have arisen.

Security/Public Access: A good basic rule about using the Web is, if you do not want the public to see a document, do not put it on the Web. Generally, the whole purpose of the Web is to facilitate the spread of information, so sensitive materials are "working against the grain" of the Web, at least as it is currently structured. Although "fire walls" and other techniques exist to limit or prevent access to computer networks, the determined hacker may be impossible to stop [7]. Thus even the most sophisticated organizations using the Web, such as the CIA, have also learned to take precautions [8].

Copyright: The ease of creating and posting materials to the Web, accessing information, and downloading text, graphics, and sounds can create copyright headaches. Be careful that materials for which copyright or trademark permission is not secured are not placed on your site. Many companies, such as Warner Brothers, have become aggressive in policing unlicensed use of their copyrighted characters on Web sites.

Similarly, your own copyrighted and trademarked materials can be easily downloaded by other users. While you may want to provide some reports, or other materials, protection of trademarks and copyrights requires diligence.

Consistency: Many corporations have design criteria for publications, stationery, etc. What about the Web? Should these decisions be made before posting to the Web, delaying access? Should there be a certain "anarchy," which will require some retrofitting to bring Web pages into line with ultimate design rules? Further, those design rules may require attention to details beyond those normally attended to by print designers. Some organizations have created style guides for their Web sites. The Yale Center for Advanced Instructional Media (http://info.med.yale.edu/caim/StyleManual_Top.HTML) has published a particularly useful manual.

Unwanted Links: The idea of the World Wide Web is to facilitate information, and the use of hypermedia allows for rapid access to documents everywhere. Much of the value of the Web has been that users have created active links to what they consider to be worthwhile sites elsewhere. Two problems have occurred because of the ease of linkage.

First, while I cannot force you to create a link to my site, I can create a link to yours. Web sites designed for a certain amount of traffic have shut down because the system cannot handle the number of calls. Some Web administrators are now advocating that permission be received before creating a link to another site. Second, problems have stemmed from employees creating links to sites that might not be something with which the organization wants to be associated. For example, one employee created a link to an adult picture Web site.

Despite these potential problems, the Web is, and will continue to be, a tool with tremendous potential for corporate communication.

References

[1] K. Hughes, "Entering the World-Wide Web," [http://www.eit.com:80/Web/www.guide/], 1995.

[2] J. Rickard, "World Wide Web traffic statistics—1814% explosion," *Boardwatch*, pp. 56–58, Jan. 1995.

[3] D. L. Hoffman and T. P. Novak, "Measuring the internet: Preliminary results of the commerce/Nielsen internet demographics survey," [http://www2000.ogsm.vanderbilt.edu/].

[4] L. Rosenfeld, "Site blueprints: The key to good Web hygiene," *Web Rev.*, [http://gnn.com/gnn/wr/design/arch/sept15/index.html], Sept. 15, 1995.

[5] L. Rosenfeld, "Structure and effectiveness," *Web Rev.*, [http://gnn.com/gnn/wr/design/arch/aug17/index.html], Aug. 17, 1995.

[6] T. Bajarin, "More than a brochure," *Web Rev.*, [http://gnn.com/gnn/wr/nov10/biz/bajarin/index.html], Nov. 10, 1995.

[7] M. Erwin, "Adding security to your Web site," *Boardwatch*, pp. 54–56, Oct. 1995.

[8] *Investor's Business Daily*, p. A8, Feb. 14, 1995.

Gary Ritzenthaler is completing the M.A. degree at the University of Florida, Gainesville. He is also a consultant to newspapers and other organizations about Web use.

David H. Ostroff is Professor of Journalism and Communications at the University of Florida, Gainesville, where he serves as Graduate Coordinator in the Department of Telecommunication.

Editing a Web Site: Extending the Levels of Edit

—Steven L. Anderson,
Charles P. Campbell,
Member, IEEE,
Nancy Hindle,
Jonathan Price, and
Randall Scasny

Abstract—*For technical editors accustomed to preparing manuscripts for print, editing in the new medium of the World Wide Web can prove challenging. This article suggests how technical editors can prepare themselves by adapting the Levels of Edit concept, long used in the technical editing of books, articles, and reports, to deal with the different requirements of this new medium.*

Index Terms—*Levels of Edit, technical editing, Web editors, World Wide Web.*

Manuscript received November 15, 1997.
The authors are with the Department of Humanities, New Mexico Institute of Mining and Technology, Socorro, NM 87801 USA.
IEEE PII S 0361-1434(98)01976-6.

THIS article describes lessons learned by an editing class at the New Mexico Institute of Mining and Technology when they attempted to edit a Web site created by others [1]. Far from being the simple text-editing project the students expected, their venture turned into a major overhaul of the site, dealing with screen design, coding, interface issues, and interactivity. The Levels of Edit concept, familiar to most editors, provided a framework to help the class organize the work. As used in this Elements of Editing class [2], the Levels of Edit look like this:

- Level Three focuses on content and structure. Its overriding concern is rhetorical: does the document achieve its objectives?
- Level Two involves stylistic changes to the prose to reduce wordiness, enhance clarity, and improve cohesion.
- Level One covers issues of convention and rule that can be decided by authorities such as style sheets, style guides, handbooks, and company policy. Its central concerns are consistency and correctness.

How the Project Started

Many first-generation Web sites have been put up hugger-mugger, in a rush. Certainly that was true for the Humanities Department at New Mexico Tech. In 1995, Jonathan Price designed the site [1], calling upon his many years of experience consulting, writing, and teaching hypertext. The structure and text (much borrowed from the college catalog) were then converted into HTML and put up on the Web by Chuck Campbell, who also teaches the editing course in the Technical Communication program.

A year later, Price and Campbell could see that the site needed work. Extra sets of pages had been attached to the site. The layout of some pages had been changed, sometimes dramatically, and with the addition of student and faculty home pages, the site had grown like a city without a planning department. Campbell decided that editing the Web site would make a good project for his class, in Elements of Editing, with students Anderson, Hindle, and Scasny. Campbell was looking for a group project like ones his editing classes had done in the past—projects that involved working together as editors and interacting with clients.

Reprinted from *IEEE Trans. Prof. Comm.*, vol. PC-41, no. 1, pp. 47–56, March 1998.

Typically, the editing class [2] spends some time working individually on Level Two issues (clarity and coherence) and Level One issues (correctness and consistency). Usually, a group project provides most of the Level Three experience that can be packed into a sophomore-level course. Price agreed to act as client, and asked the class to consider four questions about the Web site:

- Is the information adequate for the people who will visit the site?
- Is the structure clear?
- Can you navigate easily?
- Is the tone appropriate?

At first glance, the student editors concluded that the site contained enough information, in a few dozen pages; but as they explored more deeply, they discovered that there were actually 59 separate files, containing more than 8000 words. The site looked simpler than it was.

Contemplating the structure, the class spotted three interrelated problems. First, several new sets of pages had been added, dealing with the Writing Center, the student chapter of the Society for Technical Communication, plus student and faculty home pages. Second, though nominally the Humanities Department Web site, most of the pages described the Technical Communication program, which offers a Bachelor of Science degree. This program is the only major offered by the Humanities Department, which otherwise provides the liberal arts component (foreign languages, philosophy, history, and English) of science and engineering degrees offered by Tech's other departments. And third, the layout of pages varied in different areas, suggesting that the visitor had somehow left Humanities and entered whole new worlds. For these reasons, the editors felt that the structure was no longer entirely clear, and so navigation also seemed a bit uncertain.

In addition, the tone, particularly of catalog entries, seemed too academic to the class. Their concern provoked a discussion of audience, during which the editors decided to expand the intended audience beyond current students and faculty to include alumni and potential students, who might be cruising the Net looking at colleges. That change meant that we needed to modify the tone throughout, to make it more informal, conversational, and appealing.

Levels of Edit as a Conceptual Guide

Given all the concerns about the site, we found that the Levels of Edit approach, familiar to editors of print documents, offered a way of organizing and understanding the work. The Levels approach helps editors define, ahead of time, the type of editing that is to be done. Levels may be described informally as "light, regular, or heavy," or elaborately, as with the nine-level structure developed at the Jet Propulsion Laboratory [3]. Three levels seem to provide the most widely used framework. For example, Donald Samson in *Editing Technical Writing* recommends three "degrees" of edit [4]. Likewise, the central communication group at Los Alamos National Laboratory has recently moved from a four-level to a three-level system [5].

The role of the Level Three editor, as presented in Campbell's editing class, is analogous to that of an architect on a remodeling project; of the Level Two editor, to that of framing carpenters and masons; of the Level One editor, to that of the finish carpenters and trim workers.

For print documents, editing at the different levels may take place in different "shops." In the book publishing trade, for example, a general editor makes major design and content decisions; a developmental editor tends to work on the structure and prose, with perhaps a little attention to the use of visuals to augment the text; a copy editor deals with issues of correct language; and a production editor confirms the correctness of format, ensures the integrity of text and art files, and coordinates the many overlapping tasks involved in printing. The half-life of a textbook produced by this process can be measured in years.

Perhaps the print situation closest to Web sites is the manual set that comes in loose-leaf form for easy updating. For the manual set, top-level decisions about design, layout, audience, and format tend not to change much over time, though change pages may be sent out several times a year. The structure and the page numbering scheme allow for additions, deletions, and substitutions. Most of the editing is at Levels One and Two.

Though analogous to manuals, Web sites do not lend themselves so easily to this kind of compartmentalization. For one thing, a Web site is more evanescent than a book or a manual set. It is much easier (if not actually easy) to make major changes in structure and layout. Because Web sites are interactive, they can be changed more readily in response to needs expressed by visitors.

Hence, a more appropriate paradigm for Web site editing would be interactive rather than production-line oriented. An interactive paradigm for design might be based on a work such as that of Kaufer and Butler, whose *Rhetoric and the Arts of Design* [6] theorizes interactive modules in rhetorical design space: *plans*, or underlying worldview; *tactics*, or the means for achieving objectives; and most importantly for the editor, *events*, or response in real time to input from the environment. Kaufer and Butler's paradigm is intended for oral discourse, but Web sites resemble oral discourse more than books in terms of interactivity.

This interactivity makes the style of working together very different.

Publishing a book requires serial cooperation—different editors applying their particular expertise to a manuscript, one after another, with discussion occurring mainly at the intersections of tasks. Web site editing, on the other hand, requires that people with different expertise collaborate in real time: content is affected by design parameters; design is constrained by HTML coding possibilities; HTML and screen sizes affect content.

In addition, because of this interactivity, when editors turn their attention from paper documents to screen materials on the World Wide Web, the nature of editorial work changes at each of the three main levels of edit:

- At Level Three, which deals with the big-picture issues, editors may find themselves refining the definition of the audience, rethinking the categories of information, building a hierarchical model of the information on the site, tinkering with that structure, modifying the screen layout, then calling on users to report their moment-to-moment experience of the site as it undergoes revision.
- At Level Two, which in print editing aims at improving the clarity and cohesion of the prose, editors still have plenty of traditional work to do on the language, but may find themselves modifying style more aggressively than before, and trimming verbiage with a sharper blade.
- At Level One, which is concerned with correctness and consistency, editors still need a style guide but must add many new issues to their list: enforcing file-naming and layout conventions, confirming links, and correcting HTML tags.

Level Three Editing

Level Three editing of Web sites, we found, required us to ask fundamental design questions:

- Who visits the site, for what reasons?
- What kind of site structure best matches visitors' needs to the Web site's purpose?
- What kind of page layout best matches visitors' needs to the Web site's purpose?

These design questions led in turn to implementation questions:

- How is the site actually structured?
- What style conventions should we follow?
- Which version of HTML do we use?
- How can we know whether our design decisions are effective?

Design Decisions

Refining the audience definition: Redefining the audience may be the greatest challenge a Web site editor faces. In book publishing, the audience is pretty well defined when the contract is signed by the acquisitions editor; all editors downstream need only follow that lead. But the Web beckons many unexpected visitors, some of whom must be reckoned with after the initial site has been created. For example, when the student editors reviewed the Humanities Department Web site, they sensed that it was intended primarily for current students and professors. The language emphasized the mission of the Humanities Department and its academic importance in a university curriculum. The pages looked formal—almost official. The student editors concluded that the Web site ought to extend its appeal to prospective students, most of whom are in high school or other colleges, business people who might be interested in hiring our graduates, and casual surfers.

Rethinking the structure: Generally, in book publishing, the time for restructuring is early. A developmental editor may suggest changing the order of chapters, or the sequence of topics within a chapter, starting with the writer's outline, and continuing during the writer's first pass through the material. But with a Web site, the editor often faces a *fait accompli* because earlier materials have been cobbled together and posted, just to "get something up on the Web." The result is not as carefully thought out as a book. In our case, the editors faced multiple page sets added after the original design (a writing center, a student society, and many individual home pages), plus an uncertain relationship between the Technical Communication program, which had more than half the pages, and its parent, the Humanities Department, which includes many other subjects. The editors debated how far to distinguish the program from the department. Should they be separate but equal because the program is the only one within the department that actually grants a degree? Or should the program appear as a component of its department? As a compromise solution, the editors showed the program as part of the department but created distinct page layouts, using different background colors within a similar frame structure. Hence, reopening the issue of structure led to reorganization of the items on menus and redesign of the actual pages.

Redesigning the layout: Editors used to working within a fixed corporate book design may be surprised to find themselves debating background colors, frames, and tables when the constant change of Web content explodes layouts that worked fine with fewer topics or less complex relationships between topics. In our project, layout turned into an ongoing discussion, revolving around the related problems of navigation, identification, and presentation of content. To provide constant access to a high level menu, the editors decided to create a frame on the left (but what topics, exactly, would appear there?). To identify the site, the editors conceived a banner frame at the top (but should that always say "Humanities Department" or should it sometimes say "Technical Communication?"). And, for the text itself, the editors came up with a frame on the right (but that left so little room that some text had to be rechunked and reassembled). Hence, user interface problems drove the team to a fundamental redesign of the page layout.

And within this new frame structure, the editors chose a light-brown background and chocolate-colored text for the Humanities pages, to give it a somewhat warmer look, and picked a slate-gray background with black text for the Technical Communication pages, for a more professional look [1]. Hence, a concern for Level Two cohesion within each section resulted in a Level Three design decision to refine the page design even further.

Choosing a version of HTML: A major difference we found between editing print and editing Web sites was the amount of technical knowledge required. Print editors even in the age of word processors still tend to do their editing on paper; they may need computer skills only to the extent of being able to enter their edits onto a word processor file. A Web site editor, on the other hand, cannot do without a working knowledge of HTML.

Choosing a version of HTML may seem like an overly technical question for editors as a Level Three decision; indeed, it is a question that editors might not raise if they are accustomed to using a word processor or browser's automatic HTML formatting features. But it is important to consider because HTML is not the same from browser to browser. What looks nifty in one may not work on another.

Though official groups have been propounding standards over the years, the "correct" version of HTML is often that used by the currently most popular browser. First, there was Mosaic, propagated among the Unix community; then came Netscape and the commercial explosion of the Internet. Now Microsoft's Internet Explorer is the up-and-coming browser *du jour.* With competition heating up, each software company adds its own special tags to make its browser better than the competition's. The result: some features that can be viewed in, for example, Netscape Communicator are not visible in Internet Explorer, and *vice versa.*

Further, those who like standards insist that HTML follow a SGML document-type definition (DTD). SGML is Standard Generalized Markup Language, defined in ISO Standard 8879:1986 [7]. It is a meta-language for defining document structures for the application of mark-up schemes. SGML itself is not a mark-up scheme. It does not define mark-up tags nor does it provide a template for a particular type of document. Rather, it denotes a way of describing any mark-up scheme. HTML is one of the document types that have been defined using SGML [8].

So the question of which HTML version to use becomes a difficult one. The best answer is to balance the needs of a site with the desire for correctness. If adding the tag of the week does not detract from the reusability of the site and it really adds to the effectiveness of it, then by all means use it. Be aware, however, that tag may not work on all the browsers, and it may be phased out in the next release of the same browser, bringing up problems for future maintenance.

Implementation Decisions

Making a site map: As they began to think about editing individual sections, the editors realized that they did not know which files corresponded to which pages displayed in the browser. They had to find the right file by trial and error, which often took a long time. Also, several times, one editor would accidentally modify a file that someone else was working on. Such confusion would not occur in a well-run publishing house because the production editor would have imposed discipline on the file names, but in the wonderful wide-open world of the Web, many individuals can hook up to the site, without following any file conventions. The result is a directory full of weird names in no particular order with no recognizable connection to the titles displayed on screen.

As an aid to the editors, Anderson created a top-level site map, showing the screens accessible through the top few levels of the menu and their corresponding HTML files. This tree structure was such a help that the editors longed for a complete one to locate every file quickly.

Creating a style guide: As a new genre within a relatively new medium, the Web offers few established conventions, and even fewer usable style guides. Perhaps, the best to date is the one put out by Patrick Lynch and Sarah Horton, which approaches Web page and site design as "a challenge that combines traditional editorial approaches to documents with graphic design, user interface design, information design, and the technical authoring skills required to optimize the HTML code, graphics, and text within Web pages" [9]. Like the style guides posted by Ameritech [10], Apple [11], and Sun [12], the Yale guide is generic. We needed one of our own. But we did not create it at the beginning of the project, and for that we suffered. As a team, the editors agreed roughly on many issues but differed when applying those decisions on particular pages; so variations appeared in graphics, frames, background and text colors, and titling. With a real style guide, the editors could have avoided hours of guesswork and re-editing.

Testing the Effectiveness of the Redesigned Site

Touring like a user: After some changes had been made, the editors asked Price, as client, to take a tour of the evolving site. Sensing that the editors, focusing on large issues of design and organization, had lost touch with the experience of a real user moving through the site, he reported as if he were a visitor in a foreign land. Without much regard for the editors' sensibilities, he wrote down how he reacted to the text, art, and layout, moment to moment. In essence, he recorded an emotional, intellectual, and entirely personal tour, very unlike the diplomatic queries most editors have been trained to raise with authors. The point was to shock the editors into recognizing the actual, felt experience a user might have moving through the online system. Looked at intellectually, the structure may be fine, but hell to go through. Price stressed the cycle of choice, movement, adjustment to the new location, exploration, and decision to move on. Many sites seem OK in terms of information but give the user an experience something like going down a zigzagging tunnel with blinders on. No exit. Movement through is the defining experience for users, and the editors needed to get a sense of what their site felt like, to a user. Here's a sample from the narrative:

When I click the link to Technical Communications within the text on the Humanities page, the Humanities banner remains where it was, and the yellow menu stays in place, but on the right I see a list of topics. The first one, Technical Communication, seems to be a title.

Is it just a title for this list, or is it a clickable item that can take me somewhere else? If the text is a link to some other location, I wonder what information I will find there?

So, like an idiot, I click it and discover I have wiped out the banner altogether, and gotten rid of the left-hand menu. But I have not made any progress toward finding out about Technical Communication, because I am still looking at the same list. So I have gone somewhere, but I have gone nowhere; I have destroyed, but not made progress. Disconcerting!

This review shocked the team into reconsidering its working methods because the lack of coordination was clearly leading to bumps in the road for the user. The editors found that the personal narrative, internal monologue, and emotional tone of the tour made them more aware of the confusion felt by a user. That discussion led to increased efforts at improving clarity and cohesion, as well as simple consistency—in other words, to renewed work at Levels Two and One.

Level Two Editing

As in Level Three, we found that differences between print and Web site editing at Level Two put a premium on the visual. In print, Level Two editing aims to improve clarity and cohesion of prose. It also checks for overall document cohesion by verifying cross-references within the text. With a Web site, prose can be made clear and concise by familiar strategies: using direct, referential nouns and vivid verbs; avoiding sentences that sprawl across the screen so that they create a visual block, both literally and metaphorically. Text is made concise by dividing it into small units so that each screen contains one complete thought and relates clearly to other units on other pages. The pages of our site had been designed in small units in the first place, so we did not have to create many new pages. Our Level Two editing consisted mostly of making sure that links were meaningful so that a user interested in finding more information could travel deeper into the site or to linked sites, pursuing a line of thought. The

TABLE I
Level Three Differences:
Print Versus Web Site

Print	**Web site**
Cooperation: serial steps in editing and production	*Collaboration*: working together in real time
Audience Definition a given: Polishing and updating prose	*Audience Definition* refined: Rethinking site structure
Style and tools: Using mandated tools Following approved style guides	*Using any tools that create HTML*: Choosing a version of HTML Creating a style guide for the site
Document control: Tracking files related to project	*Site map*: Naming conventions for all files related to project
Design testing: Internal/external review processes	*Touring like a user*: Trial by client

ability to pursue a line of thought gives the users the impression that the site is coherent.

Improving Clarity and Cohesion Ensuring clarity and cohesion is a little different on a screen than on a printed page. We tend to think that words, more than visual attributes, dictate the message on a printed page, with each paragraph supporting the theme and providing a transition to the subsequent paragraph. Since a Web page is more a graphical than a textual medium, Web site developers often use visual attributes to communicate information or tell their story at the expense of a textual narrative. While these visual attributes can add to the message, they can also detract from the clarity of the Web page if they are overused or inconsistently applied or if they overwhelm the screen. So whether an editor is working with text or visual attributes, the same kinds of questions apply to both:

- Is there an underlying grid which organizes the page's components?
- Are components grouped by function? For example, are all menu items in the same area?
- Are all graphics in the same style?

Though these questions arise for printed pages as well as screens, readers have more tactics, such as skimming and browsing, for dealing with bad design in books than in Web sites.

For the student editors in their initial visits to the Humanities Web site, many of the pages were difficult to read because each screen covered a lot of information. They found that what may be coherent on paper may seem overwhelming on screen. This effect may occur if the screen is thought of as equivalent to a paper page.

A better way of looking at editing a screen is to think of it as a paragraph: only one main idea should be presented on each screen. Since there will be many screens to bridge these "paragraphs" together, cohesion devices must be applied to make a series of screens feel consistent and function as a group. For example, repetition of words on page headings helps users know they are still following a consistent theme within a group of pages: e.g., "What do technical communicators do?" linked to "Where do technical communicators work?"

Transitions from one screen to another become the subject of debate. Traditional prose transition devices ("as we have just seen," "therefore") do not work on a Web site because the user may not follow the intended sequence. Prose transitions to subsequent pages will work if the user can be counted on to select the "next" button. But users (as opposed to readers) cannot be counted on to follow the intended order. So named-topic links instead of "next" and "previous" were inserted.

Modifying Style to Reflect New Audience Definition Matching style to audience is a task familiar to most writers and editors. However, we quickly understood that our audience was much wider and more diverse than the audience the students had inferred from browsing. After we had some long discussions about audience, with some reluctance by some members of the class, we made some choices about a style that would appeal to an additional target audience—prospective students.

To make the Web site more appealing to prospective students, we changed to a more informal style. Here is a before and after look of a description of the purpose of humanities courses at a technical college on the Humanities homepage:

> **Before:**
> *As part of their college experience, students should grow toward critical awareness and broad understanding of the ideas and values that have characterized human history and experience.*
>
> **After:**
> *Our students take Humanities courses to give them the ethical, historical and multicultural sensitivities to create technologies that people need, want, and can use for the benefit of all.*

Our client and the class agreed the style changes made the page more appealing to our audience. Changing the style to a simple, no-frills language also improved the clarity and the impact of the page.

Compressing and reducing verbiage: Web site editors, more than editors working in print media, have to think about how the medium itself affects the way people read. If a book is interesting and well written, a reader can tolerate long paragraphs. Even if the pages on a Web site are well written, long paragraphs are likely to inspire surfers to go elsewhere because reading a typical screen is like reading a fax: the resolution, being lower than that of print, strains the eyes. While writers rely on their words and may fear that they are not being complete enough if they do not write detailed text, the reality is that if there is too much text on a screen, viewers just skip it. The point is not to delete important details, just to present them in a way that is visually appealing. It is better to write the minimum necessary on each screen, and if more is needed, to put it on the next screen or add another one.

We did not learn these lessons without some trial and error. After updating our style, and our text, we viewed it. The first thing which came to mind was, "Yeah, it's better, but wow, there are so many words!" The screen communicates more graphically than textually. We concluded that we must tell our "story" with visual content and pare the text to essential information.

Level One Editing

In print, Level One editing is concerned with correctness and consistency. With a Web site, editors must still scan for correctness in grammar, usage, mechanics, punctuation, and spelling. These issues did not take much time when we edited the Humanities Web site. Consistency issues, however, did loom large. Because of the relatively large number of pages, consistency in look was important. Once we had made Level Three decisions on page design and background color, we expedited the Level One work by creating templates and migrating the text onto them.

Following a style: Following a consistent style is as important in editing HTML as in editing print. One of the most commonly seen errors on a first-generation site is inconsistency of look and feel, caused by inconsistent coding in HTML. These lapses make the work appear either incomplete or unprofessional, just as in print media.

Style guides and style sheets for the print media are used in situations that are rhetorically fossilized, situations where conventions are so well established that it no longer seems necessary to do any additional thinking about the nature of the print medium or the needs of readers. Since the Web has barely had time enough to develop conventions, let alone fossilize them, the kinds of issues that might be enshrined in style guides are likely to be less concerned with orthographic and grammatical correctness than with standardization. One such issue has to do with the kinds of equipment users have. A frequent complaint is that Web designers create sites that work very well for people with fast computers and direct links to the Internet, but try the patience of those who must use older computers with slow modems. And in response, many sites are now designed with text-only options.

As noted earlier, we did not create a style sheet at the outset but came to wish we had. Such a style guide would have described the layout of two template pages, one for Humanities and one for Technical Communication. It would have specified background color code, heading sizes, titling, and link-button placement. It would have named any graphic files we were using for backgrounds or bullets. And it would have formalized the site's file-naming scheme.

Correcting to standards: Correcting to standards is the stock-in-trade of copy editors in publishing; far too often, it is also the main work of technical editors. The standards are published in those style guides which are ubiquitous in editing for the professions. Not only does each profession tend to have its own style guide, so does each publication within the profession. The advantage of style guides is that they save much reinventing of wheels. Their disadvantage is that effectiveness-oriented editors find them picayune and tedious; they aren't much use beyond imposing conventions consistently.

Style-guide standards for print may carry over into Web site editing for such matters as terminology and spelling. However, rules regarding the handling in print of tables, figures, and references may need modification, since a table on a Web site may provide a page's structure. Figures are usually the dominant feature of any Web page, and references may be handled by a link directly to the cited source.

Web pages' prose should follow established conventions for spelling, grammar, and usage. For spelling, people seem to rely too much on spell checkers, which are notoriously bad at selecting among homophones. ("Among the cites to be scene in Florida...") Editors still need word knowledge. For grammar, given that the Web as a whole is meant for browsing more than reading, it is best to use the natural, unforced constructions of common speech.

Enforcing file-naming conventions: File naming conventions are commonly used in both print media and computer programming. However, they appear to be uncommon in most first-generation Web sites. This is not surprising considering that many sites originate in a piecemeal fashion, creating

TABLE II
Level Two Differences:
Print Versus Web Site

Print	**Web site**
Focus mostly on text	Focus also on structure and layout
Revising style for original audience	Modifying prose style for new audience
Textual coherence devices: inchworming, topic strings in paragraphs, transitional words and phrases	Navigation tools: visual continuity devices and orienters
Compressing and reducing verbiage to improve flow and coherence	Compressing and reducing verbiage to reduce screen clutter

a trickle of new files without any consistent naming structure or file organization. Once a site has been created this way, it is quite difficult to correct. The best way we have found to correct this is to create a mirror of the original site on disk and edit the mirror files, updating the file names and links from the planned site map. Having this mirror image on disk also helps for version control and site comparison.

File-naming conventions should be laid out in the style guide. A naming scheme should reflect the hierarchical structure of the site map. For example, in our site, we had two major divisions, Humanities and Technical Communication. Thus it was natural to begin filenames with either "hum" or "tc."

Enforcing layout conventions: Layout includes the background color, font color, text placement, frames, headers, footers, and graphics. Our Level Three decision to use a similar frame structure to provide visual continuity between the Humanities and Technical Communication pages (we used two horizontal frames, the top one carrying the logo for each page set, but decided on a left-vertical frame with a Table of Contents look for the menu) resulted in our creating a template for each kind of page. The Level One work, then, involved transferring text that had survived the other two levels to the templates, then renaming the resultant files according to the file-naming scheme that was already in place.

The hardest part of the layout to enforce were the colors of background and text. Everyone was working on different computers, which translated HTML color codes into different visible hues on the computer screens. In print, it is possible to specify colors very exactly. In HTML, if the editor specifies a 256-color palette, about 210 of them will be the same regardless of whether the viewing platform is running a Mac, PC, or Unix operating system. Still, no two monitors render colors exactly the same way. Editors can only try to look at the colors on as many different platforms and monitors as possible, then modify the hexadecimal color codes so the colors look reasonably close on most of them.

Link checking: One of the greatest advantages of hypertext is that it lets the reader choose his or her own path through a series of documents. But very few things are more frustrating than choosing a link and getting an error message or a page whose subject matter is different than what the link promised. Link checking ensures that these types of errors do not occur.

There were several ways we checked links. We began with a computer-based link checker program called Linklint [13]. It is easy to use and quickly verified our links. But no matter how good a program is, a computer-based link checker cannot ensure the links point to the right places; it can only check to make sure that the destination of the link exists. For example, if a link to information about hiring practices at your company actually brings up a table of quarterly earnings instead, a computer-based link checker would say it was correct. Therefore, links must be checked manually for correct content and context.

After manually checking our links, we then used a link-checking service available on the Web called NetMechanic [14]. Services like NetMechanic have an advantage over locally installed link checkers because they do not require users to spend the time installing and setting up the software on their computers. NetMechanic will check Web sites up to 250 pages for no charge. Both Linklint and NetMechanic found similar link errors on our Web site. After we made corrections, we used both techniques through several cycles to ensure that we did not introduce any new link errors.

Correcting HTML: It is now possible to do much editing with programs such as Netscape Gold or the HTML formatting features in WordPerfect 7 or MS Word 7. With the advent of these more graphical HTML editing programs, there is a tendency to dismiss the need to understand HTML. The results produced by the graphical editors are often acceptable, but when a page just refuses to look as the

TABLE III
LEVEL ONE DIFFERENCES:
PRINT VERSUS WEB SITE

Print	**Web site**
Correcting to Standard Written English	Correcting to more informal standards
Following a style sheet for text	Following a style sheet for text and layout
Following file name conventions	Enforcing file name conventions
Verifying index, table of contents, figure and table numbering	Link checking
Verifying copy changes	Correcting HTML

editor thinks it should, the editor still needs to be able to open HTML files in a plain text (ASCII) editing program to change the codes.

In ASCII, the coded tags appear as text; any words that appear between arrows (<>) are read by the browser as commands to produce certain effects, as in this example:

<strong> This is emphasized text. </strong>

The browser boldfaces the text enclosed between the tags so that it appears thus:

This is emphasized text

Ensuring that such tagging is correct can be done several different ways. If the HTML is composed to work best on a particular browser, one obvious way to test is to look at each page in that browser to see that it displays correctly.

Another way of checking HTML is to use a validating program, such as Clark's SP [15]. Such a program checks the HTML against a standard. Also available for validating HTML are some online services as well [16]. However, even if these programs show tags to be invalid, pages may still display correctly. Not all tags produce visible effects. The DOCTYPE tag produces no effect whatsoever. Neither does the HTML, HEAD, or any of the META tags.

If a validation program sends a warning about a page, it may be best to look at the page in several browsers to see whether it displays correctly. If a page does not display correctly, the editor may need to have knowledge of HTML to diagnose the problem and correct the tags. On our site, very few pages validate without errors, but all of them display correctly in Netscape, Internet Explorer, and other browsers.

Conclusion

Our experience suggests that the original idea of Levels of Edit continues to be a useful way for editors to conceptualize the different kinds of work they must do, even when they are approaching a Web site. In this article, then, we have pointed out some of the ways in which Web site editing extends the responsibilities of the editor at each level.

- The most significant changes occur at Level Three, where Web site editors may have to refine the audience definition, reorganize the information, and redesign the page layouts—all major rhetorical challenges to the existing material, challenges that rarely arise when updating an existing paper document. These decisions, in turn, call for a thoughtful choice of a version of HTML, the quick creation of a site map, and the making of a new or drastically revised style guide. And after all Level Three edits had been made, we found we needed a new kind of testing, one that would yield not just polite queries to the makers about phrasing, but a report on the existential experience of a user, to point out where the movement through the site might get confusing.
- Level Two editing, with its concern for clarity and cohesion, also had to take into account the Web's electronic medium, which emphasizes the visual design of the page, the user's movement from one page to another, and the resultant demand for shorter and shorter texts, modified to address the newly discovered audiences.
- Level One editing, as with print materials, continues to emphasize following a consistent style, correcting to standards, and following conventions, but requires the additional chores of checking links and debugging HTML tags.

When first exploring a Web site that has been cobbled together from contributions made by many different groups of people acting independently, editors may find themselves endeavoring to answer a bewildering variety of questions involving structure, style, and design, all raised by the electronic nature of the medium, the mercurial mutability of its audiences, and the breathtaking speed at which tools, tastes, and conventions change on the Web. In this mild chaos, the editor of a Web site may be reassured to know that by following the traditional Levels of Edit approach, sanity may be regained; and that the Levels offer a reasonable way to think about the work to be done on the Web site. Thus the Web expands our definition of the activities at each level, allowing us to pursue the same ideals through a new medium.

References

[1] The "before" version at the site: <http://www.cramer.nmt.edu/Fall95>. The edited version: <http://www.cramer.nmt.edu>Fall 96. The Fall 1997 editing class, capitalizing on the experience set forth in this article, has further refined the site: (28 Jan, 98) <http://www.cramer.nmt.edu/ntc 2021>.

[2] C. Campbell, Syllabus: TC 202, "Elements of Editing" <http://www.

cramer.nmt.edu~cpc/edit/> (28 Jan. 98).

[3] R. Van Buren and M. F. Buehler, *The Levels of Edit,* 2nd ed. Pasadena, CA: Jet Propulsion Lab., 1980. In a July 1993 letter to Campbell, Buehler wrote, "I am a little concerned that people will think they have to use the Levels of Edit just as we did...People have been adapting the Levels of Edit for many years...and this is what we at JPL have encouraged people to do from the beginning."

[4] D. Samson, *Editing Technical Writing.* New York: Oxford, 1993.

[5] J. Prono, "Changing from four to three levels of edit at Los Alamos National Laboratory," presentation for STC Kachina Chapter, Jan. 11, 1997.

[6] D. S. Kaufer and B. S. Butler, *Rhetoric and the Arts of Design.* Mahwah, NJ: Lawrence Erlbaum, 1996.

[7] For more information on using SGML see C. F. Goldfarb, *The SGML Handbook,* Y. Rubinsky, Ed. Oxford: Oxford Univ. Press, 1990; see also the SGML Web Page: <http://www.sil.org/sgml/sgml.html> (28 Jan. 90).

[8] The DTD of HTML 3.2 was created and stored online. <http://www.w3.org>: the HTML 3.2 Reference Specification: <http://www.w3.org/TR/REC-html32.html> (28 Jan. 98).

[9] P. J. Lynch and S. Horton, "The Yale CAIM Style Guide," 2nd ed.: [Online]. Available HTTP: <http:/info.med.yale.edu/caim/manual/> (28 Jan. 98).

[10] Ameritech Web Page User Interface and Design Guidelines: <http://www.ameritech.com/news/testtown/library/standard/web_guidelines/> (30 Oct. 97).

[11] Apple Web Design Guide: <http://applenet.apple.com/hi/web/intro.html> (30 Oct. 97).

[12] Sun style guide: <http:// www.sun.com/styleguide/> (30 Oct. 97).

[13] Linklint: <http://www.goldwarp.com/bowlin/linklint/> (30 Oct. 97).

[14] Net Mechanic: < http://www.netmechanic.com> (30 Oct. 97).

[15] J. Clark: <http://www.jclark.com> (30 Oct. 97).

[16] HTML Validation Tools site: <http://www.cre.canon.co.uk/ neilb/weblint/validation.html>. See also Yahoo's section on HTML validation: <http://www.yahoo.com/computers_and_internet/information_and_documentation/data_formats/html/> (30 Oct. 97).

Steven L. Anderson is a senior in Technical Communication at New Mexico Tech. He has returned to college after several years working at the New Mexico Petroleum Recovery Research Center as a technical writer. He is also currently employed at the New Mexico Tech Computer Center researching and developing a documentation system. His main areas of study are online communication and structured documents.

Charles P. Campbell (A'90–M'96) chairs the Humanities Department at New Mexico Tech (Socorro, NM) and teaches editing in the Technical Communication program. A Member of IEEE, he has contributed several articles to this TRANSACTIONS. He is coauthor, with Donald W. Bush, of *How to Edit Technical Documents* (Oryx, 1995) and its companion exercise book.

Nancy Hindle, biography not available at the time of publication.

Jonathan Price is Associate Professor in the Technical Communication program at New Mexico Institute of Mining and Technology, focusing on online information design. The author of more than two dozen books, including *How to Write a Computer Manual*, and *How to Communicate Technical Information*, with Henry Korman. He frequently gives workshops and speeches at professional meetings of technical writers, designers, and managers. He is Features Editor of a Webzine at http://www.thunderbeam.com.

Randall Scasny is an undergraduate Technical Communication student at the New Mexico Institute of Mining and Technology. He is a member of the student chapter of the Society of Technical Communication. He is also the editor of the student newspaper, *Paydirt*.

Web Accessibility for People With Disabilities: An Introduction for Web Developers

—JEFF CARTER
AND MIKE MARKEL

Abstract—*This article presents an overview of the topic of web access for people with disabilities. First, we describe the four basic disabilities and explain the benefits of making sites accessible, as well as the reasons that more sites are not accessible. We review the relevant laws regarding web access, and we then discuss efforts being made by vendors and professional organizations, especially Microsoft and the World Wide Web Consortium, to encourage accessibility. Finally, we describe major resources that web developers might consult to assist them in making their sites accessible to people with disabilities.*

Index Terms—*Accessibility, Americans with Disabilities Act, disabilities, technical communication, World Wide Web.*

Manuscript received November 20, 2000; revised June 3, 2001.
J. Carter is with Marketron, Inc., 101 Empty Saddle Trail, Hailey, ID 83333 USA (email: Jcarter@marketron.com).
M. Markel is with Boise State University, Boise, ID 83725 USA (email: mmarkel@boisestate.edu).
IEEE PII S 0361-1434(01)10135-9.

As Tim Berners-Lee, World Wide Web Consortium (W3C) Director and inventor of the World Wide Web, said,"The power of the web is in its universality. Access by everyone regardless of disability is an essential aspect" [1]. Mike Paciello, author of the accessibility resource site WebABLE!, calls the introduction of the web and its subsequent evolution the near-complete "publishing paradigm shift," one that has resulted in increased access to "a global information set never before achieved" [2]. But what began as primarily a text- and number-based medium has evolved into one laden with detailed graphics, animated pictures, and complex page layouts. Although this evolution has proved a great benefit for the average user, it has created difficulties for people with disabilities.

There are four main categories of disabilities that affect a person's ability to use the web:

- mobility, including inability to move, insufficient dexterity to operate a mouse or a keyboard, inability to control unwanted movement, and lack of limbs;
- hearing, ranging from inexact hearing to diminished hearing to no hearing at all;
- vision, including partial or total blindness and color blindness;
- cognition and learning, including various difficulties reading, understanding, staying focused, remembering, and writing.

For a discussion of these disabilities and some of the major assistive technologies (software and hardware intended to help people with disabilities), see [3].

How many people have a disability? The United Nations estimates the number worldwide at half a billion [4]. The number of people with a disability in the United States has been estimated at 43–54 million [5], [6]. The number of adults who strain to see words, letters, or colors on computer screens has been estimated at 4 million. Of

Reprinted from *IEEE Trans. Prof. Comm.*, vol. PC-44, no. 4, pp. 225–233, December 2001.

those 4 million, 44% are said to be in the workforce [7]. Similarly, *The Washington Post* has cited the number of blind Americans using computers for pleasure, education, or work to be 535,000 [8]. As the web continues to become a part of everyday life for more and more people, the number of disabled persons using computers will surely increase.

Today's web, however, is mostly inaccessible to the disabled. Geoff Freed, the director of the Web Access Project for Boston-based WGBH-TV, has said that perhaps only 1% of web developers have taken any action to make their sites more accessible to the disabled [9, p. D03]. If Freed's estimate is accurate, or even if the actual number of accessible sites were to be a little higher, perhaps 3 or 5%, these figures reveal a significant problem: as the web continues to evolve, people with disabilities are increasingly finding themselves at a disadvantage. Web developers need to be aware of this problem.

This article presents an overview of the major aspects of the web-accessibility issue for web developers. First, we explain the benefits of making sites accessible: increased readership and the ability to take advantage of new technologies as they are introduced. We explain some of the major reasons web developers offer for not making their sites accessible. We review the relevant laws regarding web access, focusing on the Americans with Disabilities Act, then discuss efforts being made by vendors and professional organizations, especially Microsoft and the World Wide Web Consortium, to encourage accessibility. Finally, we describe major resources that web developers might consult to assist them in making their sites accessible to people with disabilities.

The Need for Accessibility

At first, the arrival of the web enabled many disabled persons to accomplish new tasks. It still does, but problems have arisen, mostly because web developers have begun to include increasingly complex multimedia and design elements in their sites. As one journalist puts it, "As more sites feature animated pictures and images, and home pages where clicking on a graphic is the only way to move from page to page, the web is not a friendly place for the visually impaired" [7].

Examples of the need for accessibility abound in the popular press. In September 1998, *The Wall Street Journal* carried the story of a blind teacher who found that, with the advent of the web and a speech synthesizer, he was finally able to "read" the newspaper. In this same article, however, he expresses his frustration in attempting to navigate a web that has become increasingly difficult for his speech device to decode [9]. Similar stories are common. A *US News and World Report* article featured a web user with retinitis pigmentosa, a debilitating eye disease that eventually causes blindness. Text-to-speech software once allowed her to navigate websites with relative ease; now she must struggle through the unreadable icons [7]. Likewise, a *Washington Post* article profiles the chief of international Braille and technology for the National Federation of the Blind, illustrating how difficult it is for blind users to navigate the web [8].

The accessibility barriers on the average webpage are numerous. The World Wide Web Consortium [10] lists seven common accessibility barriers:

- images without alternative text
- imagemap hot spots without alternative text
- misleading use of structural elements on a page
- uncaptioned audio or undescribed video
- lack of alternative information for users who cannot access frames or scripts
- tables that are difficult to decipher when linearized
- sites with poor color contrast

As technology continues to evolve, the web is becoming more and more exclusionary. Unless we consider universal design as we construct our sites, greater numbers of people will find themselves barred from participation and contribution. According to Cynthia J. Waddell, a California attorney and major proponent of web accessibility, "The growth and success of the emerging digital economy requires that attention be paid to the mechanism for enabling dynamic participation" [11]. This mechanism is an accessibility standard.

There are three main reasons to make sites accessible to people with disabilities.

Making Sites Accessible is the Right Thing to Do The quotation from Berners-Lee presented at the start of this article encapsulates this point. The driving force behind the World Wide Web is a desire to make information available to everyone, including people with disabilities. Access to information opens opportunities for all people by empowering them. For obvious reasons, people with disabilities, more so than other people, can benefit from the enormous resources available on the web. A United Nations report puts it this way: "Accessibility is the right thing to do. It helps achieve societal goals of full participation and equality" [4].

Making Sites Accessible Opens Vast Potential Markets Almost one in five people are disabled. That proportion will increase as the population ages because whereas only 10% of those aged 21 or under have a disability, 25% of those aged 50 do, almost half of those aged 65–79 do, and more than 70% of those aged 80 or older do [12]. People with disabilities have tremendous economic resources. According to the President's Committee on Employment of People with Disabilities, consumers with disabilities control more than $175 billion in discretionary income [13].

Making Sites Accessible Has Spillover Effects for All Users Making a site accessible to people with disabilities makes it accessible to people in noisy, poorly lit, and hands-free environments, and to people who use mobile devices with small screens without a keyboard or a mouse. Accessible sites are also attractive for people with slow modems or people who turn off images to speed downloads (most people outside the U.S. who pay for dial-up access by the minute). Accessible sites that adhere to coding standards will work well with tomorrow's technology like web telephones.

Why Most Organizations Are Not Accessible

If there are clear advantages to making sites accessible, why don't more organizations do so? Some web developers offer the following rationales.

- "*We aren't interested in this market.*" A recent survey of 30 major shopping, financial, auction, news, and search sites by *PC World* found that only a few sites were interested in the topic. An electronics retailer wrote, "That's not a market we've thought about pursuing" [14].
- "*Making the site accessible makes it boring.*" Some web developers incorrectly think that an accessible site can contain no graphics or multimedia. The accessibility features built into HTML 4.0 accommodate nearly every kind of advanced technology while still preserving the page's accessibility.
- "*We don't want to spend the money.*" Many web developers think that making a site accessible involves a tremendous investment in time and money. According to Kynn Bartlett, director of the HTML Writer's Guild Accessible Web Authoring Resources and Education Center, however, making a site accessible adds about 1 or 2% to the cost [14]. Moreover, new technology is continually reducing the cost of making sites accessible. Sun Microsystems' Java Accessibility API enables screen readers and voice-recognition software to recognize Java applets. The web-captioning editor MAGpie, from the National Center for Accessible Media and WGBH, makes it easy to add captions to video [14].

The Legal Status of Web Accessibility

Are web developers required by federal law or regulations to make their sites accessible to people with disabilities? As is the case with many aspects of law related to the Internet, the answer is not yet clear. In 1996, the Justice Department ruled that a website, like a brick-and-mortar store, is a "public accommodation" and therefore must meet the standards of the Americans with Disabilities Act [15]. As of this writing, this ruling has not been tested in court.

In the past decade, the federal government has enacted a number of laws and regulations affecting web accessibility for people with disabilities. No single statute encapsulates all of this information, and no single agency or department is charged with overseeing the government's efforts. (For an entry point on this vast and complex topic, see the General Service Administration's Federal IT Accessibility Initiative [16].)

Following is a brief overview of the major laws and regulations that affect web accessibility for persons with disabilities.

The Americans With Disabilities Act Enacted in 1990, the Americans with Disabilities Act (ADA) requires that businesses with 15 or more employees make "reasonable accommodation" for employees or potential employees with disabilities. According to the ADA, covered entities must "furnish appropriate auxiliary aids and services where necessary to ensure effective communication with individuals with disabilities" [15]. Because the ADA was drafted and passed in 1990, before the birth of the World Wide Web, there is no explicit link between the two.

However, Deval Patrick, Assistant Attorney General, ruled that the ADA does extend to the web. Patrick wrote:

> Covered entities under the ADA are required to provide effective communication, regardless of whether they generally communicate through print media, audio media, or computerized media such as the Internet. Covered entities that use the Internet for communications regarding their programs, goods, or services must be prepared to offer those communications through accessible means as well [15].

In other words, businesses with 15 or more employees that sell goods or services through the Internet are required to follow ADA accessibility guidelines. Does this ruling have the same effect as law? Advocates for people with disabilities say yes, whereas others (see [17]) say no.

Recently, some organizations have filed suits based on the ruling. For instance, the National Federation of the Blind (NFB) sued America Online (AOL), charging that AOL violates the ADA because its software cannot accommodate screen readers. However, NFB eventually dropped the suit when AOL agreed to make its software accessible by screen readers. The NFB also reached an agreement with the Connecticut Attorney General that will require four manufacturers of online tax-filing services to make their products accessible by screen readers [14].

Section 508 of the Rehabilitation Act Section 508 was amended most recently in 1998. The Department of Justice describes the main intent of Section 508 in these terms: "Section 508 prohibits federal agencies from procuring, developing, maintaining, or using EIT (electronic and information technology) that is inaccessible to people with disabilities, subject to an undue burden defense" [18]. Section 508 requires that each federal agency or department report to the Department of Justice, every two years, on the state of its own systems' accessibility to persons with disabilities.

The portion of Section 508 that refers specifically to websites makes clear that the Act applies only to "Federal web sites but not to private sector web sites (unless a site is provided under contract to a Federal agency, in which case only that web site or portion covered by the contract would have to comply)." In addition, Section 508 makes clear that the Act does not prevent the use of graphics or animation: "Instead, the standards aim to ensure that such information is also available in a format that is accessible to people with vision impairments." The Act recommends the use of text labels and descriptors for graphics [19].

Section 255 of the Telecommunications Act The Telecommunication Act, which was enacted in 1996, was amended in 1999 [20]. The overview of the amendment of Section 255 defines its intent:

> a manufacturer of telecommunications equipment or customer premises equipment shall ensure that the equipment is designed, developed, and fabricated to be accessible to and usable by individuals with disabilities, if readily achievable. Second, a provider of telecommunications service shall ensure that the service is accessible to and usable by individuals with disabilities, if readily achievable. Finally, whenever the requirements set forth above are not readily achievable, such a manufacturer or provider shall ensure that the equipment or service is compatible with existing peripheral devices or specialized customer premises equipment commonly used by individuals with disabilities to achieve access, if readily achievable [20].

As seen above, the federal government has already made it mandatory that all technology used by or created for them incorporate accessibility measures for the disabled. The scope of Section 255, as it relates to websites, however, is quite limited.

Six states—Arkansas, California, Maryland, New York, Texas, and Virginia—have enacted their own laws and regulations concerning web accessibility. In California, for example, there have been two notable cases in which students at state universities filed complaints to the Office of Civil Rights because of inaccessible computer resources [21], [22]. These cases and others were settled out of court.

A number of nations have addressed the question of web accessibility. For links to those sites, see [23].

Major Accessibility Efforts

Although most sites are not accessible, a number of vendors and industry groups are making significant efforts to help web developers make their sites accessible. This section first provides a brief overview of some of these efforts and then describes the major efforts made by Microsoft and the World Wide Web Consortium.

Apple is representative of major hardware and software vendors in its efforts to produce products that make it easier for people with disabilities to view websites. The Apple Macintosh computer [24], for example, includes screen-magnification software, system software to help people with motion disabilities, electronic documentation, text-to-speech synthesis, voice recognition, and visual alert cues.

IBM offers Home Page Reader [25], a text reader that uses the company's ViaVoice Outloud text-to-speech synthesizer. A visually impaired user can use Home Page Reader to speak text, frames, image and text links, alternate text for images and image maps, form elements, tables, graphics descriptions, text in tables and columns, and data input fields.

Adobe [26] has announced that it will support the Microsoft Active Accessibility (MSAA) Application Programming Interface (API) in future versions of Acrobat software. Microsoft Active Accessibility is an API that allows programs to expose information about their content and user interface to assistive technologies.

Microsoft's Accessibility Program Among vendors, Microsoft has perhaps the most extensive accessibility program. Because of the company's dominant position in the operating system, office-productivity, and browser markets, its position on accessible design affects many people. Microsoft's accessibility policy, called Enable, was adopted in 1995. Its four goals are to make accessible products, build strong bonds with the disabled community, equip developers, and inform customers about the accessibility of products [27].

This accessibility policy can be seen, for example, in Microsoft's Internet Explorer (IE) products. IE 5, building on accessibility features in previous versions, has new features, such as AutoComplete, AutoCorrect, and AutoSearch, that reduce keystrokes, typing mistakes, and mouse clicks. IE 5 also has a Web Accessories Kit that lets users customize features by adjusting fonts and colors for text, backgrounds, and links, using the keyboard for navigation on a page, creating their own Cascading Style Sheets for viewing pages, and using screen readers to display ALT text [28]. See [29] for Internet Explorer Accessibility, which covers principles of designing websites for people who will be using the Microsoft browser. Microsoft also presents a Checklist for Testing Your Web Pages for Accessibility, as well as examples of recommended code.

The Microsoft site contains numerous other resources, including articles, step-by-step guides, descriptions of assistive technologies, accessible documentation and support, and a valuable set of procedures that developers can use to make their products more accessible.

World Wide Web Consortium's Web Accessibility Initiative The World Wide Web Consortium (W3C), an organization interested in all aspects of the web, sponsors the most extensive set of programs and initiatives devoted to the issue of web accessibility for people with disabilities. W3C's main umbrella under which these efforts are collected is known as the Web Accessibility Initiative (WAI). According to the W3C, the WAI

> is pursuing accessibility of the Web through five primary areas of work: addressing accessibility issues in the technology of the Web; creating guidelines for browsers, authoring tools, and content creation; developing evaluation and validation tools for accessibility; conducting education and outreach; and tracking research and development [30].

The WAI has published many documents of interest to web developers. The three major sets of guidelines regarding web accessibility are the following.

- *Web Content Accessibility Guidelines.* These Guidelines [31] are based on two themes: "ensuring graceful transformation" (making Web content accessible and clear despite a person's disability and the limitations of any hardware of software he or she is using) and "making content understandable and navigable" (by using clear language and navigation so that people with disabilities can quickly and easily orient themselves in a page).
- *Authoring Tool Accessibility Guidelines* These Guidelines [32], addressed to developers of web authoring tools (including web editors, word processors, desktop-publishing software, and software for turning desktop-published documents into HTML), are intended to ensure that authoring tools be accessible to authors regardless of disability, that they produce accessible content by default, and that they assist the author in creating accessible content.
- *User Agent Accessibility Guidelines.* These Guidelines [33] are addressed to developers of browsers and other software that presents websites on a user's screen. A user agent that adheres to these guidelines will be accessible by virtue of its own interface and by virtue of its ability to communicate with assistive technologies.

Developed by the W3C as part of the WAI, the Web Content Accessibility Guidelines 1.0 is the most comprehensive and far-reaching accessibility policy created thus far. Specifically, the "Content Guidelines" presents 14 critical accessibility measures that authors and designers should be aware of when designing web content [31].

1) Provide equivalent alternatives to auditory and visual context.
2) Don't rely on color alone.
3) Use markup and style sheets and do so properly.
4) Clarify natural language usage.
5) Create tables that transform gracefully.
6) Ensure that pages featuring new technologies transform gracefully.
7) Ensure user control of time-sensitive content changes.
8) Ensure direct accessibility of embedded user interfaces.
9) Design for device independence.
10) Use interim solutions.
11) Use W3C technologies and guidelines.
12) Provide context and orientation information.
13) Provide clear navigation mechanisms.
14) Ensure that documents are clear and simple.

Each individual guideline has checkpoints that illustrate how the guideline applies to site design. The number of checkpoints per guideline varies; guideline 2), for instance, has only two checkpoints, whereas guideline 3) has seven checkpoints. Further, each checkpoint is assigned a priority.

- Priority 1 checkpoints are top priority, and to ensure that one or more disability groups do not encounter impossible situations on the web, these checkpoints must be satisfied.
- Priority 2 checkpoints should be satisfied, or the designer risks making navigation difficult.
- Priority 3 checkpoints are areas a designer might consider fulfilling to remove minor accessibility obstacles.

The Guidelines also present a conformance matrix.

- Conformance Level "A": all Priority 1 checkpoints are satisfied.
- Conformance Level "Double-A": all Priority 1 and 2 checkpoints are satisfied.
- Conformance Level "Triple-A": all Priority 1, 2, and 3 checkpoints are satisfied.

Importantly, each checkpoint is linked to the WAI "Techniques Document," allowing the web designer to view examples of how the checkpoint can be fulfilled.

In addition, the WAI includes other useful documents:

- technical documents focusing on the accessibility features included in such features and languages as Cascading Style Sheets, Synchronized Multimedia Language, and HTML 4;
- links to accessibility policies and documents from the federal government, U.S. states, and foreign nations;
- links to alternative browsers and assistive technologies popular among people with disabilities;
- links to evaluation and repair tools that help developers diagnose the accessibility of their sites and fix them;
- a comprehensive and easy-to-use self-guided tutorial, titled *Curriculum for Web Content Accessibility Guidelines 1.0*, that presents the guidelines, checkpoints, and sample code for the Web Content Accessibility Guidelines document.

The W3C Web Accessibility Initiative provides the single most comprehensive and useful set of resources for web developers who wish to make their sites more accessible to people with disabilities.

Resources for Web Developers

There are numerous resources available for web developers interested in making their sites accessible for people with disabilities. The first thing a web developer might do is determine the extent to which the site is accessible. Two sites perform accessibility audits at no charge:

- Bobby, a diagnostic program from Center for Applied Special Technology [34];
- HTML Validation Service, from W3C, checks for conformance to HTML and XHTML Recommendations and other HTML standards [35].

Also, see W3C's Evaluation, Repair, and Transformation Tools for Web Content Accessibility [36] for links to a number of other diagnostic and repair tools available on the web.

Many academic and nonprofit groups have long been involved in developing and promoting accessible technology. Following are the major sites that address web-accessibility issues.

- W3C's Web Access Initiative [37] is the motherlode of web accessibility information. Start here.
- The Federal IT Accessibility Initiative [38], a program of the General Services Administration, is the best point of entry to the federal government's information about Section 508 and other relevant federal agencies and rulings.
- The Center for Applied Special Technology (CAST) [39], founded in 1984, is a not-for-profit organization devoted to increasing educational opportunities for people with disabilities through the development and innovative uses of technology. CAST sponsors Bobby, the diagnostic program.
- The Trace Center [40] is a research organization at the University of Wisconsin-Madison. In addition to contributing to the W3C's "Web Content Accessibility Guidelines," the Trace Center has also created programs such as the Cooperative Electronic Library on Disability and technology such as the touchscreen accessibility feature called "EZ Access."
- The Web Access Project [41], founded in 1996 by the CPB/WGBH National Center for Accessible Media (NCAM), "researches, develops and tests methods of integrating access technologies (such as captioning and audio description) and new Web tools into a World Wide Web site, making it fully accessible to blind or deaf Internet users." The Web Access Project is a leading organization in researching ways to make multimedia accessible to people with disabilities.
- WebABLE! [42] is an organization promoting web accessibility through education and research. This site has an extensive accessibility-resource database (which can be searched by disability, by type of organization, and by

country) as well as workshop and conference listings and discussion boards.

- HTML Writer's Guild [43] sponsors AWARE (Accessible Web Authoring Resources and Education), a resource center for web developers interested in accessibility issues. AWARE offers online courses and links to resources about accessible design. In the Accessible Web Author's Toolkit, AWARE offers links to evaluation tools, correction and repair utilities, web-authoring software, and browsers. The Accessible Web Design Community links to organizations and online forums.
- Microsoft's Enable program [44] contains articles of interest to software developers about how to make products accessible. See, in particular, the Web Guidelines [45], which include guidelines, tools, a checklist, and examples of accessible sites.

CONCLUSION

There is no question that the World Wide Web is largely inaccessible to people with disabilities, and that it will remain so for some years. However, we are optimistic about the long-range prospects for web accessibility, not principally because we think web developers will suddenly conclude that making sites accessible is the right thing to do but because the pragmatic benefits of accessibility far outweigh the relatively modest costs. When developers begin to understand how smart it is to make their sites accessible—and how inexpensive it is to do—they will start to implement the suggestions of the W3C and other interested organizations.

The key to making the transition to accessibility, we think, lies not in the threat of legal compulsion, although there will continue to be lawsuits filed against owners of inaccessible sites. As we have seen, legal compulsion appears to be primarily a means of motivating site owners to sit down at the table with plaintiffs and work out solutions. The most promising route to full accessibility would appear to be collaboration among vendors, advocacy groups, and the government. Vendors such as Microsoft, Apple, Java, and IBM clearly see the wisdom of making their products accessible, and they are working with experts in the advocacy groups, such as W3C, the Trace Center, and WebABLE!, to create practical tools and techniques for achieving accessible sites. One example of this sort of cooperation is Microsoft's recent announcement that it will offer a series of courses to help federal IT managers and contractors who oversee federal accounts to work toward compliance with Section 508 of the Rehabilitation Act [46]. This sort of cooperation promises to create a win–win situation—not only for people with disabilities but also for all users of the web.

REFERENCES

[1] T. Berners-Lee. (2000, Oct. 10) Web accessibility initiative. World Wide Web Consortium web site. [Online]. Available: http://www.w3.org/WAI/

[2] M. Paciello. (2000, Nov. 11) People with disabilities can't access the web. WebABLE! website. [Online]. Available: http://www.webable.com/mp-pwdca.html

[3] W. Chishom. (2000, Nov. 6) Enabling your web site: A brief introduction to disabilities affecting web use. DesignShops.com web site. [Online]. Available: http://designshops.com/pace/ds/pub/1999/08/able.html

[4] L. Valdes. (1999, Oct. 11) Accessibility on the Internet. United Nations web site. [Online]. Available: http://www.un.org/esa/socdev/enable/disacc00.htm

[5] The Americans with Disabilities Act of 1990 website [Online]. Available: http://www.usdoj.gov/crt/ada/adahom1.htm

[6] National Council on Disability website [Online]. Available: http://www.ncd.gov

[7] R. M. Bennefield, "Catching a view of the web," *U.S. News and World Rep.*, pp. 68–69, May 19, 1997.

[8] P. W. Valentine, "Helping the blind handle computers; Technology allows greater accessibility," *Washington Post*, p. D03, Apr. 4, 1998.

[9] N. Wingfield, "On line: Blind web users campaign to 'see' more of cyberspace," *Wall Street J.*, p. B1, Sept. 9, 1998.

[10] World Wide Web Consortium. (1999, Oct. 11) Fact Sheet for 'Web Content Accessibility Guidelines 1.0.'. World Wide Web Consortium website. [Online]. Available: http://www.w3c.org/1999/05/WCAG-REC-fact

[11] C. D. Waddell. (1999, Oct. 17) The growing digital divide in access for people with disabilities: Overcoming barriers to participation. Washington State Department of Social and Human Services website. [Online]. Available: http://www.aasa.dshs.wa.gov/access/waddell.htm

[12] U.S. Census Bureau. (2000, Nov. 7) Americans with disabilities: 1994–95. U.S. Census Bureau website. [Online]. Available: http://www.census.gov/hhes/www/disable/sipp/disab9495/asc9495.html
[13] President's Committee on Employment of People With Disabilities. (2000, Nov. 9) Affirmative action and people with disabilities. President's Committee on Employment of People With Disabilities website. [Online]. Available: http://www50.pcepd.gov/pcepd/ztextver/pubs/ek98/affirmat.htm
[14] J. Heim. (2000, Sept. 1) Locking out the disabled. PC World.com website. [Online]. Available: http://www.pcworld.com/features/article.asp?aid=17690
[15] P. L. Deval, Assistant Attorney General. (1999, Oct. 11) Letter to Sen. Tom Harkin. U.S. Department of Justice website. [Online]. Available: http://www.usdoj.gov/crt/foia/tal712.txt
[16] Federal IT Accessibility Initiative website, General Services Administration. (2000, Nov. 13). [Online]. Available: http://section508.gov/law.html
[17] P. Thibodeau. (2000, Nov. 4) Does disabilities act apply to cyberspace?. IDG.net website. [Online]. Available: http://www.idg.net/go.cgi?id=288395
[18] U.S. Department of Justice. (2000, Nov. 4) Information technology and people with disabilities: The current state of federal accessibility. U.S. Department of Justice website. [Online]. Available: http://www.usdoj.gov/crt/508/report/exec.htm
[19] Federal IT Accessibility Initiative. (2000, Nov. 10) Proposed access standards for electronic and information technology: An overview. Federal IT Accessibility Initiative website. [Online]. Available: http://section508.gov/docs/overview.html
[20] Federal Communications Commission. (2000, Nov. 10) FCC report & order implementing Section 255. Federal IT Accessibility Initiative website. [Online]. Available: http://www.section508.gov/docs/section255.html
[21] American Association for Higher Education. (2000, Nov. 13) Equal access to software and information, Department of Education Office of Civil Rights Complaint against San Jose 1997. Rochester Institute of Technology website. [Online]. Available: http://www.rit.edu/easi/law/sjsu.html
[22] U.S. Department of Education. (2000, Nov. 12) Letter from Adriana Cardenas to Dr. James Rosser, President, California State University, Los Angeles, April 7, 1997. Rochester Institute of Technology website. [Online]. Available: http://www.rit.edu/ easi/law/csula.html
[23] World Wide Web Consortium. (2000, Nov. 12) Policies relating to web accessibility. World Wide Web Consortium website. [Online]. Available: http://www.w3.org/WAI/References/Policy
[24] Apple Computer, Inc.. (2000, Nov. 3) Disability resources. Apple Computer website. [Online]. Available: http://www.apple.com/education/k12/disability
[25] IBM Corporation. (2000, Nov. 3) The voice of the world wide web. IBM website. [Online]. Available: http://www-3.ibm.com/able/hpr.html
[26] Adobe Systems Incorporated. (2000, Nov. 3) Adobe enhances accessibility of Adobe Acrobat software for the disability community. Adobe website. [Online]. Available: http://www.adobe.com/aboutadobe/pressroom/pressreleases/200004/20000418acr.html
[27] Microsoft Corporation. (2000, Nov. 3) Accessibility policy and strategy. Microsoft website. [Online]. Available: http://microsoft.com/enable/microsoft/policy.htm
[28] Microsoft Corporation. (1999, Oct. 4) Microsoft Internet Explorer 5: Ready for action. Microsoft website. [Online]. Available: http://www.microsoft.com/enable/products/IE5.htm
[29] Microsoft Corporation. (1999, Oct. 4) Internet Explorer accessibility. Microsoft website. [Online]. Available: http://www.microsoft.com/enable/products/IE5/features.htm
[30] World Wide Web Consortium. (2000, Nov. 13) Web accessibility initiative resource: HTML 4.0 accessibility improvements.. World Wide Web Consortium website. [Online]. Available: http://www.w3.org/WAI/References/HTML4-access

[31] World Wide Web Consortium. (2000, Nov. 13) Web content accessibility guidelines 1.0. World Wide Web Consortium website. [Online]. Available: http://www.w3.org/TR/WAI-WEBCONTENT/
[32] World Wide Web Consortium. (2000, Nov. 13) Techniques for authoring tool accessibility, Note 4. World Wide Web Consortium website. [Online]. Available: http://www.w3.org/TR/WAI-AUTOOLS-TECHS/
[33] World Wide Web Consortium. (2000, Nov. 13) User agent accessibility guidelines 1.0. World Wide Web Consortium website. [Online]. Available: http://www.w3.org/TR/UAAG/
[34] Center for Applied Special Technology. (2000, Nov. 13) Bobby. Center for Applied Special Technology website. [Online]. Available: http://www.cast.org/bobby/
[35] World Wide Web Consortium. (2000, Nov. 13) HTML validation service. World Wide Web Consortium website. [Online]. Available: http://validator.w3.org/
[36] World Wide Web Consortium. (2000, Nov. 1) Evaluation, repair, and transformation tools for Web content accessibility. World Wide Web Consortium website. [Online]. Available: http://www.w3.org/WAI/ER/existingtools.html
[37] World Wide Web Consortium. (2000, Nov. 14) Web access initiative. World Wide Web Consortium website. [Online]. Available: http://www.w3.org/WAI/
[38] Federal IT accessibility initiative website (2000, Nov. 3). [Online]. Available: http://www.section508.gov
[39] Center for Applied Special Technology (CAST) website (2000, Nov. 3). [Online]. Available: http://www.cast.org/
[40] Trace Center website (2000, Oct. 31). [Online]. Available: http://www.trace.wisc.edu/world/web/
[41] CPB/WGBH National Center for Accessible Media (NCAM). (2000, Oct. 31) Web access project. CPB/WGBH National Center for Accessible Media website. [Online]. Available: http://www.wgbh.org/wgbh/pages/ncam/webaccess/wapsummary.html
[42] WebABLE! website (2000, Oct. 21). [Online]. Available: http://www.webable.com
[43] HTML Writer's Guild. (2000, Nov. 5) AWARE (Accessible Web Authoring Resources and Education. HTML Writer's Guild website. [Online]. Available: http://www.aware.hwg.org
[44] Microsoft Corporation. (2000, Nov. 10) Enable. Microsoft website. [Online]. Available: http://microsoft.com/enable/
[45] Microsoft Corporation. (2000, Nov. 2) Web guidelines. Microsoft website. [Online]. Available: http://microsoft.com/enable/dev/web/default.htm
[46] Microsoft Corporation. (2000, Nov. 2) Microsoft helps train federal IT managers to ensure government technology is accessible to people with disabilities. Microsoft website. [Online]. Available: http://microsoft.com/presspass/features/2000/04-18fose.asp

Jeff Carter is a technical writer at Marketron, Inc. in Hailey, Idaho, where he writes manuals and other documents and delivers client and in-house training. He holds a B.A. degree in history from the University of Illinois.

Mike Markel is Director of Technical Communication at Boise State University, where he teaches in the graduate and undergraduate programs. His latest book is *Ethics and Technical Communication: A Critique and Synthesis* (Ablex, 2001). From 1994 through 1996, he was Editor of IEEE TRANSACTIONS ON PROFESSIONAL COMMUNICATION.

A Conceptual Framework for International Web Design

—Fatemeh "Mariam" Zahedi,
William V. Van Pelt,
and Jaeki Song

***Abstract*—** *This paper develops a conceptual framework for exploring significant differences in how people from diverse cultural backgrounds and with diverse individual characteristics might perceive and use web documents. This is the first stage of a large multistage empirical study of user satisfaction and effectiveness of various web designs based on cultural and individual factors. We identify six cultural factors and six individual factors that could impact the effectiveness of web documents. The six cultural factors include: power distance, individualism versus collectivism, masculinity versus femininity, anxiety avoidance, long-term versus short-term orientation, and polychronic versus monochronic time orientation. The six individual factors include: demographics (age and gender), professional knowledge, information technology knowledge, flexibility, information processing abilities, and cultural knowledge. Based on the conceptual model proposed in this paper, we develop a number of testable, specific propositions on how web document effectiveness could be impacted by the cultural and individual factors in various web designs. In order to measure document effectiveness of each design, we identify components of web document effectiveness as perceived usability, reliability, clarity, and comprehension that, in turn, influence readers' overall satisfaction with web documents. Using the propositions presented here, one can measure and analyze how cultural and individual factors influence users' satisfaction, which will assist researchers, educators, and communicators working with various web designs.*

***Index Terms*—** *Clarity, comprehensibility, cultural factors, document effectiveness, individual factors, reliability, usability, user satisfaction, web design.*

Manuscript received February 1, 2000; revised March 24, 2000.
F. M. Zahedi and J. Song are with the School of Business Administration, University of Wisconsin-Milwaukee, Milwaukee, WI 53201 USA (email: zahedi@uwm.edu; jaeki@uwm.edu).
W. V. Van Pelt is with the English Department, University of Wisconsin-Milwaukee, Milwaukee, WI 53201 USA (email: vanpelt@uwm.edu).
IEEE PII S 0361-1434(01)04248-5.

The WWW has become a crucial communication medium. It is estimated that more than 100 million people will have used the web by 1998, and this figure is predicted to reach above 200 million in year 2000 [1], [2]. Since the web can now link diverse regions and communities across the globe that were relatively isolated by time and space, the growth of global communications has increased and intensified the need for learning to communicate successfully with a multitude of diverse, localized cultures.

No single model of cultural understanding is sufficient for communicating effectively with all web audiences. While the potential audience for any web document is international and intercultural, very little research has been conducted on how web documents are perceived and used by individuals from diverse national and cultural backgrounds, especially in communities and countries whose cultural tendencies differ from those where web technologies originate. We have undertaken a large, multistage research project

Reprinted from *IEEE Trans. Prof. Comm.*, vol. PC-44, no. 2, pp. 83–103, June 2001.

with the objective of addressing this research gap.

We start with two questions: "Are there significant differences in the ways that people from diverse cultural backgrounds and with diverse individual characteristics perceive and use web documents?" and "If significant cultural and individual differences exist among diverse users, what are those differences and how can web document contents be altered to increase user satisfaction and effective communications among such diverse audiences?" The first stage of answering the research questions is to develop a conceptual framework for analysis, in which the variables, relationships, and measurement methods are identified, and testable propositions are formulated. This paper reports on the development of this framework that includes specific, testable propositions concerning how users will respond to different web designs that address the various cultural factors and individual characteristics of international and intercultural users. We also discuss how to measure factors and variables presented in the model, hence making it possible to evaluate effectiveness and user satisfaction regarding specific web designs.

First, we develop the conceptual model based on the available theories in communication, cultural studies, and information systems. Then we discuss specific cultural factors and present propositions on how cultural factors may impact the effectiveness of different web designs. Next, we identify individual characteristics and suggest propositions on how individual factors may influence the effectiveness of different web designs. Afterward, we discuss how to measure the effectiveness of web documents and user satisfaction. Finally, we offer concluding remarks.

CONCEPTUAL MODEL

In information technology related research, we can approach the analysis of text data through more than one set of assumptions about the relationship between text data and reality. Lacity and Janson [3] identify three categories of approaches to text analysis: positivist, linguistic, and interpretivist. Positivist approaches assume language corresponds to an objective reality. Linguistic approaches assume that language is not a description of reality but an act of reality. Interpretivist approaches assume that language use is subjective, so that textual interpretation is influenced by personal experiences and circumstances, requiring extraneous information about the originator and interpreter of the text. Therefore, interpreting and recognizing text information involves personal biases because interpreters may bring their own emotions, attitudes, and cultures into the interpretive process.

The importance of cultural factors in communication has been reinforced by recent research on the social construction of meaning, which demonstrates that social and cultural factors dominate how readers construct meaning from texts: "Social constructionism challenges traditional epistemological assumptions... that the world is the outcome of direct and unfiltered access to reality. Rather, social constructionists argue, we view the world through a social filter: prevailing ideologies, social and cultural constructs, such as community beliefs and assumptions... direct our interpretation of reality" [4]. Social constructionist theory argues that our understanding of the world comes to us through language, which is not a neutral or transparent medium, but rather an activity already imbued with historically and locally determined cultural biases.

Postmodernist approaches to linguistic communication take social constructionism even further by suggesting that all types of knowledge are based on interpretive language games, the rules of which evolve within relatively localized cultural narratives [5], [6]. Postmodern analysis of the impact of new technologies on communication suggests that the new information economy will increasingly become decentralized and contingent on localized cultural factors, which may often include resistance to dominant socioeconomic structures in favor of localized linguistic idioms, customs, and pragmatic business practices [5], [7], [8].

If the premise of interpretivist approaches, social construction theory, and postmodern analysis is correct, then we can conclude that the processing of web documents is conditioned by differences in readers or the state of their mental programming. A web document may have different effectiveness and render different levels of satisfaction to individuals with differing cultural and individual backgrounds. If so, it becomes imperative to understand how individuals' backgrounds could impede or facilitate communication effectiveness of web documents. The next question is, "What are the categories of individual backgrounds that could impact communication effectiveness?"

Hofstede [9] identifies the forces that govern individuals' patterns of thinking, feeling, and potential acting as "mental programs," or "software of mind." He categorizes human mental programming in a three-layered pyramid, as shown in Fig. 1.

Hofstede identifies HUMAN NATURE as the most fundamental level of universal and inherited behavioral traits upon which our learned cultural conditioning, inherited characteristics, and learned individual personalities rest. The second layer of the pyramid is CULTURE, defined by Hofstede as the learned pattern of thinking, feeling, acting, and values, which are specific to a group or category of people. The third and top level of the pyramid includes personal characteristics that are unique to each individual, are both inherited and learned through experience. Hofstede's research shows that both cultural and individual factors could have significant influence in intercultural and international business exchanges [9]–[12].

Synthesizing social constructionist theory and Hofstede's categorization of differences in human mental programming in the context of web design, we posit that the effectiveness of the web communication is influenced by two sets of factors: cultural factors and individual characteristics, as shown in Fig. 2. In this model, the cultural conditioning of readers influences the effectiveness of web documents. Similarly, the unique individual mental programming, or factors of readers, also impacts the way they perceive and process web documents. One can measure the final outcome of any communication in terms of the overall satisfaction that communicators experience with regard to meeting the communication objectives in an enjoyable and easy fashion. One of the major factors in achieving communication satisfaction is the effectiveness of communication. Therefore, we posit that the perceived effectiveness of the web document impacts the reader's overall satisfaction with the content of that web document, as shown in Fig. 2.

Several studies relate cultural models and national cultural differences to problems in information systems and user-interface design [13]–[15]. Thatcher [16] connects South American history, social class, and educational differences to stark differences between the practices of communication professionals in the U.S. versus those in South America. Flint et al. [17] report the results of developing

Fig. 1. Three levels of human mental programming (adopted from Hofstede [9]).

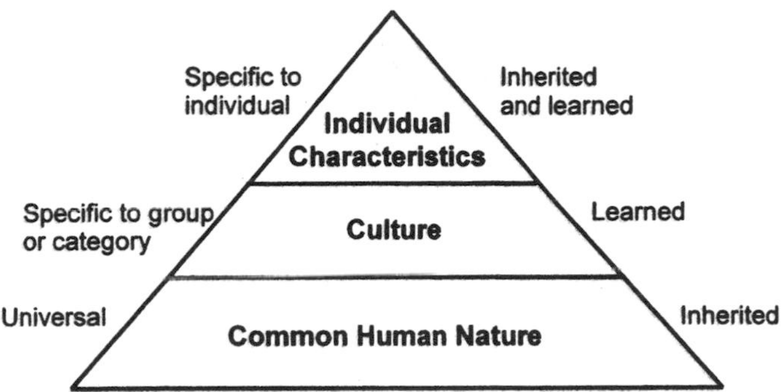

Fig. 2. The conceptual model for web design.

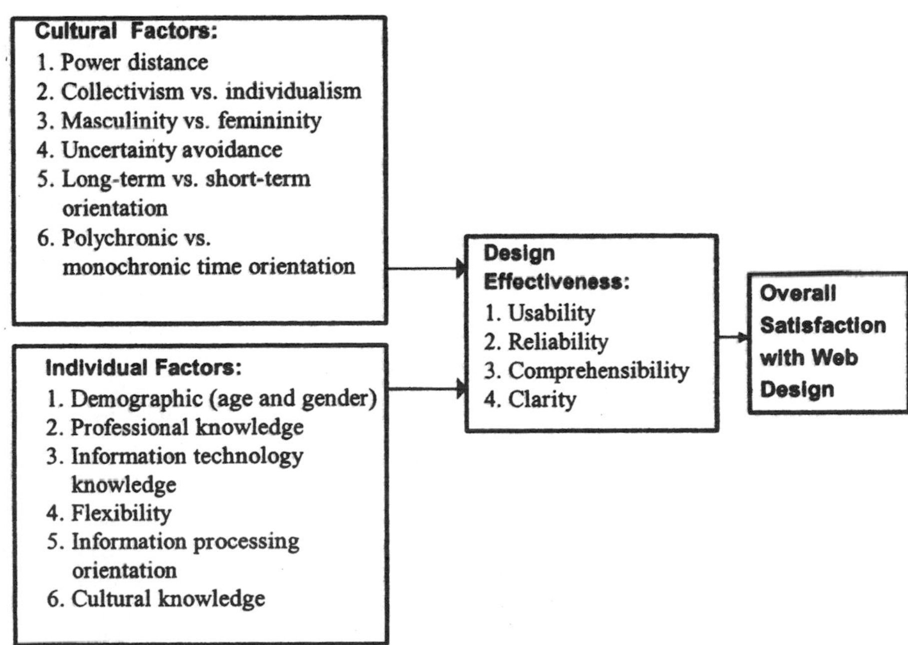

a multilingual hypertext guide to international communication; Adams et al. [18] discuss writing and design skills pertaining to global communication; and by combining Hofstede's four dimensions of culture with other cultural standards, Honold [19] investigates how people from different countries (Germany and China) learn new information. Our model, on the other hand, is one of the first attempts to identify the influence of cultural and individual differences in the perceived effectiveness of and satisfaction with various web designs.

Based in the literature in cultural studies, information systems, and organization, we have identified the cultural factors and individual factors that could impact the perceived effectiveness of web documents, as well as the components for measuring web document effectiveness, which are discussed, respectively, in the following three sections.

Cultural Factors and Related Propositions

Users from countries and cultures different than our own may make entirely different assumptions about what information is most important, how to find it, and how to present it in the most appealing and effective fashion. German business people, for example, prefer factual detail in documents and are likely to thoroughly read and absorb written documents [20]. Consequently, Germans may be likely to tolerate a substantial amount of textual material in web documents. Other cultures, such as Arabic and Latin American, place a high value on personal and oral communication [20], [15], [9]. Lengthy text-oriented webpages may not appeal to individuals from these cultures, but they might respond well to the same information punctuated strategically by sound clips and video clips presenting speakers quoting from authorities they know and respect.

Hofstede [9] identifies five dimensions of culture that can be measured relative to other cultures: power distance, collectivism versus individualism, femininity versus masculinity, uncertainty avoidance, and long-term versus short-term orientation. Hall [21] suggests monochronic versus polychronic time as a cultural dimension. These cultural dimensions have been applied in organizational and, more recently, in information systems studies. For example, Straub [22] uses Hofstede's concept of uncertainty avoidance to show that uncertainty avoidance negatively affects email use among Japanese business professionals. Adding one of Hall's cultural dimensions to Hofstede's five dimensions of culture, we have identified six cultural factors, as discussed below.

Power Distance and Web-Document Design Hofstede defines the cultural dimension of POWER DISTANCE as "the extent to which the less powerful members of institutions and organizations within a country expect and accept that power is distributed unequally" [9, p. 28]. Since social inequalities among individuals exist in all cultures to varying degrees, Hofstede was able to gather data on perceptions of employee–management relationships in 50 countries and three multicountry regions and to develop a Power Distance Index (PDI) for each country and region.

In countries where the power distance is small, such as the U.S., Great Britain, Sweden, and Denmark, an egalitarian ethos is favored. For example, in Sweden, which scores low PDI of 31, the parliament once laughed uproariously at their newly chosen King because of his heavy French accent [9]. Even today, a Swedish law stipulates that all important managerial decisions "must be discussed with all staff members before being implemented," which is deliberately aimed at leveling the ground between managers and employees by making the managers more accessible and the employees more active in decision-making [20, p. 245]. Small power distance implies a consultative style of decision-making, involving more feedback, creativity, and flexibility among managers and employees.

A large power distance or high index tends to accept power inequalities between individuals as the social norm and to respect established authority, especially in such figures as elders, teachers, experts, and those with a high degree of education and social status. Thus in Malaysia and Indonesia, which Hofstede [9] rates with very high PDI scores of 104 and 78, respectively, (PDI scores ranged from 104 at the high end to 11 at the low end), we find that "leaders are expected to be paternal," subordinates expect "Promotion must be initiated from above; better conformity and obedience than struggling for change. Age will bring progress," and "standards of deference are sky high" [20, pp. 83, 295].

A large power distance implies that decision makers are expected to be more autocratic and paternalistic and are expected to have special privileges and status symbols that announce their leadership role to others, while subordinates tend to be dependent, preferring and expecting a boss to make decisions autocratically. An ideal boss would be considered a benevolent autocrat or "father figure," who cares for his employees as a father would for his family.

In a country with a large power distance, we might expect written communications to contain references to the status and authority of leaders, professional expertise, and highly respected figures in the scientific and educational communities. Since autocratic authority works best if it is also benevolent, documents might display an understated voice of authority that is clear in direction, but show deference and respect toward the audience, avoiding a harsh imperative voice [23, p. 82]. At the same time, readers used to a large power distance would also expect communications to be one-way, detailed, exact, and followed literally, reflecting the authoritative relationships set up in the home, religious institutions, schools, and workplace [24]. It seems important that the content of the message be unambiguous for written documents in large power distance cultures. U.S. technical communicators in South America found that detailed narratives with literal, one-way scripts worked more effectively for directing employees than did abstract, hierarchical, and analytically structured documents that called for interpretations or sample contexts supplied by employees [16].

In the following proposition, we propose that aligning the document design with the readers' degree of cultural power distance could lead to more effective communication.

Proposition 1: Web documents designed for users from cultures with large power distance (as opposed to small power distance) will be more effective if they have references to characteristics associated with large power distance, such as authority, power, expertise, and wealth.

Section 1 of the Appendix contains a textual example from a document that might be more effective for cultures with large power distance since it contains references to wealth, authority, and expertise, which would make it more reliable and easy to understand for those who rely on such manifestation of power distance.

Collectivism, Individualism, and Web Design Hofstede [9] defines the cultural dimension of INDIVIDUALISM versus COLLECTIVISM as follows: "Individualism pertains to societies in which the ties between individuals are loose: everyone is expected to look after himself or herself and his or her immediate family. Collectivism, as its opposite, pertains to societies in which people from birth onwards are integrated into strong, cohesive groups, which throughout people's lifetime continue to protect them in exchange for unquestioning loyalty" [9, p. 51]. Hofstede's "individualism index" (IDV) reveals that countries such as the U.S. and Sweden ranked high (91 and 71, respectively), whereas the Arabic-speaking countries and Indonesia ranked low (38 and 14, respectively).

Collectivist cultures, such as those found in Latin American and Arabic-speaking countries, emerge out of strong extended family ties and emphasize group harmony, trust, and *we* relationships. Individualist cultures, however, emerge out of a smaller nuclear-family unit where the individual thinks in terms of *I*, and business relationships are based on well-defined contractual communications, where written regulations and well-defined tasks prevail over personal relationships. Lewis [20] confirms these cultural traits in business, identifying the high individualism among U.S. workers, who "value individual freedom above the welfare of the company" (p. 78) and tend to be very direct, with a "let's get to the point" attitude (p. 168). By contrast, in Malaysia, Indonesia, and similar Asian cultures, organizations and businesses "strongly resemble family structures" (p. 81), "deep personal relations with colleagues and family are highly prized" (p. 295), and business negotiations may be unhurried and drawn out [20, pp. 272, 298]. Similarly, Dragga [25] describes how business communication in China is often considered indirect by U.S. standards, since the Chinese focus their initial attention on establishing a personal relationship and "might start with discussion of family or social pursuits prior to addressing pertinent business issues" (p. 368).

Hofstede [9] cites Hall's concept of high-context versus low-context communications to reinforce his own emphasis on the importance of how personal relations provide most of the information for doing business in collectivist cultures versus how the lack of such personal relations requires more explicit written business communications in individualist cultures:

> A high-context communication is one in which little has to be said or written because most of the information is either in the physical environment or within the person, while very little is in the coded, explicit part of the message. This type of communication is frequent in collectivist cultures.... A low-context communication is one in which the mass of information is vested in the explicit code, which is typical for individualist cultures. Lots of things which in collectivist cultures are self-evident must be said explicitly in individualist cultures. [9, p. 60]

Therefore, business contracts in the predominantly individualist culture of the U.S. tend to be much longer than contracts in the predominantly collectivist culture of Japan. We do not identify high-context versus low-context as a separate cultural dimension since it reappears as an important aspect of culture in more than one of the dimensions that constitute our six cultural factors.

We propose that aligning the document design with the extent of cultural individualism versus collectivism of readers could lead to more effective communication.

Proposition 2: Web documents designed for high levels of collectivism (as opposed to individualism) will be more effective if they promote group cohesion and not individual self-interest.

Section 2 of the Appendix exhibits a textual example from a rejection letter from a Chinese newspaper that shows group cohesion and the preservation of harmony, rather than the direct approach of conveying a negative message.

Masculinity Versus Femininity and Web-Document Design Hofstede defines the cultural dimension of MASCULINITY versus FEMININITY as follows: "masculinity pertains to societies in which social gender roles are clearly distinct (i.e., men are supposed to be assertive, tough, and focused on material success whereas women are supposed to be more modest, tender, and concerned with the quality of life); femininity pertains to societies in which social gender roles overlap, (i.e., both men and women are supposed to be modest, tender, and concerned with the quality of life)" [9, p. 82]. It is important to recognize that masculinity and femininity are relative terms that refer to cultural characteristics that affect both individual men and women within a given culture. Masculinity and femininity constitute cultural differences that therefore do not refer to an individual's biological designation as a male or a female, terms which we, following Hofstede's lead, have reserved for the description of individual characteristics identified in a later section.

Hofstede [9] developed a Masculinity Index (MAS) in which countries such as Japan, Austria, and Venezuela scored high (95, 79, and 73, respectively) since responses from these national cultures emphasized masculine traits of assertiveness, toughness, and material success, while countries such as Denmark, The Netherlands, Norway, and Sweden scored low (16, 14, 8, and 5) since responses from these national cultures emphasized feminine traits of modesty, tenderness, and concern for quality of life. Both men and women were affected by their national cultures, so that individual women within high MAS nations scored significantly higher than women in nations with a low MAS, while men within those same high MAS nations scored slightly higher than women.

Hofstede [9], who was educated and trained in the The Netherlands, which has a very low MAS of 14, described his failure at an interview with a U.S. company (the U.S. MAS is relatively high at 62) because he was far too modest about his abilities when the interviewer expected him to show masculinity traits of self-assertiveness and tough-minded self-promotion. Lewis confirms that Swedish society, which has the lowest MAS score, embraces feminine values such as modesty, nurture, sympathy for the weak, quality of life, equality, consensus, and the welfare of all people in the society, while placing less emphasis on success, money, dominance, winning, and sympathy for the strong. He provides a telling example of a Swedish professor who explained that in order to be a powerful business manager in Sweden, one has to create an image of not being powerful [20, p. 247].

We propose that the alignment of the document design with the extent of cultural masculinity or femininity of readers could lead to more effective communication.

Proposition 3: Web documents designed for users with masculine (as opposed to feminine) cultures will be more effective if they refer to or can be associated with characteristics such as success, winning, strength, and assertiveness.

Section 3 of the Appendix exhibits a textual example from a document designed with a high level of masculinity that stresses masculine qualities of success, assertiveness, and strength. The example is excerpted from the U.S. Army's homepage.

Strong Versus Weak, Uncertainty Avoidance, and Web Design Hofstede defines the cultural dimension of UNCERTAINTY AVOIDANCE from strong to weak as "the extent to which the members of a culture feel threatened by uncertain or unknown situations" [9, p. 113]. This feeling is expressed in many ways, but more often through nervous stress and the need for predictability and both written and unwritten rules. Hofstede's Uncertainty Avoidance Index (UAI) scores countries such as Greece, Portugal, Japan, and Germany high (with scores of 112, 104, 92, and 65, respectively) and countries such as the U.S., Great Britain, Sweden, and Denmark as low (with scores of 46, 35, 29, and 23, respectively). German society, which has a relatively high UAI, maintains a high respect for punctuality, the rule of law, and the authority of expertise, especially in schools where learning is structured with precise objectives, detailed assignments, strict timetables, and one correct answer for every question. In Great Britain, which has a relatively low UAI, students tend to dislike structure and prefer open-ended learning situations with vague objectives, broad assignments, and no timetables.

Other features of strong uncertainty avoidance include a mistrust of youth, resistance to deviant ideas or innovation, little tolerance for ambiguity, and the idea that "different is dangerous," sometimes leading to a kind of xenophobic distrust of outsiders who dress, talk, and behave differently from the localized norm. Weak uncertainty avoidance, however, tends to tolerate youthful opinion, innovation, ambiguity, and tends to see people and behaviors that deviate from the localized norm as merely curious rather than dangerous. Lewis [20] confirms Hofstede's account of German business negotiators' strong uncertainty avoidance, since they, like the Japanese, prefer "to go over details time and time again" to avoid misunderstandings [9, p. 211]. In contrast to the German and Japanese tendency toward strong anxiety avoidance, British negotiators tend to display a weaker uncertainty avoidance and thus prefer to speed up discussion and introduce new or unexpected ideas when negotiations become over-rigid [20, p. 176].

We propose that aligning the document design with the readers' degree of cultural uncertainty avoidance could lead to more effective communication.

Proposition 4: Web documents designed for users from cultures with strong uncertainty avoidance (as opposed to weak uncertainty avoidance) would be more effective if they referred to precise and detailed information, referred to relevant rules and regulations, and avoided emphasizing novelty and deviating from the norm.

Section 4 of the Appendix exhibits a textual example from a document that emphasizes strong uncertainty avoidance features, such as precise and detailed information and strong adherence to known business processes and practices.

Long-Term Versus Short-Term Orientation and Web Design Hofstede [9] identifies a fifth cultural dimension of LONG-TERM ORIENTATION versus SHORT-TERM ORIENTATION. The aspects associated with long-term orientation include: adapting tradition to modern perspectives, respecting social and status obligations within limits, being thrifty and sparing of resources, persevering toward slow results, willing subordination to a purpose, and respecting the demands of virtue. Aspects associated with short-term orientation include: respecting tradition, social standing, and status, regardless of cost; "keeping up with the Joneses," even if it means overspending; expecting quick results; saving face; possessing the truth. Countries scoring high Long-Term Orientation (LTO) indexes include China, Hong Kong, Taiwan, Japan, and Brazil (with scores of 118, 96, 87, 80, and 65), while countries with lower LTO scores include Germany, U.S., Britain, and Pakistan (31, 29, 25, and 0, respectively). Hofstede developed the data for this dimension out of questionnaires and data gathered by an Asian team of social scientists [11], which developed criteria based on a Chinese value system related to Confucianism.

As an example, Hofstede [9] suggests that the Five Dragons (Hong Kong, Taiwan, Japan, South Korea, and Singapore), all of whom score high on the LTO index, have experienced tremendous long-term economic growth in the second half of the twentieth century because of their ability to adapt their traditions to the use of innovative technologies and have benefited by pragmatic management styles and the advantages possessed by cultures that can practice Virtue without a concern for Truth or put another way, by valuing "what works" over "what is true or who is right" [9, p. 172]. By contrast, he suggests that Western, Judeo-Christian, and Muslim cultures that value Truth over practical ethics, at times, have turned their obsession with the search for Truth into a liability rather than an asset, citing the examples of Muslim countries that have hindered their economic progress by viewing the new technologies as a threat to their traditions rather than an opportunity [9, p. 172].

Both Lewis [20] and Dragga [25] confirm the lasting and profound influence of Confucianism on Chinese culture, especially with regard to practical virtues of ethical behavior and self-improvement. Lewis agrees that the Confucian values have extended to Taiwan, Korea, Japan, and other East Asian countries and that these values include long-term orientation, looking beyond the deal, and being "patient, thrifty, and cautious" [20, pp. 281–282].

We propose that the alignment of the document design with the extent of cultural long-term versus short-term orientation of readers could lead to more effective communication.

Proposition 5: Web documents designed for users from cultures with long-term orientation (as opposed to short-term orientation) will be more effective if they emphasize perseverance, future orientation, resources for conservation, respect for the demands of virtue, and de-emphasize truth and falsity as a strictly binary, black-and-white relationship.

Section 5 of the Appendix exhibits a textual example from a document design that stresses perseverance, virtuous actions, and a future-oriented view. We suggest that such a design will be more effective for audiences with a long-term orientation.

Polychronic Versus Monochronic Time Orientation and Web Design We have added the cultural dimension of POLYCHRONIC versus MONOCHRONIC TIME ORIENTATION from Hall [21] to the five cultural dimensions already defined in Hofstede's work [9]. Hall [21] argues that the structure of time is formulated, used, and patterned differently in different cultures and that these culturally dependent temporal structures are unconsciously and invisibly woven into our everyday activities, deeply influencing how we work and think. Polychronic cultures prefer doing many things at a time, stress involvement with people and completion of transactions rather than adherence to schedules, emphasize commitments to people and lifetime relationships, and rely on the situational context of the message [21, pp. 42–59]. Monochronic cultures prefer doing one thing at a time, compartmentalize relationships and tasks according to strict time schedules, value promptness and adherence to plans, and rely on communications in which most of the information must be included in the message itself with details clearly spelled out [21, pp. 43–61]. Hall [21] identifies Mediterranean, Latin American, Arabic, and Asian countries (especially Japan) as largely polychronic, while he identifies North American and European countries (especially Germany and Switzerland) as monochronic.

Bureaucrats and important officials in a polychronic culture, for example, might do business with several small groups of people at once in a large reception area or other semipublic setting. In contrast, officials in a monochronic cultures would schedule individuals or separate groups one at a time in private offices, allowing each party a prescheduled amount of time. Monochronic cultures in the Western world rely heavily on law and legal contracts as a low-context communication system in which every detail of a business agreement is spelled out in advance, whereas polychronic cultures may reach business agreements based on high-context communications which involve little paperwork, but require highly developed, long-term personal relationships as the foundation of all business commitments.

We propose that aligning the document design with the readers' extent of cultural polychronic versus monochronic time orientation could lead to more effective communication.

Proposition 6: Web documents designed for users from cultures with polychronic time orientation (as opposed to monochronic time orientation) will be more effective if they have high-context personal information (as opposed to low-context personal information), tend to build lifelong relationships (as opposed to short-term relationships), offer a variety of views, issues, or topics (as opposed to consistent sets of views, issues, topics), and are oriented toward people and human relationships (as opposed to tasks or achievements).

Section 6 of the Appendix exhibits a textual example from a document designed with a polychronic cultural orientation, stressing various activities, a high degree of personal information, and human relationships.

Individual Characteristics and Related Propositions

Researchers have looked at the relationship between individual differences and the use of information systems. Zmud [26] reviews the findings of 123 empirical investigations of how individual differences (including attributes such as gender, age, experience, education, professional orientation, and organizational level) impact the success of information systems and concludes that individual differences do exert a major force in determining individual success in information systems. Other studies have shown that either individual differences in risk aversion or gender, or both, play a role in such areas as the use of email [27], decision support systems [28], learning a technology [29], and the job performance and career advancement of information systems workers [30], [31]. Very little formal research has been conducted on web use by culturally diverse groups of international users. One exception is Chu [32], whose case history addresses cultural differences to be considered when constructing a bilingual website. We have found no experimental studies published on individual or cultural differences relating to international web use. Schriver asserts that "although there are now dozens of cookbooks" on how to design websites, "there are almost no books that present empirical evidence about how people read and interpret what they encounter on the web" [33, p. 390]. Spool et al. also report that "no matter where we looked, we could not find any data—based on real user experience—about what it takes to make a usable web site" [34, p. 3].

The processing of web documents takes place at the individual level, and, if the interpretivist view is correct, the individual characteristics should play a role in the perception of the effectiveness of the document. Furthermore, recent studies (for example, [28]) show that individual characteristics even play a role in software use. We categorize individual characteristics related to web use as follows: demographic, professional knowledge, information technology (IT) knowledge, flexibility, information processing orientation, and cultural knowledge. Individual characteristics should be used as moderating factors in any study of culture and web design. They also have direct impact on the design, as discussed below.

Demographic Factors The demographic factors include age, gender, nationality, and ethnicity. We can eliminate nationality and ethnicity as separate demographic variables because Hofstede's data, gathered at the country level, already captures information about the nationality and ethnicity. He argues that "[r]egional, ethnic, and religious cultures can be described in the same terms as national cultures: basically, the same dimensions, which were found to differentiate among national cultures apply to these differences within countries" [9,

p. 16]. Gender and age, on the other hand, are more individually based and should be analyzed as separate variables.

While the cultural dimension of femininity–masculinity captures the group orientation, even within a feminine or masculine group, there are distinct differences among male and female, as reported by Hofstede [9]. Other studies have also found gender differences in nonverbal communications and cues [35], [36], conversational patterns [37], [38], and the use of models for making decisions [28]. Gender difference has been considered in IT studies. Gilroy and Desai [39] found that female college students had higher computer anxiety than male students, indicating that gender difference matters in computer-related environments. Frankel also states that "the computer culture is uncomfortable for girls and women" [40, p. 38]. In a recent study, Gefen and Straub [27], using technology acceptance model (TAM), found that gender difference affects computer-based communication and media choice. They found that women prefer to adopt networking-based communication, whereas men tend to adopt competition-based communication. Furthermore, women have a higher level of perception about ease-of-use of email than men and use email more frequently than men do.

Morahan-Martin draws on a number of research results to identify the following differences between female and male subjects using the Internet for online discussion groups and other Internet communications [41]. She reports that women tend to be more supportive and tentative while men tend to be more adversarial and status enhancing, that women include more expressions of appreciation and community building while men tend to be more contentious or self-promoting, and that women tend to give more explicit empathetic responses than men, while men tend to be more factual in their responses than women [41, p. 12].

We, therefore, consider gender to be a significant individual factor in processing web documents and propose that document designs aligned with the gender of readers will communicate more effectively.

Proposition 7: Web documents designed for female (male) users will be more effective if they are supportive (as opposed to contentious), cooperative (as opposed to adversarial), tentative (as opposed to assertive), create harmony (as opposed to status enhancing and competitive), and empathetic (as opposed to factual).

Section 7 of the Appendix exhibits a textual example from a document design that is aligned with female aspects of support, cooperation, and harmony.

Age is another individual characteristic of potential significance and Hofstede acknowledges the importance of age because "[t]he development of technology ... leads to a difference between generations" [9, p. 17]. In IT [42], [26], it has been found that older individuals take more time and seek more information in making decisions. Moreover, with the explosion of visually based media (such as video games, TV, visual objects on computers), the younger generation is more oriented toward visual cues and relies less on textual materials than the older generation. Schriver [33] observes that teenagers are sensitive to visual cues and references in processing information and are highly critical of the quality of visuals. We, therefore, propose that document design that is aligned with the age characteristics of its readers will have higher communication effectiveness. One age-related aspect is the extent of visual cues in the design as opposed to the amount of text for conveying a message. Other age-related aspects could be tested in a similar fashion as stated in Proposition 8 below.

Proposition 8: Web documents designed for younger (as opposed to older) users will be more effective if they contain less (as opposed to more) information, while using more (as opposed to fewer) visuals and less (as opposed to more) text.

Section 8 of the Appendix provides the WWW address for a document designed for youthful audiences. It has bright colors and striking visuals, but limited text.

Professional Knowledge The professional knowledge of web users impacts their attitudes and their processing of information. Zmud [26] reports that educational background influences information use and processing. Compeau et al. [43] also report a difference at the educational level in survey participation. Hofstede observes that "in most societies, social class, education level, and occupation are closely linked" [9, p. 28]. Zmud [26] reports that more knowledgeable individuals use more information and prefer aggregate information and apply more rules in integrating information.

We define the professional-knowledge factor to be indicative of the individual knowledge gained through education and work experience. Since web document processing is also affected by the web user's level of language proficiency, we have included another component in this category: proficiency in the document's language. Hence, the professional-knowledge factor consists of level of education, professional experience, and proficiency in the document's language. We posit that the alignment of the document design with the professional knowledge of its audience leads to more effective communication and hence higher level of overall satisfaction.

Proposition 9: Web documents designed for users with less (as opposed to more) professional knowledge will be more effective if they contain simpler (as opposed to more complex), common-sense (as opposed to scientific), and linguistically easier (as opposed to more difficult) contents.

Section 9 of the Appendix exhibits a textual example from a document designed to explain the concept of "fair use" for an audience with a relatively lower level of professional knowledge of law.

Information Technology (IT) Knowledge web users' experience the web and their knowledge of IT make a difference in their perception regarding the web document. The anxiety and lack of skill in accessing and using the technology itself may reduce the effectiveness of the communication contents. Krock [44] reports the cross-cultural differences in technology backgrounds for software user training. IT knowledge may be directly related to training or experience of using the web or may be related to the more general IT background. We, therefore, recognize two factors in this category: (i) web knowledge and (ii) information technology knowledge. Compeau et al. [43] found that SELF-EFFICACY, defined as a person's belief about his/her ability to perform specific tasks, influences computer use. They also report that individuals with higher level computer skills are more positive regarding the outcomes of computer use. Barker reports that the "novice basically exhibits very different degree of receptivity to different interface and media types than does the experienced user" [45, p. 60]. Kennedy [46] notes that in computer training of novice users, proficiency depended on the computer acceptance and the reduction of fear.

We posit that those who have higher level IT knowledge will use web documents more effectively because their skill with the web and technology gives them more ease in accessing what they need and prevents anxiety or distraction regarding the technology. Such individuals' familiarity with the technical terms that are inevitably used on the web gives them a better chance in understanding the document. Therefore, the alignment of the document design with the IT knowledge of its readers leads to a higher level of communication effectiveness.

Proposition 10: Web documents designed for users with less (as opposed to more) IT knowledge will be more effective if they contain less (as opposed to more) IT-related technical information.

Section 10 of the Appendix exhibits a textual example from a document designed for an audience with little knowledge of IT.

Flexibility Individuals differ in their flexibility toward changes and new technology. The difference in attitude toward change may impact the extent and the way individuals use and process the web document, since it is a new technology. We define that flexibility factor to include attitude toward risk and attitude toward new technology in particular.

Risk and uncertainty avoidance are related but different [9]. Risk is more well-defined than uncertainty because it has probability attached to it. Palma-dos-Reis and Zahedi [28] have shown that users' attitudes toward risk makes a difference in the way they use decision support systems. Geoghegan [47] has found that the faculty's aversion to risk and lack of tolerance for change contribute to the way computers are used in classrooms. Dusick [48] has also associated the use of computers by teachers with the ability to take personal risk. Using and accessing documents through the web is still a relatively new technological skill and experience for many. Documents that promote change, innovation, and new technologies may compound resistance to change and create anxiety, hence reducing the effectiveness of its communication for less flexible individuals. We, therefore, propose that the alignment of document design with the extent of flexibility of its audience will lead to a higher level of communication effectiveness.

Proposition 11: Web documents designed for users with less (as opposed to more) openness to change will be more effective if they refer to traditional and well-accepted (as opposed to innovative, new, and creative) norms, practices, ideas, and approaches.

Section 11 of the Appendix exhibits a textual example from a document designed for introducing HTML to an audience with less flexibility for learning new and unfamiliar topics by relying on familiar and well-accepted concepts of word processing.

Information-Processing Orientation Individuals vary in their information-processing orientation. Individual differences in information processing and acquisition have been studied for many years in psychology [49]. Mikulincer [50] defines the basic aspect of information processing as "the active search for new information." The integration of new information with the existing knowledge involves "decoding the acquired information, comparing it to existing schemata, and accommodating the schemata to the new data." One of the major differences in information acquisition and processing is in visual versus verbal and graphical versus textual.

The web provides both text and graphical information. Navigation on the web occurs through visual icons as well as texts, and the web has facilitated the integration of texts with graphics [51]. Kleinman and Dwyer [52] find that visual skills, including discrimination of different geometric shapes, alphabet letters, and words with different placement of letter sequences, play important role in information acquisition. This visual illustration helps the learner to identify and isolate important materials, to enhance information acquisition, and to support perceptual inferences more effectively and efficiently [52], [54]. We posit that individuals with more visual orientation are less tolerant of lengthy texts, whereas those with more text orientation prefer lengthier documents. Hence we propose that the alignment of document design with the information-processing orientation of its audience improves the communication effectiveness of the document.

Proposition 12: Web documents designed for users with greater visual orientation (as opposed to word orientation) will be more effective if they contain shorter (as opposed to longer) texts and more (as opposed to fewer) visual cues.

Section 12 of the Appendix provides the WWW address for a web design with numerous visual cues.

Cultural Knowledge The cultural aspects of the group to which the web user belongs are captured by the cultural dimensions discussed earlier in the section on Cultural Factors and Related Propositions. However, individuals differ in their knowledge of other cultures through their personal life experiences and interests. For example, persons who have multilingual proficiency, have lived in more than one country, or belong to more than one ethnic group will have more multicultural knowledge than those who know only one language, have lived in one place their entire lives, or belong to only one ethnic group. Although the multiethnicity of a country is captured in the cultural dimensions, the individual experiences within each country may vary. With the trend toward internationalization of businesses and cultural activities, some individuals may have far more cultural knowledge than others in their country.

Individuals' social standing and cultural ethos or origin may also help in creating more or less cultural knowledge. For example, individuals with high social standing may tend to have more opportunity to go abroad and be exposed to other cultures. Similarly, the cultural origin of an individual may allow for exposure to more than one culture. However, Hofstede [9, p. 17] observes that there is no standard definition of social standing and its interpretation varies from country to country. Furthermore, the individual's cultural origin is normally captured in the cultural dimensions of the country he belongs to. On the other hand, there is cultural learning that takes place through exposure to other cultures, education, and life experiences [9, p. 231].

We categorize factors related to individual cultural knowledge as knowledge of other cultures and multilanguage language proficiencies. Individuals with more cultural knowledge are able to distance themselves from their own cultural assumptions and are aware of the limitations of their inherited cultural "software" [9, pp. 231–232]. We, therefore, posit that the alignment of the document design with the cultural knowledge of its audience improves its communication effectiveness.

Proposition 13: Web documents designed for users with more cultural knowledge (as opposed to less cultural knowledge) can have less cultural specificity without loss of effectiveness.

Section 13 of the Appendix exhibits an textual example from United Nations' *Universal Declaration of Human Rights* that is designed for an audience with higher level of cultural knowledge and contains less cultural specificity.

National Factors Although cultural dimensions capture major differences in software of the mind, there are regional and national factors that have a stronger economic base and may be of importance to understanding the differences among groups of people and how they use the web. Ein-Dor et al. [55] report on the importance of the economic factors in international information systems.

We categorize the economic factors that may impact the use of web technology as **national factors**, which include **economic factors** and **technology factors**. The economic factors are related to the wealth of a nation as measured by variables such as the gross national product (GNP) of the country and average income within a country (GNP per capita). Other economic factors could also be considered, such as population growth, the level of national education, and rate of economic growth.

Hofstede [9] has found strong correlation between the IDV and the GNP per capita of 50 countries—the higher the level of individualism, the greater the wealth of the nation. On the other hand, he has found that a higher rate of population growth is correlated negatively with the IDV for the same countries. Furthermore, Hofstede [9] has found that richer countries have lower power distance indices. He reports that population, wealth, and geographical latitude account for 58% of variation in the PDI. Furthermore, the countries with long-term focus and Confucius orientation of south Asian countries (China, Hong Kong, Taiwan, Japan, and South Korea) have enjoyed economic growth in the past decades [56]. We can, therefore, conclude that to a large degree the cultural dimensions capture the economic differences among countries.

The national technology factors capture the technology infrastructure of the country, which includes communication as well as information technology exposure [57]–[60]. That is, if the web user lives in a country that has more communication facilities and IT is used more widely in the country's educational, professional, and individual activities, then one expects the web user to be more at ease with using the web. In such cases, the users of the web may not require cultural specificity.

The national technology factors could include the level of national communication and information infrastructures and the level of national exposure to IT. Even in the most technologically oriented countries, the exposure of individuals to telecommunication and IT is not uniform and one can find large discrepancies among the groups within a country. The IT knowledge and professional knowledge factors at the individual level capture the differences in technology exposures more accurately. Further more, age and gender may be associated with the knowledge of technology as well, which are also captured as individual characteristics discussed above. We, therefore, do not consider the national technology factors as separate factors in our analysis.

Interaction of Cultural Dimensions In measuring the impact of cultural and individual factors, it is important to consider the possibility of interactions among them. Hofstede [9] discusses several cases that relate to the interaction of cultural dimensions. In some cases, the correlation among cultural factors could be caused by a third variable. For example, when Hofstede [9] maps individualism versus collectivism against power distance, he observes a strong correlation between the two. Countries with a high collectivism score tend to have a high power distance score, while countries with a low collectivism (high individualist) score tend to have a low power distance score. However, Hofstede argues that this correlation is the consequence of a third variable: national wealth: "If economic development is held constant, i.e., if rich countries are compared to rich countries, and poor ones to poor ones, the relationship disappears" and there is no longer any consistent correlation between the two dimensions across cultures [9, p. 56].

In other cases, the interaction of two cultural dimensions has a multiplier effect that can create an impact greater than the sum of the two. When Hofstede [9] plots PDI scores against MAS scores, he finds that countries with both a high PDI and high MAS tend to display strongly pronounced cultural characteristics as a combined effect of both dimensions. In many Latin American countries, for example, a high power distance tends toward social organizations with both a strong patriarchal hierarchy and strong authority figures. These elements may then combine with a highly masculine culture that tends toward a family structure featuring a dominant, tough father figure and a submissive role for mothers and daughters. Consequently, a relatively strong norm of masculinity in these cultures has been dubbed "machismo," while the corresponding norm of femininity in these cultures has been described by the lesser known "term 'marianismo' for women," which means "a combination of near-saintliness, submissiveness, and sexual frigidity" [9, p. 88]. This may in turn exaggerate the impact of gender, as a component of the demographic factors, in measuring the effectiveness of web document design.

Interaction can also occur between cultural and individual factors. Hofstede [9] discusses the interaction of the cultural dimension of masculinity versus femininity with the individual factor of gender. In countries with a feminine culture, where both men and women are expected to show qualities of both masculinity and femininity, individual men scored about the same as individual women on the MAS. But in countries with a high masculine culture, both individual men and individual women scored higher on the MAS, while men tended to score somewhat higher than women [9, p. 83]. Here, we might consider the interaction to be moderate. A stronger interaction was revealed, however, between uncertainty avoidance and average age, which Hofstede [9, p. 117] describes as "circular," since one factor reinforces the other. In countries with stronger uncertainty avoidance, people changed employers less often, tended to stay in one place longer, and increased their length of service at a given job. This resulted in a higher average age for employees in countries with high uncertainty avoidance than the average age for employees at similar positions in low anxiety avoidance countries.

In our experiments, we will consider the possibility of interactions among factors and measure their impacts on the effectiveness of web designs in an exploratory fashion. If the interactions among factors show significant impacts, they will form a foundation for another set of propositions and experimental analyses.

User Satisfaction and Document Effectiveness Measures

The final outcome of using a web document is the reader's overall satisfaction with the experience. User satisfaction in a variety of computer-related activities has been based largely on the psychological studies of satisfaction in general (see, for example, [61]–[64]). Based on this literature, Bailey and Pearson define satisfaction as "the sum of one's feelings or attitudes toward a variety of factors affecting that situation" [65, p. 531]. Measuring and analyzing user satisfaction has a prominent place in information systems literature. Related to the effectiveness and productivity of the system, it enables analysts to perform comparative analysis of different systems, and is considered as one of the most important measures for the success of information systems [66]–[70]. We define satisfaction as the overall feelings of the reader regarding the experience of reading the web document. Overall satisfaction could be elicited by questions such as whether readers would be willing to read such a document again and would recommend it to others; whether the process was enjoyable and satisfactory, and whether the outcome met readers' expectations.

Satisfaction is influenced by a number of factors, which together we call web document effectiveness. There are a number of studies for identifying factors influencing user satisfaction. Based on 22 studies, Bailey and Pearson [65] develop an instrument and identify 39 factors affecting computer user satisfaction. They have found accuracy, reliability, timeliness, relevancy, and confidence in a system as the most important factors in user satisfaction. Doll et al. [69] reported that user satisfaction has five dimensions: content, accuracy, format, ease-of-use, and timeliness. Relevance, timeliness, and accuracy are identified by DeLone and McLean [68] and Seddon [70] as factors impacting system quality, which in turn influences user satisfaction.

We identify the web document effectiveness in terms of usability, reliability, clarity, and comprehensibility. We posit that the effectiveness of web documents, measured by these factors, influence the overall satisfaction of the user with the experience of reading the web document. In what follows, we present a brief discussion regarding the definition and measurement of the effectiveness factors.

Usability Usability measurement consists of perceived usefulness and ease-of-use of information systems. They have been identified as key components for predicting the acceptance and usage of information systems [69], [65], [71], [70]. Perceived usefulness relates it the enhancement of users' ability to perform their job, whereas ease-of-use relates to the format and friendliness of the system [26], [65], [67].

Since the focus of our measurement is the content of the web document, we integrate the perceived usefulness and ease-of-use into one usability metric, and we define it as the perceived usefulness and ease-of-use of the information provided in the web document. Questions that are used in this measure relate to the perception of the reader regarding how valuable, informative, useful, relevant, interesting, and easy-to-use the document is.

Reliability The reliability is another important aspect of information. The accuracy, dependability, credibility, and trustworthiness of information systems are measured under this construct [26], [65], [72], [73]. Following these studies, we define reliability as the reader's perceived extent of dependability, credibility, and trustworthiness of the web document, and questions that are used for this measure will relate to the reader's perception of these components.

Comprehensibility Comprehensibility or the readers' comprehension of a web document text refers to the readers' perception of texts' readability, understandability, organizational coherence, and the accessibility of textual meaning. Understandability of system and output as well as the readability of outputs also have been associated with user satisfaction in information systems (for example, [65]). Understandability can be measured by the readers perception of having grasped the purported meaning of the text and its purpose. If the reader can translate the text into his or her own words and understands the objectives or goals intended by the text to be fulfilled by the reading experience, then one can say that the reader has understood the meaning of the text [74], [75]. Organizational coherence depends on readers looking for and finding familiar organizational strategies and patterns in the text that remain consistent or coherent throughout the larger textual units so that they may then use those patterns as interpretive tools for understanding the text [76]. As one researcher in technical communication explains, "your readers will recognize your organizational strategy... [and] will instinctively look for a recognizable pattern of organization.... If they do not find it, they will be very uneasy after reading your document, unsure that they really understood it" [77]. Accessibility of meaning depends on whether the reader finds the diction and language of the document to be accessible to their level of knowledge and understanding [78]. The questions that measure the comprehensibility component identify the extent of the reader's perception of the readability, understandability, and accessibility of the web document.

Clarity Perception of document clarity may be defined by the users' perception of the unambiguous nature of the document's language, clear format, precise and relevant details, and references. Brusaw et al. [75] point out how linguistic ambiguity results when a word or passage is susceptible to two or more valid interpretations, causing confusion for the readers about how to choose among the alternatives. Severe ambiguity may cause a reader to abandon a text as completely incoherent. The perception of a clear document enables readers to quickly assess the document's overall hierarchy of topics and subtopics, increasing their satisfaction with the reading experience in general [45], [77]. Document clarity also depends upon the perception of precise and relevant details in the text that enables readers to visualize or concretize the meaning and thus avoid a perception of vagueness that decreases their satisfaction with a document's effectiveness. Hence, this component could be captured by questions that identify the readers' perceptions of the linguistic ambiguity, clarity of format, and the precision of details and references within the web document.

CONCLUDING REMARKS

In this paper, we synthesized social constructionist theory with cultural studies to develop a conceptual model for analyzing the impact of cultural and individual factors on the effectiveness of various web document designs. As factors influencing the communication effectiveness, we have identified six cultural dimensions as power distance, individualism versus collectivism, masculinity versus femininity, anxiety avoidance, long-term versus short-term orientation, polychronic versus monochronic orientation, and six individual factors as demographic (gender and age), professional knowledge, IT knowledge, flexibility, information processing ability, and cultural knowledge.

We have posited that the alignment of the web design with cultural factors and individual factors would improve the effectiveness of web documents and lead to higher level of overall satisfaction. Web documents effective for large-power-distance cultures would refer to authority, power, expertise, and wealth. Effective document designs for collectivist cultures would promote group cohesion and not individual self-interest. Effective document designs for masculine cultures would refer to success, winning, strength, and assertiveness; and those for strong uncertainty avoidance cultures would refer to rules and regulations and avoid emphasizing novelty and deviating from the norm. Effective document design for long-term orientation cultures would emphasize perseverance, future orientation, resources for conservation, respect for the demands of virtue, and de-emphasize truth and falsity as a strictly binary, black-and-white relationship. Effective designs for polychronic time cultures would emphasize high-context personal information, tend to build lifelong relationships, offer a variety of views, issues, or topics, and would be oriented toward people and human relationships. Effective designs for female users would be supportive, cooperative, tentative, create harmony, and empathetic; those for younger users would contain less information, more visuals, and less text; those for users with less professional knowledge would contain simpler, common sense, linguistically easier contents; those for users with less IT knowledge would be more effective if they contain less IT-related technical information; those for users with less openness to change would refer to traditional and well-accepted norms, practices, ideas, and approaches. Document designs for users with greater visual orientation would contain shorter texts and more visual cues; those for users with more cultural knowledge could have less cultural specificity without loss of effectiveness. Based on this framework, we presented specific, testable propositions for testing the effectiveness of various web designs and provided textual examples for designs that may be used in investigating the propositions. In operationalizing the framework, one needs to have a clear definition and measurement of communication effectiveness and satisfaction. The last section of the paper discussed how these constructs could be measured.

This paper is the first stage of a multistage study, and the next phases involve extensive data collection and analysis in investigating the validity of the framework and its propositions. Obviously, such an analysis should take place across cultural and multinational levels.

The findings regarding the analysis of our proposed framework and propositions could have far reaching implications. Testing various designs for web documents could provide a scientific knowledge base on how to create webpages that have maximum communication effectiveness. Since the Internet is expected to be the prime communication medium of the 21st century, such a knowledge base could be a valuable guide to researchers and professional communicators involved in web design for governments, businesses, and education, especially with regard to reaching audiences with specific cultural and individual characteristics. More importantly, such a knowledge base could also help website owners become aware of the possibility of ineffective communications with certain cultural and individual groups.

APPENDIX EXAMPLES FOR PROPOSITIONS ON THE ALIGNMENT OF CULTURAL AND INDIVIDUAL FACTORS WITH WEB DESIGN

The following sample texts have been drawn either from actual webpages, business and technical writing samples, or from textbooks. Because our study focuses on textual features of web documents, most of our examples are textual rather than graphical.

Section 1—Example for Proposition 1

This example displays obvious references to wealth, authority, and expertise:

> *A hypermedia archive sponsored by the Library of Congress and supported by the Getty Grant Program, the Institute for Advanced Technology in the Humanities at the University of Virginia, Sun Microsystems, and Inso Corporation. With additional support from the Paul Mellon Centre for Studies in British Art and the University of North Carolina at Chapel Hill. We ask you to adhere strictly to the terms under which these materials are made available. The Archive as a whole, its texts, and its images are protected under the copyright laws of the United States and the Universal Copyright Convention* [79].

Section 2—Example for Proposition 2

The following text example for Proposition 2 (collectivism versus individualism) is a rejection letter from a Beijing newspaper explaining why the editors have rejected an article from a British journalist. The letter displays indirect language that supports group cohesion and harmony through formal politeness, rather than direct, "get to the point" individual self-interest:

> *We have read your manuscript with boundless delight. If we were to publish your paper, it would be impossible for us to publish any work of a lower standard. And as it is unthinkable that, in the next thousand years, we shall see its equal, we are, to our regret compelled to return your divine composition, and beg you a thousand times to overlook our short sight and timidity* [80, p. 248.].

Section 3—Example for Proposition 3

The following text example displays language that stresses masculine qualities of success, assertiveness, and strength:

> *Be all that you can be. Become part of the best team in the world. Join the US Army or Army Reserve and we'll guarantee great training and skills to last a lifetime. Learn more and see if you're ready* [81].

Section 4—Example for Proposition 4

The following text example displays features of strong uncertainty avoidance, such as language and references that emphasize precise and detailed information and strong adherence to established business processes and practices:

> ... *SAP AG, the world's leading provider of enterprise business software solutions, announced SAP Higher Education & Research as a new industry solution. This comprehensive solution includes core SAP functionality such as fund management and human resources as well as the new SAP IQ-CAMPUS component, to help higher-education institutions become more responsive and service oriented.... Details of this best-in-class integrated solution are in the SAP Higher Education & Research solution map. Developed by SAP and higher-education customers, partners, and industry experts, the solution map promotes a common understanding of industry requirements, and details the full functionality and strategic directions SAP and its partners are taking to meet the ongoing information technology needs of higher education institutions* [82].

Section 5—Example for Proposition 5

The following text example concerning long-term orientation stresses perseverance, virtuous actions, and a future-oriented view in response to short-term economic downturn:

> *The current crisis was caused in part by distortions created during the process of rapid economic growth, and also by delays in structural reforms (including the financial sector). In the light of the fundamental conditions in Asian countries, it is firmly believed that these countries will again recover their steady economic growth in the mid- and long-term if necessary reforms are implemented* [83].

Section 6—Example for Proposition 6

The following text example for Proposition 6 shows an emphasis on polychronic (as opposed to monochronic) time orientation by stressing high-context personal information, human relationships, and family background of the president of Italy:

> *Romano Prodi, was born on August 1939 in the small town of Scandiano in the Emilia Romagna Region, one of the leading Region of Italy in all sectors: from food to culture, industry, science and politics. Its people—the Emiliani Romagnoli—are very well known for their University (the oldest of the western world), the excellent cuisine (tortellini, ravioli, parmigiano), their sport cars (Ferrari and Lamborghini), great Opera lovers (such as Giuseppe Verdi, Luciano Pavarotti, Cecilia Gasdia), creative scientists (Guglielmo Marconi) and film directors (Fellini, Antonioni, and Bertolucci) just to mention a few. The Emiliani Romagnoli are also considered by the general public as generous*

people.... Romano Prodi is one among seven brothers and sisters; he is happily married and has two children. His main hobby: Cyclism [84].

Section 7—Example for Proposition 7

The following text example shows an emphasis on supportive, cooperative, creative harmony:

> *Continuity of programming flows through all rooms in the Center. There exists a shared belief in the value of play and exploration as the major vehicle by which children learn, and a consensus about how this is best facilitated.... In group play children learn sharing, consideration and tolerance, and develop meaningful relationships with other children and the adults who care for them. Importance is placed on overall development rather than isolated parts of it, and on creative environments in which both children and adults are encouraged to learn and grow* [85].

Section 8—Example for Proposition 8

The following text example shows a sentence from a website meant to appeal mainly to a more youthful audience; the page contained bright colors and striking visuals, but limited text. The single sentence dominating the webpage is in large, bright-yellow script across the entire page and reads:

> *Give your little valentine a year of online fun and adventure* [86].

Section 9—Example for Proposition 9

The following text uses simple language and simple common sense concepts for explaining "fair use" of copyrighted materials for users with less professional knowledge of the law:

> *Follow the "Fair Use" guidelines for educational or research purposes. Fair Use is a term that refers to the limited use of copyrighted material without obtaining permission. Reprinting brief excerpts of material are considered "fair" if, for example, you use less than ten percent of a whole text or ten percent of the images at someone else's web site for educational (noncommercial) purposes such as designing your own web page for a class project* [87].

Section 10—Example for Proposition 10

The following text example attempts to reduce the amount of IT knowledge a reader would need to understand the elements of a webpage.

> *I've tried to design this page in a way that allows you to take it apart and see how it works. In the menu bar on the left, you will see a list of the major parts of any webpage. Simply (left) click your mouse on any item from that list. These items are linked to other pages (subpages) showing you the code that creates that part of a webpage. A paragraph below each line of code explains when and how to use the code. Good luck!* [88].

Section 11—Example for Proposition 11

The following text example emphasizes the well-accepted idea and practices of word processing as an analogy to webpage composing tools in order to appeal to users who may have a less openness to the new technology of HTML:

> *HTML (Hypertext Markup Language) is the language or code used to format World Wide web (web) pages. But don't worry about the idea of "coding" since you will be able to use a composing tool that writes the code for you—think of it as similar to a word processing program that lets you put images, colors, and texts into a blank page. Your composing tool, Netscape Composer, is very easy to use and will translate your webpage into the HTML language so other people can view your page on their web browsers. You can create a sample page as you read along through the following sections. It's okay if you make mistakes, since you can change things later. Just follow the examples and you'll be creating pages with paragraphs, images, and colorful backgrounds as easily as one-two-three* [87].

Section 12—Example for Proposition 12

The following website example shows short texts with many visual cues:

> http://www.consumersenergy.com

Section 13—Example for Proposition 13

The following text example lacks distinctive cultural specificity and should be effective among users with greater knowledge of cultures other than their own:

> *Everyone, as a member of society, has the right to social security and is entitled to realization, through national effort and international co-operation and in accordance with the organization and resources of each State, of the economic, social and cultural rights indispensable for his dignity and the free development of his personality* [89].

REFERENCES

[1] R. Schultheis and M. Sumner, *Management Information Systems: The Manager's View*, 4th ed. New York: McGraw-Hill, 1998.

[2] K. Laudon and J. Laudon, *Essentials of Management Information Systems*, 3rd ed. Englewood Cliffs, NJ: Prentice-Hall, 1999.

[3] M. C. Lacity and M. A. Janson, "Understanding qualitative data: A framework of test analysis methods," *J. Manag. Inform. Syst.*, vol. 11, no. 2, pp. 137–159, 1994.

[4] P. Dias, "Social constructionism," in *Theorizing Composition*, M. Kennedy, Ed. London, U.K.: Greenwood Press, 1998, pp. 285–293.

[5] J. Lyotard, *The Postmodern Condition: A Report on Knowledge*. Minneapolis, MN: Univ. Minnesota Press, 1984.

[6] W. V. Van Pelt, "Postmodernism," in *Theorizing Composition*, M. Kennedy, Ed. London, U.K.: Greenwood, 1998, pp. 218–223.

[7] R. Kasaba. (1998) *Toward a New International Studies* [Online]. Available: http://js.artsci.washington.edu/programs/is/toanewis.html

[8] R. L. Daft, *Organization Theory and Design*. Cincinnati, OH: Southwestern, 1998.

[9] G. Hofstede, *Cultures and Organizations; Software of the Mind*, 2nd ed. London, U.K.: McGraw-Hill, 1997.

[10] ——, *Culture's Consequences: International Differences in Work-Related Values*. Beverly Hills, CA: Sage, 1980.

[11] ——, "Cultural dimensions in management and planning," *Asia Pacific J. Manag.*, pp. 81–99, Jan. 1984.

[12] ——, "The interaction between national and organizational value systems," *J. Manag. Studies*, vol. 22, no. 4, pp. 347–357, 1985.

[13] J. Nielsen, *Designing User Interface for International Use*. Amsterdam, The Netherlands: Elsevier, 1990.

[14] E. M. del Galdo and J. Nielsen, *International User Interfaces*. New York: Wiley, 1996.

[15] N. Hoft, *International Technical Communication: How to Export Information about High Technology*. New York: Wiley, 1995.

[16] B. L. Thatcher, "Cultural and rhetorical adaptations for South American audiences," *Tech. Commun.*, vol. 46, no. 2, pp. 177–195, 1999.

[17] P. Flint, M. Van Slyke, D. Starke-Meyering, and A. Thompson, "Going online: Helping technical communicators help translators," *Tech. Commun.*, vol. 46, no. 2, pp. 238–248, 1999.

[18] H. Adams, G. W. Austen, and M. Taylor, "Developing a resource for multinational writing at Xerox Corporation," *Tech. Commun.*, vol. 46, no. 2, pp. 249–254, 1999.

[19] P. Honold, "Learning how to use a cellular phone: Comparison between German and Chinese learners," *Tech. Commun.*, vol. 46, no. 2, pp. 196–205, 1999.

[20] R. D. Lewis, *When Cultures Collide*. London, U.K.: Nicholas Brealey, 1996.

[21] E. T. Hall, *The Dance of Life: The Other Dimension of Time*. Garden City, NY: Anchor, 1983.

[22] W. Straub, "The effect of culture on IT diffusion: E-mail and Fax in Japan and the U.S.," *Inform. Syst. Res.*, vol. 5, no. 1, pp. 23–47, 1994.

[23] D. Andrews, *Technical Communication in the Global Community*. Upper Saddle River, NJ: Prentice-Hall, 1998.

[24] E. Kras, *Management in Two Cultures*. Yartmouth, ME: Intercultural, 1991.

[25] S. Dragga, "Ethical intercultural technical communication: Looking through the lens of confucian ethics," *Tech. Commun. Quart.*, vol. 8, no. 4, pp. 365–381, 1999.

[26] R. W. Zmud, "Individual differences and MIS success: A review of the empirical literature," *Manag. Sci.*, vol. 25, no. 10, pp. 966–979, 1979.

[27] D. Gefen and D. W. Straub, "Gender differences in the perception and use of E-mail: An extension to the technology acceptance model," *MIS Quart.*, vol. 21, no. 4, pp. 389–400, 1997.

[28] A. Palma-dos-Reis and F. M. Zahedi, "Designing personalized intelligent decision support systems: The impact of risk attitude on using security selection models," *Decision Supp. Syst.*, vol. 26, pp. 31–47, 1999.

[29] K. Proost, J. Ellen, and J. Lowyck, "Effects of gender on perceptions of and preferences for telematic learning environments," *J. Res. Comput. in Educ.*, vol. 29, pp. 370–384, 1997.

[30] M. Igbaria and J. J. Baroudi, "The impact of job performance evaluations on career advance," *MIS Quart.*, vol. 19, no. 1, pp. 107–123, 1995.
[31] J. J. Baroudi and M. Igbaria, "An examination of gender effects on career success of information systems employees," *J. Manag. Inform. Syst.*, vol. 11, no. 3, pp. 181–200, 1995.
[32] S. W. Chu, "Using chopsticks and a fork together: Challenges and strategies of developing a Chinese/English bilingual web site," *Tech. Commun.*, vol. 46, no. 2, pp. 206–219, 1999.
[33] K. A. Schriver, *Dynamics in Document Design: Creating Texts for Readers*. New York: Wiley, 1997.
[34] J. M. Spool, T. Scanlon, W. Schroeder, C. Snyder, and T. DeAngelo, *website Usability: A Designer's Guide*. San Francisco, CA: Morgan Kaufmann, 1999.
[35] J. A. Hall and J. D. Carter, "Gender-stereotype accuracy as an individual difference," *J. Personality Social Psychol.*, vol. 77, no. 2, pp. 350–359, 1999.
[36] J. A. Hall and G. Friedman, "Status, gender, and nonverbal behavior: A study of structured interaction between employees of a company," *Personality Social Psychol. Bull.*, vol. 25, no. 9, pp. 1082–1091, 1999.
[37] J. Coates, *Women, Men, and Language: Studies in Language and Linguistics* London, U.K., 1976.
[38] B. Presler, "The tentative female," *English Today*, vol. 12, pp. 29–30, Oct. 1987.
[39] D. F. Gilroy and H. B. Desai, "Computer anxiety: Sex, race, and age," *Int. J. Man-Machine Studies*, vol. 25, pp. 711–719, 1986.
[40] K. A. Frankel, "Women and computing," *Commun. ACM*, vol. 33, no. 11, pp. 34–45, 1990.
[41] J. Morahan-Martin, "Women and girls last: Females and the Internet," in *Proc. IRISS 1998 Int. Conf.*, Bristol, England. [WWW page]. Available from http://sosig.ac.uk/iriss/papers/paper55.htm.
[42] R. N. Taylor, "Age and experience as determinants of managerial information processing and decision making performance," *Acad. Manag. J.*, vol. 18, no. 1, pp. 74–81, 1975.
[43] D. Compeau, C. A. Higgins, and S. Huff, "Social cognitive theory and individual reactions to computing technology: A longitudinal study," *MIS Quart.*, vol. 23, no. 2, pp. 145–158, 1999.
[44] E. Krock, "Cultural leaning differences in software user training," in *International User Interfaces*, E. M. del Galdo and J. Nielsen, Eds. New York: Wiley, 1996.
[45] T. Barker, "Analyzing your users," in *Writing Software Documentation: A Task-Oriented Approach*. Boston, MA: Allyn & Bacon, 1998, pp. 25–85.
[46] T. C. S. Kennedy, "Some behavior factors affecting training of naïve users of an interactive computer systems," *Int. J. Man-Machine Studies*, vol. 7, pp. 817–834, 1975.
[47] W. Geoghegan, "Stuck on the barricade," presented at the The Annual Meeting of the American Association for Higher Education, Washington, DC, 1995.
[48] D. M. Dusick, "What social cognitive factors influence faculty members' use of computers for teaching?: A literature review," *J. Res. Comput. in Educ.*, vol. 31, no. 2, pp. 123–137, 1998.
[49] S. Streufert and P. Suedfeld, "Conceptual structure, information search, and information utilization," *J. Personality Social Psychol.*, vol. 2, no. 5, pp. 736–740, 1965.
[50] M. Mikulincer, "Adult attachment style and information processing: Individual differences in curiosity and cognitive closure," *J. Personality Social Psychol.*, vol. 72, no. 5, pp. 1217–1230, 1997.
[51] N. J. Muller, "Expanding the help desk through the world wide web," *Inform. Syst. Manag.*, vol. 13, no. 3, pp. 37–44, 1996.
[52] B. Kleinman and F. M. Dwyer, "Analysis of computerized visual skills: Relationship to intellectual skills and achievement," *Int. J. Instruct. Media*, vol. 26, no. 1, pp. 53–69, 1999.
[53] L. Hodes, "Processing visual information: Implications of the dual code theory," *J. Instruct. Psychol.*, vol. 21, no. 1, pp. 36–43, 1994.
[54] W. Winn, "The role of graphics in training documents: Toward an explanatory theory of how they communicate," *IEEE Trans. Prof. Commun.*, vol. 32, no. 4, pp. 300–309, 1989.

[55] P. Ein-Dor, E. Segev, and M. Orgad, "The effect of national culture on IS: Implications for international information systems," *J. Global Inform. Manag.*, vol. 1, no. 1, pp. 33–43, 1993.
[56] G. Hofstede and M. H. Bond, "The confucius connection: From cultural roots to economic growth," *Organiz. Dynamics*, vol. 16, no. 4, pp. 4–21, 1988.
[57] A. D. Meyer, "Tech talk: How managers are stimulating global R&D communication," *Sloan Manag. Rev.*, pp. 49–58, 1991.
[58] S. Mariotti and L. Piscitello, "Information costs and location of FDI's within the host country: Empirical evidence from Italy," *J. Int. Business Studies*, vol. 26, no. 4, pp. 815–841, 1995.
[59] L. A. Streeter, R. E. Kraut, H. C. Lucas Jr., and L. Caby, "How open data networks influence business performance and market structure," *Commun. ACM*, vol. 39, no. 7, pp. 62–73, 1996.
[60] H. Chen and T. Chen, "Network linkages and location choice in foreign direct investment," *J. Int. Business Studies*, vol. 29, no. 3, pp. 445–467, 1998.
[61] G. A. Churchill, N. M. Ford, and O. C. Walker, "Measuring the job satisfaction of industrial salesmen," *J. Marketing*, vol. 11, no. 3, pp. 254–260, 1974.
[62] D. Cross, "The worker opinion survey: A measure of shop-floor satisfaction," *Occupational Psychol.*, vol. 47, no. 3–4, pp. 193–208, 1973.
[63] P. Schawb and L. L. Cummings, "Theories of performance and satisfaction; A review," in *Readings in Organizational Behavior and Human Performance*, W. E. Scott and L. L. Cummings, Eds. Homewood, IL: Irwin, 1973, pp. 130–153.
[64] P. C. Smith, L. M. Kendall, and C. L. Hulin, *The Measurement of Satisfaction in Work and Retirement: A Strategy for the Study of Attitudes*. Chicago, IL: Rand-McNally, 1969.
[65] J. Bailey and W. Pearson, "Developing of tool for measuring and analyzing computer satisfaction," *Manag. Sci.*, vol. 29, no. 5, pp. 530–545, 1983.
[66] M. H. O. Ives and J. J. Baroudi, "The measurement of user information satisfaction," *Commun. ACM*, vol. 26, no. 10, pp. 785–793, 1983.
[67] W. J. Doll and G. Torkzadeh, "The measurement of end-user computing satisfaction," *MIS Quart.*, pp. 259–274, June 1988.
[68] W. H. DeLone and E. R. McLean, "Information systems success: The quest for the dependent variable," *Inform. Syst. Res.*, vol. 3, no. 1, pp. 60–95, 1992.
[69] W. J. Doll, W. Xia, and G. Torkzadeh, "A confirmatory factor analysis of the end-user computing satisfaction instrument," *MIS Quart.*, pp. 453–461, Dec. 1994.
[70] P. B. Seddon, "A respecification and extension of the DeLone and McLean model of IS success," *Inform. Syst. Res.*, vol. 8, no. 3, pp. 240–253, 1997.
[71] F. D. Davis, R. P. Bagozzi, and P. R. Warshaw, "User acceptance of computer technology: A comparison of two theoretical models," *Manag. Sci.*, vol. 35, no. 8, pp. 982–1003, 1989.
[72] W. R. King and B. J. Epstein, "Assessing information system value: An experimental study," *Decision Sci.*, vol. 14, pp. 34–45, 1983.
[73] J. Eighmey and L. McCord, "Adding value in the information age: Uses and gratifications of sites on the world wide web," *J. Bus. Res.*, vol. 41, pp. 187–194, 1998.
[74] T. Kent, *Paralogic Rhetoric*. Lewisburg, PA: Bucknell Univ. Press, 1993.
[75] C. T. Brusaw, G. J. Alred, and W. E. Oliu, *The Handbook of Technical Writing*. New York: St. Martin's, 1997.
[76] L. Flower, *Problem-Solving Strategies for Writing*. Orlando, FL: Harcourt, 1981.
[77] G. J. Alred, W. E. Oliu, and C. T. Brusaw, *The Professional Writer: A Guide for Advanced Technical Writing*. New York: St. Martin's, 1992.
[78] J. M. Lannon, *Technical Writing*. New York: Addison Wesley Longman, 1997.
[79] William Blake Archive, [WWW Page]. [Online]. Available: University of Virginia, http://jefferson.village.virginia.edu/blake/ Maint. Morris Eaves.

[80] M. E. Guffey, *Business Communication: Process and Product*. Cincinnati, OH: Southwestern, 1997, p. 248.
[81] U.S. Army Home Page, [WWW Page]. [Online]. Available: http://www.goarmy.com/ Maint. U.S. Army. 2000.
[82] SAP announces higher education & research solution, SAP AG Information Center [WWW page]. [Online]. Available: http://www.sap.com/ Maint. Software Applications and Products, Waldorf, Germany, 1999
[83] Current situation of the Asian economic crisis and Japan's responses to it, Ministry of Foreign Affairs of Japan [WWW page]. [Online]. Available: http://www.mofa.go.jp/policy/economy/asia/situ99.html Maint. Ministry of Foreign Affairs, Japan, November 1999.
[84] Central government, Republic of Italy Home Page [WWW page]. [Online]. Available: http://www.ital.com/italy/CenralGovF.htm Maint. by Italian Central Government, 2000
[85] Program goals, UWM Children's Center [WWW page]. [Online]. Available: http://www.uwm.edu/Dept/CCC/page5.html Maint. by Salvatore Librizzi, 14 Jan. 1999
[86] Club blast preview, Disney [WWW page]. [Online]. Available: http://disney.go.com/preview/index.html?clk=Hp.nav.club.ht Maint. by Disney.com. 29 Jan. 2000
[87] Univ. Wisconsin Milwaukee, *Creating Your Own Web Page*. Milwaukee, WI: English Dept., 1998, p. 22.
[88] S. Winters. The mechanics of a web site. [Online]. Available: http://www.uwm.edu/~swinters/ Maint. S. Winters, University of Wisconsin-Milwaukee, 22 May 1999.
[89] United Nations, Universal declaration of human rights: Article 22, General Assembly Resolution 217 A (III) of 10 December 1948 [WWW page]. [Online]. Available: http://www.un.org/Overview/rights.html Maint. by Information Technology Section of the Department of Public Information (DPI), United Nations.

Fatemeh "Mariam" Zahedi is the Wisconsin Distinguished Professor, MIS Area at the School of Business, University of Wisconsin-Milwaukee. She has received her doctoral degree from Indiana University. Her present areas of research include IS quality and satisfaction, e-commerce and web development, intelligent DSS, and IS-related policies and decision analysis. She has published extensively in refereed journals including: *MIS Quarterly, Decision Sciences, IEEE Transactions on Software Engineering, IIE Transactions, European Journal of Operations Research, Operations Research, Computers and Operations Research, Interfaces, International Journal of Quality and Reliability Management, Journal of Information Technology Management, Journal of Review of Economics and Statistics, Empirical Economics; Socio-Economic Planning Sciences*. She is the author of two books in *Quality Information Systems and Intelligent Systems for Business: Expert Systems with Neural Network*, and serves on the editorial board of a number of journals. Dr. Zahedi has contributed on the topic of information systems to *International Encyclopedia of Business and Management*, group decisions in *Encyclopedia of Management Science and Operations Research*, and Quality Control in *Wiley Encyclopedia of Electrical and Electronic Engineering*. She has a few years of consulting and managerial experience in developing information systems and performing policy analysis. In the Summer of 2001, she starts her tenure as the editor-in-chief of *Information Resource Management Journal*.

William V. Van Pelt is an Associate Professor of English at the University of Wisconsin-Milwaukee where he teaches technical writing, business writing, rhetorical theory, and Romantic literature. He has published several articles on technology and the writing process and coedited *Speculations: Readings in Culture, Identity, and Values, Second Edition* (Prentice-Hall: 1995) with Charles Schuster. He has worked as technical writer and consultant for many companies, including Bechtel Engineering, Intel, Motorola, and M&I Data Services.

Jaeki Song is a Ph.D. candidate in Management Information Systems at the University of Wisconsin-Milwaukee. His research interests include the implementation of information technology in the areas of e-commerce and globalization. His publications have appeared in such conferences as *AMCIS, INFORM, DSI*, and in a book chapter.

Index

About the Editor

David F. Beer earned his Bachelor of Arts in secondary education at the University of Arizona, his Masters degree in English linguistics from Arizona State University, and a Ph.D. in English from the University of New Mexico.

He taught at the University of Colorado and at Haille Sellassie I University in Ethiopia before joining the English Department at the University of Texas as an assistant professor in 1978. In 1985, he was invited to develop a technical communication program for the Department of Electrical and Computer Engineering, where he currently directs the engineering communication program. Besides teaching technical communication, he has conducted workshops at several high-tech companies in Austin, and works on a regular basis at Advanced Micro Devices, Inc.

Dr. Beer has presented papers on technical communication at IEEE and ASEE conferences and has published a number of journal articles. Besides editing the first edition of this volume, he co-authored with David McMurrey, *A Guide to Writing as an Engineer* (Wiley, 1997). He is a senior member of the IEEE Professional Communication Society and a past senior member and president of the Austin chapter of the Society for Technical Communication.